- ▶ To delete a document you no longer want, ⟨ right-click on it and choose Delete.

- ▶ To recover an accidentally deleted file, clear you can see the Recycle Bin. Double-click on document, higlight it, and choose File ➤ Restore.

- ▶ To move a document between folders, between the Desktop and a folder, or to another drive, first save the document and close it, then drag it to the destination location.

- ▶ To quickly copy a document to a floppy disk, right-click on the document and choose Send To ➤ Floppy Disk.

Folders

1996 Reports

- ▶ To see the folders in your computer, double-click on My Computer, then double-click on the drive containing the folders.

- ▶ To see a specific folder's contents, double-click on it.

- ▶ To display a larger number of documents in a folder's window, enlarge the window and/or choose View ➤ List.

- ▶ To create a new folder, right-click where you want the new folder to go (such as inside another folder or on the Desktop). Choose New ➤ Folder, name the folder, and press Enter.

- ▶ To move a folder, drag it to its new location.

System

My Computer

- ▶ To set the colors of the screen, Desktop background, or screen saver, right-click on the Desktop and choose Properties.

- ▶ To empty the Recycle Bin, right-click on the bin and choose Empty Recycle Bin.

- ▶ To make other system settings, choose Start ➤ Settings ➤ Control Panel and double-click on the related icon.

- ▶ To see the Desktop, right-click on the clock in the Taskbar and choose Minimize All Windows.

Mastering
Windows® 95

Robert Cowart

SYBEX®

San Francisco • Paris • Düsseldorf • Soest

Acquisitions Manager: Kristine Plachy

Developmental Editor: Gary Masters

Editor: Laura Arendal

Technical Editor: Arthur Knowles

Book Designer: Helen Bruno; Adapted by Jan Haseman

Technical Artist: Cuong Le

Desktop Publishers: Alissa Feinberg, Deborah Maizels, Thomas Goudie Bonasera, Debi Bevilacqua, and Lynell Decker

Production Assistants: Taris Duffié and Ron Jost

Indexer: Matthew Spence

Cover Designer: Design Site

Cover Photographer: Mark Johann

Screen reproductions produced with Collage Plus.

Collage Plus is a trademark of Inner Media Inc.

SYBEX is a registered trademark of SYBEX Inc.

TRADEMARKS: SYBEX has attempted throughout this book to distinguish proprietary trademarks from descriptive terms by following the capitalization style used by the manufacturer.

Every effort has been made to supply complete and accurate information. However, SYBEX assumes no responsibility for its use, nor for any infringement of the intellectual property rights of third parties which would result from such use.

Library of Congress Card Number: 95-67727

ISBN: 0-7821-1413-X

Manufactured in the United States of America

10 9 8 7 6

To my mother, who still *doesn't do windows*

To Rudolph Langer:

This book is dedicated by the publisher and staff at Sybex to the memory of Dr. Rudolph Langer, Editor-in-Chief at Sybex for nearly 15 years. His talent, dedication, and constant search for excellence were well-known by all who met him, worked with him, or read our titles.

Acknowledgments

I am indebted to the talented people at Sybex for their invaluable assistance in the production of this book. Special thanks indeed go to Dr. R.S. Langer for his support in acquisitional, developmental, financial, and contractual matters; Managing Editor Barbara Gordon for her central role in coordinating everything; Production Manager Jim Curran for his support; my developmental editor, Gary Masters, for assistance in fine-tuning the book's contents; to my editor, Laura Arendal, for her patience and ability to excise superfluous material and improve readability; Arthur Knowles for his technical editing; Taris Duffié, production assistant; Thomas Goudie Bonasera and Alissa Feinberg, lead desktop publishers; and everybody else who worked behind the scenes to ship the book.

Not to be overlooked are the people responsible for the distribution and sales of Sybex books, including the one you're holding. Sybex has its own independent sales and marketing force working to get these books onto shelves around the world—from small independent bookstores to the national chains. Thanks to Kip Triplett, Vice President of Sales; Julie Simmons, academic coordinator; and the rest of the crew in Alameda and around the country. I can pay my rent!

A project as ambitious and time-pressured as this book required a team effort in the writing department, too. I am indebted to several people for their research, writing, and editorial contributions. For his technical sidebars and condensation of the networking section, I greatly thank Arthur Knowles. For his elucidation of Windows 95 communications aspects, my appreciation goes to John Ross. For his extensive coverage of Windows 95 networking, heartfelt thanks to Jim Blaney. And special thanks to my multitalented friend and writing colleague Dr. Steve Cummings, whose assistance was responsible for the Accessories section.

Finally, warm thanks to my friends (especially Elizabeth and Eric) who put up with my kvetching and hair-pulling during the year of research, writing, upgrades (there were more than 490 versions of Windows 95 as it was being developed), and even traveling with laptop, that went into compiling this volume.

Contents at a Glance

Table of Contents

Part 2: Exploring Windows 95

Chapter 7: Basic Customizing with the Control Panel

Part 5: Networking with Windows 95   933

Introduction

Thank you for purchasing (or considering the purchase of) this book! *Mastering Windows 95* is designed to help you get the most out of Windows 95 with the least amount of effort. You may be wondering if this is the right book for you. I've written this book with both the novice and the experienced PC user in mind. The intention was to produce a volume that would prove both accessible and highly instructive to all Windows users.

Based on the best-selling *Mastering Windows 3.0* and *Mastering Windows 3.1*, this Third Edition uses the same time-tested approach for teaching Windows that has helped hundreds of thousands of beginners in many countries become Windows-literate.

From the outset, this book doesn't require that you have a working knowledge of Windows. All I assume is that you have a modicum of familiarity with an IBM PC. So, if you are new to Windows, a bit PC-literate, and ready to learn, this book is a good choice. I think you'll find it easy to read and not over your head. There are a lot of everyday examples to explain the concepts, and all the accessory programs free with Windows 95 are explained in detail so you can get up and running right away.

What About Power Users?

If you're a *power user*, familiar with earlier versions of Windows and the intricacies of DOS, the explanations and procedures here will quickly bring you up to speed with Windows 95 and how it's different from its predecessors. For example, the first chapter (which can be skipped by novices), is a thorough analysis of what's new in Windows 95 and how it compares to the competition and to the other members of the Windows family of operating systems. By quickly skimming the next several chapters, you'll learn how to use the new folder system, property sheets, right-click menus, the Explorer, the new OLE 2.0, and other basics.

The advanced discussions in Parts 2, 3, 4, and 6 will be extremely useful whether you're an MIS professional, an executive, an instructor, or a home user. There's significant coverage of the increasingly important area of electronic communications from the Windows workstation, be it through the Internet, over a LAN, via services such as CompuServe, or with computerized faxing. A multimedia chapter explores the possibilities for adding audio, video, CD-ROM, and MIDI elements to your Windows setup. If you want to optimize your Windows setup for high performance, that's covered as well, with discussions of hardware and software modifications, hard-disk management, video accelerator cards, and so forth.

A major section (Part 5) on networking—something you're not likely to find in the other books of this type on the market—tackles the most salient aspects of Windows 95 networking; from the initial planning stages of choosing and routing cabling, through internetworking with Windows NT, Novell, and TCP/IP, and using remote access services (RAS). Of course, simple peer-to-peer networking—which Windows 95 can do right out of the box—is covered, as is how to best manage your network.

Because laptops have become so prevalent (some say as much as 33 percent of personal computing is done on laptops as of this writing), we've given special attention to Windows 95's mobile-computing abilities. Topics such as advanced power management (APM) support, file synchronization, hot-docking stations, PCMCIA card support, and remote access—along with some tips for road warriors—are explained in Part 6.

Although for many users Windows 95 will be factory installed on the computer, this isn't always the case. So, if you haven't installed Windows yet, procedures and considerations are included in the Appendix.

This is just a sample of the topics you'll find between the covers of this book. I've addressed the topics that Windows users are likely to need, carefully chosen notable and savory value-added information, and supplied it all in one place. Please consult the table of contents for the exact topics covered.

Why This Book?

As you know, there is a manual supplied with Windows 95 and there is online Help built into Windows 95 as well. So why do you need a book? Because the Windows 95 manual is very sketchy, and often the Help system doesn't tell you what you want to know. True, great efforts have been made on Microsoft's part to simplify Windows 95 and make it more intuitive and friendly in hopes that reference tomes like this one will no longer be necessary. But until a computer can talk to you in everyday language, you will still need a good book, especially with a computer program or operating system as all-inclusive as Windows 95. If you happen to find some technical manuals from the manufacturer, explanations are often written in computerese, assuming too much knowledge. This is often true of other books as well. Either they are too technical or they speak only to the *newbie* (novice user), with nothing left for intermediate or advanced users and nothing for the novice to grow into.

Here I've done the legwork for you: I've boiled down the manuals, had discussions with many Windows 95 testers, experimented on various machines from laptops to Pentiums, and then written a book explaining Windows 95 in normal, everyday English.

The authors of this book have a wide diversity of experience with both Windows 95 and other PC software and hardware. Pooling their knowledge and working with Windows 95 since its first incarnation in alpha form more than a year before its release, I have come up with a thorough cross-section of useful information about this landmark operating system and condensed it into the book you see before you.

In researching this book, I have tried to focus on not just How To's but also on the Whys and Wherefores. Too many computer books tell you only how to perform a sample task without explaining how to apply it to your own work. In this book, step-by-step sections explain how to perform specific procedures, and descriptive sections explain general considerations about what you've learned. As you read along and follow the examples, you should not only become adept at using Windows, but you should also learn the most efficient ways to accomplish your own work.

What You Need in Order to Use This Book

There are a few things about your level of knowledge and your computer setup that this book assumes.

What You Should Know

If you are new to computers, you should at least have some understanding of PC terminology. Though Windows 95 takes much of the effort out of using your computer, it's still a good idea for you to understand the difference between things such as RAM and hard-disk memory, for example. And although I'll be covering techniques for performing typical tasks in Windows—such as copying files, formatting disks, and moving between directories—I'm assuming that you already understand why you'd want to do these things in the first place. Of particular importance is a basic understanding of the differences between data files and program files. I'll describe these things within the book, but you may also want to take some time out to bone up on these topics if your knowledge is a little shaky.

What You Should Have

For this book to make sense, and for Windows to work, it is assumed that you have the following:

▶ an IBM or compatible computer with an Intel 80386, 80486, or Pentium (or compatible CPU), with at least 4 MB of RAM and a floppy drive

▶ a hard disk with about 50 MB of free space on it (you can get away with less if you do a Compact install)

▶ optionally, a CD-ROM drive

▶ a Windows-compatible video card and monitor

▶ a printer if you want to use Windows to print out your work on paper. Some of the exercises in this book cover printing, and a whole chapter is devoted exclusively to it. Though not necessary for most of the book, it will be to your advantage if you have a printer.

▶ a mouse. Though you can operate Windows without a mouse (from the keyboard), it's quite a bit more cumbersome to do so. The mouse makes almost all Windows operations so much easier that you really should get hold of one. Most instructions will assume you have a mouse.

How This Book Is Organized

There are essentially six parts to this book. Here's the quick rundown:

Part 1 ...consists of six chapters. The first chapter is an in-depth look at what's so great about Windows 95. If you are a newcomer to Windows, you might opt to skim or skip this chapter—or you may find it interesting. Next is a discussion of some issues facing people upgrading from Windows 3.x to Windows 95. The book gets rolling with Chapter 3, where you'll find step-by-step coverage of the parts of the screen—stuff like what a window is, how to use menus and dialog boxes, that sort of thing. Then, starting with Chapter 4, you'll get started running your programs so you can get your work done rather than having to read this whole book just to write a simple letter. Following that, you'll get some lessons in organizing your work (an important issue on a computer) so you won't be searching all over the place for your projects. Finally, you'll learn how to share information between different documents with simple cut, copy, and paste techniques or with the fancier DDE and OLE methods. After reading this part and following along on your computer, you'll know how to control the Windows graphical environment, run programs, copy data between programs, and manage your files. You should definitely read these chapters if you've never used Windows before.

Part 2 ...takes you the next step in discovering, exploring, and adjusting Windows 95. The section on printing is a must for virtually all users, as everyone wants to print things out, and printers are for one reason or another (it's mostly Murphy's Law) a pain. The section on the Control Panel is great if you like to personalize the way your computer works—colors, mouse pointers, screen savers, fonts, and so on. You'll find stuff here about upgrading your computer to multimedia to use CD-ROMs and sound, the new Properties sheets, using the right mouse button, and the new version of the Windows 3.x File Manager—the Explorer.

Part 3   …is about *communications* (the buzzword these days): e-mail, faxing, working on the Internet, the Microsoft Network, CompuServe, and so forth. Windows 95 has a lot of communications features built right into it, and this section tells you how to use them to best advantage: how to set up your Inbox, your Outbox, and how use what is essentially Windows 95's central switching station—called Microsoft Exchange—to compose, organize, send, and receive e-mail, faxes, and other forms of electronic communications.

Part 4   …covers the supplied programs—the Windows accessories. There you'll learn all the ins and outs of the many helpful programs and utilities supplied with Windows 95. The list has grown considerably since Windows 3.0. The list now includes WordPad, MS Paint, HyperTerminal, Notepad, Phone Dialer, Calculator, Character Map, CD Player, Media Player, Sound Recorder, Backup, ScanDisk, and DriveSpace, among others. Though not the most sophisticated programs in their respective classes, these programs are well thought out, handy, and thrown in for free with Windows. Like me, you'll probably end up using them more than you might think at first, which is why I've included a sizable section on them. Some of the utilities such as the DriveSpace disk-compression program and ScanDisk hard-disk–checking program are extremely useful for getting the most out of your computer system.

Part 5   …is required reading if you're interested in local- or wide-area networking with Windows 95. Even home users have taken to setting up "living room networks" these days, especially as used or hand-me-down computers pile up around the house. And of course, everyone seems to have gotten networked at the office in the past few years. Windows 95 has networking built right in, so these chapters take you from the basics of what networking is through how to install, use, and manage your networking environment. Whether you are new to networks or are an MIS professional, you'll find useful information in this part.

Part 6   ...covers several diverse subjects. The first is how to best take advantage of Windows 95 on a laptop computer, including the use of plug-in cards, docking stations, external monitors, and so on. Various general tips on laptop usage and toting can be found here as well (I am a serious laptop junkie). Next, you'll see that I've come up with some tips for serious Windows 95 hackers who desire to make radical adjustments to the Windows 95 environment. Coverage of some of the more arcane areas of Windows 95 such as multiple-user arrangements, passwords, multiple language support, regional settings, use of the System applet for poking around inside and altering device-driver settings, optimizing the Recycle Bin and virtual memory settings, and an analysis of various performance determinants are discussed here.

Capping off the book, you'll find a chapter on the Windows 95 add-on product Microsoft Plus. Because many Windows 95 users are likely to purchase this product, I decided to cover this add-on package's many attractions and features even though this book is about Windows 95, not about add-ons. But Microsoft Plus dovetails so smoothly with Windows 95 (as they are both from Microsoft) that I decided a discussion of improved disk compression, Internet access, video display enhancements, and automated program control were topics worthy of a few additional pages.

Appendix   ...tells you how to install Windows 95 on your computer.

Conventions Used in This Book

There are a few conventions used throughout this book that you should know about before beginning. First, there are commands that you enter from the keyboard and messages you receive from Windows that appear on your screen. When you have to type something in, the text will be boldface: Enter **a:setup**. When referring to files and folders, the text may be on its own line like this:

```
My thesis on arthropods.doc
```

or it might be included right in a line like this: Now enter the folder name Letters to the Editor.

More often than not, responses from Windows will be shown in figures so you can see just what the screens look like. Sometimes, though, I'll skip the picture and just display the message like this:

```
Cannot read from drive A
```

Second, you'll see sections that look like this:

1. Do this...

2. Do this...

3. Do this...

These are step-by-step instructions (obviously). Although such steps are sometimes example tutorials that are a onetime deal to show you how to use, say, the word processor, more often they're the exact procedures you'll use to perform an everyday task such as formatting a disk. You might want to bookmark such a page for easy future reference.

Finally, there are many notes in this book. They are positioned below the material to which they refer. There are four kinds of margin notes: Note, Tip, Tech Tip, and Caution.

NOTE   Notes give you information pertinent to the procedure or topic being discussed.

TIP   Tips indicate practical hints that might make your work easier.

TECH TIP   Tech Tips are tips that are more technical in nature; they may be skipped by the nontechnical reader.

CAUTION   Cautions alert you to something very important. Generally, they inform you of potential problems you might encounter if you were to follow a procedure incorrectly or without careful forethought.

Before You Begin...

Before you can begin working with Windows, make sure you have correctly installed Windows 95 on your computer's hard disk. A large percentage of what appears to be software problems is often the result of incorrect installation. If your copy of Windows is already installed and operating correctly, you have no need to worry about this and can move ahead to Chapter 1. However, if you haven't installed Windows, you should do so by turning to the Appendix, which covers the Windows Setup program. If your copy of Windows is installed but appears to be operating significantly differently than what is discussed in this book, you might want to seek help from a computer professional or friend who can determine whether your Windows 95 system was installed correctly. For the purposes of this book I installed all the options in my machine, so my setup might look a little different from yours. The chapters about the Control Panel explain how you can install options you may have omitted when initially installing Windows 95 on your computer.

Happy reading. I hope this book helps you on your way to success in whatever line of work (or play) you use your computer for.

Up and Running with Windows 95

1

Chapter 1

Introducing Windows 95

FEATURING

As of this writing, there were an estimated 60 million users of Windows 3.x (3.x includes 3.0, 3.1, and 3.11). That's a lot by any standards, certainly by the standards of PC software sales. Nothing tops that number except for the users of DOS, the operating system running on virtually every IBM PC in the world.

It's likely you're upgrading to Windows 95 from one of its earlier incarnations, so this book will discuss right up front just what's so new and great about Windows 95. Please bear in mind that some terms or concepts may not make sense to you just yet. Don't worry, you'll understand them later as you work through the various chapters in the book. With that said, let's dive into the world of the latest and greatest graphical operating system for IBM PCs.

What Are Windows and Windows 95?

Windows 95 is Microsoft Corporation's latest upgrade to its phenomenally successful and ubiquitous software, which has been generically dubbed *Windows*.

Windows is a class of software called a GUI (graphical user interface). How you interact with your computer to do things like entering data or running programs like the spelling checker is determined by the *interface*. On most computers, the hardware part of the interface consists of your screen and the keyboard. But the software part of the interface determines what things look like on the screen, how you give commands such as "check the spelling" or "print this report" to the computer, how you flip between pages of text, and so forth.

In days of old, before Windows, all this was done with keyboard commands, and often very cryptic ones at that. With the advent of Windows, many everyday computer tasks—such as running programs, opening files, choosing commands, changing a word to italic, and so forth—can be done using a graphical approach that is much more intuitively obvious to people who are new to computers (Figure 1.1). Also, because all Windows programs (even ones from different software manufacturers) use essentially the same commands and graphical items on the screen, once you've mastered your first Windows program, learning others is much easier.

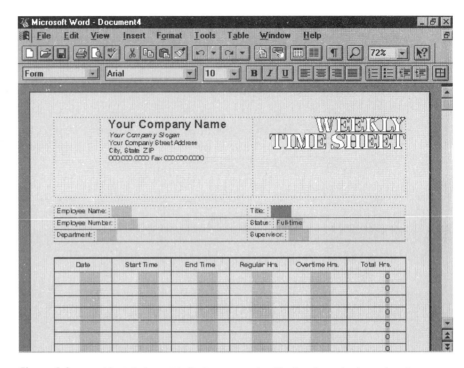

Figure 1.1   Word for Windows 6.0 displays text as it will print. Commands are found on
menus and are fairly consistent between different Windows programs.

If you've used a Mac, you know all its programs work the same way
and look much alike. Non–computer people gravitated to the Mac
over the years primarily because it is easy to use and isn't intimidating.
The problem is that up until recently the Mac's GUI could be used
only on computers made by Apple Corporation, and there weren't
any inexpensive Mac clones, either; Apple saw to that by making it
legally impossible for computer manufacturers to copy the internal
design of the Mac. So if you wanted a computer that was easy for novices to master, you had to pay top dollar for an Apple computer.

Windows changed all that by bringing the essentials of the Macintosh
interface (the mouse, the pointer arrow on the screen, the little icons
on the screen, and so forth) to the IBM PC and the thousands of super-
cheap PC-compatible brands readily available today. Really, Windows
is very much the PC's version of the Mac.

The microcomputer business is software driven. More programs are being written for the Windows platform than all other microcomputer GUIs combined (e.g., NeXTSTEP, OS/2, and variants of Unix). Windows is here to stay.

This being the case, Windows detractors have slowly had to face facts: Windows is the only big game in town, and besides, it really isn't so bad after all. Most Windows applications look and feel identical to their Mac counterparts, and because most users are running programs just to get work done, not critiquing the finer points of the operating system, the issue of Mac vs. PC is technically almost moot at this point.

About Windows 95

Targeting the needs and demands of home and small business users and hoping to keep Windows users from being wooed away by the frills of IBM's OS/2 or various Unix alternatives to DOS and Windows 3.x, Microsoft has spent the last several years developing a robust and feature-rich operating system intended to replace the somewhat glitchy Windows 3.1 and make us all (even Mac users) happy.

And of course, Microsoft thought it wise to address the needs of the burgeoning portable-computer community. Upper management, sales personnel, and technical users who have shifted from desktop systems to heavy reliance on portable computers have developed a new set of computing needs that Windows 95 caters to.

In technical terms, here are some of the features of Windows 95. I'll explain many of these later in this chapter. Windows 95:

▶ Is a graphical operating system much like Windows 3.1, with a face-lift and reliability improvements.

▶ Will run DOS, Windows 3.0 and 3.1, and some Windows NT 32-bit applications. It will be running powerful 32-bit Windows 95 programs as they appear on the market. Microsoft promises that existing Windows 3.x applications will run as fast as—if not faster than—under Windows 3.1 with 4 MB of RAM and even faster with more than 4 MB.

▶ Is not planted on top of an old version of MS-DOS, but rather on a modern DOS designed to work hand-in-hand with Windows 95. The new DOS/Windows 95 combination is finally a full-fledged graphical operating system in its own right, not a GUI tacked on top of a dinosaur. This renders it quite a bit more reliable than its predecessors and also does away with many evils, such as the large DOS "footprint" that impinged on MS-DOS programs running under Windows or the overall lack of stability of the operating system that caused erratic behavior.

▶ Is a multithreaded and preemptive multitasking operating system, which means it can run multiple applications simultaneously more smoothly than did Windows 3.1, especially if those programs are of the new breed of 32-bit applications written for Windows 95 or Windows NT. If the programs are of the older 16-bit variety designed for Windows 3.x, they will take less advantage of Windows 95's preemptive features, but overall system performance will still be smoother than in Windows 3.x.

▶ Has major portions of the operating system written in 32-bit code, taking better advantage of the Intel 80386, 80486, and Pentium processors. The memory manager, scheduler, and process manager are all 32-bit. Some sections of the operating system are still written in 16-bit code to ensure compatibility with existing 16-bit applications, however.

▶ Has a more Mac-like interface, doing away with the confusing Program Manager/File Manager design and incorporating a single integrated arrangement that allows you to place document icons and folders right on the Windows Desktop and work with them from there. A *Taskbar*, always easily accessible on screen, has buttons listing the currently running applications, letting you easily switch between them.

▶ Supports long file names rather than the severely limited eight-letter (8.3) file names used by DOS. In Windows 95, files can have names up to 255 characters long. This applies even to files used and created in DOS boxes.

▶ Stores the bulk of important hardware settings, system settings, applications settings, and user-rights settings in a central location called the Registry. These settings were previously stored in a number of different files such as `autoexec.bat`, `config.sys`, `win.ini`, and `system.ini` files. This arrangement allows for a more easily managed PC. These settings can be accessed from a remote PC on a network, allowing a network administrator to more easily maintain a network of corporate PCs.

 NOTE For backward compatibility with older device drivers and systems, the autoexec.bat and config.sys files are still used by Windows 95, so the implementation of the Registry is not as complete as it is in Windows NT. However, reliance on the older files is greatly lessened, with Windows 95 doing more system housekeeping than before and using 32-bit device drivers when possible.

▶ Lets you set up the computer for use by different people, each with their own Desktop, shared resources, user rights, and other settings.

▶ Supports installable 32-bit file systems, allowing easier future expansion of Windows 95 to incorporate other file-system schemes. It also ensures faster disk performance than the 16-bit file system used by Windows 3.1 and DOS.

▶ Is more proficient at cleaning up after a faulty application crash, thus preventing Windows from crashing altogether (i.e., you'll see fewer General Protection Fault error messages). If a program crashes, you can eliminate it from the task list without affecting other running applications. Memory and other resources the application was using are freed for use by the system.

▶ Automatically adapts more fully to the hardware it is running on and thus requires less fine-tuning to take full advantage of your particular computer setup, available disk space, amount of RAM, and so forth.

▶ Provides much more *conventional memory* space for DOS applications by implementing device drivers such as SmartDrive, mouse drivers, share.exe, CD-ROM, and SCSI device drivers as 32-bit VxDs handled by Windows 95. This means that with Windows 95 there's less chance of running out of memory space for your DOS applications.

▶ Includes built-in peer-to-peer networking, much like Windows for Workgroups, only with more-efficient 32-bit network drivers as well as support for the increasingly popular TCP/IP protocol for accessing Unix-based systems such as the Internet. It also supports NDIS 2.x, 3.x, and ODI drivers and will provide 32-bit NetBEUI and IPX/SPX as well. Redirectors for SMB and NCP-based networks will be included. (Sorry about all the acronyms!) The upshot is that a Windows 95 workstation will interface easily with most existing local- and wide-area networks such as NetWare, Banyan, LANtastic, Windows NT, LAN Manager, Windows for Workgroups, and many others. These network connections can be mixed and matched, and you'll work on these networks using the same commands and interface regardless of which one you're connected to.

▶ Incorporates Object Linking and Embedding version 2.0. This allows you to easily create fancy compound documents combining information from several different application programs, especially when using applications that support OLE 2.0 (Figure 1.2). This makes it a cinch to incorporate graphs, charts, music, video, clip art, and so forth right into your word-processing documents.

▶ Is more document-centric than Windows 3.1. This means that the new Windows user interface lets you organize your work on the computer by organizing your documents on the Desktop or in folders, then clicking on them to open them (Figure 1.3). You don't have to think about finding and running a specific application, then finding and

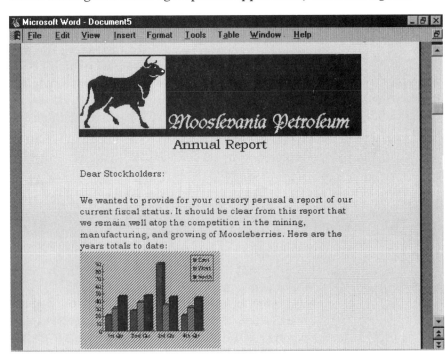

Figure 1.2   Windows 95's OLE 2.0 makes creating complex documents a simple process.

Up and Running
with Windows 95

opening a given document. You just organize your documents into folders named things like My PhD Thesis and click on each one to open it. You can create a new document simply by clicking on the Desktop and choosing New from a pop-up menu.

▶ Offers workstation security (within limits), some useful administration tools, and system tools (such as disk doublers) and comes with more than a handful of useful (though limited) accessory applications.

▶ Has Remote-Access Services, which allow Windows 95 users on the road to call into a Windows 95 network, log on, and connect just as they do from their desktop machine, sharing data and resources supplied by network servers, printers, fax modems, and other workstations.

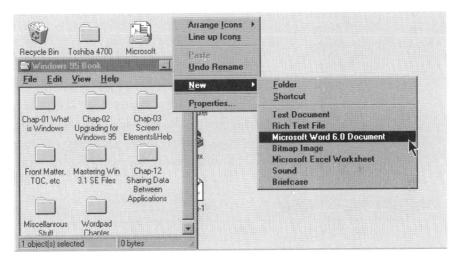

Figure 1.3   *Document-centricity means you organize and work with your computer the same way you organize and work at your desk. You simply put your documents on the Desktop or in a folder. You open the folder or find the document on the Desktop and open it. You create a new item by clicking the right mouse button and choosing New.*

▶ Supports the new Plug-and-Play standard being developed by PC makers that allows you to simply plug a new board (such as a video or network card) into your computer without having to set switches or make other settings. Windows 95 will figure out what you plugged in and make it work. No more configuration headaches!

▶ Supports PCMCIA cards for laptop computers and the use of laptop docking stations. Without rebooting the operating system, it will acknowledge what you plugged in and automatically reconfigure the system accordingly.

▶ Supports a new mail system called Microsoft Exchange for managing all the types of messages computer users typically have to deal with, such as e-mail, Internet communications, faxes, and documents. No need for separate communications programs (such as Microsoft Mail, WinCIM, or Eudora) or fax programs (such as WinFAX). Once set up, clicking a single button gets and sends e-mail from CompuServe, Internet, The Microsoft Network, or a network e-mail post office, and also sends queued-up faxes.

▶ Comes with a disk-compression program you can easily run right in Windows, essentially doubling your hard-disk space without having to purchase a new hard disk. Disk doubling can be used on floppies, too, making a 1.44-MB disk store up to 2.88 MB. The compression/decompression tool is much more facile to use than in previous incarnations of DOS or Windows, letting you *easily* change the size of compressed partitions.

These are the main new features. Now for some explanation and discussion on a few of the more salient topics listed here.

Preemptive What??

Many of the adjectives listed above probably sound like marketing hype, so let me break down the terminology a bit. Let's start with *preemptive multitasking*. Operating systems that can run a number of programs at once, such as Windows 3.1, OS/2, and Windows NT (not just software *switchers* like the DOS-based Software Carousel or Multiple Choice, which basically put one application to sleep while resuming another), need some means of servicing each of the running programs. For example, you might be typing a letter in Word for Windows while Excel is calculating a spreadsheet and you're printing a brochure you just set up in PageMaker. As you know, all these activities can occur in a typical Windows 3.1 session (though not always smoothly, of course). How can Windows do that?

Well, it's the miracle of *multitasking*, and it works much the same way you do when you're driving a car, listening to the radio, and having a conversation with a friend. The computer's "attention" switches very rapidly among the jobs it's doing. In the computer, attention to a job occurs when the CPU chip (e.g., the brains of the computer—the 486 chip, for example) turns its sights on that job and begins processing away on it. This is called giving the task "CPU time."

Now here's the catch. In Windows 3.1, this attention-switching process doesn't always behave properly. This is because of the way Windows 3.1 assigns CPU time to tasks. Ideally, no job should hog the CPU's time because this will bring other tasks to a halt. Windows 3.1 programs are supposed to be written in such a way that they use only small slices of CPU time, allowing other running applications to have the CPU, too. However, if the application was written poorly, this didn't always happen. Some programs, such as File Manager, for example, could effectively sabotage time-sensitive programs such as fax or communications programs by hogging the CPU's attention while copying files.

Windows 3.1's multitasking style is referred to as *cooperative multitasking*. On the other hand, Windows 95's *preemptive* multitasking doesn't leave control of the CPU up to the applications, but rather gives this responsibility to the operating system itself. Thus, Windows 95 can *preempt* one program's CPU time and democratically allot it to another whenever Windows 95 deems necessary. Because the operating system itself also needs attention from the CPU to keep the basics of the computer going, it can also demand CPU time as it sees fit. The overall effect of preemptive multitasking is to ensure that you can keep working with a minimum of instances of the old hourglass cursor telling you to wait. Also, application mixes that might have previously caused problems in Windows 3.1 shouldn't cause even a hiccup in Windows 95. Background communications sessions, for example, shouldn't drop data while other CPU-intensive tasks are running.

Another advantage is that in Windows 95, you'll not only find that single tasks are prevented from bringing others to a crawl, but the scheduler—the part of the operating system responsible for doling out the CPU time—can see to it that some applications are given a higher priority than others.

Multithreading?

If you've followed the reviews of Windows 95 (and NT for that matter) over the last year or two, you've probably heard the term *threading* bandied about rather glibly. Here's the scoop on threading, in everyday language.

Every task that Windows 95 performs, whether it's copying a file, calculating a statistical average, accessing the system's clock, or fetching some data from RAM, can be referred to as a *process*. During any given time period, Windows is busily performing and switching between these processes, as discussed above in the section about tasking. Thus, processes are for all intents and purposes identical to tasks.

In Windows 95 (as well as in NT), processes are further divisible into *threads*. Although most processes contain only a single thread, this isn't always the case. A single process can consist of multiple threads if the programmer writes it that way. Lost yet?

Here's an example. A typical thread would be the recalculation part of a spreadsheet program. Another thread might be the part of the program that charts a graph for you. Another two might be file saving and printing. Breaking the program down this way lets you, in Windows 95, perform these functions concurrently. By contrast, if the whole program were written as a single thread, you wouldn't be able to do the chart until the recalculation was complete or save a file until printing was finished.

The salient point is that smartly written applications can now run very smoothly—in fact much more smoothly than under Windows 3.1.

Although Windows 95 is being touted as all new and improved, what it offers the user isn't really all that new. Many of Windows 95's features have been around in other forms for some time. For example, OS/2 and the Macintosh operating system have both offered a nice object-oriented interface, one much more intuitive than Windows 3.1's. Windows NT and various forms of Unix (such as NeXTSTEP) offer sophisticated application protection and smooth preemptive multitasking. And connectivity experts such as Novell have been meeting the needs of serious corporate MIS departments with state-of-the-art networking and remote-access capabilities for years.

What *is* new is that Microsoft has done its research, fine-tuned its product, and wrapped it up neatly in one package—a package that works right out of the box. With just a little work, you can be up and running Windows 95 on a single station or set up a workgroup on a number of PCs with very little hassle. If you're upgrading a machine from Windows 3.x, all your application groups in Program Manager and the pertinent Windows settings—such as installed fonts, Desktop settings, application settings, and so forth—from the `system.ini` and `win.ini` files will automatically migrate over from Windows 3.1. All your Windows 3.x and DOS applications will run as fast, if not faster. Next, throw into the mix the ability to run the efficient 32-bit applications that'll soon appear, the support of long file names, and a more intuitive interface. Finally, mix in the facts that Windows 95 promises to work with all your existing Windows 3.1 hardware drivers (such as those for fax modems, scanners, mice, video cards, sound cards, and so on), that it has remote-access communications ability, supports Plug and Play, and allows an MIS professional to manage a Windows 95 PC from across the network, and all this adds up to a pretty spiffy package.

The Importance of Application Software

Even though the first iterations of Windows had shortcomings, the sheer number of software programs available for them ensured their success. If the demand were only for a serious operating system with most or even all of the features Windows provided, Windows 3.1 wouldn't have really caught on. Corporations heavily invested in PC-based information systems could have adopted Unix or OS/2 en masse by now, but they haven't bothered. These alternatives have been feature-rich, and each has had an advantage over Windows, but the success of an operating system, particularly in business settings, has more to do with application availability and compatibility than any other variable.

Actually, to be fair, applications aren't the only thing that matters when choosing an operating system. MIS professionals need to not only think about what's available for the platform, but whether their current hardware, software, and training investments will be jeopardized or enhanced by a specific operating-system decision.

First and foremost, Windows 95 is simply supposed to make single-user PCs and laptops easier to learn and use and easier to fully exploit. Studies have shown that the majority of PC users are confused by their computers and feel that they are not taking full advantage of the power they paid dearly for when purchasing their PC. For example, most Windows 3.1 users do not know they can run multiple programs simultaneously, don't know what happens to one program when another program's window overlaps it, and are afraid to use the File Manager.

Secondly, Windows 95 was designed to make networking easier. Workgroups that don't need serious data protection and/or security shouldn't be a hassle to set up, configure, and maintain. With Windows 95, networking is much easier both to set up and to use. It also offers remote management of the workstation. For example, a manager can connect to and alter the security settings on a Windows 95-equipped PC from anywhere on its network, even via remote access from home or another city.

Finally, Windows 95 implements some of the newest technology available (such as Plug and Play), pushing PC manufacturers into finalizing design and development of those emerging technologies in hopes of maintaining a competitive edge against other lines of computers. All three of these strategies, of course, are geared towards making PCs friendlier and thus spurring on the sales of computers and software.

This appears to be fairly true of Windows 95. As a result, if you are using MS-DOS, Windows 3.x, or Windows for Workgroups, migration to Windows 95 will be relatively easy. Most applications will work fine under Windows 95, and sometimes faster than in Windows 3.x. Windows 3.x settings will be imported into Windows 95 so your Windows 95 Program Manager, Control Panel, and applications settings will be automatically preconfigured for you.

NOTE   Actually a File Manager and Program Manager à la Windows 3.x are supplied with Windows 95, just to help veteran users get over the hump. However, the idea is that once you get used to the new interface, you won't find yourself using them much anymore. Instead, you'll use the Taskbar to launch and switch applications and the Desktop to manage your documents. To dig into the file system, you'll use the new turbocharged File Manager replacement called the Explorer.

Unlike NT, which boasts the ability to escape crashed hard drives and power outages on huge networks with nary a hiccup, Windows 95 is no Houdini. However, Windows 95 has other key features. For example, it's the first Microsoft product since Windows 3.0 to offer a significantly improved interface (one that will be incorporated into NT's Cairo version, incidentally). It was also designed to run very well without users having to do much of anything to their systems, particularly adding RAM or upgrading to a faster processor. (By contrast, Windows NT Workstation requires 8 MB *minimum* and a fast 486.) Windows 95 should run reasonably well on a 386DX 33 or better, with as little as 4 MB of RAM (though I'd suggest 8).

Windows 95 is aimed at the mass-market, non-power users, who may or may not be networked. Most new computers will be shipped with Windows 95, just as they have been with Windows 3.x. For many demanding networking needs Windows 95 will also suffice, allowing connection to other Windows 95 workstations, to NT Workstation and NT Server, to Novell, and to LAN Manager, Banyan Vines, and the Internet, among others. Support for additional networks can be easily added by the network supplier.

Which Operating System for the Desktop or Laptop?

In our opinion, Windows 95 is currently the ideal solution for the bulk of Windows users. Even OS/2 users will probably want to come back to the fold, because Windows 95 now has everything that OS/2 does (except, of course, the ability to run OS/2-specific software). In my opinion, certainly everyone currently running Windows 3.1 should upgrade, assuming they have a 386DX-based PC or higher. Judging just from my use of the Windows 95 beta software, I can say that Windows 95 runs much more smoothly and crashes less often than Windows 3.1, recovers more gracefully from an application crash, and once you get used to doing things a bit differently in Windows 95, manages your documents more efficiently.

Which Client Operating System to Choose—NT Workstation or Windows 95?

Because there are two Windows workstation operating systems (NT Workstation and Windows 95), which should you choose? And is Microsoft shooting itself in the foot by offering both?

Actually, Microsoft's strategy makes sense. There are two options because there are two markets for network workstations—high performance and low performance. If your applications require the utmost in performance or if your application mix is highly network oriented, you are using large networks, and you need top-notch workstation and network management, you should be using NT (or possibly Novell NetWare).

Windows NT provides US Government "C-2"-rated security features. For most intents and purposes, NT has essentially bulletproof security that can prevent an unauthorized user from entering the system or in other ways gaining access to files on the hard disk. Without a proper password, NT can totally protect sensitive files from being reached. Tools for assigning permission levels for various tasks are supplied, providing great flexibility in security arrangements.

If the application mix is heavy on the Windows side, I'd especially recommend NT (over NetWare) because NetWare tacked on top of DOS with Windows tacked on top of that can lead to some headaches. For one thing, it decreases the available conventional memory for DOS applications. NT removes at least one software level and has IPX/SPX drivers to connect with NetWare networks if you need to. Figure 1.4 demonstrates this. Connection to a NetWare network with Windows 3.1 and DOS requires three levels (four modules) of software. Connection with Windows 95 requires just one, with the inherent security and connectivity advantages of Windows 95. If you're running only DOS applications, stick with NetWare.

Consider that if you need to run Unix applications, NT may be able to run them because it can handle any Unix applications written to the POSIX specification.

 NOTE   To be specific, NT can only run POSIX applications written in compliance with the POSIX 1003.1 specification.

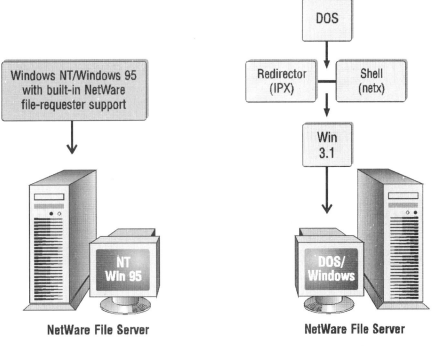

Figure 1.4   *32-bit NetWare drivers are incorporated into both Windows 95 and Windows NT, improving performance and eliminating hassles caused by loading NetWare drivers into DOS.*

It can also run many OS/2 applications. Finally, if your machines are speedy 486s or Pentiums well-endowed with RAM (and thus you wouldn't have to upgrade your hardware), why not go for NT? Just make sure that all your add-in boards and devices have NT device drivers available before you begin. Remember, NT can't use your old Windows 3.1 16-bit device drivers for your printers, video boards, mice, SCSI drives, CD-ROM drives, sound cards, and the like. It needs special 32-bit drivers written for NT.

Now for the Windows 95 argument. If the computers you are considering upgrading aren't top of the line, if having a fully 32-bit operating system with C2-level system security is nothing more than academic to you, and if you'd like to have Chicago's new object-oriented user interface as soon as possible, then Windows 95 is a sensible choice.

You can start with all Windows 95 workstations connected to one another in a peer-to-peer fashion (see Part V on networking for more about peer-to-peer networks) and then add an NT Server station later if you want more network security and performance. And remember that if you have been using or are still using a NetWare network, 32-bit NetWare client support is built in. Getting a Windows workstation up and running on a NetWare network is finally a no-brainer.

About Remote-Access Services

I've mentioned the term "remote access" (or RAS for Remote-Access Services) several times in this chapter, usually touting it as a considerable bonus to the Windows 95 user. But what exactly is RAS?

RAS allows you to dial into a network or even a single computer from a remote computer (such as a laptop) over phone lines. Each computer has a modem to connect it to the phone lines. You simply call the host machine's modem (typically back at the office) from your computer out in the field. After the host machine's modem answers, and you log onto the system with your name and password, interaction is just as if you were at the host site using the computer. For example, you could call up from home, log in, send a print job to the laser printer, use some data on a mainframe (if the network is attached to one), run applications, leave e-mail for other users, and so on. Figure 1.5 illustrates the RAS connection. Though the illustration depicts a network as the recipient of the call, you could use RAS to connect to a standalone computer as well, such as a desktop machine in your office.

You can think of a RAS connection as nothing more than a network connection made over a modem instead of through the direct cable connection that other workstations on the network use. Such a connection isn't the same as running a *remote-control* program such as PC-Anywhere with which you "take over" a remote computer. You're simply logging on as a network client.

The Windows 95 workstation that receives the call can act as a RAS server to the rest of the network, whether that network is a Windows NT, NetWare, or Windows 95-based network. RAS can also be used, incidentally, for cabled connections (through a serial port à la LapLink), infrared connections, or wireless links between two local PCs.

Setting up RAS can be a hassle. Microsoft has added a Wizard that helps the uninitiated user do this. Figure 1.6 shows the dialog box for setting up RAS for a Windows 95 PC.

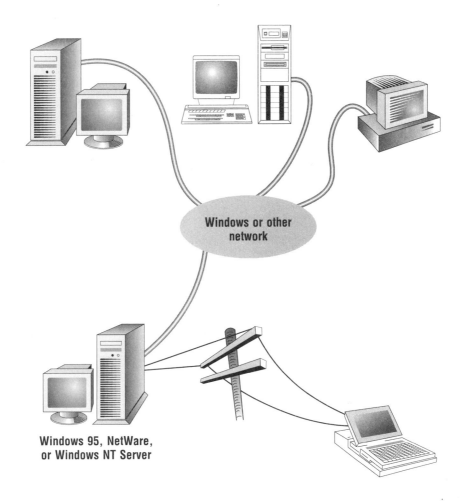

Windows or other network

Windows 95, NetWare, or Windows NT Server

Figure 1.5 Remote-Access Services in Windows 95 lets you connect to a network or an office computer as though you were there.

User Interface Problems

When you run Windows 95 for the first time, its new look and feel are evident. Windows has been given a face-lift that is as obvious as the one that marked the introduction of Windows 3.0. Previous versions looked nothing like it. Figures 1.7 and 1.8 illustrate the difference between the Windows 3.1 and Windows 95 start-up screens.

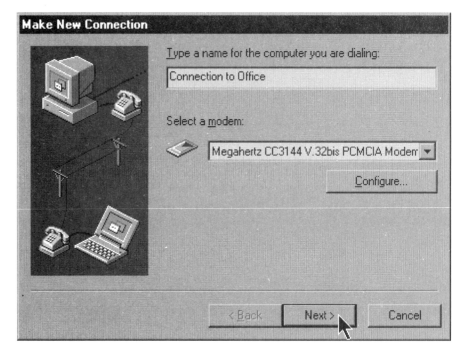

Figure 1.6   Setting up a RAS connection is fairly straightforward.

USABILITY STUDIES AND THE NEW INTERFACE

Much of the retooling of Windows for the Windows 95 release has centered on the need for a more sophisticated, robust, and powerful operating system that could keep up with the competition and could take full advantage of the hefty hardware many computer users were purchasing. From a software architectural design perspective, the internals of the 16-bit DOS/Windows combination were way more than ready for a serious upgrade.

Programmers have been chomping at the bit for a true 32-bit operating system with a "flat" memory model—an arrangement that renders programming infinitely simpler. Programmers tired years ago of writing 16-bit code simply to be backward-compatible with the ancient 8086 and 80286 microprocessors. Those chips' memory-offset requirements are a major headache.

If the success of a computer operating system or GUI is dependent on application availability, then it can also be said that application availability is tied to ease of writing for that platform. Microsoft is certainly well aware of this and is supplying programmers with Windows-related tool- and software-development kits.

Up and Running
with Windows 95

The major difference, you will note, is that there is no Program Manager window evident. Though Windows 95 sports many subtle aesthetic improvements such as more attractive menus, sunken dialog box buttons, and so forth, probably the resolution of what I call the "Program Manager/File Manager dichotomy" is the most striking advance.

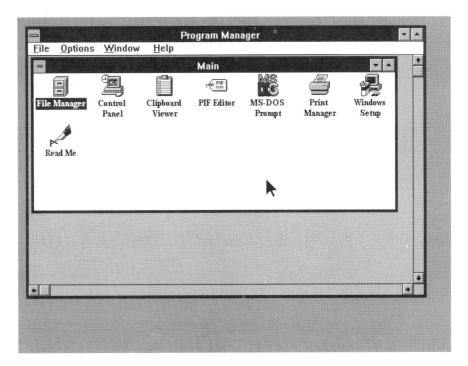

Figure 1.7   Typical Windows 3.1 start-up screen

Shells

Detractors of Windows have made a hobby of pointing out the shortcomings of the Windows *shell*. The shell refers to the control program that you use to interact with an operating system. With MS-DOS, for example, the shell is provided by `command.com`—the command-line interface. You simply type in commands at the C:> prompt and press Enter. With Windows, the big attraction is that you could point and click on icons to essentially issue commands to the command-line interpreter. Some think this is easier than typing in commands. Others think it is more abstract even than typing commands.

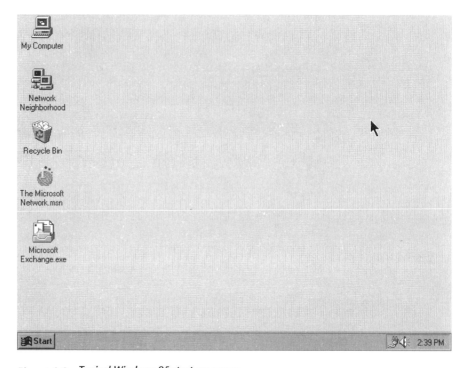

Figure 1.8   Typical Windows 95 start-up screen

Since Windows 3.0, the shell (when the MS-DOS Executive of earlier Windows versions was removed) has consisted primarily of Program Manager and File Manager. (Technically, the Control Panel, Task Manager, and Print Manager also form portions of the shell.) Program Manager allowed you to organize your favorite documents and applications into groups by adding representative icons to the group window. Then, by opening the correct group window and clicking on the desired icon, the associated document or program would open.

This was a nifty idea, but problems arose because users didn't grasp a fundamental concept: These icons were really *aliases*, not documents or programs themselves. Dragging the icons around within the shell didn't actually manipulate the object they were pointed to by the icon. And likewise, deleting one of these icons didn't actually remove the item from the hard disk—only from the group window in Program Manager. Even more challenging to figure out was how to add new icons to your program groups. Without a fairly thorough understanding of DOS's directory structure, this was next to impossible.

The only time most users saw new icons appear in groups was when they installed a new application. Application-installation programs would often mysteriously create new groups and add icons to groups, but most users didn't know how this happened.

An obvious void was created by Program Manager's lack of skills. If Program Manager couldn't perform real file operations such as copying, deleting, moving, and creating documents, how were these chores to be done? File Manager was the solution, but research at the Microsoft usability lab determined that people did not easily grasp File Manager's use of a hierarchical tree structure in the left pane and a matching "contents" pane on the right side, as Figure 1.9 illustrates.

In addition to the conceptual problems people have with File Manager, its power to wreak havoc on the operating system when put in the wrong hands is considerable! One slip of the mouse, and the unsuspecting novice can unwittingly produce such glorious effects as relegating the Windows directory to the status of a subdirectory of, say, the WordPerfect directory. After a slick move like this, Windows

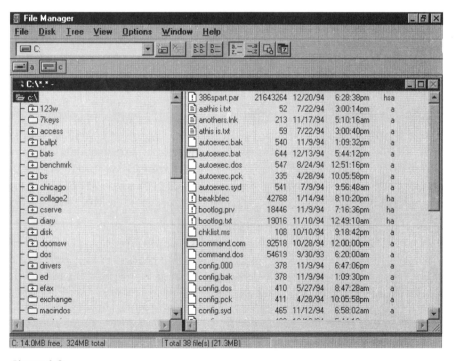

Figure 1.9 *Typical two-pane File Manager screen*

won't even boot. Because no simple utilities are provided for helping users easily and safely copy files from drive to drive (such as to make backups of critical documents on a floppy), catastrophes such as this have happened far too frequently in Windows.

Finally, consider a few other problems inherent in the Windows 3.1 interface:

▶ When Windows first boots, users are faced with numerous strange icons and no intuitively easy way to begin working.

▶ Users don't understand that icons only appear on the Desktop when applications are running and their windows are minimized.

▶ It isn't possible to leave icons representing documents on the Desktop for use the next time the users boot up.

▶ Unless there is an association set up in File Manager for a specific document type (as identified by its three-letter DOS file extension), double-clicking on the document in File Manager results in an error message. The procedure for setting up associations is too complex for most users.

▶ File names are limited to the MS-DOS "8.3" naming convention, which doesn't cut the mustard for most users. Trying to create and remember cryptic file names such as RPT4DAVE.DOC is a royal headache for everyone. This was simply a carryover from DOS days.

▶ The Task Manager, the means for switching between running applications, is little known and generally misunderstood. Pressing Alt-Tab, Ctrl-Esc, or double-clicking on the Desktop are tricks the average Windows user is ignorant of and has little likelihood of discovering. (In Microsoft's own terminology, it was "undiscoverable.") As a result, once an application window is obscured from view by another window, many users didn't realize the covered application was still running.

For power users, these shortcomings weren't tragic. People simply worked around them. Many other users scouted around for an alternative to Program Manager after deciding to ditch it. The dilemma with all the alternative approaches is that they introduce user-interface inconsistency in the computer workplace—something corporate computer professionals had hoped Windows would help eliminate!

In researching ways to improve the Windows user interface, Microsoft relied on several sources. In fact, it's quite likely that the interface of Windows 95 is the most thoroughly researched piece of software ever developed. Several phases of study were conducted in a variety of settings:

▶ *Usability Lab test groups.* Users were watched from behind mirrors and taped with video cameras as they performed tasks such as launching programs, creating new files, and printing. Their interaction at the keyboard and mouse as well as their reactions were all recorded and later analyzed by experts in learning theory and cognition.

▶ *Long-Term Testing.* Longer-term testing, also know as *summative* testing, was conducted both at Microsoft and in the field at various customer locations.

▶ *Expert consultants.* Experts in user interfaces were hired to perform a professional critique of the Windows 95 interface.

Reactions to the product design were then tabulated, digested, and fed back to the design, development, and programming staff.

Document Centrality

In addition to control issues, Microsoft claims its research findings indicated that a new interface would have to be made more *document-centric.* Recall that this means that rather than thinking about running applications and then opening documents from the application, you'll simply locate the desired document and open it.

As things stand today, Windows 3.1 and NT are primarily application-centric: Users typically first run the desired application, such as Excel, then use the File ➤ Open command and resulting dialog box to dredge through the DOS directory tree to find the document.

In a document-centric world, the computer's operating system assumes the job of appropriately linking the document and the application that created it. All the user needs do is find the document (just like in the physical world) and double-click on it. Once clicked on, the document launches the associated application and opens the document in it. Windows 95 determines the appropriate application by checking information stored in the system Registry.

There are some important features that make Windows 95 significantly more document-centric:

▶ As mentioned earlier, you can create new documents right from the Desktop by clicking the right mouse button and choosing New, or you can wander through your document folders (without using File Manager or Program Manager) and pull any existing documents onto the Desktop in icon form for super-easy access. This is done from the *My Computer* icon, which I'll discuss below. Figures 1.10 and 1.11 illustrate these two approaches.

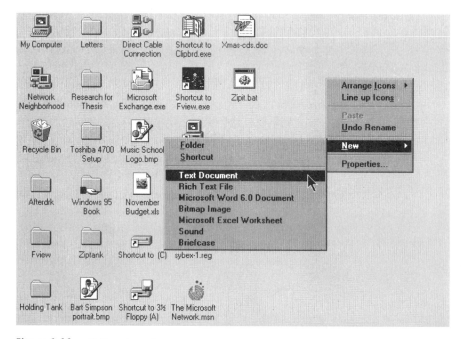

Figure 1.10 *Clicking the right mouse button on the Desktop lets you create a new document in any application that will install itself appropriately in the Registry.*

▶ Another document-centric tool is supplied as part of the Taskbar's Start button. The Start button, which is always visible on the screen and in easy reach (unless you choose to hide the Taskbar), provides a number of handy shortcuts I'll describe in detail below. Among other things, it remembers and lists the last fifteen or so documents you've been working on, regardless of application. Simply clicking on the Start button and choosing *Documents* displays the list. Then you just

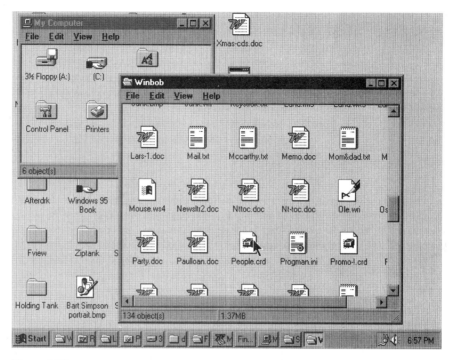

Figure 1.11   *Opening documents from the My Computer window*

select the document you want to work with. Windows 95 launches the application and loads the document (Figure 1.12).

▶ Windows 95's OLE 2 brings you a more document-centric feeling because you can edit embedded objects in place.

▶ Finally, Windows 95 gives a document window the same name as the document that was double-clicked on. Clicking on a document named *Fred's Thesis* opens a window called *Fred's Thesis* in the appropriate application. (This assumes the application was written to take advantage of long file names, which means that the application is a Windows 95 application.)

The Desktop

I've described a few of the Desktop's features above (see Chapter 3 for more detail). Take a look again at how the Desktop first appears when you boot Windows 95 (Figure 1.13).

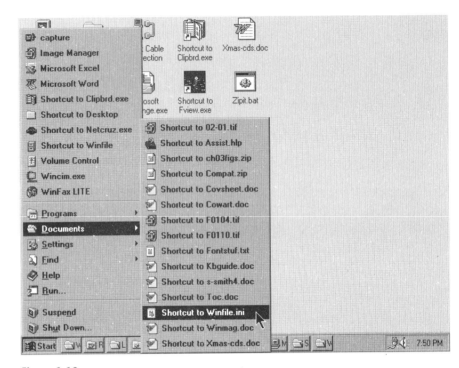

Figure 1.12   Using the Start button to open a document

Microsoft's simplifications here render access to system and network components such as disk directories (now called folders) and workstations much more graphical. Let's take a look at each of these new elements and discuss how they affect the way you'll work with Windows 95.

The Taskbar

The Taskbar (Chapter 3) can be placed at any of the four edges of your screen, and it can be set to get lost (disappear) when you don't want it and to reappear when you move the pointer to the far edge of the screen or press Ctrl-Esc. Figure 1.14 illustrates.

The Taskbar has two primary functions: it's a program launcher and a task switcher. It's also a bit of a status bar, containing a clock and little icons to indicate such things as waiting e-mail, that you're printing a document, volume settings for sound, and the battery condition

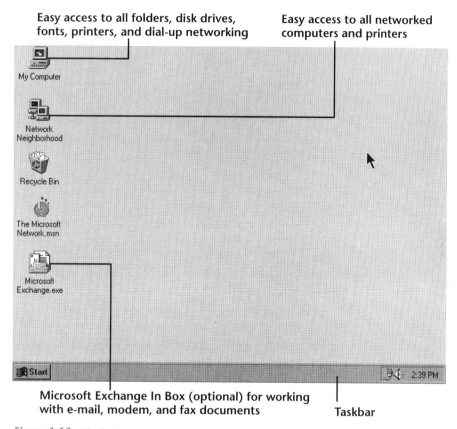

Easy access to all folders, disk drives,
fonts, printers, and dial-up networking

Easy access to all networked
computers and printers

Microsoft Exchange In Box (optional) for working
with e-mail, modem, and fax documents

Taskbar

Figure 1.13   **The basic Desktop**

for laptops. Clicking on one of the icons typically brings up a related settings box.

The Start button at the far left end of the bar (or top, when the bar is located on the side of the screen) is responsible for launching applications, opening documents, and making settings (see Figure 1.15).

Any buttons to the right of the Start button represent currently running programs or open folders and are for task switching.

The figure shows what happens when you click on the Start button— a menu appears. Notice that four of these menu choices—Programs, Documents, Settings, and Find—are *cascading* menus: choosing any one of these opens a submenu. In the case of the Programs choice, the submenu lists what amount to Program Manager groups. If you

Figure 1.14 **The Taskbar can be relocated.**

upgraded to Windows 95 from Windows 3.1, your existing Program Manager groups are ported into this new format, which is quicker and easier to use than the old Program Manager was.

If you're dual-booting Windows 3.x and Windows 95 (which is possible should you feel the need to keep Windows 3.11 around for a while), each time you boot Windows 95, a Program Group converter ensures this list of groups is up to date. This also happens when you use the supplied Program Manager to adjust the contents of your

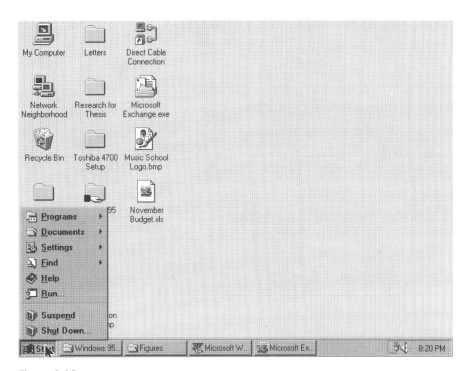

Figure 1.15 The Start button

groups. However, there's another more intuitive and more direct way to alter the contents of groups. That option is available through the Start button's *Start Menu* option. I'll get into that a little later in this section.

The Start button's Program option lets you set up groups within groups within groups, and everything is alphabetized. Figure 1.16 illustrates nesting with the Games group (we'll start calling groups *folders* soon, incidentally, so get ready), which is a subgroup of the Accessories group.

NOTE   Though the Program button is intended to help you launch your programs, actually it will display whatever *is* in existing group folders. Thus, documents such as `Readme` files that come with applications that are dumped into a program's folder will also display in the list. Such documents when double-clicked on will open in an appropriate window. You can also organize any of your own documents in this way. Thus, the Start button provides a neat, clean, and organized way for users to hierarchically arrange their documents as well as their programs.

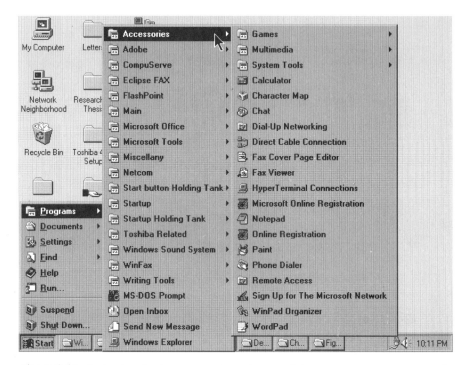

Figure 1.16 *Notice that the Games group is a subgroup of the Accessories group. Nesting of groups is possible in Windows 95, whereas it wasn't in Windows 3.x.*

One last feature of the Start button is that instead of walking through the cascading menus to reach one of your favorite applications, you can just add it to the first-level menu. For example, say you wanted Word for Windows available for launching right from the Start button. You just use the Settings option, which I'll explain in a minute. The result would look something like this:

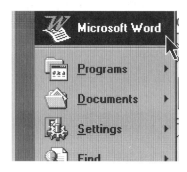

The Latest Document List

Moving along down the Start button's options, consider the next one, Documents (Chapter 4). Choose this option, and a list of the last fifteen documents you've worked with are revealed. Figure 1.17 displays an example.

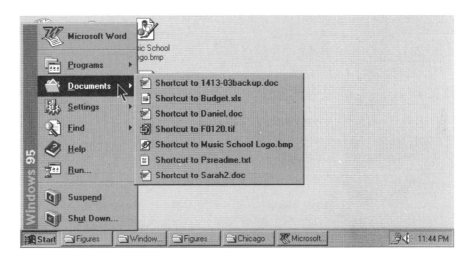

Figure 1.17   *The Document option on the Start button makes getting to the last fifteen documents you've been editing much easier.*

Just click on the document you want. The document appears in the appropriate application window. One caveat is that only selected applications know how to update this Documents list. Thus, not all of your most recently edited documents will appear there.

The Settings Option

By building a Settings option (Chapter 7) right into the Start button, the path to system customization is much more discoverable.

When you click on Settings, you'll see the menu shown here:

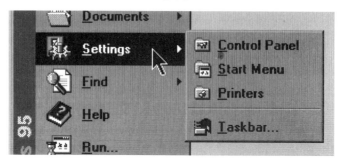

The options are Control Panel, Start Menu, Printers, and Taskbar.

Control Panel   This option simply runs the Control Panel, which operates much the same way the old one did. The only changes are a few new *applets* (icons for specific kinds of settings) and a new style of dialog boxes for each applet.

Start Menu   This displays a window somewhat similar to the old Program Manager, only with groups shown as folder icons rather than the traditional boxy-shaped Program Manager icons. Figure 1.18 shows you what I mean.

These folders are *live*, meaning you can run applications and open documents here. You can also create new folders, move applications and documents around between folders, and so on. Figure 1.19 shows an example of a folder open in a new window.

Printers   Simply click on Printers (see Chapter 8), and you'll see an icon for each installed printer and an additional icon called Add Printer, used for installing a new printer.

Double-clicking on one of the printers will give you something you wouldn't expect: a Print Manager-like window for each printer, showing print jobs currently queued up for the printer. You can make configuration changes to the printer here as well as rearrange the print queue or delete print jobs.

Now for the coup de grâce. Want to install a new printer? Microsoft's little helpful taskmasters, the Wizards, have been built into Windows 95

Up and Running
with Windows 95

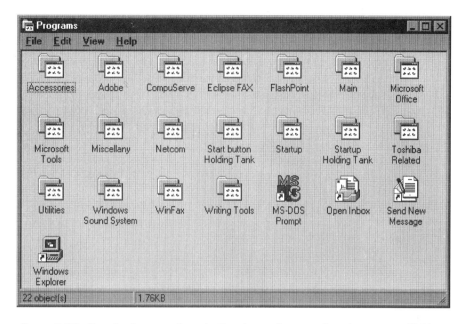

Figure 1.18   *Choosing Programs from the Start button lets you adjust the contents of folders*
(groups), including which applications will appear on the first level of the Start
menu. You can also run applications and open documents from here.

to make life easier for novices. Wizards walk you through complex
tasks and even in some cases do the whole task for you.

When you click on the Add New Printers icon, up comes a series of
Wizard dialog boxes, asking some simple questions about the printer.

Taskbar   The final option on the Settings menu is Taskbar (Chapter 7).
This lets you set up some nifty aspects of the Taskbar. Notice the new
tabular design of the dialog box. Clicking on a tab brings its page of settings to the front.

The first page lets you add your most-used programs to the top of the
Start menu. The second page is for setting some useful Taskbar options,
such as when it will disappear and whether the time and various other
indicators will appear on the bar.

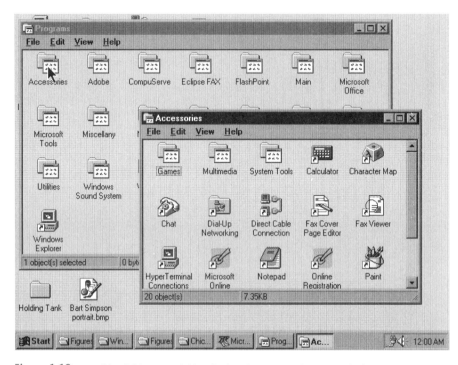

Figure 1.19   *Double-clicking on a folder displays its contents in a new window.*

The Find Button

The next item on the Start menu is the Find button (Chapter 4).
Find is a standalone program. It will search for either files, folders, or
computers:

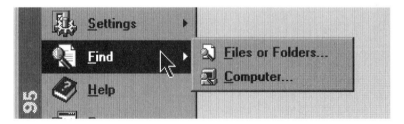

Yes, computers—that is, computers on a network. In keeping with the
new Windows 95 document-centric metaphor, the Find command
lets you search for document folders, too.

In the third tab sheet, Advanced, the *Of type* option lets you choose from the list of all registered document types. For example, on my machine, opening this list results in the following:

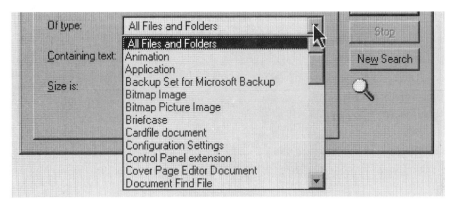

You can even search an entire hard disk for all files containing specific text. The results of a search are displayed in an extension to the bottom of the Find box.

Improved Help

Next, the Start button lets you get Help about Windows. The new interface draws on the book paradigm we're all used to: the Table of Contents and Index. Take a look at the Help system for Windows 95:

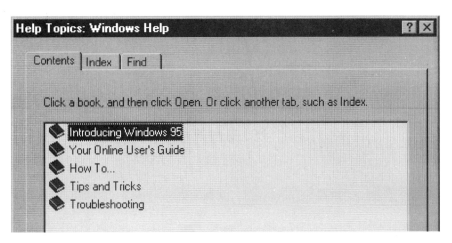

Some other points about the new Help:

▶ Help topics have been shortened whenever possible. Material has been broken down into subtopics. When you choose a topic, you're not going to be overwhelmed by too much to read. Subtopics open up like a directory when clicked on.

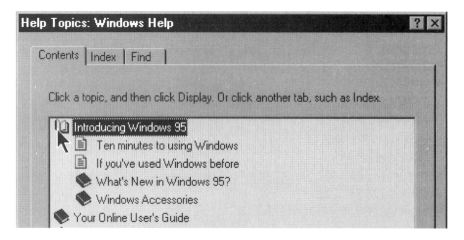

▶ Tips and tricks sections are supplied by Microsoft for Windows 95 and are encouraged by other software makers for their own Help systems.

▶ You've probably seen the ?-arrow tool: rather than just the normal question-mark–tool button, this button (called the "What's this?" button), when clicked on, changes the pointer's shape. When an object on the screen is then clicked on, an explanation appears. Developers are being encouraged to exploit this Help function in their own applications.

▶ A new type of button, called a *shortcut* button, can jump a user to the procedure he or she is reading about. For example, the Help screen for changing the system clock looks like this:

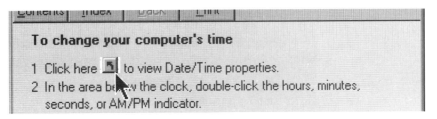

Clicking on the shortcut button will take you right to the Control Panel rather than having to read and follow any directions.

Running Applications

The Start button also lets you run a program from a Run box (Chapter 4). One improvement is that the last several commands you issued are available from the drop-down list.

Also, you can enter not only executables (application names such as wp.exe) but also the name of any document (e.g., letter.doc). If Windows 95 recognizes the extension of the file, it will be opened in a window for you.

One last nicety is that the Run box will not only run DOS applications, but like its big brother Windows NT, it will also run Windows applications. Enter **calc**, for example, and the calculator runs.

Application Switching with the Taskbar

Alt-Tab (Chapter 4) is still a part of Windows 95, but the good news is that it's been improved. Now it looks like this:

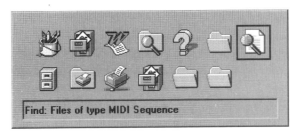

Each press of Alt-Tab advances the little box along the tasks so you can target the one you're headed for a little better. In fact, with just a press of Alt-Tab you can get a sense of how many tasks are running, even if you've decided to hide the Taskbar from view.

The even better news about task switching is that each time you run an application or open a folder, a button for it is added to the Taskbar. Simply click on the button, and the associated window jumps to the foreground ready for you to work with it.

If the task's window was minimized (iconized), it is restored to original size from the icon.

My Computer

There's one very important addition to the interface that's so obvious that nobody ever thought of it. It's called My Computer (Chapter 4). Every Windows 95 computer screen has an icon by this name in the upper-left corner. Double-click on it, and you can poke around at literally everything in your computer, hardware and software alike. Though all these services can be reached through other means, making them available in a window called My Computer makes perfect sense and is easily discoverable by even novice users. Figure 1.20 shows My Computer open and drive C, Printers, and Fonts displayed.

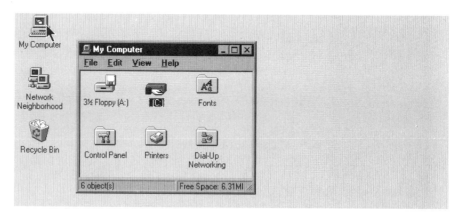

Figure 1.20   *For most users, My Computer will be the central hub of Windows 95. Through this icon you can get to any aspect of your computer from opening a document to adding a device driver or establishing remote-access dial-in connections.*

Properties and Property Sheets

Interesting and extremely powerful additions to the user interface are supplied by something called *Property Sheets* (Chapters 8 and 11). Almost every object (folders, files, Desktop, Taskbar, networked computer, etc.) has properties associated with it that can be easily examined and altered. It takes a *right* mouse click to bring up the menu from which Properties are selected.

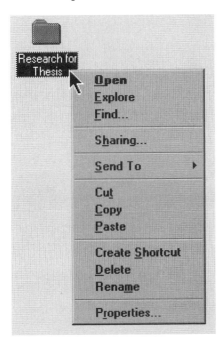

When the Properties option is selected from this menu, the associated property sheet appears. Figure 1.21 shows the property sheet for the folder above.

Just some of the many settings you can make using Properties are

▶ Share a folder on the network

▶ Change the name of your hard disk and check its free space

▶ Change a program's icon

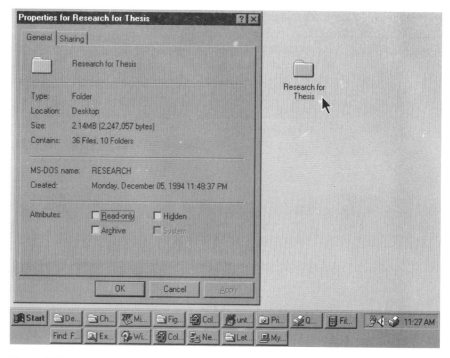

Figure 1.21   *The Properties sheet for the Research for Thesis folder*

▶ Set the Desktop's colors, background, screen saver, etc.

▶ Display a font's technical details

Right-Clicking

The right mouse button (Chapters 4 and 11) has been deemed a sort of power-user mouse button, and its application has been implemented throughout the Windows 95 user interface. In general, the right mouse button (actually the *secondary* button, which would mean the left button if you're using a left-handed mouse) implements activities that can be done using commands elsewhere in the interface, but using the mouse button provides a number of time-saving shortcuts.

Shortcuts

Shortcuts (Chapter 4) are icons that can represent almost anything in Windows 95. You can create a shortcut for almost anything, then you can drop that icon almost anywhere. Clicking on the icon then runs the application, opens the document, presents the folder window to you, and so on, depending on the type of shortcut it is.

Here's an example shortcut icon on the Desktop. Notice that it looks just like a regular icon, only with a little arrow in the lower-left corner.

Shortcut to
WinCIM

What's so great about shortcuts is that they are only pointers to objects, so deleting the shortcut above doesn't actually delete WinCIM. Nor does making a copy of a shortcut (to place elsewhere) copy the file, application, drive, or whatnot to which it points.

The New Look of Windows Elements

All your existing applications will benefit from the new, more refined look of Windows 95. Take a look at Figures 1.22 and 1.23, which are both of the same application, one shown in Windows 3.1 and the other under Windows 95.

Tab Buttons

I've already mentioned the new dialog-box design that relies on tabs (Chapter 3). A good example of this new dialog-box design is shown in Figure 1.24, from which you make screen display attributes. Notice that you can now alter the resolution of your display (e.g., from 640×480 to $1,024 \times 768$) more easily, and in many cases without rebooting Windows.

Title Bar Changes

The entire Title Bar (Chapter 3) of every document or application window incorporates a new design: the Minimize, Maximize, and

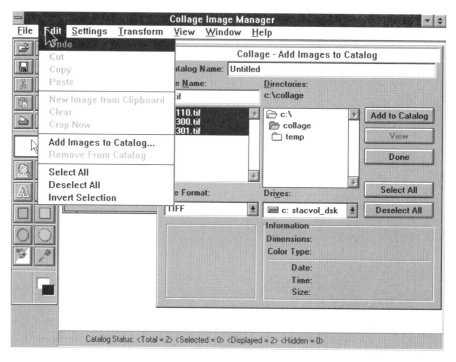

Figure 1.22 A Windows 3.x application running in Windows 3.1

Close buttons as well as the window's title have all been given a face-lift. Compare these two Title Bars, old and new:

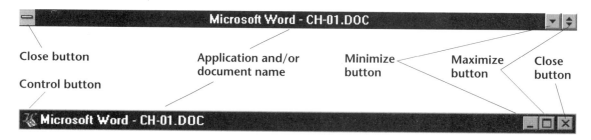

The Minimize, Maximize, and Close buttons now have more intuitive icons, and the Close button is now in the far-right corner. An X is now the universal designator for *close*. Any window can now be closed with a single click on the X.

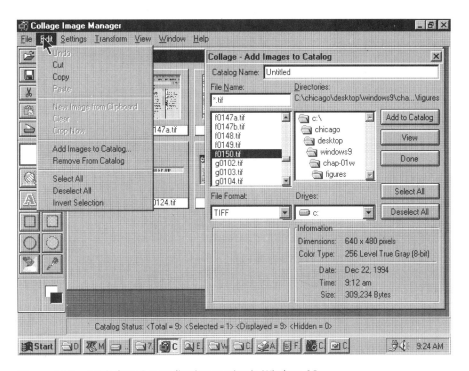

Figure 1.23   *A Windows 3.x application running in Windows 95*

The Minimize button is the shape of a button that will appear on the Taskbar or in a window when a document is iconized within an application window. The Maximize button will change to a Restore button when the window is maximized:

Restore button   This button returns the window to an intermediate size between full and iconized.

Notice, finally, that the old Control Box that was in the upper-left corner of the window is now replaced with a miniature icon. The icon that appears here is the application's personalized icon.

Shading

Shading details around buttons, menu items, borders, and so forth have been refined and standardized to produce a more coherent and

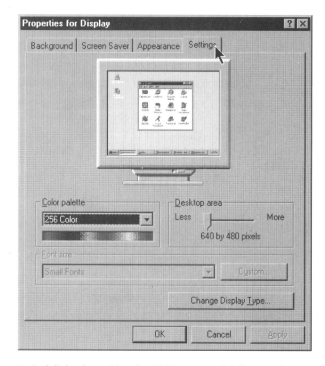

Figure 1.24   *Typical dialog box with tabs. Clicking on a tab brings up the related settings.*

integrated feel in the Windows 95 environment. Grayed-out text (options not available for some reason or other) are now displayed as sunken rather than just gray, and the new borders have a highlighted effect. Finally, the standard light source is from the upper left, and all boxes, buttons, frames, and other elements use this format, resulting in a more visually pleasing and consistent look throughout.

Easier-to-Grab Sliders

Scroll buttons (Chapter 3) are now proportionally sized to indicate the size of the document. If the document is fully displayed in the window, the button's length is the same as the whole scroll bar; if only one half of the document can fit in the window, the button will be half the scroll-bar size. More often than not, you'll have much larger scroll buttons to aim at, grab, and drag, as you see in Figure 1.25.

Figure 1.25   Scroll buttons tend to be larger in Windows 95.

Column-Heading Control

This control will likely be used whenever columns of information are displayed, allowing you to change the column width and optionally sort the data in the columns. By positioning the pointer on the division between the column heads, clicking, and dragging, the column resizes. Clicking on any column head sorts the data under the columns. Figure 1.26 illustrates this. Note that I've just sorted the listing by clicking on the Size column heading.

Video Enhancements

Microsoft has built some rather nice video stuff into Windows 95. "Live" resolution switching is one case in point; another nicety runs along the same lines, capitalizing on fancy video boards' meteoric *bit blitting* capability. (Bit blitting is short for *bit block transferring*, the kind of data juggling necessary to move a block of graphics around on the screen.) Windows 95's Control Panel offers an option that keeps the insides of your windows alive while you move them around the screen. If you purchase an add-on package called Microsoft Plus (see Chapter 32), a so-called full window drag/size option moves the guts of the window around along with its border. This works even if the

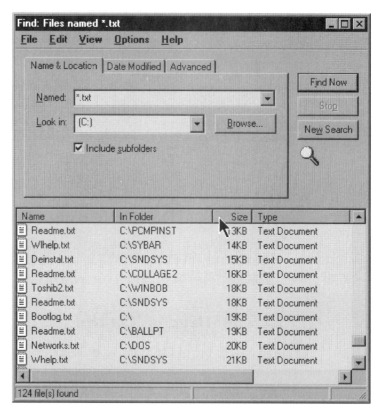

Figure 1.26 Column heads will appear in dialog boxes and applications in Windows 95.
Easy column resizing and sorting are possible with a few mouse clicks.

contents of the window is being modified at the time, such as when a
chart is being redrawn or numbers are recalculating in a spreadsheet.

Changeable System Text Sizes

Right off the bat, everyone loves to futz with their system's color scheme
(Chapter 7). The color-scheme settings in Windows 95 are far juicier
than in Windows 3.x. There's support for 256-color schemes, for starters, which means that the color schemes can be more subtle and pleasing to the eye.

But wait. There's more.

In addition to some really nice canned settings, you can also use True-Type fonts for system-related doodads such as the Title Bar and dialog boxes. Figure 1.27 shows an example scheme chosen from the Display dialog box.

Figure 1.27   *A greater degree of color and font variation for overall interface appearance are supported in Windows 95 than are available under Windows 3.x and NT. Notice the large fonts shown in this example, which could be useful for the visually impaired or for instructional purposes.*

The New File System

Windows 95 now finally gives you long file-name support (Chapters 5 and 12). A file name can be as many as 255 characters long (including spaces). But there's more to the file-system improvement in Windows 95 than long file names:

▶ The entire file system is now multithreaded protected-mode 32-bit code for improved performance and reliability.

▶ It incorporates what is essentially an enhanced MS-DOS file system called VFAT.

▶ There is a 255-character file-name limit, yet it is still compatible with MS-DOS and Windows 3.1 applications.

▶ Users don't have to see extensions in their file names unless they want to.

▶ The Explorer (an enhanced File Manager) indicates the type of file, meaning the creator of the file, such as Paint.

▶ Open architecture allows support for other file systems in the future.

▶ It has a 32-bit CD-ROM file system.

▶ Dynamic system cache doesn't require a dedicated swap file on your hard disk.

From the user's point of view, the Windows 95 file system is essentially MS-DOS. The old FAT (File Allocation Table) system continues on, albeit written in 32-bit code. The code is multithreaded as well, so, in addition to Windows 95's ability to preemptively multitask, you'll do less thumb twiddling while the system is copying files or performs other disk-related activities such as reading the CD-ROM drive, auto-saving a file you're working on, or serving a file to a workstation across the network.

In MS-DOS (and Windows 3.0), whenever the disk was accessed, the operating system had to transition into what's called *real-mode* operations. Real mode is a CPU chip operating mode that emulates the old 8086 and 80286 chips and was included for backward-compatibility with those chips. Real-mode operations are problematic, firstly because they require today's 386, 486, and Pentium CPUs to switch into real mode before they can read or write to the disk. This takes a little time, slowing down throughput.

After Windows 3.1 was around for some time, Microsoft released 32-bit protected-mode disk drivers, which, if opted for, pepped up disk performance and eliminated mode switching on supported disk drives. Still, SCSI devices often were left running on manufacturer-supplied 16-bit real-mode drivers.

Secondly, and more importantly, real-mode operations bring other operations the CPU might be handling to a halt, sort of like an adult regressing into infantile behavior where he or she can't multitask. The show stops until the CPU is done performing this real-mode task and until it switches back to its previous, more capable mode: protected mode. Another point to consider is that real-mode operations aren't as secure as protected mode. In protected mode, each task is given its own memory space in the computer's RAM, and programs can't accidentally walk on top of each other.

Windows 95's file system always runs in protected mode, so you can expect spunky and reliable performance. The only catch is that you have to be running all 32-bit programs for perfectly smooth execution of multitasking. Running a mix of 16- and 32-bit programs and/or device drivers will result in somewhat choppy performance because the 16-bit applications are not preemptively multitasked.

The 32-bit file system works hand-in-hand with a new 32-bit protected-mode disk-caching program supplied with Windows 95. If you've used Windows 3.x, you're probably aware that your system's overall speed can be dramatically improved through the use of caching, which loads frequently used hard-disk data into RAM. Once in RAM, the CPU can get to the data faster.

Because of the need for backward-compatibility, Microsoft let Windows 95 keep and utilize any 16-bit device drivers listed in your `autoexec.bat` and `config.sys` files at the time you install Windows 95. So, if you have a real-mode SCSI controller, CD-ROM driver, and MSCDEX drivers in `config.sys` and `autoexec.bat`, these will be retained by Windows 95, causing it to switch to real mode whenever the CD-ROM is accessed. Performance will suffer somewhat compared to what could be realized if you were to remove those drivers and let Windows 95 install its own 32-bit drivers for the same device(s).

Disk-Caching Improvements

Now that DOS is for all intents and purposes gone, the caching program is integrated into Windows. Dubbed VCACHE, it's written in 32-bit protected-mode code and significantly outperforms its 16-bit real-mode SmartDrive predecessor. In addition to accelerating hard-disk activities, VCACHE also does its magic on CD-ROM drives and drives you've assigned for use by networked colleagues. Finally, VCACHE uses intelligent dynamic algorithms to allocate or reduce RAM from the cache as suits the situation.

Virtual Memory

As you may know, Windows 3.x uses a portion of the hard drive to simulate RAM, acting as though your computer has more RAM than it physically does, letting it run more applications and open more documents at once than would otherwise be the case. This technique is called *virtual memory management*.

The new virtual memory manager takes the onus off the user on a number of counts. It uses more-intelligent algorithms and more-efficient 32-bit access methods (via the new file-system drivers), and determines for the user the optimal maximum and minimum file sizes. Because of the increased efficiency of the hard-disk access methods the new VMM employs, even a highly fragmented hard disk (a disk with a considerable number of noncontiguous sectors) won't result in a serious performance penalty.

Long File Names

As Windows NT, Mac, and OS/2 users (among others) will attest, the "8.3" file-name restriction (eight characters, a period, and a three-letter extension) of DOS is ridiculous.

Windows 95, now free of many DOS limitations (even though technically it's running on top of DOS 7—you can even prevent Windows 95 from loading and be dumped into the old [well, new] C> prompt), supports long file names, up to 255 characters: a terrific improvement. The 255 characters can be letters, numbers, spaces, and certain punctuation marks, but Windows 95 doesn't differentiate between upper- and lowercase letters, so Letter to Fred and LETTER TO FRED, though displayed differently on screen listing, are considered to be the same file name.

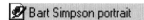

NOTE   In Windows NT, long file names are also supported in two varieties: the FAT version (like Windows 95's) and on specially formatted disk volumes called NTFS partitions. The NTFS arrangement is somewhat bothersome because it requires setting aside and reformatting part of your hard disk for use by the NTFS partition. What's more of a headache, NTFS partitions can't be seen by DOS, Windows 3.1, or Windows 95. You have to boot up Windows NT to gain access to them. The pros of that design are that NTFS partitions have numerous data-protection schemes built in, such as bulletproof security, the ability to gang multiple hard disks into a group to work faster, and the ability to recover data even if one of the drives in the group crashes. The other variety, VFAT, has been supported by NT since the release of Windows NT 3.5 Workstation and Server, allowing Windows 95 and Windows NT machines to recognize, display, and share each other's long file names on any VFAT partitions.

Unfortunately, you can't create files with long names using just any application. New 32-bit applications written for Windows 95 will eventually support this feature, but in the meantime, when you open and save files from within your old 16-bit Windows or DOS applications, you'll see the same old-style File/Save box:

Save As		
File Name:	**Directories:**	OK
hap-01w\ch-01.doc	c:\msoffice\winword	Cancel
chklist.ms	📂 msoffice	Options...
dialog.fon	📁 winword	Network...
gr_am.lex	📁 letters	Help
gram.dll	📁 macros	
hy_en.lex	📁 startup	
hyph.dll	📁 template	
intr-add.doc	📁 wordcbt	
macrode.exe		
newslast.dot	**Drives:**	
txtwlyt.cnv	💾 c:	
wdreadme.hlp		
wincim.ini		
Save File as Type:		
Word Document		

If you try to enter a long name, you'll get an error message stating that such a file name isn't valid. Only programs designed for Windows 95 will allow the actual use of long file names, so relief from DOS's naming limitation isn't going to be instantaneous.

Windows 95 will translate long names into short names for use by your old applications, so it's not as if there are any incompatibilities to worry about. When you save a file using a long name, or rename an existing file to a long name, two names are actually generated—the long one, and a short 8.3 name derived from the long one. For example, a Word document renamed to

```
My thesis on the mating behavior of arthropods
```

would show up as

```
mythesis.doc
```

under the old File Manager or in a File/Open box of a 16-bit Windows or DOS application.

As a workaround to the file-name limitation of older programs, Windows 95 allows you to do the following: You can create a document file in a 16-bit program, as usual, and save it. Then you use Windows 95's interface to rename the file to the long name of your choice. You can then open and edit the file by double-clicking on its long name or selecting the truncated name in the 16-bit program's File Open dialog boxes. After editing in the 16-bit program, when you save the file its long file name isn't truncated. Looking at it with the Explorer or in a folder also lists its full name.

NOTE   Even for long file names, Windows 95 assigns an extension. Therefore the file name above is actually `My thesis on the mating behavior of anthropods.doc`. The extension is normally hidden when displayed as a long name in the Windows 95 interface, but it reappears in 16-bit applications. (This is an option that can be defeated.) The extension is still important, however. If you have removed the extension, Windows won't know what application to associate it with.

File-Compatibility Issues: DOS, NTFS, HPFS

Windows 95 uses a superset of the old tried and true FAT file system pioneered by DOS and living on more hard disks around the world than any other. Understand that hard drives can be formatted to conform to many different specifications, depending on the needs of a particular *disk operating system* (what DOS stands for, by the way, and is a generic acronym Microsoft can't lay claim to). Thus, installing some variant of Unix on your system, such as SCO Unix or NeXTSTEP, may chop up your hard disk into sectors, directories, boot tracks, and so forth according to quite a different scheme than MS-DOS or Windows 95 will.

Who cares, you may be asking? I'm going to run Windows 95, so what difference does it make? Well, in that case, you're right—it doesn't make any difference. You will still have access to all your old DOS and Windows 3.x drives and directories just as if nothing had happened. But for those who have been running OS/2 and using that operating system's advanced disk file scheme, or NT's operating system, which is quite similar though more secure, you should sit up and listen.

Windows 95 supports only FAT- and VFAT-formatted drives. If you have formatted a drive or partition to NTFS, HPFS, or another specification, until an installable file system driver supporting that format is available for Windows 95, you'll have to use a multi-boot method to gain access to those partitions.

Luckily, a variety of installation options are built into Windows 95's setup program, so it's possible to keep two operating systems on your computer and choose from a menu the one you want at boot time. Operating-system components can be spread out across additional drives if you have them, but the boot information has to be on drive C.

Security

Windows 95 has the same level of security as Windows for Workgroups. You can sign in when booting up, or not. If you cancel the password box, you simply don't get special treatment. If you do enter the correct password, personalized Desktop arrangements, shared printers, drives, and directories can be set to automatically go into effect. This isn't much in the way of security.

What Windows 95 has to offer in the area of security comes in two flavors:

▶ Share-level security. When the user shares a disk, a directory, a printer, or other shareable resource, they have the option of requiring a password before access will be granted to a network user attempting to log onto the resource.

▶ User-level security. An administrator can give a user the right to access all shared resources on the network. As a convenience, such rights can be assigned to a group of users, which will take less time than assigning rights individually. In any case, when the user or group member logs on and supplies the correct password, the shared resources become available to him or her.

In the final analysis, the true amount of security against prying eyes and ill-intended hackers is minimal. The design of the VFAT disk system itself simply doesn't allow the kind of bulletproof security an operating system like Windows NT can muster and that government agencies' security policies mandate. However, because most businesses really don't have to concern themselves with the possibility of sophisticated hackers entering their systems, Windows 95 is the operating-system solution for the bulk of PCs in the workplace today. The lessened security of the system decreases the amount of RAM needed to run Windows 95, as well as increasing its overall speed.

Windows 95 v. the Competition

It is fairly certain among PC industry pundits that Windows 95 will take the market by storm. Market analysts are even beginning to prophesy that IBM might as well be rearranging the furniture on the Titanic as it prepares its next OS/2 release. Similarly, even though Apple has finally woken up and smelled the coffee, consenting to license its technology to wannabe Mac cloners, its days may be numbered.

So, in some very real sense, those in a position to make operating-system purchasing decisions for their business, corporation, school, or government agency shouldn't have any serious head scratching to do. Still, for anyone who's still pondering the alternatives, let's take a look at how Windows 95 stacks up against some of the competition.

Windows 95 v. DOS and Windows 3.x

Though some Windows 95 users will be making a lateral (some would say downward) move from Unix or OS/2, most newcomers to Windows 95 will be migrating upward from the DOS/Windows platform. When I say DOS/Windows, I mean typically DOS 6.x and Windows 3.11 or DOS and Windows for Workgroups 3.11.

The Importance of the DOS

Despite the enormous popularity of Windows 3.1 (some estimates put the user base as high as 60 million), this GUI is really only a shell placed on top of DOS. This is also true of other PC-based graphical user interfaces such as the now-defunct TopView from IBM, Digital Research's GEM, and VisiCorp's VisiOn.

The seed of many problems in the DOS/Windows combo is DOS itself. It truly was never designed to form the basis of a multitasking operating system, much less the underpinnings of a graphical user interface. In other words, all previous versions of Windows (with the exception of Windows NT) have been *kludge jobs*—held together with good intentions and Scotch tape. And as any veteran Windows user knows, the result of this unlikely marriage is that kinky and unpredictable anomalies arise all too frequently.

The most insidious problem is that of a single crashing program bringing your whole Windows session to its knees, including any other applications that were running quite happily. Having to reboot at this point usually meant loss of work. Windows 3.0 was particularly prone to this malady, and the state of affairs was somewhat improved in Windows 3.1. Even still, it was the limitations in the architecture of DOS itself that prevented Microsoft from building a crashproof shell.

For years it's been acknowledged that DOS as it was (single-user, non-networking, real-mode, nonmultitasking) needed to be jettisoned before a sturdy workhorse could be made of Windows. Otherwise, trying to make Windows behave was like trying to make a silk purse out of a sow's ear: thus the incentive for architecting OS/2, begun as a joint project between Microsoft and IBM, later taken over solely by IBM. It was also the seed of Windows NT.

In a nutshell, DOS was intended to run a single application at a time. That means only one program—the hard or floppy disk, the communications ports, the parallel ports, the keyboard, screen, and so on— was to have access to the computer at a time. This is called *device contention*. Once you get into running two or more programs at once, negotiation with DOS gets tricky. Windows 3.x certainly had its hands full trying to arbitrate all this, and because DOS runs in real mode, memory space was limited (real mode can only address 640K of RAM—or 1,024K if you include so-called upper memory and areas of memory where hardware devices such as video cards sometimes reside), and programs weren't protected from accidentally walking on top of each other. Because portions of Windows 3.x were written in protected mode, mode switching took up time as well.

Windows 95 and DOS Compatibility

Certainly the reason for sticking with DOS (and for many other apparently retrograde decisions at Microsoft, such as offering a real mode for Windows 3.0) was to provide backward-compatibility—the ability to run older software on newer machines—for as long as possible.

Though DOS is for all intents and purposes not available to the user at boot up, DOS applications are supported by Windows 95 in a DOS "box" just like the ones in Windows 3.x and Windows NT. In fact, the DOS in Windows 95 is, as IBM says about OS/2, a better DOS than DOS.

When Windows 95 boots up, it actually boots a fancy version of DOS that we can call DOS 7 for want of a better name. You can control the booting of Windows 95 in the following ways:

▶ Pressing F4 during bootup reloads your previous operating system (typically DOS 6.x). This is a potential way to have an older version of Windows, such as 3.1 or OS/2, still alive on your system.

▶ You can press F5 for a *fail-safe* boot into Windows 95. Fail-safe mode is a minimal system load that eliminates any unnecessary drivers that might be preventing the system from loading.

▶ Pressing F8 lets you make choices from a menu about how you want to start up, including getting to the DOS 7 prompt, stepping through the lines of your `autoexec.bat` and `config.sys` files line by line, or booting your previous version of DOS.

In any case, Windows 95's support of DOS apps is superior to Windows 3.x's. For one thing, graphics programs are better supported. Microsoft says even squirrely game programs known not to run under Windows 3.x because they attempt to directly address video hardware will run fine. These programs can even be run in a window. The intention was to make all graphics programs and games at least run under Windows and to make as many as possible run in a window.

NOTE Note however, that not all graphics programs will run in a window. Some programs—for example, DOOM (DOS version)—must be run full-screen. For super-demanding DOS programs, you can set a flag that tells Windows to switch into DOS Mode when such a program is launched. Windows 95 then automatically closes all Windows programs, temporarily giving control of the computer over to the DOS program. When you end the DOS program, Windows is reloaded automatically. This may be a solution to applications and systems developers who want to prevent users from accidentally altering files on a network server while they are concurrently running a DOS-based application such as a corporate database front end. By setting up the user's front-end program as a DOS-mode application, all Windows facilities on the user's workstation will be shut down while they are accessing the corporate database.

In addition to hard-to-run graphics programs, Windows 95 was designed to run other "ill-behaved" DOS applications that attempt to write to other pieces of hardware such as the keyboard or ports.

The Windows 95 DOS box supports all DOS commands included in the latest version of non-Windows DOS. When you launch a DOS program under Windows 95, the system creates what's called a VDM (Virtual DOS Machine). The DOS VDM fools an MS-DOS program into thinking it's running on a regular PC that it has all to itself. By default, all the settings in the `autoexec.bat` and `config.sys` files used to start up your computer are loaded into this VDM, so any device drivers such as scanner drivers, TSRs, pop-up programs, network drivers, and the like are all available to whatever DOS program you load into the box. However, custom start-up files can be assigned to a given program. In addition, a whole catalog of session-specific settings to the DOS environment can be made from the DOS window's toolbar or menu once it's running. Figure 1.28 shows one of the five tabs in this dialog box. Suffice it to say there are many options here, including all the ones you may have used in the PIF Editor in Windows 3.x.

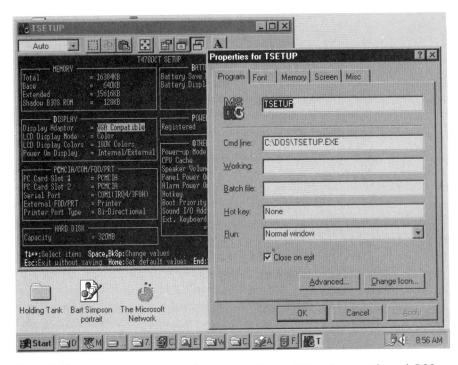

Figure 1.28   *The DOS settings dialog box lets you alter the DOS environment for each DOS session individually.*

Changes you make to one DOS VDM (say, for a running copy of WordPerfect 6) don't affect settings for other running DOS applications. What's more, such settings are automatically saved as PIF files (just like those in Windows 3.x) without the confusion of running the PIF editor and figuring out where to store the PIF file. The settings are reinstated the next time you run the specific program you've set them for. All PIF files are consolidated into one directory, the \Windows\PIF directory, which eliminates some confusion for users as well.

Though you might not think it possible, the new DOS window supports long file names. Though few DOS applications at this point will display them, developers may decide to rewrite some applications to support this feature. The replacement for the DOS editor (EDIT.COM) supplied in Windows 95 does support long names.

Unruly DOS programs that attempt to write directly to sound cards, play with the system timer, or futz with the keyboard are promised to work under Windows 95. This is possible by virtue of how the DOS VDM is set up.

Another nice feature of Windows 95's DOS support lets you display a toolbar at the top of the window (Figure 1.29). The toolbar certainly eases use of DOS under Windows, bringing a modicum of Windows ease of use to DOS. The toolbar by default is turned off, but turning it on gives you easy access to these functions:

▶ Mark, cut, copy, and paste for easy data sharing between DOS applications and between DOS and Windows applications.

▶ Change the font and resulting window size of the DOS box.

▶ Set the tasking of the box to "exclusive" for applications that need to assume control of the whole machine.

▶ Quickly set the Properties for the box (i.e., PIF settings).

▶ Quickly turn on or off background tasking for the box.

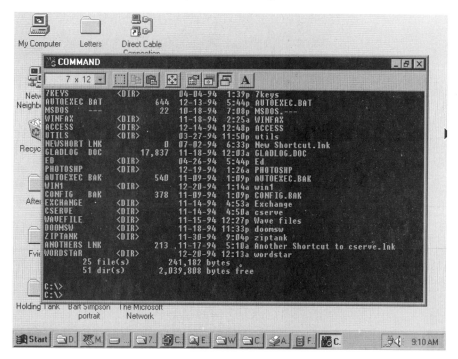

Figure 1.29   *The DOS box sports a useful toolbar.*

Significant thought on Microsoft's part went into determining the default settings for a DOS session. In Windows 3.x, background tasking was set off as a default, suspending a DOS application when it was switched away from. Now it's set on. Also, the new defaults have DOS applications come up windowed rather than full-screen.

One other little nicety is that you can now close a DOS application using the same "X" button (the one in the upper-right corner of the window) you use to close Windows applications. If you declare on its property sheet that a DOS application can be closed without having to terminate it, you'll be able to kill the DOS application with a single click. You'll want to use this option carefully because any unsaved data at the time of closure will be lost. As an option, a warning box will alert you that the application is running, warn you about possible loss of data, and ask for confirmation. Windows 95 will carefully clean up memory resources the application was using and free them for use by other programs. This is something Windows 3.x was not terribly good at doing. Figure 1.30 illustrates this.

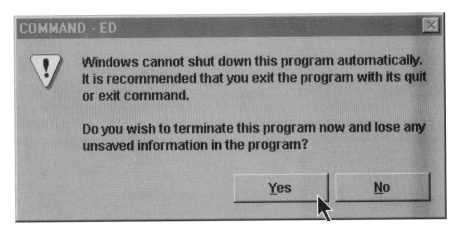

Figure 1.30   Close a DOS application by clicking on the Close button. A warning box lets you know the application is still active but you can close it anyway.

More Conventional Memory Space!

Finally, and this is a big finally, Windows 95 ups the conventional memory space available for your DOS applications.

How? Windows 95 simply uses 32-bit protected-mode driver replacements for the most popular 16-bit memory-hogging drivers used in DOS environments. These drivers provide the same functionality, but suck up zero bytes from your conventional memory map because they're supplied by the Windows 95 internals rather than the DOS VDM. Table 1.1 shows you the overall memory savings these drivers will supply you.

Description	File(s)	Conventional Memory Saved (in K)
Microsoft Network	net.exe (full)	95
client software	protman	3
	netbrui	35
	exp16.dos (MAC)	8
Novell NetWare	lsl	5
client software	exp16odi	9
	ipxodi.com	16
	netbios.exe	30
	netx.exe	48
	vlm.exe	47
MS-DOS extended file sharing and locking support	share.exe	17
Adaptec SCSI driver	asp14dos.sys	5
Adaptec CD-ROM driver	aspicd.sys	11
Microsoft/Adaptec CD-ROM extensions	mscdex.exe	39
SmartDrive disk-caching software	smartdrv.exe	28
Microsoft Mouse driver	mouse.com	17

Table 1.1   *Conventional memory saved by use of 32-bit protected-mode drivers supplied with Windows 95 (table courtesy of Microsoft)*

These savings can easily be enough to make the difference between being able to run a program and not. In severe cases, users have had to use a boot manager to load different `autoexec.bat` and `config.sys` settings for each of their major applications, loading a subset of their TSRs and drivers. Windows 95 may eliminate this need.

Windows 95 v. OS/2

Released in the fall of 1994, OS/2 version 3.0—trade-named Warp—has a 32-bit operating system that multitasks Windows and DOS programs, runs on 4 MB of memory, and costs less than $100. As Figure 1.31 shows, Warp's user interface, called *Presentation Manager*, looks much like Windows on the screen. You can run Windows 3.1,

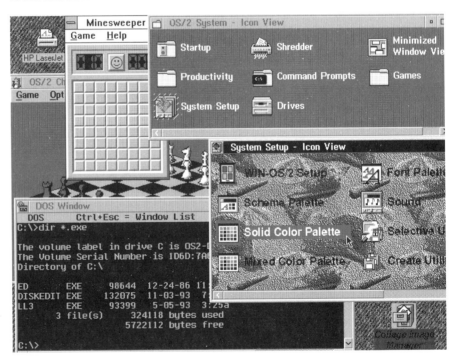

Figure 1.31   *Here's a view of the OS/2 Warp desktop. As shown here, Warp lets you choose a different appearance (background color or pattern as well as font) for each folder and for the desktop itself. In addition, you can see how Warp lets you mix OS/2, Windows 3.1, and DOS windows at will (Minesweeper is a Windows 3.1 program, while the 3-D chess game comes with Warp). The icon at the lower right is that of another running Windows program. You can print files by dragging and dropping them onto the printer icon at the upper left.*

DOS, and OS/2 programs in separate windows on the Warp desktop (at this writing, Warp can't run programs written for Windows 95, but IBM says they will add this capability if enough users request it).

For choosing system options, Warp relies heavily on tabbed dialog boxes, as shown in Figure 1.32. There's even a slick LaunchPad (Figure 1.33) that works much like the Windows 95 Taskbar.

In fact, IBM accomplished more than beating Microsoft to market—Warp actually has quite a few technical advantages over Windows 95. But whether or not these will matter to you is another story.

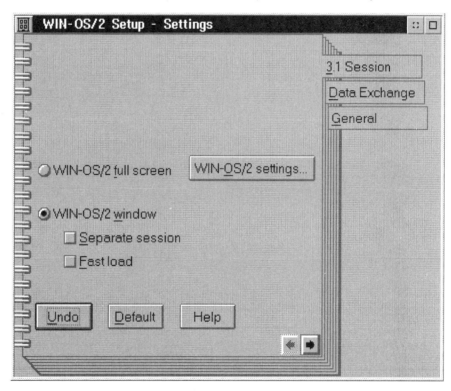

Figure 1.32 *A typical tabbed dialog box in Warp. As you can see, the Warp look is different from Windows 95's. You use the page shown here to set options for running Windows 3.1 programs. Your main choices are to run them on a separate full-screen Windows desktop or within individual windows on the Warp desktop. The Fast load check box preloads key components of Windows when you first start your computer, so individual Windows programs start up faster (often faster than in Windows 3.1).*

Figure 1.33   *The OS/2 LaunchPad. Along the right side, the buttons that have small arrow-heads let you access documents or functions related to the corresponding main button.*

IBM touts Warp as having several important advantages over Windows 95:

▶ Better crash protection. IBM claims that Warp is much more reliable—less vulnerable to failures caused by malfunctioning programs—than is Windows 95. Like earlier versions of Windows, Windows 95 provides a single address space that must be shared by all 16-bit Windows applications as well as by some key elements of the Windows core. If a program goes haywire, it may improperly modify the memory areas used by other programs or by Windows itself. As a result, other programs may stop working, or the entire system may come to a sudden halt. In Warp, on the other hand, each 16-bit program has its own separate "virtual machine." In other words, it is completely isolated from other programs and from the operating system, so if it malfunctions, nothing else is affected.

▶ True preemptive multitasking for all supported applications. Although Windows 95 can run multiple DOS and Windows applications at the same time, it often falls back on "cooperative" multitasking, a less efficient system. Preemptive multitasking is available only if *all* the programs you're running are 32-bit applications specifically developed for Windows 95. By contrast, Warp can preemptively multitask with a mix of DOS programs, older (16-bit) Windows applications, and 32-bit OS/2 programs.

▶ A more intelligent user interface. Windows 95's new system of shortcuts makes it easier to start applications or open documents. But there's a potential problem: If you move the files to which the shortcuts refer to another location on the disk, Windows will have to look around to find them. Warp keeps track of the links between shortcuts and their files, updating the shortcuts when the files are moved. Warp also provides more extensive drag-and-drop control of the user interface. For example, to change the fonts used in the interface (say in the menu bars), you can just drag the new font from the font window to the item you want to change.

▶ Better included applications. The programs in the BonusPak that comes with Warp cover more ground and have more features than the Windows 95 accessories. The core of the BonusPak is IBM Works, which includes a word processor, a spreadsheet, a charting program, a simple database manager, and a personal information manager. Figure 1.34 shows several of these components, while Figure 1.35 gives you an idea of the word processor's advanced features (read the text shown in the screen image for details). All these components share the same basic commands, and you can drag information from one component to another. Other programs in the BonusPak include: a quick-and-easy system for accessing the full range of information and services available on the Internet, a utility for streamlining access to the CompuServe information service, a communications program similar to HyperTerminal, and a faxing utility superior to the one that comes with Windows 95.

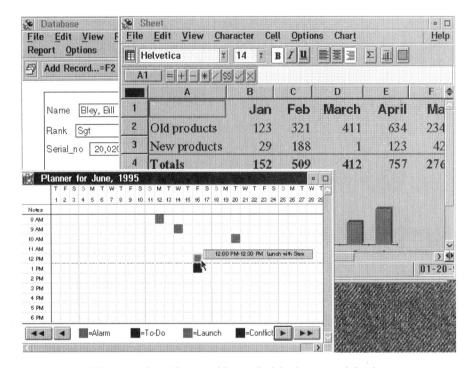

Figure 1.34 **This screen shows the spreadsheet, schedule planner, and database components
of IBM Works, part of the BonusPak that comes with Warp.**

Warp's advantages will appeal to people who drive their PCs to the
limit. But while these advantages are real, less-demanding users may
not find them compelling. Most individual users won't notice the performance boost resulting from preemptive multitasking. Similarly, system crashes are a pain, but they usually aren't so frequent as to cause
major problems. And for most people, DOS programs are fading from
memory.

The bottom line is this: While Warp is arguably a slightly better product in technical terms, Windows makes the better choice for most people just because it is so popular. So many people use Windows that
you'll find it easier to get help with problems and to share tips and
tricks with other users. Support for new hardware products like modems and CD-ROM drives appears first for Windows—just because
the market is so large—and only later for OS/2. Besides, to my eyes at
least, Windows 95 looks snazzier.

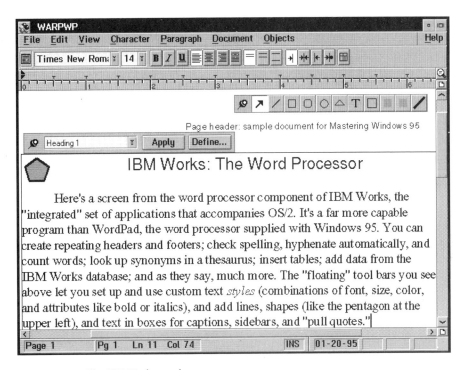

Figure 1.35   The IBM Works word processor

Windows 95 v. Unix

Unix is losing its stronghold as the champion of inscrutable operating systems usable only by academics and rocket scientists on mainframe computers. Unix popularity is rising for a number of reasons, not the least of which is the sudden fashionability of Internet. The abundance of Unix workalikes for PCs, sort of bridging the gap between the mainframe and Windows, has furthered Unix's cause as well.

NOTE   Actually, as odd as it sounds, much of Windows 95 has its origins in Unix, as filtered down through Microsoft from NT. Windows NT is more than partially based on a variant of Unix called Mach, which was developed at Carnegie-Mellon University. In a sense, though NT is a far richer operating system, much of the homework for Windows 95 was done in the NT development labs at Microsoft.

During the last few years, Unix vendors have cooperated in standardization initiatives in hopes of Unix gaining a stronger marketplace foothold. The main problem to be solved has been that the differing Unix systems don't all run the same applications because of differences in their architectures. As a result, several Unix variants now have a friendly user interface much like Windows.

Novell Corporation is a big player here because of its acquisition of AT&T's UNIX Systems Laboratory (these are the people that made Unix). Some have suspected that with Novell's upcoming Unix product, which will also be a multitasking, multithreaded, client/server network operating system, Novell might just be able to give Microsoft a run for its money. In case you haven't been following the Unix game, the other primary contenders for PC marketshare are SCO, IBM, DEC, SunSoft, and NeXT, with their products SCO Unix, AIX, ULTRIX, Solaris, and NeXTSTEP, respectively.

A major similarity between Windows 95 and Unix is how they interact with devices attached to the computer. To design an operating system that's as flexible as possible, Unix and Windows 95 both connect to the world through device drivers that allow the operating system to work on many different hardware configurations.

Another major likeness is the way Windows 95 and Unix use memory. Both can access a large, "flat" memory space of many megabytes, which makes programming easy. As mentioned above, Windows 95 offers a memory space of 2 gigabytes per application. Many Unix systems offer closer to 4 gigabytes. Both systems (assuming you're running 32-bit applications in Windows 95) prevent applications from creaming each other because memory areas are strictly separated. However, unlike Windows 95 which will run okay on 4 MB and fly on 8, Unix systems tend to require much more memory than even the older version of NT (NT 3.1). That's to say, more than 16 MB.

NOTE   Also worth considering is that a full-blown version V of Unix takes up a huge amount of disk space (almost 100 MB) and comes on close to 100 disks. It also requires significant upkeep.

Contrary to popular belief, you're not relegated to using cryptic command-line interfaces with Unix anymore. Interacting with a Unix computer used to be like using DOS on a PC. But now graphical user interfaces for Unix have appeared. However, because of the open design philosophy of Unix, standardization has proved problematic. Competing graphical interfaces such as OPEN LOOK and Motif operate differently for users and programmers alike. One of the key advantages of Windows 95 over Unix is simply that a large industry has adopted the standardized Windows interface, building thousands of applications around it.

Should You Consider Unix?

Unix competitors like NeXTSTEP and Solaris certainly have their advantages. Unix is an old, mature operating system, not something just cooked up—as, let's be honest, Windows 95 is.

However, the disparity between Unix and the PC world as we know it today is too great. Few Unixes offer the kind of DOS- or Windows-applications support that Windows 95 does, and if your company or group is well entrenched in a DOS/Windows applications mix, Unix won't cut the mustard.

Although there is a huge collection of Unix gurus the world over who have been developing Unix utilities, applications, and extensions to the operating system for many years, Unix suffers mostly from being too huge and not being fully standardized. In the final analysis, if you're looking for the kind of advanced features that Unix can brag about, you'll probably do as well, if not better, with NT, and you'll have greater Windows/DOS compatibility to boot.

Obviously, if you're already previously invested in Unix applications and networked hardware but feeling constricted when it comes to running Windows and DOS apps, it makes perfect sense to install a few Windows 95 workstations and interconnect them via Windows 95's supplied TCP/IP client drivers.

Conclusion

In this chapter, you've gotten a quick introduction to Windows 95. We've covered the most prominent new features Windows 95 brings to your desktop and laptop computer screens and contrasted Windows 95

MORE CPUS INSTEAD OF MORE RAM?

Windows 95 is designed to take intelligent advantage of additional RAM and hard-disk space you might plug into your system. But what about CPUs? If the bottle-neck in computing is often because of the CPU not having enough oomph to churn through all those bits and bytes fast enough, why not add more, you may wonder?

Unfortunately, Windows 95 isn't internally designed in such a way that can take advantage of multi-CPU machines. However, both versions of Windows NT (Windows NT Workstation and Windows NT Server) can. While the standard Workstation version supports only one or two CPUs, the Server version can take advantage of up to four. (Actually, with proprietary drivers from a manufacturer, NT can work with even more CPUs.)

Why add CPUs? Adding CPUs is the perfect solution to sluggish performance, which can develop as your network grows, as the applications load becomes heavier, or as your need for increased productivity and throughput increases. Of course, the traditional fix of adding RAM to any Windows system helps, too. But if processing power is what's suffering, only adding CPUs or increasing the speed of the existing CPU will help.

But there's a catch. Only applications that are multithreaded will benefit from multiple CPUs under NT. Without an application being divvied up into multiple threads, NT has no way of dishing out separate tasks to the individual CPU chips. But, considering the lowering cost of CPUs and the fact that now Windows 95 is multithreaded, too, we're likely to see more and more multithreaded applications. These applications will run well under Windows 95 and *will* be able to take advantage of extra CPUs under NT. You can expect to see more multiple-CPU machines, typically with 486DX 2's and 4's or Pentiums available in the near future.

with some of the other comparable PC operating systems available to-day. In the next chapter, I'll discuss what you may want to know about upgrading your computer system and your software applications for use with Windows 95. Then, in Chapter 3, we'll get down to the business of running Windows 95 (assuming you've installed it as described in the Appendix) so you can begin to understand what the parts of the screen are, how you work with them, and so forth.

Chapter 2

Getting Your Hardware and Software Ready for Windows 95

FEATURING

What software to kiss good-bye and why

What software to keep and what to upgrade

Assuming you made it through the last chapter unscathed, you should have a pretty good idea now of what Windows 95 is all about. Because this book is slated for publication at the same time Windows 95 is released in the market, part of our mission here is not only to teach you how to use Windows 95, but also what it has to offer you, how you're probably going to benefit from it, and how you can get ready for this new darling when it's finally available (most likely in the fall of 1995). But that's sort of a tall order. First let's step back for a minute and consider the landscape.

Windows Extravaganza!

Windows has had a terrific influence in spurring the computer market, both in hardware and software development. Eight years after Windows 3.0, we now have many thousands of Windows applications to choose from, many on CD-ROM (a standard enthusiastically promoted by Microsoft) and hundreds if not thousands of Windows-specific hardware devices such as mice, video accelerators, tape-backup systems, video capture and editing boards, voice-recognition systems, and so forth. With the help of price competition and the free market, an entry-level Pentium machine with CD-ROM drive and monitor can be had now for about $2,000. With an audience of an estimated 60 million Windows users/consumers, you'd expect no less.

Are We Confused Yet?

But the downside of all this Windows R&D that's making the world a better place for us is that users can't follow the technology curve without having a master's degree in science. If they're shopping, they simply don't know what to buy. How do you choose? It's not exactly like looking at a telephone, comparing a few features, and saying "I'll take the green one." There are too many decisions to make. Too many numbers, bytes, RAMs, mega this and mega that, screen sizes, CD players, and then that ever-present mouse. What's worse, people who already have computers often don't even know how best to use what they have.

Hey, sometimes even *I'm* confused, and I write computer books for a living. I've written six books on Windows and have a degree in electronics. Does it help? To be honest, not much. The technology simply changes too fast.

It's tough shooting at moving ducks. If the stuff you needed to run (applications, that is) just stayed the same, and if the operating system would hold still long enough, we could all figure out the perfect computer system, sort of like which size TV or frying pan you like best. But no such luck. On the eve of Windows 95's debut you can rest assured we'll all be barraged by a bevy of magazine articles and advertisements commanding you to run out and upgrade this or that hardware and software.

So, in this chapter, let's look at the story as best we know it at this point. What's the minimum base system you'll need to run Windows 95, really? And then how can you upgrade your system to capitalize on Windows 95's new 32-bit operating-system underpinnings, advanced processing features, display, networking, and communications options? Also, what new software will you have to (or want to) buy? What will you have to jettison or pass on to Uncle George? These considerations may affect your timing when moving up to Windows 95 and may also ease the transition.

What Software to Kiss Good-Bye and Why

First, let's look at software compatibility. As I discussed in Chapter 1, one of the cornerstones of the Windows 95 mandate was to design in backward-compatibility with existing 16-bit DOS and Windows applications. In fact, it was to provide even greater compatibility with DOS applications than Windows 3.x did. As it turns out, this seems to have been achieved; there are going to be a few bugs to work out, but that's to be expected.

The good news is that compatibility with your existing software is likely to be high. Not only that, all your Windows software will benefit from having a face-lift—nicer borders, dialog boxes, menus, and so forth. But there is some bad news, which is there will be classes of programs that Windows 95 won't be able to run, at least not in their current incarnations. Also, there will be some programs that, even though they run OK, you'll probably want to upgrade.

Applications v. Utilities

As you probably know, there are two basic categories of PC applications for the mass market: applications and utilities. Applications are programs such as dBASE, PhotoStyler, PageMaker, or Works. These programs, often called *productivity-enhancement software*, assist you in doing a certain class of work, such as generating textual documents, managing graphical images, or organizing huge amounts of data. By contrast, programs called *utilities* perform computer housecleaning of various types. For example, the Norton Utilities can help you by undeleting files you accidentally erased, defragmenting your hard disk, combing through your hard disk to find files, or determining your system's speed by putting it through its paces.

 NOTE In common parlance, the word "applications" usually includes utilities and simply means any program short of the operating system itself.

Applications programs work at the highest level of the operating system, a bit like a ship on the sea. They "ride" on top of the operating system and GUI software and don't have to interfere with the lower *primitives* of the operating system to get things done. Let me explain.

About APIs

When an application needs the operating system to do something, such as display a dialog box on the screen, accept your key press, or display letters you've typed, it does this by asking the operating system for help. This type of request is called an *API call*. (API stands for applications programming interface.) APIs are little tricks, if you will, that the operating system can do for the programmer. Sort of like saying to your dog, "Spot, roll over," the application can say: "display the Save As dialog box and ask for a file name." Then the application can say "OK, now store this file on the disk somewhere." The operating system then finds some room on the disk and saves the file.

The operating system can do these things because it is directly in touch with the operating-system *primitives,* such as writing to the hard disk, reading the keyboard, putting graphics on the screen, reading data from the COM port, and so on. Because of this, applications don't have to handle the drudgery of system housekeeping on their own. The existence of an API makes writing Windows programs much easier because the programmer doesn't have to write code to perform myriad common tasks that every program needs, such as having a window, having a menu bar, opening and closing files, and printing. The fact that Windows has a pretty good library of API calls has made life easier for Windows programmers because a lot of their work is already done for them. (Even still, 16-bit applications writing is a pain, and 16-bit DOS is a pain, which is why programmers are really going to like writing for Windows 95 and NT.)

But there's another reason why operating-system primitives are handled by API calls—it helps protect the operating-system software from failure. If every program running in the computer were allowed to have access to resources such as the screen, keyboard, hard disk, and ports, your computer could be in big trouble. For starters, your hard-disk directory could get trashed pretty quickly, and you'd in essence lose all your files. Or if you printed from two programs at the same time, both files would go to the printer at the same time (normally, in Windows, Print Manager sees to it that files are sent sequentially rather than simultaneously). The result would be a combination of, say, your 3rd Quarter Income and Expense Report with that Print Shop birthday card for Harriet, three cubicles down the hall. It wouldn't be pretty.

Here's another example. You may have used a defragmenting program such as the one in Norton Utilities or PC-Tools. There's also one supplied with DOS called defrag.exe. (It's in your DOS directory.) Though useful, these programs are in a sense dangerous because they fiddle directly with your hard disk. This is one reason you're not supposed to run them while other programs are also running on the same computer. Because they twiddle with the hard disk's directory, as well as moving your disk's files all over the place one block at a time, the whole process can be bollixed up if another program asks the operating system for disk access simultaneously.

> **NOTE**   When a file becomes too large for your computer to store in a single location on a disk, it becomes fragmented. The operating system splits it up and puts it into different sections of the hard disk. Fragmented files can still be used, but it takes the computer longer to find them because the hard-disk heads have to jump around on the disk, like the arm of a record player jumping from cut to cut. This slows down overall throughput in the computer. Defragmenting rearranges the files and free space on your computer and speeds up disk access. After defragmenting, free space is consolidated in one contiguous block and files are stored contiguously on the rest of the disk.

When programs use the prescribed Windows API calls, everything is cool. Applications that do obey the rules go sailing along minding their manners, receiving the proper help from Windows, and other programs that are running are happy too. Perhaps they will have to wait in line to gain access to the hard disk or printer, but that's OK. Spot knows how to roll over and does his job when asked.

When all the programs you're running are Windows programs, there usually isn't a problem. If a communications program needs access to a COM port, for example, it is supplied by Windows. If the particular COM port is already in use, Windows says, in effect: sorry, that port isn't available.

But things get tricky when you're running DOS programs and Windows programs simultaneously or two DOS programs at once. This is because DOS programs were written to think they are the only program running on the computer and they have the whole computer to themselves, including the hard disk, ports, screen, keyboard, printer, and any other resources. They don't know about other programs that might be running at the same time, and they might try to access the computer's hardware directly.

When programs try to bypass the API and directly access hardware that is normally controlled by the operating-system primitives, trouble can ensue. In Windows 3.x, such breaches of system security were often not perceived and prevented (especially by DOS programs), and this is one reason it wasn't a "secure" operating system. DOS-based viruses are a good case in point. Viruses make a hobby of fiddling with the innards of your operating system (typically by altering data on the hard disk), with insidious effects. Windows 3.x couldn't prevent such security breaches because it had no way of knowing they were occurring.

TROJAN HORSE VIRUSES AND WINDOWS NT

Speaking of viruses, here's a little tidbit. If you've used NT, recall that you can't even log on until you press Ctrl-Alt-Delete. Then you see the log-on box where you enter your password. You might have found this curious because these are the three keys you normally use to reboot your computer after it hangs up, not something you'd use to log on. NT uses this log-on command because what it really does is flush out any "Trojan Horse" viruses that might have loaded while NT was booting. A Trojan Horse is a program that masquerades as another in an attempt to capture information and violate either system security (capturing your password) or system integrity (wiping out your hard disk).

Protecting the System from Programs That Circumnavigate the API

Although NT is really the flagship Microsoft product when security is the issue, Windows 95's designers hoped to make it at least more secure (*robust* is the popular adjective) than Windows 3.x. There are several means to this end, but the primary approach is to disallow any program direct access to the computer's hardware. Thus, any program that tries to perform an action that the operating system thinks would jeopardize its security will be stopped from doing so.

In the case of Windows 95, the designers have achieved this kind of hardware isolation by "virtualizing" all the hardware. (This is the same approach used in Windows NT, incidentally.) Every physical piece of hardware in the computer is accessed only by virtual device drivers (called VxDs in Windows lingo). When an application wants the use of a device, it asks the operating system for it via the API call. Then the operating system validates the request and passes it along to the device driver, which in turn handles the actual communication with the device.

The 386's Device-Protection Capabilities

When a DOS program is running, all standard DOS calls (similar to Windows API calls, but invented for DOS applications way back before Windows was invented) are translated into Windows API calls and sent to the correct device. This works great until a DOS application tries to access hardware directly. Because of a nifty little feature called the *I/O permission bitmap* that is built into the Intel 386 and subsequent chips, Windows 95 can detect any illegal attempt to directly access the computer's hardware.

Each time an application is run, Windows 95 knows whether it's a DOS or Windows application. If it's a DOS application, a *virtual DOS machine* (VDM) is created. A virtual DOS machine is a software replica of an IBM PC, providing all the services that a real PC running DOS would supply to a program. Such services would include means for hardware access to the screen, keyboard, memory, and disk drives, for example. Along with this VDM, Windows 95 creates an I/O permission bitmap for the application. The bitmap is essentially a table with entries for each of the computer's internal ports (there are many, used for different things, such as the system clock, network boards, and so on), and shows which, if any, of the ports allow direct access. If the DOS application tries any funny business, it will probably generate an error message indicating your program has done something naughty and Windows will terminate it. Not only that, instead of the program crashing Windows (as in Windows 3.x's General Protection Fault error message and resultant system lockups), Windows will terminate the errant program and keep on going.

Because the designers wanted to retain as much older-DOS-program compatibility as possible, they didn't want to go overboard on this protection thing, so some direct hardware calls will be allowed. For example, if a DOS communications program wants to access COM1 and COM1 isn't currently in use by another application, Windows 95 will allow it. However, some ports, such as the hard or floppy disk's, are off limits.

So What Does This Mean to Me?

Any well-behaved Windows application or utility program is likely to run under Windows 95, no problem. However, some DOS programs, especially hard-disk utilities, may have trouble running in a Windows session. Windows 95's new "DOS Mode" (as explained in Chapter 1) lets you run particularly demanding DOS programs by temporarily exiting Windows. However, just because you can run many of your older disk utilities by forcing the issue doesn't mean that it's advisable. The new VFAT disk directory structure and support of long file names is rather magical by design, and pre-Windows 95 utility programs may indeed stomp on new long file names you create with Windows 95. Even Microsoft-supplied DOS 6.x utilities such as DEFRAG don't know about long file names and will shorten them rather crudely. Running such programs is not recommended, and I suggest you jettison them.

But don't despair. There will be new programs that do what yours did, and they'll run in Windows 95. For example, there will be multitasking and multithreading disk defragmenters with an attractive interface that will run in Windows 95. There are also some workarounds that let you use squirrely DOS programs. The numerous DOS box Property settings often provide workarounds to limitations imposed by Windows 95's DOS application defaults. But even these won't allow ambitious DOS programs access to your hard disk. Finally, realize that limitations imposed on DOS applications serve to protect your system and data against any errant programs, so in the long run it means happier computing.

The other good news is that because Microsoft has built many tricks into Windows 95 that allow far more DOS applications to run than did under Windows 3.x yet still protect the system, you should try each program first before concluding that it's history.

Which programs can and can't you run? Well, providing such a list here wouldn't be meaningful because Windows 95 is in flux. When you purchase Windows 95, you can check the software-compatibility list supplied with it.

USING UTILITY PROGRAMS UNDER WINDOWS 95

Do you have a MS-DOS utility that you just can't live without? Does it access hardware directly? Does it check to see if you are trying to run the program under Windows and fail to run if it detects that? If so, don't despair: there may be hope for the application. Just try the following steps:

1. Launch an MS-DOS box. You can use the Start ➤ Programs ➤ MS-DOS Prompt or any other method you desire.

2. Click on the system control box in the upper-left corner of the MS-DOS Prompt window.

3. Select Properties.

4. Click on the Advanced button.

5. Enable (check) the *Prevent MS-DOS-based programs from detecting Windows* check box. Now the MS-DOS application will think it is running under MS-DOS rather than under Windows.

6. Click on the OK button of the Advanced Programs Settings dialog box.

7. Click on the OK button of the MS-DOS Prompt Properties Settings dialog box.

8. In the MS-DOS box, run the **lock** command. This will give the MS-DOS Prompt exclusive access and allow direct access to the hard disk.

9. In the MS-DOS box, run the utility program.

10. When finished with the utility program, run the **unlock** command. This will remove the ability to directly access the hard disk within the MS-DOS Prompt and restore hard-disk access to other applications.

CAUTION If you run an MS-DOS disk utility under Windows 95 that is unaware of long file names, you run the risk of losing all of your long file names (directories and actual files with names greater than the 8.3 limitation) and of possible disk corruption. Before attempting to run an application like this for the first time, back up all your important data.

What Software to Keep and What to Upgrade

As you might have figured out by now, there will be at least three, possibly four, criteria on which to decide whether to keep or upgrade your software:

▶ Does it still run?

▶ Is it safe to use?

▶ Is it a Windows 3.x program that does something that Windows 95 now has built in?

▶ Do I want a faster 32-bit version of the program?

The last section discussed why programs might not run. Consider now why you might not *want* to run a particular program. Consider programs such as Norton Desktop for Windows, WinTools, or another such "shell" replacement for Windows 3.x. These are programs that improve on what was a relatively useless, annoying, and confusing shell. They also tend to include a number of useful utility programs for organizing your hard disk, finding files, recovering files, and so on.

Because Windows 95 is backward-compatible with Windows 3.x applications, you'll still be able to run your favorite shell replacements. For that matter, you'll be able to run Program Manager (progman.exe) and File Manager (winfile.exe) if you're a glutton for punishment. If you've become so accustomed to organizing your work according to the Norton view of the world that going cold turkey would be a hardship, you can stick with it. Of course, you might find that using the Windows 95 Taskbar and the Desktop arrangement is enough like Norton Desktop for Windows that you can live with it. And because the Windows 95 Desktop gives you integrated drag-and-drop capabilities, property sheets, shortcuts, and other such goodies, I'll bet my two cents on people ditching their add-on shell programs. As usual, Microsoft has learned from the competition.

Of course, better mousetraps will hit the market soon enough. And of course, Norton and all the other shell makers will be recompiling their utilities in 32-bit code so they will run faster. There will be new Norton something or other, sporting bells and whistles Microsoft opted not to include or didn't think of: stuff like password protection for all objects or a workaround for the fact that moving files to the Desktop literally means they get moved into the \Windows\Desktop directory. (This can be confusing because getting to these files in File Manager or other applications takes a little searching. Also, if you drag a program (such as `excel.exe`) to the Desktop and try to run it, it's likely not to work. This is because the application's support files will still be in the old directory (e.g., \Msoffice\Excel), while `excel.exe` is now in the Windows\Desktop directory.

> **NOTE** I'm still using PC-Kwik's Toolbox (application and document organizer) on one of my systems, just to see which interface I gravitate towards. I'm still using it for some things, and it does seem to work just fine even though it was designed for Windows 3.x. However, I'm quickly getting addicted to dropping folders and documents right on the Desktop, dragging files to a floppy drive on the Desktop, and so forth. After my first full month of heavy Windows 95 use, I noticed that I had unintentionally weaned myself from my trusty home base, File Manager. The Taskbar and Desktop have their problems, but they are well integrated and convenient.

> **NOTE** Microsoft hasn't been totally remiss on this point. Once you understand what's going on when programs and documents are dragged onto the Desktop, you can easily prevent accidental screwups through the use of shortcuts. See Chapter 5 for shortcut instructions.

Other Extinct and Unnecessary Utilities

Shells are only one class of popular Windows utilities. And we've already discussed disk managers that might be thwarted when attempting microsurgery on your hard disk. But there are scads of other utility programs for Windows, some of which you may rely on daily. For example, I have one called PowerScope that scans my hard disks and generates about five different views of where all my precious disk space went. I have others that test the speed of my Windows system, quit Windows really fast, speed up the floppy disk duplication, scour the disk for a particular file, and so on. Will you still be able to run these, and will they work?

Again, because most Windows 3.x applications were written according to Microsoft's standard Windows 3.x API, execution of these utilities shouldn't be a problem. Theoretically, only a program that goes outside the API will bomb. I've been experimenting with a lot of Windows 3.x utilities and have found that most still perform as expected. However, I've begun to rely on some utilities less. For example, the Start button's Find option is worth its weight in gold. It gives you a box like that in Figure 2.1.

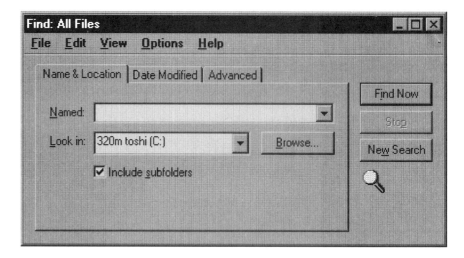

Figure 2.1 **The built-in Find utility**

It's not only always at your fingertips, but once a file, folder, or computer is found, you can manipulate the found object in a manner consistent with other objects in the Windows 95 interface. That is, with a right-mouse click you can run it, view it, cut it, copy it, rename it, create a shortcut to place on the Desktop, or alter its properties (see Figure 2.2).

This is a pretty comprehensive Find utility. It will, for example, scrutinize every file on your hard disk while prospecting for a particular string of text, or list out only files of a certain size. Windows 95's Find isn't the last word in such utilities, though, and future programs from third parties will certainly incorporate the right-mouse-button features. In fact, Microsoft is pushing developers to do just that.

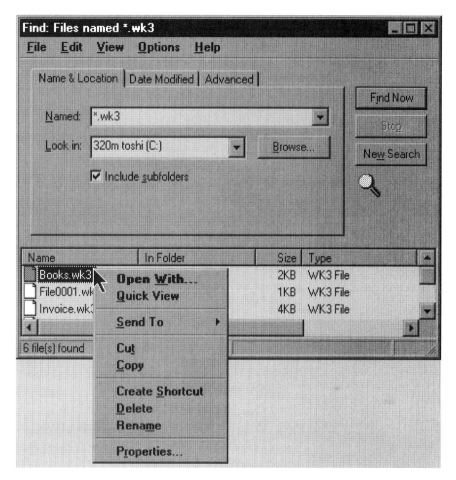

Figure 2.2   *A found object with the right-mouse-click menu open*

Many other classes of Windows 3.x utilities exist, of course, and many will not only be operable but will still supply added value to your system because their functions will not be provided by Windows 95. These include:

▶ advanced font management and translation

▶ virtual screen panning and zooming

▶ cursor shape alteration

▶ macro recording and playback

▶ mouse button assigners

▶ interesting screen savers

▶ floppy- and tape-backup programs

▶ virus checkers

▶ benchmarking programs

Again, it's difficult to prophesy just which older Windows utilities will and won't work, partially because Windows 95 is in flux and partially because compatibility will pivot on how strictly a program adheres to the Windows API. One class of utility that will certainly run into trouble, if not bomb, on Windows 95 are Windows 3.x system optimization (tune-up) programs. Tune-up utilities (e.g., WinSleuth and System Engineer, among others) are popular among power users who want to squeeze every last drop of performance from their Windows systems.

By examining computer's hardware and then thoroughly checking out its Windows configuration settings, these programs either recommend changes or actually go ahead and make them. They churn through the config.sys, autoexec.bat, win.ini, and system.ini files, examining their contents, rearranging entries when necessary, possibly deleting items, and so forth. They also typically optimize disk caching and virtual memory settings.

The problem with running these programs under Windows 95 is as follows: The configuration files that these programs fiddle with are either not actually used by Windows 95 or are used very differently by Windows 95 than by DOS and Windows 3.x. Thus, many changes such a utility makes won't be appropriate or won't make a difference in Windows 95's operation.

As mentioned in Chapter 1, Microsoft developed the Configuration Registry to provide a centralized, easily managed repository of system and applications settings. The Registry replaces or augments these Windows 3.x files:

▶ autoexec.bat, which stores start-up information for the DOS operating system pertaining to some device drivers and TSR programs, declares the system search path, and executes any start-up programs

▶ config.sys, which also loads device drivers, memory managers, and sets up system variables

NOTE   For backward-compatibility reasons, `autoexec.bat` and `config.sys` files have not been completely replaced. The operating system will boot up without them, using its own 32-bit Windows 95–supplied drivers for such things as disk-caching, CD-ROMs, drive doubling, and so forth. However, these two files will likely still be in your start-up drive's root directory and *will* be used by Windows 95 when booting. However, when you run Setup to install Windows 95, Setup will do its best to pare down the `autoexec.bat` and `config.sys` files, removing commands that are no longer valid or are not necessary, so the effect is a definite decrease in reliance on them.

▶ `win.ini`, which stores information about the appearance and configuration of the Windows environment

▶ `system.ini`, which stores software and hardware information that pertains directly to the operation of the operating system, its device drivers, and other system-specific information

▶ `*.ini`, which comprises various initialization files that store user preferences and start-up information about specific applications (e.g., `winfile.ini` for File Manager, `clock.ini` for the `clock.exe` program, and `control.ini` for Control Panel).

Compatibility with 16-bit Windows 3.x applications that expect to find and modify the `win.ini` or `system.ini` files is still present under Windows 95. Any applications that use the Windows 3.x API for making `ini` settings will still be supported under Windows 95. However, that doesn't mean Windows 95 will actually use all those settings. Application-specific `ini` files will still be used by the source application (e.g., when you run a 16-bit version of MS-Works, it'll read `msworks.ini` to load in user preferences), but `win.ini` settings and most `system.ini` settings won't have any effect on Windows 95. The only exception to this is the [enh 386] section of `system.ini`, which *will* be read. If there are any virtual device drivers in this section not already recorded in the Registry, they'll be noticed as Windows 95 boots and will be loaded.

Notwithstanding the ineffectuality of some `ini` files, utility programs conceived to fine-tune Windows 3.x do so by futzing with the SmartDrive, virtual memory, drivers, and other base system settings. Windows 95 not only incorporates new 32-bit drivers for disk caching and virtual memory management that would likely not be affected by these alterations, but Windows 95 also dynamically and intelligently scales many resources to best take advantage of the hardware and software mix on which Windows 95 is running. Therefore, for example, a utility that adjusts the permanent swap file size will have no effect because the swap file in Windows 95 is temporary and changeable in size.

The upshot of all this discussion is that system utilities for Windows 3.x optimization will need at least a face-lift, and more likely a serious overhaul, before you use them on Windows 95. No doubt their manufacturers are busying themselves doing just that even as you read this.

NOTE When you upgrade an existing Windows 3.x system to Windows 95, some application-specific `win.ini` settings *are* migrated into the Windows 95 Registry (for example, associations and OLE-related information). Any preexisting installed application packages—such as 1-2-3, Excel, WordPerfect for Windows, and so on—are noted by the Windows 95 Setup program and incorporated into the Registry so you don't have to install them again. (If you opt to install Windows 95 into its own directory rather than on top of the old Windows 3.x so that you can run either Windows version, then you *will* have to install those applications again from within Windows 95.) After this initial installation, 16-bit applications will still have their `ini` files and will use them to store their settings. 32-bit applications developers are being encouraged to use the Registry to stow applications settings in hopes that one day a preponderance of system and applications settings for each workstation will live in a central repository that can be managed from anywhere on a network.

Faster 32-Bit Applications

Obviously, as Windows 95 takes hold in the market, it will behoove software developers to recompile their applications into 32-bit versions. This will give them a performance edge over their competition and satisfy the needs of users for faster, more reliable, and more efficient programs. Windows 95's compatibility with older 16-bit applications is really only a stopgap measure on Microsoft's part, allowing users to gracefully upgrade to Windows 95 while still using their existing applications.

As a user, some of the decisions about what programs you can and cannot use with Windows 95 will become moot because the attraction to new features and faster performance of 32-bit applications will spur you to upgrade. No doubt many manufacturers will offer a variety of upgrade incentives just as they have in the past.

In the long run, though DOS and Windows 3.x applications support will probably be built into successive iterations of Windows for a long, long time, the impetus really is toward the Windows 32-bit design model. Without 32-bit applications, Windows 95 offers not much more than a face-lift for Windows 3.x. Sure, the new interface offers several key improvements, the colors and screen presentation looks snappier, and long file names are great. But until we're running 32-bit multithreaded applications that have built-in OLE 2.0 support, we're still kind of in the Dark Ages. It's going to get pretty groovy once a critical mass of OLE 2.0 network-aware multimedia applications starts running over the Internet, across your company, or even between bedrooms in your house. In the coming year or two we'll begin to see such spectacles as video teleconferencing for the average home, more very far-out multimedia CDs, interactive groupware, fancy computer-based video-editing systems, virtual-reality games, and who knows what else. Software is a sort of virtual reality in and of itself, and developers' ideas seem limited only by the box with which they have to work.

These developments will affect not only the way we work (and play) but our buying decisions and purchasing patterns. The desire for more functionality in software will lead more software writers to market their software on CD-ROMs because it's cost-inefficient (and even embarrassing) to supply a product on as many as ten or twenty floppies. All of this probably leads to your purchase of 32-bit software just as you bagged your WordPerfect 5.1 in favor of a Windows word processor.

But what does 32-bit software mean? There is a great deal of confusion about 32-bit Windows applications and what will be compatible with what. This is because of the different versions of the 32-bit API and competing versions of the 32-bit operating systems reputed to be capable of running the programs. With terms such as Win32, Win32s, Windows NT, Daytona, Cairo, and Chicago all being bandied about as 32-bit operating systems, it's no wonder.

WHAT THE TERMS MEAN

Win32s: The Win32 Subset API, generally used as the base 32-bit API for Windows 3.x. This is the minimalistic approach to writing 32-bit applications. A Win32s application will run on any 32-bit Microsoft platform (i.e., Windows 3.x, Windows 95, and Windows NT), but does not contain support for multiple threads, security APIs, or a few more APIs that are NT specific.

Win32c: Another Win32 Subset API. This approach includes support for multiple threads and will run on Windows NT and Windows 95 but not Windows 3.x. It also does not include support for security and a few other APIs that are NT specific.

Win32: The full-blown 32-bit API that is based on Windows NT. Some applications that use this API set will not run on Windows 3.x or Windows 95 if those use APIs that are not supported by the other subset versions (Win32s/Win32c).

Windows NT: Windows NT 3.5

Daytona: Windows NT 3.5

Cairo: Windows NT? Will this be Windows NT 95 or Windows NT 4.0? It's not clear. But its primary feature is that it will include an object-oriented file system. OLE 2.0–compliant applications will run unmodified on this version and be able to take advantage of some features of this object-oriented file system. This version of NT will really take the document-centric approach to the extreme.

Chicago: Has been replaced by Windows 95.

So here's the simple lowdown. There is only one 32-bit API, but it's somewhat in flux. Think of the API as a list of ingredients. Depending on which subset of the ingredients from the API a program uses, it'll be able to run higher or lower on the Windows food chain. So if a program uses all the ingredients, it can only run on NT. A slightly lesser use of the API will allow it to run on Windows 95. Even less, and it'll run in Windows 3.x.

However, according to Microsoft, by following simple guidelines, third-party developers have written 32-bit programs (not 16-bit, mind you) that will run on Windows 3.x, Windows 95, and Windows NT platforms with no modification. If this is so, these are programs with the least amount of 32-bit goodies built in, unless they have conditional code (such as multithreading) that kicks in only once they sense they're running in Windows 95 or NT. To keep the size of programs down, software makers are more likely to recompile their software into several versions, one for each platform. You'll be reading the labels on boxes much the way you read the ingredients on the back of food jars in the grocery store, I'd imagine. "Windows 95-compatible" will not mean the same thing as "Fully Windows 95 Aware" or "Multithreaded Version." Keep your eyes peeled.

What Hardware to Keep and What to Upgrade

In the context of this chapter's discussion about "getting ready for Windows 95," next I'll provide an overview of the hardware requirements and considerations pertinent to running Windows 95 successfully.

The Box

Let's start with the basic box, the computer itself, if you will. Windows 95 is going to run its fastest, of course, on fast 486 and Pentium machines. Actual performance of Windows 95 is impossible to judge at this point because optimization of the Windows 95 code (called *performance tuning*) is the last stage of software development just before a product ships. However, Microsoft's advance documentation claims Windows 95 will run reasonably speedily on typical 386 DX machines.

If you can lay your hands on a real Plug-and-Play machine (it needs a Plug-and-Play BIOS built in) *and* a fast processor such as a 486 DX/100 or Pentium, this is the formula for a Windows 95 powerhouse that'll prove effortless to upgrade when it comes time to stuff in a new card or two.

For low-to-medium performance using productivity applications such as word processors, 33-MHz 386 DX machines will likely prove adequate under Windows 95. For slightly slower—but still workable—performance, you may use an SX machine. For more demanding application mixes, such as graphics, computer-aided design, heavy database use, and particularly for networked machines that will serve as printer and communication servers, you'll want to be running Windows 95 on 486 50s, 66s, DX4/100s, and Pentiums. With the price of systems dropping like lead balls off the Tower of Pisa, it doesn't make sense to buy anything short of a DX2/66 at this point. For only a tad more you'll get a Pentium. You should purchase a system with a *local bus*, either VLB or PCI.

The jury is out as to which is better. Add-on cards for VLB are more abundant and a bit cheaper at this point. A new version of VLB (VLB 2.0) is about to hit the streets, so if you decide on VLB, you might look for a machine with this spec.

Suffice it to say that older 286-based machines are now out of the picture. They simply won't run the 32-bit code on which Windows 95 is built. If you want Windows or Windows networking compatibility on these machines, your only options are to run Windows 3.0 or Windows 3.1 in Standard mode or to run the DOS program *Workgroup Connection* (included with Windows for Workgroups) to connect to a Windows network.

RAM

Microsoft has a big-time incentive to make Windows 95 run well with 4 MB of RAM. This is simply because of the number of 4-MB machines out there and the cost of RAM chips. Just as auto manufacturers had a huge incentive (not to mention federal mandates) to make autos with higher gas mileage during the mid-seventies oil crisis, Windows 95 is going to have to do well with relatively little RAM. For the last couple of years RAM prices have hit the roof. This was particularly true in 1993, supposedly because of the accidental decimation of a major plastic fabrication plant in Japan. Prices hit as much as $100 per megabyte. Whether the fire was legitimate or trumped up is another question. Still, the vast majority of existing and new systems are endowed with no more than 4 MB of RAM. Upgrades at the time of this writing are about $40 per megabyte.

Just as with NT, even the beta version of Windows 95 scales automatically and intelligently to avail itself of any extra RAM you throw its way. I'm writing this on a Toshiba T4700 with 16 MB of RAM, and things are flying right along. Two of the other machines I've been testing the beta on have 4 MB and 8 MB respectively. The 4-MB machine does a lot more disk swapping (slowing operations as Windows 95 temporarily writes out RAM data to the hard disk or restores it from disk back into RAM). However, this impact will probably be minimized once Windows 95 is tuned. The 8-MB machine works just dandy. If there is advice to be given, it's that 4 MB is going to be acceptable, but you're really going to really appreciate 8 MB if you can find it in your budget.

Hard Disk

You'll need about 50 MB of free space to install Windows 95, so you'll want a hard disk with plenty of space. Add to this the advantage you'll get from having free disk space for the dynamically sized virtual-memory cache, and you can see why free disk space will be important when installation time comes rolling around. Whether Windows 95's Setup program will be forgiving in this regard when upgrading (many Windows 3.x files will be erased and/or replaced as part of the setup process) remains to be seen. The good news is that drives are *cheap* now. You can buy a 500-MB drive for about $300 these days if you shop. Also, the Windows 95 support files (basically everything you see in the directories) do not have to be on the boot drive. If you have a two-drive system, drive D can hold everything except the boot tracks. The Setup program sleuths around for a drive with enough space to handle the install process and suggests a drive and directory.

You'll want to use a fast hard disk. So what else is new. Well, not everyone knows that the hard disk and video card are the two most likely bottlenecks in a system. Your hard-disk system should preferably be a SCSI II system, but if not, it should at least be a SCSI or IDE type using a local bus controller. You'll want a drive with a fast access time, too, 'round about 12 ms (milliseconds) average access time. (Average access time is a specification that will likely be advertised along with the drive's price.)

Monitor/Video-Card Support

You can bet Windows 95 will be packaged with 32-bit driver support for many devices, including a wide variety of video cards. Even in the beta, support for all generic VGA cards and the more popular cards based on chip sets such as the Mach, S3, ET-4000, Western Digital, and Weitech were all on board. In fact, Setup will run around and look at your hardware, investigating the video card's identity and doing its best to load the appropriate drivers. In all four of my systems, this has worked reliably.

However, if drivers for your board(s) are not supplied with Windows 95, you won't have to fret. Unlike the situation with Windows NT, Microsoft says your old Windows 3.x 16-bit drivers happily glom right on to Windows 95. I tested this promise on a very freaky monitor, the

19-inch monochrome WYSE 1790 whose controller card is built around the Tseng Labs ET-3000 chip set. After installation, Windows 95 was running just fine using the old WYSE proprietary Windows 3.x driver I've been relying on for years.

Because slowpoke video cards can bring even the zippiest of systems to a seeming crawl, and because Microsoft has gone video happy with Windows 95, you'll want to lay your hands on a fast video card before upgrading, if possible. The full-window drag (Plus Pack option), for example, is so boss, you'll definitely want to set this option *on*. But if your video card is slow (i.e., it's on the ISA bus and/or doesn't have a coprocessor), windows will then leave trails as you move them around on screen. The only solution then is to turn off full-window drag, which only shows the outline of a window as you drag it.

Of course more and more programs and games are getting bit-blit intensive, meaning they rely on heavy-duty graphics and the ability to rapidly move images around the screen. Because some of the color schemes in such programs, and even in the Windows interface itself, call on a palette of 256 colors or more, it'll serve you to shop for a card with at least 1 MB of VRAM (not DRAM—see an explanation of the distinction in Chapter 31), resolution equal to or above that of your monitor, and a refresh rate of at least 72 Hz, noninterlaced, at the desired resolution. For really great color, you'll want the card to display at least 64 thousand colors at your desired resolution.

If your computer has a local bus, the video card should be one that plugs into one of the edge connectors attached to this bus (e.g., VLB or PCI bus) rather than into the normal, slower system-bus slots. If your system doesn't have a local bus, it's not a big deal. As far as operating Windows 95 goes, even the most prehistoric, simple VGA cards will run fine. I've been using a very old, generic VGA card on one of my systems. It's not flashy, but it works.

Plug-and-Play Items

Just plug in a board, reboot your computer, and you're off and running. All existing peripherals, sound boards, video boards, network cards, and so forth are automatically configured for you as the operating system boots up. No DIP switches to set, no IRQ conflicts, no hassles. Sounds impossible, right? Well, yes, it's currently a pipe dream, but this is the scenario which, when Plug and Play (PnP) is fully implemented, we'll all become quickly accustomed to.

 NOTE   For more about what Plug and Play is and how it works, turn to Chapter 31.

For PnP to work, three areas of technology must coordinate: the system BIOS, the operating system, and the applications. That leaves out all existing 16-bit applications, the huge majority of existing plug-in cards (with the exception of credit-card PCMCIA), and all "legacy" systems (any computer without PnP specifically built into the BIOS).

 NOTE   To gain the "Windows-95 compatible" logo, hardware and software must be PnP capable. Look for this logo when buying.

With the number of older computers around that do not have PnP-aware BIOS chips in them, such as traditional ISA and EISA machines, we've got major sticking point number one. Windows 95 itself, of course, will be PnP-aware, so the operating-system angle is covered. Then there's the applications. Well, we'll have to wait for the next generation of PnP-aware 32-bit Windows 95 applications for that.

So, in preparation for Windows 95's release, should you be considering buying PnP boards? Whole PnP computers? Definitely. Estimates are that by the end of 1995 the preponderance of new systems will be PnP-ready. Ditto for add-in cards. Purchasing systems and boards now that comply with the spec will save you precious time and Excedrin headaches later.

In addition, even though legacy systems will always be somewhat handicapped in supporting PnP, Plug-and-Play cards will still work in them and can provide you at least half the advantage of a fully PnP-aware system. How? A product called the Plug-and-Play toolkit from Microsoft can help bridge the gap. It works on ISA machines with both DOS and Windows 3.x (and eventually Windows 95) to simulate a sort of first-generation PnP. The kit helps your computer keep track of hardware in the system, using an internal database that you generate by entering various existing card settings into the database yourself. Thereafter, however, this utility manages negotiations with the operating system when you add new PnP cards. These database configuration settings will then be imported into Windows 95 when you later upgrade to it.

There's no doubt that PnP is going to become an industry standard. If implemented correctly, it will eliminate the most common headache in PC support—system-expansion incompatibilities. When shopping for new hardware at this point, you will want to look for as much PnP-awareness as possible, both for your add-on cards and complete systems. Be aware that equipment must bear the full Plug-and-Play moniker (with capital letters) to be truly compliant. And like other evolving industry standards (SCSI, PCMCIA, VLB, PCI, just to name a few) the spec for PnP is likely to fluctuate as bugs or oversights become evident over time. We're all held hostage on that account. A first-generation PnP anything may have a short half-life, but it beats shelling out good money for a system or card that's totally PnP brain-dead. Be aware also, that not all peripherals benefit from PnP awareness.

Other Upgrades

What else is there to consider? Sound cards, SCSI cards, CD-ROM drives, network boards. Don't worry about any of these. If these hardware items work with Windows 3.x, they'll operate correctly within Windows 95. If drivers for your cards aren't supplied initially by Windows 95, you can use your old ones. Eventually, every board manufacturer will supply 32-bit drivers for their hardware.

As mentioned above, if you're replacing or upgrading a board, consider a PnP-compliant one. As of this writing, finding such boards isn't easy, but this state of affairs should change in the second half of 1995.

Chapter 3

What Is Windows?

FEATURING

An overview of the Windows interface

Types of windows

Menus

Dialog boxes

The Help system

Quitting Windows

In this chapter, I'll begin explaining Windows so you can start using your computer to get your work done. If you're an experienced Windows user, you can skim this chapter just to get the gist of the new features of Windows 95. If, on the other hand, you're new to Windows, you should read this chapter thoroughly because it will introduce you to essential Windows concepts and skills that you'll need to have no matter what your line of work is or what you intend to do with your computer. A solid grasp of these concepts will also help you understand and make best use of the rest of this book.

A Brief Windows Recap

Windows owes its name to the fact that it runs each application or document in its own separate *window*. A window is a box or frame on the screen. Figure 3.1 shows several such windows.

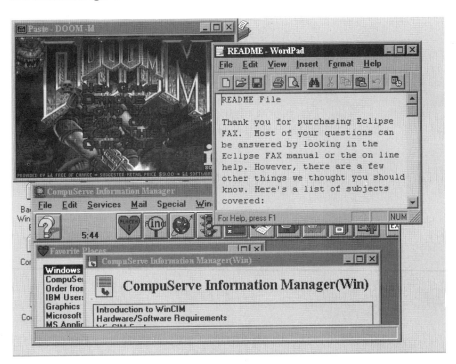

Figure 3.1   Windows are frames that hold information of some sort on the screen.

You can have numerous windows on the screen at a time, each containing its own program and/or document. You can then easily switch between programs without having to close one down and open the next.

Another feature that Windows has is a facility—called the Clipboard—that lets you copy material between dissimilar document types, making it easy to *cut* and *paste* information from, say, a spreadsheet into a company report or a scanned photograph of a house into a real-estate brochure. In essence, Windows provides the means for seamlessly joining the capabilities of very different application programs. Not only can you paste portions of one document into another, but by using an advanced document-linking feature—called Object Linking and Embedding (OLE) —those pasted elements remain *live*. That is, if the source document (such as some spreadsheet data) changes, the results will also be reflected in the secondary document (such as a word-processing document) containing the pasted data.

In addition to expediting the way you use your existing applications, Windows comes with quite a handful of its own little programs. For example, there's a word-processing program called WordPad; a drawing program called Paint; a communications program called HyperTerminal for connecting to outside information services with a modem; a couple of games; utilities for keeping your hard disk in good working order (or even doubling the amount of space on it); a data-backup program; and a mail system for communicating with the outside world—just to name a few.

Before Moving Ahead

Before going on in this book, make sure you've read the introduction and installed Windows correctly on your computer (installation is explained in the Appendix). Then, while experimenting with Windows on your computer, you should feel free to experiment (if with some caution) as I explain things you can do, offer tips, and so forth. Experimentation is the best way to learn. I'll try to warn against things you shouldn't do, so don't worry. Experience really is the best teacher—especially with computers. Contrary to popular belief, they really won't blow up if you make a mistake!

If at any time while reading this chapter you have to quit Windows to do other work or to turn off your computer, just jump to the end of this chapter and read the section called *Exiting Windows*. Also, if at any time you don't understand how to use a Windows command or perform some procedure, read the section near the end of this chapter that covers Windows' built-in Help facility.

If you truly get stuck and don't know how to escape from some procedure you're in the middle of, the last resort is to reboot your computer and start up Windows again. Though this isn't a great idea, and you may lose part of any documents you're working on, it won't actually kill Windows or your computer. You reboot your computer by pressing the Ctrl, Alt, and Del keys simultaneously (in other words, press Ctrl and hold, press Alt and hold both, then tap Del. Don't try to hit all three at once!) and then clicking on the Shut Down button. Sometimes you might have to press Ctrl, Alt, and Del again (that is, twice in a row). Other surefire ways to reboot the computer are by pressing the reset switch on your computer or turning your computer off, waiting about five seconds, and then turning it on again.

NOTE   These are last resorts to exiting Windows and can result in losing some of your work! It's better to follow the instructions at the end of this chapter.

Starting Windows

To start up Windows and get to work, follow these steps:

1. Remove any floppy disk from the computer's floppy disk drives.

2. Turn on your computer, screen, and any other stuff you're likely to use (for example an external CD-ROM drive or external modem).

3. Wait. Unlike in the old days of Windows 3.1, the DOS prompt (C:>) will not appear. Instead, after a few seconds you'll see the Windows 95 start-up logo, which may seem to sit there a long time. You'll see some action on the screen, such as some little arrows moving across the bottom or little windows flitting about. This means don't worry, your computer is still alive. Windows takes quite a while to load from your hard disk into RAM, so just wait.

TECH TIP   If you have 16-bit device drivers included in your `autoexec.bat` file, you may see a command prompt instead of the Windows 95 logo while Windows 95 loads. Also, if you press Esc while the Windows 95 logo is displayed, the logo will disappear and you'll see a listing of your `config.sys` lines as they load.

4. After about 15 seconds or so, the Windows sign-on dialog box appears and asks you to type in your user name and password.

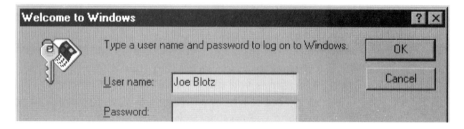

Enter your password. If this is the first time you've run Windows, then you can think up and enter your password at this point. If you upgraded from Windows for Workgroups, your old user name and password should work just as it did before. Then click on OK (or press Enter).

NOTE   *Clicking* means positioning the mouse pointer on the item in question and then clicking the left button once. Double-clicking means clicking on an item twice in quick succession.

5. If you are hooked up to a network and Windows 95 detected the network and installed itself for network activities, you'll be prompted to enter your network password, like this:

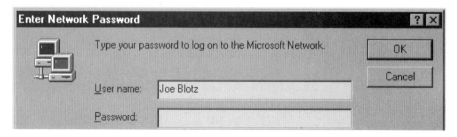

This might seem redundant, as you entered a password already. No, it's not Fort Knox. It's just that there are two possible password requirements—one that gets you into your own computer and into a workgroup, and another one for signing you onto a network domain. A typical peer-to-peer network of Windows 95 machines is considered a workgroup. If your workgroup machine is interconnected with a Windows NT Server, then the second password will be used by Windows 95 to authenticate you on the Microsoft Network domain. If you don't already have a network user name and password, enter it now. You'll be prompted to confirm it.

 NOTE   The sequence of boxes that prompt you for your user name and password the first time you run Windows 95 will likely be different from subsequent sessions. You'll have fewer steps after signing in the first time because you won't be asked to confirm your password.

6. Click on OK (or press Enter).

Now the Windows 95 starting screen—the Desktop—appears, looking approximately like that in Figure 3.2. Take a look at your screen and compare it to the figure. Your screen may look a bit different, but the general landscape will be the same. You may see a Welcome box asking if you want to take a tour of Windows or get some help about Windows. Just click on the Close button. We'll discuss the Help system and the Windows Tour later.

 NOTE   If you or someone else has used your Windows 95 setup already, it's possible that some open windows will come up when Windows 95 boots. It's also possible that you'll see more icons on the Desktop than what's shown in Figure 3.2, depending on what options you installed when you set up Windows 95.

Parts of the Windows Screen

Now let's take a quick look at the three basic parts of the Windows start-up screen: the Desktop, icons, and the Taskbar. Once you understand these three essential building blocks (and one other—a *window*—which you'll see in a few minutes) you'll begin to get a feel for how Windows works.

Figure 3.2   *The initial Windows 95 screen. This starting screen is called the Desktop—the place where you can organize your work and interact with your computer a bit like the way you use your real desk.*

The Desktop

The *Desktop* is your overall work area while in Windows. It's called the Desktop because Windows uses your whole screen in a way that's analogous to the way you'd use the surface of a desk. As you work in Windows, you move items around on the Desktop, retrieve and put away items (as if in a drawer), and perform your other day-to-day tasks. You do all of this using graphical representations of your work projects.

November Budget   Music School Logo   Letters

The analogy of the Desktop falls a bit short sometimes, but it's useful for understanding how the program helps you organize your activities.

You can put your favorite (e.g., most oft-used) items on the Desktop so getting to them requires less hunting around. Each time you run Windows, those items will be right there where you left them. This is a great feature of Windows 95.

In Figure 3.2, which displays a "virgin" system where nobody has added anything new to the Desktop, there are four items ready to go. (You may have slightly different items, depending on options you chose when installing Windows 95.) We'll get to what those items actually do later, but you get the picture. When you add your own items, such as your thesis, your recipe list, or your latest version of Doom, they'll be represented by little graphics just like these four items are.

Icons

Icons are the second basic element of the Windows screen. Along the left side of your Desktop, you'll see a few icons. Icons are small symbols with names under them. Windows 95 uses icons to represent folders, documents, and programs when they are not currently opened up and running. Below are a couple of icons.

My Computer

Research for
Thesis

Icons that look like file folders are just that—folders. Folders, just like on the Mac, are used to keep related documents or programs together. You can even have folders within folders, a useful feature for really organizing your work from the top down.

NOTE Folders, in DOS and Windows 3.x terminology, were called *directories,* or when used to group collections of programs and documents in Program Manager, *groups.* As of Windows 95, groups and directories are now called folders.

There's another kind of icon-ish sort of thing you'll need to know about. Technically, it's called a *minimized window*. When you want to get a window off the screen temporarily but within easy reach, you minimize it. This lets you do work with a document that's in another window without any extra clutter on the screen. When a window is *minimized* in this way, it's as if its program or document is shoved

to the edge of your desk for a moment and put in a little box.

There are several variations on these boxes, but the upshot is the same: the program or document's window will pop up again if you simply click or double-click on it (more about double-clicking later). Sometimes a minimized window is referred to as being *iconized*.

NOTE   Incidentally, while minimized, the program or document will actually be running. It's just that because it's shrunken, you can't interact with it. This means a spreadsheet could still be calculating, a database could be sorting, or a communications program could still be sending in your e-mail while it's minimized.

What Is a Window, Anyway?

Just in case this whole "windows" thing is eluding you, here's the scoop on what a window is and the various types of windows. Because there are different types, people can get somewhat confused when looking at a bunch of windows on the screen.

When you want to do some work, you open up a program or document with the mouse or keyboard, and a window containing it appears on the Desktop. This is similar to pulling a file folder or notebook off the shelf, placing it on the desk, and opening it up. In Windows, you do this for each task you want to work on.

Just as with a real desktop, you can have a number of project windows scattered about, all of which can be in progress. You can then easily switch between your projects, be they letters, address lists, spreadsheets, games, or whatever. This is unlike old-style PC computing under DOS where you have to "put away" one project before opening the next.

Of course, if you happen to be a neatnik, you can opt to have only one document or program open at a time and keep the Desktop clutter free, so to speak. But there are advantages to the messy-desk approach. For example, you can view two documents (such as a spreadsheet and a report you are writing about) simultaneously by placing each document side by side in separate windows that you size to fit on the screen, as you see in Figure 3.3. This approach also allows you to copy material from one document to another more easily by cutting and pasting between them.

Another feature designed into Windows is that it can be instructed to remember certain aspects of your work setup each time you quit. For example, if you use a certain group of programs regularly, you can set up Windows to come up with those programs already running—or ready to run with just a click of the mouse. Programs you use less frequently will be stored away within easy reach without cluttering your Desktop.

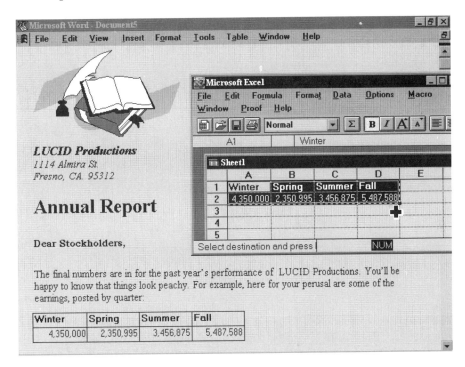

Figure 3.3   Windows let you see several documents simultaneously.

Types of Windows

Now let's look a little more closely at the various parts of the Desktop. There are three types of windows that you'll encounter while working: *application windows, document windows,* and *folder windows.*

NOTE If you want to place a window on the screen that you can play with a bit as you read the next section about window sizing, double-click on the My Computer icon.

Application Windows

Application windows are those that contain a program that you are running and working with, such as Microsoft Word, Excel, PC Paintbrush, WordPerfect, and so on. Most of the work that you do will be in application windows. Figure 3.4 shows a typical application window, sometimes called a *parent window*.

Figure 3.4   An application window is a window that a program is running in.

Document Windows

Some programs let you have more than one document open within them at a time. What does this mean? Well, take the spreadsheet program

Microsoft Excel, for example. It allows you to have several spread-sheets open at once, each in its own document window. Instead of running Excel several times in separate application windows, (which would use up too much precious RAM) you just run it once and open several document windows within Excel's main window. Figure 3.5 shows Excel with two document windows open inside it.

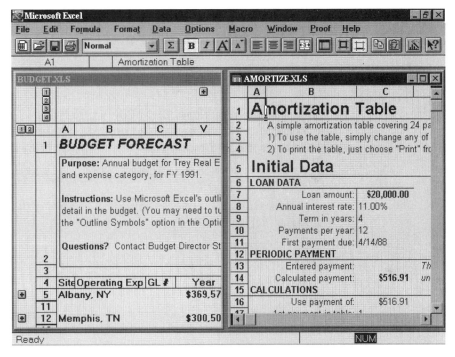

Figure 3.5 *Two document (child) windows within an application (parent) window*

 NOTE Incidentally, document windows are sometimes called *child windows*.

Anatomy of a Window

Now let's consider the parts of a typical window. All windows have the same elements in them, so once you understand one of them, the rest will make sense to you. Of course, some programs have extra stuff like fancy toolbars built in, but you learn about those things as you experiment with the particular program. Here we're talking about the elements common to any kind of window.

The Title Bar

OK. Let's start from the top and work down. The name of the program or document appears at the top of its respective window, in what's called the *title bar*. In Figure 3.5, notice the title bars read Microsoft Excel, BUDGET.XLS, and AMORTIZE.XLS. If you were running another application, such as Ventura Publisher or Paint, its name would be shown there instead.

Sometimes an application window's title bar also contains the name of the document being worked on. For example, here Notepad's title bar shows the name of the document being edited:

The title reads Notepad, followed by the name of the file being edited, `networks.txt`.

The title bar also serves another function: it indicates which window is *active*. Though you can have a lot of windows on the screen at once, there can be only one active window at any given time. The active window is the one you're currently working in. When a window is made active, it jumps to the front of other windows that might be obscuring it, and its title bar changes color. (On monochrome—black and white—monitors, the intensity of the title bar changes.) You make a window active by clicking anywhere within its border.

Minimize, Maximize, and Close

There are three small buttons at the right end of the title bar with small graphics in them—the Minimize, Maximize, and Close buttons.

Referring to Figure 3.6, the button with the skinny line in it is the *Minimize* button. The one to its right is the *Maximize* button. The third one is called the *Close* button. These are little control buttons with which you quickly change the size of a window, as I'll explain in a moment.

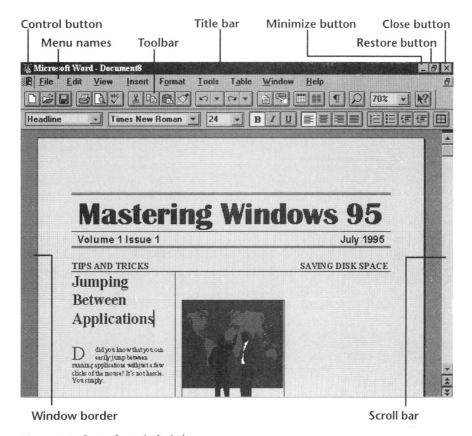

Control button   Title bar   Minimize button   Close button
Menu names   Toolbar   Restore button

Window border   Scroll bar

Figure 3.6   *Parts of a typical window*

NOTE   In Windows 3.x there were only two buttons at the right side of title bars, and they had small arrows in them. Now there are three buttons, and the graphics have changed a bit. Minimize and Maximize are still there, but a single-click Close button has been added. This new button eliminates the need for double-clicking the Control Box or choosing File/Close to close an application (these techniques varied too much between applications, confusing users). Now you can close any application (including a DOS box) with a single click on the "X" button.

After a window has been maximized, the Maximize button changes to the *Restore* button. Restore buttons have two little boxes in them. (Restored size is neither full screen nor minimized. It's anything in between.)

There are essentially three sizes that a window can have:

▶ Minimized: the window becomes an icon at the bottom of the Desktop (or of the application's window if it's a child window), where it's ready to be opened again but takes up a minimum of screen space.

▶ Normal: the window is open and takes up a portion of the Desktop, the amount of which is determined by how you manually size the window, as explained in the next section. This is also called the *restored* size.

▶ Maximized: the window takes up the whole Desktop. When you maximize a document window, it expands to take up the entire application window. This may or may not be the entire screen, depending on whether the application's window is maximized.

Here are the basic mouse techniques to quickly change the size of a window. To try these techniques, you'll first want to open a window on your screen. If you don't already have a window open, you can open one by double-clicking on the icon called My Computer. I'll explain this icon's purpose later. But just for discussion, try double-clicking on it. If nothing happens, you didn't click fast enough. Make sure you're clicking the left mouse button (on a standard right-handed mouse or trackball).

To Minimize a Window

1. First, if you have a number of windows open, click inside the perimeter of one you want to work with. This will activate it.

2. Position the mouse pointer (the arrow that moves around on the screen when you move the mouse) on the Minimize button (the one with the short line in it) and click.

The window reduces to the size of an icon and "goes" down to the bottom of the screen in the Taskbar. The window's name is shown beside the icon so you know what it is.

To Restore a Window from an Icon

OK. Now suppose you want to get the window back again. It's simple. The window is waiting for you, iconized down on the Taskbar.

1. Move the mouse to position the pointer just over the little My Computer button down at the bottom of your screen, in the Taskbar. (Unless for some reason your Taskbar has been moved to one of the other edges of the screen, in which case use that. Changing the Taskbar's location is covered in Chapter 4.)

2. Click on the button. The window is now restored to its previous size.

To Maximize a Window

You maximize a window when you want it to be as large as possible. When maximized, a window will take up the whole screen. Unless you have a very large screen, or need to be able to see two application windows at the same time, this is the best way to work on typical documents. For example, in a word-processing program, you'll see the maximum amount of text at one time with the window maximized.

1. Activate the window by clicking within its perimeter.

2. Click on its Maximize button:

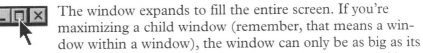 The window expands to fill the entire screen. If you're maximizing a child window (remember, that means a window within a window), the window can only be as big as its parent. So it might not be able to get as large as the screen; you'd have to maximize the parent window first. You have to look carefully to find the location of maximize and minimize buttons for child windows. Don't confuse them with the buttons for the parent application window. As an example, look at Figure 3.7.

After you maximize a window, its Maximize button changes to a Restore button.

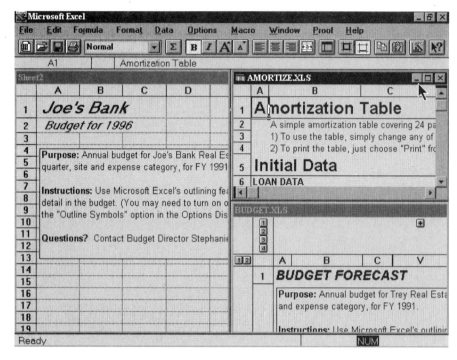

Figure 3.7   Document windows have their own Minimize, Maximize, Close, and Restore buttons. Don't confuse them with the buttons for the application they're running in.

Clicking on this button will restore the window to its "restored" size, which is neither full nor iconized; it's the intermediate size that you either manually adjusted it to (see below) or the size that it originally had when you opened the window.

To Manually Adjust the Size of a Window

Sometimes you'll want to adjust the size of a window manually to a very specific size. You might want to arrange several windows side by side, for example, so you can easily see them both, copy and paste material between them, and so forth.

TIP   Clicking on and dragging a corner allows you to change both the width and height of the window at one time.

You manually resize a window using these steps: Carefully position the cursor on any edge or corner of the window that you want to resize. The lower-right corner is easiest on windows that have a little triangular tab there, designed just for resizing. (You'll only see this feature in newer programs, though, or those supplied with Windows 95.) When you are in the right position, the cursor shape changes to a two-headed arrow, as you can see in Figure 3.8. Press the left mouse button and hold it down. A "ghost" of the window's outline moves with the arrow to indicate that you are resizing the window. Drag the window edge or corner to the desired position and then release the mouse button.

 NOTE   Dragging simply means keeping the mouse button depressed while moving the mouse.

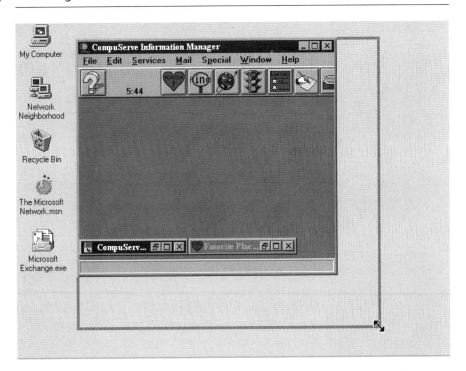

Figure 3.8   Change a window's size by dragging its corner.

The Control Box

Every title bar has a little icon at its far left side. This is the Control box. It has two functions. First, it opens a menu, called the Control menu. Figure 3.9 shows a Control box with its Control menu open. This is the same menu you get when you single-click on an iconized window. This menu only comes up from the Control box when you single-click. Most of the commands on this menu let you control the size of the window. (Menus are covered in detail later in this chapter.)

Figure 3.9   Single-clicking on the Control box brings up the Control menu.

Second, the Control box for a program or document will close the window (terminate the program or close the document) when you double-click on it.

 NOTE   Pressing Alt-Hyphen opens the Control box of the active child window; Alt-Spacebar opens the Control box of the active parent window.

Scroll Bars, Scroll Buttons, and Scroll Boxes

On the bottom and right edges of many windows, you'll find *scroll bars*, *scroll buttons*, and *scroll boxes*. These are used to "pan across" the information in a window: up, down, left, and right. This is necessary when there is too much information (text or graphics) to fit into the window at one time. For example, you might be writing a letter that is two pages long. Using the scroll bars lets you move around, or scroll, within your document to see the section you're interested in, as two full pages of text won't be displayed in a window at one time. Scrolling lets you look at a large amount of data through what amounts to a small window—your screen. Figure 3.10 illustrates this concept. Many Windows operations—such as listing files on your disks, reading Help screens, or displaying a lot of icons within a window—require the use of scroll bars and boxes.

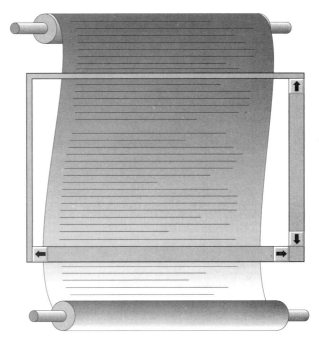

Figure 3.10 *Scrolling lets you work with more information than will fit on your screen at one time.*

Scroll bars have a little box in them called the *scroll box*, sometimes called an *elevator*. Just as an elevator can take you from one floor of a building to the next, the scroll bar takes you from one section of a window or document to the next. The elevator moves within the scroll bar to indicate which portion of the window you are viewing at any given time. By moving the elevator with your mouse, you cause the document to scroll.

Try these exercises to see how scroll bars and boxes work:

1. If you haven't already double-clicked on the My Computer icon, do so now. A window will open. (We'll discuss the purpose of the My Computer windows later. For now just use one as an example.) Using the technique explained above, size the window so that it shows

only a few icons, as shown below. A horizontal or vertical scroll bar (or possibly both) appears on the bottom edge of the window. This indicates that there are more icons in the window than are visible because the window is now so small. What has happened is that several icons are now out of view.

2. Click on the elevator with the left mouse button, keep the button held down, and slide the elevator in its little shaft. Notice that as you do this, the elevator moves along with the pointer, and the window's contents are repositioned. (Incidentally, this mouse technique is called *dragging*.)

3. Now try another approach to scrolling. Click on the scroll buttons (the little arrows at the ends of the scroll bar). With each click, the elevator moves a bit in the direction of the button you're clicking on. If you click and hold, the elevator continues to move.

4. One more approach is to click within the scroll bar on either side of the elevator. Each click scrolls the window up or down a bit. With many programs, the screen will scroll one full screenful with each click.

This example used only a short window with relatively little information in it. In this case, maximizing the window or resizing it just a bit would eliminate the need for scrolling and is probably a better solution. However, with large documents or windows containing many icons, scrolling becomes a necessity, as you'll see later.

All About Menus

The *menu bar* is a row of words that appears just below the title bar. (It appears only on application windows. Document windows do not have menu bars.) If you click on one of the words in the menu bar (called a menu *name*), a menu opens up, displaying a series of options that you can choose from. It is through menus that you tell all Windows programs what actions you want carried out.

Try this as an example:

1. With the My Computer window open and active, click on the word *File* in the menu bar. A menu opens, as you see in Figure 3.11, listing seven options. You can see why it's called a menu; it's a bit like a restaurant menu listing things you can order.

TECH TIP   You could also have pressed Alt-F to open the File menu. If there is an underlined letter in any menu's name, holding down the Alt key and pressing that letter opens the menu.

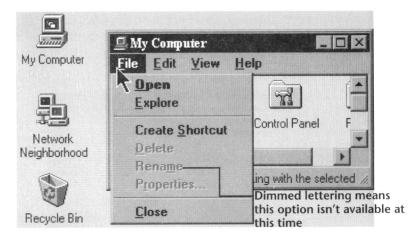

Figure 3.11   Open a menu by clicking on its name in the menu bar.

2. Slide the mouse pointer to the right to open the other menus (Edit, View, or Help) and examine their choices.

As you might surmise, each menu contains choices somewhat relevant to the menu's name. The names on menus vary from program to program, but there are usually a few common ones, such as File, Edit, and Help. It may take a while for you to become familiar with the commands and which menus they're located on, but it will become more automatic with time. In any case, it's easy enough to look around through the menus to find the one you want.

Selecting Menu Commands

Once a menu is open, you can select any of the commands in the menu that aren't dimmed (dimmed choices are explained below).

 NOTE   At this point, don't select any of the commands just yet. We'll begin using the commands in a bit.

When a menu is open, you can select a menu command in any of these ways:

▶ By typing the underlined letter in the command name

▶ By sliding the mouse down and clicking on a command's name

▶ By pressing the down-arrow or up-arrow keys on your keyboard to highlight the desired command name and then pressing Enter

You can cancel a menu (that is, make the menu disappear without selecting any commands) by simply pressing the Esc key or by clicking anywhere outside of the menu.

Special Indicators in Menus

Menus often have special symbols that tell you a little more about the menu commands. For example, examine the menus in Figure 3.12. Notice that many of these commands have additional words or symbols next to the command name. For example, the Options command has ellipses (three dots) after it. Other commands may have check marks, triangles, or key combinations listed beside them. Here are the meanings of these words or symbols:

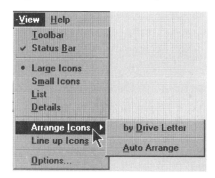
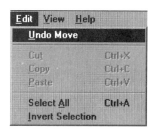

Figure 3.12   *Typical menus*

A Grayed (Dimmed) Command Name

When a command is shown as *grayed*, or *dimmed*, it means that this choice is not currently available to you. A command can be dimmed for a number of reasons. For example, a command for changing the typestyle of text will be grayed if you haven't selected any text. Other times, commands will be grayed because you are in the wrong program mode. For example, if a window is already maximized, the Maximize command on the Control menu will be dimmed because this choice doesn't make sense.

Ellipses (…)

Ellipses next to a command means that you will be asked for additional information before Windows or the Windows application executes the command. When you select such a command, a dialog box will appear on the screen, asking you to fill in the needed information. (I'll discuss dialog boxes in the next section of this chapter.)

A Check Mark (✓)

A check mark preceding a command means the command is a *toggle* that is activated (turned on). A toggle is a command that is alternately turned off and on each time you select it. It's like those old high-beam switches on the car floor that you step on to change between high beams and low beams. Each time you select one of these commands, it switches from *active* to *inactive*. If there is no check mark, then the command or setting is inactive. This is typically used to indicate things like whether selected text is underlined or not, which font is selected, what mode you are in within a program, and so on.

A Triangle (▶)

A triangle to the right of a menu command means that the command has additional subchoices for you to make. This is called a *cascading menu* (because the next menu starts to the right of the previous one and runs down from there, a bit like a waterfall of menus). You make selections from a cascaded menu the same way you would from a normal menu. The lower-left example in Figure 3.12 shows a cascaded menu. The Taskbar also uses cascading menus, but we'll get to that in a moment.

A Dot

A dot to the left of the command means that the option is currently selected and is an exclusive option among several related options. For example, in Figure 3.12, the center section of one of the menus contains the options Large icons, Small icons, List, and Details. Only one of these options can be selected at a time. The dot indicates the current setting. By simply opening the menu again and clicking on one of the other options, you set that option on.

A Key Combination

Some menu commands list keystrokes that can be used instead of opening the menu and choosing that command. For example, in the My Computer's Edit menu, shown below,

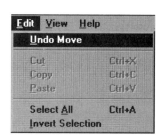

notice that the Cut command could be executed by Ctrl-X, the Copy command could be executed by pressing Ctrl-C, and the Paste command with Ctrl-V. These alternative time-saving keystrokes are called *short-cut keys*. (Don't worry if you don't understand these commands yet. They will be explained later.)

NOTE   A keystroke abbreviation such as Ctrl-C means to hold down the Ctrl key (typically found in the lower-left corner of your keyboard) while pressing the C key.

All About Dialog Boxes

As I said above, a dialog box will always appear when you select a command with ellipses (...) after it. Dialog boxes pop up on your screen when Windows or the Windows application program you're using needs more information before continuing. Some dialog boxes ask you to enter information (such as file names), while others simply require you to check off options or make choices from a list. The list may be in the form of additional sub-dialog boxes or submenus. In any case, after you enter the requested information, you click on OK, and Windows or the application program continues on its merry way, executing the command.

Though most dialog boxes ask you for information, other boxes are only informative, alerting you to a problem with your system or an error you've made. Such a box might also request confirmation on a command that could have dire consequences or explain why the command you've chosen can't be executed. These alert boxes sometimes have a big letter *i* (for "information") in them, or an exclamation mark (!). A few examples are shown in Figure 3.13.

More often than not, these boxes only ask you to read them and then click on OK (or cancel them if you decide not to proceed). Some boxes only have an OK button. Let's look at some typical dialog boxes and see how they work.

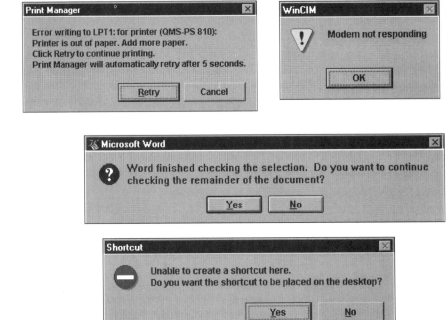

Figure 3.13   *Dialog boxes are used for a wide variety of purposes. Here are some examples of dialog boxes that are informative only and do not ask you to make settings or adjust options.*

Moving between Sections of a Dialog Box

As you can see in Figure 3.14, dialog boxes often have several sections to them. You can move between the sections in three ways:

▶ The easiest way is by clicking on the section you want to alter.

▶ If you are using the keyboard, you can press the Tab key to move between sections and press the Spacebar to select them.

▶ You can also use the Alt key with the underlined letter of the section name you want to jump to or activate. Even when you are using a mouse, the Alt-key combinations are sometimes the fastest way to jump between sections or choose an option within a box.

Notice that one of the dialog boxes here has a Preview section. This is a feature that more and more dialog boxes will be sporting as applications become more *user friendly*. Rather than having to choose a formatting change, for example, and then okaying the dialog box to see the effect on your document, a Preview section lets you see the effect in advance. This lets you "shop" for the effect you want before committing to it.

Many newer Windows programs have dialog boxes with *tab pages*, a new item introduced around the time of Windows 95. I discussed this feature somewhat in Chapter 1 but will mention it here in the context of dialog boxes. Tab pages keep a dialog box to a reasonable size while still letting you adjust a lot of settings from it. To get to the page of settings you want, just click on the tab with the correct name. Figure 3.15 illustrates this concept. I've clicked on the View menu of Word's Options dialog box.

Entering Information in a Dialog Box

Now let's consider how you enter information into dialog boxes. There are seven basic types of sections in dialog boxes:

▶ text boxes

▶ check boxes

▶ option buttons

▶ command buttons

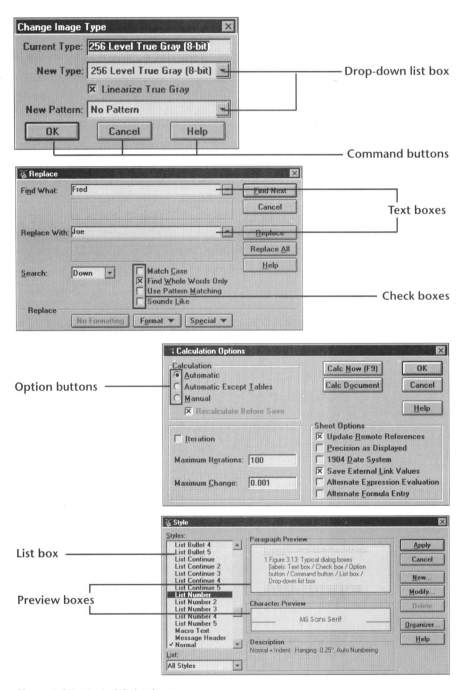

Figure 3.14   Typical dialog boxes

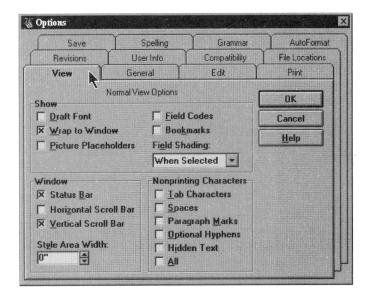

Figure 3.15   *Newer dialog boxes have multiple tabs that make the boxes easier to understand
and appear less cluttered. Click on a tab, and a new set of options appears.*

▶ list boxes

▶ drop-down list boxes

▶ file dialog boxes

Once you've jumped to the correct section, you'll need to know how
to make choices from it. The next several sections explain how to use
each kind. (Please refer to Figure 3.14 during the next discussions.)

Text Boxes

In this sort of section, you are asked to type in text from the keyboard. Sometimes there will be text already typed in for you. If you
want to keep it as is, just leave it alone. To alter the text, simply type
in new text. If the existing text is already highlighted, then the first
key you press will delete the existing entry. If it is not highlighted, you
can backspace over it to erase it. You can also edit existing text. Clicking once on highlighted text will *deselect* it and cause the *text cursor* (a
vertical blinking bar) to appear when you put the pointer inside the
text area. You can then move the text cursor around using the arrow

keys or the mouse and insert text (by typing) or delete text (by pressing the Del key). Text is inserted at the position of the text cursor. Text boxes are most often used for specifying file names when you are saving or loading documents and applications or specifying text to search for in a word-processing document.

Check Boxes

Check boxes are the small square (or sometimes diamond-shaped) boxes. They are used to indicate nonexclusive options. For example, you might want some text to appear as bold *and* underlined. Or, as another example, consider the Calculation Options dialog box from Excel shown in Figure 3.14. In this box, you can have any of the settings in the Sheet Options section set on or off. These are toggle settings (as explained previously) that you activate or deactivate by clicking on the box. When the box is empty, the option is off; when you see an ✕, the option is on.

Option Buttons

Unlike check boxes, which are nonexclusive, option buttons are exclusive settings. Sometimes called *radio buttons*, these are also round rather than square or diamond shaped, and only one option can be set on at a time. For example, using the same Calculation Options dialog box referred to above, you may select Automatic, Automatic Except Tables, *or* Manual in the Calculation section of the dialog box—not a combination of the three. Clicking on the desired button turns it on (the circle will be filled) and turns any previous selection off. From the keyboard, you first jump to the section, then use the arrow keys to select the option.

Command Buttons

Command buttons are like option buttons except that they are used to execute a command immediately. They are also rectangular rather than square or circular. An example of a command button is the OK button found on almost every dialog box. Once you've filled in a dialog box to your liking, click on the OK button, and Windows or the application executes the settings you've selected. If you change your mind and don't want the new commands on the dialog box executed, click on the Cancel button.

There is always a command button that has a thicker border; this is the command that will execute if you press Enter. Likewise, pressing the Esc key always has the same effect as clicking on the Cancel button (that's why there's no underlined letter on the Cancel button).

Some command buttons are followed by ellipses (...). As you might expect, these commands will open additional dialog boxes for adjusting more settings. Other command buttons include two >> symbols in them. Choosing this type of button causes the particular section of the dialog box to expand so you can make more selections.

List Boxes

List boxes are like menus. They show you a list of options or items from which you can choose. For example, when choosing fonts to display or print text in, WordPad shows you a list box. You make a selection from a list box the same way you do from a menu: by just clicking on it. From the keyboard, highlight the desired option with the arrow keys and then press Enter to choose it. Some list boxes are too small to show all the possible selections. In this case, there will be a scroll bar on the right side of the box. Use the scroll bar to see all the selections. Some list boxes let you make more than one selection, but most only allow one. To make more than one selection from the keyboard, press the Spacebar to select or deselect any item.

TECH TIP   You can quickly jump to an option in a list box by typing the first letter of its name. If there are two choices with the same first letter and you want the second one, press the letter again, or press the down-arrow key.

Drop-Down List Boxes

Drop-down list boxes are indicated by a small arrow in a box to the right of the option. The current setting is displayed to the left of the little arrow. Clicking on the arrow opens a list that works just like a normal list box and has scroll bars if there are a lot of options. Drop-down list boxes are used when a dialog box is too crowded to accommodate regular list boxes.

File Dialog Boxes

A dialog box like one of the three shown in Figure 3.16 often appears when you're working in Windows programs. This type of box is called a *file dialog box* or simply *file box*. Though used in a variety of situations, you're most likely to run into file boxes when you want to open a file or when you save a document for the first time. For example, choosing File ➤ Open from almost any Windows program will bring up such a box asking which document file you want to open.

> **NOTE**   If you're new to Windows, you may want to mark this section with a paper clip and refer back to it when you have to save or open a file for the first time.

File dialog boxes vary somewhat from program to program, even though they perform the same job. Some boxes, as you will note in the figure, allow you to open a file as Read Only, for example, or help you search for a file with a Find button or a Network button (if you're connected to a network). The file box went through a major redesign by Microsoft after they finally figured out that novices were thoroughly confused by it. Now the new design is much more intuitively obvious and is very similar to the file boxes used on the Mac. Because the older two boxes and new type are pretty different from one another, I'll explain the steps for each separately, starting with the two older-style files boxes.

The two older-style boxes (which 16-bit Windows 3.x applications will use) are divided into two main sections, listing files on the left and directories on the right. In most applications, directories are represented by a folder. In really old programs you only see the directory's name enclosed in brackets, like this:

```
[cserve]
```

Using Older-Style File Boxes   Here are the steps you can take to use these older boxes. If you know how to run a program (we'll cover that in the next chapter), you might try running a 16-bit program, opening its File menu, and choosing Open to experiment a bit.

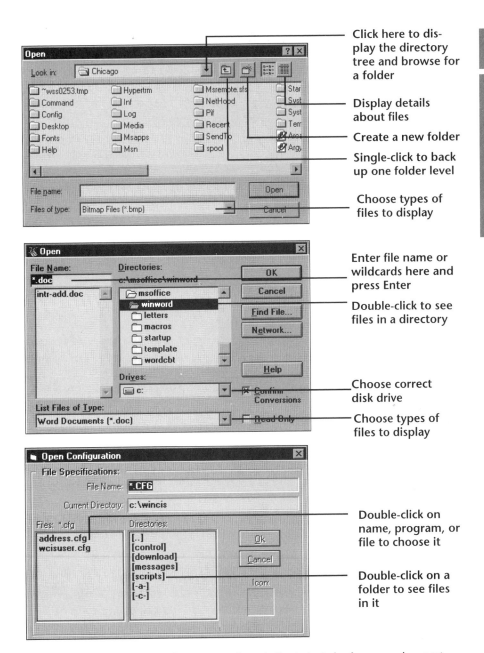

Click here to display the directory tree and browse for a folder

Display details about files

Create a new folder

Single-click to back up one folder level

Choose types of files to display

Enter file name or wildcards here and press Enter

Double-click to see files in a directory

Choose correct disk drive

Choose types of files to display

Double-click on name, program, or file to choose it

Double-click on a folder to see files in it

Figure 3.16   *A file dialog box lets you scan through directories to load or save a document. Here you see three typical file dialog box types. The upper one is the newer Windows 95 style. The middle one is the Windows 3.x style, and the lowest one is the moldy, oldy Windows 3.0 style.*

> **NOTE** In this discussion, the words *directory* and *folder* are used inter-changeably because in reality they are the same thing. In the older dialog boxes, *directory* refers to what are now called *folders* under Windows 95.

1. Make sure the correct disk drive is chosen down in the lower-right side of the box. If it's not, open the drop-down *Drives* list box and se-lect another drive if necessary. Normally, this setting will be set to drive C, which is your hard disk and should be fine. On the oldest-style file box, you don't have a drop-down list for the drive. To change drives, you scroll to the bottom of the directory list and double-click on the name of the drive (e.g., [-a-], [-b-], [-c-]) to change drives.

2. Now select a directory on the right side by double-clicking on its little folder icon or name. Whatever files are stored in the directory you just chose will then show up in the list at the left. If you don't see the di-rectory you're aiming for, you may have to move down or back up the directory tree a level or two (see Chapter 12 for a review of DOS di-rectory theory).

> **NOTE** Because these older programs were by definition written for Win-dows 3.x, their file boxes won't display long file or directory names. Long names will be converted to the "8.3" standard DOS file-name format for dis-play in these boxes. Chapter 1 covered details of how the conversion pro-cess works.

In Windows 3.1-style boxes, you'd double-click on the folder just above the one that's currently open to back up a level or on the folder below the current one to move down a level. In Windows 3.0-style boxes, you'd have to double-click on the two dots (..) at the top of the directory list to back up one directory level. Each double click backs up one directory level. To move down a level, click on any directory name enclosed in brackets.

3. If you want to see only certain types of files, open the List Files of Type box (if there is one) to select the type of files you want to see (such as programs, or all files). If the options offered don't suit your needs, or if you're using the older-style box, you can type in DOS-like wildcards in the File Name area, then press Enter to modify the file list accordingly. For example, to show only Lotus 1-2-3 worksheet files, you'd enter ***.WK?** in the File Name area and press Enter.

4. Once the file you want is visible in the file box at the left, double-click on it or highlight it, and click on OK.

When saving a file for the first time, the file won't exist on the drive yet, so it won't show up in the file list box; you'll be giving it a name. To do this, select the drive and directory as outlined above, then move the cursor to the File Name area and type in the file name and extension. Make sure to delete any existing letters in the text area first, using the Backspace and/or Delete keys. (For more information about selecting, editing, and replacing text, see Chapter 19.)

The Newer-Style File Box The newer-style file box will show up in 32-bit programs written for Windows 95 and in portions of Windows 95 itself. Here's how to use this type of file box when you're opening or saving files.

NOTE To see one of these new dialog boxes, you can run the Paint application found in the Accessories folder by clicking on the Start button, then choosing Start ➤ Programs ➤ Accessories ➤ Paint. Then choose File ➤ Open. (The ➤ symbol here indicates a chain of choices you make from the menus.)

1. First, notice the *Look in* section at the top of the box. This tells you what folder's contents is being displayed in the window below. You can click on this drop-down list to choose the drive or folder you want to look in. This will also list the folders you have on the Desktop so you can open or save files from/to the Desktop.

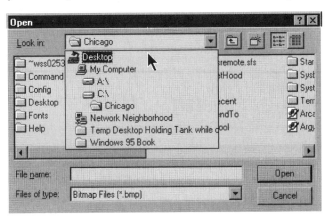

2. You can create a new folder using the Create New Folder button in the dialog box's toolbar if you want to save something in a folder that doesn't already exist. This can help you organize your files. The new folder will be created as a subfolder to the folder shown in the Look in area. (After creating the new folder, you'll have to name it by typing in a new name just to the right of the folder.)

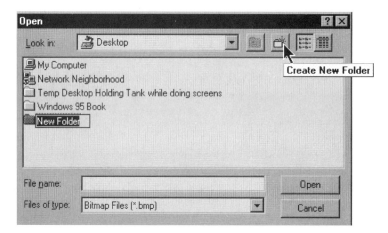

3. The object is to display the target folder in the window and then double-click on it. So, if the folder you want is somewhere on your hard disk (typically drive C), one way to display it is to choose *C:* from the Look in area. All the folders on your C drive appear in the window.

4. In the large window, double-click on the folder you want to look in. If you don't see the folder you're aiming for, you may have to move down or back up the tree of folders a level or two (see Chapter 12 for a review of DOS directory theory). You back up a level by clicking on the Up One Level button. You move down a level by double-clicking on a folder and looking for its subfolders to then appear in the window. You can then double-click on a subfolder to open that, and so on.

5. Finally, click on the file you want to open. Or, if you're saving a file for the first time, you'll have to type in the name of the file. Of course, if you are saving a file for the first time, the file won't exist on the drive yet, so it won't show up in the list of files; you'll be giving it a name. To do this, select the drive and directory as outlined above, then click in the File Name area and type in the file name. Make sure to delete any existing letters in the text area first, using the Backspace

and/or Delete keys. (For more information about selecting, editing, and replacing text, see Chapter 19.)

6. If you want to see only certain types of files, open the Files of Type box to select the type of files you want to see (such as a certain kind of document or all files). If the options offered don't suit your needs, you can type in DOS-like wildcards in the File Name area, then press Enter to modify the file list accordingly. For example, to show only Lotus 1-2-3 worksheet files, you'd enter ***.WK?** in the File Name area and press Enter.

7. Once the file you want is visible in the file box at the left, double-click on it or highlight it, and click on OK.

Getting Help When You Need It

So far, you've gotten a fairly detailed overview of the Windows interface. Some of the things covered in this chapter will be helpful as reference once you are actually using Windows, though they might seem a little academic right now. Still, it's hard for the newcomer to Windows to begin using Windows without a little orientation to the basic elements of the Windows screen, and that's why I covered these topics right up front. Perhaps you've experimented on your own with dialog boxes and windows, or perhaps you have tried running some programs supplied with Windows 95 such as Notepad or Paint, which would provide additional opportunities for experimentation. (Running programs is covered in Chapter 4.)

Regardless of the extent of your computer know-how, there will be times when you don't remember or understand how to use an operation or command, or even what an element on the screen is for. Luckily, you don't always have to drag out a book or manual to get some quick help. The people at Microsoft have done a very good job of developing a built-in Help facility for this version of Windows. Once you learn how to use it, it'll answer many of your questions.

Many computer users still find books useful, which is lucky because it keeps us writers employed and our publishers, such as Sybex, in business. Books do provide an information source and style that can't be rivaled by computers. With a book, you intuitively know how many pages of material there are on a given topic, batteries are *not* required, and they don't break if you drop them. Using them doesn't really take much know-how (except the ability to read), and you can skim through a book very easily in hopes of searching for a given topic. In my opinion, books are bound (pun not intended) to be with us all for a long, long time.

Despite my probably biased stance on the superiority of books, let's face it: We don't always have a book with us or want to pore over an index to find the right reference (assuming the book even has a decent index!). So, online help (as it's called in the computer world)—especially *context-sensitive* help in which the computer guesses what you're trying to do—can be a great boon. Windows 95 has such a Help facility, as do virtually all Windows programs by this point. Some online help is useful, and some is downright lousy, telling you no more than the obvious. The good news is that because there is a standard for how programs are supposed to dish out help to you, once you learn how to get help with one program, you'll be equipped to take on others. So let's look at how Help works in Windows 95, and if you're an old-timer with Windows, you'll find the slightly modified Help system rather interesting.

To Start Help

There are several approaches to getting help, depending on what you want help *with*. There are two categories of help you can get: You can get help about using Windows itself and help about using one of your application programs. You can always get help about Windows to pop up on your screen whenever you're running Windows 95—which is to say whenever your computer is on. To get help with an application, though, the application has to be running. So, to get help with Word-Perfect for Windows, for example, you have to be running that program. Makes sense, right?

Let's first look at how Windows 95's own built-in Help facility works. Once you learn that, you'll be able to use any new programs that comply with this design. Then, we'll look at a typical Help screen or two from other programs.

The Windows 95 Help system uses a sensible layout that lets you look things up by topic (sort of like an index in a book) or by browsing a table of contents (also like a book). A third approach will scan through all the available Help text, searching for a specific word or phrase for you.

Here's how to get help with Windows topics—that is, help with how to use Windows itself, not specifically with Windows programs you might be running. If your computer is on, you might want to follow these steps to experiment a bit.

1. Click on the Start button at the bottom of your screen and then click on Help. A large window like the one you see in Figure 3.17 pops up.

2. Each of the little purple books on the left is like a chapter. You can "open" the chapter to see subtopics by clicking on it and then clicking

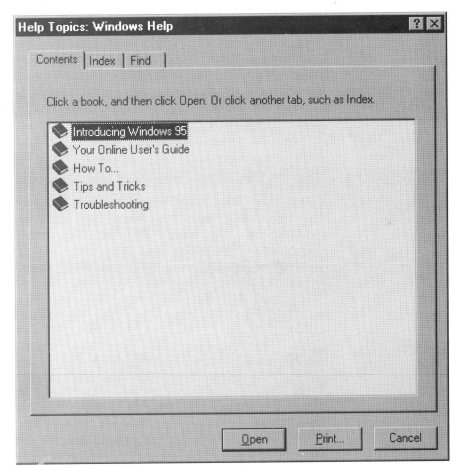

Figure 3.17   Your basic Windows Help screen. Notice the three tabs for doing three different types of topic searches.

on the Open button. (As a shortcut, you can simply double-click on the topic.) So, for example, click on Introducing Windows 95 and then click on Open. The topic opens up as you see in Figure 3.18. Some chapters will have subchapters beneath them that will open in the same way.

3. When you see a little icon that looks like a page of text, you can double-click on it (or click once and then click on Open) to read what it has to say. So, for example, try double-clicking on *Ten minutes to using*

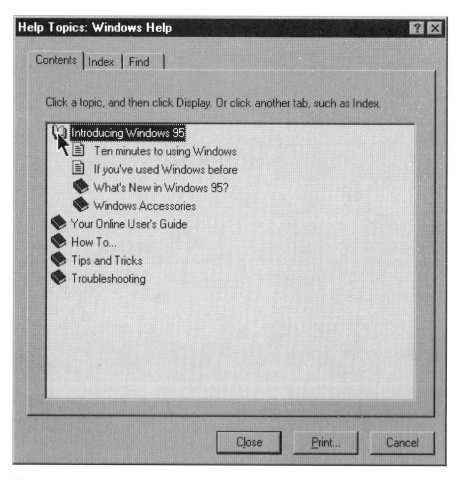

Figure 3.18   Double-clicking on a chapter opens it to display subtopics.

Windows. This brings up an illustrated Windows Tutorial that you
might find educational (see Figure 3.19).

 NOTE This is the same tutorial that's an option on the Welcome to Windows 95 sign-on screen, which you will see when Windows 95 first boots up
(unless you turned off the Welcome screen).

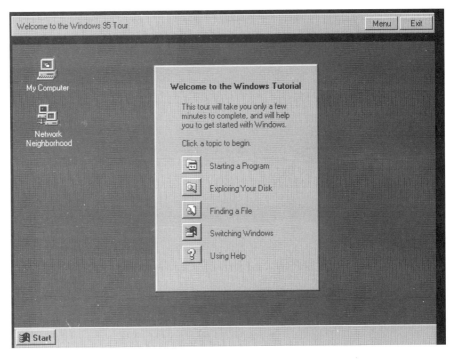

Figure 3.19 *The Windows Tutorial walks you through some of Windows 95's features. If you
get confused, you can click on Exit.*

 NOTE In this book, I'll be covering all the skills that the tutorial addresses,
but if you want to take a side trip right now, go ahead. If you want to quit
the tutorial at any point, just click on Exit up at the top of the screen.

4. Try double-clicking on one of the other Help topics, such as *If
    you've used Windows before* (or clicking once and then clicking on

Open). What you'll typically see is a little page of explanatory text, like this:

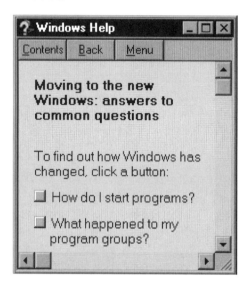

5. Notice that this little window contains buttons such as *How do I start programs?* To see how these work, you'll first have to maximize the window, otherwise you will miss the show (look back a bit in this chapter to the section on resizing a window if you have forgotten how to maximize).

6. After maximizing, click on the *How do I start programs?* button. You'll see the screen shown in Figure 3.20.

7. Try clicking on the other buttons to read related material and see additional illustrations.

8. When you're ready to return to the contents page, click on the Contents button at the top of the window:

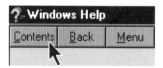

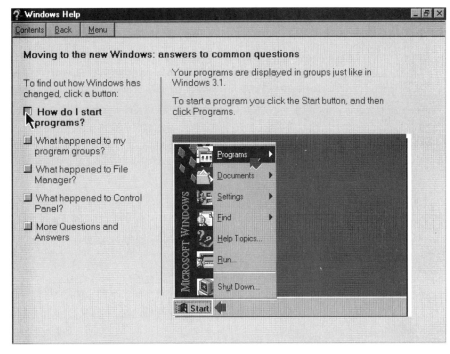

Figure 3.20 *Clicking on a topic button at the left displays an explanatory picture on the right.*

Using the Help Index

So much for the Table of Contents approach. Now check out the Index. Actually, when you're doing real work (rather than just passing the time reading about Windows and discovering new information about it), you'll use the Index. Just as in a book, the index can help you more quickly locate just the piece of trivia you need to get the job done. Of course, just as with a book index, the entry you need might not be there. It's sort of a potluck, but you're still likely to find something you need this way.

To use the index:

1. Run Help as you did in the above section.

2. Click on the Index tab this time. You'll see a new box listing a lot of topics. You can type in the topic you want information about or just click on a displayed topic and click on Display. Notice that there is a

scroll bar to the right of the list, so you can scroll the list to search for a topic.

3. However, the quicker way to find a topic is to simply start typing the topic's name. For example, suppose you were trying to print something and were having trouble. Try typing **print** as I did in Figure 3.21 and notice that the list jumps immediately to topics pertaining to printing.

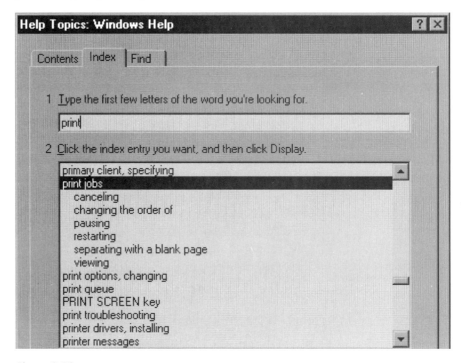

Figure 3.21 *The Index tab displays a long list of topics. Type in a topic and the list will jump to identically spelled topics as you type.*

4. Once the target is in sight, shoot! That is, double-click on it. A window will appear with helpful (you hope) information, possibly with other little buttons to click on for elaboration, and so forth. In some cases, before actually getting the help information, you'll be presented with a list of subreferences to choose from. You simply click on the one you want and click on Display.

TIP Remember, when a Help topic is being displayed, you can always get back to the main Help screen by clicking on the Contents button, as explained above.

Searching for Help with Find

The third tab page on the basic Windows 95 Help screen is *Find*. This option is a last resort if you're really bummed trying to find some help on a topic and nothing is coming up. This command actually goes through all the Windows 95 Help files (there's one for each supplied application and for all major modules of Windows 95, such as Print Manager, Taskbar, system utilities, and so forth), looking for the word(s) you stipulate.

Here's how to do a Find:

1. Click on Start and then choose Help.

2. Click on the Find tab in the Help dialog box.

3. If this is the first time you have run a Find, a Wizard will run. That's right, a Wizard. If you've never met a Wizard, you're in luck. (Actually, you probably ran into one while setting up Windows 95.) Anyway, you'll see something such as that in Figure 3.22.

4. Follow the instructions on the screen. If you're short on disk space, use the Custom option. Otherwise click on Express and then on Next, followed by Finish. The computer now creates a database of words, and as this happens a cute little picture of a pen writing in a book appears:

5. After the database is created, the Find box appears, which is like the Index box on steroids. I mean, it's pretty powerful. Just as with the Index box, you simply type in the topic you're looking for, but in this

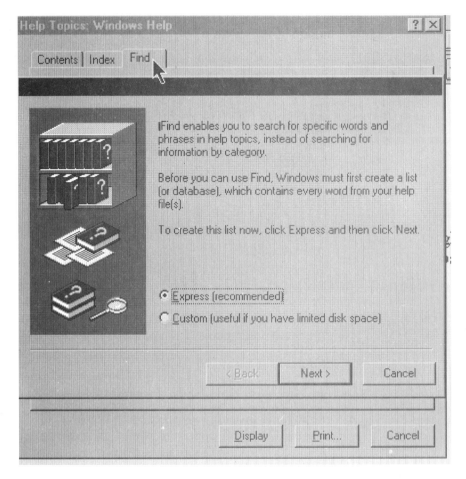

Figure 3.22 *The Wizard for setting up Find*

box you can type in multiple words and refine your search. For example, say you wanted to know how to change the speed at which the keys on your keyboard repeat. Just type in **keyboard repeat** and see what happens (see Figure 3.23).

TIP   If you type in a word followed by a space, a large list of optional words comes up that you can play with as options.

6. Now you can optionally select some additional modifiers that will narrow the search. Move to the second box (marked *2*) and click on any

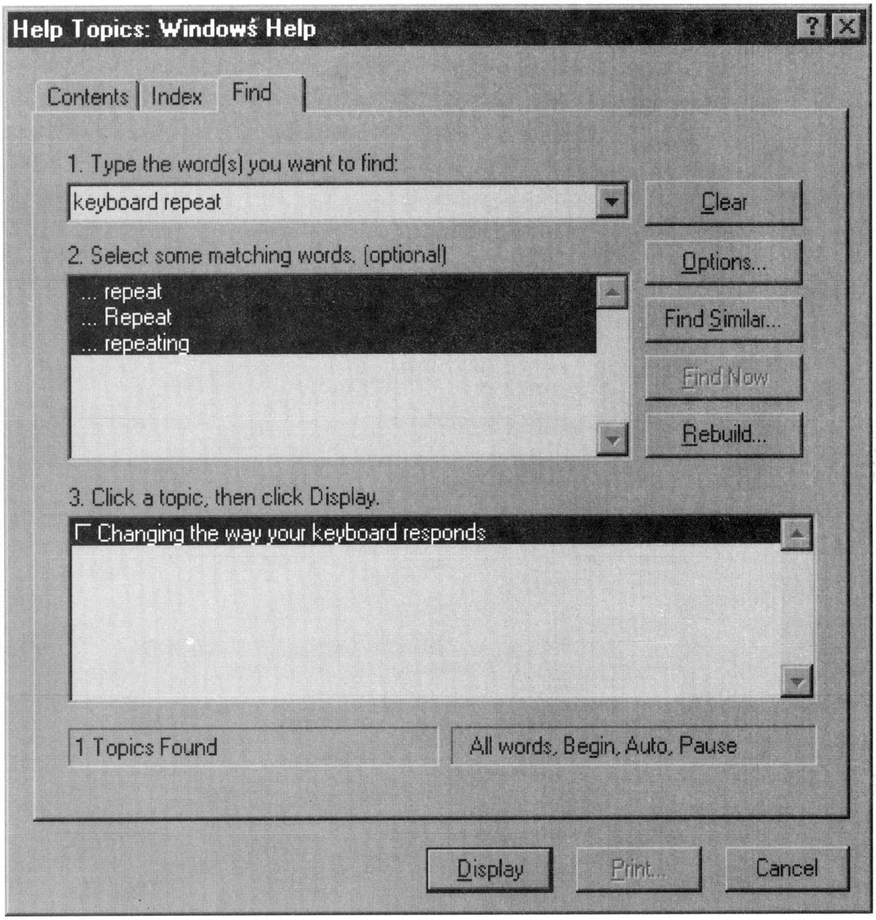

Help Topics: Windows Help [?] [X]

Contents | Index | Find |

1. Type the word(s) you want to find:

keyboard repeat ▼   [Clear]

2. Select some matching words. (optional)   [Options...]

... repeat
... Repeat   [Find Similar...]
... repeating

[Find Now]

▼   [Rebuild...]

3. Click a topic, then click Display.

☐ Changing the way your keyboard responds   ▲

▼

1 Topics Found   All words, Begin, Auto, Pause

[Display] [Print...] [Cancel]

Figure 3.23 The Find box is like the Index box but with more options.

words that have relevance to what you're looking for. By default, all
the words in this list are selected, which is why they are all blackened. If
you click on just one of these words, all others will become deselected.

7. The list of final contenders is shown in the bottom box. You can click
on any items that appear there and then click on Display to read
about the topic. You can also click in the little box to the left of a topic
to select it for printing.

> **TIP** Remember when you're reading a topic to click on the Help Topics but-
> ton in the topic's window to get back to the Find box so you can display any
> additional topics that you haven't yet viewed. Clicking on the Back button
> (when it appears) takes you back a step through the pages of information
> you have read.

8. Once some topics are check marked, you can print them by clicking
on the Print button. You can also do one other strange thing. If you
click on the Find Similar button, a list of sort-of-related topics (you'll
find some of them a little far afield) pops up as shown in Figure 3.24.

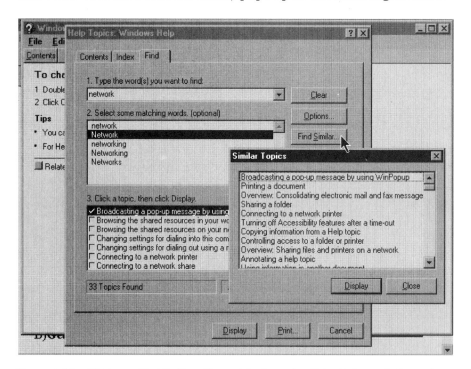

*Figure 3.24   Clicking on Find Similar will search for items that Help thinks are similar to the
checkmarked topic(s).*

Two other options in the Find box are worth noting. The first is Re-
build. This simply rebuilds the database of words in case it got trashed
or erased for some reason (like you accidentally erased the database
file). Help database files have the extension `.gid`.

The second option is called Options. Clicking on this button lets you set some of the internal details controlling how the Find dialog box works. The settings in the box are self-explanatory should you decide to play with them. However, the default settings work fine in most instances.

Using Typical Help Screens

There are features common to many Help windows. You should be able to recognize them and know how they work. One thing to keep in mind is that Help screens come in many styles and formats. Help hasn't really been standardized to the point where all programs' Help facilities are going to behave in the same way. The best I can do here is to introduce you to the variety of elements you are likely to run into and let you take it from there. The good news is that there is virtually always the word "Help" at the far right side of any Windows program's menu bar. Clicking on this menu brings up some choices pertaining to online help. For example, Figure 3.25 shows a potpourri of such Help menus.

The majority of Help menus have a *Search for Help On* command or *Help Topics* command to help you narrow the topic search. Often, choosing one of these commands will present you with an Index box like the one described above. Other options (such as *Help with Procedures*) are pretty self-explanatory.

TIP If while looking at an application's Help screen you can't remember how to use Help, just press the F1 key. You'll then see a list of topics explaining how to use the Help system.

Because many of the programs you'll be running (at least for a couple of years after the release of Windows 95) will be Windows 3.x programs, you'll be seeing older Windows 3.x-style Help screens. Here's an example. Suppose you're using NetCruiser, a program for connecting to the Internet. Figure 3.26 shows NetCruiser's opening Help screen.

Notice the underlined words and the buttons just below the menu bar. These are just some of the elements to look for on Help screens. The following list describes these and other common Help-screen elements.

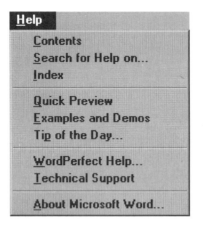

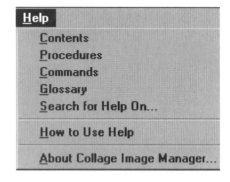

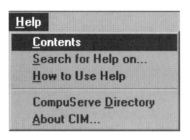

Figure 3.25   *Most Windows programs have a Help menu, though each will have its own Help options. Here are a few typical Help menus.*

▶ Any word or phrase in a list that appears lighter (or green, if you have a color monitor) and is underlined with a solid line is a *topic*. Clicking on a topic jumps you to the section in the online help that is relevant to that word or procedure. You'll then see a new Help window with information about that topic.

▶ Occasionally you'll encounter hotspots (a hotspot is any item in the Help screen text that does something special if you click on it) that are graphics rather than words. They don't look any different from other graphics in the Help windows, but the pointer turns into the hand icon when it's positioned over them, meaning it's a hotspot. View information or activate this kind of hotspot the same way you do other hotspots—simply click. There are a few key combinations that highlight the hotspots in a Help window, making it easy to locate and select them. Pressing Tab advances to the next hotspot, Shift-Tab

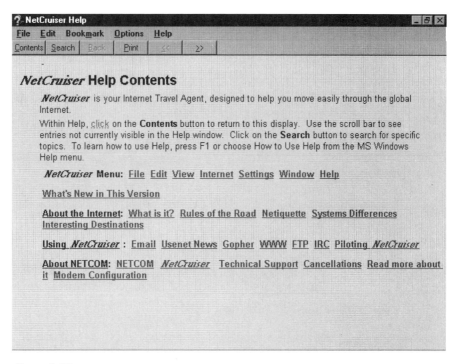

Figure 3.26 *A typical Help screen. Read the topic by clicking on an underlined word or phrase. Click on a word underlined with a dotted line to see its definition.*

moves to the previous hotspot, and Ctrl-Tab highlights all the hotspots for as long as you hold both keys down.

▶ Some words appear lighter (or green) and are underlined with a dotted line. Clicking on the word will typically bring up a box containing a definition of the word. To

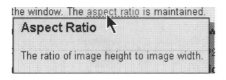

see the definition, position the pointer on the term (once again, the cursor changes to the hand icon) and click. The definition pops up in a window like that shown here. To close the box, just click again or press any key on the keyboard.

▶ The *What Is This?* button is the "?" button found on the toolbar or in the title bar of some programs. It looks like this: 🔳

or like this:

Clicking on this button turns the pointer into a question mark. Once that happens, you can click on an element on the screen that you're curious about, and you'll see an explanation of the element. For example, you could open a menu and choose a command, like this:

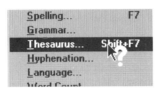

The result would likely be a screenful of information explaining the ins and outs of the highlighted command.

▶ The menu gives you a list of options you can choose from such as Annotate, Print Topic, Copy, Font, and Keep on Top. Annotation is covered below. *Print Topic* prints the currently displayed topic on your printer. Just set up your printer and click this option. You'll then have a paper version of the Help topic at hand. *Copy* puts the current page of help information on the Clipboard so you can paste it into another document. This is useful for anyone writing documentation about a program, letting them easily import Help material into their own document. (Of course, you'll want to be careful about copyright infringement.) The *Font* option lets you increase or decrease the size of the lettering in the Help boxes to get more text in the window or to increase visibility. *Keep Help on Top* prevents the Help window from being obscured by other windows on the screen as they are selected or as you open new documents or applications (see below).

The Help Buttons

Many Help screens have a row of command buttons beneath the menu bar.

Some Help screens will have fewer buttons than this. It's also possible that you'll see more than this, but not likely. Here's what the command buttons do when you click on them:

Contents   This jumps you directly to the list of Help contents for the application you are using. The Contents list is a good starting point for getting help and a good place to return to after reading Help on one item if you want to see more on another, unrelated item. Incidentally, in some programs, pressing F1 takes you directly to this list.

Search   This button lets you look for a specific word or topic. There is a list of key words for each topic in the Help system. This command shows you those words in a list box. As explained above, you can select the subject you want to read about, or you can type in a word you want Help to look up. As you begin typing, the list will scroll to the word you've entered, assuming that there's a match. See the section above about using the Index and Find tab pages in this box. If you don't find the topic you want, click on the Cancel button (or press Esc).

Back   This lets you back up through the Help topics you have already viewed in the reverse order that you viewed them (meaning the most recent first). When you have backed up as far as you can go, the Back button is grayed.

History   This brings up a little box within the current Help screen that lists the Help screens you've consulted in the reverse order that you viewed them. The most recent is at the top of the list. By using the History box, instead of backing up to a previous topic by clicking on Back until the screen you want reappears, you can just double-click on the topic in the History box. If you click on Back while the History box is open, you'll see the topics you already looked at in the order that they appear in the list. Each topic is added to the top of the list as you view it again. If there isn't a History button, try opening the Options menu. There may be a choice there called Display History Window.

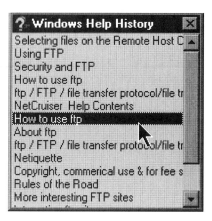

<< This is the Browse Backward button. If the Browse buttons appear on a Help screen, it means that some topics related to the current one can be viewed one after another by pressing one of the Browse buttons. Each click on the button returns you to the previous topic in the series. When you reach the first topic, the button becomes grayed.

>> This is the Browse Forward button. It advances you to the next screen in the series of related topics. When you reach the end of the series, the button is grayed.

Keeping a Specific Help Screen Handy

Help windows often "disappear" when you go back to the application that the Help screen is about. This is annoying because often you won't remember what you just read. It's not that the window really disappeared, it's simply that your application window has covered it up. With the new Help system, procedures appear in a little window that sits over to the right-hand side of your screen and doesn't go away (this is called *staying on top*) until you close it.

Sometimes the Help screen you're working with doesn't stay on top because this setting is turned off. Some older programs don't use the little Help window in the right-margin and aren't set to automatically stay on top. Even so, there are several ways to keep a windowful of specific help information in view or at least easily available.

▶ You can shrink the Help window down to a size where you can still read it but it doesn't take up the whole screen. Make it a small, wide band at the bottom or side of the screen, for example, and resize your other windows to accommodate it, as in Figure 3.27.

 NOTE Windows 95 allows Help for only one application to be open at a time. If you switch to another application and run Help from it, any Help that is already open will be closed and the new one opened. Implementing Help in this way was an economy decision on Microsoft's part. Limiting the number of simultaneously running Help files conserves memory and other resources, leaving more room for your applications and documents.

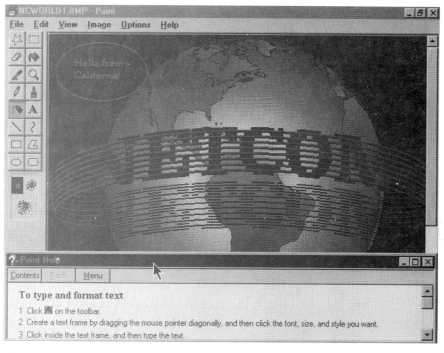

Up and Running
with Windows 95

Figure 3.27   *Keep Help windows handy while working in Windows.*

▶ Another solution is to minimize it, which puts a button for it on the Task-bar. When you need to read the Help topic again, just click on the Help button's icon. This is particularly helpful for quickly recalling lists of key commands or other information that might be difficult to remember.

Using Bookmarks

Even within a given program's Help screen, you are limited to seeing one screen at a time. That is, you can't keep several of your favorite pages of Help information on screen at once. If you want to refer to a few topics' Help screens while you're working on a project, another feature, Bookmark, is a good tool for you to become familiar with. Bookmark allows you to create a list of the topics you most often refer to. Once you find a topic the first time and add it to the Bookmark list, you can jump to that Help screen quickly the next time simply by choosing the topic from your personal list.

To define your bookmarks:

1. Run the program you want to make up bookmarks for.

2. Open the Help menu and choose either Contents, Search for Help On, or Index, depending on how you want to locate your topics.

3. When the topic Help screen is open, open the Bookmark menu by clicking on it and choose Define.

4. In the Bookmark Define dialog box, shown below, you have the option of giving the bookmark a name or leaving it with the topic name. Type in a new name if you want to. Choose OK. The dialog box closes, and you return to the topic Help screen. If you open the Bookmark menu again, you will see your bookmark listed.

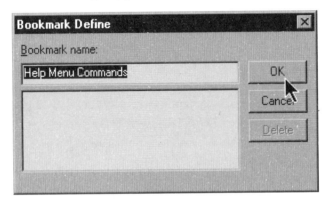

To quickly jump to one of your bookmarked topics later on:

1. Open Help for whatever program you have saved bookmarks in.

2. Up on the menu bar, click on Bookmark. The menu will list any bookmarks you have saved. Choose the desired topic by clicking on it. If more than nine topics are bookmarked, choose More from the Bookmark list, then click on the topic in the Go To dialog box.

To remove a bookmark from your list:

1. Run Help from the application in question. Then open the Bookmark menu and choose Define.

2. Click on the topic you want to delete.

3. Click on Delete. Repeat for each topic you want to delete from the list.

4. Click on OK when you're ready to close the box.

When Help Doesn't Help

In some cases, Help just won't tell you what you're interested in the first time around. In fact, probably 50 percent of the time Help doesn't help me. At least not the first time. Here's a general game plan to try when you can't seem to ferret anything useful out of Help.

First try spending some time wandering through the help screens. There is a lot of information in the Help files supplied with Windows and the Windows accessories. Sometimes the Search command won't find what you need to know, but the information is in the Help system in another context. Don't overlook playing with the Find tab page in the Contents dialog box as I described earlier.

Part
1

Up and Running
with Windows 95

TIP Though the Find tab page is a new feature for Windows 95, note that it works even with Help files from Windows 3.x applications. Any older Windows program with a standard Help file can be indexed using this command so you can search through it with a fine-tooth comb. If you're a veteran Windows user, you may want to revisit the Help files of your older applications now, searching through them in this new way. You just may discover tasty tidbits of information you didn't know existed.

Modifying the Help Screens

You can add your own notes to a Help topic. This is useful for reminding yourself of things you've figured out about an application program or of where to find information on some topic that eluded you last time you looked. Each topic can have only one annotation, but it can be quite long. An annotation is like a note that you "paper clip" to the topic. To make an annotation:

1. Get to the Help screen where you want to attach the note.

2. Open the Edit menu of the Help window and choose Annotate.

3.   Type your notes into the dialog box that appears. You can edit the text using the Backspace key, the Delete key, and the arrow keys.

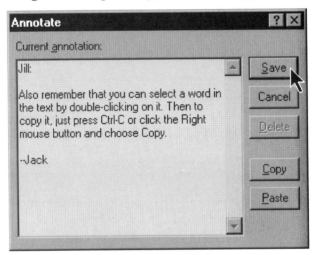

4.   When you are finished, click on Save. A paper clip now shows up before the topic title on the Help screen you're reading.

You can read the annotation on any help topic (if there is a paper clip there) by either clicking on the paper clip or choosing Edit ➤ Annotate. You can delete an annotation by opening the Annotation dialog box again and clicking on Delete.

When making an annotation, you can copy text from the Clipboard into the annotation window, or vice versa, using the Copy and Paste buttons in the box.

Copying the Help Screens

There may be occasions when you would find it useful to copy information from Help topics into a document or another application. For example, if you are preparing a training manual for employees in your company who are learning WordPerfect for Windows, you may find useful guidelines within WordPerfect's Help utility that you want to incorporate rather than retyping it all. This feature can also save you time using Help if you annotate one topic with related information from another topic.

Part
1

Up and Running
with Windows 95

Copying is done by way of Windows' Clipboard. The entire Help topic or only selected portions of it may be copied. (Graphics from a Help topic cannot be copied to the Clipboard, however.) For a complete discussion of Clipboard and text-selection techniques, see Chapter 6. I'll briefly outline the steps here for copying to the Clipboard from Help:

TIP Pressing Ctrl-Ins copies the entire contents of a Help topic to the Clipboard.

NOTE Text selection throughout Windows and in most Windows applications works the same way and is explained thoroughly in Chapter 19, which covers WordPad. The easiest way is to position the selection cursor—the blinking bar—at the beginning of the text. Then, keeping the mouse button depressed, move the mouse. Release the button when all the text you want to copy is highlighted.

1. Within the active Help topic window, use the mouse to select the text you want to copy.

2. Open the Edit menu and choose Copy (see Figure 3.28).

3. Switch to the document you want to paste the information into, open its Edit menu, and choose Paste.

TIP You can copy material from one Help screen onto the Clipboard, then paste it into an annotation box for another Help screen, as explained above. This way, you can, in essence, have the information from two Help screens in one place.

Exiting Windows

When you're finished with a Windows session, you should properly shut down Windows *before* turning off your computer. This ensures that Windows saves your work on disk correctly and that no data are lost. Even if you are running an application in Windows and you close that application, you'll have to exit Windows, too, *before* turning off your computer.

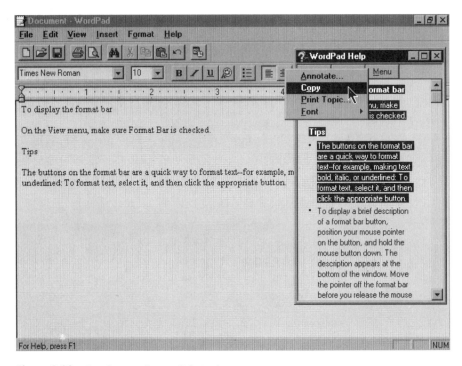

Figure 3.28   Copying text from a Help topic

 CAUTION   Exiting Windows properly is very important. You can lose your work or otherwise foul up Windows settings if you don't shut down Windows before turning off your computer.

Here are the steps for correctly exiting Windows:

1. Close any program that you have running. (This can almost always be done from each program's File menu—choose Exit from the menu—or by clicking on the program's Close button.) If you forget to close programs before issuing the Shut Down command, Windows will attempt to close them for you. This is fine unless you were working on a document and didn't save your work. In that case you'll be prompted by a dialog box for each open document, asking you if you want to save your work. If you have DOS programs running, you'll have to close

them manually before Windows will let you exit. You'll also be reminded if this is the case by a dialog box telling you that Windows can't terminate the program and you'll have to do it from the DOS program. Quit the DOS program and type **exit** at the DOS prompt, if necessary.

2. Next, click on the Taskbar and choose Shut Down.

THE SUSPEND OPTION FOR LAPTOPS

If your laptop computer has Advanced Power Manager (APM) built in, you may have a Suspend option in the Start button menu. This is like shutting down, only it lets you come right back to where you were working before you suspended. This means you don't have to exit all your applications before turning off your computer. You only have to choose Suspend. It also means you can get right back to work where you left off without rebooting your computer, finding the document(s) you were working on, and finding your place in those documents. I don't ever have to boot up Windows, run my favorite applications, and open my documents unless I want to. They are always up and running. I just pop open the lid to my laptop, enter my password, and I'm up and running right where I left off.

Though an increasing number of laptop computers now support a suspend function, they may not be APM-compatible. Also note that there is a limit to the amount of time a computer can stay in a suspended state. If the battery runs out, the computer will have to be rebooted when you turn it on, and your work may be lost.

Toshiba computers hold the record in terms of how long they will stay in Suspend mode. I have had five Toshibas thus far, precisely for their well-engineered *Auto Resume* feature. A typical Toshiba laptop will stay suspended on a full battery charge for several days to a week or more. Most other brands won't stay suspended for more than a couple hours. You'll want to check with the manufacturer of your computer about how long theirs will stay "alive" in a suspended state if you plan to use Windows 95's Suspend option.

Still, even if you have Suspend capability on your computer, you should save your work before suspending. You don't necessarily have to close the applications you're using, but you should at least save any documents you're working on.

3. You'll now see a dialog box like that in Figure 3.29. (If you are not on a network, you'll only see the first two options.)

4. Wait until Windows completely shuts down and tells you it's okay to turn off your computer. This may take about fifteen seconds.

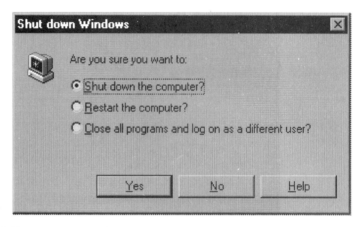

Figure 3.29 **Click on** *Shut down the computer?* **to end your Windows session.**

Chapter 4

Getting Down to Business: Running Your Applications

FEATURING

If you've just upgraded from Windows 3.1, you already know a lot about how to use Windows and Windows applications. A few things will be different with Windows 95, but you'll probably pick those up quickly. If you're new to Windows, then getting used to the turf might take a little longer, though you'll have an advantage—you won't have to unlearn any bad habits that Windows 3.x veterans have ground into their craniums.

What Can and Can't Be Run

As I discussed in the opening chapters, Windows 95 was designed to be *backward-compatible* with Windows 3.x and DOS programs and to be *forward-compatible* with most 32-bit programs designed for Windows NT. In a sense, Windows 95 is the best of all worlds when it comes to running your existing programs. You can pretty much bet that whatever is in your existing software arsenal won't be rendered obsolete by Windows 95.

Windows 95 will run your existing DOS programs quite nicely in scalable windows, offer them more conventional memory than previously possible, run many graphics programs in a window, and optionally give each DOS application its own custom DOS environment to run in. Likewise, most existing Windows programs will run just fine with smoother task switching and a more pleasant appearance, and (with a few workarounds I'll be telling you about) they can interact with the new Windows 95 Desktop. As new 32-bit programs for Windows 95 appear, you'll be able to run those, too, adding OLE 2.0 support and speedier performance. Any and all programs can be run from the DOS command line, not just DOS programs.

So, How Do I Run My Programs?

As with many of the procedures you'll want to do while in Windows, starting up your programs can be done in myriad ways. Here's the complete list of ways to run programs. You can:

▶ Choose the desired application from the Start button.

▶ Open My Computer, walk your way through the directories until you find the application's icon, and double-click on it.

▶ Run Explorer or File Manager, find the application's icon, and double-click on it.

▶ Run the old-style Windows 3.x Program Manager, open the group that contains the application's icon, and double-click on it.

▶ Find the application with the Find command and double-click on it.

▶ Locate a document that was created with the application in question and double-click on it. This will run the application and load the document into it.

▶ Right-click on the Desktop or in a folder and choose New. Then choose a document type from the resulting menu. This creates a new document of the type you desire, which, when double-clicked on, will run the application.

▶ Open the Documents list from the Start button and choose a recently edited document. This will open the document in the appropriate application.

▶ Enter command names from the MS-DOS prompt. In addition to the old-style DOS commands that run DOS programs and batch files, you can run Windows programs right from the DOS prompt.

For many users, the last three approaches will make the most sense because they deal with the document itself instead of the application that created it.

In deference to tradition, I'm going to cover the approaches to running applications in the order listed above. That is, application-centric first rather than document-centric. All the approaches are useful while using Windows, and you will probably want to become proficient in each of them.

Running a Program from the Start Button

Certainly the easiest way to run your applications is with the Start button. That's why it's called the Start button! Here's how it works.

When you install a new program, the program's name is added to the Start button's Program menu. Then you just find your way to the

RUNNING APPLICATIONS FROM THE COMMAND PROMPT

One of the nicest features of Windows 95 is that you can now run any application from the MS-DOS command prompt. If you're used to MS-DOS, you can open up a MS-DOS Prompt from the Start menu (Start ➤ Programs ➤ MS-DOS Prompt). If you use the command prompt frequently, you might want to create a shortcut on the Desktop to make access to the command prompt faster. To do this:

1. Click on the Desktop with the right mouse button.

2. Select New ➤ Shortcut.

3. In the Create Shortcut dialog box's Command line edit box enter `command.com`.

4. Click on Next.

5. As a Program-Information File already exists for this program, the *Select Title for the Program* dialog box's *Select name for the shortcut* edit box should already have *MS-DOS Prompt* listed, but if it doesn't, go ahead and enter it now. If you want another title to be displayed, you can enter that instead.

6. Click on Finish. A new shortcut should now be displayed on the Desktop.

7. At this point you can change the default start-up directory (the MS-DOS Prompt's default directory) by right-clicking on the program icon and selecting Properties. Choose the Program tab, then change the entry in the Working edit box to your desired directory. I often change this to C:\ instead of the default C:\Windows so I can browse around from the root directory.

If you use a long–file-name directory, remember to enclose the entire text string in quotes. For instance, if you want to start your command prompt in the Program Files directory, it should look like **"C:\Program Files"** in the Working edit box.

Once you have a command prompt, you can use your familiar MS-DOS commands like **CD** to change directories or **MD** to make a new directory, or you can run your programs (any `.bat`, `.pif`, `.com`, or `.exe` file). And you can run either MS-DOS or Windows programs. Just type in the program name, and it will start up. For instance, if you want to run the Windows 3.x version of File Manager, type `winfile` and press the Enter key.

program's name, choose it, and the program runs. Suppose you want to run Notepad:

1. Click on the Start button.

2. Choose Programs because you want to start a program. Up comes a list of programs similar to what's shown in Figure 4.1. Your list will differ because this is the list of programs on *my* computer, not yours.

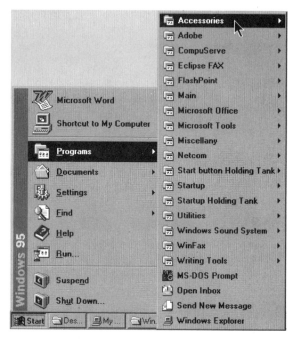

Figure 4.1   **The first step in running a program is to click on the Start button and choose Programs from the resulting list.**

Any selection that has an arrow pointer to the right of the name is not actually a program but a program *group*. If you've used Windows 3.x, you'll know that program groups are the collections of programs and related document files that were used to organize your programs in Windows 3.x's Program Manager. Choosing one of these opens another menu listing the items in the group.

3.   I happen to know that the Notepad program lies amongst the accessory programs that come with Windows 95. Slide the pointer up or over to highlight Accessories. Now the rather long list of accessory programs appears. There are a lot of accessories, as you can see. Slide the pointer down to Notepad and click, as shown in Figure 4.2.

You've successfully run Notepad. It's now sitting there with a blank document open, waiting for you to start typing. Chapter 22 covers the

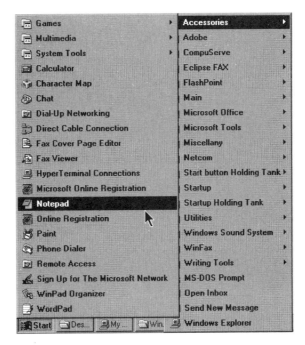

🖿 Games ▶	**Accessories** ▶
🖿 Multimedia ▶	Adobe ▶
🖿 System Tools ▶	CompuServe ▶
🖩 Calculator	Eclipse FAX ▶
🜂 Character Map	FlashPoint ▶
🕮 Chat	Main ▶
🖳 Dial-Up Networking	Microsoft Office ▶
🖧 Direct Cable Connection	Microsoft Tools ▶
🗎 Fax Cover Page Editor	Miscellany ▶
🖻 Fax Viewer	Netcom ▶
🖳 HyperTerminal Connections	Start button Holding Tank ▶
🗐 Microsoft Online Registration	Startup ▶
🗒 **Notepad**	Startup Holding Tank ▶
🗐 Online Registration	Utilities ▶
🗐 Paint	Windows Sound System ▶
🕾 Phone Dialer	WinFax ▶
🖳 Remote Access	Writing Tools ▶
🜨 Sign Up for The Microsoft Network	MS-DOS Prompt
🗒 WinPad Organizer	Open Inbox
🖋 WordPad	Send New Message
🏁Start 🖵Des... 🖳My... 🖵Win.	🖳 Windows Explorer

Figure 4.2 The second step in running a program from the Start button is to choose the program itself from the resulting Program list or to open a group such as Accessories and then choose the program.

ins and outs of using Notepad, so I won't discuss that here. For now just click on the Close button.

Because Windows 95 lets you nest groups of applications and documents into multiple levels, you might occasionally run into multiple levels of cascading menus when you're trying to launch (that's computerese for *run*) an application. For example, in the instance above, I had to open the Accessories group to find Notepad. Open it again and notice that there are a couple of groups within Accessories up at the top—Games, Multimedia, and System Tools. Sometimes because of the length of a list, the list might wrap around the screen, open to the right or to the left, or otherwise scoot around your screen in some unexpected way. None of this matters. You simply look for the program or group name you want and click on it regardless of its orientation on the screen.

TIP Sometimes spotting a program in a list is a visual hassle. Computers are smart about alphabetizing, so notice that the items in the lists are in order from A to Z. Folders appear first, in order, then programs after that. This ordering is something you'll see throughout Windows 95. To make things even simpler, you can press the first letter of the item you're looking for, and the highlight will jump to it. If there are multiple items starting with that letter, each key press will advance one in the list. This works fairly reliably unless the pointer is sitting on an item that has opened into a group.

Notice that if you open a Start button list that you don't want to look at—say, Documents—you can just move the pointer over to Programs, and that list will open. Pressing Esc also has the effect of closing open lists one at a time. Each press of Esc closes one level of open list. To close down all open lists, just click anywhere else on the screen, such as on the Desktop or another window.

Running a Program from My Computer

There are times when you might want to do a little sleuthing around using a more graphical approach as opposed to hunting for a name. The My Computer button lets you do this. My Computer is usually situated in the upper-left corner of your Desktop. Double-clicking on it reveals an interesting entry point to all the elements of your computer—hardware, software, printers, files, and folders.

The My Computer button is a little like a graphical version of File Manager, if you've used that. Getting to a program you want can be a little convoluted, but if you understand the DOS directory tree structure or you've used a Mac, you'll be able to grasp this fairly easily. Try it out.

1. Get to the Desktop by minimizing any windows that are on the screen. You can do this by clicking on each window's Minimize button (Chapter 3).

 TIP Another way to minimize all your windows and see the Desktop is to right-click on the clock in the Taskbar and choose Minimize All Windows.

2. Now double-click on My Computer. A window appears, looking something like this:

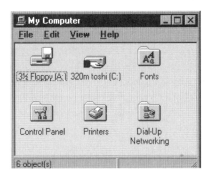

3. Typically, Drive C is where your programs will be located. Double-click on the drive icon, and your hard drive's contents will open up into another window as shown in Figure 4.3.

4. The object is to locate the folder containing the program you want and double-click on it. (Some programs are so ferreted away that it's difficult to find them. You may have to search around a bit.) The standard setting shows folders and files as *large icons*. If you want to see more folders on the screen at once to help in your search, you have several options. The large icon view can be annoying because it doesn't let you see very many objects at once. Check out the View menu.

5. Choose Small Icons, List, or Details. *Details* will show the sizes of files and other information about the files and folders, such as the date they were created. This is useful when looking for applications because the Type column will indicate whether the file is an application program.

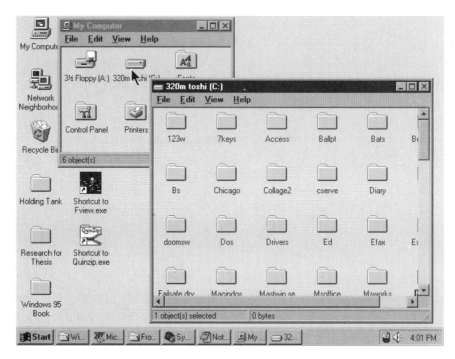

Figure 4.3   *Double-clicking on a drive icon displays its contents in a window. Here you see a portion of what I have on my C drive. Notice that folders (which used to be called directories) are listed first. Scrolling the listing would reveal any files in the folder. Here we are in essence looking at the root directory of the drive. Double-clicking on a folder will reveal its contents in another window.*

 TIP   Pressing Backspace while in any folder window will move you back one level. While in the C drive window, for example, pressing Backspace takes you back to the My Computer window. Or, if you're looking at a directory, Backspace will take you up to the root level.

6. When you see the program you want to run, just double-click on it. For example, in Figure 4.4 I've found WinCIM.

Note that many of the files you'll find in your folders are *not* programs. They are documents or other kinds of files that are used by programs. Programs tend to have specialized icons such as the one for WinCIM in Figure 4.4. Documents, as you will learn later, look a bit different.

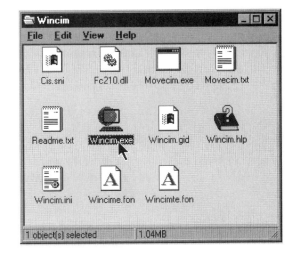

Figure 4.4 Run a program by clicking on its icon. Regardless of whether the view is Large Icons, Small Icons, List, or Detailed, double-clicking on a program will run it.

 TECH TIP   Normally files with certain extensions (the last three letters of a file's name) are hidden from display in your folder windows. Files with dll, sys, vxd, 386, drv, and cpl extensions will not display. This choice was made to prevent cluttering the display with files that perform duties for the operating system but not directly for users. If you want to see all the files in a folder, open the View menu on the folder's window, choose Options, and select the File Types tab. Then turn on the appropriate check box. In Chapter 5 I'll explain all the options you can use when displaying folder windows.

Running a Program from the Explorer or File Manager

On the Mac, all you get to work with to organize your documents and programs is folders—essentially the same arrangement the last section illustrated. This approach can be annoying when what you want is a grand overview of your hard disk's contents. Working your way through a lot of folder windows can get tedious and can clutter up the screen too much to be efficient. There are ways to reduce the clutter when using this approach, as I'll explain in Chapter 5. Even so, if you're the kind of person who prefers the *tree* approach (a hierarchical display of your disk's contents) to your PC's hard disk, you might find the File Manager and its new replacement, the Explorer, a better means of running programs and finding documents. I'll be covering Explorer in Chapter 12. But in the meantime, I'll explain how to run your programs using these two supplied applications.

The trick to using either of these two programs is that you need to know a little more about what's going on in your computer than many people care to. Principally, you'll need to know where your programs are located and what their names are. For example, Word for Windows is really called `word.exe` on the hard disk and is typically stored in the `Winword` or `Msoffice\Winword` directory.

NOTE Although not featured in Windows 95, the old-style Windows 3.x File Manager is actually supplied with Windows 95. It's not listed on the Start button menu, but it's most likely on your hard disk.

Here's how to use Explorer to run your programs (I'll explain File Manager next):

1. Because Explorer is a program itself, you have to run it before you can use it to run other programs. So click on the Start button, choose Programs, and point to Windows Explorer as shown in Figure 4.5.

TIP Another way to run Explorer is to right-click on My Computer or a drive's icon in the My Computer window and choose Explore.

2. When the Explorer window comes up, adjust the window size for your viewing pleasure. It should look something like Figure 4.6.

3. The items on the left side are folders. Scroll down to the folder that contains the program you're looking for (folders are listed in alphabetical order). If a folder has a + sign next to it, it has subfolders. Clicking on the + sign displays the names of any subfolders.

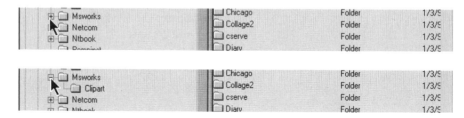

Figure 4.5   *To run Explorer, click on Start, then Programs, then Windows Explorer.*

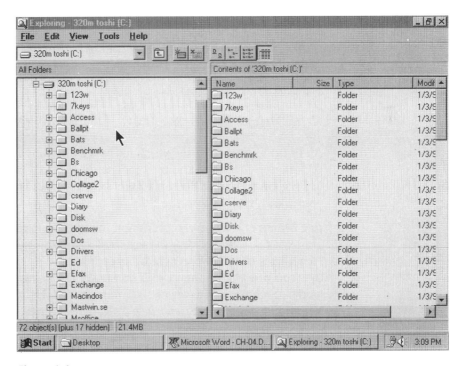

Figure 4.6   *The Explorer window*

4. Single-click on the folder containing the program you want to run. Its contents will appear in the right-hand side (called the right *pane*) of the window.

5. Then double-click on the program. Here I'm about to run Microsoft Works.

Notice that the items in the right-hand pane are displayed as large icons. Just as when using folders, you can change the appearance of listed items by opening the View menu and choosing Large Icons, Small Icons, List, or Details. It's easier to see which file is a program when the display is set to Large Icons (because you can see the icon clearly) or Details (because the third column will say *application* if the file is a program).

TIP You can also use the four rightmost buttons on the toolbar to choose how items are displayed. They have the same effect as choosing Large Icons, Small Icons, List, or Details from the View menu.

Running a Program from File Manager

As I said above, the File Manager as we all knew it and love/hated it in Windows 3.x is alive and well in Windows 95. It's just sort of hidden. It's not on the Start button's menu, but you can run it with the Run command, which *is* on the Start button's menu.

File Manager is a useful tool for a number of tasks, including running programs (aka *applications*). Although the Explorer is more supercharged, File Manager is charming because of its simplicity. It doesn't confuse the issue by displaying everything in your computer including the kitchen sink. It works much the same way as Explorer, but the display is simpler. Unfortunately, File Manager doesn't display long file names.

To use File Manager to run a program:

1. Click on the Start button and choose Run.

2. In the resulting box, type **winfile** and click on OK.

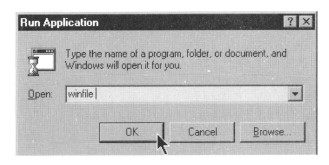

3. File Manager runs and appears in a window. Maximize the window, and File Manager will display as shown in Figure 4.7.

4. Select the folder you want by clicking on it. Normally, you won't see any indication of which folders have subfolders (subdirectories) under them. To see an indication of subfolders, you have to open the File Manager's Tree menu and choose Indicate Expandable Branches. After that, folders that have subfolders will be indicated by a + sign. Double-click on a + to display its subdirectories.

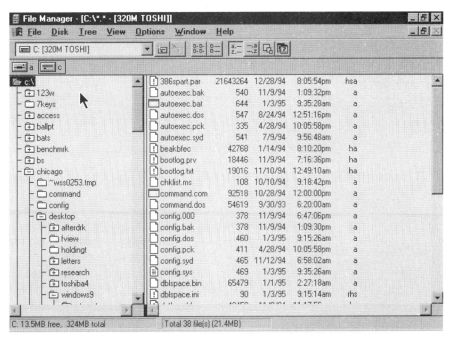

Figure 4.7   To run a program from File Manager, double-click on it.

NOTE   Even without the + sign showing, you can double-click on a folder to see any existing subfolders.

5. Scroll the display as necessary to show the name of the program you want to run. Programs have a special icon so you know which ones can be run. Here I'm about to run Works.

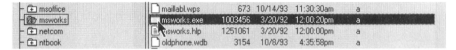

6. Double-click on the program file you want to run.

 NOTE   As a general rule to remember, four kinds of files can be run using this method: Those with extensions of `exe`, `com`, `bat`, and `pif`. All other files will either not run when double-clicked on or will run their *associated* programs and load into them. For example, files with the extension `bmp` are graphics. Double-clicking on such a file (e.g., `arches.bmp`) will run the Paint program and load the graphic into the Paint window for editing.

Running a Program from Program Manager

If you're a Windows 3.x veteran, you might be most at home running your programs from the good old Program Manager. That's the program organizer that was supplied with Windows 3.x and is now essentially replaced by the Start button's submenus. To get new Windows 95 users over the hurdle of learning the new interface, they included Program Manager in the Windows 95 package. Like File Manager, though, it's sort of hidden away.

When you install a new program onto your computer (Chapter 5), the new program usually creates what's called a *program group*. A program group is a window that contains items pertaining to the program, such as the program's icon (for running it), various Readme files, a Help file, and so forth. To run a program from Program Manager, you just open the desired window and double-click on the icon you want.

When you install Windows 95 over an existing Windows 3.x setup, it does a little sleight of hand. All your preexisting Program Manager

groups and icons end up on the Start button's Program lists. So clicking Start ➤ Programs will list your Program Manager groups.

Enough theory. Try this to run Program Manager:

1. Click on the Start button.

TIP You can press Ctrl-Esc to open the Start list from the keyboard at
any time.

---

2. Choose Run. In the Run box enter **progman**.

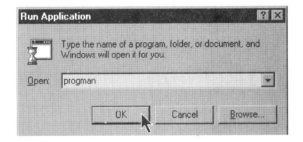

3. Click on OK, and you'll see your old familiar Program Manager. Figure 4.8 illustrates.

4. The trick with Program Manager is that you have to find and display
a group's window before you can run a program in it. If the screen is
cluttered, sometimes the easiest way to do this is simply by opening
the Window menu and choosing from there. Of course, you could just
click on the window if it's in view, but the Window menu approach is
a no-brainer.

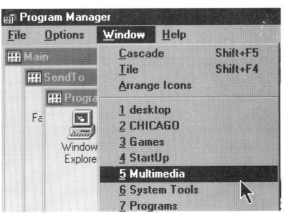

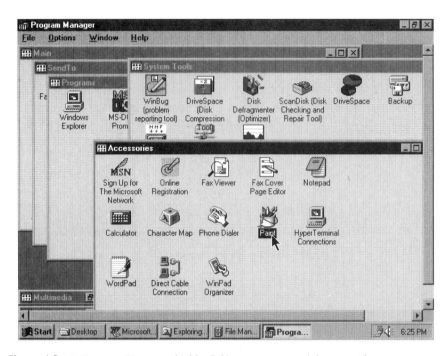

Figure 4.8   In Program Manager, double-clicking on a program's icon runs the program.

5. Once you've chosen the desired group, its window appears. Then double-click on the icon of the program you want to run. In Figure 4.8, for example, I'm about to run Paint from the Accessories group.

Running Applications from the Find Command

The Find command is covered in detail in Part V of this book, but I'll quickly mention how to use this indispensable little gadget. As with File Manager and Explorer, it helps if you know the file name of the program you're looking for, but at least Find cuts you some slack if you don't know the whole name. You can specify just part of it. Find will search a given disk or the whole computer (multiple disks) looking for something that looks like the program (or other file, such as a document) name you tell it. Once found, you can double-click on the program in the resulting list, and it will run. Pretty spiffy.

> **NOTE** The Run box technique (described above) is easier than Find if you know the exact name of the program. But the catch is that Run requires the program to be in the DOS *search path.* If it's not, the program won't run and you'll just get an error message saying the program can't be found. Of course, if you know the drive and directory the program is in, you *can* enter its entire path name, in which case it will probably run.

Here's an example. I have the program called Windsock somewhere on my computer. As it turns out, the Run command won't run this program because Windsock is stored in a folder that's not in my DOS search path. All I get when I try to find it is this message:

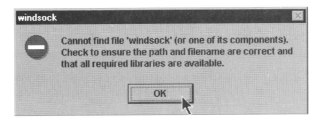

So I cancel the Run dialog box and try the Find command. Here's how:

> **NOTE** From here on out, I'll use a shorthand notation to describe making multiple menu choices. Instead of: "Click on the Start button, choose Programs, then choose Accessories, and then choose Paint," I'll say: "Choose Start ➤ Programs ➤ Accessories ➤ Paint."

1. Choose Start ➤ Find ➤ Folders and Files.

2. The Find dialog box appears, and I fill in the top part with at least a portion of the name of the file I'm looking for. (See Figure 4.9—I've maximized the Find window to show you as much information as possible.) Note that I've set the *Look In* section to My Computer. As a default it will search your C drive, which is usually fine unless you have multiple hard disks on your computer and want Find to comb through them all.

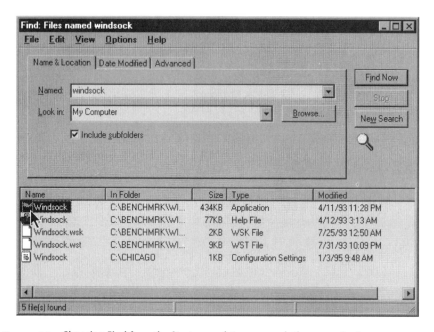

Figure 4.9   *Choosing Find from the Start menu lets you search the computer for a program.*
You don't have to enter the whole name as you do when using File Manager's
Search command.

3.   I click on Find Now. In a few seconds any files or folders matching the search request show up in the bottom pane, as the figure illustrates. Note that several Windsock files were located, but that only one is an application (a program).

4.   I double-click on the Windsock application, and it runs.

When you want to run a program or open a document by clicking on it, don't double-click on its name slowly! If you do, this tells Windows that you want to change the object's name. You know this has happened when a little box appears around the name of the file like this:

Just press Esc to get out of editing mode. To be safe, it's better to click on any item's icon (the picture portion) when you want to run it, open it, move it around, and so forth.

Running a Program via One of Its Documents

As I mentioned above, some documents will open up when you click on their icons—if they are *registered*. Windows 95 has an internal registry (basically just a list) of file extensions that it knows about. Each registered file type is matched with a program that it works with. When you double-click on any document, Windows scans the list of registered file types to determine what it should do with the file. For example, double-clicking on a bmp file will run Paint and load the file.

The upshot of this is that you can run an application by double-clicking on a document of a known registered type. For example, suppose I want to run Word. All I have to do is spot a Word document somewhere. It's easy to spot one, especially in Large Icon view, because all Word documents have Word's telltale identifying icon. Unregistered documents have no discernible icon. Check out Figure 4.10. There I'm about to double-click on a Word document I came across in a folder. Notice that the icon just above it is what a nonregistered file icon looks like.

Once the program runs, you may decide you don't want to work with the actual document that you used as a trick to get the program going.

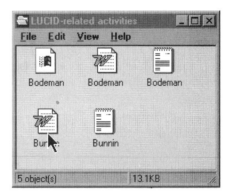

Figure 4.10   *Double-clicking on a file of a registered type runs the program that created it.*

That's OK because most programs will let you close the current document (try choosing File ➤ Close) and then let you open a new document (usually via File ➤ New) or an existing one with File ➤ Open.

TIP Try clicking on the Start button and choosing Documents to see a list of the files you've recently edited. Depending on what's on the list, you may be able to run the program you're looking for.

TECH TIP By default, file extensions of registered files are not displayed on screen. This cuts down on visual clutter, letting you see simple names that make sense, such as 1995 `Report` instead of 1995 `Report.wk3`. In later chapters I'll tell you how to turn off this option in case you always want to see and be able to change extensions at will.

How Do File Types Become Registered?

You may be wondering how documents with certain extensions become registered so they will run an application when double-clicked on. Some types are set up by Windows 95 when you install it. For example, `hlp` files (e.g., `paint.hlp`) are Help files and will open up in an appropriate window. Likewise, `txt` files will open in Notepad, `pcx` files in Paint, `doc` files in WordPad, `ht` files in HyperTerminal, and so on.

In addition to those extensions that are automatically established when installing Windows 95, some others might have been imported into your system from an earlier version of Windows. If you've upgraded to Windows 95 from Windows 3.x, then any previously registered types (called *associations* in Windows 3.x) are pulled into Windows 95.

Some programs register their file type when you install the program. So, for example, when you install Word, Windows 95 changes the registration list so that `doc` files will be opened by Word instead of by WordPad when double-clicked on.

And finally, you can register a file type yourself (Chapter 5) from any folder or Explorer window's View ➤ Options ➤ File Types command.

Running Applications by Right-Clicking on the Desktop

When you don't want to bother finding some favorite program just to create a new document, there's an easier way. How often have you simply wanted to create a To Do list, a shopping list, a brief memo, little spreadsheet, or what have you? All the time, right? Microsoft figured out that people often work in just this way—they don't think: "Gee, I'll root around for Excel, then I'll run it, and then I'll create a new spreadsheet file and save it and name it." That's counterintuitive. On the contrary, it's more likely they think: "I need to create a 'Sales for Spring Quarter' Excel spreadsheet."

Just create a new *empty* document of the correct type on the Desktop and name it. Then double-clicking on it will run the correct program. Windows 95 takes care of assigning the file the correct extension so that internally the whole setup works. Try an experiment to see what I'm talking about.

1. Clear off enough windows so you can see your Desktop area.

TIP   Remember, you can right-click on the clock in the Taskbar and choose *Minimize all windows* to minimize all the open windows. You can reverse the effect by clicking again and choosing *Undo Minimize all*.

2. Right-click anywhere on the Desktop. From the resulting menu choose New. You'll see a list of possible document types. The types in my computer are shown in Figure 4.11 as an example.

3. Choose a document type by clicking on it. A new document icon appears on your Desktop such as this one that appeared when I chose *Sound*:

4. The file's name is highlighted and has a box around it. This means you can edit the name. As long as the whole name is highlighted, whatever you type will replace the entire name. When you create a new document this way, you don't have to worry about entering the extension. For example, a sound file normally has a wav extension, but you could just type in **Blam** for the name and press Enter (remember, you have to press Enter after typing in the name to finalize it). The actual file name will be Blam.wav because Windows 95 adds a hidden file extension for you.

5. Double-click on the icon and its associated program will run. In the case of the sound, Sound Recorder will run, waiting for me to record the sound.

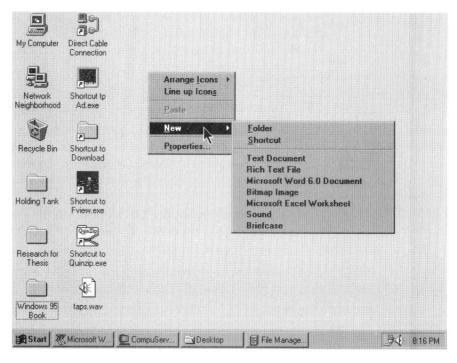

Figure 4.11   You can create a variety of new document types by right-clicking on the Desktop. This creates a blank document that you then name and run.

Using the Start ➤ Documents List

As I mentioned in a Tip above, choosing Start ➤ Documents lists the documents you've recently created or edited. It's an easy way to revisit projects you've been working on. This list is maintained by Windows 95 and is *persistent*, which means it'll be there in subsequent Windows sessions, even after you shut down and reboot. Only the last fifteen documents are remembered, though, and some of these won't be things you'd think of as documents. Some of them might actually be more like programs or folders. Check it out and see if it contains the right stuff for you. Figure 4.12 shows my list the day I wrote this section.

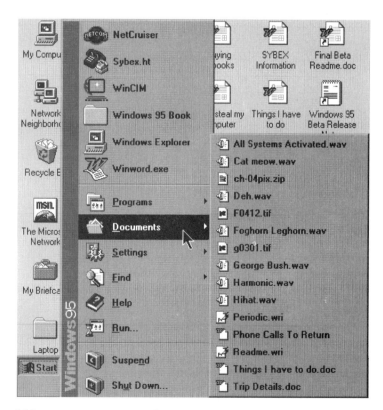

Figure 4.12 *The Document list from the Start button provides a no-brainer path to ongoing work projects.*

TIP   Many Windows programs have a similar feature that lists your most recently edited documents at the bottom of their File menus. Because many of my favorite programs sport this feature, I tend to rely on that more than on the Document list.

TIP   You can clear off the items in the Documents list and start fresh if you want to. Click on the Start button, choose Settings ➤ Taskbar ➤ Start Menu Programs, and click on the Clear button.

Running DOS Programs

Though DOS applications are by no means the preponderant genre of PC programs being sold in today's world, they certainly were for many years. Consequently, tens of thousands of useful and interesting programs exist for the IBM-PC DOS environment. Many of these programs are not easily replaced with popular Windows programs, either. This is simply because they were specialized programs custom designed for vertical market uses such as point of sale, transaction processing, inventory, scientific data gathering, and so on. It's safe to say that after a corporation invests significantly in software development, testing, implementation, and employee training, conversion to a Windows-based version just because it looks groovier isn't a very attractive proposition. As a result, much of the code that was written five to ten years ago and ran in DOS programs is still doing its job in companies and other institutions today.

The great thing about Windows 95 is that you can still run all those wonderful DOS programs, even multiple ones at the same time. And each can have its own DOS environment, tasking settings, window size and font, and so on, not to mention the ability to automate task execution and control with DOS *batch* files. Until Windows NT and Windows 95, batch files were not available for Windows users. They could be run in a DOS box but couldn't control Windows programs. Windows 95 can execute DOS programs, DOS batch files, and Windows programs from the command line. Therefore you can write batch files with Windows program command lines in them.

So How Do I Run My DOS Programs?

I'll explain briefly how you run DOS programs here.

You can run a DOS program by:

▶ clicking on the Start button, choosing Programs, and looking for the program on the resulting menus

▶ double-clicking on the program's name in a folder

▶ entering the program's name at the Run command

▶ double-clicking on the program in File Manager

▶ double-clicking on the program in Explorer

▶ running a "DOS session" and then typing in the program's name at the DOS prompt

▶ double-clicking on a document file with an extension that you've manually associated with the DOS program

I explained the first five of these techniques earlier when I told you how to run Windows programs. The only difference between running Windows programs and DOS programs using those techniques is that DOS programs don't normally have an identifying icon, such as a big "W" for Word. Instead, they tend to have a boring, generic icon that looks like:

 Therefore, you have to rely on the icon's name alone. This one is for XTREE Gold, but because the actual program's name on disk is xtgold.exe, that's what you see. Well, actually, you don't see the exe part, because as I mentioned earlier, exe extensions are normally hidden from view.

Because the last two approaches in the above list differ from running Windows programs and haven't been covered, let's check those out. Then I'll tell you a bit about how DOS programs operate in Windows and what you can quickly do to modify their behavior.

First consider the option of running a DOS program from the good old DOS prompt.

NOTE There isn't room in this book to discuss all the DOS commands and how DOS works. You should consult a book such as Sybex's *Mastering DOS 6.2* for more information about DOS commands. To get on-screen help with DOS, you can enter the command help at the DOS prompt and follow directions at that point.

To run a DOS session, do the following:

1. Click on the Start button.

2. Choose Programs, then MS-DOS Prompt, as shown in Figure 4.13.

3. The result will be what's sometimes called a *DOS box*—a window that operates just like you're using a computer running DOS. Try typing in **DIR** and pressing Enter. You'll see a listing of files on the current

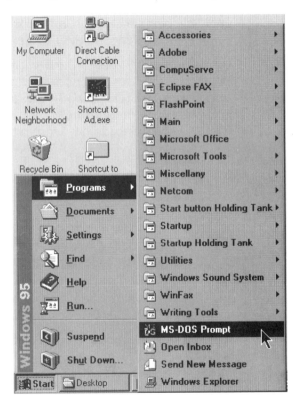

Figure 4.13   *You run a DOS session (get to a DOS prompt) by choosing MS-DOS from the Program list.*

drive, as shown in Figure 4.14. Note that short and long file names are both shown in this new version of DOS. Long file names are in the rightmost column, with corresponding short file names over on the left.

4. Enter the command **exit** when you are finished running DOS programs or executing DOS commands. This will close the DOS window and end the session.

TIP If no DOS program is actually running, clicking on the DOS window's Close button will also end the DOS session. If a DOS program is running, trying this results in a message prompting you to quit the DOS program first.

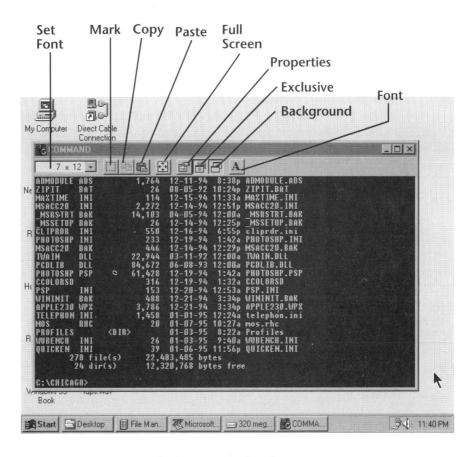

Figure 4.14   Enter any standard DOS commands at the prompt.

Options while Running a DOS Session

While running a DOS session, there are several easy adjustments you can make that are either cosmetic or actually affect the performance of the program. You can easily:

► toggle the DOS session between full screen and windowed

► turn the toolbar on or off

► adjust the font

► resize the DOS box

► allow the DOS session to work in the background

► cause the DOS session to take over the computer's resources when in the foreground

Let me briefly discuss each of these options. Refer to Figure 4.14 for toolbar buttons.

First, if the DOS window is taking up the whole screen (all other elements of the Windows interface have disappeared) and you'd like to have the DOS program running in a window so you can see other programs, press Alt-Enter to switch it to a window. Once windowed, you can return it to full-screen mode either by clicking on the Full Screen button or pressing Alt-Enter again.

Next, you can turn on the toolbar if you want easy access to most of the above features. Then you won't have to use the menus. If you don't see the toolbar (as in Figure 4.14), click in the upper-left corner of the DOS window and choose Toolbar. Choose the same command again, and the toolbar will turn off.

Once the toolbar is showing, you can set several useful options. A nice feature in Windows 95 is the adjustable font. Unlike in Windows 3.x, you can now use TrueType fonts in a DOS box. The easiest way to change the font is to open the Font drop-down list (rather than clicking on the "A" button). Fonts are listed there by the size of the character matrix (in pixels) that comprises each displayed character. The larger the matrix, the larger the resulting characters (and consequently the DOS box itself) will be. Setting the size to auto has the effect of scaling the font automatically if you resize the DOS box from its lower-left corner. When resizing, don't be surprised if the mouse pointer jumps around a bit wildly. The box is not infinitely adjustable as Windows programs are, so as you're adjusting, the outline of the window jumps to predetermined sizes.

> **TIP** The *A* button on the toolbar lets you choose whether only bit-mapped fonts, TrueType fonts, or both will show in the Fonts listing on the left.

The Properties button we'll leave alone for the time being. Selections you make here are rather complicated and require some detailed discussion. So, moving right along, take note of the Exclusive button. This button determines whether your DOS program, when in the foreground, will receive all of your CPU's attention. That is, it will be run as though there are no other programs running in the computer that might need to be serviced. Some programs—such as data-acquisition programs that expect total control of the computer, the screen, keyboard, ports, and so forth—may require this. If you want to turn this option off, (which would allow other programs in the background to continue processing while this program runs), click on this button. It should pop out rather than look indented, meaning it's turned off.

The final button, Background, determines whether the DOS program will continue processing in the background when you switch to another program. As a default, this setting is on. You can tell it's on because the button looks indented. You can turn it off if you want your DOS program to temporarily suspend when it isn't the active window (the window in which you're currently working).

> **TIP** You can of, course, have multiple DOS sessions running at the same time in separate windows. This lets you easily switch between a number of DOS programs that can be running simultaneously.

> **NOTE** You can also Copy and Paste data from and to DOS applications. See Chapter 6 for details.

Additional Property Settings for DOS Programs

DOS programs were designed to run one at a time and are usually memory hogs. They often need at least 600K of free RAM, and some may require expanded or extended memory to perform well. Running a DOS program with several other programs (particularly other DOS programs) under Windows is conceptually like bringing a bunch of ill-mannered guests to a formal dinner.

The moral of this is simply that Windows has a lot of housekeeping to do to keep DOS programs happy. When running from Windows, DOS programs don't really "know" that other programs are running, and they expect to have direct access to all the computer's resources: RAM, printer, communications ports, screen, and so on.

In most cases, Windows 95 does pretty well at faking out DOS programs without your help, using various default settings and its own memory-management strategies. However, even Windows 95 isn't omniscient, and you may occasionally experience the ungracious locking up of a program or see messages about the "system integrity" having been corrupted.

> **TECH TIP**   In reality, what Windows is doing when running DOS programs is giving each of them a simulated PC to work in, called a *VDM* (Virtual DOS Machine).

If a DOS program doesn't run properly under Windows 95 or you wish to optimize its performance, you must modify its PIF (Program Information File), declaring certain settings that affect the program within Windows. With Windows 3.x, making PIF settings for a program required using a program called the PIF Editor—a cumbersome program supplied with Windows. Things are simpler with Windows 95. The first time you run a DOS program, a PIF is automatically created in the same directory as the DOS program. It has the same name as the program but looks like a shortcut icon. Examining the properties of the icon will reveal it has a `.pif` extension.

To adjust a program's PIF settings, simply open the Properties box for the DOS program and make the relevant settings. This can be done by running the DOS program in a window and clicking on the

Properties button on the Toolbar or, without running the program, by right-clicking on its PIF icon and choosing Properties. When you close the Properties box, the new PIF settings are saved. From then on, those settings go into effect whenever you run the program from within Windows.

The PIF settings affect many aspects of the program's operation, such as, but not limited to:

▶ the file name and directory of the program

▶ font and window size

▶ the directory that becomes active once a program starts

▶ memory usage, including conventional, expanded, extended, and protected-mode memory usage

▶ multitasking priority levels

▶ video-adapter modes

▶ the use of keyboard shortcut keys

▶ foreground and background processing

▶ Toolbar display

▶ program-termination options

Some of these options were discussed above and are quickly adjustable from the DOS box Toolbar; others are not. To fine-tune the DOS environment for running a program:

▶ If the program will run without bombing:

  1. Run it as explained above.
  2. If it's not in a window, press Alt-Enter.
  3. Click on the Properties button if the Toolbar is showing or, if it isn't showing, click on the Control Box in the upper-left corner of the window and choose Properties.

▶ If the program won't run without bombing:

  1. Navigate with My Computer or Explorer to the folder containing the DOS program.
  2. Find the program's icon and click on it.

3. Open the File menu and choose Create Shortcut. A new icon will appear in the folder, called "Shortcut to [*program*]."

4. With the new shortcut highlighted, open the File menu and choose Properties.

Now you'll see the DOS program's Properties sheet, from which you can alter quite a healthy collection of settings (Figure 4.15). Unfortunately, there isn't room in this book for an explanation of all the settings available from this box. Remember, you can get some basic information about each setting via the ? button.

 NOTE In my upcoming book, *Windows 95 Secrets & Solutions* (Sybex, 1995), I'll discuss all of these settings in detail as well as the proper use of DOS device drivers and DOS TSR (terminate and stay resident) programs.

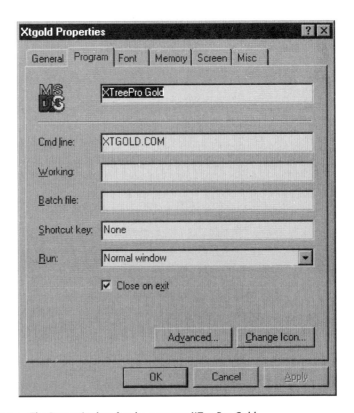

Figure 4.15   The Properties box for the program XTreePro Gold

Simply make your settings as necessary. When you're happy with them, click on OK in the Properties box to save the settings. The next time you run the program by double-clicking on the shortcut or the program's icon, the settings will go into effect.

 TECH TIP When you run a DOS program by clicking on its icon or its PIF icon, the PIF settings go into effect and the program runs. However, if you run the program from the DOS command line (by typing in a command from a DOS box), the settings *don't* go into effect. *They simply aren't used.* Two other ways to ensure they are used are to use the Run command and enter the name of the PIF, such as `ed.pif`, and to use the Start command from the DOS prompt (e.g., start ed.exe). Also, aside from the active directory, only directories listed in the search path as set up by your `autoexec .bat` file are scanned for PIFs. If a PIF isn't found when a program is double-clicked on, it won't be loaded, and Window's default PIF settings will be used instead.

 TIP If you are having trouble getting a DOS program to even check that the memory settings for the PIF match those required by the program (check the program's user manual) and if the program can't run in a window, set the screen usage to Full Screen.

 TECH TIP PIFs are one of two types of shortcut files. Shortcuts for Windows applications and documents are given the LNK extension. Only shortcuts for DOS applications actually are given the PIF extension. Even if you elect to display the MS-DOS extensions of all files (from the View ➤ Options menu in Explorer or a folder), you won't see the PIF extension in listings. Use the Find utility to look for PIFs by extension, if you need to.

What I Didn't Tell You— Shortcuts on the Desktop

A terrific feature of Windows 95 when it comes to running your programs is called *shortcuts*. Shortcuts are alias icons (icons that represent other icons) that you can add almost anywhere, such as in folders or on the Desktop. Because a shortcut is really only a link or pointer to the real file or application it represents, you can have as many as you

AUTOMATING JOBS WITH BATCH FILES

Because I am not a 200-word-per-minute typist, I like to create batch files to automate repetitive jobs or to create jobs to run at Windows start-up. For instance, if you want to automate the process of checking your hard disk for errors with ScanDisk every time you start Windows 95, try this:

1. Open up Notepad (Start ➤ Programs ➤ Notepad) or any other ASCII text editor.

2. To check just your C: drive, enter the following text:

   SCANDISK C: /n

   To check all of your local disk drives, enter the following text:

   SCANDISK /a /n

3. Save the file with a .bat file extension. For instance, you might want to save it as Check Disk Drives for Errors.bat.

4. Then add this item to the Startup folder so that Windows 95 will run it every time you start it (see Chapter 5 for complete instructions on how to do this).

5. The check will now run automatically every time you start Windows 95. You can also run it anytime you desire by selecting it from the Start menu.

The really nice part about this process is that you can do this to automate any job. And you can make the process completely automatic by adding the batch file to the Startup group (as we did above), or you can choose to manually run it whenever you select it from the Start menu. For instance, I could have created a new folder under the Programs folder, called it Batch Jobs, and placed the Check Disk for Errors batch file there. Then anytime I wanted to run this process I would select Start ➤ Programs ➤ Batch Jobs ➤ Check Disk.... You can use this same process to automate any job or start up multiple applications to create your daily working set. For instance, I could have created a batch file to launch Microsoft Mail, Schedule Plus, Word for Windows, and Excel all at once. This would save several mouse or keystroke commands because I would not have to return to the Start menu to launch them individually.

want, putting them wherever your heart desires, without duplicating your files. So, for example, you can have shortcuts to all your favorite programs right on the Desktop. Then you can run them from there without having to click on the Start button, walk through the Program listings, and so forth.

In Chapter 5 I'll explain how you make, copy, and place shortcuts. I'll also cover how you can dump shortcuts of your favorite programs onto the Start button so they are right there on the first menu when you click on Start.

Switching between Applications

Remember, Windows lets you have more than one program open and running at a time. You can also have multiple folders open at any time, and you can leave them open to make getting to their contents easier. Any folders that are open when you shut down the computer will open again when you start up Windows again.

People often think they have to shut down one program before working on another one, but that's really not efficient nor true. When you run each new program or open a folder, the Taskbar gets another button on it. Simply clicking on a button switches you to that program or folder. For the first several programs, the buttons are long enough to read the names of the programs or folder. As you run more programs, the buttons automatically get shorter, so the names are truncated. For example:

You can resize the Taskbar to give it an extra line or two of buttons if you want to see the full names. On the upper edge of the Taskbar, position the cursor so that it turns into a double-headed arrow, then drag it upwards and release. Here I've added another line for my current set of buttons.

Note that as you increase the size of the Taskbar, you decrease the effective size of your work area. On a standard VGA screen, this means you'll be cutting onto your work area quite a bit if you go to two or three lines. Still, it's possible. Another nice feature is that you can set the Taskbar to disappear until you move the mouse pointer down to the bottom of the screen. This way, you sacrifice nothing in the way of screen real estate. You do this via the Settings menu from the Start button.

TIP   If you prefer, you can also position the Taskbar on the right, left, or top of the screen. Just click on any part of the Taskbar other than a button and drag it to the edge of your choice.

Here's how to set the Taskbar options:

1. Click on Start and choose Settings.

2. Then choose Taskbar, as shown in Figure 4.16.

 TIP   A quick way to get to the Taskbar's Property settings is to right-click on an empty area of the Taskbar and choose Properties.

3. You'll now see the dialog box shown in Figure 4.15. Click on *Auto hide* to turn that option on—this is the one that makes the Taskbar disappear until you move the pointer to the edge of the screen where you've placed the Taskbar.

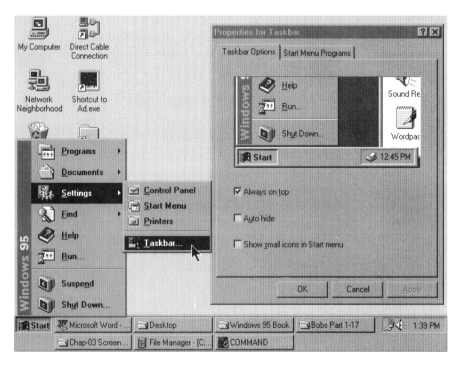

Figure 4.16   *You set the Taskbar options from this box. The mostly likely choice you'll make will be Auto Hide.*

4. If you'd like to see smaller icons in the first Start-up menu, set that option on, too.

5. OK the dialog box. Once you do so, the Taskbar will disappear. Try out the Auto Hide setting: Move the pointer down to the bottom and see how the Taskbar reappears.

TECH TIP   Even when set to Auto Hide, the Taskbar still uses 1 or 2 pixels at the edge of the screen to indicate where it is and to act as a trigger zone to pop up the Taskbar when the pointer touches it.

Switching with Alt-Tab

Don't like the Taskbar? Are you a habituated Windows 3.x user? Okay. As you may know, there's another way to switch between programs and folders—the Alt-Tab trick. Press down the Alt key and hold it down. Now, press the Tab key (you know, that key just above the Caps Lock and to the left of the Q). You'll see a box in the center of your screen showing you an icon of each program or folder that's running, like this:

Each press of the Tab key will advance the outline box one notch to the right. The outline box indicates which program you'll be switched to when you release the Alt key. If you want to back up one program (move the box to the left), you can press Alt-Shift-Tab. Note that the name of the program or folder is displayed at the bottom of the box, which is especially useful when choosing folders, as all folders look the same.

TECH TIP In Windows 3.x, pressing Ctrl-Esc brought up the Task List. It no longer does: It opens the Start menu as though you clicked on the Start button. Likewise, double-clicking on the Desktop now fails to bring up the Task List. The only time you can get the Task List is when Explorer malfunctions and causes the Taskbar to cease functioning. At that point, double-clicking on the Desktop will bring up an updated version of the Task List. You can then use that to switch tasks or to shut down.

Chapter 5

Organizing Your Programs and Documents

FEATURING

n this chapter, we'll explore the best way to organize your own work within Windows 95 and just what steps to take to do so. I'll tell you how to use the Taskbar, the Windows 95 folder system, and the Explorer to arrange your programs and documents so you can get to them easily. With the techniques I'll show you in this chapter, you'll be ready to set up new folders and move your work files into them— just like setting up a new filing cabinet in your office. You'll also learn how to put your programs and projects on the Startup menus as well as on the Desktop so they are within easy reach.

Not obvious unless you opt to install Windows 95 with the Windows 3.x user interface (an option available when you do a custom install), the old-style Windows 3.x Program Manager and File Manager are both features of Windows 95. They are included with Windows for people who want to continue using a familiar interface to organize their files and programs while they're getting used to Windows 95.

Putting Your Favorite Programs on the Start Button

One thing every Windows 95 user is bound to benefit from is knowing how to put their favorite programs and documents right on the Start button's menu. True, you can put your programs, folders, and documents right on the Desktop and just double-click on them to use them. But it's sometimes a hassle to get back to the Desktop because it can be obscured by whatever windows you might have open. Although there are ways around this (as in right-clicking on the Taskbar and choosing Minimize all Windows), dropping your favorite items on the Start button's first menu is easier. For example, Figure 5.1 shows you what my Start button's menu currently looks like.

With a single click of the mouse, no matter what I'm doing in Windows with my other programs, I can quickly see the programs, folders, and documents I use most and open them.

As with most things in Windows, there are several ways to add items to the Start menu. I'll show you the two that are the most straightforward— dragging onto the Start button, and using the Start ➤ Settings ➤ Taskbar ➤ Start Menu Programs command. The first technique is simply to drag the application, folder, or document's icon onto the

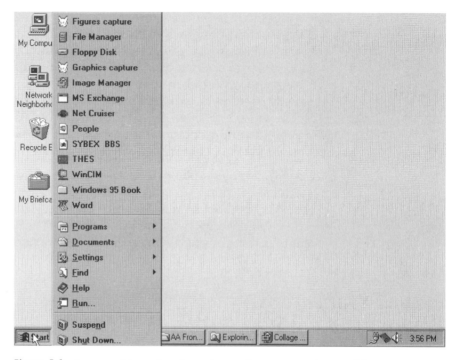

Figure 5.1   You can add your favorite projects and programs to the top of the Start menu by dragging them onto the Start button.

Start button. Windows 95 will then create a *shortcut* and place the shortcut on the Start button's opening menu.

NOTE   A shortcut is not the application, folder, or document's *real* icon, it's a pointer to that icon. The result is the same either way. Double-clicking on a shortcut has the same effect as double-clicking on the object's original icon. In the case of the start button's menu, choosing the shortcut item from the menu will run the application, open the folder, or open the document.

1. First, you'll need to find an icon that represents the object you want to put on the menu. The icon can be a shortcut icon or the original icon, either in a folder, on the Desktop, in the Find box, in Explorer, or displayed in any other window that supports drag-and-drop techniques.

The Find box is probably the easiest if you know the name of the file or document you're looking for.

2. Once you've located the object you want to add, drag it over the Start button and then release the mouse button. Figure 5.2 shows an example of adding a program to the Start button. I'm dragging a program called Wintach from the Wintac folder to the Start button.

Figure 5.2 *Dragging from a folder to the Start button is simple. Just find the object you want to add, drag it over the Start button, and release.*

3. Now when you open the Start menu, you'll see the object has been added at the top of the list.

    That's the easiest way to add new items to the Start button. When you want to remove items, you'll have to use another approach. You can't just select an item and press Del (see *Removing an Item from a Menu*, below).

Modifying the Start Button Menus

When you want a little more control over what you're adding to the Start menu, there's a command for it. This command also lets you add to and remove items from submenu folders. Here's how it works.

1. Click on Start and choose Settings ➤ Taskbar.

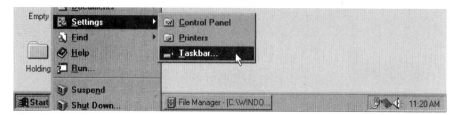

2. You now see a dialog box like the one shown in Figure 5.3. Click on the Start Menu Programs tab, then on OK.

3. Now you see a box from which you can choose Add, Delete, or Advanced. Click on Add.

4. The result is a Wizard dialog box that guides you though choosing the program you want to add (Figure 5.4).

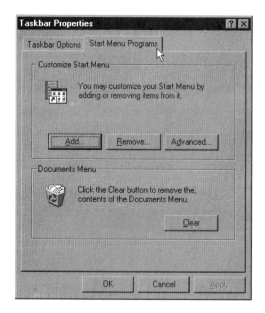

Figure 5.3   Start menu setup is reached from this tab.

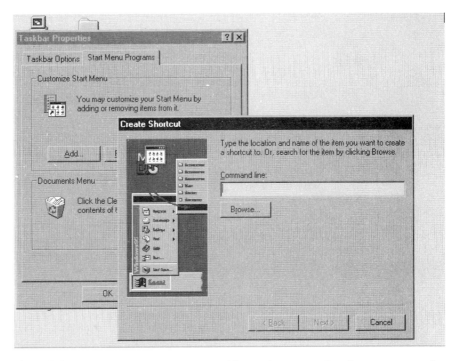

Figure 5.4   *The Wizard walks you through adding an item to your Start button menu or sub-menus. Just fill in the name of the item or use the Browse button. Browse is probably easier.*

5. If you know the name of the item, just enter it into the box. The problem is that you need to know the full path name of the item or it must be in your DOS search path. Otherwise, when you click on Next, you'll be told the file can't be found. Any program in the DOS root directory, your Windows directory, or DOS directory will work even without a full path name entered. For example, entering scandisk will work fine without specifying its full path name, which is \Windows\Command\scandisk.exe. To make life easier on yourself and cut down on possible typing or naming mistakes, click on the Browse button and browse for the item graphically. You'll see a typical File box. Normally, the box only displays *programs*. But if you're trying to add a *document* to your Start button menu, open the drop-down list and choose All Files. When you find the item you want, click on it, then click on Open.

> **TECH TIP** What if instead of adding a *program* or *document* to a Start menu you want to add a *folder?* Doing this can give you a shortcut to that folder as one of the options on your Start menu. The only catch is that you can't do it from the Browse box. You have to go back to Step 4. If the Browse box is open, close it by clicking on Cancel. Then enter the full path name of the folder.

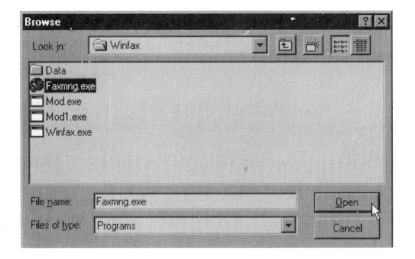

6. Now you're back to the Create Shortcut dialog box. Your item's name is now typed in. Click on Next.

7. You'll see a large dialog box asking which folder you want the shortcut added to (Figure 5.5). Note that those listed in the box are the same folders and subfolders that are included on your Start ➤ Programs menu. As you can see, there's a lot of flexibility here. At this point you can choose to add the shortcut to any existing folder, to the Desktop, or to the Start menu. You can even create a new folder if you want to by clicking on New Folder. Just scroll the list and click on the folder you want to add the item to. If you're going to create a new folder, you have decide where you want it to be added. For example, if I wanted to add a subfolder under Berneze (see Figure 5.5), I'd first click on Berneze, then click on the New Folder button. A new folder is added there, waiting for me to edit its name.

8. Click on Next.

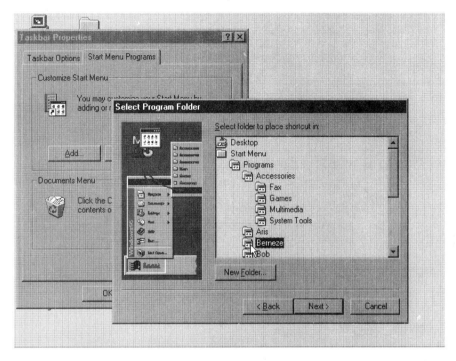

Figure 5.5 *Choose which group or other location the new shortcut will be added to. If you want the item on the Start menu, choose Start Menu. To put the folder on the Desktop, scroll up to the top of the list.*

9. Now you're asked to name your shortcut. This is thoughtful because it's more informative to have a menu item called Word Perfect 5.1 than WP51.EXE. (When you just drop an icon on the Start button, incidentally, you're stuck with whatever name the icon has.) Enter the name you want, but don't make it incredibly long because that will widen the menu appreciably, possibly making it difficult to fit on the screen.

10. Click on Finish.

11. Back at the Taskbar Properties dialog box, click on Close. The new items should now appear in the location(s) you chose.

A few points to consider: if you chose to add the item to the Desktop, it would appear there, not on one of the menus. Also, note that you can add more than one item to your lists at a time. Rather than closing the Taskbar Properties box in step 11, just click on Add and do the whole magilla over again for your next item, starting from step 2.

Removing an Item from a Menu

There will no doubt be times when you'll want to remove an item from one of your Start button menus, such as when you no longer use a program often enough to warrant its existence on the menu.

Note that moving an actual program or a document from one folder to another isn't reason enough to delete its choice on a Start menu. This is because shortcuts in Windows 95 are "self-healing." If an item that a menu item points to has been moved to another drive, directory, or computer, choosing the menu command results in a message similar to this:

Windows 95 will automatically scan your hard disk(s) looking for the item. In most cases, if you've moved rather than deleted the displaced item, Windows 95 will find it, responding with a dialog box asking whether you want to repair the shortcut path.

Just click on Yes, and the shortcut on your Start menu will be repaired. Next time it will work flawlessly.

Here's how you remove an item:

1. Choose Start ➤ Settings ➤ Taskbar.

2. Click on the Start Menu Programs tab and click on Remove.

3. Wait a few seconds as Windows 95 updates your menus.

4. In the list that appears, scroll and otherwise maneuver the list until you get to the folder and item you want (see Figure 5.6). Note a

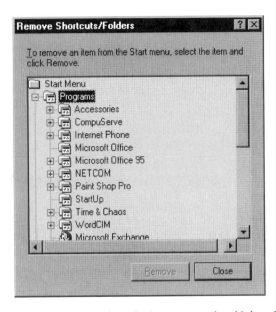

Figure 5.6   *Remove any folder or item from the Start menus using this box. Click on the item*
you want to remove, then click on Remove. Note that unless the folder is a short-
cut removing a folder deletes everything in the folder, including any subfolders it
might have.

couple of things here. All items with plus signs are folders that have
sub-items. For example, on your computer you'll certainly have an
Accessories folder. Clicking on the + sign to the left of Accessories
will display all the program items on the Accessories submenu. Clicking on the minus (–) sign closes up the folder. Items that normally list
on the first Start button menu are at the *bottom* of the list. You may
have to scroll down to see them.

5. Click on the item you want to remove. It can be a folder name or an
individual item in the folder. Note that removing a folder removes all
the sub-items in the folder.

NOTE   Just as with Program Manager icons in Windows 3.x, removing a
shortcut from the Start button menus *never* removes the actual item from
your hard disk. For example, if you remove a shortcut to Word for Windows,
the program is still on your computer. It's just the shortcut to it that's been
removed. You can always put the shortcut back on the menus again using
the Add button.

Advanced Options

If you consider yourself a hotshot, you can wreak all kinds of havoc by clicking on the *Advanced* button from the Taskbar settings dialog box. What this really does is run the Explorer and let you copy, move, delete, and *rename* items on your menus. (This is *the* place to give any goofily named menu items a new name.) Clicking on it results in a display like that shown in Figure 5.7.

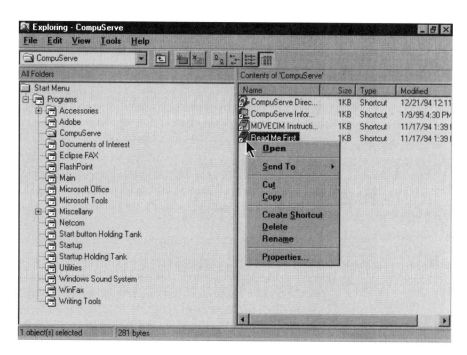

Figure 5.7   *Exploring the Start button menus lets you easily modify them. You can use right-mouse clicks for a variety of purposes. Here you see the right-click menu as it appears for a shortcut in the CompuServe menu list. You can also drag and drop items if you want to move them between folders.*

For details about using the Explorer, check out Part II of this book. For now, just note a few facts:

▶ Click on the topmost folder (Start Menu) to adjust the contents of the Start button's first-level menu.

▶ Change a name by clicking on the *name* once to highlight it, then once more. Alternatively, you can right-click on the name and choose Rename from the right-click menu.

▶ You can drag items in the right pane to destination menus in the left pane. Just drag and drop.

▶ You can create new submenus by clicking in the left pane on the menu you want to add to. Then right-click in the right pane and choose New ▶ Folder.

TECH TIP   I know it doesn't make sense to choose New and then choose Folder, because you want to create a menu, not a folder. But actually everything in Windows 95 is *folders* or *files*, and in reality this whole menu thing is based on directories. Check out the directory structure under your \Win-dows\Start Menu directory, and you'll find directories that correspond to each menu, with .lnk (link) files for each shortcut.

TIP   As a shortcut for modifying the contents of the Start button menus, right-click on the Start button. Then choose Open if you want to use the folder approach. Choose Explore if you like the Explorer approach.

Organizing Your Files and Folders

So much for adding items to the Start button menus. Now I'll show you a bit more about how you work with folders in Windows 95.

Making New Folders

As you may recall from the last chapter, you can create new documents simply by right-clicking on the Desktop, choosing New, then choosing the type of file you want and naming it. Then you double-click on it to start entering information into the document. Or, of course, you can create documents from within your programs and save them on disk using commands in the programs.

In either case you're likely to end up with a lot of documents scattered around your hard disk, or worse yet, a lot of documents lumped together in the same directory with no sense of organization. In interviewing users and teaching people about Windows over the years, I've found that most people haven't the foggiest idea where their work files are. They know they're on the hard disk, but that's about it.

TECH TIP   To some extent, Windows 95 will exacerbate this problem because every document or folder that's on the Desktop is actually stored in the `SystemRoot\Desktop` directory on the disk. Typically this will be the `C:\Windows\Desktop` directory. Even though each folder the user has on the Desktop will be a subfolder of the desktop directory, it still means that wiping out the `C:\Windows\Desktop` directory or doing a clean install of Windows by wiping out everything in the `\Windows` directory and below would wipe out anything on the Desktop. This normally won't be a problem for most people, as this kind of willy-nilly removal of whole directories or directory trees is something only power users are likely to do. If you are the kind of computer user who is going to be poking around on the hard disk, handle your `Windows\Desktop` directory with due respect.

Saving all your files in one directory without sorting them into folders makes creating backups and clearing off defunct projects that much more confusing. It's difficult enough to remember which files are involved in a given project without having to sort them out from all of Word's program and support files, not to mention all the other writing projects stored in that directory.

TECH TIP   Be cautious about storing a lot of files in the root directory of any disk. DOS and Windows 95 limits the number of file or directories in the root to 512. This limit doesn't apply to subdirectories. Also, because long file names take up additional space in the directory, economizing on name length in the root directory can be a good idea if you're pushing the 512-entry limit.

Admittedly, organizing files was a bit difficult in Windows 3.x, but with Windows 95, there's no excuse for bad organizing. And there's plenty of reasons to organize your files: You'll know where things are, you'll be more likely to make backups, and you'll be less likely to accidentally erase your doctoral dissertation because it was in the WordPerfect directory that you deleted so you could install a new word-processing program.

Probably the most intuitive way for most people to organize their work is to do it right on the Desktop. You can create as many folders as you like right there on the Desktop, name them what you like, and violà, you've done your homework.

If you want to get really tidy, you can pull all your subfolders into a single folder called something like My Work. To show you how to create folders and then move them around, I'm going to consolidate mine. First I'll create a new folder.

1. Right-click on the Desktop. Choose New from the resulting menu, then Folder.

2. A new folder appears, called New Folder. Its name is highlighted and ready for editing. Whatever you type will replace the current name. I'll enter the name *My Work*.

3. Now I'll open the folder by double-clicking on it.

   So much for creating a new folder on the Desktop.

   Incidentally, you're not limited to creating new folders only on the Desktop. You can create new folders within other folders using the same technique. That is, open the destination folder's window by double-clicking on it. Then right-click on an empty area inside the folder's window and choose New ➤ Folder.

Moving and Copying Items between Folders

Now that I've got a new folder on the Desktop, I can start putting stuff into it. Let's say I want to pull several of my existing Desktop folders into it to reduce clutter. It's as simple as dragging and dropping.

1. Open the destination folder. (Actually you don't even have to open the destination folder, but what you're about to do is more graphically understandable if you do.)

2. Size and position the destination folder's window so you will be able to see the folder(s) you put in it.

3. Repeatedly drag folders from the Desktop inside the perimeter of the destination folder's window. Be careful not to drop items on top of one another. Doing that will put the dropped item *inside* the item under it.

That's it. Figure 5.8 illustrates the process.

 NOTE   You can drag and drop most objects in Windows 95 using this same scheme. Every effort has gone into designing a uniform approach for manipulating objects on screen. In general, if you want something placed somewhere else, you can drag it from the source to the destination.

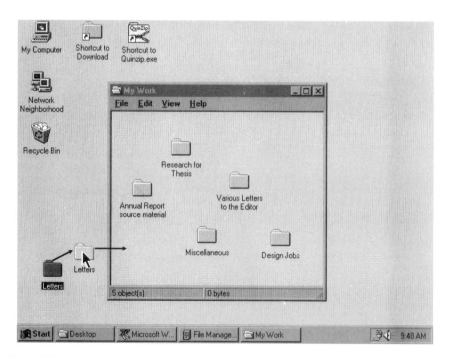

Figure 5.8   Working with folder windows and objects is as simple as dragging and dropping. Rearranging your work is as simple as organizing your desk drawer.

CAUTION   When dragging and dropping, aim carefully before you release the mouse button. If you drop an object too close to another object, it can be placed *inside* that object. For example, when moving folders around, or even re-positioning them on the Desktop, watch that a neighboring folder doesn't become highlighted. If something other than the object you're moving becomes highlighted, that means it has become the target for the object. If you release at that time, your object will go inside the target. If you accidentally do this, just open the target and drag the object out again, or, if the incorrect destination was a folder, open any folder and choose Edit ➤ Undo Move or right-click on the Desktop and choose Undo Move from the pop-up menu. Also, if you press Esc before you drop an object, the process of dragging is canceled.

Now all I have to do is close the My Work folder, and there's that much less clutter on my desktop.

Moving v. Copying

When you drag an item from one location to another, Windows 95 does its best to figure out if you intend to copy it or move it. As you might surmise, copying means making a replica of the object. Moving means relocating the original.

In the procedure above, Windows 95 assumed I wanted to move the folders from one location to another. This makes sense because it's not likely you'll want to make a copy of an entire folder. But you could.

The general rule about moving vs. copying is simple. When you *move* something by dragging, the mouse pointer keeps the shape of the moved object.

Design Jobs

But when you *copy*, the cursor takes on a + sign.

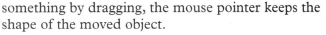

Design Jobs

To switch between copying and moving, press the Ctrl key as you drag. In general, holding down the Ctrl key causes a copy. The + sign will show up in the icon so you know you're making a copy. Pressing Shift as you drag ensures that the object is moved, not copied.

BUT ISN'T THERE AN EASIER WAY?

Here's a little technical tip you'll need to know regarding dragging. The easiest way to fully control what's going to happen when you drag an item around is to *right-click-drag*. Place the pointer on the object you want to move, copy, or make a shortcut for, then press the right mouse button (or left button if you're left-handed and have reversed the buttons) and drag the item to the destination. When you drop the object, you'll be asked what you want to do with it, like this:

Being able to create a shortcut this way is pretty nifty. Often, rather than dragging a document file (and certainly a program) out of its home folder just to put it on the Desktop for convenience, you'll want to make a shortcut out of it. There are important considerations when using shortcuts, however, so make sure you understand what they do.

Organizing Document Files

Once you've thought out how to name and organize your folders, you'll naturally want to start stashing your documents in their rightful folders.

As you might expect, moving and copying documents works just like moving and copying folders—you just drag and drop. When you want to copy files, you press the Ctrl key while dragging. If you want to create a shortcut, you right-click drag and choose Shortcut from the resulting menu (see *But Isn't There an Easier Way?*). Here's an example you might want to try.

1. Clear off the Desktop by right-clicking on the clock in the Taskbar and choosing Minimize all Windows.

2. Create a new folder on the Desktop by right-clicking on the Desktop and choosing New ➤ Folder. Name it My Test Folder.

3. Now create a couple of new documents by right-clicking on the Desktop, choosing New, and then choosing a document type. Name the documents whatever you like.

Now let's say you want to put these three files into the new folder. You could just drag them in one by one. But here's a faster approach; you can select multiple objects at once. Selecting a number of objects can be useful when you want to move, copy, delete, or make shortcuts out of them in one fell swoop.

1. First, we're going to *snap a line* around the items we want to drag. Move the pointer to an empty area on the Desktop at the upper-left corner of the three documents and press the left mouse button. Now drag the mouse down and to the right. This draws a box on the screen, outlining the items you are selecting. You know which items you've selected because they become highlighted (see Figure 5.9).

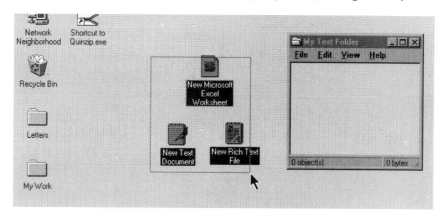

Figure 5.9   *You can select multiple objects by snapping a line around them.*

2. Once selected, you can perform a number of tasks on the group of items. For example, you could right-click on one and choose Open, which would open all three documents in their respective programs. In this case we want to move them. So while they are all selected, just drag one of them. The whole group will move (see Figure 5.10).

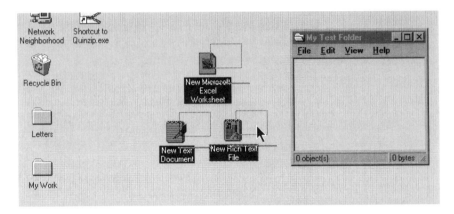

Figure 5.10 *You can move or copy a group of selected items by dragging one of them. The others will come along. Notice the outlines of all three objects are moving.*

3. Using this method, drag the items over the destination folder and release. They've all been moved into My Test Folder.

 TIP   Not all the outlines of the items you're moving need to fit into the destination folder before you release the mouse button. If just a single document's outline falls within the boundary of the target, all the selected items will move to the target folder.

Deleting Items

Of course there will be times when you'll want to delete items, like that old report from last year. Regular file deletion is very important if you don't want to become like everyone else—strapped for disk space. The same techniques will apply to deleting other objects as well, such as printers and fax machines you have installed, because all objects in Windows 95 are treated much the same way regardless of their type or utility.

To Delete a File

So how do you delete a file? Let me count the ways. Because Windows 95 has a Recycle Bin, that's one of the easiest ways, assuming you can arrange things on your screen to find the Recycle Bin. But there are other ways that are even easier though less graphically pleasing than dragging an item over the Recycle Bin and letting go.

To delete a file,

1. Just select the file in its folder, on the Desktop, in the Find box, or wherever.

2. Drag the item on top of the Recycle Bin, press the Del key on your keyboard, or right-click on the item and choose Delete from the resulting menu. Unless you drag to the Recycle Bin, you'll be asked to confirm the deletion.

3. Choose appropriately. If you choose Yes, the item goes into the Recycle Bin.

TIP If you throw something away, you can get it back until you empty the trash, as explained in the section *Checking and Chucking the Trash* later in this chapter.

To Delete a Folder

Deleting a folder works much the same way as deleting a file. The only difference is that deleting a folder deletes all of its contents. When you drag a file over to the Recycle Bin, or delete it with one of the other techniques explained above, you'll see a confirmation message warning you that all the contents—any shortcuts, files, and folders (including files in those folders) will be deleted. Take care when deleting folders, as they may contain many objects.

 CAUTION Before deleting a folder, you may want to look carefully at its contents. Open the folder and choose View ➤ Details or View ➤ List to examine what's in it, check on the dates the files were created, and so forth. Check the contents of any folders within the folder by double-clicking on them; you might be surprised by what you find.

Putting Items on the Desktop

The Desktop is a convenient place to store items you're working on regularly. Each time you boot up, the same files and folders you left there are waiting in easy reach. So how do you put things on the Desktop? You have probably figured out already that you simply drag them there from any convenient source such as a folder or the Find box.

 TIP You can also drag files and folders to the Desktop from the Windows Explorer and File Manager. See Chapter 12 for more details.

However, there are a few details to consider when using the Desktop that aren't immediately obvious. First, some objects can't actually be *moved* to the Desktop—only their shortcuts can. For example, if you open the Control Panel (Start ➤ Settings ➤ Control Panel) and try pulling one of the icons (called Control Panel *applets*) onto the Desktop, you'll see this dialog box:

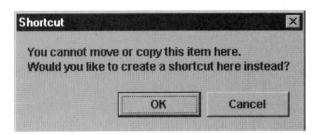

In the case of the Control Panel, setting up a shortcut is your only choice because Windows 95 won't let you move it. As you drag an icon from the Control Panel onto the Desktop or into a folder, the icon turns into a shortcut icon (it has a little arrow in it). But in some other cases, you'll have the choice of moving, copying, or creating a shortcut. How to choose? Here's a little primer about shortcuts.

Because a shortcut will work just as well as the real thing (the program or document file itself), in general shortcuts are a good idea. You can have as many shortcuts scattered about for a given item as you want. For example, suppose you like to use a particular set of programs. You can have shortcuts for them on the Start button menu, on the Desktop, and in a folder called My Favorite Programs. You still have only one copy of the program, so you haven't used up a lot of disk space.

TECH TIP Shortcuts do consume *some* disk space. Each shortcut file has the .LNK (for Link) extension and contains information about where the program, folder, or document it represents is stored. LNK files will typically use up the smallest amount of space that the disk operating system (DOS) will allow. Most LNK files consume 1K, though some you'll find to be 2K.

The same holds true for other objects, such as folders or documents that you use a lot. You can have shortcuts to folders and shortcuts to documents. For example, try dragging a folder (the folder must be displayed as an icon) onto the Start button, and you'll see that a shortcut to the folder is created. A good way to create a shortcut to a document is, as I mentioned earlier, to right-click-drag it somewhere and choose Shortcut from the resulting menu.

I have to warn you of a few things when using shortcuts, however. Remember, shortcuts are *not* the real McCoy. They are *aliases* or pointers to an object only! Therefore, copying a document's shortcut to a floppy disk doesn't copy the document itself. A colleague will be disappointed if you copy only the

Shortcut to
Bart Simpson
portrait

shortcut of a document to a floppy and then give it to him or her, because there will be nothing in it. When you are in doubt about what is getting copied, look at the icon that results from the procedure. If it has a little arrow in it, it's a shortcut.

If no arrow, then it's the actual file.

And consider this: when you move the real McCoy around—whether a program, folder, or document—it may disable some shortcuts that point to it. For example, assume you've set up a bunch of shortcuts that expect your Annual

Bart Simpson
portrait

Budget to be located in folder X. Then you move the budget document to folder Y. What happens? Nothing, until you try clicking on those shortcuts. Then you'll get an error message. Windows will try to find the missing object the shortcut is pointing to:

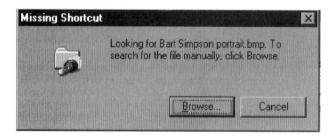

If the object is found, then the shortcut will be repaired and will work next time.

Another caution is that programs that are *installed* into Windows— these are typically big-time programs like those in Microsoft Office, Borland's or Lotus' office suites, database packages, communications packages, and so on—don't like to be moved around. Almost any program that you actually install with an install or setup program will register itself with Windows 95, informing Windows 95 of the folder it is located in. Moving the program around after that (i.e., actually moving it rather than moving the shortcuts that point to it) will bollix up something somewhere unless the program actually comes with a utility program for relocating it as, say, WinCIM (a program for working with CompuServe Information Service) does.

Saving Files to the Desktop from a Program

One of the features I like best about Windows 95 is the ability to use the Desktop as a sort of temporary holding tank. Here's one example. Suppose you want to copy some files from the floppy disk. It's as easy as opening the floppy disk window from My Computer, then dragging the desired file onto the Desktop. Violà, it's on the hard disk! (Actually, it's in a subdirectory of your Windows 95 directory, but for all intents and purposes it's simply on the Desktop.)

You can use the same kind of approach to move or copy items from one folder to another. Rather than having to open both folders and adjust your screen so you can see them both, you can just open the source folder and drag the items onto the Desktop temporarily. When you find or create the destination folder, you can later copy the items there.

But what about using the Desktop from your favorite programs? Although the Desktop is actually a subdirectory of your Windows directory, it's fairly easy to save a file to the Desktop. This is because the newer File dialog box lets you do so (Figure 5.11).

With programs written for Windows 3.x, there is no such option because the Desktop didn't exist in that version. Thus, saving a file to (or opening one from) the Desktop from a Windows 3.x program isn't so easy because the Save As dialog boxes don't have a Desktop option. Still, you can do it. Here's how:

> **NOTE** When your computer is set up for multiple users, there will be multiple Desktop directories, one for each user. They're located in subdirectories under `Windows\Profiles`. There will be one for each user who has an account. For example, for Joe, there will be a directory named `Windows\Profiles\Joe\Desktop`. These directories are *not* normally hidden and can be accessed from any program without modification.

1. Open the Save, or Save As, or Open dialog box from the File menu as usual.

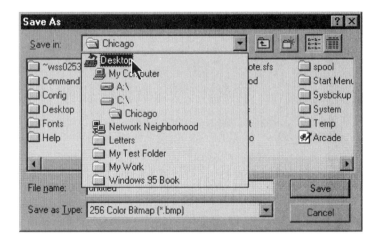

Figure 5.11   *Saving a file to the Desktop is easy with the newer File dialog box. Just scroll or click your way up to the Desktop in the Directory drop-down list box.*

2. In the dialog box, select the drive that contains Windows. This is probably your C drive.

3. Switch to the Windows directory. Then look for the Desktop subdirectory. Figure 5.12 shows an example.

4. Enter or choose the file's name or open one of the subfolders on the Desktop. Remember that subfolders that have long names will show up in the 16-bit File boxes with shortened names. For example, in Figure 5.14, notice the folder on the Desktop called holdingt. That's actually a folder called Holding Tank, something I like to use as a temporary storage area.

Copying Files and Folders to and from Floppy Disks

Whether you're sending a file to a colleague around the world, "sneaker-netting" some work down the hall, or simply making a backup of some important files, copying to and from floppy disks is one of those recurring computer housekeeping chores.

```
┌─────────────────────────────────────────────────────────────────┐
│ 🝤 Save As                                                    ⊠  │
├─────────────────────────────────────────────────────────────────┤
│ File Name:           Directories:                               │
│ ┌─────────────┐      c:\chicago\desktop          ┌───────────┐  │
│ │ch-05.doc    │                                  │    OK     │  │
│ └─────────────┘                                  └───────────┘  │
│ ┌─────────────┐▲    ┌─ windows          ▲       ┌───────────┐  │
│ │755c.txt     │     │ ⊟ desktop                  │  Cancel   │  │
│ │balloon.gif  │     │  ☐ afterdrk       ▄       └───────────┘  │
│ │compress.tif │     │  ☐ fview                   ┌───────────┐  │
│ │directca.lnk │     │  ☐ holdingt                │ Options... │  │
│ │laptopfo.txt │     │  ☐ research                └───────────┘  │
│ │mastwind.txt │     │  ☐ toshiba4       ▼       ┌───────────┐  │
│ │microsof.exe │                                  │ Network... │  │
│ │musicsch.bmp │                                  └───────────┘  │
│ │mypossib.txt │     Drives:                      ┌───────────┐  │
│ │november.xls │                                  │   Help    │  │
│ │pentium.txt  │▼   ┌─ c: 320 megger      ▼      └───────────┘  │
│ │piano.gif    │                                                 │
│ └─────────────┘                                                 │
│ Save File as Type:                                              │
│ ┌───────────────────────────────────────┐▼                     │
│ │Word Document                          │                       │
│ └───────────────────────────────────────┘                      │
└─────────────────────────────────────────────────────────────────┘
```

Figure 5.12   *Saving a file to the Desktop from Word for Windows (16-bit version)*

As you might expect, there are a number of ways to copy files to and from floppies. You can use:

▶ My Computer

▶ the Send-To option

▶ drag and drop on a floppy-drive's shortcut

▶ Explorer

▶ File Manager

▶ the Command prompt

Here I'll briefly cover the basics of the first three items. In Chapter 12 I'll cover use of the Explorer. Please refer to that chapter to learn more about copying files with that program. Refer to a book on DOS if you need help copying files by typing in copy commands at the DOS Command Prompt. Or open a MS-DOS window and type **copy /?** to read some help information about the Copy command.

Copying to and from a Floppy with My Computer

I've already explained in the sections above how to copy and move files between folders. Copying to or from a floppy disk works the same way. Your computer's floppy disk drives simply appear as icons in the My Computer window. Double-clicking on an icon brings up the contents of the floppy disk, displayed in the same format as a typical folder on your hard disk.

1. Clear off enough windows from your Desktop to see the My Computer icon.

2. Double-click on My Computer.

3. Double-click on the appropriate floppy disk icon. Typically you'll only have one, but some computers have two or more floppy disk drives. In Figure 5.13, I've double-clicked on the $3^{1}/_{2}$-inch floppy drive in my computer. (If you don't have a diskette in the drive, you'll see an error message.)

4. Once the floppy drive's window opens, you can easily work with it just as you do with other folders. Drag items from the window to other folders you might have opened on the Desktop, or vice versa.

TIP When you replace one floppy diskette with another, the computer doesn't know about it automatically, as it does on the Mac. After you change the disk, the contents of an open floppy disk window will still be the same, even though the disk holds a completely different set of files. To update the contents of the floppy disk's window, press the F5 key. (This same technique is needed with File Manager and Explorer, incidentally, whenever you change a floppy.)

Remember, you're not limited to dragging between disk and folder windows. You can drop an item on a folder's *icon*, too. Here, I'm dragging Bart Simpson's portrait from the Desktop into My Test Folder.

Sometimes when using a floppy disk you'll see an error message alerting you that the disk has not yet been formatted, that the disk can't be read, or something else, such as the disk is *write protected*.

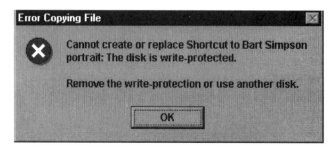

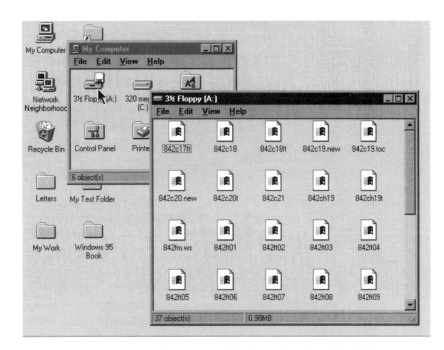

Figure 5.13   *You can examine the contents of the floppy drive by double-clicking on My Computer.*

On 3½-inch diskettes, there's a little tab on the back of the disk that must be in the closed position for the disk to be written onto (new files put on it). On 5¼-inch diskettes, if a stick-on write-protect tab covers the write-protect notch, writing will not be allowed. You should know that a disk must be *write-enabled* (have no write protection) even to open or read files with certain programs such as Word or any program that creates temporary or backup files on disk while you are editing. See Figure 5.14.

If the disk isn't formatted—because you just bought it or it was used in another kind of computer or device, such as a Mac, and you want to use it on a PC—you simply can't write anything on it, regardless of the write-protect tab setting. You can format a floppy from:

▶ the DOS prompt's Format command

▶ the File Manager (using the Disk ➤ Format command)

▶ Explorer or My Computer by right-clicking on the floppy drive's icon and choosing Format

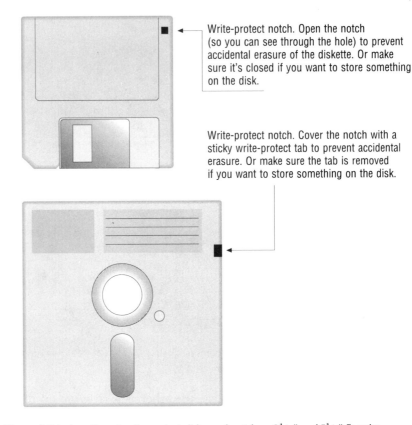

Write-protect notch. Open the notch (so you can see through the hole) to prevent accidental erasure of the diskette. Or make sure it's closed if you want to store something on the disk.

Write-protect notch. Cover the notch with a sticky write-protect tab to prevent accidental erasure. Or make sure the tab is removed if you want to store something on the disk.

Figure 5.14   Location of write-protect slider and notch on 3¹/₂″ and 5¹/₄″ floppies

▶ any floppy-disk shortcut icon by right-clicking on it and choosing Format

I'll cover formatting more in Chapter 12 when I talk about the file system.

 TIP   To see how much room is left on any disk drive, including a floppy, right-click on the drive in My Computer and choose Properties. You'll see a display of the disk's free and used space. Disk properties are described more in Chapter 11, where I discuss right-clicking and property sheets.

Copying Files to a Floppy with Send To

Realizing that people wanted an easy way to copy a file or folder to a floppy disk, Microsoft has provided a cute little shortcut to the interface that copies to a floppy from almost anywhere.

1. Just right-click on any file or folder icon.

2. Then choose the Send To option.

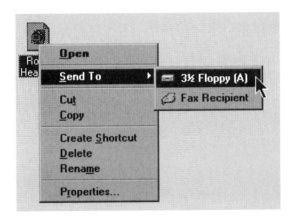

Depending on your computer's setup, you'll have differing choices in the Send To list. You'll at least have one Floppy option.

3. Insert a floppy disk that has some free space on it and choose the desired drive. The file will be copied to the drive you specify.

   The Send To option is very handy. Part III of this book, which covers Microsoft Fax, explains how you use this option to send a file to a fax recipient. You can also customize the Send To list for other purposes, such as sending a file to a viewer program, the Desktop, a file-compression program, a network destination, and so on.

Copying Files to a Floppy's Shortcut

Because a shortcut works just fine as a drag-and-drop destination, one convenient setup for copying items to a floppy is this:

1. Place a shortcut of the floppy drive on the Desktop. You can do this by opening My Computer and dragging the desired floppy drive to the Desktop.

2. Now, whenever you want to copy items to the floppy drive, insert a diskette in the drive, adjust your windows as necessary so you can see the drive's shortcut, and simply drag and drop objects on it. They'll be instantly copied to the diskette.

Of course, double-clicking on the shortcut will open a folder that displays the diskette's contents.

Setting Options
That Affect Viewing of Folders

In the interest of consistency, Microsoft has seen to it that all windows throughout the Windows 95 interface have the same menu options:

This menu provides a number of other useful features you might want to know about as you work with your files, folders, floppy disks, and so forth. I've already discussed the ways to create folders and files on the Desktop or within folders. The menu choices I want to discuss now are those found on the View menu. You can arrive at some of these commands by right-clicking and choosing View. Others are only reachable from the View menu. A couple of the settings I'll discuss here can be super useful, helping to keep your screen clear of clutter. From the View menu, you can control:

▶ The ordering of icons in the window

▶ Whether opening a new folder by clicking on it creates a new window or uses the existing one

▶ Whether file extensions (the last three letters after the period) will be displayed

▶ Which programs are associated with given file extensions

Sorting and Tidying Up the Listing

As you drag icons around, they have a way of obscuring one another, falling behind the edge of the window, or otherwise creating an unsightly mess. Once a bunch of icons become jumbled up, it's often difficult to see or find the one you want. A few commands let you quickly clean up, arrange, and sort the display of files and folders in a window.

1. If you want to tidy up the Desktop quickly, simply right-click on any free space on the Desktop and choose Arrange Icons.

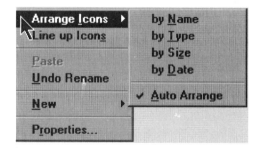

2. Then choose the appropriate command.

By Name	Sorts the display of objects alphabetically based on the name. Folders always appear first in the listing.
By Type	Sorts the display of objects according to type. (The type is only visible when you list the objects' details.) Folders always appear first in the listing.
By Size	Sorts the display of objects in increasing order of size. Folders always appear first in the listing.
By Date	Sorts the display of objects chronologically, based on the date the object was last modified.
Auto Arrange	Keeps the objects lined up nicely at all times. It doesn't ensure that they'll be in any particular order, however. This is a toggle: choose it once to turn it on and again to turn it off.

If you have the display set to show Details, a convenient feature lets you sort all the objects without using any of these commands. Simply click on the *column heading control* over the desired column. For example, to sort by Name you'd click on the Name heading:

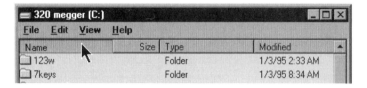

Clicking once on the heading sorts in ascending order (A to Z, 0 to 9). Clicking a second time sorts in descending order. This is particularly useful in the Size and Modified columns, letting you easily bring to the top of the list the files you've modified most recently *or* those you modified ages ago; or you can quickly find which files in a folder are very large and might be taking up significant space on your hard disk.

NOTE   Certain view settings you make in a folder pertain only to that folder. They don't affect other folders. The size, position, listing type and order, and auto-arrange setting are stored with the folder itself and will not affect other folders' settings. However, the single/multiple-window browsing option explained immediately below is global. Its setting will affect *all folder* windows.

Preventing Additional Windows from Appearing

When you're browsing around your hard disk and traversing folders, the Desktop can become cluttered with overlapping windows. If you like to nest your folders one inside another, the clutter will really become apparent as you walk your way though folders to get to a destination file or program. You can cut down on this annoyance by making a simple setting. Once set, the result will be a single window whose contents change as you browse from folder to folder.

1. Open any folder. It doesn't matter which one because this setting is *global*—that is, it affects all folders that you open in the future.

2. Choose View ➤ Options. You'll see the dialog box shown in Figure 5.15.

3. Choose the second option, as I'm about to do in the figure. Then OK the box.

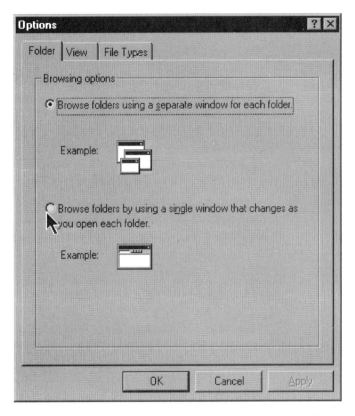

Figure 5.15   *Here you can set whether a new window will open for each folder as you browse.*

Until you change the setting again (remember you can do this from any folder window), the new scheme will stay in effect. Now when you double-click on a folder that's in a folder, a new window won't appear. Only the contents of the window will change.

File Extension Display and Other Options

If you're an old hand at Windows and DOS, you may have already

been frustrated by the fact that file names don't always appear with the extension showing. So you might see a file displayed like the example on the left, rather than the one on the right.

Extensions are normally not displayed for file types that are recognized by Windows 95. Recognized file types are referred to as being *registered.*

The reasoning behind hiding file extensions when possible is that it keeps extraneous information off the screen and makes life easier for normal mortals who don't want to be confused or hassled by file-name extensions. Once the extension is set and then hidden, you can rename a document file without fear of accidentally changing the extension and thus preventing the file from opening in the correct program when double-clicked on.

If you're a hard-core DOS type or want more control over when you see file extensions displayed in listings, folders, and whatnot, there are a few other options worth considering. Follow these steps to explore them:

1. Open any folder. It doesn't matter which one because this is a global setting.

2. Choose View ➤ Options.

3. Click on the View tab, and you'll see the dialog box shown in Figure 5.16.

4. Set the options as you see fit and OK the box. Options will stay in effect until you reset them. Here's what the settings mean:

Show all files	When set on, ensures that all files on your hard disks and floppy disks will be shown in folders, in the Explorer, in the Find box, and elsewhere.
Hide files of these types	When set on, the types of files shown in the list box won't be displayed in folders, in the Explorer, in the Find box, etc. You may want to scroll through the box to see the kinds of files that will be excluded.
Display the full MS-DOS path in the Title Bar	When set on, the entire *path name* of a document file that's open in a program will be displayed in the Title Bar at the top of the program's window. Normally, only the name of the file itself is shown. For example, a full path name might be `C:\Windows\Desktop\budget.wks`, whereas the file name alone would display as `budget.wks`.

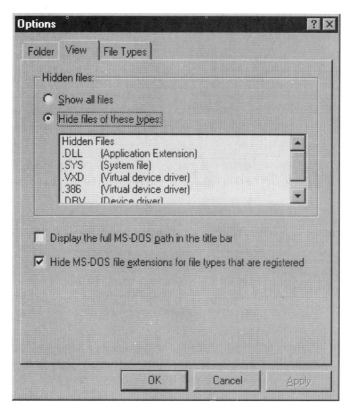

Figure 5.16 **This box, reachable from the View menu of any folder window, lets you set when**
file extensions will display. It also lets you hide altogether a preset list of file
types.

Hide MS-DOS file extensions for file types that are registered	When set on, files with recognized extensions won't have their last three letters (and the period) showing. Unrecognized (unregistered) file types will still show their extensions. Turn this off to see all extensions, even if they *are* recognized by Windows 95.

Of all these settings, the only ones I really concern myself with are the
first two and the Hide MS-DOS extensions. The first two are worth
playing with if you want to see all the files on your disk while browsing around.

Using the Cut, Copy, and Paste Commands with Files and Folders

You're probably well acquainted with the Cut, Copy, and Paste commands as they pertain to programs such as word processors. These commands let you remove, replicate, or move bits of data around while working on your documents.

> **NOTE**   If you're *not* familiar with these concepts as applied to programs, don't worry. They'll be explained in Part IV, which covers the supplied accessory programs.

An interesting Windows 95 feature is its inclusion of the Cut, Copy, and Paste commands when browsing folders, files, and other objects (such as printers, fax machines, fonts, and so forth). To veteran Windows users, these commands might not make sense at first, because cutting and copying aren't commands that have been applied to files before. They're typically used within programs and apply to portions of documents. When I first saw this menu I wondered how *cutting* a file would differ from *deleting* it and why cutting it only made a file's icon grayed out rather than making it disappear. However, once you know how these commands work, you'll use them all the time.

As I mentioned earlier, the Desktop is a useful temporary storage medium when copying or moving objects between windows or folders. Having the Desktop available means you don't have to arrange *both* the source and destination windows on screen at once to make the transfer. Well, the Cut, Copy, and Paste commands do the same thing without the Desktop.

Here's how it works, using a real-life example. Today I downloaded a file from CompuServe called editschd.doc. My e-mail program dumped the file in my Download folder, but I want it in my Mastering Windows 95 folder instead. Well, I could open both folders, arrange them on screen, and drag the file from one to the other. Or I could drag the file first to the Desktop, then to the destination folder. But instead of either of these, I'll use the Cut and Paste commands to more easily accomplish the same task. Here are the steps I used:

1. First I opened the source folder—which in this case was the Download folder.

2. Next, I located the file in question, right-clicked on it, and chose Cut (not Delete, because that command actually trashes the file instead of preparing to put it somewhere else).

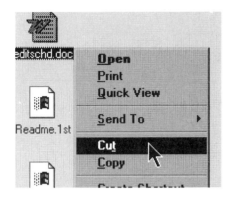

3. This turns the icon into a shadow of its former self, but it's still there in a ghostly form, which means it's waiting to be pasted into another location.

TIP At this point, failing to paste the file into a destination or pressing Esc will abort the cutting and copying process. Nothing will be lost. The file will remain in its original location.

---

4. Next, I can close the current folder, browse around to my heart's content until I find the proper destination for my file, whether it be a floppy disk, the Desktop, or another folder. In this case, I opened the Mastering Windows 95 folder.

5. I now position the pointer on an empty space within the folder, right-click, and choose Paste. The file's icon appears in its new home. That's it (see Figure 5.17).

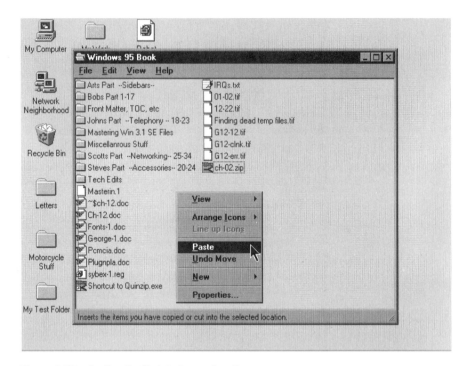

Figure 5.17   *Pasting the file into its new location*

 NOTE   If, when you go to paste, the Paste command is grayed out, it means you didn't properly cut or copy the object. You must use the Cut or Copy commands on a file or other object *immediately* before using the Paste command, or it won't work. That is, if you go into a word processor and use the Cut or Copy commands in a *document*, then the Paste command for your *files* or other objects will be grayed out and won't work. (Chapter 6 discusses use of the Cut, Copy, and Paste commands within programs such as word processors.)

Now, a few points about cutting, copying, and pasting objects in this way. First, if you want to make a copy of the file rather than move the original, you'd choose Copy rather than Cut from the menu. Then, when you paste, a copy of the file appears in the destination location.

Second, you can cut or copy a bunch of items at once to save time. The normal rules of selection apply:

▶ Draw a box around them as I described in *Organizing Document Files*.

▶ Or press the Ctrl key and click on each object you want to select.

▶ Or click on the first of the items you want to select, hold down the Shift key, and click on the last of the items you want to select. This selects the *range* of objects between the two clicks.

Once a number of items is selected (they will be highlighted), right-clicking on any one of the objects will bring up the Cut, Copy, Paste menu. The option you choose will apply to *all* the selected items. Also, clicking anywhere outside of the selected items will deselect them all.

Take a look at the Edit menu in any folder window. There are two commands at the bottom of the menu—Select All and Invert Selection. These can also be useful when you want to select a group of files. Suppose you want to select all but two files; select the two you *don't* want, then choose Edit ▶ Invert Selection.

Finally, remember that you can cut, copy, and paste complete folders, too. When you paste a folder somewhere, you get all of its contents, including any other folders within it.

TIP What if you accidentally goof and realize that you didn't want to move an object or objects to the new location after all? After you perform the Paste, simply open the Edit menu in any folder and choose Undo Move.

Checking and Chucking the Trash

When right-clicking on an object, you may have noticed the Delete command in the menu.

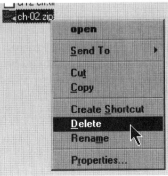

This command isn't the same as the Cut command. Delete sends the selected files, folders, or other objects to the Recycle Bin (essentially the trash can), while the Cut command puts the file on the Clipboard for pasting to another location.

When you delete a file, folder, or other item, it gets put into the Recycle Bin, which is actually a special folder on your hard disk. This folder or directory is called, as you might expect, `Recycled`, typically on your C drive.

TECH TIP   Each logical drive (drive with a letter name) has a `Recycled` directory on it. So, if you have a C and D drive, you'll have two Recycle Bins. `Recycled` directories are "hidden" system files, so they don't normally show up in Explorer or folders unless you set the View option as explained above in *File Extension Display and Other Options* You'll just have a Recycle Bin on the Desktop. If you have access to the root directory of a networked drive, whether mapped to a logical drive on your machine or not, it too will have a `Recycled` directory. CD-ROM drives, even though given a logical drive letter, do not have `Recycled` directories for the obvious reason that you can't delete their files or folders.

The Recycle Bin temporarily holds things that you delete. Because items are not actually *erased* from your computer when you delete them with the Delete command, you can get them back in case you made a mistake! This is a terrific feature. How many times have you accidentally erased a file or directory and realized you goofed? For most people even a single accidental erasure was enough. Now with the Recycle Bin, all you have to do is open its folder, find the item you accidentally deleted, and choose the File ➤ Restore command to undelete it.

Well, actually there's a caveat here. The Recycle Bin will hang onto your deleted items only until you empty the bin. Once you empty the bin, anything in it is *gone*. At that point your only hope is one of the undelete programs like those from PC Tools, Norton, or the one supplied with DOS 5 or 6. (From the Start button, check your Programs menu for a Microsoft Tools option. You may have an undelete program on it.) If that fails, look in your DOS folder (`C:\DOS`) for `undelete.exe` and run that. Or, for an easier approach, simply click on the Start button, choose Run, and enter **undelete**. If you have the program in the DOS directory, it should run. Refer to a book on DOS or the DOS help system (type **Help Undelete** at an MS-DOS prompt) for more information about how to use Undelete.

When you're doing your hard-disk housecleaning, merrily wiping out directories and files in hopes of regaining some needed disk space, you should be aware of one thing: Because files aren't actually erased until you empty the Recycle Bin, you won't increase your available disk space until you do just that.

Restoring Something You Accidentally Trashed

If there's one single thing you'll want to know about using the Recycle Bin, it's how to get back something you accidentally put there. (This page alone may make this book worth your investment!)

1. Get to the Desktop one way or another.

 TIP You can also reach items in the Recycle Bin via the Explorer. I'll discuss this approach in Chapter 12.

2. Double-click on the Recycle Bin icon. A folder will open, listing all the items you trashed since the last time the Recycle Bin was emptied. Figure 5.18 shows an example.

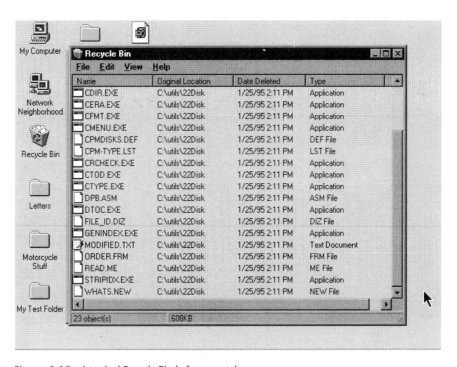

Figure 5.18   A typical Recycle Bin before emptying

3. Hunt around for the thing(s) you accidentally trashed. When you find it, highlight it by clicking on it. (You can select multiple items using the techniques I described earlier in this chapter.) If you want to know more about an item, click on it and choose File ➤ Properties. A dialog box displays when the item was created and when deleted.

TIP You can also restore an item in the Recycle Bin or Windows Explorer by right-clicking on the item and choosing Restore.

4. Choose File ➤ Restore. This will move all selected item(s) back to their original locations. Figure 5.19 shows an example.

Emptying the Recycle Bin

You've probably already noticed the command that empties the Recycle Bin. It's on the File menu. When you want to free up some disk space and are sure that all the contents of the Recycle Bin can be dispensed

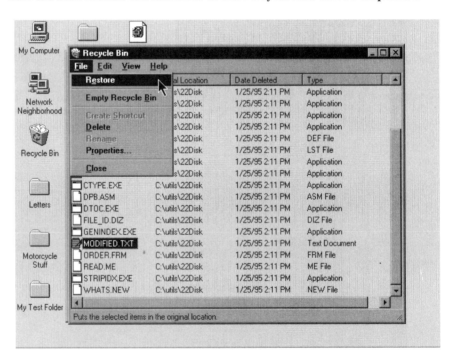

Figure 5.19   Undeleting (restoring) a file that was accidentally erased

with, go ahead and empty it. It's always a good idea to have plenty of free disk space for Windows 95 and your programs to work with, so regularly emptying the trash, just like at home, is a good practice.

Here's the easiest way to empty the Recycle Bin:

1. Get to the Desktop.

2. Double-click on the Recycle Bin.

3. Examine its contents to make sure you really want to jettison everything.

4. Choose File ➤ Empty Recycle Bin.

5. You'll be asked to confirm the process (see Figure 5.20).

 TIP You can quickly empty the Recycle Bin by right-clicking on it and choosing Empty Recycle Bin.

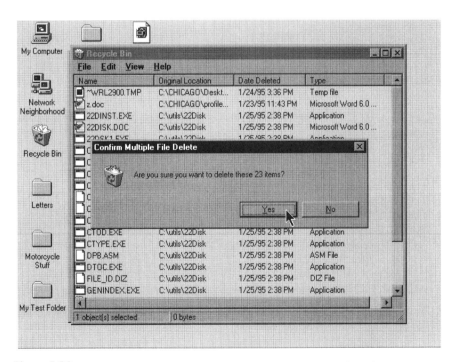

Figure 5.20   *Choosing File ➤ Empty Recycle Bin while viewing the Recycle Bin's contents results in a confirmation box. Once you confirm, the files are deleted from the disk.*

NOTE   We all love to accumulate junk on our hard disks. It doesn't matter whether the disk holds only 40 megabytes or a whopping gigabyte. It will fill up. When your hard disk can gets too crammed, Windows 95 starts to strangle. At that point, a dialog box reporting the sorry state of your disk housekeeping will pop up on your screen. If there is stuff in the Recycle Bin, the box will have a button you can click to empty the trash for you, reclaiming some precious space.

Renaming Documents and Folders

As you work with your files, folders, and other objects, you may occasionally need to rename them, either to more easily identify them later or because their purpose has changed and the current name is no longer valid. In any case, it's easy enough to change an object name. In fact, it's far easier than in Windows 3.x because you don't have to resort to the File Manager or DOS commands to do the renaming.

In general, renaming objects works similarly throughout Windows 95. The surest, though not necessarily the quickest, way is this:

1. Right-click on the object you want to rename and choose Rename from the resulting menu.

2. At this point, the name will be highlighted and the text cursor (small vertical bar) will be blinking.

3. Here's the tricky part. Because the whole name is highlighted, whatever you type now will replace the whole name. More often than not, this isn't what you want to do. Typically you'll just want to add a word or two, fix a misspelling, or something. So, just press ← (the left arrow key). This will deselect the name and move the cursor one space to the left. Now use the normal editing procedures with Backspace, Del, arrow keys, and regular typing to modify the name. (Chapter 19 details standard Windows editing procedures if you're in doubt about technique.)

4. Click outside the little text box encircling the name (or press ↵ once) when you're through; that will store the new name.

TIP A shortcut for editing a name is to do a *slow* double-click on the name. This puts the name into edit mode with the cursor blinking away and the name highlighted. Be careful not to double-click quickly or this will run the application or open the document.

If, when renaming a file, you see an error message about how changing the extension of the file may make it unworkable, you'll typically want to choose No. This message just means you forgot to give the file name an extension by typing in a period and the same three-letter extension it had before. So just rename it again, making sure to give it the same extension that it had before. So for example, let's say the file is named:

```
Budget for Winter 1995.wks
```

and you change it to

```
Budget for Spring 1995
```

You'll probably see an error message when you press the ↵ key. Renaming the file to

```
Budget for Spring 1995.wks
```

would prevent the error message.

As I discussed earlier in this chapter, extensions for registered file types are normally hidden. So a Word for Windows file named `Letter to Joe`, for example, will simply appear as:

```
Letter to Joe
```

not

```
Letter to Joe.doc
```

which is the name that's actually stored on the disk. When you change the name of a file that doesn't have an extension showing, you don't have to even think about what the extension is or about accidentally typing in the wrong one. So, when you change the name, it doesn't matter what you call the file or about typing in an extension. This is because the extension is hidden, and you can't accidentally change its name even if you tried.

Chapter 6

Sharing Data between Applications

FEATURING

A s you know, you can run several programs at one time and switch between them with a click of the mouse or a press of Alt-Tab. You may also know that you can cut, copy, and paste information between programs and documents, embedding bits and pieces of information, graphics, sound, and video from multiple sources into a single destination source to create complex documents. Previously disparate types of information are beginning to merge into a new synthesis, evidenced by products such as CD-ROM–based interactive encyclopedias, in-car electronic guidance (map) systems, and voice-controlled telephone systems. All these capabilities are outgrowths of the desire to mix and match heretofore unrelated kinds of data.

In this chapter, we'll look at data sharing on the Windows 95 platform, paying particular attention to the techniques you can use to create complex documents, including the latest in Windows data sharing—OLE version 2.0.

OLE Overview

As a result of the standardization of the Windows interface and API, users have become accustomed to being able to cut, copy, and paste not only within a given program but between Windows programs. Nowadays, thousands of applications can easily share data with one another through these commands that use the Windows Clipboard.

We still have the problem of proprietary file and data formats—the kind of thing that makes a WordPerfect file different from a Word for Windows file, or an Excel file different from a 1-2-3 file. These proprietary formats often seem to be promoted by software developers as a means of pushing their own programs by locking users into a particular file format. Unfortunately, the proprietary-file-formats marketing strategy has backfired, leaving users grumbling and feeling held hostage by a particular brand of program.

For example, just try printing out, say, a JPEG graphics file from your favorite word-processing or desktop-publishing program. The situation becomes even thornier when multimedia files are thrown in. We are now seeing competing formats for live-motion video, audio recording, MIDI files, and the like.

Software developers have finally figured this out, though, and have made working with "foreign" file formats much easier. With each new month, more applications have built-in file-format converters to allow applications to share files. For example, Word for Windows 6.0 can read and write a whole gaggle of text and graphics file formats. Ditto for PageMaker, Ventura Publisher, Microsoft Access, and many others. Standards such as Rich Text Format (RTF), Windows Metafiles, and others are now emerging to facilitate data transfers between programs. Embedded TrueType fonts and utility programs such as Adobe's *Acrobat* even allow people to see and edit documents containing fonts not in their systems.

Windows 95 and Data Exchange

Actually, much more interesting than simply being able to use one program's document in another program is the ability to mix and match a great variety of document types, such as text, sound, graphics, spreadsheets, databases, and so forth. This lets you construct complex documents previously requiring physical cutting and pasting and possibly the aid of an art department.

Windows 95 offers three internal vehicles for exchanging data between programs: the Windows Clipboard (and Clipbook, which is an extension of Clipboard), Dynamic Data Exchange (DDE), and Object Linking and Embedding (OLE). In this chapter, I'll explain each of them, discuss how Windows 95's treatment of them differs from Windows 3.1, and then describe some special considerations for data sharing across the network.

TIP   If you're new to Windows, you may only want to read the portion about the Clipboard. That's the part about the cut, copy, and paste commands. You'll use these commands much more often than the other stuff I talk about in this chapter. If you're using a network and want to share little bits of information with other people, then read about the Clipbook too. If you want to take full advantage of what Windows' OLE has to offer, read the entire chapter.

NOTE   Many of my examples in this chapter refer to Microsoft products. This isn't necessarily my endorsement of Microsoft products over other competing products! Competition in the software marketplace is a healthy force, ensuring the evolution of software technology, and I highly support it. But, because so many of you are bound to be familiar with the Microsoft product line, I use products such as Word, Excel, Graph, and Access in my examples in hopes of better illustrating the points I'm trying to make here.

The Clipboard

Though it's not capable of converting data files between various formats, such (such as `xls` to `wk3` or `rtf` to `doc`) the Windows Clipboard is great for many everyday data-exchange tasks. Just about all Windows programs support the use of the ubiquitous cut, copy, and paste commands, and it's the Clipboard that provides this functionality for you.

Clipboard makes it possible to move any kind of material, whether text, data cells, graphics, video or audio clips, and OLE objects between documents—and now, with Windows 95, between folders, the desktop, the Explorer, and other portions of the interface. The actual form of the source data doesn't matter that much, because the Clipboard utility and Windows together take care of figuring out what's being copied and where it's being pasted, making adjustments when necessary—or at least providing a few manual options for you to adjust. The Clipboard can also work with non-Windows (DOS) programs, albeit with certain limitations that I'll explain later.

How It Works

How does the Clipboard work? It's simple. The Clipboard is built into Windows 95 and uses a portion of the system's internal resources (RAM and virtual memory) as a temporary holding tank for material you're working with. For example, suppose you have cut some text from one part of a document in preparation for pasting it into another location. Windows stores the text on the Clipboard and waits for you to paste it into its new home.

The last item you copied or cut is stored in this no-man's-land somewhere in the computer until you cut or copy something else, exit

Windows, or intentionally clear the Clipboard. As a result, you can paste the Clipboard's contents any number of times.

You can examine the Clipboard's contents using the Clipbook utility supplied with Windows 95. If you've used Windows for Workgroups or Windows NT, you'll be familiar with this application. You can also use this application to save the Clipboard's contents to disk for later use or to share specific bits of data for use by others on your network.

Selecting, Copying, and Cutting in Windows Applications

In Windows 95, the Windows 3.1 standards and procedures for copying, cutting, and pasting apply because Windows 95 supports all the Windows 3.1 calls for these services. Even if you're mixing and matching 16- and 32-bit applications, the Clipboard will work just fine because in the internals of Windows 95, the 16-bit subsystem shares the same clipboard as the 32-bit section.

When running Windows 95, you simply use each application's Edit menu (or Edit menu's shortcut keys) for copying, cutting, and pasting (Figure 6.1). These tasks work just as they did in Windows 3.x.

Here are the steps for cutting, copying, or pasting within a Windows program:

1. First, arrange the windows on screen so you can see the window containing the source information.

2. Now *select* the information you want to copy or cut, such as text, a graphic, spreadsheet cells, or whatever. In many programs, simply clicking on an object, such as a graphic, will select it.

3. Once the desired area is selected, open the application's Edit menu and choose Copy or Cut depending on whether you want to copy the material or delete the original with the intention of pasting it into another location.

4. If you want to paste the selection somewhere, first position the cursor at the insertion point in the destination document (which may or may not be in the source document) you're working in. This might mean scrolling up or down the document, switching to another application using the Taskbar, or switching to another document within the *same* application via its Window menu.

Select an item and choose Cut or Copy

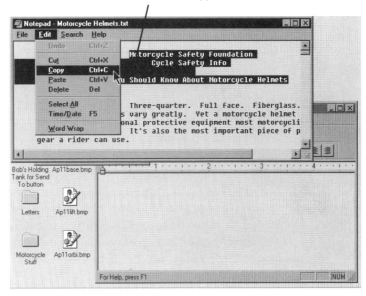

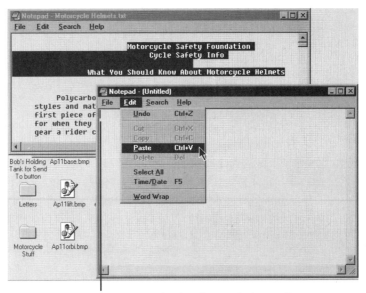

Move to a destination and choose Paste

Figure 6.1   Copying and pasting in a Windows program

5. Open the Edit menu and choose Paste. Whatever material was on the Clipboard will now be dropped into the new location. Normally, this means any preexisting material, such as text, is moved down to make room for the stuff you just pasted.

> **TIP**   There may be some shortcuts for cut, copy, and paste in specific programs, so you should read the manual or help screens supplied with the program. Generally, pressing Ctrl-X, Ctrl-C, and Ctrl-V are shortcuts for cutting, copying, and pasting, respectively.

> **NOTE**   When pasting in graphics, you'll typically have to reposition the graphic *after* pasting, rather than before. For example, Figure 6.2 shows a graphic (another copy of the Earth as taken from the moon on the Apollo 11 mission) just after pasting it into a Paintbrush window. It appears in the upper-left corner, waiting to be dragged to its new home.

Figure 6.2   Graphics applications typically accept pasted information into their upper-left corner, where they wait to be repositioned.

Copying Text and Graphics from a DOS Box

In Windows 95, as with Windows 3.x, copying selected graphics from DOS programs is also possible. This is a pretty nifty trick for lifting material out of your favorite DOS program and dropping it into a Windows document. There's only one caveat: the DOS program has to be running in a window, not full screen.

When you cut or copy selected material from the DOS box, it gets dumped into the Clipboard as text or graphics, depending on which mode Windows 95 determines the DOS box (*box* means window) was emulating. Windows 95 knows whether the application is running in character mode or graphics mode and processes the data on the Clipboard accordingly. If text mode is detected, the material is copied as characters that could be dropped into, say, a word-processing document. If the DOS application has set up a graphics mode in the DOS box (because of the application's video requests), you'll get a bit-mapped graphic in the destination document when you paste.

NOTE   As you may know, some fancy DOS programs may look as though they are displaying text when they're really running in graphics mode. For example, WordPerfect for DOS and Microsoft Word for DOS can both run in a graphics mode that displays text attributes such as underline, italics, and bold, rather than as boring block letters displayed in colors that indicate these attributes. When you copy text from such a program and then paste it into another document, you'll be surprised to find you've pasted a graphic, not text. This means you can't edit it like text because it's being treated like a bit-mapped graphic. The solution is to switch the DOS application back to Text mode and try again. Refer to your DOS program manual for help.

Because of the Windows 95 DOS box's toolbar, the procedure for copying is simple to learn. You can use the menus or the toolbar almost as if you were using another Windows program. Figure 6.3 illustrates the simple technique. Here are the steps:

1. First, switch to the DOS application and display the material you want to work with.

2. Make sure the application is running in a window, rather than running full-screen. If it's not, press Alt-Enter. (Each press of Alt-Enter toggles any DOS window between full and windowed view.)

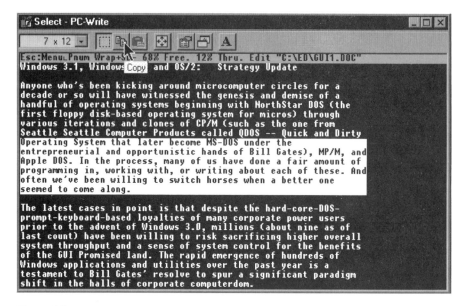

Figure 6.3   *Copying text from a MS-DOS box is now a simple procedure. Click on the Mark button, click and drag across the desired text, and click on the Copy button.*

3. If the DOS box's toolbar isn't showing, turn it on by clicking in the upper-left corner of its window (on the MS-DOS icon) and choosing Toolbar.

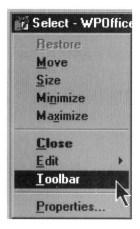

4. Click on the Mark button.

5. Holding the mouse button down, drag the pointer over the desired copy area, dragging from upper left to lower right. As you do so, the color of the selection will change to indicate what you're marking.

```
Seattle Seattle Computer Products called QDOS -- Quick and D
Operating System that later become MS-DOS under the
entrepreneurial and opportunistic hands of Bill Gates), MP/M
Apple DOS. In the process, many of us have done a fair amoun
programming in, working with, or writing about each of these
often we've been willing to switch horses when a better one
```

6. Release the mouse button. The selected area will stay highlighted.

7. Click on the Copy button. The information is now on the Clipboard.

NOTE   Notice that there isn't a Cut button because you can't cut from a DOS application in this way. Cutting has to be done using the DOS program's own editing keys, and it won't interact with the Windows Clipboard.

TIP   As soon as you click on the Mark button, the DOS box's title bar changes to read *Mark*. Once you start marking the selection, the word *Select* precedes the program's name in the title bar, indicating that you're in select mode. Typing any letter on the keyboard terminates the selection process.

That's all there is to copying information from an application that's running in the DOS box. Of course, the normal procedure will apply to pasting what was just copied. You just switch to the destination application (which, incidentally, can be a DOS *or* a Windows program), position the cursor, and choose Edit ➤ Paste to paste in the Clipboard's contents at the cursor position. (For a DOS application as the destination, you'd use the Paste button on the DOS box's toolbar. This is explained later in this chapter.)

Doing Screen Captures with Clipboard

As in Windows 3.x, you can capture all or part of the screen image while running an application. Screen captures are useful for creating program documentation, software education materials, or for putting out promotional material about software.

Clipboard is handy for capturing screen images in lieu of purchasing a special-purpose screen-capture program. The price is right, and it works, albeit with some limitations.

TECH TIP　Professional programs designed for screen capture help you organize, crop, and edit your screen captures, among other things. If you regularly do screen captures, you might want to check these programs out. I used Collage Complete for the screens in this book. Other programs you might want to explore are Tiffany, PixelPop, Hotshot, and Hijaak. These programs give you a lot of latitude with capture techniques, file formats, color settings, grayscaling, and so forth, none of which the old Clipboard workhorse affords you.

With Clipboard, you have just two options when capturing: you can capture the entire screen or just the active window. Whether you're capturing a DOS or Windows-based application, the capture is converted to bit-mapped format for pasting into graphics programs such as PageMaker, Paint, and so forth.

TIP　Though you can't edit your files or add borders and nice stuff like that using this economy approach to captures, you *can* save a file to disk for later use. The Clipboard and the Clipbook both let you save files on disk for later use. Please refer to *Saving the Clipboard's Contents in a File* and *Working with the Clipbook* later in this chapter.

To copy the active window's image onto the Clipboard, do the following (note that if a dialog box is open, this is usually considered the *active* window):

1. Get the desired application open and running in a window and adjust and size the window as needed.

2. Press Alt-PrintScreen. The image of the active window is copied to the Clipboard.

> **NOTE**   All the computers I used this technique on responded as expected when these keys were pressed. However, some older PC keyboards use slightly different codes, requiring the user to press Shift-PrintScreen instead.

Instead of just copying the active window, you might want to capture a picture of the entire screen. There is a simple variation on the above theme for this purpose.

1. Set up the screen as described above.

2. Press PrintScreen (instead of Alt-PrintScreen). The image will be copied to the Clipboard. (See the discussion below about pasting the Clipboard contents.)

> **TECH TIP**   Though object linking and embedding (OLE) is covered later in this chapter, I'll mention here briefly that you can use File Manager in conjunction with the Clipboard for embedding a file into a document. File Manager's Copy command results in a dialog box that lets you copy the file to the Clipboard instead of to another drive or directory. Then you'd use the destination application's Paste Special command to insert the object.

Using the Paste Command

Once you have some information on the Clipboard, Windows 95 offers you several options for working with it. In Windows 3.x only two of these were possible, but Windows 95 also incorporates the Clipbook facility previously part of Windows for Workgroups. Here are the three routes you'll be able to take:

▶ Paste the information into a document you're working with (or that you open subsequently).

► Save it to a Clipboard (.clp) file for using later.

► Save it on a Clipbook page for later use or for sharing over the network.

The last two choices are described later in this chapter. For standard pasting there are two options:

► You can paste information into Windows applications.

► You can paste into DOS applications (when they are in a window rather than running full-screen).

Let's look at these two individually because they require distinctly different techniques.

Pasting Information into Windows Applications As you are probably aware, the great majority of Windows applications' Edit menus include a Paste command. As the name implies, this is the command you'll use to paste material from the Clipboard into your documents. Of course, this command won't be usable unless there is something already on the Clipboard that can be accepted by the document you're working with at the time.

TECH TIP Some heavier-duty programs have their own internal Clipboard that's not connected at all to the system's Clipboard. This isn't usually the case, so you don't have to worry about it with most applications. However, to accommodate proprietary data types and large amounts of data, some programs do use their own. Word for Windows, for example, does have a so-called large clipboard that it uses when you cut or copy a sizable bulk of material. In such an application, data you thought you were making available to the entire Windows 95 system might not be. But this caveat will probably apply less to 32-bit applications than to 16-bit ones. We can expect the 32-bit internals of Windows 95—along with more intelligent memory management—to render its systemwide Clipboard both more intelligent and larger in capacity than its predecessor.

To successfully paste information from the Clipboard, here's what to do. Of course there may be some variation from application to application, but you'll figure that out as you use them. This basic approach works almost all the time.

1. First, you must set up the right conditions. That means cut or copy material onto the Clipboard.

2. Next, switch to the destination program or document—the one that will receive the information.

3. Now position the cursor or insertion point. In a text-based program this means position the I-beam cursor where you want it and click the primary mouse button.

4. Finally, choose Edit ➤ Paste or (in most programs) press Ctrl-V. The Clipboard's contents then appear in the destination window. Figure 6.4 shows an example.

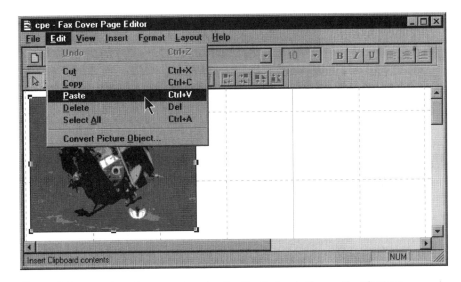

Figure 6.4 Typical pasting operation, showing the Paste selection on the Edit menu

 NOTE The Clipboard's contents remain static only until you copy or cut something new, so repeated pasting of the same material is possible. Just keep selecting insertion points and choosing Edit ➤ Paste.

Pasting into a DOS Box As weird as this seems, you can also paste into DOS applications. I say weird because most DOS applications were invented way before the Windows Clipboard was even a twinkle in

Bill Gates' eye. There are certain limitations to this technique, such as only being allowed to paste text (no graphics). This is for obvious reasons—pasting graphics into a DOS application would be a nightmare. It simply wouldn't work because there is no standard agreement among DOS applications about treatment of on-screen graphics. Even with text, the results of pasting may be less than expected because DOS applications don't all accept data the same way.

NOTE You should be aware that all text formatting will be lost when you paste text into a DOS document. This is because formatting (bold, italics, fonts, bullets, and so forth) is application-specific information (specially coded for each program), and most applications just don't speak the same language at this point.

TIP Though you can't paste graphics directly into DOS applications, here's a workaround. Simply paste the graphic into a windows-based graphics program like Paintbrush or Corel Draw. Then save the graphic in a file that's readable by the DOS graphics program. Most DOS programs can read .bmp or .pcx files, and most Windows graphics programs can save files in these formats.

When it comes time to actually do the pasting into a DOS application, here are the steps:

1. Put the desired text on the Clipboard by cutting or copying it from somewhere.

2. Toggle the destination DOS application so it's a window (this can't be done full-screen).

3. Position the DOS application's cursor at the location where you want to insert the Clipboard's material. This *must* be the location where you would next type text into the DOS document.

4. Click on the DOS box's Paste button.

Figure 6.5 shows an example in which I've inserted Clipboard text copied from a Help screen into a PC-Write file running in a window.

Up and Running
with Windows 95

```
WPOffice Editor                                          _ □ X
  7 x 12 ▼   [ ]  [ ] [ ] [ ]   [ ] [ ] [ ]   A
Esc:Menu Pnum Wrap+Sp-  68% Free.   9% Thru. Edit "C:\ED\GUI1.DOC"
various iterations and  Paste  s of CP/M (such as the one from
Seattle Seattle Computer Products called QDOS -- Quick and Dirty
Operating System that later become MS-DOS under the
entrepreneurial and opportunistic hands of Bill Gates), MP/M, and
Apple DOS. In the process, many of us have done a fair amount of
programming in, working with, or writing about each of these. And
often we've been willing to switch horses when a better one
seemed to come along.

█

The latest cases in point is that despite the hard-core-DOS-
prompt-keyboard-based loyalties of many corporate power users
prior to the advent of Windows 3.0, millions (about nine as of
last count) have been willing to risk sacrificing higher overall
system throughput and a sense of system control for the benefits
of the GUI Promised land. The rapid emergence of hundreds of
Windows applications and utilities over the past year is a
testament to Bill Gates' resolve to spur a significant paradigm
shift in the halls of corporate computerdom.
```

Figure 6.5 To paste text into a DOS application running in a window, position the cursor and click on the Paste button.

TECH TIP The internals of the process of pasting into a DOS box are interesting. The text on the Clipboard is sent to the portion of the operating system that's responsible for buffering keyboard data entry. When you paste, the application thinks you have typed in the new text from the keyboard. For the procedure to work correctly, however, the recipient program has to be written in such a way that it doesn't balk at receiving information at the speed a supernormal typist could enter it.

Right-Click Shortcuts for Cut, Copy, and Paste

As mentioned earlier, the cut, copy, and paste scheme is implemented throughout Windows 95, even on the Desktop, in the Explorer, in folder windows, and so forth. This is done using right–mouse-button shortcuts. Some applications are starting to offer this feature too.

As explained in the last chapter, right-clicking on a file in a folder window and choosing Copy puts a pointer to the file on the Clipboard. Right-clicking on another location, such as the Desktop, and choosing

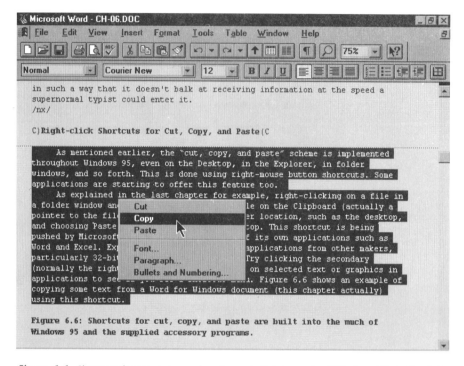

Figure 6.6   *Shortcuts for cut, copy, and paste are built into much of Windows 95 via the right-click menu. Windows applications are beginning to implement this feature, too, as you see here in Word for Windows.*

Paste drops the file there (e.g., on the Desktop). This shortcut is being pushed by Microsoft and is included in some of its applications such as Word and Excel. Expect to see it included in applications from other makers, particularly 32-bit Windows 95 applications. Try clicking the secondary (normally the right) mouse button on icons or on selected text or graphics in applications to see if there is a shortcut menu. Figure 6.6 shows an example of copying some text from a Word for Windows document using this shortcut.

Working with the Clipboard's Viewer

Once data is on the Clipboard, you may not want to paste it immediately, or you might want to see what's there. There are two programs supplied with Windows that make this really easy. One's called Clipboard Viewer, and the other is Clipbook Viewer. You can can find one or both of these in the Accessories folder (choose Start ➤ Programs ➤ Accessories ➤ Clipbook Viewer). These programs let you do some useful Clipboard-related things, such as:

➤ view the Clipboard's contents

➤ save and retrieve the Clipboard's contents to/from a file

➤ clear the Clipboard's contents

➤ set up pages of the Clipboard, each storing things you plan to use later or want to make available to networked colleagues

Let's look at each of these simple tasks in order.

Viewing the Clipboard's Contents

Sometimes you'll simply forget what information is on the Clipboard because you won't remember what you cut or copied last. And before you go ahead and paste it into an application (especially if that application doesn't have an Undo command), you might want to check out what's going to get pasted. Another time when viewing is useful is when you're trying to get a particular item into the Clipboard and don't know how successful you've been. Bringing up the Viewer and positioning it off in the corner of the screen can give you instant feedback as you cut and copy.

Here's how to view the Clipboard's contents.

NOTE   Actually, there are two different utilities that let you examine the Clipboard's contents: Clipboard Viewer and Clipbook Viewer. Either one will work. You may have both of these programs in your Accessories folder, or only one, depending on whether you upgraded to Windows 95 over Windows for Workgroups or not. The procedure below explains the Clipbook approach. If you only have the Clipboard Viewer, the steps are actually quite similar. Simply run Clipboard Viewer instead of Clipbook Viewer and skip step 2, below.

1. Click on the Start button and choose Programs ➤ Accessories ➤ Clipbook Viewer.

2. The Clipbook Viewer window comes up. Double-click on the Clipboard icon in the bottom-left corner of the window or open the

Window menu and choose Clipboard. The iconized Clipbook icon turns into a window, displaying the Clipboard's current contents. Figure 6.7 shows typical Clipboard contents; in this case, a portion of an image I had just copied from the Paint program.

Changing the View Format

It's possible that the contents of the Clipboard will look different from how they look in the application you copied or cut from. For example, graphics may appear mottled or distorted, text may appear with incorrect line breaks, fonts, and so forth. You see, graphics and text can contain substantial amounts of formatting, such as font type and size, indents, colors, resolution settings, grayscaling, and so on. But there are some limitations to the amount of information that will actually be transferred through the Clipboard. It's the job of the source application to inform Windows 95, and thus the Clipboard, of the nature of the material. The Clipboard tries its best to keep all the relevant information, but it doesn't necessarily display it all in the Viewer window.

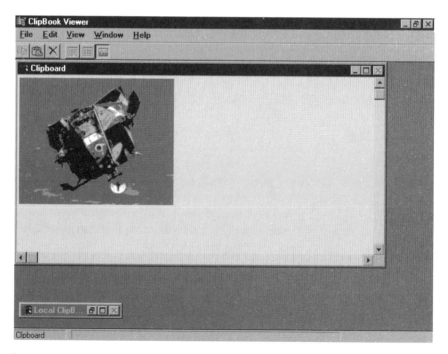

Figure 6.7 *The Clipboard's contents being displayed in a window within the Clipbook Viewer*

Let's take an example. A Paintbrush picture can be passed on to another application as what Windows 95 calls a bitmap, a picture, or a Windows Enhanced Metafile. (In addition to this, there can be information that pertains to Object Linking and Embedding, but these aspects don't appear in the Viewer window.)

When you first view the Clipboard's contents, the Viewer does its best to display the contents so they look as much as possible like the original. However, this isn't a fail-safe method, so there may be times when you'll want to try changing the view. To do this:

1. Open the View menu (or the Display menu in Clipboard Viewer).

2. Check out the available options. They'll vary depending on what you've got stored on the Clipboard. Choose one and see how it affects the display. The Default setting (called *default format*) returns the view to the original display format the material was first shown with. However, none of them will affect the Clipboard contents—only its display.

NOTE When you actually go to paste into another Windows application, the destination program tries to determine the best format for accepting whatever is currently on the Clipboard. If the Edit menu on the destination application is grayed out, you can safely assume that the contents are not acceptable. (Changing the Clipboard's view format as described above won't rectify the situation, either. In fact, it doesn't have any effect on how things actually get pasted.)

Storing the Clipboard's Contents in a File

When you place new material onto the Clipboard, reboot, or shut down the computer, the Clipboard contents are lost. Also, because the Clipboard itself is not *network aware* (meaning it can't interact with other workstations on the network), you can't share the Clipboard's contents with other networked users. You'll want to take advantage of Clipbook pages for that (see below). However, there is one trick left. You *can* save the Clipboard's contents to a disk file. Clipboard files have the extension `.clp`. Once the Clipboard's contents are stored in a disk file, it's like any other disk file—you can later reload the file from disk. If you do a lot of work with clip art and bits and pieces of sound, video, text, and the like, this technique can come in handy. Also, if you give network users access to your .clp file directory, they can, in effect, use your Clipboard.

> **TIP**   The Clipboard CLP files use a proprietary file format that is readable by virtually no other popular programs. So, to use a CLP file, you have to open it in Clipboard and *then* paste it where you want it to appear. This might all seem like a hassle, and it is. Actually, the Clipbook Viewer, explained later in this section, offers a hassle-free way to archive little things you regularly want to paste.

In any case, here's how to save a Clipboard file:

1. First make sure you have run the Clipbook Viewer or Clipboard Viewer, as explained above.

2. Activate the Clipboard window within the Clipbook Viewer. The easiest way to do this is to choose Clipboard from the Window menu. You could also double-click on the Clipboard icon if you see it at the bottom of the Clipbook Viewer window.

3. Choose File ➤ Save As. A standard Save As dialog box will appear.

4. Enter a name. As usual, you can change the folder, name, and extension. Leave the extension as .clp because Clipboard uses this as a default when you later want to reload the file.

5. Click on OK, as you see in Figure 6.8. The file is saved and can be loaded again as described below.

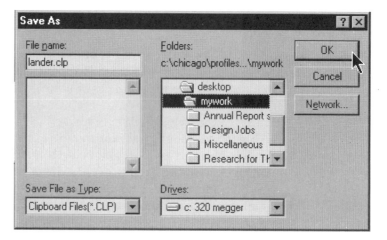

Figure 6.8 *Saving a Clipboard file*

Retrieving the Contents of a Stored Clipboard File

As I mentioned, once the CLP file is on disk, you can reload it. Use these steps.

CAUTION   When you reload a CLP file, anything currently on the Clipboard will be lost.

1. Run Clipbook Viewer.

2. Choose Clipboard from the Window menu.

3. Choose File ➤ Open. The Open dialog box will appear.

4. Select the file you want to pull onto the Clipboard. (Only legitimate CLP files can be opened.)

5. If there's something already on the Clipboard, you'll be asked if you want to erase it. Click on OK.

6. Change the display format via the View menu if you want to (assuming there are options available on the menu).

7. Paste the contents into the desired destination.

Clearing the Clipboard

You might want to keep in mind, while using the Clipboard, that the information you store there, even temporarily, can impact the amount of memory available for use by the system and other applications. If you're cutting and pasting small bits of text and graphics as most people do during the course of a workday, this shouldn't be a concern, especially because Windows 95's new memory management is more efficient than its predecessor's.

However, be aware that some items you might place on the Clipboard can be large. For example, graphics, video, sound samples, or large amounts of formatted text take up considerable space on the Clipboard. Some items are stored in a number of formats for pasting into different kinds of destinations and thus may hog more memory than you might expect.

The moral of the story is that if you're running into memory short-ages, you may occasionally want to clear the contents of the Clip-board using the technique explained below.

> **NOTE** In Windows 3.1 you could get an idea of how much system memory an item on the Clipboard was occupying by switching to Program Manager or File Manager and choosing Help ➤ About. The resulting dialog box told you how much memory and User Resources were available. Windows 95 isn't as informative. Many *About* dialog boxes that under Windows 3.x reported free memory now simply report the total amount of RAM your system has. Windows 95 utility programs that monitor and report memory usage will probably begin to appear on the market. In the meantime, you can run the *System Monitor* program from the Accessories ➤ System Tools folder if you really need to keep track of memory (and many other system resource) usages.

To clear the Clipboard:

1. From Clipbook Viewer, select the Clipboard view by double-clicking on the Clipboard icon or clicking on its window.

2. Click on the X in the Toolbar or choose Edit ➤ Delete, as you see in Figure 6.9.

3. Click on OK in the resulting dialog box to actually clear the board. The Clipboard's contents will be deleted.

Using Clipbook

Though very handy, the Clipboard does have several drawbacks. The most obvious of these are:

▶ Information on the Clipboard can't be easily shared with network users.

▶ You're limited to one item being on the Clipboard at a time. Copying or cutting a new item erases the previous one.

▶ Saving and retrieving Clipboard files is a hassle. Accessing, say, a number of small sound clips or clip art pictures requires giving each one a CLP file name and later remembering their names so you can reload them.

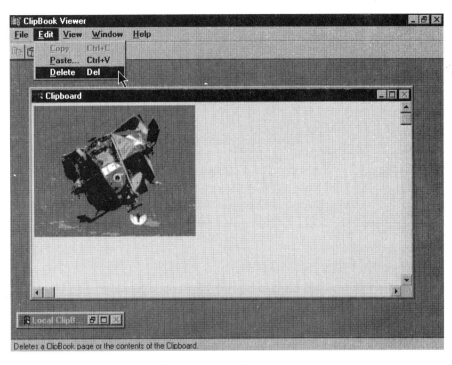

Figure 6.9   Clearing the contents of the Clipboard

So, what to do? Well, as I mentioned earlier, there's a thing called the Clipbook that works much like the Clipboard, but it's groovier. Clipbook first made an appearance in Windows for Workgroups. Then it came out in 32-bit form in NT, and now it's in Windows 95. Clipbook offers these advantages over Clipboard:

► You can store Clipboard memory on *pages* within the Clipbook. There can be as many as 127 of these pages, each one acting like a separate Clipboard.

► You can give each Clipbook page a description to help you remember what it is. The description can be up to 47 characters long. This is great for naming pages such things as *Joe's logo version 10*, and so forth.

► You can share all or selected pages of your Clipbook for use by colleagues at other network workstations.

▶ You can display thumbnail representations of each page so you can visually scan many pages of your Clipbook at once to find the one you want.

Running Clipbook

If you've been following the above section, you already know how to run Clipbook Viewer. This program is your connection to the Clipbook just as it is to the Clipboard. The only difference is that you select the Clipbook window rather than the Clipboard window. Do this from the Window menu by choosing Local Clipbook. Once you do, its window appears as you see in Figure 6.10. (It is probably empty unless you have saved some items to it in the past.)

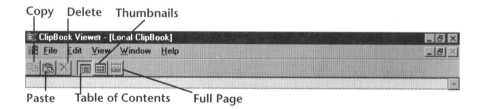

Figure 6.10   Clipbook Viewer

The following table explains the toolbar's buttons.

Button	Menu Command	Effect
	Copy	Paste selected Clipbook page to Clipboard
	Paste	Paste the contents of the Clipboard to Clipbook
	Delete	Delete contents of selected page (or of Clipboard if showing)
	Table of Contents	List the named pages in the Clipbook

Button	Menu Command	Effect
	Thumbnails	Display thumbnails of Clipbook's pages
	Full Page	Full display of selected Clipbook page

How It Works: Pasting into Clipbook

As you have probably suspected, the Clipbook doesn't actually replace the Clipboard. It simply works in concert with it. In Windows 95, cutting, copying, and pasting within and between your various applications is still orchestrated by the Clipboard. What the Clipbook supplies is a convenient repository for Clipboard items—items that would normally be wiped out of the Clipboard when you shut down Windows or copy something new onto the Clipboard. Figure 6.11 illustrates the relationship of Clipboard to Clipbook.

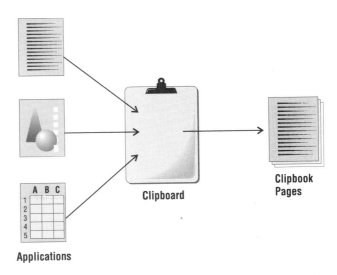

Figure 6.11 Items are added to the Clipbook by pasting them from Clipboard.

To use the Clipbook, you simply paste an item onto one of the 127 pages in your Clipbook. Then you give the page a name and description for later reference. Here are the steps:

1. First get the desired information onto the Clipboard.

2. Run or switch to the Clipbook Viewer.

3. At this point, it doesn't matter whether the Clipboard or Local Clipbook window is the active window. Just choose Edit ➤ Paste from within the Clipbook Viewer. A Paste dialog box now appears, asking for a name for the new page (Figure 6.12). Each time you paste into the Clipbook, you have to name the page. You can name the page anything you like, up to 47 characters in length. So you could name a page

   `This is a silly picture of an elephant`

4. Click on the Share Item Now box to turn it on, if you want to make the new Clipbook page immediately available to other users on the network (if you're on a network). (Sharing the item now will bring up another dialog box after you name the item, asking some things about how you want to share the item. This is explained below.)

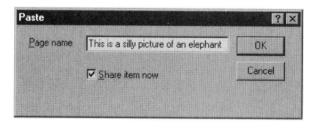

Figure 6.12   **Naming a new Clipbook page**

Using Stuff You've Stored on Clipbook Pages

Once you've got your item(s) stowed away nicely on Clipbook pages, how do you use them again? No problem. You can easily paste them into documents on your computer or later share them for use by other computers on your network. Let's take these two situations separately.

First, here's how to paste something from a Clipbook into a document you're working on. Suppose you've saved a piece of clip art on a page and now you want to paste it:

1. Run Clipbook Viewer (or switch to it, if it's already running).

2. Display the Local Clipbook window by double-clicking on it, or easier, by opening the Window menu and choosing Local Clipbook. The display can be changed from Thumbnail view to List view from the View menu or from the Toolbar (see Figure 6.10 for the Toolbar button descriptions). Figure 6.13 shows a typical listing of pages.

3. Select the page containing the information you want by clicking on its thumbnail or name.

4. Within Clipbook Viewer, click on the Paste button, or choose Edit ➤ Copy. This copies the particular Clipbook page onto the Clipboard.

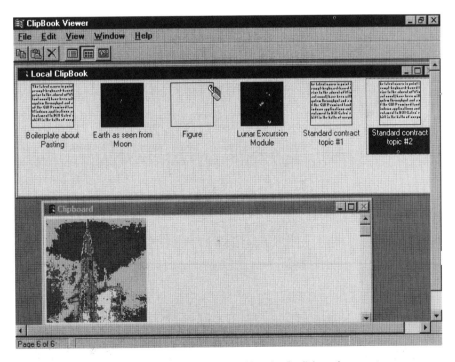

Figure 6.13   *Selecting a Clipbook page for reuse. You simply click on the page to use, copy, then paste it into the destination application. The Clipboard is used as an intermediary.*

5. Switch to the application you want to paste into. Position the cursor or do any setup in that application that might be necessary and then choose Edit ➤ Paste from that application. Windows should now paste in the item. Adjust as necessary.

Sharing Your Clipbook Pages with Network Users

When you want to share a Clipbook page so others on the network can link or copy it into their documents, do the following:

1. Run or switch to Clipbook Viewer.

2. View the Local Clipbook (via the Window menu).

3. Select the item you want to share. If you want to examine the item before sharing it, click on the Full Page button.

 TIP You can quickly toggle between full-page and Thumbnail or Table of Contents view by double-clicking on an item.

4. Choose File ➤ Share. You'll see the following dialog box:

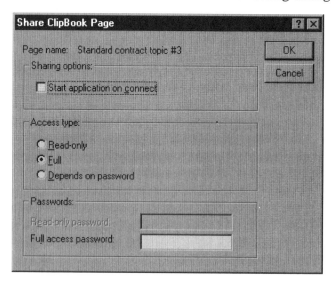

Note the *Start application on connect* check box. You have to set this check box *on* if the data on the Clipbook page is anything more complex than a bitmap or unformatted text. If you don't, network users won't be able to access the data. If you're in doubt about whether to turn this on, share the page with the setting turned *off* and let users try to use it. If this doesn't work, turn it *on*.

> **TIP**   With the switch on, the source application will run when a remote user accesses the specific page. If you don't want the running of the application to interrupt your work by opening a window on the serving workstation, set the Run Minimized check box on.

5. Fill in the other options as you see fit. Unless you specify otherwise, pages are shared with a type of Full Access. This means other people can erase or edit the page as well as copy it. If you want to prevent others from editing or erasing the page, share it either as Read-only or require a password. If set to Read-only, remote users can only paste the information into documents. They can't edit what's on your Clipbook page. If you stipulate a password, then a remote user must enter the password before gaining access to the page or before altering the page's contents.

Connecting to a Shared Page

Connecting to another network station's Clipbook to use *its* pages is a relatively straightforward process. You simply use the File ➤ Connect command in the Clipbook Viewer to browse around the network and connect to the desired station and page. Then you use it as if it were your own. Here are the steps:

1. Run Clipbook Viewer.

2. Get to the Local Clipbook window.

3. Open the File menu and click on Connect.

4. Browse to, or type in, the name of the computer whose Clipbook has the information you want.

5. Click on OK. If a password is required for the remote Clipbook, you'll be prompted to enter it. The newly available page(s) will now

appear in a new window within your Clipbook Viewer. When you attempt to access one of its pages, you may be prompted for a password.

6. When you're through using another person's Clipbook, you may want to disconnect from it. Simply activate the particular remote Clipbook's icon or window within your Clipbook Viewer and choose File ➤ Disconnect.

Object Linking and Embedding under Windows 95

The ability to run numerous programs, simultaneously switching between them at will and copying data between documents, marked a major advance in desktop computing, especially on the PC. Merely for its task-switching capabilities, Windows has been embraced by thousands of DOS diehards who don't even like Windows per se. They use Windows just to switch between multiple DOS programs!

However, the Clipboard and Clipbook impose severe limitations on truly "transparent" data sharing between applications. If you've been following Windows developments over the past several years, you'll know that post-Windows 3.0 products (Windows 3.1, Windows for Workgroups, Windows NT, and now Windows 95) have taken data sharing several steps further with schemes called *Dynamic Data Exchange* (DDE), *Network DDE,* and *Object Linking and Embedding* (OLE).

If you've followed the computer magazines at all, you've likely been as inundated as I on the topic of OLE 2.0, the latest and greatest of data-sharing schemes, which is incorporated into Windows 95. In fact, you may already be quite familiar with its predecessor, OLE 1.0, using it to create fancy documents combining bits and pieces of data from a variety of programs scattered about on your hard disk or across your company's network.

By the same token, though, many veteran Windows users have only the barest awareness of OLE, considering it some kind of black art (along with, unfortunately, such simple tasks as using a modem or getting their printer to work). So why should they care about OLE? The vast majority of folks don't understand OLE or DDE's nuances and stick instead with the tried-and-true Clipboard when it comes to passing data between applications. (Want a chart in that report? Paste it in!)

And for good reason. *Live* data sharing such as that offered by Windows OLE and DDE is the stuff computer-science conventions are made of. There are some highly technical distinctions between DDE and OLE that are a bit difficult to grasp, not to mention that not all Windows applications are *OLE aware* or implement OLE in the same way when they are. Add to this some confusion concerning OLE's use over a PC network, and you've got a topic in need of clarification!

In hopes of dispelling some of the confusion, this section offers a brief OLE and DDE primer. I'll fill you in on why you won't be using DDE, why you'd want to use OLE, and actually how easy OLE 2.0 makes creating flashy documents that really take advantage of all that power your computer has under its hood.

Advantages of OLE

Just to give you an idea of what I'm even talking about here with all this technical talk, consider an example when the regular old Clipboard doesn't cut the mustard, and where you might want to use OLE instead.

Let's assume you're applying for a grant from an arts council and they want to see a professional-looking, attractive business plan as part of your application. You'll be using a Windows word processor such as WordPerfect, Word, or AmiPro to write the text, and you'll also need to incorporate financial projections for your project using data taken from a spreadsheet. Got the picture?

Okay. So you *could* just copy numbers from the spreadsheet into your text document. But there's a problem—your projections are changing daily as you update and refine your spreadsheet. What to do? Well you can just paste in the cells at the last minute before printing the grant application. But there's a more elegant solution. You can *link* the relevant cells from the live spreadsheet directly to the document. Then, whenever you alter any numbers in the spreadsheet, they'll be automatically updated in your grant application. Figure 6.14 shows an Excel spreadsheet linked to a Word for Windows document.

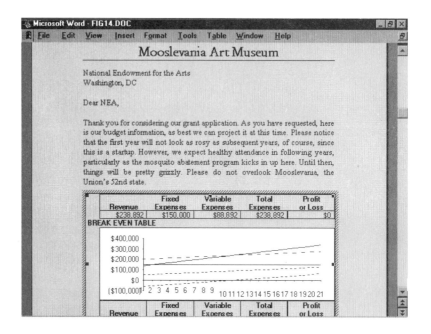

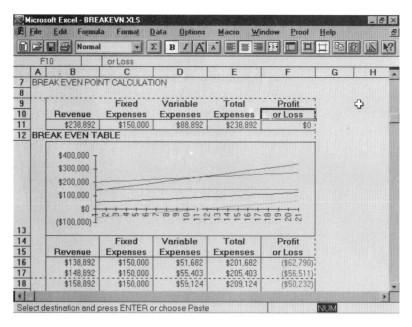

Figure 6.14   Data linked between an Excel spreadsheet and a Word for Windows document

This is basically what OLE is all about—splicing pieces of documents (called *objects*) from different applications into a single *compound* document. And this splicing (called *linking*) keeps the documents connected so editing one will affect any other documents that are linked to it.

There's one other major nicety of OLE: You can edit a linked addition to a document just by double-clicking on it. In the example above, this means if you wanted to enter new figures in the spreadsheet, there's no need to run Excel and open the source spreadsheet file. You just double-click on the portion of the spreadsheet that's in your word-processing document. Windows knows that Excel created this portion of the document and dishes up the correct tools for you to edit with. Once you've entered your changes, you save them, and you're dumped back into your word-processing document. Windows takes care of updating any related documents.

 TECH TIP Technically, in the above example, Excel becomes the active application, not Word. Excel actually runs, takes over the active window, changes the menus, and accepts the edits. When you exit, the window returns to Word. To the user, it looks as though only the menus and toolbars have changed.

The catch is that programs must be intentionally designed with OLE. But more and more of them are these days, so you shouldn't have trouble finding chart, graphics, sound, and even video programs that'll all work together. For example, you might want to add a chart from that same spreadsheet program to your business plan to communicate the numeric information graphically or a sound clip that when clicked on explains a concept in the author's own voice. And because Windows 95 supports networks so well, linked documents can be spread out all over the network. The art department's latest version of the corporate logo could be loaded into the annual report you're about to print without your having to even make a phone call.

What Is DDE (Dynamic Data Exchange)?

Though OLE is getting all the attention these days, you might run into another term while reading about Windows' data-sharing methods. An older and less ambitious means for intercommunication between applications is called Dynamic Data Exchange (DDE), and it is also included in Windows 95. Some older applications used DDE to achieve some of the same results you get nowadays with OLE. Windows 95, Windows for Workgroups, and Windows NT have included an updated network version of DDE called NetDDE that allows applications to talk to one another over the network as well as on the same machine. And actually, OLE uses DDE as its communications link between programs.

The downside of DDE is that although it provides a way for applications to share information in a *live* way as OLE does (meaning that altering one document updates any linked documents too), how you, the user, set up the link varies too much from program to program. Another problem inherent in DDE is that the links it sets up between documents are too easy to sever. Simply moving a file to a new location or upgrading one of the source applications could result in a document losing one of its objects.

Since OLE's debut (with Windows 3.1), the bulk of serious Windows applications support OLE rather than DDE for user-created data sharing. Few programs actually used DDE internally to communicate between modules of a program or between multiple documents running under the same program. DDE has essentially been left to the domain of hackers working with such tools as Excel macros—one of the few DDE-enabled tools.

Basic OLE Concepts

It's important that you have a working understanding of OLE terms and concepts before you try creating documents with OLE. Also, it's important that you understand that there are differences between OLE 1.0 and OLE 2.0. As of this writing only a handful of applications are 2.0 enabled. Although OLE 2.0 is backward-compatible with 1.0, meaning you can mix and match the two, the techniques you'll use to create compound documents differ somewhat. In this section I'll explain all you need to know to use OLE 1.0 or OLE 2.0 to put together some fancy compound documents. I'll also explain what's so great about OLE 2.0.

So let's start with objects. What *is* an object, really? An *object* is any single block of information stored as a separate bundle but incorporated into a document. An object can consist of as little as a single spreadsheet cell, database field, or graphic element; or as much as an entire spreadsheet, database, or a complete picture or video clip.

Next, there's the issue of the differences between *linking* and *embedding*. With OLE, you have the option of using either one. You either link *or* embed an object—not both. Linking and embedding are different in functionality. Also you work with linked objects differently than you do with embedded ones. Study Figure 6.15 for a moment.

In the case of linking, two separate files exist—the spreadsheet and the word-processing files. The spreadsheet data can be edited either from within the word-processor document or separately from its source file in the spreadsheet application.

By contrast, the second figure displays an *embedded* object. The embedded graphic is more intimately connected to the word-processing document. In fact, it is contained *within* the word-processing file itself. Although the embedded picture can still be edited, it doesn't have a life outside of the word-processing document that contains it.

Regardless of whether the objects in the word-processing document are linked or embedded, the resulting larger document is called a *compound* document. A compound document is any document composed of two or more dissimilar document types joined via OLE.

Servers, Clients, Containers, and other Terms

Let's look a little more closely at how applications work together to create compound documents. First consider that there are two separate and distinct roles played by programs in the process of sharing information through OLE. One program originates the object that is to be embedded or linked. This is called the OLE *server*. The other program accepts the object. This is called the OLE *client*. For example, in Figure 6.14, Lotus 1-2-3 is the originating (server) program and the word processor is the accepting (client) program.

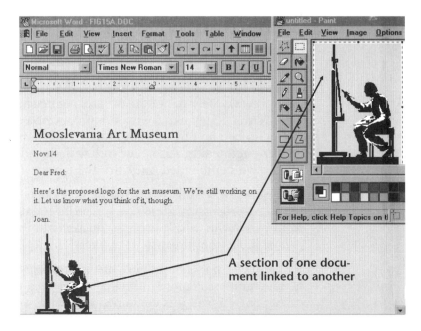

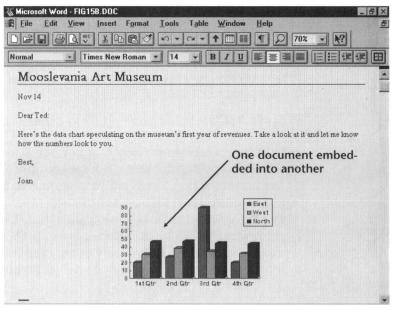

Figure 6.15   A linked and an embedded document

NOTE   To be absolutely precise, the terminology varies somewhat depending on whether you're speaking of OLE 1.0 or OLE 2.0. In OLE 2.0, the overall design model suggests the terms *container* and *component object* rather than *client* and *server.* The container is the receiver of any component object. For example, a word-processing document containing a graph would be the container, while the graph would be the component object. You'll probably be seeing these terms bandied about in the trade press, so the discussion here will incorporate these terms from time to time.

Sophisticated Windows applications usually will work both as OLE servers and as clients. As an example, consider a spreadsheet program such as Excel. This program can supply charts and worksheet objects to a word processor or desktop-publishing program—acting as an OLE server. Excel can also accept embedded database objects from, say, Access or Q+E.

This bidirectionality isn't always the case, however. For example, Windows Write, WordPad, and Cardfile can function only as clients while programs such as Paint, Media Player, and Sound Recorder can only behave as servers.

Two final terms you'll need to know are: the *source document* is the one in which an object is originally created, while a *destination document* is the one into which you place the object. I'll be using these terms in this chapter as we get into the procedures for creating compound documents.

Object Packages

In addition to the two basic OLE options I've described above—linking and embedding—there is a third variation of OLE called *packaging*. Packaging is a technique you can use to wrap up an object into a cute little bundle represented by an icon. Then you drop the icon into the destination document. For example, you might want to drop a sound clip or video clip into a document in this way. When the reader of the container document comes across the icon, he or she just double-clicks on it and it unwraps, so to speak. The video clip runs in a window, a sound clip plays, and so forth. Of course, this is only useful if the document is being viewed on a computer because nothing happens when you double-click on a piece of paper! It's particularly useful when sending e-mail messages because it keeps the messages smaller. Figure 6.16 shows an example of a WordPad document with a sound-file package embedded in it.

You add a package to a document using the Explorer, the File Manager, or the Object Packager program.

OLE 1.0 v. OLE 2.0

OLE 1.0 was a great stride forward in application integration when it was introduced with Windows 3.1. However, it still left much to be desired. For starters, creating and moving objects between applications was awkward, requiring use of the Clipboard. With OLE 2.0, you can use the ubiquitous drag-and-drop approach. By Ctrl-dragging, you can make a copy of the object.

Editing embedded objects is also much easier. In OLE 1.0, editing embedded objects confused users because double-clicking on an object brought up its source application in another window on the screen with the object loaded into that window. For example, clicking

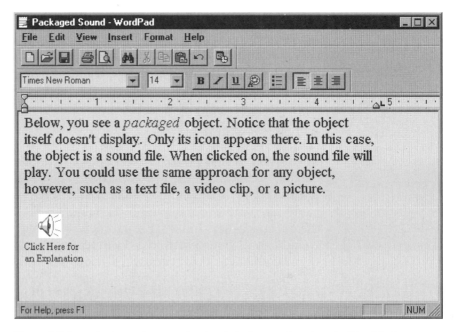

Figure 6.16 *Packaging a document iconizes it for later replay when double-clicked on.*

on spreadsheet cells embedded in a Word document brought up Lotus 1-2-3 in its own window, with the spreadsheet data loaded into it (see Figure 6.17). You'd use the 1-2-3 window to make changes to the data, then exit 1-2-3. This returned you to the original application with the data updated. This is not particularly intuitive because users feel as though they've left the report they were working on.

By contrast, with OLE 2.0 another window does *not* appear. You are still in the Word window. The two participating applications negotiate an arrangement whereby the menus, toolbars, menu commands, and palettes on the menus within the primary document's application window change. Figure 6.18 illustrates this.

This convenient arrangement has been dubbed *visual editing* and is much more intuitively obvious for users. Note however, that it only applies to editing embedded objects, not linked ones, and only works if both applications are OLE 2.0 enabled. Linked objects will be edited in separate windows, just as with OLE 1.0.

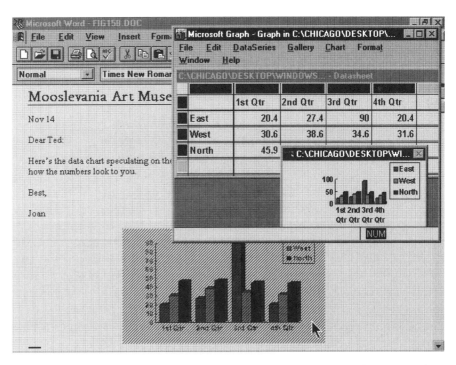

Figure 6.17   *In OLE 1.0, double-clicking on an embedded object brings up the source application in a window.*

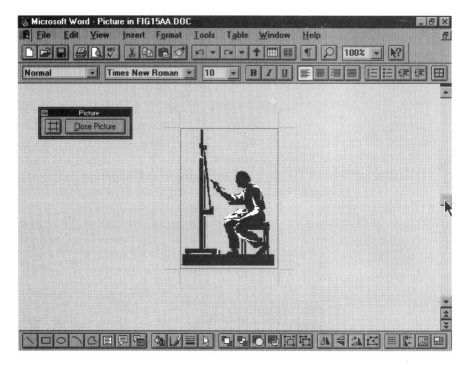

Figure 6.18 *In OLE 2.0, double-clicking on an embedded object only changes the primary application's menus and commands to those of the object's source. In this case Word takes on certain characteristics of MSDRAW that allow editing of the embedded picture.*

The other primary problem with OLE 1.0 was that moving any of the linked object files would break the link, resulting in an error message when the compound document was opened. OLE 2.0 solves these problems by allowing you to move files to other drives or directories at will. As long as all the linked files are present in the directory, the compound document will still be intact. As another workaround to having to deal with multiple files in compound documents composed of many objects, OLE 2 allows you to easily convert all the links in a compound document to embedded objects. This in essence takes all the relevant data that was previously stored in separate files and squishes it into a single (albeit larger) one. With OLE 1.0, breaking the link meant losing the object altogether and having to reestablish it.

Up and Running
with Windows 95

Another interesting feature of OLE 2.0 is that it conforms to a *transaction-based* I/O model. Thus, an OLE 2.0-enabled application can undo changes that were made to a compound document. For example, if you cut an embedded object, the application would be able to undo the cut, re-establishing the presence of the object in the file.

Next, OLE 2.0 specifies a new type of file format called the Compound File Format. This new format helps the operating system more efficiently store and edit complex documents that contain numerous objects. One advantage to this is that you can now edit a compound document object on an *incremental* basis rather than editing the entire object. For example, say you double-click on a series of spreadsheet cells embedded in your text-based report and start editing the cells. Only the cells you alter will be updated, rather than the whole series of cells. This makes for faster updating and overall performance.

Finally, the expanded OLE 2.0 specification not only allows document objects such as charts, pictures, video, and sound to communicate, but it also works with program modules. As you may know, many applications are composed of separate modules (each one usually stored in separate DLL files). A DLL typically will perform a specific function, such as spell checking, within a word-processing program. OLE 2.0 supplies a standard by which program modules can communicate with one another. As applications are written to comply with this standard, you'll have the option of mixing and matching your favorite program modules to create the "perfect" application. For example, you could buy a replacement spell checker for your favorite word processor, a favorite macro organizer for your spreadsheet, or add in some flashy graphics-manipulation tools to your favorite image-processing program.

OLE Inconsistencies

Developers, keen on building OLE compatibility into their products, are complying more and more with OLE conventions. There's been some leeway for interpretation of how an application will incorporate OLE, and so there are idiosyncrasies and slight variations in the way you work with OLE in different applications. Drag and drop isn't implemented everywhere, so it's not as simple as Microsoft might have you believe. You may have to do a little snooping in an application's manual, use online Help, or check out an application's menus to determine how to import or edit OLE items in your application.

For example, in the Windows 3.x Cardfile, you don't have to click on a linked picture before you edit it because Cardfile knows the picture is in the upper-left corner. Similarly, because you place a linked or embedded sound object in a destination document by double-clicking on the Sound Recorder icon, you can't use the double-click method to edit the object as you would in the case of, say, an embedded section of an Excel spreadsheet. Instead, you have to use the Edit menu's Sound Object command. As a general rule, one consistency you can usually count on is that an OLE-aware application has a Paste Special command on its Edit menu. If it's there, the application knows about OLE, and you'll almost certainly use this command to embed and link objects into your documents. Some applications (such as Word 6 and WordPad) also have an Insert menu that lets you embed all kinds of objects (Figure 6.19).

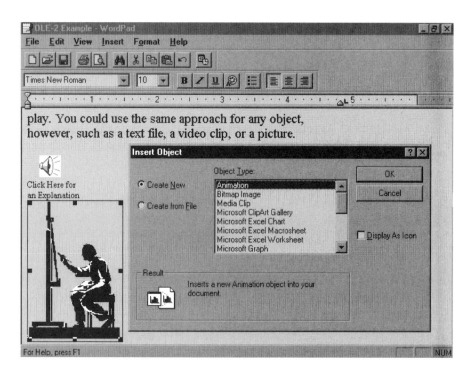

Figure 6.19   *WordPad has an Insert menu for embedding objects you create on the fly while still in WordPad. You can use the Edit ➤ Paste Special command or the Create from File option in this box for embedding and linking preexisting objects.*

You may have found the previous discussion a little daunting, what with all the hairy terms and such. Don't panic! OLE is a little confusing to everyone, especially because it's a scheme that's in flux. Once you experiment with embedding and linking a bit, you'll figure it out.

Now let's discuss the actual procedures for embedding, linking, and packaging objects in Windows 95. I'll also discuss some networking and security issues that pertain to linked objects.

Embedding Objects

The difference between linking and embedding throws people sometimes, so let's talk about that for a minute. It might help to think of embedding an object as almost identical to pasting a static copy of it from the Clipboard in a regular old non-OLE document. This is because neither embedding nor pasting involves a link to external files. Once a chart is embedded into your word-processing file, it becomes part of that file. The only difference between standard Clipboard cut and paste and OLE embedding is that once embedded, an object can easily be edited by double-clicking on it or via some other command. Even though the object (let's say a graph) isn't something the container application (let's say Word) knows how to edit, the object contains a pointer to a program that can edit it.

Here are the basic steps:

1. Open the source application and document. (The application must be able to perform as an OLE server.)

> **TIP** You might want to try this using some OLE applications, such as Word, Excel, AmiPro, 1-2-3, Wordpad, or Sound Recorder, just to name a few.

2. Select the portion of the document you want to embed in another.

3. Switch to the destination application and document. Position the insertion point and choose Paste Special. When you do so, you may see a dialog box giving you some choices about what you want to do. For example, here are two Paste Special boxes, one from Word and one from Excel.

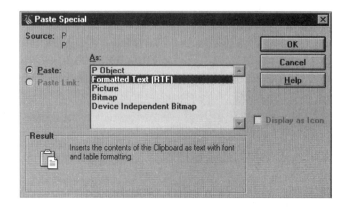

As I said before, you might have to do a little head scratching to figure out which option to choose, but here are some tips. As a rule, if the option says just plain Paste, that won't get you anything more than a normal paste job—which isn't what you want. What you want is some choice that does *not* say Link, but *does* say something about an *object*. So, for example, in Word's dialog box you'd choose the first option and click on OK. In the Excel box you'd choose Object and click on Paste (not on Paste Link, because that will link the object rather than embedding it). Some dialog boxes will let you choose to display the pasted information as an icon rather than as the item itself. For example, normally an embedded video clip will appear in a box that displays the first video frame of the clip.

After doing the Paste operation, and assuming both applications are OLE aware, you might get what looks like a static copy of the material (such as a bitmap), but the destination application will know from whence it was received and thus it can be easily edited. Figure 6.20 shows an example of an MS-Graph file embedded in a Word document.

> **TIP**   With some OLE applications you can embed an object using a command choice, such as Insert ➤ Object. This leads to a dialog box from where you choose the type of object (all the OLE-aware programs on your system are listed). When you choose, the source application runs and you can then create the object and exit. When you exit, the object is placed in the container document you were previously working in.

Editing an Embedded Object

Now assume you've got an object embedded in a document; anyone viewing the document can see it, or you can print it out, and so forth. If it's a video clip or sound clip, double-clicking on it brings up a suitable program—such as Sound Recorder or Media Player—running

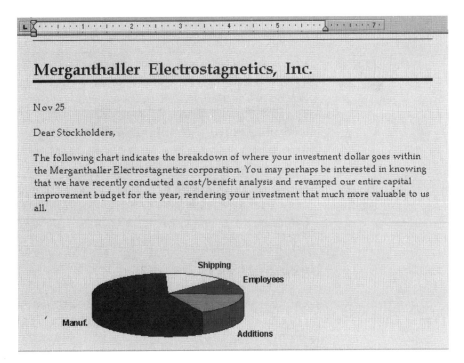

Figure 6.20   *After pasting an object into Word, the graph appears in the container document.*

the clip and allowing the reader of the document to pause, stop, rewind, and replay the clip as needed. For other types of objects, double-clicking makes the object really easy to edit. For example, say you have a graph in your Word document.

1. Double-click on the embedded item. Depending on whether the applications involved are OLE 1.0 or OLE 2.0, several different scenarios may occur. If both applications are 2.0 aware, what ideally happens is that the toolbar, menus, and commands in the application you're working with (the container application) change to those of the object. Use them just as if you were working in whatever program created the object. If one or both of the applications are only OLE 1.0 aware, the object's source application will run in its own window, and the object will be loaded into it. Edit as you normally would.

 NOTE Note that in some cases, such as a sound or video clip, double-clicking on an object will "play" the object rather than edit it. You'll have to edit it via another means, such as right-clicking on it and choosing Edit or selecting it, opening the File menu, and choosing Edit Object or some similar command.

 NOTE With some applications, double-clicking on an embedded file won't have any effect until you change modes. For example, with the Windows 3.x version of Cardfile you have to choose Edit ➤ Picture first.

2. Choose File ➤ Update and then File ➤ Exit, or just File ➤ Exit and then answer Yes to any resulting dialog boxes about updating.

 TIP As an alternative to this technique, an application may have an Edit menu option for editing the object. Select the object first, then check the Edit menu.

Linking Objects

Recall that linking an object is similar to embedding it, but there's one important difference! When linking, the object and the container both "live" in separate files on your hard disk somewhere. However, there is a connection between the linked document and the container it's linked to. This connection is called, not surprisingly, the *link*. So, instead of copying the object's data to the destination document, the link tells the destination application where to find the original source file.

As long as the link isn't broken, it is kept live by Windows, even between sessions. You can edit the linked object by double-clicking on it in the container document, just as you can an embedded object. However, the object will open in a separate window for editing—even if both the server and client applications are OLE 2.0 aware.

You can also edit the object separately using the program that created it, even if the container document isn't open. For example, if the linked item is a spreadsheet file, editing it at its source (say by running 1-2-3, opening the file, editing the spreadsheet, and saving it) will still work. What's more, any changes you make to the file independently will show up in any and all linked files. Because of this, linking is the technique to use when you want to use data that must always be identical in two or more documents.

To link two files:

1. Create or find the server document you want to link (the source document). For example, you could open Paintbrush and draw something.

> **NOTE**   Before a file can be linked, it has to be given a name and saved on disk. Windows won't let you link a file that's still called Untitled (the default name of many documents before they are saved).

2. Select the portion of the document you want to pull into the container document.

3. Choose Edit ➤ Copy to put it onto the Clipboard.

4. Switch to the destination document.

5. Move the insertion point to the place where you want to insert the linked item.

6. Open the container's Edit menu and choose Edit ➤ Paste Link (not Paste). If there isn't a Paste Link command, look for Paste Special and the relevant linking option. You'll likely see a dialog box something like one of the two on the next page.

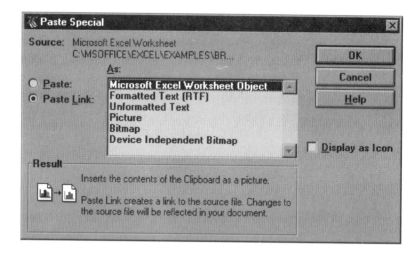

Choose options from the box as you see fit. Whatever the case, because you want to link rather than embed, choose a Paste Link option, as illustrated above.

NOTE   Some friendlier Paste Special dialog boxes explain what effect the various format options will have when you paste the link. The default choice (the one that comes up highlighted when the box first appears) is usually your best bet. However, you might prefer one of the other choices, particularly if you want the linked material to have the exact same look as the source. When linking to a spreadsheet, for example, if you want the headings, grid, and exact font in which the spreadsheet is displayed, you'd choose Bitmapped Picture. Note however, that linking data as a picture rather than text will take up much more room on the disk, making your file much larger. Importing data as formatted text is much more space efficient.

7. If you want to establish a second link, repeat steps 4 through 6, selecting a different destination document in step 4.

The linked item should now be added to the container document in the correct position. If everything went as planned, the object will appear in its original form. That is, a graphic looks like a graphic, cells look like cells, and so forth. In some cases, when OLE applications aren't communicating properly, you'll see the source application's icon instead. This can happen with older applications such as Windows 3.x's Write program and Word for Windows 2.0. If this happens, you're better off just pasting in the text as plain text. Otherwise what you get is essentially a packaged object (see the sections below on packaging).

Editing a Linked Object

Once you've successfully linked some object(s) into a container document, you can check out how well it works. Adjust both windows so you can see both sets of the same data (source and destination). Try altering the source and notice how, in a few seconds, the linked version of the data (stored in the container document) is updated as well.

But what about editing the linked stuff right from the container document? No problem. Just as with editing embedded objects, you simply double-click. The result, however, is different because changes you make to a linked object appear in all the documents you've linked it to.

Here's the basic game plan for editing a typical linked object.

1. In any of the documents the object has been linked to, simply double-click on the object. The source application will open in a window, with the object loaded. For example, Figure 6.21 shows some linked spreadsheet cells that opened in Excel when I double-clicked on them from a WordPad document.

TIP As an alternative, check the Edit menu. If you click on the object once and open the Edit menu, it may have an option such as **Edit Object** on it. Many Windows 95 applications are also supporting the right–mouse-click approach to editing. Click on the item, then click the right mouse button. You're likely to see an option such as **Edit Lotus 1-2-3 Worksheet Link**.

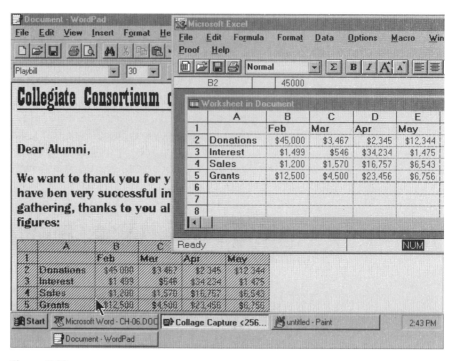

Figure 6.21   *Editing a linked object is usually as easy as double-clicking on it. You can also try right-clicking or check the Edit menu for a special editing command.*

2. In the source application's window, make your edits.

3. Choose File ➤ Save, then File ➤ Exit. Changes you made should appear in all destination documents containing links to this source material.

Maintaining Your OLE Links

As mentioned in Chapter 1, Windows 95 is better at maintaining the link between the server and client documents than was Windows 3.x. This is largely because of improvements in OLE 2.0. Still, nothing is perfect, and there are times when a link may be broken for some reason. A traditional example is when an application crashes before its links can be recorded properly. And although OLE 2.0 is intelligent about keeping your links in working order, it's not impossible to fake it out by copying source and destination files from folder to folder, erasing folders, and so forth. A broken link typically manifests itself as a hole where data was to appear in a document or as data that isn't up to date. In the next few sections I'll explain how to manually make changes to a link to modify its properties.

Manually Updating a Linked Object

Under normal circumstances, when you make changes to a server document (that is, a source document) your changes appear immediately in any other documents that contain copies of that object. (Actually, *immediate* updating requires that the other destination documents be open. If they aren't open, destination documents will be updated the next time you open them.)

In any case, there are times when you might want to delay the updating of objects linked to other documents. You can stipulate, if you want, that a given link will only update destination documents when you manually execute an update command. This might be useful when your source document is undergoing repeated revision that would cause the destination document to read inaccurately or appear unfinished or if the source document is linked to many destination documents and the automatic updating process slows down your computer too much, ties up the network (in the case of links to documents across the net), or is otherwise annoying.

To deal with this, just set up your link for manual updating. Here's how.

1. Open the destination document.

2. Click on the object to select it.

3. Choose Edit ➤ Links. You'll see a Links dialog box similar to Figure 6.22. (The box may vary somewhat depending on the application you're running.)

NOTE If the Links dialog box lists two or more links, you can select multiple consecutive links by holding down the Shift key while you click with the mouse. You can also select multiple links that don't appear consecutively by pressing Ctrl while you click.

4. The Links dialog box lists all the links in your document, identifying each link by the source-document file name. Select the link whose automatic updating you want to turn off.

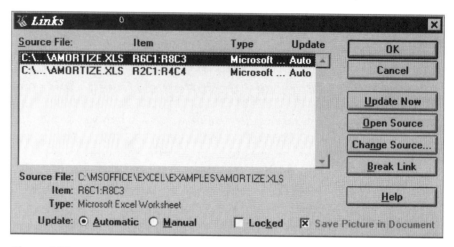

Figure 6.22 *Changing details of a link*

5. Click on the Manual button (down at the bottom of the box), then choose OK. The button should have an X or dot in it, indicating the setting is turned on.

If later you want to reset the updating to the automatic mode, open this box again and click on Automatic.

Note that once you've set a linked object to manual updating, no changes you make to the source document will be reflected in the destination until you manually update it. You'll have to open the Links dialog box, highlight the link in question, and choose Update Now.

Other Link-Management Tasks

You probably noticed that there are other buttons in the Link dialog box that suggest other possible link-related tasks. For example, you might want to break, delete, re-establish links, or alter existing links to refer to different source documents. Here's the rundown on each of these activities.

Canceling and Deleting Links

In certain circumstances you'll want to break a link between two documents. When you break a link, the data continues to appear in the destination document; it just can no longer be edited from within that document. If the destination application is capable of displaying the data, you will still see it. If it's not capable of displaying it, you will see an icon representing the material.

> **TIP**   In most cases, double-clicking on an object whose link has been broken doesn't have any effect. That is, it doesn't bring up the source application or allow you to edit the object. But here's a workaround: Select the object, copy it to the Clipboard, and paste it back into the originating program. Then edit it as you need to, copy it onto the Clipboard again, and paste it back into the destination.

But now for the obvious question. Why would you want to break a link? You'd break a link if having the link is actually more of a hassle than it's worth, such as when you are going to separate the source and destination documents. For example, suppose you want to copy the destination document onto a floppy disk to send to someone. When the recipient opens the document, they'd come up with empty sections in the document and see a dialog box saying that parts of the document are missing. Breaking the link keeps the data in the document, with the only downside being that it's no longer editable.

Okay. What about *deleting* a link? Deleting a link actually wipes out the linked material in the destination document. The source document is left intact, of course, but the previously linked object is purged from the destination document.

How do you break a link or delete a link? Just use the Links dialog box.

1. Open the document containing the object with the link you want to break or delete.

2. Select the object and choose Edit ➤ Links to bring up the Links dialog box. (In some applications, such as Word, you don't have to select the object. All linked objects appear in the Edit ➤ Links dialog box.)

3. In the list of links, highlight the one whose connection you want to break or delete.

4. To cancel the link, click on the Cancel Link (or Break Link) button. To delete the link, press Delete.

5. OK the box.

Fixing Broken Links

As mentioned earlier, links can be broken inadvertently, especially on a network. Links made from within Windows 95 are robust and can survive even when you move source and destination documents around between directories or rename files. However, links will still sometimes be broken, especially in the case of documents composed of information on different workstations across the network. When a destination document can't find the file name and path name to locate a linked object, the application gets confused and breaks the link. The data may still appear in the destination document, but you won't be able to edit it, and the connection will no longer be live. Here's how to re-establish a link so the source and destination documents are once again connected:

1. Open the document containing the object whose link is broken.

2. Select the object and choose Edit ➤ Links. The Links dialog box appears with the object already highlighted in the list of links.

TIP You can also use Change Link to replace a link with a completely different one. Just select a different file name for the source document.

3. Click on the Change Link (possibly called Change Source) button. The Change Source dialog box appears.

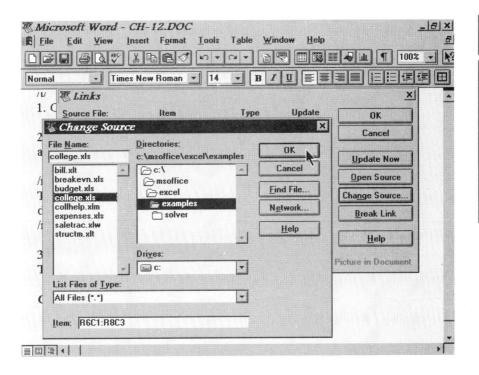

Up and Running
with Windows 95

4. Select the computer, drive, directory, and file as necessary to select the file name of the source document that contains the source material. Click on OK. The Links dialog box then reappears listing the updated location and name of the source document. If the source is on a workstation across the network, look for a Network button to click on.

5. Click on OK to finalize the new link information. When the box closes—and assuming the link is set for automatic updating—the current version of the linked object appears in the destination document.

Exploring
Windows 95

2

Chapter 7

Basic Customizing with the Control Panel

FEATURING

There are numerous alterations you can make to customize Windows to your liking—adjustments to screen colors, modems, mouse speed, passwords, key repeat rate, fonts, and networking options, to name just a few. Most of these adjustments are not necessities as much as they are niceties that make using Windows just a little easier. Others are more imperative, such as setting up Windows to work with your brand and model of printer, setting up Microsoft Exchange preferences for your e-mail, or getting your mouse pointer to slow down a bit so you can reasonably control it.

Preferences of this sort are made through Windows 95's Control Panel. Once you change a setting with the Control Panel, alterations are stored in the Windows configuration Registry. The settings are reloaded each time you run Windows and stay in effect until you change them again with the Control Panel.

A few Control Panel settings can be altered from other locations throughout Windows. For example, you can set up printers from the Start ➤ Settings ➤ Printers command, you can make MS-Exchange settings from within Exchange, and you can change your screen's settings by right-clicking on the Desktop. However, such approaches essentially run the Control Panel option responsible for the relevant settings, so the Control Panel is still doing the work. Running the Control Panel to make system changes is often easier because it displays in one place all the options for controlling your system. This chapter discusses how you run and work with the Control Panel and delves into what the multifarious settings are good for.

Opening the Control Panel

You open the Control Panel by clicking on the Start button, choosing Settings, and choosing Control Panel. The Control Panel window then opens, as shown in Figure 7.1.

 TECH TIP   The Control Panel can also be reached from My Computer or from the Explorer. From the Explorer, scroll the left pane to the top and click on the My Computer icon. Then double-click on the Control Panel in the right pane.

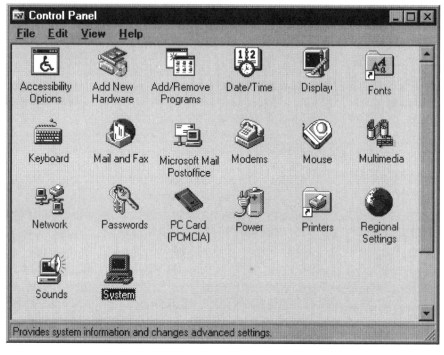

Figure 7.1   *The Control Panel window. Each item opens a window from which you can make adjustments.*

NOTE   Printers, Fonts, Multimedia, System, and Sound are not covered in this chapter. Refer to Chapter 8 for information about setting up printers, Chapter 9 for details about font management, Chapter 10 for help regarding installation and removal of video, audio, MIDI, and CD-ROM device drivers, and assigning system sounds, Chapters 15 and 16 for coverage of the Mail and Fax applet, Chapter 26 for information about the Network applet, and Chapter 31 for coverage of the System applet.

In your Control Panel there will be as many as twenty or so items to choose from, depending on the hardware in your computer and which items you opted for during installation of Windows 95. As you add new software or hardware to your system, you'll occasionally see new options in your Control Panel, too. Or your mouse icon might look different from the one you see in the figure. My computer has a

Microsoft Ballpoint mouse, so the icon looks like a trackball rather than a tabletop mouse.

Each icon in the Control Panel represents a little program (called an *applet*) that will run when you double-click on it, typically bringing up one or more dialog boxes for you to make settings in. Below is a list of all the standard Control Panel applets and what they do.

Accessibility Options   Lets you set keyboard, mouse, sound, display, and other options that make a Windows 95 computer easier to use by those who are visually, aurally, or motor impaired.

Add New Hardware   Installs or removes sound, CD-ROM, video, MIDI, hard- and floppy-disk controllers, PCMCIA sockets, display adaptors, SCSI controllers, keyboard, mouse, printers, ports, and other device drivers.

Add/Remove Programs   You can add or remove modules of Windows 95 itself and sometimes add or remove other kinds of programs. Also lets you create a start-up disk to start your computer with in case the operating system on the hard disk gets trashed accidentally.

Date/Time   Sets the current date and time and which time zone you're in.

Display   Sets the colors (or gray levels) and fonts of various parts of Windows' screens, title bars, scroll bars, and so forth. Sets the background pattern or picture for the Desktop. Also allows you to choose the screen saver, display driver, screen resolution, and energy-saving mode (if your display supports it).

Fonts   adds and deletes typefaces for your screen display and printer output. Allows you to look at samples of each of your fonts. Fonts are discussed at length in Chapter 9.

Keyboard   sets the rate at which keys repeat when you hold them down, sets the cursor blink rate, determines the language your keyboard will be able to enter into documents, and lets you declare the type of keyboard you have. Covered in Chapter 31.

Part 2

Exploring Windows 95

Mail and Fax   As explained in Chapters 15 and 16, profiles are groups of settings that control how your faxing and e-mail are handled. This applet lets you manage these profiles.

Microsoft Mail Postoffice   If you are connected to a network that has a Microsoft Mail Postoffice, this applet lets you administer the postoffice or create a new postoffice. Postoffices are used as a central repository for mail on a network. This is covered in Chapter 17.

Modems   Lets you add, remove, and set the properties of the modem(s) connected to your system. Covered in Chapter 15.

Mouse   Sets the speed of the mouse pointer's motion relative to your hand motion and how fast a double-click has to be to have an effect. You can also reverse the functions of the right and left buttons, set the shape of the various Windows 95 pointers, and tell Windows 95 that you've changed the type of mouse you have.

Multimedia   Changes the Audio, MIDI, CD music, and other multimedia device drivers, properties, and settings. See Chapter 10 for details.

Network   Function varies with the network type. Typically allows you to set the network configuration (network card/connector, protocols, and services), add and configure optional support for Novell, Banyan, Sun network support, and network backup hardware, change your identification (workgroup name, computer name), and determine the manner in which you control who gains access to resources you share over the network, such as printers, fax modems, and folders. This applet is covered in Chapter 26.

Passwords   Sets up or changes log-on passwords, allows remote administration of the computer, and sets up individual profiles that go into effect when each new user logs onto the local computer. Passwords and security are covered in Chapter 31.

PCMCIA   Lets you stop PCMCIA cards before removing them, set the memory area for the card service shared memory (very unlikely to be needed), and disable/enable the beeps that indicate PCMCIA cards are activated when the computer boots up. This applet is discussed in Chapter 31.

Power If you have a battery-powered portable computer, provides options for setting the Advanced Power Management and viewing a scale indicating the current condition of the battery charge. This is covered in Chapter 30.

Printers Displays the printers you have installed on your system, lets you modify the property settings for those printers, and lets you display and manage the print *queue* for each of those printers. Use this applet to install *printer drivers*. (Installing new printer drivers and managing the print queue are covered in Chapter 8.)

Regional Settings Sets how Windows displays times, dates, numbers, and currency (covered in Chapter 31).

Sounds Turns off and on the computer's beep or adds sounds to various system events if your computer has built-in sound capability. Lets you set up sound *schemes*—preset collections of sounds that your system uses to alert you to specific events.

System Displays information about your system's internals—devices, amount of RAM, type of processor, and so forth. Also lets you add to, disable, and remove specific devices from your system, set up hardware profiles (for instance, to allow automatic optimization when using a docking station with a laptop), and optimize some parameters of system performance such as CD cache size and type. This applet also provides a number of system-troubleshooting tools. The use of the System applet is rather complex and thus is covered in Chapter 31.

I'll now discuss the Control Panel applets in detail. Aside from the Accessibility settings, the applets here are the ones you're most likely to want to adjust.

NOTE All the Control Panel setting dialog boxes have a ? button in their upper-right corner. Remember from Chapter 3 that you can click on this button, then on an item in the dialog box that you have a question about. You'll be shown some relevant explanation about the item.

Part
2

Exploring Windows 95

Accessibility Options

Accessibility means increasing the ease of use or access to a computer for people who are physically challenged in one way or another. Many people have difficulty seeing characters on the screen when they are too small, for example. Others have a disability that prevents them from easily typing on the keyboard. Even those of us who hunt and peck at the keyboard have it easy compared to those who can barely move their hands, are limited to the use of a single hand, or who may be paralyzed from the neck down. These people have gotten the short end of the stick for some time when it came to using computers unless they had special data-entry and retrieval devices (such as speech boards) installed in their computers.

Microsoft has taken a big step in increasing computer accessibility to disabled people by including in Windows 95 proper, features that allow many challenged people to use Windows 95 and Windows programs without major modification to their machines or software. (Accessibility add-ons for Windows 3.x and NT have been available for some time, but as add-ons.)

The Accessibility applet lets you make special use of the keyboard, display, mouse, sound board, and a few other aspects of your computer. To run the Accessibility option, double-click on its icon in the Control Panel. The resulting dialog box looks like Figure 7.2.

Keyboard Accessibility Settings

Probably all of us have some difficulty keeping multiple keys depressed at once. Settings here help with this problem and others.

1. Click on the Keyboard tab (if it's not already selected). There are three basic setting areas:

StickyKeys	Keys that in effect stay pressed down when you press them once. Good for controlling the Alt, Ctrl, and Shift keys.
FilterKeys	Lets you filter out quickly repeated keystrokes in case you have trouble pressing a key cleanly once and letting it up. This prevents multiple keystrokes from being typed.

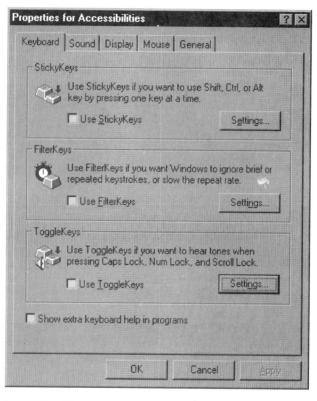

Figure 7.2 Accessibility dialog box

ToggleKeys   Gives you the option of hearing tones that alert
                              you to the Caps Lock, Scroll Lock, and Num
                              Lock keys being activated.

2. Click on the box of the feature you want your Windows 95 machine
to use.

3. Note that each feature has a Settings button from which you can
make additional adjustments. To see the additional settings, click on
the Settings button next to the feature, fine-tune the settings, and
then click on OK. The most likely setting changes you'll make from
these boxes are to turn on or off the shortcut keys.

4. After you have made all the keyboard changes you want, either move
on to another tab in the Accessibility box or click on OK and return
to the Control Panel.

TIP You can turn on any of these keyboard features—StickyKeys, FilterKeys, or ToggleKeys—with shortcuts at any time while in Windows 95. To turn on StickyKeys, press either Shift key five times in a row. To turn on FilterKeys, press and hold the right Shift key for eight seconds (it might take longer). To turn on the ToggleKeys option, press the Num Lock key for five seconds.

When StickyKeys or FilterKeys are turned on, a symbol will appear on the right side of the Taskbar indicating what's currently activated. For example, here I have the StickyKeys and FilterKeys both set on. StickyKeys is indicated by the three small boxes, representative of the Ctrl, Alt, and Shift keys. FilterKeys is represented by the stopwatch representative of the different key timing that goes into effect when the option is working.

 TIP Turning on FilterKeys will make it seem that your keyboard has ceased working. You have to press a key and keep it down for several seconds for the key to register. If you activate this setting and want to turn it off, the easiest solution is to use the mouse or switch to Control Panel (via the Taskbar), run the Accessibility applet, turn off FilterKeys, and click on OK.

Unless you disable this feature from the Settings dialog box, you can turn off StickyKeys by pressing two of the three keys that are affected by this setting. For example, pressing Ctrl and Alt at the same time will turn StickyKeys off.

Sound Accessibility Settings

There are two Sound Accessibility settings—Sound Sentry and Show Sounds (see Figure 7.3). These two features are for the hearing impaired. What they do is simply cause some type of visual display to occur in lieu of the normal beep, ding, or other auditory alert that the program would typically produce. The visual display might be something such as a blinking window (in the case of Sound Sentry) or it might be some kind of text caption (in the case of ShowSounds).

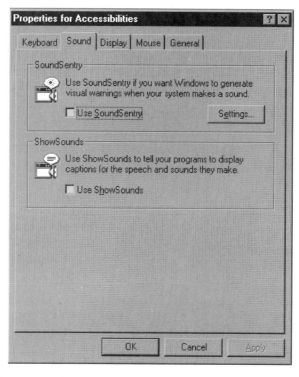

Figure 7.3   The two Sound Accessibility settings

The Settings button for Sound Sentry lets you decide what will graphically happen on screen when a program is trying to warn you of something. For example, should it flash the window, flash the border of the program, or flash the whole screen? If you really don't want to miss a beep-type warning, you might want to have it flash the window. (Flashing the whole screen doesn't indicate which program is producing the warning.)

NOTE   Not all programs will work cooperatively with these sound options. As more programs are written to take advantage of these settings, you'll see more *closed captioning*, for example, wherein sound messages are translated into useful captions on the screen.

Part
2

Exploring Windows 95

Display Accessibility Settings

The Display Accessibility settings pertain to contrast. These settings let you set the display color scheme and font selection for easier reading. This can also be done from the normal Display setting, described below, but the advantage to setting it here is that you can preset your favorite high-contrast color scheme, then invoke it with the shortcut key combination when you most need it. Just press Left-Alt, Left-Shift, Prnt-Scrn. This might be when your eyes are tired, when someone who is sight impaired is using the computer, or when you're sitting in an adverse lighting situation. Figure 7.4 displays the dialog box:

1. Turn on the High Contrast option box if you want to improve the contrast between the background and the characters on your screen. When you click on Apply or OK, this will kick in a high-contrast color scheme (typically the Blue and Black) scheme, which will put black

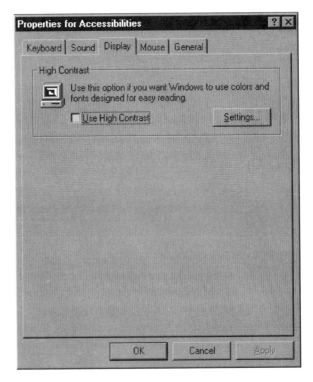

Figure 7.4   *The dialog box for setting Display Accessibility features*

letters on a white work area. (You can't get much more contrast than that!)

2. Click on the Settings button if you want to change the color scheme that'll be used for high contrast or if you want to enable or disable shortcut-key activation of this feature. This option may come in handy because some of the schemes have larger fonts than others and some might show up better on your screen than will others.

> **TIP** You can experiment more easily with the schemes in the Display applet than here. You can even create your own custom color scheme with large menus, title bar lettering, and dialog box lettering if you want. I explain how to do all this in the Display section.

3. Click on Apply if you want to keep making more settings from the other tab pages or on OK to return to the Control Panel.

Mouse Accessibility Settings

If you can't easily control mouse or trackball motion, or simply don't like using a mouse, this dialog box is for you. Of course, you can invoke most commands that apply to dialog boxes and menus throughout Windows and Windows programs using the Alt key in conjunction with the command's underlined letter. Still, some programs, such as those that work with graphics, require you to use a mouse. This Accessibility option turns your arrow keys into mouse-pointer control keys. You still have to use the mouse's clicker buttons to left- or right-click on things, though. Here's what to do:

> **TIP** This is a great feature for laptop users who are on the road and forgot the mouse. If you have to use a graphics program or other program requiring more than simple command choices and text entry, use the Mouse Accessibility tab to turn your arrow keys into mouse-pointer keys.

1. Click on the Mouse tab in the Accessibility dialog box. You'll see the box displayed in Figure 7.5.

2. Turn on the option if you want to use the arrow keys in place of the mouse. You'll probably want to adjust the speed settings for the arrow

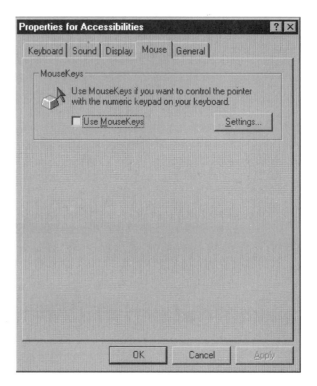

Figure 7.5   The Mouse Accessibility dialog box

keys, though, so the pointer moves at a rate that works for you. The Settings button brings up the box you see in Figure 7.6. Note that you can also set a shortcut key sequence to activate MouseKeys.

3. Play with the settings until you like them. The Top Speed and Acceleration settings are going to be the most important. And note that you have to set them, click on OK, then click on Apply in the Mouse dialog box before you can experience the effect of your changes. Then go back and adjust your settings if necessary. Notice that one setting lets you change the tracking speed on the fly while using a program, by holding down the Shift key to slow down the pointer's motion or the Ctrl key to speed it up.

4. Click on Apply if you want to keep making more settings from the other tab pages or on OK to return to the Control Panel.

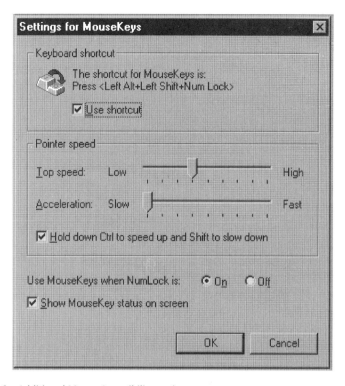

Figure 7.6   Additional Mouse Accessibility settings

TIP   The pointer keys that are used for mouse control are the ones on a standard desktop computer keyboard's number pad. These are the keys that have two modes—Num Lock on and Num Lock off. These keys usually have both an arrow and a number on them; for example, the 4 key also has a ← symbol on it. Most laptops don't have such keys because of size constraints. However, many laptops have a special arrangement that emulates these keys, providing a ten-key numeric keypad (and arrows when NumLock is off).

Other Accessibility Settings

The last tab in the Accessibility box is called General (Figure 7.7).

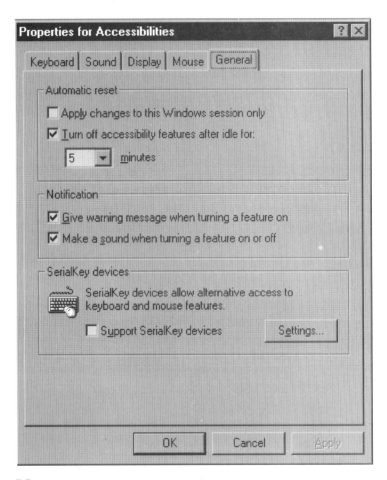

Figure 7.7 **The last of the Accessibility settings boxes**

The box is divided into three sections pertaining to:

▶ When Accessibility functions are turned on and off. Notice that you can choose to have all the settings you've made during this Windows session apply only to this session (that means until you restart Windows 95).

▶ How you are alerted to a feature being turned on or off. You have the choice of a visual cue (a little dialog box will appear) and/or a sound.

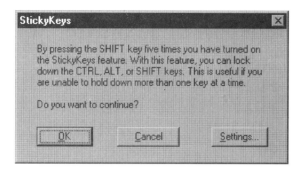

> ▶ Acceptance of alternative input devices through the serial (COM1 through COM4) ports on your computer.

Adding New Hardware

If you have a computer that is Plug-and-Play compatible, this section won't be of a lot of use to you, and you should celebrate. That's because, as I discussed in Chapter 1, Plug and Play ensures that by simply plugging a new card or other device into your computer, it will work. The Plug-and-Play software in Windows 95—in concert with software coding in the computer and add-on cards and devices—takes care of installing the appropriate hardware device driver file and making the appropriate settings so your new device doesn't conflict with some other device in the system. That's the good news.

 TECH TIP   Of course, there are a limited number of IRQs, ports, and DMAs. Plug in enough Plug-and-Play cards, and one or more is guaranteed not to be installed by the system because Plug and Play will not enable a device unless resources are available for it.

The bad news is that there are a zillion non–Plug-and-Play PC cards and devices floating around in the world and just as many pre–Plug-and-Play PCs. This older hardware isn't designed to take advantage of Windows 95's Plug-and-Play capabilities. The upshot of this is that when you install such hardware into your system, most computers won't detect the change. This will result in disappointment when you've carefully installed some piece of new and exciting gear (such as a sound card) and it just doesn't work—or worse, it disables things that used to function just fine.

Microsoft has added a nifty feature that tries its best to install a new piece of hardware for you. All you have to do is declare your new addition and let Windows 95 run around and try to detect what you've done. Luckily, the Add Hardware applet is pretty savvy about interrogating the hardware you've installed—via its Install Hardware Wizard—and making things work right. You can also tell it exactly what you have to save a little time and ensure Windows 95 gets it right.

NOTE   Notice the applet is only for adding new hardware, not for removing hardware and associated driver files. Removing drivers is done through the System applet, covered in Chapter 32. Note that there are other locations throughout Windows for installing some devices, such as printers, which can be installed from the Printers folder via My Computer. However, the effect is the same as installing these devices from this applet.

TIP   Microsoft maintains a Windows 95 Driver Library that contains new, tested drivers as they are developed for printers, networks, screens, audio cards, and so forth. You can access these drivers through CompuServe, GEnie, or the Microsoft Download Service (MSDL). You can reach MSDL at (206) 936-6735 between 6:00 AM and 6:00 PM Pacific Standard Time, Monday through Friday. As an alternative, you can order the library on disk from Microsoft at (800) 227-4679.

Running the Install Hardware Wizard

If you've purchased a board or other hardware add-in, first read the supplied manual for details about installation procedures. There may be installation tips and an install program supplied with the hardware. If there are no instructions, then install the hardware and follow the steps below.

NOTE   I suggest you install the hardware before you run the Wizard, or Windows 95 won't be able to validate that the hardware is present. Also, simply putting new hardware into your computer will rarely result in anything unless you follow these procedures. This is because Windows has to update the Registry containing the list of hardware in your system, it has to install the appropriate device-driver software for the added hardware, and it often has to reboot before the new hardware will work.

1. Close any programs you have running. You're probably going to be re-booting the machine, and it's possible that the detection process will hang up the computer, possibly trashing work files that are open.

2. Look up or otherwise discover the precise brand name and model number/name of the item you're installing. You'll need to know it somewhere during this process.

3. Run the Control Panel and double-click on the Add New Hardware applet. You'll see its dialog box, looking like the one in Figure 7.8.

Figure 7.8   *The Add Hardware Wizard makes installing new hardware pretty easy, usually.*

Part
2

Exploring Windows 95

4. There's nothing to do but click on Next. The next box, as shown in Figure 7.9, requires some action on your part, though.

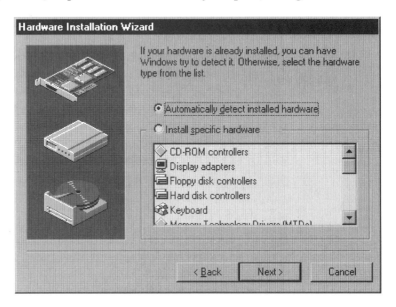

Figure 7.9   Choose the type of hardware you want to install.

5. Now, if you want the Wizard to run around, look at what you have, and notice the new item you installed, just leave the top option button selected and click on Next. You'll be warned that this could take several minutes and be advised to close any open programs and documents. Keep in mind that the Wizard is doing quite a bit of sleuthing as it looks over your computer. Many add-in cards and devices don't have standardized ID markings, so identifying some hardware items isn't so easy. The Microsoft programmers had to devise some clever interrogation techniques to identify myriad hardware items. In fact, the results may even be erroneous in some cases. Regardless, while the hardware survey is underway, you'll see a gauge apprising you of the progress, and you'll hear a lot of hard-disk activity. In rare cases, the computer will hang during this process, and you'll have to reboot. If this happens repeatedly, you'll have to tell the Wizard what hardware you've added, as explained in the next section.

6. When completed, you'll either be told that nothing new was found or you'll see a box listing the discovered items, asking for confirmation and/or some details. Respond as necessary. You may be prompted to insert one of your Windows 95 diskettes or the master CD-ROM so the appropriate driver file(s) can be loaded. If nothing new was found, click on Next, and the Wizard sends you on to step 2 in the section below.

Telling the Wizard What You've Got

If you're the more confident type (in your own abilities rather than the computer's), you might want to take the surer path to installing new hardware. Option two in the second Wizard box lets *you* declare what the new hardware is. This option not only saves you time, but even lets you install the hardware later, should you want to. This is because the Wizard doesn't bother to authenticate the existence of the hardware: It simply installs the new driver.

1. Follow steps 1 through 4 above.

2. Now choose the second option button, *Install specific hardware*.

3. Scroll through the list to get an idea of all the classes of hardware you can install via this applet. Then click on the category you want to install. For this example, I'm going to install Creative Lab's Sound Blaster sound card because that's a popular add-in item.

TIP If you don't know the class of the item you're installing, you're not sunk. Just choose the last item in the list—Unknown Hardware. Find and click on the manufacturer's brand name in the left-hand list; most popular items made by that manufacturer will be displayed in the right-hand list. Then choose your new hardware from this list.

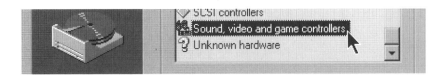

4. Click on Next. This brings up a list of all the relevant drivers in the class you've chosen. For example, Figure 7.10 lists the sound cards from Creative Labs, the people who make the Sound Blaster cards.

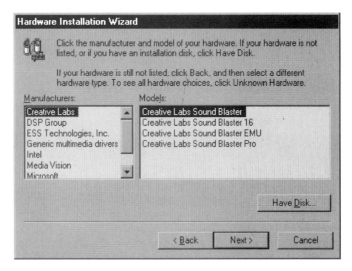

Figure 7.10   After choosing a class of hardware, you'll see a list of manufacturers and models.

5. First scroll the left list and click on the manufacturer. Then find the correct item in the Model list and click on that.

6. Click on Next. What happens at this point depends on the type of hardware you're installing:

    ▶ If the hardware is Plug-and-Play compatible, you'll be informed of it, and the Wizard will take care of the details.

    ▶ For some non–Plug-and-Play hardware, you'll be told to simply click on Finish, and the Wizard will take care of installing the necessary driver.

    ▶ In some cases, you'll be shown the settings that you should adjust your hardware to match. (Add-in cards often have switches or software adjustments that control the I/O port, DMA address, and other such geeky stuff.) For example, Figure 7.11 shows the message I got about the Sound Blaster card. Your job is to read the manual that came with the hardware and figure out how to adjust

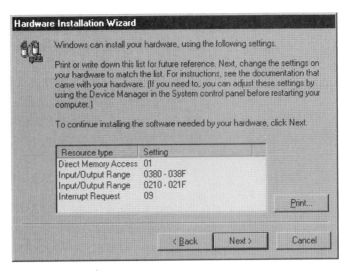

Figure 7.11 For hardware that has address or other adjustments on it, you may be told which settings to use to avoid conflicts with other hardware in the system.

the switches, jumpers, or other doodads to match the settings the Wizard gives you.

TIP If for some reason you don't want to use the settings suggested by the Wizard, you can set the board or device otherwise. Then you'll have to use the System applet's Device Manager to change the settings in the Windows Registry to match those on the card. See Chapter 31 for coverage of the Device Manager.

▶ In some cases, you'll be told there's a conflict between your new hardware and what's already in your computer (Figure 7.12). Despite the dialog box's message, you have *three* choices, not two. In addition to proceeding or canceling, you could also back up and choose a different piece of hardware, such as a different model number or a compatible make or model that might support a different port, DMA address, or whatnot. If you decide to continue, you'll have to resolve the conflict somehow, such as by removing or readdressing the conflicting board or device. In that case you'll be shown a dialog box that lets you run the *conflict troubleshooter*.

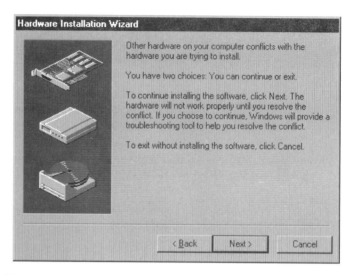

Figure 7.12   If you try to install a piece of hardware that conflicts with preexisting hardware, you'll see this message.

This is a combination of a Help file and the System applet's Device Manager. The Help file walks you through a series of questions and answers.

7. Next, you may be prompted to insert a disk containing the appropriate software driver. Windows remembers the disk drive and directory you installed Windows 95 from, so it assumes the driver is in that location. This might be a network directory, your CD-ROM drive, or a floppy drive. In any case, just supply the requested disk. If the driver is already in your system, you will be asked if you want to use the existing driver. This is okay assuming the driver is up to date and you aren't trying to install a new one.

8. Finally, a box will announce that the necessary changes have been made and you can click on Finish. If you haven't physically installed the hardware already, you'll see this message:

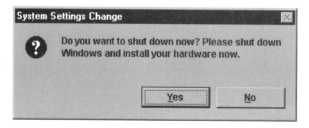

If the hardware is already installed, you'll probably see a message asking you to shut down and restart.

When Your Hardware Isn't on the List

Sometimes your new hardware won't be included in the list of items the Wizard displays. This means that Microsoft hasn't included a driver for that device on the disks that Windows 95 came on. This is probably because your hardware is newer than Windows 95, so it wasn't around when Windows 95 went out the door from Microsoft. Or it could be that the manufacturer didn't bother to get its product certified by Microsoft and earn the Windows "seal of approval." It's worth the few extra bucks to buy a product with the Windows 95 logo on the box rather than the cheapie clone product. As mentioned above, Microsoft makes new drivers available to users through several channels. However, manufacturers often supply drivers with their hardware, or you can get hold of a driver from a BBS, an information service such as CompuServe, or Microsoft Network.

If you're in this boat, you can just tell the Add New Hardware Wizard to use the driver on your disk. Here's how:

1. Run the Add New Hardware applet.

2. Click on Next, then choose the correct class of hardware.

3. Click on the Have Disk button.

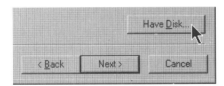

4. Enter the location of the driver (you can enter any path, such as a directory on the hard disk or network path) in this box.

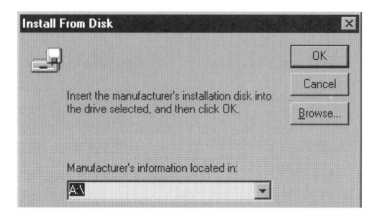

Typically, you'll be putting a disk in drive A, in which case you'd use the setting shown here. However, don't type the file name for the driver, just its path. Usually this will be just A:\ or B:\. If the driver is on a hard disk or CD-ROM and you don't know which letter drive or which directory it is, use the Browse button and subsequent dialog box to select the source drive and directory. When the path is correct, click on OK.

5. Assuming the Wizard finds a suitable driver file (it must find a file called OEMSETUP.INF), choose the correct hardware item from the resulting dialog box and follow on-screen directions (they'll be the same as those I described above, beginning with step 6).

TECH TIP   If you're not sure which ports and interrupts your other boards are using, rather than use the old trial-and-error method, Windows 95 comes with a great tool for sleuthing this out—see Chapter 31 for a discussion of the Control Panel's System applet. Double-clicking on the Computer icon at the top of the Device Manager page in that applet will reveal a list of IRQs and ports that are currently in use.

Adding and Removing Programs

The topic of adding and removing programs is discussed in Chapter 5, in the context of the Program Manager and ways to organize your programs and documents. The applet has three functions:

▶ Installing and uninstalling programs that comply with Windows 95's API for these tasks. The API ensures that a program's file names and locations are recorded in a database, allowing them to be reliably erased without adversely impacting the operation of Windows 95.

▶ Installing and removing specific portions of Windows 95 itself, such as Microsoft Exchange.

▶ Creating a start-up disk that will start your computer in case the operating system gets trashed beyond functionality for some reason. With a start-up disk, you should still be able to gain access to your files and stand a chance of repairing the problem that prevents the machine from starting up.

Installing New Programs

The applet's first tab page is for installing new programs:

1. Run Control Panel, then the Add/Remove Software applet. You'll see the box shown in Figure 7.13.

2. Click on Install. Now a new box appears, telling you to insert a floppy disk or CD-ROM in the appropriate drive and click on Next. Assuming an appropriate program is found (it must be called *install* or *setup* and have a .bat, .pif, .com, or .exe extension), it'll be displayed as you see in Figure 7.14.

3. Click on Finish to complete the task. The new software's installation or setup procedure will now run. Instructions will vary depending on the program. If your program's setup routine isn't compatible with the applet, you'll be advised of this. After installation, the new program will appear in the list of removable programs only if it's compatible with Windows 95's install/remove scheme.

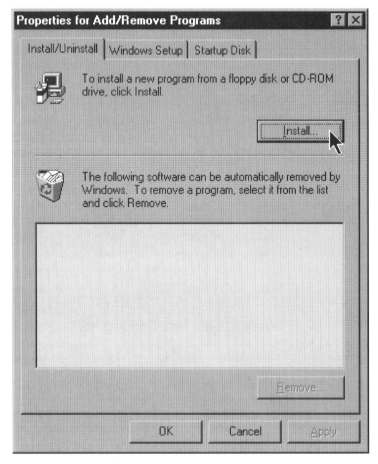

Figure 7.13   *The Wizard for adding and removing software can be reached from the Add/Remove Programs applet. Only programs that were installed using the applet will be listed in the box. Programs installed using other means (such as before you upgraded to Windows 95) will not appear here.*

Removing Existing Programs

With time, more programs will be removable via the Control Panel. This is because the PC software industry at large has heard much kvetching from users and critics about tenacious programs that once installed are hard to remove. Some ambitious programs spread themselves out all over your hard disk like olive oil in a hoagie, and there's

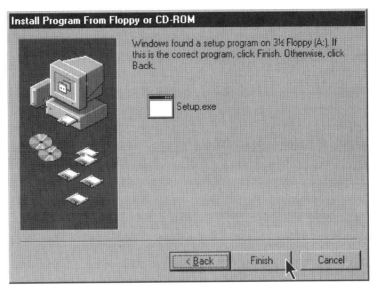

Figure 7.14 **The Wizard looks for a likely installation program on your CD-ROM or floppy
and displays the first one it finds.**

no easy way of reversing the process to return your system to a pristine state. The result is often overall system slowdown, unexplained crashes, or other untoward effects.

To this end, aftermarket utilities such as Uninstaller have become quite popular. Uninstall utility programs monitor and record just exactly what files a new software package adds to your hard disk and which internal Windows settings it modifies. It can then undo the damage later, freeing up disk space and tidying your Windows system.

In typical fashion, Microsoft has incorporated such a scheme into Windows 95 itself. Time will tell if its mousetrap is as good as the competition's. Probably not, but it will be "close enough for jazz," as the saying goes. If programmers write installation routines that work with Windows 95's Add/Remove Software applet, we'll all be in luck.

Use of the uninstall feature of the applet is simple:

1. In the bottom pane, select the program(s) you want to uninstall.

2. Click on Remove.

3. Answer any warnings about removing an application as appropriate.

NOTE   Once removed, you'll have to reinstall a program from its source disks to make it work again. You can't just copy things out of the Recycle Bin to their old directories because settings from the Start button—and possibly the Registry—will have been deleted.

Setting the Date and Time

NOTE   You can also adjust the time and date using the TIME and DATE commands from the DOS prompt.

The Date/Time icon lets you adjust the system's date and time. The system date and time are used for a number of purposes, including date- and time-stamping the files you create and modify, scheduling fax transmissions, and so on. All programs use these settings, regardless of whether they are Windows or non-Windows programs. (This applet doesn't change the format of the date and time—just the actual date and time. To change the *format*, you use the Regional applet as discussed in Chapter 31.)

1. Double-click on the Date/Time applet. The dialog box in Figure 7.15 appears.

2. Adjust the time and date by typing in the corrections or clicking on the arrows. Note that you have to click directly on the hours, minutes, seconds, or am/pm area before the little arrows to the right of them will modify the correct value.

3. Next, you can change the time zone you are in. Who cares about the time zone, you ask? Good question. For many users it doesn't matter. But because people fax to other time zones, and some programs help you manage your transcontinental and transoceanic phone calling, it's built into Windows 95. These programs need to know where in the world you and Carmen Sandiego are. So, click on the Time Zone tab and you'll see a world map (Figure 7.16).

Set month from drop-down list

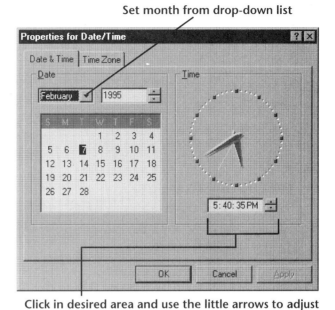

Click in desired area and use the little arrows to adjust

Figure 7.15   Adjust the date, time, and local time zone from this dialog box. A shortcut to this box is to double-click on the time in the Taskbar.

Customizing Your Screen Display

 TIP   The Display icon is accessible either from the Control Panel *or* from the Desktop. Right-click on an empty area of the Desktop and choose **Properties**.

The Display applet packs a wallop under its hood. For starters, it incorporates what in Windows 3.x were the separate Color and Desktop Control Panel applets for prettying up the general look of the Windows screen. Then, in addition, it includes the means for changing your screen driver and resolution—functions heretofore (in Windows 3.x) available only from the Setup program. If you were annoyed by getting at all these areas of display tweaking from disjunct venues, suffer no more. Microsoft has incorporated all display-related adjustments into the unified Display applet. If you

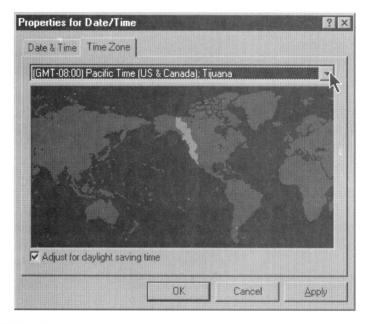

Figure 7.16   **Check and set your time zone if necessary. Some programs will use this information to help you schedule mail or fax transmissions to other time zones. For laptop users who travel, this can be a great boon. Just point to your new location
and click: The computer's time is automatically adjusted.**

are among the blessed, you will even have the option of changing
screen resolution on the fly.

Here are the functional and cosmetic adjustments you can make to
your Windows 95 display from this applet:

▶ set the background and wallpaper for the Desktop

▶ set the screen saver and energy conservation

▶ set the color scheme and fonts for Windows elements

▶ set the display device driver and adjust resolution, color depth, and
font size

Let's take a look at this dialog box page by page. This is a fun one to experiment with and will come in handy if you know how to use it.

First run the applet by double-clicking on it.

Setting the Background and Wallpaper

The *pattern* and *wallpaper* settings simply let you decorate the Desktop with something a little more festive than the default screen. Patterns are repetitious designs, such as the woven look of fabric. Wallpaper uses larger pictures that were created by artists with a drawing program. You can create your own patterns and wallpaper or use the ones supplied. Wallpapering can be done with a single copy of the picture placed in the center of the screen or by *tiling*, which gives you multiple identical pictures covering the whole screen. Some of the supplied wallpaper images cannot be used if you are low on memory. This is because the larger bit-mapped images take up too much RAM.

Loading a Pattern

To load a new pattern,

1. Click on the first tab page of the applet's dialog box.

2. Scroll the Pattern list to a pattern you're interested in and highlight it. A minuscule version of the pattern will show up in the little screen in the dialog box (Figure 7.17).

NOTE   For a pattern to show up, wallpaper has to be set to None. This is because wallpaper always sits on top of the Desktop's pattern.

3. To see the effect on the whole screen, click on the Apply button. This keeps the applet open and lets you easily try other patterns and settings. (If you want to leave it at that, click on OK. Then the applet will close, and you'll be returned to the Control Panel.)

Part
2

Exploring Windows 95

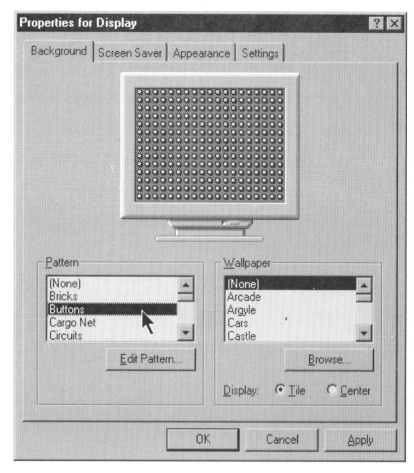

Figure 7.17   Simply highlighting a pattern will display a facsimile of it in the dialog box's tiny monitor screen.

Editing a Pattern

If the supplied patterns don't thrill you, make up your own with the built-in bitmap editor. You can either change an existing one or design your own. If you want to design your own, choose None from the Name drop-down list before you begin. Otherwise, choose a pattern you want to play with:

1.   Click on the Edit Pattern button. A new dialog box appears.

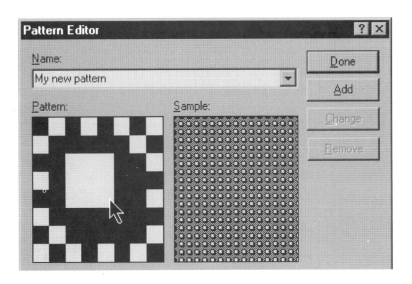

2. In the Name text box, type in a name for the new pattern.

3. Create the pattern by clicking in the box on the left. What you are doing is defining the smallest element of the repeated pattern (a cell). It
   is blown up in scale to make editing easier. Each click reverses the
   color of one pixel. The effect when the pattern is applied across a larger
   area and in normal size is shown in the Sample section to the right.

4. When you like the pattern, click on Add and the pattern will be added
   to your list of patterns.

5. Click on Done when you're through creating new patterns.

   If you later want to remove a pattern, select the pattern while in the
   editor and click on Remove. If you want to edit an existing pattern,
   get into the editor, select an existing pattern, make changes to it, and
   click on Change.

 TIP If you want to abandon changes you've made to a pattern, click on the
Close button (X) and answer No to the question about saving the changes.

Loading a New Slice of Wallpaper

The images used in wallpaper are .bmp files. These are bit-mapped
files created by programs such as Paintbrush. Other programs create

.bmp files too, so the sky's the limit as far as what you can use as wallpaper. For example, you could use a scanned color photograph of your favorite movie star, a pastoral setting, some computer art, a scanned Matisse painting, or a photo of your pet lemur. Figure 7.18 shows an example of a custom piece of wallpaper.

You can also edit the supplied .bmp files with Microsoft Paint if you want. Just load one into Paint by selecting File ➤ Open. In the Open dialog box, open the List Files of Type drop-down list box and choose BMP file (***.bmp**) to display available .bmp files. Then choose the desired file and click on OK. Also note that in Microsoft Paint's File menu there's a choice for setting the currently open bit-mapped file to Wallpaper.

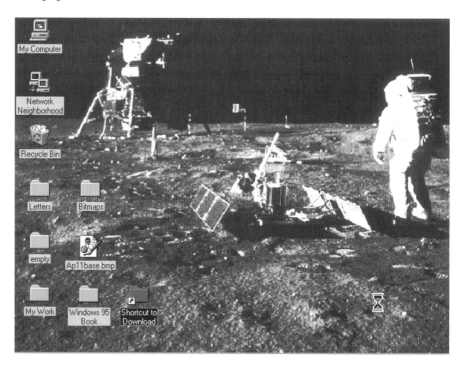

Figure 7.18   *A custom piece of wallpaper Arthur Knowles, the technical editor of this book, sent to me over the Microsoft Network. This is a* .bmp *file of the Apollo 11 base camp on the Earth's moon.*

TIP If you have some other form of picture file, such as a .gif or .pcx file that you want to use, you can, but you'll have to convert the file to .bmp format first using another graphics program such as Collage Image Manager, Publisher's Paintbrush, Paintshop Pro, or other.

Here's how to load a new .bmp file and display it as wallpaper:

1. Create or otherwise obtain the image with whatever program you want, as long as it saves the image as a .bmp file.

2. Run the Display applet and click on the Browse button in the Wallpaper section of the dialog box.

3. Switch to the directory containing your .bmp file. Select it and click on OK.

4. Click on Apply to see the effect and keep the dialog box open, or on OK to apply the new wallpaper and close the dialog box.

Setting the Screen Saver

A Screen Saver will blank your screen or display a moving image or pattern if you don't use the mouse or keyboard for a predetermined amount of time. Screen savers can prevent a static image from burning the delicate phosphors on the inside surface of the monitor, which can leave a ghost of the image on the screen for all time no matter what is being displayed.

Many modern computer monitors have an EPA Energy Star, VESA, or other kind of energy-saving strategy built into them. Because far too many people leave their computers on all the time (although it's not really true that they will last longer that way), efforts have been made by power regulators and electronics manufacturers to devise computer–energy-conservation schemes. If your monitor has an Energy Star rating and your video board supports this feature, the screen saver in Windows 95 can power the monitor down after it senses you went out to lunch or got caught up at the water cooler for a longer-than-expected break.

TECH TIP   For an energy-saving screen saver to work properly, you'll have to turn on the Energy Star option from the Control Panel ➤ Display ➤ Settings ➤ Change Display Type dialog box. Also, the monitor must adhere to the VESA Display Power Management Signaling (DPMS) specification or to another method of lowering power consumption. Some LCD screens on portable computers can do this. You can assume that if your monitor has an Energy Star emblem, it probably supports DPMS. Energy Star is a program administered by the U.S. Environmental Protection Agency (EPA) to reduce the amount of power used by personal computers and peripherals. The Energy Star emblem does not represent EPA endorsement of any product or service. If you notice that your screen freaks out or the display is garbled after your power-management screen saver turns on, you should turn off this check box.

The screen-saver options allow you to choose or create an entertaining video ditty that will greet you when you return to work. You also set how much time you have after your last keystroke or mouse skitter before the show begins.

Loading a Screen Saver

Here's how it's done:

1. Click on the Screen Saver tab. The page appears as you see in Figure 7.19.

2. Choose a name from the drop-down list. The saver will be shown in the little screen in the dialog box.

3. Want to see how it will look on your whole screen? Click on Preview. Your screen will go black and then begin its antics. The show continues until you hit any key or move your mouse.

4. If you want to change anything about the selected screen saver, click on Settings. You'll see a box of settings that apply to that particular screen saver. For example, for the Mystify Your Mind saver, this is the Settings box:

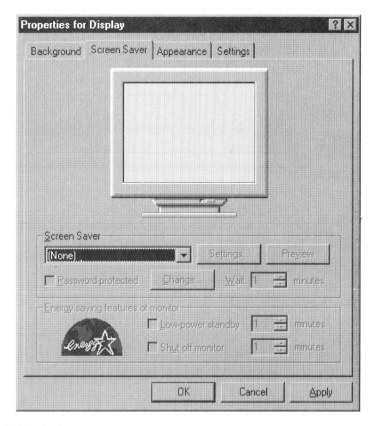

Figure 7.19   Setting up a screen saver

Most of the option boxes have fun sliders and stuff you can play with
to get an effect you like. Depending on which screen saver you chose,
you'll have a few possible adjustments, such as speed, placement, and
details pertinent to the graphic. Play with the settings until you're
happy with the results and OK the Setting box.

5. Back at the Screen Saver page, the next choice you might want to con-
    sider is Password Options. If you set password protection on, every
    time your screen saver is activated you will have to type your pass-
    word into a box to return to work. This is good if you don't want any-
    one else tampering with your files or seeing what you're doing. It can
    be a pain, though, if there's no particular need for privacy at your
    computer. Don't forget your password, either, or you'll have to reboot
    to get back to work. Of course, anyone could reboot your computer

and get back into it anyway, so this means of establishing security is somewhat limited. Click on the Password Protected check box if you want protection and go on to the next two steps. Otherwise skip them.

6. Click on the Change button to define or change your password. In the dialog box that appears, type in your new password.

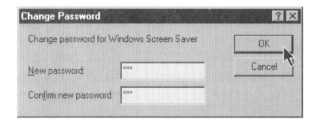

You won't see the letters, just an asterisk for each letter (to preserve confidentiality). For confirmation that you typed it correctly, *type it again* (don't copy the first one and paste it; a mistake in the first one can result in your being locked out of your computer) in the Confirm New Password text box. If there is a discrepancy between the two, you'll get an error message. Reenter the password. (If you're changing a password, the steps will be approximately the same. Enter your old password first, then the new one and its confirmation.) When it is correct, click on OK.

7. Back at the Desktop dialog box, set the number of minutes you want your computer to be idle before the screen saver springs into action. Next to Wait, either type in a number or use the up and down arrows to change the time incrementally.

8. Next you have the Energy Star options. Energy Star monitors need an Energy Star-compatible video card in the computer. If your screen setup supports this, the options will not be grayed out. Otherwise they will be. Assuming you can gain access to the settings, you have two choices: when the low-power mode kicks in and when total power off kicks in. You don't want total power down to happen too quickly because the screen will take a few seconds (like about ten) to come back on when you move the mouse or press a key, which can be annoying. So make the two settings something reasonable, such as 15 minutes and 30 minutes.

9. When all the settings are correct, click on Apply or OK.

Adjusting the Appearance

The Appearance page lets you change the way Windows assigns colors and fonts to various parts of the screen. If you're using a monochrome monitor (no color), altering the colors may still have some effect (the amount will depend on how you installed Windows).

Windows sets itself up using a default color scheme that's fine for most screens—and if you're happy with your colors as they are, you might not even want to futz around with them.

However, the color settings for Windows are very flexible and easy to modify. You can modify the color setting of just about any part of a Windows screen. For those of you who are very particular about color choices, this can be done manually, choosing colors from a palette or even mixing your own with the Custom Colors feature. Once created, custom colors and color setups can be saved on disk for later use or automatically loaded with each Windows session. For more expedient color reassignments, there's a number of supplied color schemes to choose from.

On clicking on the Appearance tab, your dialog box will look like that shown in Figure 7.20. The various parts of the Windows graphical environment that you can alter are shown in the top portion and named in the lower portion. As you select color schemes, these samples change so you can see what the effect will be without having to go back into Windows proper.

Loading an Existing Color Scheme

Before playing with the custom color palette, first try loading the supplied ones; you may find one you like:

1. Click open the drop-down Color Schemes list box.

 TIP You can always toggle a drop-down list box open and closed from the keyboard by pressing Alt-↓ or Alt-↑.

2. Choose a selection whose name suits your fancy. The colors in the dialog box will change, showing the scheme. Try them out. Some are garish, others more subtle. Adjusting your monitor may make a

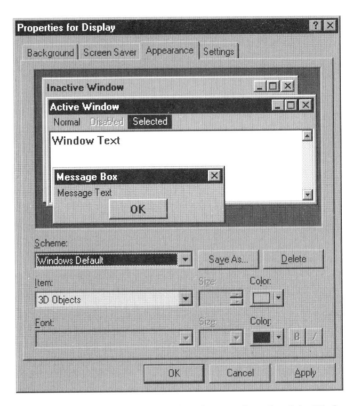

Figure 7.20   The dialog box for setting the colors, fonts, and metrics of the Windows environment

difference, too. (You can cycle through the different supplied color schemes without selecting them from the drop-down list: with the Color Schemes space highlighted, just press the ↑ and ↓ keys. The sample screen elements will change to reflect each color scheme as its name appears in the Color Schemes box.)

3. Click on Apply or OK to apply the settings to all Windows activities.

Microsoft has incorporated a few color schemes that may enhance the operation of your computer:

▶ On LCD screens that you'll be using in bright light, you might try the setting called High-Contrast White.

▶ If your eyes are weary, you may want to try one of the settings with the words Large or Extra Large in the name. These cause menus, dialog boxes, and title bars to appear in large letters.

Choosing Your Own Colors and Other Stuff

If you don't like the color schemes supplied, you can make up your own. It's most efficient to start with a scheme that's close to what you want and then modify it. Once you like the scheme, you may save it under a new name for later use. Here are the steps:

1. Select the color scheme you want to modify.

2. Click on the Windows element whose color you want to change. Its name should appear in the Item area. You can click on menu name, title bars, scroll bars, buttons—anything you see. You can also select a screen element from the Item drop-down list box rather than by clicking directly on the item.

3. Now click on the Color button to open up a series of colors you can choose from.

4. Click on the color you want. This assigns it to the item. Repeat the process for each color you want to change.

5. Want more colors? Click on the Other button. This pops up another 48 colors to choose from. Click on one of the 48 colors (or patterns and intensity levels, if you have a monochrome monitor) to assign it to the chosen element.

6. Once the color scheme suits your fancy, you can save it. (It will stay in force for future Windows sessions even if you don't save it, but you'll lose the settings next time you change colors or select another scheme.) Click on Save Scheme.

7. Type in a name for the color scheme and click on OK.

TIP   If you want to remove a scheme (such as one you never use), select it from the drop-down list and click on the Delete button.

Before I get into explaining custom colors, there are two other major adjustments you can make to your display—the fonts used for various screen elements, and Windows *metrics*, which affect how big or small some screen elements are.

In Windows 3.x this wasn't possible, but now you can choose the font for elements such as title bars, menus, and dialog boxes. You can get pretty wacky with this and make your Windows 95 setup look very strange if you want. Or, on the more practical side, you can compensate for high-resolution monitors by making your menus more easily readable by using large point sizes in screen elements. In any case, you're no longer stuck with boring sans serif fonts such as Arial or MS Sans Serif. For an example, see Figure 7.21.

1. On the Appearance page, simply click on the element whose font you want to change.

2. In the lowest line of the dialog box, the current font for that element appears. Just open the drop-down list box and choose another font if you want. You may also change the size, the color, and the style (bold or italic) of the font for that element.

3. Be sure to save the scheme if you want to keep it.

Finally, consider that many screen elements—such as the borders of windows—have a constant predetermined size. However, you might want to change these settings. If you have trouble grabbing the borders of windows, for example, you might want to make them larger. If you want icons on your desktop and in folders to line up closer or farther apart, you can do that, too.

Figure 7.21 You can use any installed fonts when defining your screen elements.

1. Simply open the list and choose the item whose size you want to adjust. Some of the items are not represented in the upper section of the dialog box. They're things that appear in other parts of Windows 95, such as *vertical icon spacing* or *selected items*. You'll have to experiment a bit to see the effects of these items.

2. Click on the up or down size buttons to adjust.

3. Click on Apply to check out the effects of the changes. You might want to switch to another application via the Taskbar to see how things look.

4. If you don't like the effects of the changes you've made, just return to the Control Panel and click on Cancel. Or you can just select another color scheme, because the screen metrics are recorded on each color scheme.

Making Up Your Own Colors

If you don't like the colors that are available, you can create your own. There are 16 slots at the bottom of the larger color palette for storing colors you set using another fancy dialog box called the color refiner. Here's how:

1. Click on the Color button and then choose Other. This opens the enlarged color-selection box.

2. In that box, click on Define Custom Colors. Now the Color Refiner dialog box appears (see Figure 7.22).

There are two cursors that you work with here. One is the *luminosity bar* and the other is the *color refiner cursor*. To make a long story short, you simply drag these around one at a time until the color in the box at the lower left is the shade you want. As you do, the numbers in the boxes below the color refiner will change. *Luminosity* is the amount of brightness in the color. *Hue* is the actual shade or color. All colors are composed of red, green, and blue. *Saturation* is the degree of purity of the color; it is decreased by adding gray to the color and increased by subtracting it. You can also type in the numbers or click on the arrows next to the numbers if you want, but it's easier to use the cursors. When you like the color, click on Add Color to add the new color to the palette.

You can switch between a solid color and a color made up of various dots of several colors. Solid colors look less grainy on your screen but give you fewer choices. The Color|Solid box shows the difference between the two. If you click on this box before adding the color to the palette, the solid color closest to the actual color you chose will be added instead of the grainier composite color.

Luminosity bar ————

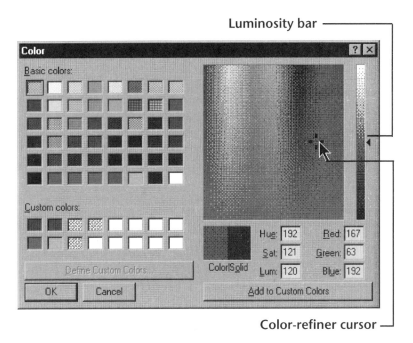

Color-refiner cursor —

Figure 7.22   The custom color selector lets you create new colors.

Once a color is added to the palette, you can modify it. Just click on it, move the cursors around, and then click on Add Color again. Click on Close to close the dialog box. Then continue to assign colors with the palette. When you are content with the color assignments, click on OK. If you decide after toying around that you don't want to implement the color changes, just click on Cancel.

Driver Settings

The last tab page of the Display applet tweaks the video driver responsible for your video card's ability to display Windows. These settings are a little more substantial than those that adjust whether dialog boxes are mauve or chartreuse because they load a different driver or bump your video card up or down into a completely different resolution and color depth, changing the amount of information you can see on the screen at once (see Figure 7.23). This option is also the

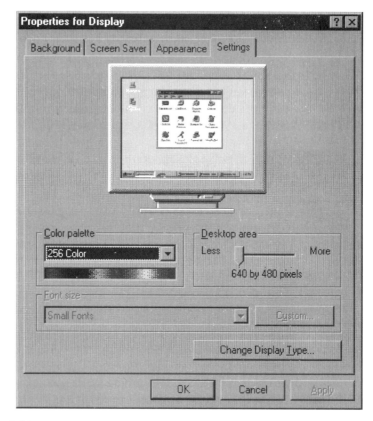

Figure 7.23   *The Settings page of the Display applet controls the video card's device driver. With most video systems, the slider lets you adjust the screen resolution on the fly. Changing color depth requires a restart, however.*

one to use for installing a Windows 3.x video driver for your video card just in case there isn't a Windows 95 driver for it.

Color Palette

Let's start with the color palette. Assuming your video card was properly identified when you installed Windows 95, this drop-down list box will include all the legitimate options your card is capable of. As you may know, different video cards are capable of displaying differing numbers of colors simultaneously. Your monitor is not the limiting factor here (with the exception of color LCD screens like those on laptops, which do have limitations); the limitations have to do with how much RAM is on your video card. All modern analog color monitors for PCs are capable of displaying 16 million colors, which is dubbed True Color.

It's possible that the drop-down list box will include color amounts (called *depths*) that exceed your video card's capabilities, in which case such a choice just won't have any effect. On the other hand, if your setting is currently 16 colors and your screen can support 256 or higher, Windows will look a lot prettier if you choose 256 and then choose one of the 256-color schemes from the Appearance tab page.

TECH TIP When you change the setting in the color palette and OK the box or click on Apply, you'll be prompted to reboot. This is because Windows 95 has to load in a different video driver altogether, not simply adjust the one currently running.

Desktop Area

The Desktop Area setting is something avid Windows users have been wanting for years. With Windows 3.x, changing this parameter (essentially the screen resolution) meant running Windows Setup, choosing a different video driver, and rebooting the machine and Windows. Now, with the right video card, you can change the resolution as you work. Some jobs—such as working with large spreadsheets, databases, CAD, or typesetting—are much more efficient with more data displayed on the screen. Because higher resolutions require a tradeoff in clarity and make on-screen objects smaller, eyestrain can be minimized by going to a lower resolution, such as 640-by-480 pixels (a pixel equals one dot on the screen). Note that there is a relationship between the color depth and the resolution that's available. This is because your video card can only have so much RAM on it. That RAM can be used to display extra colors *or* extra resolution, but not both. So, if you bump up the colors, you won't have as many resolution options. If you find the dialog box won't let you choose the resolution you want, try dropping the color palette setting to 16 colors.

To change the Desktop area:

1. Run Control Panel and run the Display applet.

2. Choose the Settings tab page.

3. Grab the slider and move it right or left. Notice how the little screen in the box indicates the additional room you're going to have on your real screen to do your work (and also how everything will get relatively smaller to make this happen, because your monitor doesn't get any larger!). Figure 7.24 illustrates.

NOTE   As of this writing, virtually all laptop computers have screens that can only display one resolution—640-by-480 pixels. (There are a few exceptions that run at 800 by 600.) Unless the computer is hooked up to an external monitor, this will be the only workable choice. If you try a higher resolution, the choice won't work, and the applet will revert to the previous setting. Check the computer's manual if in doubt about which external monitor resolutions are supported by your laptop.

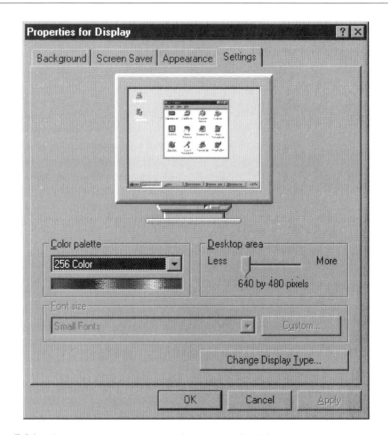

Figure 7.24   Change your screen resolution by dragging the slider. Here I've chosen 800 by 600.

4. Click on Apply. You'll now see this message:

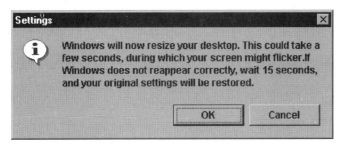

Go ahead and click on OK to try the setting. If your screen looks screwy and you can't read anything, don't worry. It will return to normal in about 15 seconds. If, on the other hand, you like what you see, there will be another dialog box asking you to confirm that you want to keep the current setting. Confirming that box makes the new setting permanent until you change it again.

TIP   If you don't change the Palette setting, you should be able to change the Desktop area without restarting Windows.

Font Size

As you may know, some screen drivers use different size fonts for screen elements such as dialog boxes and menus. When you switch to a high Desktop-area resolution, such as 1,280 by 1,024, these screen elements can get quite small, blurry, and difficult to read. For this reason, you can adjust the font size. Of course, you can do this via the Fonts settings on the Appearance page as discussed earlier. But doing it here is a little simpler. If you select a Desktop area above 640 by 480, you'll have the choice of Small Fonts or Large Fonts. Especially for resolutions of 1,024 by 768 or above, you might want to check out the Large Fonts selection from this drop-down list box. If you want, you can also choose a custom-size font by clicking on the Custom button, which lets you declare the amount that you want the fonts scaled up. The range is from 100 to 200 percent.

Display Type

Finally, the Settings box allows you to actually change the type of video card and monitor that Windows 95 thinks you have. If you install a new video card or monitor, you should update this information.

 NOTE As discussed earlier in this chapter, you can also do this from the Add New Hardware and System applets.

1. Click on the Change Adaptor button. The box shown in Figure 7.25 appears.

2. Check the settings to see that they correspond to what you have. The adaptor type may not make sense to you because it often lists the type of video chip rather than the brand of video board you have.

3. If you want to change either of the settings, just click on the Change button. In the resulting box, the Show Compatible Devices option is normally selected and will result in a list of video adaptors or monitors that are compatible with what you have. Because the computer doesn't actually know what type of monitor you have (unless it's a fancy Plug-and-Play monitor), you'll have to take its assumption with a grain of salt. You can tell it otherwise. Click on Show all Devices and choose from the resulting list. In case you don't know what kind of

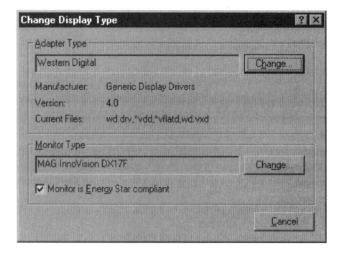

Figure 7.25   *Changing the video adaptor and display type is necessary when you install new video hardware.*

monitor you have because it doesn't have a name or the name isn't in the list of monitors (there are many no-name monitors around), choose Generic Monitor. Then narrow down the description by choosing one from the right-hand list that matches yours. You'll have to look in your monitor's manual to figure this out. Choose the highest resolution the monitor can support at the refresh rate listed. For example, if your monitor can do 1,280 by 1,024 at a refresh rate of 70 Hz, choose that.

 CAUTION   If you specify a refresh rating that is too high for your monitor, trying to expand the Desktop area to a larger size may not work. You'll just get a mess on the screen. If this happens, try using a setting with a lower refresh rate, such as 60 Hz or *interlaced*. The image may flicker a bit more, but at least it will be clearly visible.

4. If you have just received a new driver for your video adaptor card and want to use that instead of the one supplied with Windows 95 (or Windows 95 doesn't include a driver), click on the Have Disk button and follow the directions.

Adjusting the Mouse

You can adjust six aspects of your mouse's operation:

▶ left-right button reversal

▶ double-click speed

▶ look of the pointers

▶ tracking speed

▶ mouse trails

▶ mouse type and driver

Switching the Buttons and Setting Double-Click Speed

If you're left-handed, you may want to switch the mouse around to use it on the left side of the computer and reverse the buttons. The main button then becomes the right button instead of the left one. If

Part 2

Exploring Windows 95

you use other programs outside of Windows that don't allow this, however, it might just add to the confusion. If you only use the mouse in Windows programs and you're left-handed, then it's worth a try.

1. Run the Control Panel and double-click on Mouse. Then click on the first tab page of the dialog box (Figure 7.26).

2. Click on the Left-handed button as shown in the figure. Then click on Apply to check it out. Don't like it? Revert to the original setting and click on Apply again.

On the same page, you have the double-click speed setting. Double-click speed determines how fast you have to double-click to make a double-click operation work (that is, to run a program from its icon, to open a document from its icon, or to select a word. If the double-click speed is too fast, it's difficult for your fingers to click fast enough. If it's too slow, you end up running programs or opening and closing

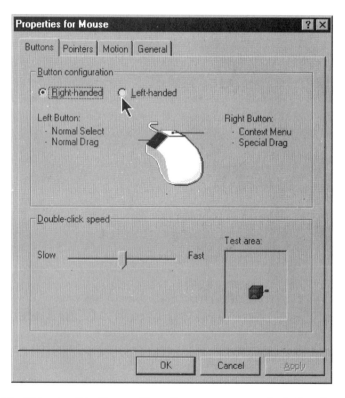

Figure 7.26   First page of the Mouse settings. Here you can reverse the buttons for use by left-handed people. You can also adjust the double-click speed.

windows unexpectedly. Double-click on the Jack-in-the-box to try out the new double-click speed. Jack will jump out or back into the box if the double-click registered. If you're not faring well, adjust the slider and try again.

> **NOTE**   You don't have to click on Apply to test the slider settings. Just moving the slider instantly affects the mouse's double-click speed.

Setting Your Pointers

Your mouse pointer's shape changes depending on what you are pointing at and what Windows 95 is doing. If you are pointing to a window border, the pointer becomes a two-headed arrow. If Windows 95 is busy, it becomes a sandglass. When you are editing text, it becomes an I-beam, and so on.

You can customize your cursors for the fun of it or to increase visibility. You can even install animated cursors that look really cute and keep you amused while you wait for some process to complete.

> **TIP**   Animated cursors don't come with Windows 95. But you can get some from anyone with Windows NT. Just copy the ANI files from the NT machine into your Windows 95 directory. You'll probably be able to find ANI files on BBSs and information services such as Microsoft Network and CompuServe. See Chapter 32 for information about the animated cursors included in Microsoft Plus.

To change the cursor settings:

1. Click on the Pointers tab page of the Mouse dialog box (see Figure 7.27).

2. The list shows which pointers are currently assigned to which activities. To change an assignment, click on an item in the list.

3. Next, if you've changed the shape and want to revert, click on Use Default to go back to the normal pointer shape that Windows 95 came shipped with. Otherwise, choose Browse and use the Browse box to load the cursor you want. When you click on a cursor in the Browse box, it will be displayed at the bottom of the box for you to examine in advance—a thoughtful feature. Even animated cursors will do their thing right in the Browse box.

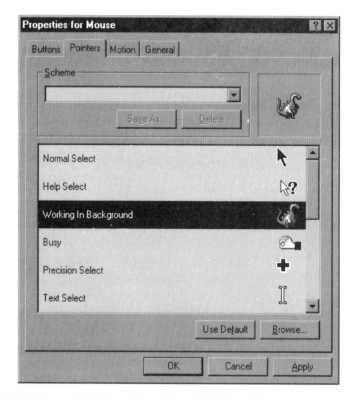

Figure 7.27   Choose pointer shapes for various activities here. As you can see, I have a couple of weird ones installed, such as the walking dinosaur instead of the sandglass.

4.   Click on Open. The cursor will now be applied to the activity in question.

You can save pointer schemes just as you can colors. If you want to set up a number of different schemes (one for each person in the house, for example), just get the settings assigned the way you like, enter a name in the scheme area, and click on Save As. To later select a scheme, open the drop-down list box, select the scheme's name, and click on Apply or OK.

Setting the Pointer Motion

Two very useful adjustments can be made to the way to the mouse responds to the motion of your hand—speed and trails (Figure 7.28).

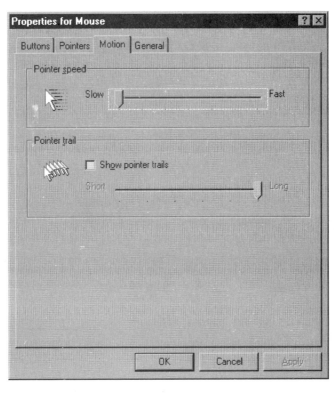

Figure 7.28   You can adjust the speed at which the mouse pointer moves and whether you'll see trails.

Pointer speed is the speed at which the mouse pointer moves relative to the movement of the mouse. Believe it or not, mouse motion is actually measured in *Mickeys*! (Somebody out there has a sense of humor.) A Mickey equals $\frac{1}{100}$ of an inch of mouse movement. The tracking-speed setting lets you adjust the relationship of Mickeys to pixels. If you want to be very exact in your cursor movement, you'll want to slow the tracking speed, requiring more Mickeys per pixel. However, this requires more hand motion for the same corresponding cursor motion. If your desk is crammed and your coordination is very good, then you can increase the speed (fewer Mickeys per pixel). If you use the mouse with MS-DOS programs that use their own mouse driver, you might want to adjust the Windows mouse speed to match that of your other programs so you won't need to mentally adjust when you use such non-Windows programs.

Incidentally, if you think the mouse runs too slowly in your non-Windows applications, there may be a fix. Contact your mouse's maker. For example, if you're using a Logitech mouse, a program called Click that is supplied with the Logitech mouse lets you easily control its tracking. See the Logitech manual for details.

The other setting—Mouse trails—creates a shadow of the mouse's path whenever you move it. Some people find it annoying, but for those who have trouble finding the pointer on the screen, it's a blessing. Mouse trails are particularly helpful when using Windows on passive-matrix or dual-scan laptop computers, where the pointer often disappears when you move it.

Here are the steps for changing these items:

1. Drag the speed slider one way or another to increase or decrease the motion of the pointer relative to your hand (or thumb in the case of a trackball) motion. Nothing may happen until you click on Apply. Adjust as necessary. Try aiming for some item on the screen and see how well you succeed. Having the motion too fast can result in straining your muscles and holding the mouse too tight. It's ergonomically more sound to use a little slower setting that requires more hand motion.

2. If you want trails, click the option box on and adjust the slider. You don't have to click on Apply to see the effects.

3. Click on OK or Apply to make it all official.

General Mouse Settings

The last tab page lets you change the mouse's software driver and possibly make changes that the driver has built in. The type of mouse is listed in the box. If this looks wrong or you're changing the mouse to another type, click on Change and choose the desired mouse type from the resulting Select Device box. See the discussion about changing the Display Adaptor, above, if in doubt about how to use the Select Device dialog box.

In some cases, you'll have an Options button on this tab page. The options will vary from mouse to mouse. They may include such things as choosing to have the mouse pointers be black rather than white or be transparent rather than opaque. For example, the Options for my Ballpoint mouse are shown in Figure 7.29.

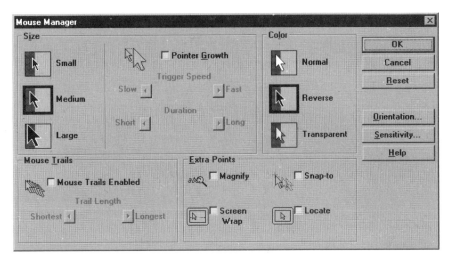

Figure 7.29   *Some mouse drivers have additional options built in. The last tab page of the Mouse applet gives you access to them.*

Chapter 8

Printers and Printing with Windows 95

FEATURING

If your printer is of the Plug-and-Play variety, your Windows 95 system will have a so-called default printer driver already installed. This means you'll be able to print from any Windows program without worrying about anything more than turning on the printer, checking that it has paper, and choosing the File ➤ Print command from whatever programs you use. If your printer isn't Plug-and-Play compatible, wasn't plugged in at the time of installation, or you weren't upgrading over a previous version of Windows for which you had printers set up already, you'll have to manually set up your printer before you can print. This chapter tells you how to do that and how to manage the use of your printer to get your work done.

As with Windows 3.1, unless you specify otherwise, Windows programs hand off data to Windows 95, which in turn *spools* the data to a specified printer. Spooling means temporarily putting on the hard disk the information that's really headed for the printer. Your document then gets sent out to the printer at the slow speed that the printer can receive it. This lets you get back to work with your program sooner. You can even print additional documents, stacking up a load of jobs for the printer to print. This stack is called a *queue*.

In Windows 3.x and Windows NT, a program called Print Manager is responsible for doing the spooling and managing the print jobs. Windows 95 nomenclature dispenses with the term "Print Manager," even though the same functionality is provided. Now you simply look at what's "inside" a printer by clicking on the printer's icon. This opens a window and displays the print queue for that printer. In reality, however, there *is* a spooler program and Print Manager-like thing in Windows 95, and that is how I'll refer to the window that displays and works with the print queue.

TECH TIP Unlike Windows NT, Windows 95 doesn't always prevent a program from writing directly to the printer port. (In Windows NT, any such attempt by programs to directly write to hardware, such as an LPT port, is trapped by the security manager.) Windows 95 offers less security in this regard. Unless a port has a printer associated with it, an application can directly access that port. Also, if you shell out of Windows 95 and run MS-DOS mode, direct port access is allowed.

NOTE   MS-DOS programs can also be spooled so you can get back to work with your DOS or Windows programs while printing happens in the background.

When you print from a Windows program, Print Manager receives the data, queues up the jobs, routes them to the correct printer, and, when necessary, issues error or other appropriate messages to print-job originators. As in Windows 3.11 and NT, you can use the Print Manager user interface to manage your print jobs. Print Manager makes it easy to check out what's printing and see where your job(s) are in the print queue relative to other people's print jobs. You may also be permitted to rearrange the print queue, delete print jobs, or pause and resume a print job so you can reload or otherwise service the printer.

In Windows 3.11, printer-driver installation and configuration (making connections) are done through the Printers applet in Control Panel, while print-job management is done through the Print Manager program. Windows 95 combines both functions in the Printers folder. (The Control Panel still has a Printers icon, but it simply calls up the Printers folder.) Each printer you've installed appears in the Printers folder, along with an additional icon called Add Printer that lets you set up new printers. Printer icons in the folder appear and behave like any other object: You can delete them at will, create new ones, and set their properties. Double-clicking on a printer in the folder displays its print queue and lets you manipulate the queue. Commands on the menus let you to install, configure, connect, disconnect, and remove printers and drivers.

This chapter explains these features, as well as procedures for local and network print-queue management. Some basics of print management also are discussed, providing a primer for the uninitiated or for those whose skills are a little rusty.

A Print-Manager Primer

Windows 95's Print Manager feature mix is quite rich. Here are the highlights:

▶ You can add, modify, and remove printers right from the Printers folder (available from My Computer, Explorer, the Start button, or Control Panel).

▶ An object-oriented interface using printer icons eliminates the abstraction of thinking about the relationship of printer drivers, connections, and physical printers. You simply add a printer and set its properties. Once added, it appears as a named printer in the Printers folder.

▶ Once set up, you can easily choose to share a printer on the network so others can print to it. You can give it a useful name such as *LaserJet in Fred's Office* so people on the network know what it is.

▶ If you're on a network, you can manage network-printer connections by displaying available printers, sharing your local printer, and connecting to and disconnecting from network printers.

▶ Because of Windows 95's multithreading and preemptive multitasking, 32-bit Windows 95 programs will print more smoothly than under Windows 3.x. You can start printing and immediately go back to work; you don't have to wait until spooling for Print Manager to finish. (This won't be true for 16-bit programs.)

▶ While one document is printing out, other programs can start print jobs. Additional documents are simply added to the queue and will print in turn.

▶ Default settings for such options as number of copies, paper tray, page orientation, and so forth are automatically used during print jobs so you don't have to manually set them each time.

▶ For the curious, a window can be opened displaying jobs currently being printed or in the queue waiting to be printed, along with an indication of the current print job's progress.

▶ You can easily rearrange the order of the print queue and delete print jobs.

▶ You can choose whether printing begins as soon as the first page is spooled to the hard disk or after the last page of a document is spooled.

▶ You can temporarily pause or resume printing without causing printer time-out problems.

Adding a New Printer

As I mentioned, the Setup program prompts you to install a printer. If you elected to do so, or if you've installed printers in Windows 3.1, you'll be somewhat familiar with the procedure. If your printer is already installed and seems to be working fine, you probably can skip this section. In fact, if you're interested in nothing more than printing from one of your programs without viewing the queue, printing to a network printer, or making adjustments to your current printer's settings, just skip down to *Printing from a Program*, below. However, if you need to install a new printer, modify or customize your current installation, or add additional printers to your setup, read on to learn about how to:

▶ add a new printer

▶ select the printer port and make other connection settings

▶ set preferences for a printer

▶ install a printer driver that's not listed

▶ set the default printer

▶ select a printer when more than one is installed

▶ delete a printer from your system

About Printer Installation

As I mention in the Appendix, before installing hardware, including printers, you should read any last-minute printed or on-screen material that comes with Window 95. Often such material is full of useful information about specific types of hardware, including printers. Because these are last-minute details, I can't include them in this book. Look for a Readme file or something else similar on your Desktop that you can open by double-clicking on it. Then look through the file for information about your printer.

With that said, here is the overall game plan for adding a new printer. It's actually a really easy process thanks to the Add a Printer Wizard that walks you through it.

▶ Run Add a Printer from the Printers folder.

▶ Declare whether the printer is local (directly connected to your computer) or on the network.

▶ Declare what kind of printer it is.

▶ Select the printer's port and relevant port settings.

▶ Give the printer a name.

▶ Print a test page.

▶ Check and possibly alter the default printer settings, such as the DPI (dots per inch) setting and memory settings.

After these steps are complete, your printer should work as expected. Once installed, you can customize each printer's setup by modifying its properties, such as:

▶ specifying the amount of time you want Windows to keep trying to print a document before alerting you to a printer problem

▶ specifying the share name for the printer so other network users can find it when they search the network for printers

▶ setting job defaults pertaining to paper tray, two-sided printing, and paper orientation

▶ stipulating a *separator file* (a file, usually one page long, that prints between each print job)

▶ selecting the default printer if you have more than one printer installed

▶ choosing whether your printer should substitute its own fonts for certain Windows TrueType fonts

▶ selecting printer settings relevant to page orientation, color matching, greyscaling, size scaling, type of paper feed, halftone imaging, and when file-header information (such as a PostScript "preamble") is sent to the printer

Part 2

Exploring Windows 95

▶ set whether you want to share the printer for use by others on the network

▶ set whether documents will go directly to the printer or will go through the spooler

The good news is that normally you won't have to futz with any such settings. The other good news is, unlike in Windows 3.x and NT, getting to any one of these settings is now a piece of cake. You don't have to wind your way through a bevy of dialog boxes to target a given setting. The Properties dialog box has tab pages, so it's a cinch to find the one you want.

> **TIP** The Properties box has context-sensitive Help built in. Click on an element in a dialog box and press F1, or click on the ? button, then on the item. A relevant Help topic will appear.

> **NOTE** Advanced printer-security issues—such as conducting printer-access auditing and setting ownership—are not features of Windows 95. Windows 95 *does* support use of a password when sharing a printer, however, which is explained later in this chapter.

About Adding Printers

Before running the Wizard, let's consider when you'd need to add a new printer to your Windows 95 configuration:

▶ You didn't tell Windows 95 what kind of printer you have when you first set up Windows.

▶ You're connecting a new printer directly to your computer.

▶ Someone has connected a new printer to the network and wants to use it from your computer.

▶ You want to print to disk files that can later be sent to a particular type of printer.

▶ You want to set up multiple printer configurations (preferences) for a single physical printer so you can switch between them without having to change your printer setup before each print job.

Notice that a great deal of flexibility exists here, especially in the case of the last item. Because of the modularity of Windows 95's internal design, even though you might have only one physical printer, you can create any number of printer definitions for it, each with different characteristics.

TECH TIP These definitions are actually called printers, but you can think of them as printer names, aliases, or named virtual devices.

For example, you might want one definition set up to print on legal-sized paper in landscape orientation while another prints with normal paper in portrait orientation. Each of these two "printers" would actually use the same physical printer to print out on. While you're working with Windows 95's manual, online help, and this book, keep this terminology in mind. The word "printer" often doesn't really mean a physical printer. It usually means a printer setup that you've created with the Wizard. It's a collection of settings that typically points to a physical printer, but it could just as well create a print file instead.

About Printer Drivers

And finally, consider that a printer can't just connect to your computer and mysteriously print a fancy page of graphics or even a boring old page of text. You need a printer *driver.* The printer driver (actually a file on your hard disk) translates your text file to commands that tell your printer how to print your file. Because different brands and models of printer use different commands for such things as *move up a line, print a circle in the middle of the page, print the letter A,* and so on, a specialized printer driver is needed for each type of printer.

NOTE Because some printers are actually functionally equivalent, a driver for a popular brand and model of printer (for example, an Epson or a Hewlett-Packard) often masquerades under different names for other printers.

TECH TIP   DOS programs require a print driver for the application, too. For instance, WordPerfect 5.1 running in a DOS session under Windows 95 will use a DOS printer driver *and* a Windows 95 printer driver to work under Windows 95.

When you add a printer, unless you're installing a Plug-and-Play–compatible printer, you're asked to choose the brand and model of printer. With Plug-and-Play printers, if the printer is attached and turned on, Windows 95 queries the printer and the printer responds with its make and model number. This is because Windows 95 can't usually detect this information on its own. Eventually all printers will be Plug-and-Play compatible, but until then, you'll typically have to tell Windows what printer you have so it knows which printer driver to install.

A good printer driver takes advantage of all your printer's capabilities, such as its built-in fonts and graphics features. A poor printer driver might succeed in printing only draft-quality text, even from a sophisticated printer.

If you're the proud owner of some offbeat brand of printer, you may be alarmed when you can't find your printer listed in the box when you run the Wizard. But don't worry, the printer manufacturer might be able to supply one. The procedure for installing manufacturer-supplied drivers is covered later in this chapter.

 NOTE   If your printer isn't included in the list, consult *When You Don't Find Your Printer in the List*, later in this chapter.

Running the Wizard to Add a New Printer

Microsoft has made the previously arduous chore of adding a printer something that's much more easily mastered by a majority of computer users. Here's what you have to do:

1. Open the Printers folder by clicking on the Start button and choosing Settings ➤ Printers. Two other paths are from My Computer and from Control Panel.

TECH TIP   Depending on the type of access control you stipulate from the Access Control tab of the Network applet in the Control Panel, you may want to password-protect your printer when you share it on the network. This helps guard against a printer being continually tied up with print jobs from an unauthorized user somewhere on the network. Just share your printer with password protection as discussed later in this chapter, or if part of an NT domain, restrict access to your resources via the Control Panel applet mentioned above (see Part V of this book).

2. Double-click on Add Printer, as shown in Figure 8.1.

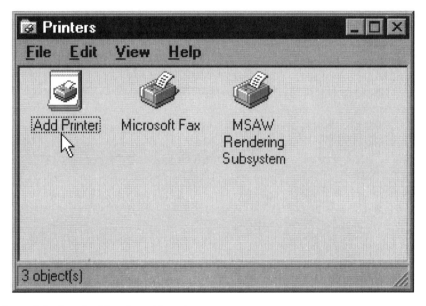

Figure 8.1   Run the Wizard to add a printer.

3. A dialog box like that in Figure 8.2 appears. Click on Next.

4. You're asked whether the printer is *local* or *network*. Because here I'm describing how to install a network printer, choose Network, then click on Next. (If you are setting up a local printer that is connected directly to your computer, at this point you should skip down to the next section, *Adding a Local Printer.*)

5. You'll now be asked two questions, as shown in Figure 8.3.

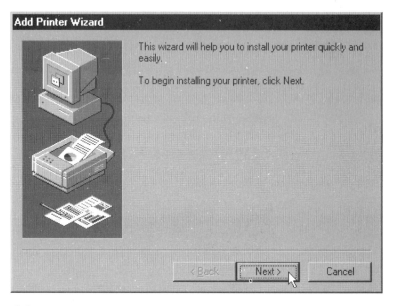

Figure 8.2   *Beginning the process of adding the printer*

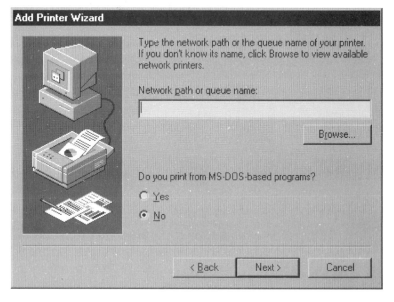

Figure 8.3   *When choosing a network printer, you have to specify the printer's path and declare whether you want to print from DOS programs.*

NOTE   For a printer to appear in the network listing, it has to have been added to the host computer's setup (the computer the printer is directly attached to) using the steps in *Adding a Local Printer*, below. It must also be shared for use on the network.

6. You don't have to type in the complicated path name for the location of the printer on the network. Just click on Browse, and up comes a list of the printers on the network. For example, in Figure 8.4 you see the network printer *Apple*. You may have to double-click on Entire Network or click on the + sign next to a computer to display the printer(s) attached to it. Either way, just highlight the printer you want to connect to and click on OK.

If the network printer is currently *offline*, you'll be told that you have to wait until it comes back online before you can use it but that you can go ahead and install it if you want. However, as long as it's offline, you'll be asked to specify the brand and model of the printer because

Part 2

Exploring Windows 95

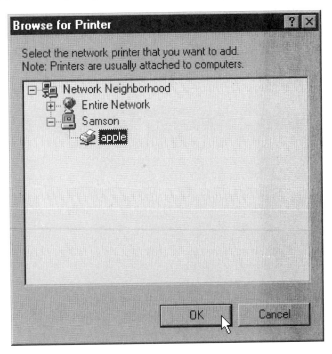

Figure 8.4   *The Browse box graphically displays computers that have shared networked printers available for others to use. Click on the printer you want, then click on OK.*

the Wizard can't figure out what kind of printer it is when it is unavailable for your computer to question. If you can alert the owner of the printer to put it online (they have to right-click on the printer's icon at their computer and turn off the Work Offline setting), then you won't have to specify these settings. If this isn't possible, just select the brand name and model from the resulting list.

7. Back at the Wizard dialog box, decide whether you want to print from DOS applications or not.

▶ If you choose Yes, click on Next, and you'll be asked to choose a printer port to associate the output with (such as LPT1, LPT2, and so on). Usually this will be LPT1. However, if you have a local printer attached to your computer using LPT1, you should choose a different port, such as LPT2. This doesn't mean the printer has to be connected to your LPT (parallel) port, it only tells Windows 95 how to fake the DOS program into thinking that it's printing to a normal parallel port. Click on Capture Printer Port, choose accordingly, and click on OK. Then click on Next.

▶ If you won't be printing from DOS applications to this new printer, choose No, and you won't be asked about the port. Just click on Next.

8. Now you're asked to name the printer (Figure 8.5). This is the name that will show up when you're setting up to print from a program such as a word processor, spreadsheet, or whatever. Type in a name for the printer; the maximum length is 32 characters. Typically, the type of printer, such as HP Desk Jet 320, goes here. There's also a description line in which you can be even more descriptive about the printer, accepting up to 255 characters. Specifying the location of the printer in this box is a good idea so network users can find a printer when browsing and will know where to pick up their hard copy when a print job is completed.

9. In this same dialog box you'll have to decide whether you want the printer to be the *default* printer. The default printer is the one that programs will assume you want to print to. Some programs don't let you choose which printer a document will print out on, so setting the default printer can be important. If you want this network printer to be the default printer, remember that the computer the printer is directly connected to (in the example here, that would be the computer called Samson) has to be up and running for the printer to work. So, if you have a local printer on your machine as well, it's better to make that the default printer.

10. Finally, you're asked if you want to print a test page. It's a good idea to do this. Turn on the printer, make sure it has paper in it, and click on Finish. You may be prompted to supply a printer driver for the printer, depending on the type of network you're connecting to and whether a driver is already on your machine. If you're told that a driver file for the printer is already on your machine, you'll be asked if you want to use it or load a new one from the Windows 95 CD-ROM or floppy disks. It's usually easier to use the existing driver. If the driver isn't on your hard disk, you'll be instructed to insert the disk containing the driver.

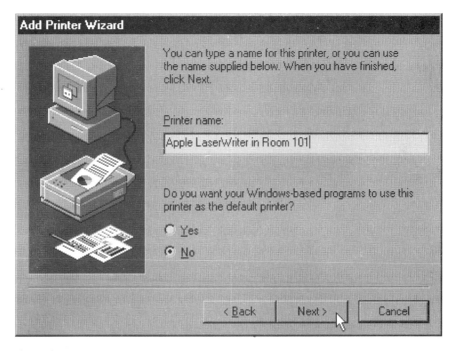

Figure 8.5 Name the printer and choose whether it's going to be your default printer.

Part
2

Exploring Windows 95

11. The test page will be sent to the printer; it should print out in a few minutes. Then you'll be asked if it printed OK. If it didn't print correctly, click on No, and you'll be shown some troubleshooting information containing some questions and answers. The most likely fixes for the malady will be described. If the page printed OK, click on Yes, and you're done.

If all went well, you now have a network printer set up and ready to go. The new printer appears in your Printers folder.

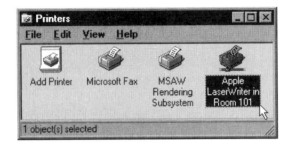

Adding a Local Printer

If you want to add a local printer rather than a networked printer, the steps are a little different from what I explained above.

1. Follow the first three steps in the section above.

2. In the box that asks whether the printer is local or networked, click on Local. Then click on Next.

3. You're presented with a list of brands and models. In the left column scroll the list, find the maker of your printer, and click on it. Then in the right column choose the model number or name that matches your printer. Be sure to select the exact printer model, not just the correct brand name. Consult your printer's manual if you're in doubt about the model. What you enter here determines which printer driver file is used for this printer's definition. Figure 8.6 shows an example for an HP LaserJet IV.

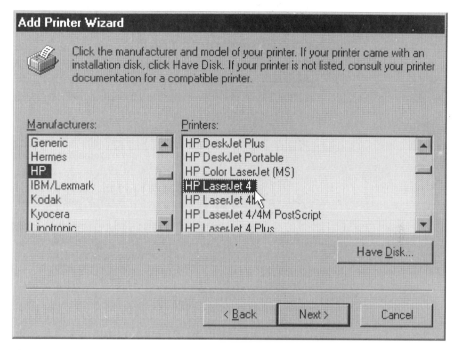

Figure 8.6 *Choosing the printer make and model; here I'm choosing a Hewlett-Packard Laser-Jet IV.*

4. Click on Next: Now you'll see a list of ports. You have to tell Windows which port the printer is connected to. (A port usually refers to the connector on the computer.)

Most often the port will be the parallel printer port called LPT1 (Line Printer #1). Unless you know your printer is connected to another port, such as LPT2 or a serial port (such as COM1 or COM2), select LPT1 as in Figure 8.7.

5. Click on Next. Now you can give the printer a name (see Figure 8.8).

NOTE If the printer will be shared with DOS and 16-bit Windows users (such as people running Windows for Workgroups 3.11), you might want to limit this name to twelve characters because that's the maximum length those users will see when they are browsing for printers.

Port	Notes
LPT1, LPT2, LPT3	The most common setting is LPT1 because most PC-type printers hook up to the LPT1 parallel port. Click on Configure Port if you want to turn off the ability to print to this printer from DOS programs.
COM1, COM2, COM3, COM4	If you know your printer is of the serial variety, it's probably connected to the COM1 port. If COM1 is tied up for use with some other device, such as a modem, use COM2. If you choose a COM port, click on Configure Port to check the communications settings in the resulting dialog box. Set the baud rate, data bits, parity, start and stop bits, and flow control to match those of the printer being attached. Refer to the printer's manual to determine what the settings should be.
File	This is for printing to a disk file instead of to the printer. Later, the file can be sent directly to the printer or sent to someone on floppy disk or over a modem. When you print to this printer name, you are prompted to enter a file name. (See the section in this chapter titled *Printing to a Disk File Instead of a Printer*.)

Table 8.1 **Printer Ports**

6. Also set whether the printer will be the default printer for Windows programs.

7. Finally, you're asked if you want to print a test page. It's a good idea to do this. Turn on the printer, make sure it has paper in it, and click on Finish. If the driver file for your printer is in the computer, you'll be asked if you want to use it or load a new one from the Windows 95 CD-ROM or floppy disks. It's usually easier to use the existing driver. If the driver isn't on your hard disk, you'll be instructed to insert the disk containing the driver.

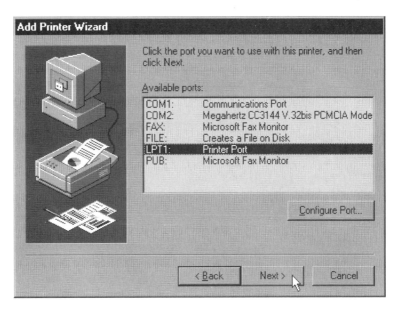

Figure 8.7 *Choosing the port the printer's connected to is the second step in setting up a local printer.*

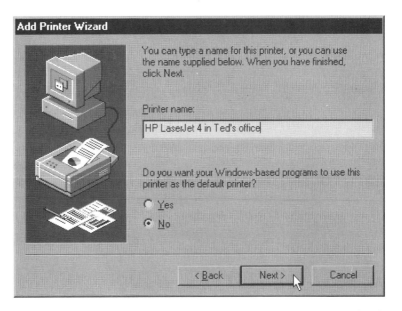

Figure 8.8 *Give your new printer a name that tells you and other people something about it.*

8. The test page will be sent to the printer. It should print out in a few minutes, then you'll be asked if it printed OK. If it didn't print correctly, click on No, and you'll be shown some troubleshooting information containing some questions and answers. The most likely fixes for the malady will be described. If the page printed OK, click on Yes, and you're done.

The new icon for your printer will show up in the Printers folder now.

TECH TIP   Windows 95 remembers the location you installed Windows 95 from originally. If you installed from a CD-ROM, it's likely that the default location for files is always going to be the CD-ROM drive's logical name (typically some higher letter, such as E or F). If you have done some subsequent installs or updates from other drives or directories, those are also remembered by Windows 95 and will be listed in the drop-down list box.

When You Don't Find Your Printer in the List

When you're adding a local printer, you have to supply the brand name and model of the printer because Windows 95 needs to know which driver to load into your Windows 95 setup to use the printer correctly. (When you are adding a network printer, you aren't asked this question because the printer's host computer already knows what type of printer it is, and the driver is on that computer.)

What if your printer isn't on the list of Windows 95-recognized printers? Many off-brand printers are designed to be compatible with one of the popular printer types, such as the Apple LaserWriters, Hewlett-Packard LaserJets, or the Epson line of printers. Refer to the manual that came with your printer to see whether it's compatible with one of the printers that *is* listed. Some printers require that you set the printer in compatibility mode using switches or software. Again, check the printer's manual for instructions.

Finally, if it looks like there's no mention of compatibility anywhere, contact the manufacturer for their Windows 95-compatible driver. If you're lucky, they'll have one. It's also possible that Microsoft has a new driver for your printer that wasn't available when your copy of Windows 95 was shipped. Contact Microsoft at (206) 882-8080 and ask for the Windows 95 Driver Library Disk, which contains all the latest drivers.

Also remember that Windows 95 can use the 16-bit drivers that worked with Windows 3.x. So, if you had a fully functioning driver for your printer in Windows 3.x (that is, your printer worked fine before you upgraded from Windows 3.x to Windows 95), you should be able to use that driver in Windows 95.

 NOTE All existing printer setups should actually have been migrated from Windows 3.x to Windows 95 when you upgraded, so if it was working under Windows 3.x, it will probably work fine under Windows 95. This is true for other types of drivers, too, such as video display cards, sound boards, and so on. However, whenever possible, you should bag any 16-bit drivers you have from Windows 3.x and use the drivers supplied with Windows 95.

Locate the Windows 3.x driver disk supplied with your printer or locate the driver file. (Sometimes font or other support files are also needed, incidentally, so it's not always as simple as finding a single file.) One source might be CompuServe, which has a listing of Microsoft's latest driver library online. Try **GO**ing WIN95, WINADV, or WDL (Windows Driver Library) for more info.

Assuming you do obtain a printer driver, do the following to install it:

1. Follow the instructions above for running the Add a Printer Wizard.

2. Instead of selecting one of the printers in the Driver list (it isn't in the list, of course), click on the Have Disk button. You'll see this box:

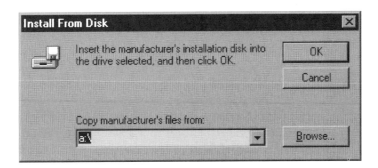

3. The Wizard is asking you to enter the path where the driver is located (typically a floppy disk). Insert the disk (or make sure the files are available somewhere), enter the path, and click on OK. Enter the correct source of the driver. Typically, it'll be in the A or B disk drive.

Part
2

Exploring Windows 95

TECH TIP   The Wizard is looking for an file with an `.inf` extension, incidentally. This is the standard file extension for manufacturer-supplied driver-information files.

4. Click on OK.

5. You might have to choose a driver from a list if multiple options exist.

6. Continue with the Wizard dialog boxes as explained above.

TECH TIP   If none of the drivers you can lay your hands on will work with your printer, try choosing the Generic *text-only* driver. This driver prints only text—no fancy formatting and no graphics. But it will work in a pinch with many printers. Make sure the printer is capable of or is set to an ASCII or ANSI text-only mode, otherwise your printout may be a mess. PostScript printers don't have such a text-only mode.

Altering the Details of a Printer's Setup—The Properties Box

Each printer driver can be fine-tuned by changing settings in its Properties dialog box. This area is difficult to document because so many variations exist due to the number of printers supported. The following sections describe the gist of these options without going into too much detail about each printer type.

The settings pertaining to a printer are called *properties*. As I discussed earlier, properties abound in Windows 95. Almost every object in Windows 95 has properties that you can examine and change at will. When you add a printer, the Wizard makes life easy for you by giving it some default properties that usually work fine and needn't be tampered with. You can change them later, but only if you need to. It may be worth looking at the properties for your printer, especially if the printer's acting up in some way when you try to print from Windows 95.

1. Open the Printers folder.

2. Right-click on the printer's icon and choose Properties. A box such as the one in Figure 8.9 appears.

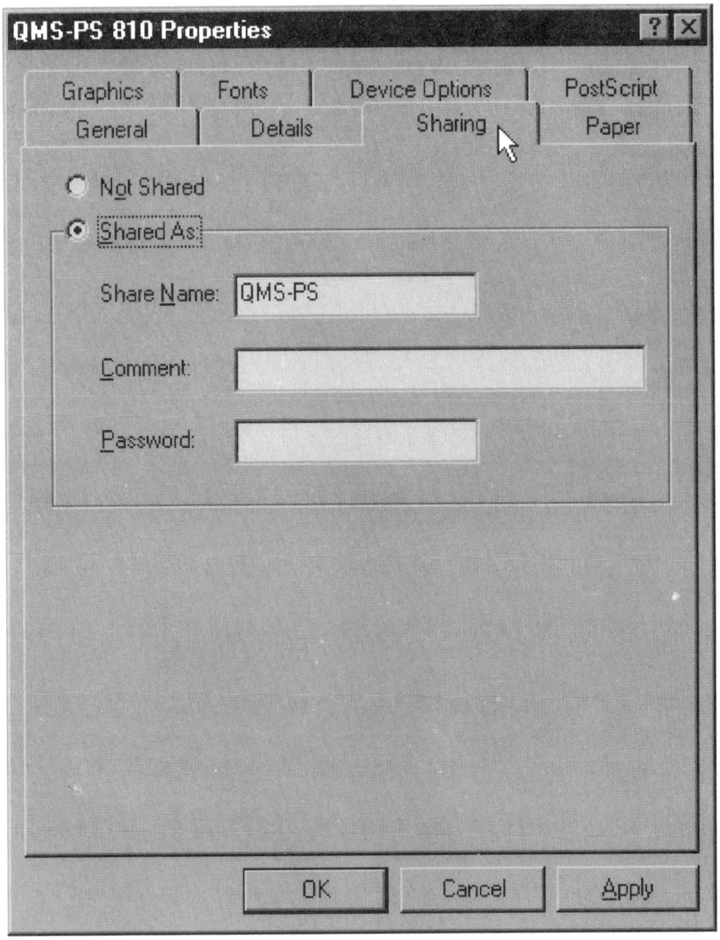

QMS-PS 810 Properties

| Graphics | Fonts | Device Options | PostScript |
| General | Details | Sharing | Paper |

○ Not Shared

◉ Shared As:

Share Name: QMS-PS

Comment:

Password:

[OK] [Cancel] [Apply]

Figure 8.9 *Each printer has a Properties box such as this, with several tab pages. Options differ from printer to printer.*

TIP You can also type Alt-Enter to open the Properties box. This is true with many Windows 95 objects.

3. Notice that there is a place for a comment. This is normally blank after you add a printer. If you share the printer on the network, any text that you add to this box will be seen by other users who are browsing the network for a printer.

Part
2

Exploring Windows 95

4. Click on the various tab pages of your printer's Properties box to view or alter the great variety of settings. These buttons are confusing in name, and there's no easy way to remember what's what. But remember that you can get help by clicking on the ? in the upper-right corner and then on the setting or button whose function you don't understand.

Sharing a Printer for Network Use

You have to *share* a printer before it becomes available to other network users. Sharing is pretty simple: First you add the printer as a local printer. Then you share it by right-clicking on it and choosing Share, or via its Properties box. Here are the details:

1. Add the printer as described earlier in this chapter.

2. Right-click on the printer's icon and choose Properties or Sharing.

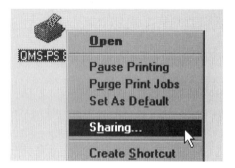

3. Now you'll see the box in Figure 8.9. Click on the Sharing tab if it's not selected.

4. On the Sharing page, click on Shared As.

5. A *share name* based on the Printer Name is automatically generated. You can leave the share name as is or give it another name. DOS-based network users see this name, which must conform to DOS file-naming rules. Other users will see this name, too, though some may see the other comments about the printer. This name can't be more than twelve characters long and mustn't contain spaces or characters not acceptable in DOS file names, such as ?, *, #, +, |, \, /, =, > , < , or %.

6. Fill in a comment about the printer, such as the location of the printer so users know where to pick up their printouts.

7. Fill in a password only if you want to restrict the use of the printer. If a password is entered here, other network users will be prompted to enter it at their machine before they can print to your printer. Make a list of people whom you want to give printer access to and tell them what the password is. This is one way to prevent overuse of a given printer. If you don't enter a password, protection is not in effect.

> **TIP** Another approach to preventing overuse of a given printer (at least temporarily) is to right-click on its icon and choose Pause Printing. Not a very elegant way to deter people from printing to your printer, but it *will* stop print jobs.

Part
2

8. Click on OK. If you entered a password, you'll be prompted to verify it by reentering. Then click on OK, and your printer is shared! Its icon now has a hand under it. Pretty soon you'll start to see unexpected print jobs rolling out of your printer.

QMS-PS 810

To unshare your printer, open the Properties box again, choose the Sharing page, and click on Not Shared.

> **TIP** If you forget the password, don't worry. You can change it by simply entering a new password from the Share tab page.

Connecting to a Network Printer

Assuming your Windows 95 network system is successfully cabled and running, network printing should be possible. Before a network user can access a network printer, the following must be true:

▶ The printer must be cabled to the sharing computer.

▶ The printer must be created and working properly for local use.

▶ The printer must be shared.

▶ The printer's security settings and network users wishing access must match.

Exploring Windows 95

> **TIP** By default, new printer shares are given a security setting that gives all users access for printing. Only the creator and administrators can *manage* the printer, however. Managing the printer means rearranging the print-job queue: starting, stopping, and deleting print jobs.

How to Delete a Printer from Your Printers Folder

You might want to decommission a printer after you've added it, for several reasons:

▶ You've connected a new type of printer to your computer and you want to delete the old setup and create a new one with the correct driver for the new printer.

▶ You want to disconnect from a network printer you're through using.

▶ You've created several slightly different setups for the same physical printer and you want to delete the ones you don't use.

In any of these cases, the trick is the same:

1. Open the Printers folder (the easiest way is using Start ➤ Settings ➤ Printers).

2. Right-click on the icon for the printer setup you want to delete and choose Delete (or just press Del).

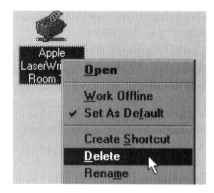

You will see at least one confirmation box before the printer is deleted. You may see another warning if there are print jobs in the queue for the printer.

> **NOTE** If you have stipulated that the computer can keep separate settings for each user (via Control Panel ➤ Passwords ➤ User Profiles), the removal process removes only the printer setup from Windows 95's Registry for the currently logged-in user. Also note that the related driver file and font files are not deleted from the disk. Therefore, if you want to re-create the printer, you don't have to insert disks, and you won't be prompted for the location of driver files. This is convenient, but if you're tight on disk space, you might want to remove the printer fonts and drivers. To remove fonts, use the Fonts applet in the Control Panel, as described in Chapter 9.

How to Print Out Documents from Your Programs

By now your printer(s) are added and ready to go. The procedure in Windows 95 is really no different from Windows 3.x, Windows NT, or even Mac programs. Just open the document, choose File ➤ Print, and make a few settings, such as which pages to print. (You might have to set the print area first or make some other settings, depending on the program.) If you're already happy with the ways in which you print, you might want to skim over this section. However, there *are* a couple of conveniences you might not know about, such using drag and drop to print or right-clicking on a document to print it without opening the program that created it.

About the Default Printer

Unless you choose otherwise, the output from both Windows and DOS programs are shunted to the Print Manager for printing. If no particular printer has been chosen (perhaps because the program—for example, a DOS app or Notepad—doesn't give you a choice), the default printer is used.

> **NOTE** The default printer can be set by right-clicking on a printer icon and choosing Set as Default.

Exactly how your printed documents look varies somewhat from program to program because not all programs can take full advantage of the capabilities of your printer and the printer driver. For example, simple word-processing programs like Notepad don't let you change the font, while a full-blown word-processing program such as Ami Pro can print out all kinds of fancy graphics, fonts, columns of text, and so forth.

> **TIP** Here's something to consider. If you choose as a default a printer that your DOS programs can't work with, your print jobs could bomb. Suppose you're running WordPerfect 5.1 for DOS and have it installed to print to an HP LaserJet, but the default printer is a Postscript laser printer. This would cause your printouts to be nothing but a listing of PostScript commands, such as `ERROR: undefined`, `OFFENDING COMMAND: |ume STACK {-pop-`, and so on. On another type of printer, you might see garbage printouts such as `@#$@$%G$V%B^YB&M(OM` instead of readable text. Just make sure your DOS 95 programs can work with your default printer (or change the default printer).

When you print from any program, the file is actually printed to a disk file instead of directly to the printer. Print Manager then spools the file to the assigned printer(s), coordinating the flow of data and keeping you informed of the progress. Jobs are queued up and listed in the Print Manager window, from which their status can be observed; they can be rearranged, deleted, and so forth.

Printing from a Program

To print from any program, including Windows and Windows 95 programs, follow these steps (which are exact for Windows programs but only approximate for other environments):

1. Check to see that the printer and page settings are correct. Some program's File menus provide a Printer Setup, Page Setup, or other option for this. Note that settings you make from such a box temporarily (sometimes permanently, depending on the program) override settings made from the Printer's Properties dialog box.

2. Select the Print command on the program's File menu and fill in whatever information is asked of you. For example, in WordPad, the Print dialog box looks like that in Figure 8.10.

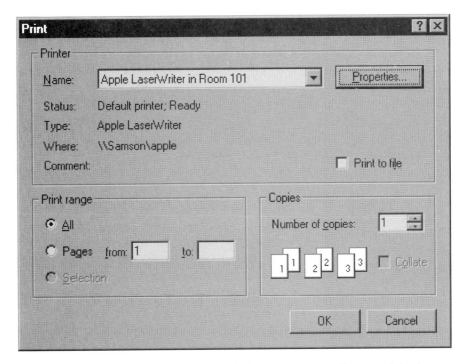

Figure 8.10 *When you choose Print from a Windows program, you often see a dialog box such as this that allows you to choose some options before printing. This one is from WordPad, a program supplied with Windows 95.*

Some programs have rather elaborate dialog boxes for choosing which printer you want to print to, scaling or graphically altering the printout, and even adjusting the properties of the printer. Still, you can normally just make the most obvious settings and get away with it:

▶ correct printer

▶ correct number of copies

▶ correct print range (pages, spreadsheet cells, portion of graphic, etc.)

▶ for color printers, which ink cartridge you have in (black & white or color)

3. Click on OK (or otherwise confirm printing). Windows 95 intercepts the print data and writes it in a file, then begins printing it. If an error

occurs—a port conflict, the printer is out of paper, or what have you—
you'll see a message such as this:

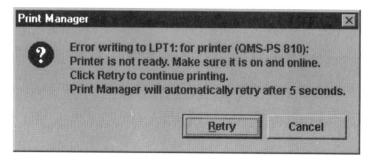

Check the paper supply, check to see that the printer is turned on,
that it's online (there may be a switch on the printer for this). If it's a
network printer, make sure it's shared and that the computer it's connected to is booted up and has shared the printer for use.

TIP When printing commences, a little printer icon will appear in the Taskbar next to the clock. You can double-click on this icon to see details of your
pending print jobs.

Printing by Dragging Files onto a Printer Icon or into Its Window

You can quickly print Windows program document files by dragging
them onto a printer's icon or window. You can drag from the Desktop,
a folder, the Find box, the Explorer, or the File Manager window into
the running Print Manager. This will only work with documents that
have an association with a particular program. (See Chapter 3 for a
discussion of associations.) To check if a document has an association,
right-click on it. If the resulting menu has an Open command on it
(not Open With), it has an association.

1. Arrange things on your screen so you can see the file(s) you want to
print as well as either the printer's icon or its window (you open a
printer's window by double-clicking on its icon).

> **TIP** You can drag a file into a shortcut of the Printer's icon. If you like this way of printing, keep a shortcut of your printer on the Desktop so you can drag documents to it without having to open up the Printers folder. Double-clicking on a shortcut provides an easy means of checking its print queue, too.

2. Drag the document file(s) into the Print Manager icon or window (Figure 8.11 illustrates). The file is loaded into the source program, the Print command is automatically executed, and the file is spooled to Print Manager. The document isn't actually moved out of its home folder, it just gets printed.

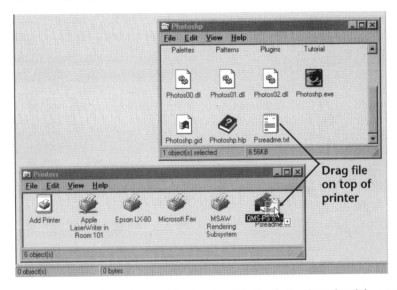

Figure 8.11   *You can print a document by dragging it to the destination printer's icon or window.*

If the document doesn't have an association, you'll see an error message:

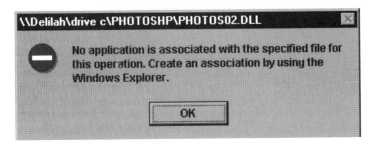

Part
2

Exploring Windows 95

Also, a nice feature of this approach is that you can drag multiple files onto a printer's icon or open window at once. They will all be queued up for printing, one after another, via their source programs. You'll see this message asking for confirmation before printing commences:

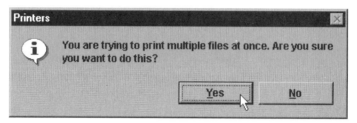

One caveat about this technique: as you know, some programs don't have a built-in facility for printing to a printer other than the default one. Notepad is a case in point: Try to drag a Notepad document to a printer that isn't currently your default printer, and you'll see this message:

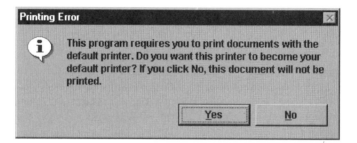

TIP   The drag-and-drop method can be used with shortcuts, too. You can drag shortcuts of documents to a printer or even to a shortcut of a printer, and the document will print.

Printing by Right-Clicking on a Document

Finally, you can print some documents using another shortcut that doesn't even require you to have a printer icon in view; instead, you use the right-click menu. Here's how:

1.   Right-click on the icon of any document you want to print and notice whether the right-click menu has a Print command on it.

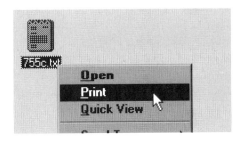

2. If there's no Print command, press Esc to cancel the menu. You can't print the document using this technique. If there is a Print command, choose it. The file will open in its source program and start printing right away. Once spooled to the Print Manager, the document will close automatically.

Working with the Print Queue

If you print more than a few files at a time, or if you have your printer shared for network use, you'll sometimes want to check on the status of a printer's print jobs. You also might want to see how many jobs need to print before you turn off your local computer and printer if others are using it. Or you might want to know how many other jobs are ahead of yours.

You can check on these items by opening a printer's window. You'll then see:

Document Name: Name of the file being printed and possibly the source program

Status: Whether the job is printing, being deleted, or paused

Owner: Who sent each print job to the printer

Progress: How large each job is and how much of the current job has been printed

Start at: When each print job was sent to the print queue

Figure 8.12 shows a sample printer with a print queue and related information.

To see the queue on a printer:

1. Open the Printers folder.

2. Double-click on the printer in question.

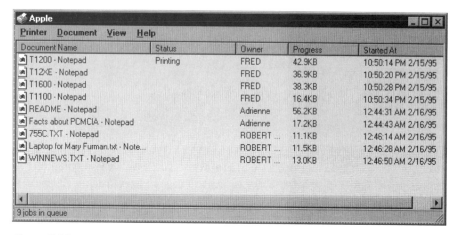

Figure 8.12 *A printer's window with several print jobs pending*

3. Adjust the window size if necessary so you can see all the columns.

NOTE   If the print job originated from a DOS program, the Document Name will not be known. It's listed as Remote Downlevel Document, meaning that it came from a workstation that doesn't support Microsoft's RPC (Remote Procedure Call) print support. Additional cases in point are Windows for Workgroups, LAN Manager, Unix, and Netware.

TIP   You can resize the columns in the display to see more data in a small window. Move the pointer to the dividing line in the header display and drag the line left or right.

TIP   If the printer in question is a network printer, and the printer is offline for some reason, such as its computer isn't turned on, you'll be forced to work *offline*. An error message will alert you to this, and the top line of the printer's window will say *User intervention required—Work Offline*. Until the issue is resolved, you won't be able to view the queue for that printer. You can still print to it, however.

Refreshing the Network Queue Information

The network cabling connecting workstations and servers often is quite busy, so Windows 95 usually doesn't bother to add even more traffic to the net by polling each workstation for printer-queue information. This is done when necessary, such as when a document is deleted from a queue. So, if you want to refresh the window for a printer to get the absolute latest information, just press F5. This immediately updates the queue information.

Deleting a File from the Queue

After sending a file to the queue, you might reconsider printing it, or you might want to re-edit the file and print it later. If so, you can simply remove the file from the queue.

1. Open the printer's window.

2. Select the file by clicking on it in the queue.

 NOTE I have found, especially with PostScript laser-type printers, that after deleting a file while printing, I'll have to reset the printer to clear its buffer or at least eject the current page (if you have a page-eject button). To reset, you'll typically have to push a button on the printer's front panel or turn the printer off for a few seconds, then on again.

3. Choose Document ➤ Cancel Printing, press Delete, or right-click and choose Cancel Printing. The document item is removed from the printer's window. If you're trying to delete the job that's printing, you might have some trouble. At the very least, the system might take some time to respond.

 NOTE Of course, normally you can't delete someone else's print jobs on a remote printer. If you try to, you'll be told that this is beyond your privilege and that you should contact your system administrator. You *can* kill other people's print jobs if the printer in question is connected to *your* computer. But if you want to be able to delete jobs on a remote computer, someone has to alter the password settings in the remote computer's Control Panel to allow remote administration of the printer. Remote administration is covered in Part V.

NOTE   Pending print jobs will not be lost when computers are powered down. Any documents in the queue when the system goes down will reappear in the queue when you power up. When you turn on a computer that is the host for a shared printer that has an unfinished print queue, you will be alerted to the number of jobs in the queue and asked whether to delete or print them.

 TIP   When an error occurs during a print job, Windows 95 tries to determine the cause. For example, the printer might be out of paper, or the printer might be offline or unplugged from the AC outlet. You may be forced to work offline until the problem is resolved. Opening the printers queue should display an error message approximating the nature of the problem to the best of Print Manager's capabilities. Check the printer's File menu to see if the Work Offline setting has been activated. When you think the problem has been solved, turn this setting off to begin printing again.

Canceling All Pending Print Jobs on a Given Printer

Sometimes, because of a megalithic meltdown or some other catastrophe, you'll decide to bail out of all the print jobs that are stacked up for a printer. Normally you don't need to do this, even if the printer has gone wacky. You can just pause the queue and continue printing after the problem is solved. But sometimes you'll want to resend everything to another printer and kill the queue on the current one. It's easy:

1. Select the printer's icon or window.

2. Right-click and choose Purge Print Jobs, or from the printer's window choose Printer ➤ Purge Print Jobs. All queued jobs for the printer are canceled.

CAUTION   Make sure you really want to cancel the jobs before you do this. This is a good way to make enemies if people on the network were counting on their print jobs being finished anytime soon.

Pausing (and Resuming) the Printing Process

If you're the administrator of a printer with a stack of jobs in the print queue, you can temporarily pause a single job or all jobs on a particular printer at any time. This can be useful for taking a minute to add paper, take a phone call, or have a conversation in your office without the noise of the printer in the background. The next several sections explain the techniques for pausing and resuming.

Pausing or Resuming a Specific Print Job

You can pause documents anywhere in the queue. Paused documents are skipped and subsequent documents in the list print ahead of them. You can achieve the same effect by rearranging the queue, as explained in the section titled *Rearranging the Queue Order*. When you feel the need to pause or resume a specific print job:

1. Click on the document's information line.

2. Choose Document ➤ Pause Printing (or right-click on the document and choose Pause Printing as you see in Figure 8.13). The current print job is temporarily suspended, and the word "Paused" appears in the status area. (The printing might not stop immediately because your printer might have a buffer that holds data in preparation for printing. The printing stops when the buffer is empty.)

3. To resume printing the document, repeat steps 1 and 2 to turn off the check mark next to Pause Printing.

Pausing or Resuming All Jobs on a Printer

In similar fashion, you can temporarily pause all jobs on a given printer. You might want to do this for a number of reasons including:

▶ to load paper or otherwise adjust the physical printer

▶ to alter printer settings from the printer's Properties dialog box

Part 2

Exploring Windows 95

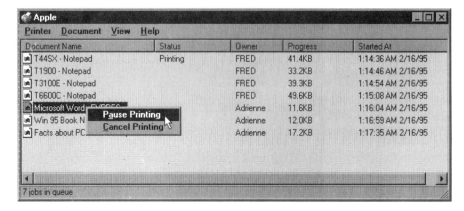

Figure 8.13 Pause the printing of a single document with the right-click menu. Other documents will continue to print.

Follow these steps to pause or resume all jobs for a printer:

1. Deselect any documents in the printer's window; press the Spacebar if a document is selected.

2. Choose Printer ➤ Pause Printing. The printer window's title bar changes to say "Paused."

3. To resume all jobs on the printer, choose Printer ➤ Pause Printing again to turn off the check mark next to the command. The *Paused* indicator in the title bar disappears, and printing should resume where the queue left off.

Rearranging the Queue Order

When you have several items on the queue, you might want to rearrange the order in which they're slated for printing.

1. Click on the file you want to move and keep the mouse button depressed.

2. Drag the file to its new location. The name of the document moves to indicate where the document will be inserted when you release the mouse button.

3. When you release the mouse button, your file is inserted in the queue, pushing the other files down a notch (see Figure 8.14).

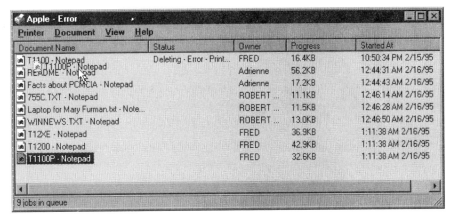

Figure 8.14   *You can shift the order of a document in the queue by dragging it to the desired position and dropping it.*

Printing to a Disk File instead of a Printer

There are times when you may want to print to a disk file rather than to the printer. What does this mean? When you print to a disk file, the codes and data that would normally be sent to the printer are shunted off to a disk file—either locally or on the network. The resulting file typically isn't just a copy of the file you were printing; it contains all the special formatting codes that control your printer. Codes that change fonts, print graphics, set margins, break pages, and add attributes such as underline, bold, and so on are all included in this type of file. Print files destined for PostScript printers typically include their PostScript preamble, too—a special file that prepares the printer to receive the instructions that are about to come and the fonts that are included in the document.

Why would you want to create a disk file instead of printing directly to the printer? Printing to a file gives you several options not available when you print directly to the printer:

▶ Print files are sometimes used by programs for specific purposes. For example, printing a database to a disk file might allow you to more easily work with it in another application. Or you might want to print an encapsulated PostScript graphics file to be imported into a desktop-publishing document.

▶ You can send the file to another person, either on floppy disk or over the phone lines, with a modem and a communications program such as Terminal. That person can then print the file directly to a printer (if it's compatible) with Windows or a utility such as the DOS **copy** command. The person doesn't need the program that created the file and doesn't have to worry about any of the printing details—formatting, setting up margins, and so forth. All that's in the file.

▶ It allows you to print the file later. Maybe your printer isn't hooked up, or there's so much stuff on the queue that you don't want to wait, or you don't want to slow down your computer or the network by printing now. Print to a file, which is significantly faster than printing on paper. Later, you can use the DOS **copy** command or a batch file with a command such as **copy *.prn lpt1 /b** to copy all files to the desired port. This way you can queue up as many files as you want, prepare the printer, and then print them without having to be around. Be sure to use the **/b** switch. If you don't, the first Ctrl-Z code the computer encounters will terminate the print job because the print files are binary files.

In some programs, printing to a disk file is a choice in the Print dialog box. If it isn't, you should modify the printer's configuration to print to a file rather than to a port. Then, whenever you use that printer, it uses all the usual settings for the driver but sends the data to a file of your choice instead of to the printer port.

1. In the Printers folder, right-click on the printer's icon and choose Properties.

2. Select the Details tab page.

3. Under *Print to the following port*, choose FILE:

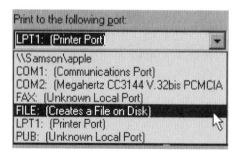

4. OK the box. The printer's icon in the Printers folder will change to indicate that printing is routed to a disk file.

Epson LX-80

Now when you print a file from any program and choose this printer as the destination for the printout, you'll be prompted for a file name.

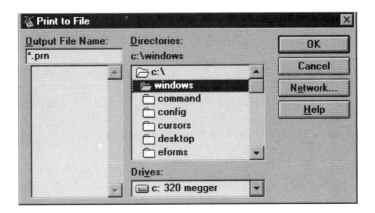

 TIP If you want to print the file as ASCII text only, with no special control codes, you should install the Generic/Text Only printer driver. Then select that as the destination printer.

 TIP If you want to print to an encapsulated PostScript file (`.eps`), print to a printer that uses a PostScript driver (the Apple LaserWriter or the QMS PS-810, for instance) or set up a phony printer that uses such a driver. (No physical printer is needed.) When prompted for a file name, specify an EPS extension.

Chapter 9

Using Fonts Effectively

FEATURING

One of the most compelling characteristics of Windows—possibly even the single ability that most ensured the acceptance of Windows as *the* PC standard GUI—is the convenience of having a single system for displaying and printing text that works with all Windows programs. Though at the time Windows 3.0 appeared some ordinary MS-DOS programs could display and print high-quality fonts, they have had to rely on a bewildering hodgepodge of different printer drivers and font formats to achieve any success in this arena. Worse yet, each program solved font dilemmas in its own way, not sharing their wealth of fonts or font-management utilities with other MS-DOS programs.

By contrast, Windows programs (especially as of Windows 3.1, when True Type fonts were introduced) need only a single printer driver and one pool of fonts. Thus, Lotus 1-2-3 for Windows, Ami Pro, Paradox, Microsoft Access, Power Point, and Ventura Publisher programs on a Windows system can all share the same fonts and print with them to a number of printers without difficulty. Because fonts are so readily available at this point—in shareware packages, on BBSs, or on those economy CD-ROM packages down at the local computer discount store—getting your paws on some interesting fonts is a cinch.

Like other Windows versions, Windows 95 comes with a set of stock fonts such as Courier New, Times New Roman, and Arial. You may be happy with these relatively banal, though useful, choices and possibly never feel the need to add to them. More likely, though, you'll want to augment these rudimentary fonts with a collection of your favorites to spruce up your documents. In this chapter I'll explain how to add and remove fonts from your system, how to choose and use fonts wisely, ways to procure new fonts, and even how to create fonts of your own.

Font Management in Windows 95

Fonts are highly desirable to most users. Suddenly having the Gutenbergian power to lay out and print aesthetically sophisticated correspondence, books, brochures, newsletters, and the like is one of the great joys of computerdom. But installing, removing, and managing fonts threw a kink in the works for many Windows 3.x users, especially once they installed a zillion fonts and realized how much that slowed down their system. Windows 3.x initially loads much more slowly once you've hyped up your system with a lot of fonts because all the fonts, font names, and font directories have to be checked out and loaded.

Once font-related boondoggles became common knowledge, font-management programs started popping up in the marketplace. These programs improved on the rudimentary Font utility supplied in the Windows 3.x Control Panel. For example, they'd display all your fonts, let you print sample pages of your fonts, manage fonts in groups that could be easily installed and removed from the system, and so on. Some of these packages also had built-in font-conversion capabilities, producing TrueType fonts from other types such as Adobe Type 1 or bit-mapped fonts, and could create novel display type by applying special effects to fonts you already had installed.

Microsoft has included much-improved font management in Windows 95. It's not perfect, but it's better. Choosing Fonts from the Setting menu or My Computer, or selecting the Fonts directory in Explorer will present options such as:

▶ installing and removing fonts

▶ viewing on screen or printing an example of each font in various point sizes

▶ listing only font families rather than each variation of a font, eliminating redundant listings (for instance, Times New Roman, Times New Roman Bold, and Times New Roman Italic)

▶ listing all fonts similar in appearance to a given font, such as all fonts similar to Arial

▶ toggling between a listing of actual font file names and the font's common name

What Are Fonts and What Is TrueType?

Fonts are the various type styles that you can use when composing a document, viewing it on the screen, or printing it on paper. Fonts add visual impact to your documents to help you express your words or numbers in a style that suits your audience. They can also increase readability.

As an example of some fonts, Figure 9.1 shows several popular type styles. Fonts are specified by size as well as by name. The size of a font is measured in *points*. A point is $\frac{1}{72}$ of an inch. In addition, fonts styles include **bold,** *italic*, and <u>underlining</u>.

Times New Roman

12 point

Brush Script

33 point

Times New Roman Italic

12 point

Gill Sans

28 point

Shelley Allegro

30 point

Casper Open Face

20 point

Figure 9.1   Various fonts and point sizes

Windows comes supplied with a reasonable stock of fonts, some of which are installed on your hard disk and integrated into Windows during the setup procedure. The number and types of fonts installed depend on the type of screen and printer you have. When you install a printer into your Windows setup (see Chapter 8), a printer driver is installed. The printer driver includes a set of basic fonts for your printer.

Some programs, such as word processors, may have additional fonts supplied with them—fonts not included with Windows—that you may want to use. Fonts can also be purchased separately from companies that specialize in typeface design, such as Bitstream, Inc., Adobe Systems, Inc., and Microsoft.

Font packages usually come with their own setup programs, which will automatically install the fonts into your Windows system for you. When installing fonts with these programs, just follow the instruction manual supplied with the font package. If there is no such installation program, use the Control Panel's Fonts applet as explained later in this chapter.

General Classes of Fonts

There are several basic classes of fonts that are used in Windows, and an understanding of them will help you manage your font collection. Windows fonts break down into the following groups:

Screen fonts control how text looks on your screen. They come in predefined sizes, such as 10 points, 12 points, and so forth.

Printer fonts are fonts stored in your printer (in its ROM), stored on plug-in cartridges, or downloaded to your printer by Windows when you print. Downloaded fonts are called *soft fonts*.

Vector fonts use straight line segments and formulas to draw letters. They can be easily scaled to different sizes. These are primarily used on printing devices that only draw lines, such as plotters.

TrueType fonts are generated either as *bitmaps* or as soft fonts, depending on your printer. The advantage of TrueType fonts is that they will print exactly as seen on the screen. (TrueType fonts were first introduced with Windows 3.1 to solve problems associated with differences between how fonts appear on screen and how they print.)

Before Windows 3.1, both printer and screen fonts often had to be added for each type style you wanted to add to your setup. TrueType fonts simplify matters because adding a TrueType font installs both printer and screen fonts simultaneously. In addition, TrueType fonts will look identical (though perhaps with differences in smoothness or resolution) regardless of the printer with which you print them.

When you print a document, Windows checks your printer driver file to see if it includes the fonts you put in the document. If the printer or printer driver does not supply the font, Windows attempts to find a happy solution. In most cases, Windows will handle day-to-day printing jobs just fine. If your printer has a soft font already in it (from plug-in font cartridges or in its ROM) and Windows doesn't have a screen font of that type, Windows will usually substitute another, similar screen font with the correct size for displaying your work on screen. Even though it might not look exactly like the final printout, the line length and page breaks on your screen should be accurate.

About TrueType Fonts

With the addition of TrueType fonts in Windows several years ago, typefaces could be scaled to any size and displayed or printed accurately on virtually all displays and printers—without the addition of any third-party software. And because of the careful design of the screen and printer display of each font, TrueType provides much better WYSIWYG (What You See Is What You Get) capabilities than previous fonts. Furthermore, you no longer have to ensure that you have fonts in your printer that match the fonts on screen.

In the past, if you used a printer like the LaserJet II, you might have been limited to the two fonts that come standard with that printer (Courier and Line Printer). If you wanted to print any other fonts, you had to buy a cartridge containing a few additional fonts, or you had to buy soft fonts. These fonts had to be individually rendered by the vendor in each size that might be required. This was often costly and required a tremendous amount of hard-disk space. If you wanted to display the fonts on screen, you had to create yet another set of screen fonts that matched the printer fonts.

With TrueType, any printer that can print graphics can print the full range of TrueType fonts—all orchestrated by Windows 3.1. And the results will look more or less the same, even on different printers. Although different printers provide different resolutions, the essential characteristics of a TrueType font will remain consistent whether it is printed on a 9-pin dot-matrix printer or a high-resolution image setter.

TrueType also allows users of different computer systems to maintain compatability across platforms. For example, because TrueType is also integrated into System 7, the Macintosh operating system, a document formatted on a Macintosh using TrueType fonts will look exactly the same on a Windows 3.1-equipped PC.

Finally, because TrueType is an integrated component of Windows, any Windows program can make use of TrueType fonts. These fonts can be easily scaled (increased or decreased in size), rotated, or otherwise altered.

TECH TIP   You can only use TrueType fonts if you have a Windows 3.1 or later printer driver.

Comparing TrueType Fonts to Bit-Mapped and Vector Fonts

So much for TrueType fonts. Now let's consider other types of fonts, namely bit-mapped and vector fonts. First let's see how these two kinds of fonts work as screen fonts. Then I'll discuss printer fonts.

NOTE   Recall from the list above that printer fonts are those built into the printer or those sent to the printer by the computer to print a document. Screen fonts are the fonts Windows uses to display text on the screen.

There are two types of screen fonts: bit-mapped and vector. Each is quite different from the other and serves a distinct purpose.

Bit-Mapped Fonts

Bit-mapped fonts are essentially a collection of bitmaps (pictures), one for each character you might want to type. These bitmaps cover the entire character set and range of styles for a particular typeface in a limited number of sizes. Examples of bit-mapped fonts in Windows 3.1 are Courier, MS Serif, MS Sans Serif, and MS Symbol. When you install Windows, these fonts are automatically copied to the appropriate Windows FOLDER by Setup. Windows comes with a number of versions of these fonts. Based on the resolution of your video adapter, Windows chooses the font files that take best advantage of your particular display. Figure 9.2 shows a character map of a bit-mapped font (MS Serif).

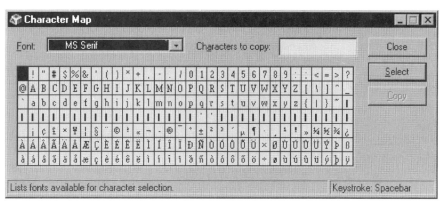

Figure 9.2 *A bit-mapped font*

NOTE   Some of your programs may not display the list of bit-mapped fonts in their Font boxes. They may only show a list of TrueType fonts. This doesn't mean they aren't there, only that your program isn't displaying them. If you try other programs, such as MS Paint (when using the Text tool), you'll see a larger list, including such bit-mapped fonts as MS Serif.

Because bit-mapped fonts are dependent on the bitmaps included in their font files, you are limited to displaying these fonts in the sizes provided or in exact multiples of their original sizes if you want the font to look good. For example, MS Serif for VGA resolution includes bitmaps for display at 8, 10, 12, 14, 18, and 24 points. Opening the Size box for a bit-mapped font will display a limited list of sizes such as this list for Courier:

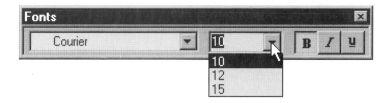

Even though the list of sizes for a bit-mapped font is usually limited, you can type in any number you want. Windows will do its best to scale the font to the approximate size you ask for, but it will likely look pretty icky. There's one exception to this: bit-mapped fonts can scale acceptably to exact multiples. So if 10 is on the list (as in the example above), you could get decent-looking 20-, 30-, or 40-point renditions, although the results will not look as good as a TrueType font at the same size.

Vector Fonts

Vector fonts are more suitable for devices like plotters that can't use bit-mapped characters because they draw with lines rather than dots. Vector fonts are a series of mathematical formulas that describe a series of lines and curves (arcs). They can be scaled to any size, but because of the process involved in computing the shape and direction of the curves, these fonts can be quite time consuming to generate. PostScript fonts are actually vector fonts, but because the PostScript printer itself is optimized to do the computing of the font sizes and shapes, performance is fairly good. Examples of vector fonts are Modern, Roman, and Script.

Variations of Printer Fonts

Just as there are different types of screen fonts, there are also several different types of printer fonts:

▶ device fonts

▶ printable screen fonts

▶ downloadable soft fonts

Device fonts are those fonts installed in your printer, either factory defaults or members of a font-cartridge collection. Printable screen fonts are bit-mapped and vector fonts that can be used not only on screen but also sent to the printer. Downloadable soft fonts are fonts that, like TrueType, are stored on your PC's hard disk and can be sent to the printer as needed. Unlike TrueType fonts, though, they are specific to your printer and are generally provided in limited styles and sizes.

How Does TrueType Work?

TrueType fonts are similar to both bit-mapped and vector fonts. They contain a description of the series of lines and curves for the typeface—like a vector font. When you press a key in a Windows word processor, for example, that application asks Windows to generate the bitmap of the appropriate character in the right font and size at a particular spot on screen. Windows' Graphical Device Interface (GDI) creates a bitmap in memory that best represents that character. But the job of creating the character is only half done.

Like bit-mapped fonts, TrueType fonts include a number of bit-mapped "hints" that help Windows when rendering the font in smaller point sizes. Hints are an extremely important element of TrueType. Because the resolution of a VGA monitor is considerably less than that of a 300-dpi laser printer, many fonts simply don't look right on screen. There just aren't enough pixels to accurately reproduce the font at smaller point sizes.

When Windows displays a character at a small point size, it uses the hinting instructions located in a TrueType font to cheat a bit by reshaping the character so lines or curves aren't missing or misshapen. But hints are not just important for screen display. Look closely at a page of small text generated by your printer. If it prints 300 dots per inch, chances are you'll notice slight imperfections in characters. An *O* may not be perfectly round; the slant of a *W* may not be truly straight. Hinting ensures the highest possible quality of fonts despite the resolution limits of most common output devices.

You may notice that when you select a different font or a new point size that Windows pauses for a moment. During this delay, it creates bitmaps for the entire character set in the new size or style. This happens only once during a Windows session. After first generating the bitmaps, Windows places them into a memory cache where they can be quickly accessed the next time they are required.

> **TIP**　If you have a number of documents you created using fonts that you no longer have, you don't need to go through the documents and change your formatting. You can force Windows to substitute appropriate replacements. Load `win.ini` into an editor like Notepad. If you look at the [FontSubstitutes] section of the file, you'll notice lines like `TmsRmn=MS Serif`. Add any associations you like, keeping the old name on the left of the equation and the new name on the right. Windows will automatically fill requests for the old font with the new font.

Elements of TrueType Typography

As discussed earlier, *font* is now used freely to describe a number of different typographical elements. Font is often used to mean the same thing as *typeface*, a group of fonts that are closely related in design. Technically, a font is a specific set of characters, each of which shares the same basic characteristics. For example, Arial is a typeface. In turn, Arial comprises the fonts Arial, Arial Bold, Arial Bold Italic, and Arial Italic. When you pick Arial from your word processor's font dialog box and then choose to italicize text, you are selecting the font Arial Italic.

Basic TrueType Font Families

As with other types of fonts, all TrueType fonts can be generalized into font families. These are a group of typefaces with similar characteristics but that are much more loosely related than the members of a typeface. Windows recognizes five font families: Decorative, Modern, Roman, Script, and Swiss.

The most common of these families are Roman and Swiss. The Roman font family contains the majority of serif fonts. Sans-serif fonts like Arial are generally members of the Swiss family. Figure 9.3 shows fonts from the Roman and Swiss families. (Serifs are discussed below, in *Classes of Font Styles*.)

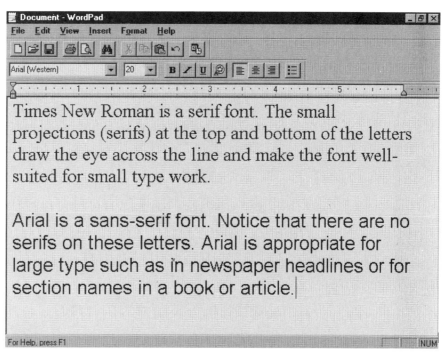

Figure 9.3   A Roman font (Times New Roman) and a Swiss font (Arial)

Special Characters

Each TrueType font contains a number of special characters like trademark (™) and yen (¥), punctuation such as the em dash (—) and curly quotes (""), and foreign (æ) and accented (ñ) characters. But Windows 95 also includes two special fonts you should become familiar with: Symbol and WingDings.

Symbol contains a number of mathematical symbols such as not-equal-to (≠) and plus or minus (±). It also contains a complete Greek alphabet for scientific notation.

WingDings is quite a bit more versatile. It contains a wide range of symbols and characters that can be used to add special impact to documents. Instead of printing *Tel.* next to your phone number, why not place a telephone symbol? WingDings includes several religious symbols: a cross, a Star of David, and a crescent and star, as well as several zodiac signs. Figure 9.4 displays all of the characters of these two fonts.

You can access these special characters in several different ways. The easiest is to select WingDings or Symbol in any TrueType-compatible application, then type characters from the keyboard. For example, the universal symbol for *airport* corresponds to a *Q* in WingDings. This method requires a bit of memorization or a handy reference chart to keep the associations straight.

Alternately, you can enter keys by using the Alt key with your numeric keypad. Each character in a font is associated with a numeric value between 0 and 255. By holding down the Alt key while entering that number, you can insert the appropriate character. For example, to insert an em dash (—), hold down the Alt key and press the numbers 0151 on the keypad. This will not work with the number keys at the top of your keyboard, and you must remember to preface the number

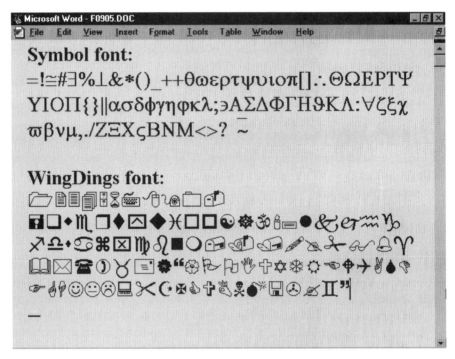

Figure 9.4   *Symbol and WingDings are two TrueType fonts worth checking out. They contain characters you might find useful in your documents. You may even want to use one of these for your personal or corporate logo.*

with a 0. Again, you will need a reference chart for the particular font you're using to take advantage of this method.

 TIP The Fonts option from the Control Panel lets you examine all the characters in a font, too. You can read about that later in this chapter, under *Adding and Removing Fonts Using Control Panel* .

Many word processors include a function called Insert Symbol. This feature allows you to choose a character from a table of all the characters in a particular font. You just highlight the character you want and click on OK (or double-click on the character), and it appears instantly in your document. This is not the quickest way to enter a symbol, but it is the easiest if your word processor offers it. Figure 9.5 shows the Insert Symbol table in Word for Windows 6.0.

If your application lacks an Insert Symbol feature, you can open the Character Map accessory discussed in Chapter 22 and copy the symbols you want to the Clipboard. Then switch back to your application and paste the symbols where you want them. While not the easiest way to insert symbols, this method is adequate for most uses. However, sometimes the font "loses" its font family name when it's copied in this way; once pasted, you may have to select the character and reset its font.

Part 2

Exploring Windows 95

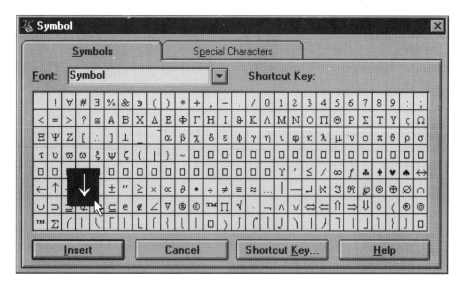

Figure 9.5 *A typical Insert Symbol table in a word-processing application*

TrueType Font Embedding

What if you get a document from a friend or a business associate that was formatted with TrueType fonts you don't have on your system? One of the most important features of TrueType is the ability to *embed* fonts in documents. So when you send a document to someone else, the fonts you use go with it.

NOTE Beware: although Windows itself supports embedded TrueType fonts, not all Windows applications do. Most programs will be able to display embedded TrueType fonts, though an occasional program won't be able to embed them.

When you load a document that contains embedded TrueType fonts, Windows copies those fonts into memory temporarily. They can then be used in conjunction with that document specifically. Depending on the attributes set by the font vendor, a font can have one of three embedding options—read-only embedding, read-write embedding, or no embedding at all.

The most common type of font will most likely be read-only. If you load a document containing read-only fonts—and you don't have those fonts yourself—you will only be able to print or view the document. You won't be able to alter it. This prevents nonowners of a font from using it without paying for it.

However, the fonts supplied by Microsoft in Windows 95 as well as those in Windows 3.x and Microsoft's TrueType Font Pack are read-write fonts. Documents containing these fonts can be printed, viewed, and edited regardless of whether the fonts themselves are installed on the system. Also, Windows provides the ability to save the fonts themselves for use with future documents. Obviously, this approach is not popular with commercial developers who make their livings selling their fonts, but a quick scan of public-domain TrueType fonts that have popped up on online services like CompuServe and GEnie shows that most free fonts are read-write enabled.

On the other end of the spectrum, vendors may choose to disallow embedding of their fonts. If you try to save a document that contains one of these typefaces, your word processor will simply not include the fonts.

Essentially, this would create documents similar to those containing no font information other than the name of the original font.

TrueType's greatest advantage is that it ensures that the fonts you see on screen are the fonts you get on paper. Embedded TrueType takes this one step further by ensuring that the fonts used to create a document are the ones used to view, edit, and print it.

 TECH TIP   If when you send another person a document, you want to ensure that he or she will be able to actually edit the document using the fonts you have used to create it, either use popular fonts that all Windows users have on their systems, such as Times New Roman, Arial, or Courier New; or check that your application is set to embed fonts. For example, in Microsoft Word this is done with the Tools ➤ Options menu.

Which Fonts Should I Use?

You can install bit-mapped, vector, and scalable fonts into Windows. But as long as your printer can print graphics and is not a plotter, you should stick to scalable fonts like TrueType and ignore bit-mapped and vector fonts entirely—in fact, you can remove them from your system, as discussed later.

Bit-mapped fonts look good on your screen, but only at the particular size they're designed for; when you display them at another size, they appear distorted and jagged. In addition, because you need one file for every size of a given typeface you want to display, one set of bit-mapped fonts can consume a great deal of valuable territory on your hard disk. It's also inconvenient to keep track of all the files involved.

Vector fonts are worth using only if your output device is a plotter. While the files aren't overly large, and while you can print vector fonts at any size, they have an unattractive, noticeably angular appearance. One plus: vector font files are quite small.

TrueType and other scalable fonts, by contrast, look great when displayed or printed at any size. If you decide that a particular document requires, say, a 13.5-point rendition of Times, all you have to do is request it, and Windows will generate it automatically. Although True-Type font files are fairly large, typically around 60K, you only need one file for each typeface. Font files of other scalable font formats such as Type 1 PostScript and FaceLift tend to be somewhat smaller.

How Your Fonts Get Used by Windows

Most Windows programs that print text let you specify the font you want.

In some cases, as in most word-processing programs, you can change fonts with every text character, while other programs restrict you to one font for each block of text or field or impose some other limitation. For example, in the accessory program Paint, once text is laid into a picture, its font can't be altered.

Ideally, Windows should let you select only from the fonts your printer can actually print. Unfortunately, this isn't always the case if you install more than one printer driver. In this situation, many Windows programs offer you all the fonts available with every installed printer driver, leaving it to you to figure out which ones are appropriate for your printer. Or they might switch the list of fonts available when you change the default printer to a new printer, but a list of MRU (most recently used) fonts may still display fonts from the previous default printer. Word 6 has such a list at the top of its font list.

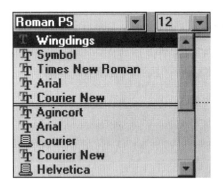

All the fonts above the double line are recently used fonts.

In any case, once you've chosen a font, what you see on the screen depends on the class in which the font falls. If you've selected a True-Type or other scalable font, Windows will generate the appropriate screen font for you so you'll always get a close match between the screen and the final printout. On the other hand, if you're using a nonscalable font, Windows must look for a screen font that corresponds to the one you'll be printing with. If it can't find a match, Windows will substitute the most similar screen font it can find. Depending on the font you've chosen and your screen font collection, this substitute screen font may not look anything like the printed version. Nevertheless, at least the line lengths and page breaks you see on your screen will be accurate.

When you print the document, Windows checks your printer driver file and the win.ini file, looking for the fonts you specified. If the fonts exist, Windows will know whether they're already resident in the printer or must be scaled or downloaded from the hard disk. If a font is missing, Windows will again make an effort to substitute a similar one.

Building a Font Collection

Windows comes with a set of very attractive TrueType fonts that will serve you well in most situations, whether you're writing letters, preparing reports or grant proposals, or adding text to charts or graphics. So why buy more fonts?

Broadly stated, the reason to enlarge your font collection is simple: to improve your ability to communicate. Typographers claim the fonts you use can influence the impact of your message on your readers, even if they're not consciously aware of their reactions. With more fonts to work with, you'll be better able to select ones that suit the mood of whatever document you're preparing. Some fonts, such as Bodoni or Times New Roman, have a decidedly formal appearance, ideal for serious business correspondence. But these same fonts are just too stuffy for a letter to a friend; for this you'd be better off using a font with a casual look, such as Dom Casual or Tekton.

In addition, looking beyond the stock Windows fonts helps you create an identifiable style for your printed documents. Like a logo, the typefaces you choose become associated with you or your business in the minds of those who read your documents regularly. Using the same typeface that everyone else does will make it harder to establish your own typographic identity.

What About Other Scalable Type Alternatives?

TrueType fonts are the most convenient kind of scalable fonts for anyone who uses Windows because TrueType technology is built right into the Windows environment. However, you have several other choices in scalable-font formats.

TrueType's biggest competitor is the Type 1 or PostScript format. Type 1 fonts produce very high quality screen fonts and printed output. Vast numbers of fonts are available in the Type 1 format from many different manufacturers, including some of the most respected typographic houses, and they cover an extremely wide range of beautiful designs.

> **NOTE** PostScript fonts used with Adobe Type Manager are referred to as Type 1 fonts to distinguish them from another PostScript font format, Type 3. Don't get Type 3 fonts unless you have a PostScript printer or a way to convert them to Type 1.

Since the release of Windows 3.1, TrueType has become very popular, even to the point of being implemented widely on the Macintosh. Although the selection of TrueType fonts was limited only a few years ago, this is no longer the case. Still, there is at least one other reason to consider using Type 1 fonts instead of TrueType fonts: PostScript is still the established standard for very high resolution typesetting devices used in professional publishing. If you stick with Type 1 fonts, you can use the exact same fonts for printing drafts on a desktop laser printer and outputting final typeset copy on a Linotronic or other digital typesetter. This means you can be confident that, aside from lower resolution, your draft will look exactly like your final document.

To use Type 1 fonts to your best advantage, you need a utility program called Adobe Type Manager (ATM). ATM scales Type 1 fonts to the requested size faster than Windows does. It also provides a number of useful options for handling the fonts that you don't get with Windows' built-in font manager.

Other scalable font choices for Windows are less attractive, though you might want to consider them in special circumstances. If you have access to a library of fonts in another scalable font format, it may make sense to purchase a font-scaling utility that allows you to use your font collection with Windows. Like ATM, other font-scaling utilities take over from Windows the job of creating the correctly sized final fonts for the screen and printer.

The runner-up font-scaling utility with the broadest appeal for Windows users is probably Intellifont-for-Windows (by Hewlett-Packard). It works with the Intellifont scalable-font format designed for the LaserJet III family of printers. If you have a LaserJet III, IIID, or IIISi and use Intellifont fonts with your non-Windows programs, it may make sense to use Intellifont-for-Windows and stick with a single set of fonts.

Another choice is Bitstream's FaceLift. Although FaceLift produces high-quality output, the only reason to prefer it to TrueType is if you have already purchased a large FaceLift font library for use with the non-Windows programs that require this format.

SuperPrint (by Zenographics) is the Rosetta stone of font-scaling utilities. It works interchangeably with most of the major font formats—including Type 1, FaceLift, Intellifont, Fontware, and Nimbus Q—although reviews have judged output quality to be lower than that from ATM or FaceLift. As a bonus, SuperPrint speeds up Windows graphics printing significantly and allows you to print sophisticated graphics on non-PostScript printers.

Finally, if you have a limited font budget, consider Publisher's Powerpak for Windows (by Atech Software) and MoreFonts (by Micro-Logic Software, Inc.). The fonts that work with them are much, much less expensive than most TrueType, Type 1, and FaceLift fonts.

NOTE As of this writing, all of these products were available in versions for Windows 3.11 but had not yet been rewritten for Windows 95. Though Windows 3.11 versions may work correctly under Windows 95, you should acquire up-to-date versions.

Choosing Specific Fonts

Once you've settled on the font format you're going to use, your next task is to decide which specific fonts to buy. The number of typeface designs available for Windows totals in the thousands and is still growing. With that much variety, selecting a set of fonts that's right for you can be a daunting proposition.

For this reason, it makes sense to stick to the tried-and-true favorites of typographic professionals when you're starting to build a font library. Figure 9.6 offers a few suggestions; you can't go wrong with any of the fonts shown here. Another simple solution is to buy one of the font sets available from vendors such as Adobe Systems and Monotype. Each of these packages comes with several fonts chosen for a specific type of document, along with design tips for using the fonts appropriately.

Classes of Font Styles

As Figure 9.6 suggests, fonts can be classified into various styles, or looks, too. Even if you choose your fonts from a style chart, such as Figure 9.6, a basic understanding of the classifications is a good idea before you start buying fonts and designing your own documents.

The simplest division in the font kingdom is between serif and sans-serif designs. As a look at the table will show you, serifs are the little bars or lines that extend out from the main parts of the characters. A

Serif typefaces for body text

| Baskerville | Caslon |
| Garamond | Palatino |

Sans-serif faces for general use

| Futura | Gill Sans |
| Optima | Univers |

Display and decorative faces

| Benguiat | Bernhard Modern |
| LITHOS | Peignot |

Figure 9.6   *The typefaces in the top two groups are proven designs that work well in many types of documents. To be safe, start with these faces. It's more difficult to recommend display faces because you must choose them carefully for the particular mood you want to convey. Still, they are high-quality designs, popular among professional designers, and they cover a considerable range of moods.*

sans-serif font lacks these lines. It's important to choose a few fonts from each category because almost any combination of a serif and a sans-serif font will look good together, but two sans-serif or two serif fonts will clash.

Another simple classification for fonts depends on the space allotted to each character. In a *monospaced* font, every character occupies the same amount of space in the horizontal dimension. That is, an *i* takes up just as much room on a line of text as a *w*. In a *proportionally spaced* font, characters occupy differing amounts of space. Proportional fonts are easier to read and allow you to fit more text in a given space. (The typefaces in this book are proportional.) The only reason to use mono-spaced fonts is when you're printing reports or tables in which the alignment of columns is determined by spaces (by pressing the space-bar on the keyboard).

NOTE   The numerals in most proportionally spaced fonts are monospaced, allowing you to line up columns of numbers easily.

Still another way to classify fonts has to do with their intended purpose, such as for:

▶ body text

▶ headlines

▶ ornamental special effects

▶ nonalphabetic symbols

Body fonts have highly legible characters and work well for long blocks of text. Although any body-text font can be used for titles and headlines, display or headline fonts are specifically meant for that purpose (such as those used in this book). They boast stronger, more attention-getting designs, but for that reason don't work well for body text.

Two remaining font types—*ornamental* and *display* fonts—aren't shown in Figure 9.6 because they don't have universal application. The distinction between ornamental (or novelty) fonts and display fonts is arbitrary. Still, the idea is that an ornamental font is so highly stylized that it might distract the reader's attention from your mes-sage. Use ornamental fonts with care when you want to set a special mood. Symbol or pi fonts contain special symbols such as musical notes, map symbols, or decorations instead of letters, numbers, and punctuation marks, as explained earlier.

Procuring Fonts

The explosion of interest in typography generated by desktop-publishing technology has, in turn, resulted in a proliferation of font vendors. Even Microsoft is offering its TrueType Font Pack, a $99 collection of 44 fonts designed by the same group that produced Arial, Courier New, and Times New Roman—the TrueType fonts included with Windows 95.

Many other leading font vendors, including Bitstream and SWFTE, have brought out TrueType versions of their font collections. You can find these in most software stores. Shareware sources of TrueType fonts abound. Be aware though, that not all TrueType fonts have sophisticated hinting built in and may not look as good as fonts from the more respectable font foundries. Also, some users report that badly formed TrueType fonts can sometimes wreak havoc on your system.

If you're looking for fonts on the cheap side, check out one of your local BBSs or an online service like CompuServe or GEnie. The Windows sections of these networks hold a number of free fonts that are yours for the taking. Many of the fonts are PostScript Type 1 fonts that have been converted to TrueType. The quality of these fonts is generally not as good as the commercial fonts, but in most cases, you'll be hard-pressed to notice the difference. I've seen numerous cheapie CD-ROMs that pack hundreds of TrueType fonts on them in several computer stores.

Adding and Removing
Fonts Using Control Panel

Now that you have the basics of fonts under your belt, let's get down to the business of managing and maintaining your font collection. As mentioned earlier, the Control Panel's Fonts applet (also available from Explorer if you display the \Windows\Fonts directory) is the tool for the job. The Fonts applet lets you:

▶ add fonts to your system so your programs can use them

▶ remove any fonts you don't use, freeing disk space

▶ view fonts on screen or print out samples of each font you have

▶ display groups of fonts that are similar in style

Adding Fonts

If no installation program came with your fonts or if you want to add some TrueType fonts to your system that you downloaded from some BBS or otherwise acquired, here's how to do it.

1. Run Control Panel by clicking on Start ➤ Settings ➤ Control Panel.

2. Double-click on the Fonts icon. A window now appears as shown in Figure 9.7. All your installed fonts appear in a folder window that

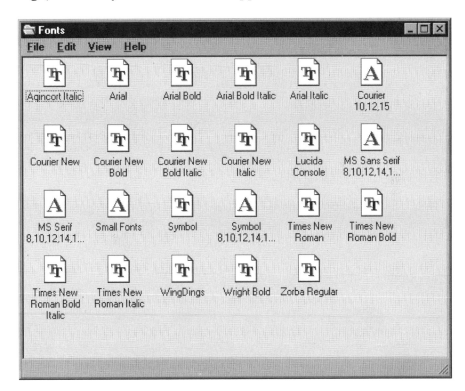

Part 2

Exploring Windows 95

Figure 9.7   *All of your installed fonts are displayed when you choose Fonts from the Control Panel. Because fonts are actually files, they appear the same way other files on your disks do. The TrueType fonts have the TT icon. The fonts with the A icon are bit-mapped or vector fonts.*

looks like any other folder. (This is a departure from Windows 3.x, which had a nonstandard Font dialog box.) You can choose the form of the display from the View menu as with any other folder, too. There are a couple of extra menu options, though, as you'll see.

 NOTE If you have installed special printer fonts for your particular printer, these fonts may not appear in the Fonts folder. They will still appear on font menus in your programs. They just won't show up in the Fonts folder because they probably aren't stored in that folder.

 NOTE Bit-mapped and vector fonts are stored on disk in files with the extension .fon; TrueType font files have the extension .ttf.

3. Open the File menu and choose the Install New Font option.

A file dialog box appears, as shown in Figure 9.8. Choose the correct drive and directory where the fonts are stored. Typically the fonts you'll be installing are on a CD-ROM or on a floppy disk drive, so you'll have to select the correct drive by clicking on the drive selector.

4. Choose the fonts you want to add. If you want to select more than one, extend the selection by Shift-clicking (to select a range) or Ctrl-clicking (to select individual noncontiguous fonts). Noticed that I have selected several fonts to install at once. If you want to select them all, click on Select All.

 NOTE If the fonts you want to install are on a network drive somewhere, you have to choose the correct network drive from the Drive list. If the drive isn't in the list, this means you have to *map* the network drive to a local hard-disk name (D, E, F, and so forth) by clicking on Network and filling in the resulting box (mapping drives is covered in Part V).

5. When fonts are installed, they're normally copied to the \Windows \Fonts directory. However, font files are pretty large. If the fonts you're installing are already on your hard disk in another folder, you

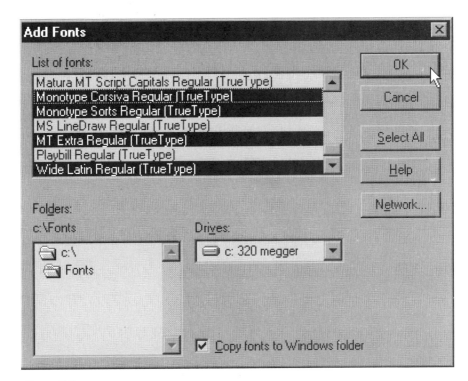

Figure 9.8 *Choose the drive, directory, and fonts you want to install. Consider whether you want the fonts copied into the Windows font directory, typically* \Win-dows\Fonts. *You can select multiple fonts to install at once, using the Shift and Ctrl keys.*

might want to leave them in their current home, especially if your hard disk is low on space. If this is the case, turn off the Copy Fonts to Windows Folder check box. The fonts will still be installed, but they'll be listed in the Fonts folder with shortcut icons rather than normal font file icons.

> **TIP** You should *not* turn off this box if the files are being installed from a CD-ROM, a floppy, or from another computer on the network (unless the network drive is always going to be available). You'll want the fonts on your own hard disk so they'll always be available.

6. Click on OK. The font(s) will be added to your font list, available for your Windows applications.

If you try to install a font that's already in your system, the installer won't let you, so don't worry about accidentally loading one you already have.

TrueType Options

As mentioned above, TrueType fonts take up a fair amount of disk space. They can also be slower to print than fonts that are built into your printer. For example, PostScript printers often have 35 or so built-in fonts that are very similar to popular TrueType fonts like Courier, Times New Roman, and Arial. If you use the basic cast of True-Type fonts a lot, you may be able to speed your print jobs by telling Windows 95 to use a font-substitution table that uses the printer's built-in fonts rather than downloading TrueType fonts to the printer each time you print something. The substitution table will, for example, use the internal Helvetica font in place of the TrueType font Arial. Line breaks and page appearance should print as you see them on the screen, though minute details of the font may differ a bit. Some other kinds of printers, such as HP LaserJet's for example, have TrueType options too.

For examples of typical dialog boxes with options that affect TrueType printing, study Figure 9.9. It shows the TrueType options for a Post-Script printer (such as an Apple Laserwriter) and for an HP LaserJet IV.

These dialog boxes are reached via the Printers folder. Open the folder, right-click on a printer, choose Properties, and then choose the Fonts tab.

NOTE   Font options will vary from printer to printer, depending on the printer driver. Some printers won't even have a font tab page.

TIP   Normally you will do just fine by not even adjusting the settings in these boxes. If you are curious, you can click on the buttons such as the Edit Substitution Table button or Send Fonts As button. You'll see a lot of options, many of which may be confusing at first. You can always click on the ? button on the title bar of the dialog box, then on the item in question to learn about the options. Some interesting bits of information about the options will pop up, including advice about how best to set them.

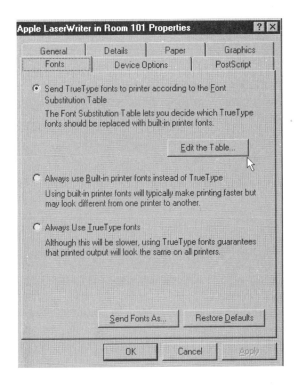
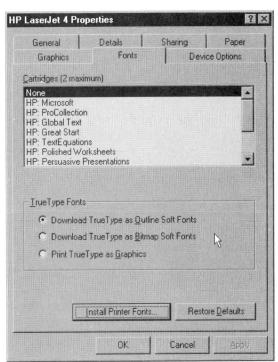

Figure 9.9 *Options for TrueType printing are available for some printers. Setting these correctly can speed up printing. As a rule, these settings have already been optimized when you install Windows 95.*

One last point about TrueType font options: in Windows 3.x, the Fonts applet in the Control Panel gave you two systemwide options controlling TrueType fonts. You could disable TrueType fonts to economize on RAM usage, and you could elect to show only True-Type fonts in your applications, eliminating confusion on the font menus by hiding vector and bit-mapped fonts. Both of these options have been dropped in Windows 95, mostly because of improvements in Windows 95's memory management and the standardization of TrueType fonts industrywide. Windows 95 just doesn't bog down as much when TrueType fonts are enabled, and because the majority of Windows machines these days are using TrueType fonts, disabling other fonts isn't as advantageous as it once was.

Part
2

Exploring Windows 95

Displaying and Printing Examples of Fonts with the Font Viewer

Once you have a large selection of fonts, it can be difficult to remember what each looks like. Windows 95's built-in font viewer provides an easy way to refresh your memory.

1. Open the Fonts folder.

2. Double-click on any icon in the folder. The font will open in the font viewer. In Figure 9.10 I've displayed a font called Desdemona and maximized the window.

3. You can open additional fonts in the same manner and arrange the windows to compare fonts to one another.

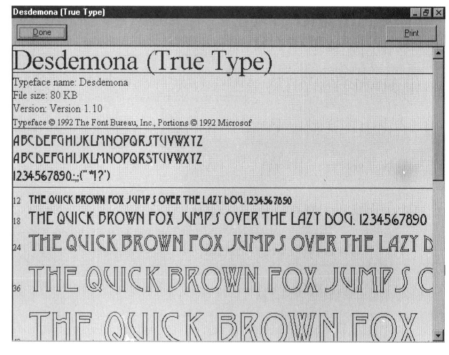

Figure 9.10   *The font viewer kicks in when you double-click on any font in the Fonts folder. The small numbers in the left margin indicate what point size is displayed to the right. Information about the font's maker appears in the upper portion of the window.*

4. Sometimes it's useful to have a printout of a font. You can compile a hard-copy catalog of all your fonts for easy reference if you work with a healthy stable of fonts regularly. To print a single font, double-click on it and click on Print (or right-click on it and choose Print).

 TIP To print all your fonts (or multiple fonts) in one fell swoop, select them in the Fonts window with Edit ➤ Select All. Then choose File ➤ Print (or right-click on one of the selected icons and choose Print). You'll get a one-page printout for each font.

 TIP Actually, the font viewer will work from any directory. So, if you have a floppy with some fonts you're thinking of installing but you want to see each font first, just open the floppy disk folder and double-click on the fonts one at a time.

 TIP Like other objects in Windows 95, fonts have properties. Right-click on a font's icon and choose Properties to view details about the font's size, creation date, location, type, DOS attribute settings, and so forth. Chapter 11 discusses object properties in detail.

Viewing Font Families

Each variation on a typeface is stored in a separate file. That means a separate font file is required for normal, bold, italic, and bold italic versions of each font.

When you're viewing the contents of the Fonts folder, it can be helpful to see only one icon per font family instead of four. This way, you can see more clearly and quickly just which fonts you have. To do this, open the View menu and choose Hide Variations:

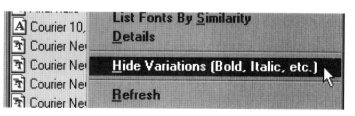

Try it with your fonts and notice how it clears up the display. Unless all four files required for a complete font family are installed, a name won't appear in the listing now. So, if you've installed only Garamond Bold but not Garamond, Garamond Italic, and Garamond Bold Italic, you won't see Garamond listed at all. You will still see an icon for the one type you installed, but such icons won't be named. Double-clicking on an unnamed icon will still display the font in the font viewer so you can identify it.

To return the view to showing all font files listed separately, choose the command again to toggle the check mark off in the menu.

Viewing Fonts by Similarities

Many TrueType fonts contain within them something called *Panose* information. Panose information helps Windows 95 classify a font by indicating a font's general characteristics, such as whether it is a serif or sans-serif font. Based on this information, Windows 95 can group together fonts that will appear somewhat similar on screen and when printed. It can be a boon to have Windows 95 list the fonts that are similar in look to, say, Arial, in case you're looking for an interesting sans-serif font that everyone hasn't seen already.

NOTE   Some older TrueType fonts, as well as all bit-mapped and vector fonts, won't have Panose information stored in them. This is also true of symbol fonts, such as WingDings and Symbol. The font folder will simply display *No Panose information available* next to the font in this case.

To list fonts according to similarity:

1. Open the Fonts folder, one way or another. You can do this most easily from the Control Panel, as described earlier, or from Explorer.

2. Choose View ➤ List Fonts by Similarity. If the folder's toolbar is turned on, you'll have a button that will render the same effect.

3. The folder window will change to include column headings and a drop-down list. The list box is for choosing which font will be the model to which you want all the others compared. Open this list box and choose the desired font. The font must be one endowed with Panose information, otherwise Windows 95 will have nothing with which to compare other fonts. The results will look like Figure 9.11.

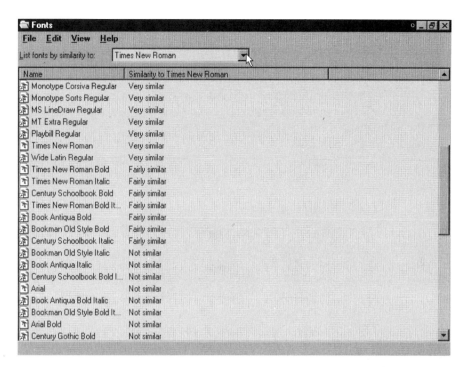

Figure 9.11 Font listing by similarity. Notice three categories of similarity: Very similar, Fairly similar, and Not similar.

4. You may want to turn off the Hide Variations setting on the View menu to eliminate unnamed icons in the window.

Removing Fonts

Fonts consume space on your hard disk. A typical TrueType font consumes between 50 and 100K (one thousand bytes) of disk space. Deleting individual fonts or font sets increases the available memory in your computer, letting you run more programs and open more documents simultaneously. If you are having memory-limitation problems, you could gain some room by eliminating fonts you never use. If you never use the Italics versions of some fonts, for example, you might want to remove the Italic and Bold Italic versions specifically, leaving the normal version installed. A little-known fact is that even if an italic or bold font has been removed, Windows 95 can still emulate it on the fly. It won't look as good as the real thing, but it will work.

Part
2

Exploring Windows 95

To remove a font, follow these steps:

1. Open the Fonts folder. All the installed fonts are displayed.

2. To remove an entire font family (normal, Bold, Italic, and Bold Italic), turn on the View ➤ Hide Variations setting. If you want to remove individual styles, turn this setting off so you can see them.

3. Select the font or fonts you want to remove.

4. Choose File ➤ Delete or right-click on one of the selected fonts and choose Delete.

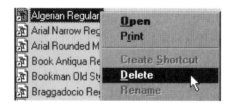

 CAUTION   Don't remove the MS Sans Serif font set; it's used in all the Windows dialog boxes.

5. A dialog box asks you to confirm the removal. Choose the Yes button. The font is moved to the Recycle Bin.

 CAUTION   You shouldn't remove or install fonts just by dragging them from and to the Fonts folder. Using the Install command from the File menu ensures that the fonts will be registered properly in the Windows 95 Registry and the internal list of fonts that applications draw on for displays in their menus and dialog boxes. Always use the Install New Font command to add fonts and the Delete command to remove them.

Some Basic Guidelines for Using Fonts

Whether you rely on the fonts supplied with Windows or put together a sizable font collection, you should follow a few simple guidelines when formatting your documents. Attractive fonts by themselves aren't enough—the chief goal is readability:

▶ Allow plenty of space between lines. The space between two lines of text should be about 20 percent greater than the size of the font. Thus, if you're using a 12-point font, you should set the line spacing or *leading* to 14 points. This guideline doesn't hold true for headlines, in which the line spacing should usually be about the same as the font size.

▶ Don't mix too many fonts in one document. It's often best to stick with one font for the main body of your text and a larger, bold version of the same font for headlines. If you want to mix fonts, use a serif font for the body of your text and a sans serif for the headlines, or vice versa. You can get away with using a third font for sidebar text, but you'll run the risk of clashing font designs.

▶ If you use two or more font sizes, be sure they contrast adequately. If your main text is in 12-point Times New Roman, use at least 14-point type for the subheadings.

▶ Use italics or boldface type to indicate emphasis. Avoid underlining and capitalizing letters, both of which make it harder to read your text.

▶ Make your margins generous. One of the most common mistakes that causes an amateurish-looking document is text that crowds too closely to the edge of the paper. Allow plenty of space between columns as well.

Following these few guidelines will help you avoid the most glaring errors of document layout. For more detailed advice, consult your bookstore or library for treatises on the topic of desktop publishing or graphic and printing design.

Part 2

Exploring Windows 95

Deleting Font Files from Your Hard Disk

While a variety of high-quality fonts can definitely lend a professionally typeset look to your printed documents and make it easier to understand the information on your screen, a big font collection isn't necessary to run Windows. In fact, you don't even need all the fonts that come with Windows.

In Windows 3.x there were three critical system fonts you had to have on your hard disk; Windows simply wouldn't work if you deleted certain important fonts used in dialog boxes, menus, and DOS boxes. In Windows 95, because you can use TrueType fonts for just about every aspect of a window, including DOS boxes, you can bag any fonts you're not using. Remember, however, that I don't just mean fonts you're not using in your documents; your Windows 95 screen display (set or checked via the Control Panel's Display applet) uses fonts as well. But if disk space is at a premium and the appearance of your text isn't critical for the work you do with Windows, you can remove unused fonts from your Windows setup, saving valuable disk space in the process.

Using Control Panel's Fonts applet, you can remove all the fonts you find unnecessary from your Windows installation and delete their files on disk at the same time. The procedure is detailed in *Removing Fonts* in Chapter 5. However, I recommend you keep at least the fonts that have the *A* icon (bit-mapped fonts)—such as all the ones that start with *MS*, as in MS-Sans Serif—in the dialog box because various error dialog boxes and some programs will use these from time to time. If they are missing, Windows 95 will substitute a system font that you may find harder to read.

After removing all the fonts from the Control Panel list, you can then check your disk for any remaining `.fon` or `.ttf` files. They may be scattered around in different directories. You can use Start ➤ Find to assist you in the search.

Font Utility Programs

If you are a font nut, you might like to know about a few classes of font programs that can assist you in managing and expanding your type library. This section describes some of them.

Managing Large Numbers of Fonts

Font aficionados and typography professionals typically have no trouble acquiring a bevy of typestyles that range from the sublime to the absurd. The upside of this method is that you'll always have just the right typestyle available when you need it. But managing hundreds of fonts can be tedious, and Windows' performance can be negatively impacted if you have a large number of fonts installed in the system and active at one time. Windows start-up time can become sluggish, and some applications may also be bogged down by too many installed fonts. Aside from performance issues, scrolling through a gargantuan font list in your word-processing program just to find a common font such as Times New Roman is a nuisance. If you have a healthy font collection (more than 50 fonts), you'll want to lay your hands on a good font-organizer program. There are a number of programs on the market for Windows 3.x as of the time of this writing, and those for Windows 95 are appearing.

TECH TIP   Some Windows 3.x font-utility programs expect to find fonts in the \Windows\System directory. Windows 95 now places fonts in the \Windows\Fonts directory, which could throw a wrench into some font-manager programs. You should contact the manufacturer of a font-utility program about its compatibility with Windows 95 before purchasing or using it.

Although there are shareware font managers available that you might hunt around for if you're on a budget, Ares Software's FontMinder at $79 probably offers the most attractive commercial font-management product. In fact, Ares provides just about anything you could want in the way of font utilities. But I'll get to that later.

Ares FontMinder gives you several advantages over manually managing font installation and removal. First, it lets you preview fonts and print type samples before loading them onto your hard disk. Second, you can create font *packs*—predefined groups of fonts that can contain any number of fonts in the TrueType or PostScript Type 1 format. A single font can be included in any number of font packs without duplicating the font file itself. Typically, a professional would have font packs associated with a given design job or area of work, such as word processing, database, spreadsheet, CAD, and so forth. Once packs are set up, FontMinder lets you install or uninstall them on the fly (without having to reboot Windows). Most applications will recognize the changes to the system font arsenal as they occur. You can even associate a font pack with a given document so installing the pack automatically launches the application and document (such as a design job), ready to go to work. A font pack can be moved to a floppy disk, too, so you can take it to a service bureau in preparation for typesetting.

As discussed above, Windows 95's Font Viewer lets you print out samples. But the printout is rather pedestrian. FontMinder prints six different styles of font summary pages, including complete characters sets, font capabilities, sample text in a variety of user-definable sizes, and a "family" page showing columns of each font in the family (bold, italic, and so on). You can easily print batches of font samples (something I've had trouble getting Windows 95 to do).

As another benefit, you can sort all your fonts, arranged by six preset categories: serif, sans serif, script, monospaced, symbol, and decorative. If a font isn't already assigned to a category, you can add it using the included properties editor. You can create additional custom categories should you need to.

Finally, because so many people in the document-design field work on a LAN, a Network Administrator option for FontMinder is designed to help control and manage burgeoning font libraries on client/server networks. TrueType, PostScript Type 1, and PostScript multiple master fonts can be controlled on three different levels of network support, depending on your needs. The upshot is that management of shared fonts over the network is possible, eliminating unnecessary duplication of fonts and the resulting loss of disk space.

NOTE   Some fonts are copyrighted and not in the public domain. It is illegal to copy and use these fonts without buying them or buying site licenses for them.

The other primary font-management program of note is called FontHandler, from Qualitype. This program also lets you set up packs (groups) of predefined fonts and subgroups of fonts, much like the Explorer has folders and subfolders. It provides an elegant means for viewing, printing, searching for, installing and uninstalling, and viewing details about each of your fonts. Four different sample page styles can be printed. Figure 9.12 shows one of the installed fonts being displayed.

Figure 9.12 *FontHandler lets you quickly scroll through and display fonts.*

Up to nine fonts can be displayed at once, which is a nice feature, allowing quick comparison. ATM, Printer, and TrueType fonts are supported.

Beyond this, FontHandler offers something not found elsewhere. Unless a document has embedded TrueType fonts, a problem arises when you try to open a document that includes a font not currently installed in your system. Windows will do its best to locate a font that will suffice as a replacement, but it rarely looks very good. If the font called for in the document is actually on your computer, but not installed, a utility in FontHandler called *Font Sentry* can save the day. It sits in the background, quietly watching and waiting for any program or document to request a font that is not currently available. When a request for a missing font is detected, Font Sentry goes out and *AutoInstalls* the needed font on the fly, with the application or document never missing a beat or being aware of anything having been wrong.

Once a font is installed in this way, it will appear as available in all Windows programs. Such AutoInstalled fonts can be declared *temporary* or *permanent*, defined by the user, so that AutoInstalled fonts are either automatically forgotten when Windows is restarted or fully installed as if you'd done it from the Control Panel's Fonts applet or Explorer.

Font Conversion and Modification Utilities

The other general category of font programs deals with conversions of one sort or another. For example, you may have aquired fonts other than TrueType ones. If you've used type managers like Adobe Type Manager, you probably have a number of PostScript fonts that you use frequently. If you own a copy of CorelDRAW or another program that comes with Adobe fonts, you have more than a hundred fonts at your disposal. You can convert such fonts to TrueType format using various conversion tools, salvaging your font investment. Some other popular tools are available that will help you manage your fonts by organizing them into collections or create variations of your existing TrueType fonts. The sections below describe a few of the available programs.

Ares FontMonger can convert fonts—and it does a great job at it. It also provides support for TrueType, PostScript Type 1 and Type 3, Nimbus Q, and Intellifont; as well as CorelDraw WFN and Laser-Master formats.

But FontMonger goes far beyond simple format conversion. Font-Monger is a full-featured type-manipulation and editing tool. It becomes clear after just a few minutes with the product that format conversion is just a side benefit of FontMonger.

Fonts can be converted by FontMonger as a batch or individually. When you select File ➤ Convert Batch, you are presented with a batch list containing the names of the fonts in your last conversion batch (see Figure 9.13).

When you press the Find button, FontMonger will scan the directories you specify for all the font types it knows. You just select the files you want to convert, tell FontMonger what format to convert them into, and off it goes.

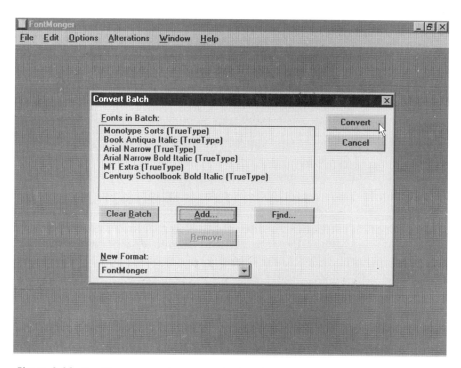

Figure 9.13 *FontMonger eases font conversion by allowing you to convert a batch of fonts in one fell swoop. Here's a list of fonts about to be converted.*

FontMonger provides facilities to set font information such as font name and family relationship (normal, bold, italic, bold italic, or other). Once you've set the selections appropriately, you can set the font-protection level (meaning whether your font should have read-only or read-write embedding). Unless you want to customize further, you can then choose File ➤ Build Font to create a new font. Select the new format for the font, and you're done.

FontMonger looks at the font itself and generates new hinting rules based on the characteristics of the font. The result is clean, crisp-looking screen fonts that can be recognized as distinct designs even at small point sizes.

But the real strength of FontMonger is its full complement of font-editing tools. FontMonger will easily perform a number of alterations to a font, including Small Caps, Slant (italicize), Superior (superscript), and Inferior (subscript). You can even create your own custom alterations by simply dragging the font's outline in an editing box. FontMonger also lets you import characters designed in Adobe Illustrator or saved in Encapsulated PostScript. You can develop a logo or symbol in a drawing package such as Illustrator, Micrografx Designer, or CorelDRAW and assign your logo to a key in a standard font.

NOTE FontMonger is available for about $149 from Ares Software in Foster City, California. Call 415-578-9090.

Two other font products also from Ares are worth noting. The first, dubbed Font Fiddler, has some of the capabilities of FontMinder, handling three font-related chores: renaming and changing the properties of fonts, printing samples without installing the font, and setting the kerning pairs of any TrueType or Postscript Type 1 fonts.

The second, Font Chameleon, is a positively reviewed program that lets you easily create custom fonts. And you don't have to do this meticulously, character by character. Instead, Chameleon comes with a number of flexible highest-quality, hinted fonts and lets you combine them (sort of like morphing photographs) in millions of different combintations, tweaking weight, width, x-height, and ascender and descender sizes as you go. The upshot is that you can have an incredibly small type library (each flexible font takes up only 4K of disk space) rather than tie up tons of disk space with hundreds of fonts. When you need a new font, just create it on the fly with Font Chameleon. Then save it as a Type 1 or TrueType font and install it. The fonts you design can also be used under OS2/Warp or on a Mac. As of this writing, Font Chameleon was priced at $55 with 45 flexible fonts, or $295 with 200 fonts.

Finally, here's an interesting category of font manipulation: what the marketing people call *special effects*. If you have Microsoft Office or Word, you'll have a font special-effects program called WordArt that lets you create fun and interesting shadow effects, rotated text, 3-D looks, and such. An example of some WordArt is shown in Figure 9.14.

Another font-effects product is TrueEffects from MicroLogic. This program works differently than WordArt. Like Chameleon, it generates whole new TrueType fonts based on existing TrueType fonts in your system. WordArt just lets you insert a small snippet of text into

Figure 9.14   *Microsoft's WordArt add-on to Microsoft Office lets you insert fancy text into any OLE-aware document. In Word, for example, choose Insert ➤ Object and click on WordArt.*

an otherwise normal document. With TrueEffects, you choose which of a zillion effects you want to apply to an existing TrueType font. For example, effects such as 3-D shading, patterned fills, and various thicknesses of outline can be applied. You then give the new font a name, save it on disk, and install it into your system. This is a convenient way to generate novel display fonts for posters, flyers, banners, or newsletters. For information, call MicroLogic at (800) 888-9078 or (510) 652-5464.

Part 2

Exploring Windows 95

Chapter 10

Windows Multimedia

FEATURING

A s of version 3.1, Windows has been *multimedia-ready*. Though it could be argued that Windows' multimedia capabilities are still a bit sketchy, PC-based multimedia has nevertheless grown dramatically in the last several years and affords users impressive benefits by this point. Even mainstream products such as Lotus 1-2-3 and Paradox for Windows, when purchased in their CD-ROM format, provide online multimedia help. Multimedia PCs, which are very affordable and highly compatible, are capable of:

▶ displaying television-quality video

▶ recording, editing, and playing stereo CD-quality sound

▶ responding to voice commands; playing MIDI sequences on your synthesizer or other MIDI device

▶ playing fancy CD-ROM titles such as interactive encyclopedias that talk, play music for you, and have moving pictures

All such considerations and the hardware and software that make them work fall into the category of *Windows multimedia*. This chapter will answer your questions about Windows 95's multimedia abilities and how you can best take advantage of them. Please keep in mind while reading that talking about Windows multimedia is like shooting at a moving target. Changes are taking place so rapidly in the field that book publishers would need unrealistically brisk turnaround times (akin to that of magazines) to accurately reflect the state of the industry. Therefore, in the interest of sparing you the annoyance of reading out-of-date material, I'll focus this chapter on the multimedia features of Windows 95 itself and deal only fleetingly with issues of secondary, aftermarket products.

What Is Multimedia?

Multimedia—alias *interactive media* or *hypermedia*—is difficult to define, which accounts for much general confusion on the topic. At the simplest level, in today's use of the term, it simply means adding sound to your programs. At the most advanced level, it is the amalgamation of animation, graphics, video, MIDI, digitally recorded sounds, and text—with all of these presentation media controlled by a single PC.

Some multimedia applications are *interactive* and some are not. Interactivity means that through some input device such as keyboard, mouse, voice, or external controller—for example a Musical Instrument Digital Interface (MIDI) keyboard—you interact with the system to control aspects of the presentation. Most of today's software is still primarily based on text display, perhaps supplemented by simple graphics such as a chart or piece of clip art. With the added capabilities of stereo sound, animation, and video, multimedia computing offers a much richer and more efficient means for conveying information.

As an example of a simple interactive program, consider the Windows tour, which demonstrates Windows fundamentals for the newcomer, reachable from the Start ➤ Help button. The tutorial demonstrates rudimentary multimedia, integrating small moving graphics and text. It does not incorporate speech or live-action video clips. Now imagine expanding such a tutorial to include spoken instructions, music, realistic animation, and moving video images just as if you were watching TV. As you probably know by now, animators, musicians, designers, writers, programmers, audio engineers, industry experts, and video producers are beginning to join forces to create multimedia applications such as:

▶ A WordPerfect document that lets you paste in video clips (with audio) from a VCR tape; instead of displaying just a still graphic, the document will be "alive" with sight and sound.

▶ A music-education program on a CD-ROM from Microsoft that plays Beethoven's Ninth Symphony while displaying informative and educational text about each passage and about the composer.

▶ A dictionary, thesaurus, book of quotations, and encyclopedia on a CD-ROM from Microsoft that not only contains a huge amount of textual information but actually pronounces the dictionary entries; reads quotations aloud in the voices of Robert Frost, Carl Sandburg, T.S. Eliot, e.e. cummings, Dylan Thomas, and JFK; and illustrates scientific phenomena with animation.

▶ Programs that teach you how to play the piano using a MIDI keyboard connected to your PC. The computer senses whether you play the lesson correctly and responds accordingly with a recorded high-quality voice. Similar programs teach music theory.

▶ Multimedia magazines on CD-ROM that let you choose what news topics you want to read. News is displayed like television, with high-fidelity sound and video.

▶ Interactive company annual reports, product demonstrations, presentations, or corporate training manuals for new employees.

▶ Interactive real-time video conferencing (*videotel conferencing*) on your desktop computer, where you can see your colleagues at several remote office locations while working interactively on your company's newsletter, also displayed on the screen.

▶ *Moving catalogs* from mail-order houses, displaying everything from cars to coats via high-quality video and audio.

▶ An interactive geography test used at the National Geographic Society Explorer's Hall in Washington, D.C.

▶ Interactive high-speed, random-access books, newspapers, or catalogs for the blind, using high-quality voice synthesis or recorded voices.

▶ Interactive training for hard-to-teach professions such as medical diagnosis, surgery, auto mechanics, and machine operation of various types.

▶ Complex interactive games that incorporate stereo sound effects, flashy visuals, speech synthesis, and speech recognition, where you interact with the game by speaking.

▶ A program that uses popular sound cards to record your voice, then compresses it on the fly and pumps it across the Internet, allowing two-way conversations with users around the globe without the phone charges.

Most of these applications (often called *multimedia titles*, *information titles*, or simply *titles*) already exist. Others are still in the making. The explosion of multimedia CD titles has been enormous in the last two years, and mail-order CD-ROM catalogs are becoming ubiquitous. One PC Magazine disk includes an entire year's articles, easily searchable.

Upgrading to Multimedia

With Windows 3.0, working with multimedia required purchasing Microsoft's Multimedia upgrade kit or buying an expensive and hard-to-find MPC (multimedia PC). MPCs were manufactured by several vendors and were not generally available on the clone market. Whether upgrading an existing computer or buying an MPC, the results were about the same: you got the Microsoft multimedia extensions (drivers), a CD-ROM drive, audio card, and a good VGA video card.

Either solution was pricey, often amounting to thousands of dollars. Some people didn't want to shell out for the hardware because they only needed a specific hardware addition, such as a sound card. More often than not, people just wanted the software drivers so they could use the hardware they already owned. In response to this interest, Microsoft decided to bundle some popular drivers and a couple of utility programs with the Windows 3.1 package in the hopes that this would accelerate the development of multimedia Windows applications. Microsoft also included the programming *hooks* (called APIs—Application Programming Interfaces) in Windows 3.1 that allow multimedia applications to run on it.

The MPC specification helped set some standards for what a multimedia PC should look and act like, and the PC add-on market did the rest. A vast profusion of multimedia hardware, applications, and utilities have subsequently become prevalent. The magazines now inundate us with ads for newer and faster CD-ROM drives, 64-bit co-processed video cards, high-resolution energy-efficient monitors, and fancy sound cards—even ones with samples of real orchestral instruments built in. The MPC moniker has sort of fallen by the wayside, and now what's really more important is whether a system is Windows 95-compatible or not. After that, the rest is icing on the cake: How big is the screen, how good do the speakers sound, how clear is the image, and overall, how fast does the *whole system* (not just the CPU chip) perform. You'll have to rely on the magazines for these kinds of test comparisons. Don't rely on the guys in the store. One brand of 50-MHz 486 machine might actually be faster than another one that's got a 75-MHz 486 under the hood, due to the vagaries of hard-disk controllers, type of internal bus, memory caching, or speed of the video card.

If you're already in possession of a multimedia-ready machine with a couple of speakers and a CD-ROM drive, you might as well skip this section and move down to the next major section in this chapter, *Supplied Multimedia Applications and Utilities*. But if you're thinking about endowing your machine with the gift of gab, some fancy video graphics capabilities, and the ability to run all those groovy-looking CD-ROM-based games or educational packages your kids are bugging you about, read on.

There are three basic ways to upgrade your computer: buy a whole new computer, buy an "upgrade-in-a-box," or mix and match new components that exactly fit your needs. As of this writing, there were about twenty upgrade-in-a-box products to choose from. You'll typically get a CD-ROM drive, speakers, a sound card, and maybe some CDs in the package. The sound card has the SCSI connector that hooks the CD-ROM drive to the computer. Mixing and matching is for us total control-freak geeks who must have the best or who don't like the idea of other people controlling our purchase decisions. The obvious downside is that sorting through the sea of components in the marketplace is a big waste of time. I've spent too many hours testing video boards, trying to get a SCSI upgrade to my sound card to work with my CD-ROM drive, or running around listening to speakers. In any case, here are a few points about the pros and cons of the three upgrade routes:

NOTE   You might want to check out Chapters 2 and 31 for more about choosing and adding hardware to your system because some of those topics apply to multimedia.

In your shopping, you may wonder what the minimal requirements of a multimedia system should be. With the technology changing so quickly, it's hard to predict what the pickings will look like a year from now and what the latest and greatest version of Star Trek (the interactive CD-ROM game) or Myst will want your system to have. As a rule, though, the best balance between price and performance lies just in the wake of the technology wave. Don't bother being on the cutting edge. Brand new cutting-edge gear is too expensive and usually still has some bugs to be worked out or ends up being dropped by the industry at large. When a product hits the mainstream, that's the time to buy; prices usually take a nosedive at that point, often about 50 percent.

Question	New Computer	Kit in a Box	Mix and Match Components
What is it?	A whole computer that is designed for multimedia Windows 95 from the ground up and includes a fairly zippy computer, color screen, speakers, sound card, and CD-ROM drive.	A box of stuff you get at a computer store or by mail order. Everything works together and costs less than $500. Includes a sound card, CD-ROM drive, and speakers.	CD-ROM drive, sound board, speakers, cabling, and any necessary software drivers that you research and purchase separately.
Who should buy?	Owner of a mid-level computer who has already decided to purchase a new computer either because existing computer isn't worth upgrading to a faster CPU and larger hard disk or because an additional computer is needed.	Average owner of nonmultimedia computer that's well endowed in the CPU and hard-disk area (e.g., a 486 and 250-MB hard disk or larger) but needs multimedia capability to run multimedia games and standard productivity applications.	Power user who wants the best selection of components—or who already has one or two essential components, such as a CD-ROM drive, and now wants the rest. May be a professional such as a musician, application developer, or graphic artist who needs one element of the multimedia upgrade to be very high quality.
How much hassle?	No hassle. Everything is installed and working. Get the system with Windows 95 installed and working if you can, and you're really set.	You'll have to remove the cover to the computer, remove some screws, insert a couple of cards, hook up some cables and the CD-ROM drive if the drive is the internal type then hook up the speakers. If the cards and computer are not Plug-and-Play compatible, you'll have to make IRQ and DMA settings.	About the same amount of hassle as a box upgrade, but you'll have to deal with separate documentation for each component and figure out how to get everything working together, unless they are Plug-and-Play components.

Table 10.1   Approaches to Multimedia Upgrading

Question	New Computer	Kit in a Box	Mix and Match Components
		This may take some homework. You might have conflicts with existing hardware; then you have Windows 95 detect and install drivers for the new hardware, or you use supplied drivers.	IRQ and DMA conflicts are likely otherwise.
Advantages?	Low hassle factor. You can start getting work done instead of poring over magazines and manuals. Your church (or kid) gets your old computer, you get a tax write-off, and you get more sleep.	You don't have to sell your existing computer. You might even get some free CD-ROM software in the box.	You can have exactly what you want. 24-bit TrueColor graphics, direct video capturing, video conferencing, great sound, superfast display at 1,600 by 1,280—you name it.
Disadvantages?	You have to buy a whole new system. You'll probably be compromising somewhat on the components for the low hassle factor.	It will take some work to install it, unless it comes from the same people who made your computer (e.g., a Dell computer). Again, some compromise on the components is likely. You may not have the best-sounding speakers, fastest video, greatest color depth, or CD-ROM drive.	Price and installation hassle is high.
Price?	Not much more for a multimedia system than for those without multimedia. A few hundred additional dollars is typical.	Typically between $200 and $500, though some high-class upgrades are closer to a thousand.	Difficult to predict. Bottom-of-the-line but functional clone parts could run you as little as a few hundred dollars. Or you could pay well into the thousands for the best brands.

Table 10.1 *Approaches to Multimedia Upgrading (continued)*

What does that mean in the current market? Well the MPC specification requires at least a machine with 4 MB of RAM, a 130-MB hard disk, and a fast processor such as a 486 or Pentium. Here are my thoughts when you're shopping for multimedia components and systems:

Computer   I'd suggest at least a 486DX2/50 CPU, a local bus video card, and a 500-MB hard disk (E-IDE or SCSI), with 8 MB (preferably 16 MB) of RAM. SCSI is the better bet because you can also hook up as many as seven devices to a SCSI controller, not just hard disks.

CD-ROM Drive   Get at least a double-speed drive. Double-speed drives will do most anything you need, albeit slower than triple- or quad-speed drives. Windows 95 caches your CD-ROM drive, so that will help with slower drives. Quad-speed drives are getting cheap and you will notice the difference, so get one if you can afford it. If you want to be able to connect to a laptop or move the drive between computers, get a lightweight portable external job. You'll pay more for it, but prices are plummeting anyway, so the difference won't be that much. If you change disks a lot, get the *caddyless* type. Make sure the drive supports *multisession* Kodak photo format. This lets you not only view photographs in CD-ROM format on your computer but also take an existing photo CD-ROM to your photo developer down at the pharmacy and have them add new pictures to it. You might want up-front manual controls on the player so you can listen to audio CDs without running the CD Player program.

Speakers   The larger the better, usually. Little speakers will sound tinny by definition. Listen before you buy if possible. Listen to a normal, speaking human voice—the most difficult instrument to reproduce. Does it sound natural? Then hear something with some bass. If you're going to listen to audio CDs, bring one with you to the store and play it. Speakers that are separate (not built into the monitor) will allow a nicer stereo effect. Separate tweeter and woofer will probably sound better, but not always. It depends on the electronics in the speaker. Magnetic shielding is important if the speakers are going to be within a foot or so of your screen; otherwise, the colors and alignment of the image on the screen will be adversely affected. (Not permanently damaged, though. The effect stops when you move the speakers away.) Of course, instead of buying speakers you can use your stereo or even a boom box if it has high-level (sometimes called *auxiliary*) input. Some boom boxes and virtually all stereos do have such an input. Then it's just a matter of using the correct wire to attach your sound card's *line* output to the stereo's or boom box's Aux input and setting the volume appropriately. The easiest solution is to purchase a pair of amplified speakers designed for small recording studios, apartments, or computers. For about $150 you can find a good pair of smaller-sized shielded speakers (4- or 5-inch woofer, separate tweeter) with volume, bass, and treble controls. For $300 you can get some that sound very good. If you like real bass, shell out a little more for a set that comes with a separate larger sub-woofer you put under your desk.

Sound Board   This should have 16-bit 44.1-KHz sound capability for CD-quality sound. You'll want line-in, line-out, and microphone in jacks at least. Typical cards also have a joystick port for your game controller. The card should be compatible with Windows 95, with the General MIDI specification, and with Sound Blaster so it will work with popular games. This means it should have protected-mode 32-bit drivers for Windows 95 either supplied with Windows 95 or with the card. If it doesn't, you'll be stuck using 16-bit drivers that take up too much conventional memory space, preventing many DOS-based games and educational programs from running. I've seen this problem with cards, such as the Sound Blaster Pro, prevent a number of games such as the Eagle-Eye Mystery series from running. Fancy cards such as those from Turtle Beach don't sound like cheesy synthesizers when they play MIDI music because they use samples of real instruments stored in *wave tables* instead of using synthesizer chips, but you'll pay more for them.

Video Card and Monitor   (The video card goes inside the computer and produces the signals needed to create a display on the monitor. A cable runs between the video card and the monitor.) For high-performance multimedia, you'll want a *local bus* video card (typically VLB or PCI) capable of at least 256 colors at the resolution you desire. Local bus cards only work in computers that have a local bus connector slot, so check out which kind of slots your computer has. Standard resolution (number of dots on the screen at one time, comprising the picture) for a PC is 640 (horizontal) by 480 (vertical). Most new video cards these days will support that resolution at 256

Part
2

Exploring Windows 95

colors. If you have a very sharp 15-inch screen or a 17-inch screen, you may opt for a higher resolution, such as 800 by 600 or 1,024 by 768. When shopping for a video card, make sure they display at least 256 colors (and preferably in the thousands of colors) at the resolution you want *and have at least 70-Hz noninterlaced refresh rate at that resolution and color depth.* The correct refresh rate ensures the screen doesn't flicker and give you a headache. Video cards with graphics co-processor chips on them will run faster than those that don't. Fast speed is necessary when you move objects around on the screen or display video clips. Make sure the board will work well with Windows 95, preferably with the 32-bit video driver that comes with Windows 95, not an old driver designed for Windows 3.x. You don't have to worry about any monitor's ability to display colors because any color monitor will display all the colors your card can produce. What you have to check out are the monitor's dot pitch, controls, and refresh rate. The monitor should ideally have a dot pitch of .25 or .26, be at least 17 inches (though 15 inches will do), and run all your desired resolutions at 70-Hz refresh or higher to avoid flicker. Beware of the refresh-rate issue: False or misleading advertising is rampant. Many monitors and video cards advertise 72-Hz or higher refresh rates, but the fine print reveals that this is only at 640 by 480. Bump up the resolution, and the refresh on cheaper cards or monitors drops to a noticeable 60 Hz. Get a monitor that has low radiation emissions, powers down automatically when isn't being used (a so-called green monitor), and has a wide variety of controls for size, picture position, pincushion, and barrel, brightness, contrast, color, and so forth.

That's the basic rundown on multimedia upgrading. Now let's look at what's supplied with Windows 95 in the way of multimedia programs and utilities.

The Supplied Multimedia Applications and Utilities

Here's what you get in the way of multimedia programs and utilities with Windows 95:

Sound Settings   This Control Panel applet lets you assign specific sound files (stored in the .wav format) to Windows system events such as error messages, information dialog boxes, and when starting and exiting Windows.

Media Player This application, which you'll find in the Accessories ➤ Multimedia folder from the Start button, lets you play a variety of multimedia files on the files' target hardware. In the case of a device that contains data, such as a CD-ROM or video disk, Media Player sends commands to the hardware, playing back the sound or video therein. If the data are stored on your hard disk (as are MIDI sequences, animation, and sound files), Media Player will send them to the appropriate piece of hardware, such as a sound board, MIDI keyboard, or other device.

TECH TIP   The Media Player only works with MCI devices (Media Control Interface) and thus requires MCI device drivers.

Sound Recorder This is a little program for simple recording of sounds from a microphone or auxiliary input and then editing them. Once recorded, sound files can be used with other programs through OLE or used to replace or augment the generic beeps your computer makes to alert you to dialog boxes, errors, and so forth. It is also the default program used to play back WAV files.

CD Player Assuming your computer's CD-ROM drive and controller card supports it (most do), this accessory program lets you play back standard audio CDs. This can be great boon on long winter nights when you're chained to your PC doing your taxes or writing that boring report. You'll find coverage of this program in Chapter 22 along with the other Accessory odds and ends.

Adding Drivers The System and Add New hardware applets in the Control Panel let you install drivers for many add-in cards and devices such as CD-ROMs, MIDI interface cards, and video-disk controllers. Drivers for most popular sound boards such as the Sound Blaster (from Creative Labs, Inc.) and Ad Lib (Ad Lib, Inc.) and popular MIDI boards such as the Roland MPU-401 (Roland Digital Group) are supplied. Other drivers can be installed from manufacturer-supplied disks using this option. Even if your hardware is physically installed, it won't work unless the proper driver is loaded.

A few programs have either been covered elsewhere in this book or were seen in Windows 3.x but have been dropped from Windows 95. They are:

Volume Control The volume control accessory, available from the Taskbar, simply lets you control the balance and volume levels of the various sound sources that end up playing through your computer's speakers. This is covered in Chapter 22.

MIDI Mapper This was included as a separate Control Panel applet in Windows 3.1 and NT but has been hidden in Windows 95 because it is rarely used. Its purpose was to declare settings for your MIDI device, such as channel assignment, key remapping, and patch-number reassignment for nonstandard MIDI instruments. The assumption now is that most MIDI instruments comply with the General MIDI standard for these parameters and thus the Mapper is rarely needed. If you have a nonstandard MIDI instrument that you're running from Windows programs (this won't affect DOS programs), check out the Control Panel's Multimedia ➤ MIDI ➤ Add New Instrument button. It will lead you to the rather complex remapping facilities.

Assigning Sounds with the Control Panel's Sound Utility

The Control Panel's Sound utility is for designating sounds to system events, such as warning dialog boxes, error messages when you click in the wrong place, and so on. Once you've installed a sound board, you can personalize your computer's beep to something more exciting. If your computer had a sound card when you installed Windows 95, it's likely Windows 95 established a default set of rather boring sounds for your system, most of which you're probably tired of already. Aside from making life more interesting, having different sounds for different types of events is also more informative. You know when you've made an error as opposed to when an application is acknowledging your actions, for example.

Of course, to add basic sounds to your Windows setup, you need a Windows 95-compatible sound card. The sounds you can use must be stored on disk in the .wav format. Most sounds you can download from BBSs or get on disk at the computer store are in this format. Also, the Sound

Recorder program explained later in the chapter records sounds in WAV format. Windows 95 comes with more than a few sound files now, a big improvement over the measly assemblage of WAV files supplied with Windows 3.x. In fact, just as with the color schemes you can create and save with the Control Panel's Display applet (covered in Chapter 7), you can set up and save personalized sound schemes to suit your mood. Microsoft has supplied us with several such schemes, running the gamut from happy nature sounds to futuristic, mechanistic robot utterances to the sonorities of classical musical instruments.

> **NOTE** You have to do a Custom installation to get all the sound schemes loaded into your computer. You can do this after the fact by running Control Panel ➤ Add/Remove Programs ➤ Windows Setup. Then click on Multimedia to select it and click on the Details button. The sound schemes are located near the bottom of the list.

Despite this diverse selection, you may still want to make or acquire more interesting sounds yourself or collect them from other sources. To record your own, you'll need a sound board such as Sound Blaster or another digital sampler board. I have messages in my own voice, such as, "You made a stupid mistake, you fool," which—for a short time—seemed preferable to the mindless chime. If your system lets you play audio CDs, you should be able to directly sample bits and pieces from your favorite artists by popping the audio CD into the computer and tapping directly into it rather than by sticking a microphone up to your boom box and accidentally recording the telephone when it rings. Check out the Volume Control applet and adjust the slider on the mixer panel that controls the input volume of the CD. Then use the Sound Recorder applet to make the recording.

Like any good sound-o-phile, I'm always on the lookout for good WAV files. You'll find them everywhere if you just keep your eyes open: cheap CDs at the local Compu-Geek store, on the Internet, on CompuServe, even on other people's computers. Usually these sound files aren't copyrighted, so copying them isn't likely to be a legal issue. Most WAV files intended for system sounds aren't that big, either. But do check out the size, using the Explorer or by showing the Details view in a folder, before copying them. Sound files *can* be super large, especially if they are recorded in 16-bit stereo. As a rule you'll want to keep the size to a minimum for system sounds because it can take more than a few seconds for a larger sound file to load and begin to play.

Once you're set up for sound and have some WAV files, you assign them to specific Windows events. Here's how:

1. Open the Control Panel and run the Sounds applet. The dialog box shown in Figure 10.1 appears:

2. The top box lists the events that can have sounds associated with them. There will be at least two classes of events—one for Windows

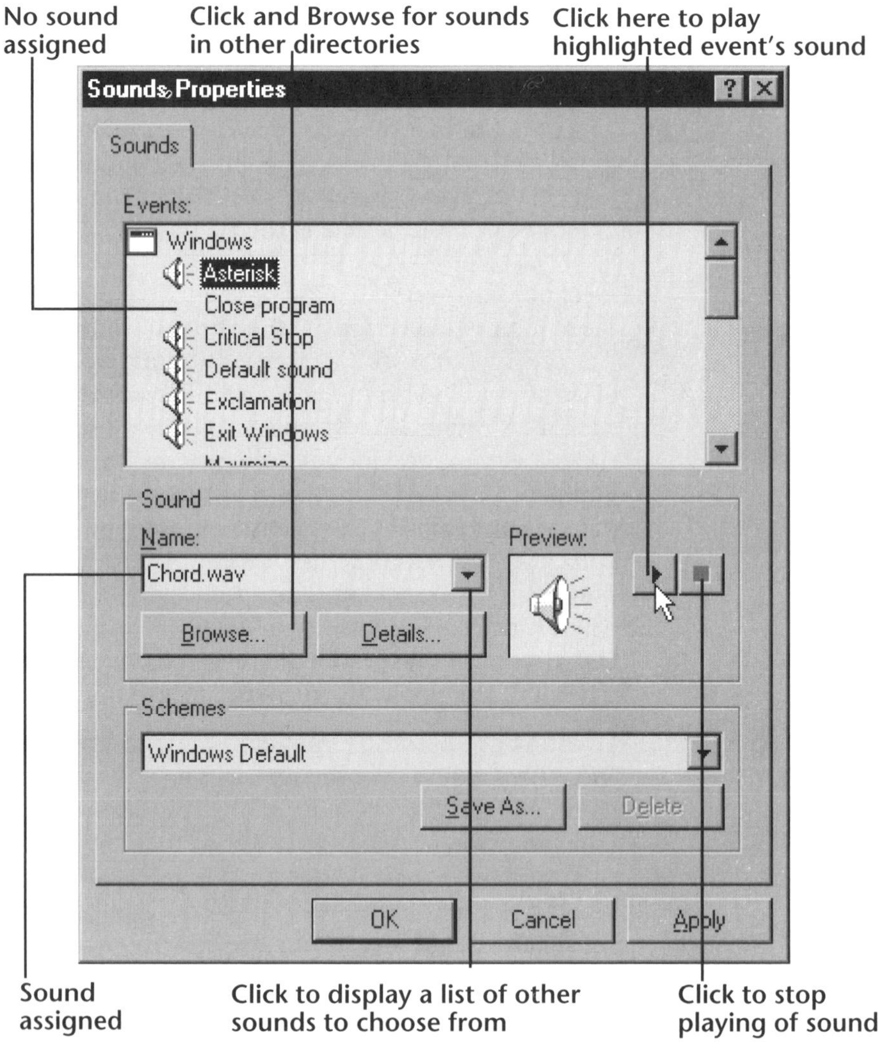

No sound assigned **Click and Browse for sounds in other directories** **Click here to play highlighted event's sound**

Sound assigned **Click to display a list of other sounds to choose from** **Click to stop playing of sound**

Figure 10.1   Use this dialog box to choose which sounds your computer makes when Windows events occur.

events and one for Explorer events. (Scroll the list to the bottom to see the Explorer events.) As you purchase and install new programs in the future, those programs may add their own events to your list. An event with a speaker icon next to it already has a sound associated with it. You can click on it and then click on the Preview button to hear the sound. The sound file that's associated with the event is listed in the Name box.

3. Click on any event for which you want to assign a sound or change the assigned sound.

4. Open the drop-down Name list and choose the WAV file you want to use for that event. Some of the event names may not make sense to you, such as Asterisk, Critical Stop, or Exclamation. These are names for the various classes of dialog boxes that Windows 95 displays from time to time. The sounds you're most likely to hear often will be Default beep, Menu Command, Menu Popup, Question, Open Program, Close Program, Minimize, Maximize, Start Windows, and Exit Windows.

TIP   The default directory for sounds is the `\Windows\Media` directory. That's where the WAV files that come with Windows 95 are stored. If you have WAV files stored somewhere else, you'll have to use the Browse button to find and assign them to an event. I find it's easier to copy all my WAV files into the `\Windows\Media` directory than to go browsing for them when I want to do a lot of reassigning of sounds.

---

5. At the top of the list of available sounds there is an option called <none> that has the obvious effect—no sound will occur for that event. Assigning all events to <none> will effectively silence your computer for use in a library, church, and so forth. You can also quickly do this for all sounds by choosing the No Sounds scheme as explained below.

6. Repeat the process for other events to which you want to assign or reassign sounds.

7. Click on OK.

Keep in mind that different applications will use event sounds differently. You'll have to do some experimenting to see when your applications use the default beep, as opposed to the Asterisk, Question, or the Exclamation.

Clicking on the Details button displays information about the WAV file, such as its time length, data format, and copyright information (if it's copyrighted).

Loading and Saving Sound Schemes

Just as the Control Panel's Display applet lets you save color schemes, the Sounds applet lets you save sound schemes so you can set up goofy sounds for your humorous moods and somber ones for those gloomy days—or vice versa. The schemes supplied with Windows 95 are pretty nice even without modification.

To choose an existing sound scheme:

1. Click on the drop-down list button for schemes, down at the bottom of the box:

2. A list of existing schemes will appear. Choose a sound scheme. Now all the events in the upper part of the box will have the new sound scheme's sounds. Check out the sounds to see if you like them.

3. If you like them, click on OK.

   You can set up your own sound schemes by assigning or reassigning individual sounds, as I've already explained. But unless you *save* the scheme, it will be lost the next time you change to a new one. So, the moral is: once you get your favorite sounds assigned to system events, save the scheme. Then you can call it up any time you like. Here's how:

1. Set up the sounds the way you want. You can start with an existing scheme and modify it or start from scratch by choosing the No Sounds scheme and assigning sounds one by one.

2. Click on the Save As button.

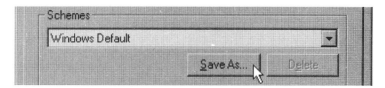

3. In the resulting dialog box, enter a name for the scheme. For example, here's one I made up and saved:

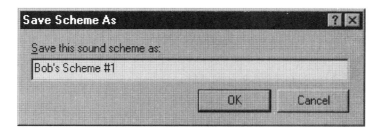

4. OK the little dialog box, and your scheme is saved. Now you can create additional schemes and save them or just OK the large dialog box to activate the new scheme.

You can delete any existing sound schemes by choosing the doomed scheme from the list and then clicking on the delete button. You'll be asked to confirm the deletion.

Playing Multimedia Files with Media Player

Media Player is a little application that plays multimedia files, such as digitized sounds, MIDI music files, and animated graphics. It can also send control information to multimedia devices such as audio CD players or video disk players, determining which tracks to play, when to pause, when to activate slow motion, and so on.

Obviously, you can only use Media Player on devices installed in your system and for which you've installed the correct device drivers (see *Installing New Drivers*, below), so first see to that task. Then follow these instructions for playing a multimedia file:

1. Run Media Player from the Start ➤ Programs ➤ Accessories ➤ Multimedia folder. The Media Player's control panel appears, as shown here:

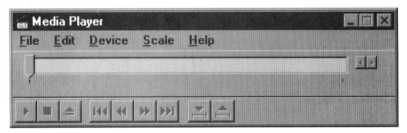

2. Open the Device menu and choose the type of device that's going to receive the information.

3. If the type of device you've chosen has an ellipsis (...) after it, a File Open dialog box will appear, asking for the name of the file you want played and displaying the files with the correct extension for the selected device. This only happens with devices that play a file stored in a disk file (this type of device is called a *compound* device). Choose the file you want played. If the device you selected has no ellipsis after it, it's a *simple* device. This means the data to be played are already in the drive—as in the case of a CD-ROM or video disk—and don't have to be chosen (no File Open box will appear). When you load a file for a compound device, the Media Player's appearance will change slightly to display a scale and tick marks indicating the length of the item:

TIP You can jump to a particular location in the piece by dragging the scroll bar, clicking at the desired point in the scroll bar, or using ↑, ↓, ←, →, PgUp, and PgDn. Also, check the Device menu for options pertaining to the device you are using.

4. Now you can use the buttons in the dialog box to begin playing the piece. The buttons work just as on a VCR or cassette deck; if in doubt, the buttons have pop-up descriptions. The Eject button only works for most devices with an Eject feature, like an audio CD player. However, not all devices will respond to the eject button. It depends on the device and the driver.

5. If you want to open another file for the same device (in the case of compound devices), use the File ➤ Open command to do so. If you want to play a file intended for another device, you'll have to change the device type first from the Device menu, which will then bring up the File ➤ Open command for you to open a new file.

6. You can change the scale (tick marks) above the scroll bar to show *tracks* instead of time. Track display may be useful when you're playing audio CDs or video disks arranged by track. Do this from the Scale menu. Track tick marks will then replace the time tick marks. To change tracks, drag the scroll bar, click on the scroll buttons, or use →, ←, PgUp, and PgDn.

7. When you're done playing, close the application from the Exit menu.

NOTE Compound devices will stop as soon as you quit Media Player; simple devices will continue to play.

Media Player has a few options worth noting. Check out the Edit ➤ Options and Device ➤ Configure options. Choose Device ➤ Volume control to bring up the volume control and mixer for your particular sound board.

NOTE Use of the Volume Control is covered in Chapter 7 of this book.

Recording and Editing Sounds with Sound Recorder

Sound Recorder is a nifty little program that lets you record your own sounds and create WAV files. To make it work, you need a digital sampling card such as the Sound Blaster with a microphone. The program also lets you do some editing and manipulation of any WAV files you might have on disk. You can do this even if you don't have a microphone.

The resulting WAV files can be put to a variety of uses, including assigning them to system events or using them with other multimedia applications, such as Media Player. Once a file is recorded, you can edit it by removing portions of it. Unfortunately, you cannot edit from one arbitrary spot to another, only from one spot to either the beginning or the end of the file. You can also add an echo effect to a sample, play it backwards, change the playback speed (and resulting pitch), and alter the playback volume.

Playing a Sound File

Follow the steps below to play a sound file:

1. Make sure you've installed the correct driver and that your sound board works (Chapter 7 discusses how to add new hardware and drivers).

2. Run Sound Recorder by choosing Start ➤ Programs ➤ Accessories ➤ Multimedia ➤ Sound Recorder. The Sound Recorder window will appear, as shown here.

3. Choose File ➤ Open and choose the file you want to play. Notice that the length of the sound appears at the right of the window and the current position of the play head appears on the left.

4. Click on the Play button or press Enter to play the sound. As it plays, the wave box displays the sound, oscilloscope style. The Status Bar also says *Playing*. When the sound is over, Sound Recorder stops and the Status Bar says *Stopped*. Press Enter again to replay the sound.

You can click on Stop during a playback to pause the sound, then click on Play to continue.

5. Drag the scroll button around (see below) and notice how the wave box displays a facsimile of the frequency and amplitude of the sample over time.

You can also click on the rewind and fast-forward buttons to move to the start and end of the sample or press the PgUp and PgDn keys to jump the play head forward or backward in longer increments.

Recording a New Sound

This is the fun part, so get your microphone ready. Suppose you want to make up your own sounds, perhaps to put into an OLE-capable application document such as Write or Cardfile so that it talks when clicked on. Here's how:

1. Choose File ➤ New.

2. You may want to check the recording format before you begin. Choose File ➤ Properties. Select Recording Formats, then click on Convert Now. A dialog box appears, asking some details about the recording format as shown in Figure 10.2. A combination of data-recording format (e.g., PCM, Microsoft's ADPCM, and so forth) and sampling rate (e.g., 8-KHz 4-bit mono) are shown. Together these comprise a *format scheme*.

Part 2

Exploring Windows 95

Choose a pre-existing format scheme here

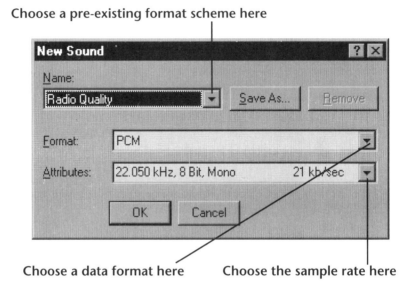

Choose a data format here   Choose the sample rate here

Figure 10.2   *Choosing a data scheme for a new sound recording*

NOTE   The Attributes list shows the amount of disk space consumed per second of recording. You'll want to consider this when making new files, as recording in high-fidelity stereo can suck up precious disk room, rendering sound files quite unwieldy. Also, for most purposes, you are best served by choosing one of the preexisting sound schemes—CD-Quality, Radio Quality, or Telephone Quality—for your recordings. All three use the PCM recording technique but employ different sample rates. If you are recording only voice, use either the Radio or Telephone setting. The CD-quality setting will only use up more disk space than you need to. If you are planning to record from an audio CD player, you'll probably want to choose the CD-quality setting unless you want to conserve disk space. If you accidentally record at a higher quality level than you wanted to, don't worry. You can convert to a lower quality and regain some hard disk space via the File ➤ Properties ➤ Convert Now button. You can save recording and playback settings with the Save As button in the dialog box if you want or not save it if you don't mind choosing a setup each time you want to change from the default settings.

3. Click on the Record button. The clock starts ticking, counting the passing time. Begin talking into the microphone that's plugged into your sound card, playing whatever is connected to your AUX input (aka *line in*) on the sound card, or playing the audio CD that's in the CD-ROM drive. You'll have to use the volume control applet to set the relative balance of the various devices. Typically you'll be able to mix these disparate audio sources into a single recording if you use the mixer deftly. The maximum recording time will vary, depending on your recording format. In the default setting (PCM, 22.050-KHz 8-bit mono) you can record for up to one minute. Be cautious about the length of your sounds, as they tend to take up a large amount of disk space. For example, a one-second sample at CD Quality in stereo consumes about 172K.

4. Click on Stop when you are finished recording.

5. Play back the file to see if you like it.

6. Save the file with File ➤ Save As. You'll see the familiar File dialog box. Enter a name (you don't have to enter the WAV extension; the program does that for you).

When recording a voice narration, make sure to speak loudly and clearly, particularly if you notice that playback is muffled or buried in noise.

TIP A simple way to create a new sound file is to right-click on the Desktop and choose New ➤ Sound File. Name the file, then double-click on it. Then click on the Record button.

Editing Sounds

You can edit sound files in several ways. For instance, you can:

▶ add echo to a sample

▶ reverse a sample

▶ mix two samples together

▶ remove unwanted parts of a sample

▶ increase or decrease the volume

▶ increase or decrease the speed and pitch

NOTE   You may run out of memory if your file becomes very long because of inserting files into one another. The amount of free physical memory (not virtual memory) determines the maximum size of any sound file.

To edit a sound file:

1. Open the sound file from the File menu.

2. Open the Effects menu to add echo, reverse the sound, increase or decrease volume, or increase or decrease speed. All the settings except echo are undoable, so you can experiment without worry. You undo a setting by choosing its complementary setting from the menu (e.g., Increase Volume v. Decrease Volume) or by choosing Reverse. Some sound quality can be lost by doing this repeatedly, however.

3. To cut out the beginning or ending of a sound—i.e., to eliminate the lag time it took you to get to the microphone or hit the Stop button—determine the beginning and ending points of the sound, get to the actual starting position of the sound, and choose Edit ➤ Delete Before Current Position. Then move the scroll button to the end of the desired portion of the sample and choose Edit ➤ Delete After Current Position.

4. To mix two existing sounds, position the cursor where you'd like to begin the mix, choose Edit ➤ Mix with File, and choose the file name. This can create some very interesting effects that are much richer than single sounds.

5. To insert a file into a predetermined spot, move to the spot with the scroll bar, choose Edit ➤ Insert File, and choose the file name.

6. To put a sound on the Clipboard for pasting elsewhere, use Edit ➤ Copy.

7. To return your sound to its original, last-saved state, choose File ➤ Revert.

Note that not all sound boards have the same features. Some won't let you save a recording into certain types of sound files. Also the quality of the sound differs from board to board. Some boards sound "grainy," others less so. This is determined by the sampling rate you've chosen, the quality of the digital-to-analog converters (DAC), and the analog amplifiers on the board.

Playing Tunes with CD Player

The CD Player accessory turns your computer's CD-ROM drive into a music machine: With it, you can play standard audio CDs with all the controls you'd expect on a "real" CD player, and then some. Of course, you'll need speakers (or at least a pair of headphones) to hear the music. Here's what CD Player looks like:

With CD Player, you can:

▶ play any CD once through or continuously while you work with other programs

▶ play the tracks in sequential or random order, or play only the tracks you like

▶ move forward or in reverse to any desired track

▶ fast forward or rewind while a track is playing

▶ stop, pause, and resume playback, and (if your CD-ROM drive has the capability) eject the current CD

▶ control play volume if you're playing the CD through a sound card (this only works with some CD-ROM drives)

▶ control the contents of the time display (you can display elapsed time, time remaining for the current track, or time remaining for the entire CD)

▶ catalog your CDs (after you've typed in the title and track list for a CD, CD Player will recognize it when you load it again, displaying the titles of the disk and the current track)

Getting Started with CD Player

To run CD Player, begin from the Start menu and choose Programs ➤ Accessories ➤ CD Player. Load your CD-ROM drive with an audio CD, turn on your sound system or plug in the headphones, and you're ready to go.

CD Player can tell when your CD-ROM drive is empty or doesn't contain a playable audio CD. In this case, it will display the message:

```
Data or no disc loaded
Please insert an audio disc
```

in the Artist and Title areas in the middle of the window.

Basic Playing Controls

The CD Player window looks much like the front panel of a typical CD

player in a sound system. The large black area at the top left displays track and time information. On the left, the faux LED readout tells you which track is currently playing, while on the right it keeps a running tally of how many minutes and seconds have played in the track (you can change the contents of the time display as detailed below).

If you've ever worked a standard CD player, the control buttons (to the right of the track and time display) should be immediately familiar.

On the top row are the essential stop/start controls:

Play: The largest button with the big arrow starts or resumes play.

Pause: The button with the two vertical bars pauses play at the current point in the track.

Stop: The button with the square stops play and returns you to the beginning of the current track.

On the second row, the first four buttons have double arrows pointing to the left or right. These let you move to other parts of the disk.

TIP You can move directly to a specific track by choosing it from the list in the Track area near the bottom of the CD Player window. See *Playing Discs with the Play List* later in the chapter.

Previous and *Next Track:* At either end of this set of four buttons, the buttons with the vertical bars move to the beginning of the previous or next track. The one at the left end—with the left-pointing arrows—moves to the beginning of the previous track (or if a track is playing, to the beginning of the current track). The one at the right—with the right-pointing arrows—moves to the beginning of the next track.

Skip Backwards and *Skip Forwards:* The two center buttons in the set of four have double arrows only; these are for moving quickly through the music while the disc plays in the reverse or forward direction.

The *Eject* button is the last button at the far right of the second row, with the upward-pointing arrow on top of a thin rectangle. Click here to pop the current disk out of your CD-ROM drive. Of course, this will only work if your drive is capable of ejecting automatically.

Display Options

Modern Windows program that it is, CD Player has a *Toolbar* with buttons for other common commands (we'll cover these in a moment). The Toolbar may not be visible when you first run the program. Choose View ➤ Toolbar to turn it on and off. Here's how the CD Player window looks with the Toolbar visible:

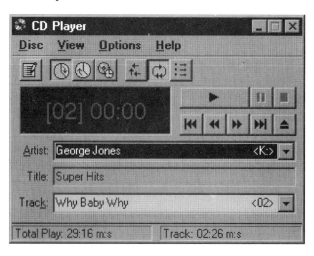

Part 2

Exploring Windows 95

When the Toolbar is on, you can get a brief description of each button's function by placing the mouse pointer over the button.

Two other elements of the CD Player window can also be turned off and on via the View menu. These are the Status Bar and the area displaying the artist and disc and track titles.

When visible, the Status Bar runs along the bottom of the window. It offers Help messages when the mouse pointer passes over a menu choice or rests over a button on the Toolbar for a few moments. Otherwise, it displays the total play time for the disc and current track. To turn the Status Bar off or on, choose View ▶ Status Bar.

Once you've cataloged a disc, CD Player displays the artist, disc title, and title of the current track in the middle of its window. If you want to hide this information, perhaps to make the window small enough to stay on your screen while you work with another program, choose View ▶ Disc/Track Info.

TIP You can choose between two font sizes for the numerals in the track and time readout. See *Setting CD Player Preferences* below.

You can also control what time information appears in the main readout of the CD Player window. The standard display setting shows elapsed time for the track currently playing. If you prefer, you can instead see the time remaining for the current track or for the entire disk. To select among these options, open the View menu and choose one of the three relevant options: Track Time Elapsed, Track Time Remaining, or Disk Time Remaining. The currently active choice is checked on the View menu. Or, if the Toolbar is visible, you can click on the button corresponding to your time-display choice.

Other Play Options

You have several commands for determining the play order for a disc's tracks. Three of these are available as items on the Options menu or as buttons on the Toolbar:

Random order: Plays the tracks randomly. This is often called *shuffle* mode on audio-only CD players.

Continuous play: Plays the disc continuously rather than stopping after the last track.

Intro play: Plays only the first section of each track. You can set the length of this intro with the Preferences command, covered below.

 NOTE If you have a multiple-disc CD-ROM drive, you'll find an additional Multidisc Play choice on the Options menu. Select this if you want to hear all the discs loaded in the drive rather than just the currently active disc.

You can select these playback options in any combination. To turn them on or off, open the Options menu and choose the desired item; they are active when checked. Alternatively, click on the button for that command (the button appears pressed when the command is active). Here are the buttons you use:

 If none of these commands are active, CD Player plays the tracks in full and in sequence, stopping after the last track.

Other play options include whether or not the current disc keeps playing when you close CD Player (covered in *Setting CD Player Preferences*, below) and playing a custom list of tracks, covered in the next section.

Cataloging Your CDs and Creating Play Lists

If you're willing to do a little typing, CD Player will keep a "smart" catalog of your disc collection. Once you've entered the catalog information, such as the disc title, the artist, and the track titles, CD Player automatically displays these details whenever you reload the disc:

Note that if you have a multidisc CD-ROM drive (or more than one unit), you can choose from the available drives by letter using the list in the Artist area.

Cataloging a Disc   When you load a disc that hasn't been cataloged, CD Player displays generic disc information. The Artist area reads *New Artist*, and the Title area says *New Title*. Tracks are titled by number (*Track 1*, *Track 2*, and so on).

To enter the actual information for the current disc, choose Disc ➤ Edit Play List, or, if the Toolbar is visible, click on the corresponding button (the one at the far left, shown here on the left). The dialog box shown in Figure 10.3 will appear.

The top area in this dialog box, labeled Drive, identifies the location of the disc being cataloged. If you have a multidisc player, you can double-check whether you're working with the correct disc here.

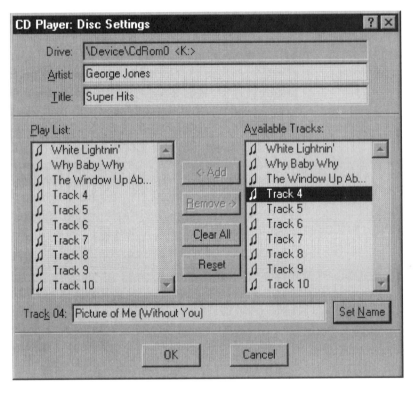

Figure 10.3   *The Disc Settings dialog box*

Type in the artist and title of the CD in the appropriate areas at the top of the dialog box. To type in track titles:

1. Select a track in the Available Tracks box (the one at the *right* of the dialog box).

2. Type in the track title in the Track area at the bottom of the dialog box.

3. Click on the Set Name button to change the current name.

You can change any of this information at any time. When you're satisfied with your entries, go on to create a play list as described below or click on OK to return to CD Player. The disc information will appear in the appropriate areas of the window.

Creating a Play List   The typical CD has some great songs, a few that are good to listen to but aren't favorites, and one or two that are just terrible. CD Player lets you set up a custom play list for each disc so you never have to hear those dog songs again. If you like, you can even play your favorites more often than the others (be careful, you might get sick of them).

Here's how to create a play list:

1. In the Disc Settings dialog box (Figure 10.3), the Play List box on the left side of the window displays the tracks in the play list. Initially, the box displays all the tracks on the disc in order.

2. If you just want to remove one or two tracks, drag each track off the list as follows: Point to the track's icon (the musical notes) in the Play List box, hold down the mouse button, and drag to the Available Tracks box. Alternatively, you can highlight each track in the Play List box and click on the Remove button. To remove all the tracks and start with an empty list, click on Clear All.

3. You can add tracks to the play list in two ways:

   ▶ Drag the track (or tracks) to the Play List box using the same technique for deleting tracks but in the reverse direction: Starting from the Available Tracks box, drag the track to the desired position in the play list. You can add a group of tracks by dragging across them to highlight them, releasing the mouse button, then dragging from the icon area to the play list.

Part 2

Exploring Windows 95

> ▶ Use the Add button: Highlight one or more tracks in the Available Tracks box and click on Add. In this case, the added track always appears at the end of the list.

4. If you want to start again, click on Reset. The Play List box will again show all the tracks in order.

5. Click on OK when you've finished your play list to return to the main CD Player window.

Playing Discs with the Play List   CD Player always selects the tracks it plays from the play list. Before you make any modifications, the play list contains all the tracks on the disc, and you'll hear every track when you play the disc. Once you've created your own play list, though, CD Player plays only the tracks on the list. If you select Random Order play, the program randomly selects tracks from the play list, not from all the tracks on the disc.

The play list tracks are accessible individually in the Track area near the bottom of the CD Player window. To move to a particular track, just select it in the list. If the disc is already playing, the selected track will start. Otherwise, click on the Play button to start it.

Setting CD Player Preferences

Use the Preferences dialog box to change miscellaneous CD Player settings. To display it, choose Options ➤ Preferences. Here's what the Preferences dialog box looks like:

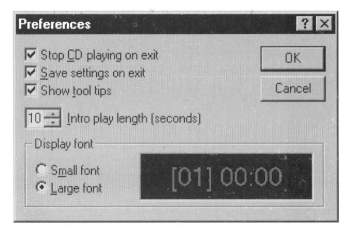

Here are the available preferences settings and their effects:

Stop CD playing on exit: When this box is checked, CD Player stops the CD-ROM drive, halting audio playback. If you clear this box, the current disc plays through to the end.

Save settings on exit: When this box is checked, the settings you make on the View and Options menu and in the Preferences dialog box are saved when you close the program. If you clear this box, changes in settings affect only the current session—the previous settings are restored the next time you start CD Player.

Show tool tips: Check this box if you want pop-up descriptions and Help messages in the Status Bar when the mouse pointer rests on a button for a few moments. Clear it if you find these messages annoying.

Intro play length: Use the arrow controls to set the number of seconds at the beginning of each track that CD Player will play when you activate the Intro Play command.

Display font: Choose a large or small font for the LED-like track and time readout by choosing the appropriate radio button.

Managing Multimedia Drivers

When you add a new piece of hardware to your system, such as a sound board, CD-ROM controller, MIDI board, or other piece of paraphernalia, you'll have to alert Windows to this fact by installing the correct software device driver for the job. Some drivers simply control an external player as though you were pushing the buttons on the device's control panel by hand. These types of devices are called Media Control Interface (MCI) devices and include audio CD players, video disc players, and MIDI instruments. Other drivers actually send the sound or video data to the playback card or hardware, as well as control the playback speed and other parameters.

You use the Add New Hardware option in the Control Panel to install the device driver. Drivers for popular multimedia items are included with Windows and will often be detected when you've added the hardware, especially if the hardware is Plug-and-Play compatible.

Chapter 7 covers the use of the Add New Hardware applet; refer to that chapter if you have added new multimedia hardware to your system and it isn't being recognized.

Part 2

Exploring Windows 95

If you are having trouble running your multimedia hardware or need to make adjustments to it, you'll have to examine the Properties of the item and its driver. Device property dialog boxes can be reached from several locations. For example, the Edit menu in the Sound Recorder applet will take you to your sound card's Properties settings, though you could also use the System applet in the Control Panel to get there. Properties are discussed in Chapter 11.

Information Sources

Magazines are great sources of quickly changing computer-product information. Visit your local smoke shop or magazine rack to look for multimedia intelligence. One magazine speaks directly to the issues herein—*MPC World*, available nationwide.

For online assistance, files, and general chitchat on multimedia, try CompuServe's Multimedia Forum (**GO MULTIMEDIA**) and Multimedia Vendor Forum (**GO MULTIVEN**); they contain the latest gossip, hints, trivia, and tips on the subject. Also try the Windows Advanced Forum (**GO WINADV**) and The Microsoft Network.

Windows Information Manager (*WIM*) is a periodical that's offered in a hypertext multimedia format, incorporating sound and animation.

Finally, there is at least one book that looks at Microsoft's multimedia development tools and discusses the processes involved in integrating image, sound, and text within a multimedia title. *Microsoft Windows Multimedia Authoring and Tools Guide* (Microsoft Press) is intended for publishers, managers, and developers who are considering writing their own multimedia titles. It doesn't touch on other vendors' authoring languages (of course). Still, it should be required reading when planning and preparing your sound, MIDI, graphics, animation, text, and CD-ROM data for use with any authoring language front end. Logistics of project planning and coordination are also covered.

Multimedia PC Marketing Council

These are the companies involved in establishing multimedia standards for PCs. They also market multimedia products and are good sources of information on MPC systems and software:

AT&T Computer Systems
1 Speedwell Ave.
Morristown, NJ 07960

CompuAdd Corp.
12303 Technology Blvd.
Austin, TX 78727

Creative Labs, Inc.
2050 Duane Ave.
Santa Clara, CA 95054

Media Vision, Inc.
47221 Fremont Blvd.
Fremont, CA 94538

Microsoft Corp.
One Microsoft Way
Redmond, WA 98052-6399

NEW Technologies, Inc.
1255 Michael Drive
Wood Dale, IL 60191

Olivetti
Via Jervis 77
10015 Ivrea
ITALY

Phillips Consumer Electronics Co.
1 Phillips Drive, P.O. Box 14810
Knoxville, TN 37914

Software Publishers Association
1730 M St. N.W., Suite 700
Washington, DC 20036

Tandy Corp.
700 One Tandy Center
Fort Worth, TX 76102

Video Seven
46221 Landing Parkway
Fremont, CA 94538

Zenith Data Systems
2150 East Lake Cook Road
Buffalo Grove, IL 60089

Part
2

Exploring Windows 95

Chapter 11

Object Properties and the Right-Click

FEATURING

Right-clicking to reveal quick menu choices

Object Properties boxes

In this chapter, I'll discuss Properties boxes and the use of the right-click as a means for getting your work done faster and for adjusting object properties. Let's start with a brief recap of right-clicking.

Right-Clicking around Windows

As you are well aware by now, right-clicking on objects throughout the Windows 95 interface brings up a shortcut menu with options pertaining to the objects at hand. The same options are typically available from the normal menus but are more conveniently reached with the right-click.

> **NOTE** These button names will, of course, be reversed if you are left-handed or have reversed the mouse buttons for some other reason. If you have a trackball, a GlidePoint, or other nonstandard pointing device, your right-click button may be somewhere unexpected. You may have to experiment a little to find which one activates the right-click menus.

Right-clicking isn't only part of the Windows 95 interface; it's being incorporated into recently written Windows programs, too. For example, Microsoft Office programs such as Word 6 and Excel have had right-click menus for some time. Some of the accessory programs supplied with Windows 95 have context-sensitive right-click menus, too. In general, the contents of the right-click menus change depending on the type of object. Options for a table will differ from those for a spreadsheet cell, frames, text, graphics, and so on.

As a rule, I suggest you start using the right-click button whenever you can. You'll learn through experimentation which of your programs do something with the right-click and which don't. Many 16-bit Windows programs won't even respond to the click; others may do the unexpected. But in almost every case, right-clicking results in a pop-up menu that you can close by clicking elsewhere or by pressing Esc, so don't worry about doing anything dangerous or irreversible.

A good example of a right-clickable item is the Taskbar. Right-click on an empty place on the Taskbar, and you'll see this menu:

Now right-click on the Start button, and you'll see this menu:

Here are a few other right-clicking experiments to try:

▶ Right-click on My Computer and notice the menu options.

▶ Right-click on a document icon. If you right-click on a DOS batch file (any file with a BAT extension), you'll have an edit option on the menu. What an easy way to edit a batch file!

▶ Right-click on a program file, such as Pbrush.exe in the Windows directory or on a DLL (Dynamic Link Library) file. The Quick View option lets you read information about the program, such as how much memory it requires to run and when it was created. A Properties option may tell you even more.

▶ When you right-click on a printer in the Printer's folder, you can quickly declare the printer to be the default printer or to work offline (not actually print yet even though you print to it from your applications) or go online with accumulated print jobs. Right-click on the Desktop to set the screen colors, screen saver, and so forth.

▶ Right-click on any program's title bar and notice the menu for resizing the window or closing the application.

▶ Right-click on a minimized program's button down in the Taskbar. You can close the program quickly by choosing Close.

▶ Right-click on the time in the Taskbar and choose Adjust Date/Time to alter the date and time settings for your computer.

Right-click menus will often have Cut, Copy, Paste, Open, Print, and Rename choices on them. These are discussed in Chapters 4, 5, and 6.

Many objects such as folders, printers, Network Neighborhood, and Inbox have a right-click menu called Explore that brings up the item in the Explorer's format (two vertical panes). This is a super-handy way to check out the object in a display similar to the Windows 3.x File Manager. You'll have the object in the left pane and its contents listed in the right pane. In some cases the contents are print jobs; in other cases they are fonts, files, folders, disk drives, or computers on the network. The Explorer is covered in Chapter 12.

Sharable items, such as printers, hard disks, and fax modems will have a Sharing option on their right-click menus. The resulting box lets you declare how an object is shared for use by other users on the network. Sharing a printer is covered in Chapter 8, and those general rules apply here. Additional discussion of sharing can be found in Part 5.

Property Sheets

Just as most objects have right-click menus, many also have property sheets. Properties pervade all aspects of the Windows 95 user interface, providing you with a simple and direct means for making settings to everything from how the screen looks to whether a file is hidden or what a shared printer is named.

Virtually every object in Windows 95—whether a printer, modem, shortcut, hard disk, folder, networked computer, or hardware driver—has a *property sheet* containing such settings. These settings affect how the object works and, sometimes, how it looks. And property sheets not only *display* the settings for the object, but usually allow you to easily *alter* the settings.

You've probably noticed that many right-click menus have a Properties choice down at the bottom. This choice is often the quickest path to an object's property sheet—not that there aren't other ways. Many dialog boxes, for example, have a Properties button that will bring up the object's settings when clicked on. And the Control Panel is used for setting numerous properties throughout Windows 95. Still, as you become more and more comfortable with Windows 95, you'll find the right-click approach most expedient.

Who Will Use Property Sheets?

The majority of Windows 95 users will rarely bother viewing or making changes to property-sheet settings because Windows 95 is well-enough behaved to govern itself (for example, repairing shortcuts when the target file or folder has been moved) and to prompt you when necessary for details about objects. As a case in point, when you install Windows 95 for the first time, or when you add new hardware or create a new printer, Wizards conscientiously assume the responsibility of setting up properties appropriately. The upshot is that tweaking Windows 95's internals and objects isn't nearly as necessary as it was in Windows 3.x. And in those rare instances when it is, unearthing the required dialog box for the job isn't an exercise reminiscent of dismantling a Chinese box puzzle.

Certainly any self-respecting power user will want to know all about properties for easily performing tasks such as sharing a folder on the network, changing the name of a hard-disk volume, checking the status of the computer's ports, displaying a font or other file's technical details, or checking the amount of free disk space on a hard disk.

> **TIP**   To even more quickly see an object's properties, highlight the object and press Alt-Enter.

Trying Out a Few Properties Boxes

The Properties option is always the last command on a right-click menu. For example, if you right-click on My Computer, you'll see this menu:

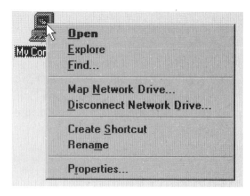

Or right-click on the clock in the Taskbar, and you'll see this:

Just choose the Adjust Date/Time command to easily set the time, date, and time zone for your computer, ensuring that all your files are properly date and time stamped and your Taskbar displays the time correctly.

Here's another everyday example. Suppose you're browsing through some folders (or the Explorer) and come across a Word document. Wondering what it is, when it was created, and who created it, you just right-click and choose Properties. The file's property sheet pops up, as shown in Figure 11.1. Notice that there are several tab pages on the sheet. That's because this is a Word file, and Word stores information in such files.

Property sheets for other kinds of files may only have a single tab page with less than a copious amount of information. In fact, most document property sheets are truly useful only if you want to examine the history of the file, determine its shorter MS-DOS file name, or set its DOS attributes such as whether it should be read-only (to prevent others from using it), hidden from view in folders, or if its *archive bit* should be set. (A check mark in the Archive box means the file hasn't been backed up since it was last altered or since it was created.) My point is that you can usually only *view* the status of the document, not *alter* it.

Property sheets for objects other than documents often let you make more substantive changes to them. A shortcut's property sheet, for example, lets you adjust some goodies about how the shortcut works, the file it points to, and so on, as shown in Figure 11.2.

Part 2

Exploring Windows 95

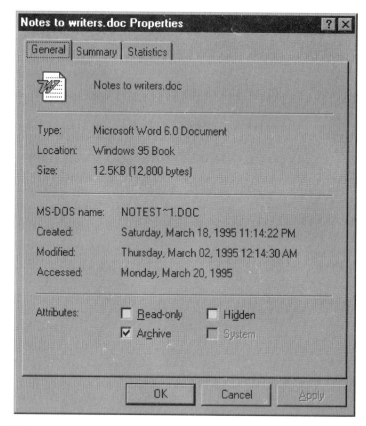

Figure 11.1 *A typical property sheet for a document file. This one is for a Word 6 file, so it has several pages listing its editing history, who created it, keywords, title, and so forth.*

TIP There is now a way to ensure that a program (whether DOS *or* Windows) defaults to a certain directory. In the dialog box shown in Figure 11.2, you can use the Start In field to set the default directory for a program. When you start the application from the shortcut, the File ➤ Open and File ➤ Save As commands will then default to this directory. In Windows 3.x, setting this variable was only possible for DOS programs. Now it's possible for Windows programs too.

This property sheet is somewhat similar to the old PIF files in Windows 3.x, though those only affected the running of DOS programs.

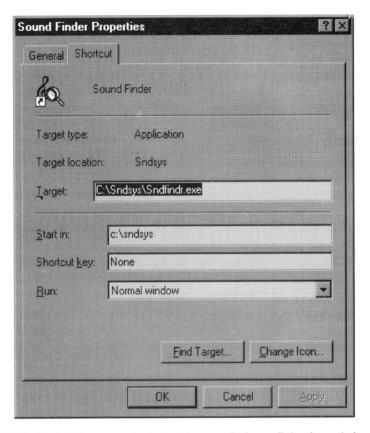

Figure 11.2 *Shortcuts have property sheets with a second tab page listing the particulars of the shortcut and allowing modification. Here you can change settings that control how the document or program will run when the shortcut is double-clicked on.*

Shortcut property sheets can affect any program or document. You can use the ? button for help on any of the options, but I'll just say that the two handiest items here are Shortcut Key and Run. Shortcut Key lets you assign a key combination that will run the shortcut from anywhere. For example, to jump to My Computer without having to minimize all your other windows first:

1. Get to the Desktop. Then right-click on My Computer and choose Create Shortcut. This creates a new shortcut on the Desktop called Shortcut to My Computer.

2. Right-click on the new shortcut and choose Properties.

3. In the Properties dialog box, click on the Shortcut tab, then click in the Shortcut Key field.

4. Press Ctrl-Alt-C to assign the shortcut key to Ctrl-Alt-C.

5. OK the box.

Now whenever you want to open My Computer, just press Ctrl-Alt-C. It takes a little manual dexterity, but it's quick. Use the same trick for any object you use regularly and find you're fishing around to open.

The Run field in a Shortcut's property box just determines whether the object will open in a maximized, minimized, or normal (floating) window.

Another interesting property sheet belongs to the Recycle Bin. See Chapter 31 for details.

Making Property Settings from My Computer

Probably the most powerful property sheet is reachable directly from My Computer. Clicking on My Computer and choosing Properties brings up the box shown in Figure 11.3.

Examine the four tab pages here. The first page tells you some useful information about the version of Windows 95 you are running, how much memory your computer has, and what type of CPU chip is in your machine. This will come in handy the next time someone asks you what's in the computer you're running: Instead of drumming your fingers on the desk, feeling like a dufus, you can open this box and read what it says.

The second tab page lists all the devices in the whole computer, many of which you probably didn't even know you had. Clicking on a + sign opens up a device to display more attributes about it. Clicking on a device and then on the Properties button tells you more about the highlighted device.

The third and fourth tab pages are about setting up specialized system profiles (collections of settings to match different hardware arrangements, such as when a laptop is docked into a base unit or running around in the field) and for fine-tuning your system's virtual memory management, file system, and video graphics display speed. These are covered in Chapter 31.

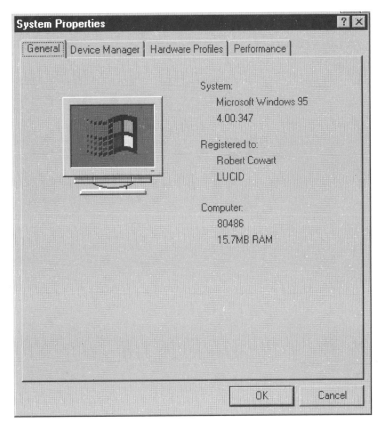

Figure 11.3   *A grand overview of your computer's attributes is available by right-clicking on My Computer and choosing Properties. Use some caution with these settings. This box is also available from the System applet in the Control Panel.*

CAUTION   As a rule, don't toy with the System Properties settings unless you know what you're doing. Examining all the dialog boxes is fine if you just cancel them. But adjusting the file system and virtual memory settings will more likely negatively impact your system's performance than accelerate it.

Chapter 12

Working with the File System and Explorer

FEATURING

Most application programs nowadays consist of numerous files. Add to this the plethora of documents and programs you're likely to collect, and suddenly your hard-disk directory looks like that ugly snake-filled chamber in *Raiders of the Lost Ark*. With the advent of affordable high-capacity hard disks (300 MB, 500 MB, even 1 or 2 gigabytes), one of the more challenging maintenance issues with any computer operating system is the job of managing your files.

If you find that the folder system is a nuisance because of the circuitous routes it takes you through at times, read on, because in the following pages, I'm going to reveal the pleasures of the Windows Explorer—a sort of supercharged Windows 3.x File Manager. It's a very powerful tool that does almost any Windows 95 system task, from making Control Panel settings to adding printers, viewing and mapping network drives, creating and managing folders and documents, and running programs. If you want to truly master Windows 95, the Explorer is *the* vantage point from which to do it. You'll benefit greatly in your day-to-day tasks by understanding how to use it.

A Review of DOS Directories

But first a little review. For the most part this chapter assumes you understand the basics of the DOS directory structure. However, if you're a little rusty on the topic, here's a thumbnail primer of directory (folder) workings.

> **NOTE**   Keep in mind that although Microsoft would like us all to forget we ever heard the terms "directory" and "subdirectory," any discussion of the Explorer has to at least acknowledge that most of what the program does is display and manipulate your DOS directories. In Windows 95 lingo we're now to think of these as *folders* and *subfolders*, as those terms conform more with the new paradigm of the file/folder approach to organizing your work. If it serves you to think in the new terms, have at it. As a compromise, I'll use the terms "folders" and "directories" interchangeably, though I'll favor the new terms.

DOS stores all files in folders on your disk. As you know, a folder is simply a collection of files, whether they are programs, documents, fonts, or what have you. Even Windows with all its bells and whistles is nothing but a bunch of files spread out across many folders. As you also know, folders let you keep related files nested together. With occasional limitations imposed by specific programs, you can organize your files however the spirit strikes you.

Folders are organized in a system analogous to a tree, as illustrated in Figure 12.1. In fact, the organization of folders is called the *directory tree*. The folders are organized in a hierarchical manner, from the *root* (the most basic level) to various branches off the root (folders) and branches off those branches (subfolders).

It is possible that you've never used folders before, because, theoretically, you can put all your files in the default folder (aka the *root directory*), though there is a limit to the number of files you can store in

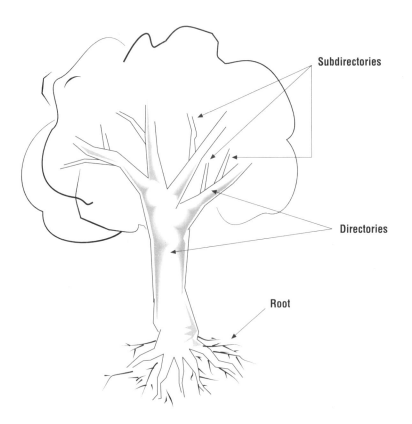

Figure 12.1   *The DOS directory-tree structure. Folders are organized from the root outward.*

the root folder (512 using short files names, fewer with long names). If you've never created a new folder, it's possible (though not likely) that all your files are stored in the root folder. However, as discussed in Chapter 5, it's much wiser to divide things up according to projects.

The root folder in DOS and File Manager was indicated by a single backslash (\). In Explorer it's indicated by the drive's icon:

 All other folders have names that you or some program (such as a program's installation program) create. For example, the Windows Setup program created a folder branch called Windows. Subordinate to Windows, it created another branch called System. The official name of the system folder is C:\Windows\System. This is called the folder's path name. The name describes the path you'd take to get to the folder, just as if you were climbing the tree—from the root up to the particular branch. Notice that the \ (indicating the root) precedes the folder name and that branches in the path name are also separated by a backslash.

In working with folders, the main thing to keep in mind is the *you can't get there from here* rule. To switch between distant branches, there are times when you have to remember their relationship to the root; I explain this in Chapter 3 in *File Dialog Boxes*. For example, if you were working in the \Windows\System folder and wanted to save a file in the \Letters\Personal folder, you'd typically have to back up to the root level first, select the Letters folder, and finally select the Personal folder. Just like when climbing a tree, if you want to get from one branch to the next, you have to go back to the trunk, *then* out the other branch.

Exploring the Explorer

To run the Explorer, click on the Start button and choose Programs ➤ Windows Explorer. The Explorer will load. Maximize the window and it will look something like Figure 12.2. Of course, the folders in your window will be different from those shown here.

Unlike the File Manager, Explorer doesn't let you open multiple windows. On the other hand, it's not necessary because Explorer is more flexible in design. You can actually copy files, folders, or other objects from anywhere to anywhere without needing multiple windows.

Part 2

Exploring Windows 95

Click on a + to
open a folder

Click on an icon to see its contents in
the right pane

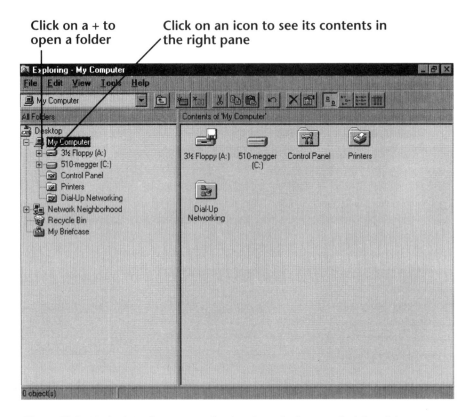

Figure 12.2 *The basic Explorer screen, showing the major items on the left and the contents on the right*

TIP   Actually, there are two workarounds that will give you multiple windows for a drive or folder. The first is to put multiple shortcuts for a drive on your Desktop. Then you can double-click on them all and adjust the size and placement of the windows as necessary. This uses the folder system, not Windows Explorer, though. If you prefer to use Explorer, you can run it more than once and adjust the windows as necessary to see the multiple instances of it.

Displaying the Contents of Your Computer

When you run the Explorer, all the objects constituting your computer appear in the list on the left. Some of those objects may have a plus sign (+) next to them, which means the object is *collapsed*; it contains sub-items that aren't currently showing. For example, my hard disk drive in Figure 12.2 is collapsed. So is Network Neighborhood (which you won't see unless you're on a network) and the floppy drive (drive A). Here's how to check out the contents of such an item:

1. Click on the item itself, not on the + sign. For example, click on your C drive's icon. Now its contents appear in the right pane as a bunch of folders.

2. Another approach is to click directly on the + sign. This opens up the sublevels in the left pane, showing you the relationship of the folders in a tree arrangement as in Figure 12.3.

Part 2

Exploring Windows 95

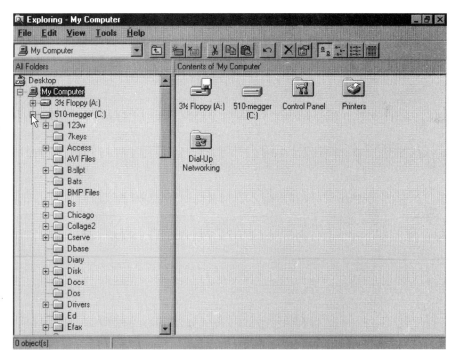

Figure 12.3 **Click on a + sign to display folders and other sub-objects.**

3. Notice that the + is replaced with a − sign, indicating that the object's display has been *expanded*. Click on it again, and it collapses.

4. To collapse everything, click on the − sign next to My Computer.

5. Click on the Desktop icon up at the top of the tree. Notice that all the objects on your Desktop appear in the right pane.

The tree is a graphical representation of your disk layout. Each file folder icon symbolizes one folder, and the straight lines connecting them indicate how they're related. The name of each folder appears after the icon. If you have more folders than can be seen at one time, the window will have a scroll bar that you can use to scroll the tree up and down. Notice that there are two scroll bars—one for the left pane and one for the right. These scroll independently of one another, a feature that can be very useful when you are copying items from one folder or drive to another.

Also notice that a Toolbar just like the one in the My Computer window is at the top of the Explorer window. Refer to Chapter 4 for a discussion of the buttons' functions.

TIP   You may or may not see a status line at the bottom of the window displaying information about the item(s) you have selected in the right or left panes. You can turn this on or off through the View menu. Turning it off frees up a little more space for displaying folders and files. The same is true of the Toolbar.

TIP   Change the view in the right pane just as you do in any folder. Click on the Toolbar icons over to the left or use the View menu to display large icons, small icons, list view, or details.

Working with Folders

To work with folders and files, the first task is to select the correct drive, whether a local hard disk, a floppy drive, or a networked drive. Once you have the correct drive selected, you can drag and drop files, run programs, open documents that have an association, and use right-click menu options for various objects. For example, you can right-click on files or folders and choose Send To ➤ 3^1/$_2$ Floppy to copy items to a floppy disk.

Selecting the Correct Drive and Choosing a Folder

To select the drive whose contents you want to work with:

1. Scroll the left pane up or down until you see the drive you want. Use the scroll bar in the middle of the window to do this. If the drive you want isn't showing, you may have to expand the My Computer icon by clicking on its + sign. At least one hard drive (and probably a floppy) should be visible.

2. Click on the name or icon of the drive whose contents you want to work with. The right pane then displays its contents. On a hard disk, you'll typically see a bunch of folders there, not files. (Floppies often don't have folders on them.) Folders are always listed first, followed by files. If you scroll the list a bit, you'll reach the files. Remember, at this point you are in the root directory of the selected drive. You have to find a specific folder before you get to see what's in it.

3. If the drive has folders on it, you now have a choice. You can double-click on one of the folders in the right pane, or you can expand the drive's listing in the left pane by clicking on its + sign. Which option you choose doesn't really matter. You can get to the same place either way. The advantage of expanding the drive in the left pane is simply that it gives you more of a graphical view of how your disk is organized and also lets you drag items from the right pane into destination folders. Go ahead and click on the drive's + sign if it's showing (Figure 12.4). Note that I've changed the right pane's view to show small icons so I can see more items at once.

4. Now suppose you want to see which fonts you have in your Fonts folder. This folder is a subfolder of the Windows folder. Finding it from My Computer would take a little hunting around, but with Explorer it's easy. If necessary, scroll the left list down, using the scroll box in the left pane's scroll bar, until you see the Windows folder.

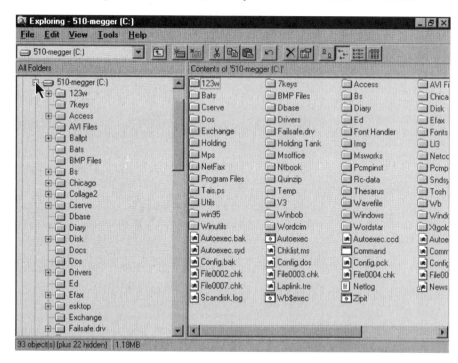

Figure 12.4 **Clicking on a drive's + sign opens it. Here you see my C drive.**

5. Because the Windows directory has subfolders, click on the + sign. Its subfolders now show.

6. `Fonts` is one of the subfolders under `Windows`. Click on it to see which font files are in the directory and consequently which fonts are installed on your system. The Fonts directory works a little differently than other directories, letting you install and display fonts by similarity. You'll notice some menu commands that are different from other directories.

7. Click on the Cursors folder to see which cursors are in your system. These are the shapes Windows has available for your mouse pointer.

Here are a few tips when selecting folders:

▶ Only one folder can be selected at a time.

▶ When a folder is selected, its icon changes from a closed folder to an open one.

▶ You can select a folder by clicking on it, typing its first letter, or moving the highlight to it with the arrow keys. When selected, the folder icon and name become highlighted.

▶ You can jump quickly to a folder name by typing its first letter on the keyboard. If there is more than one folder with the same first letter, each press of the key will advance to the next choice.

▶ Click on the + sign to expand a folder tree one level down. Click on the - sign to collapse a folder's tree up a level.

▶ The fastest way to collapse all the branches of a given drive is to click on the drive's − sign.

Notice that every time you select a folder, its contents are displayed in the folder-contents side of the window. The contents will include subordinate folders (listed first and looking like little folders just as they do in the left window), followed by the list of files.

If you want to change the order in which files are sorted (by name, extension, etc.), you can only do it in Details view. Change to Details view via the View menu, the right-click menu, or the Toolbar, then click on the appropriate column heading. For example, to sort files by size, click here:

All Folders	Contents of 'Windows'			
	Name	Size	Type	Modified
⊞ 🗀 Tosh Utils	🖾 Win386.swp	20,992KB	SWP File	3/22/95 1:1
🗀 Toshiba	🖾 Msn.pst	801KB	PST File	3/20/95 5:3
⊞ 🗀 Utils				

The first time you click, the files list in ascending size. A second click reverses the order. And just as with most column headings of this style, you can resize any column by dragging the dividing line between two column headings.

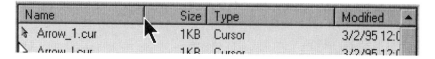

Creating a New Folder

As explained in Chapter 5, organizing often involves making up new folders. You already know how to do this using My Computer. In keeping with Windows 95's consistency, Explorer uses the same techniques.

TECH TIP   Technically, the folder system is also the Explorer. They both are part of the same program.

Creating a folder is easy, and because of the graphical nature of the folder tree, for many people it's easier to visualize what you're doing in Explorer than when creating folders from My Computer when you have windows scattered all over the screen.

1. From the left (tree) pane, select the folder in which you want to create a subfolder. If you select the A drive icon at the top of a tree (the root), the folder will be created directly off of it. Make sure you click on the folder, not just on its + or − sign. The folder icon has to open up, and the name must be highlighted.

2. Now here's the trick. Click in any empty space in the *right* pane, then create a new folder just as you do from My Computer. That is, choose File ➤ New or right-click and choose New ➤ Folder.

3. Type in the name for your folder, replacing the default name *New Folder*, which is really only a placeholder. When you finalize the name by pressing Enter, it will show up in the left pane when you expand its parent folder branch.

Deleting a Folder

As you may know, deleting a folder in DOS can be a pain. You have to remove all the files first, then delete the folder. After DOS 6, the **deltree** command made this much simpler. And in Explorer, just as from My Computer, it's even more simple; you can do it in one step. But because it's so easy, you should be careful—you can easily trash an entire directory. The good news when using Explorer or My Computer rather than DOS is that you can reverse the action with the File ➤ Undo command—at least until you delete something else. And of course, you can examine the Recycle Bin and return individual items to their former locations until you empty the trash.

CAUTION   You should know that only programs designed to take advantage of the Recycle Bin will safely move files there rather than irrevocably deleting them. Deleting a file in the old File Manager or from the MS-DOS prompt, for example, will definitely erase the file.

You'll be asked if you want to delete an item or group of items before it gets trashed; you have the option of turning the confirmation request off, but it's a reasonable safeguard. Techies who don't want to be bothered with the Recycle Bin or confirmation messages may turn off from the Recycle Bin's property sheet (Global Settings tab page).

TIP   To quickly erase an entire floppy, right-click on the drive's icon and choose Format ➤ Quick erase ➤ Start.

1. In the left pane *or* the right pane, right-click on the folder you want to delete and choose Delete. As an alternative, left-click on it, then

choose File ➤ Delete or press Del. A confirmation box such as this will appear, asking for your permission:

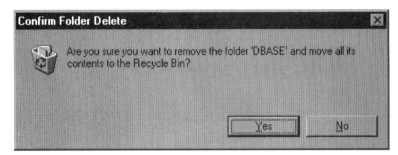

2. If you really want to delete the folder and all its files, click on Yes. The contents of the folder (*including* any and all subfolders!) will be moved to the Recycle Bin.

    If you click on Yes in the above dialog box with the confirmation messages set on, you will need to keep clicking on Yes for each file before it is deleted. If you click on *Yes to All*, all files will be deleted with no further ado, with one exception. When Windows 95 detects that you are trying to erase an application program (any file with an EXE, COM, or BAT extension), it will ask for additional confirmation:

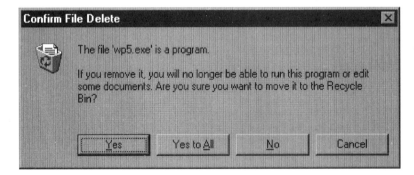

    Click on Yes to delete the named program. Click on Yes to All to not be hassled by such messages for the duration of the folder's deletion.

Moving Folders

In addition to enabling you to move files easily, the Explorer lets you move complete folders or folder branches. When you move a folder, all the files in the folder are moved automatically.

You can select the folder to be moved either from the tree pane or from the folder (file) pane. Just drag the folder from either pane to the new destination:

▶ When you move a folder to another folder, Windows adds it below the destination folder.

▶ When you move a folder from one drive into another drive's icon, it gets added below the current folder in the destination drive.

More often than not, people want to move folders around on the same drive, a bit like rearranging their living-room furniture. This is extremely easy with the Explorer. After using this feature, you'll wonder how you ever did without it:

1. Select the folder you want to move (in either pane) and drag it to its new location. As you slide the mouse over possible targets, the target becomes highlighted, indicating where the folder will land if you release the mouse button.

2. When you release the mouse button, the folder will be added as a subfolder one level below the destination folder (and any subfolders will be arrayed below it as before).

Moving Multiple Folders Simultaneously

You can move the contents of more than one folder at a time, but unless they are connected by a descending branch, you have to do this from a folder (file) pane, not from the tree pane. For example, suppose you wanted folders named 1994 Reports, 1995 Reports, and 1996 Reports to be subfolders under a folder called All Reports. You could do this by dragging one folder at a time as explained above. But it's faster to do it in one fell swoop. Select the three folders in the folder pane. Drag them as a group to All Reports in the tree pane. Figure 12.5 shows one way of doing this and the resulting dialog box.

Part 2

Exploring Windows 95

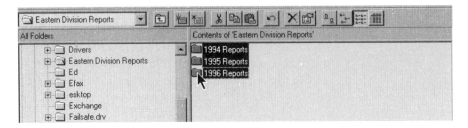

Figure 12.5 *Dragging multiple folders into a destination folder. The source folders will become subfolders of the destination folder.*

Figure 12.6 shows the change to the folder tree. Notice that 1994 Reports, 1995 Reports, and 1996 Reports were added under All Reports
as subfolders.

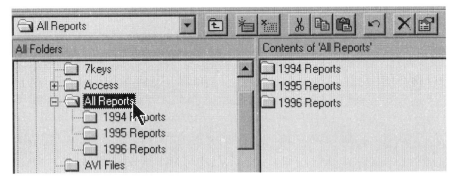

Figure 12.6 *The result of moving* 1994 Reports, 1995 Reports, *and* 1996 Reports *into* All Reports. *Notice the altered folder tree.*

> **TIP** Though not a skill often needed, you *can* copy a complete directory. Sim-
> ply click on a folder (either in the left or right pane) and choose Edit ➤ Copy.
> Then click on the destination drive or folder icon and choose Edit ➤ Paste.

Working with Files

So what about working with files? It's simple. All the rules of working with files in standard folders (as discussed in Chapter 5) apply to Explorer. Once you've selected the correct drive and folder, you do all your work with files by selecting them in the right pane. Just select the file(s) and then cut, copy, paste, run, open, print, quick view, or change properties of the files using the right-click menu or commands from the File and Edit menus. You can also drag files around to relocate them or right-click-drag them to move, create shortcuts, or copy them.

All these techniques were covered in Chapter 5. But to give you a feel for dragging a file from one folder to another, here's a little exercise. Try moving a file, using the drag-and-drop approach.

1. In the left pane, click on the Windows folder. Then make sure it's expanded to show its subfolders.

2. Then click on the Media folder, which is a subfolder of Windows. In the right pane, you should see a lot of sound (WAV) files.

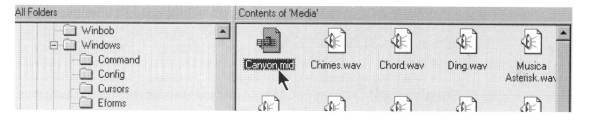

3. Now scroll the right pane until you see the file Canyon.mid. We can experiment with this file because it's not terribly important. It's a MIDI sound file.

4. Now let's say you wanted to move this file to the Cursors folder. Scroll the left pane up or down until you see Cursors (another subfolder of Windows).

5. Now drag Canyon.mid *on top* of the Cursors folder. The Cursors folder is the *target* folder and must be highlighted before you release the mouse button, so keep the mouse button depressed until the word *Cursor* is highlighted, then release.

Part
2

Exploring Windows 95

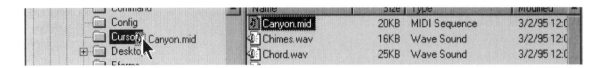

6. Just to check that it worked, now view the contents of the `Cursors` folder by clicking on it. In amongst all your icon files you'll now have the Canyon file.

7. Now, for purposes of good housekeeping, you should return the file to its origin. Choose Edit ➤ Undo Move (or drag the file from the right pane onto the `Media` folder in the left pane).

Refreshing the Directory

Sometimes other programs will affect the contents of an open drive window. For example, you might switch away from Explorer into an application window such as Word, Paradox, or whatever, and create a new document in a folder that's displaying back in the Explorer. Or you might edit a file that's also displayed in the folder's window, changing its size (in bytes). Normally Windows takes care of updating the information in the display; however, there are times when this doesn't happen reliably. Particularly when you are connected to a network, Windows may have trouble detecting that a folder's contents have changed. This will also be an issue if you change floppy disks and want to see the folder on the new disk. If you suspect that a folder may have been changed in some way that isn't reflected in the folder pane, just choose Window ➤ Refresh or press F5.

Selecting Files

Before you can work with the files in a folder, you have to select one or more of them. As with other objects in Windows, you select files by highlighting them. Here are various methods of selecting (and deselecting) files:

To select one file: Click once on the file. Notice that the status line (the last line in the File Manager window) indicates that one file is selected.

To select multiple nonconsecutive files: Click on the first file to select it and Ctrl-click on additional files.

To select a group of consecutive files: (This is easiest in the List or Details view because objects are in a list.) Click on the first file in the series, then Shift-click on the last item you want to select. As an alternative, you can draw a box around the files you want to select.

To select several groups of consecutive files: Select the first group as described above. To select the second group, hold down the Ctrl key and click on the first file in the second group. Press the Shift and Ctrl keys simultaneously and click on the last file in the second group. Repeat for each additional group.

To select all the files in a folder: Choose File ➤ Select All. You can then deselect specific files by Ctrl-clicking.

To invert the selection of files: Select the files you want to omit from the selection. Then choose Edit ➤ Invert Selection.

Once highlighted, a file or group of files can be operated on via the mouse or by using the commands on the File and Edit menus. For example, you can drag a group of files into another folder, delete them, copy and paste them somewhere else, or print them (assuming they are documents). All these commands are covered in Chapter 4, but here's a quick recap of the commands and clicks:

▶ *Run* a program or *open* a document by double-clicking on it. Alternatively, highlight a file and press Enter.

▶ *Print* a document by choosing File ➤ Print. Alternatively, right-click and choose Print.

▶ *View* a file (document, program, font, etc.) with File ➤ Quick View or by right-clicking and choosing Quick View.

▶ *Edit* a BAT file with File ➤ Edit or by right-clicking and choosing Edit.

▶ *Send* selected file(s) to a floppy drive, fax recipient, or your Briefcase with File ➤ Send To or by right-clicking and choosing Send To. (Briefcase is covered in Chapter 30.)

▶ Create a *new* document or shortcut or certain types of registered documents with File ➤ New or by right-clicking and choosing New. You can also create a new shortcut for the selected item(s) with File ➤ Create Shortcut.

▶ *Paste a shortcut* for the selected item(s) by first copying, then choosing Edit ➤ Paste Shortcut. Alternatively, right-click-drag and choose Shortcut from the pop-up menu when you release the mouse button.

Part 2

Exploring Windows 95

▶ *Delete* the selected item(s) with File ➤ Delete, the Del key, or by right-clicking and choosing Delete. This sends items to the Recycle Bin. Clicking on the X button in the Toolbar has the same effect.

▶ *Rename* items with File ➤ Rename, by right-clicking and choosing Rename, or by a slow double-click on their name. Edit the name with the edit keys, then press Enter to finalize the new name.

▶ Check a file's *Properties* with File ➤ Properties or highlight it and press Alt-Enter. (Properties are covered in Chapter 11.)

▶ *Copy* a file by choosing Edit ➤ Copy, selecting the destination (folder or drive), and choosing Edit ➤ Paste. You can right-click and choose Copy followed by right-clicking and choosing Paste as a shortcut or use the Copy and Paste buttons in the Toolbar.

▶ *Move* selected item(s) from one location to another by dragging and dropping or with Edit ➤ Cut followed by Edit ➤ Paste. (Again, the Cut and Paste buttons on the Toolbar will work.)

▶ *Undo* your last action with the Edit ➤ Undo command or the Undo button on the Toolbar.

For viewing options, setting up associations, or refreshing the directory listing, please refer to Chapter 5.

> **TIP**   In Explorer and in My Computer folders, pressing Backspace always moves you up a level in the folder hierarchy. This is an easy way to move back to the parent directory of the current folder. After several presses, you'll eventually end up at the My Computer level, the top level on any computer. At that point, Backspace won't have any effect.

When moving files around, keep these points in mind: The new destination can be a folder window that you opened from My Computer, a folder in the left pane of Explorer, or a folder in the right pane. Many programs that support drag and drop will let you drag from Explorer into them, too. To open a Word file in an existing Word window, for example, drag the file onto the Title Bar of the Word window. You can even drag a document onto a printer's window, icon, or shortcut. The general rule is this: If you want to move it, try selecting it and dragging it to the new location. If the action isn't allowed, Windows will inform you and no damage will have been done. If you're trying to move the item and get a shortcut instead, right-click-drag the item and choose Move from the resulting menu.

Moving Files to Another Disk Drive

Moving or copying files to another disk drive uses much the same technique as when moving or copying to another folder on the same drive. The basic game plan is that you select the source files and drag them into the destination drive icon as described below.

1. Open the source drive and folder and select the files in the right pane.

2. If it's not showing, scroll the tree pane so you can see the destination drive's icon.

3. Click open the drive if you need to target a particular folder on it.

4. Drop the files on the target. If you're moving the folders or files to a floppy drive, make sure you have a formatted disk in the drive, or you will get an error message.

> NOTE   When you drag files (or folders) between *different* drives, Windows 95 assumes you want to copy them, not move them. That is, the originals are left intact. When you drag files between folders on the *same* drive, Windows 95 assumes you want to move them, not copy them.

Working with Disks

Explorer has a few features that apply specifically to managing your disks, particularly floppy disks. These commands make the process of formatting disks and copying disks a bit simpler. There's also a way to easily change the volume label of a disk, the optional name that each floppy or hard disk can be assigned (typically for archival purposes).

Formatting Disks and Making System Disks

> CAUTION   Formatting erases all data from the disk! Reversing the process is difficult if not impossible.

As I mentioned in Chapter 5, floppy disks must be formatted before they can be used in your computer. Many disks you buy in the store are preformatted, so this isn't an issue. Some are not, however. Also, you more than likely have many disks with old defunct programs and files on them that you'd like to re-use. To gain maximum room on such a disk, you'll want to erase all the old files, something you can most efficiently achieve with a *quick format*. Finally, you may want to create a disk that is capable of booting the computer. In this section I explain how to do all these things.

> NOTE   What with the myriad disk capacities and sizes around these days, formatting a floppy disk from DOS can turn out to be quite an exercise. The DOS manual is usually not much help either. There are enough options to the format command to choke a rhino. You might become a real fan of Windows just for its formatting command.

Here's how to format a disk:

1. Put the disk to be formatted in the floppy drive.

2. Right-click on the floppy disk in the My Computer window or in Explorer and choose Format.

3. The dialog box shown in Figure 12.7 appears. Use the drop-down lists to set the drive and disk capacity of the floppy.

4. In the *Format type* and *Other options* section of the box, choose the appropriate options.

    ▶ *Quick:* simply deletes the file-allocation table and root folder of the disk, but the disk is not scanned for bad sectors. It doesn't actually erase the whole disk and reinitialize it or check for errors in the disk medium itself. Quick formatting can only be done on a disk that has been formatted in the past.

    ▶ *Full:* checks the entire disk's surface to make sure it's reliable. Any bad spots are omitted from the directory table and won't be used to store your data. This kind of format isn't fast, but it better ensures that valuable data is stored properly on the disk.

Choose the capacity of your floppy disk here

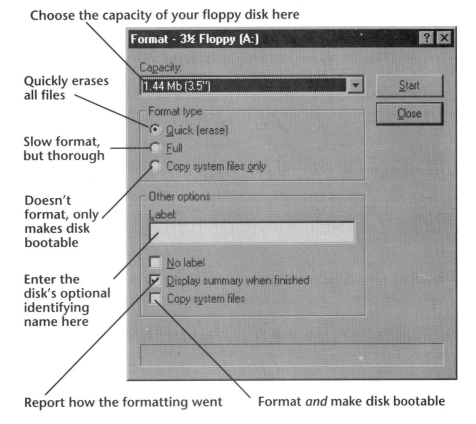

Quickly erases all files

Slow format, but thorough

Doesn't format, only makes disk bootable

Enter the disk's optional identifying name here

Report how the formatting went

Format *and* make disk bootable

Figure 12.7 *Right-click on a floppy drive and choose Format to reach this dialog box. A disk must be formatted before you can store files on it.*

NOTE Disks can actually lose some of their formatting information with time. If you are going to use an old disk, it's better to full format it rather than quick format it to prevent data loss down the road. And if you do not know where it has been, it's a good idea to full format it to prevent any possible viruses from spreading.

▶ *Copy system files only:* doesn't format the disk. It just makes the disk bootable. That means it can start up your computer from the A drive in case your hard disk is having trouble. The necessary hidden system files will be copied to the floppy disk.

➤ *Label:* lets you enter a name for the diskette if you're really into cataloging your disks. All floppy and hard disks can have a volume label. This is not the paper label on the outside, but a name encoded into the folder on the disk. It shows up when you type **DIR** at the DOS prompt and in some other programs. The label really serves no functional purpose other than to identify the disk for archiving purposes. You can change the label from the disk's Properties box at any time.

➤ *No Label:* clears any existing label from the disk.

➤ *Display summary when finished:* causes a dialog box listing particulars of the diskette, such as how much room is available on it, bad sectors found, and so on, after formatting.

➤ *Copy system files:* works similarly to Copy system files only, except that you use this option when you want to copy the system files in *addition* to formatting the disk.

5. Click on Start. You may see a confirmation message. A gas gauge at the bottom of the dialog box will keep you apprised of the progress of the format. A typical full format will take a minute or so.

Copying Disks

You can make copies of disks four basic ways—from My Computer, Explorer, the DOS prompt, and the old Windows 3.x-style File Manager.

For many, the DOS-prompt approach is probably the easiest way.

1. Choose Start ➤ Programs ➤ MS-DOS prompt.

2. Type the following command:

```
diskcopy x: y:
```

where *x* is the drive that contains the disk you want to copy and *y* is the drive that contains the disk you want to copy to. For example:

```
diskcopy a: b:
```

TIP   You can use the same drive letter for both drives if you have only one floppy drive. For more information, type diskcopy /? at the command prompt.

Using Explorer or My Computer will work fine as well. Just right-click on a floppy drive's icon, and you'll see a Copy Disk command. Choose it, and a little dialog box pops up asking for the destination drive. If you only have one drive, that's okay. You may have to swap the source and destination disks, but you'll be prompted if this is necessary.

Finally, you can also use the Windows 3.x File Manager to copy disks if the disk formats and sizes are the same. Run File Manager by choosing Start ➤ Run and entering **winfile** in the Run box. Click on the floppy drive up in the menu bar and choose Disk ➤ Copy Disk. If you have two drives, you'll have to choose the destination drive from the dialog box. If you only have one drive, you'll have to swap the disks a few times.

CAUTION   Be aware that all of these methods erase everything on the destination disk before creating an exact copy of the source disk.

The Explorer has no built-in command for copying a disk. However, you could do it by creating a directory on your hard disk, copying the files from the floppy there, switching floppies, then copying from the hard-disk directory to the floppy.

Making Sure There's Enough Room on a Floppy Disk

When you are moving files about, particularly to a floppy disk, there may not be enough room on the floppy for all the source files. Explorer shows you how many bytes you've got selected in the Status Bar of its window. So, select the files you're going to copy, then look at the Status Bar.

`8 object(s) selected        619KB`

Remember this number for a moment. Then in the left pane, click on the destination drive and check its properties before doing the copy.

Part
2

Exploring Windows 95

Using Network Drives, Files, and Disks

Assuming you are on a network, the Explorer lets you browse around and explore it, too. This is a brilliant feature of Explorer. Networks are covered in great detail in Part 5, but here I'll just introduce you to simple use of Explorer for examining and working with networked objects.

Here's the general game plan. You can *share* your drives and folders (printers and fax machines, too, as discussed in Parts 3 and 5) for use by coworkers on the net. Likewise, you can hook up to the resources other people have shared. With Explorer, scanning the network to see what's available is straightforward. It's just like looking at your own hard disk or computer's contents.

Many everyday tasks such as using a document or program on another workstation's hard disk can be done right from the folder system or the Explorer without any fancy footwork. You just open Network Neighborhood from the Desktop or from the Explorer (open the drop-down list in Explorer or any folder and choose Network Neighborhood) and see who's on the net:

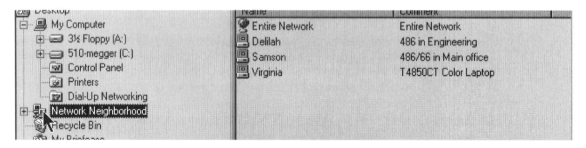

Then double-click on a computer and start browsing. Examining someone else's drives and folders is *exactly* like looking at your own. For example, I double-clicked on Samson and saw the contents of Figure 12.8.

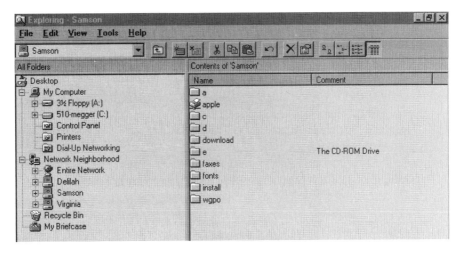

Figure 12.8 *Here you see the shared folders and drives on the networked computer named Samson.*

Note that you'll only see *shared* items on any networked computer, not *everything* in or on that computer. This scheme allows users to protect confidential items. Password protection is another option, limiting access of shared objects to specific users. Each of the folders in Figure 12.8 (as well as the printer) were intentionally shared by the person who maintains Samson.

Another point about using Explorer on the network concerns *connecting* to networked drives. If you are familiar with Windows for Workgroups 3.11, you'll note that with Explorer you don't have to connect to a networked drive before you can examine it. You simply browse any networked computer to see what's been shared on it. Some programs may need you to *map* a shared folder to a drive letter so you can open a document or perform some other action, but there's an easy way to do this from Explorer, from folders, and from some older-style Windows 3.x File dialog boxes that have a Network button on them.

Virtually all Windows 95 programs will let you use networked drives and folders with no hassle. For example, say I wanted to open a Notepad file that's stored on someone else's computer. I simply find the file and double-click, just as if it were on my computer. If I'm already in, say, WordPad and I want to use its File ➤ Open command to open a file, no problem. Consider this dialog box:

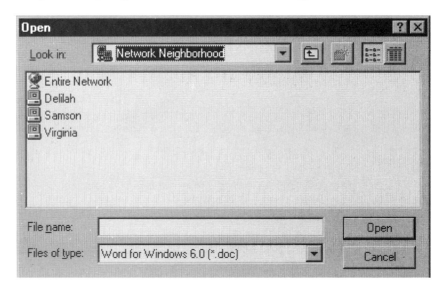

Notice that I've selected Network Neighborhood in the drop-down list, and the stations on the net show up. Just double-click on a workstation and look for the document you want. Of course, the same approach applies to saving a document with File ➤ Save.

Mapping a Drive from a Windows 3.x File Dialog Box

With Windows 3.x-style applications, you won't have the same luxuries because the File dialog boxes aren't as savvy about networking. You'll more often see something like the dialog box on the following page.

To gain access to a workstation's shared folder, you first have to map the network folder to a drive letter (such as D, E, F). Basically, mapping is just a way to fake your computer and your applications into thinking it has another hard disk on it so you can use older File dialog boxes with networked folders. Mapping is also necessary for some other procedures such as when an application expects to find support files on a logically lettered drive. In any case, the necessity is a throwback to DOS days.

Click on Network, then fill in the dialog box below. In the lower text area, type in the network path name of the shared directories. You can also use the drop-down list of previous mappings, assuming you've made this connection before. Then select or choose the disk letter you want to assign this folder to.

When you OK this box, you'll have a new disk-drive letter to choose from when you open or save a document from any application. Here's what happened when I mapped Delilah's drive C to my local drive D:

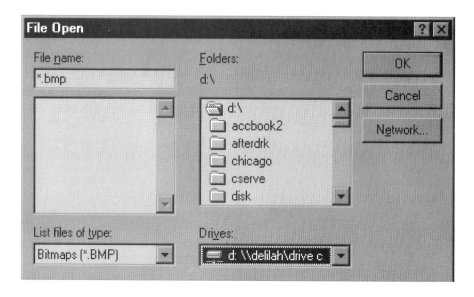

 NOTE   Now even Explorer and My Computer will show the newly mapped drive as a "network" drive D until you disconnect it as explained below.

Mapping a Drive from Explorer—The Easy Way

The approach explained above is necessary at times, and it's handy because many dialog boxes have a Network button right there. But it's sometimes a hassle to remember the network path name of a particular folder and to enter it. Notice above that the path name syntax is `\\computer name\path`. In a complex path name there are a lot of slashes to enter and potential for typos. Also, there's no Browse button to let you cruise the network and find a folder to map.

Opening Network Neighborhood from the Desktop or Explorer makes mapping a network drive way simpler.

1. Open Network Neighborhood.

2. Browse to the folder you want to map.

3. Right-click on it and choose Map Network Drive (or click on the Map Network Drive icon in the Toolbar).

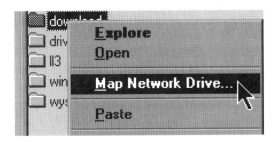

4. Choose the drive letter.

5. Click on Reconnect at Logon if you want to always have this mapping made when you boot up your computer. Of course, the remote workstation will have to be running when you boot up for this to work properly, but it won't harm anything if it isn't. You just won't have access to the drive.

> **NOTE** If the folder you're trying to connect to is password protected, you'll be prompted to enter a password.

Now you'll have an additional icon in Explorer and in your My Computer folder, representing the new drive letter. For example:

Network drives have their own style of icon, similar to the hard-disk icon but with a network cable attached. Not that it will behave as a local drive would. For example, open its Properties box to see how much free space is left on it.

Disconnecting from a Network Drive or Folder

When you're through with a mapped network drive, you'll probably want to disconnect from it. There's no sense in staying connected unless you regularly use the drive and expect to always have the setup available. Use the following steps to disconnect a network drive:

1. Click on the mapped networked drive either from My Computer or Explorer.

2. Choose Tools ➤ Disconnect Network Drive, right-click and choose the same, or click on the Disconnect Network Drive icon in the Toolbar.

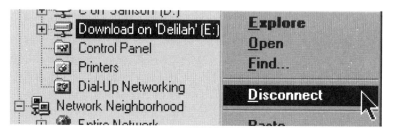

If you currently have any files open on the mapped drive, attempting to disconnect will result in a warning. Make sure you're not running a program, editing a file, or otherwise accessing the logical drive that you're about to disconnect. If you get such a warning, cancel the box, close any suspicious programs or documents, and try again. In my experience, this warning can actually be erroneously triggered (i.e., when no files are open). As long as you know you're not going to lose data, go ahead and disconnect.

Sharing Folders and Drives

As implied above, you and others can share folders on the network for others to use. Before other workgroup members can use your files, though, you have to share the directory containing them. Shared directories can have passwords, and they also can have specific privileges (read-only or read-write). If you have a bunch of files that you want people to be able to see but not alter, just put them into a new folder and share it as read-only. If you want only specific people to be able to alter the files, share them protected by a password. The following section discusses how to share your folders.

1. In My Computer or Explorer, right-click on the folder or drive you want to share.

> **CAUTION**   Because sharing a hard disk itself allows network users into all directories on the disk, doing so can be dangerous. Clicking on a disk icon in the Explorer or My Computer and sharing it is certainly the easiest way to share all files and folders on your computer. However, it allows any connected user to alter or erase everything you have on your hard disk.

2. Choose Sharing. A dialog box appears, as shown in Figure 12.9. Click on Shared As.

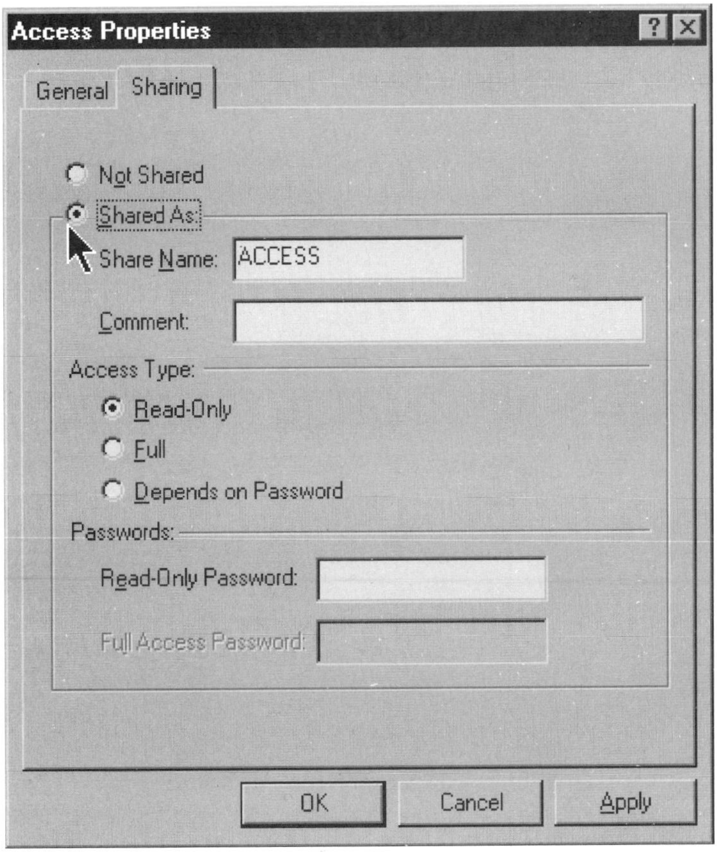

Figure 12.9   To share a folder or drive, just click on Shared As and OK the box.

3. You don't have to do anything other than click on OK. The icon of the folder or drive will change to include a little hand under it, a suggestion of sharing.

The other options in the dialog box are useful to better control details of how the object is shared. Here's some discussion on each of those settings:

▶ The Share Name is, by default, the same name as the directory itself. This should be limited to a DOS 8.3-character name if others on the network will be using an operating system that doesn't display long file names, such as Windows 3.11 or DOS.

> **TIP**   Even if you choose to limit the Share Name to the DOS 8.3 file-naming convention, you might want to elaborate on the directory name a bit. For example, while still conforming to DOS file-naming conventions (spaces and some characters are illegal), you could lengthen `Reports` to `Reports.96`.

▶ You can add a comment line that network users will see, perhaps explaining who the file is for or what is in the shared folder. This will show up when someone checks out your computer in Network Neighborhood or Explorer in the Details view. This line can be approximately 50 characters long and include spaces and punctuation.

▶ Next, you have the option of setting specific permissions to restrict the use of the directory by others.

> **TECH TIP**   If you don't manually set the permissions, although anyone can access the directory, nobody will be able to edit the files in it or make other changes that an application might require, such as recording changes to a style sheet or creating a temp file in the directory. If you are sharing a folder that has applications in it for use by workers on the net, this could cause a problem. Consider carefully whether you should share the directory with Full permission to prevent potential application or document problems.

▶ Set the Access Type by clicking on the appropriate button. You have three choices:

Read   Enables viewing file names, copying information, running applications in the directory, and opening document files.

Full	All permissions listed above, plus the ability to delete files, move files, edit files, and create new subdirectories.
Depends on Password	The type of access will be determined by which password option is chosen and which password is entered by the person attempting to use the disk or folder.

 CAUTION   Note that a user has the same rights to all the subdirectories of a shared parent directory. Be careful not to share directories that have subdirectories unless you want those to become accessible with the same level of restriction.

▶ Finally, there are the password settings.

With Read-Only or Full selected, you can enter a password in the appropriate spot. Anyone trying to use the folder will be prompted to enter a password. If you choose the Depends on Password option, the level of access the remote user is granted (Read-only or Full) is determined by the password he or she enters.

 NOTE   Access to shared objects can be further controlled from the Network applet in the Control Panel. Using this applet, you can control whether access is granted on a user-by-user basis or on a group basis. Group access control is discussed in Part 5 of this book.

Changing a Share's Properties

You can change permissions or other settings pertaining to the share after the fact, if necessary. For example, you might decide to limit the number of people who use the shared folder by requiring passwords to be entered. You might want to change the passwords on a regular basis to ensure security. Or you might decide to stop sharing a folder altogether.

1. Right-click on the directory or disk in Explorer or My Computer's File Manager and choose Sharing.

2. The Share dialog box that appears, letting you make changes, is the same one that appeared when you originally shared the directory.

3. Click on Not Shared to stop sharing the object. If workgroup users are currently connected to the directory, you see a message indicating this and warning you against terminating the share. If you really want to terminate, click on Yes, but be aware that other users might lose their data—particularly if the dialog box indicates that files are open. Closing a shared directory like this is a great way to lose friends, so normally you would click on No, get the other user to sign off from your directory, then try again later.

 TIP   You might want to contact users of the directory to alert them of your intention to remove the drive from the network.

If you want to know what's really going on with a directory (that is, who's using it and whether files are open), run the NetWatcher program found in the Programs ➤ Accessories ➤ System Tools folder. This program isn't installed by default, so you might have to load it from your master Windows 95 disk(s).

Working with Other Objects in Explorer

As I mentioned at the top of this chapter, Explorer has many talents. You can explore and set properties for not only files, folders, and disks, but also Printers, Control Panel, the Recycle Bin, Dial-Up Networking (an option with Microsoft Plus; see Chapter 32), and Briefcase. Try experimenting with each of these objects by clicking on them. You'll find most of them at the bottom of the Explorer's tree in the left pane. As you'd expect, the Explorer simply provides another view of these items, even though functionally the effect is no different from working with them in ways discussed elsewhere in this book. For example, look at Figure 12.10, which shows the result of clicking on

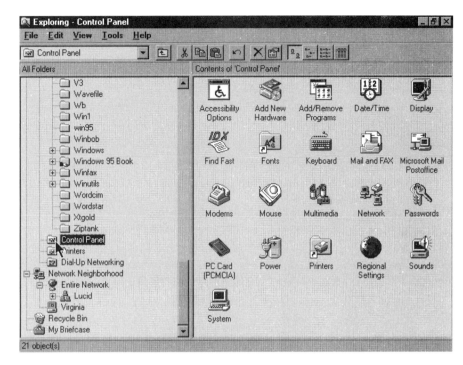

Figure 12.10 *Other computer-related objects such as the Control Panel can be accessed via Explorer, too.*

the Control Panel. You can run the Control Panel applets from the right pane by double-clicking as usual.

Part
2

Exploring Windows 95

Managing Communications with Windows 95

3

Chapter 13

Introduction to Windows Communications

FEATURING

When you first got your computer, you probably planned to do things like word processing, financial record keeping and analysis, and maybe play some games. You would tap information into the keyboard, the computer would do its thing, and after a while, it would print the result on a piece of paper or display it on your screen. At that point, your computer was probably a standalone device, not connected to any other computers. If you needed to exchange data with somebody else, you could use a floppy disk to move files from one machine to the other (this technique is sometimes called "sneakernet").

But when you start connecting them together, standalone computers become extremely flexible communications tools. Relatively early in the development of computer technology, people figured out that it wasn't particularly difficult to transfer information through a wire from one computer to another. As long as the computers on both ends use the same technical standards, you can move messages, programs, text, and data files back and forth. And when you connect a *lot* of computers together through a network, you can communicate with any other computer on the same network, just as you can reach any other telephone connected to the global telecommunications system from the one on your desk.

Under the broad category of "communications," your PC can send and receive text, program files, sounds, and images. It can also exchange images of fax pages with a distant fax machine. This data can enter and leave your PC through a modem, a network interface card, or a direct cable connection to another computer.

Communications capability has been part of DOS and Windows since the earliest IBM PCs. Windows 95 includes an extensive set of communications tools that can allow you to exchange electronic mail with other computers, to send and receive faxes, and to use your computer to control telephone calls. This chapter contains information about the communications features of Windows 95 and tells you how to configure Windows to work with your modem. You can find more specific information about communications applications, Microsoft Exchange, and Microsoft Network in the remaining chapters of this section. HyperTerminal, the new communications program, is discussed in Chapter 20. Finally, Chapter 17 describes how to use Windows 95 to connect your computer to the Internet.

What's New in Windows 95 Communications?

Windows 95 includes some major improvements over the way Windows 3.x handled communications—it's a lot happier about sending and receiving data at high speeds, transferring data in the background doesn't interfere with other applications, and you don't have to shut down a program that waits for incoming messages or faxes before you try to use the same modem to place an outgoing call. In addition, Microsoft has replaced the old Terminal program in Windows 3.x with a completely new set of applications for connecting to distant computers through a modem; for sending, receiving, and managing messages, data files, and faxes; as well as a "Telephony Applications Program Interface" (TAPI) that integrates your PC with a telephone system. Microsoft has also included access to its own online information service, called the Microsoft Network. Overall, Windows 95 goes a long way toward turning your standalone computer into a tool that can be linked to other computers, fax machines, and other communications devices anywhere in the world.

The Windows Telephony Interface

Windows 95 includes a new set of software "hooks" to applications that control the way your computer interacts with the telephone network. TAPI is an internal part of the Windows 95 operating system rather than a specific application program—it provides a standard way for software developers to access communications ports and devices such as modems and telephone sets to control data, fax, and voice calls. Using TAPI, an application can place a call, answer an incoming call, and hang up when the call is complete. It also supports things like hold, call transfer, voice mail, and conference calls. TAPI-compliant applications will work with conventional telephone lines, PBX and Centrex systems, and with specialized services like cellular and ISDN.

By moving these functions to a common program interface, Windows prevents conflicting demands for access to your modem and telephone line from multiple application programs. Therefore, you no longer need to shut down a program that's waiting for incoming calls before you use a different program to send a fax.

Windows Telephony is part of the base Windows 95 operating system; it's not a separate program. Unless you're planning to write your own communications applications, you won't ever have to deal directly with TAPI, but you will see its benefits when you use the communications programs included in the Windows 95 package—such as HyperTerminal, Microsoft Exchange, Phone Dialer, and Remote Access—and when you use new, Window 95-compatible versions of third-party communications programs such as ProComm and WinFax. In addition, Microsoft is planning a separate Windows Telephony application product (code name Tazz—short for Tasmanian Devil) that will use TAPI to integrate your PC with the telephone network.

Windows 95 includes a relatively simple telephony application called Phone Dialer, but that just scratches the surface of what TAPI will support. In the same way that Windows 95's faxing capabilities are not as extensive as those of a program like WinFax or that WordPad has fewer bells and whistles than Word for Windows, Phone Dialer is much simpler than some of the other programs that will appear in the near future.

Eventually you can expect to see a lot of new Windows Telephony products that will move control of your telephone to the Windows Desktop; for example, you might be able to use the telephone company's caller ID service to match incoming calls to a database that displays detailed information about the caller before you answer, or use an on-screen menu to set up advanced call features like conference calling and forwarding that now require obscure strings of digits from the telephone keypad.

Installing a Modem

Every time you installed a new communications application in Windows 3.x, you had to go through another configuration routine—you had to specify the port connected to your modem, the highest speed the modem could handle, and so forth. Because there was no central modem control, each program required its own setup.

Part
3

Managing
Communications

This has changed in Windows 95, which uses a *universal modem* driver called *Unimodem*. Unimodem is the software interface between all of your computer's 32-bit Windows 95-compatible communications applications (including the ones that use TAPI) and your modem or other communications hardware. It includes integrated control for port selection, modem initialization, speed, file-transfer protocols, and terminal emulation. The modem configuration is handled by Unimodem, so you only have to specify setup parameters once.

If you're using third-party communications applications left over from earlier versions of Windows, they'll work with Windows 95, but you'll still have to configure them separately. When you replace them with newer, Windows 95-compatible updates, they'll use the settings already defined in Windows.

In most cases, you will need a modem to use Windows 95's communications features. Your modem might be an internal expansion board, an external modem plugged into a serial port, or a credit-card-n-sized PCMCIA modem. If the modem is already in place when you install Windows, the Windows Setup routine will automatically try to detect your modem for you. To install your modem later, you can use the Windows Control Panel, or you can configure it from a communications application such as Phone Dialer or HyperTerminal.

Follow these steps to install a modem from the Control Panel:

1. Click on the Start button and open the Control Panel from the Settings menu.

2. If you're using an external modem, turn it on and make sure it's connected to both the telephone line and a serial port on your computer.

3. Double-click on the Modems icon. The Modems Properties dialog box in Figure 13.1 will appear.

4. Click on the Add button to open the Install New Modem wizard.

5. Because you turned on the modem in step 2, you can let the Modem Wizard try to identify your modem type. Click on the Next> button.

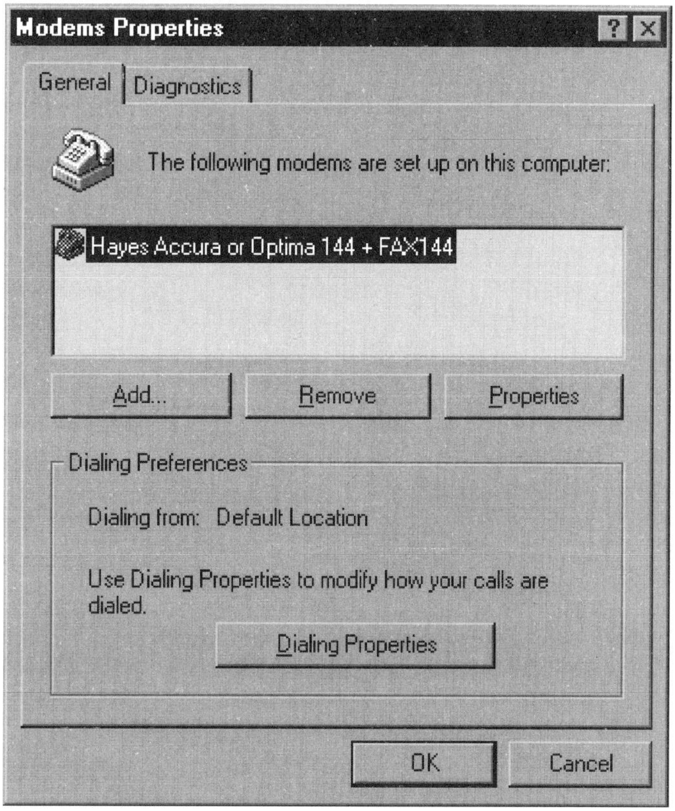

Figure 13.1 *This is the Modems Properties dialog box: click on the Add button to install a new modem.*

6. If you have an external modem, you will see the lights flash on the front panel while the Wizard tests it. When the tests are complete, the Wizard in Figure 13.2 displays the Verify dialog box.

7. If the Wizard is not able to identify your modem, click on the Change button and choose its make and model from the list. If your modem is not listed, look in the modem manual for an equivalent type or select the Generic Modem Drivers item in the Manufacturers list. When Windows 95 is in wide use, modem manufacturers will probably supply drivers on diskette with their modems. In that case, use the Have Disk button to install the driver.

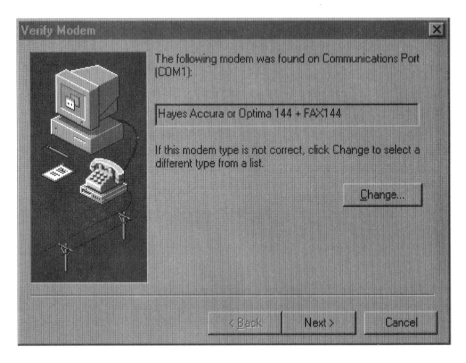

Figure 13.2 **The Verify Modem dialog box: if the modem type is correct, click on the Next> button.**

8. Click on the Next> and Finish buttons to complete the modem installation. If you haven't already entered your location and area code, the Location Information dialog box in Figure 13.3 will ask for this information.

   If your modem is connected to a line that uses Touch-Tone™ dialing, choose *Tone*. If not, choose *Pulse*.

Changing Modem Properties

Once you've installed your modem, all of your Windows 95 communications programs will use the same configuration settings. When you change them in one application, those changes will carry across to all the others. In general, you won't want to change the default modem properties, which specify things like the loudness of the modem's

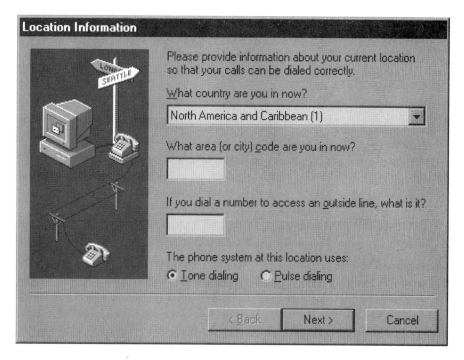

Figure 13.3   *The Location Information dialog box: choose your location from the drop-down menu and type in your area code.*

speaker and the maximum data-transfer speed. If you replace your modem, or if you use different modem types in different locations, you can install an additional modem from the Control Panel.

To change the modem properties after installation is complete, open the Control Panel and double-click on the Modems icon. When the Modems Properties dialog box appears, click on the Properties button to display the dialog box in Figure 13.4.

General Properties

The General tab has three settings:

Port   Use the drop-down Port menu to specify the COM port to which your modem is connected.

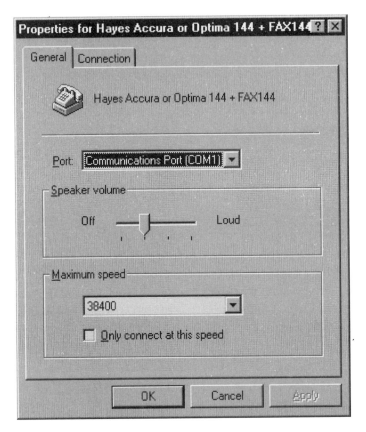

Figure 13.4 *Use this Properties dialog box to change your modem configuration.*

Speaker Volume The Speaker Volume control is a slide setting that sets the loudness of the speaker inside your modem.

Maximum Speed When your modem makes a connection, it will try to use the maximum speed to exchange data with the modem at the other end of the link. As a rule, if you have a 9,600 bits-per-second (bps) or faster modem, the maximum speed should be three or four times the rated modem speed (e.g., set your modem speed to 38400) to take advantage of the modem's built-in data compression.

If you don't want to accept a slower connection, check *Only connect at this speed*.

Choose the Connection tab to display the dialog box in Figure 13.5.

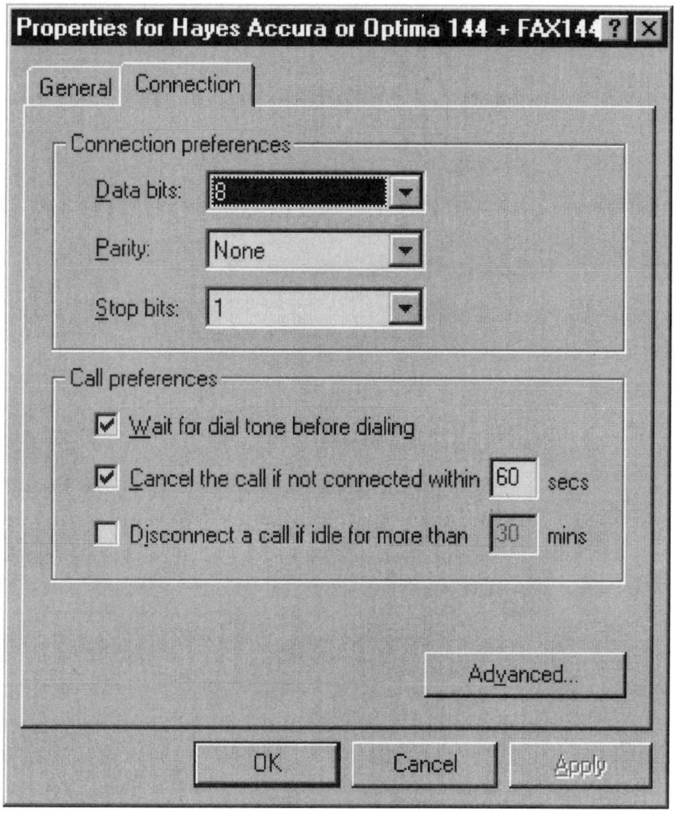

Figure 13.5   **Use the Connection dialog box to change communication parameters.**

The Connection dialog box has several options:

Connection Preferences   The Data bits, Parity, and Stop bits settings must be the same at both ends of a data link. The most common settings are 8 data bits, no parity, and one stop bit.

Call Preferences   The three *Call preferences* options control the way your modem handles individual calls. Place a check mark in each box if you want to use that option.

Advanced Options   The Advanced Connection Settings are options that you will probably set once and then leave alone. They manage error control, flow control, and additional special settings.

Figure 13.6 shows the Advanced Connection Settings dialog box.

The *Extra settings* section is a place to send additional AT commands to your modem. In most cases, you won't need to add any special commands. Because different modem manufacturers use slightly different command sets, you'll have to consult your modem manual for specific commands.

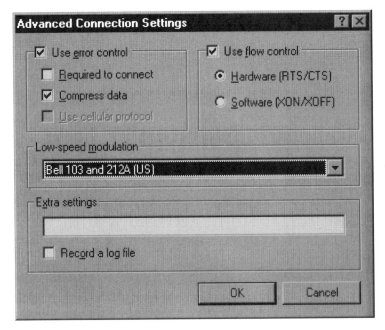

Figure 13.6 Use the Advanced Connection Settings dialog box to specify error control and flow control.

Diagnostic Properties

Click on the Diagnostics tab back in the original Properties for Modems dialog box to display the dialog box in Figure 13.7. The Diagnostics dialog box identifies the devices connected to each of your COM ports.

Click on the Driver button to see information about the Windows communications driver program. Highlight a COM port and click on

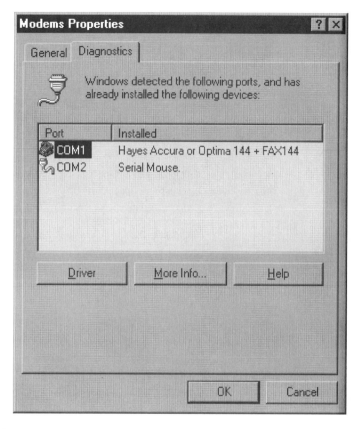

Figure 13.7 *Click on the Diagnostics tab to see the devices connected to your COM ports.*

the More Info button to display the information in Figure 13.8. This information can be extremely useful when you are trying to configure additional communications devices.

Dialing Properties

If you're using a portable computer, you may need to change the information about your location. You can open the Dialing Properties dialog box in Figure 13.9 from any Windows 95 communications application.

Part
3

Managing
Communications

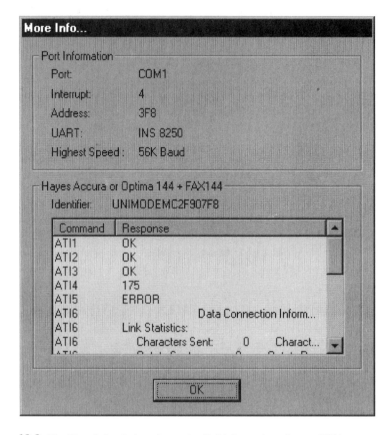

Figure 13.8   **The More Info window shows detailed information about a COM port configuration.**

The Dialing Properties dialog box includes these fields:

I Am Dialing From   This field specifies the name of each configuration set. To create a new configuration, use the New button and type a name in the Create New Location dialog box.

The Area Code Is   Type your own area code in this field.

I Am In (Country Code)   This field contains a drop-down menu that lists the international dialing codes for most countries of the world. Choose the name of the country from which you will be originating

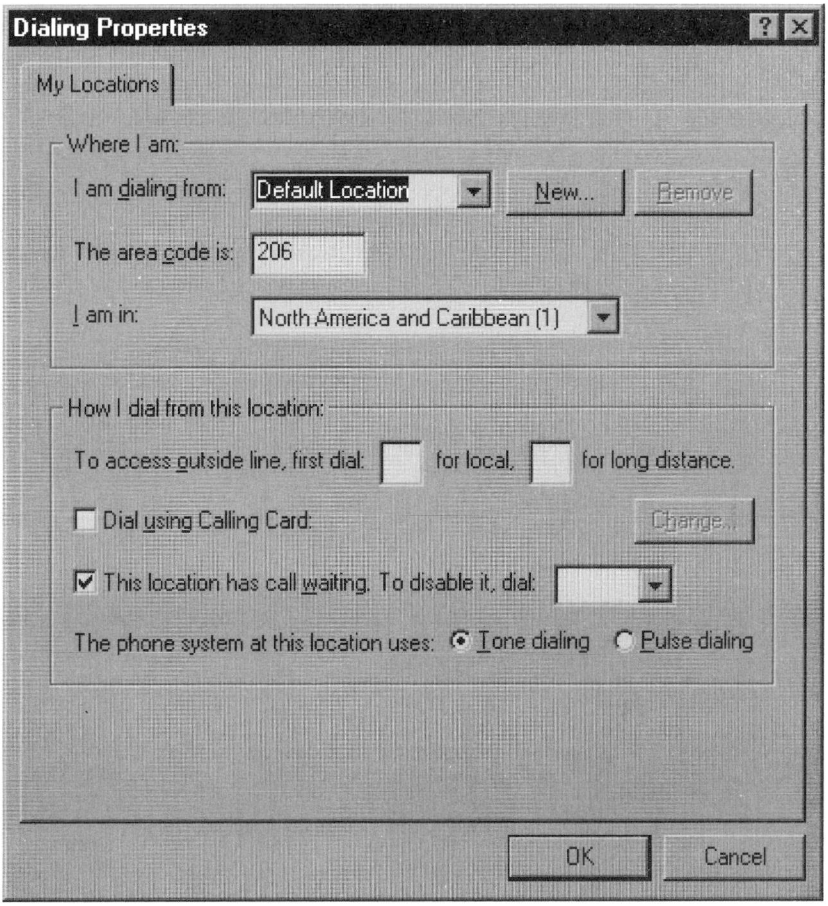

Figure 13.9 *The Dialing Properties dialog box controls the way communications programs place telephone calls.*

calls. The United States, Canada, and many Caribbean countries all use the same Country Code.

How I Dial From This Location   If your modem line is in an office where you must dial **9** for an outside line or some other code for long distance, type those number in these fields. If you have a direct outside line, leave these fields blank.

Part 3

Managing Communications

NOTE   The only time you will need to use the *long distance* field is when your modem is connected to a PBX or other telephone system that uses a special code for toll calls. Do not use this field for the "1" prefix that you dial before long-distance calls. The dialer will add that code automatically.

Dial Using Calling Card   To pay for a call with a calling card (a telephone company credit card), you must dial a special string of numbers that includes a carrier access code, your account number, and the number you're calling. In some cases, you have to call a service provider, enter your account number, and wait for a second dial tone before you can actually enter the number you want to call.

To use your calling card, select the Calling Card option to display the Change Calling Card dialog box in Figure 13.10. Either select your calling-card type from the drop-down menu or type the name of the card in the *Calling Card to use* field. Enter your complete calling-card number or account number in the *Calling Card number* field.

The drop-down Calling Card to use menu includes the most commonly used telephone credit cards in the United States—those issued by AT&T, MCI, and Sprint. If you choose a calling card from the menu, the program automatically uses the correct calling sequence for that long-distance carrier. But if you need a special calling sequence,

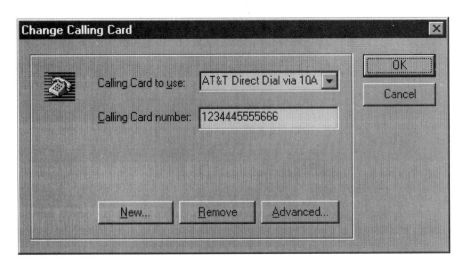

Figure 13.10   *Use the Change Calling Card dialog box to specify your telephone credit-card type and number.*

choose the Advanced button and type the sequences for local, long distance, and international calls in the Dialing Rules dialog box.

Use these codes for variables within a calling sequence:

E	Country Code
F	Area Code
G	Destination Local Number
H	Calling-card number
W	Wait for second dial tone
@	Wait for a ringing tone followed by five seconds of silence
$	Wait for a calling-card prompt tone (the "bong" tone)
?	Display an on-screen prompt

For example, the default calling sequence for long-distance calls using an AT&T calling card is 102880FG$H:

10288	specifies AT&T as long distance carrier
0	specifies a credit-card call
F	specifies the area code
G	specifies the local telephone number
$	specifies a wait for the calling-card prompt
H	specifies the calling-card number

This Location Has Call Waiting   Call waiting is an optional service offered by many local telephone companies to let you know that a second call has arrived while you are on the telephone. Unfortunately, the call-waiting signal can break a modem connection, so you must disable call waiting before placing a call through your computer.

If your telephone line uses call waiting, click on the call-waiting option to disable it. Look in the front of your local telephone directory or call your telephone business office to find out which code you need to use and select that code from the drop-down menu.

Part
3

Managing
Communications

Tone v. Pulse Dialing

Most push-button telephones use tone dialing (known in the United States as Touch-Tone™ dialing). However, older dial telephones and some cheap push-button phones use pulse signaling instead. Tone dialing is a lot more efficient because it takes a lot less time. Chances are, your telephone line will accept tone dialing even if there's a dial telephone connected to it. Therefore, you should go ahead and select Tone dialing and place a test call to see it if works. If it doesn't, choose Pulse dialing instead.

Because all Windows 95 application programs use the same modem-configuration information, you'll probably have to worry about the stuff in this section only once, when you install your modem for the first time. After that, TAPI uses the existing information when you load a new program.

In the next couple of chapters, you can find more specific information about using the communications applications that are included in the Windows 95 package, including the Phone Dialer, Microsoft Exchange, and The Microsoft Network online service.

Chapter 14

Using
Phone Dialer

FEATURING

Phone Dialer is a simple application that places outgoing voice telephone calls through your modem. You can tell Phone Dialer what number you want to dial by typing the number, choosing it from a Speed Dial list, or clicking numbers on an on-screen keypad. After you've called a number, you can select it from a list of recent calls. After it dials the call, Phone Dialer connects the line through to the telephone set plugged into the phone jack on your modem so you can pick up the handset and start talking.

You'll have to decide for yourself whether pressing keys on your computer keyboard is any improvement over pressing buttons on a telephone, but the speed-dial feature can be quite convenient for frequently called numbers. Of course, you're out of luck if you normally use separate telephone lines for voice and data.

Starting Phone Dialer

Phone Dialer is in the Windows Accessories menu, so you can start it by clicking on the Start button and then choosing Programs ➤ Accessories ➤ Phone Dialer. If you use Phone Dialer frequently, you can create a shortcut for this application.

When you start the program, the main Phone Dialer screen in Figure 14.1 appears. To make a call, either type the number or click on the numbers on the on-screen keypad. If you want to call a number you've called before, you can display recently dialed numbers in a drop-down menu by clicking on the arrow at the right side of the *Number to dial* field. When the complete number you want to dial is in this field, click on the Dial button.

Dialing a number with Phone Dialer is exactly like dialing the same number from your telephone. Therefore, you must include all the prefixes required by the phone company for this kind of call, such as a **1** for prepaid long-distance calls or a 0 for operator-assisted calls. On the other hand, if you're using an office telephone that requires **9** or some other access code for an outside line, you can use the Dialing Properties dialog box to add the code for all calls. You can open the Dialing Properties dialog box from Phone Dialer's Tools menu (Chapter 13).

Figure 14.1   The Phone Dialer screen offers several ways to enter a telephone number.

Programming the Speed Dial List

The eight entries in the Speed Dial list are push buttons. Click on one of the names in the list to dial that person's number. When you click on an unassigned button, the Program Speed Dial dialog box in Figure 14.2 appears. Type the name you want on the button in the *Name* field and the complete telephone number in the *Number to dial* field. Click on the Save button to save the new number and return to the main Phone Dialer screen or the Save and Dial button to call the number from this dialog box.

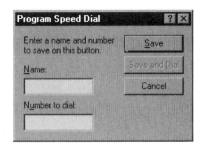

Figure 14.2   Use the Program Speed Dial dialog box to assign names and numbers to the Speed Dial list.

You can program several Speed Dial buttons at one time or change the name or number of a previously assigned button by choosing Speed Dial from the Edit menu. When the Edit Speed Dial dialog box in Figure 14.3 appears, click on the button you want to change and then type the name and number you want to assign to that button. After you have configured as many of the eight buttons as you want to use, click on the Save button.

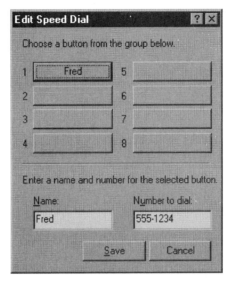

Figure 14.3   *Use the Edit Speed Dial dialog box to add or change Speed Dial items.*

Placing a Call

When you place a call through Phone Dialer, the Dialing dialog box in Figure 14.4 appears. If you entered the number from the Speed Dial list, the dialog box will display the name of the person you're calling. Otherwise, it will report the call destination as *unknown*. If you wish, you can type the recipient's name and a few words about the call to keep a record of this call in the Phone Dialer log.

As Phone Dialer places the call, you will hear the dialing tones (or pulses) and the ringing signal or busy signal through the modem's speaker. A *Call Status* window will let you know when the call has gone through. To transfer the call to your telephone set, click on the Talk button and pick up the handset or click on Hang Up to break

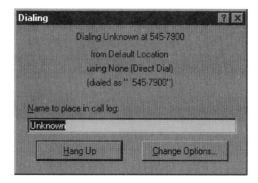

Figure 14.4 **This dialog box appears when you place a call with Phone Dialer.**

the connection. If the modem detects a busy signal, you will see a *Call Failed* window instead.

After you pick up the receiver and click on the Talk button, your call passes through the modem to your telephone set. At this point, there's no real difference between a Phone Dialer call and one placed directly from the telephone itself. To end the call, hang up the telephone.

Chapter 15

E-Mail and Microsoft Exchange

FEATURING

The Microsoft Exchange client is the central control point for Windows 95's messaging components, including electronic mail and fax. When you use Microsoft Exchange instead of separate application programs, a list of all of your messages and faxes appears in one window, regardless of the way your computer received them. You can send and receive messages, files, and faxes through several different services while using just one common on-screen client window.

Initially, the Exchange client supports three messaging services: Microsoft Mail, the Microsoft Network online service, and direct fax transmission through a fax modem. Microsoft will offer Exchange support for additional messaging services, including CompuServe and the Internet, in the Microsoft Plus accessory (see Chapter 32) and in their planned quarterly upgrades to Windows 95.

It's likely that other messaging services such as America Online and MCI Mail will offer add-on integration with Microsoft Exchange. And as new technologies such as voice mail become available, Microsoft Exchange will support them as well. The ultimate goal is to handle all kinds of messages through a single front end.

The Exchange client is a trade-off between the convenience of a single control center for many kinds of messages and the flexibility and features offered by single-purpose programs like WinFax and Lotus Notes. If you're committed to using the built-in Windows 95 messaging services, you may think of Exchange as the heart of Windows messaging. On the other hand, if you prefer using third-party messaging applications and services, you don't need to use Exchange at all.

In addition to the message-handling front end in Windows 95, Microsoft also uses the name *Exchange* for the separate network-messaging product that will probably be released some time in 1996 as Microsoft's answer to Lotus Notes. The Exchange client in Windows 95 will work seamlessly with the Exchange server product.

The Microsoft Exchange client is the most visible part of Windows 95's Messaging Subsystem, but it's just one piece of the puzzle. The Messaging Subsystem in Windows 95 also includes these elements:

The Messaging Applications Program Interface (MAPI)   MAPI is the interface between Microsoft Exchange or other compatible applications and the drivers that communicate with many information services.

Personal Address Book   Your Personal Address Book contains names, e-mail addresses, telephone and fax numbers, and other information about potential recipients of messages, even if you reach them through different services. E-mail and fax applications consult the Personal Address Book through MAPI, so you can keep a single address book for all the people to whom you send messages.

Personal Folders   Personal Folders is a database that contains messages, forms, and documents. Microsoft Exchange uses Personal Folders to store incoming and outgoing messages. If more than one user shares the same PC, each can use a separate Personal Folder.

Microsoft Mail Postoffice and Drivers   The Microsoft Mail Postoffice server is similar to the one in the separate Microsoft Mail product except that it does not provide access to Microsoft Mail gateways, it only supports a single post office, and it has fewer, less-extensive administration tools. The Microsoft Mail drivers are the interface between Microsoft Mail and MAPI.

Fax Drivers   In addition to conventional e-mail messages and files, Exchange can also handle fax pages to and from standalone fax machines or fax modems. Chapter 16 describes Windows 95's fax functions in detail.

Drivers for the Microsoft Network   The Microsoft Network is the new online information service that Microsoft is introducing along with Windows 95; Exchange can automatically connect to the Microsoft Network (MSN) to send and receive e-mail messages. And because MSN has gateways through the Internet to most other electronic mail services, you can use Exchange and MSN to process e-mail to many other destinations.

Windows 95's messaging architecture is similar to the telephony architecture described in Chapter 13: It uses an application programming interface (API) between the front-end programs the user sees and the individual drivers for various messaging services. The software flow looks like this:

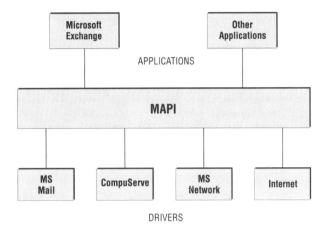

This modular structure allows outside software developers to create new drivers to work with existing applications or new front-end applications that will work with existing drivers. As a user, you can install new features and services without the need to completely relearn the messaging system.

Microsoft Exchange

All the messaging applications in Windows 95 use Microsoft Exchange to process inbound and outbound messages. The advantage of this approach is that it provides a single point of access.

Installing Microsoft Exchange

There are two ways to install Microsoft Exchange: during Windows 95 Setup or separately. If you want to load the Messaging System (including Microsoft Exchange) when you load the rest of Windows 95, you must select Custom rather than Typical setup. If you took the program's on-screen advice and used Typical Setup, you'll have to figure out where you've put the Windows 95 software disks before you can load Microsoft Exchange and the other communications programs.

To perform a separate installation, click on the Control Panel's Add/Remove Programs icon and choose the Windows Setup tab. If you're installing Windows from scratch, choose the Custom Setup option. Either way, you'll see a list of components like the one in Figure 15.1.

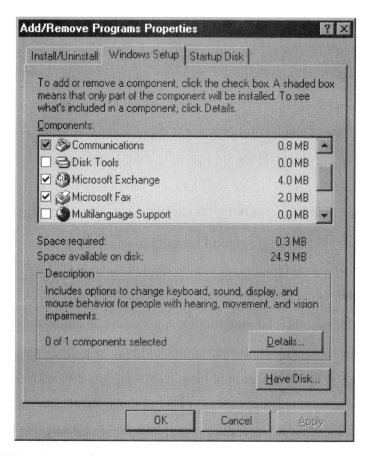

Figure 15.1   *Choose applications from the Windows Setup tab of the Add/Remove Programs Properties dialog box.*

Check the services you want to install. If you choose one or more of the messaging applications, such as either Microsoft Fax, Microsoft Network, or both, the Wizard will also force you to install Microsoft Exchange.

After you specify the services you want Microsoft Exchange to manage, the Wizard completes the installation for you.

Working with User Profiles

Microsoft Exchange uses configuration profiles to specify each user's messaging services and other options. If more than one person shares a single computer, or if you use the same computer in more than one location, it's a simple matter to create multiple profiles.

A single profile may include one or more messaging services, and each profile manages the features of all of the services in that profile. Depending on the way you want to manage your mail, you can either create one central profile that handles all your mail, or you can create separate profiles for different services.

The first time you run Exchange, a Configuration Wizard creates a profile for you. When you install the Microsoft Network software, Windows automatically creates a new profile.

To modify an existing profile or create a new one, follow these steps:

1. Open the Control Panel and double-click on the Mail and Fax icon.

2. When the Properties dialog box appears, click on the Show Profiles button. The Exchange Setting Properties dialog box in Figure 15.2 will appear. It will display a list of all the profiles that have previously been created on your system.

3. Highlight the name of a profile and choose one of these options:

   Add: creates a new profile.

   Remove: deletes the profile whose name is highlighted.

   Properties: defines the way Exchange will handle messages in the currently highlighted profile.

   Copy: creates a new profile with the same properties as the currently highlighted profile. After you copy a profile, you can use the Properties option to personalize the new profile.

 NOTE If you create more than one profile, you should assign a name to each profile that describes the way you plan to use it, such as the name of the person using it or the name of the service that the profile controls.

4. When you open Microsoft Exchange, it will start with the default profile active. To change the default profile, drop down the menu in the *When starting, use this profile* field and highlight a profile name.

Part
3

Managing
Communications

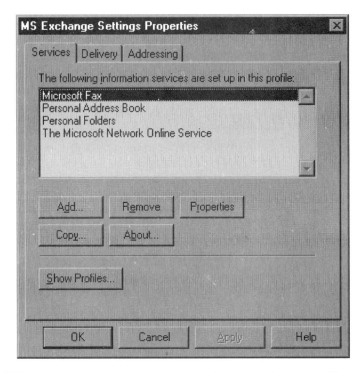

Figure 15.2 *The Exchange Setting Properties dialog box shows all current profiles.*

Defining Properties in an Exchange Profile

Each of the services in a profile has a specific set of properties that defines the way Exchange uses that service. To view or change the default settings, double-click on the Mail and Fax icon in the Control Panel to open the Properties dialog box. Highlight the name of the service whose properties you want to view or change and click on the Properties button.

Fax Properties

The Microsoft Fax Properties dialog box in Figure 15.3 controls the way Exchange handles fax messages. Chapter 16 contains detailed information about configuring Fax Properties.

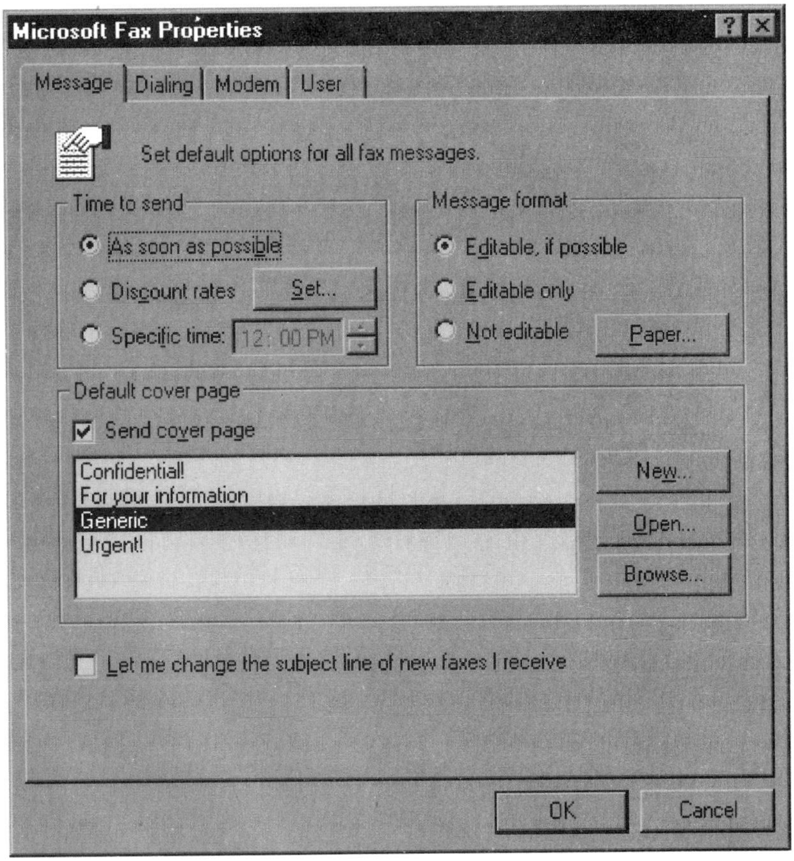

Figure 15.3 *Use the Fax Properties dialog box to select features of outbound faxes.*

Microsoft Mail Properties

To send and receive messages through a Microsoft Mail post office, you must add Mail to your Microsoft Exchange profile. The Microsoft Mail dialog box has eight tabs:

Connection To use Microsoft Mail, you must specify the full path for the post office that handles your messages on the Connection tab page shown in Figure 15.4. The post office may be located on your computer or on another computer connected to yours through a network.

Part
3

Managing
Communications

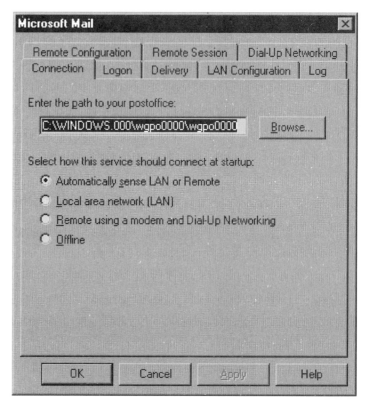

Figure 15.4   *The Connection tab defines the connection to your post office.*

You can connect to your post office through a LAN or a modem and telephone line. Select the radio button that describes the type of connection you're using.

Logon   Use the Logon tab to specify the name and password that your post office uses for your account.

Delivery   The Delivery tab in Figure 15.5 controls the way messages move between your post office and the Exchange client.

The *Enable incoming* option must be active to receive mail. The *Enable outgoing* option must be active to send mail.

Many Microsoft Mail installations have gateways to other messaging services, including fax and MCI Mail, among many others. If you don't want to use Mail to send messages to one or more of these

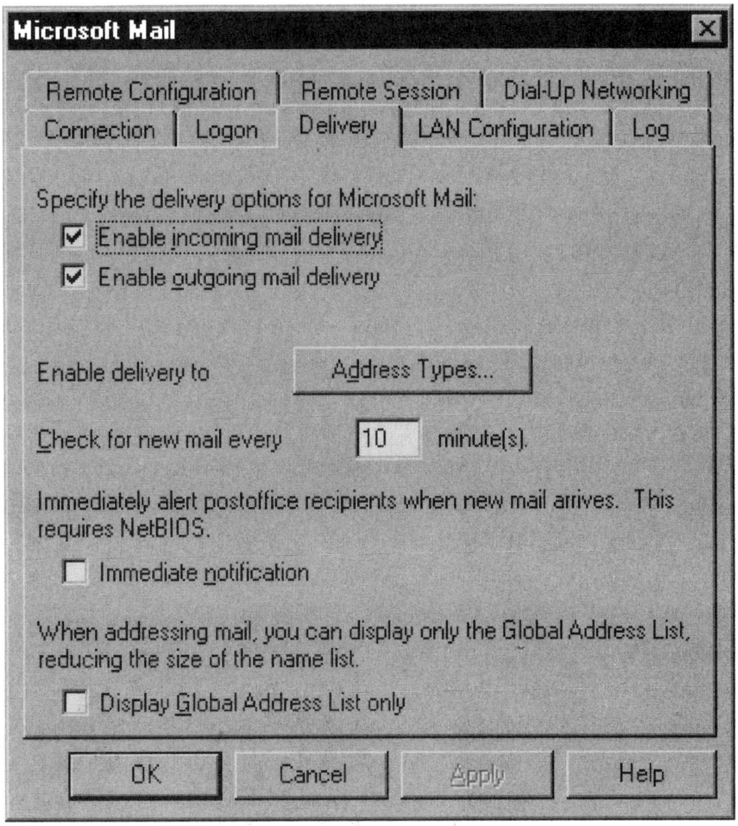

Figure 15.5 *Use the Delivery tab to specify delivery options.*

services, click on the Address Types button and remove the check mark from the name of the service. For example, if you want to send faxes through your fax modem rather than through your LAN, remove the check mark next to Fax.

LAN Configuration The LAN Configuration options all require a connection to a LAN. If you connect to your post office through a modem, you can ignore these options.

When *Use remote mail* is active, Exchange automatically transfers the headers of new incoming messages rather than the full text of the messages. When you want to read a message, use the Remote Mail command in Exchange's Tools menu.

Part 3

Managing Communications

When the *Use local copy* option is active, Exchange stores a copy of the post office's address book on your local hard drive and uses that list rather than connecting you to the post office every time you request an address.

If your connection to the post office is extremely slow, the external delivery agent may reduce the amount of time needed for mail delivery.

Log   Use the options on the Log tab to create a history file for Microsoft Mail activity.

Remote Configuration   The Remote Configuration tab controls options that apply when you're using a modem connection to your post office. These options are similar to the ones on the LAN Configuration tab.

Remote Session   Use the Remote Session tab to specify when and for how long you want Exchange to connect to the post office through a modem. When the *Automatically start* option is active, Exchange will dial out to your post office as soon as you start Exchange. The *Automatically end* options specify when Exchange breaks the connection.

Dial-Up Networking   The options in the Dial-Up Networking dialog box control the way Exchange connects to a remote network through a modem. These are the same options you can reach through the Dial-Up Networking icon in the My Computer window.

Personal Address Book Properties

Your Personal Address Book is a combined listing of people to whom you send messages, regardless of the service that you use to reach that person. When you choose a name from your Personal Address Book, Exchange automatically routes the message through the service specified for that name. For example, your address book might include some people with Microsoft Network addresses, others with fax numbers, and still others who are on your Microsoft Mail system. By using the address book, you won't have to specify which service to use every time you send a message.

You can use as many separate Personal Address Books as you want. For example, if you share the computer with somebody else, each of you might want your own address book. Or you might want to use separate address books for personal and business purposes.

The Personal Address Book dialog box in Figure 15.6 specifies the file that contains your Personal Address Book and the order in which Exchange displays the contents of the address book (first name first or last name first).

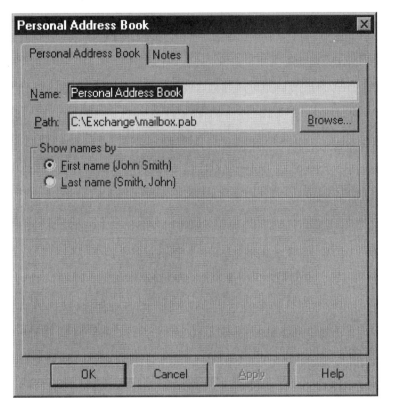

Figure 15.6 *The Personal Address Book dialog box controls the location and format of address books.*

The Notes tab displays any comments you might want to save about each Personal Address Book on your computer. If you have more than one address book, you can use these comments to remind yourself what each one contains. If you have only one address book, you can leave the Notes field blank.

Personal Folders Properties

Personal Folders are folders on your hard drive where you store messages. The Personal Folders dialog box shown in Figure 15.7 controls the way Exchange manages these folders. Most of the fields in the Personal Folders dialog box are fixed.

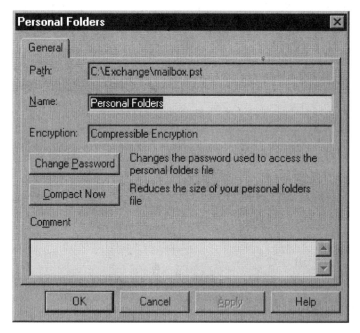

Figure 15.7   The Personal Folders dialog box specifies the way Exchange stores messages.

Microsoft Network Properties

The Microsoft Network Properties dialog box controls the way Exchange sends and receives messages from MSN. Use the Transport tab shown in Figure 15.8 to specify when you want Exchange to retrieve your MSN mail.

The Address Book tab turns address verification on and off. If *Connect to MSN to check names* is active, Exchange will automatically call MSN to confirm that names in your Personal Address Book with MSN addresses are current MSN subscribers.

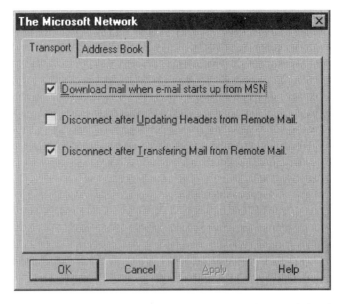

Figure 15.8 *The MSN dialog box lets you choose when Microsoft Network downloads your messages.*

Adding New Services to an Exchange Profile

To add a new service to an existing profile, click on the Add button to open the Add Service dialog box in Figure 15.9.

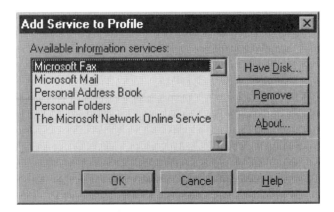

Figure 15.9 *Use the Add Service dialog box to add a messaging service to an Exchange Profile.*

Part
3

Managing
Communications

The services in the *Available services* field are the ones included with Windows 95. To add one to the current profile, highlight it and click on the OK button.

Over time, Microsoft and other software developers and service providers will integrate other messaging services into Exchange. To add a new service to an Exchange profile, place the diskette or CD-ROM that contains the software in a drive and click on the Have Disk button to specify the location and name of the directory that contains the software.

Other Exchange Profile Options

Use the Remove button to delete a service from a profile.

If you have more than one Exchange profile, you can copy a messaging service, including its configuration, from one profile to another by clicking on the Copy button.

The About button opens an information window that shows details about all of the DLL files that control the currently highlighted messaging service.

The Delivery tab controls the location where Exchange will deliver new messages and the order in which Exchange polls messaging services.

The Addressing tab specifies the address book that Exchange uses as a default and the order in which Exchange consults address books when you send a message.

Using the Exchange Client

There are several ways to open the Exchange client:

▶ Click on the Start button to open the menu bar and choose Microsoft Exchange from the Programs menu.

▶ Double-click on the Inbox icon on the Windows Desktop.

▶ Connect to the Microsoft Network and click on E-Mail in the MSN Central screen.

The default Exchange screen in Figure 15.10 shows a list of messages in the current folder. You can customize the way Exchange organizes information in folders and the specific information that appears on your screen. I'll talk about other screen layouts later in this section.

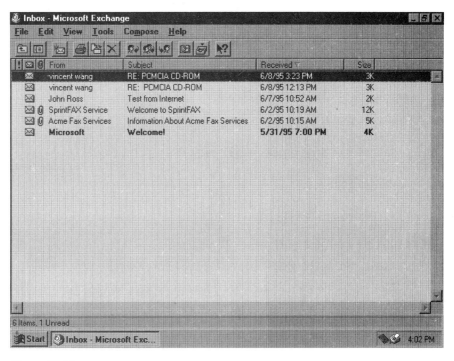

Figure 15.10   Microsoft Exchange uses an Explorer-like screen layout.

When you click on the Show/Hide Folder List button in the Toolbar or select the Folders command in the View menu, a graphic display of Exchange folders appears to the left of the list of messages. This layout is very similar to the Windows Explorer. Figure 15.11 shows a folder list.

Exchange calls each user's mailbox a *Personal Folder*. Each Personal Folder may contain an unlimited number of subfolders, but at a minimum they all must include an Inbox, an Outbox, and folders for deleted items and sent items. You can use the subfolders in a Personal Folder to hold the items that you send and receive through Exchange,

Part 3

Managing Communications

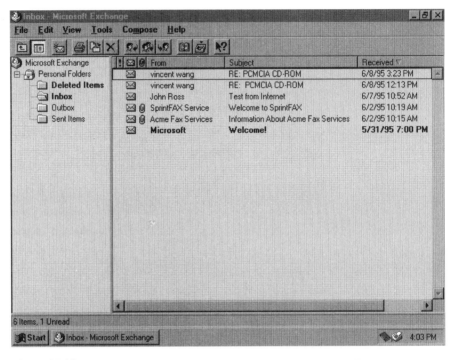

Figure 15.11   The Exchange folder list is similar to the list in Windows Explorer.

including e-mail messages, files, and faxes. As a general rule, you should have one Personal Folder in each user profile.

Like Explorer screens, the Exchange Viewer shows folders on the left and the contents of the currently highlighted folder on the right. You can move a message or other item to a new folder by dragging it to the destination folder or by highlighting it and using the Move or Copy command in the File menu or the menu that appears when you click the right mouse button. If you have more than one Personal Folder, it's also possible to move or copy an entire subfolder from one Personal Folder to another; however, you can't move or copy one subfolder to another subfolder within the same Personal Folder.

There are several possible ways to arrange the display of files and messages in the right pane of the Exchange Viewer: You can define the specific information that will appear in each column, the order in which the columns appear, and the way the Viewer sorts messages and other items.

The headings across the top of the pane identify the information in each column. Click on a heading button to sort the messages according to that heading; for example, click on the From heading to arrange the messages and other items by source. To change the order from ascending (earliest or smallest first) to descending (latest or largest first), use the Sort command in the View menu or right-click on the column heading.

To change the set of headings in the Viewer or the order in which the headings appear, use the Columns command in the View menu to open the dialog box shown below. To add a heading, choose it from the *Available columns* list and click on the Add button; to remove a heading, highlight it in the *Show the following columns* list and click on the Remove button. The columns appear in the Viewer in the same order they appear in the list; to change the order, highlight an item and use the Move Up or Move Down button.

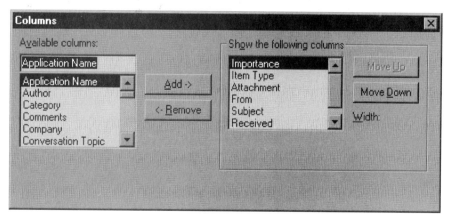

Searching for a Message

If you send and receive a lot of messages, you will eventually have either a bunch of folders with many messages in each one or one folder with a huge amount of stuff in it. Finding a month-old memo by looking through subject lines could take hours; fortunately, there's an easier method. Exchange has a message finder that can search through all the messages in a folder or in an entire Personal Folder to find messages that match one or more search criteria.

Follow these steps to search for messages:

1. Choose the Find command in the Tools menu.

2. When the Find window in Figure 15.12 appears, fill in the fields you want to use to search for messages:

   Look in: This field specifies the folder whose contents you want to search. Use the Folder button to choose a different folder.

   Find items containing: Use one or more of these fields to specify the contents or other characteristics of the message you want to find.

   Advanced: Click on the Advanced button to display the dialog box shown on the next page. You can use this dialog box to specify the size, date, and other characteristics of the messages.

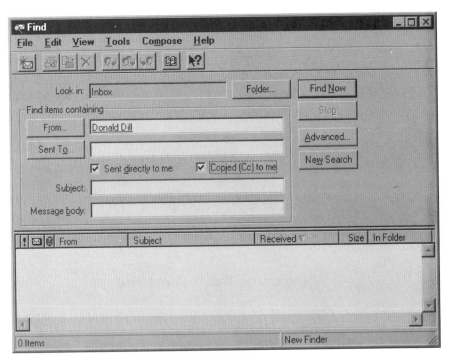

Figure 15.12 Use Find to search for messages.

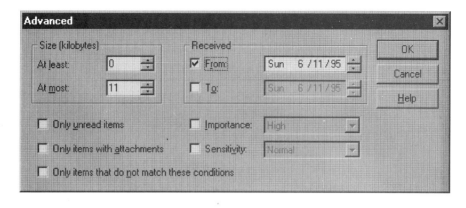

3. Click on the Start button to begin the search.

4. If the Finder locates any messages that match your search criteria, it will list them in the bottom half of the Finder window.

5. To cut off a search before it is complete, use the Stop button.

   You can work with messages in the Finder the same way you work with them in the Exchange Viewer window. Double-click on a listing to display the contents of the message. Use the commands in the menu and the Toolbar to arrange columns; sort messages; use groups, filters, and views; and compose new messages.

Changing the Exchange Window

Most of the elements of the Exchange screen can be adjusted to meet your own needs and preferences. The Customize Toolbar command in the Tools menu opens a dialog box that controls the set of buttons in the Exchange Toolbar. The Services and Options commands in the Tools menu open the same dialog boxes that you used to configure Exchange from the Control Panel. And the commands in the View menu display, hide, or rearrange many specific screen elements.

Address Books

An address book is a list of names of potential recipients of Microsoft Exchange messages. Because each address-book entry specifies the messaging service you use to reach that person, you can create a single list that includes people with whom you communicate through several services.

When you want to send a message, you can choose the recipient by name and let Exchange worry about the transmission details.

If several users share the same machine, each user can have one or more personal address books. In addition, many messaging servers—such as Microsoft Mail and Microsoft Network—also provide directories of their subscribers in the same address-book format.

You can open an address book from the Compose Message window by clicking on the To or Cc buttons, or directly from the Microsoft Exchange screen by using the Address Book command in the Tools menu or clicking on the Address Book button in the Toolbar.

Figure 15.13 shows the Address Book window. The Type Name field is a smart search tool that will home in on the name you want as you type it. In most cases, it will find the name you want by the time you

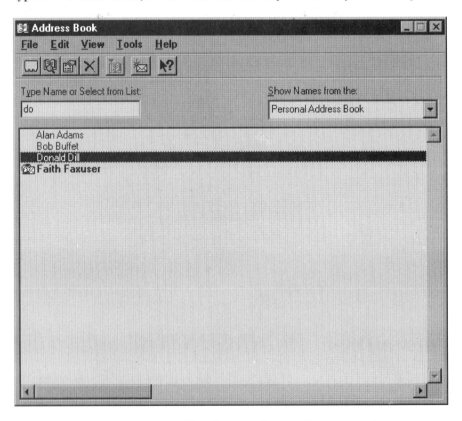

Figure 15.13 *A single Exchange address book can list subscribers to several messaging services.*

type three or four letters. If you prefer, you can point directly to a name in the list and click to highlight it. Double-click on an address-book listing to change the properties assigned to that name. To select a different address book, drop down the menu in the Show Names field.

To add a name to your address book, use the New Entry command in the File menu or on the Toolbar. Choose the service you want to use to communicate with this person and click on OK to open a Properties dialog box. The Exchange client in Windows 95 does not support direct connection to the Internet, but you can send e-mail to Internet addresses through the Microsoft Network.

The Properties dialog box asks different questions for each type of messaging service. For example, if you specify an MSN e-mail address, the dialog box in Figure 15.14 will appear.

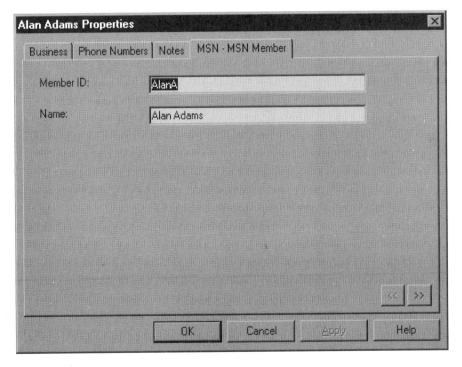

Figure 15.14   *The Properties dialog box for a Microsoft Network address includes space for the recipient's name and MSN Member ID.*

Part
3

Managing
Communications

The other tabs provide space for you to add additional information about this party, including full name and address, up to eight different telephone numbers, and other notes.

Besides using Address Book listings to send messages through Microsoft Exchange, you can also use the Address Book to set up voice telephone calls through Phone Dialer. To place a call, double-click on the name of the person you want to call and click on the Phone Numbers tab to display the dialog box in Figure 15.15. Choose the location you want to call and click on the Dial button next to that telephone number. When the call goes through, Phone Dialer will tell you to lift the handset and start talking.

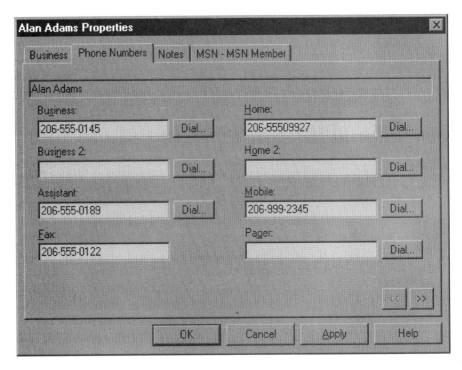

Figure 15.15 *The Exchange Address Book may contain multiple telephone numbers for the same person.*

Creating and Sending Messages

Everything I've talked about so far in this chapter is about getting Microsoft Exchange organized. In this section, I'll explain how to use it to do something actually useful. It's easy to forget that Microsoft Exchange isn't really about profiles or address books—it's a tool for sending and receiving messages. All of its other features and functions support those activities.

Here's the procedure for sending a message through Microsoft Exchange:

1. Start Microsoft Exchange from the menu bar or the Desktop Inbox icon.

2. When the Inbox - Microsoft Exchange screen appears, choose the New Message command from either the Compose menu or the Toolbar.

3. When the New Message screen in Figure 15.16 appears, either type the names of the recipients in the To field or click on the To button to select names from an address book. If you want to send this message to more than one person, use semicolons to separate the names.

   ▶ If you want to send duplicate copies of this message, tab or mouse to the Cc field in the New Message box and type the names. Alternatively, in the Address Book dialog box click on the Cc-> button to select from the list.

   ▶ If you want to send a blind copy of this message, use the Bcc Box command in the View menu.

4. Point and click on the Subject field and type a subject line for this message.

5. Move your cursor to the large box at the bottom of the screen and type the text of your message. You can find more detailed information about formatting messages, adding inserts, and attaching files in the next part of this chapter.

6. When the text and format of your message are complete and ready to go, use the Send command in the File menu or the Send button in the Toolbar to place the message in the Exchange Outbox.

Part 3

Managing Communications

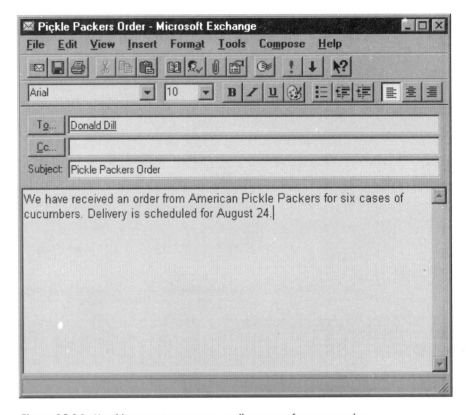

Figure 15.16   Use this screen to compose e-mail messages for many services.

7. After you have finished composing messages, open the Outbox folder and choose the Deliver Now command in the Tools menu. If all the messages in your out box are for the same message service, you can choose that service from the Deliver Now submenu, but it's generally easier to use the All Services command.

8. After Exchange has uploaded your message, it automatically transfers the message from the Outbox folder to the Sent Items folder. You can move the message to a different folder by dragging and dropping it in the Exchange window.

Formatting Messages

The message editor in Microsoft Exchange uses the same formatting tools as WordPad, including a Toolbar with buttons to control font, character size, style, color, indentation, and justification. To change the format of all or part of a message, highlight the text you want to format and click on the appropriate button in the Toolbar.

Just because it's possible to do all kinds of fancy formatting tricks with your messages, it doesn't mean you have to use them in every message. In most cases, you send a message to communicate information, and a screen with three different colors and four different typestyles doesn't contribute anything to the reader's understanding of your message—it's just hard to read. Sending an e-mail message that looks like a ransom note does not convey a businesslike image, but it might be exactly what you want when you send a birthday greeting to a ten-year-old.

It's also a good idea to think about the type of hardware and software the person receiving your messages will use. Unless the recipient is also using Microsoft Exchange, all your special effects will be lost if the other mail reader does not recognize formatting information.

Attaching a File to a Message

In addition to new text, you can also include existing text files in the body of your message and accompany your message with one or more binary files. An attached file can appear in the body of your message as an icon with a name. As in the Explorer and the Windows Desktop, clicking on an icon in a message opens the attached file.

It's also possible to create a link to a file that already exists on the recipient's computer or network. For example, you might have a program on your computer that reports your company's daily sales volume. If other people on the same LAN have access to your computer through the network, you could send them a message like the one in Figure 15.17.

Part
3

Managing
Communications

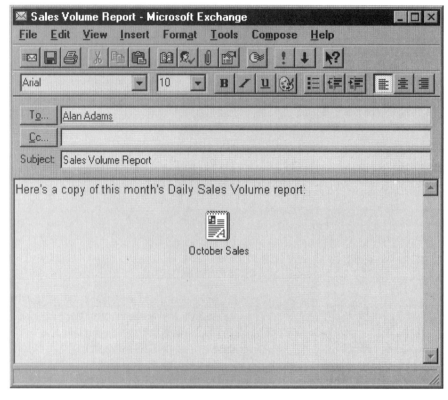

Figure 15.17 Microsoft Exchange messages may include embedded files.

Follow these steps to include a file with a message:

1. Move your cursor to the place in the message where you want the file.

2. Select the File command in the Insert menu. The Insert File window in Figure 15.18 will appear.

3. Locate the file you want to attach and highlight it.

4. Choose a method from the Insert As box:

   Text only: inserts the text contained in the file into your message as text.

   An attachment: attaches a copy of the file to your message and places an icon in your message at the current cursor location.

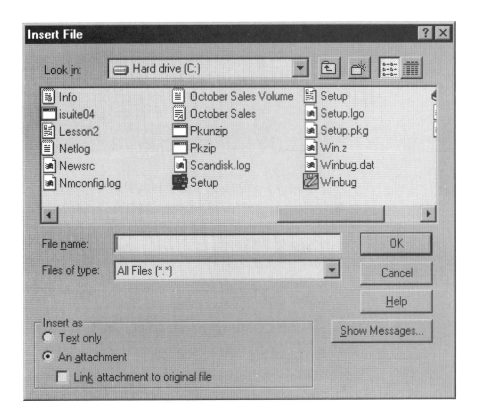

Figure 15.18   Use the Insert File dialog box to attach a file to a message.

Link attachment to original file: inserts an icon that points to the file's location rather than making a copy of it. A linked file must be located in a place where the recipient can get to it. Therefore, you should generally limit linked files to recipients who are on the same computer or network.

5. Click on the OK button or double-click on the icon for the file you want to insert.

6. If you want to insert or attach another file, repeat steps 3, 4, and 5.

7. To close the Insert File dialog box, click on OK.

Part 3

Managing Communications

Embedding an Object in a Message

An object is a data file that contains information formatted for a particular application. When the recipient reads a message with an embedded object, Microsoft Exchange uses the application to open the file. Therefore, an embedded object could be any kind of data file, such as a graph, spreadsheet, or picture. Like an attached file, an object may be either pasted directly into the message or displayed as an icon.

You may use an existing data file as an object or create a new one especially for your message. If you choose to create a new object, Exchange will open the application program associated with the type of object you specify.

Here's the procedure for embedding an object in a message:

1. Move your cursor to the place in the message where you want the embedded object or icon to appear.

2. Select the Object command from the Insert menu.

3. The Insert Object dialog box shown below has two options:

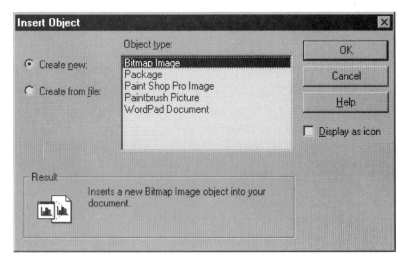

Create New: Use this option if the object does not already exist.

Create from File: Use this option to select an existing object.

4. If you want the object to appear in the body of your message as an icon, check Display As Icon.

5. If you're creating a new object, select the object type from the list. The application associated with that object type will open.

6. If you're embedding an existing file, choose Create from File to display the dialog box shown below. Either type its full path and name in the File field or use the browser to find the file you want.

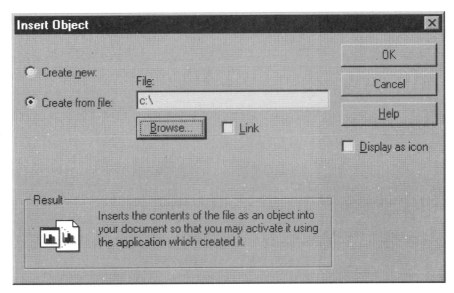

7. When the Link option is not active, the embedded object is part of the message you actually send. When Link is active, Exchange displays the latest version of the file, even if the file changes after you send your message.

 NOTE   A linked object file must be located in a place where the recipient can get to it. Therefore, you should generally limit linked objects to recipients who are on the same computer or network that you use.

8. Click on the OK button to embed the specified object file.

Part
3

Managing
Communications

Receiving Messages

Exchange checks for new mail at the same time it delivers outgoing messages to the messaging services that relay them to their ultimate destinations. To connect to your messaging services, use one of the Deliver Now commands in the Tools menu.

When Exchange receives new messages, it stores them in the Inbox folder. It displays descriptions of unread messages in boldface type. After you read a message, the description changes to normal type. To read a newly received message, open the Inbox folder and double-click on the description.

Fax messages are a special case. Unlike most e-mail services, which are store-and-forward systems that hold your messages until you go looking for them, fax messages might arrive at any time. Chapter 16 contains detailed information about using Exchange to send and receive faxes.

Moving Messages and Files to Other Applications

Microsoft Exchange is an OLE-compatible application. Therefore, you can drag messages and other items in the Exchange Viewer to and from other applications, including the Windows Desktop. When you drag a message from an Exchange folder to a drive or directory on the Desktop, Windows will save the message as a file with an .msg file extension.

It's also possible to drag files from other applications into Microsoft Exchange. If the file was created with an application that uses Summary Info dialog boxes, you can use the Summary fields as column headings for sorting, searching, or filtering in Microsoft Exchange.

Microsoft Mail

Microsoft Mail is one of the information services that can use MAPI and Microsoft Exchange to move messages to and from your PC. Microsoft Mail uses a post office located on one of the computers in a workgroup to hold messages until the Mail client on the recipient's own machine retrieves it. You may know Microsoft Mail as a separate product or as an element of Windows for Workgroups. Windows 95 includes both a Microsoft Mail client and a Mail post office that are completely compatible with other products that support Mail. Therefore, you can operate a mixed workgroup that includes both Windows 95 and Windows 3.x systems along with Microsoft Mail clients for other platforms.

It's important to remember that a workgroup may have only one post office, so you should not create a new post office if you're adding a new Windows 95 machine to an existing workgroup. The post office in Windows 95 is limited, which means that it can't communicate with other post offices. If you're planning to move mail through more than one post office to other workgroups, you'll have to use the complete version of Microsoft Mail. This version comes as a separate product, and it will be included with the standalone Microsoft Exchange product.

Earlier in this chapter, I explained that Microsoft Exchange uses a Personal Folder to hold messages from many different information services. A Microsoft Mail post office is a similar information store that holds messages for all the members of a workgroup. When the recipient receives a message, the post office removes its copy of the same message. If a message is addressed to more than one recipient, the post office deletes it after the last recipient retrieves it.

Microsoft Mail can deliver mail to three kinds of Windows 95 clients:

▶ a Personal Folder located on the same computer that holds the post office

▶ a Personal Folder located on a computer connected through a network to the computer that holds the post office

▶ a Personal Folder located on a mobile or remote computer that makes a temporary connection to the computer that holds the post office

Installing a Microsoft Mail Post Office

The first time Exchange runs, it will ask for the location of your post office. If your workgroup already has a post office, you should not install another one from Windows 95. If you don't have access to an existing post office, you should create one on your PC. All Microsoft Mail users must use a post office, even if they are not connected to a LAN.

Part
3

Managing
Communications

Follow these steps to create a new post office:

1. From the Control Panel, click on the Microsoft Mail Postoffice icon to start the Postoffice Admin Wizard.

2. Choose the Create a New Postoffice option and click on the Next button.

3. Type a path for the post office folder.

4. When the dialog box shown below appears, fill in the details for your Administrator account. You will need this name and password to add or remove additional accounts in this post office.

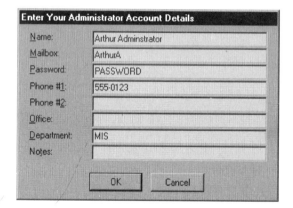

5. When the Administrator account is set up, go back to the Control Panel and click on the Microsoft Mail Postoffice icon again. This time, choose the Administer radio button and click on Next. The Wizard will display the location of your post office. Click on Next.

6. Type your Administrator password in the Password field and click on Next.

7. When the Postoffice Manager window in Figure 15.19 appears, click on the Add User button to create new accounts for the other people in your workgroup. Use the Details button to see information about existing users.

8. After you have created an account for every user in your workgroup, click on the Close button.

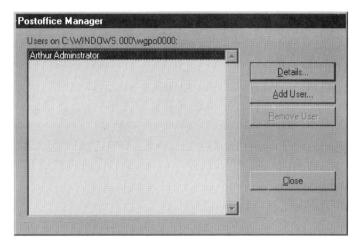

Figure 15.19   *Use the Postoffice Manager dialog box to add, remove, or modify user accounts.*

Shutting Down Microsoft Exchange

Once you start Microsoft Exchange, it will run in the background, waiting for incoming messages, until you use the Exit or the Exit and Log Off command in the File menu.

By this time, you're thinking that Microsoft Exchange seems incredibly complicated. You're right. Because Exchange and MAPI can control so many different message services, it has a very large set of configuration options. But in practice, you will probably use no more than a few services at the same time—maybe just fax and Microsoft Network or Microsoft Mail. It's really not as complex as it looks.

The great advantage of Microsoft Exchange over a separate application for each service is that you can store and manage all your messages in one place and use the same set of commands to send and receive messages through many services. Once you've got Exchange configured the way you want it, you can spend your time thinking about the content of your messages.

In the next two chapters, I'll explain how to use two specialized communication services: fax and the Internet. Both of these services can use Microsoft Exchange as a front end, but that's just one of several options—there's a lot more to sending and receiving faxes and to connecting your PC to the worldwide Internet.

Chapter 16

Sending and Receiving Faxes

FEATURING

If you're in business today, a fax machine is as essential as an office copier or a coffeepot. The most common tool for facsimile communication is still the standalone fax machine, but there are some real advantages to using your PC as a personal fax machine instead.

Here's what you need to do to send a fax through a fax machine: create the document; print a copy on paper; write up a cover sheet; carry the document and cover sheet to the fax machine; wait for your turn to use the machine; dial the recipient's fax number; feed the document and cover sheet through the fax machine; and finally, walk back to your office. When somebody sends you a fax, it spills out of the machine and waits for you to come get it—meanwhile, everybody who walks past the fax machine has a chance to read your messages before you do.

On the other hand, you can send and receive faxes through your PC and a fax modem without leaving your chair. If you have a home office or a *really* small business with a tight budget, you can do PC-based faxing without spending two-hundred dollars or more for a separate machine. And when you're traveling with a portable computer, you can use it to exchange faxes with your office and your customers.

In this chapter, you can find out how to use Microsoft Fax to send faxes from Microsoft Exchange, from the Windows 95 desktop, and directly from application programs. You'll also learn how to create cover pages for your outgoing faxes, how to receive faxes through your modem, and how to use the Fax Viewer program.

Installing Microsoft Fax

Before you can send or receive faxes, you must configure Windows 95 to recognize Microsoft Fax as a virtual printer. You can load the fax software when you install Windows 95 by choosing Custom Setup and checking Microsoft Fax from the list of components. Since the fax program uses the Microsoft Exchange client, you'll also have to load Exchange if it's not already present on your computer. If you've already installed Windows 95 without the Microsoft Fax component, you can add it by using this procedure:

1. From the Control Panel, double-click on the Add/Remove Programs icon.

2. Choose the Windows Setup tab.

3. Scroll down the list of components until you see the listing for Microsoft Fax in Figure 16.1.

4. Check the box for Microsoft Fax and click on the OK button.

5. Insert and remove the Windows 95 software disks as the on-screen Wizard instructs you to do so.

6. Open the Control Panel again and double-click on the Mail and Fax icon. The dialog box in Figure 16.2 will appear.

7. Either click on the Add button to create a new Exchange profile for fax messages or highlight the name of an existing profile and click on Properties to add Fax to an existing profile.

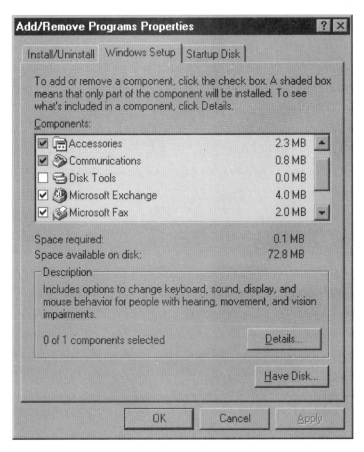

Figure 16.1   **Check Microsoft Fax to send and receive faxes.**

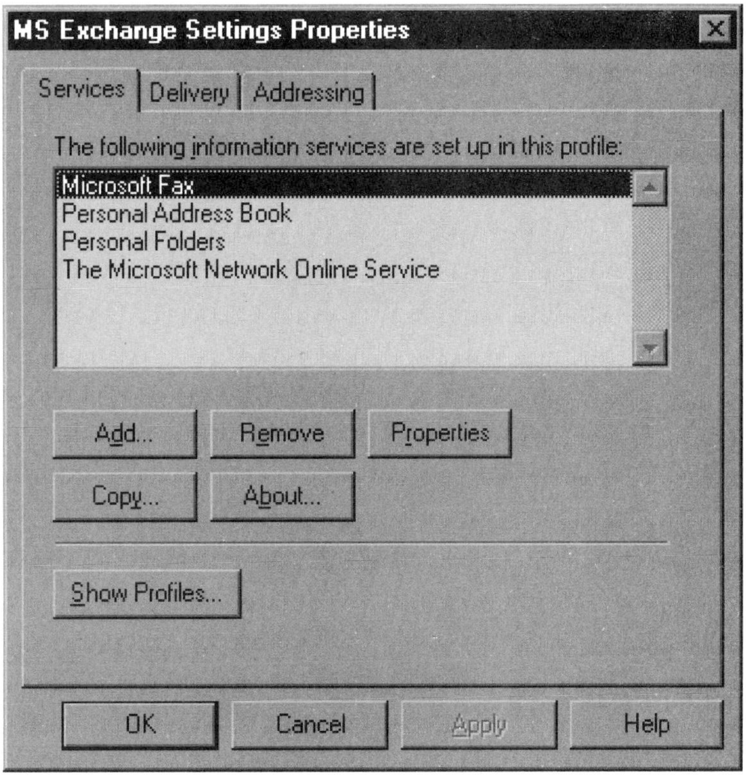

Figure 16.2 You may add Microsoft Fax to an existing profile or create a new one.

8. If you're creating a new profile, the Exchange Setup Wizard will ask you to identify the services you want in this profile. Check the box next to Microsoft Fax.

9. Click on the Next button and fill in each field as the Wizard asks for information about this new profile.

To add Microsoft Fax to an existing profile, follow these steps:

1. Open the Control Panel and double-click on the Mail and Fax icon or use the Shortcut to Mail and Fax icon on your Desktop. The Properties dialog box in Figure 16.2 will appear.

2. Click on the Show Profiles button to display a list of profiles.

3. Highlight the name of the profile to which you want to add Fax and click on the Properties button. The dialog box in Figure 16.2 will

appear again, this time with the name of the profile you just selected in the title bar.

4. Click on the Add button to display the dialog box below.

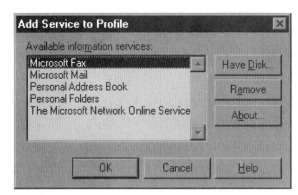

5. Highlight Microsoft Fax in the list of available Information Services and click on the OK button.

6. A warning message will appear advising you that Microsoft Fax needs information about your fax number. Click on OK in the warning message window to open the Fax Properties dialog box.

7. The Microsoft Fax Properties dialog box has four tabs: Message, Dialing, Modem, and User. You can accept the default settings under the Message, Dialing, and Modem settings, but you'll have to type the name and fax number that you want on your fax cover sheet in the User dialog box.

8. The Message tab opens the dialog box in Figure 16.3. It includes these fields:

> **Time to send:** These radio buttons control the time of day when Microsoft Fax will send your faxes. The three options are:
>
> *As soon as possible:* Microsoft Fax tries to send your fax immediately.
>
> *Discount rates:* Microsoft Fax holds your faxes until the long-distance rates are lower, usually in the evening. Use the Set button to specify the times of day when discount rates begin and end.
>
> *Specific time:* Microsoft Fax waits for the specified time before sending your faxes. To change the time, highlight the hour or minute and use the up and down arrows.

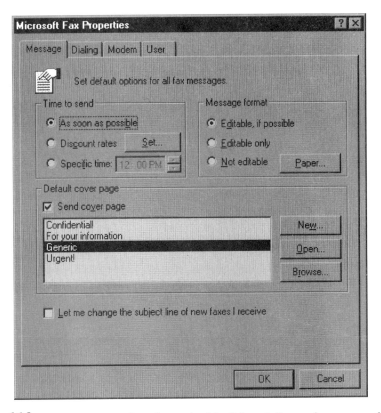

Figure 16.3   *Use the Message tab to change the default format, time, and cover page of your faxes.*

Message format: The message format is not only the layout of the page, as you might expect, but it's also the way Microsoft Fax sends the message: as either a binary file that the recipient can edit with a word processor or text editor, or as a bit-mapped image.

Editable, if possible: Microsoft Fax will automatically use the binary editable format when the receiving system can recognize it.

Editable only: Microsoft Fax will try to send all faxes as binary files and refuse to send the message if the receiving system can't accept that format.

Not editable: Microsoft Fax will send faxes as bit-mapped images.

Paper: This button opens the dialog box on the next page, which controls the layout of the fax page.

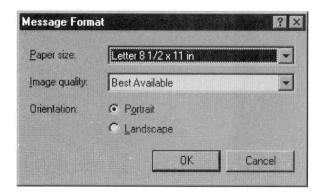

Default cover page: This section controls whether Microsoft Fax normally sends a cover sheet with every fax message, and if so, which one. Each time you prepare to send a fax, you will specify the name and fax telephone number of the recipient. The cover sheet may include information about both the sender and the recipient of each fax message.

9. The Dialing tab opens the dialog box in Figure 16.4.

    Dialing Properties: This button opens the same Dialing Properties dialog box as most other communications applications. Chapter 13 explains this dialog box.

    Toll Prefixes: This button opens the dialog box in Figure 16.5. If you must dial your own area code when you dial an in-state long-distance call, you can use this dialog box to specify the telephone numbers that require an area code.

    If Microsoft Fax does not successfully connect and send your fax on its first attempt, it will use the Retries information to make additional attempts.

10. The Modem tab opens the dialog box in Figure 16.6. The top half of the dialog box contains the same information that you saw when you ran the modem-setup routine. The other options are:

    Set as Active Fax Modem: If you have more than one modem attached to your computer, highlight the one that you want to use to send and receive faxes, and click on the Set as Active button.

    Let other people on the network use my modem to send faxes: If your PC is connected to a LAN, you can allow other people to send faxes through your fax modem by making this option active.

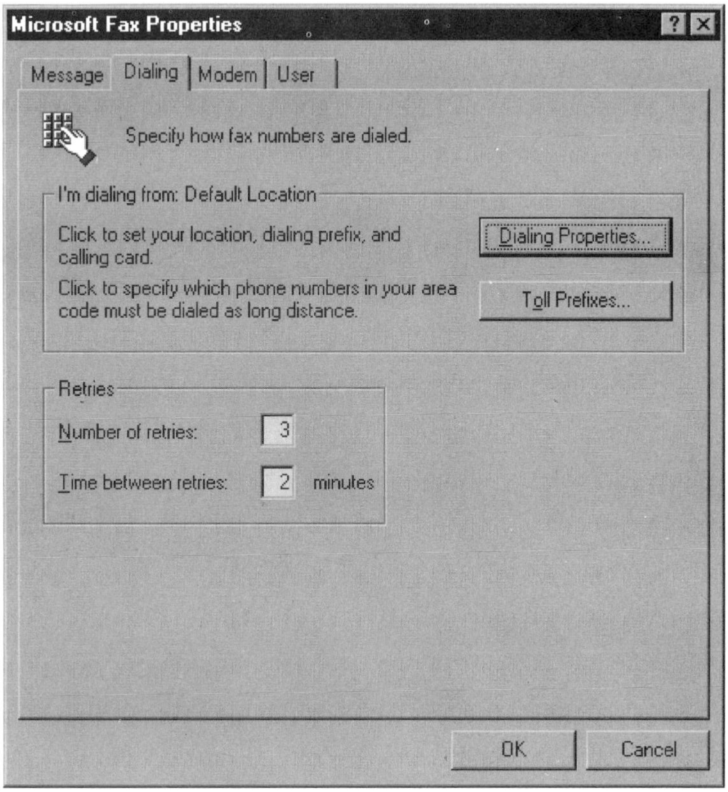

Figure 16.4   *Dialing properties control the way Microsoft Fax places fax calls.*

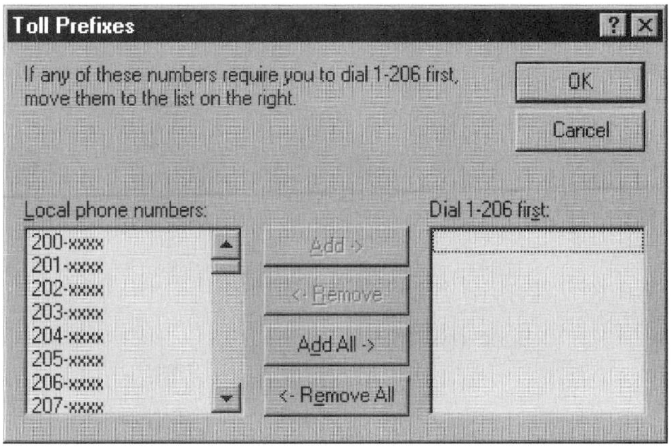

Figure 16.5   *Use the Toll Prefixes dialog box to identify nearby telephone numbers that require an area code.*

Part
3

Managing
Communications

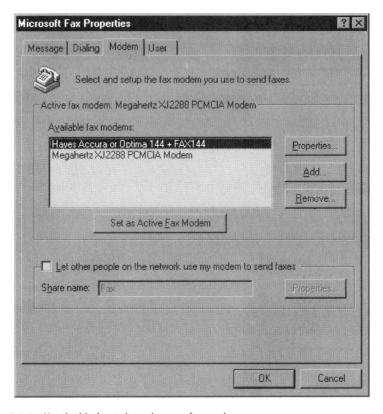

Figure 16.6   Use the Modem tab to choose a fax modem.

Work offline: When this option is active, Microsoft Fax will not send or receive fax messages, but you can still create new faxes and store them in Exchange. This option could be useful to portable computer users for creating faxes when no telephone line is available.

11. The User tab opens the dialog box in Figure 16.7.

12. Click on the OK buttons in the Fax Properties dialog box and the Settings Properties dialog boxes and the Close button in the Exchange Profiles dialog box to save the changes to this profile and return to the Control Panel.

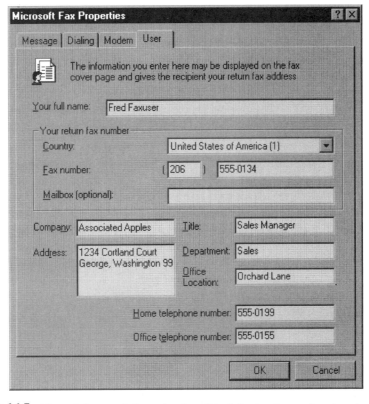

Figure 16.7 *Microsoft Fax uses information from this dialog box in your fax cover sheet.*

Sending Faxes

There are four ways to send faxes from Windows 95:

▶ Drag a text or graphics file to the Microsoft Fax icon in the Printers folder.

▶ Right-click on an icon and choose the Send to Fax Recipient command.

▶ Select Microsoft Fax as the printer in any application program.

▶ Fax from Microsoft Exchange.

All of these methods lead you to the Compose New Fax Wizard. However, if you use the Message Editor in Exchange, you won't see the Wizard if you choose a fax recipient from your address book.

Part 3

Managing Communications

The Print to Fax Wizard

When you "print" a document to the fax driver, Windows 95 uses the Compose New Fax Wizard to take you through the steps needed to specify the recipient's fax telephone number and add a cover sheet to the document.

When the Compose New Fax Wizard opens the dialog box in Figure 16.8, either type the recipient's name in the To field and the fax number in the Fax # field or click on the Address Book button to choose a recipient from your address book. Click on the Add button to place this name in the list of recipients. You can send the same fax message to more than one recipient by adding more names to the list. Click on the Next button to move to the next dialog box.

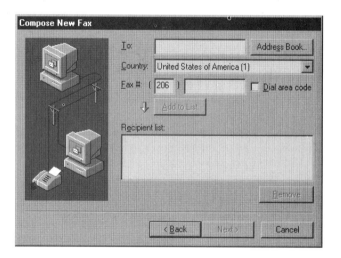

Figure 16.8 *Use the Compose New Fax Wizard to choose a fax recipient.*

The dialog box in Figure 16.9 specifies the cover sheet that will accompany this fax, if any. To add a cover page, click on the *Yes, Send this one* radio button and highlight the description of the cover page you want to use. To schedule delayed transmission or change any of the other default options, click on the Options button.

If you chose to include a cover page, the next dialog box in the Compose New Fax Wizard (Figure 16.10) includes space to type a subject header and message.

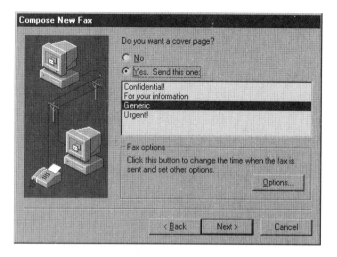

Figure 16.9 Use the Compose New Fax Wizard to add a cover sheet to your fax message.

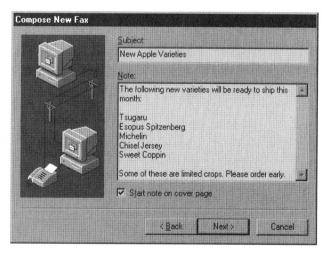

Figure 16.10 Type your subject line and cover-page message in this dialog box.

It's possible to attach a file to a fax message, but people who use standalone fax machines won't be able to receive them. If you know that the recipient of your fax is using a PC with a fax modem and software that can handle attached files, use the Compose New Fax function in Exchange. The New Fax Wizard dialog box in Figure 16.11 specifies the file you want to send with your fax message. Click on the Add File button to open a File Selector window.

Part
3

Managing
Communications

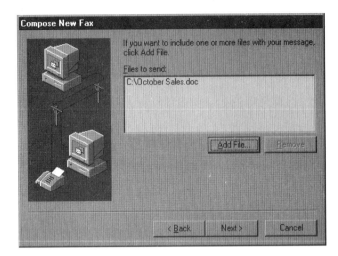

Figure 16.11 **Use this dialog box to attach one or more files to your fax message.**

Some users may find that attaching files to fax messages is easier than using a data communications program such as HyperTerminal, especially if the recipient is not familiar with file-transfer protocols.

Dragging an Icon

Because Windows treats the fax driver like a printer, you can drag and drop a file to the *fax printer* in the Printers window to send that file as a fax. When you drop a text file or image file on the fax printer, Windows automatically starts a Fax Wizard where you can specify the recipient and create a cover page.

If you plan to use this technique frequently, you might want to create a Microsoft Fax shortcut icon on the Windows 95 Desktop rather than opening the Printers window every time you want to send a fax. To create a shortcut, right-click on the Microsoft Fax icon in the Printers folder and select the Create Shortcut command.

Follow these steps to send a fax by dragging an icon:

1. Open the folder that contains the file you want to send as a fax.

2. Move your mouse to the icon for the file you want to send and hold down the left mouse button while you drag the icon to the Microsoft Fax icon in the Printers window or on the Desktop.

3. Windows will open the application associated with the file type you want to send, format the file, and print it to Microsoft Fax. The Print to Fax Wizard will start.

Right-Clicking on an Icon

As you know, clicking the right mouse button opens a menu that contains a set of commands appropriate to the current location of the cursor. If the file is an object that can be printed (such as a document or a bit-mapped image), the right-click menu includes the Send To command shown below, which opens a submenu with a list of destinations.

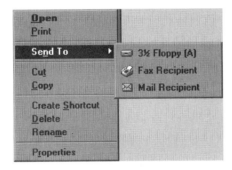

When you click on Fax Recipient, Windows starts the Compose New Fax Wizard. If you have more than one profile, or if you have defined a profile as your default, Windows asks you which Messaging Profile you want to open.

Sending a Fax from Within an Application

Because Windows treats Microsoft Fax as a printer, it's a simple matter to send a fax by designating Microsoft Fax as your printer in an application. For example, when you enter the Page Setup command in WordPad and then click on the Printer button, it displays the dialog box in Figure 16.12. To send a fax, drop down the Printer Name menu to select Microsoft Fax. In other applications, such as Notepad, you must use the Print Setup command to specify the Fax printer driver before you enter the Print command.

The Properties button opens a set of dialog boxes that control details about printing. Most of the tabs are common to many printers, as

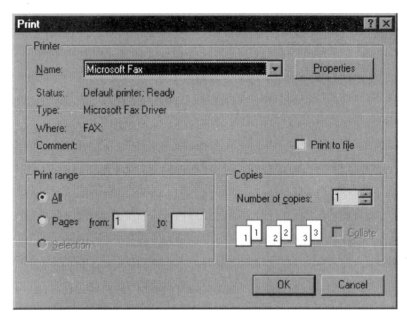

Figure 16.12   *Use the WordPad Print dialog box to choose Microsoft Fax as a printer.*

detailed in Chapter 8, but the Graphics tab in Figure 16.13 is specific to the fax driver.

The Graphics Properties dialog box includes these options:

Dots Per Inch: The number of dots per inch determines the resolution of the transmitted document. If you use a higher resolution, the fax will look better, but it will take longer to transmit. If the fax machine at the receiving end can't handle 300 dpi, Microsoft Fax will step down to 200 dpi.

Grayscale - Halftoning: Choose one of the radio buttons in this option to define the way Microsoft Fax will handle colors other than either solid black or solid white. As a general rule, Patterned Grays is a good choice, because an image with big solid black areas will be very hard to read.

Darkness: If you want the fax to appear darker or lighter at the receiving end, use the slide control to increase or decrease darkness. For most faxes that you send from a PC, you should leave the slider in the middle, which is the default setting, but if you have a particularly muddy bit-mapped image, or if the recipient asks you to re-send the page, you might want to experiment with other settings.

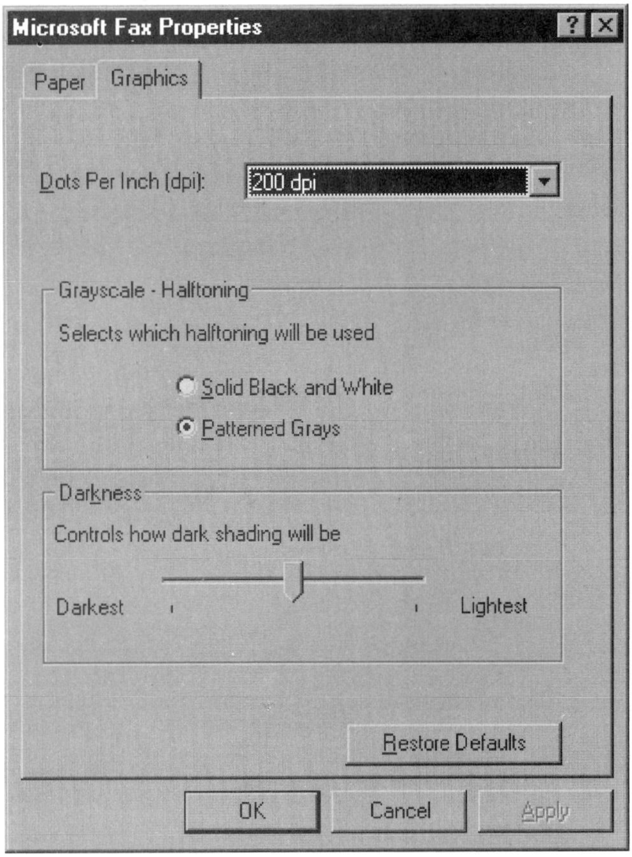

Figure 16.13 *Graphics Properties dialog box*

The exact command may be different from one program to another, but every Windows application that can print to paper can also print by sending a fax. When you specify Microsoft Fax as your printer, the application's Print command will start the Compose New Fax Wizard.

Sending a Fax from Microsoft Exchange

In most cases, you'll want to send faxes from your word processor or other application, but you can also originate faxes from Microsoft.

There are two ways to send a fax from Exchange:

▶ Use the New Fax command in the Compose menu to open our old friend the New Fax Wizard. After you complete the Wizard, Exchange will open the Message Editor.

▶ Use the New Message command in the Compose menu to open the Message Editor and choose one or more fax recipients from your address book. This technique is especially convenient when you want to send the same message to some recipients via e-mail and others by fax.

Write your message in the Message Editor, format it, and use the Send command in the File menu.

This is probably a good place to point out that it will do absolutely no good to send somebody a multicolor message by fax if the recipient is using a fax machine; regardless of the colors going in, the image that spews out of the fax machine at the receiving end will be in boring black and white.

Sending Binary Files

When you send a fax from a fax machine, three things happen:

1. Your fax machine converts the image on the paper to digital form.

2. Your fax machine connects to a distant machine and transmits the digital data.

3. The distant fax machine converts the digital data back to an image, which it prints onto paper.

A fax modem connected to a PC is really only concerned with step 2 of this process—it receives digital data from the PC and transmits it to a distant fax machine (which may be a standalone machine or another modem). Your PC converts the image to digital form before it gets to the fax modem.

The fax modem doesn't care where that digital data came from—it could just as easily have been from a data file or a program file instead of a fax image. As long as there's similar software at the receiving end to convert it back to its original form, you can send any kind of binary data file by fax. Some fax software, including Delrina's WinFax Pro, calls this method *binary file transfer*.

Binary file transfer via fax is a technology whose time has not yet come; no standalone fax machines and few fax programs will accept binary files. Unless you know that the recipient has a fax modem and software that knows how to deal with binary files, your transmission will fail.

Exchange treats fax transmission as just one more type of e-mail, but fax protocols are completely different from the protocols used for other kinds of data transfer, even if they use the same modem. You can't use a terminal program (such as HyperTerminal) to receive a binary fax message. Therefore, you will probably find it easier and more consistently reliable to use HyperTerminal or some other data communications program to move programs or data files over a telephone line.

That said, if you know that the recipient can receive and process binary files, you can attach any file to a fax message just as you would attach it to an e-mail message. There are three ways to do it:

▶ Right-click on the icon and choose the Send to Fax Recipient command.

▶ Drag the file icon to the Fax icon in the Printers folder.

▶ Open Microsoft Exchange and use the Compose New Fax command in the Fax menu. When the message-editor window appears, select the File command in the Insert menu.

Cover Sheets

A cover sheet serves several purposes: in an office where several people receive faxes through the same machine, it identifies the intended recipient; it tells recipients how many pages to expect; and it lets them know who to call if there's a transmission problem. A cover sheet can also contain a comment about the document that it accompanies.

Unless it's absolutely obvious who is supposed to receive your fax and who sent it, you should include a cover sheet as the first page of every fax you send. Your cover sheet should include this information:

▶ the name, fax number, and voice telephone number (or extension) of the recipient

▶ the name, fax number, and voice telephone number of the sender

▶ the number of pages in the fax message

▶ the date and time of transmission

Part
3

Managing
Communications

Windows 95 includes a handful of standard cover pages and a Cover Page Editor program that produces *templates* that automatically insert information about the sender, the recipient, and the message into information fields. You can choose the cover page you want to add to each fax in the Compose New Fax Wizard. After Windows 95 is released, there will probably be an assortment of additional fax cover-sheet templates available for downloading from Microsoft Network, CompuServe, and other online information services.

To create a new cover-sheet template, follow these steps:

1. Start the Cover Page Editor program from the Programs ➤ Accessories ➤ Fax menu.

2. Use the Insert commands to add the information fields you want to include in your cover sheet. Figure 16.14 shows the Cover Page Editor screen.

   Click on a menu item to add it to your cover-sheet template. Don't worry about the position right now; you can move items around the page after you have chosen them.

   When you send a fax, Windows will use information from your Fax Setup dialog box and address book to fill in the information fields.

   The Insert menu includes these fields:

Recipient:	Name	Zip Code	Home Telephone
	Fax Number	Country	Number
	Company	Title	Office Telephone
	Street Address	Department	Number
	City	Office Location	To: List
	State		CC: List
Sender:	Name	Title	Home Telephone
	Fax Number	Department	Number
	Company	Office Location	Office Telephone
	Address		Number
Message:	Note	Time Sent	Number of
	Subject	Number of Pages	Attachments

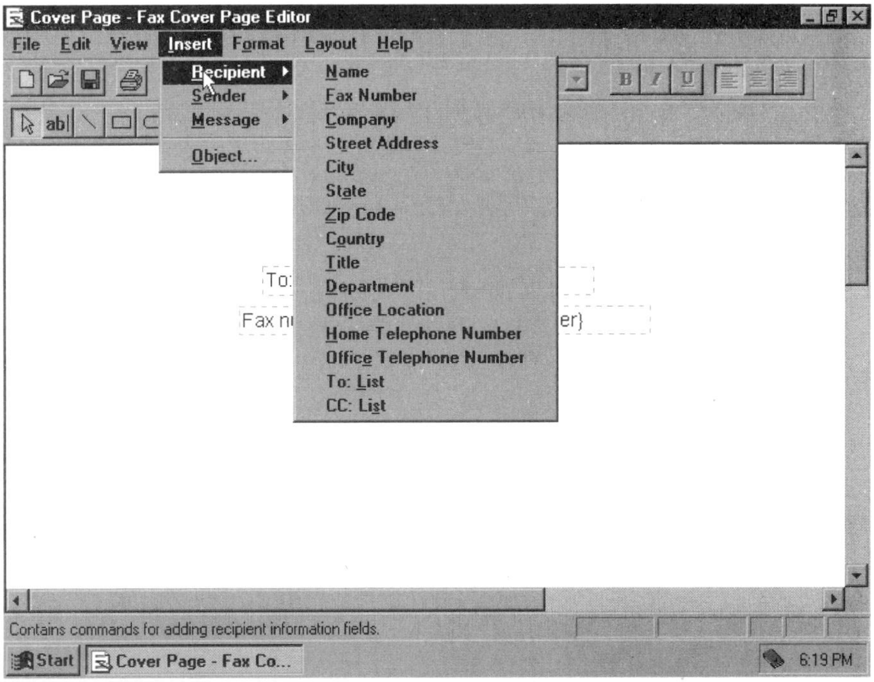

Figure 16.14   Use the Insert commands to place information fields in your fax cover sheet.

3. Drag each information field to the position you want it to appear in on the page.

4. To add text to your cover-sheet template, click on the arrow key in the Drawing Toolbar and drag your mouse to create a box, click on the text button, and then click inside the new box to create a cursor. Type the text at the cursor. If you need more space, move your mouse to the edge of the box and expand the box by dragging one or more edges. Don't worry about the exact position of your text; you can fix it later.

5. To add new graphics to your cover page, click on the arrow key in the Drawing Toolbar and drag your mouse to create another box. Use the line, rectangle, polygon, and ellipse buttons in the Toolbar to choose a shape and place the figure in the new box. You can change the characteristics of a figure with the Line, Fill, and Color command in the Format menu.

Part
3

Managing
Communications

6. To import an existing text file or graphics object into your cover sheet, use the Insert ➤ Object command. You can also use this command to create a graphics object with another application.

7. Drag each element to the location you want it to appear in on the page.

8. Highlight each text element of your cover page and use the buttons in the Style Toolbar to change the typeface, size, style, and alignment of each item.

9. Use the commands in the Format menu and the toolbars to change the typeface, type style, and alignment of your text.

10. Save the cover sheet with the Save command in the File menu.

To attach a cover sheet to a fax message, answer *Yes* when the Fax Wizard asks, or use the Send Options command in the Message Editor's File menu. When the Send Options dialog box in Figure 16.15 appears, check the *Send cover page* option and either drop down the cover page menu or use the browser to choose a template.

Receiving Faxes

If you plan to use your PC to receive faxes as well as send them, you will probably want to leave your computer and modem on all the time, with Microsoft Fax running in the background, because it's not always possible to predict when somebody will try to send you a fax. If you share the same telephone line for voice, data, and fax calls, you must either use a line-sharing device to direct voice calls to your telephone set and fax/data calls to the modem, or you will have to accept calls manually when you hear a fax calling tone through the handset.

To set up Microsoft Exchange to automatically receive fax calls, follow these steps:

1. If it is not already set up, add Microsoft Fax to the active Exchange Profile. See Chapter 15 for information about configuring your Exchange Profile.

2. Start Microsoft Exchange. Within a minute or two, the minimized Fax Modem Status button will appear in the Taskbar. When the Fax Modem Status is Idle, Microsoft Fax is ready to accept incoming calls.

Figure 16.15   Use the Send Options dialog box to choose a cover page.

3. Click on the Fax machine icon in the Taskbar to open the Status window shown below.

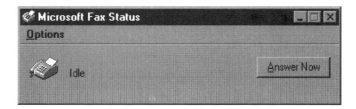

4. Select the Modem Properties command in the Options menu to open the Fax Modem Properties dialog box in Figure 16.16.

5. If you have a dedicated fax/data telephone line, click on the *Answer after* radio button. If you use the same telephone line for incoming voice calls, click on the Manual radio button. If you use this computer for

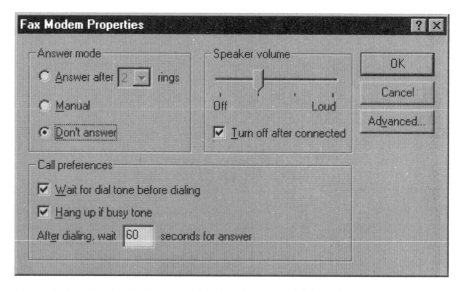

Figure 16.16   *The Fax Modem Properties dialog box controls inbound and outbound Microsoft Fax calls.*

sending faxes but not receiving them, choose the *Don't answer* radio button.

6. Click on OK to close the Fax Modem Settings dialog box and then minimize the Fax Modem Status window.

If Microsoft Fax is set to automatically answer, it will show the progress of incoming and outgoing calls in the Status window or button. If Manual Answer mode is active, Microsoft Fax will display a message when it receives a call.

When Microsoft Fax receives an incoming message, it places the message in your Microsoft Exchange inbox. Like any other message in Exchange, you can open a fax message by double-clicking on it. Most of the faxes you receive will be bit-mapped images from fax machines, but others may be binary files from other computers with fax modems. When you double-click on a bit-mapped image, Exchange opens the Fax Viewer; when you double-click on a binary file for which an association exists, Exchange opens a program that can read and edit the file. Because Exchange automatically recognizes both types of fax messages, you can open all fax messages the same way.

Using Fax Viewer

Fax Viewer is a tool for viewing and printing bit-mapped fax pages. Fax Viewer opens automatically when you double-click on a bit-mapped image entry in Microsoft Exchange. Figure 16.17 shows the Fax Viewer window.

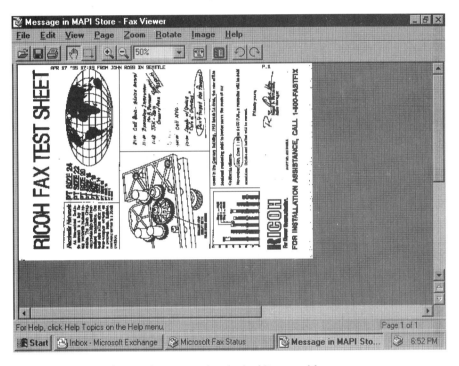

Figure 16.17   Use the Fax Viewer to read and print bit-mapped fax pages.

When you open Fax Viewer from Exchange by double-clicking on the name of a fax, Fax Viewer automatically loads the first page of the fax message. To load a different message, use the Open command in the File menu. Almost all of the commands in the Fax Viewer menus and Toolbar control the way the Viewer displays fax images.

Part 3

Managing Communications

Fax Viewer Command Summary

File Menu

Open	Loads a new fax message. Choose the fax file (with a .awd or .dcx file extension) from the browser.
Save	Stores the current fax message with the original name.
Save As	Saves the current image with a new file name.
Automatically Save View	Saves the zoom, rotation, and image settings.
Print	Prints the current image.
Print Preview	Displays the current page.
Print Setup	Selects a different printer or print option.
Recent File	Re-opens the current page from the version on disk.
Exit	Closes the Fax Viewer.

Edit Menu

Copy	Copies the currently selected portion of the image to the Windows Clipboard.
Copy Page	Selects the entire current page.
Select	Highlights an image.
Drag	Moves the image in the Viewer to a new position. Because the Viewer window is smaller than the fax page within the window, you will need the Drag command to read an entire page.

View Menu

Toolbar	Displays or hide the Fax Viewer Toolbar.
Status Bar	Displays or hide the Status Bar at the bottom of the Fax Viewer window.
Thumbnails	Displays small "thumbnail" views of several pages of a fax message, rather than a larger view of a single page.

Page Menu: Use the commands in the Page menu to move between pages in a multiple-page fax message.

Zoom Menu

Fit Width	Expands the image horizontally to the full current width of the Viewer window.
Fit Height	Expands the image vertically to the full current height of the Viewer window.
Fit Both	Distorts the shape of the image to fit the current dimensions of the Viewer Window.
25% 50% 100%	Expands or contracts the size of the image in the Viewer window. The percentage numbers are the relative sizes of the image that will appear when you choose one of these commands.
Zoom In	Changes the view to the next larger size.
Zoom Out	Changes the view to the next smaller size.

Rotate Menu

Right	Rotate the current image 90 degrees to the right.
Left	Rotates the current image 90 degrees to the left.
Flip Over	Turns the current image upside down.

Image Menu

Invert	Replaces the current image in the Viewer with a mirror image of the same page.

Most of the faxes you will receive will be images of pages, which Windows stores as bit-mapped files. Even though a page may contain text and graphics, it is really a picture of the page that the sender placed in his fax machine or printed to her fax modem. Sometimes it would be nice to be able to export text from a fax to an editor or word processor, either to make changes to the text or to incorporate it into another document. Likewise, you might want to use a picture or diagram from a fax in another document.

Unfortunately, the Windows 95 fax utility does not include any tools for exporting or modifying received faxes. However, there are many separate fax programs that provide these services. Among others, Delrina's WinFax Pro has an extensive set of fax-management features, including converting images to Paintbrush, TIFF, and Windows Bitmap formats and converting words to ASCII text.

Part 3

Managing Communications

Chapter 17

The Microsoft Network

FEATURING

The Microsoft Network (MSN) is the software giant's new entry in the online information-service wars currently dominated by CompuServe, America Online, and Prodigy. Like its competitors, MSN offers electronic mail, conferences about a wide variety of subjects, technical support from Microsoft and other hardware and software vendors, data files and programs available for downloading, general and specialized news services, and live *chat* channels where you can exchange messages with other users and with experts and celebrity guests. In addition, MSN offers a gateway to the Internet, including access to Usenet news groups and e-mail. MSN is closely integrated with the Windows 95 user interface, so you can use online resources as if they were located on your own PC.

Even more than the rest of Windows 95, the Microsoft Network is still a work in progress. At this stage in its development, MSN does not include many of the features and services that will (Microsoft hopes) make it attractive to millions of users. By the time Windows 95 is actually released, MSN will probably have signed up a long list of additional information providers. This chapter explains how to connect your PC to MSN and how to use its features and services. It is not a definitive guide to content areas, because most of them are not yet in place at the time of this writing. But by using the tools and procedures you find here, you will be able to explore MSN and take advantage of everything it has to offer.

The only way to connect to MSN now is through a modem and telephone line, but eventually you can expect it to be accessible through the same cable TV service that brings you all those wrestlers and music videos today. TCI, the largest American cable company, owns 20 percent of the Microsoft Network.

Installing and Signing Up for the Microsoft Network

To join MSN, you must have a modem connected to your PC. Chapter 13 describes the procedure for installing Windows 95 modem support.

You can install the Microsoft Network support when you install Windows 95 by choosing Custom Setup; you can also install it after Windows 95 is running. To add the Microsoft Network to an already installed system, double-click on the Add/Remove Programs icon in the Control Panel and choose the Windows Setup tab. Either way, when the dialog box in Figure 17.1 appears, scroll down the Components list until you see the listing for the Microsoft Network.

Check the box next to the Microsoft Network listing. If you haven't previously installed Microsoft Exchange, Setup may force you to install it at the same time. When you click the OK button, Setup will ask you to load the disks that contain the MSN software.

After the software is loaded, follow these steps to set up your account with the Microsoft Network:

1. Click on the Microsoft Network icon on your desktop. An MSN start-up screen will appear.

2. Click on the OK button to move to the screen in Figure 17.2.

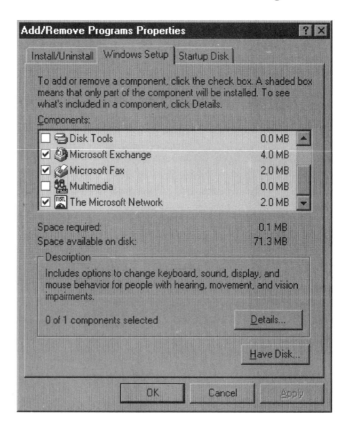

Figure 17.1   Use the Windows Setup dialog box to install the Microsoft Network.

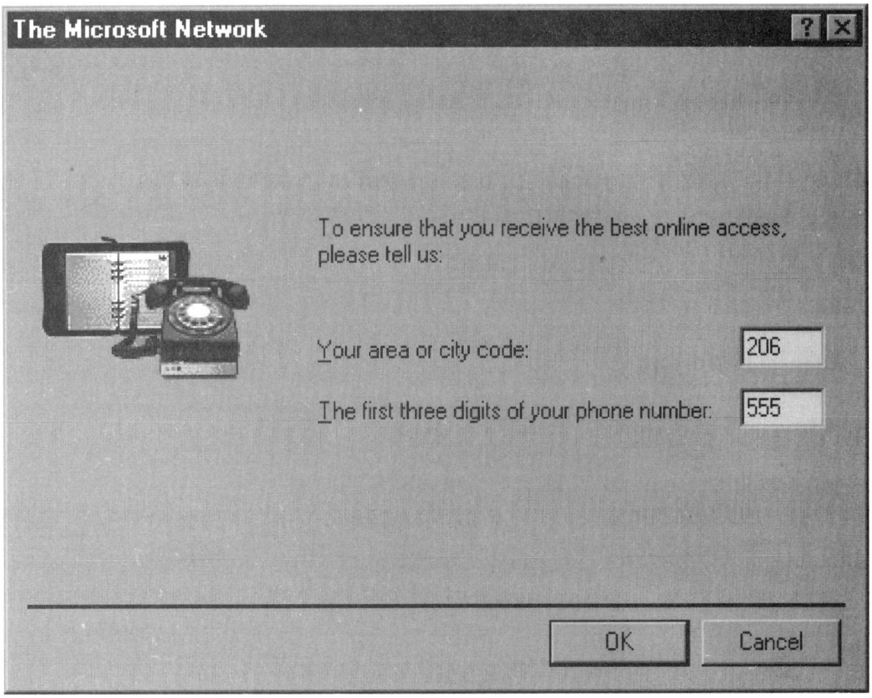

Figure 17.2   Use this screen to find the nearest local telephone number for the Microsoft Network.

3. Fill in the area-code portion of your own telephone number (or if you're outside North America, your city code) and the first three digits of your telephone number. This information will guide the program to find the nearest access telephone number for MSN. Click on the OK button.

4. If you have an external modem, make sure it is turned on and connected to your PC. If you have an internal modem, it's always on. Make sure the modem is connected to your telephone line.

5. Click on the Connect button in the Calling screen. The program will call Microsoft and download the current list of access numbers for your area and the current subscription rates.

6. Your computer will display the window in Figure 17.3 with the three steps needed to join MSN. Click on the *Tell us your name and address* button.

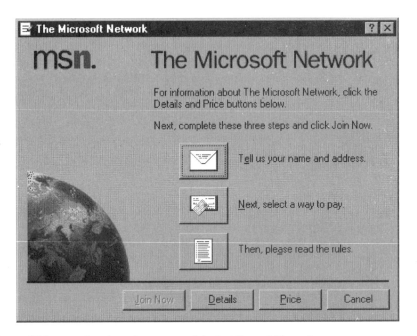

Figure 17.3   Complete these three steps to join the Microsoft Network.

7. Complete all of the fields in the next dialog box, shown in Figure 17.4, and click on OK.

8. Click on the *Next, select a way to pay* button and fill in your credit card number or other billing information in the dialog box shown in Figure 17.5. Click on OK to return to the previous screen.

9. Click on the *Then, please read the rules* button. After you have read the fine print, click on the I Agree button.

10. When you have big check marks next to all three steps, click on the Join Now button. Based on the telephone number you specified in Step 3, two nearby access numbers will appear in the dialog box in Figure 17.6. If the number is a local call, the software will ignore the area code even though it appears in this dialog box.

    If there's no local number for your area, it might be less expensive to use a number different from the one the program automatically assigns you. For example, the rates for calling across a state line might be cheaper than an in-state call. To choose different access numbers,

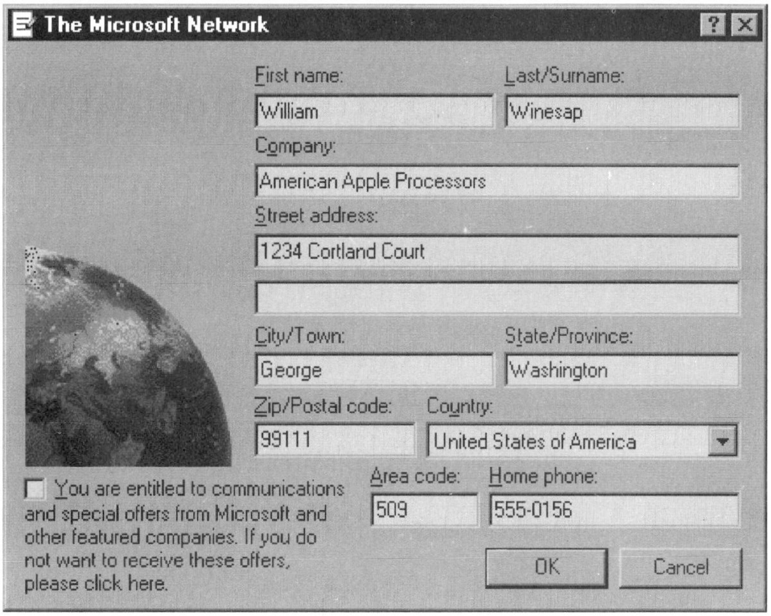

Figure 17.4   Fill in your name and address in this dialog box.

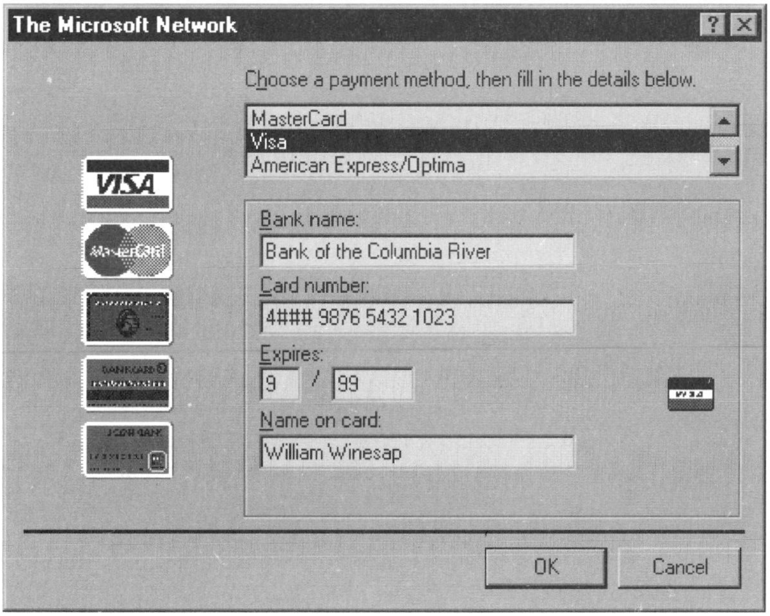

Figure 17.5   Use this dialog box to send MSN your credit card number.

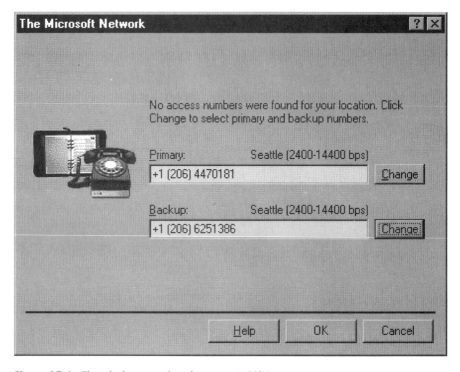

Figure 17.6   **The telephone numbers for access to MSN**

click on the Change buttons and find the location you want to call from the drop-down menus.

11. Click on the OK button and then the Dial button to call MSN and set up your account.

12. When the connection goes through, MSN will ask for a member ID (log-in name) and password using the dialog box in Figure 17.7. Because you will need both of these items to sign in later, you should write them down somewhere. But don't paste them on your computer or put them someplace where other people can see them.

Connecting to the Microsoft Network

Follow these steps to connect your PC to the Microsoft Network:

1. Make sure your modem is turned on and connected to a telephone line.

2. Double-click on the Microsoft Network Icon on your Desktop.

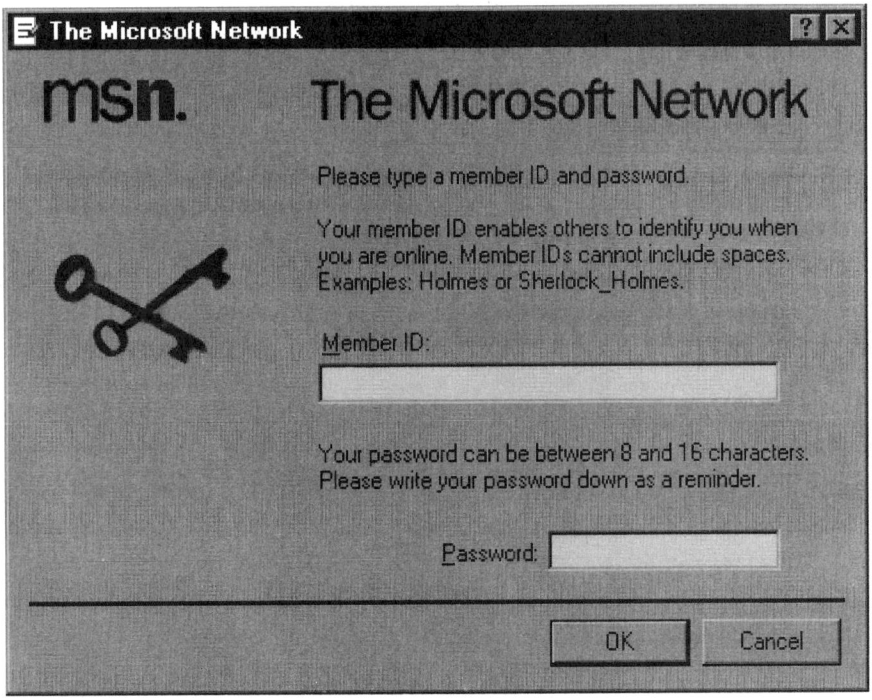

Figure 17.7   **Type your log-in name and password in this dialog box.**

3. When the Sign In screen in Figure 17.8 appears, type in your member ID and your password. If you are the only person using your PC, you can check the *Remember my password* box so you won't have to type it again the next time you log in.

4. Click on Connect to start dialing. The Sign In window will show the progress of your call as it dials and verifies your account. When it completes the log-in, it will display the MSN Central screen in Figure 17.9.

    While you're connected to MSN, a little modem icon with two red dots is visible on the lower right side of the Taskbar. The left dot duplicates the RD (Receive Data) light on an external modem. It turns green when your PC is receiving data from MSN. The right dot corresponds to the SD (Send Data) light on your modem. It turns green when your PC is sending data to MSN. If you move your cursor to

Part 3

Managing Communications

Figure 17.8   Type your ID and password to log into MSN.

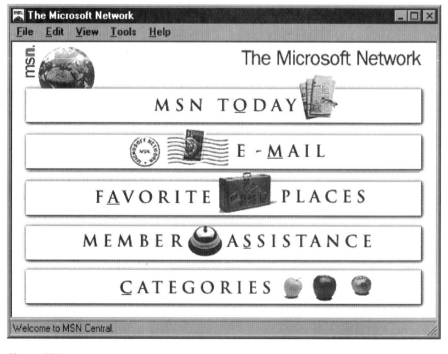

Figure 17.9   The MSN Central screen

the modem icon, MSN will display the number of bytes received and sent during the current online session as shown below.

For more details about your connection to MSN, double-click on the modem icon to display the window shown below.

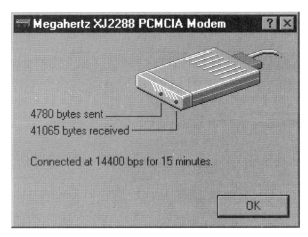

When Microsoft Exchange transfers a message to or from MSN, a tiny envelope with an arrow pointing in the direction the message is traveling appears between the MSN icon and the modem icon. When Exchange has received one or more messages, it shows envelope icons without any arrow.

When you're connected to MSN, you can right-click on the MSN icon in the Toolbar (next to the time of day) to open the menu of shortcuts shown below.

Navigating the Microsoft Network

The first window you see when you connect to Microsoft Network is called *MSN Central* and contains links to various online areas. When your cursor is on a link, it changes from the usual arrow to a pointing finger. To link to one of the areas listed in the MSN Central window, click on the area's name.

The Options command in the View menu is the same as the Options command in other windows used for browsing folders on your computer. The Folder tab offers a choice of either using a separate window for each new folder you open or using a single folder that changes when you move from one folder to another.

There are five areas you can reach from MSN Central:

MSN Today

MSN Today is a daily list of special events and services that MSN wants to promote, such as scheduled live appearances and new resources. Figure 17.10 shows a typical MSN Today window. To jump to one of the items promoted in MSN Today, move your cursor to the icon and single-click your mouse. To return to MSN Central, close the MSN Today window.

E-Mail

The E-Mail button in MSN starts Microsoft Exchange and downloads any messages that might be waiting for you at MSN. The E-Mail command starts the default Exchange profile, including any other message services that might be in that profile. Therefore, you might want to make sure that MSN is the first item in the profile so Exchange doesn't waste your time trying to set up fax or other online services while you're connected to MSN.

MSN E-Mail is closely integrated with Exchange. The Options for Microsoft Network command in Exchange's Tools menu opens the dialog box in Figure 17.11.

Figure 17.10 MSN Today offers jumps to other MSN resources.

The Transport dialog box includes these options:

Download mail when e-mail starts up from MSN	When this option is active, MSN automatically opens Exchange and downloads your messages when you start the MSN E-Mail program.
Disconnect after updating headers	When this option is active, Exchange copies the headers of any waiting messages and then disconnects from MSN. When you select a message header, Exchange will reconnect to MSN and download the whole message. This allows you to reduce your connect-time charges because you can preview messages offline before deciding to transfer them to your PC.

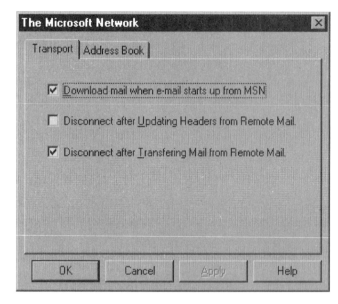

Figure 17.11 **Open the Transport tab of the Microsoft Network dialog box from Exchange's Tools menu.**

Disconnect after Transferring Mail	Make this option active to break your connection to MSN after Exchange has downloaded your mail.

Favorite Places

Favorite Places is an area you can use to place shortcuts to the MSN services you regularly use in a single convenient window. When you join MSN, your Favorite Places area will be empty. To include an area in your list of Favorite Places, use the Add to Favorite Places command in the File menu, the right mouse button menu, or the MSN toolbar.

To add a forum, BBS, or other MSN area to your Favorite Places list, use the Add to Favorite Places command in the File menu or toolbar, or right-click on an icon and select the Add to Favorite Places command.

If you have multiple MSN windows open, you can also drag and drop icons from other parts of MSN to your Favorite Places window or to the Windows Desktop.

Member Assistance

Member Assistance is a specialized set of conferences and documents directly related to MSN itself. If you're looking for online help in using MSN, Member Assistance is a good place to start looking for help.

Categories

The Categories window in Figure 17.12 is the subject guide to MSN services. Each category icon opens a set of conferences, kiosks, chat areas, file archives, additional subcategories, and other resources related to that category. Double-click on an icon to open a category.

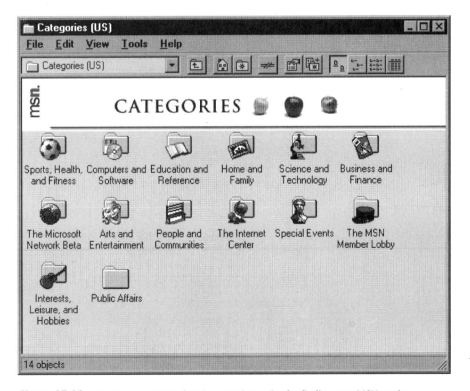

Figure 17.12   The Categories window is a starting point for finding new MSN services.

Moving Around MSN

Microsoft Network has a hierarchical file structure that will be familiar to anybody who has used DOS and Windows. MSN Central takes the place of the root directory, and each subdirectory may contain many different kinds of files and services, including additional sub-subdirectories. To move to a subdirectory or open a file or service, double-click on the icon. The icons in MSN work exactly the same way as those in Windows 95; you can create shortcuts and place MSN icons on your Desktop or in folders.

MSN navigation commands are like the ones in other Windows toolbars. The two unfamiliar buttons are: one that moves you back to MSN Central and one that adds an item to Favorite Places.

If you find yourself hopelessly lost, you can always return to MSN Central by clicking on the toolbar button with the house on it. You can also open a new MSN Central window by clicking on the MSN icon on your Desktop. When you right-click on the MSN icon in the Taskbar at the bottom of your screen, you will open a menu with several common commands, including jumps to MSN Central and Favorite Places, as well as sign-out.

The MSN navigation windows have menu bars with these commands which are not in other windows:

File Menu

Add to Favorite Places   This command copies the currently highlighted icon into your Favorite Places window.

Sign In   This command is active if you are not currently connected to MSN. Click on it to dial MSN and log yourself in.

Sign Out   This command is active when you are connected to MSN. When you choose it, Windows disconnects your PC from MSN.

Edit Menu

Go To   Use this command to jump directly to a specific MSN service. Go Words in MSN are like GO commands in CompuServe or keywords in America Online. To find the Go Word for any MSN service, highlight the icon for that service and use the Properties command in the File menu or the right-mouse-button menu. For example, Figure 17.13 shows the Properties for the Windows 95 forum. In this example, the Go word for this forum is "Windows."

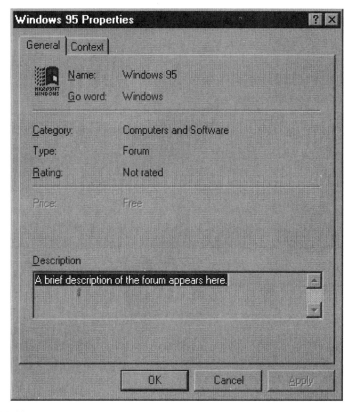

Figure 17.13 **The Go Word for the Windows 95 Forum is "Windows."**

View Menu

Options   The General tab within the Options dialog box opens the dialog box below. You can use this command to set the number of minutes MSN waits before shutting down automatically and specify whether you want to see the MSN Today message every time you connect to the Microsoft Network. The Content view menu lists groups of bulletin boards, chat rooms, files, and other services organized by language or geographical region. If you want to see content groups for a region other than your own, click on that content view item. The next time you connect to MSN, it will display the new content view.

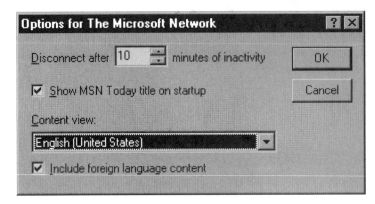

Tools Menu

Password   Use to change your MSN password.

Billing Payment Method   Choose to view or change the credit card number or other information that MSN uses to bill you for service.

Billing Summary of Charges   Choose to see the current status of your account, including the current monthly charge.

Billing Subscriptions   This command displays information about your subscription plan. At the bottom of the dialog box, you can set a maximum amount for any single transaction. If you try to download something that costs more than this amount, MSN will ask for confirmation.

At the time this was written, Microsoft had not yet announced how it plans to charge for MSN, so this dialog box may change by the time Windows 95 is released.

Connection Settings   Use to choose a different access telephone number or modem configuration. You can also get to the Connection Settings dialog box before you log into MSN by clicking on the Settings button in the Sign In window. If you are running MSN on a portable computer, this is the place to set up access after you arrive at a different location. Figure 17.14 shows the Connection Settings dialog box.

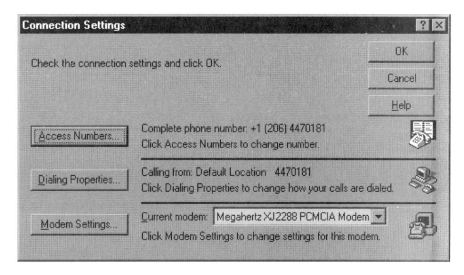

Figure 17.14   *Use the Connection Settings dialog box to change details about your MSN connection.*

Help Menu

Member Support Numbers   If you need assistance, choose this command to display a list of telephone numbers for Customer Service and Technical Support. Of course, if you can't log into MSN, you won't be able to reach MSN Central, so it won't be possible to use this command when you need help making the connection. However, you can also display the same list of telephone numbers by clicking on the Settings button in the MSN Sign In window, clicking on the Help button, and choosing the Customer Service Phone Numbers item at the bottom of the MSN Member Support Help window.

Right-Click Menus   Like those in other windows, the icons in MSN windows all display context-sensitive menus when you move the cursor to an icon and click the right mouse button.

Conferences and File Libraries

Many of the items you will see in MSN windows are conferences (which MSN calls Bulletin Boards or BBSes) and file libraries devoted to a particular topic, such as household improvements or Windows communication. When you double-click on one of these icons, you will see a message folder window like the one in Figure 17.15. The commands and toolbar buttons that control the appearance of the screen have special functions in a message folder window—the three options are Conversation view, List view, and Attached Files view. In all three views, listings change from boldface type to normal type after you view them, but you can display a listing again by clicking on the message description.

When you visit a BBS, MSN will display a list of all messages and downloadable files that have been added since the last time you looked at that BBS. It will also show you older items for which there are new replies. To display message listings you've seen before, use the Show All Messages command in the Tools menu.

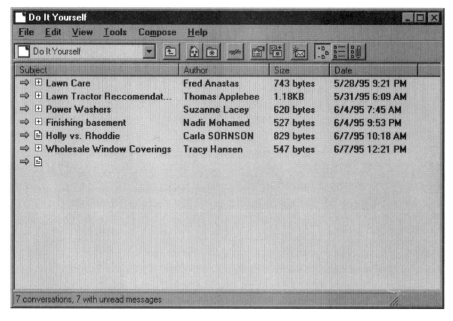

Figure 17.15   *The Conversation view is the default layout for message folder windows.*

In Conversation view, you only see the top item in each thread until you click on an icon, which displays all the items that are replies to the original item. If there are replies to replies, you will see another plus sign inside the icon, which you can click to expand the list. You can expand all the lists at one time with the Expand All Conversations command in the View menu. An arrow at the left side of a listing indicates that there are unread messages in this thread. Figure 17.16 shows the same BBS with all replies visible.

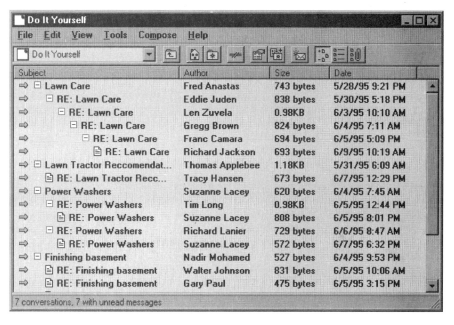

Figure 17.16 *Expand the conversations in a BBS to see all replies.*

In the List view shown in Figure 17.17, all messages and files appear in a single column. To rearrange the order in which entries appear, click the heading you want to use to sort the listings—subject, author, or date. Items with attached files appear in the list with a paper-clip icon at the left side of the description instead of a piece of paper.

Attachment view, shown in Figure 17.18, limits the display to items that have embedded files. If you're looking for a file to download, Attachment view is probably the easiest way to find it.

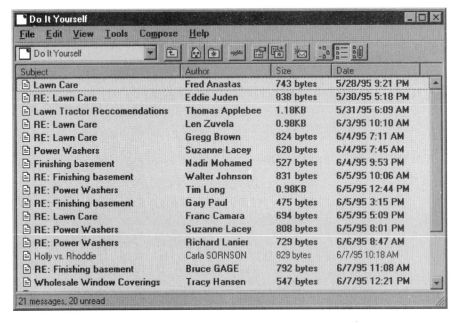

Figure 17.17   List view displays all messages in a flat list.

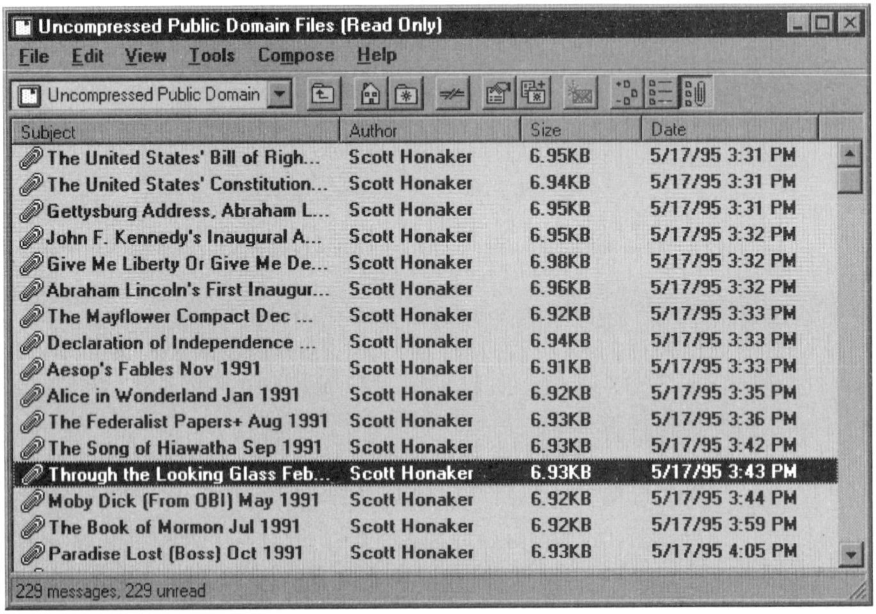

Figure 17.18   Attachment view shows only those messages with attached files.

Adding a new message to a thread or creating a new message is very much like creating a message in Microsoft Exchange: Use the Compose ➤ New menu command to open a message editor. Chapter 15 contains detailed information about the Message Editor.

Message Folder Commands

The menu bar in a message folder window includes these special commands:

File Menu

Open   This command opens the currently highlighted message.

Save As   Use to save a message as a file.

Properties   This command opens a panel with more detailed information about the currently highlighted item, including the additional cost, if any.

Up One Level   This command moves you to the parent window for the current window.

Edit Menu

Go to   These commands move you directly to MSN Central, Favorite Places, or to any other location in MSN using a Go Word.

View Menu

Conversation   This command displays messages in a threaded list, with replies indented under the original message.

List   This command displays all messages in a flat list, arranged alphabetically by subject or author, or chronologically by date.

Attached Files   This command displays a flat list of only those messages with attached files.

Arrange Messages   These commands specify the order in which MSN displays the messages in a BBS—by subject, author, size, or date.

Expand All Conversations   This command displays all the threads of all conversations in nested form, with replies indented under original messages. This command only works in Conversation view.

Collapse All Conversations   This command is the opposite of Expand All Conversations. It hides listings of message replies and shows only the top-level message in each conversation.

Refresh   Use to obtain a new copy of the current message list.

Tools Menu

Use one of these commands to change the status of one or more messages.

   Mark Message as Read

   Mark Message as Unread

   Mark Conversation as Read

   Mark Conversation as Unread

   Mark All Messages as Read

Show All Messages   Use to include messages that you've seen before in MSN's display of a BBS, even if there are no new replies to those messages.

Compose Menu

New Message   Use to open the Message Editor. To send a reply to an existing message, open the message and use the Reply command in the Compose menu.

Reading Messages

To read a message, double-click on the listing. The Message Viewer window in Figure 17.19 will appear. The Message Viewer looks and works very much like the Message Editor; you can change the

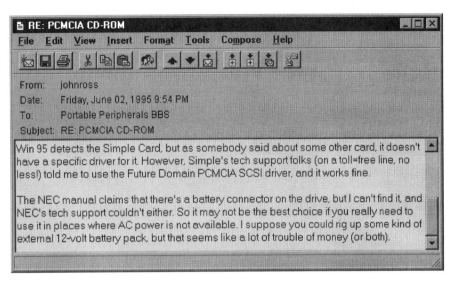

Figure 17.19   The Message Viewer displays messages from MSN conferences.

typestyle, size, color, or alignment of the text as it appears on your screen.

To reply to a message, use the Compose ➤ Reply to BBS command. If you prefer to send a private reply, use the Reply by E-mail command. A Message Editor will appear, and you can type your text, attach a file, or copy text from another message or other document.

The Message Viewer includes these commands that don't appear in other Windows menus:

View Menu

Previous Message   Use to close the current message and open the preceding message immediately before it in the message folder.

Next Message   Use to close the current message and open the next message.

Next Unread Message   Use to close the current message and open the next message that you haven't read yet.

Previous Conversation   Use to close the current message and open the first message in the previous conversation.

Next Conversation   Use to close the current message and open the first message in the next conversation.

Next Unread Conversation   Use to close the current message and open the first message in the next conversation that you haven't already seen.

Tools Menu

Member Properties   Use to display information about the person who wrote the current message.

Compose Menu

New Message   Use to create and post a message that is not related to the current message.

Reply to BBS   Use to create a new message and send it as a public reply to the current message.

Reply by E-Mail   Use to send an e-mail message to the person who posted the original message.

Forward by E-Mail   Use to send a copy of the current message to another user as an e-mail message.

The Message Viewer also has two optional toolbars. The first contains commands related to sending and receiving messages. The message toolbar is shown in Figure 17.20.

Downloading Files from MSN

Figure 17.21 shows a message with an embedded file icon. You can obtain more information about a file by double-clicking on its icon to open the Properties window for that file. Figure 17.22 shows a typical Properties window. Notice the information in the Price field; some files cost additional money to download.

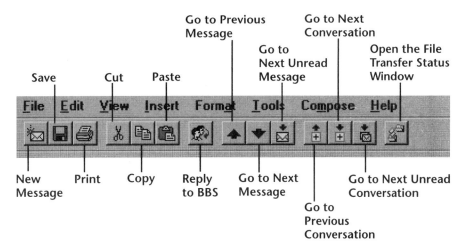

Figure 17.20   The message toolbar

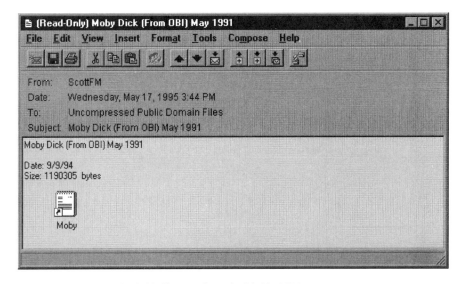

Figure 17.21   Downloadable files may be embedded in MSN messages.

There are several ways to download a file:

▶ Use the Save As command in the File menu or the toolbar.

▶ Right-click on the icon and select Download from the File Object submenu.

Part
3

Managing
Communications

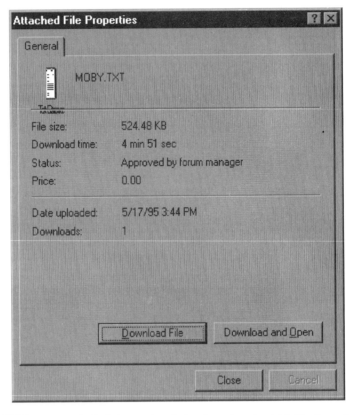

Figure 17.22   The Attached File Properties window for a downloadable file shows detailed information about that file.

▶ Click on the Download or Download and Open button in the Properties window for that file.

Live Chat Areas

The Message Folders described in the previous section are a store-and-forward method for sending and receiving messages and files. The Microsoft Network also supports real-time conversations in which other people see your messages as soon as you type them.

MSN calls these conversations *chats*. Some chats are dedicated to informal conversation around a specific topic, while others provide an opportunity to ask questions of experts who presumably know what they're talking about. Chat rooms are identified in MSN subject windows by icons with speech balloons.

Figure 17.23 shows a chat window. The text of the ongoing conversation appears in the Chat History pane in the upper-left part of the window. The Member List on the right side of the window shows the names of the current participants in this chat room. At the bottom of the screen there's a Compose Pane where you can type your own comments or questions. When you click on the Send button, you transmit the text in the Compose Pane to the chat room, and you should see it in the Chat History pane within a few seconds.

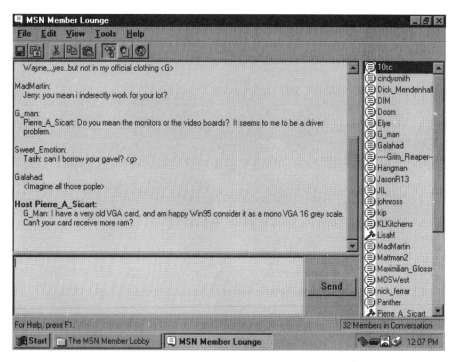

Figure 17.23   *Chat rooms contain live online conversations.*

Managing
Communications

You can change the relative sizes of panes by moving the cursor to the space between the panes and dragging the border. If you like, you can even make one or more of the panes disappear from the window completely.

The Member List displays an icon next to each name. This icon identifies the person as a host, a participant, or a spectator. The Host is generally the first person to enter a chat room. Participants can send and receive comments, but spectators may only read comments from other people. The Host can change a user's status from Participant to Spectator and back again.

Sometimes it's useful to learn more about the other people participating in a chat with you. To see information about a person listed in the Member List, highlight the name and either click the Member Profile button in the toolbar or choose the Member Profile command in the Tools menu.

Chat rooms have these commands in their menus that aren't in other windows:

File Menu

Save History　　Use to store the current conversation in a text file.

Save History As　　Use to assign a new name to the text file that contains the current conversation.

Edit Menu

Clear History　　This command deletes all of the text in the Chat History Pane.

View Menu

Move Split Bar　　Use to change the relative sizes of the panes within the chat window. You can do the same thing by moving your cursor to the boundary between panes and dragging the edge to a new position.

Show Spectators   When active, the member list shows both participants and spectators. When it is not active, it lists participants only.

Ignore Members   Highlight one or more names and use this command if you don't want to see postings from certain people who are participating in a chat.

Member Properties   Use to open the dialog box below for the currently highlighted name. If you check the Ignore Messages box, you will not see messages from this person.

Tools Menu

Select Members   This command opens a submenu with options for selecting all names in the Member List and for inverting the current selection. When you invert a selection, all of the currently unselected names will be selected, and the selected names will be unselected.

Host Controls   You can't use this command unless you're host of the current conference. If you are a host, you can use the command to change the status of other members from Participant to Spectator or Spectator to Participant.

Options   This command opens the Options dialog box on the next page. Use this dialog box to change message spacing, automatically save a conversation when you leave a chat room, and see notices when a member joins or leaves the chat room.

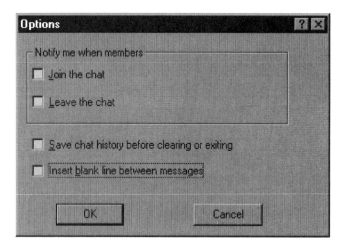

The chat room toolbar has three icon buttons that are not in other windows:

Show Spectators   Use this button to display the names of spectators as well as participants in the Member List.

Member Properties   Use this button to display information about the currently highlighted name in the Member List.

Ignore   Use the Ignore button to omit messages from the currently highlighted name in the member list. When you Ignore a name, that name appears in the Member List with a line through it.

Internet Access through the Microsoft Network

In addition to its own services, Microsoft Network will also incorporates a variety of Internet functions. MSN's Internet services are now limited to e-mail and newsgroups. By early 1996, Microsoft has promised to in-corporate a World-Wide Web browser into MSN. (See Chapter 32 for a discussion of the Web browser available with Miscrosoft Plus.)

Internet Newsgroups

MSN treats Internet newsgroups as one more source for bulletin-board conferences. In the main Categories window, there's a folder called *The Internet Center*. You may also see an icon in many folders, labeled *Related Internet Newsgroups*. When you click on one of these icons, you open sub-folders that eventually lead you to individual newsgroups.

MSN displays the contents of Internet newsgroups exactly the same way as it shows the bulletin boards and conferences that originate within the Microsoft Network. The important difference is that messages posted to an Internet group will be distributed to readers on many other networks around the world.

Sending and Receiving Internet E-Mail

The only difference between e-mail to another MSN user and messages to foreign addresses is the address format. Follow these steps to send a message through the Internet from MSN:

1. Starting at MSN Central, click on the E-Mail button.
2. Click on the compose button and choose the New Message option.
3. Type the Internet e-mail address of your intended recipient in the To field.
4. Compose and send the message just as you would for any other service.

Disconnecting from the Microsoft Network

To disconnect your PC from the Microsoft Network, use the Sign Out command in either the File menu, the toolbar, or the menu that appears when you left-click on the MSN icon on the Taskbar.

Because Microsoft wants you to spend as much time as possible on MSN with the meter running, the final version will have all kinds of interesting areas to occupy your attention and tempt you to download files and use special services for a "slight additional cost." Unless you have an unlimited budget, you will want to keep a close eye on the amount you spend online each month, or you'll have a *really* unpleasant surprise when you receive your credit card bill.

Part
3

Managing
Communications

Chapter 18

Internet Access Tools

FEATURING

Connecting to the Internet

Internet utilities

Other Internet applications

A s you probably know by now, the Internet is the worldwide interconnection of computers and computer networks that permits exchange of messages and files among millions of users around the world. Windows 95 includes the networking utilities necessary to connect your PC to the Internet, along with a couple of very basic Internet application programs.

This chapter will tell you how to connect to the Internet, how to use the built-in applications, and how to use those applications to obtain some free or almost-free applications that will make your life online a great deal more pleasant.

Connecting Your PC to the Internet

There are at least four common methods for connecting a PC to the Internet: as a remote terminal on a host computer already connected to the Internet, through a Network Interface Card (NIC) to a local-area network, through a dial-in TCP/IP connection to an Internet access provider, and through an online information service such as America Online or Microsoft Network.

 NOTE An Internet access provider is a business or nonprofit organization that supplies dial-in or private line connections to the Internet.

To understand the differences among these connection methods, it's helpful to know that the Internet uses a common set of rules, commands, and procedures called TCP/IP (transmission-control protocol/Internet protocol), which allows many different kinds of computers to communicate with one another. To send and receive data through the Internet, you must either use TCP/IP software on your own computer or move the data through another computer that converts it to and from TCP/IP.

Figure 18.1 shows a remote-terminal connection. Your PC uses a conventional communications program such as HyperTerminal or Pro-Comm to exchange data with a second computer, called a *host*, that is connected to the Internet. As far as the host is concerned, your PC is just like a terminal that does not have its own computer processor. For this reason, communications programs like HyperTerminal are also called *terminal-emulation* programs. Unless the host is located in the same building, you probably use a modem to connect to the host through a telephone line. You may also see this kind of Internet access called a *shell account* because many host computers use a user interface called a *shell*.

Remote-terminal access to the Internet has both advantages and disadvantages. It's frequently less expensive than other types of Internet connection because a single host can support many remote terminals at the same time. And because the TCP/IP programs are located on the host, not on your PC, you can use a slower modem and less powerful computer (but if your computer has enough power to run Windows 95, it should have no trouble with TCP/IP software). However, remote access generally uses a command line (like the DOS prompt) rather than a graphic interface, it limits you to the Internet tools loaded on the host, and it takes a lot longer to transfer files from a distant computer because you have to relay it through a host.

Figure 18.2 shows a connection through a local-area network (LAN), and Figure 18.3 shows a direct TCP/IP link through a SLIP (serial-line Internet protocol) or PPP (point-to-point protocol) connection. The Internet tools that control such functions as mail, news, and file transfer all run on your own PC. If you're already connected to a LAN, it's generally more efficient to connect the whole network to the Internet because a network connection is faster than a modem link.

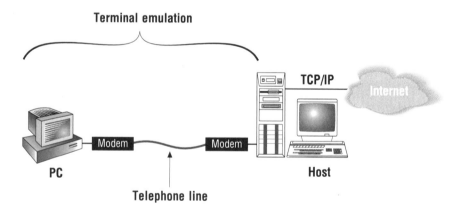

Figure 18.1   A remote-terminal connection to the Internet uses TCP/IP programs on a host computer.

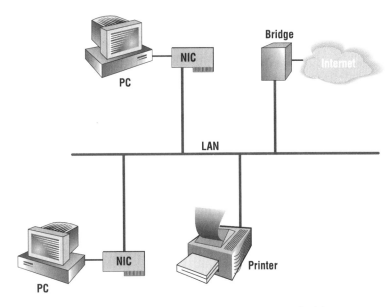

Figure 18.2 A LAN connection to the Internet provides access to all of the computers on a local-area network through NIC (the Network Interface Card).

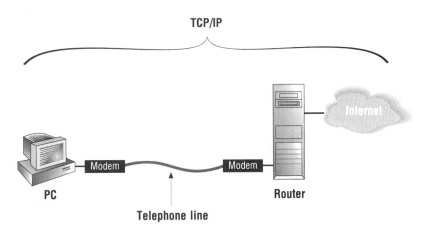

Figure 18.3 SLIP and PPP connections to the Internet communicate directly to the Internet using TCP/IP protocols.

The advantages of a direct TCP/IP connection to the Internet are speed and flexibility. There are many Windows application programs that provide graphical displays, drag-and-drop file transfer, and other features that are not available through a remote-terminal connection.

Part 3

Managing Communications

On the other hand, TCP/IP connections are usually more expensive than shell accounts, and they require high-speed modems (at least 14,400 bps) or other kinds of (usually costly) data links between your PC and an Internet *point of presence.*

Internet Addresses

Every computer on the Internet has a unique identity in the form of a four-part numeric address. For example, a typical address would look like this:

```
132.163.135.130
```

In most cases, that address also exists as a name, with a *domain* that shows either the type of business or other institution that uses this address (such as .com for commercial, .edu for educational, or .gov for government), or the country in which it's located. For example, Microsoft's domain address is microsoft.com, while Mindlink, an Internet service provider in Vancouver, British Columbia, Canada, uses mindlink.bc.ca as its address. Your Internet access provider uses a database called a *Domain Name Server* to convert from domain names to numeric addresses.

Regardless of the access method you choose, you will need to obtain an account from your network administrator or service provider. In the same way that every computer connected to the Internet has its own address, every user has a distinctive account name. Therefore, if the same business employed both Frances Smith and Fred Smith in the same department, only one could have the account name fsmith. When you combine the user name with the domain name, the two are separated by an *at* sign (@) so you can identify (and send mail to) anybody with an account on any Internet system in the format *name@address.domain.* So, for example, some typical Internet account names would be

```
bluebottle@finchley.uk
yokum@dogpatch.com
snorkel@swampy.mil
```

In addition to your own account name, address, and password, your service provider or network administrator may also give you several other pieces of information that you will need to set up your Internet account. These may include the dial-in Internet host's telephone number and the numeric addresses of the servers for name conversion, mail, and network news.

Connecting as a Remote Terminal

When you use a communications program such as HyperTerminal to dial into a host computer, your PC becomes a terminal on that host. If the host is connected to the Internet, you must use Internet programs resident on the host.

The most common remote-terminal access to the Internet is through a Unix host, or a host that recognizes Unix-like Internet commands such as telnet, ftp, and so forth.

NOTE Unix is a widely used computer operating system that is available for many different kinds of computers, including desktop systems, mainframes, and everything in between. Unix allows more than one program to run at the same time and multiple users to share a single computer.

As far as Windows is concerned, when you use a shell account, your PC is running a modem communications program to move ASCII characters or binary files through a modem. All the TCP/IP activity is happening at the host. In other words, when you type commands on your PC's keyboard, those commands pass through your computer to the host, which runs the programs that communicate with the Internet.

If you have a remote-terminal connection to the Internet, you don't need to worry about network configuration, because the administrator of the host has taken care of all those things for you. Once you know your own account name and password and the host's Internet address, you're ready to go.

Configuring Windows for TCP/IP Internet Connection

Windows 95 includes support for dial-in TCP/IP access to the Internet through a PPP account. To use this function, you must have a PPP account with an Internet service provider. If you have a SLIP account, you will have to install SLIP support separately. I'll explain how to do that later in this chapter.

This kind of connection is not your only option for connecting to the Internet. There are many add-on Internet access products, including Microsoft Plus (Chapter 32), that offer easier ways to set up a TCP/IP connection.

When you set up your Internet access account, you will need to obtain the following information from your service provider:

▶ your log-in name and password

▶ the service provider's access telephone number

▶ the service provider's host name and domain

▶ the numeric IP address of your service provider's name server

If your service provider does not use dynamic address assignment (most do), you will also need to obtain your IP address, subnet mask address, and gateway address from the service provider.

With this information in hand, follow these steps to load and configure dial-in Internet access:

1. If you haven't yet installed Windows 95, run Setup and choose Custom Setup. If Windows has already been installed, open Add/Remove Programs from the Control Panel and click on the Windows Setup tab.

2. Click on Communications to put a check mark in the box and then click on the Details button.

3. Check the Dial-Up Networking option in the component list shown in Figure 18.4 and click on the OK button. Insert the disks as Windows asks for them.

4. After loading the software, double-click on the Network icon in the Control Panel.

5. When the Network dialog box in Figure 18.5 appears, click on the Add button.

6. Click on the Protocol option and the Add button.

7. When the Select Network Protocol menu in Figure 18.6 appears, choose Microsoft from the Manufacturers menu and TCP/IP from the Network Protocols menu. Click on OK.

8. When the Configuration dialog box appears again, highlight the Dial-Up Adapter and click on the Properties button.

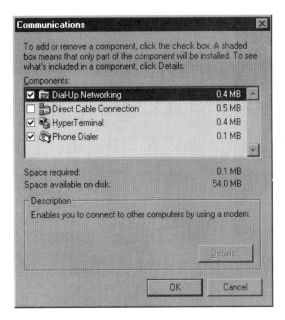

Figure 18.4   Check Dial-Up Networking to install the Internet access software.

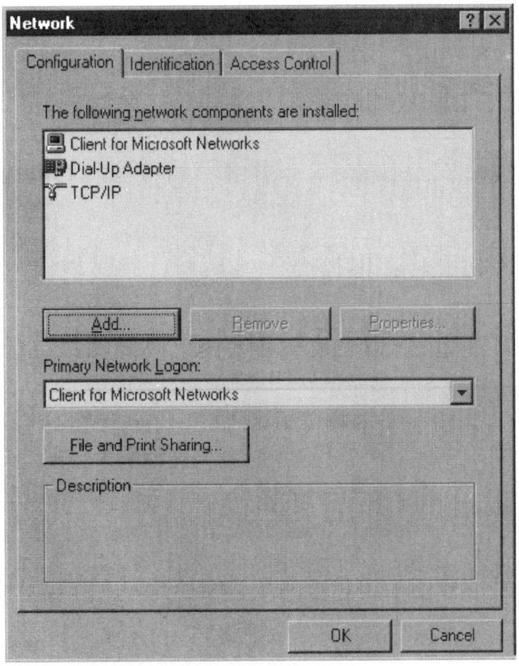

Figure 18.5   Click on the Add button to install TCP/IP support.

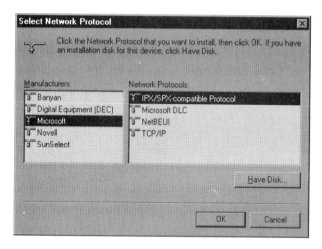

Figure 18.6   Choose the TCP/IP network protocol to set up a PPP connection to the Internet.

9. Click on the Bindings tab to display the list of protocols in Figure 18.7. Confirm that there's a check mark next to the TCP/IP protocol listing. Click on OK.

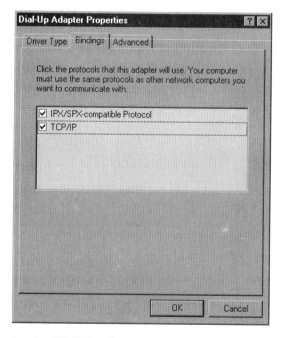

Figure 18.7   Confirm that TCP/IP is active.

10. Once again, the Configuration dialog box appears. Highlight TCP/IP in the Network Components menu and click on the Properties button.

11. Choose the IP Address tab to display the dialog box in Figure 18.8. If your Internet access provider supplies a different IP address each time you log in, choose the *Obtain an IP address automatically* radio button. If your service provider has given you a permanent IP address, choose the *Specify an IP address* radio button and type your address and subnet mask (if any) in their respective fields.

12. If your service provider gave you a gateway address, click on the Gateway tab and type the gateway address in the New Gateway field.

13. Click on the DNS Configuration tab to display the dialog box in Figure 18.9. Click on the Enable DNS radio button and type your service provider's host name and domain. Type the Domain Name Server's IP address in the *DNS server search order* field and click on the Add button.

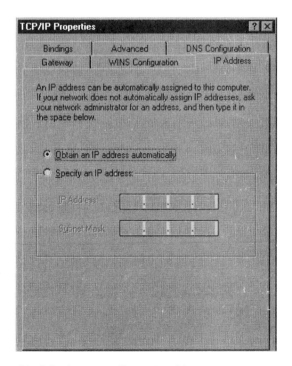

Figure 18.8   *Use this dialog box to specify your IP address.*

Part
3

Managing
Communications

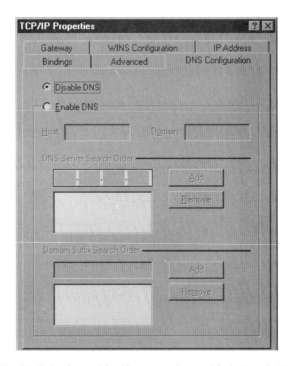

Figure 18.9 Use this dialog box to identify your service provider's Domain Name Server.

14. Click on OK to return to the Network dialog box and OK again to return to the Control Panel. Windows may ask you to load one or more disks at this point.

15. Close the Control Panel and restart Windows 95.

16. After Windows has restarted, double-click on the My Computer icon and choose the Dial-Up Networking icon, or click on the Start menu, open the Programs menu, and choose Dial-up Networking from the Accessories menu.

17. If you haven't already installed a modem, the program will give you a chance to install it now.

18. Double-click on the Make New Connection icon to start the New Connection Wizard. In the first screen of the Wizard, shown in Figure 18.10, replace "My Connection" in the *Type a name for the computer you are dialing* field with the name of your service provider or with something like *Internet Access*. Click on the Next> button.

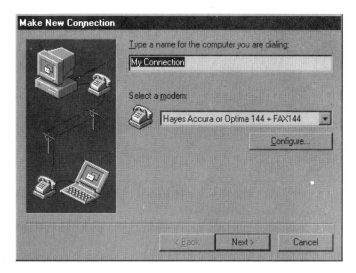

Figure 18.10   Type a name for the command that connects you to the Internet.

19.   In the next screen of the New Connection wizard, type your service
provider's telephone number for dial-in access.

20.   The Dial-Up Networking window will now have a second icon with
the name you specified, as shown below. Right-click on the new icon
and select the Properties command.

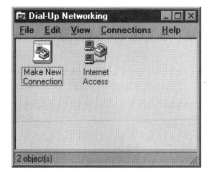

21.   Click on the Configure button and select the Options tab to display
the dialog box in Figure 18.11. Under *Connection control*, make the
Bring up terminal window after dialing option active.

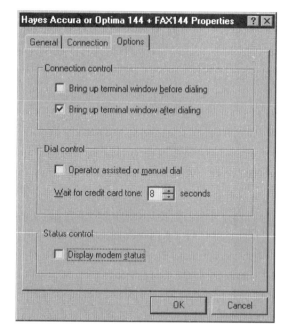

Figure 18.11   *Be sure to choose the After Dialing option and not Before Dialing.*

Configuring a SLIP Connection

If your TCP/IP connection to the Internet uses SLIP rather than PPP, you'll need a separate setup information file called `rnaplus.inf` that is not automatically installed during Windows setup. If you have the CD-ROM version of Windows 95, you can find the file in the directory `\admin\apptools\slip`. If you don't have a CD-ROM, you'll have to download the file from Microsoft. It should be available on Microsoft Network, CompuServe, and other online information services, as well as from the Microsoft Download Service at 206-936-6735. Look for a file called `rnaplu.zip`.

Follow these steps to install a SLIP connection:

1. Copy the `rnaplus.inf` file to a floppy disk. Leave the diskette in the drive.

2. Open the Windows 95 Control Panel and select Add/Remove Programs.

3. When the Add/Remove Programs Properties dialog box appears, choose the Windows Setup tab and click on the Have Disk button.

4. When the Install from Disk dialog box shown below appears, make sure the path of the drive that contains the `rnaplus.inf` file is in the Copy From field and click on OK.

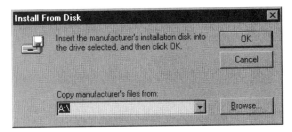

5. The Have Disk dialog box in Figure 18.12 lists setup information files in the path you specified in step 4. Click on the box next to Unix Connection for Dial-Up Networking to put a check mark in the box and click on Install.

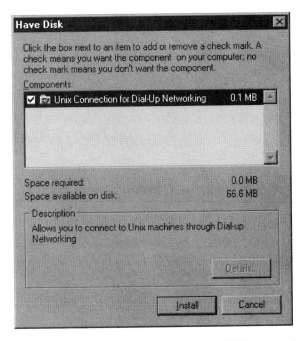

Figure 18.12 *The Unix Connection item adds SLIP access to Dial-Up Networking.*

6. Windows will copy the Unix Connection component from the diskette. When the Add/Remove Programs Properties dialog box appears again, scroll to the bottom of the Components list and make sure there's a check mark next to Unix Connection for Dial-Up Networking.

7. Close the Control Panel and restart your computer.

8. When the Windows Desktop re-appears, click on the Start button, open the Programs menu, and choose Dial-Up Networking from the Accessories submenu.

9. Double-click on Make New Connection.

10. Step through the New Connection Wizard until you see the screen in Figure 18.13.

11. Click on Next and then Finish to complete the New Connection Wizard.

12. Click on My Computer in your Desktop and open the Dial-Up Networking Window.

13. Right-click on the new icon for Internet Access (or whatever you chose to name it) and select the Properties command.

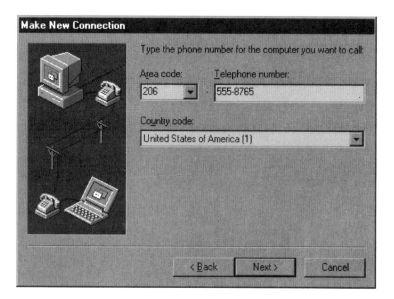

Figure 18.13   **Type your Internet service provider's access number in this screen.**

14. Click on the Server Type button to open the dialog box in Figure 18.14.

15. Drop down the Type of Dial-Up Server menu and choose either the CSLIP or SLIP option, depending on the kind of connection your service provider supplies. If you're not sure which option to choose, ask your service provider.

16. Click on OK to save your configuration and again to close the Properties dialog box.

Making the Connection

The good news about network configuration is that you only have to do it once. After that, you can make your Internet connection by simply making a network connection.

Follow these steps to connect your computer to the Internet through a PPP or SLIP account:

1. Make sure your modem is turned on.

2. Open the Dial-Up Networking window from either My Computer or the Programs Accessories menu.

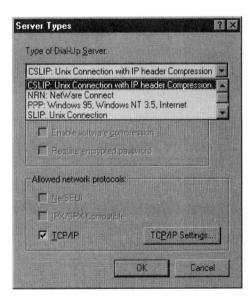

Figure 18.14 *Specify either CSLIP or SLIP as your server type.*

Part
3

Managing
Communications

3. Double-click on Internet Access (or whatever you named your Internet-access command).

4. When the Connect To dialog box in Figure 18.15 appears, fill in any blank fields and click on Connect. Windows will start dialing.

5. When your modem connects to the network host, Windows will open a Terminal window like the one in Figure 18.16. If the host asks for your log-in and password, type the information requested and press the Enter key.

6. If you're using a SLIP account, the host may tell you your IP address for this session. Make a note of the address; you'll need it in a minute.

7. Click on the Continue button or press the F7 key.

8. If a dialog box asking you to confirm your IP address appears, type the number you copied from the host and click on the OK button.

9. Your computer now has an active connection to the Internet. When you start an Internet application, such as ftp, Mosaic, or telnet, the application will automatically send and receive data through this connection.

When you have finished your interaction with the Internet, click on the Disconnect button to take your computer offline.

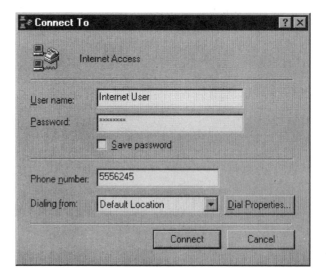

Figure 18.15   *The Connect To dialog box*

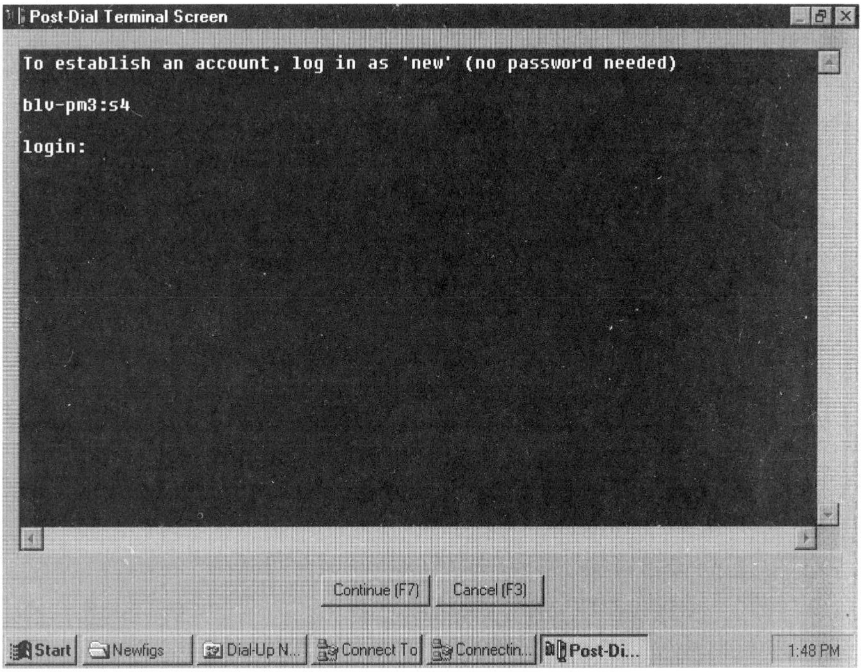

Figure 18.16   Type your name and password in the Terminal window.

If you have access to the Internet through a LAN, follow these steps to make your connection:

1. Click on the Network Neighborhood icon in the Windows Desktop.

2. Select the icon for your Internet connection.

3. Start the Winsock-compatible application you want to run. The application will communicate to the Internet through `winsock.dll` and your network connection.

Regardless of the type of connection you're using, your Winsock applications will automatically find your connection to the Internet. If you close one application and start another or run more than one application at the same time, the second (and subsequent) application will use the same Winsock connection to the Internet.

If you're using a dial-in connection, remember to break the connection when you're finished doing whatever you're doing online.

Internet Utilities

Window 95 includes several Internet utilities—an FTP (file-transfer protocol) program, a telnet program for remote log-in to distant computers, and a handful of programs for testing Internet connections. Both the FTP and the telnet programs are *clients*, which means they can communicate with computers configured as FTP and telnet servers. Most of these applications are character-based programs that operate from within a DOS window. Therefore, you need to use the DOS Prompt command in the Program menu before you can use them.

Some of these utilities may not work with other Winsock stacks, such as the ones in Internet Chameleon, Internet in a Box, or Trumpet Winsock. This really isn't a problem because most Internet packages include other utilities that do the same job as the ones in the Windows 95 package, only better.

File-Transfer Protocol

FTP is the standard TCP/IP file-transfer protocol used for moving text and binary files between computers on the Internet. If you have an account on a distant computer on the Internet, you can use FTP to download files from the other computer to your PC and to upload files from your PC to the host. In addition, there are hundreds of *anonymous* FTP archives all over the Internet that accept log-ins from anybody who wants copies of their files.

The Windows 95 FTP program is located in the \Windows directory, which is in your Path statement. Therefore, you don't have to specify the path when you enter an ftp command. To connect to an FTP server, follow these steps:

1. Use the Run command in the Start menu to enter this command: **ftp <host name>**.

2. A terminal window will open with an ftp> prompt.

3. When FTP connects to the server, the server will ask for your user name and password. If you're connecting to an anonymous FTP server, type **anonymous** as your user name and your Internet address as your password. Use the standard *name@address.domain* format.

Most FTP servers use the same system of directories and subdirectories that you know from DOS and Windows. To see the contents of the current directory, type **dir** at the ftp> prompt. Figure 18.17 shows an FTP directory.

A "d" as the first letter in a listing indicates that the item in that line is a directory. If there's a dash as the first character, the item is a file. The name of the file or directory is at the extreme right.

To move to a subdirectory, use the command **cd** *name*.

To move up to the next higher level, use the command **cd ..**

When you download a file from an FTP server, you must specify that it is either an ASCII text file or a binary file. As a general rule, binary files that you can read on a PC will generally have a DOS file extension (other than .txt for a text file or .ps for a Postscript print file), but you really can't be certain. ASCII text files may or may not have a file extension.

When you make your initial connection to an FTP server, you're in ASCII mode. Before you try to transfer a binary file, you'll have to change modes. To switch to binary mode, use the command **binary**.

Figure 18.17   The FTP directory shows files and subdirectories.

To switch back to ASCII mode, use the command **ASCII**. The host will acknowledge your mode-change command.

To download a file from the server, use the command **get** *filename*. If you want to store the file on your PC with a different name, use the command **get** *filename newname*. When the file transfer is complete, the host will send you another message, shown below.

```
ftp> get index.txt
200 PORT command successful.
150 Opening ASCII mode data connection for index.txt.
226 Transfer complete.
860 bytes received in 0.88 seconds (0.98 Kbytes/sec)
ftp>
```

When you are finished with your FTP session, use the command **disconnect** to break the connection to the server. You can connect to another host by typing the new server's address.

To close the FTP utility, type the command **quit**.

Telnet Remote Log-In

When you connect through a telnet connection, your PC becomes a terminal on the distant system. In most cases, a telnet log-in requires an account on the host (remote) machine, but there are also many systems that accept log-ins from anybody who wants to connect. Among the most common public telnet sites are online library catalogs. Other public telnet sites let you use character-based Internet services that may not be available on your own computer, such as *Gopher* or *Finger*.

To set up a telnet connection, follow these steps:

1. Click on the Telnet icon in the Windows directory. The Telnet window in Figure 18.18 will open.

2. Open the Connect menu and select the Remote System command to display the Connect dialog box shown below.

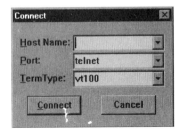

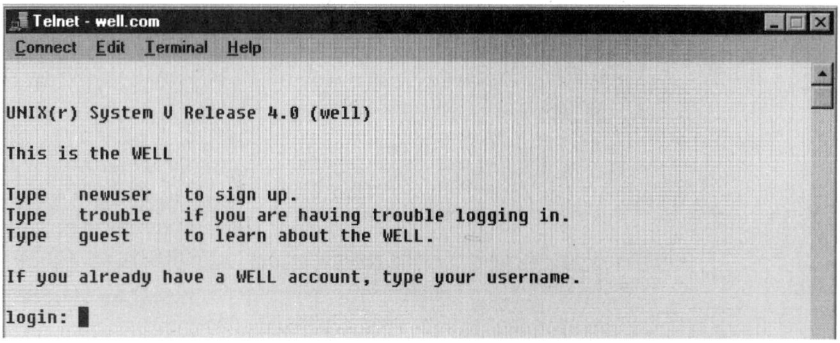

Figure 18.18   Use the Telnet window to connect to remote computers across the Internet.

3. Type the name of the host to which you want to connect in the Host Name field. Click on the Connect button.

   If you prefer, you can use the Run command in the Start menu and type **telnet** *hostname*, using the domain name or IP address of the computer to which you want to connect in place of *hostname*.

   Telnet will connect your computer to the host whose name you supplied and display messages from that host in the Telnet window.

   Most telnet hosts display a series of log-in prompts as soon as you make the connection. If you're connecting to a public telnet host, it will probably tell you how to log in.

Ping

Ping is a diagnostic utility that tests your ability to connect your computer to another device through the Internet by sending an echo request and displaying the number of milliseconds required to receive a reply.

To set up a Ping test, follow these steps:

1. Use the MS-DOS Prompt command in the Start ➤ Programs menu to open a DOS window.

2. At the C:\Windows> prompt, type **ping** *destination*. Use the domain name or the IP address of the host you want to test in place of *destination*.

Part
3

Managing
Communications

3. Ping will send four sets of Internet Control Message Protocol (ICMP) echo packets to the host you specify and display the amount of time it took to receive each reply, as shown in Figure 18.19.

    The important part of the Ping display is the "time=*nnn*ms" section of the Reply lines. The fact that Ping was able to connect to the distant host at all tells you that your own connection to the Internet is working properly; the number of milliseconds can tell you if you have an efficient connection to this particular host (anything less than about 800 milliseconds is usually acceptable).

Network Configuration

The Network Display diagnostic command opens an information window that shows your current TCP/IP configuration values. To open the information window in Figure 18.20, type **winipcfg** at the DOS prompt or the Run window. For additional details, click on the More Info>> button.

Protocol Statistics

Use the **netstat** command to display a list of currently active connections to other computers across the Internet.

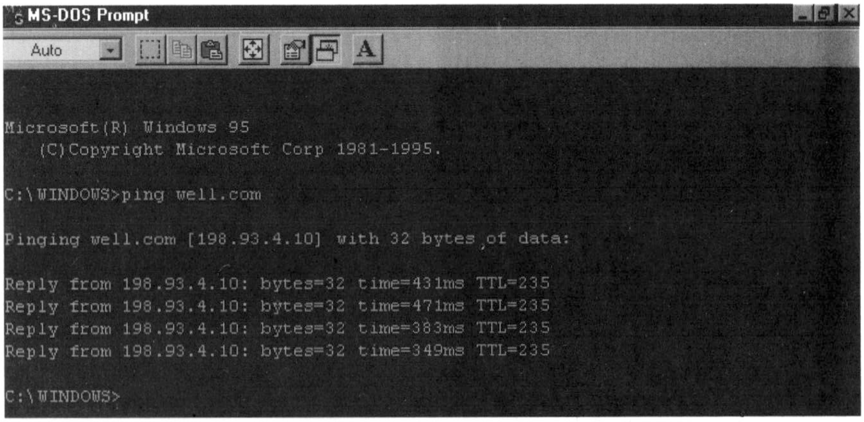

Figure 18.19   A successful Ping test shows the amount of time needed to send and receive several echo packets.

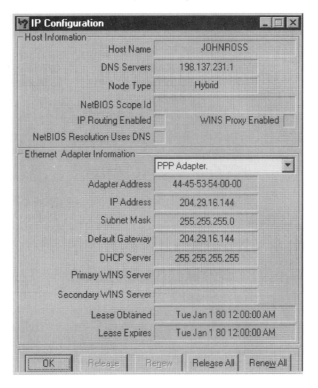

Figure 18.20   *The IP Configuration window shows the current TCP/IP configuration values.*

1. Use the MS-DOS Prompt command in the Start ➤ Programs menu to open a DOS window.

2. At the C:\Windows> prompt, type **netstat**. A list of connections similar to the ones shown below will appear.

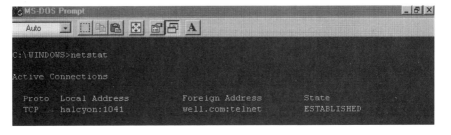

A Netstat report includes the following information:

Proto   Shows the networking protocol in use for each active connection. For PPP or SLIP connections to the Internet, the Proto column will always be "TCP," which specifies a TCP/IP connection.

Local Address   The identity of your PC on the network.

Foreign Address   Shows the address of each distant computer to which a connection is currently active.

State   Shows the condition of each connection.

Trace Route

In most cases, when you set up a connection to a distant computer through the Internet, your signal path passes through several routers along the way. Because this is all happening in a fraction of a second, these intermediate routers are usually invisible. But when you're having trouble making a connection, the trace route command can help isolate the source of the problem.

To run a trace route test, complete these steps:

1. Use the MS-DOS Prompt command in the Start ➤ Programs menu to open a DOS window.

2. At the C:\Windows> prompt, type **tracert <*target*>**. In place of *target*, type the address of the distant system. A trace route report will appear in the DOS window.

In many cases, your connection will pass through one or more backbone networks between your own connection to the Internet and your ultimate destination. For example, the tracert report in Figure 18.21 shows a route from a PC in Seattle to The WELL, near San Francisco. In this case, the connection passes through backbone networks operated by Sprintlink and AlterNet.

Tracert steps through the connection route, one step at a time. For each step, it shows the amount of time needed to reach that router, in milliseconds. If an intermediate router, or a connection between two intermediate routers fails, tracert will not display any steps beyond that point in the route. If that happens, you can assume that the failed site is the reason that you are unable to connect to your intended destination.

Obtaining Other Internet Applications

With the exception of telnet and e-mail through Microsoft Network, the Internet tools included with Windows 95 are pretty primitive. They're all character-based programs that use the klunky old DOS command line. If you plan to use the Internet more than once every three or four months, you really ought to replace them with some of the Windows-based graphic applications that are available from several software archives on the Internet. You can use the Windows FTP program to obtain another, easier-to-use FTP program, and then use that program to download other Winsock-compatible Internet application programs. If you prefer, you can use the Internet Tools in Microsoft Plus (see Chapter 32) or one of the commercial all-in-one

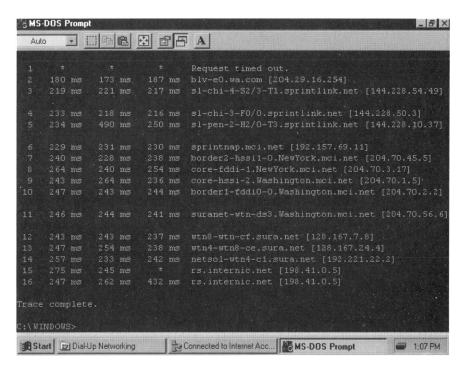

Figure 18.21   *The* tracert *command produces a list of intermediate routers between your PC and an Internet host.*

Managing
Communications

Internet-access products, such as Internet in a Box or SuperHighway Access.

Winsock FTP is a free FTP application that is a lot easier to use than the one included with Windows 95. Figure 18.22 shows the main Winsock FTP window. You can obtain it via anonymous FTP from `ftp.usma.edu`, in the directory `/Pub/Msdos/Winsock.files`. The file is called `ws_ftp.zip`. You'll need an unzip program such as PK-Zip to uncompress the file after you download it. Winsock FTP includes a list of other FTP archives that contain additional Winsock applications.

A few *whiteboarding* programs are available, which let you and other users exchange drawn or hand-printed ideas in real time in a manner similar to using the whiteboard at your company's conference center. When a user draws on his or her screen, the other's screens are all updated to show the new addition. Typically, each connected user can have a different color "marker," and pictures or documents can be loaded into the whiteboard when needed.

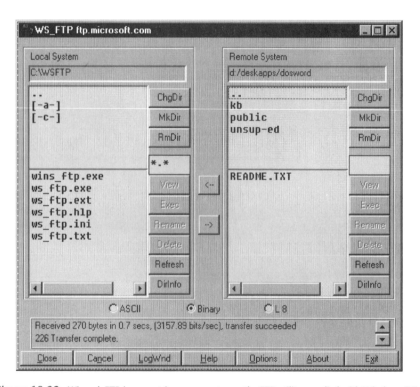

Figure 18.22   Winsock FTP is a great improvement over the FTP utility supplied with Windows 95.

If you literally want to chat across the network, try VocalTec's IPhone (see Figure 18.23) or Camelot's Digiphone. These products let you talk with anyone else over a TCP/IP connection and require only the software, almost any sound card, and an inexpensive microphone. The amazing thing about these products (aside from the fact that they actually work) is their relatively low bandwidth; for example, you can be chatting with someone while simultaneously viewing Web pages with Mosaic or Netscape over even a 14.4K Internet connection.

Taking the above ideas a step further, video-conferencing applications—such as CU-SeeMe and VidPhone—let you send still or motion video to other users. Besides the software, you will need either a camcorder (usually on a tripod) or a small designed-for-videoconferencing camera that perches on your monitor. In addition, you will need a video capture card, typically used to convert video from a VCR or camcorder into a signal you can display on your computer monitor, which can also be used to create movie or graphics files. For less-than-full-motion video, even a 14.4K modem connection can be used to send a few frames a second; on a faster network connection, these video-conferencing applications can meet or exceed movie-quality video.

Another relatively new arrival in the multimedia-over-TCP/IP category is RealAudio. This product gives you the equivalent of AM-radio–quality continuous (but one-way) sound across a TCP/IP connection. Currently the Deutsche Welle (national radio of Germany), Radio Canada, a few U.S. radio stations, and other individuals are experimenting with simulcasting parts of their normal radio broadcasts over

Figure 18.23 Internet Phone (IPhone) from VocalTec lets you communicate with voice over any TCP/IP connection.

Part 3

Managing Communications

the Internet. Again, the bandwidth is low enough that you can receive their broadcasts even over a 14.4K audio connection.

As you can see, the Internet is a virtual hotbed of new multimedia and client-server technology, and by adopting TCP/IP as your network protocol, you can ensure easy expansion into a wide-area network, plus have the freedom to assimilate Internet media technologies to your own network, even if you decide not to connect your company's network to the Internet.

Coming Attractions: Accessing the Internet through Microsoft Network

It won't be available until the end of 1995 (or later), but Microsoft has announced that it plans to offer full Internet access through the Microsoft Network, including a licensed version of NCSA Mosaic. This version of Mosaic won't look exactly like the screen in Figure 18.24, but it will provide a similar set of graphical Internet navigation tools, including browsers for FTP, Gopher, and the World Wide Web.

The advance publicity for the MSN Internet service describes it as "seamless access," which suggests that the user interface will be an extension of the Microsoft Network architecture. You can expect to see Internet tools in Home Base and Internet resources in other MSN screens and menus. It won't be necessary to find a separate Internet service provider because an Internet connection will be closely integrated with MSN.

Obviously, this kind of Internet access will be a great deal easier to use than the primitive TCP/IP tools bundled with the earliest release of Windows 95, but because Microsoft hasn't revealed how much going to charge for Internet access, it's too soon to know if MSN will be a better deal than any of the other ways to connect to the Internet. In the meantime, there are about half a dozen shrink-wrapped products and several shareware programs available today that provide easier Internet access than the tools in Windows 95.

Microsoft also includes a World Wide Web browser and a mail reader that uses Exchange in the add-on Microsoft Plus package (see Chapter 32).

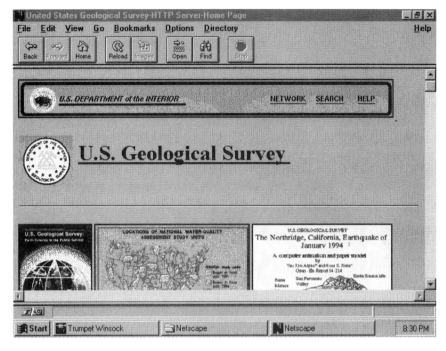

Figure 18.24   Microsoft Network will eventually include an Internet browser similar to this one.

The Internet can connect you to a huge and growing number of resources, including thousands of programs and data files, newsgroup discussions on almost every imaginable subject, and much more. For a more detailed guide to exploring the Internet, check out *Access the Internet!* (Sybex, 1995) or *The Internet Roadmap* (Sybex, 1994).

Part
3

Managing
Communications

The Supplied Applications

4

Chapter 19

Using WordPad for Simple Word Processing

FEATURING

I f you're like most people, you'll end up using Windows for writing more than for any other task. Writing letters, memos, and reports with your computer is much more efficient—and much more fun—than banging them out on a typewriter. To get you started, Windows 95 comes with a simple yet capable *word processor*, called WordPad, for editing and printing text documents.

WordPad lacks the frills of the hefty word-processing programs like Microsoft Word for Windows, WordPerfect, or Ami Pro, but it works fine for most everyday writing chores. WordPad gives you all the essential tools you'll need for editing word-processing documents of virtually any length; it is limited only by the capacity of your disk drive. Like the high-end programs, it even lets you move text around with the mouse, a feature called drag-and-drop editing. WordPad accepts, displays, and prints graphics pasted to it from the Clipboard; it also lets you edit those graphics right in your document using OLE (see Chapter 6 for more about OLE). WordPad may not offer all the bells and whistles of the market leaders, but it's no toy—and besides, the price is right.

This chapter begins with a tutorial that gives you the opportunity to learn how to create and edit a word-processing document. Along the way, you can experiment with the major procedures involved in a simple Windows-based word processor. Many of the techniques discussed in this chapter are applicable to other Windows programs as well.

After entering and editing your document, I'll discuss the various formatting features you can easily apply to your documents. Included in the discussion is information on how to

▶ format individual characters with font, style, and size alterations

▶ format paragraphs by changing line spacing, indents, and margins

▶ set the tab stops to aid you in making tables

▶ quickly search for and replace specific text

▶ include headers and footers

▶ paginate your document correctly

▶ incorporate and edit graphics

▶ copy text between two WordPad documents

▶ save and print files

TIPS FOR WINDOWS 3.1 USERS

If you have ever used Windows Write, the word processor included with earlier versions of Windows, you know how crude it seems compared to WordPad. But while WordPad would clobber Write in a beauty contest and WordPad's fancier button bars make it easier to use, Write actually has several important features that WordPad lacks. If your word-processing needs don't justify buying a high-end program such as WordPerfect or Microsoft Word, you should consider keeping Write handy in case you need these capabilities.

Present in Write but missing from WordPad are:

▶ Repeating headers and footers for information you want to display on every page. Write lets you insert a page-number marker that automatically numbers each page for you.

▶ Full paragraph justification (so that text is flush on both the left and right sides of a paragraph).

▶ Double-spacing and $1^1/_2$-spacing for paragraphs (WordPad permits only single-spaced paragraphs).

▶ Decimal tabs, allowing you to line up columns of decimal numbers.

▶ Superscript and subscript character formats.

▶ A *Regular* character format command, allowing you to remove all styles (bold, italic, underlining, super- and subscripts) from selected text with a single command.

▶ A *page break* command, allowing you to force text that follows to the top of a new page, regardless of how you edit previous text (useful for creating documents with sections).

▶ The ability to find text that matches the capitalization (case) of your entry in the Find dialog box and the ability to find text that is found only if it occurs as a separate word (not as part of a longer word).

▶ The ability to search for paragraph markers, page breaks, and tabs with the Find command. Among other uses, this lets you reformat DOS-style plain text documents much more easily.

By the way, you should know that although WordPad can open Write documents, items that WordPad doesn't recognize are converted or discarded. For example, WordPad converts decimal tabs to ordinary tabs, and it simply discards headers or footers.

Creating a Document

To start a new WordPad document, begin from the Taskbar. Choose Programs ➤ Accessories ➤ WordPad. Within a few moments, the WordPad window will appear with a new, empty document window open for you. If the WordPad window isn't already maximized, maximize it so it fills the whole screen. Your screen should now look like that shown in Figure 19.1.

Getting Help in WordPad

Before going any further, it bears repeating that on-screen help is always a mouse-click or key press away while you're working in WordPad. To activate WordPad Help, press F1 or choose Help ➤ Help Topics. When the standard Windows Help application appears, choose the Contents, Index, or Find tabs, then locate the topic you need help with and double-click on it.

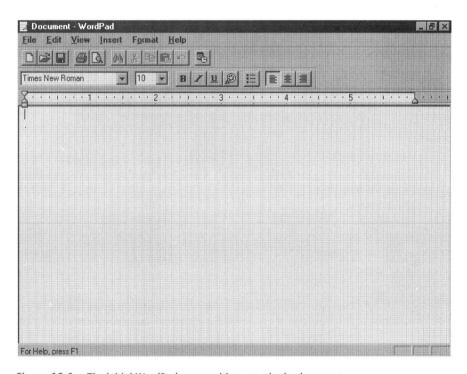

Figure 19.1   The initial WordPad screen with no text in the document

You can also get help for any item in a dialog box by using the right mouse button. Click over the item with the right button to pop up the *What's this?* button. Click on the button to display a short help message.

Finally, WordPad displays brief help messages when you pass the mouse pointer over certain items on the screen. These include menu choices and the buttons on the Toolbar and Status Bar (those rows of buttons at the top of the screen).

Working with the WordPad Window

There are several things to notice on your screen. As usual, up at the top of the WordPad window you see the menu and Title bars. The menu bar offers options for writing, editing, and formatting text.

Referring to your screen or to Figure 19.1, notice that the Title Bar shows *Document* as the file name because you haven't named the document yet.

The Toolbar

Just below the menu bar you should see a row of buttons, each with a small graphical icon. This is the *Toolbar*, shown below. (If you don't see the Toolbar, someone has turned it off. Display it by choosing View ➤ Toolbar.)

Clicking on the Toolbar buttons gives you one-step access to some of the most common WordPad commands. For instance, the first button (on the far left) shows a single sheet of blank paper. Clicking on this button creates a new, blank document. About halfway across the row of buttons, the Find button—the one showing a pair of binoculars—lets you search for specific passages of text.

In WordPad, you don't have to memorize what each button does. Just position the mouse pointer over the button and wait a few seconds. WordPad will display a small text box with a one- or two-word description of the button's function. In addition, the Status Bar at the bottom of the screen displays a longer help message.

Displaying and Hiding Control Bars with the View Menu

WordPad offers several other bar-like sets of controls and readouts to speed your work and give you quick information on your document. The View menu lets you display or remove each of these control bars individually. If the item isn't currently visible, choose its name from the View menu to display it. Do exactly the same to remove the item if it's already displayed (if, for example, you want more space for editing text).

Notice that when you display the View menu, you'll see a check mark to the left of each control bar that is currently visible. If there's no check mark, the corresponding bar is currently hidden.

The Format Bar

Like the Toolbar, the *Format Bar* offers a set of graphical buttons, but it also contains (at the far left) two drop-down list boxes for selecting font and type size:

All of the Format Bar's controls affect aspects of your document's appearance. Besides the font and type-size controls, various buttons let you set such characteristics as type style (such as boldface and italics) and paragraph alignment (such as left aligned or centered).

The Ruler and the Status Bar

The *ruler*, another control bar available from the View menu, lets you see and modify paragraph indents and tab stops. See *Formatting Paragraphs* below for instructions on working with the ruler. The *Status Bar* is a thin strip at the very bottom of the WordPad window. It displays messages from WordPad on the left. On the right are indicators showing when the Caps Lock and Num Lock keys are depressed.

Repositioning the Toolbar and Format Bar

You can reposition the Toolbar and Format Bar if you like. Just position the mouse pointer over any part of the bar that's not a button and drag the bar where you want it. If you drag the bar to the bottom of the WordPad window, the bar will merge with the lower portion of the window. You can also drag the Toolbar to the right side of the window so it becomes a vertical strip fused with the right window edge (this won't work with the Format Bar because the list boxes for typeface and size are too wide to fit in the narrow strip). If you drag either bar into the document area or outside the WordPad window altogether, it becomes a separate moveable window with its own title bar (as shown in Figure 19.2).

Entering Text

Notice the main document area of the WordPad window. Because you haven't typed in anything yet, the only item to look at here is the blinking cursor in the upper-left corner. This *insertion point* indicates the place where new text will appear when you type.

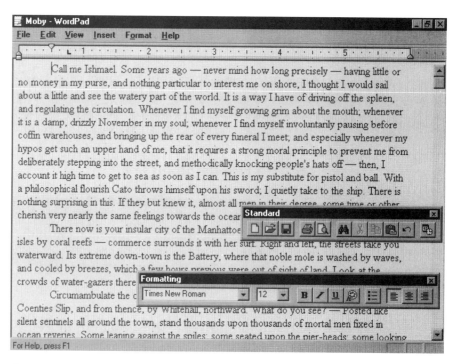

Figure 19.2   Here's how the Toolbar and Format Bar look when you "tear" them from their standard locations, thereby turning them into separate, moveable windows.

Now begin creating a document. Of course, you're free to type in anything you want. However, to establish a consistent text to refer to later on in this chapter, try entering the following text, a hypothetical news story. (For later steps in the tutorial, keep the two misspelled words, *Pizza* and *sight*, as they are.) If you are at all unfamiliar with word processors, first read the steps that follow this text:

NEWS FLASH

Society for Anachronistic Sciences
1000 Edsel Lane
Piltdown, PA 19042

The Society for Anachronistic Sciences announced its controversial findings today at a press conference held in the city of Pisa, Italy. Pizza was not chosen as the sight for the conference because of its celebrated position in the annals of Western scientific history. The Society has made public its annual press conferences for well over 300 years and, as usual, nothing new was revealed. According to its members, this is a comforting fact and a social service in an age when everything else seems to change.

Begin entering the text into your new file, following the steps outlined here. If you make mistakes while you are typing, use the Backspace key to back up and fix them. If you don't see an error until you have typed past it, leave it for now—you'll learn how to fix any mistakes later:

1. Type **NEWS FLASH** on the first line.

2. Next, press Enter twice to move down a couple of lines to prepare for typing the address. Notice that pressing Enter is necessary to add new blank lines in a word-processing document. Pressing the ↓ key will not move the cursor down a line at this point or create new lines; you will only hear an error beep from your computer if you try this.

TIP Don't double-space between sentences as you would with a typewriter. WordPad will automatically add enough space to clearly separate each sentence. If you double-space, your text will print with unsightly gaps between sentences.

3. Enter the first line of the address, then press Enter to move down to the next line. Repeat this process for the last two lines of the address.

4. Press Enter twice to put in another blank line.

5. Begin entering the body of the story. Don't forget to leave in the spelling mistakes so we can fix them later on. When you get to the end of a line, just keep typing. You shouldn't press Enter because WordPad will automatically move text that overflows to the next line for you. This is called *word wrapping*. All you have to do is keep typing—and leave only one space between sentences, not two.

When you've finished entering the sample text, the WordPad window should look something like Figure 19.3.

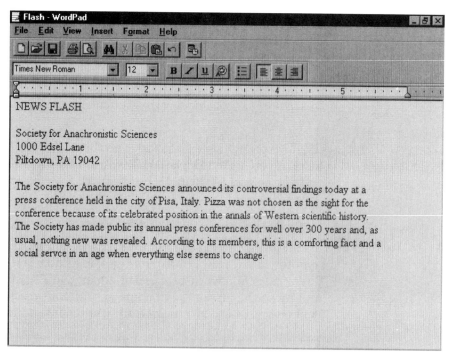

Figure 19.3 *The WordPad window after you've entered the sample text*

Editing Your Text

The first step in editing is learning how to move around in the text. If you followed the instructions above, you moved the cursor only by pressing Enter and, perhaps, by pressing Backspace to delete a character or two after you had mistyped. For the most part, you left the cursor

Part
4

Supplied Applications

alone and it moved along by itself as you typed. But now you'll want to move up and down to fix misspelled words and make other changes. After all, it's the ability to move around freely in your document and make changes at will that makes a word processor so much more capable than a typewriter.

Moving the Cursor

The *cursor* marks the position where letters appear when you type—the *insertion point*. Editing your text involves moving the insertion point to the correct location and then inserting text, removing words, fixing misspellings, or marking blocks of text for moving, copying, or deletion.

The easiest way to move the cursor is just to point and click. When the mouse pointer is over the document window, it looks like a large letter *I* or a steel beam (this shape is often called the *I-beam pointer*). Move the I-beam pointer so that the vertical line is over the place in the text where you want to begin editing or typing. When you click, the blinking insertion point will jump from wherever it was to this new position.

NOTE   After positioning the cursor with the mouse, don't forget to click; otherwise, you'll end up making changes in the wrong place.

You can also use the arrow keys to move the cursor. This is often quicker than using the mouse when you only need to move the cursor by a few characters or lines.

Here are some exercises in cursor movement using both the mouse and the keyboard:

1. Move the mouse pointer to the second line of the story and click immediately to the left of the *t* in the word *sight*.

2. Press → and hold it down for a few seconds. Notice that the cursor moves one character to the right, pauses briefly, and then moves rapidly to the right. When it gets to the end of the first line, it wraps around to the start of the second line, continuing to the right from that point. Now press ← and hold it down. The cursor moves steadily to the left until it reaches the beginning of the line, then jumps to the end of the previous line. When the cursor gets to the beginning of the document, your computer starts to beep because the cursor can't go any farther.

3. Press ↓ to move the cursor down a line. If you hold down the key, the cursor will keep moving down until it reaches the last line in the text. (If a document has more text than will fit in the window, the text will scroll up a line at a time until the document end is reached.) To move up one line at a time, press ↑. Again, the text will scroll when you get to the top of the window until the cursor reaches the very first line.

4. Press Ctrl-→. Each press of the arrow key moves the cursor ahead one word. Ctrl-← moves it a word at a time in the other direction.

5. Press Ctrl-Home. The cursor jumps to the very beginning of the document. To jump to the end of the text, press Ctrl-End.

    Because writing relies heavily on the keyboard, WordPad provides several keyboard combinations that can be used to move the insertion point. These are listed in Table 19.1.

Key combination	Moves the insertion point...
↑	Up one line
↓	Down one line
←	Left one character
→	Right one character
Ctrl-←	Left one word
Ctrl-→	Right one word
Ctrl-Home	Beginning of document
Ctrl-End	End of document
Ctrl-PgUp	Top left of current window
Ctrl-PgDn	Bottom right of current window

Table 19.1   **Keyboard Combinations for Moving the Insertion Point**

Scrolling in the Document

Like other Windows programs, WordPad gives you a variety of ways to scroll through your document when the entire text doesn't fit in the window. Depending on the size of your WordPad window, the sample press release you've typed in probably does fit.

With the mouse, you scroll using the scroll bars. You can also use the arrow (cursor) keys to move right and left a character at a time or up and down a line at a time. Use the PgUp and PgDn keys to scroll your text a screen at a time.

Scrolling with the Mouse

When your entire document won't fit in the WordPad window, scroll bars appear in the work area along the right edge or at the bottom. A vertical scroll bar indicates the text is *longer* than the window, a horizontal bar means the text is *wider*. Because the sample document you've entered in this chapter fits in the maximized WordPad window, scroll bars will only be visible if you make the window smaller, as shown in Figure 19.4.

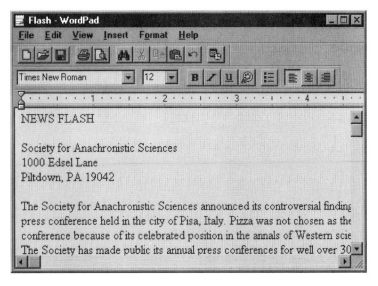

Figure 19.4 *This resized window has both horizontal and vertical scroll bars.*

Consider the vertical scroll bar to be a sort of measuring stick for your document, with the top of the bar representing the beginning of your document and the bottom of the bar the end. The elevator, that rectangular object that you slide along the scroll bar, shows you the relative position of the current window's text within the document.

By dragging the elevator to the approximate relative position you want to scroll to, you can get close to your desired spot quickly. You can also scroll by clicking in the scroll bar above or below the elevator.

The horizontal scroll bar works the same way as the vertical bar but is only useful if your document is more than a page wide.

Scrolling with the Keyboard

Scrolling with the keyboard can be more efficient than using the mouse because you don't have to take your hands off the keyboard.

1. Hold down the ↑ or ↓ key to move one line at a time. When you reach the top or bottom of the window, the text scrolls a line at a time as long as you hold down the key.

2. Press the PgUp key. Pressing PgUp moves you up one window toward the beginning of your document. Pressing PgDn has the opposite effect.

Making Selections in WordPad

Much of editing with a word processor centers around manipulating blocks of text. A *block* is a section of consecutive text characters (letters, numbers, punctuation, and so on). Blocks can be of any length. Many of the commands in Windows programs use this idea of manipulating blocks of information.

You must *select* a block before you can work with it. When you select a block, it becomes the center of attention to WordPad. As shown in Figure 19.5, WordPad highlights the block. Until you deselect it, WordPad treats the block differently than the rest of the document. For example, some menu commands will affect the selection and nothing else.

There are two main ways to select a text block: with the mouse, by dragging over the area you want to select, and with the keyboard, by holding down the Shift key while you move the cursor. We'll cover

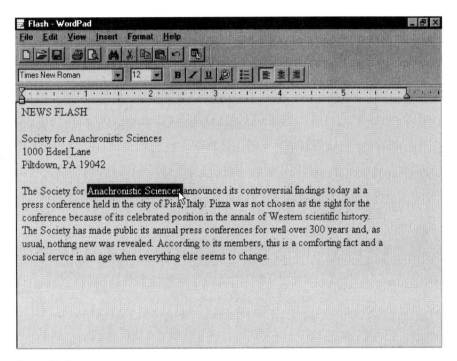

Figure 19.5   **The highlighted passage is a selected block of text.**

both methods in detail in a moment. You *deselect* when you click else-where, select elsewhere with the mouse, or move the cursor after let-ting up on the Shift key.

Once you've selected a block, be careful about the keys you press. If you type **A**, for example, the text of the whole block (the *selection*) will be replaced by the letter *A*. If this happens accidentally, choose Edit ▸ Undo or click on the Undo button on the Toolbar *before doing any-thing else*, and your text will be returned to its previous state.

After selecting a block of text, you can manipulate it in any number of ways: you can cut or copy it, change its font size, alter the paragraph formatting, and so forth. Try the following exercises to get the hang of selecting blocks.

Selecting an Arbitrary Text Area with the Mouse

Selection is particularly intuitive and simple with the mouse. Try this:

1. Deselect any possible selections you may have made already by clicking anywhere in the text.

2. Move the pointer to the beginning of a word somewhere (you may have to scroll the window).

3. Hold the left mouse button down and move the pointer down several lines. As you move the mouse, the selection extends. You'll notice that as soon as the pointer touches any part of each word in turn, the entire word becomes selected (unless someone has changed the relevant setting—see *Selecting Measurement Units and Controlling Word Selection* below). When you let up on the button, the selection is completed.

4. Click anywhere again to deselect the selection.

   The *anchor point* is the point you first clicked on. Dragging downward extends the selection downward from the anchor point. If you were to keep the mouse button down and drag *above* the anchor point, the selection would extend from the anchor point upward.

Selecting an Arbitrary Text Area with the Shift Key

You can also use the Shift key in combination with the arrow keys or the mouse to select an arbitrary amount of text:

1. Deselect anything you have already selected.

2. Move the cursor to the beginning of any word in the first paragraph. Now press Shift-→. The selection advances one letter with each press (unless you hold the key down too long, in which case it moves by itself and selects several letters).

3. Press Shift-↑ five times. Notice that as you move up past the anchor point, the selection reverses, moving upward in the text.

4. Press Shift-Ctrl-→. As the cursor jumps a word to the right, WordPad removes the selection highlighting from the characters it passes over.

5. Release the keys and click somewhere to deselect.

6. Click on the first word in the second paragraph (with the method you're testing now, this sets a new anchor point there).

7. Hold down the Shift key.

8. Click on a word in the middle of the paragraph. This changes the selection: It now extends from the new anchor point to the point where you clicked.

Selecting a Word or a Paragraph at a Time

Often you'll want to select a word or paragraph quickly, either to delete it or to change some aspect of it, such as its font size. You can do this easily by double-clicking (to select a word) or triple-clicking (for a paragraph). If you keep clicking rapidly, the selection alternates between the whole paragraph and the word under the pointer.

Selecting a Line or Series of Lines

There's a shortcut for selecting an entire line or quickly selecting a series of entire lines:

1. Move the mouse pointer into the left margin. It changes into an arrow pointing to the top right. This margin is called the *selection area.*

2. Position the pointer to the left of the first line of the first paragraph and click the mouse to select the entire line.

3. Starting from the same place, hold down the mouse button and drag the pointer down along the left margin. This selects each line the pointer passes.

Selecting an Entire Paragraph: An Alternative Method

Here's another shortcut for selecting an entire paragraph:

1. Move the cursor into the selection area (left margin) next to the first paragraph.

2. Double-click. The entire paragraph will be highlighted.

Holding down the Shift key while you drag the pointer in the margin selects additional paragraphs.

Selecting an Entire Sentence

If you need to change a particular sentence in its entirety, you can do so easily:

1. Hold down the Ctrl key.

2. Click anywhere in the document. The whole sentence containing the location you clicked on will be selected.

Selecting an Entire Document

Sometimes you'll want to select the whole document. This can be useful for changing the font size or type of all the text or changing other attributes, as discussed below. You have several choices for selecting an entire document. From the menu, you can choose Edit ➤ Select All. But try these simpler methods as well:

▶ Move the pointer into the selection area (the left margin of the document window). Hold down Ctrl and click the mouse. The entire document will be selected. Click anywhere in the text to deselect it.

▶ Move the pointer back to the selection area. This time, triple-click to select the whole document. Again, deselect it by clicking elsewhere.

▶ The keyboard shortcut for selecting the whole document is Ctrl-A.

Making Some Changes to the Text

Now that you know how to get around and select portions of text, you can begin to correct some of the typos in your letter.

Deleting Letters

Let's start with the second sentence of the first paragraph, where the word *site* is misspelled as *sight*:

1. Position the cursor between the *i* and *g* in *sight*.

2. Press Del. This removes the misplaced *g*. Notice also that the space closed up where the *g* was when you deleted the letter, pulling the letters to the left to close the gap.

3. Press Del again to remove the *h*.

4. Move the cursor one character to the right and add the *e*.

Notice that the line opened up to let the *e* in. Unlike on a typewritten page, lines on a computer screen are flexible, letting you insert the letter—in fact, so flexible that you may have noticed that WordPad re-wraps all the lines of the paragraph almost instantly as you insert text.

Many simple errors can be fixed using the Del or Backspace key. But suppose you wanted to delete an entire word, sentence, or paragraph. You could do this by moving to the beginning or end of the section you wanted to erase and then holding down Del or Backspace, respectively, until the key repeated and erased all the words, letter by letter. But this is a slow and potentially risky method. If you're not careful, you may well erase more than you intended to. This where selecting a text block comes in.

Deleting Words

For our second change, find the word *not* in the second sentence, the one that now begins "Pizza was not chosen..." So the paragraph makes more sense, delete the *not* as follows:

1. Select the word *not* with one of the techniques you learned earlier.

2. You have several choices for removing the word. You can press Del or Backspace to remove the offending word permanently. Choosing Edit ➤ Clear has the same effect, it just takes a little longer.

> **TIP** If you delete a word accidentally with any of these techniques, you can retrieve it by choosing Edit ➤ Undo or clicking on the Undo button before you make any other changes. And if you want to remove a word but save it on the Clipboard for later use, you would cut it—you'll learn how to cut selected blocks a bit later.

But what if you want to *replace* a word, not just delete it? WordPad gives you a shortcut method for doing just that.

1. Select the misspelled *Pizza* in the first sentence.

2. With *Pizza* highlighted, type in **Pisa**. Notice that as soon as you type the first letter, *P*, it replaces the entire selection. This saves the extra

step of pressing Del or choosing Clear from the Edit menu. (You may have to add a space after the word, depending on how you selected *Pizza*.)

All of this may seem like a lot of work just to change a few letters, but for larger selections you will find it's worth the effort.

Inserting Letters

You can insert any number of letters, words, or paragraphs wherever you want within a document. This is called *inserting* because as you type new characters, they appear within the existing text, which is pushed to the right as you type.

Some word processors allow you to deactivate insertion in favor of *overwriting*, where newly typed letters replace the old ones instead of pushing them to the right. WordPad does not let you do this. The advantage is that you will never accidentally type over some text you want to keep. The disadvantage is that you will have to take action to delete unwanted text.

TIP   If you need to insert characters that aren't available on your keyboard—such as ™, ©, or ¥—use the Character Map accessory, covered in Chapter 22.

Moving Selected Blocks

The editing process often involves moving large portions of text, such as sentences and paragraphs, within a document. Rather than inserting a block of text by retyping it, you can pick it up and move it from one place to another with the Cut, Copy, and Paste commands covered here. And WordPad also gives you a snazzy drag-and-drop method for moving text around with the mouse.

Moving Blocks with Cut and Paste Commands

Here's an example of the Paste command that will reverse the order of the first two paragraphs in our letter:

1. Move to the top of the document.

2. Select the "News Flash" line (this is a one-line paragraph) with what-ever technique you prefer—and carefully select the blank line immedi-ately below the paragraph, too, because you want a blank line between the paragraphs after the move. This second line is also a *paragraph* as far as WordPad is concerned. If you're selecting by dragging, just drag the mouse a little further down. If you double-clicked in the margin to select the first paragraph, press Shift to retain the paragraph selec-tion and then double-click to the left of the blank line. You'll know the blank line is selected when a thin strip at the left margin becomes highlighted (this is the normally invisible *paragraph mark* associated with the blank line):

TIP Every paragraph has a paragraph mark. Paragraph attributes such as alignment, tab settings, and margins are contained in it. Copying this mark is an easy way of copying attributes from one place to another.

---

3. Now it's time to cut the block. You have three choices: You can choose Cut from the Edit menu, click on the Cut button on the Tool-bar, or press Ctrl-X on the keyboard.

4. Move the insertion point to the place where you want to insert the paragraph, which happens to be just before the *T* of the word *The* in the first main paragraph.

5. Paste the paragraph back into your document. You can click on the Paste button on the Toolbar (the one that shows a small piece of paper and a clipboard), choose Edit ➤ Paste, or press Ctrl-V.

Sometimes after moving paragraphs around, you may have to do a lit-tle adjusting, such as inserting or deleting a line or some spaces. You can always insert a line with Enter. If you have extra blank lines after a move, you can delete them by putting the insertion point on the first space of a blank line (the far-left margin) and pressing the Backspace key.

Just a reminder: once you've placed text (or any other information) on the Clipboard, you can reuse it as many times as you like because it stays on the Clipboard until you replace it with new information by using the Cut or Copy commands.

Moving Blocks Using the Right Mouse Button

In WordPad, clicking the right mouse button over the document pops up a small menu offering immediate access to the most common editing commands, as shown in Figure 19.6.

Here's how to move the paragraph back with this method:

1. Select the paragraph again.

2. Click the right mouse button anywhere over the selected block. The pop-up menu shown in Figure 19.6 appears.

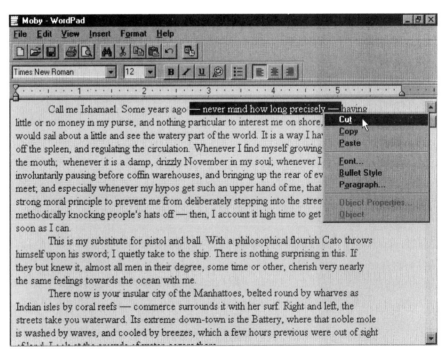

Figure 19.6   *WordPad's pop-up menu, displayed when you click the right mouse button*

3. Choose Cut from the pop-up menu.

4. Position the pointer where you want the text to go and click, again with the right button. From the pop-up menu, choose Paste.

Copying Blocks of Text

There are times when you want to move existing text to a new location without deleting the original. That's when you need the Copy command. After selecting a block of text, use Copy instead of Cut to place a copy of the passage on the Clipboard. Then move the cursor to the spot where you want the copy and Paste it in. As usual, you have several alternatives for copying a selected block to the clipboard. You can

▶ click on the Copy button, the one that shows two overlapping pieces of paper

▶ click the right mouse button, then choose Copy from the pop-up menu

▶ choose Edit ➤ Copy

▶ press Ctrl-C

After you've copied the text to the Clipboard, you paste it in just as you would when moving a text block.

Moving Blocks with Drag and Drop

WordPad gives you yet another method for moving a block of text within a document. With drag-and-drop editing, you *pick up* the block with the mouse and *drop* it into place without ever having to fuss with menus, buttons, or keyboard commands.

This time, move the third full paragraph in the story to the very end of the document. Here's how:

1. Select the paragraph.

2. Click anywhere within the selection and hold the button down.

3. Very slowly (just for this exercise), begin to move the pointer while holding the button down. Notice that the pointer becomes a white arrow with a dotted line at its tip and a small dotted rectangle at its base as soon as you begin to move it.

4. Move the pointer so that the dotted line is over the very end of the document (when you get to the bottom of the window, the text will scroll automatically if the end isn't visible) and release the button. The paragraph reappears at its new location.

A couple of points about drag-and-drop editing bear mentioning. First, no matter where you click on a selected block as you start to drag it, the entire block will appear—beginning at the pointer location—when you let go of the mouse button.

Second, don't panic if you realize you've made a mistake after you've started dragging a block. One way out is to press the Esc key before releasing the mouse button. You can also move the pointer back to the original block, releasing it anywhere in the block. The insertion point moves to the spot where the pointer is, but the block itself remains in place. Finally, you can let up on the mouse button wherever you happen to be when you discover your mistake and immediately use Undo to restore the block to its original location.

Inserting the Date or Time in a Document

One of WordPad's few frills is a special command that automatically inserts today's date or the current time into your document. For dates, you have many choices for the style WordPad uses. Depending on the document's intended audience, you can pick an abbreviated format such as 12/12/95 or let WordPad write out the full date, as in December 12, 1995. For the time, you can choose between two versions of the 12-hour AM/PM format that most people use and the 24-hour military format.

 NOTE WordPad always records the complete current time—down to the second—in your text. You probably won't want the seconds to appear in most documents, so you'll need to delete them after the Insert Date and Time dialog box has closed.

To insert the date or time:

1. Choose Insert ➤ Date and Time; or, if the Toolbar is visible, click on the Date and Time button shown below. The Insert Date and Time dialog box appears.

2. In the dialog box, choose your preferred style for the date or time from the list. The list offers more choices than will fit in the box, so you should scroll through if you don't see the style you want.

3. Click on OK to insert the chosen information in your document.

Formatting Paragraphs

Paragraphs are the most essential division of your text when it comes to *formatting*, which simply means controlling the looks of your document. A paragraph is defined by WordPad as any text terminated by pressing the Enter key. So even a single letter, line, or word will be treated as a paragraph if you press Enter after typing it. For that matter, pressing Enter on a completely blank line creates a paragraph, albeit an empty one.

WordPad handles each paragraph as a separate entity, each with its own formatting information. The press release you created early in the chapter uses a standard block-paragraph format typical of many business letters. In that format, a paragraph's first line is not indented, so you separate paragraphs with an empty paragraph. Also notice that the right margin is *ragged*, rather than aligned evenly—or *justified*—as it is on the left.

These and other qualities affecting the looks of your paragraphs can be altered while you are entering text or at any time thereafter. As you change the format settings, you immediately see the effects. Bold letters will look bold, centered lines centered, italic letters look slanted, and so forth.

For most documents, you may find that you are happy with WordPad's default format. WordPad applies the standard default format for you, carrying it from one paragraph to the next as you type. If you decide you'd rather use a different format for a new document, just alter some settings before typing anything. Then everything you type into the new document will be formatted accordingly until you change the settings again.

The *ruler* helps you keep track of where you are typing on the page, much like the guide on a typewriter. It also lets you alter the format of paragraphs by clicking on various symbols displayed within its boundaries. These alterations can also be made from the Paragraph menu and from the pop-up menu displayed when you click the right mouse button, but making changes on the ruler is probably easiest. The ruler and its sections are shown below.

The ruler may be off (*hidden*), but you can turn it on or off at will: Choose View ➤ Ruler. This command is a *toggle*: if the ruler is off, choosing the command displays it; if it is already on, choosing this command hides it.

Hiding the ruler lets you see extra lines of your text in the document window, but the ruler is useful to have around. The ruler has markings on it to help you gauge where your text will fall across the printed page and to help you set up tab stops. Each inch is marked with a number, and each tenth of an inch is marked by a small line. (You can change the ruler to show centimeters or other units via the Options dialog box.)

Notice the small markers at either end of the ruler. On the left are two triangular shapes: one along the top of the ruler, the other along the bottom; the lower one rests atop a small block. At the right side of the ruler, there's a single upward-pointing marker.

The lower markers at either end indicate the current paragraph's left and right indents (these are sometimes called *margin settings*, but remember that they affect the current paragraph, not the whole page). The upper marker on the left indicates the setting of the first-line indent for each paragraph. Actually, these markers do more than mark the current settings—you can use them to change the settings as well.

The ruler also shows tab settings. WordPad's built-in tab stops are marked by tiny gray dots along the lower border of the ruler. When you set your own tab, it appears on the ruler as a heavy black L-shaped mark in the ruler proper.

Viewing and Altering Paragraph Settings

Paragraph formatting falls into three categories with WordPad: *alignment*, *spacing*, and *indents*. The following sections explain and illustrate these categories. Unless otherwise noted, the examples here use inches as the basic unit of measure. If you wish to indicate another unit, such as centimeters, you can use the View ➤ Options command to do so.

Alignment

Alignment refers to where the text in a paragraph sits within the margins. *Left* is the default, causing text to be flush with the left margin (and ragged right). *Center* centers every line of the paragraph. *Right* causes text to be flush with the right margin (and ragged left).

Figure 19.7 shows three paragraphs, each one with a different type of alignment. To display or modify the settings for a given paragraph, click anywhere on it and then view or change the setting either from the Format Bar or from the Format Paragraph dialog box. Anytime you position the insertion point in a paragraph, the rulers and menu will reflect that paragraph's current settings.

> **CAUTION**   WordPad does not permit you to create fully justified paragraphs, that is, paragraphs whose text is flush on both the right and left. If you need justified paragraphs, you'll have to use another word processor.

Viewing Paragraph Alignment

1. Move the insertion point to the paragraph in question and click.

2. If the Format Bar is visible, look at it. The alignment buttons will indicate the current setting—the button for that setting looks like it has been pressed, as shown below.

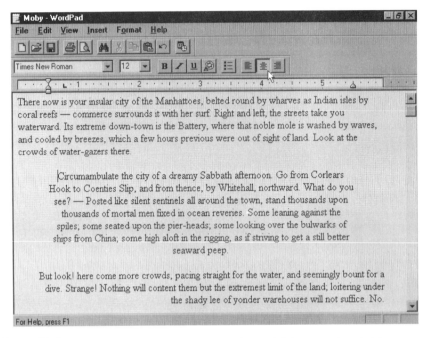

Figure 19.7   Three types of alignment (from top to bottom): left, centered, and right

3. To open the Format Paragraph dialog box (Figure 19.9) you can choose Format ➤ Paragraph or click the right mouse button with the pointer over the paragraph and then pick Paragraph from the pop-up menu. At the bottom of the Format Paragraph dialog box you'll see the current paragraph's alignment setting. On the next page you can see how the dialog box looks for a centered paragraph with a first-line *outdent* (true, that's an unlikely combination, but notice that outdents are specified by typing negative numbers).

Changing Paragraph Alignment

You can change the settings for a paragraph almost as easily as you can display them:

1. Move the insertion point to the paragraph or select several paragraphs (even a portion of each paragraph will suffice).

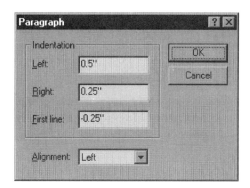

2. Open the Format Paragraph dialog box (choose Format ➤ Paragraph or right-click and choose Paragraph). In the Alignment drop-down list box, choose the alignment setting you want.

3. As an alternative, if the Format Bar is showing, click on one of its three alignment buttons (this is faster).

Indents

Indents fall into three categories: *right*, *left*, and *first-line indent*. Every paragraph has settings for each, and each paragraph's settings can be different. As with the other paragraph settings, these are carried from one paragraph to the next as you type, or you can change them after the fact. You set indents via the Paragraph menu's Indents command or by dragging the indent symbols on the ruler shown below to change the left, first line, and right indents.

The settings determine how far in from the left and right margins your text will appear. (They do not determine how far from the edge of the page the text will appear, however. That's established by the *margins,* discussed later in this chapter.) The first-line indent determines the starting position of the first line of each paragraph.

Setting the Left or Right Indent

You can change the left or right indent by either typing new settings into the Format Paragraph dialog box or using the ruler. Here's the first method:

1. Place the insertion point in a paragraph or select several paragraphs whose settings you want to change.

2. Choose Format ➤ Paragraph or right-click and choose Paragraph from the pop-up menu. The Format Paragraph dialog box (shown in Figure 19.9) will appear. Type in the desired indent and click on OK. If you just type in a number, it's assumed to be in inches. You can type **cm** after the number to indicate centimeters, **pt** to indicate typesetter's points, or **pi** for typesetter's picas.

    If the number you enter isn't acceptable, WordPad will tell you. This usually happens when you accidentally enter a value that is too large for the paper your printer driver is set up for.

    You can also use the ruler to change the left or right indent:

1. Place the insertion point in the paragraph or select several paragraphs whose settings you want to change.

2. Turn on the ruler, if it's off, by choosing View ➤ Ruler.

3. Drag the left-indent marker in the ruler—the lower triangular symbol—to its new position. First, try grabbing the block *underneath* the triangular portion of the marker. This moves the block, the triangle that rests on it, *and* the other triangular marker, the one at the top of the ruler. When you let go of the mouse button, the paragraph's left indent moves to the new location. Notice that the first line has moved too, even if it had been indented or outdented. It retains its indent relative to the left indent of the other lines.

4. Now try dragging the left-indent marker by grabbing the lower triangle. This time, the top triangle remains where it is; when you release the button, all the other lines move to align with the new left indent.

Setting the First-Line Indent

On a typewriter, you have to hit the Tab key if you want to indent the first line of each paragraph. It's easier to let WordPad do it for you with its first-line indent setting. This also lets you modify the look of a letter after you've written it because you can adjust the first-line indents.

The first-line indent setting establishes the relative indent for the first line of each new paragraph. Note that the setting is *in addition to* the left indent. So if the left indent is 1 inch and the first-line indent is 0.5 inch, the first line will start 1.5 inches from the left margin. Incidentally, setting the first-line indent to a negative number, such as -0.5, will cause it to hang out that amount from the left indent. This is sometimes called a *hanging indent* or an *outdent*. To change the first-line indent:

1. Place the insertion point in the paragraph—or select several paragraphs—whose settings you want to change.

2. Choose Format ➤ Paragraph or right-click and choose Paragraph. The Format Paragraph dialog box will appear. Type in the first-line indent amount and click on OK.

As an alternative, drag the first-line indent marker (the upper triangle on the left side of the ruler) to the new indent position.

In either case, WordPad will immediately reformat the paragraph in accordance with the new settings. Figure 19.8 shows examples of three different indent setups.

Creating Bulleted Paragraphs

One of the most common conventions in business and technical writing is the use of *bullets* to set off the items in a list. The standard bullet—and the one WordPad uses—is a heavy circular spot, though a bullet can be any symbol offset to the left of a paragraph. Bulleted text is useful for, and illustrated by, the following items:

▶ calling attention to the individual benefits or features of a product or service

▶ listing a set of options

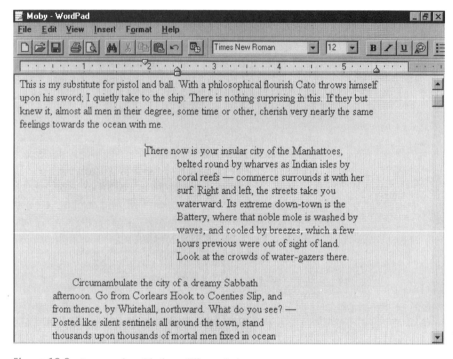

Figure 19.8   **Paragraphs with three different indent setups**

▶ itemizing the parts or supplies needed for a given job

WordPad can automatically add a bullet to any paragraph or to each paragraph in a selected block of text. WordPad places the bullet at the original left indent of the paragraph, shifting the rest of the paragraph to the right (the position changes are accomplished by adjusting the left indent and first-line indent settings, as you can see on the ruler).

The Bullet Style command works as a toggle: If the paragraph already has a bullet, the Bullet command removes the bullet.

To apply bullets to an unbulleted paragraph or group of paragraphs:

1. Place the cursor in the paragraph to be bulleted or select a group of paragraphs.

2. Choose Format ➤ Bullet Style or, if the Format Bar is visible, click on the Bullet button shown below.

Reformatting the Whole Document

You'll often want to reformat an entire document. That is, you'll print out the document, look at it, and realize you should have used larger (or smaller) type or perhaps that it should have smaller (or larger) first-line indents.

Select the whole document first, then change the settings.

Formatting Characters

WordPad includes commands for altering the look of the individual letters on the printed page. This is called *character formatting*. You can use character formatting to emphasize a section of text by making it bold, underlined, or italicized, or you may want to change the size or the font.

> NOTE   As with all Windows programs, WordPad measures character sizes in *points*. Typical point sizes are 9 to 14 for ordinary text. (This book is printed in 11 point Plantin.) Newspaper headlines may appear in anything up to 60 points or so.

Just as with paragraph formatting, WordPad starts you off with a standard character format: a conventional, unobtrusive font (Times New Roman) at a standard size (10 points). But you can change character formatting to your heart's content. WordPad gives you three ways to modify character formatting:

- from the Format bar
- from the Fonts dialog box
- with shortcut Ctrl-key combinations to change type styles

You can change the formatting of individual characters, selected blocks of text, or the whole document. Character formatting applies to paragraphs as a whole only if they're actually selected.

Formatting Existing Characters

To change the formatting of characters you've already typed, begin by selecting the text character(s) to be altered. You can select a single letter, a sentence, a paragraph, the whole document, or any arbitrary sequence of characters. Now you have three choices:

▶ Use the controls on the Format Bar to alter individual format characteristics (font, size, and so forth). This is a quick way to control any aspect of character format.

▶ Use keyboard shortcuts to modify the text style (boldface, italics, or underlining). This is the quickest way to change these styles, but you have to memorize the shortcuts and you can't control other aspects of character format.

▶ Use the Fonts dialog box to set all the format characteristics from a single window. This lets you see a sample of how your text will look as you experiment with different formatting choices.

CAUTION   Expect lower print quality if you add boldface or italics when you don't have separate fonts installed for those styles. Windows lets you add boldface or italics to any installed font, even if you haven't installed the bold or italics versions of the font. When the actual bold font is missing, Windows just makes the characters thicker. When the italics font is missing, it simply slants the regular font. See Chapter 9 for details on how fonts work in Windows 95.

Changing Character Format with the Format Bar

Here's how to use the Format Bar to change character formatting:

1. If the Format Bar isn't already visible, choose View ▶ Format Bar to activate it.

NOTE   The icon next to the font name tells you whether it is a TrueType or Printer font. Note that the type of font you choose affects the range of available sizes. Scalable fonts such as TrueType and PostScript (Type 1) fonts can be used in virtually any size, while other fonts have a set number of specific font sizes available.

2. To change the font of the selected text, choose the new font name from the drop-down list box at the left side of the Format Bar.

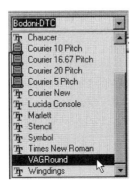

3. To change the text size, you can pick a new size from the next list box or type in the size you want (WordPad only allows integer font sizes—fractional values won't work).

4. To turn styles (boldface, italics, or underlining) on or off, click on the appropriate button. When the style is active, the appropriate button looks like it has been pressed.

Finally, to change the color of the selected text, click on the button that displays an artist's palette and pick your color from the list that appears.

Note that you can change these settings in any combination. For example, a single selection can be italicized, underlined, and displayed in fuschia—if you're willing to take some serious liberties with typesetting etiquette.

After you've returned to your document and deselected the block, the Format Bar shows you the current formatting of the character or selection. If the character or selection has been italicized, for example, the button for italics appears pushed.

You can see at a glance if a selected block contains more than one style, font, or font size. For example, if only part of the block is set to bold, the Format Bar button for bold appears translucent. If the block contains two or more different fonts, the entry in the box for fonts will be blank.

Changing Character Format with the Fonts Dialog Box

If you're willing to give up the space on your screen to display the Format Bar, you might want to use the Fonts dialog box to see a sample of your character-formatting choices before you apply them. Otherwise, if your formatting experiments prove unsuccessful, you'll have to reset all the settings for the selected block individually.

To modify character formatting with the Fonts dialog box:

1. With the text selected, choose Format ➤ Fonts or right-click and choose Fonts. You'll see the Fonts dialog box.

2. In the dialog box, you can make changes to any of the character-formatting settings you wish. When you're through, click on OK.

Changing Character Formats with Keyboard Shortcuts

You can also use keyboard shortcuts (these also are toggles) to modify the character styles (bold, italics, and underlining) of a selected block. Use Ctrl-B for bold, Ctrl-I for italics, and Ctrl-U for underlining.

Formatting Characters as You Type

You can also change the appearance of text as you type. Subsequent characters will be entered with the new settings—and the settings will remain in force until changed. For instance, you would press Ctrl-B once to start typing bold characters and then press it again when you're ready to type more unbolded text.

Working with Tabs

As with a typewriter, you can vary WordPad's tab settings to suit your needs. For complex multicolumn tables, you'll probably want to set up your own custom tab stops. Default tabs are already set up across the page in half-inch increments. If you haven't set tabs yourself, the half-inch markers—small gray dots on the ruler's lower border—indicate the locations of the default tabs.

For each paragraph—or any selected group of paragraphs—you can also place as many as 32 of your own tabs. These show up as heavy L-shaped markers in the ruler, as you can see in this detailed view:

NOTE   When you set a tab manually, WordPad automatically eliminates all default tab stops to its left.

You can set and alter tabs from the Tabs dialog box or from the ruler.

Setting Tab Stops from the Ruler

If you're good with the mouse, setting tabs is much easier and faster with the ruler. Here's how to do it:

1. Get the ruler on screen (choose View ➤ Ruler if it's not already visible).

2. To position a tab, click inside the ruler at the place where you want the tab. You can drag the tab marker left and right to adjust its placement any time. The text affected will be adjusted immediately.

Setting Tab Stops from a Dialog Box

To set tabs from a dialog box, choose Format ➤ Tabs or right-click over the paragraph or selection and choose Tabs from the pop-up menu. A dialog box appears, as shown below.

All you need to do is type in the exact location for each new tab stop and choose Set. You can set tabs in any order (for example, you could set a tab at 4.5 inches, then set a second at 2.5 inches). When you choose Set, WordPad inserts the tabs in order.

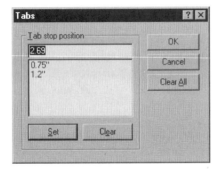

Type the position in inches (or whatever measurement unit you're using in the Options dialog box). Three custom tabs are shown above: .75 inches, 1.2 inches, and 2.69 inches.

After you click on OK, the tabs will be set. The ruler will have new tab markers in it to indicate the new tab positions, and the text will be adjusted immediately.

Repositioning Existing Tab Stops

It's easy to adjust existing tabs to improve the layout of a table or list without ever having to retype columns or add or delete spaces between them. The quickest way to change a tab's location is with the ruler. Just drag the tab to its new location. If you want more precision, you can use the Tabs dialog box—but you have to first clear the existing tab stop, then set a new one at the desired location.

Clearing Custom Tab Stops

You can clear any of your custom tab stops at any time, either from the ruler or from the dialog box. To clear a tab from the ruler, simply drag the tab marker from the ruler down into the document as though you were pulling it off the ruler. It will disappear.

Any text formerly aligned at that tab will move right to the next custom tab stop. If there are no remaining custom tab stops, the text moves to the appropriate default tab.

To clear tabs from the dialog box:

1. Choose Format ➤ Tabs. The Tabs dialog box appears.

2. Find the tab stop you want to clear in the list box and click on it. It will appear in the entry box above the list.

3. Choose Clear to zap the tab stop, removing it from the screen.

4. Click on OK. Any text aligned at deleted tabs will move right to the next one.

To remove all your custom tab stops in one step, choose the Clear All button in the Tabs dialog box.

Using Undo to Reverse Mistakes

WordPad makes allowances for our imperfections via the Undo command. In a split second, a slip of the mouse—choosing Clear instead of Cut—can send a large block of text to oblivion instead of to the Clipboard.

Undo is, quite understandably, the first selection on the Edit menu. But you can access Undo even faster if the Toolbar is visible: Just click on the button showing an arrow with a curved stem.

Undo can reverse the following:

▶ block deletions made with the Delete command from the Edit menu or the Del key on the keyboard

▶ individual or multiple letters that you erased using the Del or Backspace keys. Unfortunately, it will return only the last letter or series of letters erased. Once you move the cursor to another location using any of the cursor-movement keys and delete again, the text in the previous deletion is lost.

▶ selected blocks directly deleted and replaced by typing new text on the keyboard

▶ new text you typed in. This can be undone back to the last time you issued a command.

▶ character- and paragraph-formatting changes (if you select the Undo command immediately after making the change)

When you realize you've done something that you regret, select Edit ➤ Undo or click on the Undo button on the Toolbar. Remember, though, that the Undo command can only recall the last action. If you decide you have made a mistake, either while entering or deleting, you must undo the damage before using any other editing or formatting commands.

Searching for and Replacing Text

WordPad offers Find and Replace commands to look for specific letters, words, or series of words in your text. Once the word processor finds the text, you can have it automatically replace that text with other text if you wish. Though WordPad calls these searching commands Find and Replace, this type of operation is also referred to as *search and replace*.

You can also use searching to get to a particular place in your document quickly. If you put unique markers (for example, *##1* or *aaa*) in your text, you can search for them to move from one part of a document to another specific point.

Using Find and Replace together, you can replace abbreviations with words. For example, in preparing the manuscript for this book, I replaced *W* with *Windows* and *wp* with *word processor*. This eliminated a lot of repetitive typing.

Finding a Specific Word or Text String

Here's how to use Find to locate a specific word or group of words:

1. Choose Edit ➤ Find, press Ctrl-F, or, if the Toolbar is visible, click on the Find button (the one showing binoculars). The dialog box you see in Figure 19.9 will appear.

2. Type the text you're searching for and press Enter or click on Find Next. The cursor moves to the next instance of that text.

3. To find out if there are any other occurrences of the text, click on Find Next again or just press Enter. WordPad will try to find the text again. WordPad always remembers the last word you searched for so you can repeat the action more easily. It also scrolls the document for you so you can see the text if and when it's found.

> **TIP** Here's a shortcut for finding other occurrences of text in your document: Select the text, then bring up the Find dialog box. WordPad will have entered the text for you in the *Find what:* area, so you can immediately click on Find Next.

When there are no further occurrences of the text you're searching for and the entire document has been searched, a dialog box will appear saying:

    WordPad has finished searching the document.

Just press Enter or click on OK.

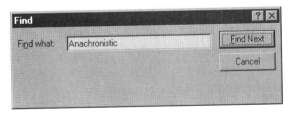

Figure 19.9   *The Find dialog box. Type the word you want to find—here, it is Anachronistic.*

The Find command always starts at the current cursor location and searches to the end of the document. Then it wraps around to the beginning and continues until it reaches the cursor again.

Keep in mind that you can move the Find dialog box around the screen. Although WordPad automatically moves the Find window so you can see text that has been found, you may want to move the Find window so you can see other parts of the document. The Find window stays on the screen, ready for searching, until you close it.

Another handy command lets you repeat the previous search without the Find dialog box. After using Find to search for your text the first time, close the box. Now whenever you want to repeat the search, either choose Edit ➤ Repeat Last Find or simply press F3.

Replacing Specific Words

To replace a text string with another text string, you use the Replace dialog box:

1. Choose Edit ➤ Replace or press Ctrl-H. A Replace dialog box appears, slightly larger than the one for Find. There is an additional text area in the dialog box called Replace With. This is where you type in the text that you want the found text to be changed to.

2. Now click on Find Next, Replace, or Replace All. Here's what each does:

Find Next	Finds the next occurrence of the word, but doesn't change anything.
Replace	Changes the next or currently highlighted occurrence of the word and then moves on to find and highlight the next occurrence.
Replace All	Automatically finds and changes all occurrences of the word. You don't get to see what's happening.

3. Depending on which option you chose, you may want to continue the process by clicking again on a button.

4. Close the window when you're through by clicking on Close.

Copying between Two Documents

You may often need to copy portions of text between two documents. Many professionals use word processors because they can use *boiler-plate text* to piece together new documents from existing ones. This is particularly useful for constructing legal documents or contracts that regularly include standard clauses or paragraphs. A more domestic example is creating a series of somewhat similar letters to a number of friends.

Because Windows lets you have multiple programs running at once, you have a fair amount of flexibility here. Though WordPad doesn't let you open more than one *document* at a time, Windows *will* let you run more than one *session* of WordPad. So you can run WordPad for each document you want to open.

Once your documents are open, you can select text from one, copy or cut it, and then open another window, position the cursor, and paste it in. Adjust the windows so you can see enough of each document to easily select and insert text. Figure 19.10 shows an example of two WordPad documents open simultaneously.

Of course you can use the multiple WordPad windows for simply writing or viewing more than one document at a time, too. For example, you may be working on several news stories, several letters, or several chapters of a book. Just minimize the documents you're not actively working on but want to have close at hand.

Here are the general steps for opening two WordPad documents and transferring material between them:

1. Minimize any other running applications. The quick way to do this is to click with the right button over any empty part of the Windows Taskbar and choose Minimize All Windows from the pop-up menu that appears.

2. Run WordPad and open the first document (or just leave the window as is if you're creating a new document).

3. Run another copy of WordPad from the Start menu and open the file from which you're going to be cutting or copying.

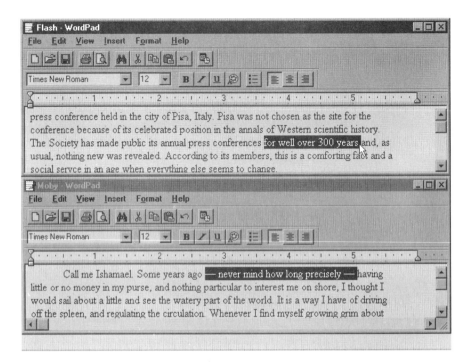

Figure 19.10   *You can run multiple copies of WordPad and load a different document into each window. This lets you transfer material easily between them or switch between writing tasks.*

4. Adjust the windows so you can see both. Again, the quick way is to right-click on the Taskbar, then choose Tile Horizontally from the pop-up menu.

5. You can now move information between the windows to your heart's content.

Hyphenating

WordPad does not hyphenate your text automatically. As a result, some lines will be too short because WordPad has to push an entire large word to the next line. In WordPad, the only cure for such layout problems is to insert the missing hyphens manually. You should do this as the very last step you take before printing a document. Otherwise, if you make any further changes in your text—whether it's adding or deleting text or changing paragraph or character formatting—the line layout will likely change, and the entire word you hyphenated will now appear on a single line with the hyphen still visible (if this happens, just delete the hyphen).

Here's what you should do:

1. Find the optimal hyphenation point in the long word at the beginning of the next line, move the cursor to that point, and type a hyphen.

2. Then move the cursor to the beginning of the line and press Backspace. The newly hyphenated word will split, with the first section being pulled up to join the last word on the previous line. Press the Spacebar to separate the two words again.

You may find that when you press Backspace, the last word from the previous line jumps down to join the hyphenated word. If this happens, it means that even the first part of the hyphenated word will not fit on the previous line. Go back to the word and remove the optional hyphen.

TIP If you edit your text or change the formatting after hyphenating it, be sure the changes don't cause hyphenated words to move to locations where the hyphens are inappropriate. The easiest way to check for this is to use the Find command to search your document for all occurrences of a hyphen.

Adding Graphics to Your WordPad Document

Although it's sort of a bare-bones word processor, WordPad *does* allow you to insert pictures or graphics—and all kinds of other *objects* such as charts, video sequences, and sounds—into your documents. We'll focus on graphics for the moment, but the steps you'll learn here apply to other types of objects as well.

With this insertion feature you can add your company logo to every letter you print, put your picture on your letterhead, or put a map on a party announcement. Figure 19.11 shows examples of graphics inserted into WordPad documents.

You can't *create* graphics with WordPad itself—you have to get them from other Windows applications such as Paint. But you can use just

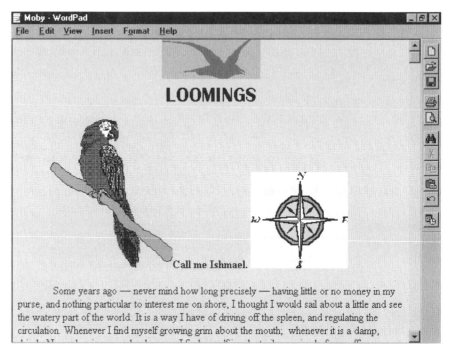

Figure 19.11   Examples of graphics in WordPad documents. Graphics are imported from the Clipboard and then can be moved and sized.

about any kind of image in your WordPad documents. To add a photo, for example, you would have the photograph digitized with a scanner, then copy the picture onto the Clipboard and paste it into WordPad.

Once you've inserted graphics in the document, you can then cut, copy, or paste them. You can also change a graphic's size or move it around.

The simplest way to handle graphics in WordPad is to treat them as isolated items copied as independent chunks directly into the document via the Clipboard. But with a little more effort, you can maintain a connection between the graphic and the other application that created it. That way, you can edit the graphic from within WordPad— you don't have to return to the application that created the picture to make changes and then recopy the graphic to WordPad. Windows calls this feature *object linking* and *embedding*, or OLE. Chapter 6 covers object linking and embedding in detail.

Importing a Graphic from the Clipboard

To import a graphic into your document, follow these steps:

1. Place the picture on the Clipboard by switching to the source application, such as Paint, and choosing the Copy or Cut commands (in Paint and many other applications, you'll have to select the portion of the image you want before you copy or cut). You can then paste almost any image that can be cut or copied into WordPad.

2. Open the WordPad document or activate its window.

3. Position the insertion point on the line where you want the picture to start and select Edit ➤ Paste.

   The graphic will be dropped into the document at the insertion point. Figure 19.12 shows an example. Now you can move it or resize it with the methods explained next.

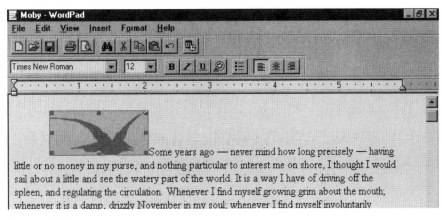

Figure 19.12   *A graphic copied from Paint into a WordPad document. The small squares at the corners and along the edges are the handles.*

Positioning the Graphic

Once you've pasted a graphic into WordPad, you have only crude control over positioning it where you want it in the document. You can't move a graphic around with the mouse, and there's no menu command for this purpose. Instead, you must "push" the picture around in your document with ordinary typing.

NOTE   WordPad automatically adjusts the spacing between lines so that the graphic fits without overlapping the line above it—just as it does if you change the text size.

It helps to know that WordPad treats an inserted graphic or other object as if it were a single text character. The bottom edge of the graphic sits on the line of text marked by the insertion point.

If you insert a graphic into a separate paragraph—so that it's the only "character" in the paragraph—you can use WordPad's paragraph alignment commands to position the image. With the insertion point on the same line as the graphic, click on any of the alignment buttons on the Format bar or use the Format ➤ Paragraph command to choose the correct alignment.

Otherwise, you can move the graphic by typing characters to the left or right on that same line. If the right edge of the graphic passes the right-indent setting for the current paragraph, WordPad wraps the graphic down a line, repositioning it on the left side just as when wrapping text.

To move a graphic, then, begin by positioning the insertion point to its left. Now:

▶ Press Backspace to move it to the left (or up a line, if it's already at the left side of the paragraph).

▶ Press the Spacebar or Tab to move it to the right.

▶ Press Enter to move it down in the file.

Another way to change the *vertical* location of a graphic is to select it (by clicking on it), cut it to the Clipboard, click where you want to move the graphic, and paste it into place.

Sizing the Graphic

You can resize a graphic, too. Here's how:

1. Select the graphic by clicking on it. The rectangular frame indicating the boundaries of the graphic appears, with small black squares called *handles* at the corners and at the center of each side.

2. Drag the handles to resize the graphic. You can resize in both the horizontal and vertical dimensions by dragging a corner handle. Drag a side handle if you want to resize in one dimension only.

3. When you're finished stretching or shrinking the image, release the mouse button. If you don't like the results, Undo will return the graphic to its previous size.

   Notice that you can distort the picture if you want to by making it long and skinny or short and fat. In general, you'll get best results by trying to maintain its original proportions, or *aspect ratio*, by changing both width and height by the same percentage.

> **TIP** To avoid distortion when the picture is printed, keep the x and y values (in the status line) the same and keep them in whole numbers rather than fractions.

Also, be aware that bit-mapped images, such as Paint pictures and scanned photos, never look as good when resized. If you shrink them, you lose detail; if you stretch them, curved edges look blocky.

Inserting Graphics as Objects

When you place a graphic into a WordPad document using the Clipboard, the connection between the image and Paint (or whatever application created it) is broken. If you need to edit the graphic, you'll have to delete it from WordPad, then start all over in Paint.

Unless you're sure the graphic is final, it makes more sense to insert it using Windows' OLE (object linking and embedding) capability. That way, the graphic remains *live* in your document—you can edit it in place without having to leave WordPad at all. See Chapter 6 for step-by-step instructions on how to link and embed objects into your documents.

Saving Your Work

WordPad stores your document in memory while you work on it. However, memory is not a permanent storage area; you will lose your work when you turn off your computer unless you first save it.

You save your documents with two commands: File ➤ Save and File ➤ Save As (there are two shortcuts for the Save command: the Save button on the Toolbar and the Ctrl-S keyboard shortcut). The first time you save a document, WordPad will ask you for a name to give your document—in this situation, the Save and Save As commands work the same. After the initial save, WordPad assumes you want to use the current name unless you indicate otherwise by using the Save As command.

Remember to save your work frequently. Nothing hurts like losing forever an afternoon's inspired writing. Taking a few moments to save your document every five or ten minutes is much easier on the psyche.

Again, there are three ways to save a file: File ➤ Save, the Save button—the one with the picture of a floppy disk—and Ctrl-S.

No matter which of these methods you use to start the process, the Save As dialog box (Figure 19.13) appears because this is the first time you've saved this file. WordPad has assigned a generic name, Document, but you can change it. Finish saving your file as follows:

1. Type in a more descriptive name in the File name box.

2. Ensure that the correct drive and directory are selected.

3. If you wish to change the type of file you'll be saving, do so by picking a new choice from the *Save as Type* drop-down list box.

4. Click on OK.

The Save as Type drop-down list box is normally set to store your document in the Word for Windows 6 format. Different programs use different coding systems, or *formats,* to store the document's text, its character and paragraph formatting, any graphics or other objects, and other miscellaneous information.

NOTE   There are two distinct uses for the term "format": It can refer to the way a document is stored in a disk file or to the appearance of text in a document.

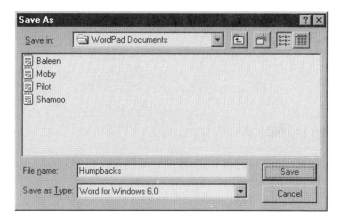

Figure 19.13 *The Save As dialog box. After making sure the drive and directory are right,
type in the file name.*

The various formats in which you can save a document are discussed
below. You shouldn't alter this setting unless you want to create a
document that other word processors or other types of programs
can read:

Word for Windows 6.0

This choice stores the document in the same format used by
Microsoft Word for Windows, version 6.0. This full-featured word
processor is the most popular Windows application. If you open the
document with Word, all the text, character and paragraph formatting, graphics, and other objects will be preserved.

Rich Text Format

The Rich Text Format is used as a common format for exchanging
documents between word processors, but none of them use it as their
primary format (it's sort of like Esperanto for word processors). The
Rich Text Format preserves the appearance as well as the content of
your document. Graphics and other objects are saved in the file along
with the text but may be lost when you open the file with another
application.

Text Files

Files saved with this option contain only text without any of the character and paragraph formatting you've added. Such files are also

known as *plain* text files. They can be opened by a text editor such as Notepad. You can also open them with DOS text editors such as PC-Write, WordStar, or Sidekick, though you may have to add line breaks, and special characters—such as bullets—will not display or print properly.

Opening Other Documents

Once a WordPad document has been saved on disk, you can come back to it at any future time. To *open* a document—moving the information stored on disk into RAM so you can work with it again—use the Open command.

Keep in mind that in WordPad, unlike fancier word processors, you can only work with one document at a time. When you open a document, it replaces the one you were working with, if any. If you want to keep the changes you made in a document, you must save that document before opening a new one. But don't worry—WordPad will remind you to save before it lets you open another document.

As usual, you have several options for opening existing documents: choose File ➤ Open, press Ctrl-O, or on the Toolbar click on the Open button, which shows a picture of a file folder opening.

Regardless of which technique you use, you'll see the Open dialog box. After listing any subdirectories, this dialog box shows you all the files in the current directory matching the setting in the *Files of type* drop-down list box. Unless someone has changed the entry, you'll see a list of all files stored in the Word for Windows format, WordPad's preferred format.

To open a document, double-click on it in the list or click once on the document and then click Open. At this point, if you haven't already saved the previous document, WordPad asks if you want to do so. Choose Yes or No, as you prefer.

A Shortcut for Opening Recent Documents

WordPad lists the last four documents you've opened on the File menu. If you want to reopen any of these documents, do it the quick way: Open the File menu, then choose the document by name from the menu. WordPad will open the document immediately without displaying the Open dialog box (you'll still receive a message asking if you want to save the current document if you haven't done so yet).

Opening Documents Stored in Other Formats

Although WordPad's standard format for storing documents on disk is the Word for Windows 6.0 format, WordPad can also open documents stored in several other formats. Formats WordPad can open include:

▶ the Windows Write format (Write was a simple word processor included with earlier versions of Windows)

▶ the Rich Text Format

▶ *text only* files

If you know the format of the document you want to open, select that format in the Files of Type drop-down list box. If you're unsure of the format, choose All Files instead—Windows will now display all the files in the current directory. Once you locate the correct document in the list, double-click on it to open it.

WordPad automatically opens Word for Windows, Windows Write, and Rich Text Format files, even those incorrectly named. If someone has improperly renamed say, a Word for Windows-format document, the Open dialog box may not show it even when the Files of Type setting is correct. However, WordPad can still open the document if you locate it with All Files selected in the Files of Type box (or if you type in the document's name at *File name*).

All other documents are opened as text-only files. If the document contains formatting information from some other application, WordPad will display the entire document, including the formatting information, as ordinary text. You'll likely see gibberish mixed in with intelligible text.

Converting ASCII Files

When opening most text-only files created by DOS programs, WordPad interprets each line of text as a separate paragraph (in these *ASCII* files, paragraphs are typically set apart by a blank lines).

The only way to fix the problem is to delete the unwanted paragraph dividers once you open the document into WordPad. It's best to do this systematically immediately after opening the document.

Follow these steps to fix each paragraph. Skip paragraphs that are only one line long:

1. Move the cursor to the end of the first line of the paragraph. Press Del to remove the paragraph division. This will pull up the previous line to the cursor.

2. Press the Spacebar to add a space between the two words on either side of the cursor, if necessary.

3. Repeat the above steps on all lines of the paragraph *except* the last one.

Opening a New Document

Whenever you start WordPad, the program opens a new, empty document for you. To create a new document after working with an existing one, however, you need the New command. Here's how to do it:

1. Choose Edit ▶ New, press Ctrl-N, or click on the New button on the Toolbar—it's the one that looks like a blank sheet of paper.

2. If you haven't already saved the current document, WordPad gives you a chance to do so.

3. WordPad now asks you what format you want to use for the new document: Word for Windows, Rich Text, or Text Only. Select the desired format in the list and choose OK. The new document will appear in the window.

Display Options

You have some choices about the way the WordPad window looks and works. As you learned earlier, the View menu lets you turn on or off any of the individual control bars (the Toolbar, the Format Bar, the ruler, and the Status Bar). Other display options are available via the Options dialog box.

To open the Options dialog box, choose View ➤ Options. You'll see the window shown in Figure 19.14.

The Options dialog box is tabbed. One tab covers general options, while the remaining tabs apply to the various document types (file formats) that WordPad can handle.

Selecting Measurement Units and Controlling Word Selection

Click on the tab labeled Options in the Options dialog box to set measurement units for your document. You can choose from inches, centimeters, points, and picas (the last two units are used by typesetters). If the ruler is visible, it will be displayed with the selected measurement units. In addition, spacing settings in the Paragraph Spacing and Page Setup dialog boxes will be listed in the chosen unit.

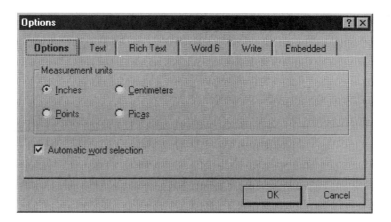

Figure 19.14 *The Options dialog box. It lets you set measurement units for the ruler and for spacing settings, among other choices.*

TIP   Regardless of the *Measurement units* setting in the Options tab, you can enter new settings in the Paragraph Spacing and Page Setup dialog boxes in any unit by typing the unit abbreviation after the value. For example, type 1.5 in to enter a left margin of 1.5 inches, 2.3 cm to enter a right margin of 2.3 centimeters.

The only other choice on the Options tab is a check box labeled Automatic Word Selection. With this setting checked, the mouse selects entire words when you drag the pointer across two or more words. You can still select a group of characters within a single word by holding down Shift while pressing the arrow keys.

Uncheck the Automatic Word Selection box if you want the selection to cover only the characters you actually drag the pointer across.

Choosing Display Options for Each Type of Document

Aside from the page labeled Options, the other pages in the Options dialog box pertain to the various types of documents that WordPad can open—Word for Windows 6.0, Windows Write, Rich Text Format, and Text-only files, as well as WordPad documents embedded via OLE in other documents. Each of these pages offers identical choices, shown in Figure 19.15.

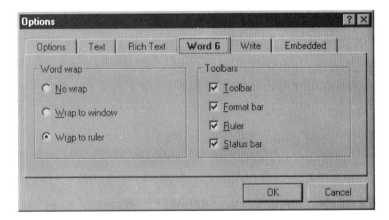

Figure 19.15   *The Options dialog box offers these choices for each type of file WordPad can handle.*

Check boxes on the right of each tab let you select which of the control bars (the Toolbar, Format Bar, ruler, and Status Bar) WordPad will display automatically when you open a document of the type indicated by the tab.

On the left side of each tabbed panel are radio buttons for selecting the way WordPad wraps your text from line to line on the screen. Note that none of these choices affects the way your document prints:

No Wrap   If this button is selected, WordPad doesn't wrap your text at all. As you add text anywhere within a line, the line keeps expanding toward the right regardless of the right indent and right margin settings. On printed copies, though, the text still wraps according to the indent and margin settings.

Wrap to Window   With this button selected, WordPad wraps the text to fit within the document window, ignoring the right indent and margin settings. Choose this setting to see all your text even when the WordPad window is narrower than the paragraph width set by the ruler. Again, this doesn't affect printed documents.

Wrap to Ruler   When this button is selected, the displayed text wraps according to the right indent and right margin settings as shown on the ruler (whether or not the ruler is visible).

Printing Your Document

Generally speaking, the ultimate goal of all your typing and formatting is a printed copy of your document. Printing a WordPad document is a straightforward process. Like the major-league word processors, WordPad lets you see a preview of your document as it will appear in print, and you can fix your mistakes before they appear on paper.

Seeing a Preview of Your Printed Document

Instead of wasting paper on a document with an obvious layout mistake, use WordPad's *print preview* command to inspect your work before you print. The print preview command displays your document on screen just as it will look when printed. You can look at entire pages to check the overall layout or zoom in on a particular portion to check details.

To use print preview, choose File ➤ Print Preview. (Alternatively, you can click on the Print Preview button if the Toolbar is visible—it's the button with the picture of a magnifying glass over a sheet of paper.)

The WordPad window fills with a mock-up of your document, fitting two full pages into the available space, as shown in Figure 19.16. A special Toolbar offers quick access to a number of special commands, and the mouse pointer becomes a magnifying glass.

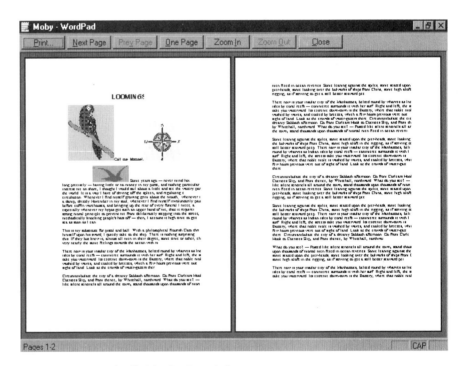

Figure 19.16 *WordPad's Print Preview window*

At this level of magnification, you can't read ordinary-size text, but you can check for problems with page margins, paragraph alignment, and spacing. Clicking anywhere on the document window changes the magnification, cycling through the three available levels. Starting from the full-page view, the first click zooms you in on the portion of the page you clicked on, the second gives you a life-size close-up of a still smaller area, and the third click returns you to the full-page view. You can also change the magnification by clicking on the Zoom In or Zoom Out buttons in the Toolbar.

To page through the mock-up of your document, click on the Next Page button. You can move back toward the beginning with the Prev Page button. To display only a single page of the document instead of two, click on the One Page button; you can switch back to the two-page view by clicking on the same button, which will now read Two Page. You can also page through the mock-up with the PgUp and PgDn keys.

When you're satisfied that the document looks as you expected, click on the Print button to begin the actual printing process, covered in the next section. On the other hand, if you find mistakes, click on the Close button to return to editing the document.

Printing

When you are about ready to print, don't forget to save your file first just in case the computer or the printer goes berserk in the process and you lose your file. If you want to print only a portion of your document, select that portion. And don't forget to turn on the printer and make sure it has paper and is ready to print (in other words, that it is *online*).

Then, to print just choose File ➤ Print (or you can press Ctrl-P or click on the Print button from Print Preview). You'll be presented with a dialog box asking you about the following options:

Name (of Printer)   If the printer you plan to use isn't already chosen in this box, choose it from the drop-down list of your installed printers.

Properties This button takes you to the Printer Properties dialog box for the selected printer. From this dialog box, you can choose the paper orientation (portrait or landscape), paper size and feed, print quality (for text) and resolution (for graphics), and other options available for your printer. See the discussion of printer properties in Chapter 8 for full details.

Print Range If you want to print all the pages, click on All. If you want to print specific pages only, click on Pages and type in the range of page numbers you want to print in the *From* and *to* boxes. If you want to print only text that you selected, click on Selection.

Copies The number of copies of each page to be printed.

Collate Whether each complete copy should be printed one at a time, in page order (more convenient but slower), or all copies of each page should be printed before moving on to the next page (quicker but requires you to hand collate). Applies only if you're printing more than one copy of the document.

When you've made your choices, press Enter or click on OK. If the printer is connected and working properly, you should have a paper copy of your document in a few moments.

The Print Button

If you're sure the settings in the Print dialog box are already correct and you want a copy of the entire document, you can streamline the printing process via the Toolbar's Print button. It's the one showing the picture of a printer ejecting a page.

When you click on the Print button, WordPad immediately begins sending your document to the printer via Windows' Print Manager—you won't have to deal with the Print dialog box.

Chapter 20

Communicating Using HyperTerminal

FEATURING

The HyperTerminal program supplied with Windows lets you and your PC make contact with other computers to exchange or retrieve information. With HyperTerminal and the right hookups, you can communicate with other computers whether they are in your own house, around the block, or on the other side of the world. The kinds of information you might share in this way run the gamut from electronic mail through instant stock quotes to complete document files (such as word-processing or spreadsheet documents). More and more people use communications programs to connect to their company's computer so they can work from home—a style of work called *telecommuting*.

There are countless types of information you can access with your PC and a communications program such as HyperTerminal. You've probably heard of the Internet, a web-like international network of computers that has become the most talked-about telecommunications phenomenon of the '90s. If you subscribe to an Internet access service, you can tap news, scientific data, and commentary and discussions on almost any topic imaginable via HyperTerminal. Commercial information (online) services such as CompuServe, Prodigy, and Genie offer a lot of information, too, but they also provide shopping, investing, and even dating services. Nowadays, many clubs and organizations have their own dial-up Bulletin Board Systems (BBSs) where members can leave messages and read notices of interest. Numerous BBSs also provide a wide variety of public-domain software and shareware that anyone with a computer, a modem, and a communications program can have just for the taking.

Working with HyperTerminal

We'll get into the details of how to operate HyperTerminal in a moment, after a summary of the steps required to set up your system for telecommunications. For now, I owe you a quick answer to a question you may have: Why is the choice on the Start menu called HyperTerminal *Connections*, instead of plain HyperTerminal? The reason is that HyperTerminal needs a different setup to communicate with each different connection (information service, BBS, computer, or what have you). But after you've set up for a given connection, connecting again is as simple as double-clicking on its icon in the HyperTerminal Connections folder. In the example on the next page, I'm just a double-click away from the Internet, CompuServe, MCI Mail, and the chemistry lab at the university.

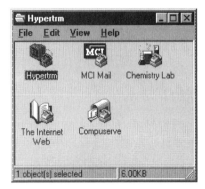

HyperTerminal is usually set up to display its Dial dialog box (or the prerequisite setup dialog boxes) when the program starts. For this reason, you may not see HyperTerminal's *main window* for a while. Just so you'll know, Figure 20.1 shows how the main window looks. Like many other Windows programs, it has a Toolbar at the top full of buttons for one-click access to common commands. At the bottom is the Status Bar, which keeps you informed of the progress of your

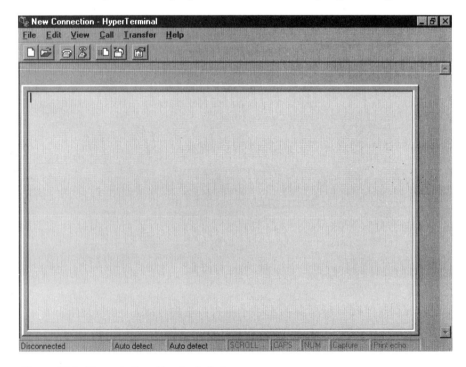

Figure 20.1　The main HyperTerminal window

communications session. (You can shut the Toolbar and Status Bar off if you prefer—we'll talk about that below.)

Within dialog boxes, you can click on the Help button at the upper right and then on a button or setting of interest to get a quick help message.

Finally, an apologetic explanation is in order here: The information in this chapter is necessarily somewhat general. Because a communications program such as HyperTerminal can be used to connect to an almost endless variety of information services and computers, it's impossible to cover all the specific situations. What's more, each service typically has its own way of logging on, transmitting and receiving files, and so on. So, instead of demonstrating exact procedures, I'll discuss all the aspects of the HyperTerminal program and explain the general steps you'll have to understand to use it effectively.

FOR WINDOWS 3 USERS

If you've been relying on the Terminal program supplied with previous versions of Windows, making the transition to HyperTerminal will be easy. But before you decide to switch to HyperTerminal, you should compare the two programs to see which really fits your needs best. You may find that sticking with Terminal makes more sense, especially if you're already very familiar with how it works.

While HyperTerminal offers a few meaty improvements over Terminal, most of the changes have to do with making your communications sessions easier and better looking. On the other hand, some of Terminal's most useful features aren't available in HyperTerminal.

One thing you won't sacrifice if you stick with Terminal is speed: When it comes to telecommunications, the limiting factor is modem speed, always far less than the speed of your software.

For my money, the most important additions to HyperTerminal are the new file-transfer protocols, especially Zmodem. Zmodem's speed, its ability to communicate the name and size of a file, and its talent for recovering gracefully from interruptions make it the best of the widely used protocols. Zmodem's absence from Terminal is that program's Achilles heel.

Another substantive improvement is in the area of complicated dialing sequences. While Terminal can remember a phone number in each setup file, there is no way to configure it to automatically access outside lines, dial credit-card numbers, or shut off call waiting. HyperTerminal does all this with aplomb.

(continued on next page)

Other new features address convenience and cosmetics. For example, the Toolbar buttons are a nice addition for one-click access to commands, and the reorganization of the various settings into a set of concise tabbed dialog boxes is much less confusing for the newcomer.

Now comes the bad news. If you're used to Terminal, here's what you'll miss in HyperTerminal:

▶ Function key commands. In Terminal, you can assign sequences of commands and typed characters to the function keys on your keyboard and then play back the command sequences by pressing the keys. For example, you can assign to a function key the sequence of characters you have to type each time you log on to an online service or BBS (usually your name or ID number and a password). This can be a big time-saver if you telecommunicate frequently. HyperTerminal has no comparable feature.

▶ The ability to view text files from within the program. HyperTerminal lacks Terminal's View Text File command, meaning you have to switch to another application such as Notepad or WordPad to examine disk files (so you can figure out which one to send, for example).

▶ The ability to send selected text without copying it to the Clipboard first. Terminal's Edit menu has a Send command for selected text, but HyperTerminal lacks a counterpart.

▶ Tabular text format for received text. Terminal can be set up to recognize incoming text as a table and format it accordingly; HyperTerminal can't.

▶ Some advanced communications settings. A number of the settings available in Terminal have been dropped in HyperTerminal. These include Carrier Detect, Flow Control for text files, word wrap for outgoing text files, and the ability to set the number of columns in the window. While these aren't necessary very often, they do come in handy from time to time.

If you do plan to switch to HyperTerminal, you can make the transition as efficient as possible by importing the settings from your Terminal setup (.TRM) files. To open a Terminal setup file:

1. Choose File ➤ Open.

2. At the bottom of the Select Session File dialog box, choose Terminal files from the list in the *Files of type* box.

3. Locate the Terminal file you want, select it, and click on Open. HyperTerminal reads its settings.

4. Make any necessary adjustments to the settings via the Properties dialog boxes.

5. Choose File ➤ Save As to save the settings as a HyperTerminal connection (session file).

Once you've completed these steps, you can use the new settings just as you would any other HyperTerminal connection.

Setting Up Your Communications System

In most cases, you'll be using HyperTerminal to communicate across a telephone line. You might connect to the Internet, to a commercial dial-up service such as CompuServe, Dow Jones News/Retrieval, the Source, or MCI Mail, or you might call up a friend's or colleague's computer to exchange files. The other computer can even be of a different type, such as a Macintosh.

 NOTE *Telecommunications* is the term used for communication over telephone lines or via cellular phone systems.

To communicate in this way from a distance via the telephone line (as opposed to communications between computers connected directly together with a cable), you'll need a modem. A *modem* is a device that provides the electronic connection between a computer and the phone line. The modem attached to your computer converts digital information from the computer into an *analog* signal that travels over the phone line. On the other end of the line, the receiving modem does just the reverse (see Figure 20.2). The word *modem* stands for *modulator/demodulator*, as the process of converting digital information to an analog signal is called modulation.

Though you can always run the HyperTerminal program to experiment with it, you can't use it over the phone line without a modem.

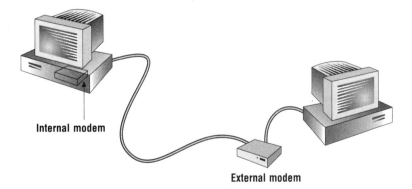

Internal modem

External modem

Figure 20.2   *A telecommunications setup, which consists of two computers, two modems, and interconnecting wires*

To connect a modem, you'll need either:

 an external modem, a cable, an unused serial port (where you plug in the cable), and an unused COM port (the electronics that permit communications at a specific computer *address*)

 an internal modem installed inside your computer plus an unused COM port

In either case, the general installation procedures are similar. You install the modem, plug your telephone line into it, and run a communications program (in this case, HyperTerminal).

The main distinguishing factor among modems is the speed at which they can transfer data over the phone lines. As of this writing, modems that transmit data at 14,400 bits per second are the most popular, though many slower modems are still in use and faster ones are available. (When it comes to bits-per-second ratings, the larger the number, the faster the transmission.)

 NOTE You're likely to see the word *baud* used as a synonym for bits per second as a rating of modem speed. Technically, the two terms aren't strictly synonymous, and you can avoid confusion by sticking with *bits per second*.

Because I can't cover all the ins and outs of modem purchasing here, I'll leave the purchase and installation details to you. Comparative reviews in computer magazines are a great source of up-to-date consumer information. A few quick pointers: in theory, of course, the faster the modem, the better. But buying a brand-new superfast unit won't do you any good unless the modem on the *other* end of the line is equally fast—so don't overspend. And don't let anyone sell you a modem that's not *Hayes compatible*. Fortunately, though, most modems are.

On the other hand, if you somehow acquire a modem that isn't Hayes compatible, you can probably still use HyperTerminal because other popular modem types—such as MultiTech and TrailBlazer models—are also supported.

 NOTE *Hayes compatibility* lets you take advantage of some useful features of HyperTerminal (and most other communications programs) such as the ability to dial the phone for you automatically, redial busy numbers, and so on.

Make sure you have your modem connected to, or installed in, your computer properly, following instructions in the modem's manual, before continuing. Incorrect modem installation (most often caused by improper switch settings) is a frequent cause of communications problems.

Once the modem is installed, Windows should be able to set it up properly for you. If there's a glitch in the setup process, the most likely solution will be to manually change the settings for the COM port to which you've connected the modem. Of course, you'll need to know which COM port that is. Beyond that, Chapter 26 will point you in the right direction when it comes to manually configuring the ports.

Setting Up a HyperTerminal Connection

Your most basic rule in communicating holds true in HyperTerminal: You have to know how to reach the other party. Before doing anything else, find the telephone number your modem must dial to connect to the information service, BBS, or computer you're trying to reach. Be sure you have the number for modem communications—in printed material it may be labeled the *modem* or *data* number. *Voice* or *fax* numbers won't work.

While you're looking for the number, see if you can locate any details on the communications setting in force at the computer you want to connect to. Your system must be set up to match, as detailed later in this chapter.

Starting HyperTerminal

To access HyperTerminal, begin from the Start menu and choose Programs ➤ Accessories ➤ HyperTerminal Connections. This will display the contents of the HyperTerminal folder. This window will look like the one shown earlier in this chapter except that the first time you use it, the HyperTerminal icon is the only icon you'll see.

Double-click on the HyperTerminal icon to run the program and pre-pare to set up a new connection. Once a specific connection has been set up, you'll be able to double-click on its icon to start a communications session with that connection.

Defining a New Connection

When you start from the program icon (rather than from an existing connection icon), HyperTerminal asks you to define a new connection in the dialog box shown here:

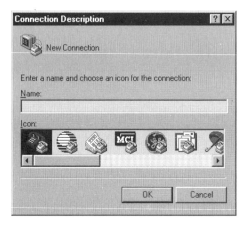

You can also set up a new connection once you're working with the main HyperTerminal window by choosing File ➤ New Connection or clicking on the New button on the Toolbar to display the above dialog box.

Your first step is to give the new connection a name. Keep it simple—something like *MCI* or *Bill's office PC* will do. Then pick out an appropriate icon for the connection from the scrolling list and click on OK to go on.

Entering a Phone Number

Next you must supply the phone number your modem should dial to make the connection. HyperTerminal displays the Phone Number dialog box, shown on the next page.

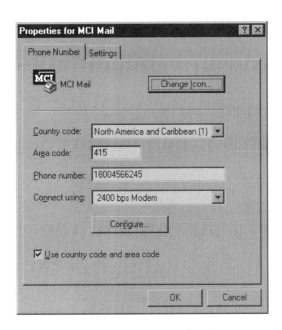

Type in the phone number for the new connection. You have your
choice of styles:

1-(510)-555-1111

1-510-555-1111

15105551111

555-1111 (if you are calling a local number)

In case you're wondering, HyperTerminal ignores dashes and parentheses in the main phone number.

If the phone number for the new connection is local, that's all you have
to do—Windows has already entered your settings for the country code
and area code. If you're dialing out of the area or out of country, use the
first two boxes to set the correct country and area code. And if you have
more than one modem connected to your computer, choose the one you
want to use for this connection from the list at the bottom of the dialog box.

OK the Phone Number box when all the settings are correct.

Setting Dialing Properties

Once you've set the phone number, HyperTerminal assumes you want to dial it and presents you with the following dialog box:

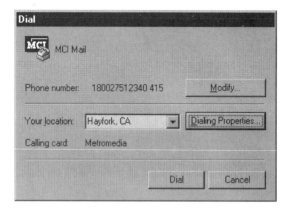

At this point, it's safe to go ahead and click on OK to see if the setup works. But don't be too surprised if nothing happens. In many cases, you'll need to change other settings before you can connect successfully.

Take a look at the area labeled *Your location*. Here, you should select the choice that describes where you are at this moment. The first time you use HyperTerminal, the only choice available is the nondescript selection *Default location*. This corresponds to the area code and country you entered when you set up Windows itself, so if you haven't moved, it may well be correct for those items.

If you use a portable computer, however, you may be thousands of miles from your default location. And besides, there are other considerations: Do you have to dial 9 to get an outside line? Are you dialing from a customer's office, so it will be necessary to use your telephone credit card? Or are you at a friend's place who doesn't believe in high technology and never installed a push-button phone? If so, tone dialing won't work.

To change any of these properties for the default location or to set up new locations from scratch, click on Dialing Properties. You'll see the dialog box shown in Figure 20.3.

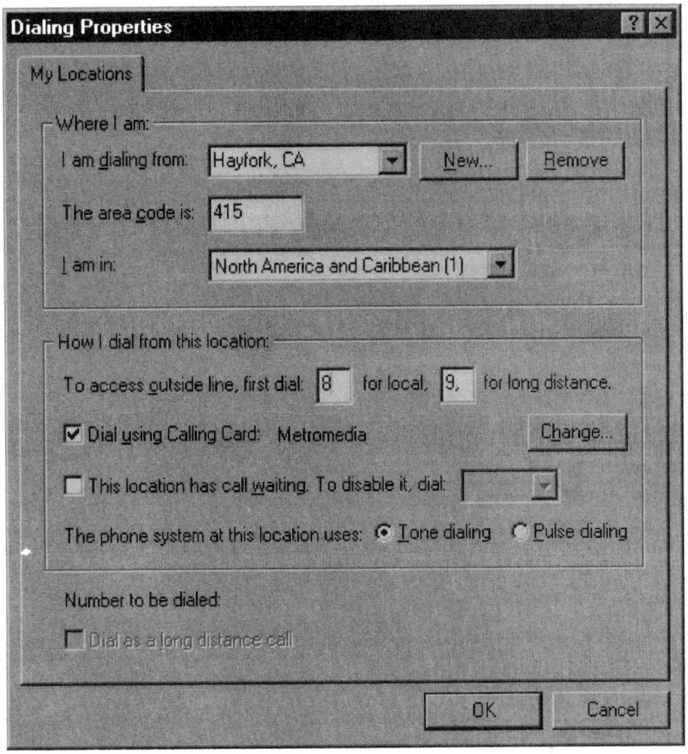

Supplied Applications

Dialing Properties   ? X

My Locations

Where I am:

I am dialing from: Hayfork, CA   ▼   New...   Remove

The area code is: 415

I am in: North America and Caribbean (1)   ▼

How I dial from this location:

To access outside line, first dial: 8   for local,   9,   for long distance.

☑ Dial using Calling Card: Metromedia   Change...

☐ This location has call waiting. To disable it, dial: ▼

The phone system at this location uses: ⦿ Tone dialing   ○ Pulse dialing

Number to be dialed:

☐ Dial as a long distance call

OK   Cancel

Figure 20.3   **The Dialing Properties dialog box**

 NOTE The Dialing Properties dialog box controls dialing settings for the Phone Dialer accessory, too. Phone Dialer is covered in Chapter 14.

Follow these instructions to set up or change a location and its dialing properties:

1. First comes a group of settings collectively titled *Where I am*. In the area labeled *I am dialing from*, choose the name for the location settings you want to work with. To create a new location, click on New and type in the name. For example, if you move around from place to place with your computer, you'll want to create locations, say, for your home, for your office, and for each customer site. After you create a new location, it will automatically appear in the *I am dialing from* area.

2. In the next area, type in the area code for the location you're setting up. Remember, you're identifying *your* location—the location where you'll be when you use these settings. (Don't type in the area code of the number you're dialing.)

3. Likewise, choose the location's country code from the list in the *I am in* area.

> **TIP**   Insert commas into the phone number to tell your modem to pause before moving ahead to the next digit. On Hayes-compatible modems, each comma results in a two-second pause. At least one comma is necessary when you have to dial a special number to reach an outside line. So a typical entry in the boxes for accessing an outline line would be **9 , .**

4. Next comes a group of settings titled *How I dial from this location*. On the first line in this group, type the numbers you must dial to reach an outside line for local and long-distance calls. By the way, the dialer knows enough to add a 1 before long-distance numbers—you don't need to enter it here.

5. If you use a calling card to dial from this location, check the box on the next line. When you do—and if the location wasn't previously set up for calling-card dialing—the Change Calling Card dialog box appears:

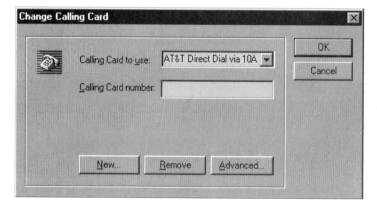

Here, choose the type of calling card you have from the list. Then type in your card number (your *PIN*), the number you must dial so the phone company can bill you. If your card isn't listed, use the instructions in *Customizing Calling Card Settings* below.

> **TIP**   Again, you may need to add one or more commas in a calling-card dialing sequence to create pauses. Often it takes several seconds for the second dial tone to come on after the connection to the service is made.

6. If the phone line at this location has the call waiting "service" (I regard call waiting as a punishment), be sure to check the box labeled *This location has call waiting*. Then choose the sequence of characters that must be dialed to disable call waiting at this location (if the correct sequence isn't available in the drop-down list, just type in the characters yourself). If you don't disable call waiting, calls that come in during a communications session will likely interrupt the connection, forcing you to start the session all over again.

7. Click on the radio button for the type of phone line at the location, tone or pulse (pulse is the type of dialing used by rotary-dial phones). If you're dialing from a location with a rotary phone, you will still be able to use tone dialing—which is faster—if the line is set up properly. If you don't know, you can always try tone dialing first and switch to pulse if tone doesn't work.

8. Check the display at *Number to be dialed*, which shows the actual digits that will be dialed. If you find an error, go back to the appropriate section and re-enter the correct codes.

9. The last option in the Dialing Properties dialog box is the check box labeled *Dial as a long distance call*. This choice is available only if the number you're dialing has the same area code as your current location. If you check this box, the dialer adds a 1 before the number and any other special access numbers you've specified for long-distance calls. When the box is unchecked, the number is dialed as a local call.

10. Click on OK to close the Dialing Properties dialog box and return to the Dial dialog box.

    At this point, you may be ready to proceed with making the connection to another computer. On the other hand, there is a reasonable chance that you will need to modify one or more of the rather technical settings that pertain to communicating via a modem. See the next major section, *Choosing Communications Settings*, if you want to check your settings now or if your attempt to connect fails.

Customizing Calling-Card Settings

The dialer comes set up for several popular telephone calling (credit) cards, but with so many different carriers, yours may not be on the list. Here's how to set up your own calling card or modify the settings for an existing card:

1. Display the Dialing Properties dialog box (Figure 20.3) by clicking on the Dialing Properties button on the Dial dialog box in HyperTerminal (or by choosing Tools ➤ Dialing Properties in Phone Dialer).

2. Check the *Dial using Calling Card* box if it's not already checked. If the Change Calling Card dialog box appears automatically, go on to step 3; otherwise, click on the Change button to display the new dialog box.

3. If you're adding a new calling card—one that's not on the list at *Calling card to use*—click on the New button. In the little dialog box that appears, type in the name of your card and click on OK. The new name appears as the selected card in the Create Calling Card dialog box.

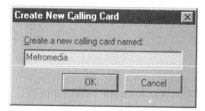

4. To customize the dialing sequence for the currently selected card, click on Advanced in the Change Calling Card dialog box. Another small dialog box appears:

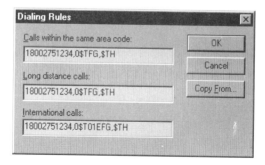

You use the Dialing Rules dialog box to enter the sequence of numbers that you must dial to place a call using your calling card. There are three entry areas allowing you to enter different dialing sequences (*rules*) for local, long-distance, and international calls. You can enter the actual digits that must be dialed, plus codes for various sequences such as the calling-card number (the PIN) and the phone number itself. Table 20.1 summarizes the entries you can make in a dialing rule. An example of a typical rule is shown below.

5. Click on OK to return to the Dialing Properties dialog box. If you're working in HyperTerminal, the calling-card sequence is added to the actual digits to be dialed displayed at *Number to be dialed*. For a bit of security, however, your private calling-card number is indicated by the name of the card in brackets. Check to ensure that the sequence shown is correct; if not, click on the Change button again to edit the calling-card settings. When the sequence is right, click on OK to close the Dialing Properties dialog box.

Here's an example showing how to build up a custom dialing rule using the characters in Table 20.1. Let's say your card requires the following dialing sequence: You begin by accessing your long-distance carrier by dialing 1-800-555-2000. After you hear the bong tone, you dial the phone number, beginning with the area code. You then wait for a second bong tone and finally dial your calling-card number.

Your entry in the Dialing Rules dialog box would look like this:

    18005552000TFGH

Here's a breakdown of the entry's parts, in order:

▶ First comes the access number.

▶ After the access number, the first *$* tells the dialer to wait for the bong tone.

▶ The *T* tells the dialer to switch to tone dialing at this point in the dialing sequence. That way, you can when necessary set the dialer to initiate calls with pulse dialing on the main Dialing Properties dialog box. With the T command, your calling card—which depends on tone dialing—will still work.

▶ The *F* tells the dialer to dial the area code of the phone number you're calling.

Character(s)	Results
0-9	Dialed as typed
★	Dialed as typed (works only on tone dialing lines)
#	Dialed as typed (works only on tone dialing lines)
A–D	Dialed as typed (the letters A-D are used to control some phone systems; they work only on tone dialing lines)
E	Dials the country code for the phone number you're calling
F	Dials the area code for the phone number you're calling
G	Dials the phone number (without the area code or country code)
H	Dials the calling card number (PIN)
T	Dials digits that follow via tone dialing
P	Dials digits that follow via pulse dialing
,	Pauses for a fixed time (2 seconds on most modems)
!	*Flashes* the connection (same as hanging up for half a second or pressing the Flash button on your phone)
W	Waits for a second dial tone
$	Waits for the bong tone that indicates the system is waiting for a calling-card number or other entry
@	Waits for an answer followed by 5 seconds of silence as required by some systems

Table 20.2   Valid Entries for Calling-Card Dialing Rules and Their Effects

▶ The *G* tells the dialer to dial the phone number itself.

▶ The second *$* tells the dialer to wait again for another dial tone.

▶ The *H* at the end tells the dialer to dial your card number.

Choosing Communications Settings

Unfortunately, there are no set standards covering all aspects of the technology required for modem communications. But look on the bright side: Once you've figured out the correct settings for a given connection, HyperTerminal will remember them. From then on, all you have to do is start up the connection, and you're guaranteed success.

If you are in doubt about how to set these options, there's a simple solution. Just find out what the settings are on the computer at the other end of the line and set yours accordingly. If you can't find out what those settings are, go ahead and try the standard settings by dialing the connection and seeing if you can communicate. If that doesn't work, then start systematically altering the settings one at a time, testing for a good connection each time.

To change the communications settings, choose File ➤ Properties or click on the Properties button on the Toolbar.

This works even if the Dial or Dialing Properties dialog box is active. You can also click on Modify in the Dial dialog box. After any of these steps, you'll see the Properties dialog box showing settings for the current connection, as shown in Figure 20.4.

NOTE   To alter settings for another connection, you must open the Properties dialog box for that connection first. You can set the Properties for any connection from the HyperTerminal folder (the fast way: right-click on the connection's icon and choose Properties from the pop-up menu). Alternatively, when HyperTerminal is already running, switch to another connection by choosing File ➤ Open, then choose File ➤ Properties or click on the Properties button on the Toolbar.

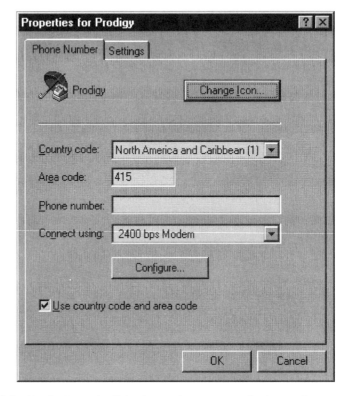

Figure 20.4   Use the Properties dialog box to change communications settings

Changes you make here apply only to the specific connection you're working with at the time. As you can see, the Properties dialog box has two tabs, one called Phone Number, the other called Settings.

The settings you may need to change to connect successfully fall into the following categories:

Basic Communications	For setting the speed and format for commands and data sent between the two connected computers.
Terminal Emulation	For choosing between the types of terminals that HyperTerminal can simulate (terminals are defined below). Both the remote computer and your software must be set to the same terminal type to communicate correctly.

In addition, you can control a variety of settings that are a matter of preference, detailed at the end of this section.

Choosing Basic Communications Settings

What I'm calling basic communications settings control the fundamental "language" of modem-to-modem communications. They determine such critical characteristics as how fast information flows between the modems, how they signal each other, and how each modem can tell one nugget of information from another.

One fundamental principle bears repeating: Most of these settings must be identical on both ends of the communications link (I'll note the exceptions as they come along). Because you probably have no control over the settings at the other end of the line, you're stuck with making sure your settings match. Actually, most connections will work without any changes—HyperTerminal's standard settings are the most popular ones, in use by most of the major commercial information services. But if you experience problems or if you know the other computer's settings are different, you'll need to alter the standard settings.

All the basic communications settings are controlled via the modem Properties dialog box. Access it as follows:

1. Display the Properties dialog box for the connection you're working with (Figure 20.4).

2. In the list labeled *Connect using*, choose the modem you want to use for the connection.

3. Click on the Configure button. You'll see the Properties dialog box for this particular modem, as shown in Figure 20.5.

   The modem Properties dialog box has three tabbed pages: General, Connection, and Options.

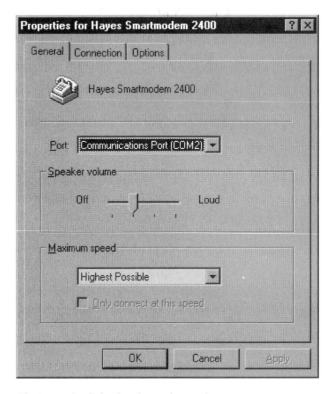

Figure 20.5   *The Properties dialog box for modem settings*

The Port Setting

NOTE   There's a subtle but important distinction between the communications or COM ports, which are circuits that permit communications at a particular computer address, and the *serial* ports on the back of your computer, which are the physical receptacles into which you plug devices like external modems. Each serial port is assigned to a specific COM port. On the other hand, you may not have a serial port for every COM port—devices such as internal modems can access a COM port directly.

The first setting on the General page of the modem Properties dialog box is Port. Here, you tell HyperTerminal which *port* your modem is connected to. Most PCs have at least two communications ports, called COM1 and COM2. Many systems have COM3 and COM4 ports as well. Each modem is assigned to one of these ports when you first install the modem. If the port has changed, you can change the setting to match by choosing from the list here.

CAUTION   Don't change this setting unless you know what you're doing. It's uncommon for the port to which your modem is connected to change—often, you would have had to plug the modem into a different place on the back of your computer or change little switches on the modem. If you change the port setting incorrectly, HyperTerminal won't be able to access your modem at all.

This is an exception to the rule about your settings needing to match those of the other computer. The port setting pertains exclusively to communications between *your* computer and *your* modem, and doesn't affect interactions between your system and another modem.

Setting Modem Speed

The speed at which your modem transfers information makes a big difference in how much work you can get done during a communications session. Just how fast information can travel between two modems depends on two things: the top speed of the *slower* modem and the quality of the telephone line.

NOTE   As discussed before, modem speed is measured in bits per second, or *bps*. Typical modem speeds at this writing range from 1,200 and 2,400 bps at the low end through 9,600 and 14,400 bps, available with most modems now being sold, to 28,800 bps for the latest reasonably priced models. At any given speed, some modems achieve even faster transmission rates by *compressing* the data. When you set the modem speed in Windows, use the value for the actual speed (with compression turned off).

In any connection, the theoretical speed limit is set by the slower modem—obviously, it won't do you any good to have a super-fast modem when you're communicating with an old, slow unit. Usually, though, you don't need to worry about the speed of the other modem. Because most modems can sense the speed of the other modem, automatically adjusting themselves to match, you may be able to leave yours set to its maximum speed. If your modem cannot auto-adjust, though, you'll have to set its speed to match the other unit (consult your modem's instruction manual to see if it can auto-adjust). If the two modems are mismatched for speed, you will fail to get a connection, or you may see weird characters or punctuation marks on your screen instead of normal text.

In practice, the top speed you actually achieve may be less than the theoretical limit, depending on the quality of the phone line. If there's much static or distortion on the line—still a problem on some long-distance calls—you may need to drop your speed setting down a notch (from, say, 14,400 bps to 9,600 bps or from 2,400 to 1,200) to avoid data loss.

Also, many information services, such as CompuServe, charge more for your connection time when you use a fast modem. You'll save money if you take advantage of the faster communications speed to get your work done quicker. On the other hand, if you just like to dial up and browse through the available options, you may save money at a slower speed.

To change the speed setting, display the modem Properties dialog box (Figure 20.5). Then:

1. In the Maximum speed area, choose the speed you want. The setting is labeled *Maximum speed* on the assumption your modem can auto-adjust to lower speeds to match its counterpart on the other end of the line. If your modem lacks that feature—this is unlikely—the speed you choose here will be used exclusively. If you choose the Highest Possible option, Windows will try to connect at the fastest speed your modem and computer can handle.

2. If you're sure you don't want to connect at a slower speed than the one you've set, check the box labeled *Only connect at this speed.* This can be useful if you'd rather call back later to take advantage of a higher speed if the receiving modem is too slow at the moment. This choice is available only if your modem's auto-adjust feature can be turned off.

Specifying the Data Format Settings

Three key settings pertain to the way the two modems in a connection define and detect individual chunks of data. The two modems must agree on the same format for data, or they will speak completely different languages.

The individual data-format settings—data bits, parity, and stop bits—are described in separate paragraphs below. To change any of these settings:

1. Display the Properties dialog box for the connection you're working with (Figure 20.4).

2. In the list labeled *Connect using*, choose the modem you want to use for the connection, then click on the Configure button. In the Properties dialog box for this modem (Figure 20.5) click on the Connection tab. The dialog box should now display the page shown in Figure 20.6.

3. For each of the three settings in the *Connection preferences* area, select the choice you want from the list.

Setting Data Bits   The *Data bits* setting refers to the number of *bits* (the smallest division of computer information) you want to send out in each separate chunk of data. For example, each letter is typically

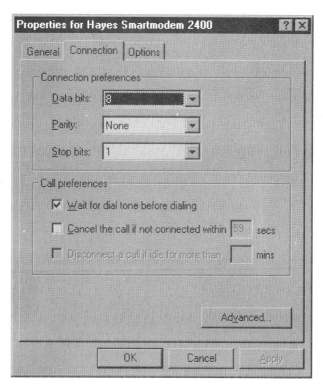

Figure 20.6 *The Connections page of the modem Properties dialog box*

stored in your computer as eight bits. (Eight bits is called a *byte*.) Suffice it to say that this setting is almost always going to be 8 and must be 8 if you are intending to transfer binary files between computers. Binary files include all programs and any documents that consist of more than plain ASCII characters. Thus, formatted word-processing documents, spreadsheets, and graphics documents are binary files. The other popular standard is 7 bits, which allows you to send plain text files slightly faster. The 4-, 5-, and 6-bit options are rarely used. Change this setting only if you are specifically told that the other system uses a setting other than 8 bits.

Setting Parity   *Parity* is a means by which the communications software can perform a rudimentary check to see if an error has occurred in the transmission of each byte of data. Parity checking isn't commonly used, and the standard setting is None. If you are specifically told that the system with which you're communicating uses parity checking, change this setting to match.

Setting Stop Bits   *Stop bits* are used by the computers on both ends to indicate the end of one character and the beginning of the next. You can probably leave this set to 1. Change this setting if you are specifically told that the other system uses 2 or 1.5 stop bits.

Special Dialing Settings

NOTE   Because they only affect your own modem, these dialing settings are an exception to the rule about matching your settings to those at the other end of the line.

Two settings control the way your modem interacts with the telephone line. You'll need to change these settings if your modem is unable to dial for you even when other settings are correct. This can happen with certain types of phone systems that have nonstandard dial tones—or no dial tone at all—or that require you to dial outside calls via the operator.

The two settings are:

Wait for dial tone before dialing: This check box is located on the Connection page of the modem Properties dialog box. It's available only if Windows knows how to control your modem's ability to recognize the dial tone. The box should be checked if there's a delay before the dial tone comes on—otherwise HyperTerminal will start dialing too soon. Clear the box if the system uses a nonstandard dial tone, if there is no dial tone at all, or if you will be dialing yourself or with the operator's help.

Operator assisted or manual dial: This check box is located on the Options page of the modem Properties dialog box. Check it only if you need to dial the phone yourself or via the operator. When this box is checked, HyperTerminal displays a message telling you to dial the number after you click on Dial on the Dial dialog box:

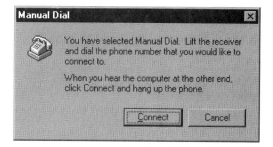

As the message indicates, you should then dial the number (directly, or with the operator's help). When you hear the modem at the other end of the line answer, click on the Connect button and hang up the receiver.

Specifying Advanced Settings

A number of the basic communications settings are accessible in a separate window for advanced settings. These settings are perhaps more technically complex than the ones described above, but they can be just as critical to successful communications. They include:

▶ error-control settings

▶ flow-control settings

▶ low-speed settings

▶ custom-initialization commands

To access these settings, begin from the Connection page on the modem Properties dialog box (see Figure 20.6). Click on the Advanced button to display the Advanced Connection Settings dialog box, shown here.

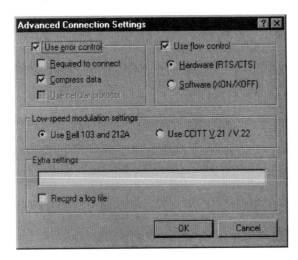

When you're through making changes to the advanced settings, click on OK to return to the modem Properties dialog box. From there, you can change other settings or click on OK again to return to HyperTerminal.

Selecting Error-Control Settings   Some modems come with built-in circuits that detect and correct errors in transmission and that *compress* data, reducing the amount of information that must be sent and, in turn, speeding up the transfer process. If your modem has these features, you can turn them on or off in the Advanced Connection Settings dialog box. Use the four check boxes in the area labeled *Use error control*.

To access any of these error-control features, you must first check the *Use error control* box. The remaining choices are:

> *Required to connect:* Even if your modem has error-control features, you may not be able to use them for a given connection—the modem at the other end of the line may not have them or some other problem may interfere. Check this box if you don't want to proceed with a connection unless the error-control features are working. If the box is clear, HyperTerminal will go ahead and connect even if error control isn't available.

Compress data: Check this box if you want to use the data-compression feature if it's available. At each end of the connection, information is compressed by the sending modem and then *decompressed* by the receiving modem. Data compression speeds up transmission significantly and appears to work reliably, so this box should be checked unless you have some specific reason to do otherwise.

Use cellular protocol: Some modems include a special error-control method for cellular communications, which are prone to more glitches than communications over standard phone lines. If you're communicating "cellularly," checking this box may be necessary for a successful connection. On the other hand, the extra error-control procedures will slow you down, so clear the box when you return to a regular phone line.

Setting the Flow-Control Method

> **NOTE** This setting has no effect on the interaction between your modem and the remote computer, so you don't need to match the other computer's setting.

In the process of receiving and sending data, your computer often has to attend to other tasks as well, such as storing information on disk. Sometimes these tasks can distract the computer from handling incoming data. The *Use flow control* setting in the Advanced Connection Settings dialog box determines how *your* computer interacts with *your* modem to manage such situations. It provides a way for the computer and the modem to agree when to stop and start the sending process so other contingencies can be dealt with.

Unless you know the system will work otherwise, leave the *Use flow control* box checked. Beneath the check box, choose one of the available flow-control protocols. The hardware method is more reliable, so choose its radio button unless your modem isn't able to respond via hardware.

Setting the Low-Speed Modulation Protocol At speeds above 2,400 bps, modems use a standard international signaling (modulation) protocol. At 1,200 bps and 2,400 bps, however, there are two sets of signaling protocols in wide use: Bell and CCITT. The Bell protocols are the ones to use in the United States, while the CCITT are for Europe and many other parts of the world (outside the United States and

Europe, you'll need to check locally). Choose the appropriate radio button in the Advanced Settings dialog box.

Specifying Initialization Settings

NOTE The initialization command may or may not pertain to settings in effect at the other end of the line.

If you need to send special commands to your modem before you begin a communications session—*initialization* commands—type them into the area labeled *Extra settings* in the Advanced Connection Settings dialog box. For example, you may want to tell your modem how many rings to try before giving up trying to connect with the remote computer. Or, if you don't have Touch Tone™ service, you can tell the modem to use pulse dialing instead. Check your modem's manual for the commands it uses.

By the way, you can send commands to your modem at any time from the main HyperTerminal window. Just type the command and press Enter. As an example, you can set up the modem to answer an incoming call after four rings with the command ATS0=4.

Choosing Terminal Settings

Before PCs were invented, people used *terminals* to communicate with large mainframe computers. Terminals are essentially nothing but a screen and keyboard with which data can be entered and displayed. They have no internal computing power or disk storage as does your PC. Because more than one manufacturer made terminals, conflicting standards developed regarding how data were displayed on the terminal screens and how keyboards worked.

These standards remain valid today. They apply to communications setups using PCs as well as to terminals. As its name implies, HyperTerminal can make your PC act like an old-style terminal. But because your computer has more brains and storage capabilities than a terminal, your PC is something of a chameleon—it can *emulate* more than one type of terminal with a change of options in a dialog box.

NOTE Some of the settings on the Settings page have more to do with personal taste than ensuring successful communications. Still, because HyperTerminal lumps them together, I'll cover them in this section.

For successful telecommunications, two computer systems must use the same terminal standard. This almost always means that you'll be setting up your connection to match the terminal standard used by the remote system.

To set or check the settings pertaining to *terminal emulation* and related attributes in HyperTerminal, begin by choosing File ➤ Properties or clicking on the Properties button on the Toolbar. In the Properties dialog box for this connection, click on the Settings tab to display the page shown in Figure 20.7.

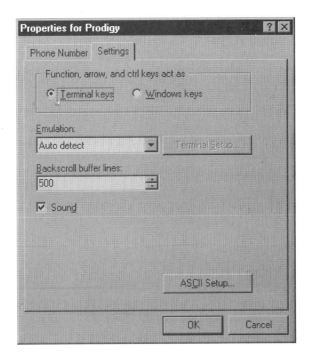

Figure 20.7   The Settings page for a HyperTerminal connection in the Properties dialog box

Controlling the Function, Arrow, and Ctrl Keys

HyperTerminal gives you a choice around how some of the keys work when you're communicating with another computer. In the area labeled *Function, arrow, and ctrl keys act as,* choose the Terminal keys radio button if you want HyperTerminal to send the codes for these keys to the other modem. Choose the Windows keys radio button to have HyperTerminal *trap* these keys so they're still available to control Windows. For example, pressing Ctrl-Esc would still work to open the Start menu.

Selecting a Terminal-Emulation Setting

The Emulation setting lets you choose which type of terminal Hyper-Terminal should emulate (work like) for this connection. The standard setting, Auto detect, usually works—HyperTerminal can tell what type of terminal the remote computer expects and sets everything up for you automatically. If the Auto detect setting doesn't work or if you simply want manual control over your system, choose the correct terminal type from the drop-down list.

Here are descriptions of some of the more popular terminal standards:

TTY (for teletype): is the least sophisticated choice and therefore has the highest level of compatibility. It makes your PC emulate what's known as a *dumb* terminal, meaning that the only formatting codes it uses in communicating to the remote computer are carriage return, Backspace, and Tab characters. If you do not know which terminal emulation to use or if you see strange characters on your screen during a session, try this.

VT52: emulates the DEC VT-52 terminal. Use this for information services such as CompuServe, BBSs, electronic mail services, and so on.

VT100: emulates the DEC VT-100 terminal. Select this for communicating with mainframes as though you were using a DEC VT-100, VT-220, or VT-240 terminal or compatible.

ANSI: recognizes a set of standard commands, or *escape sequences,* governing screen displays. Most BBSs optionally allow you to use these ANSI escape sequences to display their menus and other screen elements in color. ANSI stands for American National Standards Institute, an industry body that establishes voluntary standards for many products.

Choosing Options for a Specific Terminal Emulation   If you choose a specific type of terminal in the Emulation area, you can then set various options concerning its operation. To do this, click on the Terminal Setup button. The available options are different for each terminal-emulation setting. Here's an example:

Often, as in the above example, you can choose whether the Hyper-Terminal cursor appears as a block or underline and whether or not it blinks. When you change the cursor setting, it changes for all the other terminal emulations. Settings unique to a given terminal emulation remain even after you select a different emulation; when you change back to the first emulation, the previous settings are restored.

Setting the Backscroll Buffer Size

HyperTerminal records all the text that it displays in its main window, storing it so you can scroll back to see earlier material at any time. The recorded text is preserved in a backscroll buffer even when you exit HyperTerminal so you can see text from a previous day's communication sessions.

You can control how many lines of text the program records on the Settings page of the Properties dialog box for the current connection. The standard setting is the maximum, 500 lines. To change it, type in a new number or click on the small arrow controls to increase or decrease the value.

Turning Sound On or Off

The Sound check box at the bottom of the Settings page toggles Hyper-Terminal's beep off and on. Sometimes the remote computer will send your computer the code that causes a beep sound. You may want to disable this if you find it annoying. To do so, clear the Sound check box.

Controlling How Text Is Sent and Received

Five settings control the way HyperTerminal handles text transferred between your modem and its counterpart at the other end of the line. To access these settings, click on the ASCII Setup button, found on the Settings page of the Properties dialog box. The ASCII Setup dialog box appears, as shown here:

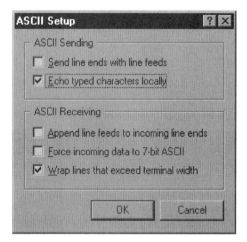

All five choices are check boxes, meaning you can turn them on or off individually by checking or clearing the box. Here's how they work:

Send line ends with line feeds: Computer systems differ in how they register the end of a line of text. Sometimes the system you're sending text to won't be able to detect the end of a line unless HyperTerminal sends a special character called a *line feed* after each line. If that turns out to be the case, check this box.

Echo typed characters locally: When this box is checked, the characters you type on your keyboard appear on your screen so you can see what you're typing. It may sound strange, but in some communications sessions you may find you can't see what you're typing unless this setting is turned on. That's because the remote computer isn't sending the characters it receives from you back to your screen. On the other hand, if you see double characters on the screen (such as *HHEELLLLOO!!*), clear this box.

Append line feeds to incoming line ends: If all the incoming text appears on a single line that gets continually rewritten, or if the cursor moves to the right margin and seems to get stuck, try checking this box. What's happening is that the other computer isn't sending the special line-feed character to move the cursor down after each line is complete. When you turn this setting on, HyperTerminal moves the cursor down every time it receives a finished line. If this box is checked and the text you receive is double-spaced, clear the box.

Force incoming data to 7-bit ASCII: On a PC, each character is represented by 8 bits of data, providing a total of 256 different characters. Although the first 128 characters have been standardized internationally, characters numbered 128 and above (*high-ASCII characters*) vary from country to country and from computer system to computer system (in fact, they are different in DOS and Windows). So if you see strange characters on your screen, it may help to check this box. HyperTerminal will then translate high-ASCII characters according to the International Standards Organization (ISO) 7-bit codes. Normal letters, numbers, and punctuation marks are left as is.

Wrap lines that exceed terminal width: Checking this box causes incoming text that is longer than the width of your screen to wrap to the next line.

Setting Other HyperTerminal Preferences

A smattering of other settings control various aspects of HyperTerminal's operation according to your preferences—these settings don't affect your ability to transfer information successfully. You can:

- control your modem's speaker volume
- control how long HyperTerminal waits to make a connection
- have HyperTerminal hang up automatically if no information is being transferred
- control the display
- change the font for the main window

Setting Speaker Volume

Many modems are equipped with speakers, allowing you to monitor the progress of a call audibly. If your modem has a speaker and Windows knows how to control the speaker (this varies by type of modem), you can change the volume as follows:

1. Choose File ➤ Properties or click on the Properties button to display the Properties dialog box for this connection (Figure 20.4).

2. Click on Configure to display the Properties dialog box for the selected modem (Figure 20.5).

3. Change the volume with the sliding *Speaker volume* control.

Setting Call Preferences

Two settings let you set waiting periods governing HyperTerminal's behavior in certain calling and communications situations. When dialing, you can specify the number of seconds HyperTerminal waits for a connection before giving up. After a connection is made, you can tell HyperTerminal to disconnect if no information has been transferred after a specified number of minutes.

Change these settings as follows:

1. Choose File ➤ Properties or click on the Properties button to display the Properties dialog box for this connection (Figure 20.4).

2. Click on Configure to display the Properties dialog box for the selected modem (Figure 20.5).

3. Click on the Connection tab.

4. To have HyperTerminal stop trying to connect after a given waiting period, check the box labeled *Cancel the call if not connected within* and type in the number of seconds. To have HyperTerminal disconnect after a period of inactivity, check the box labeled *Disconnect a call if idle for more than* and type in the number of minutes. (If Windows can't control the settings in question, they will be unavailable.)

Controlling the HyperTerminal Display

Several settings are available for controlling what you see in HyperTerminal and when.

For one thing, you can choose whether or not to display the Toolbar or the Status Bar. Just choose the appropriate item on the View menu to turn either bar on or off.

You can also decide whether the Dial dialog box appears when you first start HyperTerminal and whether to view a window showing modem status when HyperTerminal dials a number. To access these settings:

1. Choose File ➤ Properties or click on the Properties button to display the Properties dialog box for this connection (Figure 20.4).

2. Click on Configure to display the Properties dialog box for the selected modem (Figure 20.5).

3. Click on the Options tab. You'll see the settings shown in Figure 20.8.

4. The check boxes in the area labeled *Connection Control* determine whether or not HyperTerminal displays the terminal window (the main portion of the HyperTerminal display) before dialing the connection or after the call is concluded. In the *Status control* section, the check box labeled *Display modem status* turns on and off the message

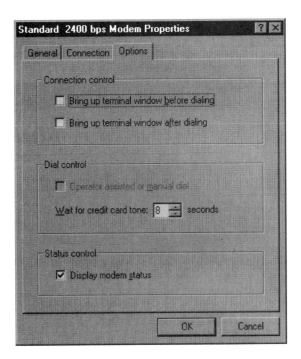

Figure 20.8 **The Options page of the Properties dialog box**

window (shown below) that tells you how a connection is progressing when HyperTerminal dials. (The *Dial control* settings on the Options page are covered earlier in this chapter.)

Choosing a Font

Another cosmetic option, this one determines which font and type size HyperTerminal will use to display both incoming and outgoing characters. This is actually a thoughtful feature, giving tired eyes a break when you're doing a lot of telecommunications. If you increase the font size beyond a size that will allow a complete line of text to fit in the window, scroll bars will allow you to scroll horizontally to see it. However, it's rather a nuisance to do this, and it's better to stick with a smaller size, such as 12 or 14 points.

To make a font change, choose View ➤ Fonts. Select the font, style, and size in the standard Fonts dialog box that appears, then click on OK.

Saving Your Settings

HyperTerminal automatically saves the changes in settings you make as soon as you click on OK in the Properties dialog box for the current connection as well as in the modem Properties dialog box. However, you can save the settings yourself just to be sure they're recorded. More practically, you can save the current settings as a new connection. That makes it easy to use existing settings to connect with a different service or computer—all you have to do is change the phone number and then use the Save As command.

To save the current settings for the connection that's already active, just choose File ➤ Save. To save them as a new connection, choose File ➤ Save As. The familiar Save As dialog box will appear. Give your connection a name, preferably one that will help you remember which information service or computer the settings are for, and click on OK.

Making Connections

 NOTE By the way, if HyperTerminal has displayed the Dial dialog box but you don't want to make the connection at this time, just click on Cancel to go to the main HyperTerminal window.

Assuming you've completed all the setup steps properly, the process of actually making a connection couldn't be simpler. All you do is click on the Dial button on the Dial dialog box:

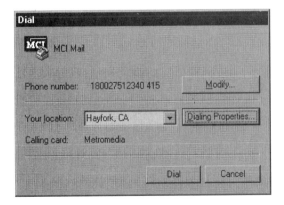

HyperTerminal displays the Dial dialog box first each time you start the program from an existing connection. There are other ways to bring up the Dial dialog box to start a new communications session:

▶ When you're creating a new connection, the Dial dialog box will appear after you've named the connection, chosen its icon, and typed in a phone number.

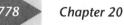

▶ Once you're working with the main HyperTerminal window—perhaps after completing a previous communications session—you can display the Dial dialog box again by choosing Call ➤ Connect or clicking on the Dial (Connect) button.

 TIP   If you want to stop the dialing process, click on Cancel in the Connect window.

When you click on the Dial button, HyperTerminal immediately starts the dialing process. You'll see the Connect message window, informing you of the progress of the call:

Behind the scenes, HyperTerminal begins by sending a series of commands to the modem to prepare it for dialing. These are determined by the settings you've chosen, as detailed in the previous section.

Then HyperTerminal sends the command to dial the number. At this point, if your modem's speaker is on, you'll hear the telephone being dialed. When the phone on the other end is answered, you may hear some high-pitched tones indicating that the modems are "talking" to each other.

If the connection is successful, the message *Connected* will appear briefly in the Connect window and you'll hear three quick beeps. The Connect window will then disappear. If you have the Status Bar visible, you'll see the message *Connected* at its far left followed by a time indicator showing how long your computer has been connected to the remote machine in hours, minutes, and seconds.

At this point, if both modems are set up properly, and depending on how the other computer is programmed, you're likely to see messages from the connection on your screen. From now on, everything you type on the keyboard will be sent to the other computer. You can respond to these messages—or initiate messages of your own—by simply typing whatever you like. And you're now ready to transfer files from disk in either direction, as discussed later in the chapter.

What Might Go Wrong

A variety of problems can prevent you from successfully communicating. Here are the broad categories and some brief tips on how you can track down the specific problem:

▶ If you receive a message that no lines are available, or if the Connect window never displays the *Dialing* message, something is wrong with your modem or its connection to your computer. The modem may not be connected properly, it may not be turned on, or the COM port settings may be incorrect. Your modem could even be broken, though this is by far the least likely problem.

▶ If HyperTerminal is able to dial your modem, but can't establish a connection, it will eventually give up. You'll see the message *Busy* in the Connect window. Typical reasons for failure at this point are the following:

  ▶ There was a busy signal.

  ▶ The call didn't go through. Check to be sure the phone number is correct and that you've set up the Dialing Properties dialog box to dial the proper numbers to connect you to an outside line and to dial using your calling card, if you're using one.

  ▶ The other phone never answered.

  ▶ The other phone was answered, but not by a modem (you dialed a voice line or a standard fax machine, or the other modem was turned off). You may have entered the wrong number or area code.

  ▶ The modems are set at different speeds so they didn't recognize each other.

When any of these problems occur, the Connect window remains on your screen. The Dial Now button becomes active, so if you want to try again, just click on it.

▶ If a connection is made but you see gibberish on your screen, your modem settings don't match those of the other party. See *Choosing Communications Settings* above for details on changing modem settings.

Disconnecting

After you've completed a communications session, it's time to break the connection between your system and the other modem. When possible, the graceful way to do this is by telling the other computer you want to end the session. Most information services and BBSs let you type a command such as **EXIT** or **BYE** for this purpose. When you do, the other computer sends the *disconnect* command to your modem, and you are disconnected automatically.

Sometimes, though, it's necessary to break off a connection manually. All you have to do is click on the Disconnect button on the Toolbar or choose Call ➤ Disconnect.

When HyperTerminal disconnects, you'll hear three quick beeps. The message *Disconnected* appears at the far left of the Status Bar.

Making a Different Connection

Of course, after opening HyperTerminal from one connection icon and completing your communications session with that computer, you don't have to shut down the program to call a different destination. All you need do is choose File ➤ Open or click on the Open button on the Toolbar. Pick the connection (session) file you want to open, click on Open, and click on the Dial button to place the call.

Connecting via Cable

> **TIP** If you are connecting two computers directly to each other (without using modems), you might want to refer to *The RS-232 Solution (Second Edition)* (Sybex, 1994).

While you'll usually use HyperTerminal to communicate over the telephone lines, the program will also work to transfer information when you connect your computer to another computer directly, via a *serial cable*. All you need is the right type of cable: a *null-modem* cable, with jacks that fit the serial ports on the backs of the two computers (a modem is not required and shouldn't be used).

When you plug in the cable to your computer, be sure you know which COM port you've connected it to. Then, in HyperTerminal, proceed as follows:

1. Open the Properties dialog box for this connection to set up the program for that port. On the Phone Number page, select the correct COM port from the list at *Connect using*.

2. Click on the Configure button. You'll see the dialog box full of settings for this COM port shown in Figure 20.9. Select the maximum speed the two computers can reliably handle—direct connections are usually much faster than modem-based connections. The other settings work the same as they do for modems and are described earlier in the chapter. All of them should be set the same on both computers.

3. Click on OK twice to return to the main HyperTerminal window.

4. Click on the Connect button or choose Call ➤ Connect to establish the connection. HyperTerminal immediately proceeds with the connection—you won't see a Dial dialog box or anything similar. If all the settings are correct, you should be able to send messages back and forth between the two computers by typing on their keyboards. You can now send and receive text and files just as in a modem-based connection.

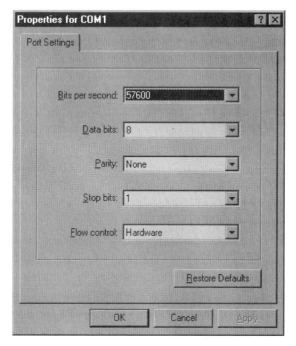

Figure 20.9 *Configure the COM port with the settings in this dialog box.*

Sending and Receiving Data

Once you've made a successful connection, you can begin to transfer data between the two computers. What you do now depends entirely on what the other computer expects from you. If you are calling an information service, BBS, or a mainframe computer, you will typically have to sign on to the remote system by typing your name and possibly a password. If you are calling a friend's or associate's computer, you can just begin typing whatever you want to say. In any case, once the initial connection is made, there are several ways that you can begin to transfer data between the two computers. The next several sections describe these techniques and how to use them.

Communicating in Interactive Mode

The simplest way to communicate information is directly from your keyboard. As mentioned earlier, once you're connected to the other computer, everything you type is automatically sent to the other end of the connection. Conversely, characters typed at the other computer will be sent to your computer, showing up on your screen. Sending and receiving data this way is called working in *interactive* or *terminal* mode. Communication sessions often begin in terminal mode, with each person typing to the other's screen.

Terminal mode is often used, too, when connecting to many of the information services and electronic-mail services that are interactive in nature. With these, you type certain commands to the host computer, and it responds by sending you some data. As information comes over the line to your computer, it will appear on the screen, as shown in Figure 20.10. As you type, your text will appear on the screen as well.

How HyperTerminal Displays and Stores Text

As each new line of text is received or typed in by you, the cursor moves down a line in the HyperTerminal window. Once it reaches the

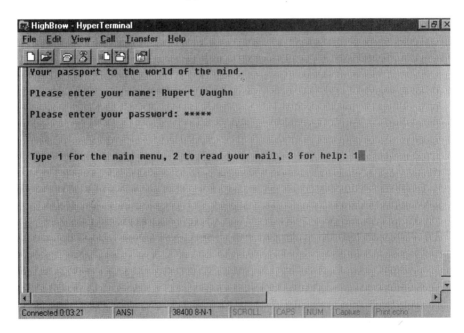

Figure 20.10   *A typical interactive session. Notice that the user entered the number 1 at the bottom of the screen in response to the prompt from the sender.*

bottom of the window, each new line shifts the previous text up so the oldest line disappears from view. This is just as text behaves in a word-processing program such as WordPad (Chapter 19).

But the older text isn't gone forever. HyperTerminal remembers the last 500 lines in its *backscroll buffer*. To see text that has scrolled off the screen, use the vertical scroll bar or the standard cursor-movement keys. Then scroll back down to continue interacting with the other computer. (You can scroll through previous text when you're not connected, too.)

Capturing Text

There will be times when you'll want a way to save data you see on your screen while you're working in terminal mode so you can work with it later. You can *capture* incoming text at any time during a communications session with the Receive Text File command on the Transfer menu and save it in a disk file for later reading, printing, or editing. Here is the basic procedure for capturing text:

1. Choose Transfer ➤ Capture Text.

2. A small dialog box appears, asking you to name the file in which you want the captured text stored. Type in the name (you can use the Browse button to select a new directory) but don't press Enter yet.

3. Click on OK. The file will be opened. If the Status Bar is visible, the Capture message becomes highlighted, indicating the capture is in progress.

4. Continue with your session. All incoming text, along with whatever you type as well, will be captured in the file you chose. When you want to stop capturing text, choose Transfer ➤ Capture Text again to display a new submenu (only available when a capture is currently in progress). Here, choose either:

   ➤ *Stop* to close the file or

   ➤ *Pause* to temporarily discontinue capturing text while leaving the file open for more. To resume the capture, choose Transfer ➤ Capture Text ➤ Resume.

By the way, after you stop a capture, you can add or append more text to the same file by simply restarting the capture process and specifying the file again. If you don't want the new text to go into the previous capture file, you must enter a different file name when you restart the capture process.

Capturing Selected Portions of Text

During text capturing there may be sections of text you don't want to save interspersed with portions you do. There are two ways to selectively capture portions of the text that appears in the HyperTerminal window:

▶ You can use the Pause feature of the Capture command to stop the capture process whenever you're receiving information you don't want to keep. When you expect more "good" information, use Resume.

▶ Alternatively, you can dispense with the Capture command and just allow HyperTerminal to store the text in its backscroll buffer. You can then scroll through the buffer to copy the information you want to keep to a document in a text-editing program such as Windows Notepad. See *Manipulating Text in the HyperTerminal Window* below for details.

Sending and Receiving Text Files

Receiving text files sent from the other computer is easy: You just use the Capture command described in the previous section. When you're connected to a BBS or information service, you'll first have to type whatever commands are needed to get the other computer to send you the file you want.

It's convenient to *send* short messages by typing them on your keyboard, but obviously, this would be an inefficient way to send larger quantities of text. HyperTerminal gives you an alternative: You can send documents already prepared by a word processor or other program and stored on disk. By composing your messages first with a word processor or text editor, you can drastically reduce the connection time (and resultant cost). And it's much easier than typing them using the primitive editing features of HyperTerminal.

There are two ways to do it. One method uses error correction to ensure that the other computer receives your file without any loss of data, and it also allows you to transfer complete documents. This is discussed in the next section. The other technique does not use error correction and can send *only* text, but it is compatible with a wider variety of computers.

> CAUTION   You cannot use the Send Text File command to send formatted documents or to send programs. Send such files as binary files as described in the next section.

The Send Text File command on the Transfer menu is the method for sending text only, *without* error correction. Use this command to send memos, letters, and so forth when the content alone of your text, without any fonts or formatting, will suffice.

Files you can send with this command are called, of all things, *text-only* files, also known as ASCII files. (Sometimes they're just called *text files*, but this can be a little confusing because a word-processing document might also be considered a text file.) Text-only files are standard means of communicating on most electronic-mail services such as MCI Mail. There are several ways to create text-only files:

▶ You can use a text editor such as Windows Notepad (see Chapter 22).

▶ Most word-processing programs, including WordPad, let you save a document as a text-only file. Remember that when you save a word-processing document as a text-only file, all formatting—including fonts, type styles, and spacing settings such as margins and indents—are lost.

▶ Files stored with HyperTerminal's Capture Text File command (described in the previous section) are also text-only files, and they'll work too.

Checking Settings for Text-File Transfers

Before sending or receiving a text file, you might want to check the pertinent settings for this connection. To do so:

1. Choose File ▶ Properties or click on the Properties button on the Toolbar. When the Properties dialog box for this connection appears, switch to the Settings page.

2. Click on the ASCII Setup button. A small dialog box appears.

Supplied Applications

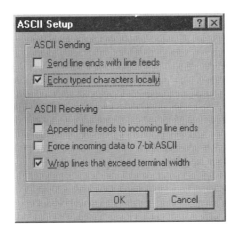

Only the first choice, *Send line feeds with line ends*, pertains to sending text-only (ASCII) files. If you need to add a line feed to the end of each line of text you send, check this box. You might have to talk with the person running the other computer to determine whether line feeds should be added or not. The three choices in the section labeled *ASCII Receiving* pertain to receiving text-only files. You can figure out which settings are correct based on the appearance of the text you receive.

3. Click on OK twice to close the dialog boxes.

Sending a Text File

Once you've selected the correct settings, you're ready to actually send the text file. Connect to the other computer if you haven't already done so. Then follow these steps:

1. Prepare the other computer to receive the text. If you're sending an e-mail letter via a BBS or commercial service, for example, type whatever command the service requires to prepare itself for the message. You might need to enter a command such as *Create* or *Send mail*, and then enter the name and electronic address of your recipient. Consult the service for details.

2. When the other computer is ready to receive your text, choose Transfer ➤ Send Text File.

3. A standard Windows file dialog box will appear. Select the file you want to transfer, then click on OK. The text from the file will appear on your screen as it is sent to the other computer.

4. When the entire file has been sent, type whatever command the other computer requires to indicate the end of the message or go on to send another file.

Sending and Receiving Documents and Other Files

Most of the files stored on your computer's disks do *not* consist of only text. Instead of simple sequences of characters arranged in lines, the typical file—whether it's a document created by your word-processing or spreadsheet program or the program itself—contains all sorts of information in encoded form. This information is perfectly understandable by your computer (with the right software), but it usually looks like complete gibberish to you and me.

TIP   There is a way, with a little legwork to send non-text files to another person through an electronic-mail service that only accepts text-only files. You have to use a utility program that converts binary files into a special type of encoded 7-bit "text" file before sending it. The receiving party will then have to reconvert the file on their end with the same utility program. Such utilities are available as shareware on many BBSs.

That's why you can't transfer most files with HyperTerminal's Capture Text and Send Text File commands. You need the Send File and Receive File commands instead. These commands transfer the entire document just as it is, without trying to interpret it as text. In the bargain, they detect and correct errors that have crept in during the transfer.

TIP   By the way, it's perfectly okay to send and receive text-only files via the Send File and Receive File commands to get the benefits of error correction. The only drawbacks: you won't see the text on your screen, and the process takes a tad longer.

It's not uncommon for data to be lost or corrupted during the transmission process over telephone lines, particularly when long distances are involved. As we all know, long-distance lines often suffer from noise, static, or even other people's conversations accidentally being crossed with ours. Usually we just put up with the noise, asking the other party to repeat their last sentence, or we redial the call.

Computers are less tolerant of such maladies. Noise on the line between two computers can cause a plethora of erratic data alterations during a file transfer. In response to this, computer scientists have devised numerous error-detection and error-correction schemes to determine whether errors have occurred in transmission and to correct them if possible. These schemes are referred to as *file-transfer protocols* because they also manage other aspects of the file-transfer process. HyperTerminal lets you choose from several of the most popular of these file-transfer protocols with its Receive File and Send File commands.

Understanding File-Transfer Protocols

To detect and correct errors, file-transfer protocols divide a file into a series of small sections, called *blocks*. The blocks are then sent sequentially, and each one is accompanied by a mathematically calculated code based on the contents of the block. After getting the block, the receiving computer sees whether its contents match this calculated code. If they do, the sending computer is advised to send the next block. If there is a discrepancy, the receiving computer asks the sending computer to retransmit the block until it's received properly. This process continues until the entire file is transmitted error free.

Some file-transfer protocols, such as Zmodem, keep track of how far along the file transfer is from moment to moment. If the connection is broken, they can pick up the file transfer where it left off so that you don't have to start all over again from scratch.

Choosing a File-Transfer Protocol

When you transfer a file with the Send File or Receive File commands, HyperTerminal lets you choose which of several file-transfer protocols to use for the transfer. Although each of the file-transfer protocols has its own characteristics, the critical point should sound familiar by now: To send or receive a file successfully, you need to use the same protocol as the other computer.

Often, when you're transferring files to or from a commercial service or BBS, you'll be able to tell the other computer which protocol to use. Whether or not you select the other computer's protocol, just be sure to set HyperTerminal to match.

Here's a list of the file-transfer protocols available in HyperTerminal:

Xmodem was the first widely used error-detection and correction scheme. It was devised by Ward Christensen, who placed it in the public domain in 1977 for use on microcomputers, which were just then becoming available. Xmodem is available on most information services, such as CompuServe. The 1K version is a bit faster than the standard version.

Ymodem is similar to Xmodem but a little faster and more reliable.

Kermit may be the only protocol available when you communicate with some larger computers such as the minicomputers at a university. It's usually slower than the others, so this protocol would be a second or third choice.

Zmodem is the fastest and most capable of HyperTerminal's protocols. Use this choice if the other computer permits it.

Sending Files

NOTE　You can't pause a binary transfer, but you can stop it in midstream by clicking on Stop or choosing Stop from the Transfers menu.

To send a file, follow these steps:

1. Make sure you're online (connected).

2. Make sure the receiving computer is ready to receive the file. How you do this depends on the computer system, BBS, or information service to which you are connected. If you are sending a file to another PC, you may want to type a message in HyperTerminal mode telling the operator of the other computer to do what is necessary to prepare for receiving the file.

3. Choose Transfer ➤ Send File or click on the Send button on the Toolbar.

A small dialog box appears:

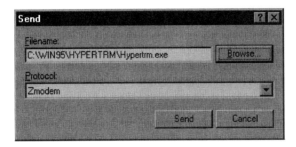

4. Enter the name of the file you want to send (or click on Browse, locate and select the file, and click on OK to go back to the Send dialog box). Then choose the error-detection protocol you want (the one in use by the receiving system).

5. Click on OK to begin the file transfer.

> NOTE By the way, you won't see the contents of the file on the screen (if it's not all text, it would look like garbage anyway).

You'll now see a large window reporting the progress of the transfer as shown in Figure 20.11. At the top, the name of the file being sent is displayed. Next come several readouts on the error-checking process—these are pretty technical, and you can usually ignore them. If something goes seriously wrong, HyperTerminal will halt the transfer. At that point, you may be able to diagnose the problem by reading the message displayed at *Last error*.

The (slightly) more interesting part of the display is the lower half. Here, HyperTerminal shows you graphically and in numbers how quickly the transfer is going. The bar graph at File expands to the right giving you a quick sense of how much of the file has been sent so far, relative to its total size. Next to the graph, you're shown how much of the file has been sent in numbers. Below are counters showing how much time has elapsed since the transfer began, how much time is remaining (assuming all goes well, and if HyperTerminal is able to calculate this), and, in the Throughput area, your current "speed." By clicking on the cps/bps button, you can set the display units for throughput speed: characters per second (cps) or bits per second (bps). Characters per second is actually a measure of the number of bytes (8-bit information units) being transferred each second.

To cancel a file transfer before it has finished, click on the Cancel button at the bottom of the window. If the transfer completes normally, you'll hear a single beep as the window disappears.

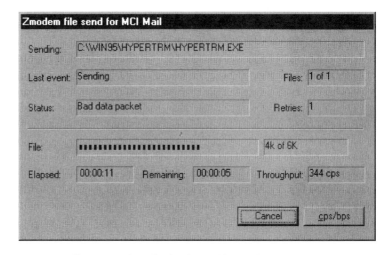

Figure 20.11 You'll see a window like this during file transfers.

As a recap of sending binary files, consider the following: a binary file will arrive just as you sent it, with no modifications (for example, no adding or stripping of line feeds). All types of files, including program files, can be sent and received as binary files. Formatted text as well as program files must be transmitted as binary files, or information will be lost.

Receiving Files

You'll want to use the Receive File command to transfer document and program (non-text) files to your computer from the computer at the other end of the line. The process of receiving such a file is very similar to sending one:

1. After connecting to the other computer, tell the sending computer to send the file and which file-transfer protocol to use in the process. How you do this depends on the computer and program(s) involved. If you're connected to a BBS or information service, you can usually

control the process from your computer. If you're connected to another individual's computer, you ask the person at the other end of the line to type in the command to send you the file.

2. Choose Transfer ➤ Receive File or click on the Receive button on the Toolbar.

The Receive File dialog box appears. Choose the *directory* where you want HyperTerminal to store the received file (not the actual file name, which will be set by the other computer). Type in the directory name or use the Browse button to find it. Then select the file-transfer protocol that matches the one used by the other computer. And do all this quickly because the other computer is already trying to send the file. It will wait, but usually not too long.

3. Click on OK or press Enter, and the transmission should begin.

Once the transfer is underway, a window that looks and works very similar to the one you see when sending files (Figure 20.11) will appear. See the previous section for details on its use.

CAUTION   Depending on the file-transfer protocol you're using, HyperTerminal may not know the size of the file being sent to it. In this case, you won't be able to check to see whether you have enough disk space for the file, and you may run out of disk space while receiving it. This is a real hassle, particularly if you've spent half an hour receiving most of a large file only to get an error message saying there isn't enough room on your disk for the rest of it. When this happens, HyperTerminal will abort the receiving process. So make sure the disk you choose to store the file on has enough free space on it before you begin the transfer.

Manipulating Text in the HyperTerminal Window

You can manipulate the text in the document window in various ways while in a HyperTerminal session. You can:

▶ copy it to the Clipboard

▶ transmit selected text or the Clipboard's contents to the other computer as though you were typing it

▶ print incoming or selected text

▶ clear all the text in the window

Copying Text to the Clipboard

Any text you can see on screen or that is still in the backscroll buffer can be copied to the Clipboard. Once there, it can be pasted into other applications or sent to the other system:

1. Select text with the mouse, just as in any other program, such as WordPad or Notepad. (Refer to Chapter 19 for instructions on selecting text in WordPad.) To select all the text in the buffer, choose Edit ➤ Select All.

2. Choose Edit ➤ Copy.

   The text is now on the Clipboard, and you can place it in any open document in another application with the Paste command.

Transmitting Text from the Clipboard

Sometimes you'll want to send text from a different application to the other computer you're currently connected to. If the document containing the text is open in a window, this is very easy. You don't have to create and send a new file. Just follow these steps:

1. In the other application, copy the text to the Clipboard. It can be text in any other application window, such as Microsoft Word, Excel, Write, Ami Pro, PageMaker, and so forth. You can also copy text from the HyperTerminal window.

2. Switch back to the HyperTerminal window (if you're not already there) and choose Edit ➤ Paste to Host. The contents of the Clipboard will be sent, unchanged, to the other computer. If the other computer is using Windows, the user could then select the information, copy it to the Clipboard, and paste it into another document.

CAUTION Only text can be transferred in this way. If a graphic is on the Clipboard, you cannot paste it.

Printing Incoming Text

If you want to print text as it comes onto your screen from the remote computer, follow these steps:

1. Set up your printer and put it online. If necessary, select the correct printer by choosing File ➤ Print and then choosing the printer by name.

2. Choose Transfer ➤ Capture to Printer. A check mark will appear next to the menu selection. All received text will be printed. (If you've set up the connection to echo characters you type to the screen, everything you type will be printed, too.)

3. Choose Transfer ➤ Capture to Printer again to turn off this function.

Printing Selected Text

You can't print selected text directly from HyperTerminal. However, here are two ways you can print what's come over the line:

▶ Select the text you want to print and copy it onto the Clipboard. Then open WordPad, Notepad, or another word processor and paste the text into the document, edit it, and print it as usual.

▶ Save the incoming text as a file, as explained earlier. Exit HyperTerminal and then open the text file in a word processor and print it.

Background Communications with HyperTerminal

Like other Windows programs, HyperTerminal remains active even when you switch to another application. Not only does the HyperTerminal program itself continue running, but any communications connection you've made remains *live*. In other words, information can continue to flow between the two computers in the background while you're working with other programs.

This is a great feature because it allows you to do constructive work with your computer while HyperTerminal transfers files, conducts on-line searches, or carries out other time-consuming communications chores. Otherwise you'd just have to twiddle your thumbs during such activities.

To take advantage of background communications, just start your file transfer or other procedure as you normally would and switch out to whatever other application you want to use. HyperTerminal notifies you when a file transfer is complete by sounding a quick beep. If the connection is broken while you're working with another program, you'll hear the three-beep disconnect signal.

 NOTE   Of course, you can hear these audible messages from HyperTerminal only if the Sound setting is turned on. You'll find this check box on the Settings page of the Properties dialog box for this connection.

Running Multiple Communications Sessions

There probably aren't too many times that you'd want to run multiple communications sessions, but it is possible to have two sessions connected at the same time. To do this, run HyperTerminal a second time by double-clicking on a different connection icon while you still have the first session open. Change any settings as necessary and dial. You must *not* use the same communications port as you're using for the first session. From the Communications dialog box you'll have to select the unused COM channel (1 or 2) as the port for the second session. Of course, you'll need another modem (or cable in the case of direct connection) connected to the second port, as well. By using the Pause command wisely and jumping between windows, you could juggle the two communications sessions.

Ending a Communications Session

Once you've finished your work (or play) during a session, you should end it by following some simple rules:

1.   If you want to save the settings you've made, choose File ➤ Save and name the file.

2. If you are logged on to an information service, electronic mail provider, or BBS, follow the system's instructions for signing off. This may be important to free up a connection for other users or to ensure that the service will cease billing you for connect time.

3. Choose Call ➤ Disconnect.

4. Close HyperTerminal by double-clicking on its Control box.

Troubleshooting

Despite great strides in the field of communications, mostly due to conveniences spurred by the personal computer market, communications is still a bit of a black art. Chances are good that you'll run into some problem or other while transferring files, sending mail, or whatever it is you end up doing with HyperTerminal. The fault will not necessarily lie with HyperTerminal (or yourself), but much more likely will be the result of improper wiring, faulty modems, noisy telephone lines, incorrect log-on procedures, or incompatible software on the other end of the line. If you're trying to connect to a BBS or information service, don't hesitate to call them (the old-fashioned way) for help with making things work right. You can also get help from your company's computer expert, your computer store, or an experienced friend.

Chapter 21

Painting Pictures with Windows Paint

FEATURING

Basic painting techniques

Manipulating areas of a picture

Zooming in for detail work

Editing the color scheme

Printing

Paint is a program for the artist in you. It's a simple but quite capable program for painting and drawing images on your computer screen. You can brush on colors free-form, draw lines and geometric shapes, and even add text to your pictures. A variety of nifty special effects are at your command, too.

Here are some ideas for things you can do with Paint:

▶ create printed signs

▶ create illustrations for printed matter

▶ create images for use in other Windows programs

▶ design invitations

▶ enhance digitized images or photographs

▶ draw maps

▶ make wallpaper images for your Windows Desktop

▶ edit clip art (pre-drawn images you can buy in collections)

▶ clean up "digital dust" from scanned images

▶ edit graphics embedded or linked into documents created by other programs (see Chapter 6)

Starting a New Document

To bring up Paint:

1. Beginning from the Taskbar, choose Start ➤ Programs ➤ Accessories ➤ Paint.

2. The Paint window appears. Maximize the window. Figure 21.1 shows the Paint window and its component parts.

The *work area* is the main part of the window where you do your painting. Along the left side, the *Tool Box* provides a set of buttons for activating the tools you use to paint. You choose colors from the *Color Box* at the bottom of the window. The Status Bar offers help messages on menu choices and displays the coordinates of the mouse pointer.

FOR WINDOWS 3.X USERS

Compared to its Windows 3.x predecessor, Paintbrush, Paint has more features, it looks a little snazzier, and some of the commands and buttons have changed. Still, Paint will seem very familiar if you've worked with Paintbrush. The one big difference that you might not notice is this: You can paint with the *right* mouse button, not just the left (using the right button paints with the background color). Aside from that, most of the tools work about the same as they did in Paintbrush.

Though they aren't earth shattering, new features are plentiful in Paint. You get two new tools: the eyedropper and the pencil. Manipulating selections is much easier now that they have resize handles, and you can rotate them or even use them as a brush shape. Print Preview lets you check your work before you print, saving paper and time. It's easier to work with text by virtue of the Text Toolbar (for setting font, size, and style). And you can Undo three previous commands, not just one.

You give up some features, too. The color eraser tool is gone. You can't save files in the PCX (PC Paintbrush) format, and you can't use shadow or outline styles with text. Paintbrush let you print headers and footers, Paint does not. But if you are enamored of any of these features, you don't have to give them up. Because both programs can open the same files, you can keep Paintbrush on your hard disk and use it when the need arises.

Here's a list of some of the tools and menu commands that have changed:

In Paintbrush	In Paint
Paint roller	Paint Can
Shrink and Grow	Stretch
Tilt	Skew
Inverse	Invert Colors

Understanding Computer Art

Before going any further, let's pause a minute for a little background on how Paint works—it will help you to get the results you want from your artistic creations. In the personal-computer world there are two basic classes of pictures, or *graphics*: *bit-mapped* and *object-oriented*.

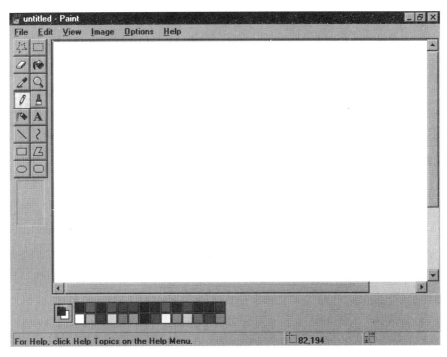

Figure 21.1   *The Paint window*

Paint can create and edit only bit-mapped graphics, so let's focus there (more on object-oriented graphics in a moment).

In programs like Paint, you create a picture on the computer screen as if you were painting on a canvas with paint. Imagine yourself painting the Mona Lisa. With each stroke of the brush, the paint you apply to the canvas sticks irreversibly, covering up whatever was there before.

In Paint, you use colored dots on the screen as your paint, but the process is otherwise quite similar. Once you've placed anything on the screen (and unless you use Undo immediately), it becomes an integral part of the image. It remains there until you cover it up with something else.

Here's why Paint works this way. Your computer's screen is divided into very small dots (*pixels* or *pels*) that are controlled by the smallest division of computer information—bits. A bit map is a collection of bits of information that creates an image when assigned (*mapped*) to dots on the screen. This is similar to a sports scoreboard that can display the score, a message, or even a picture by turning on and off specific lightbulbs in a grid.

The point is, the only thing Paint knows about the image on your screen is which dot should be displayed in which color. When you change the picture, Paint doesn't keep track of whether you paint a line, draw a circle, or type some text. Instead, it simply changes its map of colored dots—the new dots blend into all the other ones.

What all this means is that bit-mapped graphics can be incredibly detailed because you can control the color of each and every dot in your picture if you want to (with the Zoom command). That's why bit-mapped graphics are used to create artwork with the rich detail of a real painting and to store photographic images that have been recorded by a scanner.

On the other hand, there are some limitations to keep in mind. Once you paint a shape, you can't move it independently. True, you can use the computer to remove an area of the painting and place it somewhere else—as if you were cutting out a piece of the canvas and pasting it elsewhere. But *all* the dots in the area get moved, not just the ones in the shape you're interested in. Also, because a bit-mapped graphic has a fixed number of dots, its resolution is fixed—you can't make it look sharper by printing it on a higher-resolution printer, for example.

By contrast, in object-oriented graphics, the computer stores each shape as a separate entity—it's something like those felt boards you used in grade school. Each line, circle, and text character retains its identity as a separate object. These objects can later be moved, sized, cut, copied, and otherwise altered without affecting anything else in the picture. In addition, object-oriented graphics always display and print at the maximum possible resolution of the device you're using.

With object-oriented graphics it's harder to do detailed work, especially involving random shapes and color blends, than with bit-mapped graphics. On the other hand, this type of computer art is great for line drawings, logos, and poster-like illustrations.

Windows 95 doesn't come with an object-oriented graphics program. Popular programs of this type include Corel Draw, Adobe Illustrator, and Micrografx Designer. Also, simple object-oriented graphics modules are included in many word processors and spreadsheets.

Enough theory.

Opening an Existing Picture

To open, or *load*, an existing picture, do the following:

1. Choose File ➤ Open.

2. Select the picture by name in the Open dialog box. Windows 95 comes with many Paint-style pictures in the main Windows directory. Figure 21.2 shows a picture of weightless chess pieces open in Paint.

   Now you can edit the picture and save it again or copy any part of it to the Clipboard for use with other programs.

> **TECH TIP** Paint remembers the last four pictures you've opened or saved, listing them by name at the bottom of the File menu. To open one of these pictures without slowing down for the Open dialog box, just choose the picture from the File menu.

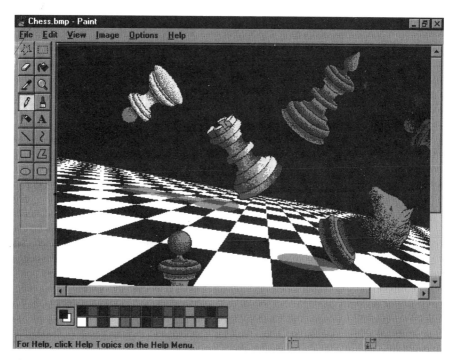

Figure 21.2 *A picture file opened and displayed in the work area*

Paint can only open pictures stored in its own format (also known as the BMP format). If you want to open pictures stored in other formats, such as PCX or TIF, you'll have to translate them to the BMP format with conversion software first.

Seeing More of the Picture

If the picture is too big to fit in the work area, you can, of course, scroll to see any part of the image. But scrolling is a nuisance. You can also take steps to see more of the picture all at once, as detailed in the following sections.

Removing and Tearing Off the Tool and Color Boxes

The simplest method to increase your viewing area is to remove the tools along the left side and bottom of the Paint window. Actually, you don't have to give them up entirely—you can "tear them off" as floating windows that are easy to reposition on the screen.

To tear off the Tool Box or the Color Box, click on any part of the box's background. Hold down the mouse button and drag the window outline that appears into the work area. As shown in Figure 21.3, the box becomes a separate floating window that you can move around as needed to work with your picture.

If you don't need the Tool Box or Color Box—not very likely, but once in a while this may be the case—you can turn them off altogether. Open the View menu and choose the corresponding menu command. You can also remove the Status Bar at the very bottom of the screen this way. To turn on an item back on, just choose its command again from the View menu.

NOTE   When a screen item (Tool Box, Color Box, or Status Bar) is visible, the View menu displays a check mark beside the item's command; there's no check mark if the item has been turned off.

Alternatively, if you've torn off a box, making it a separate window, you can remove it from the screen by clicking on its close box. To turn

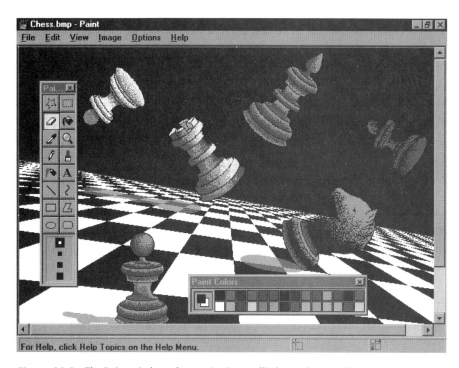

Figure 21.3   The Paint window after you've "torn off" the Tool Box and Color Box

it on again, choose the corresponding item on the View menu. It will
appear on the screen in its last location.

Displaying Only the Picture

If you just want to look at as much of your picture as possible, choose
View ➤ View Bitmap. The picture fills the entire Paint window—all
the other screen elements, including the title bar, menu bar, and scroll
bars disappear. You still may not be able to see the whole picture, of
course, but this is as good as it gets. And all you can do is look at the
picture—you can't make any changes. Clicking anywhere on the
screen or pressing any key returns you to the working screen.

Creating a New Picture

To start a new picture, choose File ➤ New to erase the previous image, then choose Image ➤ Attributes to set the picture size and select *color* or *black and white*.

If another picture is open, choose File ➤ New to begin work on a new, blank "canvas." If you haven't already saved the previous picture, Paint will ask if you want to do so. The existing image will then disappear, leaving the work area empty.

> **TIP** You can start a new picture with a background color other than white. Just before creating the new picture, use the Color Box to change the background color setting (see *Setting the Foreground and Background Colors* below). When you then choose File ➤ New, the blank new picture comes up in the work area in the chosen color.

Setting a Picture's Basic Characteristics

Before you actually start painting, decide whether you want to change any of Paint's standard settings governing the picture's basic characteristics: its size and whether it's a color or black-and-white image. When you use Paint for the first time, it sets up each new picture as a color image with a size equal to that of your screen (not the Paint work area, but the entire screen).

To change the settings for either of these characteristics, choose Image ➤ Attributes to display the Attributes dialog box shown below. You can also change a picture's size with the mouse.

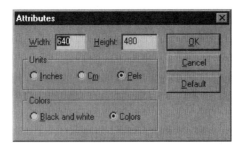

Setting Picture Size

The first thing you should decide when starting a new picture is how big it should be. If you're creating a picture to fit snugly into another document, or if you have an idea of how much room you'll need to express your ideas, defining the picture's size now may save you some work down the road. It's easy to change the size of a picture, so don't spend much time on this decision.

Keep in mind that the size of the image you see is tied to the resolution of your screen. Actually, the size settings control only the number of dots in the picture (even though you can set the size in inches or centimeters in the Attributes dialog box). If you increase the resolution of your screen (see Chapter 7), the picture will look smaller because each component dot is smaller.

Likewise, the image will almost certainly print smaller than it appears on your screen because most printers have much higher resolution than even a Super VGA monitor.

TIP   If you're planning to print the image, choose size settings according to the printed size you plan, not the screen size. For example, if you want the image to be 3×5 inches on the printed page and your printer's resolution is 300 dots per inch, you would enter a width of 900 pixels and a height of 1,500 pixels. Remember too that if your picture is wider than it is tall, and if its printed width is more than about 8 inches, you'll need to change the page orientation for printing from Portrait to Landscape. Choose File ➤ Page Setup and select the appropriate button.

NOTE   The maximum size of a picture is limited by the amount of memory available in your computer. Maximum size also depends on the color scheme: black-and-white pictures use far less memory than color pictures do, so they can be much larger. Paint will let you know if you set a picture size that's too large to fit in memory.

NOTE   When you change the size of a picture, Paint remembers the new dimensions. From then on—until you make further size changes—Paint uses these dimensions whenever you choose File ➤ New to create a new picture. This is so even if you open other larger or smaller pictures in the meantime.

You can resize a picture with the mouse or by typing entries in the Attributes dialog box. Using the mouse is easier if the entire picture fits in the work area, but many pictures are bigger than that. Besides, the mouse isn't very accurate, whereas you can type exact dimensions. At any rate, you use the same resizing techniques whether you're working with a brand new picture or an existing one.

To set the size of your picture with the Attributes dialog box:

1. Choose Image ➤ Attributes. The Attributes dialog box appears.

2. Decide on the measurement units you want to use and click on the corresponding radio button. Pixels (screen dots) is the standard unit, but you can choose inches or centimeters instead.

3. Type in new width and height values. At any time, you can return to the standard size values—equal to the size of your screen—by clicking on Default.

4. Click on OK to return to Paint. The size of your canvas will change according to your entries, though you can only see this if the entire canvas fits within the work area.

To resize a picture with the mouse:

1. Find the picture's sizing handles, the small squares at the bottom-right corner of the picture and along the bottom and right edges. If the picture is larger than the work area, you'll have to scroll down or to the right to see the sizing handles. (The handles at the other three corners and along the other edges do nothing.)

2. To change the picture's width, drag the handle on the right edge to the left (to make the picture narrower) or to the right (to make the picture wider). To change the height, drag the bottom-edge handle up or down. To change both dimensions simultaneously, drag the handle at the bottom-right corner.

Setting the Image to Color or Black and White

NOTE   Paint's black-and-white setting restricts you to two "colors" only, black and white (the speckled-looking choices on the color palette are patterns of black and white dots). A black and white image is *not* the same thing as a grayscale image, in which you can paint with 16 or more separate shades of gray. To create a grayscale image, you must place the desired shades of gray on the palette—see *Editing the Color Scheme* later in this chapter.

Paint can handle both color and black-and-white images. Of course, if you want to create a cartoon or line drawing, you can do it with a color picture by painting with a black brush only. The only real reason to set the picture itself to a black-and-white "color" scheme is to save memory or disk space. Black and white pictures consume one-fourth as much memory and disk space as the simplest color pictures. If you need a very large image, and memory or disk space is limited, black and white may be your only choice.

You're not likely to get great results when converting an existing color image to black and white. Paint converts light colors to white and darker colors to black, and you have no control over the process. In most cases, you'll lose much of the image detail.

CAUTION   You can't undo a change from color to black and white. Be sure you want to make the change. If you're working with an existing color picture, make a backup copy before you convert it to black and white.

To set up a new black-and-white picture, or to convert an existing color picture to black and white:

1. Choose Image ➤ Attributes to open the Attributes dialog box.

2. Choose the *Black and white* radio button and click on OK. Any existing colors in the picture will be converted to either black or white.

Remember, this change is permanent.

> NOTE   New pictures always open in color, even if you changed a previous picture to black and white.

Basic Painting Techniques

Once you've created a new, empty painting, you're ready to try your hand at computer art. Feel free to play with the tools as much as you want—you can't hurt anything, and the learn-by-doodling approach is fun.

In this section I'll explain each of the on-screen controls in the Color Box and Tool Box and suggest some tips and tricks to make your work easier. You might want to sit at your computer and work with each of the tools as you read, changing colors to suit your fancy along the way. Pretty soon you'll have a good high-tech mess on your screen, at which point you can just choose File ➤ New again to clear it and be ready for more experimentation. (When asked about saving your work, click on No unless you really like it.)

Setting the Foreground and Background Colors

> NOTE   The term *color* describes either a color or a colored pattern selected from the Color Box. If you are using a black-and-white screen, colors in the Color Box may appear as shades of gray or varying densities of dot patterns.

One of the most fundamental techniques to learn is selecting a color to paint with. In Paint, you control both foreground and background colors independently.

Understanding Foreground and Background Colors

The foreground or drawing color is the main color you paint with. For example, when you add strokes with Paint's paintbrush, draw lines or shapes, or even when you type text, these items appear in the currently selected foreground color.

The term *background color* is somewhat misleading. True, if you select a background color just before you start a new painting, this will be the color of the canvas or backdrop for the entire picture.

NOTE   It may help to understand that creating a new picture with a specific background color is exactly equivalent to painting the entire picture with that color. There's nothing special about the background color as far as Paint is concerned—a picture is just a set of dots that happen to be all one color when you first create it.

On the other hand, once you have a picture on your screen, many of the tools (such as the Brush, Pencil, and the shape tools) let you paint with the so-called background color just as you would with the foreground color. All you have to do is hold down the right mouse button instead of the left one as you paint. The background color also determines the fill color for circles, squares, and other enclosed shapes, the fill color inside text frames, and the color with which you erase existing parts of the picture.

The key thing to remember: after you've started work on a picture, changing the background color doesn't affect the picture directly in any way. If any of the original background color is still visible, it remains the same.

Choosing a Color Scheme: Basic Tips

You'll get the best results if you stick with solid colors. Here's the scoop: the number of separate solid colors you can use depends on the capabilities of your display hardware and the specific software driver setting you've chosen. A standard VGA screen can display only 16 discrete colors, while more sophisticated displays can handle 256 on up to 16.7 million colors.

Paint uses patterns made up of dots of different colors to represent hues that it can't display as solid colors. These patterns tend to look murky or fuzzy in your pictures. Avoid them when possible.

Also, keep in mind the color capabilities of your printer when you choose colors for your picture. An image that looks great on your screen can become a blurry gray soup when you print it out on a black-and-white printer. When Windows prints to a black-and-white printer, it attempts to translate colors into contrasting shades of gray (actually, gray shades are simulated with different densities of black dots). Sometimes the translation gives you good results, but if not, experiment with the color scheme until you find one that produces a clear image in print—even if the colors clash horribly on the screen. If that doesn't work, just stick with painting in black on a white background.

Viewing and Changing Color Settings

The current settings of the foreground and background colors are shown in the area at the left side of the Color Box. In this area, the box on top toward the upper left shows the foreground color. The box in back, toward the lower right, shows the background color. The default colors are a black foreground on a white background, and they always come up that way when you open a new or existing picture.

You choose new foreground and background colors by selecting them in the Color Box, as described below. Alternatively, you can use the Eyedropper tool, described later, to use a color from the picture as the new foreground or background color.

Setting the Foreground Color

Set the foreground color as follows:

1. Point to the color or pattern you want.

2. Click the *left* mouse button. Now whatever you paint with the tools using the left mouse button will appear in this color. Notice that the foreground color box at the left side of the Color Box reflects your color choice.

Setting the Background Color

To set the background color:

1. Point to the color or pattern in the Color Box.

2. Click the *right* mouse button. The background color box at the left side of the Color Box changes accordingly.

If you want to apply a background color to an entire picture, you must choose the desired background color, then immediately choose File ➤ New to create the new picture. Note, though, that the background color becomes white again as soon as Paint creates the new picture.

CAUTION   You can't change the color of an existing picture's actual background by changing the background color with the Color Box.

TIP   If you start a new picture with the wrong background color, there's an alternative to starting all over again. Before painting anything on the picture, choose the correct background color and click anywhere over the work area with the Paint Can tool, described below. The entire picture area will change to the background color. Alternatively, after choosing the desired background color, choose Image ➤ Clear Image.

Selecting Colors with the Eyedropper Tool

We haven't yet covered the use of the Tool Box—that's the subject of the very next section. Still, this is the appropriate place to mention an alternative technique for selecting colors: the Eyedropper tool.

The Eyedropper lets you "suck up" a color that already appears in the picture. That color becomes the new foreground or background color for use with any of the painting tools.

Be aware, though, that the Eyedropper can only detect solid colors. If the shade you're interested in is a composite of two or more solid colors, the Eyedropper will select only one of those colors, not the shade.

Here's how to use the Eyedropper:

1.   Click on the Eyedropper tool in the Tool Box. When you move the mouse pointer into the work area, the pointer becomes an eyedropper.

2.   In the picture, locate the color you want to use. Click over that color with the left button to select it as the foreground color, with the right button to make it the background color. The Color Box display changes accordingly.

You can now paint with the chosen color using any of the painting
tools as detailed in the next section.

Using the Painting Tools

To use any of the tools in the Tool Box:

1. Click on the tool you want to use. This selects the tool.

2. Position the pointer in the work area where you want to start painting, selecting, or erasing and then click and hold the mouse button.

3. Drag to paint, select, or erase. Release the mouse button when you
   are through.

Paint's Tool Box offers a slew of useful controls to help you realize
your artistic vision. Here's the Tool Box:

To choose a tool, you simply click on its button in the Tool Box. The
tool is then activated (and highlighted), and the pointer changes
shape when you move back into the work area. In most cases, the tool
stays selected until you choose another one.

Most of the tools are for making modifications to your picture, but one lets you select colors (the Eyedropper), and one is for zooming, or magnifying, the screen image of the picture (the Magnifier tool). Two other tools let you select areas that you can then move around in the picture or modify with other commands. These selection tools and the commands you can use with them are covered in *Manipulating Areas of a Picture.*

When some of the tools are selected, the area below the grid of buttons provides options for the selected tool. The options are different for each tool. For example, if you're drawing with the line tool, you can choose how thick the line should be by clicking on an icon in this area. If there are no options associated with a tool, this area is empty.

The following sections will describe each of the painting tools, referring to the names in Figure 21.4.

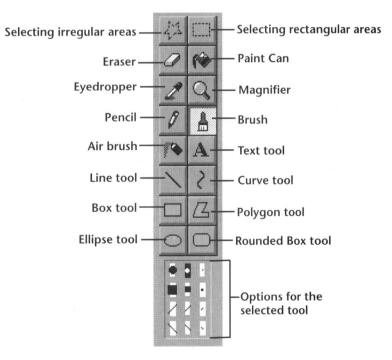

Selecting irregular areas — Selecting rectangular areas
Eraser — Paint Can
Eyedropper — Magnifier
Pencil — Brush
Air brush — Text tool
Line tool — Curve tool
Box tool — Polygon tool
Ellipse tool — Rounded Box tool
Options for the selected tool

Figure 21.4 The Paint Tool Box with its many tool buttons

The Brush

The Brush is the basic painting tool.

It works like a paint brush, pen, or marker. Use this tool to create free-hand art.

With the Brush, you can paint in either the foreground or the background color, switching between the two by simply changing which mouse button you press. All of the painting tools that add lines, strokes, or enclosed shapes work this way.

Here's how to use the Brush:

1. In the Color Box, select the foreground and background colors you want to paint with by clicking on them with the left button and right buttons, respectively.

2. Choose the Brush button in the Tool Box.

3. Pick a size and shape for your brush from the tool options area in the bottom of the Tool Box. The diagonal brush shapes produce lines that vary in width depending on which direction you move the brush—it's a calligraphic pen effect.

4. Move the pointer over the work area so it becomes a crosshair. Press and hold the left button to paint with the foreground color, the right button to paint with the background color. Paint by dragging the mouse around in the work area. Release the button when you want to stop painting. Repeat the process as often as you like.

Figure 21.5 shows a simple brush design.

NOTE You can also paint with a custom brush that you create by copying it from the picture. This brush can be any shape and can contain multiple colors. You don't use the Brush tool for this—see *Sweeping* later in this chapter for the technique.

Doing Precision Work   Although painting is usually a free-form act of creativity, there may be times you want to position your work with precision, perhaps to align a series of shapes along an imaginary horizontal

Figure 21.5 **A freehand design made with the brush**

line. You can use the Status Bar for this purpose. To the right of center, the Status Bar always displays a readout of the mouse pointer's location in pixel coordinates. The first value represents the horizontal location, in pixels, from the left edge of the picture. The second number is the vertical location from the top.

A second readout farther to the left is only active when you're drawing shapes such as boxes, ellipses, and polygons or when you're selecting an area of the picture. This set of coordinates tells you where the mouse pointer is relative to the location where you started drawing the shape or where you began selecting.

Undoing Mistakes   Each addition you make to a picture ultimately loses its identity, blending seamlessly into the rest of the image. However, Paint does keep track of the most recent additions as separate items, giving you a chance to undo your mistakes. Otherwise, if you accidentally covered up part of the picture you wanted to keep, you'd be stuck having to recreate it—if you could.

You can use the Undo command to eliminate the last *three* additions to the picture. Each time you make a new change, Paint "forgets" the fourth most recent change, and it becomes permanent.

To activate Undo, choose Edit ➤ Undo or press the keyboard shortcut, Ctrl-Z.

Paint will even let you redo changes you've removed with Undo. To restore what you previously undid, choose Edit ➤ Repeat or press F4. Again, you can restore as many as three changes.

Here's another way to undo your mistakes: If you realize something is wrong in the middle of any painting operation, such as using the Brush, drawing a line, or even using the Eraser, click the *right* mouse button *before* you release the left button. Whatever changes you were in the process of making disappear—it's as if you never started.

> **TIP**   This little trick gives you a fourth level of Undo: You can erase whatever you're currently drawing by clicking the right mouse button—and still undo three previous changes.

The Eraser

The Eraser works like the eraser on a pencil—only you don't have to rub.

Just pass it across an area, and it erases whatever it touches, leaving nothing but the background color behind. Use the Eraser whether you want to obliterate a major section of your picture or just touch up some stray dots or lines.

Actually, of course, the Eraser doesn't remove anything from your picture—it just replaces the existing dots with dots of another color. In fact, you can think of the eraser as just another brush tool, but one that paints with the background color (that is, the background color that's currently selected—the Eraser doesn't know what background color you started the picture with).

Of course, there's nothing that special about the Eraser—after all, the other tools apply the background color if you paint with the right mouse button instead of the left. It's just that with the Eraser, you

Supplied Applications

access the background color with the left button, which you're probably more used to (the right button has no effect with the Eraser). The Eraser can paint wider lines than the brush, too.

Here's how to use the Eraser:

1. Set the background color (in the Color Box) to the color you've chosen for the background (of your picture) or to the color you want to paint wide strokes with.

2. Select the Eraser.

3. In the tool options area at the bottom of the Tool Box, set the eraser size. For fine work, use the smallest setting.

> **TIP** Even the smallest Eraser size covers more than a single dot in your picture. To erase (change) individual dots, use the Pencil tool (see the next section), setting the *foreground* color to the desired erasure color.

4. The mouse pointer will change to a hollow box when moved into the work area. Drag it over the material you want to erase. Hold the Shift key down while moving the mouse if you want to limit your movement to just the vertical or horizontal direction.

Below you can see the effect of dragging the Eraser over a solid colored area.

The Pencil

The Pencil works much like the Brush for freehand art, except that it only paints lines that are one dot (pixel) wide.

You can produce essentially the same effect with the Brush by choosing the smallest circular shape for the Brush (at the top right of the Brush-shape display), but the Pencil is often a convenient way to draw fine lines freehand while leaving the brush for wider swaths.

In addition, you can force the Pencil to draw straight vertical, horizontal, or diagonal lines, something you can't do with the Brush. After selecting the Pencil tool, hold down the Shift key while you drag the mouse. The direction you initially move establishes the line's direction—as long as you hold down Shift, you can only lengthen the line, not change directions (this is different from the way the Line tool works, as described below).

The Pencil is your best bet for doing fine touch-up work, including erasures. To erase individual dots with the pencil, set either the foreground or background color in the Color Box to the background color of your picture. Then click with the corresponding mouse button on stray dots one at a time to erase them. (Like the Brush, the Pencil applies the foreground color when you paint with the left button, the background color when you paint with the right.)

TIP   For precise, dot-by-individual-dot editing, make it easy on yourself—zoom in on your picture to see the detail. See *Zooming In for Detail Work* below.

The Airbrush

Here's a tool that's a legal outlet for repressed graffiti artists.

The Airbrush works like the real thing, or like a spray can, spraying a mist of paint that gets thicker the longer you hold it one place. Think of the mouse button as the button on the top of the spray can:

1. Set the foreground and background colors to taste.

2. Click on the Airbrush tool (the button with the spray-can icon).

3. Select the spray size in the tool options area at the bottom of the Tool Box.

4. Position the cursor in the work area—it now looks like an airbrush—and press the mouse button for the desired color (left for foreground color, right for background color). Hold it down.

5. Move the mouse around and spray the color onto the work area. Note that the speed of movement affects the density of the spray, just as it does with a real spray can: moving the mouse quickly results in a finer mist, while letting it sit still or moving very slowly plasters the paint on.

Figure 21.6 shows an example of some airbrushed painting.

Figure 21.6 **The Airbrush works like a spray can. Just point and spray.**

The Line Tool

Use the Line tool to draw straight lines (and only straight lines):

TIP   Hold the Shift key down to force the line to be vertical, horizontal, or at a 45-degree angle.

---

1. Select the foreground and background colors you want to draw with.

2. Select the Line tool.

3. Choose from one of the five line widths offered in the tool options area at the bottom of the Tool Box.

4. Move into the work area. The cursor becomes a crosshair.

5. Press and hold one of the buttons and move the mouse. Use the left button to draw with the foreground color, the right button for the background color. A straight line will appear between the point you started drawing (the anchor point) and the current location of the mouse pointer. (Actually, the line won't look perfectly straight because computers can't draw straight diagonal lines.)

6. Move the endpoint around until you are satisfied with its location (you can make a full circle around the anchor point if you like). Release the button.

Below is an example of a drawing made up only of lines.

The Curve Tool

Use the Curve tool for drawing curves, of course.

But don't expect to master this tool quickly—it will seem downright strange at first.

You start by laying down a straight line, just like you would with the Line tool. Then you get two chances to "stretch" that line into a curve—once from one location and once from another. The result might be an arc, an *S* curve, or even a pretzel-y shape:

1. Select the foreground and background colors you want to draw with.

2. Choose the Curve tool.

3. Select the line size from the tool options area at the bottom of the Tool Box.

4. Begin the curve with a straight line, using the same techniques as you would with the Line tool covered earlier. When the line is finished, release the mouse button.

5. Move the cursor to one side of the line, hold down the mouse button, and drag the cursor away from or towards the line. As you do so, the line will stretch like a rubber band. Release the button when the bend is correct. (How will you know when it's correct? That's another book...)

6. If the curve already looks right, finish it by clicking on the endpoint (the end opposite where you started the line). If you do want to stretch it some more, move to another position in the work area, perhaps on the other side of the line, and drag the mouse again. The line will stretch further. When you are satisfied with the final shape—or give up—release the mouse button.

Figure 21.7 shows the process of drawing a curve.

The Box Tool

The Box tool draws, well, boxes—or rectangles, if you prefer.

You can draw three types of boxes:

Hollow boxes with borders only: In this type of box, the border is the only addition to the picture, enclosing whatever was already there in the picture. The border appears in the currently selected foreground color.

Filled, bordered boxes: This type of box has a solid-color interior that covers up whatever had been there plus a surrounding border. The solid interior appears in the currently selected background color, while the border appears in the foreground color.

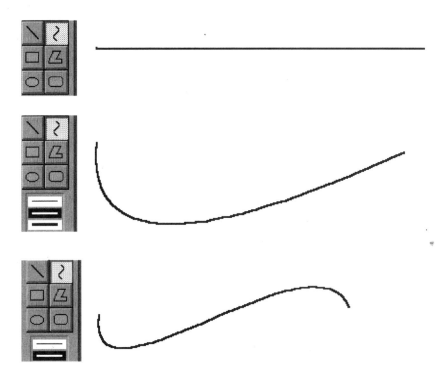

Figure 21.7   **The three steps in creating a curved line: draw a straight line, bend it one way, then bend it another.**

Solid boxes without borders: This type of box appears as a solid rectangle drawn in the currently selected background color.

The above descriptions apply if you use the left mouse button to draw the box. If you use the right button instead, the border and interior colors are reversed. This applies to the other tools for drawing enclosed shapes as well.

Here's how to create boxes of any type:

 TIP   To constrain boxes to be perfect squares, hold down the Shift key as you draw. This applies to filled boxes as well as to hollow ones.

1. Set the background and foreground colors to taste, as necessary (see the discussion above).

2. If you're drawing a bordered box, select the Line tool and then set the line width from the choices in the tool options area at the bottom of the Tool Box.

3. Select the Box tool.

4. Click where you want one corner of the box to start. This sets the anchor.

5. Drag the crosshair down and to one side. As you do, a rectangular outline will appear.

6. Release the mouse button when the size is correct.

The Rounded Box Tool

The rounded Box tool works exactly like the regular Box tool described in the previous section, but it creates boxes with rounded corners, rather than crisp right angles.

The Ellipse Tool

This tool also works just like the Box tool, except that it creates ellipses (ovals).

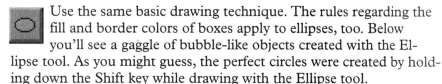
Use the same basic drawing technique. The rules regarding the fill and border colors of boxes apply to ellipses, too. Below you'll see a gaggle of bubble-like objects created with the Ellipse tool. As you might guess, the perfect circles were created by holding down the Shift key while drawing with the Ellipse tool.

The Polygon Tool

With the Polygon tool you can create an endless variety of polygonal shapes.

It works something like the Line tool and something like the Box tool.

As with the Line tool, you manually draw straight lines—the difference being that you keep adding endpoints until you complete the polygon's edges. Paint then connects all the endpoints into a single shape with an unbroken boundary.

As with the Box tool, you can choose from three types of polygons: hollow ones (with borders but no solid filling); filled, bordered polygons; and solid polygons with no border.

TIP   To constrain any line of the polygon to be vertical, at 45 degrees, or horizontal only, hold down the Shift key as you draw.

---

1. Select the colors you want for the polygon's border (the foreground color) and filling (the background color) as appropriate.

2. If you're drawing a bordered polygon, select the Line tool and choose a line width for the border.

3. Select the polygon tool and choose the type of polygon you want to draw (border only, filled and bordered, or solid with no border).

4. Click where you want the anchor point of the first side and hold the button down.

5. Drag the mouse pointer to the endpoint for the side and release the button. The line you've drawn defines the first side of the polygon.

6. Press and hold the mouse button again as you drag to the endpoint of the next side (or just click over this next endpoint). Paint draws the second side. Continue adding sides in this way, but *double-click* to mark the endpoint of the next-to-the-last side (for example, the fourth side of a pentangle). Paint connects this endpoint with the original anchor point, filling in the polygon if appropriate.

Note that a polygon's sides can cross. The polygons don't have to be symmetrically shaped the way hexagons or octagons are. You can haphazardly click all over the screen, and, until you double-click, Paint will keep connecting the dots regardless.

You can create a cubist artistic effect with this tool because of the way Paint calculates an enclosed area. It starts at the top of the screen and begins filling areas. If your polygon has a lot of enclosed areas from multiple lines overlapping, Paint alternates the fills. Thus adjacent enclosed areas will not all be filled. Using the tool with the cutout tools and the Invert command can lead to some rather interesting geometrical designs (inverting is covered later in the chapter). Figure 21.8 shows an example of the possibilities.

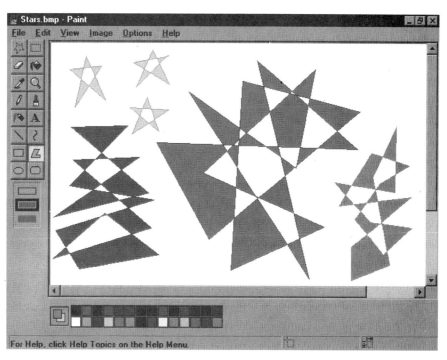

Figure 21.8 *A geometric design created with the Polygon tool using filled polygons*

Filling Areas with the Paint Can

 The Paint Can will fill in any enclosed area with the foreground color. An *enclosed area* can be defined by any lines or curves in the work area. So three separate lines set up to form a triangle constitute an enclosed space just as much as a box's border does. Because the entire work area is also considered an enclosed space, you can use the Paint Can to change the background of the picture. Letters you create with the Text tool (discussed next) can be filled, too:

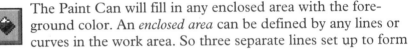 **CAUTION** There's one situation where the Paint Can doesn't work as expected. If you've previously filled an enclosed area with one of the "grainy" shades, Paint Can may not be able to replace the current filling or may do so inaccurately. The problem is that these grainy colors are actually made up of a pattern of two or more other colors. Because of the complexity of the pattern, Paint Can has trouble locating the boundaries of the area.

---

1. Choose the foreground and background colors you want to use for fills.

2. Select the Paint Can tool. The pointer becomes a spilling paint can when you move it over the work area.

3. Point the tip of the spilling paint into the area to be filled and click with the button for the desired color. The enclosed area will be filled with the foreground color if you click with the left button, with the background color if you click with the right.

   Note that the color flows to fill the entire enclosed area. If there is a leak in what you thought was an enclosed area, the paint will seep through the crack, so to speak, and fill everything until it is stopped by a complete boundary. You may accidentally fill the entire work area. If this happens, just choose Undo.

The Text Tool

The Text tool lets you add words to your pictures, which is great when you're designing flyers, invitations, maps, instructions, and the like.

Before you actually start typing, you define a rectangular *frame* for the text. You can resize or reposition this frame or change its color at any time until you finalize your text entry by clicking elsewhere in the picture.

Oh yes, about the color of the text frame. You can add text in two ways: as text only, so that only the characters you type are added to your picture; and as text on a solid rectangular background that covers up whatever was there in the picture. These two styles are also called *transparent* and *opaque*.

1. Choose the color for the text by clicking in the Color Box with the left button (text always appears in the selected foreground color). If you plan to add opaque text (on a solid-color background), choose the color for the background by clicking on it with the right button.

2. Choose the Text tool in the Tool Box.

3. In the tool-options area at the bottom of the Tool Box, choose the icon for opaque or transparent text. The top one turns on the opaque style. Alternatively, you can switch between opaque and transparent styles by choosing Options ➤ Draw Opaque. When the Draw Opaque menu choice is checked, the opaque style is active.

4. Draw your text frame using either mouse button. When you let go, *handles* appear on the dashed rectangular frame at the corners and along the edges, and, if you chose the opaque text style, the frame fills with the background color. In addition, a large flashing vertical bar (cursor) marks the text-insertion point. And a small window titled Paint Font Tool (also known as the Text Toolbar) appears. Figure 21.9 shows a text frame and the Text Toolbar.

5. Choose the font, size, and styles for your text from the Text Toolbar. You can use bold, italic, and underline in any combination.

TIP If the Text Toolbar isn't visible, choose View ➤ Text Toolbar to restore it to the screen.

6. Click again over the new text frame to make the insertion-point cursor reappear. Now type whatever you like. When your text reaches the right edge of the text frame, Paint wraps down to the next line. You can use standard Windows text-editing techniques to move the insertion point, select characters or words, and cut, copy, and paste (see the section on Notepad in Chapter 22 for a summary).

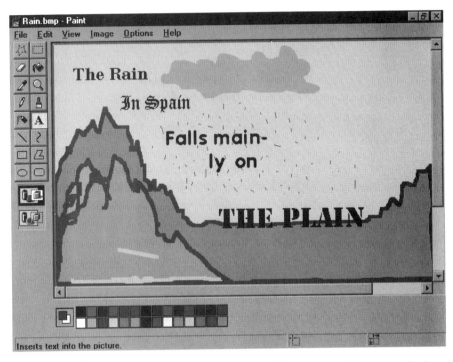

Figure 21.9   *Some type styles produced with the Text tool on my system. They may differ from yours.*

 NOTE   Even though you can select individual words in a text frame, Paint permits only one font, size, and style combination for *all* the text within the frame.

---

7. As long as the rectangular outline of the text frame remains on the screen, you can change its size and location and the colors of the text and the frame background:

> *To resize the frame:* Drag any of the handles, the little squares at the corners and along the sides of the frame. The mouse pointer becomes a double-headed arrow when it's directly over a handle, indicating that you can move the handle.
>
> *To move the frame:* Drag any part of the frame outline that isn't a handle. The mouse pointer becomes an arrow when it's over the outline. As you drag, a solid gray rectangle represents the moving frame, which appears at the new location when you release the button.

To change colors: On the Color Box, click the left button to change the color of the text, the right button to change the frame background's color. You can also switch between a transparent and opaque text frame by clicking on the appropriate icon in the tool-options area or by choosing Options ➤ Draw Opaque.

8. Click outside the text frame to finalize your text entry.

Once you've completed a text entry, it loses its separate identity, becoming just another set of dots in the picture. While you can select the text area for other operations (as described in the next section), you can't select, cut, copy, or otherwise manipulate the individual characters as such.

Manipulating Areas of a Picture

So far, you've learned how to add and change colors and shapes with the various painting tools. But your creative options don't stop there. Paint gives you a variety of tools and commands for working with a specific portion of the picture as a unit. Of course, you must first define, or *select*, the area you want to work, as detailed in the next section. If you don't select an area (see Figure 21.10), many of the commands covered in this section will affect the entire picture.

Selecting an Area

The Tool Box offers two tools for selecting specific portions of a picture for further manipulation. Appropriately enough, they're collectively called the *selection tools*. They are the top two buttons on the Tool Box. The one on the left with the star-shaped outline is for selecting irregular shapes; it's called the Free-Form Selection tool. The one on the right with the rectangular outline, the Select tool, is for selecting rectangular areas.

Once you've selected an area with either tool, you can "cut out" the area, either by cutting it to the Clipboard or simply by moving it around in the picture. For this reason, selections are also called *cutouts*. You can also perform many other manipulations on a selection, such as inverting its colors or rotating it.

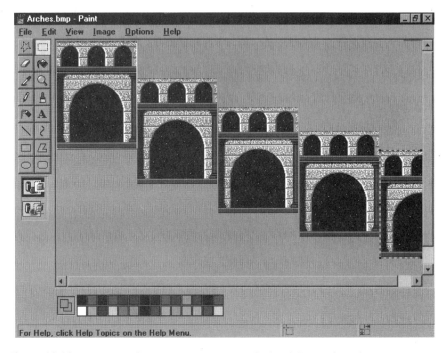

Figure 21.10 *Once you select an area, you can manipulate it in a variety of ways. Here you see brick archways copied and placed across the picture.*

Selecting Rectangular Areas

The easiest way to select an area—or define a cutout, if you prefer—is with the Select tool, the one with the dotted rectangular outline at the top right of the Tool Box.

All you have to do is drag the mouse to define a boxed area. You can easily select the entire picture if you need to:

1. Select the Select tool (how's that for computerized English?).

2. Move to the upper-left corner of the boxed area you want to select. Click and hold down the left mouse button.

3. Drag the mouse down and to the right. As you draw, a dotted rectangular outline indicates the selection area.

**Part
4**

4. Release the button. After a moment, the dotted outline reappears, but it now has handles on all four corners and along each edge (see Figure 21.11). Don't use the handles to redefine the selection area—they're for resizing the image within the area.

Once you've selected an area, it remains selected until you click outside the dotted outline around it (the *selection rectangle*) or until you choose another tool.

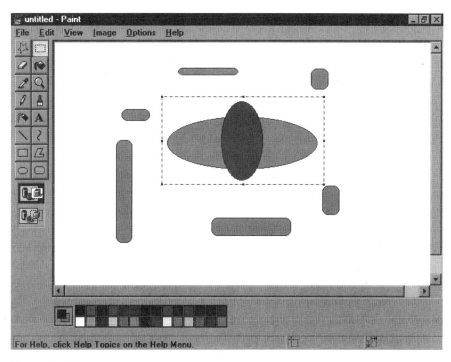

Figure 21.11 *A selection is marked by this dotted outline, the selection rectangle.*

Selecting Irregular Areas

The Free-Form Select tool lets you select any area of the picture by drawing a line freehand around the area.

It allows you to select exactly the part of the picture you're after, hugging the edges of the element that interests you.

That way, the commands you use on the selection affect only that element, not the nearby dots. And if you plan to cut or copy an area and then paste it elsewhere, using this tool to select the area ensures that you won't paste an unwanted border that might overlap other items. The only drawback: it's hard to draw the selection outline accurately.

To use this tool, select it and move to the spot where you want to start defining the area. As you hold the mouse button down, draw a line completely around the area. When you're through, Paint displays a dotted rectangular outline large enough to contain the entire selection. This works just like the selection rectangle described in the previous section. Again, you'll see handles for stretching the selected part of the picture. If you make a mistake in defining the selection, press the right mouse button and make the selection again.

Moving a Selected Area

Once you've selected an area, the simplest thing you can do with it is to move it elsewhere in the picture. All you have to do is drag it where you want it to go: Press the left mouse button down anywhere within the selection, or cutout, move to the new location, and release the button.

If you try this, you'll immediately see why they call a selection a cutout: The selection is neatly removed from its original location, just as if you'd cut it out with a straightedge and tacked it down in the new spot. Again, it remains selected until you click outside the selection rectangle, so you can move it again or perform other manipulations.

TIP   Actually, this is both a tip and a caution, depending on the results you're after. When you move a cutout by dragging it, without leaving a copy behind, Paint colors the area you cut it out from. The area is covered with the currently selected background color. So if you want to move a cutout and leave behind a colored "shadow" at the same time, change the background color first (*before* you select the area). On the other hand, if you previously changed the background color for an interim operation, be sure to change it back to the "real" background color, or you'll get shape of an unwanted color in your picture.

To move a *copy* of the selection, leaving the original in place, just hold down the Ctrl key while you drag the cutout to its new home. Figure 21.12 shows the results of moving a copy of the selection by dragging it.

> **TIP** There's even a way to create special effects by dropping multiple copies of the cutout along the path you move the mouse on as you drag. See the *Sweeping* section below.

Opaque v. Transparent Placement

When you move a selection by dragging it, you can choose between *opaque* and *transparent* placement at the new location. In opaque placement, the selection will completely replace whatever you place it on top of in the picture—nothing of what was previously there will show through.

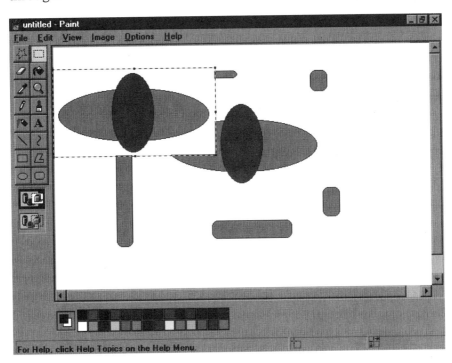

Figure 21.12   In this picture, a selection has been copied to another location, leaving the original intact, by dragging it with the Ctrl key held down.

In transparent placement, the selection's background disappears, so only the foreground elements in the selection appear at the new location. But this only works if you select the background color of the cutout as the background color in the Color Box (by clicking in the Color Box with the right button). Select the correct background color before you move the selection.

> NOTE   In transparent placement, what actually happens is this: Paint ignores all parts of the selection having the background color currently active in the Color Box. Of course, you're free to set the Color Box background color to match part of the selection's *foreground*. In that case, these elements, not the selection's background, would drop out when you place the selection.

Sweeping

Sweeping a selection is a neat trick that deposits multiple copies of the cutout across the picture as you move the mouse. You can use this technique to suggest motion of an object or to create interesting artistic effects. Figure 21.13 shows an example of sweeping.

There are two ways to perform this special sweeping effect. The first method is just a modification of the standard technique for moving a selection with the mouse. With the second technique, you convert the selection into a brush, more or less, that remains active until you choose another tool.

Just as when you move a single copy of a selection, you can do opaque or transparent sweeping. Again, the background color of the cutout and the current background color have to be the same for transparent sweeping to work as you'd expect.

To try the first technique:

1.   If you plan to do a transparent sweep, set the background color in the Color Box to match what you consider to be the background color in the selection.

2.   Choose either of the selection tools and set it to opaque or transparent operation.

3.   Select the area.

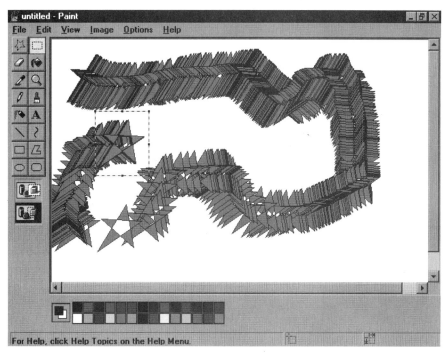

Figure 21.13 *Sweeping a cutout makes numerous copies on a single sweep of the mouse.*

4. Drag the selection while holding the Shift key down. Copies of the cutout are made as you drag the cursor around.

   In the second sweeping technique, you use the selection as if it were a brush tool:

1. Choose the background color in the Color Box, choose a selection tool, and choose a setting: opaque or transparent.

2. Select the area.

3. Press Ctrl-B. A copy of the selection appears on the screen, slightly offset from the original selection.

4. Paint with the left mouse button to sweep with the actual colors you see in the selection. If you paint with the right mouse button, the Brush paints with the background color selected in the Color Box. Details of how this works are complicated to explain, so if you're interested, just try it.

Copying or Cutting a Selection to the Clipboard

You can also move parts of your picture around using the Windows Clipboard as an alternative to dragging a selection directly to a new location as described above. The latter method is usually easier, but there may be times when you want to place a selection on the Clipboard for later use. For example, you might want to cut a design from one picture, then open another picture and paste it in.

To cut or copy a selection to the Clipboard, define the area with one of the Selection tools, then choose Edit ➤ Cut or Edit ➤ Copy, or just press the standard Windows keyboard shortcuts for these commands (Ctrl-X and Ctrl-C, respectively).

 NOTE   When you cut a selection to the Clipboard, Paint fills in the space left behind with the currently selected background color.

Pasting from the Clipboard

Once you've placed a selection on the Clipboard, you can paste it back into any picture at any time. To paste the Clipboard contents, choose Edit ➤ Paste or press Ctrl-V. The selection appears in a selection rectangle at the top left of the work area, and you can drag it into place wherever you want it. Just as with new selections, pressing Ctrl while you drag leaves a copy of the original selection behind.

Saving and Retrieving a Cutout

You can save a selection as a disk file for later use. Using this technique, you can create a stockpile of little graphics (like clip art) that you can call up from disk to drop into new pictures. Here are the steps to save and retrieve a selection:

1. Define the selection with either of the selection tools.

2. Choose Edit ➤ Copy To. A file box pops up. Name the file as you wish.

3. When you want to reload the cutout, choose Edit ➤ Load From and click on the picture file containing the selection from the file box. It will appear in the upper-left corner of the current picture on screen.

4. Reposition the selection by dragging it.

Flipping and Rotating Selections

Paint lets you rotate any selected area within the plane of the picture or *flip* the selection on its vertical or horizontal axis. Flipping reverses the pattern within the selection, producing a mirror image. If you flip horizontally, the pattern is still right-side up, while if you flip vertically, it's upside down. Rotating simply turns the pattern on its side or turns it upside down, but it doesn't create a mirror image.

You'll understand better how these commands work if you just play with them:

1. Select an area with one of the selection tools.

2. Choose Image ➤ Flip and Rotate. The Image Flip and Rotate dialog box appears.

3. Choose the appropriate radio button: Flip horizontal, Flip vertical, or Rotate. If you choose Rotate, an additional set of three radio buttons becomes available. Choose 90° to lay the area on its side, rotating to the right; 180° to stand the selection on its head, so to speak; or 270° to lay the image on its left side.

4. Click on OK to close the box. Paint transforms the selection according to your choices.

You can use these commands to create symmetrical patterns by defining a selection, copying it to the Clipboard, and then pasting it repeatedly into the same picture. Each time you paste, position the new copy where you want it, then flip or rotate it. Figure 21.14 shows an example.

Inverting Colors

The Invert Colors command *reverses* the colors in the selected area (or, if nothing is selected, in the entire picture). Black turns to white and white will turn to black. If you're working in color, the colors will turn to their complements. *Complementary colors* are defined here as being the color on the opposite side of the RGB (Red, Green, Blue) color wheel. This is a really fun tool. Try selecting several slightly overlapping squares of a picture and inverting them in sequence. An example is shown in Figure 21.15.

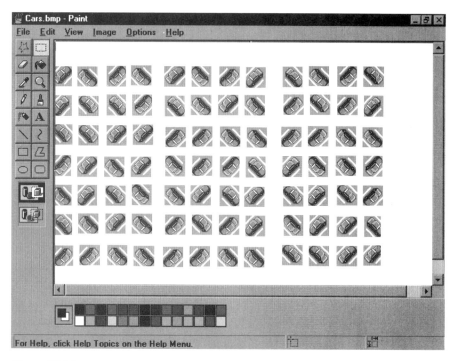

Figure 21.14   **Cutouts flipped horizontally and vertically**

To try this:

1. Select the area to have its colors inverted.

2. Choose Image ➤ Invert Colors.

Stretching and Shrinking a Selected Area

Paint lets you change the size of a selection with the mouse, for convenience, or by typing values into a dialog box, for accuracy. Figure 21.16 shows a selection that has been stretched and shrunken to several different sizes. (Using the dialog box, you can slant the selection at the same time you resize it, as described in the next section.)

You can repeatedly resize a selection as many times as you like until you click elsewhere to deselect the area. Just remember that the more you stretch or shrink the area, the more distorted it will look.

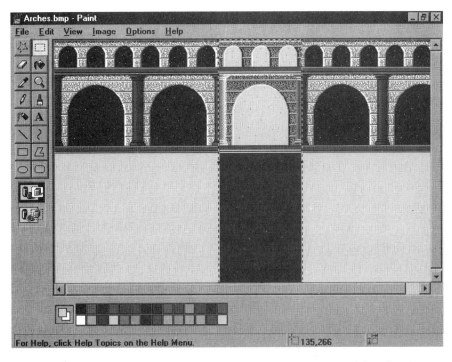

Figure 21.15   *Invert a section of a picture by selecting the cutout area and then choosing Image Invert ➤ Colors.*

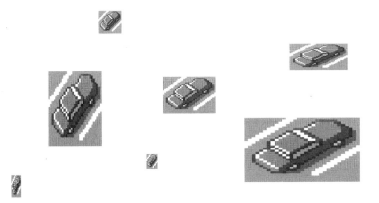

Figure 21.16   *In this picture, a selection has been pasted in several times, with each copy stretched or shrunken to a different size.*

CAUTION When you change the size of a bit-mapped image (or any part of it), you create unavoidable distortions in the image look. Even if you maintain the area's proportions perfectly, shrinking it will result in loss of detail and a coarse appearance, while enlarging it will make curved lines appear more jagged.

To change a selection's size with the mouse:

1. Select the area whose size you want to change. The selection rectangle appears as an outline around the area.

2. Drag any of the eight handles on the selection rectangle (located at the four corners and along each side). Dragging a side handle lets you stretch or shrink the selection in one direction only, while dragging a corner handle lets you change both dimensions at once.

3. Release the mouse button when you're satisfied with the size change.

To resize a selection with the dialog box:

1. Select the area you want to resize.

2. Choose Image ➤ Stretch ➤ Skew. Select one of the top two radio buttons, Horizontal or Vertical, then type in the percentage by which you want to resize the selection in that dimension. Negative numbers make the area smaller.

3. If you also want to slant the selection, enter values in the Skew area now (see the next section for details).

4. Click on OK.

You can only change the size in one dimension each time you use the dialog box. If you want to resize the area in both dimensions, you must enter the value for one dimension, then choose Image ➤ Stretch ➤ Skew again to repeat the process for the other. To maintain the area's proportions, type the same value for both dimensions.

Slanting a Selected Area

You can slant, or *skew*, a selection horizontally or vertically, as shown in Figure 21.17. Here's how:

1. Select an area.

2. Choose Image ➤ Stretch ➤ Skew. The Image Stretch and Skew dialog box appears.

3. Choose the radio button for Horizontal or Vertical skewing. Horizontal skewing slants the selection to the right; vertical skewing slants it upward.

4. Type in the skew angle in degrees. You can type any integer between 1 and 89 (negative numbers aren't allowed).

Zooming In for Detail Work

Sometimes you need a magnified view of your picture, either to see fine detail or to make precise changes more easily. In Paint, you can choose from five magnification levels: normal, 2×, 4×, 6×, and 8×. Figure 21.18 shows a picture at highest magnification, 8× (800%).

Figure 21.17 Examples of skewing. Notice that skewing can distort the appearance of text as well as graphics.

At the normal level, a dot on the screen corresponds to a dot on your picture. At the magnified levels, a dot in the picture is represented by a group of four or more dots on your screen that act as a unit. At any zoom level, the tradeoff is between how much you can see of the whole picture versus how detailed a view you have.

You can use any of the standard painting tools at any magnification level. By viewing things close up, you'll be able to do more precise work. But for the ultimate in precision, you can edit individual dots with the Pencil tool, covered earlier, which lets you change the color of one dot at a time.

The highest magnification is best for editing individual dots. This kind of microsurgery is useful for smoothing out lines, creating minute patterns, and eliminating single stray dots that often appear in scanned images.

You can change the magnification level with the Magnifier tool or the Zoom command.

Using the Magnifier Tool

To zoom in on your work using the Magnifier tool:

1. Click on the Magnifier tool, the one with the magnifying glass.

2. At this point, you have two choices:

   ▶ You can move into the work area. The mouse pointer displays a rectangular outline, which you position over the area you want to magnify. When you click, Paint displays this area at 4× (400%) magnification.

   ▶ You can click on one of the magnification levels in the tool-options area at the bottom of the Tool Box. Paint immediately displays your picture at that magnification.

When the picture is magnified, you can restore it to the normal, unmagnified size by selecting the Magnifier tool and clicking anywhere in the work area.

Magnifying with the Zoom command

To change the magnification level with the Zoom command:

1. Choose View ➤ Zoom to open a submenu of Zoom commands.

2. To display the picture at 4× (400%) magnification, choose Large Size. To display it at any other level, choose Custom to display the View Zoom dialog box. Click on the radio button for the desired magnification, then click on OK.

When you're zoomed in, you can go directly back to the normal, un-magnified view by choosing View ➤ Zoom ➤ Normal.

Seeing the Big Picture When You're Zoomed In

Although magnifying your picture lets you see and work with the fine details, you can lose your sense of how the picture will look at normal size. That's why Paint provides a little window that displays a normal-size view of the magnified area. This Paint View window is visible in Figure 21.18.

You can move the Paint View window around as necessary, and you can turn it off or on at will. To close the window, just click on its close box. To turn it on again, choose View ➤ Zoom ➤ Show Thumbnail.

Displaying a Grid for Precision Editing

At higher magnification levels (4× and above), Paint lets you display a grid of lines that indicates the location of each individual dot in your picture. With the grid visible, you'll find it easier to do very detailed, accurate work with your painting tools.

To turn the grid on, choose View ➤ Zoom ➤ Show Grid. The grid is shown in Figure 21.18.

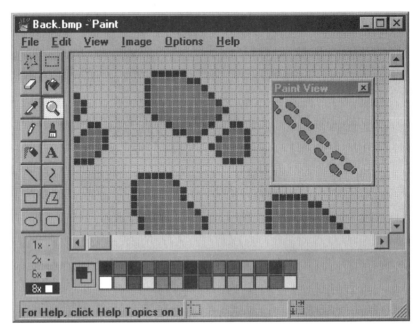

Figure 21.18   *Here's a screen image showing what a magnified picture looks like. The network of horizontal and vertical lines is Paint's grid, designed to make precision editing easier. The little Paint View window shows some of the magnified area at its normal, unmagnified size.*

Editing the Color Scheme

If you are working in color, you may want to create custom colors. If you are working in black and white, you may want to create a new pattern. To do either:

1. Start by selecting the color you want to change in the Color Box. Click on the chosen color to make it the foreground color.

    TECH TIP   Double-click on a color in the Color Box to open the Color dialog box.

2. Choose Options ➤ Edit Colors (or you can just double-click on the chosen color in the Color Box). The Color dialog box, shown in Figure 21.19, appears.

3. The Basic Colors area shows more colors than are available in the Color Box. If you find a suitable color in the grid, click on it to select it and then click on OK to close the dialog box. The chosen color replaces the previously selected color in the Color Box.

4. If none of the basic colors will do, click on the Define Custom Colors button. The dialog box expands to show a color-editing area.

5. In the large color-editing area, drag the crosshair cursor to choose the desired color (it appears in the smaller area below). Once you have the basic hue, you may find it easier to select the exact shade you want with the slider at the far right.

6. When you're satisfied, click on the Add to Custom Colors button. The new color appears in the area for custom colors. When you click on OK, it also appears as a choice in the Color Box.

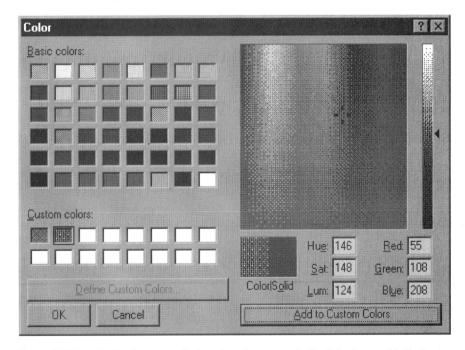

Figure 21.19   *Here's where you edit the colors that appear in the Color Box. In this illustration, the Define Custom Colors button has already been clicked on; when the Color dialog box first appears, you'll see only the left half.*

Note that the changes you make do not affect the picture's existing colors.

A custom color set remains active only with the current picture. When you open a different picture, Paint uses the color set that was active when the picture was last saved. If you start a new picture, Paint restores the standard, or default, color set.

Saving and Loading Your Own Color Schemes

Once you've created a custom color set, you can save it for use with other pictures using the Options ➤ Save Colors command. And once you've saved a custom color set, you can use it again in other pictures with the Options ➤ Get Colors command.

Saving Your Work

If you're painting for posterity—or at least have some use in mind for your work other than doodling—remember to save your work to disk regularly. Of course, you can open pictures you've worked on before for further editing—or just to admire them.

Saving Files

You can save pictures as disk files in several formats, all of them variations of the basic Paint (BMP) format. Normally, you can just let Paint choose the correct format for you. But there may be times when knowing which format to use comes in handy.

Here are the available formats and their descriptions:

Monochrome Bitmap: Use when you have only two colors (black and white) in your picture.

16-Color Bitmap: Use when you have 16 colors or fewer in your picture.

256-Color Bitmap: Use when you have more than 16 and fewer than 257 colors in your picture.

24-Bit Bitmap: Use when you have more than 256 colors in the picture.

Why change a picture's format? The most common reason: you have a picture and you like its design, but it looks cartoon-ish because it has too few colors. By saving it in a format with more colors, you'll be able to modify it with a much richer, more realistic color palette. But this only works if your screen can display the additional colors and is set up in Control Panel to do so (see Chapter 7 for instructions). Note that the more colors you save, the larger the files become and the more disk and RAM space they'll need.

CAUTION Saving a picture with a format that has fewer colors may ruin it. When you save (for example, if you save a picture with 16 colors as a monochrome bit-mapped file), Paint translates each color in the original picture into the closest match in the new format. Clearly, you're likely to lose a significant amount of detail, especially when going to the monochrome format—the picture may well come out looking like a sea of black with a few white dots, or vice versa.

Using Your Picture as Windows Wallpaper

After you've saved a new picture, or if you're working with a picture you opened from disk, Paint can tell Windows to use the picture as wallpaper. From then on, the picture will appear as the backdrop for your Windows Desktop. Paint handles the details for you—you don't need to use the Control Panel at all. (See Chapter 7 for more on wallpaper.)

To set the current picture as wallpaper:

1. Save the picture to disk if you haven't already done so.

2. Choose File ➤ Set as Wallpaper (Tiled) if you want multiple side-by-side copies of the image on your Windows Desktop. Choose File ➤ Set as Wallpaper (Centered) if you want a single copy of the image centered on the Desktop.

Printing

Finally, you might want to print out your artwork! Here's how you do it:

1. Open the picture document, if it's not already open.

2. Turn on the printer and get it ready to print.

3. If you want to change the page margins or paper orientation, choose File ➤ Page Setup and make the necessary entries in the dialog box.

4. To see how the picture will look on the printed page, choose File ➤ Print Preview. You'll see a mock-up of the printed page on your screen. This works exactly like the Print Preview function in WordPad (see Chapter 19).

5. When you're ready to print, choose File ➤ Print, or, from Print Preview, click on the Print button. The standard Windows Print dialog box will appear, allowing you to choose the correct printer, specify which pages should print and how many copies, and change the printer's settings (by clicking on the Properties button).

Chapter 22

The Other Windows Accessories

FEATURING

Reading and writing text files with Notepad

Using the Calculator

Entering special symbols with Character Map

Adjusting Volume Control

In this chapter, you'll learn about the miscellaneous accessories included with Windows 95. These accessories are fairly modest programs, but each is genuinely useful in its special niche. If you take the time to acquaint yourself with their basic functions, you'll know where to turn when you need help with a problem they can solve.

Jotting Down Notes with Notepad

Like WordPad, Notepad lets you type and edit text. But the two programs have different missions. Notepad is a tool for text editing *only*, while you use WordPad to make the text you type look good (that is, to *format* your text). To use the appropriate jargon, Notepad is a *text editor*, while WordPad is a *word processor*. (WordPad is covered in Chapter 19.)

In Notepad, you can type text, but you can't change the fonts, add bold, italics, or color, modify the tab settings, center a paragraph—well, you get the point. So why bother with Notepad? After all, you could type your text in WordPad and simply not use that program's formatting features.

Notepad's main advantage over WordPad is that it's *lean*—it takes up much less memory than WordPad, and it starts up faster, too. It's small enough to keep open all the time so you can jot down quick notes whenever you need to. And it's a perfect tool to call up whenever you need to view a text file. So what's a text file?

Understanding Text Files

Notepad can only open and save *text-only* files—files that contain only text characters. That is, text-only files *don't* contain any of the formatting codes used by word processors to store information about the looks and layout of a document. Text-only files are also known as plain text files, ASCII or plain ASCII files, or simply as *text files*, which is what Windows calls them.

Before I explain more about text files, here is some practical information: Windows recognizes a text file as such only if it is stored on disk with the file-name extension .txt. Files having the .txt extension appear in your folders with the text-file icon, shown to the left. Text files often have other extensions, however. Note that Windows will recognize files having the .doc extension as WinPad documents even if they actually contain plain text only. You may wish to rename such files to avoid this conflict.

Though text files look fairly boring, they do have some important advantages over fancier, formatted text documents. The most important one is their universality: Text files provide the lowest common denominator for exchanging text between different programs and even between different types of computers. Every system has a way to create and display text files. That's why they remain the medium for most of the electronic-mail messages passed back and forth on the Internet and other information services, as well as those posted to electronic bulletin boards.

In addition, most programs have text files on the installation disk named something like READ.ME, README.TXT, or README.DOC. Such files usually contain important information about the software that was added after the manual was printed, including tips on installation, details on new features or bugs in the software, and corrections of errors in the manual. Again, these messages are stored as text-only files because that way, everyone can read them.

Text files are also good for storing the "source code" used to generate computer programs. When a programmer writes the source code, he or she types it in using a text editor such as Notepad, saving the work in a text file. That way, the instructions needed to create the final program aren't mixed up with extraneous formatting information that would confuse the *compiler* (software that converts the source code into a working program).

You may not be a programmer, but you do sometimes deal with program files of a sort—your system-configuration files, including win.ini, sys.ini, protocol.ini, config.sys, and autoexec.bat. These text files qualify as programs because they tell your system how to operate. You can edit them with Notepad.

Notepad's Limitations

Just so you won't use it for the wrong tasks, here's a summary of Notepad's limitations:

▶ It has no paragraph- or character-formatting capability. It can wrap lines of text to fit the size of the window, however, which is a nice feature.

▶ Files are limited to text only. Notepad can't open formatted documents created with WordPad, Microsoft Word for Windows, WordPerfect, or any other word processor (actually, it can open the files, but they won't look right).

▶ Files are limited in size to about 50K. This is fairly large, accommodating approximately 15 pages of solid single-spaced text—20 or so pages of regularly spaced material.

▶ It doesn't have any fancy pagination options, though it will print with headers and footers via the Page Setup dialog box.

Running Notepad

TIP If you have Notepad files that you use regularly—for example, a file for your random notes—you might want to put them into a folder for easy access. If you use them very regularly, put them into the start-up folder so they are loaded when you start up Windows. You can assign each one a shortcut key for rapid access.

To run Notepad, double-click on the Notepad icon; it's in the Accessories group. Notepad will appear on your screen, and you can immediately begin typing in the empty work area (Figure 22.1).

Alternatively, you can double-click on any document that Windows recognizes as a text file. As it starts up, Notepad will open that file automatically, and you'll see the text in the work area.

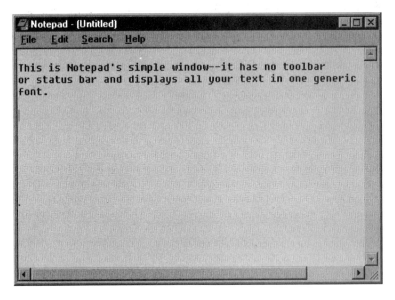

Figure 22.1   **The Notepad window**

Opening Files

NOTE   Of course, you can choose File ➤ New to start a new file at any time. If you've made changes in the previous file, Notepad gives you the expected opportunity to save it before creating the new file.

Once Notepad is up and running, opening another text file is as simple as choosing File ➤ Open and selecting the file you want from the Open dialog box.

Keep in mind, though, that Windows may not recognize the file you want to open as a text file. When you initially bring up the Open dialog box, it's set to display only files stored with the .txt extension (note the setting in the *Files of type* area). To locate a text file with another extension, choose All files in the Files of type area.

If you try to open a file that is too large, Notepad will warn you with the message:

```
This file is too large for Notepad.
Would you like to use WordPad to read this file?
```

Clicking on Yes will automatically run WordPad, which will open the chosen file.

> **CAUTION** Be careful about opening non-text files with Notepad. While it's fine to browse through a non-text file to see if you can make sense of it, don't make any changes and, above all, *don't save the file*. If you do, the file may be unusable even by the program that originally created it.

Notepad will go ahead and open any file you specify, even if it doesn't contain only text. If you open a non-text file, it will probably look like unintelligible garbage.

Entering and Editing Text

You can enter and edit text in Notepad as you would expect, with a few exceptions. To enter text, just start typing. The insertion point will move, just as it does in WordPad. However, as you reach the end of the window, the text will not wrap. Instead, Notepad just keeps adding new text to the same line, scrolling the window to the right so that the insertion point is always visible. When you press Enter, the window will pan back to the far left again, ready for the next line of text. Figure 22.2 shows an example of text in this state.

This is a rather inconvenient way to enter your text because you can't see much of what you just typed. To fix the problem, choose Edit ➤ Word Wrap. When you do, the text will wrap within the constraints of the window. If you resize the window, the text will rewrap to fit the available space. Figure 22.3 shows the same long line of text reformatted with Word Wrap turned on.

> **NOTE** Certain types of program files, such as .bat, .ini, and config.sys files, are line-oriented and are better edited with Word Wrap off. This allows you to distinguish more clearly one line from the next in the case of long lines.

Note that the word-wrap setting doesn't affect the text file itself. That is, Notepad does not insert line feeds or carriage returns at the points where the lines wrap.

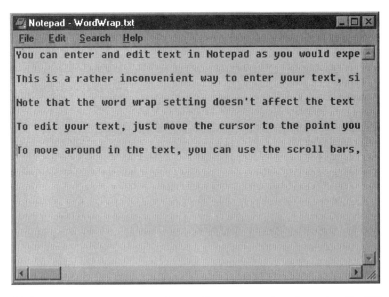

Figure 22.2   Each paragraph of text will normally stay on one long line unless Word Wrap is turned on.

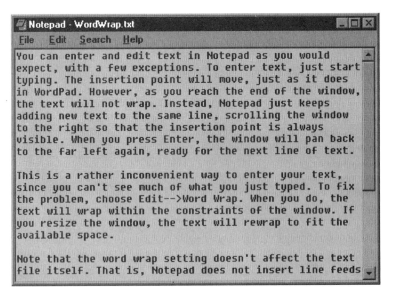

Figure 22.3   Text will wrap within a window if Word Wrap is turned on.

To edit your text, just move the cursor to the point you want to change. You can select, cut, copy, and paste text with the mouse, using the same techniques described in Chapter 19. To select all of the text in the file, choose Edit ➤ Select All.

To move around in the text, you can use the scroll bars, of course. You can also use the following keys:

Key	Moves Insertion Point to
Home	Start of the line
End	End of the line
PgUp	Up one window
PgDn	Down one window
Ctrl-Left Arrow	Start of previous word
Ctrl-Right Arrow	Start of next word
Ctrl-Home	Start of the file
Ctrl-End	End of the file

Entering the Time and Date in Your Text

A common use of a Notepad-type program is to take notes pertaining to important phone conversations or meetings with clients or colleagues, or to type up memos. Typically, you'll want to incorporate the current time and date into your notes to document developments as they happen. The Time/Date command on the Edit menu does this quickly.

To enter the time and date at the cursor:

1. Position the insertion point where you want the time and date inserted.

2. Choose Edit ➤ Time/Date or press F5.

Searching for Text

You can search for specific text in a Notepad file, but you can't replace it automatically. Follow these steps to search:

1. Choose Search ➤ Find. The dialog box shown on the next page will appear.

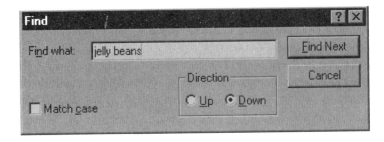

2. Type in the text you want to search for.

3. Check the Match Case box if you want to find text only having the same capitalization as your text. If you want the search to ignore capitalization, leave the box clear.

4. Click on Up if you want to search the portion of text above the current insertion point. Down is the default setting—Notepad searches from the insertion point to the end of the file and stops. Unlike Word-Pad, Notepad does not wrap around to the top of the file and continue the search down to the insertion point.

5. If you want to search again for the same word, choose Search ➤ Find Next or, better yet, press F3.

Setting Margins and Adding Headers and Footers

While its formatting capabilities are crude, Notepad does let you change the page margins and set up headers and footers. Here's how:

1. Choose File ➤ Page Setup command. You'll see the small dialog box shown here:

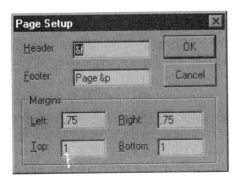

2. To change the margins, type in the new settings in inches.

 NOTE   Margin changes and header and footer settings aren't visible on the screen but will show up in your printed document.

3. To add a header or footer, type in any text you want to appear on every page. You can also use special codes to have Notepad place various information in the header or footer for you. Note the standard header and footer settings in the Page Setup dialog box shown above. These standard settings print the file name at the top of the page and the page number at the bottom. Here's a list of the codes you can enter:

Code	Effect
&d	Includes the current date
&p	Includes the page number
&f	Includes the file name
&l	Makes the subsequent text left align at the margin
&r	Makes the subsequent text right align at the margin
&c	Centers the subsequent text
&t	Includes the time of the printing

You can enter as many of these codes as you like.

Printing a Notepad File

To print a Notepad file, do the following:

1. Make sure the printer is ready.

2. If you're not sure that the correct printer is selected or if you want to make changes to its settings, choose File ➤ Page Setup, then click on the Printer button. You can now choose a different printer (if more than one is installed) or change settings by clicking on the Properties button.

3. Choose File ➤ Print to print the file. Notepad immediately starts the printing process and always prints the entire document—you don't have an opportunity to select which pages will print or how many copies.

Performing Calculations with the Calculator

The Calculator is a pop-up tool that you can use to perform simple or complex calculations. There are really two calculators in one—a Standard Calculator and a more complex Scientific Calculator for use by statisticians, engineers, computer programmers, and business professionals.

To run the Calculator, find it in the Accessories group on the Start menu and select it from the menu. A reasonable facsimile of a handheld calculator will appear on your screen, as shown in Figure 22.4. If your Calculator looks larger, it's the Scientific one. Choose View ➤ Standard to switch back to the basic calculator. The program always remembers which type was used last and comes up in that mode.

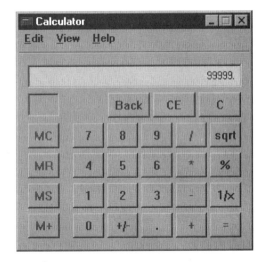

Figure 22.4 **The Standard Calculator**

Getting Help with the Calculator

For quick tips on how to use any calculator button, just click the right mouse button over the calculator button of interest. A little *What's this* button appears. Click on this, and you'll see a pop-up Help window. Of course, you can also choose Help ➤ Help Topics to display the main Help text.

Calculating a Result

> **TIP** To add up a series of numbers or to find their mean, you may prefer to use the statistical functions on the Scientific Calculator. This way, you can see all the numbers in a list before you perform the calculation instead of having to enter them one at a time. And don't let the idea of statistics make you nervous—the technique is very simple.

To perform a typical calculation, follow these steps:

1. Clear the calculator's display by pressing Esc or clicking on the C button.

2. Enter the first value in the calculation by clicking on the numbers or using the keyboard. (If you set the keypad's Num Lock setting on, you can use it to enter the numbers and the four mathematical operators. This is easier than using the number keys across the top of the keyboard.) You can use the Backspace key to fix mistakes, click on C to clear the calculator and start again, or click on CE to clear only the current entry but preserve the previous result.

3. After entering the first number, click on the mathematical operator you want to use. (The asterisk represents multiplication, SQRT calculates the square root, and 1/x calculates the reciprocal. The others are self-evident.)

4. Enter any additional numbers followed by the desired operators. In this way, you can perform a sequence of operations using the result of each computation as the beginning of the next.

5. Press Enter or click on the calculator's equals (=) button. The answer appears in the display.

Most of the operations on the standard calculator are self-explanatory, but a couple of them—square roots and percentages—are just a bit tricky. They are explained below, as are the functions of the scientific calculator.

Using the Memory Keys

The memory keys work just like those on a standard calculator. MS stores the displayed number in memory, MR recalls the memory value to the display for use in calculations, M+ adds the current display value to the existing memory value, and MC clears out the memory, resetting it to zero.

When the Calculators' memory contains a value, an *M* appears in the small area just above the MC button. If no value is in memory, this area is empty.

Copying Your Results to Other Documents

To enter the number displayed in the Calculator readout into another document, just use the standard Windows copy and paste commands. Use the Calculator for your computations, and then, when the result you want is in the display, choose Edit ➤ Copy (or press Ctrl-C). The value will be copied to the Clipboard. Then switch back to your document, position the cursor where you want the result, and paste it in.

Copying Calculations from Other Documents to the Calculator

Although the Calculator doesn't keep records of your computations for reference or reuse, you can get around that limitation via the Clipboard and a text editor such as Notepad or your word processor. Here's what to do:

1. In the text editor, type in the entire equation using the special symbols listed in Table 22.1.

2. Copy the equation to the Clipboard.

3. Switch to Calculator.

4. Click on the C button to clear the Calculator, then press Ctrl+V or choose Edit ➤ Paste.

If you've written out the equation correctly, the Calculator will compute the answer for you.

Calculator button	Equivalent keyboard key
%	%
(	(
)	)
⋆	⋆
+	+
+/−	F9
−	−
.	. or ,
/	/
0–9	0–9
1/x	r
=	= or Enter
A–F	A–F
And	&
Ave	Ctrl-A
Bin	F8
Byte	F4
Back	Backspace
C	Esc
CE	Del
cos	o
Dat	Ins
Dec	F6

Table 22.1 **Keyboard Shortcuts for the Calculator**

Calculator button	Equivalent keyboard key
Deg	F2
dms	m
Dword	F2
Exp	x
F–E	v
Grad	F4
Hex	F5
Hyp	h
Int	;
Inv	i
ln	n
log	l
Lsh	<
M+	Ctrl-P
MC	Ctrl-L
Mod	%
MR	Ctrl-R
MS	Ctrl-M
n!	!
Not	~
Oct	F7
Or		
PI	p

Table 22.1   Keyboard Shortcuts for the Calculator (continued)

Calculator button	Equivalent keyboard key
Rad	F3
s	Ctrl-D
sin	s
SQRT	@
Sta	Ctrl-S
Sum	Ctrl-T
tan	t
Word	F3
Xor	^
x^2	@
x^3	#
x^y	y

Table 22.1 **Keyboard Shortcuts for the Calculator (continued)**

Here's how a simple calculation might look, ready for copying from the text editor to Calculator:

    ((2+4)+16)/11=

or

    (2+(4+16))/11=

Note that you must surround each pair of terms in parentheses to indicate the calculation sequence. This is true even if you would have gotten the right answer had you typed in the numbers into the Calculator without the parentheses.

If you don't like the parentheses, you can try this format instead:

    2+4=+16=/11=

Note that this time you have to insert a = after each arithmetic operation; the Calculator gets confused if you don't.

You can use the following special characters in an equation to activate various Calculator functions:

:c	Clears the Calculator's memory
:e	If the Calculator is set to the decimal system, this sequence indicates that the following digits are the exponent of a number expressed in scientific notation; for example, 1.01:e100 appears in the Calculator as 1.01e+100
:m	Stores the number currently displayed in the Calculator's memory
:p	Adds the number currently displayed to the number in memory
:q	Clears the calculator
:r	Displays the number stored in the Calculator's memory
\	Places the number currently displayed into the Statistics box, which must already be open

Computing Square Roots and Percentages

To find a *square root,* just enter the number whose square root you want and click on the SQRT button. That's all there is to it—the only thing to remember is that this is a one-step calculation. You don't need to click on the = button or do anything else.

Percentages are a little trickier. Let's say you want to know what 14 percent of 2,875 is. Here's how to find out:

1. Clear the Calculator of previous results. This is a key step—you won't get the right answer if you leave a previous result in memory when you start.

2. Enter the number you're starting with, 2875 in this case.

3. Click on or type * (for multiplication) or *any* of the arithmetic operators. It actually doesn't matter which one you use—this step simply separates the two values you're entering.

4. Enter the percentage; in this case, 14. Don't enter a decimal point unless you're calculating a fractional percentage, such as 0.2 percent.

5. Now click on or type %. The Calculator reports the result.

Using the Scientific Calculator

In the Standard view, the Calculator may seem a fairly simple affair, but wait 'til you see the Scientific view—this is an industrial-strength calculating tool that can handle truly sophisticated computations. Figure 22.5 shows how the Scientific calculator appears on your screen. To display it, choose View ➤ Scientific.

The term "scientific" is somewhat misleading because the functions available here cover programming and statistics as well as the operations traditionally used by scientists. With the Scientific Calculator, you can:

▶ perform complex computations, grouping terms in up to 25 levels of parentheses

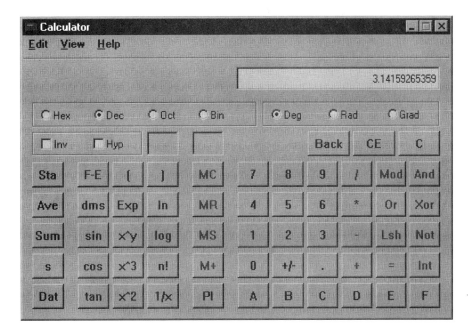

Figure 22.5   The Scientific Calculator

▶ display and perform calculations on values expressed in scientific (exponential) notation

▶ raise numbers to any power and find any (nth) root

▶ calculate logarithms and factorials

▶ perform trigonometric functions such as sine and cosine, displaying values as degrees, radians, or gradients

▶ insert the value of pi into your calculations

▶ perform calculations in four bases (hexadecimal, octal, and binary, in addition to decimal) and translate values between the bases

▶ perform bitwise operations (logical and shift operations on individual bits in a value) such as And, Or, Not, and Shift

▶ calculating standard deviations and other statistical computations

Details on the individual functions of the Scientific Calculator are beyond the scope of this book—if you're rocket scientist enough to use them, you probably don't need me to explain them to you. An introduction to operating the program is in order, however.

Accessing Additional Functions with the Inv and Hyp Check Boxes

The Inv check box at the left side of the Scientific Calculator functions something like the Shift key on your keyboard: checking it alters the function of some of the Calculator's buttons. This means you have access to additional functions that aren't obvious from the button labels.

For example, to find the arcsine of the value currently displayed in the readout, you would check the Inv box, then click on the sin button. Similarly, to find a cube root, enter the number, check the Inv box, and then click on the x^3 button. Instead of raising the value to the third power, you've calculated the cube root.

As you can guess, Inv stands for *inverse*, and it causes most buttons to calculate their inverses. With some buttons, though, checking the Inv box simply accesses a related function.

The Inv box is automatically cleared for you after each use.

Immediately to the right of the Inv box is the Hyp (for hyperbolic) check box, which works similarly. Its function is to access the corresponding hyperbolic trigonometric function when used with the sin, cos, and tan buttons.

Working with Scientific Notation

To enter a number using scientific (exponential) notation:

1. Begin by entering the significant digits (the base number).

2. When you're ready to enter the exponent, click on the Exp button. The display changes to show the value in exponential notation with an exponent of 0.

3. If you want to enter a negative exponent, click on the +/– button.

4. You can now enter the exponent. The Calculator accepts exponents up to +/– 307. If you enter a larger number, you'll get an error message in the display and you'll have to start over.

You can switch back and forth between exponential and standard decimal notations for numbers with absolute values less than 10^{15}. To do so, just click on the F–E button.

Working with Different Number Bases

The Scientific Calculator lets you enter and perform calculations with numbers in any of four commonly used number base systems: decimal (base 10), hexadecimal (base 16), octal (base 8), and binary (base 2). To switch to a different base, click on the appropriate radio button from the group at the upper left. The value currently in the display will be translated to the new base.

Many of the Scientific Calculator's operators and buttons work only while the decimal numbering system is active. For example, you can only use scientific notation with decimal numbers. The letter keys (A–F) at the bottom of the Scientific Calculator's numeric button pad are for entering the hexadecimal digits above 9 and only work in hexadecimal mode.

You have three display options when each number base system is active. The choices appear as radio buttons at the right side of the Calculator.

When the decimal system is active, you can display values as degrees, radians, or gradients. These are units used in trigonometric computations, and for other work you can ignore the setting.

> **NOTE** If the display is set for Degrees, you can use the dms button to display the current value in the degree-minute-second format. Once you've switched to degrees-minutes-seconds, you can translate back to degrees by checking the Inv box, then clicking on the dms button.

The choices for the other three bases are:

Dword, which displays the number as a 32-bit value (up to 8 hexadecimal places)

Word, which displays the number as a 16-bit value (up to 4 hex places)

Byte, which displays the number as an 8-bit value (up to 2 hex places)

When you switch to an option that displays fewer places, the Scientific Calculator hides the upper (more significant) places but retains them in memory and during calculations. When you switch back, the readout reflects the entire original number, as modified by any calculations.

Grouping Terms with Parentheses

You can use parentheses to group terms in a complex calculation, thereby establishing the order in which the various operations are performed. You can *nest* parentheses inside other parentheses to a maximum of 25 levels.

Aside from the math involved, there's nothing tricky about using parentheses—except keeping track of them as your work scrolls out of the display area. In this regard, the Scientific Calculator does provide one bit of help: It displays how many levels "deep" you are at the moment in the small area just above the right parenthesis button.

Performing Statistical Calculations

The Scientific Calculator can also perform several simple statistical calculations, including standard deviations, means, and sums. Even if you're not savvy with statistics, the statistical functions provide a good way to add or average a series of values. You get to enter the numbers in a list, where you can see them all, and then click on a button to get the result.

You access the statistical functions via three buttons at the left of the Scientific Calculator: Ave, Sum, and s. These buttons only work when you display the Statistics box, as detailed in the general instructions below. The functions of each button are listed after the instructions.

Now you're ready for the general method for performing any statistical calculation:

1. Click on the Sta button to display the Statistics box, shown here:

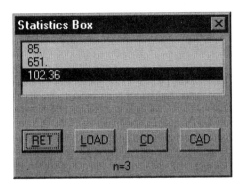

2. Position the Statistics box and the Calculator on your screen so you can see the box and have access to the Calculator buttons and readout.

3. Place each value in the Statistics box by entering the value and clicking on Dat. Repeat this for all the values you want to perform the calculation on.

4. To delete an entry in the Statistics box, highlight it, then click on CD (clear datum). You can delete all the entries by clicking on CAD (clear all data).

5. When you've entered all the correct values, click any of the three statistics buttons to perform the selected calculation. The answer appears in the Calculator's main readout.

Each of the statistical function buttons performs two functions: one "regular" function and a second function if you check the Inv box above before clicking on the button. Here are the buttons' functions:

Button	Normal function	Function with Inv
Ave	Calculates the mean	Calculates the mean of the squares
Sum	Calculates the sum	Calculates the sum of the squares
s	Calculates the standard deviation using $n-1$ as the population parameter	Calculates the standard deviation using n as the population parameter

Never heard of the population parameter? You're not alone....

Entering Special Symbols with Character Map

The Character Map program lets you choose and insert into your documents those oddball characters such as foreign alphabetic and currency symbols and characters from specialized fonts such as Symbol and Wingdings. With Character Map, you can easily view and insert these symbols even though there aren't keys for them on your keyboard.

Here are some everyday examples. Suppose that instead of the standard straight quotes (like "this") you'd prefer to use real open and close quotes (like "this") for a more professional-looking document. Or perhaps you regularly use the symbols for Trademark (™), Registered Trademark (®), Copyright (©); Greek letters such as α, β, δ; or the arrow symbols $\uparrow$, $\downarrow$, $\leftarrow$, and $\rightarrow$ that we use in this book. These, as well as fractions and foreign-language accents and the like, are included in your Windows fonts and can most likely be printed on your printer.

Character Map is a small dialog box that displays all the symbols available for each font. You select the symbol(s) you want, and Character Map puts them on the Clipboard for pasting into your document. Figure 22.6 displays some examples of special characters.

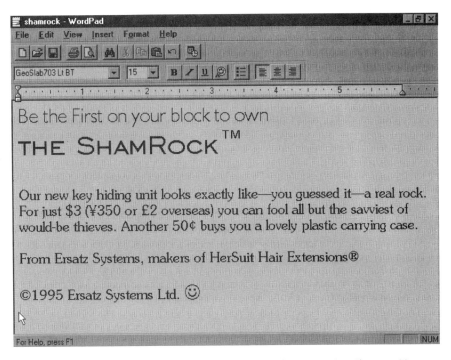

Figure 22.6   Sample characters inserted into a WordPad document using Character Map

Using Character Map

Here's how to use Character Map:

1. Run Character Map (it's in the Accessories group). The Character Map table comes up, showing all the characters included in the font currently selected in the Font list (a font can contain up to 224 characters).

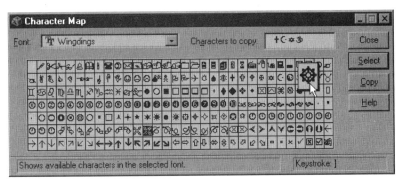

2. In the Font list, choose the font you want to work with. Most of the fonts have the same characters, but some special fonts have completely different *character sets*. For example, the Symbol font includes all sorts of special math and Greek symbols, while the Wingdings font consists of a wacky set of little pictures.

3. To make it easier to see the individual characters, you can click on a character box and hold the mouse button down to magnify the symbol. You can accomplish the same thing with the keyboard by moving to the character using the arrow keys. With this technique, each character is magnified as you select it.

4. Double-click on a character to select it, transferring it to the *Characters to copy* box. Alternatively, once you've highlighted a character, you can click on the Select button or press Alt-S to place it in the Characters to copy box.

> **NOTE** You can change fonts at any time. Just be aware that this will affect the characters you previously placed in the Characters to copy box, not just new characters.

5. If you want to grab more than one character, keep adding them in the same way. Each new character is added to the end of the string in the Characters to copy box.

6. Click on the Copy button. This places everything in the Characters to copy box onto the Clipboard.

7. Switch back to your destination application and use the Paste command (typically on the application's Edit menu) to insert the characters into your document. You may then have to select the inserted characters and choose the correct font to format the characters correctly.

Of course, once you've entered a character in this way, you're free to change its font and size as you would any character you typed in.

Entering Alternate Characters from the Keyboard

Notice that the bottom of the Character Map dialog box includes a line that reads

```
Keystroke:
```

When you click on a character in Character Map, this line displays the keys you would have to press to enter the character directly from the keyboard rather than from Character Map. For the characters in the first three lines—except the very last character on the third line—the keystroke shown will be a key on your keyboard. If you're working with a nonstandard font such as Symbol, pressing the key shown will enter the selected symbol into your document. With Symbol, for example, pressing the *a* key enters α. With Wingdings, pressing *J* enters the cheery symbol shown at left.

For all the other characters, Character Map instructs you to enter a sequence of keys in combination with the Alt key. For example, say you wanted to enter the copyright symbol (©) into a Windows application document. Note that with a standard text font like Arial or Times New Roman selected in Character Map, the program lists the keystrokes for the copyright symbol as Alt-0169. Here's how to enter the character from the keyboard:

1. Press Num Lock to activate the numeric keypad on your keyboard if the keypad is not already active.

2. Press Alt and as you hold it down type 0 1 6 9 (that is, type the 0, 1, 6, and 9 keys individually, in succession). When you release the Alt key, the copyright symbol should appear in the document.

Not all Windows application programs accept characters in this way, but it's worth a try as a shortcut to using the Character Map.

Character Sets: ANSI v. IBM

Normally you'll be using Character Map with Windows applications. However, you may have some success dropping special characters into non-Windows applications. The basic technique is simple:

1. Copy the desired characters to the Clipboard.

2. Display the non-Windows application in a window if it isn't windowed already.

3. Paste the Clipboard contents into your application using the application window's Control menu (choose Edit ➤ Paste or click on the Paste button).

That's easy enough, but whether or not you see the desired characters depends on several factors. Here's the situation: Windows uses the American National Standards Institute (ANSI) character set to display characters on the screen and assign them to the keyboard. This includes 256 characters, numbered 0 to 255. By contrast, when your PC runs DOS *text mode* or *character-based* programs, the computer uses a different character set called the IBM extended character set.

In the United States, at least, the ANSI and IBM sets are identical for the characters numbered between 32 and 127, which correspond to the letters, numbers, and symbols on a standard U.S. keyboard. However, the two sets differ dramatically when it comes to the other characters. For example, in the ANSI set the British pound symbol (£) is character 163, whereas in the IBM extended character set it is 156.

With me so far? Okay, here's how Character Map and your non-Windows programs interact. When you copy a character from a standard Windows text font to a non-Windows application, Windows tries to translate the character into one that the non-Windows program can display. Sometimes this works, sometimes it doesn't. Here are the possible scenarios:

▶ If the symbol is present in the IBM character set, you may be in luck—it should appear in the non-Windows document as is. For example, if you select and copy the British pound symbol, Windows translates it to the correct code for that same symbol in the IBM character set. So far so good. But what happens when that code gets pasted into your non-Windows program is up to the program. Some programs can accept any character code you throw at them. Others display some codes as expected but react strangely to others, perhaps by executing some menu command. Still others ignore all characters except the standard ones.

▶ If Windows has no exact equivalent in the IBM character set, Windows converts it to the character it thinks is the closest. Thus, a copyright symbol becomes *c*, the registered trademark becomes *r*, and so on. Again, depending on the character code after the conversion, your non-Windows application may or may not accept it when you paste it in.

By the way, Windows performs these translations on all Clipboard text you paste to a non-Windows program, not just characters copied from Character Map.

It's usually easier to enter the non-keyboard characters into a non-Windows application directly, rather than copying them from Windows—that way, you'll avoid all the pitfalls I've just described. Check your non-Windows application's manual to see whether it includes information about entering non-keyboard characters from the keyboard. If you don't find any specific advice, you can try entering them as follows:

1. Look up the code for the character you want to insert. There are several places to look:

   ▶ In Character Map's Font box, select the font called Terminal, which is used to display text in your windowed non-Windows programs. This font includes all the characters of the IBM set, although Character Map doesn't display the first 31 of them. Again, the necessary code appears at the bottom of the Character Map window.

   ▶ Character codes are usually listed in your computer's manual or your DOS manual.

   ▶ You can get pop-up utilities (I'm talking non-Windows utilities) that display the characters and their codes on the screen. Usually referred to as *ASCII tables*, these utilities are available as shareware or freeware from many bulletin boards and shareware distributors.

2. Once you've found the code, press Num Lock to activate the numeric keypad on your keyboard if the keypad is not already active.

3. To enter the character, press the Alt key, hold it down, and type the three-digit code on the numeric keypad. Note that these are *three*-digit codes, not four-digit codes as in Windows. All Windows key-codes require entry of an initial 0, the fourth digit. For example, to enter the British pound symbol in a non-Windows program, you would enter Alt-156, *not* Alt-0156. If the three-digit code does start with a 0, go ahead and enter that.

Note that you can use a Windows program such as WordPad or Notepad to open text files saved by a non-Windows application, even if they contain extended characters. In general, however, the extended characters will be represented by small solid or hollow boxes—in other words, you'll lose them. The rest of your text should remain intact, however.

Audio Control

This accessory is a pretty simple one. When you run it, it pops up volume controls, balance controls, and the like for controlling your sound card, if you have one. If you don't have a sound card, this accessory won't be available, or won't do anything. There are two sets of controls—one for recording and one for playback.

1. Run the accessory from Start ➤ Programs ➤ Accessories ➤ Multimedia ➤ Volume Control. You can more easily run it by double-clicking on the little speaker icon in the Taskbar. Your sound system's capabilities will determine the format of the volume control(s) you'll see. On first running the accessory on my machine, I see:

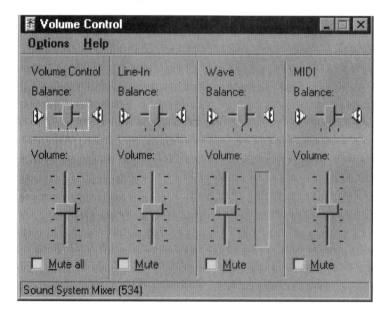

Part
4

2. Change any volume control's setting by dragging the volume up or down. Change the balance between right and left channels by dragging the Balance sliders left or right.

3. Check out the Properties menu. It may have options that will provide an expanded view of the volume controls. The graphic below shows a typical Properties box allowing alteration of which volume controls display.

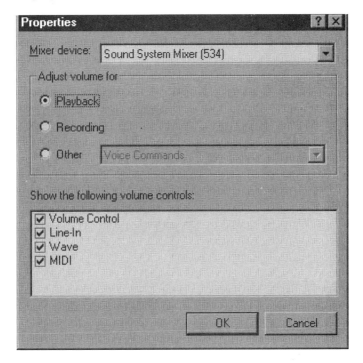

 NOTE Some of the sliders in one module are linked to sliders in other modules. Adjusting the Volume setting on one will affect Volume settings on the other mixers, for example.

Because audio controls operate differently for different sound cards, check out any Help files that might be available from your audio controls. Typically there will be a Help button to press.

Two little tips here: if you're using the Microsoft sound system, you can adjust the recording volume by clicking on the microphone or line slider and speaking into the microphone. As long as you keep the mouse button depressed, the input signal will be displayed in the VU meter bar.

Second, to quickly kill the sound output from your system (useful when the phone rings), click on the little speaker icon in the Taskbar:

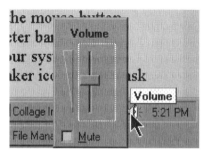

You'll be able to adjust the master volume from here and even mute the sound by clicking on the Mute box.

Chapter 23

Using the System Tools

FEATURING

Correcting disk errors with ScanDisk

Backing up files with Backup

Increasing disk capacity with DriveSpace

Disk Defragmenter

Tracking system resources with System Monitor

Windows 95 comes with a full set of software tools designed to improve the performance of your system and protect your vital information against breakdowns, damage, theft, or loss. The tools include:

ScanDisk: for detecting and correcting errors on your disks that might otherwise cause you to lose information or waste disk space.

Backup: for making backup copies of the files on your hard disks onto floppy disks or tape. If your computer or hard disks ever break down or get stolen, you'll be able to retrieve the files using Backup and the backup copies.

DriveSpace: for increasing the amount of storage space available on your disks by compressing the information in your files.

Disk Defragmenter: for speeding access to the files on your hard disks. It works by reorganizing the disks so each file is stored as a single block on one area of the disk instead of in sections scattered over different parts of the disk.

System Monitor: for displaying technical information about the activity of your system, showing you how your system resources are being used on a moment-to-moment basis (this is only available if you install Network Administrator Tools).

Correcting Disk Errors with ScanDisk

While your PC's disks give you a reliable place to store vast amounts of information, they are vulnerable to glitches of various types that can make the information unusable or reduce the space available for storing new data. The ScanDisk accessory can find these problems and take remedial action either by correcting the problem directly or locking out problem areas on the disk. It can't fix all possible errors, but it will notify you of every problem it discovers.

NOTE   This version of ScanDisk performs functions similar to those of the non-Windows programs SCANDISK and CHKDSK (SCANDISK was included with MS-DOS 6, and CHKDSK is available in every version of DOS and comes with Windows 95 as well). The big difference is, you can use the new version of ScanDisk while you're working with Windows.

To run ScanDisk, begin from the Start menu and choose Programs ➤ Accessories ➤ System Tools ➤ ScanDisk. You'll see the main Scan-Disk window, shown in Figure 23.1.

> **TIP** If something has gone seriously wrong with your hard disk, it may help to run ScanDisk more than once. In some cases, the program is able to find and repair additional errors on each of several passes.

You have only a few choices to make in this window. Choose the disk you want to analyze from the list at the top of the window. Check the Automatically Fix Errors box if you want ScanDisk to correct the errors it finds for you without any further input from you. Clear this box if you want a chance to determine how ScanDisk handles each error.

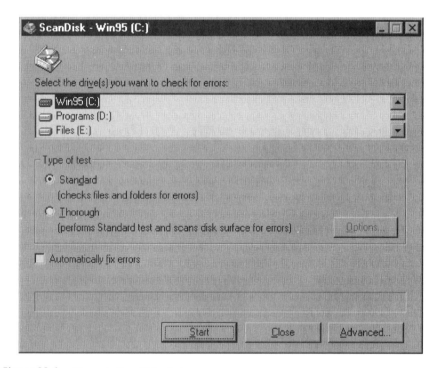

Figure 23.1   *The main ScanDisk window*

The two radio buttons in the center let you select either a standard test, which simply checks for errors and inconsistencies in the records Windows keeps on folders (directories) and the files they contain; or a "thorough" test which in addition checks the actual disk surface itself for problems with the magnetic media on which information is stored.

I'll explain more about the various types of checks that ScanDisk performs and why they're necessary in a bit. For now, a quick word of advice on how to choose between these two options is in order. The standard test is *much* faster than the thorough test, and the problems it detects occur far more frequently than flaws in the disk surface. You should run the standard test regularly—every day when you start your PC, if you're a heavy user, or once a week if you only use your computer occasionally. Running the thorough test once a week (for heavy users) to once a month (for occasional users) should be enough to catch most disk-surface errors before you lose data.

Testing a Disk

To begin a disk test, click on the Start button at the bottom of the ScanDisk window. As the program analyzes your disk, it reports its progress in the area above the buttons near the bottom of the window. You'll see messages explaining what ScanDisk is doing at the moment plus a graphical meter of how much of the analysis is complete.

You can stop a test at any time by clicking on the Cancel button. Otherwise, ScanDisk displays the message "Complete" when it finishes the analysis. Depending on how you've set the display options, you may see a summary of its findings.

Setting ScanDisk Options

ScanDisk's standard settings are best for most users, and you probably won't need to change them. But choice is the name of the game. ScanDisk lets you select settings for a variety of options pertaining to both standard and thorough tests.

To review and change the settings for standard disk tests, click on the Advanced button in the ScanDisk window. You'll see the Scan-Disk Advanced Options dialog box, shown here:

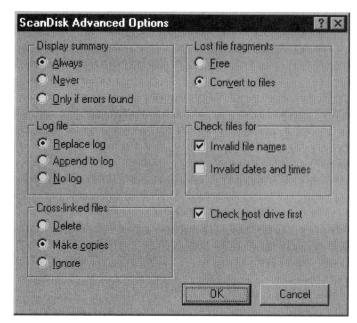

The dialog box is divided into four main areas: one for specifying display options, one for controlling how files are analyzed, and two for specifying how ScanDisk handles specific types of errors. In addition, there's a check box near the bottom of the dialog box that pertains only to compressed drives.

Setting Display Options

The Display Summary area offers radio buttons for three settings that determine when you will see a summary of ScanDisk's findings. Choose:

Always: if you want to see the summary when ScanDisk finishes testing a disk, whether or not it finds any errors.

Never: if you never want to see the summary.

Only if errors found: if you want to see the summary only if ScanDisk found any errors.

Handling Cross-Linked Files

One long-familiar PC problem that can still bedevil your Windows disks is *cross-linked files*. Because of quirks in the way DOS and Windows store information about files, errors can creep into the master record that shows where each file is located on the disk. When files are cross-linked, the record shows that two or more files share a common part (cluster) of the disk. Files are always supposed to be independent entities, so this is clearly a mistake. When the system tries to access a cross-linked file, it will likely read the wrong information. Your documents may open looking like garbage, or your whole system may come to a halt.

ScanDisk lets you decide how to handle the cross-linked files it discovers as it combs through the disk's master record. However, these settings only apply if you have checked Automatically Fix Errors in the main ScanDisk window (if not, ScanDisk will let you decide how to handle each cross-linking problem on a case-by-case basis as described just below).

Choose one of the radio buttons in the Cross Linked Files area as follows:

Delete: if you want ScanDisk to erase the cross-linked files. You won't have to worry about them again, although you'll lose the data they contain.

Make copies: if you want ScanDisk to copy each cross-linked file to a new location on the disk in hopes of preserving the original information. When two or more files are cross-linked, the disk cluster they have in common contains valid information from only one of the files, at most. (In some cases, all of the information in the shared cluster is garbage.) If you're lucky, copying the files will restore one of them to its original condition. In any case, you may be able to retrieve some of the contents if they are copied word-processor or database files. To try this, open them in a text editor or word processor and copy any valid information you find to a new file.

Ignore: if you want ScanDisk to leave the cross-linked files as is. This is a choice for advanced users who may wish to use other disk tools to examine the contents of the problem files in hopes of retrieving more of their data. Normally, you shouldn't select this option—if you leave the cross-linked files in place, you're very likely to lose even more of the information they contain, and the problem may spread to other files.

If Automatically Fix Errors is not checked, ScanDisk displays a dialog box similar to this one when it detects cross-linked files:

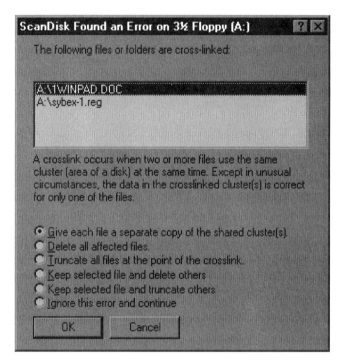

Handling Lost File Fragments

Lost file fragments are portions of the disk containing information that doesn't belong to any specific file. Somehow, the master record for the disk has gotten muddled. While the record indicates that these areas hold data, it doesn't show which files they belong to. As Scan-Disk checks the master record, it finds these free-floating chunks of information by checking the entry for each cluster against the list of files and their locations.

If you have checked the Automatically Fix Errors box in the main ScanDisk window, ScanDisk will deal with the lost file fragments it finds according to the setting in the Lost File Fragments area. Choose:

> *Free:* if you want ScanDisk to delete the lost file fragments, freeing up the space on disk for other files.

Convert to files: if you want ScanDisk to convert the fragments to valid files. Scan-Disk names the files according to the pattern `file0000.chk`, `file0001.chk`, and so on, placing them in the top-level folder (the root directory) of the current disk drive. After you finish with ScanDisk, you can use a file-viewing program to examine their contents.

If the Automatically Fix Errors box isn't checked, you'll receive a message when ScanDisk encounters lost file fragments, allowing you to decide then how to deal with the situation.

File-Checking Options

The Check Files For area has two check boxes having to do with the types of errors ScanDisk checks for when analyzing individual files. You can check them in any combination. Choose:

Invalid filenames: if you want ScanDisk to find files with invalid characters in their names.

Invalid dates and times: if you want ScanDisk to find files whose date and time information is invalid.

If you have checked the Automatically fix errors box on the main ScanDisk window, ScanDisk will fix the types of errors you've chosen automatically. If not, you'll be shown a message describing the problem and giving you options for dealing with it, as in this example:

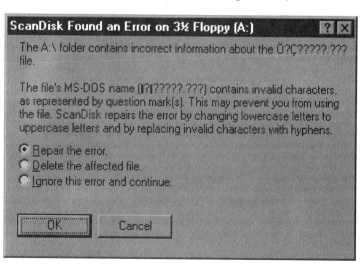

Options for Compressed Drives

The check box labeled *Check host drive first* in the ScanDisk Advanced Options dialog box applies only to compressed drives. If you're testing a drive that has been compressed for more storage space by DriveSpace (included with Windows 95) or DoubleSpace (included with DOS 6), you might want to change this setting.

When the box is checked, ScanDisk tests the actual disk—the *host* drive—where the compressed drive is located before checking the files and folders of the compressed drive. You should leave this box checked for most work because the host drive may be hidden and because errors on a compressed drive are commonly caused by problems with the host drive. Clearing the box will make the test run faster.

Options for Thorough Disk Tests

If you select a thorough test on the main ScanDisk window, the Options button becomes available. Click on it to display the Surface Scan Options dialog box, shown here:

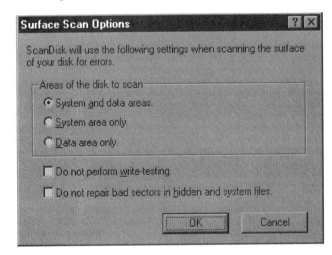

In the bordered area labeled *Areas of the disk to scan,* choose the radio button for the type of test you want to perform:

> *System and data areas:* if you want to scan the entire disk.

System area only: if you want to scan only the sections of the disk that store system information, such as the boot (start-up) programs and the master records of the file and folders. Much of the information stored here cannot be moved, so Scan-Disk will be unable to fix problems here. If errors in the system area are found, the disk probably should be junked.

Data area only: if you want to check the bulk of the disk area, where your files can be stored, but not the system area. This choice scans the entire data area, including areas not currently storing files. When it finds a faulty location, ScanDisk can often preserve the information stored there by moving the data elsewhere. The faulty location is then marked as "bad" so it won't be used in the future. If the problem isn't caught early enough, however, data at the faulty location may be unreadable, in which case it's gone for good (ScanDisk will still mark the bad spot).

Because the system area occupies only a small part of the entire disk, testing the system area only takes much less time than testing the data area or the full disk.

The Surface Scan Options dialog box also has two check boxes:

Do not perform write-testing: when this box is cleared, ScanDisk tests each location on the disk exhaustively. It reads the data stored at that location, writes the data back to the same spot, then rereads the information to check it against the original copy. If you check the box, ScanDisk simply checks to be sure it can read the data. This may not be enough to catch and correct some errors before the information becomes unusable.

Do not repair bad sectors in hidden and system files: when this box is cleared, Scan-Disk attempts to relocate the data stored in all damaged locations on the disk, even if the information belongs to a hidden or system file. The problem is, some programs expect to find certain hidden system files in a specific disk location. If these files (or any part of them) are moved, the program stops working. In the early days of the PC, this was a fairly common *copy-protection scheme,* a technique to keep people from making unauthorized copies of software. If you have such programs, you may wish to check this box. ScanDisk will then leave hidden and system files where they are even when they are found on damaged areas of the disk. The programs will find their special files in their expected locations—but because of the disk problems, they may not work anyway.

Backing Up Your Files with Backup

You're probably sick of people telling you how important it is to back up the work you do with your computer. Well, as far as I'm concerned, whether or not you back up is your business. My job is to tell you how to do it with the Backup program included with Windows 95.

> **NOTE** In case you're new to computers, you should know that backing up is a critical everyday task. Any information you store on a disk is vulnerable to damage or loss from a host of dangers, ranging from theft, fire, and water to magnetic or mechanical failure of the disk itself. The greatest threat to your data is you—choosing the wrong command can wipe out hours of work in an instant. Your most effective weapon in the battle to protect your data is to make backup copies of everything you keep on your disks, especially the documents and other files you create yourself. Should disaster strike and wipe out your frontline data, you can fall back on the backups—but only if you've made them.

Backup simplifies the process of backing up your disks and of *restoring* the backed-up files should the originals ever be lost. With Backup you can:

▶ back up to floppy disk or on tape

▶ specify which files are backed up

▶ create sets of files for repeated backup as groups

▶ compress the backed-up files so fewer floppy disks or tapes are required

▶ restore the backed-up files to their original folders or to new locations

▶ compare the backed-up files with the current versions on disk

One caveat is important to mention here: don't rely on your backups until you've tested the entire process of backing up and restoring data. Back up a set of files including programs and some data. After restoring them, check that the programs still run properly and that the other files will still open and still contain valid information. This is the only way you can be sure that Backup and your backup hardware are working properly.

Also, be aware that backup tapes and floppies can go bad as they age. Although it should be fine if your daily backup sessions only back up files that are new or have changed, I urge you to back up *all* your files at regular intervals.

Running Backup

To run Backup, begin from the Start menu and choose Programs ➤ Accessories ➤ System Tools ➤ Backup. Backup's window appears on your screen as shown in Figure 23.2.

> **TIP**   If you install a new tape drive after running Backup for the first time, you must choose Tools ➤ Redetect Tape. Backup will re-initialize itself, repeating the search for a working tape drive.

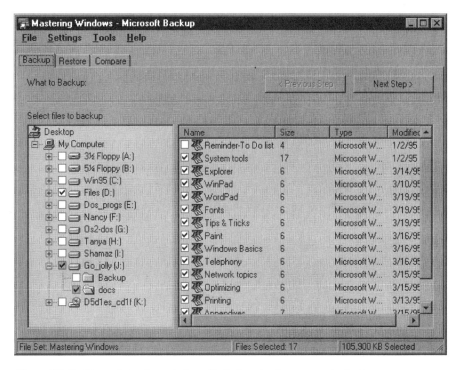

Figure 23.2   *The main Backup window, displaying the first step on the Backup page*

The first time you run Backup it examines your system, looking for a working tape drive. You may hear some gruesome noises from your floppy drives as Backup probes to see just what kind of devices they really are. If Backup can't find a working tape drive, you won't be able to access the tape-related commands.

The main window is tabbed and has three pages: one for backing up files, one for restoring them, and one for comparing the versions on disk with their backed-up counterparts.

Backing Up Your Files

The first page of the Backup window is the Backup page, appropriately enough. You use this page to choose the information you want to back up and where you want to store it as well as to initiate the actual backup process.

 NOTE   Backup lets you set a variety of optional settings controlling details of the backup process. See *Setting Backup Options* below.

Begin by selecting the items you want to back up: entire disks, their folders, or individual files, in any combination. The display works just like the one in Explorer, showing disks and folders in a tree view on the left and listing subfolders and individual files in the currently selected disk or folder on right. Unlike Explorer, however, Backup displays a small check box next to each item. To select an item for backup, click on the square for that item (in either side of the window) so a check mark appears there.

As you can guess, checking a disk selects all the folders and files on that disk for backup. If you select specific folders rather than an entire disk, Backup places a check mark in the disk's box, too, but on a gray background. Similarly, if you pick out separate files within a folder, the folder's box will be checked and will turn gray.

Specifying the Backup Destination

When you've chosen all the information you want to back up, click on Next Step to select the destination for the backups. The Backup window changes, as shown in Figure 23.3.

Here, use the tree on the left to locate the disk and directory in which you want to store your backups. When you click on your choice, it will show up in the Selected Device or Location area at the right.

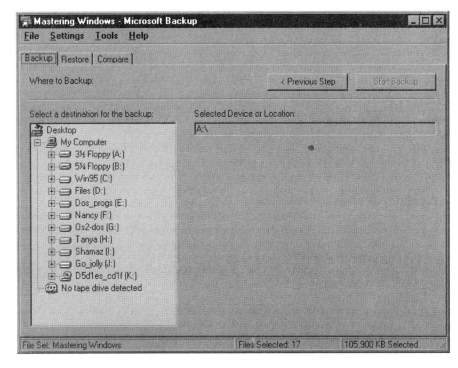

Figure 23.3 *The Backup page lets you choose a destination for your backups after you click on Next Step.*

 NOTE Although the File menu offers a Save As choice when you're select-ing the files to back up, you can't save a file set until you specify a backup destination.

Saving and Using Backup File Sets

Once you've selected the information you want to back up and the backup destination, you have the option of saving these choices in a reusable *file set*. When you want to back up the same files again—a common necessity—just open the file set and proceed with the backup.

To save a file set, choose File ➤ Save As, type in a name, and click on OK. To open a file set you previously saved, choose File ➤ Open File Set.

Finishing the Backup

Before you go any further, prepare the disks or tapes you'll be using for the backup:

1. Get out enough of them to hold all the data. (Backup displays the total size of all the selected files at the bottom right. If you turn the compression option on, you may need half this much capacity or less on your backup tapes and disks.)

 TIP If you need to format your tapes or erase existing data from tapes or disks, use the commands on the Tools menu described in *Formatting and Erasing the Backup Media* below.

2. Label the first tape or disk with the date, a set name, and the number 1.

To proceed to the actual backup step, click on Start Backup at the upper right. Backup first asks you to type in a descriptive name for the backed-up files as a unit:

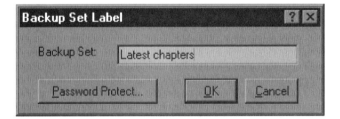

Before you go on, you have the option of protecting the whole set of files with a password. If you assign a password, Backup will ask you to enter it again before you can restore files in the set to replace a damaged or missing original.

To set a password, click on Password Protect in the Backup Set Label dialog box. You are required to type in the password twice to ensure that you've entered it correctly.

Back at the Backup Set Label dialog box, click on OK to proceed. Backup creates a new file on the destination device and begins copying the information from your files there. You'll see a series of message windows that keep you posted on how far along the backup has gone from moment to moment.

NOTE If Backup encounters any problems during the backup process, you'll see error messages describing the glitch.

If all the files won't fit on the first floppy disk or tape, Backup notifies you and asks you to insert another disk or tape (before you do, label it with the date and set name and number it in proper sequence). The process continues in this way until all the files in your file set have been backed up.

Formatting and Erasing the Backup Media

Backup can format blank tapes for you. To format a tape, insert it in the drive and choose Tools ➤ Format Tape, following the instructions provided. If you always back up to new, blank tapes, you can set up Backup to format all the tapes automatically. See *Changing Backup Settings* below.

You can also use Backup to erase existing data from the tape currently in the tape drive by choosing Tools ➤ Erase Tape. By the way, you can set up Backup so that it *always* automatically erases existing data from tapes and/or from floppy disks before each new backup operation. See *Changing Backup Settings* below.

Quick Backups from the Desktop

Once you've created a backup file set, you can back up the files in the set directly from the Desktop without starting the Backup application first. You can set up and perform these quick backups in two ways:

▶ You can place a shortcut for the Backup application on the Desktop. Then, whenever you want to back up a given file set, just locate the set in any file display, drag it to the Desktop, and drop it onto the Backup shortcut.

▶ Alternatively, you can place a shortcut for one or more particular file sets on the Desktop. To start the backup, you just double-click on the shortcut.

Use the first approach if you've created a number of Backup file sets and want to keep the Desktop from becoming too crowded. If you use only one or two sets, the second approach is faster. Of course, you can combine the two methods, placing a shortcut for your most commonly used file set on the Desktop and using the drag-and-drop technique for the sets you back up only occasionally.

With default settings, you never see the main Backup window when you start a backup using either quick method. Instead, you're simply informed that the procedure is starting and asked whether you want to continue. As the backup proceeds, other messages let you monitor Backup's progress as it finds and selects the files in the set and then backs them up. Error messages appear if anything goes wrong.

Setting Drag-and-Drop Options

You have three simple choices for controlling the way Backup operates during quick backups from the Desktop. You can:

▶ decide whether or not Backup runs minimized so you never see the main Backup window on your screen during a quick backup

▶ choose whether or not you'll be asked to OK the backup before it begins

▶ decide whether or not Backup closes after carrying out the backup

To change any of these settings, choose Settings ➤ Drag and Drop and, in the resulting dialog box shown below, clear or check the relevant box.

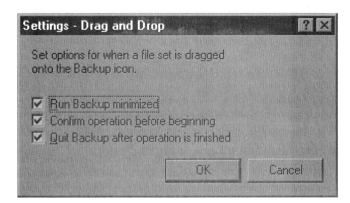

Restoring Files from Your Backups

You may never need the backups you've so diligently made, day after day, week after week. If your hard disk never breaks down, if you never delete a file by mistake, if your computer never gets stolen, consider yourself lucky and the time you spent backing up as inexpensive insurance.

But if you ever do lose data, your backups suddenly will seem to you precious jewels of infinite value. After your computer is running again—or you've gone out and bought another—slip the backup disk or tape into the machine, and a few minutes later your vanished files will be miraculously restored.

With Backup, restoring files is a piece of cake. Find the set of tapes or disks containing the lost files and insert disk or tape #1. Then, in Backup:

1. Switch to the Restore page, shown in Figure 23.4.

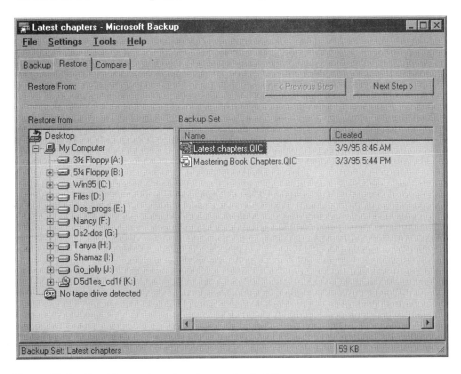

Figure 23.4 *Use this page to restore damaged or lost files.*

2. Navigate in the disk-and-directory tree on the left to the disk or tape drive containing the backups. When you're there, Backup finds and displays on the right the backup file set or sets (there may be more than one if you back up fairly small files in separate sets).

3. Double-click on the set you want to restore from. After Backup checks the set, the window changes to show the set's disks and folders (Figure 23.5). To select the information you want to restore, click in the little boxes next to each displayed item just as you did to select files for backup. If you check the box of the top item in the left-hand list, all the disks, folders, and files contained in the set will be restored. Otherwise, you can check individual disks, folders, and files in any combination. To display an item's contents in the right side of the window, click on the item (not its check box).

4. When you've selected the correct files, click on Start Restore to proceed. If you assigned a password when you created the backup, you'll be asked to type it in now. Depending on the option settings, you may

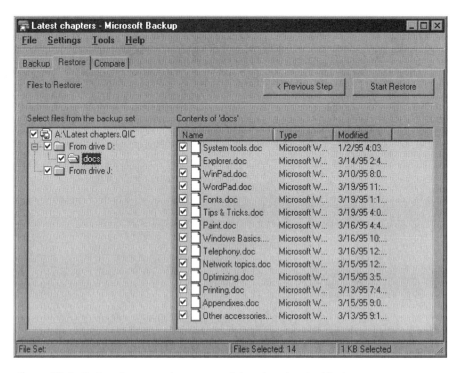

Figure 23.5   Backup shows you the contents of the selected set in this view.

also need to specify a destination for the restored files (if the standard settings are active, Backup restores the files to their original disks and directories, if possible).

5. The restoration begins. You'll be informed of its progress and notified when it completes. Depending on how you've set the options, you may be asked for permission to overwrite existing files with the same names as the ones you're restoring.

Comparing Backups against the Originals

Once you've backed up a set of files, use the Compare function to ensure that the backup copies contain exactly the same information as the originals. This step takes a significant amount of time, but without it you can't be sure the backup copies are actually protecting you against data loss.

Here's how to compare backups and their originals:

1. Insert the tape or floppy disk containing the backed-up files you want to compare into the proper drive.

2. On the main Backup window, switch to the Compare page (see Figure 23.6).

3. Use the disk-and-directory tree on the left to locate the backup set containing the files you want to compare and click on it so it is listed on the right.

4. Click on the desired backup set, then click on Next Step at the top right. The Backup window changes to display the set you've chosen on the left.

5. Now select the specific folders or files in the backup set you want to compare:

    ▶ If you want to compare the entire contents of the set, just click in the box to its left.

    ▶ To select individual folders, click on the icon for the set so folder icons appear, then click on the boxes for each folder you want.

    ▶ To pick out individual files, open the folders one at a time to display their contents on the right side of the window, then click on the box for each file.

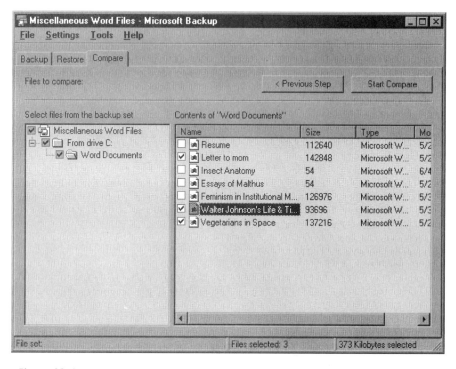

Figure 23.6 Backup's Compare page

6. Click on Start Compare at the top right. Backup displays its progress in the Compare window, shown below.

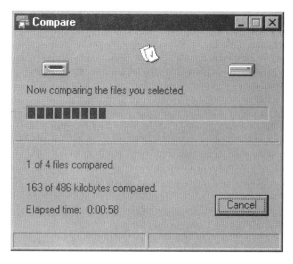

7. When the comparison is complete, you'll see a little message box to that effect. Click on OK to return to the Compare window, where you'll see a summary of the operation.

Using Filters to Select Files and Folders

To speed file selection for a Backup, Restore, or Compare operation, you can use a *filter* to automatically select or reject files that match criteria you specify. You can exclude particular types of files, even if they're in a selected folder, or specify a range of dates for the files to be selected. Choose Settings ➤ File Filtering to display the dialog box shown in Figure 23.7.

The top portion of the dialog box lists many common types of files. To exclude a particular type, select it in the list and click on Exclude.

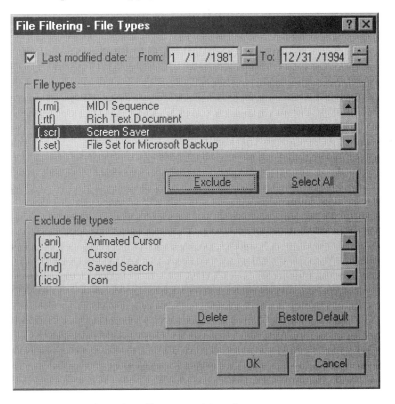

Figure 23.7   Set filters for various file types and dates here.

It will appear in the exclude list in the lower part of the dialog box. To specify a date range for selected files, check the Last Modified Date box and then set the From and To dates as desired.

Changing Backup Settings

You can control Backup's operating characteristics by choosing Settings ➤ Options to display the Options dialog box.

The Options dialog box is tabbed and has four pages, one each for General settings and for options pertaining to the Backup, Restore, and Compare functions. Here are the settings on the General page:

Turn on audible prompts: Check this box if you want Backup to sound a tone when your input is required.

Overwrite old status log files: Check here if you want Backup to replace the contents of the status log with a report on the most current session each time you use the program. With this box cleared, Backup saves a new status log each time so you can go back and view reports on previous sessions.

The settings on the Backup page of the Options dialog box include:

Quit Backup after operation is finished: Check here to have Backup close automatically once it completes a backup operation. This frees the memory and resources Backup uses as soon as the program has finished its work without further intervention from you.

Type of Backup: Choose between a *full* backup, which backs up all files in the file set, or a *differential* backup, in which only the files that have changed since the last backup are backed up anew each time.

Verify backup data....: Check here to ensure that the backup copies created during a session exactly match the originals. Backup runs its Compare function as soon as the backups have been made.

Use data compression....: This check box lets you decide whether or not the backed-up data will be compressed. Compression saves space, but it can have drawbacks: If even a little of the compressed data goes bad, your backups may become completely worthless, whereas you might be able to salvage uncompressed files.

Always format tape backups: If you know you'll be using fresh, blank tape every time you back up, check this box. That way, Backup will automatically format the new tape before it starts copying information to it. If you clear this box, you'll need to format new tapes with the Format Tape command on the Tools menu.

Always erase on....: The last two check boxes let you specify whether Backup erases all existing data on your backup tape or floppy disk before proceeding with a new backup.

Options on the Restore page include:

Quit Backup after operation is finished: Check this box to have Backup close automatically after any restore procedure finishes.

Restore backed up files to: The three radio buttons here tell Backup where to put the restored files: in their original disks and folders (directories); in an alternate location (disk and folder) of your choice, preserving the original hierarchy of subdirectories; or in an alternate location, with all the restored files placed in a single directory.

Verify restored data....: Check this box if you want Backup to perform a Compare operation after it completes the restore to ensure that the restored files match the data stored on the backup tapes or disks.

<Overwrite options>: The last three radio buttons on this page let you tell Backup what to do when a file it is restoring is already present on the destination disk. Choose *Never overwrite* to preserve the disk file no matter what; *Overwrite older files only* to replace only those disk files that are older than the ones being restored; or *Overwrite files* if you want Backup to replace the disk files with those from the backup set. If you pick the last choice, you can then check the box beneath it, *Prompt before overwriting files.* When this box is checked, Backup will ask you for permission before replacing an existing disk file.

Here are the options on the Compare page:

Quit Backup after operation is finished: Check this box if you want Backup to close automatically after completing any compare operation.

Location of Compare: These three radio buttons tell Backup where to find the disk files it compares to the files in the backup set. Select the radio button for the desired choice: in the same disks and folders that were used to create the backup set; in another location (disk and folder) that otherwise has the same subfolder hierarchy as the original; or in another location with all the files in a single folder. The two latter options are especially useful for comparing a backup set against copies of the files you've already restored from backup disks.

Increasing Disk Capacity with DriveSpace

The DriveSpace system tool helps you stay ahead of the ever-increasing demand for information storage capacity. DriveSpace *compresses* the files on your disk, storing them in an encoded form so they take only about half as much space as they normally would.

No matter how big a hard disk you buy, it always fills up faster than you expected. It's easy to see why. Windows 95 itself takes up 50 MB of hard disk space or more, depending on which components you install—that's roughly five times as much as Windows 3.1. Programs are constantly growing larger, too. And if your system software and programs haven't eaten up all the available room, wait 'til you save a few of those multimedia files everybody talks about. A high-resolution still image with a color palette of 16-million-plus colors can easily consume many megabytes of disk space. And when you're talking about full-motion video sequences or CD-quality digital sound files, look out (remember, an audio CD that plays only an hour of music holds about 600 megabytes).

With DriveSpace, there *is* a free lunch: It roughly doubles the available space on any disk, leaving you with a compressed disk that operates exactly as normal and *maybe even faster*. Of course, you'll still run out of disk space faster than you planned.

FOR WINDOWS 3.X USERS

Windows 95's version of DriveSpace recognizes and works fine with existing compressed disks created by the non-Windows version of DiskSpace that came with MS-DOS 6.22 or the DoubleSpace utility included with MS-DOS 6.0 or 6.2. You'll no longer need your DOS-based tools to manage these disks because DriveSpace can handle compression-related chores, while ScanDisk (covered earlier in this chapter) can check for and repair errors on the compressed disks.

Windows 95 will recognize disks compressed with other compression software such as Stacker. However, keep two limitations in mind: ScanDisk can't check these "foreign" compressed disks for compression errors, and you can't use DriveSpace and another compression utility at the same time.

NOTE   See Chapter 32 for a discussion of DriveSpace 3, the enhanced version of DriveSpace in Microsoft Plus.

Using DriveSpace

To run DriveSpace, begin from the Start menu and choose Programs ➤ Accessories ➤ System Tools ➤ DriveSpace. You'll see the main DriveSpace window, consisting simply of a menu bar and a list of the disk drives on your system:

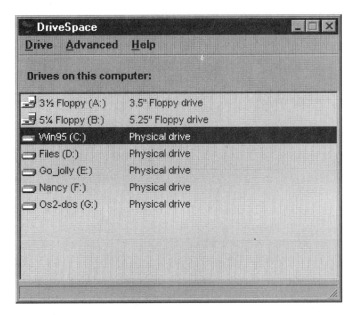

The DriveSpace menu choices let you compress new disks, activate and deactivate them, remove existing compressed disks, and adjust various settings. These options are covered in detail below.

To see information about any disk in the list, double-click on the entry for the disk or choose Drive ➤ Properties. You'll see the window shown in Figure 23.8.

The window tells you whether or not the disk is compressed and displays a pie graph showing how much space is in use and how much is

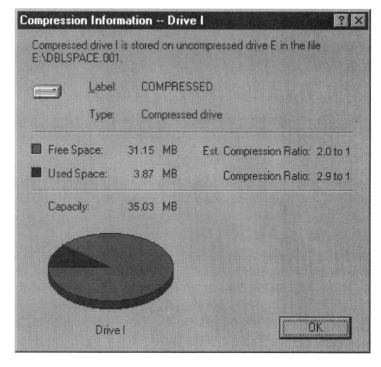

Figure 23.8   The Compression Information window

free for new programs and documents. You also get a numeric readout of the used and free space and of the total disk capacity. OK the window to close it.

How DriveSpace Works

Disk compression is essentially a coding system for the information in your files. As it stores a file on disk, DriveSpace examines the data for repeated sequences that it can represent with shorter codes. Files containing long repeating sequences wind up more compressed than files in which the information has no consistent pattern. When it reads a compressed file, DriveSpace translates the codes back into the original sequences. DriveSpace works with all your files, programs and documents alike.

> **NOTE** Compression utilities such as PKZIP and LHA work by encoding and decoding files the way DriveSpace does, but only when you specifically tell them to. Such utilities can create significantly smaller compressed files than DriveSpace does, which is great for storing large files you rarely use. Because you have to operate them manually, though, these utilities are far too time consuming and inconvenient for ordinary use.

DriveSpace works behind the scenes without any intervention on your part. When you run a program, copy a file, or save or open a document, Drive-Space steps in automatically to handle the compression or decompression. In the jargon of the day, DriveSpace provides *on-the-fly* compression.

As the discussion implies, DriveSpace actually compresses files, not disks. When it "compresses" a disk, it creates one large special file on the disk to hold the compressed files it then stores there. This special file is set up to act just like a real disk in Windows. It is assigned a letter, just like any other disk drive. The original disk that contains the special file is called the *host* drive.

The file containing the compressed disk must exist on a single unbroken area of the hard disk (that is, it must not be *fragmented*—see *Disk Defragmenter* later in this chapter for more on fragmentation). For this reason, DriveSpace must defragment the hard disk to consolidate its free space before the actual compression process. It also checks the disk for errors before proceeding.

When to Use DriveSpace

My advice is to go ahead and use DriveSpace on all your hard disks, but to preserve some uncompressed space—say about 10 to 20 megabytes—on the C drive that's used to boot your computer. Disk compression really does work, it's very reliable, it doesn't slow your system down, and it's free—so why not take full advantage of it?

Although DriveSpace can compress floppy disks, keep in mind that you can only use these floppies on computers that also have DriveSpace.

Compressing a Drive

Before you compress a disk for the first time, it makes a lot of sense to back up the entire disk just in case something goes wrong during the compression process. After all, you should be backing up regularly anyway, so just think of this as a good time to do your regular backup. You can use the Backup utility, covered earlier, to do the job.

CAUTION   Be prepared to wait a long time—possibly many hours—if you compress a disk that already contains a lot of files. And don't think you can walk away from your computer while it works because you may need to respond to messages from the program many times during the process. Why does it take so long? DriveSpace starts by creating a small, uncompressed disk from the available free space. It then goes through a cycle of copying some uncompressed files to the compressed disk, erasing them from the uncompressed disk, and enlarging the compressed disk, repeating this sequence over and over. The best time to compress a disk drive is *before* you install programs other than Windows.

When you use the standard method for compressing a drive, DriveSpace converts nearly all of the original (host) drive to the new compressed drive. All existing files are copied to the compressed drive, leaving only about 2 megabytes of free space uncompressed on the host. If you like, however, you can control how much free space is left uncompressed. You can also use an alternative method, covered later, to create a compressed drive using only the remaining free space on the host.

To compress a drive using the standard method, select the drive from the list in the DriveSpace window, then choose Drive ➤ Compress. You'll see the window shown in Figure 23.9.

This before-and-after window shows you graphically and in numbers how much more room you'll have on the disk after you compress it.

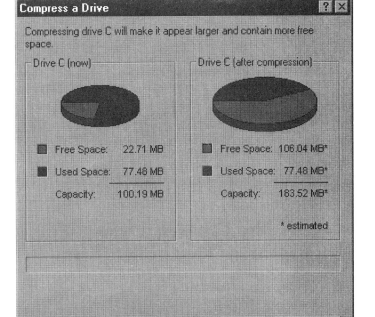

Figure 23.9   The Compress a Drive window

To go ahead and compress the drive using the standard settings, click on Start.

When DriveSpace compresses a drive with this standard method, the new compressed drive is assigned the drive letter that had been used by the original uncompressed drive, the host. The host receives a new letter but is then *hidden* so it won't appear in Windows Explorer, My Computer, and File dialog boxes such as Open and Save As (after all, the host hardly has any usable space).

Setting Compression Options

To review the compression settings and change them if you like, click on Options in the Compress a Drive window. You'll see the small dialog box shown here:

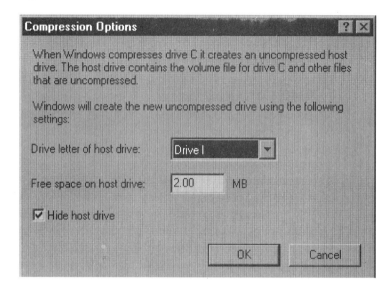

Your choices include:

Drive letter of host drive: DriveSpace will automatically assign the next available drive letter to the host drive. If you want to assign a different drive letter, select it from this list. For example, if you know the letter DriveSpace has chosen will be used by a network drive or a new, real hard disk you plan to install, you would select another letter.

Free space on host drive: If you want to change the amount of uncompressed free space DriveSpace automatically preserves on the host drive, type in the new amount here.

TIP I recommend that you keep at least 5 MB uncompressed on the drive used to start your system (originally drive C). After the compression process is complete, you should copy some essential utility programs such as a non-Windows text editor and a disk manager such as Xtree to the noncompressed drive, just in case something ever goes wrong with DriveSpace and you need a way to get at your machine without Windows. (As a safeguard against even more serious problems, make sure you have made two or more start-up diskettes). If you're using a program that requires uncompressed disk space for its work files, as some do, you'll need to increase this amount. The other host drives require little or no free space.

Hide host drive: Check this box to have DriveSpace hide the host (the uncompressed original drive) in Windows. The host won't appear in Explorer, dialog boxes, and other lists of available disk drives. Clear the box if you don't want the host drive hidden.

TIP To "unhide" all hidden drives, choose Advanced ➤ Options and click on Show all hidden drives.

Click on OK to confirm any new settings you've made and return to the Compress a Drive dialog box, then click on Start to compress the drive.

Adjusting the Amount of Free Space

After you've compressed a drive, it may turn out that you need more uncompressed free space on the host. Or perhaps you realize that you don't need as much uncompressed space as you thought you would and you really should compress the surplus to get more capacity. Fortunately, DriveSpace lets you shift unused capacity back and forth between a compressed drive and its uncompressed host.

To change the distribution of free space, highlight either the compressed drive or its host in the main DriveSpace window. Then choose

Drive ➤ Adjust Free Space. You'll see a window like the one shown in Figure 23.10.

The window shows you graphically and in numbers how much free space is currently available on the two drives. Use the slider control at the bottom of the window to shift free space between them. You can set the slider with the mouse or by pressing the → and ← keys. As you do, the graph changes to show you how free space would be distributed with the new settings.

When you're satisfied, change the setting in the *Hide this host drive* box if you like and then click on OK. DriveSpace makes the necessary adjustments and returns you to its main window.

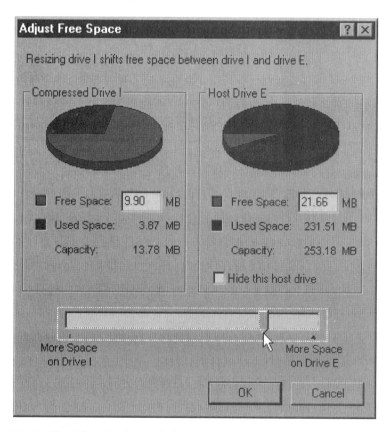

Figure 23.10   The Adjust Free Space window

Uncompressing a Compressed Drive

Just in case you ever need to, you can restore a compressed drive to its original, uncompressed state. (Actually, what you would be doing is removing the compressed drive from its host, but let's not get bogged down in technicalities.) DriveSpace will transfer the files contained on the compressed drive to the host, reset the host to its original drive letter, and show the host if it was hidden.

There's only one potential fly in the ointment, but unfortunately it's rather large: If you've been using the compressed drive for its intended function—storing files—there's a good chance those files won't fit on the uncompressed drive. In this case, if you want to go through with uncompressing the drive, you'll need to move the excess files to another disk somewhere before uncompression can proceed. If your computer is connected to a network, a drive somewhere else on the network may be a good place to try.

To uncompress a compressed drive, highlight it in the main DriveSpace window, then choose Drive ➤ Uncompress. DriveSpace displays a window showing a before-and-after graph of the used and free space on the compressed drive and the host. If the projected results meet your expectations, click on Start to proceed.

Creating an Empty Compressed Drive from Free Space

If you prefer, you can have DriveSpace compress only the free space on an existing drive rather than compressing the entire drive. This is often a *much* quicker way to get more space because DriveSpace doesn't have to copy all the existing files to the new compressed drive. On the other hand, if the existing disk contains a lot of files, you won't have much free space to work with and the compressed drive will be relatively small.

Because it is created from free space, the new compressed drive is empty. The host drive retains its original letter while the compressed drive is assigned a new letter. This is the opposite of the way things work when you compress a drive with the standard method as described above.

To create an empty compressed drive from free space, select the un-compressed drive where the free space is located in the main DriveSpace window. Choose Advanced ➤ Create Empty. You'll see the dialog box shown in Figure 23.11.

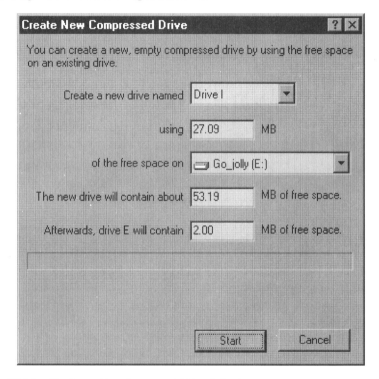

Figure 23.11   The Create New Compressed Drive dialog box

DriveSpace assumes you want the new drive to occupy all but 2 MB of the free space now available on the uncompressed drive. You can change the new drive's size in any of the three areas listing megabyte amounts. The first of these three areas, labeled *using*, indicates the amount of uncompressed free space to be compressed; the second area, *The new drive will contain about*, gives an estimate of how much space will be available on the compressed drive; while the third area, *Afterwards, drive "X" will contain*, shows you how much free space will be left on the host. Typing a new number into any of these areas changes all three areas. If you enter a value that's too large, DriveSpace adjusts it to the maximum valid value.

Supplied Applications

You can choose a different drive letter for the new drive if you need to in the first area. When you're through making changes, click on Start to create the new compressed drive.

Deleting a Compressed Drive

If you know you won't ever need the information on a compressed drive, or if you've backed up all the files you want to preserve, you can summarily delete the drive. This is a quicker way of restoring the host drive to its original state than using the Uncompress command because DriveSpace doesn't have to copy all the compressed files back to the host.

To delete a compressed drive, select it in the main DriveSpace window, then choose Advanced ➤ Delete. DriveSpace will warn you that this command will delete all the information on the drive. To proceed, click on Yes.

Mounting and Unmounting Compressed Drives

Mounting a compressed drive means to activate it so that the drive and the files it contains are accessible. Normally, DriveSpace automatically mounts all compressed drives, including those on floppy disks and removable hard-disk cartridges. If you turn off this automatic mounting feature, however, you'll have to mount the drives yourself. This doesn't make much sense for most people.

To mount a compressed drive, select its uncompressed host drive in the list in the main DriveSpace window. Then choose Advanced ➤ Mount. DriveSpace will search the disk for the special files that contain compressed disks. If it finds any unmounted compressed drives, it displays them in a list box (if there are two or more of these files, you can pick the one you want to mount from the list). DriveSpace shows you which drive letter it plans to assign to the selected disk. You can select a different letter by clicking on Options and choosing the desired letter from the list box that appears at the bottom of the same window.

Of course, you can *unmount* any compressed drive any time you like. Each mounted compressed drive uses a small amount of system memory, so if you're not using the drive, you may want to unmount it. You might also unmount a drive to keep other people who use the computer from accessing it, though anyone familiar with DriveSpace could find and mount the drive. The best reason to unmount a drive is when you need to change its letter designation, because you can't select a new letter for a drive that is currently mounted.

Changing the Estimated Compression Ratio

Because the amount of compression varies from file to file, Drive-Space can only estimate how much free space is available on a compressed drive. When you store an average mix of files, DriveSpace's standard estimate is about as good as you can expect. If you store many files of a particular type, however, you can improve on the estimate's accuracy. This will help you figure out how much more information the compressed drive will hold.

Select the compressed drive and choose Advanced ➤ Change Ratio. DriveSpace displays this window:

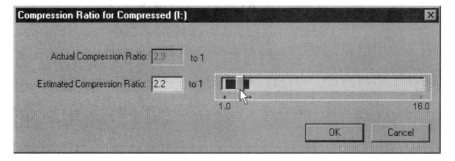

Here you can see the actual compression ratio for the files currently stored on the drive, along with DriveSpace's current setting for the estimated ratio it uses to calculate the remaining free space. If the actual ratio varies from the estimate and you're pretty sure you'll be using the disk in about the same way, you should change the estimated ratio. Use the slider control, dragging it to the new value with the mouse or pressing the ← and → keys.

Automatic v. Manual Activation

Choose the Advanced ➤ Options command to display the following dialog box:

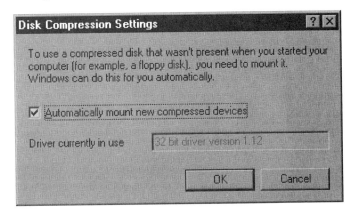

Normally, DriveSpace automatically activates, or mounts, new compressed drives immediately after you create them. If you want to mount new compressed drives manually, clear the *Automatically mount new compressed drives* box.

The *Driver currently in use* box simply lists the version number of the DriveSpace software installed on your system. Before installing a new version, check to make sure it has a later version number—if not, leave the existing driver in place.

Disk Defragmenter

Disk Defragmenter keeps your system performing at its best by detecting and correcting *fragmentation* on the hard disks. The term "fragmentation" sounds a little scary—after all, who wants their hard disk to break into little pieces? Actually, though, it refers to the files stored on the disk, not the disk itself.

When Windows stores information on your disk in a file, it begins *writing* the information onto the first place it can find that isn't already occupied by another file. If the disk already contains a lot of other files, however, that location may not be large enough for the whole file Windows now wants to store. If this is the case, Windows must search for another open spot on the disk for the next section of the file. The process goes on in this way until the entire file has been written to the disk into as many pieces, or fragments, as necessary. Of course, Windows keeps track of the location of all the fragments, and when you need the file again, it can find all the pieces for you without your ever knowing where they are stored.

Actually, this system for breaking files up into fragments when necessary has important performance benefits. If Windows had to stop and find a single section of the disk big enough for each entire file, your system would steadily slow down as the hard disk filled up. Also, you would wind up with less usable disk space. Eventually there would come a time when the disk still had many free areas, but none of them big enough to fit a reasonably sized file.

So what's the problem? Well, fragmentation also slows your hard disk down. To access information stored on a disk, the disk drive must move mechanical parts over the location where the information is stored. It takes only a fraction of second to move these parts, but those fractions add up when a file is broken into many fragments. As more and more files become fragmented, you may begin to notice the slowdown, especially when Windows opens and saves files.

Disk Defragmenter remedies the problem by reorganizing the disk so that each and every file is stored as a complete unit on a single area of the disk. To do this, it identifies any remaining free areas, moves small files there to open up more space, and uses this newly opened space to consolidate larger files. It continues to shuffle files around in this manner until the entire disk is defragmented. All of this takes place behind the scenes. Though the files have been moved physically on the disk, they remain in exactly the same place "logically"—you'll find all your files in the same folders they were in before running Defragmenter.

When Should You Use Disk Defragmenter?

After wading through this long technical explanation, you may feel let down when I tell you that you may not ever really need to defragment your hard disk. Yes, it's true that fragmentation puts a measurable drag on file access if you time the system electronically. But in real life, you'll probably detect a slowdown only if you have very large, very fragmented data files. The reason is simply that today's hard disks are so fast.

Keep in mind also that the defragmenting process itself can take quite a bit of time (on the other hand, you can run Disk Defragmenter overnight or while you're out to lunch). Anyway, the point is simply that you shouldn't worry about a drastic performance loss if you don't defragment your disk regularly.

All that said, here are some tips for deciding when to use Disk Defragmenter:

▶ Disk Defragmenter itself can help you decide when to defragment. When you run the program, it analyzes the disk to detect fragmentation and offers a recommendation about whether or not to proceed (more on that in a moment).

▶ The slower your hard disk, the more you'll notice the performance hit caused by fragmentation and the more often you should defragment it. If you're still using a disk with an access time of 25 milliseconds or greater, you'll probably detect an improvement after defragmenting a heavily fragmented disk.

▶ The greater the percentage of data files (documents, pictures, database files, and so on) on your hard disk—as compared to program files—the more likely you'll need to defragment. After you install them, your program files stay put. Data files, on the other hand, are constantly being revised and saved anew, and are much more vulnerable to increasing fragmentation. (If you frequently install and then remove programs, the risk for significant fragmentation also rises.)

Running Disk Defragmenter

To run Disk Defragmenter, begin from the Start menu and choose Programs ➤ Accessories ➤ System Tools ➤ Disk Defragmenter. A small Window appears:

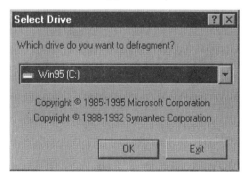

Choose the hard disk you want to defragment from the drop-down list and click on OK. You can switch to another disk later as necessary.

Disk Defragmenter analyzes the chosen disk for fragmentation, then displays another small window informing you of its findings:

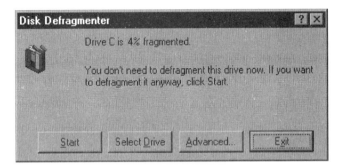

This dialog box has four buttons:

Start: begins the defragmentation process. If Disk Defragmenter recommends against defragmenting the disk at this time, the button will be labeled *Defragment Anyway*, but it does the same thing.

Select Drive: returns you to the Select Drive dialog box shown above so you can choose another drive to defragment.

Advanced: lets you set defragmentation options.

Exit: closes Disk Defragmenter.

The Defragmentation Process

Click on Defragment (or Defragment Anyway) in the Defragmentation dialog box to begin the process. You'll see yet another little dialog box informing you of the program's progress:

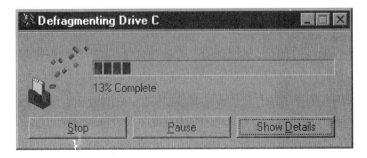

As Disk Defragmenter does its work, the indicator at the right shows you graphically how far along you are in the process, and the percentage complete is displayed as well. Three buttons are available:

Stop: stops the defragmenting process and returns you to a dialog box titled Are You Sure. The choices are similar to those of the Defragmentation dialog box: You can click on Resume to return to defragmenting, Select Drive to pick another drive to defragment, Advanced to set defragmentation options, or Exit to close Disk Defragmenter.

Pause: temporarily stops the defragmenting process. The Pause button appears pushed in while Disk Defragmenter remains paused. To continue where you left off, click on it again.

Show Details: displays a large window showing you exactly what's going on during the defragmentation process (Figure 23.12). This window represents the disk contents as a grid of little colored boxes, each of which stands for a single *cluster* (usually 2,048 bytes). The various colors signify the status of each cluster: those containing information that needs to be moved, those that are already defragmented, those that are free (containing no file information), and so on. To see a legend showing the meanings of the block colors, click on the Legend button:

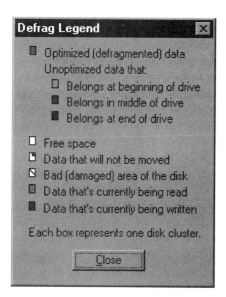

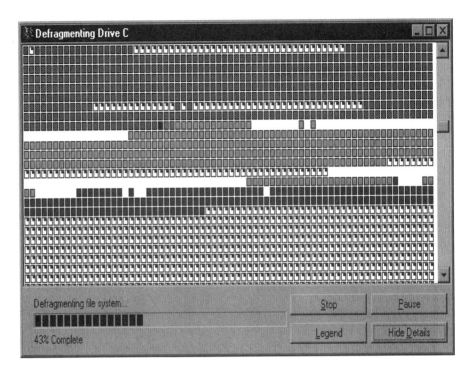

Figure 23.12   This is the window you'll see if you choose Display Details during defragmentation.

As Disk Defragmenter moves information around, the map gives you a moment-by-moment readout of which clusters are being read and written to, and the resulting disk organization. The bottom of the window displays a progress indicator and readout and includes Stop and Pause buttons. You can close the large map window at any time by clicking on Hide Details.

Because Disk Defragmenter continues its work whether or not the program window is visible, you can switch to another program to continue your work. You'll hear the hard disk chattering more or less continuously during the defragmentation process, and your system will probably seem a little sluggish at times when it waits for Disk Defragmenter to give it access to the disk. Otherwise, however, you can use Windows just as you normally would.

Setting Disk Defragmenter Options

Disk Defragmenter's standard settings ensure that your disk is fully defragmented, which can take quite a while. You can often speed things up considerably with a partial defragmentation targeted for the characteristics of your disk. You should get most of the performance benefits of a full defragmentation.

To change the defragmentation settings, click on the Advanced button in the Defragmentation dialog box (or in the dialog box you see when you stop an earlier defragmentation). You'll see the Advanced Options dialog box, shown in Figure 23.13.

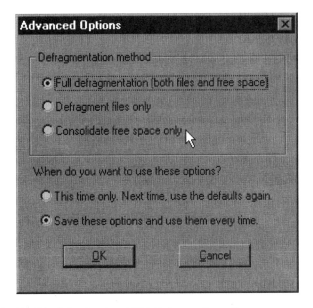

Figure 23.13   *Use this dialog box to set Disk Defragmenter options.*

In the top part of the dialog box, choose the radio button for the type of defragmentation you want:

Full defragmentation (both files and free space): This is the standard setting. All the files are defragmented, and, in addition, they are placed one after another on the disk so all the remaining free space is available on a continuous section of the disk.

Defragment files only: When this choice is selected, Disk Defragmenter moves information on the disk only enough so every file is stored in its entirety on a continuous area of the disk. Free space between these continuos files is left where it is. This setting is faster than a full defragmentation because the files don't have to be rearranged as much. But depending on how much free space there is between the files, files you save in the future will be vulnerable to fragmentation.

Consolidate free space only: Use this option to move existing files around just enough so all the available free space on the disk is placed in one continuous area. Files you save from now on will be less likely to become fragmented. Again, this is quicker than a full defragmentation. The downside is that fragmented files remain fragmented and the existing files may be more vulnerable to fragmentation when they are changed and saved again. This can be a good choice if you know you're about to save some large files that would otherwise be broken up into fragments. It can also be useful if you have just copied many files to a new disk (or installed a number of programs); the files are unlikely to be fragmented, but there may be gaps of free space between them.

The two radio buttons in the lower portion of the Advanced Options dialog box let you specify whether the defragmentation method you select is stored for future use or is used only for the current session. Choose the appropriate button before you OK the dialog box.

Tracking Your System Resources with System Monitor

System Monitor is a *real-time* analysis tool that lets you monitor Windows' activities from one moment to the next. If you are trying to track down a performance problem, say with unexpected memory shortages, or if you just want to keep tabs on what Windows is up to, try System Monitor. You can use it on your own system or across a network to monitor other computers.

There's a good chance System Monitor is not yet installed on your hard disk. If you need to install it, begin by placing the install disk in your floppy or CD-ROM drive, choosing Add/Remove Programs in the Control Panel, and switching to the Windows Setup page. Highlight Accessories, then click on Details. In the list that appears, check the box for System Monitor. When you click on OK, the program will be installed.

Once System Monitor has been installed, run it by choosing Programs ➤ Accessories ➤ System Tools ➤ System Monitor from the Start menu. You'll see the System Monitor window, as shown in Figure 23.14.

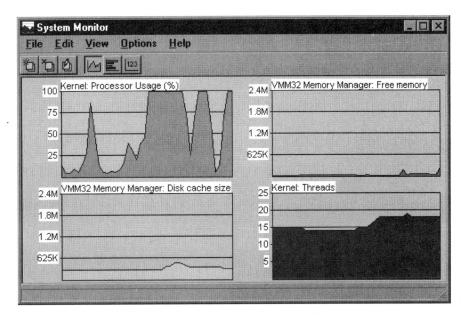

Figure 23.14   *The System Monitor window. The specific items displayed when you first start the program will be different from those shown here.*

The main part of the window is divided into areas for each type of information you choose to monitor. When you first run the program, it displays its reports as shaded line graphs, but you can select bar graphs or numeric displays instead. You can click on any displayed item to get a report of its last and peak values in the Status Bar at the bottom of the window.

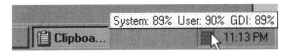

Note that System Monitor has its own little button bar for quick access to commonly used commands. The buttons are displayed in two groups of three buttons each. The first group (on the left) includes buttons for adding, removing, and editing individual items on the display; the second group lets you pick between the two graph types and a numeric readout.

System Monitor continuously updates the information it displays at a rate you can control. To change the frequency of updates, choose Options ➤ Chart and use the slider to set the Update Interval.

Choosing Items to Display

You have your choice of twenty-odd types of system information you can track with System Monitor. To add a new item, click on the Add button or choose Edit ➤ Add Item. You'll see the dialog box shown here:

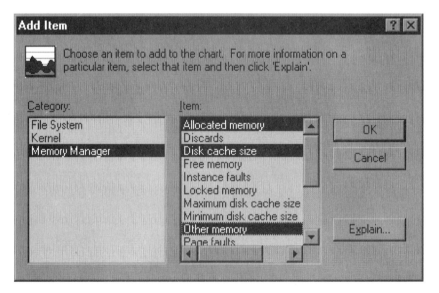

Select a category of system information from the list on the left. When you do, a list of the individual items available for display appear on the right. Be forewarned: Unless you're technically oriented, the terms you see here may look completely foreign to you. You can learn something about what an item means by selecting the item and clicking on Explain. System Monitor will then display a slightly longer— but also highly technical—description of the term.

When you're ready to choose one or more items, select them in the list. You can select more than one item at a time by dragging across consecutive items with the mouse or by holding down the Ctrl key while you click on individual items anywhere on the list. However, you can only select items from one category at a time.

Click on OK to return to System Monitor. The items you chose will now appear, each in its own area on the screen. As you add more items, System Monitor reduces the size of each item's graph.

Editing an Item's Display Properties

System Monitor lets you control some aspects of the graphical display of each item. To see or change the current settings:

1. Click on the Edit button or choose Edit ➤ Edit Item. You'll see a list of all the items currently displayed.

> **TIP** You can double-click on the item you want to edit to move directly to the Chart Options dialog box for that item.

2. Select the item you want to work with and click on OK. A Chart Options dialog box appears:

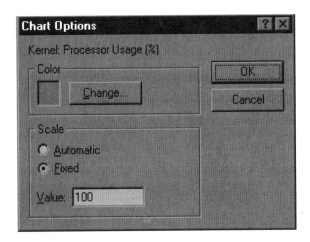

3. Here you can choose the graph color and control its scale. The pair of radio buttons on the left let you switch between letting System Monitor adjust the scale automatically based on the current values for the item and fixing the scale to cover a range you specify by typing in the

scale maximum at Value. The right pair of radio buttons switches between linear and logarithmic display.

4. Click on OK to confirm your choices. System Monitor adjusts the item's graph to match.

Choosing the Display Type

To select a different type of display for all the items in the window, click on the button for the type of display you want (line graph, bar graph, or numeric). Alternatively, you can choose the desired type from the View menu.

Removing Items from the Window

To remove an item from the System Monitor display, click on the Remove button or choose Edit ➤ Remove Item. You'll be presented with a list of all the items currently displayed. Choose the item or items you want to remove and click on OK.

Other Display Options

To reset all items to zero, removing all the current graphs and starting the analysis again from scratch, choose Edit ➤ Clear.

You can control whether the Toolbar and Status Bar are visible. Choose the corresponding command on the View menu to turn either item off or on.

To remove System Monitor's title bar, menu bar, Toolbar, and Status Bar so only the graphs remain visible, press Esc or choose View ➤ Hide Title Bar. To restore the window to its normal state, double-click anywhere in the window or press Esc again.

To keep the System Monitor visible no matter what other programs you use, choose View ➤ Always on Top. If you choose this option, you may wish to resize the window so it won't block your view of your other programs.

Networking with Windows 95

5

Chapter 24

An Overview of Windows 95 Networking

FEATURING

The OSI reference model

The Windows 95 networking model

Windows 95 has been endowed with all the features necessary to make it the perfect network citizen. Right out of the box—with no additional software required—your PC with Windows 95 installed is capable of connecting to and interoperating with all major network operating systems (NOSs) and can function either as a client, a server, or as both simultaneously. Because of its modular approach to networking software and its true multitasking ability, it is capable of simultaneously speaking multiple network languages (called *protocols*) and even using multiple network interface cards. You could, for example, simultaneously access a database on your company's mainframe, print a report on your office's Novell print server, and cruise the Web on the Internet, all while one or more other users are accessing files located on your PC's hard drive. Moreover, these various network connections can be made via any combination of the following: standard network adapters and cable, high-speed digital phone lines, "normal" phone lines and modem, or even directly attached to your PC via either a serial or a parallel port. And because the networking features are truly integrated parts of Windows 95, you can access drives and printers located on a variety of different networks from any Windows application—always in the same way, regardless of the type of computer or network you are connected to. Being able to network—or rather, *internetwork*—with other computer systems in exactly the same manner, whether you're at the office, at home, or even on the road using your laptop, opens almost endless possibilities for extending the usefulness of your computers.

These networking possibilities supplied by Windows 95 truly are exciting—never before have so many ways to so easily network with other computers been brought together like this in one product—let alone within a popular, graphical, operating system. In this and following chapters, we will look closely at the networking capabilities of Windows 95 and discuss step by step how to install, configure, and use them. If you are interested less in the details and more in how to quickly set up your networking components, just skip ahead to the "how-to" sections in the following chapters.

Windows 95, as I have said, can share your local hard drive(s) and printer with other users, acting as a server on a peer-to-peer network. In this role, a Windows 95 workstation allows other computers to use its resources such as files, printers, and (in certain respects) modems. Additionally, Windows 95 can act as either a Dial-Up Networking client or as a host so you can use regular phone lines to extend the reach of your network. This allows you to be on the road (or at home—or anywhere) and dial into your office network and have the same resources available as if you were sitting right at your desk.

If your computer supports Plug and Play, when you install a Plug-and-Play–compatible network adapter card, Windows 95 will automatically load and configure all the necessary software to place your computer on a network—all with no user intervention apart from selecting the desired protocols.

Roughly, protocols can be thought of as the various languages that different networks use to communicate. The protocol implementation manages such tasks as requesting data from file and application servers, providing resources to other workstations, and placing data onto the network. Each of these tasks uses a specific protocol or layer of a protocol, and Windows 95's networking software ensures that it uses the correct protocol at the correct time. While this may sound complex (and behind the scenes, it is), Windows 95 makes it very easy to choose, install, and make use of the protocol(s) you will need. In the next section, we will discuss protocols in more detail. You *can* configure and use Windows 95 without a thorough knowledge of networking protocols, but having at least a passing familiarity with networking protocols and related concepts will be helpful in getting the best performance out of your network.

A protocol, in general, is really nothing more than a set of rules and conventions for accomplishing a specific task. In the case of computer networking, a protocol defines the manner in which two computers will communicate with each other. As an analogy, consider the protocol you use to place a phone call. Before you dial, you first make sure no one else is using the phone line. Next you pick up the phone and listen for a dial tone. If you are at your office, you might have to dial 9 and again wait for a dial tone. Then you can dial either a 7-digit number for a local call or a 1 followed by a 10-digit number for a long-distance call. You then wait for the other person to answer. But if you do not follow this protocol correctly—for example, you do not dial a 9 for an outside line when at the office—you will be unable to place your phone call.

In the world of computers, a protocol works exactly the same way. If a client does not structure and send a request in the exact manner in which the server expects it—and we all know how particular computers can be—it will never establish the connection.

When you first activate the networking component on your computer, Windows 95 installs the NetBEUI and IPX/SPX protocols by default. Besides these two, Windows 95 allows you to install several other protocols that—depending on the design of your network and type of applications you run—might provide better performance or have other advantages. To help you make the best choices possible for your Windows 95 network, I will next present an overview of how LANs work—both in theoretical and practical terms. I will do this by first talking about networking models and then looking at how Windows 95 implements these concepts. Finally, I will delve into the most common protocols themselves and help you choose which is or are the best for your particular environment.

The OSI Reference Model

In the early years of networking, each vendor defined its own standard for communication between its computers. The primary goal was to maximize the performance on a particular vendor's hardware (and lock you into their products) rather than to provide compatibility with other vendors' products. This caused problems as these systems did not share a common protocol and so could not interact with each other. In the late 1970s, the networking community came together in an effort to replace these closed systems with open systems. This would allow IS (Information Systems) shops to mix and match their hardware so end users could access the desired resources on other vendors' products. The end result was the Open System Interconnect (OSI) model developed by the International Standards Organization (ISO). While no network fully implements this model in the exact manner described by the ISO committee, it is a very common framework for discussing networking in theoretical terms. Its strongest asset is that it provides an excellent way of comparing two different networking technologies because it provides a common measuring stick.

The OSI reference model (often referred to simply as the OSI model) takes a modular approach to networking by identifying and defining seven separate processes that any network—whether local- or wide-area—must accomplish. In OSI lingo, each process is a layer. Figure 24.1 shows the seven layers of the OSI model.

Each of these seven layers is responsible for a specific and discrete aspect of networking. The OSI model describes the flow of network data from the top layer—the user's application—to the bottom layer—physical connections of the network. Because no network follows the OSI model exactly, some networks may use only four separate pieces to cover the same functionality as the seven layers of the OSI model. Others may segment it into nine parts.

As data flow across a network, the OSI model stipulates that each layer only communicate with the layers immediately above and below it. This serves two purposes. First and foremost, it creates modularized layers. Each layer needs to know none of the details of how the other layers work; it only needs to know what its input will look like and how it must format its output so the next layer can understand it. Second, modularizing prevents *feature creep*—layers growing excessively complex and taking on the functions that other layers should accomplish.

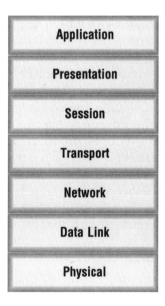

Figure 24.1 *The seven layers of the OSI reference model*

When creating a message, each layer assumes that it is in direct communication with its peer layer on the other side. For example, when the transport layer needs to send an error across the network, it sends the message directly to the transport layer on the other side. This virtual communication further streamlines the process.

Before we delve into the individual layers of the OSI model, let's look at the process of network communication in everyday terms. A good way to look at network communication is simply as a message: requesting a database row, opening a file for access, or sending someone an e-mail note. Now imagine that this message is nothing more than a letter to Gramma Gertrude that needs to pass through several layers to get from you to her.

After deciding to write the letter, you need to get out some paper and a pen and write the message: "Thanks for the lovely dress, I wear it to church every Sunday." Now you must place it in a container—an envelope. Next you place a stamp on the envelope. After that, you address it so it can get to the correct place. Finally you drop it into the mailbox and from there the post office bundles it with all the other messages and delivers it. If you want to ensure that the letter was delivered, you might send it via certified or registered mail with a return receipt; otherwise, you have no guarantee that the letter will be delivered.

The Application Layer

The application layer is at the top—closest to the end user—of the OSI model. This layer directly supports any application that wants to access a network resource for any reason—be it a file, a printer, or another application. In other words, anytime any user's application—regardless of type—needs to communicate with any resource across the network, it must begin here.

In the example of the letter to Gramma Gertrude, this layer systematically encompasses your decision to write the letter thanking her for the dress. Explorer, Exchange, and Dial-up Networking provide application-layer services in Windows 95.

The Presentation Layer

The presentation layer acts primarily as a translation agent. In doing so, it determines the best way for two computers to communicate with one another. When data are going down to the physical layer, the application layer relies on the presentation layer to translate the data sent from the application layer into an intermediary format. Here the presentation layer resolves character set (ASCII, EBCDIC, Unicode) differences, adds any security, and compresses the data. Conversely, when data come up from the physical layer, the presentation layer reverses the process and removes the encryption, re-expands the data, and gives it to the application layer using a data set that the application layer can directly use.

Back in the Gramma Gertrude example, translating the message content from your mind to written words represents the activities of the presentation layer. When you first start up your computer and log into an NT network, Windows 95 encrypts your password so no one can steal it as it goes across the network wire—this is the presentation layer at work.

The Session Layer

The session layer manages the dialogue between two logical addresses. It allows applications on a network to initiate, use, and terminate a connection—called a session—with another computer or another process. The layer also is responsible for name recognition between computers.

Once two computers have established a session, the session layer synchronizes the communication between them. Essentially, it sets the ground rules defining whose turn it is to send data and sets a limit on how long one side may monopolize the communication before it must yield to the other computer.

When you place the letter to Gramma Gertrude in the envelope, you are, in OSI terminology, *initiating a session*—passing control over to the session layer.

The Transport Layer

The transport layer ensures end point–to–end point data integrity by managing error recognition and, if necessary, correction and recovery throughout the data transfer. This layer ensures accuracy by adding Error Correcting Code (ECC), typically a Cyclic Redundancy Checksum (CRC). This CRC is a calculated value based on an accumulation on a byte-per-byte basis of the data being sent.

Once the transport layer receives a packet, it first calculates the Cyclic Redundancy Checksum (CRC). If the CRC calculated in real time does not match the CRC the other side originally placed in the data packet, it knows there has been an error in the transmission. If an error occurred, the data will be sent again until an acknowledgment is received. If several attempts to transmit the data fail, an error message will be displayed.

In our letter example, placing a stamp on the envelope and requesting the return receipt is the proxy for the transport layer. Here you are providing a means of ensuring the message gets through snow, sleet, and rain. If it encounters an error along the way, you will get the message back; otherwise, you will get a signed receipt indicating that your grandmother received (and hopefully read) your letter.

The Network Layer

The network layer manages addressing the message. Once it has resolved the address, it routes the message using a cost-based algorithm. On the addressing side, the network layer translates the logical address it originally received from the session layer into a physical address the data layer can understand. When data come back up the chain, the network layer reverses the process, replacing the physical address with a logical one. By doing so, it provides connections between two open systems regardless of the type of physical link between the two. Packages coming from the upper layers need only contain the logical address, thus freeing these layers from concerning themselves with the peculiar addressing schema of various network technologies.

In your letter to Gramma, you performed the task of the network layer when you put the address on the letter. If you wanted to send it via the U.S. Postal Service, you would include a zip code and possibly the carrier route.

The Data Link Layer

The data link layer is responsible for providing error-free transmission of this frame between any two destinations over the physical layer. (This differs from the data integrity provided by transport layer. The transport layer, remember, is concerned with the data throughout the transmission.) As a data frame flows down to the physical layer, the data link layer takes the frames sent to it from the network layer and places them bit by bit onto the physical layer.

The address in the data link layer differs from that in the network layer in that it is a simpler address, one that the data link layer on the other side will recognize. To understand the difference between the addresses, you can think of the network layer address as the street name and the data layer address as the street number.

The Physical Layer

The physical layer's job is to send individual bits—usually impulses of light or electricity—from one end of the physical medium (the wire) to the other. The physical layer defines the data-flow rate, the type of cable over which the data flow, the topology, the number of pins, and the voltage flowing through those pins. Common specifications for the physical layer include 10Base-T Ethernet, Token Ring, and FDDI (optical fiber). In the letter example, the mail carrier would be considered our network physical layer as he or she drives down to your grandmother's house to deliver your letter.

The Windows 95 Networking Model

Now that I have covered networking on the theoretical level, I can discuss the networking architecture built into Windows 95 and the protocols it supports. Just like the OSI model, Windows 95 takes a layered approach to networking as shown in Figure 24.2.

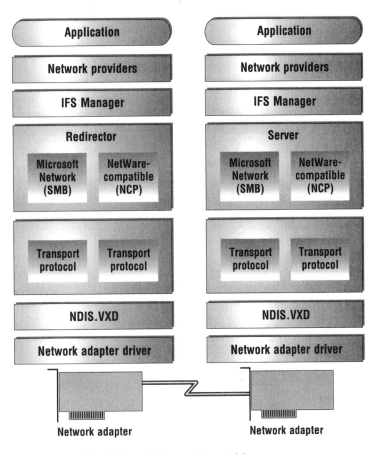

Figure 24.2   Layers of the Windows 95 Networking model

The Network Drivers Interface Specification (NDIS) is key to Microsoft's layered network. It provides the vital link between the protocol and the network interface card driver. While the protocol and the network interface card drivers provide separate functions, they remain fundamentally linked. The protocol (discussed in more detail in a later section) determines how your computer structures data sent across the network. The network adapter card drivers define how your computer interacts with the card, which, in turn, actually places the data on the network.

Network Drivers Interface Specification (NDIS)

A network interface card fulfills the most basic requirement of networking—a physical connection to the other computers. Before your computer can use this card, you must load a device driver for it just as you would load a driver for your video card or CD-ROM drive. The driver is a piece of software that instructs the computer how to interact with the network card; how to drive it, if you will. Because each vendor's cards differ from those of another vendor, each type of card requires a driver tailored to its peculiarities. This driver takes the data packets sent from the upper layers of the network architecture and packages them for the physical layer.

There are two types of NDIS drivers provided by Microsoft. The first is NDIS 2.0, and the second is NDIS 3.1. The primary difference between these drivers is that an NDIS 2.0 driver is a real-mode driver and is loaded in your `autoexec.bat` or `config.sys` files, while an NDIS 3.1 driver is loaded in Windows 95 as a 32-bit protected-mode driver. This protected-mode driver is designed as a dynamically loadable virtual device driver (VxD) and will perform better than the real-mode NDIS 2.0 drivers.

Open Datalink Interface (ODI)

As a universal client, Windows 95 also supports the Open Datalink Interface (ODI) standard put forth by Novell and Apple in addition to NDIS. Essentially, ODI and NDIS provide the same functionality in different ways. The only practical difference from an end-user perspective is that Windows 95 implements ODI as a real-mode device driver where NDIS is a 32-bit protected-mode driver. If you plan to connect to a NetWare server, you might need to stick with the ODI drivers for compatibility reasons as some network applications are very particular about the network drivers. I would recommend trying NDIS drivers first, though, keeping in mind you may need to change to ODI if any of your networking applications begin misbehaving. The performance gain of using the 32-bit protected-mode NDIS drivers makes having to use ODI (which executes in real-mode) rather undesirable, but if you absolutely need the most compatibility, the ODI drivers are there and can be installed just as easily as the NDIS drivers can.

With an understanding of Windows 95's networking model, we can now go on to look at the various transport protocols available to you as you set up your Windows 95 network.

Which Protocol to Use?

Right out of the box, Windows 95 gives you a choice of twelve transport protocols. These protocols fall into two broad groups. First, there are the open-systems protocols such as NetBEUI and IPX/SPX that you can use to connect to several vendors' networks. With them you can communicate over a Windows 95 peer-to-peer network or over another vendor's network. The second type are the proprietary protocols used to support specific vendors' networks such as Banyan Vines and DEC Pathworks. Because the choice of protocols only becomes important in open systems (if you have DEC Pathworks for example, you already know what protocol you are going to use), I will discuss the open protocols in this chapter. In Chapter 28 I will cover these other (proprietary) protocols.

> NOTE   Although it is somewhat confusing, when a network manager refers to a *transport protocol*, he or she usually means the functions provided by both the transport and network layers. The reason these two layers are combined into one term (besides sloppiness) is that they are interrelated; between the two of them they are responsible for transporting your data through the network. The upper layers are more closely tied to the application requesting the network services. The lower physical layer, because it is the only layer with a tangible presence (unless you are using a wireless net where there is no tangible presence except for the network interface card), is not lumped into *transport protocol*.

Whenever you are installing Windows 95 Networking support (either initially or at any later point), Windows 95 allows you to select protocols as shown in Figure 24.3. Here Windows 95 gives you the choice of five built-in, open protocols: IPX/SPX, DLC, NetBEUI, TCP/IP, and IPX/SPX with NetBIOS.

Before I go into more detail on the particulars of each protocol, I'll quickly look at the typical uses of each protocol.

▶ IPX/SPX is the protocol used by Novell to connect to their NetWare file servers.

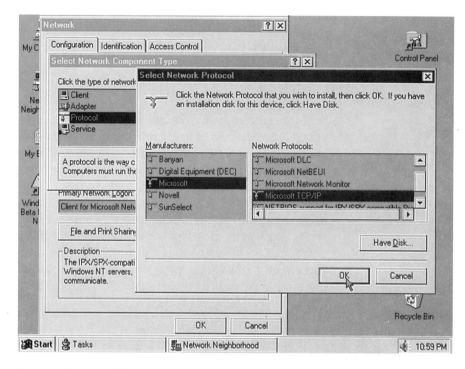

Figure 24.3   List of Microsoft-supplied protocols when installing a network

▶ IPX/SPX with NetBIOS adds support for the NetBIOS application programming interface (API) to the standard IPX/SPX protocol stack.

▶ DLC (data link control) provides an interface between Windows 95 machines and mainframes as well as network printers.

▶ NetBEUI is a protocol originally developed by IBM and used by Windows for Workgroups and LAN Manager.

▶ TCP/IP is a protocol often used over wide-area networks and for communicating with computers running some flavor of the Unix operating system.

IPX/SPX and IPX/SPX with NetBIOS Protocols

Xerox originally developed the Internetwork Packet Exchange/Sequenced Packet Exchange (IPX/SPX or just IPX) protocol as part of its XNS protocol suite. Novell decided to use it as the base protocol for connecting to its NetWare file servers and currently maintains the specifications and ongoing enhancements to the protocol. In Windows 95 you can use the IPX protocol to connect to NetWare 2.x, 3.x, and 4.x (with bindery emulation) servers. You can also use it to connect to Windows for Workgroups 3.x, Windows NT 3.x, and of course Windows 95 computers running the IPX protocol.

> **NOTE** Windows 95 allows you to install either Microsoft's own version of IPX/SPX or one supplied by Novell. I will discuss the ins and outs of these two flavors in Chapter 28; for the time being, however, we will treat them both as simply IPX/SPX.

Where NetBEUI used to be the default protocol in Windows 3.x, Windows 95 now uses IPX as the default. IPX works for small to medium-size networks because it is small and fast, besides being *routable*. A routable protocol is one that you can use to send data to computers on different LAN segments. (I will discuss what constitutes a LAN segment in the following chapter.)

The IPX protocol can support larger networks than can other non-routable protocols because it allows network managers to break down larger networks into smaller segments to achieve significant performance gain, with packets being automatically forwarded (routed) to the correct segment. However, IPX is not suitable for networks consisting of more than 500 workstations or networks connected over a WAN, because IPX workstations regularly send out "hey, I'm still here" messages, called broadcasts, which tell other servers and stations on the network that their connection is still active. On large networks, these broadcasts alone generate quite a bit of network traffic and thus reduce the performance of the network as a whole.

Network Basic Input/Output System (NetBIOS) is a programming interface that implements many of the functions provided by the session layer. Sytek originally developed it for IBM's broadband computer networks and included it in the ROM of its network adapter cards. Since then, many other companies have developed their own version of NetBIOS, making it a de facto standard.

NetBIOS allows applications to communicate over any protocol that is compliant with NetBIOS. Many server-based applications, such as Lotus Notes, use NetBIOS to communicate with clients over a network. Because IPX does not directly support NetBIOS, you must load it separately. Previously, to use NetBIOS over the IPX protocol, you had to use a Novell-provided terminate-and-stay-resident (TSR) driver called netbios.exe. Like all other TSRs, you had to load it before starting Windows if you wanted any of your Windows applications to take advantage of it. As such, it not only took up valuable conventional memory (below the 640K limit), but it also forced Windows to switch into real mode to communicate with NetBIOS applications.

Fortunately, Windows 95 provides a full 32-bit protected-mode implementation of NetBIOS for use with the IPX protocol called NWNBLink (NetWare NetBIOS Link). It is fully compatible with the Novell version and provides significantly improved performance simply because it is 32-bit and executes in protected mode. In addition, Windows 95 can support Windows *Sockets* over IPX. (Like NetBIOS, Windows Sockets is another network programming interface—in this case, based on the sockets standard used on several other operating systems, Unix in particular.) When communicating with other computers using NWNBLink, Windows 95 can support sliding windows and PiggyBackAck (acknowledging previous frames in later response frames).

In Windows NT 3.5 (both flavors), the service that allows it to act as a peer-to-peer server (not to be confused with the product NT Server) supports IPX without NetBIOS. The service that provides peer-to-peer *workstation* support (not to be confused with the product NT Workstation), however, does *not* support IPX without NetBIOS. Therefore, a Windows 95 client running IPX without NetBIOS can connect to a Windows NT *server*; however, a Windows NT *workstation* will not be able to connect to a Windows 95 machine running IPX without NetBIOS. If you install IPX with NetBIOS support on both sides, you will always be able to communicate over the IPX/SPX protocol.

Advantages of IPX/SPX	Disadvantages of IPX/SPX
Compatible with Novell products	Not as fast as NetBEUI
Routable	Not as routable as TCP/IP
Single protocol support for mixed NetWare and Microsoft networks	More overhead than NetBEUI
	Regular broadcasts take up limited bandwidth

DLC (Data Link Control)

Networks based on IBM Token Ring claim most of the users of the Data Link Control protocol. Actually, DLC really is not properly a transport protocol; rather it is a data link layer protocol that behaves much like a transport protocol. You cannot, for example, use DLC to share files and printers on Windows 95 networks; however, Windows 95 machines can use DLC to send print jobs to printers located directly on the network (rather than attached to a printer server), such as HP LaserJet IVs with a JetDirect card installed. And Microsoft has also included DLC to enable your Windows 95 machines to connect directly to IBM mainframe computers.

Advantages of DLC	**Disadvantages of DLC**
Compatible with IBM mainframes	Not compatible with standard Microsoft file and print services

NetBEUI

The NetBIOS *Extended User Interface* (or NetBEUI), first introduced by IBM in 1985, is a protocol written to the NetBIOS interface. Microsoft first supported NetBEUI in MS-Net, its first networking product, when it introduced the product in the mid-1980s. It used to be the default protocol for all Microsoft networks from Windows for Workgroups to LAN Manager up through Windows NT 3.1. NetBEUI is a small and very fast protocol—in fact, the fastest protocol shipped with Windows 95—because it requires very little overhead. Overhead in this context refers to the additional network-control information such as routing and error checking that the protocol adds to the data that the application layer wishes to send across the network.

NOTE NetBEUI is not NetBIOS. It is easy to confuse NetBIOS and NetBEUI (NetBIOS Extended User Interface). The confusion stems not only from the similar naming but from the fact that earlier implementations of NetBEUI provided NetBIOS as an integral part of the protocol driver. When I refer to NetBEUI here, I am referring to the transport-layer protocol, not the NetBIOS programming interface. NetBEUI is a sufficient but not a necessary requirement for using NetBIOS because other protocols also support NetBIOS. In other words, if you use NetBEUI, you can run NetBIOS applications. On the other hand if you have another protocol such as IPX *with* NetBIOS (which obviously includes support for NetBIOS), you can completely remove the NetBEUI protocol and still run your NetBIOS applications.

One reason for NetBEUI's lower overhead is that NetBEUI only provides what is called *unreliable communication*. Don't worry, unreliable is something of a misnomer; the connection is still reliable. Unreliable communication means that the protocol does not require an explicit acknowledgment (ACK) of each frame before it sends the next. Rather, the receiving computer bundles up several acknowledgments and sends them all at once. In our example of the letter to Gramma Gertrude, you would have had unreliable communication had you decided not to send the letter registered but waited to hear that she had received your card as part of some future message like a holiday card.

Were a protocol to require an ACK for each packet, it would waste the majority of the networks' resources because an ACK is so small it would use very little of the network's bandwidth. Rather than require an acknowledgment for each frame, NetBEUI dynamically determines (through a process called Sliding Windows) the number of frames the sender can transmit before receiving an ACK, based on the current network conditions.

NOTE   Actually, the NetBEUI shipped with Windows 95 and Windows NT is not really NetBEUI. Rather, it is a NetBIOS Frame protocol (NBF), sometimes referred to as NetBEUI 3.0. NBF is completely compatible with the "real" NetBEUI used in Windows for Workgroups and LAN Manager. In addition to supporting the NetBEUI specification, NBF is completely self-tuning, provides better performance across slow links such as telephone lines, and eliminates the 254-session limit of the original NetBEUI. Because the Windows 95 documentation refers to NBF as NetBEUI, we will too; for all practical purposes, they are identical.

Because of its speed and ability to self-tune through Sliding Windows, NetBEUI provides an excellent protocol for small networks such as regional sales offices. While NetBEUI is fast on small networks, you cannot use it effectively on large networks. The main reason for the poor performance over large networks is its addressing scheme. For NetBEUI, your computer's address is the very name you entered as your computer's name in the Network Identification dialog. Obviously, this prevents a network from having two computers with the same name—something quite difficult to achieve on a large network while still giving computers meaningful names. Another, not quite as obvious, implication is that you cannot route it although you can bridge it. A bridge provides the same basic functionality as a router by providing the ability to combine multiple network segments into one logical segment.

Advantages of NetBEUI	Disadvantages of NetBEUI
Compatible with Windows for Workgroups and LAN Manager	Not routable
Small memory footprint	Poor performance on large networks
Good error checking	Difficult to give meaningful names to computers on large networks
Fastest protocol in Windows 95	Tuned for small networks

TCP/IP

Quite simply, Transmission Control Protocol/Internet Protocol (TCP/IP) is the most complete, most widely accepted protocol in the world. And strictly speaking, TCP/IP is not a single protocol but a suite of protocols, usually referred to singularly as TCP/IP, that defines various interactions between computers sharing the protocol. TCP/IP originated as the protocol the U.S. Department of Defense developed in the late 1970s to connect computers to the Advanced Research Projects Agency Network (ARPANet), the precursor to the Internet. In 1983, in an effort to ensure that all its computers could talk to one another, the Department of Defense mandated that all its new networking products support TCP/IP. Overnight, it created an instant market for TCP/IP. Soon after, one of the three major Unix vendors, Berkeley Software Distribution (BSD), released Unix version 4.2BSD, which incorporated TCP/IP into its core operating system, thus making it the lingua franca of midrange computers.

Until recently, that's where TCP/IP stayed—on midrange computers. In the last few years, however, the PC began to replace the dumb terminal as the standard in desktop computing. This forced network managers to find ways of integrating PCs into the rest of their corporate network, which included TCP/IP-based midrange computers.

Because PCs use an open architecture rather than the proprietary ones in legacy systems, the obvious choice was to bring the PCs to the legacy systems via TCP/IP. Thus, just like the Department of Defense, many network administrators began demanding TCP/IP support for all their new PCs.

Windows 95 includes an easy-to-configure version of all the standard TCP/IP connectivity applications (FTP, telnet, etc.) as well as the diagnostic tools (arp, ipconfig, ping, route, etc.).

NOTE For an in-depth discussion of TCP/IP, see Chapter 18.

While TCP/IP has a reputation as a difficult protocol to configure and manage, new implementations are making it easier. In the TCP/IP arena, support for servers running Dynamic Host Configuration Protocol (DHCP) represents probably the most important advance in Windows 95 over Windows 3.x. Without DHCP, network managers have to manually assign the four-byte IP addresses to each machine. With DHCP enabled, a DHCP server manages a range of IP addresses and assigns one to each workstation as it logs onto the network.

NOTE Currently only Windows NT Server 3.5 provides the Dynamic Host Configuration Protocol server required by the DHCP client in Windows 95. Windows NT Server 3.5 also provides the Windows Internet Name Service (WINS) server to resolve NetBIOS computer names to IP addresses. WINS provides the same functionality as the Unix Domain Name System (DNS) service.

The TCP/IP protocol included with Windows 95 supports Windows Sockets 1.1. Windows Sockets is a programming interface similar to NetBIOS but specifically designed for client/server applications because of its scalability. Microsoft TCP/IP supports NetBIOS by encapsulating—providing a wrapper—around the NetBIOS request within the TCP/IP protocol.

Advantages to TCP/IP	Disadvantages to TCP/IP
Most widely used	More overhead than NetBEUI
Routable	Can be difficult to administer
Interoperates across hardware and software platforms	Not as fast as NetBEUI on small networks
Provides Internet connectivity	
Supports Windows Sockets 1.1	

Subsequent chapters examine many of the networking features in much more detail to help you either to design a new network around Windows 95 workstations or to integrate Windows 95 clients into your existing network.

Chapter 25

Planning Your Windows 95 Network

FEATURING

Ethernet networks and cabling technologies

Which LAN topology to implement

Choosing your cards

This chapter is a fast track to designing your Windows 95 network. While there are several network-technology choices you can make, I am only going to look at Ethernet networks. This is because Ethernet networks are less expensive to implement than token ring and easier to manage. Token-ring networks require more hardware than Ethernet, are more expensive to implement, and are only advantageous if you have to interface your network clients with IBM mainframes.

I will first take a look at the two most likely network-cable topologies that will be used by home consumers and small-business owners, and then I will help you pick the best network interface card (NIC) for your computer.

If you are setting up a brand new Windows 95-based network, one of the first things you will have to decide on is the technology you will use to physically connect your computers. If you are integrating Windows 95 computers into an existing network (or if someone else has specified the network technology), you can skip ahead to the section on selecting your network adapter card.

If your network will have more than 30 or 40 workstations, you will probably need to split it into multiple sections, called *segments*. You then connect each segment to the other segments of the network through a series of routers or bridges. While I will mention the implications your decisions will have on both segmented and nonsegmented networks, segmented networks are outside the scope of this book. While there are indeed several excellent books on the subject, I have found that enterprise-wide network specialists design more successful networks than network managers who try to do everything themselves. Because these sorts of networks are exceedingly complex and there are no clear guidelines, many consultants resort to trial and error as a design methodology. When looking for a network consultant, try to find one who has done a trial-and-error period with a previous client.

Ethernet Networks and Cabling Technologies

Ethernet is what network professionals call a Carrier-Sense Multiple Access with Collision Detection (CSMA/CD) network. The University of

Hawaii developed this model in the late 1960s when it was trying to place multiple computers on a campus-wide wide-area network (hence *Multiple Access*). Their network controlled access by requiring each computer to listen to the wire and wait until no one else was transmitting (the *Carrier Sensing* part). Once the network was free, a station could go ahead and send its data. If another station tried to send at the same time and the transmissions collided, the computers realized this (*Collision Detection*), and each waited a random period of milliseconds before trying to resend. Whichever computer had the shorter random period of time got to transmit first.

When designing the physical side of your local-area network (LAN), you have two main decisions to make. You need to select which type of cable you will use to connect your computers together, and you need to choose which LAN technology you will employ to send data over this cable. In the next section I will deal with the first question—the wiring. After that I will discuss in more detail each of the technologies I highlighted above.

Which Type of Cable to Use?

In the past decade or so, network managers have installed LANs that run on every type of wiring imaginable. We will limit our discussion to looking at coaxial cable, often referred to as Thin Ethernet, and un-shielded twisted-pair cable. These two cabling mediums are most widely used today and each offers unique strengths and weaknesses.

Coaxial Cable

Up through the late 1980s, almost every LAN (at least every one that I saw) used coaxial cable, usually referred to as coax. Coax has only a single center conductor—usually solid copper wire—with a thick insulation surrounding the center and a layer of wire-mesh braid over this insulation. A final, outer layer of plastic insulation covers the wire braid and is what you normally see when you look at a piece of coax. The purpose of the wire-braid layer is to further insulate the inner conductor from possible interference. As you can see on the next page, this coax looks very much like the round cable that connects your TV set to your antenna. In fact, network coax (especially thin coax) is quite similar to the coax used by ham and CB radio and TV antennas.

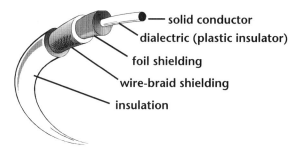

- solid conductor
- dialectric (plastic insulator)
- foil shielding
- wire-braid shielding
- insulation

Coax is fairly inexpensive and very easy to install. One complicating factor, however, is that each LAN technology uses a slightly different specification (called an RG number—such as RG-58). As a result, your existing cabling may or may not work with a new technology. However, for a home consumer or small-business owner this technology will provide usable network services for many years to come.

Advantages of Coax	Disadvantages of Coax
Simple to install	Low security, easy to tap
Good signal-to-noise ratio, particularly over medium distances	Difficult to change topologies
Low maintenance costs	Limited distance and topology
	Easily damaged

Unshielded Twisted Pair

Unshielded twisted pair (UTP) is similar to the cable that connects your phone to the wall jack. Each pair of wires is twisted around each other, as shown below, to create a magnetic field that provides better transmission capabilities. Because the wire is unshielded, it is open to

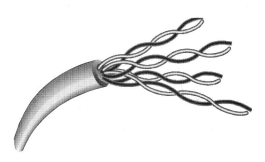

electrical interference, so you should be careful about how you route the cable. For instance, never run your cables next to a power transformer or an overhead lighting system.

You should never use a low-quality cable type for your network. For instance, never use a telephone patch cord in your network segment. While a telephone cable looks just like a network cable (RJ-45), they have different properties. Telephones will run on almost anything that carries a current; high-speed data networks, however, are very finicky. If the cable is not perfect, the data will garble up and bring your network to its knees. A single six-foot patch cable constructed from the standard untwisted telephone cabling that runs between your wall jack and phone (called *silver satin*) will usually prevent the entire LAN from sending any data across the entire segment.

To clean up the confusion over what constitutes acceptable network cable and to prevent installation mistakes, the Electronics Industries Association/Telecommunications Industry Association (EIA/TIA) released a system differentiating the varieties of unshielded twisted pair. The EIA/TIA system ranks cable from Grade 1 at the low end to Grade 5 at the high end.

▶ Levels 1 and 2: These grades are not appropriate for high-speed digital transmissions and should only be used for voice.

▶ Level 3: You can safely use Level 3 for low- to moderate-speed data such as 4-Mbps token ring and 10-Mbps 10Base-T. If your network is in a location where it will be subjected to a great deal of electrical interference, you probably will want to use at least Level 4 even for speeds of 10 Mbps.

▶ Level 4: When you start getting up above 10-Mbps speeds such as 16-Mbps token ring, you must use at least Level 4.

▶ Level 5: This top-of-the-line cable can be used for all transmission speeds, even up to the 100-Mbps rate of Fast Ethernet. One word of caution: when you start using the new, high-speed technologies, be sure to use a top-rated cable-installation firm; a high-quality installation becomes essential at these speeds.

So what level should you choose? For the past year or so, I have been recommending nothing other than Level 5. Because installing cable is labor-intensive (at least three-quarters of the total installation cost is directly related to labor; even more in complex, multifloor jobs), it only makes sense to make sure that whatever you use will last as long as possible. By saving a few hundred dollars in cable costs, you run the risk of having to rip it all out and pull all new cable if your cable is not up to supporting the newest LAN technologies. Remember, like any physical plant, you would like your cable to last at least ten years, so it behooves you to plan for your network's future traffic.

> **NOTE** Every now and then one of my clients tells me that one of their (usually previous) vendors told them they could not use Level 5 for token ring and 10Base-T because the specification called for Level 3. This misunderstanding is due to a misreading of the spec that sets the minimum acceptable EIA/TIA grade rather than the required grade. You can—and usually should—use a higher grade anytime a lower grade is specified.

The following table lists the maximum data-transfer rates for each of the EIA/TIA grades for unshielded twisted pair.

EIA/TIA Level	Maximum Data-Transfer Rate
1	0 Mbps
2	1 Mbps
3	10 Mbps
4	10 Mbps
5	100 Mbps

Advantages of Unshielded Twisted Pair	Disadvantages of Unshielded Twisted Pair
Easy to add additional nodes to the network	Limited bandwidth
Well-understood technology	Limited distance
Inexpensive	Low security, easy to tap
Can be used to support phones	Requires hubs
Supports many topologies	

All told, unshielded twisted pair is probably your best choice if you are using a cabling contractor to install your network cable in a business office or if you are building a new home and can have the cable installed before you put the wallboard up. If you are just trying to connect several computers in the same room or have short cable runs between rooms, coax cable is the better choice.

Which LAN Topology to Implement

Now that you understand the physical media, you need to decide which LAN topology you will use to create your network. There are basically two types to be considered in our discussion: either a bus topology for thin Ethernet or coax cabling, or a star topology for unshielded twisted pair.

Thin Ethernet (10Base-2)

Thin Ethernet uses the main network cable, or bus, to connect each person's PC to the network. Each PC connects to this main cable by splicing the cable and terminating it with a bayonet nut connector (BNC), which is then connected to a T connector on the back of the network card. This essentially creates a single network cable that runs from the first PC to the last PC on the network.

You can create a Thin Ethernet segment for up to 185 meters (about 600 feet) and connect up to 30 stations to it. The cable itself must have an impedance of 50 ohms and be terminated with a $\frac{1}{2}$-watt 50-ohm (±1 ohm) resistor at each end. To prevent ground loops, you should also ground one (and only one) end of the cable as shown in Figure 25.1.

Thin Ethernet quickly became one of the most popular LAN technologies primarily because of its high performance-to-cost ratio and also because of its relative ease of installation. In the early 1990s it began to lose favor to a newer variant of Ethernet, which runs on twisted pair rather than coax.

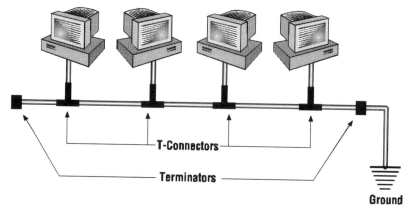

Figure 25.1 *A typical Thin Ethernet segment*

The real problem with 10Base-2 comes not from the coax cable but from the bus topology, where every computer is connected to a single cable. Whenever a computer wants to send data, it places a signal on the wire. This signal or *bus* then travels the length of the cable. As the bus passes each computer, the computer checks the destination address to see if it matches its own. If it matches, it reads the message; otherwise, it ignores it. If the cable breaks or otherwise becomes inoperable, suddenly every computer between the break and the terminator can no longer communicate with any of the stations on the other side of the break.

This is the primary reason I no longer recommend Thin Ethernet for business use outside of training rooms. If you only have three or four computers to connect or the network cable can be easily routed from computer to computer and is very accessible, thin Ethernet is a good choice. Otherwise, by all means go with 10Base-T.

Twisted-Pair Ethernet (10Base-T)

In the late 1980s, LANs moved out of the domain of the tightly controlled corporate MIS departments and into the departmental workgroup where everyone was connected to the network. Not only did the likelihood of the cable breaking increase as more computers were put on the network but so did the costs of downtime as more and more users began to depend on consistent network access.

In an effort to address these problems, vendors began offering Ethernet running on twisted pair using a star bus topology. In a star bus network, each workstation is connected directly to a multiport repeater, sometimes called a *hub* or a *concentrator*. The concentrator basically acts as a traffic cop, directing incoming messages out to the correct computer. Each hub usually supports either eight or sixteen computers, but some hubs can handle up to 128. If you need to add more computers than your concentrator can handle, or if you want to segment network traffic, you can connect several concentrators together.

The benefit of a star topology (see Figure 25.2) is that if the cable fails at any point, only the computer directly served by that cable loses its connection. The downside, however, is that if the multiport repeater (*hub*) fails, then all the workstations attached to it lose their

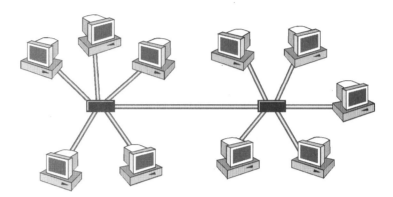

Figure 25.2 *A network based on the star bus topology*

connection to the network also. In my opinion, you should not view this as a deterrent to installing a star bus rather than a bus network.

A failed hub in a star bus topology has the same effect as a cable break in a regular bus-style network: a lot of people lose their connection to the network. However, a failed hub is almost always easier to troubleshoot than a broken cable. With bus-style networks, you have no idea where your cable might have broken; it may be right at someone's computer or it may be up in the ceiling between the third and fourth floors. Once you have located the point of failure, hub problems are easy to fix—just swap in a new one. It is not that easy with cable because you cannot replace it; you need to fix it by splicing in a good piece of cable.

While twisted-pair Ethernet only requires two pairs, typical networks use 8-pin (four pairs) cable with an RJ-45 connector. Some networking professionals suggest using the extra wires for voice so you do not have to pull separate cables for your phones. While this is technically possible, I don't think it's a good idea. Rather than use the extra wires for voice, use them for future expansion or as a backup in case a wire breaks. Better yet, you may be able to use them as part of your new 100-Mb Ethernet cabling.

With twisted-pair starting to catch on, computer managers quickly jumped at the opportunity to upgrade their cables to twisted-pair Ethernet, and the IEEE 802.3 committee created a new specification for Ethernet called 10Base-T. Among other things, this specification stipulates that a workstation running 10Base-T must be within 100 meters (330 feet) of a concentrator and connected to it by cable meeting or exceeding the EIA/TIA UTP Level 3 grade.

As for the hubs themselves, you are better off sticking with the eight- or sixteen-port variety rather than going with the larger ones. By using more hubs, you can reduce the workload on each one. As of this writing, you can get these hubs for around $20 per port. In addition to the RJ-45 jacks for the twisted pair, each will usually have a BNC or AUI (attachment unit interface) connector on the back so you can attach it to ThickNet or fiber backbones.

As your network grows, you will want to look at hubs with built-in management features. While costing more, they are a great benefit to the harried network manager because they allow him or her to remotely check the status of and administer each port on the hub.

I would recommend 10Base-T for your Ethernet network; unless you have a huge investment in thin Ethernet, or you have a small network with an even smaller budget, the other options just are not worth it.

The following table summarizes the specifications of each of the LAN technologies discussed.

	ThinNet (10Base-2)	Twisted Pair (10Base-T)
Topology	Bus	Star Bus
Cable	RG-58	UTP
Impedance	50 ohm	N/A
Termination	50 ohm ± 2 ohm	UTP 85–115 ohm
Maximum length per segment	185 m	100 m
Maximum segments	5	N/A
Maximum stations per segment	30	N/A
Minimum distance between stations	.5 m	2.5 m (between hub and station)

Choosing Your Cards

Now, with the LAN, protocol, technology, and topology decisions behind you, you only have one more decision to make before you can start installing your network: How will you connect your PCs to this physical network you have just designed?

Four years ago network designers agonized over this decision. They would pore over manufacturers' spec sheets, then dutifully design a whole set of tests so they could compare the performance of various cards from various manufacturers. Finally, they would spend days laboriously putting the cards into each model computer on site and running the tests.

Why put forth such an effort for a $300 (that's what they cost then) piece of silicon? Well, while the costs of cards only varied by about 25 percent, the performance difference between a good card and a bad card could vary as much as 300 percent. Nowadays, most manufacturers use standard chip sets so the performance difference is quite small.

When choosing a card, by far the most important factor should be whether there is an NDIS 3.1 driver available for the card. If not, you will either not be able to use the card with Windows 95, or you will have to use 16-bit real-mode drivers rather than the faster 32-bit protected-mode drivers.

Really, if the card does not have a NDIS 3.1 driver available, don't even consider buying the card. Using 16-bit real-mode drivers will deprive you of one of Windows 95's major benefits—the speed of 32-bit protected-mode drivers—every time you need to access the network.

Microsoft ships Windows 95 with drivers for many of the most popular token ring and Ethernet cards on the market. But if you find that Windows 95 does not have a driver for an existing card, you do have a few options. First, check to see if Microsoft has recently released a driver. You can get all the latest Microsoft drivers from the following sources:

▶ CompuServe: Windows 95 Driver Library

▶ CD-ROM: \Drivers subdirectory (some but not all drivers)

▶ Internet: FTP to ftp.microsoft.com (131.107.1.11)

▶ Microsoft Download Servers: Data (206) 936-6735 (N81)

▶ Microsoft Product Support Services: Voice (206) 637-7098 if you do not have a modem

In addition, you will probably be able to download the drivers from the Microsoft Network.

If Microsoft does not have a driver available, you can contact your card's manufacturer directly. Be warned, however, this is a real hit-or-miss prospect. In some cases, the hardware manufacturers produce excellent drivers for their hardware—they, after all, know its ins and outs better than anyone else. In other cases, the manufacturer will have put very little effort into producing a quality driver. Rather, it simply wants to say Windows 95 supports its hardware with little regard for how buggy the hardware is and how often it crashes your system.

You will also want to consider the flexibility of your cards. You want a card that supports multiple network media and one you can configure with software. Until recently, manufacturers made separate cards for Thin coax and twisted pair. Now many manufacturers offer cards that support both of the popular media. If your network runs on multiple technologies, you definitely want cards that will support all of them.

I refuse to purchase a manufacturer's cards if I cannot configure them on the fly with software. As recently as two years ago, you could only change a card's configuration—interrupt, I/O address, DMA channel—by getting the forceps out and changing the jumpers. Most leading manufacturers now allow you to either hard configure your NIC with jumpers or soft configure with software. Until all your cards are Plug-and-Play compliant, soft configuration is the best available option.

You also need to match your network adapter card to your computer's system bus. Bus types are fairly easy to identify as there are only five from which to choose:

▶ 16-bit Industry Standard Architecture (ISA)

▶ 32-bit Extended Industry Standard Architecture (EISA)

▶ 16- and 32-bit Micro Channel Architecture (MCA)

▶ VESA (VL-Bus) Local Bus

▶ Intel Peripheral Component Interconnect (PCI) Local Bus

If you are not sure what type of bus you have, chances are it is an Industry Standard Architecture (ISA) machine. Currently ISA (sometimes called AT-bus or AT-compatible because it originated when IBM first released the IBM Personal Computer AT) is by far the mostly widely used architecture. ISA machines have both 8- and 16-bit slots. If you have any 16-bit slots still available, get a 16-bit network adapter card. While it will not double your throughput, switching from an 8- to a 16-bit card will produce a noticeable improvement.

The Extended Industry Standard Architecture (EISA) standard was *supposed* to be the successor to the ISA standard. In addition to the standard 8- and 16-bits slots used in ISA machines, EISA adds support for 32-bit cards. Unfortunately, it never gained market acceptance because the additional performance failed to justify the (substantial) extra cost. These days you only see EISA machines in file and database servers. While you can use both 8- and 16-bit ISA cards in an EISA machine, you should take advantage of the EISA bus and use 32-bit EISA cards. (But see the comments below about EISA network cards.)

IBM also tried to create the successor to ISA with MCA. Like EISA, the costs outweighed the benefits. To make matters worse, if you have an MCA machine, you *must* use MCA cards (unlike EISA, which supports ISA cards). If you have an IBM P/S or any other computer that requires a reference disk, you probably have an MCA bus and therefore must use MCA cards.

If you purchased your computer in the last year or two, you might have local bus slots in addition to ISA or EISA slots. A local bus interface card can send and receive data at the full speed of your system bus (usually 25 or 33 MHz); it doesn't have the 8-MHz limit of standard ISA and EISA slots. Because of their faster throughput, local bus slots are a perfect candidate for I/O-intensive interface cards such as video and disk controllers.

There are two types of local bus machines on the market; those adhering to the VESA local bus standard (VL-Bus) and the PCI bus produced by Intel for its Pentium machines. If you have a VL-Bus machine, the benefits of a local bus network card are unclear. For reasons outside the scope of this discussion, the VL bus requires a great deal of your CPU's resources. In some cases you may even get slightly better performance from a standard EISA or even an ISA network card. Besides the possible performance hit, a computer can only have a maximum of three VL bus cards. Because of this limit and the ambiguities surrounding VESA performance, I recommend you save your local bus slots for other cards such as video accelerators, where you know you will get improved performance.

Pentium machines built around the PCI local bus show much more promise when it comes to increasing network performance. First off, they support a full 64-bit data path, as opposed to the VL Bus' 32-bit path. Second, you can have any number of PCI local bus cards in your computer. Lastly, there is no uncertainly about the performance of PCI: it is definitely faster. If you have a PCI machine and find network cards that Windows 95 supports, buy them.

When choosing a manufacturer, I recommend that all my clients purchase a card from a leading vendor. For Ethernet you cannot go wrong with 3Com, Eagle, Intel, National Semiconductor, or SMC. These are the market leaders: almost all software supports them, and they have the widest variety of drivers available. While you might save a bit purchasing the GarageTech clone, it is not worth the possible incompatibilities to save 20 percent on a $100 card.

Now that you have your physical network planned, in the following chapter we will take a look at setting up a simple-yet-complete Windows 95 peer-to-peer network.

Chapter 26

Setting Up a Simple-Yet-Complete Peer-to-Peer Windows 95 Network

FEATURING

Getting acquainted with peer-to-peer networking

Setting up the network

Network Neighborhood

In this chapter I will walk through setting up a simple peer-to-peer network of Windows 95 workstations. I will start with obtaining, configuring, and installing a network adapter card, then installing and configuring the correct network drivers, go on to discuss pros and cons of installing Windows 95 before or after installing your network card, and finally set up a small workgroup of at least two Windows 95 stations, which will be able to easily access each other's disk drives, printers, and modems.

Getting Acquainted with Peer-to-Peer Networking

Peer-to-peer refers to the fact that each station on the network treats each other station as an equal or a peer. There is no special station set aside to only provide file and print services to all the other stations. Instead, any printer, CD-ROM drive, hard drive, or even a floppy drive located on any one station can (if you wish) share access with all the other stations on the network. When you share a resource, such as a disk drive or printer, the computer that shares the resource becomes the server, and the computer that accesses the shared resource becomes the client. In a peer-to-peer network you can both share resources and access shared resources equally. In effect, your computer can be both a server and a client at the same time. Figure 26.1 illustrates a peer-to-peer network arrangement.

 NOTE A modem, too, can be shared with other stations on the network— but only when configured as a dedicated fax server. In this way, stations without a fax modem can both send and receive faxes. For detailed instructions on configuring and sharing a fax server, see Chapter 16.

Of course, there are security features as well, which will allow you to grant or remove access to shared resources on your computer. But first let's get the network up and running.

 NOTE For step-by-step instructions on setting up a direct-cable network connection, see Chapter 28.

Figure 26.1   A typical peer-to-peer network topology: notice that no particular station is designated as a standalone server.

NETWORKING WITHOUT A NETWORK CARD

Amazingly, with Windows 95, it is *possible* to set up a peer-to-peer network of two computers with no additional hardware except a $5 cable! By installing the Direct Cable Connection (DCC) network driver supplied in Windows 95 and connecting a cable between available printer or serial ports on two PCs, you can quickly set up a simple yet full-featured, two-station network, actually sharing drives and printers just like the bigger networks.

The main drawback to this approach is that it is slow—copying a 1-MB file, for example, takes about one minute via a null-modem serial cable or about 25 seconds via a parallel cable. While this is much faster than networking via modem (an option that is also supported), it is significantly slower than most network interface cards (NICs). Generally, if you want to network two or more PCs on a regular basis, it will be worth the money to just buy network cards and cable and network the normal way. But whenever you need a convenient but temporary network connection, DCC provides you with a slick and easy built-in solution.

I was *amazed* the first time I connected my laptop to desktop via parallel port and discovered I suddenly had several "neighbors" in my Network Neighborhood. Not only could I access resources such as my Desktop's CD-ROM drive and 5¼-inch floppy drive, I also could print from my laptop directly to any network printer at the office, send faxes using another station's fax modem, and send and receive e-mail from the network mail server—all of this just using the parallel (printer) port. (The serial port could be used just as easily but is somewhat slower than using the parallel port, and it's usually easier to find an available printer port as serial ports tend to be already occupied by mice and/or modems.) In Chapter 28 I discuss DCC and its cousin—Remote Access Service (RAS)—in greater detail.

Setting Up the Network

By way of example, let's assume in this chapter that we are setting up a new Windows 95 peer-to-peer network from scratch. For now, our goal will be to connect two or three stations together so we can share various drives and printers from each station to its peers. Based on our reading of the previous chapter, we have decided to go with a 10Base-2 (coax) configuration. Accordingly, here is our shopping list of equipment and hardware we will need—other than Windows 95 and our soon-to-be-networked computers:

▶ one network interface card (NIC) for each station we want on the network

▶ one premade coax (RG-58) cable with BNC connectors on each end for each workstation to be connected. Cable-length requirements will be based on the distance between workstations, between 6 and 50 feet.

▶ one T-connector per network card

 TIP Look in your local computer store for a Microsoft Windows 95 starter kit. Currently Microsoft sells just such a kit for Windows for Workgroups 3.11, and I expect that when Windows 95 is made available to the public, Microsoft will continue these starter kits. The kit includes everything you need, aside from the computer, to get your network up and running: two software-configurable network cards, two T-connectors, a 25-foot roll of coax cable, two licenses for your operating system, and complete instructions. You can purchase additional add-on kits that include another network card, T-connector, coax cable, and software license to add additional single workstations as well.

Let's take a closer look at each of these items.

Buying Your Network Cards

First you'll need a network card for each station. If you're buying network cards for the first time, please note that these are also frequently referred to as network adapters or network interface cards (NICs). Your network cards will have a thin Ethernet connector (also called a BNC connector) on them, and you might want the flexibility of also having RJ-45 connectors and/or thick Ethernet connectors, if you foresee ever having to use these types of cable. You may find that the two- or three-connector cards cost almost as much individually as buying two separate single-connector network cards. But again, if you think you need the flexibility, nothing beats the convenience of being able to change cable type without (in many cases) even having to change software or card settings. Figure 26.2 shows what a typical NIC (network interface card) looks like.

At the time of this writing, typical 16-bit single-connector network cards range from $45 to $60 or more, with dual-connector (and triple-connector) cards ranging from $120 to $140, and high-speed PCI, VESA, and other 32-bit cards selling for around $130 or more. Be sure your cards either come with NDIS 3.1 drivers on diskette or (ideally) are supported with a Windows 95 built-in driver. Last, remember you want Plug-and-Play adapter cards (if available) or at least software-configurable cards, as these can save a lot of grief and aggravation when you start installing and configuring driver software.

Installing the Network Hardware

In this section I'll describe how to install and connect the basic hardware elements of your peer-to-peer network—the NIC and the cables.

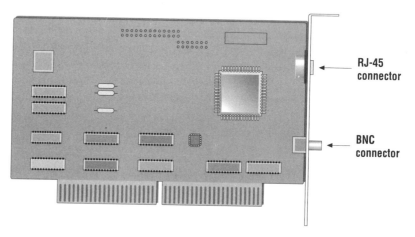

Figure 26.2   *This is a typical Network combo-card, sporting both RJ-45 and BNC thin coax connectors.*

TIP   If you happen to be adding a non–Plug-and-Play network card (or any other hardware, for that matter) *after* Windows 95 is already running on your system, first use Windows 95 to print out a current System Summary Report, then shut down your system. This report can be printed by going into My Computer ➤ Control Panel ➤ System applet and clicking on the Device Manager tab. Click on the Print button, choose System Summary for report type, and click on OK. This will give you a handy listing of all current IRQs, DMA channels, port I/O addresses, and upper memory the memory between 640K and 1024K) currently being used in your system.

Installing the Network Interface Card (NIC)

In the unlucky event you are working with a network card that still uses jumpers to configure it, we have a little work to do. First, open the card's manual to where it shows how to set the jumpers or switches to configure the card's settings. For now, don't make any changes, but do write down the current IRQ (interrupt) number, DMA channel, and memory address, as you will need these to configure the driver. Even if you have a card that doesn't have switches but lets you make changes to settings via software, you'll have to install the card. Follow these steps to do so:

Part 5

1. Select your first PC "victim," make sure the power is turned off, unplug it to be really safe, and remove the PC's case. If you have questions about how to remove your computer case, refer to your owner's manual for a complete description.

CAUTION   Don't forget to unplug your PC from the AC outlet before opening up the cover. This ensures you have the PC's power turned off, plus reduces to zero any chance of electric shock. Having come this far, I don't want to lose you. Also, before you install the network card, be sure to ground yourself by touching the metal case of the computer to eliminate the possibility of static electricity zapping your network card.

2. You likely have all too much experience inserting and removing cards, but in any case, you'll have to remove the screw that holds the thin metal slot cover behind the connector you intend to use for your card. Don't drop the screw into the machine! If you do, you must get it out one way or another, such as by turning the machine over.

Networking with Windows 95

3. Insert the card gently but firmly until it is completely seated in the slot. You may have to wiggle the card a bit from front to back to ensure it seats firmly into the connector.

4. Next, store the metal slot cover somewhere for future use and screw the card in securely (this can be a hassle sometimes as the screw may not line up with the hole too easily).

> **CAUTION** After installing your network card, it is imperative that you take the time to put the screw back in the bracket and tighten the card down securely. Otherwise, once you have the network cable attached to the card, a little tug on the cable could easily uproot the NIC, damaging it and your computer's motherboard (if the power is on). This is not fun. So take the extra time to put the screw back in.

5. If the PC in question is a laptop computer or a desktop that accepts PCMCIA cards, your chores are much easier. Simply plug the card into an available PCMCIA slot. Your computer (and Windows 95) can even be running while you do this. (You might want to verify this first, however, by reading the manual or asking the salesperson, as there are a few early PCMCIA cards that should only be inserted when the unit is off.) And, of course, it won't hurt to insert the card before turning on the laptop. If the card is in next time Windows 95 starts up, the appropriate driver will be loaded immediately. But the ability to insert the card *while* Windows 95 is running is Plug and Play at its finest. If all goes well, network drivers appropriate to your card will get automatically loaded when you insert the card and unloaded when you remove it. The first time you plug the card in, however, you may be prompted to insert one of the master Windows 95 diskettes (or the CD-ROM) to load the correct network card driver.

> **NOTE** Some network cards may come with updated Windows 95 drivers included on a diskette. Read the documentation that came with your card (or call the manufacturer) to determine whether this is the case, and if so, insert this driver diskette into your drive when you are prompted to do so.

6. Repeat the above process with each PC you intend to network. When finished, place each PC's cover back on but do not put all the screws back into the case yet—anyone who's done this before will tell you that screwing the case back on before making sure everything works is

the best way to ensure that things will *not* work. Unfortunately, even with Plug-and-Play network cards, you may still end up having to get back inside your PC to reconfigure that Sound Blaster or some other card that happens to be using a needed IRQ or DMA channel and is not itself Plug-and-Play compatible. (In my experience, sound cards are the most frequent problem.)

Installing the Cables

Connect the T-connectors to the back of each network card, then connect each workstation to the next with lengths of coax cable. The first and last stations must have a terminator attached to the free end of their T-connector. Be sure to ground one, and only one, terminator to prevent ground loops.

With a network card installed in each of your stations and each card connected via cable to the next, you are now ready to install and configure your Windows 95 software for networking. If all goes well, the hard part of your job is already complete.

Installing and/or Configuring Windows 95 for Networking

If you have not yet installed Windows 95 on your stations, you'll need to do so before continuing (see the Appendix for installation instructions). If all goes well, Setup will automatically detect your newly installed network card and, if you're lucky, will even determine the type of card and configure it for you. If it does neither, you have two choices—either manually tell it during setup which network card you have or wait until Windows 95 is finished installing and then add the network drivers. If you take the opportunity during setup to configure your network drivers, use the following procedure. Otherwise, skip down to *Installing Network Drivers After You've Installed Windows 95.*

Installing Network Drivers During Windows 95 Install If you want to declare the settings for your network while you are installing Windows 95, start the normal Windows 95 Setup program and follow these steps as Windows 95 is installing:

1. When you get to the Select Components screen, make sure the *accessories* option is checked. If you are certain you do not want the accessories, you may still at least want the Communications features, which include

Microsoft Fax, Dial-Up Networking, and Direct Cable Connect. If you think you will need these, either include the accessories or double-click on accessories and enable the Communications check box.

 NOTE If you leave out an option during installation, don't worry—it can be added quite easily after Windows 95 is installed and running.

2. When you get to the Network Configuration part of the setup (see Figure 26.3), you will want to verify that the following network components get installed:

▶ Client for Microsoft Networks

▶ a driver specific to your network card (if not listed, just let Setup finish for now)

▶ NetBEUI

▶ File and Printer Sharing for Microsoft Networks

If you need to add anything to this list, just click on the Add button, select Client, Adapter, Protocol, or Service, then select the manufacturer and type. Don't worry about IPX/SPX and other protocols now, these can easily be added later. And unless you want them immediately, the Dial-Up and Direct-Cable connection can probably wait

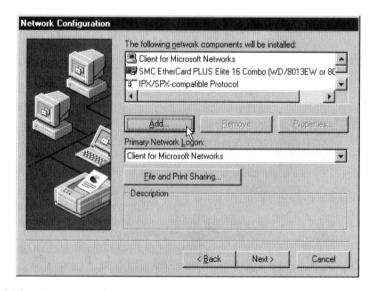

Figure 26.3 **The Network Configuration dialog box**

and be added later as well. Keeping your network components to a minimum right now may make it easier to get your initial network connections operating.

3. Click on the File and Print Sharing button and make sure both options are checked: *I want to be able to give others access to my files* and *I want to be able to give others access to my printer(s)*. These will probably be on by default, but check to make sure. Again, if you accidentally skip this step, you can do it later. Just remember that file and printer sharing will not even appear on menus if these options are not enabled.

NOTE   Because Windows 95 (unlike Windows for Workgroups) includes support for Novell networks right out of the box, the Client for Novell Networks as well as IPX/SPX (its default protocol) will probably show up in your *network components to be installed* list. To keep things simple, remove the Client for Novell Networks and the IPX/SPX for now—unless you plan to connect to a Novell Network—and make sure NetBEUI is selected as the only protocol to be installed. Installing additional clients and protocols can only complicate matters right now, and can also slow down your network to a small degree.

4. When asked for your machine name, choose a name descriptive of the computer—the important thing is to make this name different for each station. Fortunately, the machine name can be very easily changed later, so don't worry too much about being creative at this point. Select a descriptive name for your workgroup: this *does* need to be the same for each station—in Chapter 8 I discussed making multiple workgroups.

5. Continue through the rest of the install process, and if you've configured the networking components appropriately, you can skip ahead to *Network Neighborhood*.

Network operability should be complete now. However, if you already have Windows 95 running but have not installed your network card yet, shut down Windows (perhaps print out a system-configuration report first), then turn off the computer and install the network card. (See *Installing the Network Interface Card*, above, for details on installing your card.) You'll want to note the IRQ, I/O, and memory address of your card in case you need to manually enter these settings later. Most likely, however (especially if your card is new), after turning your computer back on, Windows 95 will come up and detect that you've added a network card, detect what kind it is, and configure it for you. If this is the case, you can skip down to *Network Neighborhood* now.

Installing or changing Network components after Windows 95 is up and running is also quite easy. You can access the network-configuration options in Windows 95 via the Control Panel by choosing My Computer ➤ Control Panel ➤ Network, as shown in Figure 26.4.

Installing Network Drivers After You've Installed Windows 95

Assuming you have opened the Network applet under the Control Panel, you should see the Network Properties dialog box (see Figure 26.5).

1. Under *The following network components are installed* on the Configuration tab, make sure you have the following:

   ▶ Client for Microsoft Networks

   ▶ a driver specific to your network card

   ▶ NetBEUI

   ▶ File and Printer Sharing for Microsoft Networks

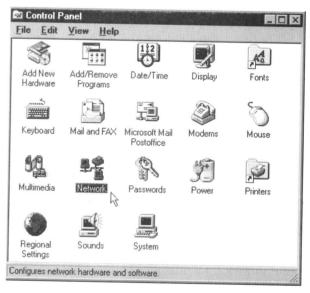

Figure 26.4   Accessing network options once Windows 95 is installed

Because Windows 95 includes support for Novell networks right out of the box, the Client for Novell Networks and IPX/SPX (its default protocol) will show up in your *network components to be installed* list if you didn't uncheck them earlier. Remove the Client for Novell Networks and the IPX/SPX for now—unless you plan to connect to a Novell Network—and make sure NetBEUI is selected as the only protocol to be installed.

If you need to add anything to this list, just click on the Add button, select Client, Adapter, Protocol, or Service, then select the manufacturer and type.

NOTE   Sometimes the diskette that shipped with your network card will contain drivers for a variety of different operating systems, each in a different subdirectory. If Windows 95 cannot find the correct drivers in the root directory of the diskette, you may have to help it along a little. Click on the Browse button and double-click on the correct subdirectory before letting Windows 95 continue.

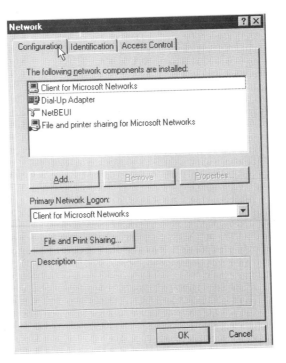

Figure 26.5   *The Network Properties dialog box*

IF WINDOWS 95 DOESN'T DETECT YOUR NETWORK ADAPTER TYPE

If Windows 95 did not detect your adapter correctly (or at all), do the following, making sure you have the diskette containing your network card's drivers:

1. Choose Control Panel ➤ Network and click on the Configuration tab.

2. Click on Adapter. If you see an incorrect network card driver installed, remove it by selecting it and then clicking on the Remove button.

3. Press the Add button to add your new driver.

4. Now click on Have Disk in the Select Network Adapters dialog box.

5. When prompted, insert the driver disk and press Enter.

6. For some cards, you will next be shown the desired settings for your network card. Make sure you write these down, because as soon as the drivers are installed, you will need to shut down Windows 95, remove your card, and make sure all the jumpers are set to configure the card for the required settings. If your card is software configurable, just run the card's configuration program and verify that the settings are what Windows 95 wants them to be.

7. Windows 95 will probably let you know it needs to restart (reboot) to load your network drivers. Choose Yes to restart.

When Windows 95 comes back up, the newly installed drivers will hopefully detect your network card and be able to communicate with it. If you do not see any error messages, you can proceed with the Network configuration procedure already in progress. (If you do have problems—an error message comes up, for example—first see if the message points to anything obvious you can fix; otherwise, flip to Chapter 29.)

Continuing with the network-configuration procedure, next do the following:

2. Again, on the main Network Configuration property sheet, make sure for now that the Primary Network Logon says Client for Microsoft Networks (shown in Figure 26.5).

3. Click on the File and Print Sharing button and make sure both options are checked; when finished, the dialog box should look like the one on the next page.

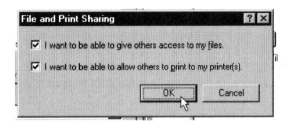

4. Now click on the Network Identification tab (see Figure 26.6). For the computer name, enter something descriptive of the computer—the important thing is that this name be different from others on the network. Select a descriptive name for your workgroup: This name needs to be the same for each station. Finally, add a computer description, if you like.

Part
5

Networking
with Windows 95

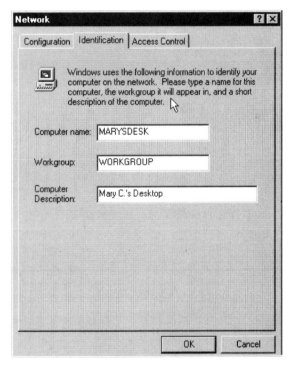

Figure 26.6   *The Network Identification Properties sheet lets you specify how your computer will be known to other users and which workgroup you are a member of.*

TIP   When configuring large numbers of Windows 95 machines, you may want to give more attention to the machine name you assign to each workstation. While the machine name itself is easy to change later, doing so can confuse all the other workstations that used to know the workstation under a different name. Also all resource sharing is based on the computer name. Therefore, if your office has a high turnover rate, you do not want to be naming machine names after employees using each machine; rather, give each machine a name descriptive of its function within the workgroup it belongs to.

5. Now click on the Access Control tab. Again, at least for now, select the share-level access control. We'll look at user-level access control at the end of this chapter, under *Security Features*.

When finished setting these options, be sure to click on the OK button at the bottom of the Network Property dialog box. After the dialog box closes, you may be prompted to shut down and restart Windows 95. If so, go ahead and do this.

Repeat this network-configuration procedure on any other stations that need it.

If all goes well, either you or Windows 95 has successfully installed the appropriate network drivers on each of your peer-to-peer stations, and you are now ready to begin testing and configuring your network. (If all has *not* gone well, the most likely problem will be incorrect network-card settings. Check Chapter 29.)

Network Neighborhood (aka The Hood)

Start up Windows 95 on each of your stations, and you should now see the Network Neighborhood icon on each station's Desktop. Double-click on the icon, and you should see a number of computer-shaped icons with names matching those unique machine names you assigned to each station.

Each station on your network should appear in this Neighborhood folder. If any are missing, or worse, if you do not *have* a Network Neighborhood on your Desktop, you'll have to do some troubleshooting. The most common problem, aside from missing protocol(s) and incorrectly configured network cards, will be that one or more of your stations are not set to the same workgroup as all the others.

Sharing Resources on the Network

To make the resources from one station accessible to other stations on the network, you need to *share* the drive or printer. First we will look at sharing drives, then sharing printers, and, finally, we will look at how to use security features to restrict access to your shared resources.

NOTE   File and Print Sharing must be enabled before you can share files or printers to your network.

Sharing Drives and Subdirectories

Using the Explorer and manipulating folders both provide an easy way to share information with other people on your network. In the following example, I'll share a station's hard drive. (If you are not currently on a station that has a hard drive, you may wish to switch to one on your network that does so you can try the example.)

Sharing from a Folder   The easiest way to share a folder object is to point to an object in the folder you wish to share and right-click on it. As shown on the next page, this will bring up the right-click menu for that object, and you will see a menu option labeled Sharing. Select this, and you will go to the Properties dialog box (see Figure 26.7). Then just follow these steps.

Part
5

Networking
with Windows 95

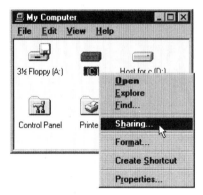

1. Click on the Sharing tab.

2. Type in a share name or just keep the default share name. If you like, you may add a comment describing the contents of this share.

3. Next you need to set the access type. Note the default is read-only, which only allows other users to open and view the contents but not to change them. The Full option lets anyone on the network both read and make changes to this folder. Keep in mind, by the way, that sharing a drive or folder shares all the subfolders below it as well.

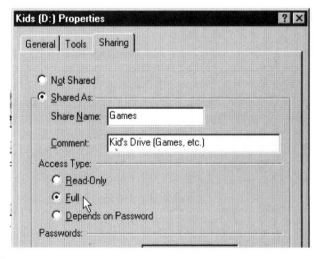

Figure 26.7   *The Sharing dialog box lets you specify how a shared drive (or folder) will be known to others on the network. It also allows you to specify a password and even which users and groups of users will be allowed to access the shared resource.*

4. If you want to restrict access to the share, assign a password. For now, let's leave access set to Full. We'll cover security shortly.

Another way you can bring up the share options is via the File menu. If you click on the drive or folder to be shared, then select the File menu option, you will see Sharing on this menu as well. Selecting this sharing option produces the same results as right-clicking and selecting Sharing.

Note the change in appearance of your drive or folder. When it is shared, the same icon appears, but as if held out in someone's hand.

Sharing from Explorer   If you understand the above-mentioned ways to share from a folder, then you also know how to share using Explorer. Both sides of the Explorer window support right-clicking to bring up property sheets (and from there you can select Sharing), and the File menu will also have the Sharing option, provided you've selected an object on the right side of the Explorer window (see Figure 26.8).

Before you go to another station to see if you can access the shared drive, bring up an MS-DOS prompt and type **NET VIEW *Com-puterName*** where *ComputerName* is the name of your computer. This will display a list of all the resources you have shared on your computer. If you can see the new shared resources, then go to another workstation and open Network Neighborhood, then open the computer that has the shared drive. If you now see the shared resource,

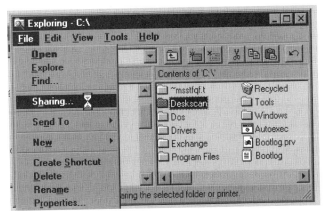

Figure 26.8 *Resources can also be shared via the Explorer applet—either using the menu or via the right-click method just mentioned.*

congratulations. You can now go to each station and add shares to any local drive you want accessible from the network.

Don't forget you can also share floppy drives and CD-ROM drives in exactly the same way. Perhaps only one station has a $5\frac{1}{4}$-inch floppy or a CD-ROM drive. Share it via the network, and anyone now has access to both sizes of floppy drive and the CD-ROM drive. Of course, network etiquette will likely preclude frequent use of someone else's floppy or CD-ROM drive, but for occasional use—installing software, for example—having the ability to share even removable media drives can be wonderfully helpful. Here, I am about to share a CD-ROM drive:

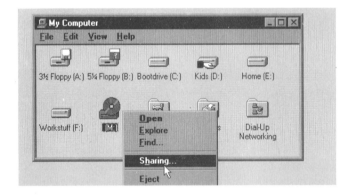

 NOTE If you are going to share a read-only resource such as a CD-ROM drive, be sure to set the network access to read-only (the default). This will prevent a remote user from attempting to write to the CD-ROM drive. If you do not do this, your remote software may hang while attempting to write to read-only media, so it's best to make sure that read-only access is enabled.

Sharing Printers

Sharing printers is just about as easy—and is certainly as much fun—as sharing drives and subdirectories. Before a printer can be shared, of course, its driver must be installed on the station to which the printer is physically attached. Additionally, other stations needing to use this printer across the network must have the same printer driver installed on their stations. Therefore, let's next look at how to install the printer driver.

Installing the Printer Driver for a Shared Printer   Go to a station that has a local printer attached. If you haven't yet installed the driver for this printer, you will need to do this first. To install it, just open My Computer ➤ Printers ➤ Add printer, and select the appropriate printer brand and model. If you are asked whether this is a network or local printer, select local. Depending on which printer you have, you might be asked for a Windows 95 driver diskette.

Once the printer driver is installed, the printer should show up in the Printers folder (located in My Computer). Using the right-click method, share the printer. Note that printers can also be shared from Explorer, just as drives and folders can.

Now, to share the printer, do exactly what you did to share a drive—namely, after right-clicking on the printer's icon, select the Sharing menu option. You have a set of sharing options quite similar to those for drive sharing. Type the name you want your printer known as on the network, provide a descriptive comment, if you like, and note the option to provide a password. If you do enter a password, your printer will only be available to users on the network who know the password. For now let's leave the password off, as this will make testing easier.

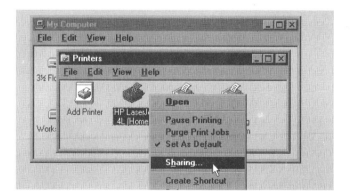

After you've shared the printer, go to another station—preferably one that has no local printer attached—and open Network Neighborhood. Double-click on the computer icon that has the shared printer, and you should now see the printer, plus any shared drive(s) for that station. If so, congratulations are once more in order. You can now go to any other stations that have a local printer and share those as well. Here's an example of what a shared printer will look like:

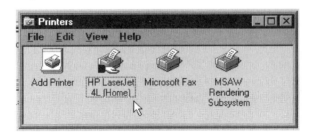

Having shared those printers you want accessible on the network, your users will now be able to print to any of them simply by choosing the Print option from any Windows application that supports printing. Of course, with more than one printer on the network, the desired printer can also be selected from any Windows application, usually by selecting File ➤ Print Setup from the application's menu. Additionally, note that any printer (local or network) can be set on each station as that station's default printer.

Now that your network printers are printing correctly (at least I hope they are!), I'll discuss using security features to control access to your shared drives and printers. For more about printers and printing with Windows 95, refer to Chapter 8.

Security Features

Although we've disabled all of them for clarity's sake, Windows 95 does have several means of restricting access to a station's shared resources.

Hiding Share Names

Let's start with the easiest (but not a very well known) technique. In any Share As name, if you add a dollar sign ($) to the end of the share name, that resource becomes invisible but still accessible to those who know both its existence and name. For example, if you want to make your CD-ROM drive accessible anywhere on the network but not have everyone using it, you might type CDROM$ as the drive's share name. Then, whenever you need to access this drive from another station, you would need to specify the share name and the machine name to map to the drive or otherwise access it. The access path would look similar to this: \\CD_STATION\CDROM$.

Obviously this technique is only as secure as the knowledge of the resource's share name (and location).

Share-Level and User-Level Access Control

A second means of restricting access is to use passwords with share-level control. This means you supply one password for each shared resource, and that password remains the same for all users who access the resource. Again, there are limitations to this.

Although the simple effectiveness of the above two methods might be all that is needed on smaller networks, eventually you will need to consider using user-level access control. This more-sophisticated security relies on Windows 95 verification of users by their log-on password. In other words, you specify exactly which users and groups of users are to have access to a given network resource, and then those users, once they have logged in, automatically gain access to that network resource. For Windows 95 to make use of user-level access, it must use a Windows NT Server user database.

Read-Level and Read-Write-Level Access Control

Both the user- and share-level control methods also allow read-only access as distinct from read-write access. Read-only access makes perfect sense for memoranda, static databases (perhaps a zip code database?), and backups.

Obviously, any such security is only as good as the confidentiality of the passwords. If security is of more than passing interest to you, you should encourage proper choice of user passwords. There are several good computer security books that discuss guidelines for selecting difficult-to-guess passwords. Additionally, keep in mind that you may want to combine share-name hiding with share-level or user-level passwords. In this way, even if someone logs on with a stolen ID and password, he or she may not know a particular resource exists. I wouldn't

Part 5

Networking with Windows 95

count on this, but on the other hand, I wouldn't discredit or overlook even small additional layers of security where they are called for.

Please bear in mind that Windows 95 was not designed to be a really secure operating system. If you do need something more secure, strongly consider using Windows NT—it is one of only a few operating systems that has security incorporated in it at every level, earning it a C2-level security rating. We will look at these and other features of Windows NT in the next chapter.

Chapter 27

Internetworking Windows 95 Workstations with NT

FEATURING

Domains

Adding Windows 95 workstations to the network

As you connect more stations to your Windows 95 peer network, you will sooner or later want to interconnect with one or more Windows NT Workstations or Servers. My goal in this chapter is to learn how to network Windows 95 stations with one or more Windows NT stations functioning as a server for files, printers, and applications. Adding one or more Windows NT servers to your network provides you with an array of powerful options and tools that can help maximize the usefulness and productivity of your Windows 95 workstations—especially in the areas of security, performance, and network administration.

Some Networking Philosophy

In the preceding chapter you saw how each networked peer showed up in the Network Neighborhood as a computer icon. Each station's shared printers and folders were available to anyone who double-clicked on a particular computer or created a map to one of the shared drives or printers. This is great as far as it goes, but consider how it would be if you had two hundred, a thousand, even several thousand stations on the network all appearing in Network Neighborhood. Clearly, the neighborhood concept would become very confusing to use and a *nightmare* for the network administrator. What is needed then is a way to organize these stations into groups, and perhaps groups of groups, so visualizing and working with the stations becomes both more manageable and efficient: thus the concept of *workgroups*. First introduced in the Windows for Workgroups product, the subdividing of Windows workstations into workgroups helps free the members of each workgroup to maintain, support, and use only those resources needed by their workgroup. All other network resources may still be *physically* connected, but the workgroup sees and makes use of only those resources directly relevant to their area. From the user's vantage point, 95 percent of the clutter is removed from Network Neighborhood, and the neighborhood becomes a familiar metaphor once more. And where security is needed, passwords can be assigned within the workgroup on either a per-resource or a per-user and groups-of-users basis.

Smaller networks—say fifty or fewer workstations total—might find that this workgroup approach is a sufficient and easy enough means of organizing the network resources and users, assuming subdivision into multiple workgroups. But with very large networks, workgroups are not adequate either because there's no way to oversee all the different workgroups. Management of at least the centralized networking resources on larger networks requires being able to access and configure user accounts and network resources in a way that transcends the boundaries of individual workgroups.

Domains

For ease of organizing and managing larger networks, Microsoft came up with the idea of *domains*. Domains are similar to workgroups but provide the ability to group all users in a single user database. This database resides on the Windows NT Server domain controller. For more specific information on NT Server, take a look at *Mastering Windows NT Server 3.5* (Sybex, 1995). When you log onto a domain from the Windows 95 log-on dialog box, you are authenticated as a specific user with specific access rights. These access rights are the basis for your ability to access shared resources on the network such as a directory or printer.

 NOTE Throughout this chapter, I am speaking of NT version 3.5 or later. If you are still running NT or NT Advanced Server version 3.1, you will notice a marked performance increase by upgrading to version 3.5 or later.

NT Workstation v. NT Server

Although in this chapter I will be primarily concentrating on Windows NT in its capacity as a server, NT can also be used as a workstation and as a peer of Windows 95 stations. In fact, Microsoft emphasizes these dual uses by currently selling two different "flavors" of NT, appropriately labeled NT Workstation and NT Server. While both can be used as servers and both can be used as workstations, each has certain optimizations that better suit it to one of the two uses. Why, you may wonder, would you want to use NT on a workstation? If you plan to run NT services software or certain high-end graphics software, need beefed-up security or support for non-FAT file systems, or have a non–Intel-compatible workstation, you will need Windows NT rather than Windows 95. Software developers, CAD users, and scientists doing math-intensive work might need or prefer Windows NT over Windows 95 for a combination of these features. Some programmers, for example, will have both Windows 95 and Windows NT installed on their stations and can boot to either operating system to develop and test their software. So without further ado, let's look at the differences between NT Workstation and NT Server.

While NT Workstation can certainly function as a server, it (unlike NT Server) has the following limitations:

▶ It cannot function as a domain controller.

▶ It has a maximum of ten simultaneous client connections.

▶ It does not provide gateway services to Novell Netware.

▶ It does not provide network services for Apple workstations.

▶ It has a limit of two CPUs (for Symmetric Multiprocessing).

Let me clarify these briefly. First, and perhaps most notably, NT Workstation cannot be used as a domain controller. As mentioned above, a domain controller is where the user database resides. NT Workstation can, however, log onto a domain and can function as an additional server within an existing domain. Despite this limitation, I do want to emphasize that NT Workstation can perform very ably as a server for a workgroup of Windows 95 stations. Where cost is an issue and the ten-client limit is not a problem, NT workstation might well be the best choice. The ten-connection limit, by the way, does not prevent NT Workstation from having more than ten user accounts or from recognizing more than ten other stations on a network. It simply means that no more than ten other workstations or servers can be *simultaneously* connected to its disk and printer resources. If you do have one or more Novell Netware servers, consider installing NT Server.

NT Workstation (and of course Windows 95 stations themselves) can easily connect to and use Novell resources—and Windows 95 can even share files and printers back to Novell stations. But for the ultimate in all sorts of connectivity options between Windows and Novell network resources, you definitely want NT Server. And if you have Apple workstations connecting to your network or have a server computer with more than two CPUs, you will need NT Server. NT Server also provides for centralized administration because all the user accounts and groups reside on the domain controller rather than on each individual NT workstation. The above differences between NT Server and Workstation are by no means the only differences, but they are the main points to keep in mind if you're considering buying NT. For the rest of this chapter, I'll be discussing NT Server unless otherwise mentioned.

> **NOTE**   One other interesting point about Windows NT Server is that it can operate as a super workgroup server. When NT Server is configured to run in server mode, instead of as a domain or backup controller, it does not perform any user authentication. In this mode it essentially works just like NT Workstation but with unlimited user connections, and it still includes the rest of the NT Server functionality, like the Novell Gateway Service and Macintosh Services.

Adding Windows 95 Workstations to the Network

To allow your Windows 95 stations to communicate with an NT server, you must make sure they are using one of the protocols used by the NT server. In most cases, this will probably be either NetBEUI or IPX/SPX—or if you have a really big network, you may be using TCP/IP. Remember, on a small Windows-only network (where no connections to Novell or other systems are needed) NetBEUI will be your fastest protocol. Again, you just need to make sure the Windows 95 stations are talking the same language as your server.

Adding Windows 95 Workstations to an NT Server

Once the protocols have been configured, you need to take the following steps so your Windows 95 stations can share network resources with an NT server.

1. Use the right-click ➤ Share Properties dialog box on your Windows 95 stations to share any printers, drives, and/or folders that you want the NT station (and the other Windows 95 stations) to be able to access. Add any security restrictions (either share level or user level) desired.

NOTE To use user- or group-level access rights, you must be part of a Windows NT domain.

2. Use NT's File Manager applet to share any drives or folders you want your Windows 95 stations to access.

3. Use NT's Print Manager applet to share any printer(s) you want your Windows 95 stations to access. Note that NT can share not only any locally attached printers, but also any printers it has access to if they are located on another NT station (either Workstation or Server).

4. If the NT server is a domain server, you will also need to create a user account on the NT server for each Windows 95 user needing access to resources on the NT server. Use NT's User Manager for Domains to create these accounts and then set any desired file restrictions using NT's File Manager and any desired printer or printing restrictions using NT's Print Manager.

5. Choose as appropriate:

   ▶ If you are using NT Server, set each Windows 95 station to log onto the NT domain and enter the correct domain in the domain field at each station. To do this, open Control Panel ➤ Networks and double-click on Microsoft Client for Windows Networks. Click on the Domain check box and type in the name of your NT domain (see Figure 27.1).

   ▶ If you are using NT Workstation, simply make sure you have the same workgroup name specified on the NT workstation as you do for each Windows 95 station that will be part of this workgroup.

After performing these steps, you should be able to open Network Neighborhood on any Windows 95 stations in the workgroup (or domain) and see an icon for the NT server. Using the server browsers in either NT's Print Manager or File Manager, you should now also see your Windows 95 stations appear as additional servers in the workgroup (or domain).

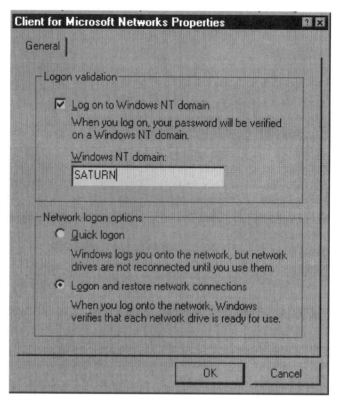

Figure 27.1   Configuring a Windows 95 station to log onto an NT Server domain

    NOTE   If your office has one or more Novell Netware print servers and you are running NT Server, you can use Print Manager to share Netware print servers as well. You must first install and configure the Netware Gateway Services software (supplied with NT Server) and then connect to the Netware print queue before trying to share it. In this way, Windows 95 stations (and even DOS, Windows 3.1, and Windows for Workgroups stations) will not need Novell-specific network drivers loaded to print on the Novell print queue, although you will need to use a printer driver for each printer you use.

Using Shared Printers

One of the major benefits of using Windows NT or Windows 95 is that they both provide the ability to connect to a network printer without installing a printer driver. You will of course need to install a printer driver on the computer that has the local printer attached to it, but your NT and Windows 95 clients do not need to have a printer driver installed. Instead, they will access the remote printer and use the printer driver installed on the remote computer. The only time you will need to install a printer driver is when you connect to a different type of print server, such as a Windows for Workgroups, Novell Netware Server, or Unix server. If you are unfamiliar with how to install a printer or connect to a networked printer, take a look at Chapter 8.

Mapping Windows 95 and Windows NT Shared Drives

You might also at this point wish to establish *persistent* drive mappings on either the NT server or your Windows 95 stations, or both. This will allow you to always have the same drive letters assigned to shared drives (or folders).

For Windows 95 stations, the fastest and easiest way (in my opinion) to map to any drive is simply to right-click on Network Neighborhood's icon, then select the Map Network Drive option. Just select the drive letter you want to refer to the drive as, type in the correct *machine name\drive name*, and press the OK button. Note that the Reconnect on Login option is enabled by default; this is probably what you want. If not, you can also disconnect from a shared drive quite easily. Right-clicking on Network Neighborhood is again one way to do this, but for disconnecting mapped drives, I find the most straightforward way is to open Network Neighborhood and right-click on the shared drive's icon. Choose the Disconnect option, and you're done.

For NT stations, mapping drive letters to network (shared) drives is accomplished using (again) NT's File Manager. The disk-connecting and mapping procedure for NT is as follows:

1. Open File Manager.
2. Click on the Drives menu option.
3. Select the Connect option.

4. Select the drive letter you want to map to, then use the server browser (the list box in the lower half of the dialog box) to select which server and which shared drive to connect to. Or just type in the *machine name\drive name*.

5. Press the OK button.

6. At this point you may also need to enter a password if the directory share includes share-level password protection.

   Assuming your NT station is going to function primarily as a server, you will probably place some or all of your workgroup's most frequently accessed data on the NT server, both to free up your workstations' loads somewhat and also to get the best performance because you now have a dedicated server. Just keep in mind that NT Workstation can only provide ten simultaneous connections, so its use as a dedicated server will only work well for very small networks.

Chapter 28

Extending Your Networking with Dial-Up Networking

FEATURING

Remote access

Windows 95 and Dial-Up Networking

DCC using a serial or parallel port

In the past few years, the number of mobile computer users has increased dramatically. Both advances in computer technology—in both the hardware and software arenas—and changes in the business climate have driven this sea change. Improved manufacturing techniques have allowed miniaturization only dreamed of ten years ago—clearly, there would be far fewer mobile users if everyone still had to carry around a seventeen-pound Compaq luggable. And improved communication interfaces have allowed users to access other computers without having to memorize obscure Unix or AT modem commands.

On the business side, the near-universal reliance on computers has driven the cost of being disconnected from the network so high that technology managers have had to provide remote access to their off-site users. That, coupled with the downsizing and reengineering trends that forced users out of the office and off to client sites, created the demand for remote access at about the same time advances in computer technology provided the means.

Mobile users are everywhere. Because computer-toting travelers are so ubiquitous these days, few self-respecting motels and hotels fail to provide RJ-11 data jacks on their phones. I no longer ask if a hotel is modem-friendly; I simply assume that because they are still in business they provide data jacks. While I still carry a telephone patch cable with alligator clips on one end, it has been more than a year since I stayed in a hotel so far in the Dark Ages that I actually had to splice their phone cord and use it.

In this chapter, I will first cover the options Windows 95 provides for remote connections and help you choose the best one for your particular circumstance. Next, I'll examine the hardware requirements for effective remote commuting over phone lines and take an in-depth look at *Dial-Up Networking*, as Microsoft Plus' remote-node client is called. Finally, I will cover specific issues you need to address when using remote access, such as security.

NOTE   Dial-Up Networking is an option available in Microsoft Plus, an add-on product for Windows 95. Please see Chapter 32 about procuring and installing this product.

Remote Access, Your Computer, and You

If you need to allow off-site users to connect to your network, you essentially have two choices: remote control or remote node.

Remote-control programs use standard telephone lines and provide on-demand connections. Remote control works just as you would expect from the name. You sit down at the remote computer, it dials into a host computer, and then you can actually control the computer you dial into from the computer you have dialed in from. The leading remote-control products include Norton PCAnywhere, Carbon Copy, and Co-Session. When you type or move the mouse on the remote computer, the software sends the keystrokes and mouse movements to the host computer for processing. In turn, the software transmits any screen updates such as dialog boxes or drop-down menus from the host back to the remote computer for display. If the user wants to run an application, he or she launches the application on the host computer.

Remote node works on an on-demand basis just like remote control, but rather than taking over the host computer, the remote computer uses the host computer as a server. This places the remote node directly on the network. In other words, the phone line becomes an extension of the network cable. This allows the user to request file and print services just as if he or she sat right next to the file server. When a user starts an application, it runs on his or her local computer, not on the host computer as in remote-control systems.

Remote node and remote control both provide network connectivity, but they use two entirely different approaches to providing remote access. The primary difference between these two types of remote-access software is that remote-control software actually takes over complete control of the host system, while remote-node software just uses the modem to provide a network interface to the host system.

Windows 95 and Dial-Up Networking

A mobile user can use Dial-Up Networking, Microsoft Plus' remote-node software, to seamlessly connect remote resources. While early versions of Windows included a version of Dial-Up Networking, called Remote Access Services (RAS), it was clearly an add-on feature. To use it, you had to start it separately before accessing shared resources on a remote computer. Installing Dial-Up Networking from Microsoft Plus (see Chapter 32) places the remote-node software directly into the core operating system so you can access remote resources just as you can local ones. Whenever you try to open a remote file (whether through the File ➤ Open dialog box or by double-clicking on the file), Windows 95 automatically starts Dial-Up Networking and establishes the remote connection with the host computer.

Dial-Up Networking uses the Telephone Application Programming Interface (TAPI), Microsoft's proposed standard for integrating telephones and computers. Because TAPI allows multiple applications to share a single line, one application can wait for a call while another dials out.

What is the point, you may ask; when one application dials out the line is busy, so waiting applications can't receive a call anyway. Suppose, for example, you have Microsoft Fax waiting to receive incoming faxes and you want to use Dial-Up Networking to download a file from a computer in a satellite office. In earlier versions of Windows, you would have had to shut down the fax software before you could use the modem for any other purpose. Because Dial-Up Networking uses TAPI, you can leave Fax running in the background as you connect to a remote computer. As soon as you finish with Dial-Up Networking, Fax will pick up any incoming faxes.

Another benefit of TAPI is its support of Dial Helper, shown below, which allows you to define phone numbers in location-independent fashion.

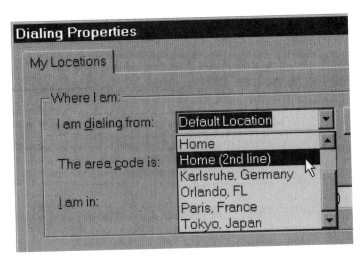

This way, you can associate a single number with any resource. If you change locations, you simply change the Dial Helper location rather than having to reenter the number. When you want to call that number from the office, Windows 95 will prefix it with a 9 so your PBX can distinguish it from an internal call and thus give it an external line. When at home, Windows 95 will prepend a *70 to turn off call waiting. Finally, when on the road, it will enter your calling-card information for you.

Along with its support of TAPI, Windows 95 further simplifies Dial-Up Networking by supporting the unimodem infrastructure. You can think of unimodem as the modem equivalent of the Windows printer subsystem. Rather than require each application to manage its own printing, Windows 95 allows the application to send a print job to the printer subsystem, which then passes the job to a printer driver specifically designed for the printer in use. Unimodem does the same thing; it provides a single interface for any application requiring communication services. When an application wants to access a modem, it sends a packet or *communication job* to Unimodem. Unimodem then passes the packet off to the modem-specific driver.

Anytime you want to connect to a remote computer, you must keep three questions in mind. What type of server or host do you want to connect to, how will you connect with it, and what communication protocol will you use? Luckily, Windows 95 supports the majority of the options available. Better yet, Dial-Up Networking will negotiate with the host and automatically configure itself using the best set of options that both it and the host support.

Windows 95 supports the following remote-node servers:

- Windows 95 Dial-Up Server
- Windows NT 3.x RAS
- Novell NetWare Connect
- Microsoft LAN Manager Remote Access Servers
- Windows for Workgroups 3.x RAS (if you have the separate WFW RAS server installed)
- Shiva LanRover (and compatibles) dial-up router
- Third-party PPP and SLIP servers, including Internet access providers

NOTE At the time this was written, Dial-Up Server support was removed from Windows 95. It will be provided as an add-on package in Microsoft Plus (see Chapter 32).

If you are like the vast majority of Windows 95 users, you will use standard modems to establish asynchronous connections over Plain Old Telephone Service (POTS)—residential and business phone lines. To accommodate users with additional requirements, Dial-Up Networking also supports:

▶ PBX modems

▶ Integrated Systems Digital Network (ISDN)

▶ Parallel port or null modem over a serial connection

Just as you have a choice of protocols when plugging directly into your local-area network, Dial-Up Networking can communicate with any of the following protocols:

▶ NetBEUI

▶ TCP/IP

▶ IPX/SPX

If your network has either an NT Server or NetWare server, Windows 95 will fully support user-based security, allowing you to grant different users varying levels of access to your computer and the rest of the network. If your server is running NT, Windows 95 additionally supports domain-trust relationships and centralized network security administration.

 TIP If you plan to dial into a computer running either Windows NT 3.x (Advanced) Server or Workstation, make sure the computer's owner or the network administrator has granted you dial-in access. When you first install Remote Access Services (RAS) it does not give dial-in privileges to anyone, not even the administrator. You can start up the RAS server and, unless you have explicitly granted someone dial-in rights, it will be useless.

Once you have connected to a remote computer, you can use any of its shared resources, be they files, printers, or other modems (for faxing), just as if you were in the same office building connected with Ethernet or Token Ring.

Besides the resources on the single computer you're dialed into, you may also use the services of any other computer in the workgroup (or the NT domain)—assuming you've been given access. In other words, if you dialed into your office computer from home, you could copy the files from any computer that your office computer can see or print a report on any printer your office desktop can access. You can, of course, restrict access to the rest of the network if you choose.

Setting Up Your Modem for Dial-Up Networking

As with all other hardware, Windows 95 provides a Wizard for installing your modem(s). You can activate it either through the Hardware Installation Wizard or by double-clicking on the Modems icon in the Control Panel. The following steps use the Hardware Installation Wizard:

1. If you have an external modem, make sure it is properly connected to your computer and turned on.

2. Open up the Control Panel by selecting it from the Start ➤ Settings menu.

3. Double-click on Add New Hardware.

4. This will bring up the Hardware Installation Wizard welcome screen. Select Next.

5. From the next screen, select Modem from the list of specific hardware, then press Next.

6. The next window asks you whether you want Windows 95 to automatically detect the modem type or select from a list of modems. I usually let Windows 95 try to detect the new modem, so go ahead and press Next. (This is the first screen you would have seen had you double-clicked on the Modems icon in the Control Panel.)

7. Once the Hardware Installation Wizard has finished, it will ask you to verify the modem type. If Windows 95 failed to detect your modem correctly, press the Change button and the Hardware Installation Wizard will take you to the window shown in Figure 28.1. If Windows 95 correctly identified your modem, which is usually the case, skip to step 11.

8. First, select the manufacturer of your modem. If it is not listed and you have an installation disk from the manufacturer, press the Have Disk button. If you do not have a disk, try using the Generic Modem driver appropriate for your modem speed. These drivers will work for most Hayes-compatible modems.

9. Next choose the specific model or modem speed.

10. Press OK.

11. Press Finish, and you are done.

Part 5

Networking with Windows 95

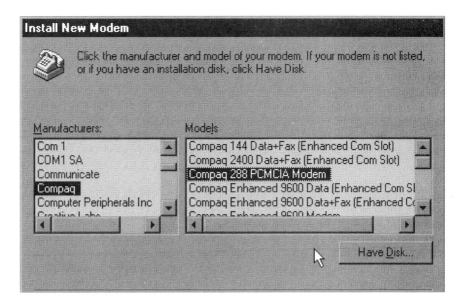

Figure 28.1 *Selecting a specific modem*

NOTE   If you have a PCMCIA modem, you may find that Windows 95 installs a generic modem driver for it. This is because many modem manufacturers use modems designed by someone else.

Now that you have installed your modem, you can install and set up both a Dial-Up Networking client and server. The client allows you to dial into other computers. The server portion allows other computers to dial into yours.

Setting Up Dial-Up Networking on Your Computer

To install Dial-Up Networking, choose it when you install Microsoft Plus (see Chapter 32). Once you have the Dial-Up Networking component installed, you need to set it up.

1. Select Dial-Up Networking from the Start ➤ Programs ➤ Accessories menu. Alternatively, you can double-click on the Dial-Up Networking folder in My Computer. Either way, you get to the screen below.

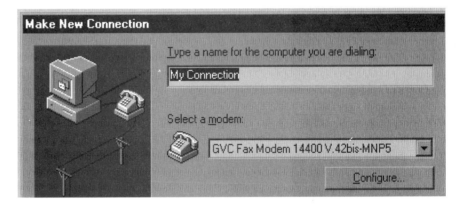

2. Give your connection a name, such as *Al's Desk in the East Wing*.

3. If you have more than one modem, select the modem you want to use.

4. Press Next. This leads you to the screen shown on the next page where you enter the particulars for this connection.

5. Enter the area code and phone number.

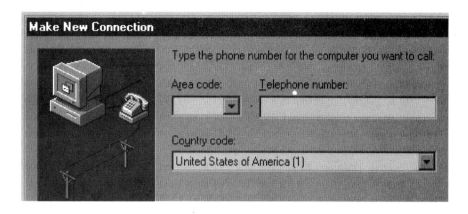

6. If necessary, change the country code.

7. Press Next.

8. You are now done. Verify the name and press Finish to save the connection.

   Now that you have set up Dial-Up Networking, whenever you open up the Dial-Up Networking folder there will be two icons: the connection you just created—Al's Desk in the East Wing in my example—and Make New Connection. If you select this second icon, Windows 95 will use the same Wizard to lead you through setting up a connection to another remote-node server.

   Now that you have Dial-Up Networking installed and configured, you can use the Dial-Up Networking client to dial into other computers. You are now ready for the next section where you will learn how to take full advantage of Dial-Up Networking.

Using Dial-Up Networking

As noted earlier, Dial-Up Networking allows you to leverage the near-universal reach of the phone system to extend your network to any location with a phone line. But just because you can, it does not mean you should. You will need to exercise some caution when using remote resources over a dial-up connection because your connection is much slower than a normal network connection. While you might not think twice about SUMing an XBase table (DBF) across a Token

Part 5

Networking
with Windows 95

Ring connection, trying this over a Dial-Up Networking link will produce a very disappointing performance. The same goes for starting up applications that reside on the remote computer. In both cases, the cause of the poor performance is the same: Dial-Up Networking must transfer the entire file over the phone link. For example, starting Fox-Pro from a remote computer requires the transfer of the entire 2.5-MB executable. Instead of taking a few seconds to load from a local hard disk, it takes about 20 minutes over a 14.4K modem connection.

> **TIP** Whenever you want to run any application during a Dial-Up Networking session, make sure you have the application on your local hard drive *and* in your path. This will ensure that you run the local version and avoid passing the entire executable across the wire.

With Windows 95 you have three ways to establish a remote connection:

▶ explicit

▶ application initiated

▶ implicit

With an explicit connection, you must manually initiate the connection. As you might expect, an application-initiated connection is started by an application calling the remote-node software. As for implicit connections, Windows 95 starts these when it can find a resource neither locally nor on the physical network (i.e., via your network adapter card).

Explicit Connections

Connecting to a remote computer with an explicit connection is very similar to creating a RAS connection with Windows for Workgroups 3.11 or Windows NT.

When you create an explicit connection, you manually dial up the remote computer and log on. Once you have done this, the remote computer and all its share points show up in your Network Neighborhood.

You can manipulate these resources just as you would any other computer's resources—except that it's much slower.

To use Windows 95 Dial-Up Networking to explicitly connect to a remote computer:

1. Open up the Dial-Up Networking folder by selecting Dial-Up Networking from the Start ➤ Programs ➤ Accessories menu. Alternatively, find the Dial-Up Networking folder in My Computer and double-click on it.

2. Double-click on the icon you created in the previous section. This will bring up a dialog box like the one shown in Figure 28.2.

3. Enter the password, if any, for this resource. If you are connecting to a computer with user-based security, enter your log-in name and password.

4. Click on the Connect button.

Part 5

Networking with Windows 95

Figure 28.2   Connecting to a remote network

Windows 95 will now initiate a process that will result—if all goes well—in a connection to the remote computer. As the negotiation between the two computers progresses, Windows 95 gives you periodic updates to reassure you the process has not gone awry.

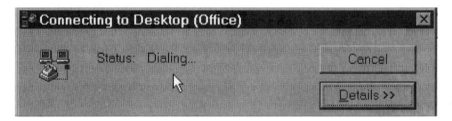

Now that you have manually initiated the connection, you will remain connected until you click on the Disconnect button or time out your session connection.

Application-Initiated Connections

Windows 95 also allows application developers to create programs that will establish Dial-Up Networking connections themselves rather than forcing the user to initiate the session manually.

A Dial-Up Networking-enabled application will take responsibility for automatically connecting to a Dial-Up Networking server as needed. The application uses Windows 95's Remote Access Session API to select a server, initiate a connection, and later disconnect the session. Besides allowing applications to initiate their own connections, the Remote Access Session API also reports the status back to the calling application. This way, if the server is unavailable for some reason (like the line being busy), the application can try again later.

The Exchange client provided with Windows 95 serves as an excellent example of an application that takes advantage of the Remote Access Session API. If you have configured Exchange for remote access, it will automatically use Dial-Up Networking to connect to your mail server anytime you try to access your mailbox. You can change Exchange's connection method by opening up Microsoft Exchange Profiles in the Control Panel and then selecting Properties ➤ Microsoft

Mail ➤ Properties ➤ Connection (for more information on Exchange, see Chapter 15). As soon as it is connected to the mail server, Exchange will send all your outgoing mail, retrieve any new messages, and then disconnect.

Implicit Connections

Establishing a Dial-Up Networking implicit connection to a remote computer is just like connecting to that same computer in the office—simply double-click on the network object. Depending on the type of object you clicked on, Windows 95 may try to automatically create an implicit Dial-Up Networking connection. Whenever you have Dial-Up Networking installed, the following circumstances will cause Windows 95 to establish an implicit connection:

▶ You double-click on a link pointing to a remote resource.

▶ You try to use a network resource while disconnected from a network.

▶ Either you or an application you are using specifies a resource using a Universal Naming Convention (UNC) name (i.e., \\serve name\share point), and Windows 95 cannot find it on the local-area network. Remember that Windows 95 references printers via their UNC names (\\server name\printer name), so printing to a remote printer will also trigger an implicit connection.

▶ You try reconnecting to a remote OLE object not located on the local network.

▶ An application tries to connect to a named pipe.

Whenever you try to access a resource either by directly double-clicking or through an application request, Windows 95 first tries to find it locally on your computer or out on your LAN. If it fails to locate the resource, Windows 95 gives you the dial-in dialog box shown in Figure 28.3, asking if you want to connect to the resource through Dial-Up Networking.

It then checks the Registry for the Dial-Up Networking entry for the server associated with the object. If it finds a server, it establishes the connection automatically. If it cannot find a server associated with the object, it prompts the user to either select the proper Dial-Up Networking connection for the object or to enter a new one, as shown

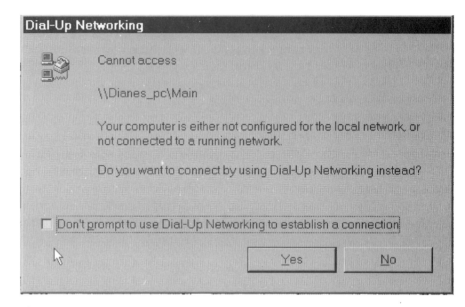

Figure 28.3   *Windows 95 asks the user if it should connect to a remote resource via Dial-Up Networking.*

below. With this information, Dial-Up Networking tries to establish a connection to the server.

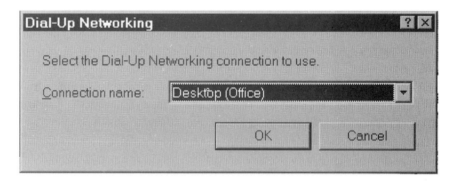

If it succeeds and successfully establishes a Dial-Up Networking connection, Windows 95 stores the name of the connector in the Registry so the next time you click on the object or enter its name in a File ➤ Open dialog box, it does not have to prompt you to select the server.

NOTE According to the documentation, when prompted for the name of a remote server, you can either select an existing server or enter a new one. (In the beta used to write this book, however, there is no means to enter a new server save for going back to the Dial-Up Networking folder and double-clicking on New Connection.)

Which of the three connection modes you use most often depends on the type of work you do. If you are a network manager and your job requires you to manage several remote networks, you will probably find yourself using explicit connections most often, as they give you the greatest amount of control over your remote session. Less technical users will probably rely on implicit connections because they are less hassle. Whether you use application-initiated connections depends on whether you purchase any remote-access–enabled applications. Even so, you might end up establishing the connections yourself rather than relying on the application to do it for you; this way, once you have a connection to a remote server, you can do several tasks online rather than having the enabled application simply hang up when it is done with the first task.

Advanced Configurations for Dial-Up Networking

In this section I will cover the advanced settings you will find most useful. When configuring Dial-Up Networking, there are three sets of parameters you can edit:

▶ dialing locations

▶ server type

▶ modem configurations

You can select a dialing location each time you establish a connection. Whenever you change locations, your location selection only remains in effect for that one connection. You set the other two parameters— server type and modem configuration—in the Connection property sheet. Any change you make there affects all subsequent connections to that server. Modem configuration is covered in Chapter 13.

Server Type

Changing the server type is the last of the Dial-Up Networking settings we will discuss. With the exception of ensuring you have the line speed set to the modem's maximum data rate, the Server Type options will have the greatest impact on the performance of Dial-Up Networking.

To bring up the Server Type Properties:

1. Open the Dial-Up Networking folder from My Computer.

2. Right-click on the connection you want and select Properties from the drop-down menu. This brings up the Dial-Up Networking Connection Properties box.

3. Select the modem whose Properties you wish to edit. Remember, Dial-Up Networking will use whichever modem you select to establish your connection. As with the Modem Configuration Properties, you can set the Server Type options on a per connection, per modem basis.

4. Click on the Server Type button to open up the dialog box shown in Figure 28.4.

As you can see, Windows 95 allows you to configure three properties:

Server Type: Windows 95 will connect to four types of Dial-Up Networking servers: NetWare Connect; Point-to-Point Protocol (PPP) servers such as Windows 95, Windows NT 3.5, and Internet access providers; Serial-Line Internet Protocol (SLIP) hosts; and Windows for Workgroups 3.x and Windows NT 3.1. By default, whenever Windows 95 establishes a Dial-Up Networking connection, it assumes the computer on the other end is a PPP server. If it isn't, Windows 95 cycles through the other three possibilities until it succeeds in making a connection or fails on all four. If you know the type of server to which you will connect (and you probably do), you will reduce connection time by selecting the proper type in this field. A warning, however: if you select the incorrect type of server, Windows 95 will not cycle through the other options. Rather, it will give up after trying your selection.

Enable software compression: As a rule, data compression will increase the effective data-transfer rate. These days, most modems support compression themselves, so you can have either the software (your computer) or the hardware (the modem) compress the data for you. For almost all types of data, software compression will

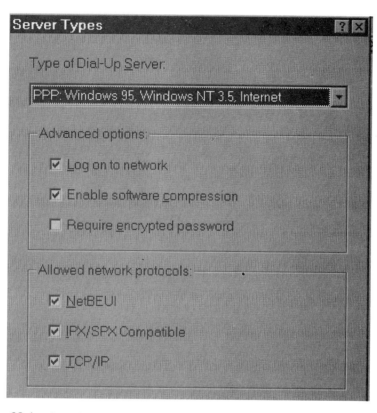

Figure 28.4 **Editing the Server Type Properties**

provide superior performance to hardware compression. As you probably know, data compression works through a pattern-recognition algorithm that reduces redundancies in the data. Because Windows 95 provides more memory for storing patterns than your modem, software compression has a better chance of recognizing complex patterns and thus of compressing the data as much as possible. The only time data compression does not increase performance—and in fact may reduce it—is when you transfer already highly compressed data such as ZIP files. If you plan to transfer ZIP files in a given Dial-Up Networking session, turn off software compression. Along the same lines, if you choose to use software compression, be sure to turn hardware compression off.

Require encrypted passwords: This is a security feature. By checking this box, Windows 95 will scramble your password as it transmits it across the phone lines so no one tapping your line can steal your password. (For additional information about

Dial-Up Networking and security, see the following section.) If you check this box, make sure the server can understand and decrypt the password.

Dial-Up Networking and Security

Whenever you allow dial-in access to your network, you open it up to everyone who has a modem. Before you set up a Dial-Up Networking host, you need to take a good look at the risks involved and design your security model to minimize them. Some network managers go so far as to forbid dial-up access to any of their machines, regardless of the circumstances. While this is a Draconian step, you do need to give security some thought.

Before setting up a Dial-Up Networking server, your first level of network security was not the user accounts and log-ins, but the more difficult hurdle of gaining physical access to your network. Dial-Up Networking effectively removes this first (and probably most effective) deterrent.

For a system with remote access, your first line of defense becomes the relative obscurity of your modem's phone number. Before anyone can gain remote access to your network (at least through the telephone lines), the would-be hacker must know your data phone number. Accordingly, you should keep a tight grasp on who knows this number. You cannot, however, keep your modem number a secret. Hackers can (and will) set their modems to dial every number in a given prefix just looking for modems.

The next level in your security model is supplied by the user accounts and passwords. Regardless of how open your company is with its data, instituting a policy of secure log-ins and passwords on any network is a good precaution. This becomes essential when physical access is no longer a requirement for logging onto your network.

You can add security to your network by using Dial-Up Networking's callback feature. When using a Windows 95 Dial-Up Networking server with the callback facility turned on, as soon as the server authenticates a user, Windows 95 drops the line. It then calls the user back at a prearranged phone number. The obvious advantage being that simply figuring out the modem number and guessing the log-in and password combination is not enough to gain access to your network. An unauthorized user must also be at the prearranged phone number.

This scenario also has an obvious drawback: It will not work for users, such as members of your sales force, who move around and thus do not have a consistent phone number. There is also a less obvious security hole: The phone system is not all that secure, and talented phone hackers (phreakers) can reroute a phone call to any location.

NOTE   Many companies implement RAS callback features primarily as a means of controlling phone costs. Callback enables you to control who pays for the call and therefore provides a means of tracking costs. With callback, companies are able to centralize their telecommunications costs to one line (or a group of lines) so they can easily tell how much money they are spending to provide their free-spirited users with ready access to corporate resources. Additionally, callback allows them to route calls through the least-expensive channels available, whether it be WATS lines or lines purchased though a reseller.

On top of these security measures, you can use several third-party security devices such as random-number generators and encrypted-access modems with Dial-Up Networking to further bolster your security.

The best method for maintaining a secure environment is to regularly monitor your network's activity; not only the dial-in portion, but *all* activity. When you notice something unusual, such as repeated (yet unsuccessful) log-in attempts or abnormally high traffic at strange times, investigate it at once to find out the cause. While the answer may be simply an employee working late or someone who forgot their password, it may also be someone trying to break into your system.

Direct Cable Connect (DCC)
Using a Serial or Parallel Port

When you installed the Dial-Up Adapter in your Control Panel ➤ Networks dialog box, you may not have realized that this same driver is used for both RAS and for Direct Cable Connect (DCC) support. Windows 95's DCC is a wonderful little feature that lets you have a fully operational network connection between any two PCs connected only by their serial (modem/mouse) ports or parallel (printer) ports.

If you find working over a RAS connection at 14.4K usable but still really slow, you may be pleasantly surprised at the networking performance DCC provides—considering you are not actually using a networking card. To be sure, RAS and DCC were designed for different uses, and each can be an ideal tool for the job, depending on the circumstances. RAS is great when you need to connect to a computer (or network) that is some distance away and your only connection can be via phone line or digital or leased line. DCC, on the other hand, is most helpful when you need a temporary network connection between two PCs where one or both of them do not have network interface cards installed.

If you're one of the growing numbers of laptop users, you probably appreciate having the mobility of the laptop but still find times when you could really use a $5\frac{1}{4}$-inch floppy drive, or a CD-ROM drive, or just wish you could copy files up to the network or down to your laptop faster than with floppies. Using DCC, you can very easily and quickly connect that laptop to any other computer running Windows 95 as long as you have either a serial-to-serial or a parallel-to-parallel cable designed for data transfer between two computers (LapLink-style cables). There's a place near where I live that sells nice, long parallel cables for only $5, and if you find a similar deal, I'd recommend buying at least a few. Leave one cable connected to a parallel port on your desktop PC at home and another at the office, and when you go on trips with your laptop, pack a cable along with it. It is really a joy to simply connect the cable to the printer port on your laptop, start DCC on both PCs, and within seconds actually have a network connection, allowing you to access any shared resources on whichever PC is configured as the host.

The first thing you will need to do to set DCC up on your system, if you haven't done so already, is add the Dial-Up Adapter driver to your list of network components. Just open My Computer ➤ Control Panel ➤ Networks, click on Add, click on Adapter, select Microsoft, and select Dial-Up Adapter. Click on OK, and you're all set. To start up the DCC applet, look in your Accessories folder or click on Start ➤ Programs ➤ Accessories, then choose Direct Cable Connect.

When you start up DCC for the first time, it will ask you to select whether this PC will be configured as a Guest or Host PC, as shown in Figure 28.5. Usually it makes sense to make your desktop PC the host and the laptop the guest, but remember that the guest PC is the

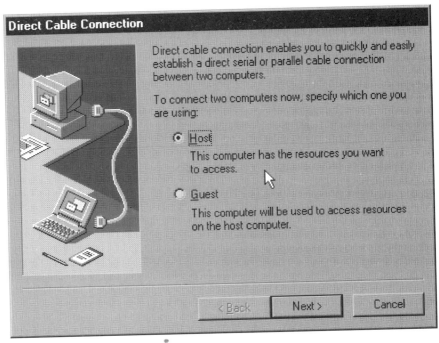

Figure 28.5   *Configure one PC as Host, the other as Guest. The guest PC is the one that will access the host PC's shared resources.*

one that will need to use the folders, drives, and/or printers located (and shared) on the host PC. Also, if one PC happens to be on a network, you might want that one to be the host because it will allow the guest to access any resources the host normally can.

Finally, you have to select which port you want to use with DCC (see Figure 28.6). If at all possible, you want to use a parallel port. Not only is it quite a bit faster, it will also usually be easier to find an available parallel port on the computers you'll be connecting to.

TECH TIP   One time I was installing DCC, no parallel ports showed up in the ports list. After checking out my Device Manager list in Control Panel ➤ Devices, I discovered that the parallel port was disabled because it conflicted with a sound card. After reconfiguring the sound card to a different IRQ, the printer port showed up in DCC's list of available ports.

Part 5

Networking with Windows 95

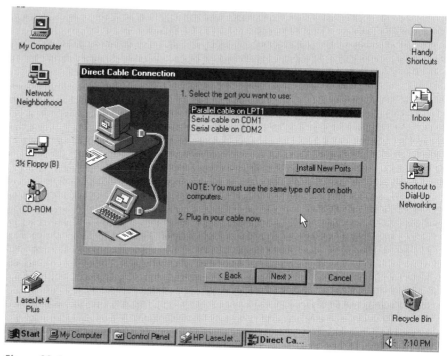

Figure 28.6   *Configuring DCC to use a parallel port. Note that both PCs will need to be using the same type of port (either serial or parallel).*

Now that you've configured one PC, you need to do the same on the other one, of course making sure you choose the same port type (either serial or parallel), and set one PC to Host and the other to Guest. Then, connect your cable between the two ports, click on Listen on the host PC, and click on Connect on the guest PC. After a few seconds, you should see a message similar to this:

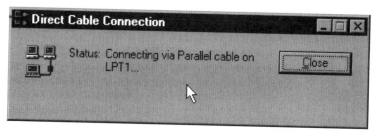

If you've entered a password (on both sides), you will next see *Verifying user id and password*, and then the connection will be established. Once the connection has been established, you can minimize the DCC status dialog box on both PCs to get them out of the way.

At this point, you will be able to access the host PC from Network Neighborhood and thus can map drives, install a printer driver corresponding to any printers on the host side, and so on—just like we did back in Chapter 26 while setting up the peer network.

TIP   If you will be using DCC frequently on a particular PC, you may want to drag the DCC icon onto your Desktop for easy access. Or, if you prefer, drag and drop the DCC icon onto your Start button; the next time you click on Start, you will have DCC as one of the Start menu options.

By now you should have a good understanding of the many options Windows 95 gives you for interconnecting (networking) your computers. In the next chapter I'll discuss troubleshooting.

Chapter 29

Troubleshooting Your Windows 95 Network

FEATURING

Aside from reducing your system bottlenecks, running backups, and dealing with daily user issues—such as creating new accounts, setting up new stations, adding servers, and so on—much of a network administrator's time is typically spent fixing various network problems. In this chapter, I will look first at the process of troubleshooting network problems, then step through several of the most frequent types of problems and show how to resolve them. At the end of this chapter, I'll discuss some procedures for getting a Windows 95 station back into operation after a hard-drive failure.

Not only are networking problems sometimes difficult to track down, they also typically require a quick resolution because frequently a network problem means downtime for one or more network users. When you first learn of a problem, it helps to assign it a priority by taking into account criteria such as the following:

▶ How many users are (or will be) affected?

▶ What type of work (emergency, critical, or lower priority) is affected?

▶ How difficult does the problem appear to be?

▶ Does the problem have a known solution (at your organization) or are you dealing with something new?

TIP   It is a very good policy to always log problems as they occur. Include the time and date, who reported the problem, initial prognosis, and estimated time to resolution. And, most importantly, be sure to add a detailed description both of the problem and the steps taken to fix the problem. While such a log requires a certain time (and discipline) investment, it can pay off significantly the next time a problem occurs. Be sure to make frequent backups of your log—including regular printed copies. (Keeping it on the computer gives you the ability to do quick searches.)

Dealing with networking problems—and with computer problems in general—is largely a matter of deduction, eliminating possibilities through questioning, trial and error, and adverting to past experience. This is why keeping a problem-and-resolution log can be so effective. If someone else is reporting the problem to you, write down what they say and ask questions while the situation is still fresh in their memory. Almost always, the first thing you should ask is, "When was the last time this equipment, software, or whatever, worked correctly?"

The second most helpful question to ask—assuming someone else is explaining the problem to you—is, "What were you doing when you noticed the problem?" (Avoid giving this question an accusatorial tone—you just want to know what led to the problem.) Besides helping to narrow your focus, these questions sometimes point you directly to the root cause of the problem. Sometimes, for example, users will try tightening the keyboard or mouse cables and end up loosening the network cable. Perhaps they turned off the computer without first shutting down. About half the time, the problem was caused by operator error, but if so, rather than chastising the user, show them how to avoid this problem in the future. As much as you may enjoy using computers, don't forget that to some users, they are probably a mystery and even an object of fear. Try to pass on your appreciation of computers whenever possible. A thorough and positive introduction to the computer and occasional user training can go a long way toward eliminating accidental damage to cables, keyboards, and other hardware and software.

Troubleshooting is also helped by having a good memory (or a good set of notes). When was the software on this station upgraded? Which network adapter (and drivers) is it using? When was this cable run? Again, knowing what to look for greatly reduces the number of possibilities you need to look at.

Certain applications may indirectly cause extra troubles for your organization. Maybe an older communications program insists on using an earlier version of Winsock, thus conflicting with Windows 95's built-in version of Winsock. Perhaps some application is opening files in exclusive mode, preventing other users from opening the same file.

Has a new piece of hardware or software recently been added to the station? If so, this is a good place to start looking. Until every system is fully Plug-and-Play aware and has only Plug-and-Play components installed, interrupt and I/O address conflicts will be an ongoing source of problems. The best weapons against such conflicts are these: using identical hardware for all workstations, using the same interrupts and I/O addresses for the same devices in each workstation as much as possible, documenting the card settings on a sheet of paper taped inside each computer, and lastly, making use of a POST (power-on self test) diagnostics card. Such a card fits into the bus of a problem PC and can perform a large array of tests on the computer, reporting the results via LEDs on the card. The Discovery Card from

JDR Microdevices costs about $99 and can find IRQ- and DMA-related conflicts, while a more complex card may cost $1,200 to $1,500 and can identify all devices set to the same IRQ, bad SIMMs, errors on the motherboard, as well as problems with the power supply, serial and parallel ports, and so on. Such errors might otherwise take half a day or longer to diagnose, besides the productivity time wasted while the system is down. I have seen completely configured systems delivered with two serial ports configured to the same address, a network card conflicting with video memory, and even two parallel port adapters, both configured to LPT1, in the same PC. Obviously whoever configured these systems was not using a POST diagnostics card.

For the rest of this chapter, I'll look at some of the most common problems that can plague your Windows 95 network and how you can resolve them most efficiently.

Diagnosing Cable Problems

One of the nicest things about star-topology networks (such as 10BaseT) is the relative ease of diagnosing and fixing cable problems. If all stations on a particular hub suddenly lose their network connection, you should check out your hub. Check the connection from the hub to the server, in particular—assuming you have a dedicated server. If none of the cable connections have pulled loose, try swapping in a different hub. If the stations now connect to the network again, you've found the problem. You can see the practicality of keeping a spare hub around—ideally one identical to what's in use so you can immediately replace the hub if it ever becomes necessary. For diagnostic purposes though, even a hub with a small number of ports lets you try connecting a few stations. If it works, you know there's a problem with the other hub.

On a network using thin coax, however, things are a bit more hairy. First of all, it's much more likely for the whole segment to go down, because of the nature of the connection. Typically what you'll have to do then is perform *binary searching* for the location of the cable break by splitting the network segment in half, seeing which half still works when you connect it to the server, then splitting the bad subsegment in half and repeating this process until you locate the offending cable portion.

On a thin-net coax network, some additional things you'll want to check include making sure the terminators are still connected to each end and that one end is properly grounded, and verifying that the complete length of cable has the same RG number. I have seen strange connection problems surface only months later, and then only intermittently, when someone used a length of cable somewhere in the network that had slightly different impedance than the rest of the network cable.

When single stations lose their connection on a star-type configuration, again the problem-solving process is much easier. The first thing to do (obvious, but frequently effective) is to check that both ends of the cable are connected tightly. If this doesn't take care of the problem, try connecting the hub end of the cable to a different jack on the hub.

> NOTE   One thing I really appreciate about Windows 95 and NT is their ability to auto-reconnect when a connection is temporarily broken. This may seem like a small thing, but it's nice not to have to reboot the station each time; I can just double-click on Network Neighborhood or reopen a folder on a network drive.

If you still aren't able to establish a connection, try whichever of these is less trouble: either swap in a different cable or connect a different PC to the end of the existing cable (use a PC known to have no trouble getting on the network). Using these two tests, you can determine either that the cable is bad (if the new cable worked or the new PC did not) or that the original PC has a network-card problem (if the new PC worked, but the new cable did not work with the original PC). If you determine that the cable is the problem, you might try replacing the cable connector if you are adept at this and think it's a quicker solution than running a new length of cable.

Finally, if you are able to connect to the network, but transferring data across the network seems slow as molasses, you are likely dealing with an inferior quality (or damaged) network cable. Remember, nowadays you want level 5 cable, if possible (and at least level 3); otherwise, you can expect all sorts of problems with throughput on your network.

Diagnosing Network Interface Card (NIC) and Driver Problems

If you have reason to believe a network card may not be functioning properly, here are several things you can try in the order in which you'll most likely want to try them. First, if Windows 95 is already running, go into Control Panel ➤ Networks and check that all network components that should be installed actually are. If not, add them, shut down and restart Windows 95, and again try to get on the network. If this doesn't work, then just to get everything working, you could remove any network (software) components other than these three:

▶ the driver for the installed network card

▶ the protocol(s) you need to get on the network

▶ the appropriate client service (for example, Client for NetWare Networks or Client for Microsoft Networks)

The most important thing is to verify that the card settings match those configured on the driver. To do this, double-click on the card driver (while looking at the installed–network-components list). This should bring up the network card's Properties dialog box (see Figure 29.1). Click on the Resources tab and verify that the settings are correct. Also write down these settings in case you need to pull your network card later to verify that its settings correspond to these.

Another common problem is that the memory-address settings required by the adapter card are not excluded from use by the expanded memory manager. In our example above we would also want to make sure that the `DEVICE=EMM386.EXE` line in `config.sys` also included an `X=E000-E3FF` entry. Otherwise the expanded memory manager would map the NIC memory address to be used as upper memory and could cause connectivity problems. As a quick and easy test to determine an upper memory block (UMB) problem, comment out the expanded memory manager in `config.sys`. This can be accomplished by placing a REM statement in front of the `DEVICE=EMM386.EXE` if using Microsoft's expanded memory manager or `DEVICE=QEMM386.SYS` if using Quarterdeck's QEMM.

Part 5

Networking
with Windows 95

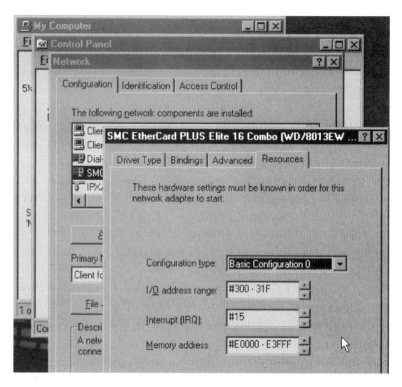

Figure 29.1   Verifying and configuring network-card settings

Next, click on the Driver Type tab. In almost all cases, you'll want the first radio button, *Enhanced mode (32 bit and 16 bit) NDIS driver*, selected—the only reason you ever need real-mode drivers is if you happen to be using a network card for which you cannot find Windows 95 protected-mode drivers or if you want to test network-connectivity problems. For instance, when attempting to solve a connectivity problem, you can install an NDIS 2.0 (real-mode) driver, boot Windows 95 to a command prompt, then try and log onto the network with a **NET LOGON** command. If that works, but the NDIS 3.1 (protected-mode) driver failed, you have at least identified the problem and can begin troubleshooting the protected-mode driver installation. In any case, make sure the setting matches what you need. Also, click on the Bindings tab and verify that a check mark is placed next to the protocol(s) you will need to get on your network.

If you notice any incorrect settings, after changing these you will next want to restart Windows 95 and see if you are now able to connect to the network. Otherwise, the next thing I'd recommend doing is printing out a handy list of equipment and resource settings, which can be done by going to Control Panel ➤ System ➤ Devices and clicking on Print.

If your network card is one that lets you software-configure the IRQ and I/O address, open a DOS window and run this software now. If the settings match what they should be, good. Otherwise, adjust them accordingly.

> **NOTE** Some cards that let you run a software-configuration utility also have one or more jumper settings that need to be set to enable this feature. If your card is like this, you may find your configuration software will not work: either it won't run at all, or when you try to make changes, they won't stick. In this case, refer to your card's documentation for information on enabling the software-configuration option.

If your network card is not software configurable, you'll need to remove the network card to visually inspect it and possibly make changes to it. Again, first print out the system summary report, as it will definitely be helpful in setting your card. Next, shut down Windows 95, turn off the PC and unplug it, remove the PC's cover, and take out the network card. If you're lucky, the network card will have the jumper settings silk-screened near the jumper pads. Otherwise, dredge up your card's documentation and flip to the jumper-settings diagram. Verify that the settings match what your driver is configured to. If not, make changes to the jumpers.

> **NOTE** If your network-card settings match your network-driver settings and you are *still* not able to connect to the network, it's likely either the IRQ or I/O address conflicts with another card. In this case, refer to your system-configuration report and select a different (unused) IRQ and I/O address for your network card.

When you've got your network card configured, gently reinstall it and tighten down the edge bracket with a screw. Replace the PC's cover (you don't want to replace all the screws holding the cover just yet—wait until your network card is verified operational). Then turn the computer back on and make any changes to the network-card driver to synch it with the changes you've made to the card. If you're prompted to shut down and restart Windows 95, do so.

> **NOTE**   When attempting to get network support operational, you may want to start Windows 95 in *safe mode with networking support*. This disables other drivers that may conflict with your network card, reducing the number of factors that can interfere with initially connecting with the network. To boot Windows 95 in this mode, press the F6 key when the computer is first starting (when you see the Starting Windows 95 prompt), before you see the logo screen. (Alternatively, you can press F8, then select Safe Mode with Network Support.)

If you've got any patience left, and you're *still* not able to talk to the network at this point (you're probably a saint!), you might try swapping this network card into a PC that is talking to the network—and perhaps swap that PC's card into the problem PC. This, finally, will tell you one way or another what you need to know. Either the NIC from the bad PC will now work in the good PC, meaning there's still a conflict with another card in the bad PC, or the bad card will also refuse to work in the good PC. If it's a conflict, start removing other cards from the bad PC one by one, bringing up Windows 95 after each time, until you're able to get back on the network. If you're with a large-enough organization to have a POST diagnostic card, you will have put it to use before now, I am sure. Otherwise, you'll be wishing you had one at this point.

If you continue to have no success after futzing with IRQs and I/O addresses some more, try installing a different network card, preferably from a different vendor. If the first card was a jumpered card, do yourself a favor and try a newer card. By the time you're reading this, just about any new network card should at least be software configurable, if not fully Plug-and-Play. Just choose one of the top five or six brands, and you should be up and running again in no time. If not, your problems are way outside the scope of this book and you certainly deserve a prize of some sort for having come this far.

Restoring from a Downed Hard Drive

When you have a station that has undergone a disk crash or for other reasons has damaged system files, you will likely find the system refuses to get further than the initial logo screen before issuing an error message and then hanging at the system prompt. Of course the ideal thing at this point is to simply restore the system files from those back-ups you make every night. Here are the files you will need most if you need to restore from a damaged drive:

From the root directory of the boot drive:

▶ config.sys (if used)

▶ autoexec.bat (if used)

▶ io.sys (hidden, read only, system)

▶ msdos.sys (hidden, read only, system)

▶ command.com

From the \Windows directory (the directory where Windows 95 is installed):

▶ win.ini

▶ system.ini

▶ protocol.ini

NOTE   These next two are the most important (or the most likely to be damaged).

▶ user.dat (hidden, system)

▶ system.dat (hidden, system)

Try booting Windows 95 using the boot menu and selecting Safe Mode. To bring up the boot menu, press the F8 key while the system is first booting. The first thing I usually try running is the *logged to file* option, which tries starting Windows 95 again normally and also creates a file in the Windows 95 directory called BOOTLOG.TXT, which shows each step as it's trying to boot.

Part
5

Networking
with Windows 95

NOTE   If BOOTLOG.TXT isn't in your Windows 95 directory, look in the root directory of the boot drive. If you find it here, it will be marked as a hidden file.

If your system fails again while starting Windows 95, reboot, select *System Prompt only*, go into the Windows 95 directory, and check BOOTLOG.TXT for clues to why Windows wouldn't start. If this doesn't help, try booting using Safe Mode. As a last resort, try booting using *safe mode with command prompt only*. This will at least let you try the following technique.

TECH TIP   When a Windows 95 station will not start Windows 95, the single most likely way to get the station up again fast is to go to the directory Windows 95 is installed in (usually \Windows or \Win95), run attrib -s -h on SYSTEM.* and USER.*, and then make a backup of SYSTEM.DAT and USER.DAT. Finally, copy SYSTEM.DA0 to SYSTEM.DAT, and USER.DA0 to USER.DAT. What this does is restore the backup copies of the system Registry files. If you're lucky, rebooting after doing this will allow you to get back into Windows 95.

If you still cannot get Windows 95 to start, and you've tried replacing the Registry files SYSTEM.DAT and USER.DAT from the backups automatically made by Windows 95, it's looking rather grim. You need to start thinking about reinstalling Windows 95. If you do have a recent full-system backup, try restoring all the files from the Windows 95 directory and all directories under it. If restoring from a backup won't work, your best bet is to dust off your Windows 95 CD-ROM or disks and run the install again.

TIP   If you are only able to boot to a system prompt, do not have a CD-ROM drive locally attached, but have been (up 'til now) part of a network and using an NDIS 2.0 (real-mode) network driver, try going into the Windows 95 directory and typing NET START WORKSTATION. With luck, this will get you on the network and allow you to copy the Windows 95 install files from some other station on the network that *does* have a CD-ROM drive. Of course, you will need to have sufficient disk space (around 35 MB) available, plus space for installing Windows again.

TIP   For those systems on your network that can afford 30-some MB of disk space better than they can afford to be down for some time, copy the contents of the \Win95 install directory from your CD-ROM or diskettes into a unique directory on the hard drive and then reinstall from this directory if you ever need to reinstall Windows 95. You will find this to be noticeably faster than even the fastest CD-ROM drives. And if you want to save even more time, look at creating a setup script file so you can run the reinstall without any prompting for options. (This is an advanced option; you will need to run the NetSetup program, click on Make Script, and then set all the options as you would normally set them interactively.)

When reinstalling Windows 95, first try installing to the same directory you originally installed to. This usually works fine and will let you keep most of your system settings (assuming they haven't been damaged).

What to Do If You Cannot Even Boot to a System Prompt

While rather rare, it is possible to have your system in such a state that it won't even boot but says *invalid system* or some such message. Before taking the extreme measure of reformatting your drive, try booting with the Windows 95 start-up disk you made during setup. If you don't have one of these, go to another station on the network and make one. In case you're not familiar with the process, open Control Panel ➤ Add/Remove Programs, click on the Startup Disk tab, and click on the Create Disk button (after inserting a blank diskette).

Once you've booted with the Windows 95 start-up diskette and are at the command prompt, do the following:

1. Change to the System directory, which is under the Windows 95 directory.

2. Copy the file sys.com to your Windows 95 start-up diskette.

3. Switch to drive A (or B if appropriate) and type **SYS C:**—this should allow your hard drive to at least boot to a Windows 95 command prompt.

4. Remove the diskette and attempt to reboot system.

5. If Windows 95 doesn't start normally, reboot and use the Safe Mode with command prompt only.

At this point, follow the above instructions for restoring the SYS-TEM.DAT and USER.DAT Registry files. If this doesn't work, read the above section about reinstalling Windows 95.

Ideally, you are reading this before any troubles arise and can see some ways to practice preventive medicine, such as keeping an extra hub, cables, and network cards handy for quick replacements in time of failure. You may realize that it makes more sense to use several smaller hubs rather than one or two large ones. And I'm sure you can now better see the utility of making Windows 95 start-up diskettes and regular backups of the system Registry files.

Customizing and Traveling with Windows 95

6

Chapter 30

Using Your Laptop with Windows 95

FEATURING

Power management with APM

Using PCMCIA cards

Using a docking station

Deferred printing

Using the Briefcase to synchronize your files

Portable computing tips

An increasing premium is being placed on portability in the computing arena. Whether you are a traveling salesperson, writer, programmer, teacher, student field scientist, or corporate manager, the freedom that portable computing affords in achieving your goals is hard to rival. As a freelance writer, I've been an advocate of portable computing since its inception. The idea of being chained to a desk is tantamount to incarceration—merely an extension of the oppressive office cubicle that I quit my nine-to-five job years ago to escape.

I went portable as soon as the first viable mobile computer hit the streets sometime about ten years ago. It was the Radio Shack Model-100. With its puny 8-line display (and only 40 characters wide at that) and performance-challenged programs, it wasn't much to write home about. On the other hand, at least you *could* write home *with* it. You could even write home via *e-mail*, using the built-in 300-bps modem and the free CompuServe starter account that came with the machine.

Portable-computing technology has come a long way since then; experts estimate that at the end of 1995, 33 percent of PC computing will be performed on mobile machines. Nowadays a clear majority of PC sales are of the mobile variety. The competition is fierce, the technical developments rapid. Thanks to the feeding frenzy, the last year has brought us high-capacity lithium-ion batteries, 28.8-Kbps cellular modems, a wide array of PCMCIA cards, impressive display panels (that we'll also benefit from as flat-screen TVs), Plug-and-Play cards and computers, miniature pointing devices such as the "eraser head" and the GlidePoint, portable CD-ROM drives, and tiny high-capacity backup devices, just to name a few.

Windows 95 and Portable Computing

So, as a laptop or potential laptop user, what special goodies does Windows 95 have to offer you? Recognizing that computers are leaving the desktop in droves, Windows 95 doesn't just offer a few add-ons for portable users, such as a version of LapLink or specialized LCD color schemes. Much of the overall design concept of Windows 95 was influenced by portable computing needs and the desire of portable computer owners to stretch their (considerable) investment beyond the point of the forced obsolescence that rapid technological evolution often causes.

The basic advantages of running Windows on a portable are obvious: If you have a laptop with enough disk space on it, simply being able to run Windows 95 and your favorite programs anywhere you go is quite benefit enough. Many portable users are rarely in the office or have no office at all, so simply having the use of a computer, however crippled its performance, is terrific. But beyond that, consider some additional mobile abilities of Windows 95:

▶ You can plug and unplug your PCMCIA cards, serial mice, and pointing devices without rebooting Windows. The changes are detected and the correct drivers activated. (You can't plug or unplug bus mice or PS/2 mice, however.)

▶ Have a PCMCIA fax modem? From your hotel-room phone jack you can send and receive e-mail and faxes, surf the Internet, or, using RAS, log onto the network back at your office.

▶ Got a cable to connect your cellular phone to your fax modem? Then do all the above from the beach rather than your hotel room.

▶ If your laptop has a built-in or portable CD-ROM drive, you'll really be in hog heaven. You can run Myst on the beach in Bora Bora. Windows has built-in SCSI drivers to work with most portable CD-ROM drives.

▶ Have a docking station? Windows 95 reconfigures itself appropriately the moment you insert or remove the portable from its docking station, taking best advantage of what's in it.

▶ You can use Drive Space, Stacker, and DOS 6.x-compatible disk compression to double the size of your portable's hard disk.

▶ You can use Advanced Power Management (APM) to wring the most performance out of your battery.

▶ You'll be able to keep files on your desktop and laptop computers synchronized so the most up-to-date files are on the computer you're working on.

▶ You can transfer files between computers quickly via parallel or serial cable and the *direct-cable connect* program.

▶ You can send a file to print from programs even when no printer is available or attached. When you find a printer, your print jobs are all queued up, ready to print.

Notice that all these points fall into one of three general categories: squeezing more out of your hardware, staying connected to the world, and keeping your work organized.

Several of the points listed above are discussed in these other chapters:

▶ For coverage of e-mail, faxing, and Microsoft Exchange, see Part III.

▶ For coverage of the direct-cable connection for transferring files and connecting to the network, see Part V.

▶ For coverage of remote-access services with Dial-Up Connection, see Part V.

▶ For coverage of the disk-compression program, see Chapters 23 and 33.

Power Management with APM

In Chapter 7, I referred to the Power applet in the Control Panel. This applet is for managing the way your laptop uses power. Microsoft and Intel worked together to develop something called APM (Advanced Power Management) to help stretch rundown times on laptop batteries. Windows 95 implements APM version 1.1. The extent to which APM is successful depends on the design of the computer, which CPU it's running (such as whether it's an SL chip or not), whether the hard disk and screen can power down, and so forth. Many laptops have built-in utilities that you run to set up such energy-saving features. Also, because the way energy-saving features are implemented varies from machine to machine, most portables these days come with a custom version of APM designed for them. On some machines, a line in the config.sys file such as

```
devicehigh=c:\dos\apm.sys
```

loads the APM driver so power management is activated. Only APM version 1.0 is loaded this way. If you have such a line, leave it there. It's important.

Some computers (such as many from Toshiba) have APM built into their BIOS chip. In this case, you don't have to have your config.sys load APM for you. In fact, if you try to load APM, you'll get an error message saying your computer has APM built in.

The Power applet's options will vary depending on your computer, the type of processor, and APM. Suffice it to say, however, that you'll probably have a few options to choose from. Figure 30.1 shows the applet's dialog box:

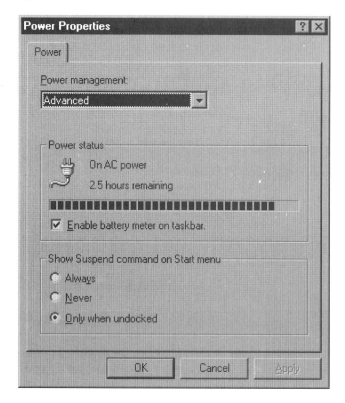

Figure 30.1   *The Power applet in the Control Panel brings up this dialog box from which you can change some settings pertaining to your laptop's power-conservation features.*

The gas gauge is particularly useful if your computer doesn't have another means of informing you of the state of the computer's battery (only laptops with voltage- and current-sensing circuitry will have such a gauge).

Tip   You can also open the Power dialog box by double-clicking on the battery or AC-plug in the *system tray,* which is at the right side of the Taskbar.

Let's take the settings one at a time.

Power Management   The first setting offers a drop-down list from which you choose the type of power management you want active. The options are Advanced, Standard, and Off. Choose Advanced to take advantage of special power-conservation features built into Windows 95. The Standard setting simply uses whatever conservation features you have built into your computer. The Off option deactivates any and all power-saving features of Windows 95.

> **NOTE**   The settings you make in this dialog box don't affect your computer's internal hardware settings. They only affect the degree to which Windows 95 detects any power-saving features of your computer that you've activated. See your computer's manual for instructions on how to adjust such features. For example, for the greatest battery efficiency, you'll still have to use the switches or software utilities that turn on various power-down features.

Normally, you'll want to use Advanced. Windows does some spiffy power-management tricks such as putting a Suspend option on the Start button (see Chapter 3). On some computers, the Shut Down command actually powers off the computer for you without having to touch a switch (having Windows perform the shut-down procedure can prevent data loss and can correctly power down peripheral devices such as PCMCIA cards). Finally, the accuracy of the battery meter is enhanced.

When would you want to turn APM off? Well, some energy-saving features can be annoying. Particularly when you are plugged into the wall outlet, there will be times when you won't want your screen's backlight to turn off or hard disk to power down. You may always want the CPU running at full speed (another trick APM does is to power down the CPU, ports, and keyboard after a period of inactivity). Some computers sense when you're plugged into the wall and then run full bore. Others use a switch or keyboard combination that allows you to manually set conservation options on the fly. You might want to check your computer's manual on how it uses APM and what your options are.

Power Status   Here's your gas gauge, showing remaining battery time. When the option box is turned on, the battery icon (AC plug icon) appears on the Taskbar. Just position the mouse pointer on the little

Part 6

Customizing Windows 95

Taskbar icon and wait a second. The remaining battery time will display. On some machines the setting will display a percentage instead of time.

Suspend Options   If your computer supports this feature, there will be a Suspend option at the bottom of the Start Button, just above Shut Down.

As I mentioned in Chapter 3, this option lets you quickly put the com-

puter into a hibernation state, then pick up where you left off when you power up the computer again. It's a terrific feature. However, not all computers will support it; even if yours does, make sure you save any work before you suspend just in case your laptop's battery runs down before you resume your work. If you leave the computer plugged into the AC outlet, this isn't an issue, obviously.

The three options in the Power dialog box pertaining to Suspend let you choose when the Suspend option will appear on the Start button's menu. Normally, this is set to *Only when undocked*. When the computer is docked, suspending it might not work because any cards and other jazz you might have hooked up to in the docking station may not come back to life when you restart the computer. When docked, just as with desktop machines, save your documents, close your applications, choose Shut Down, and then turn off your computer the normal way.

Using PCMCIA Cards

Great strides in miniaturization in the past year or two have brought us plug-in cards that are no larger than a credit card. Soon to be gone are the days when add-in cards require a toolbox and the nerve to dig inside your PC, where you wind up with little puncture wounds on your fingertips from the metal points on the back of the card. The new little cards plug in effortlessly and are standardized in size, shape, and function. They even identify themselves to your operating system.

They're called PCMCIA cards. It doesn't stand for People Can't Memorize Computer Industry Acronyms, though it should; it stands for Personal Computer Memory Card International Association, a group created in 1989 as a standards body and trade association consisting of manufacturers of semiconductors, connectors, peripherals, systems, and devices, and software developers. The end result for users is a selection of PCMCIA cards ranging from video capture cards to hard disks, network adapter cards, SCSI adapters, and, of course, modems. The cards were at first designed for portables but are now finding their way into desktop systems. Some journals and companies are beginning to call the cards simply *PC cards*.

There are three designations for the PCMCIA cards—Type I, Type II, and Type III. The only difference between the cards is their thickness: Type I devices are the thinnest (3.3 mm thick) and are primarily used for memory devices like flash RAM (cards that are like a low-capacity hard disk without moving parts). Type II cards are 5 mm thick; modems and LAN adapters are the most common of these type. Type III cards are 10.5 mm thick and are used for devices that require more space; for example, hard-disk drives and wireless communication devices. Any PCMCIA slot will accept its own size card as well as smaller cards. Thus, a Type II slot will accept a Type 1 or Type II card, but not a Type III.

There are two major versions of the PCMCIA standard. The first spec was version 1.0, released in September 1990 with only hardware addressed. The second release was version 2.0, issued September of 1991. This version added software specs for input/output cards like modems and hard drives. Release 2.01 contains typographical corrections and no new technical specs. Some of what the specs cover include the hardware configurations for pin assignments (they all have 68 pins), some electrical specifications, and the ability to detect the insertion and removal of the cards to promote *hot swapping*.

> **NOTE** A new PCMCIA spec is under development; it will include 32-bit I/O (currently it is 16-bit) as well as add DMA support (not supported in 2.01), and it will be backward-compatible with current standards.

Adding and Removing Cards

Windows 95 is the first operating system to have Plug-and-Play support for PCMCIA cards. Just insert a card, and it will be detected. You don't have to power down before inserting. And it doesn't matter which slot you insert the card into. Once inserted, assuming Windows 95 properly recognizes the card (this doesn't *always* happen), it will load the proper software driver and activate the card. If the applicable driver isn't on your computer, you'll be prompted to insert the appropriate Windows 95 installation disk. If this is the first card you've inserted into your machine, it's possible that the PCMCIA Wizard will run. This only happens if the 32-bit PCMCIA support isn't already installed on your computer. Simply answer any questions when prompted. You may be instructed to insert disks and/or restart your machine.

Once your card commences running, you'll see a PCMCIA icon in the Taskbar's system tray.

The icon only appears if PCMCIA cards are inserted, recognized, and running. Double-click on the icon to bring up details about the status of your cards. For example, on my machine, the status is as follows:

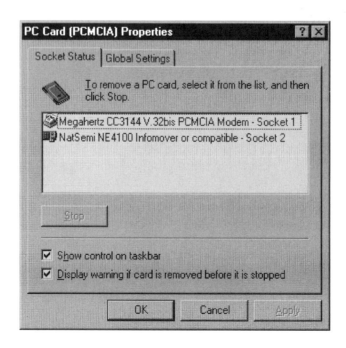

You can see here which card is in which slot. Notice the check boxes. One lets you turn off the PCMCIA icon that appears in the Taskbar. The other suppresses the warning message as explained below.

Notice that the Properties box also lets you *stop* a card by selecting it and clicking on it. What does this mean? These things are supposed to be completely Plug and Play, which means you should be able to run amuck with impunity, right? Well, not exactly. Microsoft suggests that you should stop a card before ejecting it. I've had pretty good luck simply ejecting the cards without stopping them. It won't crash your system. However, using the Stop button is a good idea because it lets Windows 95 and/or a program using the card warn you first if there is some reason you shouldn't eject it. For example, a networked user might have a file open on your machine or your modem might be in the middle of downloading your mail. If you fail to stop certain cards before ejecting, you might see this message:

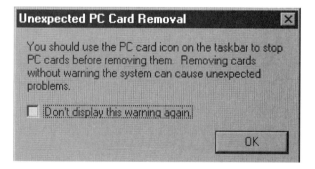

TIP If you are having trouble with an SRAM card (Static RAM card), check the Windows Help system under PCMCIA for some tips.

The Global Settings tab page in the Properties dialog box lets you turn off the little two-beep sounds that your computer makes when you boot up or resume from a suspended state. Each card when initialized will make such a sound. The sounds have signatures: if the second beep is higher, the card was recognized and initialized properly. If the second of the two short beeps is lower, it wasn't. I find that having the sounds on provides useful feedback, but I'm a geek. When resuming or booting up in a library, the beeps can be annoying to other people. You might want to turn off the sounds.

USING CELLULAR PHONES WITH YOUR LAPTOP FAX MODEM CARD

Getting a cell phone to work with your laptop isn't as easy as it could be. I've been trying to get mine to work for some time now and have had the runaround from more than a few companies on the issue.

There are a few things you should know. First, when shopping for both the phone and the modem, make sure they will work with each other. Call the people who make the phone and see which modems if any, support it; ditto for the modem supplier. If you already own the phone, call various modem vendors to see who supports your phone. Talk to the technical people, not the salespeople, and state the exact modem and phone make and model.

If you don't have a phone or modem yet or you're looking to upgrade, here's the scoop:

Some PCMCIA fax modems are designed for use with cell phones. They have a *direct-connect* port that lets you cable the phone and modem directly to each other without an intermediary connector module. (To connect a non–cellular-ready modem to a cell-phone, you'll need such a box; they cost about $200.) So, it makes sense to purchase a fax modem that's ready for prime time (cell-time, that is, which is always prime time when you consider the connect charges), such as the AT&T Keep in Touch PCMCIA card and the Megahertz CC, with an optional $25 to $70 cable. (The AT&T card supports a large number of phones.) There are two major functions such modems provide that non–cellular-ready cards don't: they fake the modem into thinking it's connected to a land line with dial tone; and they do compression and error detection so your cell phone can reliably cram more data across typically noisy channels.

External module boxes provide dial-tone compatibility, and some will do compression and error detection. Spectral, the most popular maker of the add-in boxes, claims the box arrangement with a non–direct-connect PCMCIA card actually works better than a fancy PCMCIA card because each box is fine-tuned for a specific brand and model of phone. I can't vouch for that, but it makes sense. Generic cellular-ready fax modems work with any number of phones, and input and output voltages and signals may vary among them. I'd say judge by the results. Try a system on spec, with return privileges, if you can. Try to get a modem with upgradable BIOS. Because the BIOS in the card stores the error-correction and compression algorithms, you'll be able to update the card as standards evolve.

Compression and error detection is another issue. As of this writing, there are two standards contending for the market: ECT and MNP-10. Both have their advantages, though neither will net you any gain unless the modem at the other end of the connection uses them. So far, most services only support the standard V.34bis that every desktop modem uses.

(continued on next page)

As for speed, getting a superfast 28.8 job isn't worth it if all your connects will be by cell phone. At this point, the highest connect speed you can expect is 9,600 bps anyway. Cell channels just won't run faster because of noise and bandwidth limitations. Don't expect that shelling out extra bucks for a digital cell phone will help either. Digital channels are quite limited and won't support data—only voice. You'll have to get a phone that is at least analog/digital with manual switching to analog when you want to transmit data.

Using a Docking Station

Laptop owners have had to make certain compromises for portability. We accept smaller, lower-resolution (albeit sharper) screens; smaller hard disks; and cramped keyboards in trade for freedom. Docking stations and port replicators are hardware solutions that provide users the best of both worlds. Whip out the computer and take it with you into the field. When you return to the office, plug your computer back into the docking station (see Figure 30.2), and you've got your favorite monitor, keyboard, pointing device, hard disks, CD-ROM, and printer at your beck and call. In some ways a docking-station

Figure 30.2   *Docking stations give you the best of two worlds—lightweight portability and desktop-style peripherals.*

Part
6

Customizing
Windows 95

arrangement beats having multiple computers because you don't have the problem of maintaining duplicate hard disks and synchronizing multiple files.

A port replicator is similar to a docking station, but it doesn't provide internal slots for standard PC cards (ISA cards, not PCMCIA), hard disks, and so on, just a single quick-connect for all the junk you might want to attach to your parallel, serial, SCSI, video, sound, or other ports on the laptop.

Docking stations are great if you really need to supercharge your laptop and you don't minding sitting at a desk. Still, one of the hassles of docking stations is that you typically have to adjust a lot of settings in the operating system when you dock or undock. Like telling the computer you want to run in 800 by 600 video resolution instead of 640 by 480. Or that your CD-ROM, humongous hard drive, and Mega-Decibel sound card are now available.

Enter Windows 95. Working in conjunction with popular laptop and docking-station makers such as Toshiba and Compaq, Microsoft built in some Plug-and-Play smarts. Some computers know when you've docked or undocked. If your machine is so equipped, docking and undocking is a no-brainer. Windows 95 applications and hardware developers are being encouraged to support the standard, so even programs in the future will know what to do when you are about to undock, such as closing certain files, issuing warnings, and so forth. Even if you're using non–Plug-and-Play equipment, there's a workaround.

With Plug-and-Play stuff, simply use your computer in each configuration as you'd expect. When docked, set up your video support and map network drives as you like. When you are about to undock, tell Windows 95 about your intentions. Your Start button will have an option called Eject PC on it. Choose it, and you'll be instructed or warned as necessary. Windows will then reconfigure itself, manage any conflicts about files in use on other drives, and load the drivers needed for going mobile. You may not even have to power down!

 NOTE Not all machines will support what's called *hot docking*, and may require that you turn off your machine and reboot before reconfiguration will occur. You should consult your computer's manual to determine the proper strategy for docking and undocking.

Non–Plug-and-Play Docking Stations

Windows 95 will detect and set up a separate hardware profile for a great majority of docking stations and port replicators. However, if yours isn't detected, or if you want to set up your machine with temporary external hardware—such as a monitor or mouse—without a port replicator or docking station, and you want to easily switch between such setups, it's possible. Just set up a *hardware profile* for each arrangement, then switch between them.

 NOTE   Use hardware profiles for any computer where you alter the physical setup regularly in a predictable manner, such as switching between two monitors.

Tucked away within the Control Panel you'll find the hardware-profile settings option that lets you name and save hardware setups just as you can color or sound schemes. Here's how.

1. Get your system running with a superset of the hardware you're going to want to use. That is, as much external stuff—such as hard drives—as possible. This may require using the Control Panel's Add/Remove hardware applet as well (see Chapter 7).

2. Run Control Panel and choose System. Click on Hardware profiles.

3. Select the profile you want to use as a basis for your scaled-down (undocked) profile and click on Copy.

4. Name the new profile something meaningful such as *Undocked Laptop*.

5. Switch to the Device Manager tab page in the System dialog box.

6. Click on the + sign next to any piece of hardware whose inclusion/exclusion in one of your profiles you want to alter. Highlight the specific item and click on Properties.

7. At the bottom of the resulting dialog box, turn off or on the appropriate boxes.

8. Repeat this for each device whose usage will be affected by a given profile.

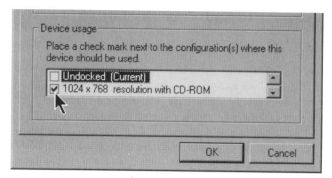

If you have more than one profile set up, you'll be prompted to choose one on booting up. This isn't as neat as an automatic switchover, but it works.

> **TIP**   You might want to check the Help system under *Hardware Profiles* **for more information.**

Deferred Printing

If you regularly print out documents, working out in the field without a printer can be annoying. If you've worked on a number of projects during the course of the day, you are likely to forget what to print once you get back to the office or find a printer. Also, you have to run each application, load each document, and set up the Print dialog box before you print. This is a hassle that Windows 95 lets you circumvent by printing *offline*.

When you work offline, print jobs simply get stored up in the print queue (a disk file on your hard disk). When you find a printer, just plug it in and run the queue. If you're in the field, it's possible you won't even know what kind of printer you'll find. No problem—you can even change the driver type of the printer before printing. Here are the steps:

1. From My Computer or Explorer, right-click on the printer in question and choose Work Offline. The check mark should now be turned on.

2. Print whenever and whatever you want as though there were a printer connected. Printing to the same printer each time will help consolidate your print queue.

3. When you get to a printer, plug it into the appropriate port.

4. From My Computer or Explorer, right-click on the printer in question and choose Work Offline to turn the check mark off.

TIP Actually this works with any computer in case you want to stack up a bunch of print jobs for printing later.

TECH TIP If the printer you found in the Kopy Korner store in Wakeegan, Illinois, isn't the same kind you printed your queue to, open the queue window, choose Printers ➤ Properties ➤ Details, and change the driver type. Unless you've installed the new type of printer before, the print driver won't be on your hard disk and you'll be prompted to insert a disk. This is a bummer if you don't carry copies of your Windows 95 disks with you. One workaround is to create a Generic Text Only printer (see Chapter 8) and print to that when you're in the field. A generic printer driver will print to many printers one way or another, though you won't get any fancy fonts or graphics with such a driver and you might have to set the printer into a "dumb" text-only mode. Another option is to figure out which diskette(s) you're prompted for each time you create a new printer and copy the contents (it will have a single `.cab` file on it) to a dedicated folder on your hard disk. When prompted for a disk, tell Windows 95 to look in this directory.

Using the Briefcase to Synchronize Your Files

Many people have more than one computer that they use regularly. For example, you may have a laptop for use on the road or at home and a desktop machine in your office. This poses a problem: how do you keep often-used files up to date on both machines? You can manually copy files back and forth via a floppy disk, but you have to remember what file is where and which copy has the latest edits in it. The solution is Windows 95's *Briefcase*, a little utility program that provides for file synchronization between two machines.

In essence, the Briefcase is just a folder that contains copies of all the files you want to keep up to date. When you switch from your desktop computer to your laptop, you drag the briefcase to a floppy disk or to your laptop's hard disk if your laptop is networked via a network card, Remote Access Services (RAS), or Direct Cable Connect. This copies the files onto the floppy or directly onto the hard disk of the portable. If you used a floppy, you then insert the floppy into your laptop machine, hit the road, and do your work on those files. If you went direct to hard disk, you're just ready to roll. You reverse the process when you return to the office. The Briefcase program takes care of determining which copy of a given file has the latest changes in it and where they should be copied to.

Of course, the Briefcase can be used between any two computers even if they are both laptops or desktop machines. And you can have as many briefcases as you like (in case you have a number of computers or diverse tasks, each of which rely on different files).

The following steps explain how to use the Briefcase between a desktop computer and a portable computer by way of a floppy disk. The next section explains how to use a direct connection (the preferred method) rather than a floppy disk.

1. First, if you don't have a Briefcase on your Desktop, you'll have to add one. Right-click on the Desktop and choose New ➤ Briefcase. If that doesn't work, it means the program isn't installed. You'll have to install the Briefcase utility from your Windows 95 master CD or floppies using the Control Panel's Add/Remove Programs applet. Click on Start ➤ Help and search for help about installing the Briefcase.

My Briefcase

2. Once you have a Briefcase icon on the Desktop or in a folder (you can create a Briefcase in any folder by right-clicking and choosing New ➤ Briefcase), you're ready to roll. Figure out which documents you want to keep up to date and drag them (not their shortcuts) into the Briefcase. (You can just drop them onto the Briefcase icon, or you can open its window and drag the files into that.)

3. Insert a floppy disk into your desktop machine.

4. Using My Computer or Explorer, drag the Briefcase to the floppy disk.

5. After some copying, all the contents of the Briefcase are now on your floppy disk. (You may be prompted to insert multiple disks if the Briefcase contains copious amounts of data.) Remove the disk and insert it into your portable.

6. Edit the document files stored in the Briefcase folder using the programs in your laptop. Editing the files from the floppy is the easiest way to manage them. You can move them off the floppy and onto the portable's hard disk, but you'll have to remember to move them back into the Briefcase before the next step.

7. When you return to your desktop computer, remove the floppy containing the Briefcase from the portable and insert it into your desktop computer.

8. Open the floppy drive's window from My Computer or Explorer. Find the Briefcase icon and double-click on it.

9. Open the Briefcase menu and click on Update All. Or select the files you want to update and choose Update Selection. In Figure 30.3 I have chosen Update All. Notice the dialog box that appears.

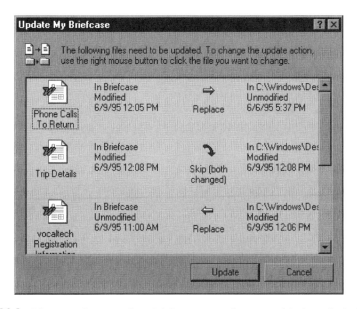

Figure 30.3 *When you choose Update, Briefcase reports the status of the items in the briefcase and what effect the update will have on each of them.*

You can also select individual files and choose Update Selection if you want to limit the update to certain files. In either case, the matching files on both machines are compared to see which has been modified and when modifications were made. The results of the comparison appear in the box. Typically, the arrows will all point to the right, indicating that items in the Briefcase have been changed and that updates should be made to the originals in the desktop computer. Arrows will point to the left when you've made changes to the Desktop's copy of a file but not to the copy in the Briefcase. The Trip Details file in Figure 30.3 shows what happens when both files have been changed. The Update procedure will normally skip this file, letting you decide which update you want to keep. You can right-click on such a file and choose its fate from the resulting menu.

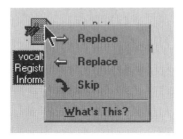

NOTE   Files that haven't been modified on either machine won't appear in the Update list.

Adjust any file's settings as you see fit and then click on the Update button. Files will be synchronized and progress reported in a box like the one shown below.

Options and Tips with Briefcase

Briefcase has some options worth noting. You can, for example, use it *without* a floppy disk if you have your computers directly connected or networked.

 NOTE Briefcase works best over a network, RAS, or with Direct Cable Connect (see Chapter 28). Using the floppy intermediary imposes some limitations because of the limited amount of storage space and potential for conflict between the Briefcase databases on the hard disk and on the floppy.

For directly connected machines, the procedure is slightly different from above.

1. On your desktop computer, share the folders containing the files you want to put in your Briefcase.

2. Then from your portable computer, copy those files to your laptop's Briefcase. (You can drag the files to the My Briefcase icon on your laptop's Desktop.)

3. Work on your files on your portable or laptop computer, even if it's disconnected from the desktop computer.

4. When you're finished working on the files, connect the two computers, double-click on the My Briefcase icon, choose Briefcase ➤ Update All (or click on the files you want to update and then click on Update Selection).

If at some point during the process a source file is moved or deleted, the link between the file in Briefcase and your main computer will be broken—Windows 95 won't be able to figure out what to update in this case. This creates an "orphan" file. Trying to update it will result in this message:

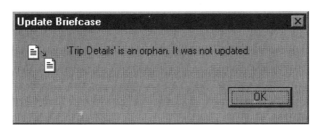

It can still be worked with directly from the briefcase, but if you want to synchronize files again, you'll have to copy the file from Briefcase to the same folder it was in when you added it to the briefcase originally. Updating should now work. Alternatively, select the orphan file, then choose File ➤ Properties. In the Update Status box, click on the Find Original button to find the original file. You can now synchronize again.

Conversely, if you want to break the link between the file in the Briefcase and its source, click on it in the briefcase and choose Briefcase ➤ Split from Original.

Portable Computing Tips

Portable computing is a black art that you only get good at with some experience. Here is just a brief smattering of my findings that you might find meaningful.

> **TIP**   Steve Cummings, who authored a portion of this book, also wrote a terrific book on the subject, covering all manner of laptop know-how, including where to buy your solar battery recharger for that trip to the Andes. It's called *The Little Laptop Book* (Peachpit Press, 1993).

▶ If you use the Suspend command, you should save your work before suspending just in case your batteries die or Suspend doesn't work right.

▶ If you take your computer out of the house a lot, purchase a laptop insurance policy. Some policies will cover not only theft but any kind of damage, and compared to your laptop's price, they're a bargain.

▶ Get a decent padded bag to carry your computer in.

> **TIP**   You might want to use a bag that doesn't look like a laptop computer bag. Those make an easy target for thieves.

▶ If you work outside and have trouble reading the screen, try wearing a dark shirt so your reflection on the screen is minimized. Monochrome and dual-scan screens work best in outdoor light, in that order. Active-matrix screens, though expensive and great indoors, appear black in strong sunlight.

▶ When shopping, buy a lithium-ion–batteried machine if possible. Short of that, get a nickel-metal hydride one. Nickel-cadmium (Nicad) batteries are a pain to care for because you have to regularly run them down all the way before you charge them back up to keep them healthy. Otherwise they die, and they aren't inexpensive. If you do have Nicads, make sure you cycle them regularly.

TECH TIP For longest life, you should cycle all batteries once a month regardless of type, particularly if you are connected to AC most of the time. Even though nickel-metal hydride batteries are supposed to be memoryless, they do seem to be susceptible to trickle overcharges.

▶ In your laptop you can actually install drivers for several pointing devices, such as a trackball, desktop mouse, GlidePoint, and so forth. When you change pointing devices, Windows 95 will detect it.

▶ If you use a modem, carry an extra telephone cord and possibly some connectors such as a Y connector and a coupler (female-to-female) so you can reach a distant outlet and/or share a telephone on the same line.

▶ Always have a floppy disk around for transfers to other computers.

▶ If you're a hardcore road warrior and occasionally need to transfer large files between computers, don't assume the other computer has Windows 95 on it. Besides, the direct-cable-connection program is slow at transfers. Purchase the latest version of LapLink, install it, and carry a serial LapLink cable with you. Only the serial cable lets you directly install LapLink on another computer you run into even though the parallel cable in faster.

NOTE For coverage of Direct Cable Connect, please refer to Chapter 26.

Chapter 31

Heavy-Duty Customizing

FEATURING

Advanced Control Panel settings

Adjusting other performance determinants

Troubleshooting

The best-laid plans of mice and men oft gang agley, as the saying goes. And so, despite the tens of thousands of work hours invested in designing and coding Windows 95 to brilliantly sleuth out your computer's hardware endowments and make the most intelligent use of them, it doesn't always pan out. True, Windows 95 beats Windows 3.x by a country mile when it comes to automated installation, hardware detection, and optimization on various counts. Still, human intervention can be advantageous at times. If you're a systems administrator, computer jock, or power user and want to tweak your computer for optimal performance, read through this chapter.

 NOTE Unfortunately, there isn't room in this book for all of the tricks. Check out my book *Windows 95 Secrets & Solutions* (Sybex, 1995) for more inside know-how on Windows and for tips, tricks, workarounds, and hardware-optimization angles. In that book you'll find in-depth discussions on Windows' inner workings; how to best upgrade your computer hardware for use as a desktop, workstation, or client/server-based system; how to choose monitors, hard disks, backups, UPS, RAM, CD-ROM, PCMCIA, and Plug-and-Play items; how to integrate Windows 95 into other brands of networks; how the Registry works and how to edit it; how to optimize your configuration files; and a variety of other meaty topics.

Keyboard Options

Without modifying anything via the Control Panel's Keyboard applet, your keyboard will likely work just fine. But the applet's settings determine several important behavioral characteristics of your keyboard and can be modified. Running the applet reveals what they might be (see Figure 31.1).

Most likely to be used is the character-repeat rate. Most keys repeat when you hold them down for a while. Because this setting not only controls the rate for normal keys but also affects the rate at which the Spacebar, arrow keys, and PageUp and PageDown keys work, you may have reason to make adjustments. On the first tab page, simply drag the slider to a faster or slower setting. You can test the effect of a given setting by clicking in the test text box and holding down a letter key. If it's too slow or fast, adjust and try again.

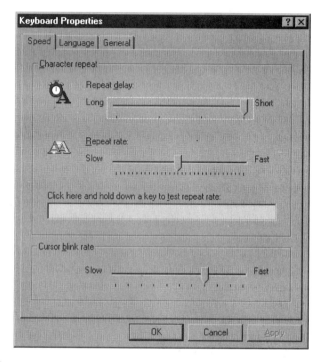

Figure 31.1 **The Control Panel's Keyboard Properties dialog box**

The *Repeat delay* setting determines how long you have to hold down a key before it starts repeating. If you tend to hesitate more than the average typist and find your screen responding with *tthhee* instead of *the*, you should lengthen the repeat delay.

At the bottom of the first tab page, you can change the cursor blink rate. This setting determines how fast the insertion point (or *I-beam*) blinks when you're editing text. Setting this too slow can cause the cursor to vanish for too long, too fast can be annoying. Drag the speed slider, then click in the test area to observe the effect.

Multiple Language Support in Windows 95

Because of differences in language and alphabet, computers marketed abroad have different key assignments than your computer. Key assignments for special characters such as accented characters, umlauts, and the like are determined in Windows 95 by choices you can make on the Keyboard applet's second tab page. During installation of

Windows 95, you're asked to confirm the language that setup has assumed is correct for your location, so typically this will be already correct. If your line of work calls for text in several languages, no problem; you can install any number of language drivers into your system, switching between them very quickly. A click on the Taskbar or a key press is all you need to switch from one driver (and thus keyboard layout) to another.

Typically you'll have only one driver showing when you open the dialog box. To add a new one, click on Add and choose a language from the resulting list. You may be prompted to insert a disk or CD-ROM so the applet can locate the proper driver. Then you'll have a second listing in the installed languages box. Here I've installed Swedish in addition to English.

Once set to another language, some keys (shifted and unshifted) will type different letters than printed on your keyboard's key caps. You'll have to experiment a bit to determine where your new keys are. Unfortunately Windows 95 doesn't include a utility that'll display a keyboard map for each language driver.

If you check Enable Indicator on the Taskbar, your Taskbar will indicate which language driver is active at any one time. Clicking on it brings up a menu that lets you easily switch between languages.

If you want to get super efficient at switching between installed languages, just activate either the Left Alt-Shift or Ctrl-Shift option. Then simply pressing that key combination toggles between languages.

If you want to remove a language driver, simply select it in the dialog box and click on Remove. Likewise, setting the default language is as easy as clicking on Set as Default. This determines which language will be used when you start up your computer.

Part
6

Customizing
Windows 95

General Keyboard Settings

Finally, on the last tab page, you'll find the General settings. Here you set the actual hardware driver that Windows 95 should use with your keyboard. I say *actual hardware driver* to distinguish from keyboard layout or language characters that will be produced when you press a key. Some keyboard brands require a special driver or have additional keys on them, such as number pads and the like. During Windows 95 setup, your keyboard was likely recognized and the correct driver installed. Should you purchase a new keyboard that is acting squirrely after you plug it in, you might want to select this tab page and click on the Change button. Your keyboard will then be checked for compatibility, and you'll have the option of installing a different type of driver. Click on Change, then Show All Devices to see a list of all the possible keyboard hardware drivers.

Working with Passwords

The Control Panel's Password applet lets you change log-on passwords, allow remote administration of the computer, and set up individual profiles that go into effect when each new user logs onto the local computer. The Passwords dialog box is shown in Figure 31.2.

Use the first page of this dialog box for typical password adjustments. More often than not you'll use the first button to change your log-on name—the password that's used when you log onto Windows. The second button lets you set other passwords—such as your password to log onto another LAN such as a Novell network. If you want, you may use the same password for each to simplify things. Passwords can be as long as 127 characters, although that's a bit more than anyone would want to bother with. You may use letters, numbers, and punctuation marks.

 NOTE The maximum password length on other networks may be different. For example, NT and Novell passwords must be shorter. Check the documentation with those networks.

To change your password, click on the upper button, then in the resulting box fill in your old password, the new password, and then repeat the new password.

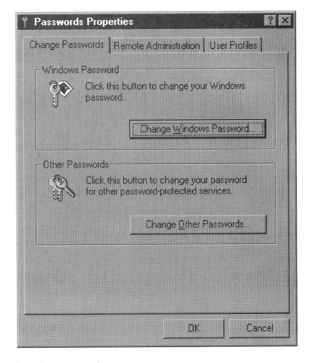

Figure 31.2 *Changing passwords*

CAUTION   You should not use Cut and Paste commands (Ctrl-X and Ctrl-V) to enter the passwords. Always manually enter them to prevent accidentally introducing a typo into your password and then being unable to access your hard disk or change your password.

Remote-Administration Passwords

The second tab page of the dialog box is only used for setting up passwords to allow someone at another workstation to access your computer. Recall from Part 5 that a network administrator can manage shared folders and printers on this computer and see who connects to them. Settings on this page determine which password the remote administrator has to enter remotely to create, change, or monitor shared resources on your computer. Remote administration is covered in Part 5, so I won't go into that here. However, to set up the computer for remote administration, you have to enable it first by checking the box. Then enter the password you want to require for remote administration of your shared resources. Remember to inform your network administrator of the password.

Multiple-User Passwords

Windows NT introduced the concept of multiple users on a given computer workstation, (aka PC) each with his or her own settings. In NT such an arrangement is necessary because NT's security model necessitates that each user be given a set of security privileges controlling the use of network-shared resources. Windows 95 isn't based on as ambitious a security model, but it still includes a decent functional subset of NT's user-by-user customizability. By creating an entry in the configuration Registry for each user on the system, Windows 95 can accommodate any number of different people on the same computer, each having many of their own settings. When a user signs in, the Registry is accessed and the appropriate settings go into effect.

User Profiles

The collection of settings each user creates is called a *user profile*. A typical user profile might include Desktop colors, screen saver, shortcuts and icons, and program groups.

As it comes from the factory, Windows 95 is set up in single-profile mode. Each user that logs on will get the same settings regardless of the user name and password they enter. You have to enable the multiple-user mode before logging in as a new user; this will create a new profile in the Registry. Here are the steps to follow to enable the multiuser arrangement.

You should start with a pretty ordinary setup. Any settings that are currently in effect, such as icons on the Desktop, colors, etc., will be cloned into all subsequent profiles that get created. Then get to the Password Properties User Profiles tab page shown in Figure 31.3.

By default the top radio button is on. Click on the second one (*Users can...*); this activates the lower portion of the dialog box.

You have two options in the lower half of the box: You can check either, both, or neither of these two. The options declare which settings are stored in your new profile when you make changes from the

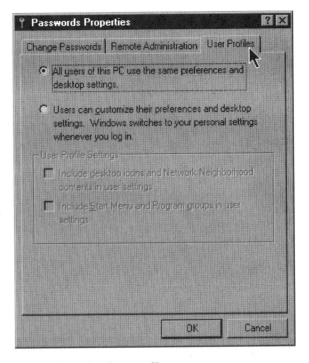

Figure 31.3 Enabling differentiated user profiles

Control Panel, property sheets, and so forth. If you elect *not* to turn
on an option, you'll *share* that setting with other users. When you OK
the box, you'll be told that you must restart your computer for the
changes to take effect.

Once you're set up for multiple users, the machine will reboot and
work just as you would expect. You have to sign in as usual. However,
when someone else signs in with a name not recognized by the system, they'll see the following dialog box:

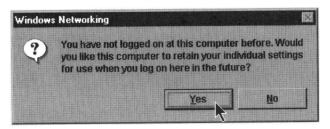

Click on Yes. They will then have to verify their password. A copy of the settings currently in effect is made and assigned to the new user's environment, so the Desktop and all the other settings will come up looking like nothing new happened. But any changes the new user makes to system settings will have *no effect* on other user's settings.

There's one ramification of all this multiple customization that you might bump into. Having separate profiles on the machine might tip off certain programs that there are additional users around. Programs that previously assumed you were the only user may now ask you for some identification such as a password before performing some task that requires security of some sort. Here's an example: Microsoft Exchange, even if set to remember your password automatically, will now prompt you to re-enter the password when you attempt to log onto services such as the Microsoft Network. This prevents other users of the computer from logging on under your name, running up a bill, and reading your mail.

CAUTION   Even though certain system settings that other users make on the computer won't affect yours, this doesn't mean other users can't affect your data files, folders, hard disks, and so forth. Unlike the password protection you can assign to printers or folders that you share with users over the network, you can't password protect or specify user permissions for resources that are on your computer. Thus, once a user logs onto the system,, they are able to gain access to any files on your hard disk. If you want to more thoroughly protect individual disks, folders, and files, you'll have to use another operating system such as Windows NT.

Switching Users without Rebooting

You may have noticed when shutting down Windows that you have the option of logging on as a different user.

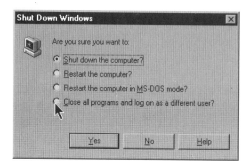

Choosing this option is an easy way to switch to another user's settings without having to wait for shutdown and reboot. It is the preferred approach, especially if resources on your machine are in use by other networked users.

Removing User Profiles

At the time of this writing, the internal procedures for adding and removing individual system settings was not always reliable nor straightforward. For example, not all of the folders on the Desktop were imported into each new user's settings. Also, a series of hard-disk subfolders are set up for each user. Turning off the multiuser settings didn't erase these folders, leaving them consuming disk space. In future releases of Windows 95, this process may be smoothed out and/or automated as it is in Windows NT.

In any case, if you decide you want to remove all but the default profile, just run the Control Panel again, choose Passwords, select the User Profiles page, and choose the first option, which will turn off the multiple-user setting. OK the box and reboot. Now, regardless of who you log in as, you'll get the same settings.

TECH TIP   You can't remove just a single profile; multiuser capability is either on or off. However, even after turning off the multiuser option, all the subfolders for individual users will still be in the `\Windows\Profiles` folder just in case you reactivate the multiuser setting. The only way to get rid of all the potential junk in these folders is to manually delete them using Explorer or some other file-deletion program such as File Manager or XTREE. Make sure you're not deleting any important documents or programs stored in a user's subfolders.

Regional Settings

The Regional settings customize Windows for use in other countries. If you're using Windows in English in the United States, don't bother making any changes. The settings made from this box pertain exclusively to Windows and Windows applications; other programs won't take advantage of them. Even some Windows applications won't. You should do some experimenting with the settings to see if they make

Part 6

Customizing Windows 95

any difference or read the application's manual for information about how to set the formats for it.

Choosing Regional from the Control Panel displays the dialog box you see in Figure 31.4. The settings and their explanations are shown below.

NOTE   Windows may ask you to insert one of the floppy disks when making changes.

Regional Settings selects which country you're in. All other settings change in accordance with the accepted practices in that country. Only bother changing the other options if necessary.

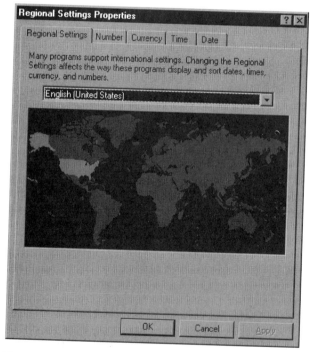

Figure 31.4   *The Regional Settings Properties dialog box. Changes you make here affect only the applications that use the internal Windows settings for such functions.*

Number displays numbers with or without decimals, commas, or leading zeroes and with different decimal separators. It also determines whether to display measurements in metric or English units and what your *list separator* should be. For example, in the now-famous sentence, "Well, it's one, two, three, what are we fighting for...," the list separator is a comma. In other languages, items listed in a sentence are separated by other punctuation marks.

Currency sets the currency indicator and the location and number of decimal digits.

Time allows for 12- or 24-hour time indication, AM or PM indicators, choice of separators, and leading zeros.

Date sets dates from a myriad of formats such as 3/6/53; 03/06/53; 3/6/1953; 06-03-1953; March 6, 1953; and others. This is useful for programs that pop the date into text at the touch of a key or translate dates from one format to another.

To change the settings, simply click on the appropriate tab page, then on the drop-down list box for the setting in question. Examples of the current settings are shown in each section, so you don't need to change them unless they look wrong.

The System

The Control Panel's System applet is quite capable. If you're a power user who digs around in the computer, goofing around with boards and various upgrades, you'll probably be using this applet a lot. It displays information about your system's internals—devices, amount of RAM, type of processor, and so on. It also lets you add, disable, and remove specific devices from your system, set up hardware profiles (for instance, to allow automatic optimization when using a docking station with a laptop), and optimize some parameters of system performance such as CD cache size and type. This applet also provides a number of system-troubleshooting tools.

Using the Device Manager

The first tab page of the System Properties dialog box simply reports the system type, registered owner, and version of Windows. The second page, Device Manager, provides a powerful overview of your entire system, displaying the classes of hardware in the computer (see Figure 31.5).

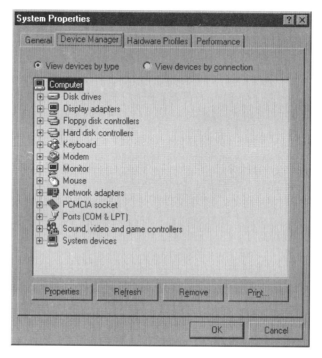

Figure 31.5   *The Device Manager displays the hierarchy of system components.*

Basic components are listed in alphabetical order by type unless you click on the *View devices by connection* radio button at the top of the window. Clicking on a plus sign displays specifics about the class of component. For example:

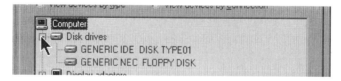

An X through an icon means the hardware has been disabled. A circled exclamation point through the icon means the hardware has a problem. The type of problem will be displayed in the hardware's property sheet.

You can click on a specific sub-item and learn more about it by clicking on Properties (or simply double-click on the sub-item). The resulting box will tell you whether the component is working properly, possibly who the maker of the device is, and what its version number is. Many components will have three or four property sheet pages, such as General, Settings, Driver, and Resources. The available options vary depending on the type of device. From these pages you can examine and declare a great variety of settings for your hardware devices. For example, the Settings page for your floppy drive(s) lets you reassign logical drive letters. Pages for sound cards and network cards will report DMA, IRQ, and port settings.

NOTE   Many components' Properties boxes have a Device Usage section that determines which hardware configuration the components will be used in (such as when a laptop is docked or undocked; see Chapter 30 for more on multiple configurations for laptops).

You might have noticed the Remove button on the Device Manager's first page. Use this button to remove support for any device in your system that you've decided to bag and that Windows 95 didn't automatically remove for you. Windows 95 is pretty good at detecting hardware-configuration changes and will often remove unnecessary or redundant drivers when you remove a piece of hardware. But in case it doesn't, use this button.

CAUTION   Many devices will have Resources and Drivers tab pages. As a rule, you'll not want to mess with the Resources and Driver settings unless you know what you're doing. Changing the address, IRQ, DAM, and other down-and-dirty system settings can lead to problems, such as a device not working or Windows not booting. If the Properties' General tab page indicates a device is working properly and doesn't report conflicts, you're probably best off leaving the component's settings alone.

TECH TIP   For systems integrators who find they are altering a system's configuration regularly, are trying to get some new hardware working and having trouble with it, or want to catalog the hardware configuration of a number of systems for inventory or comparison purposes, the Print button comes in handy. In the Device Manager's dialog box, click on Print. You'll have three options determining the content of the printout, including Print to File.

Making COM Port Adjustments

If you've ever used the DOS **MODE** command to set up the communications parameters of your computer's serial COM ports, you know that it's a hassle to remember the exact syntax and *arguments* (the numbers and letters you type after the command) required for a specific setup. Because most programs that use the serial ports (such as communications programs, mouse drivers, or slow-speed networks) take care of setting the COM ports, it's rare that you need to deal with these directly anyway. But should you need to, the Device Manager lets you configure the serial (COM) ports on a machine. Under Computer, click on Ports. You'll see a dialog box for making the settings for baud rate, parity, and stop bits. The settings should match the settings of the equipment you are connecting to the port. If you're in doubt about them, consult the manual supplied with the external equipment. You may also want to refer to a book specializing in the use of asynchronous serial communications interfaces, such as *The RS-232 Solution* (2nd Edition) (Sybex, 1994).

> **TIP** Try double-clicking on Computer at the top of the Device Manager page. This is a great troubleshooting tool to help you resolve port, IRQ, and DMA conflicts.

Optimizing Performance

The last page of the System applet is for checking and altering settings that affect the optimal performance of your system. Though Windows 95 optimizes as best it can, you may have need for or simply an interest in knowing what's going on in terms of virtual memory management, disk caching, and other performance determinants. All these settings now live in one place—on the Performance page of the System applet. Clicking on this tab brings up the screen shown in Figure 31.6.

Notice that this figure indicates my system is optimized about as much as it's going to be. I'm using 31-bit file-system, PCMCIA, and virtual-memory drivers.

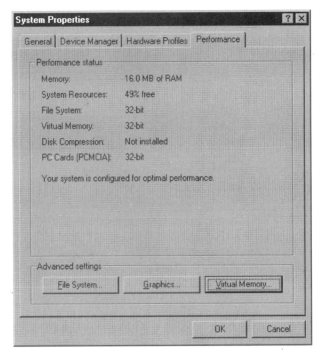

Figure 31.6   You can set and check system optimization from this page of the System applet.

There are three major performance sections you can examine using the buttons at the bottom of the dialog box:

▶ file system

▶ graphics acceleration

▶ virtual memory

I suggest you examine each dialog box carefully, read the help files, and use the ? button in the dialog boxes to get some tips about each setting before making any changes. Note that in Windows 95, the virtual memory file size is dynamically sized—and is best left that way— rather than being set to a static size. However, if you have multiple disk drives and want to ensure specific amounts of virtual memory on each or disable virtual memory swapping altogether, you can.

Part 6

Customizing Windows 95

Other Tweaking Angles

Chapter 2 touched on some basic Windows 95 software and hardware compatibility issues, some of which will affect system throughput and overall performance. Although Windows 95 is, in many ways, a radical departure from Windows 3.x, a genie in a bottle isn't bundled in. The old tried-and-true performance essentials are still applicable. I could write a hundred pages about keeping your hardware doodads up to snuff, your hard disk organized, and other tricks for squeezing the most out of every CPU cycle. But in the end, most people don't bother, and it doesn't really net you much. In reality there are really only a few truly beneficial performance tricks worth the hassle or price.

▶ First off, always keep a bunch of free space available on your hard disk. This is essential. You should have at least 20 (some people say as much as 50) MB free on your disk for use by Windows for virtual memory. If you have too little, you'll start getting messages about running out of memory when you try to switch between programs. If you use only a few small programs at a time, this is less of an issue.

▶ Next, you should defragment your hard disk once in a while (see Chapter 23). Once a month is a good idea.

▶ If you are unhappy with the performance of your system and it's a pretty fast 486 already, increase the amount of RAM. You probably have 8 MB. 16 MB will dramatically improve things.

▶ If you don't have a local-bus hard-disk controller, switch to one. SCSI II is best, IDE on the VLB or PCI bus is good. You may be able to keep your existing drive, but make sure it's large enough and has a fast step rate (18 milliseconds or lower).

▶ Your video controller should be on the local bus too. If you're now using 256 or more colors and you can live with only 16 colors, use the Display applet in Control Panel to reduce the colors. Screen redrawing will speed up significantly.

▶ Do what you can to remove 16-bit drivers from your system. In simplest terms, this means only install and use devices that are recognized and supported by Windows 95 right off the shelf. Network cards, video controllers, CD-ROMs, PCMCIA cards, and the like should all be running with 31-bit drivers. Refer to the installation guide supplied with the product or contact the manufacturer to determine how best to do this. (It may require removing or *remming* out statements in your autoexec.bat and/or config.sys files.)

 TECH TIP When you install Windows 95 over an existing copy of DOS and Windows, all of the network drivers, device drivers, and utilities in your existing config.sys, autoexec.bat, and system.ini files are pulled into your new configuration—including files it doesn't need or can't work with. This duplication doesn't usually prevent Windows 95 from running, but it can slow it down and decrease the amount of conventional RAM available for DOS sessions.

Setting the Recycle Bin's Properties

A few final settings worth considering affect how your Recycle Bin works. Recall that when you delete files, they aren't actually erased. They get moved to the Recycle Bin, which is a directory on your hard disk. If your hard disk is modest in size or getting crammed, decreasing the size of the Recycle Bin might be in order. In some cases, you might even want to *increase* its *size*. The options in the Recycle Bin's property sheet are therefore worth a gander.

To get to the setting, right-click on the Recycle Bin icon, either on the Desktop or in Explorer, then choose Properties. The Recycle Bin settings appear as shown in Figure 31.7.

There are number of settings here to contemplate. Firstly, notice that each of your local hard disks will have a tab. If you choose *Configure drives independently*, you'll use those pages to make individual drive settings. Otherwise you'll just use the Global page.

If you don't want to be able to reclaim deleted files, check the *Do not move files...* option. This will speed up deletion. It will also free up disk space immediately on deletion of files.

As a default, 10 percent of each drive is used for the Recycle Bin. When you delete a file on drive C, it goes to drive C's Recycle Bin until you empty the bin. When you delete from drive D (if you have a second hard drive), it goes into drive D's Recycle Bin. As a Recycle Bin reaches capacity, newly deleted files will push older files off the bottom of the list, deleting them permanently. In practical terms, the

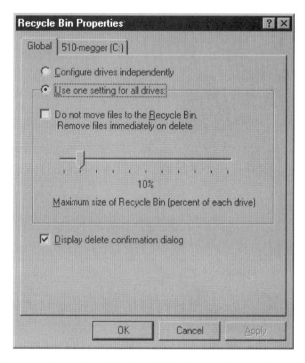

Figure 31.7   You can set specifics of the Recycle Bin's behavior from its Properties box.

Recycle Bin's size simply determines how long a file will be recoverable before it's pushed off the list. It also determines the maximum size file that will be recoverable after an accidental deletion. If a file is larger than the maximum size of the Recycle Bin, then it just won't be recyclable. As of this writing, you won't be warned of this, either. It will just be erased.

If you want to alter the size of your Recycle Bins, use the percentage slider. As a rule, the default of 10 percent works just fine. If you work with very large files, you may want to increase this percentage to accommodate them. If you're short on disk space and don't tend to make deletion mistakes, decrease it.

TECH TIP   When you empty the Recycle Bin, all bins are flushed. You can't empty them on a drive-by-drive basis unless you use a file-management program other than Explorer, such as File Manager (click on Start ➤ Run and enter winfile). You *can* delete specific files from the Recycle Bin using Explorer if you select and delete them individually, however.

The final check box is normally set on, requiring you to confirm before Windows 95 will empty the bin. If you find the confirmation boxes annoying, turn off this check box.

 TIP If you delete a folder, only the files within that folder appear in the Recycle Bin. If you restore a file that was originally located in a deleted folder, Windows recreates the folder and then restores the file to it.

Troubleshooting Windows 95

Getting help about troubleshooting: Assuming your computer boots up, there is substantial troubleshooting help in Windows 95. Choose Start ➤ Help and double-click on Troubleshooting.

Windows 95 doesn't start up when you turn your computer on: Remember, booting up can take up to a minute. Don't assume there is trouble unless there is no activity on the screen. Check that power is connected, the monitor is on, the brightness isn't turned down, the monitor cable is secure, and no floppy disk is inserted in drive A. If the problem persists, press the reset switch or turn the computer off, wait a second, and turn it on again. Still no go? Insert your start-up disk in drive A and turn the computer off and on again. If you see *Starting Windows 95...* but things get stuck after that, restart and press F8 the next time you see those words. Then choose Safe Mode from the resulting menu. Use Safe Mode to sleuth out which setting (such as screen driver) was wrong.

You are running out of memory: Try closing some programs and/or documents. Empty the Recycle Bin. Remove any unnecessary programs from the Startup folder. Use the Explorer or My Computer to delete some files. Empty the Recycle Bin again. Make sure you have at least several (preferably 10) megabytes of free space on your hard disk. Let Windows manage your *virtual memory* settings (use the Control Panel's System applet to set these). If you only have 4 MB of RAM in your computer, it's a good idea to upgrade to 8, 12, or 16.

You are running out of disk space: Empty the Recycle Bin. Delete files you don't need. Remove whole components of Windows that you never use, such as wallpaper, Exchange, sound schemes, or accessories (some of these consume large amounts of space—see Chapter 7). Remember to empty the Recycle Bin again. Use a compression program such as PKZIP to compress directories you don't use often. Use DriveSpace to compress your drive and double your available disk space (Chapter 23). Upgrade a compressed drive to DriveSpace 3 format (Chapter 32). Use ExtraPack to further compress a compressed drive (Chapter 32).

Part 6

Customizing
Windows 95

Increase the DriveSpace compression settings on your drive if the drive is already compressed. Purchase a higher-capacity hard disk.

Printing doesn't work at all: Check that the printer is on, online, filled with paper, and wired securely. Try printing a test page by running Help's printer troubleshooter (click on Start ➤ Help ➤ Troublehsooting) or by opening the Printers folder (Start ➤ Settings ➤ Printers), right-clicking on the printer, choosing Properties, and clicking on Print Test Page. If the page prints, the problem is with your document or application program, not the printer or Windows 95. If the page doesn't print, make sure Properties ➤ Details shows the correct port for the printer (typically LPT1).

Printing looks wrong: If a partial page printed, check the page orientation. It may be set to Landscape. Check the page-layout command in the program you are printing from *and* in the Properties box for your printer (click on the Details tab, then on Settings). If just the edges of the printout are missing, decrease the margins for your document and try again. Make sure the paper size you are using matches the document size you are printing. If you get PostScript error codes instead of normal text and graphics, either you are trying to use a PostScript printer driver with a non-PostScript printer or the printer needs to be set to PostScript mode. Add the printer to your computer again using the Add Printer Wizard; choose Start ➤ Settings ➤ Printers ➤ Add Printer (Chapter 8).

Fonts don't print correctly: Use TrueType or printer fonts whenever possible. Screen fonts—such as MS-Sans Serif or System—aren't good choices. Change the font in the document and try printing again. If your printer has plug-in font cartridges, you may have the wrong one installed. In the printer's Properties box, click on the Fonts tab and ensure the correct Fonts cartridge is selected. You may have to Install Printer Fonts if the cartridge isn't listed. If TrueType fonts still aren't printing right, as a final resort you can try printing them as bitmaps instead of outlines (select this option from the Fonts tab of the Properties box).

Color printing comes out black and white: Check that you have installed the right print cartridge by looking inside the printer. In the printer's Properties box, choose Details ➤ Setup to check for a possible cartridge-selection option (it might also be available for the program you're using; select File ➤ Printer Setup).

Printing is slow: Open the Properties box for the printer, click on the Details tab, and check the spool settings (spooling should be turned on). If you're waiting a long time for a printout to appear, open the printer's Properties box, click on the Details tab, and click on Spool Settings. Try changing the spool setting from EMF to RAW.

The computer seems "stuck": First, press Esc once or twice. If it's still stuck, try Ctrl-Alt or use the Taskbar to switch to another program to see if Windows 95 is really dead. If the Taskbar is in Auto-Hide mode and doesn't appear, try Ctrl-Esc to bring up the Start list. Use these techniques to get to and save any documents you are working on, then close all programs if possible. If you suspect only one program is having trouble (such as being stuck), press Ctrl-Alt-Del *once*, then wait. In a few seconds a list of programs should come up. Select the program listed as not responding and click on the End Task button; repeat for each stuck program. Save your work and reset the computer as soon as possible.

Chapter 32
About Microsoft Plus

FEATURING

Also known as Plus Pack, Microsoft Plus is a collection of add-on programs, utilities, and other useful doodads for Windows 95. Microsoft Plus isn't supplied with Windows 95—you'll have to buy it separately. At this writing, the exact contents of the Microsoft Plus package were not finalized because the product was still in testing.

The current beta product at the time included the following options.

Option	Description	Hard-Disk Space Required
DriveSpace 3	Enhanced version of the disk-compression software supplied with Windows 95, giving you additional compression	2,649K
System Agent	For setting up automated system maintenance—such as defragmenting and file backup—during periods of system inactivity	1,509K
Internet Plus	Add-ons for Microsoft Exchange, giving you an Explorer interface and mail services for the Internet	1,429K
Master Themes	Collections of flashy sound schemes, color schemes, and cursors	18,193K
Dial-Up Network Server	Lets you set up your office computer so you can call it from home	32K

Option	Description	Hard-Disk Space Required
3-D Pinball	A pinball game with fancy graphics and sound, an example of the kind of flashy Windows 95 games we'll be seeing more of	2,288K
Visual Enhancements	Full-window drag, font smoothing, wallpaper stretching, fancy animated cursors, and additional TrueType fonts for DOS boxes	417K

If you choose to install all the options, you'll need approximately 26 MB of hard-disk space, so make sure you have enough before beginning. If you choose to install fewer options, the Setup program will tell you the amount of disk space needed for them. Master Themes takes up a whopping 14 MB, so if you are short on space, this might be the option to pare down or eliminate (especially if you only work with a 256-color video adaptor); approximately half the themes require a high-color (64-thousand-color) adaptor and look terrible on anything less.

You should read any supplied notes that came with the product, especially any Readme files on Disk 1 of the disk set. As of this writing, the primary warning in the Readme file was:

Plus requires a 486 or higher processor, 8 MB of memory, and a display that's capable of displaying at least 256 colors. A high-color (16-bit) display and sound card are recommended.

Installing Microsoft Plus

Installation is similar to other Microsoft Windows products. Simply do the following:

1. Insert the first floppy disk in drive A.

2. Click on Start and choose Run.

3. Type in **A:setup** (replace A: with B: if that's the disk drive you inserted the diskette into. If you have purchased the CD-ROM version, use that drive's letter instead). The Setup screen appears (see Figure 32.1).

4. Follow the instructions. Choose Custom setup if you want to install all possible goodies, or select specific ones. Feed in the disks as necessary.

5. Depending on which options you choose to install, you may see additional instructions.

 CAUTION Do not install Plus disk compression if you are using third-party disk-compression software, such as Stacker. Use Custom mode to disable installation of Plus compression.

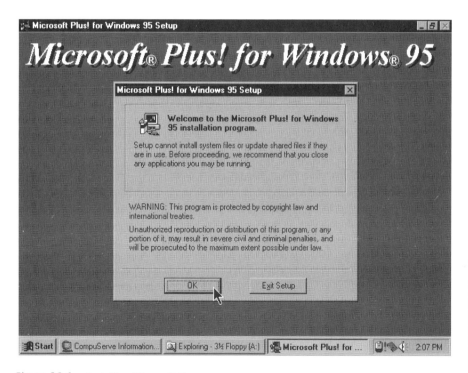

Figure 32.1   Installing Microsoft Plus

Running Microsoft Plus

Microsoft Plus isn't a single program; thus, after installation, you won't have a single new program icon in one specific place. Instead, your new goodies will be scattered about in their appropriate locations. Full-window drag and font smoothing will simply be built into your graphical user interface. The Pinball game will be found via Start ➤ Programs ➤ Accessories ➤ Games. DriveSpace 3 is reachable by choosing Start ➤ Programs ➤ Accessories ➤ System Tools, and so on.

The following sections will cover each of the Microsoft Plus add-ons. Remember that because the product is in flux, there may have been changes to some of the commands or features since this was written.

    NOTE   Dial-Up Networking is covered in Chapter 28.

DriveSpace 3

DriveSpace 3 is an enhancement to the DriveSpace program that was supplied with Windows 95. The major advantage of the updated version is that it uses more-advanced compression algorithms for providing even more space on your hard disk. On installing this part of Microsoft Plus, DriveSpace will be updated to DriveSpace 3. Open its program folder with Start ➤ Programs ➤ Accessories ➤ System Tools, and you'll see the DriveSpace 3 icon.

The new enhancements of DriveSpace 3 let you:

▶ Customize the type of compression used to save files to a compressed drive. You can save files uncompressed, in the Standard compression format, in the new HiPack format, or double-compressed in the new UltraPack format.

▶ Create compressed drives that are up to 2 gigabytes in size.

    NOTE   To create a 2-gigabyte compressed drive, you need an uncompressed drive that is at least 900 MB in size.

- Recompress a currently compressed drive using a single compression method or compress each individual file and folder using a separate method for each with ExtraPack.

- Uncompress an entire disk or only specific files and folders.

- Specify highest compression for files you seldom use, medium compression for files you use more frequently (access will be quicker).

TIP   Likely candidates for highest compression are all Help files (HLP) and setup-information (INF) files. These files are not often used; the Help files are particularly large, sometimes as much as 2 MB.

Compressing an Uncompressed Drive

To run DriveSpace 3, open its program folder as described above and choose DriveSpace 3. See Chapter 23 for a discussion of creating, sizing, removing, and uncompressing hard-disk volumes with Drive-Space. Once you have those instructions under your belt, return to this section and read on.

To gain access to the additional compression options, click on the Advanced menu and then click on Settings. A slider lets you choose various amounts of compression:

No Compression: Files will not be compressed.

Depends on Free Space: When available disk space drops below a certain amount, compression will begin. Standard compression is used.

Standard Compression: The normal method of compression used by Windows 95. Files are typically compressed to a little more than 50 percent of original size. After installing Microsoft Plus, Standard compression is improved a bit, providing even more compression while maintaining good performance when opening and saving files.

HiPack Compression: This option searches your disk for repetitive data and provides better compression than Standard while still giving you minimal slowdowns when opening files. However, because a larger portion of your disk is searched for repetitive data, compressing your drive may take longer. HiPack files are, on average, compressed to one-half their original size—a little smaller than Standard.

**Part
6**

Customizing
Windows 95

A utility called ExtraPack provides an additional compression type:

UltraPack Compression: This option uses optimal compression technology to provide the most space savings on your hard disk. To use this feature, first upgrade your compressed drives to the DriveSpace 3 format by running DriveSpace 3 and choosing the Drive ➤ Upgrade command. You can then use UltraPack by running ExtraPack, which recompresses drives compressed in the DriveSpace 3 format to about one-third their original size. However, accessing UltraPacked files may be slow if you are using a 486-based computer because the file crunching takes advantage of certain Pentium-processor abilities.

Further Compressing Previously Compressed Drives

Unless you specify otherwise, on installing Microsoft Plus, the System Agent program (explained below) is automatically activated to run ExtraPack on any preexisting compressed drives, giving you additional space without your intervention. This process will normally kick in after the computer has been on and left idle for twenty minutes. You can change this time setting, turn off the automatic conversion altogether, or run the ExtraPack program manually if you want.

To upgrade a compressed drive, suppose you have a compressed drive such as the one in Figure 32.2.

To further compress the drive:

1. First, you have to upgrade the drive from the DriveSpace format to DriveSpace 3. Select the drive in the DriveSpace program and choose Drive ➤ Upgrade.

Now you can do a couple of things:

▶ If the System Agent is set to do extra compression automatically, just turn on your computer and let it sit idle. Recompression with ExtraPack should start after twenty minutes.

▶ You can run ExtraPack manually by choosing Start ➤ Programs ➤ Accessories ➤ System Tools ➤ ExtraPack. You'll see a box such as the one shown on the next page.

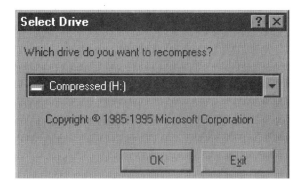

Choose the drive you want to further compress and click on OK.

NOTE   Only drives already compressed will be selectable from the drop-down list. If you want to compress an uncompressed drive, use DriveSpace 3 instead of ExtraPack.

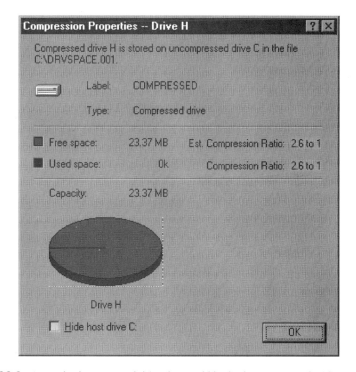

Figure 32.2   A standard compressed drive that could be further compressed with ExtraPack

2. You can change a number of defaults that affect ExtraPack's choices about compression. Click on the Settings button in the ExtraPack dialog box, and you'll see:

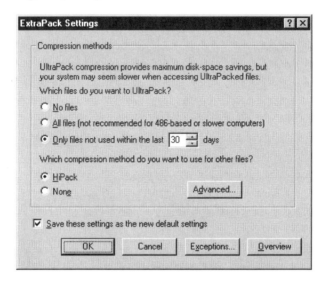

Study these options carefully before changing them; the default settings work for most users. You can click on the Advanced button for a few more. The Exceptions button lets you specify files (or complete folders) you don't want compressed or want compressed using a specific compression technique. Use this option when you want to accelerate access to files you use frequently, particularly if you have noticed a performance penalty after compression. (You can revisit this dialog box later if you find there are files whose compression properties you need to alter.)

3. Click on Start in the main ExtraPack dialog box. A progress gauge will keep you posted on the recompression.

Creating New Compressed Drives Using DriveSpace 3

Chapter 23 explains the use of DriveSpace to compress your drives. Essentially, DriveSpace 3 works the same way as DriveSpace. The major differences are that HiPack and the Settings button shown above have been added, allowing Exceptions and the other advanced settings discussed above. When you are about to create a new compressed drive, check the Advanced menu's Settings options and set the compression method. Then go ahead and create the compressed drive.

The System Agent

The System Agent is a program that runs programs automatically! It's designed with automatic execution of system-maintenance programs—such as defragmenters, compressors, and backup programs—in mind. However, it could be used for any program you want to run at a predefined time or after a predetermined period of inactivity.

Using the utility is a two-step process: first you decide which program(s) you want to run and when, then you run System Agent and leave it running in the background. The rest is automatic. Each program you add to the System Agent's list of tasks can be set to run at a different time or under different conditions.

After installing Microsoft Plus, the System Agent will already be installed and activated. You'll know it's running because you'll see a little icon in the Taskbar:

Point to it to find out whether the System Agent is awake or asleep. Double-click on it to see what programs are currently in the list of tasks and to make adjustments.

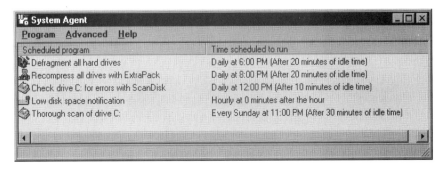

The list on the previous page should look like yours. These are the programs that Microsoft Plus added by default to the Agent's tasks. They all pertain to hard-disk maintenance; primarily to tasks we all should do anyway but usually don't bother about until it's too late. Keep in mind that ExtraPack only works if you have compressed drives.

Most of the options you'll be concerned with are on the Programs menu. From there you add or remove programs, change the schedule for a program, change settings that apply to a program, or change the properties for that program. Settings and properties will be different for each program, but they typically allow you to change the description that appears in the System Agent's window, determine things such as which drive(s) will be affected, whether the program runs in a window or minimized as an icon, and whether the time of running and possible results of a given program are stored in a log file. You can view the log with the Advanced ➤ View Log command.

TIP You can disable any program from running by clicking on it and choosing Programs ➤ Disable. *Disabled* then appears next to the program. To reactivate the program, toggle the command off.

You can immediately run a single program in your list by clicking on it and choosing Programs ➤ Run Now.

There may be times when you want to temporarily stop the System Agent (you may be working late and not want ScanDisk to kick in while you're out getting that midnight pizza). Just choose Advanced ➤ Suspend System Agent. Toggle the command to reactivate the System Agent.

TECH TIP Don't like the System Agent concept at all? Well, it's possible: It takes up memory and some computing power, it might interfere with some other program you have, or you may want to run all of these system utility programs manually. In any case, you can prevent System Agent from loading when you boot Windows. Just choose Advanced ➤ Stop Using System Agent. If you want to reactivate it in the future, choose Start ➤ Programs ➤ Accessories ➤ System Tools ➤ System Agent.

Internet Plus

This option gives you an Explorer-like interface for the Internet and provides an Internet mail service. When installing this function, you'll be asked whether you want to connect to the Internet via the Microsoft Network or via your own service provider:

▶ If you choose the Microsoft Network option, you'll be asked if you want to sign up or if you already have an account.

▶ If you indicate that you have an account with another service provider, you'll be asked to provide information relevant to your account such as area code, phone number, user name, password, IP address of your DNS server (e.g., 128.8.5.1), e-mail address, Internet server, and so forth. Research this information before attempting to set up your connection.

After installing Internet Plus (even if you don't know your Internet-provider information), you'll have a new folder under Accessories called `Internet Tools`.

If you bail out of the Internet install, you can always run the Wizard again to set up your account.

Once installation is complete, you can get onto the Internet by choosing the Internet Explorer option. This launches what is essentially a World Wide Web browser, much like the popular program Mosaic. In fact, it's called Microsoft Mosaic and looks like Explorer crossed with Mosaic (see Figure 32.3).

The upshot here is that you have a version of Mosaic that is licensed by Spyglass Inc. to Microsoft.

What About My Internet Mail?

Internet Explorer doesn't do mail; the Web doesn't, so the Web browser can't. So, the other half of Internet Tools is an extension to Microsoft Exchange. This extension lets you send and receive mail over the Internet by adding a few features to Microsoft Exchange that

Figure 32.3 *The Internet Explorer is a Web browser. Though only representing a portion of what the Internet has to offer, the Web is quickly becoming the most traveled lane of the information superhighway. However, this Internet tool doesn't support some Internet services (such as FTP, Finger, IRC, telnet, Gopher, or newsgroups).*

tell it how to call up your Internet provider (IP). Your IP may be a separate company such as Netcom or it might be Microsoft (via the Microsoft Network). After setting up your Internet connection, you'll be prompted to choose which Microsoft Exchange profile your connection will be added to. You'll then have a few additional items in your Microsoft Exchange setup; for example, the Tools ➤ Deliver Mail Now menu will have a new option:

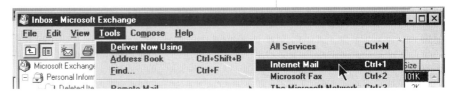

Please refer to Chapter 15 for details about Microsoft Exchange mail services and to Chapter 18 for related details about FTP and other Internet tools.

> **TECH TIP** Unless you're dead set against using Microsoft as your Internet provider, you can eliminate some hassles by simply using the Microsoft Network as your provider. If you use another provider, be sure to purchase an account that works with Microsoft Exchange for Windows 95. Providers will begin to understand what this means in the months after the release of Windows 95. If you want to use the Web browser, you will have to have a SLIP or PPP account; if you want mail, your IP will have to provide a mailbox with a standard Internet mail address.

Master Themes

Master Themes combines sound schemes, color schemes, screen savers, and cursors for your Windows 95 system. It isn't much different

from what you can achieve using the Sounds, Display, and Mouse applets from the Control Panel. The advantage of Master Themes is that settings from these three areas are pulled into one applet called Desktop Themes, making it easy to recall many settings at once. You'll find Master Themes in the Control Panel.

Master Themes isn't just a tool for organizing your own settings into groups. You also get some great sounds; Desktop backgrounds; and cute new icons for My Computer, the Recycle Bin, and Network Neighborhood.

Running the applet brings up the dialog box shown in Figure 32.4.

You can create your own schemes by setting up the screen saver, sounds, cursor, and Desktop the way you like and then saving them using the Save As button at the top of the box. However, you might find that the supplied themes give you all the variation you need. Choose a theme from the drop-down list box to see what it looks like. You can preview the screen saver, pointers, and sounds using the two Preview buttons in the upper-right corner.

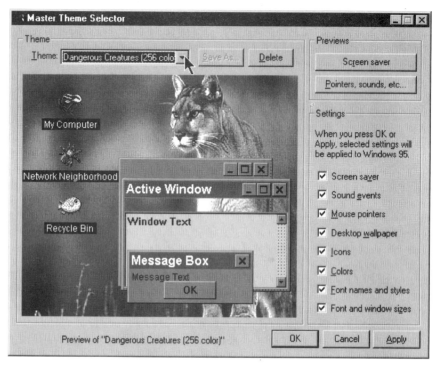

Figure 32.4   *Desktop Themes provides a means for coordinating various elements of the Windows 95 environment and saving them under a single name. An interesting variety of master themes is supplied with Microsoft Plus.*

TIP   Some of the schemes look pretty bad even in 256 colors. Because some of the visuals are actually photo-realistic, switching to a high-color or true-color setting will give you more impressive results. High-color themes are marked as such. If you *don't* have a high-color video driver, you might as well remove these schemes; it will save a significant amount of disk space.

In the Settings portion of the box, you'll see eight check boxes for things like Screen Saver, Sound Events, and so on. Each scheme includes settings for all these options. However, you might not want to load all these features when you change schemes; for example, you might like the sounds you already have but want everything else from one of the master themes. To do this, turn off the Sound Events option before clicking on Apply or OK.

To switch back to the ordinary Windows 95 settings, choose the Windows Default master theme at the bottom of the list of themes.

3-D Pinball

This is an entertainment program based on the classic time waster—the pinball machine. But it looks great. You'll find it in the Games folder (choose Start ➤ Programs ➤ Accessories ➤ Games). Once you run it, press F8 for a listing of keys that control the flippers, bump the table in different directions, and so forth. You can press F4 to switch between windowed and full-screen display. The game's physics and sound effects are realistic. It beats Solitaire and Minesweeper by a country mile!

> **TIP** The longer you hold down the spacebar, the farther back the plunger is pulled, which affects the force applied to the ball as you launch it. I also suggest setting the flippers to the F and J keys as that's where index fingers usually feel at home.

> **CAUTION** Be careful who you show the game to. Little did I know that my friend Niel is a pinball wizard. The game sucked him in so much, he kept slapping my laptop around, instinctively trying to tilt it.

Visual Enhancements

In addition to master schemes, a couple of visual enhancements are added to your system when you install Microsoft Plus:

- ▶ sliding Taskbar
- ▶ full-window drag
- ▶ font smoothing
- ▶ wallpaper stretching
- ▶ fancy animated cursors
- ▶ additional TrueType fonts for DOS boxes

**Part
6**

Customizing
Windows 95

Sliding Taskbar

If you have the Taskbar set to Auto Hide (from Start ➤ Settings ➤ Taskbar), it now slides away smoothly rather than just disappearing. A subtle touch.

Full-Window Drag and Resize

Next, there's the full-window drag option. If Microsoft Plus senses that your system can take it, it installs a driver that keeps the insides of your windows alive while you move them around the screen. Recall that in Windows 3.x and in the stock version of Windows 95, when dragging or resizing a window you see a little empty frame moving around. After installing Microsoft Plus, contents of the window move along with its border, even if the contents of the window are being modified at the time (such as when a chart is being redrawn or numbers are recalculating in a spreadsheet).

Font Smoothing

TrueType fonts in Windows actually comprise two font files on the hard disk: the screen fonts and the printer fonts. The screen fonts are responsible for showing you how the printed font will look and are actually only a close facsimile of the final printed font, close enough to give you a sense of the font's appearance and display accurate line breaks, pagination, and so forth.

Screen font files don't actually have all the possible sizes (2 to 127 points in Windows 3.x and to 999 points in Windows 95) built in. Instead, they are rendered via a formulaic description of the font. With smaller point sizes, this works fine. With larger sizes, the extrapolated display looks edgy, and fonts get the *jaggies* (meaning rough around the edges). A new Windows 95 feature called *font smoothing* or *anti-aliasing* mitigates this problem, in effect smoothing off the rounded edges on large fonts.

On installation of Microsoft Plus, a 32-bit font rasterizer is loaded into your system. It's optimized to *antialias* by filling in the rough spots with softer colors than the one the font is displayed in; for example, shades of gray are used for black letters. Font smoothing is compatible with any TrueType fonts, including the ones you may already have from Windows 3.x. Notice the difference between the two letters below; the one on the left uses smoothing.

NOTE For support of TrueType font smoothing, you need a video setup that supports 256 colors or greater. Also, smoothing has no effect on characters larger than 190 points.

NOTE Font smoothing is nothing new. Adobe's Display PostScript technology, implemented on the NeXT computer (among others) has had it for some time. But Microsoft opted not to support PostScript, developing its own TrueType instead.

Wallpaper Stretching and Animated Cursors

Stretching attractively increases the size of wallpaper images intended for standard VGA monitors (640 by 480) so they display on higher-resolution monitors such as 800 by 600 or 1,024 by 768.

Animated cursors are pointers (such as the frustrating hourglass) that put on a little show rather than just sitting there. Windows NT has animated cursors, and now Windows 95 does, too. Actually, you can use the cursors from NT or ones you download from a BBS even if you don't have Microsoft Plus. Animated cursors have an .ani extension. Microsoft Plus installs a small collection of new ANI files for you to choose from when customizing your system from the Mouse applet in the Control Panel (see Chapter 7).

Part 6

Customizing Windows 95

New TrueType Fonts for DOS Boxes

Before installing Microsoft Plus, a DOS box in Windows 95 will have six possible TrueType font sizes for displaying DOS programs in a window: 6×12, 7×14, 7×15, 8×16, 10×20, and 12×22.

After installing Microsoft Plus, you'll have fourteen TrueType font options for displaying character-based DOS applications in a window: 2×4, 3×5, 4×7, 5×8, 5×9, 6×10, 7×11, 8×13, 8×14, 9×15, 10×16, 11×18, 12×20, and 13×22.

See Chapter 4 for a discussion of adjusting fonts in a DOS box.

Appendix

Installing Windows 95 on Your Computer

FEATURING

Running the Setup program

Chances are good that your computer came installed with Windows 95 already, in which case reading this appendix isn't necessary for you. On the other hand, if you are still using Windows 3.x or have no version of Windows on your computer at all, you'll want to read this appendix.

There are two basic scenarios when installing Windows 95. You're either upgrading over a previous version of Windows or on top of DOS. Either way, you'll be able to install Windows 95 using the same easy-to-follow installation program. Just so you know, there are two versions of Windows 95: an update version and a full version. The update version assumes you have a copy of Windows 3.x, OS/2, or NT on your computer and won't install unless you do. If you have an upgrade-only version of Windows 95 and for some reason you have to reinstall over a botched installation of Windows 95, you may have to reinstall your previous operating system first. If you have the full version of Windows 95, you can install over any operating system, such as DOS or an unsuccessful install of Windows 95, with no trouble.

NOTE If you have a previous version of Windows on your computer, you can install from a DOS prompt, though Microsoft recommends installing from within Windows.

During installation, you can choose to install Windows into a directory other than the existing Windows directory. This lets you keep a previous version of Windows to go back to as well as install a clean version of Windows 95. Although this might make you feel safer about trying out the new version, it will be a hassle in the long run. I highly recommend upgrading *over* your existing Windows directory, meaning into the same directory, typically C:\Windows. When you opt to install over Windows 3.x, various important settings—such as program INI settings, file locations, program associations, program groups, and so forth—are transferred into your new version. The most important advantage of replacing Windows 3.x is that you won't have to install all your applications (such as Microsoft Office) again for Windows 95. Things get pretty complicated with two separate versions of Windows on the same computer because changes you make in one version don't carry over to the other.

TECH TIP Unfortunately, you can't install Windows 95 over Windows NT or vice versa. While you could install NT over Windows 3.x and share settings, associations, and so forth, Windows 95 does not work this way. As a result, though you can have NT and Windows 95 on the same computer and boot either operating system as you like, they won't share INI settings, installed applications, and other settings. This may change in the future, but in the meantime, it's simply an annoyance. You'll have to install most applications twice—once for NT and once for Windows 95.

When you install over Windows 3.x, your existing settings are imported into Windows 95, and you'll have the least amount of hassle getting used to the new operating system because the turf will be familiar. All your familiar programs will still be installed and easy to get to.

Microsoft has done a laudable job of making the Windows 95 installation process pretty painless, thanks to the setup Wizard, which provides a pleasant Q&A-type interface. Therefore, I'll spare you the boredom of walking you through every step here on paper. Rather I'll get you going and discuss some of the decisions you'll have to make along the way.

Running the Setup Program

First off, you'll need to decide whether you are going to install from floppy disks or the CD-ROM. I highly recommend the latter if you have a drive. It will save you a lot of time and disk swapping. With the CD-ROM you can get things going, then take a coffee break while the necessary files are copied in. Otherwise you have to stay by the computer for about half an hour. Before beginning, make sure you have at least 30 MB of free hard-disk space on the drive you're going to install Windows on. Use File Manager or the DOS **dir** command to check this. The CD-ROM drive needn't be on your local computer. You can also install from a shared directory or drive that you are attached to by way of a local-area network. You simply switch to that directory (say via File Manager in Windows for Workgroups 3.11) and run Setup.

TECH TIP   If you do have the floppy-disk version and you have enough free disk space (an additional 1.8 MB or so per floppy), you can copy all the disks into a directory on your hard disk and run Setup from there. This will speed up the process considerably.

To begin the setup process,

1. Boot your computer either to the DOS prompt or, if you have Windows, into Windows.

2. Insert the first diskette into the appropriate floppy drive or, if you have a CD-ROM drive, put the CD into that.

 TECH TIP   You can't install from a CD-ROM unless your CD-ROM driver is installed, functioning, and has a logical letter name (such as D). When installing from a CD-ROM, simply inserting the CD-ROM in the drive and switching to it may run a program that presents you with a simple means of running the installation program. This wasn't finalized at the time of this writing.

3. I recommend you read through two text files that contain last-minute information about Windows 95. These files might provide special tips about your brand of computer or cards, printers, and other accessories. The files are called `readme.txt` and `setup.txt`. They can be found on Disk 1 of the floppy set or in the `\Win95` directory on the CD-ROM. To read these files in Windows, just get to them via the File Manager, then double-click on them. From DOS, use a text editor that can read ASCII or DOS text files.

4. If you're in Windows, switch to the File Manager or Program Manager, open the File menu, and choose Run. If you're in DOS, get to a DOS prompt. Then enter the following command, depending on whether you're installing from a CD-ROM or floppy:

    Floppy: **a:setup** ⏎

    CD: **d:\win95\setup** ⏎

    Replace a: or d: in the above statements with the appropriate drive letter for your machine. (Alternatively, in File Manager you can scroll to `setup.exe` and double-click on it.) In a few seconds you'll be greeted with a fancy blue screen and some directions about installation (as in Figure 1).

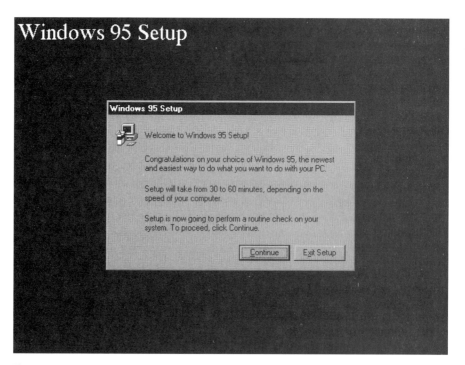

Figure 1   *The first welcome screen when installing*

5. Click on Continue to let Setup check out your computer. If you have too little disk space or there's some other problem, the program lets you know, then the Setup Wizard is whipped up and runs.

6. You'll see a license agreement. If you agree to the terms, move the mouse pointer on top of the Yes button and click the left mouse button.

7. You'll be alerted to quit other programs if they are running. This is because Setup might bomb, in which case any work you were doing could be lost. Switch to any program in which you have open work, save the work, close the program, and switch back to Setup.

8. Now the Wizard begins Phase I of three phases. The first phase checks out what hardware is in your computer. Click on Next.

9. You're now asked where you want to install Windows.

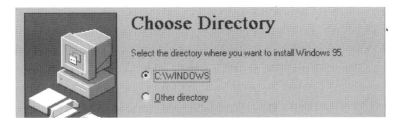

10. Your current Windows directory (if you have one) is shown as the default choice. This is the best bet. Click on Next.

11. Now Setup sleuths around for quite a while, checking out what operating system is currently in your computer. After awhile you'll see this box asking which type of installation you want to perform:

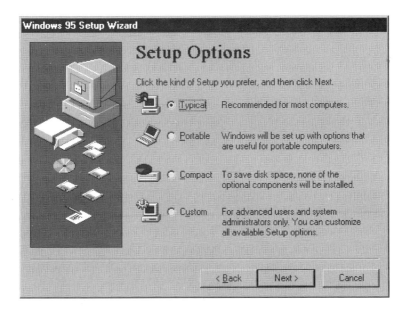

There are four basic types of installation: Typical, Portable, Compact, and Custom. The option you choose determines which accessory programs and utilities get installed. If you want full control over what gets loaded onto your machine, choose Custom. The Typical option will work fine for most users. Regardless of which you choose, the basics of Windows 95 will be identical, and you can add or delete any accessories later. If you're short on disk space, use Compact. If you choose an option for which you don't have enough disk space, don't worry. You'll be alerted and allowed to change choices.

> **TECH TIP**   If you choose Custom, you'll be shown a screen that lets you choose which options to install. A grayed check mark next to a component means that only some of its suboptions are selected. Double-click on a component to see a list of its subcomponents or uncheck the gray check, then wait a second and click again to get a black check mark. The black check mark means all subcomponents are selected and will be installed. To ensure you install every possible component, just make sure all the check marks are black.

12. Click on the radio button next to the type of installation you want and then click on Next.

13. When asked to enter your user information, enter your name and company (if there is no company, leave it blank). After entering your name, click on the company line to skip down to it, then click on Next. (These lines may already be filled in for you if you're upgrading from an older version of Windows, in which case just click on Next.)

14. Now Setup sleuths around again, this time looking for hardware. It does a pretty exhaustive search, scouting for almost every known brand of add-on card, hard disk, SCSI controller, and so on. This can take some time; a little gas gauge keeps you informed of the progress. You *must* wait until the search is through. Don't cancel the search unless your computer sits idle for a good long time, like about five minutes, with no hard-disk activity (this means Setup has crashed). If that happens, reboot the machine by turning it off (*not* by pressing Ctrl-Alt-Del) and then on again. Then choose Safe Recovery when prompted. The Setup program will then pick up where it left off.

15. Now you'll be asked about setting up communications:

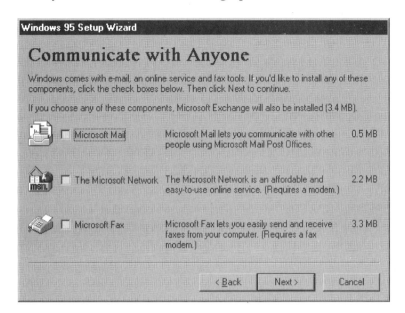

Choose which if any of these options you want to install. If you don't install them now, you can later. If you have a fax modem, you'll at least want Fax so you can send and receive faxes from your computer.

16. Depending on the type of install you're doing, you may now see a box asking if you want to install the most common components automatically or choose from a list. It's up to you. The first choice is faster because you don't have to think about it. The second choice shows you the whole shooting match, and you make choices from there. If you choose the latter, see the Tech Tip above. Click on Next.

17. Next you may be asked about your network ID, including your computer's name as it will appear to others on the network, which Workgroup you're in, and a description of the computer. Fill it in as you like. It may be already filled in if you're upgrading. Ensure the Workgroup name is accurate, or you won't be let into your own Workgroup. Click on Next.

18. When asked about creating a start-up disk, choose Yes (unless you don't have a spare disk around). A start-up disk can come in handy in case your operating system gets messed up in the future somehow. Click on Next.

NOTE   You can create a start-up disk later using the Add/Remove Programs applet on the Control Panel.

19. Now Setup goes into Phase II, copying a zillion files onto your hard disk. This is where the floppy-disk swapping, or simply waiting, comes in. Just click on Next.

20. When asked to insert a floppy to make the start-up disk, do so. It must be at least a 1.2-MB disk and must be in drive A (it can also be a 1.44-MB or 2.8-MB disk). Just follow the instructions; the floppy will chug along for a while.

 TECH TIP   It's possible you will be prompted with a version-conflict message about a DLL or other support file that Setup is installing being older than the one on your hard disk. In most cases you should keep the newer version of the DLL.

21. When all the copying is over, you'll be prompted to begin Phase III, in which your computer is restarted. Just click on Finish.

22. Now your computer will seem to sit there forever with the little flashing Windows logo doing its thing. Finally, the Welcome to Windows log-on box will appear. Enter a password (you may have the option of not entering a password) and click on OK.

23. Windows 95 now sets up Plug and Play, installs Help, and does some housekeeping. Then you'll be asked to set the home time zone. Use the ← and → keys to move to your time zone. Then click on Date and Time and check for accuracy (see Chapter 7 for more about the Date and Time box).

24. Finally, you'll be prompted to restart your computer. You're done! Windows reboots, and you're up and running. Turn to Chapter 1 and begin reading *Mastering Windows 95*. We hope you enjoy the book!

Index

Note to the Reader:

Main entries are in **bold**. **Boldface** numbers indicate pages where you will find the principal discussion of a topic or the definition of a term. *Italic* numbers indicate pages where topics are illustrated in figures.

Numbers and Symbols

3-D Pinball game, 1086, **1099**
10Base-2 (Thin Ethernet) topology, 960–961, *960*
10Base-T (twisted-pair Ethernet) topology, 959, 961–963, *962*
16-bit applications
compatibility of, 89–90
file dialog boxes in, 132–135, *133*
long file names and, 53–54
saving files to the Desktop from, 227–229, *228*, *229*
upgrading to 32-bit applications, 90–93
16-bit device drivers, 104, 1078–1079
32-bit applications
file dialog boxes in, 135–137
upgrading to, **90–93**
32-bit device drivers, 89–90
32-bit processing, 6, 20
286-based computers, 94
386 device-protection capabilities, 81
.386 files, 173
➤ **(arrow)**, in menus, *123*, 124
@ **(at sign)**, in Internet addresses, 652

\ **(backslash)**, root directory and, 497
<< >> (chevrons)
in dialog boxes, 131
in Help screens, 154
● **(dot)**, in menus, 124
… **(ellipses)**
in dialog boxes, 131
in menus, 124, 125
- **(hyphen)**, Alt-— (minus) (open Control box), 118
– **(minus sign)**, in Explorer, 499–500, 502, *502*, 503
() **(parentheses)**, in Calculator, 872
+ **(plus sign)**
and copying objects, 219
in Explorer, 499–500, 502, *502*, 503
? **(question mark)**, Help ?-arrow tool, 38, 151–153

A

About dialog box, 272
Accessibility Options applet, 311, **314–323**. *See also* Control Panel
Display tab, 318–319, *318*
General tab, 321–323, *322*, *323*
Keyboard tab, 314–316, *315*
Mouse tab, 319–321, *320*, *321*

Sound tab, 316–317, *317*
accessories, **853–882**, **1055–1060**. *See also* applications; HyperTerminal; Paint; system tools; utilities; WordPad
Briefcase, **1055–1060**
Calculator, **862–874**
accessing scientific functions, 870–871
calculating results, 863
copying calculations to and from other documents, 864–868
entering numbers in scientific notation, 871
grouping terms with parentheses, 872
Help, 862
Inv and Hyp options, 870–871
keyboard shortcuts and equation symbols, 865–867, 868
memory keys, 863–864
percentages, 868–869
Scientific calculator, **869–874**, *869*
square roots, 868
Standard calculator, **862–869**, *862*
statistical calculations, 863, 872–874
using different number base systems, 871–872

NetBEUI protocol, 949–951
NetBIOS Frame (NBF) protocol, 950
NetBIOS protocol, 947–948, 949
Network Drivers Interface Specification (NDIS) and, 943–944, 1036
Open Datalink Interface (ODI) standard and, 944–945
TCP/IP protocol, 951–953
v. Windows NT networking, 15–18, *17*
newsgroups, 647
NICs. *See* network interface cards
notebook computers. *See* laptop computers
Notepad, 853–861. *See also* accessories; text files; WordPad
creating files, 856
entering date and time, 859
entering and editing text, 857–859, *858*
finding text, 859–860
headers and footers, 861
limitations of, 855
margin settings, 860–861
navigating in, 859
opening files, 856–857
printing files, 861
starting, 855, *856*
understanding text files, 853–854
word-wrap option, 857, *858*
v. WordPad, 853
Novell
NetWare v. Windows NT, 16
Unix operating system, 70
NTFS partitions and file names, 53, **55**
null-modem cables, 781, *782*. *See also* Direct Cable Connection
number base systems, in Calculator, 871–872
number formats, 313, **1071–1073**, *1072*

O

Object Linking and Embedding (OLE), 8, *8*, 27, **251–252**, 280–305
advantages of, 281–283, *282*
component objects, **287**
compound documents, 283, 285
Compound File Format, **291**
containers, **287**
v. Dynamic Data Exchange (DDE), 280–281, 283–284
embedding, **285, 293–296**
defined, **285**, *286*
editing embedded objects, 295–296
embedding objects, 293–295, *295*
files with File Manager, 261
objects in e-mail, **584–585**
TrueType fonts, 420–421
inconsistencies in, 291–293, *292*
linking, **285, 296–305**
canceling and deleting links, 303–304
defined, **285**, *286*
editing linked objects, 299–300, *300*
fixing broken links, 304–305
linking files, 296–299
manually updating links, 300–302, *302*
Paste Special dialog boxes and, 297–299, *298*
Microsoft Exchange and, 586
objects defined, **283, 285**
OLE clients and servers, **285–287**
packaging, **287–288**, *288*
version 1.0 v. version 2.0, 284, 287, **288–291**, *289*, *290*
object-oriented graphics, 800–802
objects. *See also* documents; files; folders; property sheets

copying between folders, 217–220, *218*
copying v. moving, 219
defined, **283, 285**
moving and copying between folders, 217–220, *218*
packaging, **287–288**, *288*
renaming, 248–249
renaming on Start button menus, 215
selecting multiple objects, 221, *221*
undoing object moves, 219
online services. *See* CompuServe; GEnie; Microsoft Network
opaque placement of selections, in Paint, 835–836
Open Datalink Interface (ODI) standard, 944–945
Open System Interconnect (OSI) reference model, 937–942. *See also* networks
application layer, 939
data link layer, 942
network layer, 941–942
physical layer, 942
presentation layer, 940
session layer, 940
transport layer, 941
opening. *See also* loading; running; starting
address books, 576–577, *576*
Clipbook, 274, *274*
Control Panel, 309, *310*
documents, 26–27, *27*, *28*, 31
latest-document-opened list, 33, *33*
in Notepad, 856–857
with Open dialog boxes, 132–137, *133*
folders, 34, *36*
graphics in Paint, 803–804, *803*
menus, 121–122, *122*, *123*
Microsoft Exchange, 570–571, *571*
Printers folder, 374

EXPERIENCE
SUITE SUCCESS
WITH OFFICE

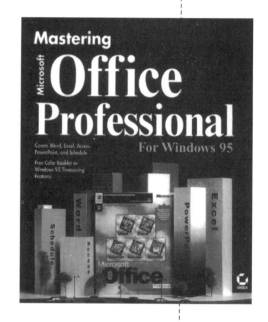

Learn how Windows 95, Word, Excel, PowerPoint, Access and Mail/Schedule+ can work together to solve real-world problems. Using a business process approach, the author focuses on accomplishing tasks, rather than individual program features. A practical book for savvy business people who want meaningful results, fast. Includes a pull-out color guide on Windows 95, revealing all the new time-saving features.

1,000 pages
ISBN: 1747-3

SYBEX

SYBEX Inc., • 2021 Challenger Drive • Alameda, CA 94501 • 800-227-2346 • 510-523-8233

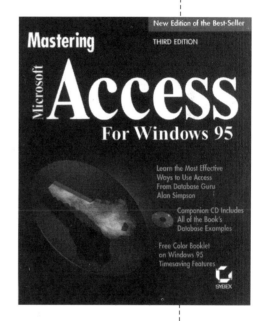

SYBEX · NEW · SYBEX · HOT!

Roadmaps for Travelers on the Information Superhighway

The Pocket Tour™ Series

What's your interest?

Sports? Games? Music? Travel?
Money? Health and Fitness?
Whatever it is, the Internet's
crammed with everything you
could ever want to know on
the subject.

Knowing where to look, however,
is another matter. That's why
Sybex has developed the exclusive
Pocket Tour™ series—to guide
you every step of the way through
the often confusing
Internet maze.

Watch for additional
Sybex Pocket Tours of:

- *Celebrities*
- *Food & Drink*
- *Kidstuff*
- *Law*
- *Shopping*

SYBEX

Games	Health & Fitness	Money	Music	Sports	Travel
1694-9	1711-2	1696-5	1695-7	1693-0	1760-0

FOR EVERY COMPUTER QUESTION,
THERE IS A SYBEX BOOK THAT HAS THE ANSWER

ach computer user learns in a different way. Some need thorough, methodical explanations, while others are too busy details. At Sybex we bring nearly 20 years experience to developing the book that's ht for you. Whatever your needs, we can lp you get the most from your software d hardware, at a pace that's comfortable you.

e start beginners out right. You will learn by seeing and doing with our **Quick & Easy** series: friendly, colorful idebooks with screen-by-screen illustrations. r hardware novices, the **Your First** series ers valuable purchasing advice and stallation support.

ften recognized for excellence in national book reviews, our **Mastering** titles are designed for the intermediate advanced user, without leaving the beginner hind. A **Mastering** book provides the most tailed reference available. Add our pocket- ed **Instant Reference** titles for a complete idance system. Programmers will find that ı new **Developer's Handbook** series ovides a more advanced perspective on veloping innovative and original code.

ith the breathtaking advances common in computing today comes an ever increasing demand to remain technologically up-to-date. In many of our books, we provide the added value of software, on disks or CDs. Sybex remains your source for information on software development, operating systems, networking, and every kind of desktop application. We even have books for kids. Sybex can help smooth your travels on the **Internet** and provide **Strategies and Secrets** to your favorite computer games.

s you read this book, take note of its quality. Sybex publishes books written by experts—authors chosen for their extensive topical knowledge. In fact, many are professionals working in the computer soft-ware field. In addition, each manuscript is thoroughly reviewed by our technical, editorial, and production personnel for accuracy and ease-of-use before you ever see it—our guarantee that you'll buy a quality Sybex book every time.

 o manage your hardware headaches and optimize your software potential, ask for a Sybex book.

FOR MORE INFORMATION, PLEASE CONTACT:

Sybex Inc.
2021 Challenger Drive
Alameda, CA 94501
Tel: (510) 523-8233 • (800) 227-2346
Fax: (510) 523-2373

SYBEX

GET A FREE CATALOG JUST FOR EXPRESSING YOUR OPINION.

Help us improve our books and get a **FREE** full-color catalog in the bargain. Please complete this form, pull out this page and send it in today. The address is on the reverse side.

Name _____ Company _____

Address _____ City _____ State ____ Zip _____

Phone ( )_____

1. How would you rate the overall quality of this book?

- ❏ Excellent
- ❏ Very Good
- ❏ Good
- ❏ Fair
- ❏ Below Average
- ❏ Poor

2. What were the things you liked most about the book? (Check all that apply)

- ❏ Pace
- ❏ Format
- ❏ Writing Style
- ❏ Examples
- ❏ Table of Contents
- ❏ Index
- ❏ Price
- ❏ Illustrations
- ❏ Type Style
- ❏ Cover
- ❏ Depth of Coverage
- ❏ Fast Track Notes

3. What were the things you liked *least* about the book? (Check all that apply)

- ❏ Pace
- ❏ Format
- ❏ Writing Style
- ❏ Examples
- ❏ Table of Contents
- ❏ Index
- ❏ Price
- ❏ Illustrations
- ❏ Type Style
- ❏ Cover
- ❏ Depth of Coverage
- ❏ Fast Track Notes

4. Where did you buy this book?

- ❏ Bookstore chain
- ❏ Small independent bookstore
- ❏ Computer store
- ❏ Wholesale club
- ❏ College bookstore
- ❏ Technical bookstore
- ❏ Other _____

5. How did you decide to buy this particular book?

- ❏ Recommended by friend
- ❏ Recommended by store personnel
- ❏ Author's reputation
- ❏ Sybex's reputation
- ❏ Read book review in _____
- ❏ Other _____

6. How did you pay for this book?

- ❏ Used own funds
- ❏ Reimbursed by company
- ❏ Received book as a gift

7. What is your level of experience with the subject covered in this book?

- ❏ Beginner
- ❏ Intermediate
- ❏ Advanced

8. How long have you been using a computer?

years _____

months _____

9. Where do you most often use your computer?

- ❏ Home
- ❏ Work

- ❏ Both
- ❏ Other _____

10. What kind of computer equipment do you have? (Check all that apply)

- ❏ PC Compatible Desktop Computer
- ❏ PC Compatible Laptop Computer
- ❏ Apple/Mac Computer
- ❏ Apple/Mac Laptop Computer
- ❏ CD ROM
- ❏ Fax Modem
- ❏ Data Modem
- ❏ Scanner
- ❏ Sound Card
- ❏ Other _____

11. What other kinds of software packages do you ordinarily use?

- ❏ Accounting
- ❏ Databases
- ❏ Networks
- ❏ Apple/Mac
- ❏ Desktop Publishing
- ❏ Spreadsheets
- ❏ CAD
- ❏ Games
- ❏ Word Processing
- ❏ Communications
- ❏ Money Management
- ❏ Other _____

12. What operating systems do you ordinarily use?

- ❏ DOS
- ❏ OS/2
- ❏ Windows
- ❏ Apple/Mac
- ❏ Windows NT
- ❏ Other _____

13. On what computer-related subject(s) would you like to see more books?

_____

_____

_____

_____

14. Do you have any other comments about this book? (Please feel free to use a separate piece of paper if you need more room)

_____

_____

_____

_____

- - - - - - - - - PLEASE FOLD, SEAL, AND MAIL TO SYBEX - - - - - - - - - -

SYBEX INC.
Department M
2021 Challenger Drive
Alameda, CA
94501

Let us hear from you.

**T**alk to SYBEX authors, editors and fellow forum members.

**G**et tips, hints and advice online.

Download magazine articles, book art, and shareware.

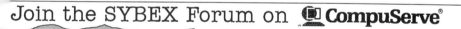

Join the SYBEX Forum on **CompuServe**®

If you're already a CompuServe user, just type **GO SYBEX** to join the SYBEX Forum. If not, try CompuServe for free by calling 1-800-848-8199 and ask for Representative 560. You'll get one free month of basic service and a $15 credit for CompuServe extended services—a $23.95 value. Your personal ID number and password will be activated when you sign up.

Join us online today. Type **GO SYBEX** on CompuServe.
If you're not a CompuServe member, call Representative 560
at **1-800-848-8199**.

SYBEX

(outside U.S./Canada call 614-457-0802)

TIPS AND SHORTCUTS

Disks

3½ Floppy (A:)

▶ To format a disk, open My Computer, right-click on the drive, and choose Format.

▶ To copy a disk, open My Computer, right-click on the drive, and choose Copy Disk.

▶ To scan, compress, or defragment a disk, click on Start ➤ Programs ➤Accessories ➤ System Tools. Then choose ScanDisk, DriveSpace, or Disk Defragmenter.

Mail

Inbox

▶ To e-mail a document you have open, choose File ➤ Send (if the program has this function), and respond to the prompts.

▶ To e-mail a document from a folder, right-click on the document and choose Send To ➤ Mail Recipient.

▶ To send a fax from within a program, choose File ➤ Print, choose Microsoft Fax as the printer, and begin printing.

Printing

HP DeskJet 540 Printer

▶ To print a document you have open, turn on the printer and choose File ➤ Print.

▶ To check the print queue for a printer, click on Start ➤ Settings ➤ Printers. Double-click on the printer.

▶ To pause, rearrange, or cancel a print job, click on Start ➤ Settings ➤ Printers, click on the job, and choose Document ➤ Pause or Document ➤ Cancel.

ENGLAND, THEIR ENGLAND

ENGLAND, THEIR ENGLAND

**The definitive story of foreign footballers
in the English game since 1888**

Nick Harris

ENGLAND, THEIR ENGLAND

The definitive story of foreign footballers in the English game since 1888

Published by:
Pitch Publishing
10 Beresford Court
Somerhill Road
Hove
East Sussex BN3 1RH
Email: info@pitchpublishing.co.uk
www.pitchpublishing.co.uk

10 9 8 7 6 5 4 3 2 1

A catalogue record for this book is available from the British Library.

ISBN: 0-9542460-1-2

Editor: Jo Hathaway
Cover design: Swallow Company
Book design: Jigsaw Design
Printed and bound by Mackays Chatham

Contents

Author's note and acknowledgements

As THE title of this book suggests, only England's history of foreign players is considered, although some of Scotland's legionnaires are mentioned in passing. Every overseas-born player to have appeared in at least one English Football League or Premier League match since 1888 is included in the appendices, although some non-League players are mentioned in passing in the narrative. Some of the players in the appendices are overseas-born Britons but are included for the record.

Foreign players, for this book's purposes, are defined as those born outside Britain and Ireland. Though Scotland, Wales, Northern Ireland and the Republic of Ireland are all distinct from England in international football, they all share a heritage and role with English football as old as the game itself. In that sense, they are not considered foreign. On a practical level, including them would have trebled or quadrupled the size of the book.

I am grateful to hundreds of people in dozens of countries for their help and co-operation. First and foremost all the players, managers and other football folk who gave freely of their time and their memories and/or took the trouble to compile a personal 'All-time Foreign XI' especially for this book. They include Ossie Ardiles, Jimmy Armfield, Brendon Batson, Clyde Best, Craig Brown, Keith Burkinshaw, Barry Davies, Lindy Delapenha, Alec Eisentrager, Sir Tom Finney, Eddie Firmani, Denis Foreman, Steve Gibson, John Giles, Ron Greenwood, Johnny Haasz, John Hewie, Hans Jeppson, Juninho, Graham Kelly, Joe Marston, Gary McAllister, Lawrie McMenemy, Steve Mokone, Jan Molby, John Motson, Michael Parkinson, Ces Podd, Claudio Ranieri, Sir Bobby Robson, Graham Taylor, Peter Taylor, Bert Trautmann, Martin Tyler, Rolando Ugolini and Howard Wilkinson.

I am also indebted to Michael Joyce and his database of every match in English football history. That marvellous piece of software deserves a wider audience and has been a huge help with the statistics. My thanks also go to all the statisticians and historians who helped compile the appendices, and to all the supporters who provided anecdotal colour for the narrative. A more comprehensive list can be found on pages 365–66.

Thanks also to Colin Jose, a fountain of knowledge about the game in North America; Colin Cameron of Charlton, who has been tirelessly helpful; Jack McInroy, for his painstaking research into the life of Hassan Hegazi; Leigh Edwards, for his encyclopaedic knowledge; Tom Egbers, for helping to throw light on the complicated life of Steve Mokone; and my good friend Jon Roberts for his generosity, experience and unstinting enthusiasm. I am also grateful to the varied expertise of Steven Bridge, Alex Fynn, Miriam Sutter and Brian Sears. And to all those journalistic colleagues whose work has in turn informed and inspired, not least Richard Williams, Phil Shaw, Glenn Moore, Henry Winter, James Lawton, Grahame Lloyd and Paul Hayward.

Thanks to Karen Hobden at Jigsaw Design for being a complete star. Thanks to everyone at Pitch for having faith, and Jo Hathaway for her absolute dedication.

Above all thanks to Helen, Daisy and Isabel, who never fail to inspire.

Nick Harris, 30 June 2003

Preface

WITHIN A generation England has become the most cosmopolitan footballing nation on earth.

Twenty-five years ago, in the summer of 1978, it was deemed extraordinary that Tottenham had signed two Argentineans, Ossie Ardiles and Ricky Villa. Nowadays it's unusual if a top-flight team doesn't sign at least a couple of foreign players a year.

Fifteen years ago, in the 1988–89 season, it was still absolutely normal that Arsenal should win the League title without using a single foreign player. They were the last team to do so. It is unlikely that any team will ever again win it using players only from Britain and Ireland.

Ten years ago, in 1993–94, Manchester United were on their way to the first League and FA Cup Double in their history. Eric Cantona was in his second influential season at Old Trafford but established foreign internationals in England were still few and far between. In the run-up to the 2003–04 season, few transfer stories were without one.

One day in June threw up the following. Ronaldinho, the Brazilian whose goal eliminated England from the 2002 World Cup, was telling the world he wanted to sign for Manchester United. United were also reportedly interested in Ronaldinho's international team-mate, Lucio, and Leeds United's Australian international, Harry Kewell, who was also attracting interest from Arsenal and Liverpool.

Arsenal's French manager, Arsène Wenger, fresh from denying that he was about to leave Highbury for Real Madrid, was said to be interested in Lazio's Argentinean striker, Claudio Lopez. Wenger's compatriot, Gérard Houllier of Liverpool, was reportedly on the trail of the French striker Djibril Cisse and the Turkish midfielder Yildiray Basturk.

Everton, who had produced the home-grown hero of 2002–03 in teenager Wayne Rooney, were in talks to retain the services of Li Tie of China. Other clubs were looking towards another emerging source of foreign talent: Scotland's Old Firm. Italy's Lorenzo Amoruso, who scored the winning goal for Rangers in the 2003 Scottish Cup final, was reportedly on the verge of a move to Blackburn or Manchester United. Michael Mols, Rangers's Dutch international striker, was being pursued by Leicester City. And so it went on, England as a multi-national merry-go-round.

Foreign players and managers will play a major part in the 2003–04 season, not least in the upper reaches of the Premier League. Wenger, Houllier and Chelsea's Claudio Ranieri all led their teams to top-five finishes in 2003 and vowed to do better next time.

Whoever wins the League (or the FA Cup or the League Cup) will probably do so with key foreign players. If recent history repeats itself, the Premier League's highest goalscorer will probably be foreign, as will the Footballer of the Year.

Consider the personnel who dominated the 2002–03 season. Arsenal won the FA Cup final against Southampton by a single goal. France's Thierry Henry (England's Footballer of the Year in 2003) was crucial in setting it up, flicking the ball to Dutchman Dennis Bergkamp (the 1998 Player of the Year). Bergkamp crossed to Sweden's Freddie Ljungberg, who tried a shot, looking for a goal in a third consecutive FA Cup final. The ball fell to France's Robert Pires (the 2002 Footballer of the Year), who scored.

Southampton's goalkeeper that day, Antti Niemi of Finland, was one of 22 foreign keepers who appeared in the 2002–03 season in the Premier League, where 60 per cent of clubs had a first-choice goalkeeper who was foreign. They included Blackburn's Brad Friedel (USA), Chelsea's Carlo Cudicini (Italy) and Manchester City's Peter Schmeichel (Denmark). When Schmeichel announced his retirement, Niemi called him "the

Michael Jordan of goalkeepers", a reference to the great Dane's record of having stayed at the top of his game for so long. He chose to do so in England.

Schmeichel's former employers Manchester United won the League after a tremendous run-in that saw Dutchman Ruud Van Nistelrooy take his season's goal tally to 44. He scored 25 goals in the League to win the Golden Boot. United's manager, Sir Alex Ferguson, has always had a strong home-grown contingent in his sides but has also augmented his teams with foreign players, nine of whom featured in the 2002–03 season. Five of them – Fabien Barthez and Mikael Silvestre (both from France), Juan Sebastian Veron (Argentina), Ole Gunnar Solskjaer (Norway) and Van Nistelrooy – played in a majority of United's League games in 2002–03.

Arsenal, who were pipped to the title, used 18 foreign players in the League, including Henry, Pires, Bergkamp, Ljungberg, Patrick Vieira, Sylvain Wiltord, Gilberto Silva, Lauren, Kolo Toure and Kanu. Their campaign saw a sublime summer and autumn and then a setback in the spring that meant they to settle for 'only' the League runners-up spot and their FA Cup success.

Even as Arsenal faltered in the season's run-in, they did so at the hands of foreign opponents. Arsène Wenger pinpointed a 2–2 draw at Bolton on 26 April as the match in which his title dream was fatally damaged. Bolton started that game with 11 foreign players hailing from eight different countries – Denmark (2), Finland, France (3), Iceland, Jamaica, Nigeria, Senegal and Spain.

Bolton's Player of the Year was Jay-Jay Okocha of Nigeria, who produced some stunning moments as his side secured Premier League safety. Okocha moved to England after the 2002 World Cup, as did another major African footballer, El Hadji Diouf of Senegal, who joined Liverpool, who won the first trophy of the 2002–03 season, the League Cup.

That success came under the managerial guidance of a Frenchman, Houllier. Significant performances came from Poland's Jerzy Dudek (who revived his reputation with vital saves after a bad run), a Swiss-Finnish defensive alliance, Germany's Dietmar Hamann (who returned from injury to be influential in midfield) and England's Steven Gerrard and Michael Owen, who scored the goals in the 2–0 win after

Houllier had applied his Gallic academic touch to counsel them both through recent personal crises.

The historic questions about foreigners have been answered. After England gave football to the world in the 19th century it spent more than 100 years being institutionally opposed to foreigners playing in England. Navel-gazing logic was consistently applied to support this stance. What did foreigners know about football? Very little. What could they teach? Nothing. What could they bring to the English game? Job losses and confusion. What would an acceptance of foreign players say about England? That England could not produce enough good players of her own.

The answers are different now. The best of the foreign players are exemplary professionals who prepare meticulously, eat properly, train hard, possess superb technical skills and draw people through the turnstiles to watch them. They are dedicated to football for its own sake and have been teaching England how to play the game, on and off the pitch, for years. Gianfranco Zola springs to mind as the prime example.

The debate has moved on. The questions now are not what foreign players can offer but how English football can move forward, accommodating them to the best effect, in the age of cosmopolitan maturity.

The birthplace of the game has already passed through an age of superiority (1888–1939) when the English authorities refused to believe foreigners had anything to offer. Chapter One tells the stories of the pioneers who fought against that mentality and came anyway.

Next came the age of post-war revival, when competitive football resumed in England after a seven-year break with a new international cast (Chapters Two, Three and Four). Then came the age of extreme prejudice (Chapter Five) as England – and English football – became truly multi-cultural. From 1978, European law ushered in the age of legislative expansion, when the barriers to free movement started to come down (Chapter Six).

The Premier League era (Chapters Seven to Twelve), the era of television riches and Bosman, has seen a rapid acceleration of imported talent, from Cantona, the fiery French catalyst of Old Trafford, to the multi-national legions in towns and cities from Birmingham to Blackburn to Bolton to London to Liverpool to

Middlesbrough. Reliable Scandinavians, brilliant Brazilians, sexy Dutchmen, classy Italians, world-class Frenchmen – the English game has become planet football's most diverse melting pot.

So what comes next?

Has the volume of imported players peaked? The number of foreign players appearing in England's four professional divisions actually fell in 2002–03 to 457 from 497 the previous season. Arguably this was because the economic climate forced clubs to look to home-grown players before opening their chequebooks and buying off the peg from abroad. But maybe there was also a wider realisation that successful shopping overseas should be about quality not quantity.

Sir Alex Ferguson, England's most successful manager of the past decade, has achieved consistent success by blending home-grown players with a minority of well chosen imports. And while Arsène Wenger has prospered in recent years by fielding teams with a majority of foreigners, he has also claimed that his long-term ideal is to utilise local players and then add from overseas, not vice versa. The team building of Sir Bobby Robson at Newcastle is a rather more convincing case of someone who feels the same.

Are the days of spiralling transfer fees and wages, which were fueled largely by the post-Bosman 'foreign invasion', over? Certainly a period of reassessment has begun. Football clubs are starting to realise they must be more accountable to their backers, their shareholders and their fans. But not *that* accountable because the clubs are steadfastly against independent regulation, as are the football authorities, who are essentially comprised of vested interests inextricably linked to the clubs. Which means that the murkier aspects of football's recent past – bungs, irregular transfers, dodgy passports, player poaching and corrupt agents – could yet continue to haunt the game.

Maybe, in the near future, an age of complete transparency will dawn. Maybe clubs will be obliged to state publicly how much they paid, and to whom, at every stage of every deal. Such transparency is required especially in cross-border transfers. It seems an unlikely scenario at the moment.

Equally unlikely, on recent evidence, is that English football will reassert a consistent authority in Europe that has not been seen since English clubs won the European Cup seven times in eight years between 1977 and 1984. But then why should it? Success in Europe has always been cyclical, with Spain, Italy, Germany, England and The Netherlands dominating in turn.

The more pertinent question is whether English football can redefine itself in a truly contemporary form. This involves accepting the most progressive thinkers and the best ideas from wherever in the world they hail, be it the powerhouses of Europe and South America or one of the emerging nations.

It involves aspiring to the attacking flair of Real Madrid (2003 vintage) and the defensive nous of Milan (ditto) but with the acceptance that the two are not easily reconciled.

Above all, it involves educating the upcoming generations of home-grown players so that proper preparation and technical advancement become the norm not the exception. Only then can English football really claim to have come home, to a home frequented by foreign visitors for almost as long as the game has existed.

Arrivederci Isolation

Date: *26 December 1999*

Place: The Dell, Southampton
Southampton v Chelsea, English Premier League match

Chelsea's starting line-up: Ed De Goey; Albert Ferrer;
Emerson Thome; Frank Leboeuf; Celestine Babayaro;
Dan Petrescu; Didier Deschamps; Gustavo Poyet;
Roberto Di Matteo; Gabrielle Ambrosetti; Tore Andre Flo

One historic day at The Dell

CHELSEA'S 2–1 win was less significant than the fact they fielded
the first all-foreign XI in the history of the English Football
League. Gianluca Vialli couldn't understand the fuss. There he
was, sitting at a small table in the pokey post-match pressroom
at The Dell, expecting to give his thoughts on how his Chelsea
side had beaten Southampton, and all the questions were about
his team selection.

"Was it deliberate?" asked one of the assembled journalists.

"Did you know it's never been done before?" asked another.

"How do you feel to be the first manager ever to pick a team
entirely made up of foreign players?"

That afternoon, after 111 years, 3 months and 17 days of
Football League history, when British players had featured on
both sides in every one of its 150,000-plus fixtures, the Italian

1

had become the first manager to select a team with none. His goalkeeper was a Dutchman and his defenders hailed from Spain, Brazil, France and Nigeria. His midfield quartet included a second Frenchman, a Romanian, a Uruguayan and a Swiss-born Italian. Another Italian played a support role in attack to a Norwegian.

"We had a few players out," shrugged Vialli. "Unfortunately, some of them were English."

He said that nationality was "not important"...

"Whoever we play, wherever we play and in whatever competition, everyone – British or foreign – must be capable of adapting. We are an English team made of English and foreign players. It doesn't matter as long as we speak the same language on the field."

The Londoners scored twice in the first half with Tore Andre Flo getting both goals after skilful passes respectively from Gustavo Poyet, his captain for the day, and Didier Deschamps, a 1998 World Cup winner. Southampton, whose starting line-up was slightly more typical of the lesser top-division sides of the day – a Welshman, six Englishmen, two Norwegians, a Moroccan and a Latvian – pinched a late consolation through their Sheffield-born forward, Kevin Davies. Chelsea's win moved the expensively assembled legionnaires up to ninth place in the table.

In England, where foreign players were hardly rare, Vialli's landmark selection was flagged in the next day's newspapers with little more import than a trivia question stashed for the future. Outside Britain, away from the Premier League's made-for-TV world of exotic names and seven-figure contracts, Chelsea's team was seen as extraordinary.

> Imagine if the Baltimore Orioles came out to play at Camden Yards with not a single American in the starting line-up,

wrote one columnist in *The Washington Times*.

> Sounds crazy, doesn't it? ...The club's [*Chelsea's*] 30-man roster reads like the United Nations, with players from 12 different nations, including seven Italians and four Frenchmen.

It was ironic that observers in America, a nation about as distant from England as it gets in footballing geography, should seem alarmed. By 1999, even in America – melting pot America, home throughout the 20th century to a series of leagues based on imports, often from Britain – there were limits. Teams in the Major Soccer League had a ceiling of four foreign players.

It was simple enough to trace the chain of events to Chelsea's all-foreign line-up.

Glenn Hoddle, one of the most stylish and creative midfielders of the 1980s with Tottenham and England, had been appointed as player-manager of Chelsea in summer 1993. He was one of the rare Englishmen to have had success abroad, in his case in France between 1987 and 1991 with Monaco. It was there, under the tutelage of the Frenchman, Arsène Wenger, that Hoddle first thought of himself as management material. And there that he gained continental experience as part of a blended multi-national squad.

As manager of Chelsea, when the chance arose in July 1995 to import a player who would grace any such set-up, Hoddle did so. Enter Ruud Gullit, a 32-year-old former European Footballer of the Year with his own ambitions of management and a bulging contacts book. The seeds were sown.

In summer 1996, when Hoddle departed to manage England, Gullit took the reins in one hand and opened the Chelsea chequebook with the other. In came Roberto Di Matteo, Frank Leboeuf and Vialli. Then a Norwegian goalkeeper, Frode Grodas, and the chirpy Italian striker, Gianfranco Zola. Then Celestine Babayaro, Poyet, Ed De Goey and Flo among others, before Gullit was sacked in February 1998.

Vialli took up the baton, signing another 13 foreign players between his appointment and December 1999, by which time an alien XI was almost inevitable.

Chelsea's approach, of attempting to jigsaw together from myriad nations a team capable of fighting for honours, at home and in Europe, was pioneered enthusiastically by Ken Bates, the club's chairman…

"There is a suggestion that so-called foreign mercenaries are driving out English footballers, destroying the grass roots," Bates had said in 1997, a year that saw Chelsea win the FA Cup, their first major silverware since 1971. "What actually happens is that the foreign players bring new ideas, new ways of living and new attitudes to training which brush off on the youngsters."

Certainly by 1999, the cream of the imports had made their mark, domestically and in Europe, not least in Arsenal's Double-winning team of 1998 under Wenger, in Chelsea's European Cup Winners' Cup-winning team of the same season and in Manchester United's unique Treble-winning side of 1999. Imports had also made a clean sweep of the prestigious Footballer of the Year award for five consecutive years, from Tottenham's Jurgen Klinsmann in 1995 to Manchester United's Eric Cantona in 1996, Zola in 1997, Arsenal's Dennis Bergkamp in 1998 and Tottenham's David Ginola in 1999.

But these were just a handful among the 800 foreign players who had entered the English game's four professional divisions during the 1990s alone. This particular influx – the biggest if not the first – started with a couple of dozen foreign players in 1991, becoming 100 by 1995 and more than 200 by the end of 1996. Another 450 new faces arrived in the three years leading up to Vialli picking 11 of them to face Southampton. Like the language expansion at Chelsea, the 1990s influx can be mapped.

The genesis of the multi-national Premiership

In one sense, it originated in the 'dark days' of English football in the 1980s. Hooliganism – 'the English disease' – was commonplace, at home and abroad. The 1985 European Cup final between Liverpool and Juventus at the Heysel Stadium in Brussels on 29 May became an irrelevance after 39 people, mostly Italians, died when a wall collapsed on them during a riot involving supporters. Eighteen days earlier, on the last day of the domestic season, 56 people died when a fire, possibly caused by a discarded cigarette, swept through the aged, wooden main stand at Bradford City's Valley Parade ground. And then, on 15 April 1989, at the semi-final of the FA Cup between Liverpool and Nottingham Forest at Sheffield Wednesday's Hillsborough ground, came Europe's worst ever football tragedy. Errant policing and poor sign-posting led to a fatal crush in a fenced terrace pen that cost 96 people their lives.

The official report into the Hillsborough disaster was published at the end of January 1990. English football, it said, was blighted by old grounds, poor facilities, hooligans, a lack of adequate leadership and a frequent disrespect for the people who funded the industry – the supporters. It was recommended that terracing be banned from all grounds, starting with the top clubs. Within months the Football Association, under the stewardship of a new chief executive, Graham Kelly, was considering other fundamental steps forward.

By August 1992, English football had radically reshaped, with the leading 22 clubs – each housed in or planning refurbished or new all-seater stadiums – embarking on their inaugural season in the Premier League, the new all-singing, all-dancing, breakaway top division, funded by television receipts from Rupert Murdoch's Sky TV. England's performance at the 1990 World Cup, drenched in the tears of a young Paul Gascoigne, had already re-awakened a wider interest in the national game. Now the hard cash from Murdoch to the Premier League clubs – up to £304m between them over five years from 1992 – enabled a round of unprecedented spending on transfer fees and wages. English football had turned into a honey pot.

Déjà vu... with spending power

The advent of the Premier League, crucial though it was in attracting foreign players, was arguably only the stimulus for a *revival* of imports after a hiatus that, due to the state of the English game, effectively spanned most of the 1980s. Foreign footballers had been effectively excluded from playing in England between 1931, when the FA introduced a two-year residency rule to deter imports, and 1978, when European Community legislation dictated that national associations could not, by law, ban players from Common Market countries. As we shall see, this 47-year period was not without imported players, many of them prominent, some of them involved in momentous matches in English football history. They came and played in England despite the insular mentality of the game's rulers and the Government, either because they arrived before 1931, or came from colonial territories, or were refugees or amateurs or prisoners of war who never went home. But the period between 1931 and 1978 was nonetheless an era when all obstacles possible were placed in the way of aspirant immigrants.

From 1978–79 onwards this was no longer the case. The English authorities were forced to open their doors and did so to players from outside Europe as well. That season Tottenham sensationally signed two Argentinians, Osvaldo Ardiles and Ricky Villa, who had just been involved in their country's success at the 1978 World Cup. At Ipswich, Bobby Robson signed the Dutchmen Arnold Muhren and Frans Thijssen. Manchester City signed Poland's most-capped international, Kazimierz Deyna. Southampton signed Ivan Golac, a Yugoslavian international defender. These half-dozen were joined the same season by others from around the world following moves that a year before would have been outlawed by the authorities' isolationist rules. And they came not for money *per se* but because English football was seen as a vibrant and potentially successful place to work.

It was during the 1978–79 season that Trevor Francis became Britain's first £1m footballer after a move from Birmingham to Nottingham Forest. Kevin Keegan, then with SV Hamburg in Germany, won the European Footballer of the Year award and would soon return to England. Nottingham Forest won the European Cup, the second of six consecutive successes by English clubs in the competition and one of 11 European trophies won by English clubs between 1976 and 1985.

Foreign internationals arrived steadily in the early 1980s – and mostly at top-division clubs – from Argentina and Poland and Yugoslavia, from Belgium and The Netherlands and from across Scandinavia. But by the mid-1980s, when hooliganism was rife and English clubs were indefinitely banned from European competition because of the Heysel tragedy, the attraction of England had dramatically diminished. Why come when you couldn't aspire to European football? To dodge policemen as they tried to break up crowd disturbances at the final whistle? To play in front of dwindling crowds in crummy stadiums?

Not until the European ban was lifted, in the 1990–91 season – when Manchester United won the Cup-Winners' Cup, incidentally – was there really any incentive again for a foreign player to come to England. The end of the following season then saw the end of the old Football League structure and the start of the Premier League. The international players started to come back, only this time circumstances meant they came in numbers.

Back in Europe, back on track

English football was being screened, live via satellite television, to a wider international audience than ever before. The marketing men projected a fan-friendly environment that had shaken off its grubby, thug-ridden image of a decade before. There was no ban on English clubs playing in Europe, so players could move with legitimate hopes of international club football as well as good money. And the money, of course, was an incentive in itself, not only to the players but to agents. The most infamous of the 1990s, the Norwegian Rune Hauge, saw profits to be made – legitimately and otherwise – and personally brokered the transfers of countless players, mostly Scandinavians, more than 200 of whom moved to England. Agents proliferated at a global level and so did the moves to England, where home-grown players became increasingly more expensive than imports.

By December 1995, the imports of the early 1990s were already well established. The Norwegian defender, Henning Berg, for example, had been part of a title-winning team with Blackburn in 1995. The Danish midfielder, John Jensen, had featured as Arsenal won the FA Cup and Coca-Cola Cup in 1993 and the European Cup-Winners' Cup the following season. Stig Inge Bjornebye, Liverpool's Norwegian defender, had helped his side to the Coca-Cola Cup in 1995. Peter Schmeichel, the Danish goalkeeper, and Andrei Kanchelskis, the Ukrainian winger, had both won two league titles with Manchester United, the second coming as part of a League and FA Cup Double in 1994. That quintet of players, incidentally, had all been represented by Hauge during their moves to England. A third foreign player at Manchester United, France's Eric Cantona, had been part of the club's recent triumphs as well as a title-winner with Leeds in 1992.

The Bosman ruling

Yet it wasn't until the end of 1995, and the so-called 'Bosman ruling' in the European courts, that overseas markets became the primary source of talent, including for clubs lower down the leagues. Like Murdoch and Hauge before him, Jean-Marc Bosman, a journeyman midfielder from Belgium, was to become another outsider who would never play football in England yet influence the landscape of English football dramatically.

His legal action began when he took the Belgian FA and his club, RC Liege, to court in 1990 after they had combined to stop him moving to a minor French side, US Dunkerque, when his contract with Liege, who wanted to retain him on a quarter of his former salary, expired. Unemployed but unable to move to Dunkerque because his registration had not been transferred, as was mandatory, he took action through the local courts, a process that led, almost five years later, to a momentous decision in the European Court of Justice in Luxembourg. Out-of-contract players became free agents, no longer at the mercy of clubs, who had previously been allowed to stop them moving unless fees were paid.

On the face of it, the decision was a boon for footballers across Europe. They could see out their contracts and then move for nothing to another club who would, in all probability, pay higher wages because there was no transfer fee payable. In a sellers' market, the wage spiral cranked ever higher. New Premier League deals with Sky TV and the BBC in 1996 – worth £743m over four years from 1997 – gave the clubs yet more money. This in turn enticed more players from overseas. And as foreign managers, including Arsène Wenger at Arsenal, Gérard Houllier at Liverpool, Jean Tigana at Fulham and Claudio Ranieri at Chelsea became more prevalent, so the number of foreign players rose ever faster. The international market, revitalised by the formation of the Premier League, fuelled by Sky and staffed by Bosman, was well and truly open.

England's gift to the world

England first codified the rules of football and then played an integral part in its global dissemination. It should have been a natural melting pot for a heterogenous footballing culture during the 20th century. Yet throughout those 100 years the game's governors and administrators – often with the assistance of the Government – had done almost everything in their power to stop it being so.

Never mind that codified football had spread around the world since the English FA had formed in 1863 and lain down its rules. Nor that, after the English Football League kicked off in 1888, clubs and leagues with British roots were hastening the development of a truly international game. If Empire was ultimately about expansion of territory to utilise resources,

English football's hierarchy wanted none of it. It was a blinkered approach founded on the ignorant supposition that football should be controlled from the centre and that the centre was England. Not that such attitudes curtailed expansion.

In The Netherlands, where English textile workers took the game in the 1860s and clubs still carry names marking their British roots (Go Ahead Eagles in Deventer and Gronigen's Be Quick, for example), there was an FA by 1889. By 1889 there was also an FA in Denmark, where that country's first club, KB, had been started by Englishmen 11 years before. By 1908 the Danes had the strongest international side outside the British Isles, a fact illustrated by their progress to the Olympic final of that year. They lost 2–0 at the White City Stadium to Great Britain – actually an English side, selected by the FA – but not before trouncing France's 'B' team 9–0 and their 'A' team 17–1. Denmark reached the next Olympic final too, and again met Great Britain in the final, only to lose 4–2.

In Switzerland, a playground for wealthy British students in the latter half of the 19th Century, the St Gallen club was formed in 1879 by locals who had learnt the game from English visitors. The same team eliminated Chelsea from the UEFA Cup 121 years later. History is littered with such continental wins over English clubs by teams started by Englishmen a century or more before. Another Swiss team, Grasshoppers, was also founded by Englishmen, in 1886, the same year that a footballing pioneer, Vittorio Pozzo, was born in Italy. He would later play for Grasshoppers on his travels in search of football knowledge across Europe, which included time in Manchester. Later he would be the coach of Italy as they won the World Cup in 1934 on home turf and retained it in France four years later.

Italy's oldest club, the Genoa Football and Cricket Club – which like AC Milan, retains its English spelling in testament to its founders – was started by Englishmen in 1893, the same year that Argentina established the first FA in South America. The game had been taken there in the 1860s by English sailors, leading to the formation in 1867 of Buenos Aires FC, the first constituted club outside of Britain or North America. By 1898 when Italy founded an FA, the first club in Spain, Athletic Bilbao, was being formed in the wake of the game's introduction there by British businessmen. The Spanish took the game to Mexico, where the first league in North America started in 1902.

By the start of the 20th Century, football had spread throughout Europe. Germany formed an association in 1900, some 20 years after Bremen had been formed under English influence. One early team in Hamburg, a forerunner of the SV Hamburg of today, even kept their minutes in English. Uruguay's FA was also formed in 1900, where 18 years earlier English students had started the first club. Hungary formed an FA in 1901 with the game's dissemination largely down to pioneer Karoly Lowenrosen, who had lived for years in Britain.

In Austria, the Vienna Cricket and Football Club was formed by English ex-pats, soon to spark a rival, First Vienna, staffed by locals but retaining the English spelling. Direct English influence came through Mark Nicholson, a defender in West Bromwich Albion's FA Cup-winning side of 1892. He moved to Vienna to work in the city's Thomas Cook travel agency and was instrumental in the formation of the early Austrian FA.

So it went, a game passed on, invariably by Englishmen and Scots and then from neighbour to neighbour. To Sweden, Finland, Russia, Brazil, Portugal, just a few of which had associations before the First World War. Often, as in France, the game took hold many years before any formal organisation was formed to administer it. France's FA was formed in 1919 but its first club, Le Havre Athletic Club, was founded by English students in 1872. By the turn of the century there were numerous clubs in Paris, including The White Rovers, primarily made up of Scotsmen, and Standard FC, a British invention and such a success that citizens in the Belgian town of Liege copied the name.

Football was, by any measure, a truly international game and arguably the only one. And it had come largely via England. And yet, in official terms, there was little more than arrogance, distance and superiority from the country where it started. Indeed when the idea was first mooted by broadminded nations for an international association, the English dragged their heels to such an extent that they missed the boat.

The establishment of FIFA

Wanting to involve the English body, in acknowledgement of its role in the game, Carl Hirschmann, the secretary of The Netherlands FA, asked the English FA to help create an international organisation. Time passed. Not much happened.

The FA's committees said they needed more time to discuss it. Not much happened. Eventually, Robert Guerin of France took the initiative and invited the other major nations to a meeting to sort something out.

The Fédération Internationale de Football Association – FIFA – was founded in Paris on 21 May 1904. Its founding members were The Netherlands, France, Belgium, Denmark, Spain, Sweden and Switzerland. But not England or any of the home nations. Provisional statutes were laid down. The member nations would recognise each other's rights, including upholding suspensions of players across borders. No player would be allowed to represent two nations simultaneously. FIFA's members would adhere to the Laws of the Game of the English FA. FIFA alone would have the power to organise international competitions. The founding members decided that these statutes would come into force on 1 September 1904. The ambition was catching. Before sundown on 21 May, the German FA had even cabled to say it was on board. There was no communication from London.

Guerin was elected FIFA's first president at the inaugural Congress two days later. It was agreed that the English needed to be courted and brought on board, and they were, in April 1905. Other nations followed, including Austria, Italy and Hungary but the ensuing decade was not always conciliatory even after, in 1906, England's Daniel Burley Woolfall began a tenure as FIFA president that would last until his death in 1918. England, for example, arranged – and won – the 1908 Olympic football tournament, but only six teams took part and it was not deemed a great success. Similar problems beset the 1912 event. Then came the Great War, which did nothing but foster bitterness and acrimony, not least from the English. So much for the power of the beautiful game, the catalyst for the famous truce on the Western Front on Christmas Day 1915 when soldiers on both sides downed their weapons to share food, beer and a 40-a-side kickabout in No Man's Land.

After Woolfall's death FIFA survived largely through the efforts of Hirschmann, who worked tirelessly from Amsterdam to keep it alive. At the end of the war he made contact with all members on the initiative of President of the French FA, Jules Rimet. Congress was convened but, with the war not long finished, relations were strained. The English opted out in 1920, not able to get on with the others. In 1920, Rimet was elected chairman of the FIFA board and ascended to the presidency the following year. His 33-year reign would see two Olympic Games under FIFA's jurisdiction (1924 and 1928, England staying away from both), five World Cups including the first in 1930 (England stayed away) and an increase in membership from 20 nations to 85 by 1954. By then the English FA and the other home nations had rejoined FIFA (1924), left again (1928) and rejoined for good (1946) but not before they had made it clear for several decades that they, and by extension the English game, had nothing to learn and everything to lose by fraternising too closely with foreigners.

The voice of little England

If there was one voice that epitomised this stance, it was that of Charles Edward Sutcliffe, a driving if not universally popular force within the Football League for some 45 years from the 1890s onwards. No-one would disagree he was dedicated to the game although few could agree where his priorities lay. A solicitor from Lancashire, he was renowned for his blunt manner. He was the chairman of Burnley, a leading Football League official, a League delegate on the International board, an FA councillor and later the League's president.

"Who does he represent?" someone once asked Sutcliffe at an international match, pointing to another FA official, a button-holed, white haired, revered figure of the stock exchange.

"The Public Schools," said Sutcliffe.

"Who do we represent?" asked his companion.

"The public houses," came the reply.

And yet Sutcliffe was a lifelong teetotaller. The contradictions stretched to his relations with players. A thorn in the side of the Professional Footballers' Association for years despite having been a player once himself, he fought consistently to keep wages down but campaigned vigorously against foreign players, whom he maintained would cost English footballers their jobs. Some said he typified a generation of power barons and mill owners who wanted nothing but to profit from the game. And yet there are anecdotes that portray him as a man of honour striving to maintain the principles of sport. One Christmas Day in the 1890s he is said to have cancelled his family's festivities at short notice to make a six-hour round trip on a slow, freezing cold train to stand in as referee for a game at Darwen. When the hosting secretary came to pay him, he said he never pocketed such fees and asked that it be put in the players' box.

What was never in dispute was Sutcliffe's authority, actual or perceived, nor his ability to send out messages about what the FA, or the League, believed to be the final word. As the author John Harding noted in his official history of the PFA, *For The Good Of The Game*:

> He was a one-man propaganda machine on behalf of the League and his influential and prominent articles in popular magazines helped shape the outlook of the average fan and thus, in turn, the attitude of the general public towards the professional player.

What Sutcliffe said and wrote carried weight. So the view below, expressed on 14 January 1928 in his column for the weekly sports paper, *Topical Times*, where he was regularly billed as 'C. E. Sutcliffe, The Famous Football Legislator', can be taken as official policy on international matters, as if the actions of the FA were not sufficient.

> Continental football has no appeal to me. It takes me all my time to study things at home and the clubs have enough on hand to keep things going here and bring about the necessary improvement in the game without wasting time by overseas worries. I don't care a brass farthing about the improvement of the game in France, Belgium, Austria or Germany. The F.I.F.A does not appeal to me. An organisation where such football associations as those of Uruguay and Paraguay, Brazil and Egypt, Bohemia and Pan Russia, are co-equal with England, Scotland, Wales and Ireland seems to me to be a case of

magnifying the midgets. If central
Europe or any other district want to
govern football let them confine their
powers and authority to themselves,
and we can look after our own affairs.

A fortnight later, writing about the disagreements between the
home nations associations and FIFA, Sutcliffe added:

I can foresee nothing other than a
lot of Associations who are still
learning the game and with little
experience of government, and of
no concern to us, seeking to make
laws and lay down the law, to play
the game and make the laws of
the game, no matter whether we
approve or not. The British
Associations previously severed their
connection with the Federation and
then joined up again and though the
Continental Associations talk of a
desire to respect our wishes and work
amicably, they have the power to do
as they like; and my experience is that
inexperience with power leads us to
the improper exercise of such power.

Referring to the fact that many teams enjoyed touring
overseas, and disregarding the possibility that some clubs and
supporters might enjoy or benefit from continental contact,
he added:

I think the clubs of this country have
done more to reduce their efficiency
by Continental tours and picnics than
many of them are aware of.

Two weeks after publication, the British associations officially
withdrew from FIFA.

Such an insular mentality was being displayed at a time when
football's other nascent powers in Europe were spreading their
recruitment nets, and not just to neighbouring countries.
Hundreds of South American players were taking their skills

and knowledge from Argentina, Brazil and Uruguay to Europe, around 120 of them to the professional league in Italy in the 1930s and early 1940s alone. The only players born in Argentina, Brazil or Uruguay to play in England before the 1970s were sons of Britons who had temporarily migrated for work. Barriers had been erected, by the League, the FA, the PFA and various Government departments, to keep any others out.

Against the tide

Those foreign-born players who did get into England often paid a price, as later chapters will show. Among the many were Max Seeburg, born in Germany in 1884, who came to London as a child and went on to play for Tottenham, among other teams, and suffered for his nationality into adulthood. Nils Middleboe, a renowned Olympian who played for Chelsea before the Great War, was forbidden from earning from his labours. Hassan Hegazi and Tewfik Abdallah, Egyptian international regulars who played either side of the war for Fulham and Derby respectively, found themselves torn between studies and football. Gerry Keizer, a Dutch international goalkeeper who played briefly for Arsenal in the 1930s, saw his move lambasted via one of Charles Sutcliffe's columns. It is no surprise he did not stay there long. There were others who were refused even entry to the country by immigration officials.

The Second World War went some way to dismantling the barriers, with English football every bit as much in need of manpower as the rest of society. But with the FA's two-year residency rule in place and no willingness on the part of the League or FA to consider paying professional foreigners to play, the imports were restricted largely to refugees and amateurs. Or in the case of Bert Trautmann and Alec Eisentrager, German POWs who stayed on after the war to forge long and contrasting careers at Manchester City and Bristol City respectively. Needless to say, they encountered discrimination from opponents and fans, and not only those of the opposition.

Johnny Haasz was a refugee who fled Hungary after the 1956 uprising. Warmly welcomed by his adoptive nation, his main obstacle was that FIFA banned him from playing for 'deserting' his country of origin. Other imports who had largely successful experiences in the 1950s before eventually hankering for their country of birth were Joe Marston, an Australian lifesaver who swapped the beaches of Sydney for Preston, and George Robledo, a World Cup star for Chile in 1950.

There were other notable international players who were denied long-term contracts due to the rules. Albert Gudmundsson of Iceland had played in Glasgow for Rangers during the war but his time at Arsenal was limited. Milan were more than happy to make him a professional. Hans Jeppson of Sweden, who like Robledo had starred in the 1950 World Cup, was another who found fame and vast fortune in Italy because the English authorities would not allow a change in amateur status.

Sources of foreign talent were largely limited to territories with colonial ties. South Africa alone was the provider of dozens of talented players between the 1930s and 1950s. Charlton recruited dozens of South Africans, many of whom made League appearances in that period. Many others settled elsewhere, and indeed still live in Britain. There were also 16- and 17-year-olds who spent weeks on Atlantic liners only to feel homesick or isolated on arrival, then fail to make the grade and return home.

Throughout the 20th Century there were also players from the West Indies and Africa who, because they were black, faced not only the travails of migration but the psychological lacerations of often vicious racial prejudice. 'Darkie' was a common nickname for any black player into the 1960s. The language of the 1950s, peppered with phrases defining what were or were not 'Negro sports', typified the age. Monkey chants were the norm, not the exception, well into the 1980s. And as for the logic of the racist supporter, it stretched little beyond theorising that 'the blacks' couldn't function in cold weather and had no place in the game.

Arthur Wharton, born in Ghana, was the first black player in the Football League in the 1890s. Despite a long athletic career as a champion sprinter and goalkeeper, he died in poverty, his contribution quickly forgotten. Steve Mokone, the first black South African to play outside that country when he joined Coventry in 1956, also had a depressing time in England before finding great success elsewhere. Albert Johanneson, a compatriot, the first black player in an FA Cup final, with Leeds in 1965, stayed in England, only to die alone in a Leeds tower block in the 1990s.

Institutional insularity

More than any other footballing authority, the British Government has had a chequered history of relations with non-white immigrants. The *British Nationality Act 1948* allowed Commonwealth citizens to live and work in the UK, allowing a number of players careers in the League. But then the *Commonwealth Immigrants Act* of 1962 effectively reversed the decision, designed as it was to restrict migration from the Caribbean. Into this society came such socially influential figures as the Bermudan striker Clyde Best, who eventually swapped West Ham for America in search of a more peaceful life, and Brendon Batson, who arrived as a boy from Grenada and became one of Ron Atkinson's 'Three Degrees' at West Bromwich and later the deputy chief executive of the players' union, the PFA.

Given the laws of the land and the restrictions of the football authorities, it is little surprise how few native players, relatively, came to England from colonial territories. While the appendices in this book list every player born outside the British Isles who has played at least one game in the Football League, a few countries (India being the best case in point) feature a majority who were born of British parents working overseas either in the military or in commerce.

Despite the expansionism that saw such people work overseas, Britain has always been reticent to accommodate the indigenous from her conquered territories. Clearly they had nothing much to offer… Other nations took a different view, as a brief glance at the birth certificates of numerous French and Dutch footballers to have played in England would confirm. They are almost as likely to read Senegal or Surinam as Marseille or Maastricht.

Cometh the hour, cometh the Swede

But despite there never having been any prospect that an England team would be staffed primarily by players born in India or Kenya or Hong Kong, the colonisation of the domestic game by other players from overseas has been completed. And the clearest evidence that the game's rulers are now prepared to accept that the world outside has something to offer came in 2000 with the historic appointment of the Swede Sven Goran

Eriksson as the first non-English manager of the English national side.

This was largely down to the then chief executive of the FA, Adam Crozier, a Scot with no previous experience in football administration, who took a fresh approach to an old institution. When Kevin Keegan walked away from his post as England manager on 7 October 2000, after a 1–0 World Cup qualifying defeat to Germany in the last ever match at the old Wembley Stadium, it was Crozier who decided to consider a foreign manager as a replacement.

Arsène Wenger had been considered and rejected as a possibility because he had already made it clear he was not going to leave Arsenal. David Dein, the vice-chairman at Highbury and also on the FA's head-hunting committee, was probably relieved he would not have to ask himself for permission to approach his manager about the England job. Bobby Robson, at Newcastle, was another in the frame, although it quickly became apparent that Newcastle would not allow the FA to make an approach. And there was also Eriksson, Crozier's preferred choice from the start. He was such an outsider in the days after Keegan's resignation that he did not even feature in the bookmakers' lists. As bookmakers tend to list umpteen managers, available or not, for every major job that comes up, it was indicative of how far-fetched his appointment seemed.

Within a fortnight things had changed. Major bookmaking chains started phoning the sports desks of newspapers to announce they'd suspended betting on the new manager. They'd had a cluster of significant wagers in the west London area not far from the headquarters of the FA in Lancaster Gate. Eriksson's the man, they said. Within a week, he was. Crozier flew to Rome where Eriksson was the coach of Lazio, and on 30 October offered a five-year contract, worth £2.5m a year plus bonuses. The Swede accepted at the first time of asking. "As for my heart, it will become more and more English," he said in early November 2000, presumably meaning he would become more attached to his life and work in England as opposed to more insular and suspicious.

It was little surprise that he faced a wall of doubt from some of the game's leading figures…

"I will stand to be corrected on this, but I don't think he is going to start," said Gordon Taylor, the chief executive of the

PFA. "He will wonder what has hit him when we have the first bad result. A five-year contract? I do not think so. I think there is going to be tears before bedtime."

Sir Bobby Charlton and his brother Jack, who had both won World Cup medals in 1966, were similarly sceptical...

"Sven Goran Eriksson knows nothing about English football," said Jack, a former manager of the Republic of Ireland. "He has done a good job with a couple of clubs abroad but suddenly he becomes our Messiah and I don't agree with it. The job is an unenviable task because there are very few high quality players available to him. I believe an Englishman would do a lot better at selecting an English team to play against the best teams in the world."

Sir Bobby pointed out that the French were managed by a Frenchman, the Germans by a German and the Italians by an Italian. "Who do we get? Someone who has never managed in this country before. I think it is a terrible mistake by the FA."

The Sun, a newspaper owned by Rupert Murdoch, the man who bankrolled the multi-national Premier League, was more scathing still.

> What a climb-down. What an admission of decline. What a humiliation. What a terrible, pathetic, self-inflicted indictment. What an awful mess.

Jeff Powell of the *Daily Mail* waded in with:

> We've sold our birthright down the fjord to a nation of seven million skiers and hammer throwers who spend half their lives in darkness.

In the 21st Century, it seemed, in a multi-cultural Britain where foreign experts were managing or administrating in all walks of life from the London Underground to the Stock Exchange to Marks & Spencer to the Royal Ballet, it was still too much to expect wholehearted approval of a foreigner in charge of an England football team. So what if sushi had become a supermarket staple and Cuba a common destination for holidays? So what if Britain's champion rowers were coached by a German, England's cricketers by a man from Zimbabwe and the head of the Lawn Tennis Association was French? A foreigner in charge of the English football team? Perish the thought.

> Bobby Robson was persecuted for his white hair, Glenn Hoddle for his beliefs, Terry Venables for his business dealings, and Graham Taylor for just about everything. Welcome to the world's toughest job, Svennis

said the Swedish newspaper, *Aftonbladet*.

With this Eriksson set out on his own voyage of discovery, the latest footballing foreigner in a long, long line.

CHAPTER ONE

Pioneers Against The Tide

THE LONGEST match report in England's newspaper of record on Monday 10 September 1888 did not involve any of the teams in the new Football League. Its first-ever fixtures had been staged on 8 September but *The Times* led its small section on football with news from Glasgow of an international touring side. One of the players involved, Walter W. Bowman, born and raised in Canada, would later become the first foreign player in the League.

On the Saturday morning, the newspaper's front page, with its usual assortment of announcements, personal ads and miscellany, provided a snapshot of the era. 'A Lady' had advertised that she would be glad to travel abroad.

> Has spent two years in Italy.
> Expenses only. Highest references.

Readers interested in modern gadgets could buy a wonderful 'literary machine' described as being

> used by the late Emperor of
> Germany for holding a book, lamp,
> etc, in any position over an easy chair,
> bed or sofa. Deliciously luxurious.
> Price £1 1s.

And there were plenty of distractions for the hoi polloi, including an afternoon at Alexandra Palace to witness Professor Baldwin's 1,000ft jump from the clouds at 5.30pm.

> The Press of Great Britain, the Continent and America unite in describing this feat as the most remarkable of this or any past century.
> One shilling.

This was the England of Queen Victoria, in her 52nd year on the throne. London, a sprawl of seven million people, lay at the heart of a burgeoning empire expanding towards its ultimate hinterland of a quarter of the world's land mass. And the 'Latest Intelligence' in *The Times* dedicated as much space to news from overseas as it did to events at home.

From the United States came word that General William Terry, the former commander of the Stonewall Brigade in the Confederate Army, had drowned attempting to cross a swollen creek. In China there had been rioting in Canton and Peking, where locals were incensed that America wanted to restrict immigration of their labour. From Zululand came a report that

> the pacification of the country is believed to be making rapid progress.

From Paris came news of a French Government inquiry into alleged slave trading between Lindy and Madagascar. And so on, from the West Indies to Albania, Germany to Zanzibar, Servia [*sic*], Spain, Samoa and Belgium, where the correspondent's dispatch, in its entirety, read:

> An international congress of otology will be held here shortly.

The 'Sporting Intelligence' section on 8 September ran to a column and a half and dealt solely with horse racing and cricket. The previous day, Dr W. G. Grace had opened the batting for Lord Londesborough's Eleven against the Australians at the Scarborough Festival.

> Extraordinary cricket has been a frequent occurrence this season [*the report said*]. However, yesterday's play must certainly rank among the most remarkable events of the

summer. In the Colonial innings, 90
went up with only two wickets down;
yet the whole side was out for 96...'

But the first round of matches to be played in the new Football
League were not mentioned at all. The sports column finished
abruptly and the reader moved on to the Trade Union Congress
in Bradford, Naval Military Intelligence reports, Foreign
Commercial Intelligence and the Latest Shipping Intelligence.

The lack of a preview for the hatching League can be
attributed to two factors. First, that the competition was untried
and untested. No impartial observer would have had any idea
that the new structure, retaining the same fundamental shape,
would evolve to such an extent over the next 100 years that its
cast of players would one day infiltrate all sections of most
newspapers, not just those dealing with sport. Second, that
while football had undoubtedly grown in popularity, not least
since the widespread adoption of the Saturday half-day holiday,
the League in 1888 was a preserve of a northern clique, and not
necessarily an attractive one. Not so long ago, football had been
just a game. Now, in the minds of gentlemen amateurs, it was
becoming slightly vulgar.

Until 1888, football clubs had largely relied on local
tournaments and friendly matches for their income, the
exception being ties in the FA Cup, which had steadily grown in
popularity, with clubs and fans, since the inaugural tournament
in 1871–72. The legalisation of professionalism had come on 20
July 1885 after 18 months of bitter arguments between the
largely amateur south and the predominantly reformist north.
This paved the way for the formation of the League, which
would guarantee the major fixtures necessary to pay the players.
Thus when William McGregor, an Aston Villa committee
member, sent a letter in March 1888 to a select band of clubs
floating the idea, the response was positive.

The number of free weekends in the season dictated that
membership be limited to 12 clubs. A series of meetings
through the spring and summer determined which they would
be. The process ended with six from Lancashire and six from
the Midlands, and thus Accrington, Blackburn Rovers, Bolton
Wanderers, Burnley, Everton, Preston North End, Aston Villa,
Derby County, Notts County, Stoke, West Bromwich Albion

and Wolverhampton Wanderers became the founder members of the Football League.

From being a game played solely for fitness and recreation by amateurs, and dominated by Oxbridge gentlemen of the south, its power base had shifted to the industrial north. Four years of FA Cup wins by teams from Blackburn between 1883 and 1886 had already signalled the way the wind was blowing. But then the League – increasingly to be staffed by salaried Scottish ball artists, widely acknowledged as the architects of the passing game as opposed to the kick 'n' run approach – formalised the transition.

It was into such a footballing landscape that Bowman, born in Ontario in 1862, first set foot in Britain in August 1888, as a forward in the Canadian side. At home he had played his football for Berlin Rangers, Berlin being the former name of the city now known as Kitchener and the centre for Canadian football at the time. It is likely that he attended Berlin High School, whose alumni formed the Rangers. Primarily a right-sided player, he was good enough to represent his country and is recorded playing internationally, including against the United States in East Newark, New Jersey, on 25 November 1886, which the US won 3–2.

By 8 September 1888, Bowman's Canadians had already played four games on their tour, all in Ireland. The first, on 1 September, had been against County Antrim. The visitors won 6–2. The result filtered back across the Atlantic at the same time as reports of the third in a series of gruesome murders in London's Whitechapel district.

> All three murders have taken place in the same district, at about the same hour, and have been categorised by the same inhuman and ghoul-like brutality

reported *The Globe* in Toronto on its front page on Monday 3 September.

> The police have concluded that the same man did all three murders and that the most dangerous kind of lunatic is at large. Excitement is intense over the matter.

By the time the Canadians began their fifth tour fixture, in Glasgow on 8 September, Jack the Ripper, as he would later become known, had struck again. *The Times*, on the Monday, carried lengthy reports of the savage dismemberment of the latest victim, Annie Chapman, a prostitute. Elsewhere in the paper, latest intelligence came from India, Afghanistan, Burmah, Mexico, Hayti, Egypt, St Petersburg and Constantinople, to name a few. The 'Sporting Intelligence' was dominated again by horse racing and cricket (another 'startling' collapse for the Australians) but there was also lawn tennis, with news of the annual tournament at Devonshire Park, Eastbourne. And finally, there was football.

The first League matches were there, not as scores but as single-sentence reports, mixed together with other football games of the day, from both the rugby and association codes. Hence the report of the first League meeting between two of the Midlands' major teams read:

> Aston Villa v Wolverhampton Wanderers – played on the ground of the latter at Wolverhampton and ended in a tie, with a goal to each side.

This was listed above York v Hull…

> played under Rugby Union rules at York. Hull won by a goal and a try to a try

which in turn was listed higher than West Bromwich Albion v Stoke…

> The winners of the National Cup visited Stoke and gained a victory over the home side by two goals to none.

But the leading item in the section, consisting of the fixture in capital letters plus three whole sentences, was dedicated to the touring internationals.

> THE CANADIANS v GLASGOW RANGERS – Having played four matches at Belfast, three of which they won, the Canadians on Saturday

25

engaged in a contest with the powerful Scotch club, the Glasgow Rangers, at Ibrox Park. After some spirited play the result was a tie match, each side kicking a goal. The Canadians continue their tour with a match at Aberdeen today.

In Scotland, the game was discussed in two lengthy articles in the Monday edition of the *Glasgow Herald*. One writer, no doubt mindful of the start of the English League, a competition that would lure the best Scots south, noted that

our national pastime, instead of being on the wane, as some captious critics would have it, is in as flourishing a condition as ever.

The Canadians' draw with Rangers, in front of a reasonable crowd of 2,000, despite there being plenty of alternative games to choose in the city that day, was used as evidence. There had been 'considerable misgiving' before the match whether the tourists would have anything to show. But they secured their draw

after displaying form which was admitted on all hands to have far exceeded expectations. They play the game as it should be played, in a true, gentlemanly spirit, and in every respect they will prove themselves foemen worthy of the steel of any organisation.

And so, tentatively, the concept that alien footballers might actually be able to play football, began, like the League in England, to evolve. As *The Globe*'s pseudonymous tour reporter, The Parson, wrote after the game with Rangers:

The eyes of all the football world are on us — we feel it and our chests protrude about 2½ inches accordingly … The idea that Canada can produce something in the way of football worth going to see is growing

26

gradually on the mind of the canny Scotchman.

As Bowman and co progressed south, so illusions were shattered about their talents and countenance alike. After the Canadians had beaten Lincoln City 3–1 on 29 September, The Parson wrote:

> Some queer ideas have been dispelled as to the colour, language and manners of the inhabitants of Canada as shown by its representatives on the football team. In this old fashioned city of Lincoln, one of the ministers told the secretary of the city club that he was going to see these blacks play football. On being told this it was suggested that we blacken our faces for the first half-time then come out from the dressing room like the Nigger boy that used Pears' soap. Everywhere we are called Yankees and told that we speak through our noses. What a sad blow to the swell members of the party to be told that they speak with a down-east Yankee twang! And [*that despite*] trying to acquire the English accent, not to mention the frequent use of that peculiarly English word, 'jolly'…

In Nottingham, at the start of October, the tourists took a break from the delights of the famous Goose Fair –

> menageries and side shows; shows where fat women, skeletons and 'real' American cowboys could be seen, all for the small sum of a penny. Fakirs and thieves of all kinds were in abundance

– to head to the Trent Bridge grounds and face the Notts County team. They lost 2–0 but not without heart.

Then at Newton Heath – who would later become Manchester United – the Canadians won 2–0, with Bowman on the score

27

sheet. The game was watched by 7,000 admiring spectators and the post-match banquet was hosted by a knight called Ferguson, Sir James to be precise, the Political Secretary at the Foreign Office.

Other opponents came from both sides of the amateur-professional divide, from Blackburn Rovers to Oxford University, from Aston Villa and West Bromwich to the Old Carthusians, concluding, on 31 October 1888, with a 1–0 defeat to the Swifts at the Kennington Oval, with the Prince of Wales in the crowd. After 23 matches in two months, the visitors had won nine, lost nine and drawn five. And as observers even in the heartland of the League acknowledged, they had given a decent account of themselves.

> Before the Dominion team came over their chances against our best English teams appeared rather remote

the *Blackburn Telegraph* reported.

> But the visitors have given ample proof that they know how to play clever and scientific football out in Canada... There is an impression abroad that the Canadians are merely imported Scotchmen but that is a fallacy for we are able to state positively that every man in the team was born in Canada.

Historic first

Despite the success of the tour, Bowman's League debut was not to come immediately. *The Globe* reported that he and two team-mates, Kranz and Brubacher, headed next to 'the Fatherland'. Bowman is later recorded back in Canada, playing in Toronto, from where he returned to England on a second tour in 1891. It was after this voyage that he signed for Accrington. And it was for Accrington, on 23 January 1892, that he first played – and scored – in a League match as his side beat West Bromwich Albion 4–2. An alien player, born and raised to adulthood in a country so far removed from Britain that some people were unaware what colour its inhabitants were, let alone that they played international football, had started the process of reverse colonisation.

Bowman's time with Accrington was brief. He played five games and scored three goals at the tail of the 1891–92 season, which saw an expanded 14-team League. By the start of the next season he had joined Ardwick, one of 14 new teams in a further expanded two-division competition. On his League debut for Ardwick, on 18 February 1893, he scored as Crewe Alexandra were beaten 3–1. Although Ardwick were later forced into bankruptcy, Bowman remained with the club as they re-emerged in 1894 as Manchester City. In seven years, he would play 47 games in the League with them, his outings dwindling as his age ticked past 30.

Among the most notable games Bowman played with Ardwick was a club record-defeat, 10–2 at Small Heath – later Birmingham City – on 17 March 1894. There was also an 11–3 win, then a record for Manchester City, against Lincoln City on 23 March 1895. By that time Bowman was playing alongside the legendary outside-right, Wales's 'Wizard of the Wing', Billy Meredith. And towards the end of his time at City, the club signed Jimmy Ross, previously with Burnley and Liverpool but best remembered as a member of the Preston North End 'Invincibles' who won the first ever League and FA Cup Double in 1888–89 without losing a match.

To keep such company, Bowman was evidently a decent player. He was also versatile. Records even show him turning out as a goalkeeper, in an emergency capacity, against Newton Heath in a reserve match in November 1898. The result was 1–1. It was one of his last appearances in English football.

What happened next remains something of a mystery. Indeed not much is known about Bowman's life away from football, nor what work he undertook outside the game, if any. It is known, however, that he returned across the Atlantic and settled in America when his playing days were over. A story in a Kitchener newspaper in April 1929 reported on a reunion in Canada of the touring side of 1888. It appears that Bowman did not attend. He was said to have been living in the United States and had last been heard of in Butte, a copper mining city in western Montana. Investigations via the local archives office have not proved conclusively what became of him. Entries in a residents' directory for his most probable neighbourhood during the period throw up two possible theories. One shows a Walter Bowman, a chef, married to a woman called Dixie. Given Bowman's advancing years, he would probably have retired by then. Another shows a widowed teacher, Marie Bowman, whose deceased husband had been called Walter. Whichever of these men had the footballing past, his journey from Toronto to Accrington to Manchester to Montana was the earliest international career path of a foreign Football League player.

Captain of history

While the final resting place of Walter Bowman is not certain, it is known where another significant overseas-born player, Edward Hagarty Parry, is buried. He never played League football – his career came too early for that – but his place in English footballing history warrants a mention.

Like Bowman, Parry was born in Canada, in Toronto on 24 April 1855, the son of Edward St John Parry and Lucy Susanna Parry (nee Hagarty) and baptised in St James' Cathedral in Toronto on 10 June 1855. His grandfather, Thomas Parry, a former missionary, once served as the Bishop of Antigua, typifying the nomadic lifestyle of the era's travelling classes.

Unlike Bowman, Parry left Canada with his family when he was young and moved to England. A fine scholar and sportsman, he attended Charterhouse School and later Oxford University, where he was formally admitted on 17 October 1874. He obtained second-class honours in Classical Moderations in 1876 and third-class honours in Modern History in 1878. In between, he played for Oxford University in the 1877 FA Cup final as they lost 2–1 to the prolific winners Wanderers.

Parry, who played at inside left, was a fast dribbler with a fair shot. He went on to play three times for England, once in 1879 against Wales, and twice in 1882, in Glasgow against Scotland and in Wrexham against Wales. But it was in the 1881 FA Cup final, when the Old Carthusians – former students of Charterhouse – beat the Old Etonians 3–0, with Parry scoring one of the goals, that he secured an historic first.

The significance of Parry's role is clearly marked, both in the publication *Bell's Life in London*, on the morning of the game, 9 April 1881, and in the match report in *The Times* on the following Monday. Both list the teams and identify Parry as the captain. So it was, more than 100 years before Eric Cantona, in the 1990s, was widely claimed as the first foreign-born captain of an FA Cup-winning side, that Edward Parry actually became the first overseas-born player to achieve the feat.

Parry was later a teacher, becoming a headmaster in Slough between 1892 and retiring in 1918. He died on 19 July 1931 in West Bridgford, Nottingham, aged 76. His funeral was held at Plumtree, a few miles outside the city, and he was buried there, in the village churchyard, where he remains today, alongside his wife, Amelie Marthe.

Opening the door

While it had taken three seasons from the League's inception for Bowman to take his bow as the first foreigner, the incidence of overseas-born players increased markedly as the 19th Century drew to a close. James Dalton, a team-mate of Bowman's in Canada's 1891 touring side, stayed on in England and eventually signed for Sunderland. The extent of his career was a few games in the League in the 1893–94 season. As such, he was an early example of a transient visitor who either didn't make the grade or decided England wasn't for him.

The 1893–94 season also saw the League debut of Arthur Wharton from Ghana. A sportsman of considerable ability, he had already played for Preston North End in occasional cup matches. But he did not play League football until later, with Rotherham Town. Thanks to a detailed biography, *The First Black Footballer* by Phil Vasili, we know much about his triumphs, troubles and ultimately depressing end, although the title of that book no longer strictly applies.

The first black footballer now commonly accepted to have played for a league club in Britain was Andrew Watson, a Guyana-born warehouseman. He started playing in Glasgow in 1874 – pre-dating Wharton's football career by about a decade – and later went on to play for the famous Queen's Park club. He also represented Scotland three times. It was only in very recent times that curators at the Scottish Football Museum at Hampden Park discovered 19th-century references to Watson as a 'coloured gentleman'.

"For years, I had looked at our pictures of Watson in his Queen's Park and Scotland strips but never had the facts to back up the evidence of my own eyes," Ged O'Brien, the museum's director, said.

The census of 1881 shows Watson living in Govan, the working-class shipbuilding district of Glasgow that later produced such footballers as Sir Alex Ferguson. There is no record of why or when Watson came to Britain but his birth date on the census is given as 1857 and the place as Georgetown, Guyana, which was then a British colony. Watson was therefore, as far as has been established, not only the first black player but the first foreign-born player of note anywhere in Britain. But despite records showing he also ventured south of the border, he never played in the English Football League. Indeed he would have been ending his career as it started.

Keeping up appearances

The same was not true of Wharton, born in 1865 in Accra (then in the Gold Coast), the son of the Rev Henry Wharton, a Wesleyan Methodist Missionary from Grenada. Arthur's paternal grandfather had been a Scottish merchant. Arthur's mother, Annie, also had Scottish ancestry, being the daughter of another Scottish trader, John Grant, and Ama Egyiriba, a Fante royal.

Wharton's middle-class background meant he had the benefit of a good education. Some of it came in London in the late 1870s, and then, after time back in Ghana, at two missionary schools, in Cannock and Darlington, where he studied to become a missionary teacher. A remarkable all-round athlete, he came to prominence as a sprinter in the 1880s, winning the Amateur Athletic Association national sprint title at Stamford Bridge in 1886 in a time of 10 seconds flat. Had official international records been kept at the time he would likely have been deemed the fastest man in the world. He retained his title in 1887 and then won the unofficial professional championships of 1888 in Sheffield.

In the summer of that year Wharton was featured in the popular *Athletic Journal*. The article recalls an occasion when he was resting between races at an event in Yorkshire.

> He was lying down completely hidden from view by a rug. A couple of competitors were discussing their chances with the dark 'un, unaware of his near presence. One says to the other something to this effect, 'Who's he, that we should be

frightened of him beating us? We can beat a blooming nigger any time.' Wharton, who had been taking it all in, jumped up from amongst his coverings and said, 'Allow me to give you to understand that I not only run but I do a little boxing when it is required.' The two friends were terror-stricken for the moment and made it their business to retire as early as possible. Moral: rugs, as well as walls, have ears sometimes. Wharton is a genuine sportsman, and is a good all-round man, not omitting the swimming, cricket and football branches of sport.

Speed was evidently Wharton's forte, but all his football was played in goal. He made his League debut for Rotherham in the 1893–94 season, playing for them 19 times before stints at Sheffield United, Rotherham (again) and non-league Ashton North End. He returned briefly to the League with Stockport County in the 1901–02 season.

One of Wharton's legacies was the spirit of entertainment he brought to football. Often eccentric on the pitch, he was known to hang from the crossbar to catch the ball with his feet. He was also a fine puncher – as any good boxer would be – although opponents' heads were as likely as the ball to feel the weight. There are also recorded incidents of him lying on the goal line during quiet spells only to jump up at the last moment to foil an approaching attacker.

But while such buoyancy of spirit gave him and his supporters some good times, his essential 'other-ness' – his phenomenal talents as well as his origins – did little but work against him. Black people were not supposed to excel, let alone enjoy doing so. And for every *Athletic Journal* writer who saw him, albeit patronisingly, as 'a good all-round man', there were plenty who thought he was playing above his station.

Wharton's private life was also complicated and he fathered one, possibly two, children by Martha, the sister of his wife, a local girl, Emma Lister. In later life, he became a pub landlord and a heavy drinker, and his sporting achievements were rapidly

– but never prominently – consigned to history. He spent some of the remains of his working life as a haulage hand at Yorkshire Main Colliery, Edlington, and died, aged 65, after a lengthy illness, on 12 December 1930. Two causes of death were noted on his death certificate, syphilis and epithelioma (a form of skin cancer). He was buried in a municipal cemetery in the local pit village. Only in 1997, after a memorial campaign was launched by the 'Football United, Racism Divides' campaign, was a headstone provided. The largest single donation came from the Professional Footballers' Association.

Success and skullduggery

Around the turn of the century came League debuts by various other players, who, like Wharton, were 'firsts' from their countries of birth. Not all were the children of colonials. Cornelius Hogan, the first player from Malta, joined New Brighton Tower in 1899 and later moved to Burnley. Wilfred Waller, a goalkeeper, was the first of more than 100 South Africans to join the League when he played for Bolton from 1899. Either side of that he played outside the League for Tottenham, Southampton and Watford among others. By 1907 he was back in South Africa, playing for a Springboks side against a touring party from Corinthians, another of his former English clubs.

The second South African, Alec Bell, had more of an impact. Born in Cape Town in 1882 of Scottish ancestry – which later earned him a Scotland call-up – he played 278 League games for Manchester United from 1902–03. His first four seasons saw United finish 5th, 3rd, 3rd and then 2nd in the Second Division. The last of these seasons, 1905–06, featured the renowned half-back line of Dick Duckworth, captain Charlie Roberts and Bell instrumental as United reached the quarter-finals of the FA Cup. More significantly, 12 years after relegation (at the end of the 1893–94 season as Newton Heath) the club went back up to the top division.

United then signed Walter Bowman's old Manchester City team-mate, Billy Meredith, from their city rivals. Meredith's years at City had ended in acrimony after he had been involved in bribery accusations and the club had suspended him for a year. He reacted by blowing the lid on a raft of illegal payments City had made to their players, himself included. The FA banned several City directors for life and most of City's team from playing for the club ever again. United stepped in and signed Meredith and several others.

In 1907–08, with the Wizard's goals and the half-back line's resistance crucial, United won the League title for the first time. United took a second trophy, the inaugural Charity Shield, in 1908, a third with the FA Cup of 1909, and a fourth, with Bell still involved, when they took their second title in 1911. The last of those successes was deemed a fitting way to mark the end of a first season in a new home, Old Trafford. The following year the League was won by Blackburn Rovers, for whom Bell would briefly play before ending his career as the most successful foreign-born player of the era.

Not long after Bell left Manchester, United signed George 'Cocky' Hunter, one of 20 Indian-born players to feature in the League before the Second World War. Needless to say, none of them were Indian. The first was Jimmy Pass, a forward whose career at Stockport began a couple of years after Arthur Wharton's had ended there. Among the others was Alf Quantrill, who played for Derby, Preston, Bradford Park Avenue, Nottingham Forest and England; Les McDowall, who played, among other clubs, for Manchester City, who he would later manage; and Jack Dugnolle, who played for Brighton and Plymouth and later wrote an authoritative coaching manual.

Hunter, born in Peshawar in 1885, was a half-back who won the League title with Aston Villa in 1910. He also played for Oldham and Chelsea before his £1,300 move to Old Trafford but the deal ultimately proved poor value. The daring play which brought him admirers was often interpreted by neutral eyes as recklessness. This did not stop Manchester United making him their captain – nor has it stopped them in the face of similar criticism since – but the 1913–14 season proved a flop. United finished well down the table and Hunter, having fallen out with his directors, was suspended *sine die* for failing to comply with training regulations. He took his attitude and military background into the Great War and saw active service in France and Gallipoli.

Among the other 'firsts' of the era was John Cuffe, born in Sydney in 1880. He was the first Australian in the League, a full-back who had a lengthy career at Glossop from 1905. He also played cricket for Worcestershire. Billy Andrews, born in Kansas City in 1886, was the first League player born in the

USA, although he had Irish roots and played for Glentoran before becoming a wing-half at Oldham, Stockport and Grimsby. He was also capped by Ireland.

Another early player with connections to America was Tom Wilcox, the only League player known to have been born at sea. The son of a sea captain, he entered the world on board the four-masted *Grassendale* en route to America in 1879. His ability as an athlete became apparent across the Atlantic, where he reportedly excelled at punchball. After moving back to England at the turn of the century, he became a goalkeeper, attached at various times to Millwall Athletic, Woolwich Arsenal and Norwich, but made his League debut for Blackpool in 1906–07. He was a non-playing member of Manchester United's first championship-winning squad in 1907–08 and played for them twice the following season. After serving in the Great War, he ran a tobacconist's shop in Preston before retiring to Blackpool, where he died in 1962.

Most of the earliest foreign-born players – Wharton excepted – faced few, if any, problems with prejudice. For all the distance they had travelled they were white, they spoke English and they could mostly claim links to Britain or her Empire. This was not true of the first League player from continental Europe, Max Seeburg.

Going Continental

Born in Leipzig, Germany, in 1884, Max Seeburg moved to London as a boy but his country of birth would affect him throughout his life. Seeburg's father, Franck, arrived in England in the late 1880s to work as a furrier at a shop within sight of Tower Bridge. The family settled in Tottenham, where the young Max soon showed talent on the pitch. Despite his father disapproving of a career in the game – he felt his son, an apprentice carpenter, would be better served by a 'proper' trade – Max began playing for local side Cheshunt. Later he moved to Chelsea, then Tottenham, where he made his League debut in 1908–09. His other clubs in a nomadic career included Leyton, Burnley, Grimsby and Reading, who were then in the Southern League.

Seeburg's daughter, Margaret, was born in 1923, some 10 years after he hung up his boots to manage a pub. Yet in 2002, aged 79, she could still recall with clarity her father's stories of his time in the game. Grimsby had been a special place, she recalled.

"My parents weren't far from the sea, so they could get in the water and strengthen their legs. There was none of these gymnasiums in those days." And settling in Reading after moving around the country for years had been a source of relief to her mother, Ellen. "She was quite delighted when they eventually came back to stay. She wasn't enthralled by the life, moving from town to town, finding somewhere new to live all the time."

The first repercussions for Seeburg of his birthplace came shortly after the start of the Great War.

"Father had assumed that that he and his brother, Franck Jnr, had been naturalised but they hadn't," Margaret recalled. "Franck was already fighting for Britain in France when they came and took dad away. He said to mother 'I've got to go' and he was taken to the POW internment camp in Newbury. The police in Reading knew him well and he was well liked so they sorted it all out quickly. He only stayed there a week before being released."

But the damage had already been done. Despite all his good relations with his employers and neighbours, the week he spent in Newbury cost him his job.

"They lost the pub and everything," said Margaret. "Tipped out, because my father had been born in Germany. Mother was absolutely shattered. Because of this blessed business with the war my parents spoke very little of the past. They blocked it out, the fact he was born a German."

Some 20 years later, in 1939, Margaret applied for her first job, at Berkshire County Council.

"I remember going to the post box with my application one evening. The next day, the very day it arrived, there was a policeman on the doorstep asking for father's naturalisation papers."

Seeburg, who died in 1972, owned a succession of Reading pubs including the one in Kings Road where Margaret was born.

"I used to go with him in the old days to watch Reading. He was always there and I took an interest, when football was football. I wouldn't go now. In those days you mixed with the people you saw playing."

Flair from afar

Arguably the most flamboyant import of the pre-1915 period was Hassan Hegazi. Born in Kremlah, on the east side of the Nile delta in September 1891, he was the spoilt son of a wealthy rural aristocrat, Mohammed Bey Hegazi. As a boy, he was rarely without a ball at his feet and played competitively from primary school onwards. Later, as a member of National Sporting Club, he spent his mid-teenage years competing against teams drawn from the British army bases and government offices stationed in the Middle East.

He arrived in London in the summer of 1911 to study engineering at University College and joined Dulwich Hamlet FC as a forward at the same time. His approach to the game was a revelation. Central attacking players at the time were, typically, burly individuals who hung around the goal. Finesse was an affliction. Bundled conversions were the norm. Hegazi was different, agile and quick. He was a sprinter, playmaker and dribbler. His ball control was superb, his passing second to none. True, he had an inclination, on occasion, to wander around and indulge his gifts. He would have been known perhaps, in later parlance, 'a luxury player'. A Le Tissier perhaps, or a Gascoigne. The kind of man who would seemingly be doing nothing until a shimmy, a flick and a shot ended with a bulge in the net. Hegazi ran the show and his goals were sweet and plentiful.

> The way he makes openings for himself and his wing men shows much brain work,

said the *South London Press* in September 1911...

> He should make quite a name for himself.

He did. The fans soon dubbed him 'Nebuchadnezzar'. And it wasn't long before Fulham of the Second Division saw his potential as an architect of their own Babylon. Their manager, Phil Kelso, asked him to play in a League match against Stockport County. The date could not have been more auspicious: 11 November 1911. Hegazi opened the scoring in a 3–1 win and was asked to play at Leeds the following week.

The authorities at Dulwich, not best pleased at potentially losing their man, went to see Hegazi at his lodgings in Gower Street, Bloomsbury.

"I was in a difficulty," Hegazi said. "For I wanted to play very much in League football, and at the same time I did not want to leave Dulwich Hamlet who have been very good to me. So I have decided to play for the Hamlet. I am sorry if Fulham are disappointed." Pa Wilson, the esteemed Dulwich manager, said that Hegazi's decision made him "as honourable a man as ever stepped onto a football field". And with that his League career was over.

Two days after his solitary outing for Fulham, a report on the match, with a photograph of the player and a few biographical details appeared in the *Athletic News* under the headline 'An Egyptian Centre Forward'. His goals were lauded as 'brilliant'. By the following week, the same publication's resident bard had been moved to write a long poem in dedication. It began:

> *Hussein Hegazi, by birth an Egyptian,*
> *Djinn of the leather and wizard of wiles,*
> *Do not imagine, though, by this description,*
> *That he is fictive, and not in these isles.*

If nothing else, Fulham's attempt to secure Hegazi's full-time services provoked an intense debate about the poaching of players. And although, in all the furore, his nationality was not an issue, it was only a matter of time before players such as Hegazi provoked not awe but suspicion.

Hegazi remained with Dulwich until 1913 and also represented Middlesex county five times. He toured in The Netherlands with Dulwich, and in France and Bohemia with his University. He subsequently enrolled at St Catherine's College, Cambridge, where he won a Blue on 7 January 1914 as Oxford University were defeated 2–1. He returned to Egypt in the summer of 1914.

Within weeks of his departure, Lord Kitchener, the Proconsul of Egypt, returned to London to take up his role as Secretary of State for War, in which he masterminded the recruitment drive with his 'Your Country Needs You!' campaign. Virtually every one of Hegazi's British male friends – students and fellow footballers – were to be involved in the Great War. Many lost their lives, including some of his team-mates from Dulwich.

Hegazi himself continued his football career at home, going on to play for his country in the Olympic Games of 1920 and

1924. In 1932, at the age of 40, he hung up his boots, his reputation as a sportsman beyond doubt. In his latter years, when married with five children, he developed a new reputation as a socialite and ladies' man. An affair with a prominent actress of the day, Naima Almassreya, gave early evidence that although you can take a maverick out of football, you can't remove the maverick from the man.

Hegazi died in Egypt in 1958 and has a street named after him, Sharia Hassan Hegazi, in the Garden City area of Cairo.

A first Great Dane

Two other players with international pedigrees also played in the League before the First World War. Isaac Van Den Eynden of Belgium played for Clapton Orient in the 1913–14 season. And Nils Middleboe, of Denmark, was attached to the Casuals and Newcastle before playing League football for Chelsea. He played 41 times for them from the 1913–14 season onwards. Photographs from the time show an awkward, apparently shy man with long skinny arms and a concave chest. But as his lengthy international career and authorship of coaching manuals showed, he lacked nothing in skill or mental application.

He came to the attention of English clubs through his involvement in two Olympic tournaments, in 1908 and 1912. The first, in London, saw the hosts prevail, beating Denmark – and Middleboe – in the final. By the 1912 Games in Stockholm he was captain, playing in the final as Denmark lost again to England having earlier steered his side to resounding wins over Norway and The Netherlands. While the likes of Chelsea were happy to employ Middleboe – albeit as an amateur – England's authorities would take a dimmer view of the Olympics after 1912. The 1924 and 1928 tournaments, both won by Uruguay, were ignored, as was the inaugural World Cup in 1930, also won by the South Americans. And as the 1920s unfolded, creating a new order of international football, so England became ever less willing to embrace it.

The resumption of organised football after the Great War saw more 'firsts' but most were by dint of colonial connections. Jack Butler, born in Sri Lanka, had a lengthy career with Arsenal. Frank Burton, born in Mexico, where his father had been working, played for West Ham. Francisco Enrique

Gonzales (aka Frank Peed), born in Argentina of a native father and Wolverhampton mother, would play for a succession of clubs in the 1930s. And Edward Laxton, born in Brazil, the son of a British engineer, made his league debut in 1920–21 for Norwich City. The next Brazilian-born player would not arrive in England until Mirandinha at Newcastle in the late 1980s.

A Cantona for the 1920s

An exception was the French international Eugene Langenove. Without exhaustive non-league records that do not exist, it is impossible to chart the movement of every player at every level around the world. But certainly numbers of Englishmen crossed the Channel to play professionally in France early in the 20th Century while Frenchmen played in England below national level around the same time. Goalkeeper Georges Crozier at Fulham, before their elevation from the Southern League, was among them. But it was Langenove, one of the star players of the French giants Olympique de Paris from 1919 to 1921, who was the first Frenchman in the Football League. Like one his most eminent successors, Eric Cantona, he was a man with a soupçon of attitude.

A right-sided defender, he won two caps for France in 1921, in one defeat against Italy in Marseille and another in Brussels against Belgium. An eventful year also saw an appearance in that year's French FA Cup final against Olympique's Paris rivals, Red Star, in the Stade Pershing. But then he got himself in the *merde*. He was suspended for three years in July 1921 for kicking another player in the eye during a friendly match. It is not recorded whether he used the kung fu style...

Undeterred by his sentence, he had a one-game trial with Le Havre in 1922, in the hope of an amnesty that never came. Banned from playing in France, he made his way across the Channel to find another employer. Walsall, then a Third Division (North) side in the tough industrial West Midlands, took him on near the start of the 1922–23 season. His debut came on 7 October 1922 against Crewe in a 1–1 draw, in which he played as an inside-right. Possibly the position did not suit him – he'd made his name at home as a defender – but after he played there again the following week against Rochdale, he was dropped.

He returned to France, where another year was added to his suspension for having played professionally in England. He eventually resumed his career in 1925–26 with Red Star. Not a chap to learn his lessons quickly, he kicked another opponent during a friendly in March 1926. Red Star expelled him. As history would later show, bad behaviour is not necessarily a hindrance to a player as long as he does the business on the pitch. Langenove went on to play for SC Draguignan, AS Cannes and Nice before ending his career with a string of minor clubs dotted around the suburbs of Paris. He left behind no record of speeches about seagulls, trawlers or sardines.

The Pyramid effect

Throughout the 1920s, the trickle of colonial-born players from South Africa and India continued, and the second Egyptian arrived. He was Tewfik Abdallah and was the last international from his country to sign for a League club before Ibrahim Said briefly joined Everton of the Premier League in 2003.

Born in Cairo in 1897, Tewfik moved to Derby, aged 23, in 1920, probably as a result of knowing the club's Scottish full-back, Tommy Barbour, who had served in Egypt, where Tewfik had often played against the British Army. Tewfik's main aim in migrating was to find experience in the engineering trade but his arrival caused a stir.

The front cover of the *Topical Times* in November 1920 featured a photograph of him grinning as he ran with a ball. This cheery-looking chap was set against a line-drawn backdrop complete with a pyramid, the Sphinx and palm trees. 'Derby's Dusky Dribbler' said the billing. There was a brief mention of him inside, but only in passing in a news item about the 'new fashion' of 'going far afield for players'.

Sheffield United had just secured the services of a young Canadian outside-left, Jack Coule, who had resigned from his job as a Mountie to travel to the steel city. The article reported that although he'd been born in England, he'd lived in Canada since the age of five.

> He is a magnificent specimen of manhood, standing 6ft 1in and weighing 13st 2lbs. He formerly played for the Mounted Police team,

every member of which was at least
6ft and 13 stones!

Clearly, the appreciation of Canadian football had grown since Walter Bowman's day even though Coule ultimately failed to make the grade.

Tewfik had what it took, although it would be later, in America, that he was most appreciated. An inside-right of no little technical ability, he made his Derby debut at home to Manchester City in October 1920. He was the subject of numerous jibes about his quirky style and trademark chewing – which earned him the nickname 'Toothpick' – not to mention his struggles with the language. One probably apocryphal tale of his first game saw him take to the field asking: "Where's me camel?". Mick Hamill, it transpired, was an Irishman making his City debut and Tewfik had been assigned to mark him.

Derby won the game 3–0, with Tewfik scoring. It was first of 15 appearances for Derby but his first and only goal. The club were relegated and although he was retained, he fell out of favour and was sent on loan to Cowdenbeath in the Scottish Second Division. The fans took him to their hearts, nicknaming him 'Abe'. According to local legend, he also won the ultimate accolade when a prominent local miner named his greyhound 'Abe' in his honour. Hampered by injury, he lasted a season before moving to non-league football in Wales with Bridgend Town. His last spell in Britain was at Hartlepools at the end of the 1923–24 season.

The American dream

In the summer of 1924, Tewfik left England for the American Soccer League, which was causing quite a stir in Britain, from where players were being lured with good prospects and hard cash. The economic downturn in the early 1920s had already seen waves of emigrants in all professions heading west to America. Now the dollar was enticing 'freebooter' footballers to break their contracts at home and join the rush.

Is American Football Menace Real?

asked one typically hysterical headline of the day.

The threat of a talent drain was seen as ever more likely because the United States was not bound by any international agreements on transfers.

One of the biggest names to move – and fuel the mid-1920s panic – was the Everton and England outside-right, Sam Chedgzoy. A strategist and tactician, he was also famous for having exposed a flaw in the law regarding corners. The law made provision for goals to be scored directly but did not outlaw the kicker playing the ball twice. In a game against Arsenal in 1924, Chedgzoy took a corner, passed to himself, dribbled inside and scored. The referee, who'd dropped his whistle in amazement, almost penalized Chedgzoy but was persuaded to check the rulebook at half-time. The FA changed its laws within 48 hours, heralding the innovation of the 'short corner' of today.

Another high-profile migrant was a certain Mick Hamill of Manchester City and Ireland. Tewfik and Hamill both went to clubs in New England, the Providence Clamdiggers and Boston Wonder Workers respectively.

Tewfik played in the ASL until 1928, first with the Clamdiggers, where he scored a goal every other game, then the Fall River Marksmen, Hartford Americans and New York Nationals. He also played for the ASL all-star team against Nacional of Montevideo at the Polo Grounds in New York on 2 April 1927. Later he had a stint in Canada with Montreal Carsteel who were then under the managerial reigns of Chedgzoy. Tewfik was later a coach himself, in the US, although it is thought he finally left America after becoming disaffected at the racial divide where he, being black, was often not allowed to stay in 'white hotels' with his team. It is thought Tewfik returned to Egypt, although the Football Association there has been unable to confirm what became of him.

Tewfik's time in Britain, and his subsequent move to America, were symptomatic of the growing international market in players. Even though the United States had passed an Immigration Act in 1921, which was the first real attempt to ration the number of people coming in, football was different. The British were not only about to intensify the rules governing players going out but also to tighten the regulations to stop any foreigners coming in.

Banning foreigners

The pivotal event that spurred this action was an attempt by Arsenal to sign an Austrian goalkeeper, Rudy Hiden, in the late summer of 1930. The Gunners' manager, Herbert Chapman, and Hiden's club, Vienna, had agreed a fee and a two-month contract was prepared that included the option for an extension. Arsenal had even gone to the trouble of finding Hiden suitable supplementary work as a chef. His boat duly arrived in England, where he was promptly refused admission to the country. Hiden's was not a singular case. The Ministry of Labour said allowing such people into the country would restrict employment opportunities for British workers.

Signs that the authorities would not back Hiden's cause had first come, resoundingly, in the *Topical Times* column of the game's most vocal administrator, Charles Sutcliffe, earlier in August. He said that the Management Committee of the League would discuss the matter, if it arose, on the 25th of that month.

Under the headline 'This Foreign Player Business', he wrote:

> If and when a registration form with the accompanying memorandum of the contents of the player's agreement arrived at the league office, the Management Committee can then take such action as it thinks fit and consistent with its rules.

> I hope we may be spared giving an official opinion, not because I fear anyone would shirk it but merely because I feel the idea of bringing 'foreigners' to play in league football is repulsive to the clubs, offensive to British players and a terrible confession of weakness in the management of a club.

> If the report of the Arsenal's intention is accurate, I cannot see why the authorities should refuse admission to players engaged or proposed to be engaged by three other clubs and then favour the Arsenal. If such importations are allowed, where will it end? The difficulties are innumerable and if the opportunity arises I hope the

> Management Committee will decline
> to register continental players.

Sutcliffe, and by extension the authorities, could not have made their stance clearer had they gone to Dover themselves, waited for Hiden to disembark, given him two fingers and told him to clear off back where he'd come from.

Sure enough, when the Football Association's various committees met at the FA's Lancaster Gate HQ on Monday 25 August, the opinion was voiced that the Government should be encouraged to stop imports before they became common. This became official policy, as laid out in the minutes of the FA's International Selection Committee meeting of that day. Minute No. 11 was as follows:

> 11. – Alien Professional Players. The Committee having considered a letter from the Minister of Labour, decided to make the following recommendation to the Council:–
>
> In reply to an enquiry of the Minister of Labour, the Council of The Football Association is not in favour of granting permits for alien players to be brought into this country for the purpose of being employed as football players and would desire a continuance of the present practice of the Minister of Labour.

The minute was submitted to the FA Council that day and the recommendation immediately adopted. Sutcliffe then used his *Topical Times* column of 6 September 1930 to explain precisely how united the authorities and the Government had been on the issue.

> The Football Association have sounded the death-knell of the proposal to engage alien football players

he trumpeted. He quoted the Minister of Labour as saying:

> Why should an alien be permitted to land to keep a Britisher out of a job?

He said the Player's Union, which also represented coaches, was initially afraid that stopping foreign players might see retaliatory measures that would limit opportunities for British coaches abroad. And yet he said the PFA ultimately resolved:

> We don't care, keep the aliens out.

Sutcliffe ended his piece with a double flourish.

> It may now be assumed that the Austrian will finish his chef education in another country.

Then:

> It will be a bad day for club managers when they have to cultivate team spirit in a team of players where some would not understand a word said to them.

The matter did not finish there. Arsenal, having been thwarted in their attempt to sign Hiden, had gone and secured the services of another foreign goalkeeper already resident in the country. His name was Gerry Keizer and he became the first Dutch international at Highbury some 65 years ahead of Glenn Helder and Dennis Bergkamp in 1995. Charles Sutcliffe was almost apoplectic. The steam from his ears could almost be imagined as he wrote his column for 13 September 1930. Not only had Arsenal already played Keizer – who had been attached to Millwall and Margate previously – but they had circumvented the spirit of the FA's new 'anti-professional foreigner' stance with a bizarre arrangement. Keizer, it seemed, had been offered a professional contract and accepted it. But Arsenal, knowing the authorities would refuse a work permit, had torn it up. Instead, Keizer was offered terms as an amateur and duly received a permit to play without pay.

Sutcliffe wrote:

> Thus we had a club of untold wealth who could well afford to get a professional [British] goalkeeper, who, in turn, would make room for another unemployed [British] professional, playing a player with an alien permit and without pay.

With his disgust barely disguised, he added that he was 'British to the bone' and that if the time ever came when the country could not find British players for its teams there would be something seriously amiss.

In the event, Keizer, who had a reputation for being something of a bruiser, only played 12 times for Arsenal, moving down a division to join Charlton the next season. Chapman's Arsenal, largely without him, went on to utterly dominate English football in the 1930s, winning the League five times between 1931 and 1938.

In the months following Hiden's non-arrival and Keizer's appointment at Arsenal, the debate intensified within the FA about what else could be done to stop foreign players. Clearly the Government was on side but that would not necessarily be permanent. In any case, the authorities wanted control of their own affairs. By December 1930, the FA Council was considering a proposal that would ban non-British players from playing in FA Cup matches. This could effectively be achieved by introducing a two-year residency rule to deter impulse buying. But by the time the FA came to formalise this notion, in June 1931, the game's authorities took more draconian action still. They changed the Rules of the Association.

The following amendment to the rules concerning the eligibility of players was formally approved by the FA Council at Lancaster Gate on 1 June that year.

> A professional player who is not a British-born subject is not eligible to take part in any competition under the jurisdiction of this Association unless he possesses a two years' residential qualification within the jurisdiction of the Association.

To much of the world, the door was closed. Between 1931 and 1939, only players with colonial ties came in.

Alf Charles was notable as the first player born in Trinidad. A magician by trade, he was attached to Burnley, Nelsen, Darwen and Stalybridge but only played League football for Southampton, and then only one game in the 1936–37 season. Otherwise, the biggest single country of origin was South Africa, with 24 League players arriving between the wars. Some were sons of servicemen, such as the Osborne brothers, Frank, Reg and Harold, who had returned to England as children, then played through the 1920s with a series of clubs. Reg was with Leicester and Frank with Fulham, Tottenham and Southampton. Both had long League careers and were capped for England. Frank was later secretary-manager at Fulham from 1948 to 1964.

Other players were born and raised to adulthood in South Africa and were either spotted by British teams, many of whom toured that popular location, or came to Britain on tours themselves and stayed on. Liverpool's Arthur Riley, a goalkeeper, and Gordon Hodgson, who would become one of Anfield's greatest ever goal-scorers, arrived by the latter route after a Springbok tour to the UK and Europe in October and November 1924.

Hodgson scored 232 goals for Liverpool in 359 League games, all in the First Division, an astonishing ratio in any era. It was no surprise he was capped by England. He also played cricket for Lancashire and football for Aston Villa and Leeds before turning his hand to management with Port Vale. After taking charge in 1946, he oversaw the club's move to their current stadium, Vale Park, in 1950. He died the next year, aged 47.

And so these 'non-foreign' overseas players came through the 1930s to Liverpool, Aldershot, Fulham, Millwall, Southampton, Chesterfield and elsewhere. Umpteen destinations from few ports of origin. What a difference another war would make.

CHAPTER TWO

Back In Business

Soccer kicked off after seven years in pelting rain, on slippery grounds—and with sensations in plenty. Wolves routed Arsenal 6—1, Brentford took away points from Everton. Villa lost at home to 'Boro. Bury piled up seven against Fulham. Luton trounced Sheffield Wednesday. Newport v. Southampton was postponed through floods...

Crowds of close on a million saw the League games. Highest was at Chelsea—61,461. Everton drew 55,000. Sunderland 53,000. Wolves and Villa 50,000. A Third Division match drew 25,000 to Frank Buckley's Hull City. Gates closed at Chelsea, Millwall, Swansea. Total for League matches, 847,000. Add the few smart ones who dodged the turnstiles...

Goals a-plenty. Jesse Pye, Wolves' capture from Notts County, got three. So did Barnsley's Robledo.

The Daily Mirror
Monday 2 September, 1946

TAKE THAT. A debut hat-trick. What a way to bid *adios* to the war.

Seven years on from the last official League matches in England, 16 months on from VE Day and 363 days since VJ Day had marked the cessation of hostilities in the Pacific, football was back in business. On 'F Day', as the tabloids had dubbed Saturday 31 August 1946, the national game, like the nation itself, started to return to its feet. And George Robledo, born in Chile, ended his first 90 minutes in the League with three goals to his exotic name.

Robledo wore the No9 shirt for Barnsley of the Second Division that afternoon. Their match against Nottingham Forest at Oakwell drew a crowd of 17,317. Forest scored twice. Robledo went one better. He scored another two in a 4—2 win at Sheffield Wednesday in his next game, all of two days later. The players were obviously hungry after a seven-year wait. Two outings, five successful strikes, four points.

Robledo played 42 games that season and racked up 23 goals. Before his time as a Tyke was up, he made 114 appearances and scored 47 goals. Later, with Newcastle – 164 games, 91 goals – he scored the winner in an FA Cup final. It was his second FA Cup success in two years, in the second of six consecutive FA Cup finals that featured landmark contributions by players born overseas.

In August 1946, football in the post-war era faced exactly the same crises as society at large. Manpower was insufficient, rebuilding was the key. Many of the men walking onto pitches for the 3.15pm kick-offs had never played League football before. Numerous players had been killed in the war. Others had been more fortunate, losing only the best years of their careers.

Britain had not been totally devoid of war-time competitions, often staffed by visiting players, but as *The Times* noted in the countdown to 'F Day', war-time football

> served its purpose [*but*] was unreal
> and may be forgotten gracefully.

Now it was back to points and prizes; promotion, relegation, honours; the drama of the FA Cup, and all without an ample reservoir of youth upon which to draw. The League, resuming with the same teams in the same divisions as during the abandoned 1939–40 season, was facing the sternest test in its history.

There were signs that wider society was returning to some kind of normality, albeit after a process of re-evaluation. Comedian Charlie Chaplin, for example, was again able to displace more solemn stories from the front pages, even if it was to announce that he was throwing away his moustache, bowler hat and walking stick "because the funny little man I always portrayed has no meaning to the present generation".

And the footballers' union, intent as ever on casting off its own shackles, was again lobbying for an increase in the maximum wage, from £10 a week to £12. This latest campaign came as US baseball players secured their own new deal – in less than two hours – of a minimum annual salary of £1,250 plus pension plan, expenses and representation on their governing body.

But the world at large was still distracted by post-war dilemmas. An opinion poll in Berlin showed that 1.9 per cent of people thought the Nazi war criminals at the Nuremberg trials, which had been going on for 10 months, should be unconditionally released. This 1.9 per cent of 'incorrigible fanatics' made the headlines in the British press ahead of the 49.8 per cent of Germans who wanted those on trial to hang or the 48.3 per cent who favoured the softer option of lifelong detention in hard labour camps.

In London, the newspapers were dominated by the court martial of Major Cecil Boon, on trial facing 11 charges of 'aiding the Japs' while a prisoner in Hong Kong. His defence team said he'd been put in an 'unenviable position' of being asked to carry out the orders of his captors. His critics said he had been unduly harsh in doing so, and that he had received extra cigarettes for his work.

The letters' pages of newspapers and magazines were still dominated by matters relating to the war.

> Children under two years should have a bigger sugar ration [*wrote one correspondent*]. I would rather do without my four-months-old baby's bacon ration – he doesn't need that – in exchange for more sugar.

Another reader, not atypically, had written asking why his house, blitzed in 1940, had still only received 'first-aid' repairs. Others he knew had been almost patched up.

Even popular adverts required amendments for the times, with Cadbury's taking extra space to inform consumers:

> Although milk chocolate is one of the most nourishing foods made from milk, Cadbury's are allowed only a very small proportion of the surplus summer milk allocated each year to manufacturers. This is why Cadbury's milk chocolate is in short supply. When you are lucky please save it for the children. There's a glass and a half of full-cream milk in every half pound.

Talent from another planet

As for football, the country's major leisure-time solace, it was on the verge, through necessity and accident and circumstance, of its most multi-national era to date. The rules and regulations designed to keep foreigners out would remain in place – and indeed be strengthened yet again – but the League soon featured 'firsts' from, among other places, Bermuda, Jamaica, Hungary, Italy, Iceland, Latvia, Norway, Poland, Sweden, Spain and Switzerland. And, in the wake of their pre-war pioneer compatriots, more players would arrive from Germany, Denmark, Belgium, Australia and South Africa. Some of this new wave were refugees, others civil servants or students or servicemen or businessmen. Some were professionals, others amateur. Some stayed a few games, others for decades. What George Robledo did, on 31 August 1946, was announce their arrival in emphatic fashion.

"I just thought he came from another planet, another world," recalled Sir Bobby Robson, a boyhood fan of Robledo. George moved to Newcastle in 1949, the year before Robson left his hometown for London to begin his own career with Fulham.

"Thick-set, swarthy, he had a Chilean countenance, half sunburnt. Good-looking chap actually. Compact, solid player, a goal-scorer. He got in with the centre-forward, he saw the crosses, he got in the box. He worked very hard, he could turn on the ball, he could play the good pass."

Robson was in attendance at Wembley, as a fan, for both Robledo's FA Cup successes in 1951 and 1952.

"He was a bit like Alan Shearer, really, a good solid body, good legs, strong thighs, he got up and down and he played in that attacking half. He could turn on the ball and he was adept in the air. I just thought he was a pretty good player."

Robledo's mother, Elsie, had been born and raised in South Yorkshire. Aged 18, she travelled to Argentina to work as a governess to the children of an English mine manager. When her employer was later transferred to northern Chile, she moved too. It was there, in Iquique, that she met Aristides Robledo, an accountant, and there she had three children, including George, in 1926, and Ted, who also played for Barnsley, and Newcastle, in 1928. Not long after the arrival of a third son, Walter, in 1932, Elsie decided to return to England. Aristides stayed behind, never to see his wife or two of his sons again. George, on a later trip back home to play internationally for Chile, was the exception.

Elsie and the boys settled in West Melton, Yorkshire, where George, having developed into a fine athlete, played amateur football for Huddersfield and Barnsley in the war. He joined the latter professionally in April 1943, the month of his 17th birthday. Three years later he made the national papers with his debut League hat-trick. He went on to become a huge favourite with the fans, even inspiring a local poet to immortalise him in verse.

> *Relentlessly he surges on; Intrepid, fearless, cool,*
> *The foeman cannot stem the tide; Engulfed in this whirlpool.*
> *With desperation in their hearts; They give a cry of pain,*
> *Then – crash – the ball is in the net; Robledo strikes again.*

Such prowess in front of goal was bound to attract attention. Thus in January 1949, Newcastle United, on their way to becoming regular top-four finishers in the First Division, tempted George away to the north-east. They paid £26,500, with George making a condition that Ted move too. He did, and they took Elsie and Walter for good measure.

George, or 'Pancho' as his team-mates nicknamed him, went straight into the Newcastle side, forming an attacking partnership with Jackie Milburn that was to become the country's most feared combination. By the end of the 1949–50 season, his form had even earned a call-up to the Chilean national side for the 1950 World Cup in Brazil. There he played in all Chile's group matches, including a 2–0 defeat to an England team featuring Alf Ramsey, Tom Finney, Stan Mortensen and Wilf Mannion. In Chile's third and last match of the tournament, George opened the scoring in a 5–2 win over the USA, who three days earlier had pulled off one of the greatest-ever World Cup shocks by beating England 1–0.

Returning as a hero in both Chile and England, George helped Newcastle to fourth place in the League in 1950–51. The season was crowned when Newcastle beat Blackpool – a side that included Stanley Matthews and Mortensen – in the FA Cup final. Milburn scored both goals, with George the provider of the crucial opener, five minutes into the second half.

The following season Newcastle finished eighth in the League but scored more goals – 98 – than any other side. Another 15 were scored in the Cup. George scored 39 in all competitions, with 33 coming in the League, making him the country's leading marksman. By this point, Ted was also in the Newcastle team and the brothers played together in the FA Cup final of 1952, against Arsenal.

The match was remembered for the Londoners' valiant display after being reduced to 10 men after 27 minutes by an injury to Walley Barnes, their right-back. "We have won the cup but the glory is yours," said Stan Seymour, the Newcastle director-manager, to the Arsenal players afterwards. But the glory was also George Robledo's, having been the man, five minutes from time, who attached himself to a cross from Bobby Mitchell and headed home the decisive goal. The decider in the final the following year would also be scored by an overseas-born player, Bill Perry of South Africa, as Blackpool beat Bolton 4–3 in the famous 'Matthews Final'. But more of that later.

The 1952–53 season saw Arsenal win the League and Newcastle finish seventh from bottom. After repeated approaches from Chilean clubs, George and Ted ultimately joined Colo Colo of Santiago. The chance of playing in their country of birth, not to mention earning salaries that far exceeded the kind of money they could earn in wage-capped England, had proved irresistible. The brothers both went on to win League titles with Colo Colo and regularly played for Chile, where they were known as 'Jorge' and 'Eduardo' despite having been baptised with anglicised names.

After his playing days were over George went into coaching and later teaching, while Ted returned to England for a brief spell with Notts County. Ted later worked on oil rigs, only to die in mysterious circumstances in 1970 after going missing from a ship in the Persian Gulf.

"I heard Ted was on a banana boat," Bobby Robson said. "The body was never found. I think he was thrown overboard. Disappeared off the boat. Obviously murdered. That's the message I got."

No-one, in fact, was ever found guilty of Ted's murder. There had been talk of a fight between him and the captain. But although the captain was charged with murder, he was acquitted.

George died in Chile of a heart attack in 1989, age 63, never knowing what had happened to his brother. George's Chilean widow, Gladys, stayed in touch with Bobby Robson and indeed travelled to Newcastle at the end of 2002 to unveil a plaque at St James' Park in honour of her late husband.

The Robledos, especially George, made the kind of footballing contribution to the post-war years that would later be held up as trademarks of the best foreign players. Their professionalism was unquestioned, on or off the pitch. They trained well and looked after themselves as full-time athletes, not twice-weekly entertainers who could spend five nights a week in the pub. They sought new experiences, and ultimately better money, befitting their talents. And George, while adapting to whatever system of play he was asked to be a part of, also liked innovation. Players who could execute the 'bicycle kick' were a rarity and he was one of them. Above all, through their looks, style and George's flair, they compelled people to pay good money to walk through the turnstiles and watch them play. And on numerous occasions those same people would leave two hours later having seen something just a little bit different, a little bit magical.

Journeymen and trailblazers

While Arnold Woollard could not claim to have had quite such an effect, he nonetheless won many admirers. He was the first Bermudan to play in the League – and the first Bermudan to play anywhere in the world professionally – after joining Northampton in 1949 on the recommendation of Bermuda's High Commissioner. After being converted from a winger to a full-back, he then moved to Peterborough from where Newcastle, impressed by his displays in the giant-killing FA Cup run of 1952–53, signed him for £4,000, then a record fee to a non-League club. He played only 10 times alongside the likes of the Robledos and Milburn but considered his time at St James' Park, which included a part in the successful FA Cup run of 1955, a highlight in his career. He later gave long service to Bournemouth, where he played a part in FA Cup upsets over Wolves and Tottenham, before a second short spell with Northampton, helping them win the Third Division in 1962–63. He returned to Bermuda to work in a bank. In 1964, aged 33, he was a member of his country's first international side ever to play outside Bermuda. They lost to Iceland.

Newcastle did not have a monopoly on foreign players in the north-east of the 1950s. Sunderland had two South Africans, Ted Purdon, a forward who also played League football for Barrow, and Don Kitchenbrand, another attacker. There was also the long-serving Australian-born goalkeeper, Willie Fraser, although as his name suggests, his roots were in Scotland, a country he represented.

Middlesbrough also had an overseas goalkeeper, Norman Malan from South Africa, but he played just twice before moving to Scunthorpe and Bradford Park Avenue. Another more significant foreign-born goalkeeper at Ayresome Park was Rolando Ugolini, the first Italian to play in the League. And strictly speaking, despite having moved to Britain – Glasgow, to be precise – with his parents as a toddler, he *was* Italian when he played his first League match for Boro against Chelsea at the start of the 1948–49 season. The reason was that he had never been naturalised. Quite why this was, Ugolini has never been certain, although it may have been because his father wanted Rolando to retain that key part of his Italian heritage. Or it may have been that Ugolini Snr did not feel especially predisposed to British officialdom, having been interned on the Isle of Man during the Second World War because he was Italian, and Italy had sided with Germany.

"It was only for three months," Rolando recalled. "Although during that time me and my mother were sent to live in an unprotected area of Glasgow where we spent every single night in a bomb shelter as Clydebank was blitzed."

Whatever the reasons, Ugolini was officially Italian when he first played for Middlesbrough. And that meant the football authorities deemed him to have broken their rules. His first major club had been the Glasgow giants, Celtic, from where he moved in May 1948 for £7,000. Therefore, when he made his Boro debut not only was he an Italian, but he was an Italian who had not lived within the jurisdiction of the English FA for two years before playing a League game. And as the FA rules – changed in 1931 (see Chapter One) – stated at the time, he was therefore ineligible to play in any competition within the jurisdiction of the English FA. His time in Scotland did not count.

Matters only came to a head before the third round of the FA Cup in the 1948–49 season. Possibly the protectionist FA, still keen on keeping foreigners out despite the labour situation of the post-war period, had taken its hawkish eyes off the ball before then. Thus this 'foreigner', born in Lucca but raised almost entirely in Britain, had been allowed to slip through the net. But come the FA Cup, and no doubt a flurry of media interest in Ugolini's fine and often theatrical displays, the authorities decided to clamp down. It was clear evidence that the anti-foreigner stance was still well and truly in place.

"It was approaching the first Cup tie I was due to play in and the FA said that I could only play if I was British," Ugolini said. "They said I wasn't British, and until I was, I wouldn't be able to play."

Middlesbrough, faced with an intransigent FA but an important Cup match looming on 8 January 1949, at Brentford, did the only thing they could.

"They put me in a taxi, sent me up to the appropriate office in Linlithgow in Scotland and got me to become a naturalised British subject."

As luck would have it – bad luck, in this case – Middlesbrough of the First Division, complete with Ugolini, went to Brentford of the Second Division, and lost 3–2. The winner was scored by a Scotsman, Peter McKennan, who wrapped things up with a 40-yard scorcher. "Like a bullet it was," said Ugolini.

Middlesbrough signed McKennan a few months later. Ugolini stayed with Boro until 1957, playing 334 matches, before four years with Wrexham. He retired in Edinburgh to a life of golf.

Winging in from Jamaica

Most of Ugolini's time at Middlesbrough was spent in the same team as Lindy Delapenha. He was the first Jamaican ever to play League football and the first black player to be part of a championship-winning team, with Portsmouth in 1948–49.

Born in Kingston in 1927, the young Delapenha excelled at school in a variety of sports, winning trophies at youth level in athletics, cricket and tennis.

"But football was what I liked," he recalled. "Academically I wasn't going to be a doctor or a lawyer so when my sports master said he thought I might make something as a player, I thought I'd give it a go. And England was the only place I could try."

The 18-year-old's parents funded the cost of a one-way ticket, £40. It bought a berth on a ship transporting British POWs on a circuitous route home after years of captivity at the hands of the Japanese.

"Most of them had had an awful time, but they looked after me and gave me some good advice," said Delapenha. "I knew I wouldn't be able just to go over and start playing football straight away so the idea was to join the army, the physical training corps, spend some time playing some football there and see what happened. I arrived in November 1945 in Southampton. My first night was spent in a Nissan hut made for 5,000 people. I was the only one there. I hadn't really thought about the situation I'd find but it wasn't that – being in Jamaica one minute and then in this strange place, washing in freezing water – the next."

It quickly became apparent that part-time enlistment would not be possible. That left two options: find a club immediately despite having no experience, or sign-up full-time in the army and take his chances down that route.

"Before signing up I thought I'd just go and see Arsenal and show them the letter of recommendation from my sports master. Tom Whittaker, who was assisting at Highbury at the time [*and would soon become the manager*], put me up and played me in a few reserves trials. He said I just wasn't ready for it but to come back and see him when I got out of the army.

"I did service for two years at a barracks in Brentford and then got posted overseas. It was a blessing in disguise. I blossomed in the heat of Egypt, played football, cricket, ran 10.1 seconds for the 100 yards. I made a bit of name for myself. During one game against the Egyptian national side, a scout spotted me and said I might be useful to Chelsea or Portsmouth. He wrote me a letter of recommendation. When I was demobbed in 1948 I had nowhere to live but I had a friend who lived not far from Portsmouth who said I could stay with him. That's why I went to see the Portsmouth manager, Bob Jackson. I gave him the letter. He said he'd give me a trial to see what I was worth. We went to Bristol Rovers with the reserves. He signed me at half-time. He said he'd seen enough."

That was in April 1948. In the 1948–49 season, Portsmouth, in their golden jubilee season, won the first of their back-to-back League titles, ahead of Manchester United in second.

In 1949–50, they won again, finishing level on points with Wolves but taking the League by dint of a better defensive record. The second title-winning side had involved, for five games, the Swedish international forward Dan Ekner, who was the first man from his country in the League. He'd come to England to read business studies at college and was only allowed to play short-term as an amateur. He later went on to forge a long and successful professional career in France, Italy, America, Spain, Germany and The Netherlands.

Like Ekner, Delapenha only featured sporadically in Portsmouth's championship-winning seasons but he did enough to earn the chance of moving centre-stage elsewhere. The catalyst for his transfer to the north-east was a dynamic performance for Portsmouth against Boro on 3 September 1949, which Pompey won 5–1. Two days later, at Aston Villa, he would suffer serious ankle-ligament damage in a challenge with Villa's wing-half, Amos Moss. While he was recuperating, and trying to fight his way back into the team, Middlesbrough's manager, David Jack, approached Bob Jackson and asked what had happened to the lad who'd played so well against his team. Jackson explained and Jack made an offer. Jackson agreed to sell on the informal condition that Delapenha be guaranteed first-team football. The deal was completed in April 1950.

On arrival at Ayresome Park, Delapenha, who favoured the inside-right position in the forward line, found himself in the reserves.

"You're not playing me in the first team," he told Jack, who didn't need to point out that he already had a rather decent inside-right in Wilf Mannion. Along with four other giants of the era – Stanley Matthews, Stan Mortensen, Tommy Lawton and Tom Finney – Mannion helped comprise the 'Famous Five' England forward line, regarded by many as the best attacking line-up that England ever fielded.

"Can you play outside-right?" Jack asked Delapenha, who replied that he'd give it a go. Some go. His combination with Mannion brought the house down and eventually led to Delapenha becoming Middlesbrough's biggest name of the mid-50s and their highest-paid player. In 270 games, he scored 93 goals, a magnificent return for a winger. His ball control was superb and the fans delighted in his flicks and tricks, innovative at the time.

His favourite memories revolve around games where for one reason or another he was not expected to do well, but he confounded his critics. The notion that a man from Jamaica would struggle in snow irked him.

"When it was so cold and snowy that the lines had to be marked out in blue, I set out to be extraordinary," he said. "And I was. I remember one cup-tie against Derby, January 1952, which we drew at Ayresome Park and then won the replay away in four climates – frost, sun, quagmire, wind, the lot."

Away from match days he was also an asset to his team-mates, introducing extra skills drills and head-tennis tournaments after regular training, which was often tedious in the extreme. One of the players to benefit was a young man called Brian Clough, then progressing into the side.

"We never saw a ball from one week to another," Delapenha recalled. "So the head tennis especially became popular. At one stage, word got around that we were doing this and me and Brian Clough were invited to go on stage at the local Empire Theatre and do it as a routine in support of a fella who was doing a Houdini-style variety act. We did it every night for a week."

Delapenha, being the only Boro player at the time who had a car, was also enlisted to take Clough and his wife-to-be, Barbara, to buy their engagement ring in his Morris Minor.

There were also difficult times, not least the abuse he received because he was Jamaican.

"My complexion is quite light, maybe that's why I didn't get all that much," he said.

Certainly there were no problems with home supporters or team-mates, of whom he counted Clough, Ugolini and Peter Taylor – later Clough's assistant in the glory years at Derby and Nottingham Forest – among his closer friends. But it did happen, and often it came from opponents.

"You got called names. It happened a lot. Remarks about going back where you belong. But my greatest asset was to take it all, on all occasions, and then turn around and laugh straight at whoever said it. I'd smile and then say: 'It's okay, I'll be on the next banana boat home.' I did that over and over."

The message soon got through that he wasn't going anywhere, except up the right wing and onto the score sheet.

After Middlesbrough, Delapenha moved on, in June 1958, to Mansfield, where he played 120 games and scored 27 goals. He had a spell in the non-league, including at Burton under Peter Taylor, before returning to Jamaica in 1964 to coach a sugar estates team.

"But sugar went bad and they paid me off. They gave me a ticket to England but I didn't really fancy the weather any more."

He sold insurance for a while before carving out a new career as a commentator with the Jamaica Broadcasting Corporation. Like Ugolini – and countless others in the game – he retired to a life of golf.

"It's the one game that anyone who plays any kind of sport wants to play."

Refugees and soldiers

Along with Delapenha, Ekner and Ugolini came a group of other 'firsts' in the post-war years. Emilio Aldecoa was the first Spaniard in the League, playing for Coventry in the 1946–47 season. He had arrived in England in 1937 as one of 4,000 Basque refugee children fleeing General Franco's fascism in the Spanish Civil War. He came to prominence in a Basque Boys side in December that year as they beat a team from Yarmouth 9–0. He played war-time football in attack for Wolves, who he joined in 1943, moving to Coventry two years later as a winger. He played one season of League football before returning to Spain, where he starred for Atletico Bilbao, Real Valladolid and Barcelona, where he won two league titles. He was capped by Spain shortly after he returned there from England. Two other refugees from 1937, the Gallego brothers, Tony and José, also played League football after the war. Tony played for Norwich, while José played for Brentford, Southampton and Colchester.

The first Polish players also made League debuts in 1946–47. Eryk Kubicki, an outside-left, and a goalkeeper, Edouard Wojtcazk, a former tank commander and champion ice skater, had been members of the Second Polish Army Division stationed at Sand Hutton, near York, after the war. The pair impressed in a friendly game when a Polish side beat York 7–3 in October 1946. Both went on to play for York that season. Stan Gerula, a Polish amateur international goalkeeper, made 30 League appearances for Leyton Orient around the same time. He later played for Walthamstow Avenue as they twice won the

Isthmian League and earned national attention by taking Manchester United to an FA Cup replay. Two other Poles, Konrad Kapler and Adam Wislewski, had short spells with Rochdale. A third, at Northampton, was Felix Starocsik, a winger who played 50 times and scored 13 goals. He later settled in Bedford, where his son became a local golfing celebrity.

The first Icelandic player also made his League debut in 1946–47. Albert Gudmundsson, born in Reykjarvik in 1923, had already played as a forward for Rangers in Scotland, where he had been studying marine biology, before he moved to Arsenal. But as with a variety of others in the era, he was only allowed to play amateur football in England. He played just twice in the First Division before seeking paid employment elsewhere. He went on to play professionally for Milan in Italy and for Nancy and Racing Club de Paris in France before an illustrious career in business, politics and football administration. He was the president of the Icelandic FA between 1968 and 1973. There is no knowing what he might have achieved had he stayed in England, but the authorities were in no mind to find out. Who knows, his son, Ingi Bjorn Albertsson, who was born in 1952, might even have ended up a British citizen and been in contention for honours in an adoptive country rather than in Iceland, where he became one of the most prolific strikers of the 1970s. But it was never to be, because of the effective ban on professional foreigners via the two-year residency rule. Amateurs, so the rationale went, would only come to England if they had a non-footballing primary purpose. Why would they stay if they could not earn from the game, as they could elsewhere? Thus, Gudmundsson and Dan Ekner and others plied their trades in other countries and the English game passed up chance after chance of allowing the possibility of fresh ideas from outside.

Amateur dramatics

Another international player with a short League career was the defender Willi Steffen, the first Swiss in the League, with Chelsea in 1946–47. Again, he was an amateur and he stayed for just one season. Clearly he was a player of note, appearing in the famous 'Match of the Century' at Hampden Park, Glasgow, on 10 May 1947, when the return of the British associations to FIFA was celebrated with a game between Great Britain and a

Rest of Europe XI. Some 135,000 fans contributed receipts of £35,000 to watch the British side win 6–1. As a gesture of good will, the money was placed at FIFA's disposal to help the world body recover from the financial hardships of the war years. No such gestures headed in the direction of Steffen or others wanting to earn a living in England.

Other 'firsts' in the decade after the resumption of football included Arthur Atkins, born in Japan, albeit of British parents. He played for Birmingham and Shrewsbury. The first Japanese national would not debut in the League until November 2001, when Yoshi Kawaguchi played in goal for Portsmouth. At the same time Junichi Inamoto and Akinori Nishizawa were playing for Arsenal and Bolton respectively, but not in the hothouse of the League.

Eddie Freimanis was the first Latvian in the League, in 1948–49 at Northampton. He had come to England to work as an interpreter after the war. He later changed his name to Freiman and then Freeman. Moving into the mid-1950s, Mauno Rintanen, the first League player from Finland, joined Hull from HJK Helsinki in September 1956. Rintanen was Finland's international goalkeeper and a former Finnish Player of the Year but was only allowed amateur terms with Hull and stayed only a few months.

The first League player born in Hungary was Mick Nagy, very briefly with Swindon in the early 1950s. Next came Bela Olah at Northampton, from December 1958, and then Johnny Haasz, in the early 1960s with Swansea and Workington. Olah and Haasz were both among the 21,000 Hungarians who fled their country following the 1956 uprising against the Communist regime.

Prior to leaving, Haasz had been involved in some gruesome guerilla activity against the Soviet occupiers. On the run he once even found himself hiding in a graveyard, inside an occupied coffin. He eventually fled first to Austria and then to England, where a friend owned a transport café. Despite having been a footballer at home, he was unable to play immediately in his new country because the Hungarian FA deemed such players 'deserters' and banned them. FIFA decided to uphold the Hungarian FA's ruling and helped to enforce the edict internationally. Olah escaped a ban, not having been a prominent footballer before his escape from Hungary.

Puskas, the impossible purchase

In some cases, after lobbying from the Communist nations, FIFA extended the bans. Such a fate befell the legendary Ferenc Puskas – the captain of the Hungarian side who had beaten England 6–3 in astonishing fashion at Wembley in 1953 – after he fled Hungary in 1956. Matt Busby, the manager of Manchester United, considered trying to sign this 'Magical Magyar' when he was rebuilding his team after the Munich air disaster of February 1958. The possibility was ultimately ruled out. Earlier, as Busby had lain in hospital in Germany, his assistant, Jimmy Murphy, desperate for players, had thought of signing Puskas. But firstly, Puskas was still banned; secondly, Murphy reasoned that the maximum wage and the FA's restriction on foreign players would make such a move impossible. Even when Puskas's ban expired, the latter two factors still worked against United. So Puskas ended up in Spain, with Real Madrid. His enforced lay-off was followed by an awesome renaissance that was capped with four goals in the European Cup final of 1960. That match, a 7–3 crushing of Eintracht Frankfurt at Hampden Park, Glasgow, was Real Madrid's fifth European Cup win in the five years since the tournament began. Things might have been quite different but for FIFA's rules and the English authorities' barricades.

Haasz returned from his own ban in the less rarified surroundings of Swansea Town before moving on to another League club, Workington, and then Cambridge and Corby.

"There were never any problems as far as the English were concerned," he said. "The government found us [*refugees*] jobs. We were warmly received and quickly accommodated."

Haasz eventually settled in Doncaster, the home town of Edith, the woman he married.

Another foreign player who had settled in England before Haasz even arrived was the first post-war Belgian, Marcel Gaillard, who played for Crystal Palace soon after the war and later for Portsmouth. A classy winger, he played more games for Pompey than Lindy Delapenha and Dan Ekner combined, appearing in 58 League games and scoring seven goals in the First Division. He also played in six FA Cup games in the 1951–52 season, scoring six Cup goals in a run that ended in the sixth round. The 4–2 home defeat that saw Portsmouth eliminated came – in a thrilling encounter – at the hands of the Newcastle side of George Robledo, who scored the winner to lift the trophy that May. Gaillard later moved to Yeovil Town and managed Dorchester Town. He died, aged 49, in 1976.

From Down Under to Deepdale

For some imports of the 1950s, England provided years of rich memories but did not hold a lifelong allure. Australia's Joe Marston was such a player. After George Robledo in 1951 and 1952 and Bill Perry in 1953, Marston, in 1954, saw the FA Cup final graced with a foreign presence for a fourth consecutive year. He was the first Australian to appear in a showcase that was a world away – or in literal terms, half a world away – from his previous life 'Down Under'.

Marston was doing his shift as a lifesaver on Whale Beach on Sydney's north shore on 31 December, 1949, when he got a message to get in touch with Percy Sewell, a scout from England who'd settled in Australia. Sewell had seen Marston, a sturdy centre-half, playing for Leichardt Annandale in Sydney. Impressed with his attitude and composure, he'd written to Blackpool and Preston with a recommendation.

"Blackpool said they were fixed up for centre-halves," Marston recalled. "And then I didn't hear anything until that New Year's Eve, when Percy told me Preston wanted to give me a trial. They paid the fares, £665 one way for me and my wife Edith. We flew on BOAC Qantas and it took four days. We stopped in Singapore, where we stayed at Raffles, then Karachi, in another wonderful hotel, and then Cairo."

The couple landed at Heathrow on 2 February 1950, where two directors from the Deepdale club met them and whisked them straight to Windsor for a look at the castle.

"The deal was effectively tied up before I arrived and I went straight into the reserves after a week," Marston said.

The weather took some getting used to – he'd never seen snow before – and the English landscape differed markedly from his pre-conceived idea of an urban tableau.

"On the train to Preston, I couldn't believe how much vacant land there was – farms, rural areas, quite an eye opener."

His starting wages – £7 a week, £2 bonus for a win, £1 bonus for a draw – were also lower than he'd earned at home in a paint factory. But football came first and these were small quibbles. He made his League debut, in October 1950, at right-back, where he failed to make an impression. Fate then intervened when Preston's regular centre-half, Harry Mattinson, broke his leg and Marston was switched to replace him. He would go on to make 185 League appearances and be a Preston ever-present between 1951 and 1954.

"I don't think there were any bad times," he said. "A footballer's life, even then, was on a higher level. People thought of you as something special, you got recognised. They were good times."

The high points included being part of the side that won the Second Division title in 1950–51, and being ever present in the 1952–53 team who had a neck-and-neck battle with Arsenal for the League championship.

"We went 14 games undefeated at one stage and our run-in included two away games on consecutive days, at Burnley and then Sunderland, that we managed to draw."

The same run-in saw Preston beat Arsenal 2–0 at Deepdale but the Londoners took the title by the narrowest of margins. Both teams ended with 54 points but Arsenal, despite conceding more goals than Preston, had scored the few more required for the championship.

"That was hard," said Marston. "We gave them a hammering and knew we were better. But fair play, they'd done enough to win it."

Over the following season, yearning for the beach and more sunshine, Marston considered going back to Australia. But then someone offered him tickets to go and see the 1953 FA Cup final, which turned out to be a classic.

"I went with Edith. After seeing all that razzmatazz and the rendition of *Abide With Me*, I turned around to her and said 'Wouldn't it be amazing if we were here again next year, only with me playing?', and as it turned out, we were."

Indeed they were. Edith proudly watched from the stands while Joe, alongside team-mates who included Tom Finney, was on the pitch to face West Bromwich Albion. Despite a spirited performance, in which Finney, who had been voted Footballer of the Year that week, was man-marked out of the action by two opponents, Preston lost 3–2.

"I'm not one for big emotions," Marston recalled, still moved by the day almost 50 years on. "But I did have to take a few really big breaths out there at the end to cope. It was a bitter pill, actually."

The day was also memorable for the post-match sentiments of team-mate Willie Forbes.

"He was a heavy smoker, Willie, and he took out his match box and emptied it onto the floor. Then he used it to scrape the mud and bits of turf off his boots and he stuffed the box with the proceeds. 'This is what I'll keep, this is my souvenir from today,' he said. He was right. We all took something away."

The following season would be Marston's last in England. Before he left, though, he was party to another big occasion, being selected to play for the English League against the Scottish League at Hampden in March 1955. The Scots won 3–2, thanks to an own goal by Joe. His abiding memory of the trip, however, was sharing a room with Duncan Edwards, the young Manchester United and England wing-half, later to lose his life in the Munich air disaster. Many believed he would have gone on to be one of the finest footballers the world had ever seen. Marston remembers him most fondly as a mate with whom he saw a Frankie Vaughan concert on a free night in Glasgow in March 1955.

By 1955, Joe and Edith had a young daughter, and for all the good times, they missed Australia, their families and the weather. They went home. Marston continued playing, semi-professionally, in a career that spanned 22 years, and then coached for another 16. He retired to the central coast.

Among the other Australians in the League around the time were Frank Mitchell and Ken Grieves. Mitchell was the first Australian in the top division, post-war, after he settled in England following war service with the Australian navy. He played for Birmingham, Chelsea and Watford. Grieves, one of numerous footballer-cricketers – who often hailed from Australia or South Africa – originally came to England to play cricket in the Lancashire League. He'd made a name for himself representing New South Wales in cricket and baseball. But it was as a goalkeeper for Bury, Bolton and Stockport that he earned his living. On one occasion he and Marston played for opposing sides in the League, when Preston beat Bolton 3–1 in September 1953.

A struggle for identity

Another notable Antipodean – the first Australian of Aboriginal descent in the League – was Peter Baines, who played at Wrexham during and after the war, and later, briefly, for Crewe, Hartlepool and New Brighton. He is not recalled in great detail by any Wrexham archives. At one time, a (now deleted) reference on the club's official website, said, in its entirety:

> Peter 'Darkie' Baines is believed to be the first coloured player to have represented the club, making 55 appearances and scoring some 35 goals during and just after WW2. Unfortunately, soon after his professional career was over Peter was sent to prison at Manchester Crown Court for receiving stolen goods – the first of many appearances before the courts.

Baines's story was infinitely more complex than those two sentences relate. Indeed, even his birthplace is a subject of conjecture. Some sources claim he was born in Manchester, where he was raised in an orphanage. But it seems he was quite possibly born in Australia and only later transported to the orphanage as a result of the repugnant 'Make Australia White' policy. This official government programme was in place in Australia in 1919, the year of Baines's birth, and saw mixed-race children with one Aboriginal parent forcibly removed from their families and taken to institutions – religious or otherwise – to be raised as 'civilised' members of society. In most cases, the father was white.

By taking those children and effectively making them orphans (their mothers were left behind, their fathers were mostly unwilling to have anything to do with them), the powers-that-were made headway towards their aim of a segregated society and also shortened the odds on embarrassing the fathers in the process. It is possible that Baines was the product of a relationship between an Aboriginal woman and a white man who would have been extremely embarrassed if any knowledge of his illegitimate half-Aboriginal son had ever become public. Official records at the time were regularly fudged to protect white men who preferred others did not know of their associations with black women. If Baines's father fell into this category, and his standing and finances had allowed it, it could be that strings were pulled to send Baines as far from Australia as possible, in his case to Manchester. It was there, after his playing career fell apart, that he turned to crime, served his prison sentences, and ultimately died, in 1997.

Benchmark for a trusty Scandinavian

Alienation for Baines and other black players would long be a common experience in England, as we will see in later chapters. Conversely, it was players from nations of cultural and linguistic proximity who often fared best and stayed longest. In the 1930s and the 1950s, such individuals mostly came from South Africa and Australia. By the 1990s, the biggest recruitment grounds were in Scandinavia, where most professionals spoke English and followed the English game. They became seen as good value, adaptable and dependable, all qualities found in Viggo Jensen of Denmark, who could not have done more to propagate such an image in the immediate post-war years.

Jensen was born in Skagen in 1921 and was working as a Danish government official when he signed for Hull City in October 1948 as an amateur. Although he was an established Danish international at the time – he played for Denmark against Great Britain in the 1948 London Olympics – these were the only terms Hull were allowed to offer. After spending two years living in England, however – thereby fulfilling the criteria set down by the anti-foreign FA – he was able to sign professional terms in December 1950. He was a mainstay in the Hull side, in a variety of positions, from 1948 to 1957, making 335 first-team appearances and scoring 54 goals.

Jensen's longevity at Hull was matched by his versatility. He started his career at left-back, ended it at right-back and played in positions across midfield and attack en route. His Hull career featured one hat-trick, in February 1949. The club won promotion that year to the Second Division under player-manager Raich Carter, one of England's greatest players. Jensen scored on both his League and FA Cup debuts and there was only one season, 1950–51, when he did not score at all. His best remembered goal came in a fifth-round FA Cup match in 1954 against Tottenham, who'd been First Division champions in 1951 and runners-up the following year. Hull played most of the game with 10 men after they lost a player through injury. Spurs took the lead but Hull equalised with a Jensen penalty. Hull lost the replay but many of those in the 47,000-strong crowd say the original tie was among the most memorable ever staged at Boothferry Park. Jensen retired from playing in late 1956 and returned to Denmark as a coach.

"He can be regarded as a truly great player in the annals of Hull City but, equally as important, he will be remembered as a gentleman as well," said Mike Petersen, a club historian.

Another Scandinavian who had an enormous impact around the time, albeit in a short tenure at Charlton, was Hans Jeppson. The Swedish centre-forward was known to English supporters because he'd scored against England on his international debut, a 3–1 win, in 1949. He had also made a splash at the 1950 World Cup – being part of the team who had shocked Italy 3–2 in their opening game of the tournament – before his arrival in London in January 1951 for a three-month business course. Jimmy Seed, Charlton's manager, knew about Jeppson's trip because he had been informed by Sigge Anderson, the secretary of a Swedish side that Charlton had played against during a 1938 tour. Jeppson knew something about Charlton because a family friend, a Mr Borg (father of the tennis legend, Bjorn) had started following the London side's fortunes after the same tour.

Charlton were in the mire at the wrong end of the First Division. Seed knew Jeppson wanted to play in the League, as an amateur, while studying. He also knew Arsenal were interested and that Jeppson had arranged a meeting, at the FA's headquarters, to discuss his options. Seed turned up unannounced and persuaded the Swede to share lunch. Jeppson was initially unsure about moving to The Valley but Seed asked him to go and meet Charlton's vice-chairman, Stanley Gliksten, even though the latter was in bed with flu. He got up pretty quickly when Seed told him Jeppson was downstairs. A short-term amateur contract was signed the following day.

Charlton's transformation during Jeppson's sojourn was extraordinary. He played only 11 League games but scored nine League goals, including a hat-trick at Highbury against Arsenal. He remains one of an elite band to have achieved that feat. 'Now It's Hats Off To Hans' said the headline in the *Daily*

Mirror on 26 February 1951, the Monday after the game. The accompanying article said:

> Hans left the ground with the white ball used in the second half. It was inscribed: 'To Hans Jeppson with congratulations on a great game at Highbury, Tom Whittaker'... Hans will take the ball back to Sweden when he returns home on April 1 on completion of a salesmanship course here. He certainly seems to have learned how to sell the dummy.

Jeppson stored the ball for safekeeping in his summer house in Sweden, where it remains.

Jeppson also scored vital winning goals against Sheffield Wednesday (an 89th-minute strike on his debut), Liverpool and Chelsea. He scored two against Wolves in a 3–2 win and four in a 5–1 friendly win over West Ham. In short, he saved Charlton from relegation and provided thrilling entertainment in the process. By the time it came for him to return to Sweden, Gliksten had become so enamoured with the 'Handsome Swede' that he tried to charter a helicopter to whisk him away from his final game. He failed, but instead paid 30 guineas to transport him in a launch along the Thames to Tilbury docks, where he boarded the Swedish ship, Suecia, that would take him home.

When his football days were over, he turned his hand to business, working in Italy for ten years before postings to Chile and Belgium. He later worked for the Swedish Export Council in Milan and retired to Rome. It was there he came to know compatriot Sven Goran Eriksson, who managed Lazio and later England.

"I was only at Charlton for three months," Jeppson said, speaking on his 77th birthday in summer 2002. "But I worked well with my team-mates, people like [*legendary goalkeeper*] Sam Bartram and [*club captain*] Benny Fenton. I had some proposals that were seen as fantastic. Like keeping the ball on the ground. Or playing one-twos with my centre-half that left defenders confused. Players marking me had no idea where I was going.

Little tricks like that worked well. It was a special time in my career."

For the football authorities it had been a little too special. The Football League, unhappy that Charlton had imported a foreign player to save their season, subsequently refused an application by Hull to sign Jens Hansen, a compatriot of Viggo Jensen, even on amateur terms. By December 1952, temporary transfers of 'foreign well-known players' had been banned under League rules. Not until European law dictated, in 1978, that the two-year residency rule be dropped and the ban lifted, could such high-profile foreign players think about returning to England.

Not that this mattered to the talented, genial Jeppson, who turned professional on the back of his exploits in London, securing a lucrative move to Italy with Atalanta. He received a signing-on fee of £18,000, which was a huge amount of money at the time. Later he moved to Napoli for a record 105 million lira fee (about £60,000, of which Jeppson received another £18,000 signing-on payment). It was the first time anyone had moved for a fee of more than 100 million lira. The English game, as ever, was unable to compete. And the authorities, of course, were unwilling to let it happen anyway.

Foreign players were not good news, even if one of them, as we will see in Chapter Four, was on his way to becoming one of the most renowned and best-loved players of the 1950s.

CHAPTER THREE

From South Africa To The Valley And Beyond

Buying in bulk

ONE MANAGER above all others decided that his post-war staffing problems could be solved by importing from abroad. The man was Jimmy Seed of Charlton and his country of choice for recruitment was South Africa. Fifty-two footballers who were born there made League debuts between 1946 and the end of the 1950s alone. A quarter of those did so at Charlton. This influx bears examination for several reasons, not least the sheer numbers involved, which caused more eyebrows to be raised in the players' country of origin than in England. The individual players' stories also represent a cross-section of migrant experiences, from those who spent less time playing football than in transit to those who went on to fame and sometimes fortune at the highest level, elsewhere.

Seed found the transitional season after the war hard. Charlton finished 19th in the First Division in 1946–47. Given the three consecutive top-four placings in the three seasons before the war, it was deemed quite unsatisfactory.

In his 1958 autobiography, Seed wrote:

> I realised something had to be done to strengthen the side. The war had left the country short of young and ambitious players. I discovered sadly that my happy hunting ground in the north-east of England, which had provided me with so many youngsters in the 30s was now barren soil.

> Where could I discover promising talent without paying ridiculous transfer prices plus personal inducements that infringed Football League law? Where, oh where! I suddenly thought of South Africa.

In 1929 Seed, who'd played more than 350 times for Tottenham and Sheffield Wednesday, had captained an English team who toured the Union. On that trip he'd made the acquaintance of George Brunton, a South African defender, and Frank Bonniwell, a scout. He enlisted their help in the search for talent.

Word soon came back that Syd O'Linn, a Cape Town inside-forward (and also a South African Test-level cricketer) was a player worth considering. He agreed to travel to London for a trial if his friend, Dudley Forbes, could go too. They arrived in England on 6 December 1947, the first pair from a cheap and a cheerful conveyor. Players often came, like animals to Noah's ark, two by two. "And just for their boat fare," Seed was fond of saying, time and time again.

Next to arrive was goalkeeper Albert Uytenboogaardt, in October 1948. His opportunities were limited as a reserve to the long-serving Sam Bartram and he played just six League games before returning home to become the South African national goalkeeper.

At the end of the 1948–49 season, Seed travelled to South Africa himself, ostensibly to look at Johnny Hubbard, an outside-left. He decided against taking him and Hubbard went on to play for Rangers in Glasgow. Seed did return, though, with another player he'd seen on the same trip, Norman Nielson, a big defender who didn't stay long at The Valley but went on to play for Derby, Bury and Hull. And Seed also scouted Bill Perry, a "go-ahead, speedy and goal-scoring winger".

In a meeting with Seed, Perry said he wanted to come to England but needed time to think about the move. Seed went back to England, leaving behind a furore about the poaching of South African players. Undeterred, he and his chairman, Stanley Gliksten, who was originally from South Africa, went back to Johannesburg in September 1949. Their trip had made the front pages in England and they were mobbed by local journalists on arrival. The South African Football Association had already made a statement saying Seed's arrival was the worst possible news for the country's footballers:

> At the moment we are powerless to
> stop South African footballers being
> taken away, but we are determined to
> fight tooth and nail against this latest
> threat.

Seed remained unbowed and contacted Perry again, who told him he was awaiting a call from Blackpool. The next time the pair met was when Charlton lost 3–2 to Blackpool – and Perry – at The Valley in December 1950. Perry had signed for the seaside club in November 1949.

Seed's September 1949 trip had not been without dividends. He took the chance to look at a 16-year-old Cape Town schoolboy, Stuart Leary, who had been recommended by Syd O'Linn. And he also picked up a 21-year-old defender, John Hewie, who signed within minutes of meeting him in a Pretoria café. That deal, however, was overheard by the restaurateur, a local football official, who reported it to the authorities. The next day it was announced that any player wanting to leave the country would need to give seven days' notice of their intent. If they failed to do so, they could face being banned from South African football in future. Hewie travelled anyway, disembarking at Southampton on 14 October 1949.

Before returning to England, Seed moved on to Cape Town to see Leary in action again. The teenager scored twice in a 9–2 win and the other seven goals were scored by another 16-year-old, a forward called Eddie Firmani. Impressed with both youngsters, Seed talked to the boys' parents and promised that if they were allowed to travel to England they could both turn professional for Charlton. They duly arrived in February 1950. It was only then that Seed 'discovered' they were both still short of their 17th birthdays and were not yet allowed to sign professional forms. He signed them both anyway, earning nothing more than a warning from the English FA for his "impulsive" behaviour.

In the following years, Charlton would also entice Ken Chamberlain, Peter Firmani (Eddie's brother), Ron Oosthuizen, Brian Tocknell, Cliff Durandt, Leslie Fourie, Henry Griesel, Kenneth Kirsten and Karel Blom. Some would make the grade, others not, but all were born and raised in South Africa. As a sign of how significantly the influx was regarded, Seed was invited by the Scottish FA to select a South African XI to face Scotland at Ibrox in the 1955–56 season. A crowd of 50,000 turned up to watch, Scotland winning 2–1.

Leary, Hewie and Firmani

Of all the South Africans at Charlton, three of them – Eddie Firmani, Stuart Leary and John Hewie – stand out for their broad achievements. Firmani set a British transfer record when he moved from Charlton to Sampdoria in Italy. He remains the only player ever to have scored 100 League goals in both England and Italy. He later returned to Charlton twice more as a player and then as the manager. Later still he would manage in the USA, at one stage for the famous New York Cosmos side that included Pele and Franz Beckenbauer.

Leary, a marvellous all-round athlete, scored more League goals for Charlton – 153 – than any player before or since. He also played cricket for Kent for 20 years, scoring 16,517 first-class runs, including 18 centuries, taking 146 wickets, and once took a record six catches in one innings in 1958. After returning to South Africa to coach cricket he committed suicide in 1988 by throwing himself from Table Mountain.

Hewie, by his own admission, was such a rough diamond when he got off the boat in 1949 that Jimmy Seed didn't want to play him in the first-team in case he damaged himself or, more likely, an opponent. And yet, after making his break-through, he was rarely out of the side for almost 15 years, making 495 first team League appearances and scoring 37 goals from defence. Capped for Scotland by dint of his ancestry, he took his first-ever trip to that country to make his international 'B' debut. He later played for Scotland in the 1958 World Cup.

"Cape Town to England was a long way to travel," said Firmani, recalling his first journey aboard the Union Castle liner.

"My mother didn't want me to go. My father convinced me I should. In the end the boat trip was like a two-week holiday for Stuart and I, entering the daily sporting competitions, training on the deck every day.

"I didn't have any preconceptions about England. I just wanted to do my best. When I got off the boat and took the train to London, George Robinson [*Seed's assistant, whose daughter Pat would become Firmani's first wife*] was waiting at Waterloo station. He had a taxi to come to fetch us. As we drove through London, we didn't know what we'd let ourselves in for. Bomb damage, ruined houses, barricades. We wondered what the hell we were coming into. It was like a desolate area. In South Africa we'd had green grass and then in England we had slush and rain, heavy pitches.

"But Charlton was the right club, absolutely. Very close. It was a family club, a family team, no bickering, no fighting, no animosity, even in training. Jimmy Trotter did the training but Jimmy Seed was the boss, did the paperwork and signings and every Friday pinned the team up on the board."

It was on 3 November 1951, a Saturday, that an 18-year-old Firmani first saw his name there, in an unfamiliar wing-half-back role as a replacement for an injured colleague. In a 3–3 draw with Derby, Firmani made an error that gave the visitors a share of the points. He returned to the reserves not with recriminations but encouragement to work on his game.

The following season started with Firmani being played as a defender rather than in his preferred attacking role. After requesting a chance to play at inside-left, he scored twice for the reserves against Coventry, earning a first-team call-up at Manchester City on 15 November 1952. Charlton lost 5–1.

"I thought that was the end," said Firmani. But Seed kept faith with his team. The following week Firmani scored a hat-trick in a 5–1 win over Stoke. "That was the beginning," he said.

From then on Firmani stayed at inside-left, with Leary at centre-forward.

During his first spell with Charlton, Firmani played 100 League games and scored 50 League goals, a strike rate that attracted admirers from Italy. It was in July 1955 that Seed called Firmani into his office and told him that Sampdoria wanted to sign him. A meeting was arranged at Claridges hotel with officials from the Italian club. At that lunch Firmani had his first-ever glass of wine but it was the numbers that really made his head buzz.

The lure of the lira

Sampdoria paid Charlton a £35,000 transfer fee, then a record amount for an English club. Firmani got a £5,000 signing-on fee and a weekly wage of £18, double what he was earning in London. The bonuses were phenomenal. In England they were £2 for a win and £1 for a draw. At Sampdoria it was £50 for an away win, £25 for a home win or away draw and £12 10s for a home draw. There was also assistance with a flat and a car and the promise of more bonuses if he received an international call-up. He did, for Italy, the land of his grandfather's birth. Firmani went on to play in Milan for Internazionale, who paid £88,000 for him, and for Genoa before being sold back to Charlton, in October 1963, aged 30, for £10,000.

Firmani later played for Southend before a final playing spell at Charlton from March 1967. This ended when he was offered the manager's job, which he kept until being sacked in 1970. Some time away from the game, selling insurance, was followed by a managerial career in the USA and elsewhere. He took the Tampa Bay Rowdies to the US championship in his first season. In 1977 he moved to the New York Cosmos, where his players included Pele, Beckenbauer and Carlos Alberto.

"Carlos Alberto told us he was 36. He might have been 46, who cared?" said Firmani. "He was the greatest defender I have ever seen in my life, no doubt. And the others were class guys. First class."

Firmani had a second spell as manager of the Cosmos in the mid-1980s, and was the coach at New York MetroStars in the mid-1990s. He also spent six years in the Middle East. Most dramatically, in 1990, he returned home to Kuwait just as Saddam Hussein's Iraqi army was invading. Using his football contacts, he was helped to Baghdad by a former Iraqi international and secured a visa to flee to safety. These days he lives in Florida, working for Field Turf Inc, a company that sells artificial pitches to sports stadiums around the world and to Premier League academies in England.

Such a rich tapestry of experience, as a player and manager, has given Firmani a rare perspective. He recalls the differences between English and Italian football in the 1950s and how those differences remain apparent into the 21st century.

"In England the training was hard, very hard, the aim being to instill toughness. If someone hit you, you needed to get up and get on with it. Develop resistance. Increase your stamina. In Italy there were more exercises, more stretching and drills. We actually trained with the ball as you would in a match. And Italy was where I learned about tactics.

"English soccer was a different game. It was about being strong and powerful and playing at the very highest speed, getting long balls to the forwards. In Italy they passed the ball on the floor. It was better to watch along the floor too. In Italy we played possession football going forward. We played to feet, not to zones unless someone was making a specific run into that area. In England they played fast, too fast. They still do. When you consider the time that's elapsed, it hasn't changed a hell of a lot."

If one player embodied the application of strength and power in the 1950s it was Firmani's team-mate John Hewie. He wasn't a bulky player but he was tall, rangy and resolute. Watching him in action would give the impression he was a hard man, a persona apparently affirmed by his memory of leaving South Africa.

"The Northern Transvaal association suspended me [*for leaving without notice*], not that I gave a damn because I had a contract in England. Jimmy Seed organised the ticket for the boat. I got an overnight train to Cape Town to catch it. That was it."

But away from a football pitch, as soon as he was outside the boundary of play, he was a different, quieter person.

"I was an introvert when I arrived in England. So shy that for the whole two weeks on the boat, the Athlone Castle, I did not speak a single word to anyone at all until the day before we docked. I went for meals alone, walked around deck by myself. And I slept. The day before we docked I saw someone who seemed in a similar position and went up and said hello to him. He was Italian. He didn't speak a word of English."

As with Firmani, the taxi ride across London came as something of a shock.

"The only thing I'd heard about London was that there were pickpockets and prostitutes all over. I was told 'Keep your hands in your pockets'."

He soon settled in, lodging with a Mr Wright, a former steam-train driver, and his wife. He caught the bus from Bexleyheath to training and back. He hung out with the other South Africans, playing snooker or going to the cinema in his free time. And he tried to tame his game, so he'd have a chance of playing in the League.

"I was in the third team for one and a half seasons, I didn't even get a reserve game. I was too wild. Anything that moved, I kicked it. A person, a ball, whatever. That'd been the way I'd played in South Africa. I was wild, rushing about. Raw and crude. Really quite physical. And then at Charlton I was told 'If you keep flying into tackles like that you'll get hurt'. I was still quite shy off the pitch and I gradually calmed down when I was on it. That got me into the reserves."

In August 1951, Hewie got his chance in the first team.

"Jock Campbell, our full-back, was injured. I got in. And I stayed in, for 15 years, never out of the team unless I was injured."

His debut came away from home against Portsmouth. He was played as a right-back and given the job of marking Pompey's Belgian winger, Marcel Gaillard. "He was a decent player," Hewie said. Portsmouth won 1–0 and Hewie didn't like the taste of defeat.

Over the next decade and a half, he gained a formidable reputation, as Sir Bobby Robson testifies.

"He was at Charlton the same time I was at Fulham," said Robson, who includes Hewie in his all-time League 'foreign XI', compiled especially for this book. "He was a big guy, very tall. A very good defender. What amazed us at the time was how he'd come from South Africa, not really a footballing nation, and how they should supply somebody like him. Good defender, long legged. I wouldn't quite say like Jackie Charlton but he was tall and slender like Jackie Charlton. Good in the air, and a really combative player. He took no prisoners, he didn't. He rattled you. Very combative. Good solid defender. Didn't like playing against him. Didn't like him. I liked him because I didn't like him. You went past and he kicked you."

Such a style, in the physical combat of the 1950s, gained Hewie admirers, including the England manager, Walter Winterbottom.

"England were grooming me, Winterbottom was interested and I played three games for an FA team. But then our club physician, Dr Montgomery, noticed my father had been born in Scotland. He told the Scots and I was drafted in for a 'B' game in Edinburgh."

His first full cap came in a 1–1 draw against England in 1956. He played for Scotland 19 times, becoming Charlton's most-capped player. His record was only overtaken when John Robinson, born in Zimbabwe, gained his 20th cap for Wales, in summer 2000.

Hewie's time with Scotland saw him play in the 1958 World Cup in Sweden, a tournament where Bobby Robson played for England and where Brazil were the eventual winners with a team including Garrincha, Didi, Vava and Zagallo. The undisputed star was a 17-year-old, Pele, who scored two goals in the final after a hat-trick in the semi-final against France. The French team included the Moroccan-born forward, Juste Fontaine, who scored 13 goals in the tournament, still a World Cup record. One of Fontaine's goals came in a 2–1 win against Scotland, precisely 22 minutes after Hewie had smacked a penalty against the post and missed an opportunity to give his side a sniff of victory.

"I only took it because our captain, Tommy Younger, and Tommy Docherty, who was about to leave Preston for Arsenal, neither of whom played that day, said 'Hewie takes them for Charlton, he can do it'."

The most incredible scoreline in the League

He couldn't "do it" on that occasion but there were plenty of times he did. There were umpteen other matches where he kept attackers at bay, and not just as an outfield player. Due to a goalkeeping crisis in 1961–62, he played four consecutive First Division matches between the posts. Charlton won two and drew two. Hewie also played in one historic game where Charlton showed such dogged determination in adversity that the result has entered English football folklore. The scoreline alone, 7–6 to Charlton against Huddersfield in December 1957, remains one of the most incredible in League history. Indeed, no team before or since has scored six goals away from home in the League and lost. The outcome is more fantastic still when you know that Charlton were losing 5–1 at half-time, having been reduced to 10 men by injury.

Derek Ufton, a centre-half, was the player who went off after only 15 minutes. With no substitutes in those days and the defence weakened, it was a one-sided contest until the interval. The second half was one-sided too, in the other direction. And as forward Johnny Summers started clawing back the deficit – he scored five times, all with his right foot, his "wrong 'un" – so every Charlton fan in The Valley and every one of their players believed they would achieve the impossible.

"It was the most remarkable game of my life," said Hewie.

The whole team, led by Summers, were asked afterwards to climb to the directors' box and take their applause.

As Summers explained to newspapermen who found him the next day celebrating with his family and team-mates in The Arrow, his local pub:

"I just hit the ball and the goals went in… I'm a great one for singing a song and after I'd said thanks to the fans they asked me for a tune. But I was so choked that I couldn't even give them my favourite, 'I'm Going to Sit Right Down and Write Myself a Letter'."

The match was obviously the talk of the weekend although an Arsenal player, Danny Le Roux, was also gaining a few headlines for his performance in a 3–0 win over Sunderland.

> Dan Le Roux, a strong, fast right-winger from South Africa is Highbury's new pin-up boy

said one report.

> He made two of Arsenal's three goals even though he didn't get the service he deserved. Le Roux goes straight, cutting out all unnecessary frills and follies. He's a favourite with Arsenal fans.

Le Roux would play only five League games for the Gunners. Genuine longevity was the preserve of men of granite, like Hewie. Among all the overseas-born players in the history of the League, no outfield player has yet made more League starts for one club than Hewie's record of 495 for Charlton. Ces Podd, a St Kitts-born defender, played 502 League games for Bradford from the early 1970s onwards but started in a mere 494 of them.

Only two overseas-born goalkeepers have made more starts for one club than Hewie. They were Norwich City's Kevin Keelan (born in India to a British father and Indian-Portuguese mother), who started 571 League matches for the Canaries, and Germany's Bert Trautmann, who started 508 League games for Manchester City.

Hewie's stay at The Valley, despite the rough 'n' tumble start, was happy.

"Moving to England meant I was playing in front of 30,000 or 40,000 people. When I played at Hampden that could be 120,000. It brought me out of my shell. I lost the shyness. I just wanted to be a Charlton player and gave my best to be one."

The Charlton South Africans faced no problems with discrimination although Hewie recalled one match at Bury when he was abused.

"Someone shouted 'Get back to South Africa you black bastard.' I thought it was a strange thing for someone to be shouting. It was even stranger because I'm not black."

Such insults would later be common for black South Africans. But all Seed's recruits from there were white. It wasn't until October 1956 that Steve Mokone became the first black South African footballer to be allowed to play outside his country (see Chapter Five). Seed had parted company with Charlton the month before.

Hewie finished playing for Charlton after the 1965–66 season. He returned to South Africa to coach a former club, Arcadia Shepherds, but returned to England in 1968 and became the player-manager of non-league Bexley United. He then lived in South Africa between 1969 and 1994 working variously in football, and as a car salesman and a garage owner. He retired in 1994 to Lincolnshire.

While Firmani and Hewie both played international football, and the likes of Brian Tocknell gave Charlton great service – almost 200 League games – many Charlton supporters of the 1950s regard Stuart Leary as the most naturally gifted footballer of them all.

The statistics tell their own story. He played 376 League games for Charlton and scored 153 goals. He stayed with the club from 1950 until 1962 even though, aged 24 in 1957, Charlton were relegated and Leary's prowess as one of the country's finest centre-forwards meant he could have spent his prime at a higher level. In the summers he played first-class cricket for Kent. He amassed his thousands of runs with a light but stealthy touch. He took most of his wickets with leg breaks and was also a brilliant fielder.

But that was just part of it. On a football pitch he appeared to have more time and space than anyone, his mind ahead of the game so he'd already have stolen the advantage when his feet caught up. Not that he was slow. He delighted in running to the corner flag as time ran down, seemingly time-wasting, only to turn and flick the ball across to a team-mate. His touch was teasing, patient, light. His passing was divine, and he was great in front of goal.

In January 1954 he was picked for the England Under-23 team to face their Italian counterparts in Bologna. What should have been, by widespread consensus, the start of a long international career to the highest level for his adopted country turned out to be his last appearance in an England shirt.

The FA introduced a ruling that stated that a player's father had to be born in England for the player to represent England. Leary's international career was over. A barrage of criticism, led by the Press, had no effect. Why, they wondered, could a man who had willingly done national service, as Leary had in the RAF, be asked to be ready to fight for England but not be allowed to play football for her? It was to no avail. But then with the FA's track record it was never going to be.

Leary stayed with Charlton until 1962, when he fell out with his manager, Frank 'Tiger' Hill. After a draining season at The Valley and a summer playing cricket for Kent, he went home on holiday to South Africa against Charlton's wishes. He missed pre-season training. There was a furious row and by December that year he'd moved across London to Queen's Park Rangers, where he played until 1965–66.

He continued to play cricket for Kent until 1971, with a benefit year there in 1967. He received proceeds of £9,100, then a Kent record. Sir Alf Ramsey, who had led England to World

Cup success in 1966, contributed to one of the programmes issued in connection with Leary's benefit year. He wrote:

> Leary will be remembered as one of
> the stylish forwards of his day… As a
> player, he graced the game with a
> combination of skill, intelligence and
> hard work. His behaviour on the field
> speaks for itself and is an example to
> all who play football; in 16 years he
> was never suspended or sent off. He
> contributed a great deal to our game.

Leary returned to South Africa to do some coaching work. In August 1988 it was reported that he had been missing from his home and that his car had been left near the base station of the cable-car system that ascended Table Mountain. Poor weather and high winds had been hampering the search for him. His body was eventually found five days after he disappeared. At the summit, from which he jumped, there is a plaque in dedication.

"In my opinion, Leary was the best player, of any nationality, to have worn a Charlton shirt, certainly since the war," said Colin Cameron, a lifelong fan and also the club's official historian.

Other supporters have their own abiding memories of the South Africans. A request by Cameron for submissions prompted a deluge of correspondence from Croydon to North America to Australia. Leary is recalled time and time again.

"I will always remember when I heard of his death," said Phil Haynes, a lifelong supporter. "I'd turned on the radio at 3 o'clock one Saturday when Charlton were playing Liverpool, and the commentator announced: 'Before the kick-off there will be a minute's silence for the former Charlton centre-forward…'. I assumed he was going to say someone like Sailor Brown or Charlie Vaughan. But…"

Another fan, Ian Burden, who left Bexleyheath for Sydney in 1967, wrote:

> I lived for Saturday afternoons, to
> stand on the vast terrace at about the
> halfway line and watch Stuart Leary
> lead the team out to 'Red Red Robin'.

There was a touch of class about him, his appearance, his demeanour. I remember being in the queue at Bexleyheath station one Monday morning waiting for my train ticket. Stuart was in front of me in the line. He was suntanned and smart. Even in a ticket queue he looked too good for the rest of us.

There were also recollections of Eddie Firmani's sportsmanship, exemplified by a quote from John Charles, the peerless Welsh forward who will forever be loved in Italy – where he played at the same time as Firmani, as the 'gentle giant'. After a match in 1963, in which Charlton won 5–2 against Cardiff, for whom Charles was then playing, Firmani and he left the pitch to a huge ovation. Charles said afterwards of Firmani: "He is always there, always fair." A tribute indeed.

And then there were the minutiae, the day-to-day incidents that still have resonance some five decades later. Norman Renouf, born in London but now a trans-Atlantic fan who travels as often as he can from Virginia in the US, remembers Brian Tocknell persuading Jimmy Seed to allow fans on the team bus back from away games. Sheila Drake, another ex-pat, now resident in Canada, remembers Hewie's stand-in appearance in goal.

"We won the game and I remember clearly the headline in the *Sunday Express* the following day: 'Hewie the Stop Gap Hero.'

She also recalled a time when Firmani, then Charlton's manager, gave her and a group of friends tickets for an evening away game at Preston and how they had to wangle some time off work to sneak away to catch an afternoon train.

The same kind of memories, of course, are shared by fans of all clubs about players of all nationalities. But there is no doubt that, as a group, those South African players of the 1950s, and others in later chapters, left their mark.

The Matthews Final

For Bill Perry, that mark was to score the winning goal in what is probably the most famous FA Cup final ever, the so-called 'Matthews Final' of 1953. The world's most famous footballer,

Stanley Matthews, finally won the medal that had eluded him as Blackpool beat Bolton 4–3. Bolton had been 3–1 ahead after 55 minutes before Stan Mortensen made it 3–2. Mortensen's equaliser came, like much else that afternoon, through Matthews's persistence and passing. It arrived in the last minute of normal time. At the death, after a pass from Matthews, Perry converted the decider from 10 yards.

Perry played 394 League games for Blackpool, winning three England caps. He was not prevented from doing so by the FA's 'parent' rule because his father had been a British soldier, posted to South Africa in the Great War. Perry also played briefly with Southport, had a short spell in Australia and then came back to England to open a shop selling kitchen equipment. He retired to Blackpool.

Golden glory, journeymen and cricketers

The most successful South African player of the 1950s, in terms of medal-winning feats, was Eddie Stuart, a defender who travelled from Johannesburg to sign professional terms with Wolverhampton Wanderers in January 1951. He would later play a part in three title-winning campaigns, a triumphant FA Cup run and one of the most famous European club matches of the decade.

His Wolves career took a while to get started. He didn't make his League debut until April 1952, when he was used as a forward against West Bromwich Albion. He scored that day, his only goal in 11 years at the club. That summer, while back home visiting his family, he contracted a serious, mystery virus. He returned to England only to be hospitalised, his future in doubt. It wasn't until late 1952 that he was playing regularly again, and then only in the reserves at full-back.

When his chance arose to return to the first team, he did so in that position, playing the last 12 games of the 1953–54 season, the year Wolves won their first League title. By that point Stuart had developed a reputation as a tough, no-nonsense operator, not unlike John Hewie. Stuart's other strength was his passing.

He stayed in the first team for the best part of eight years, a fixture in the side that finished second in the League in 1955, third in 1956 and sixth in 1957. During the championship-winning season of 1957–58 he missed only two games. During the following season, when the title was retained, he missed only four. He would later play four times in the FA Cup run that led to Wolves winning the trophy in 1960, but did not play in the final.

Alongside all their domestic success of the 1950s, Wolves won admiration for their performances against European opposition, not least during their mid-50s floodlit friendlies at Molineux. The popularity of these matches, against some of the Continent's leading sides, would help lead to the establishment of the European Cup.

Wolves' most significant win, for English football as well as the club's supporters, came in December 1954 with the visit of Honved of Hungary, who were billed at the time as the best club side in the world. Their players included six internationals, Ferenc Puskas and Sandor Kocsis among them. That pair had both been part of the 'Magical Magyars' side who had beaten England 6–3 at Wembley a year before and then 7–1 in Budapest six months later.

Although Wolves went 2–0 down within 14 minutes, they staged an epic comeback to win 3–2 in front of an ecstatic crowd of almost 55,000. The result made headlines around Europe and Stuart had played his part. Old photographs show him leaving the pitch afterwards, shaking hands with Puskas.

Stuart left Wolves in 1962, moving to Stoke, who he captained to the Second Division title in the spring of 1963. He later played for Tranmere and then Stockport, where he was part of the team who won the Fourth Division in 1967. He then became the player-manager at non-League Worcester City before retiring from the game to run a successful hairdressing business in the West Midlands.

Another long-serving player of the era was the prolific forward Alf Ackerman, who scored between 21 and 62 goals during each of six separate stints at five different League clubs – Hull (twice), Norwich, Derby, Carlisle and Millwall – between 1950 and 1961. At the other end of the appearance scale were players like Ron Tulloch, who spent 34 days in total travelling between South Africa and Hull for less than five hours of first-team football.

And there were others, like Denis Foreman, who'd stood on a 10-gallon drum in Cape Town to get a peep of a touring

Wolves side in the late 1940s and vowed to play in England one day. He achieved it and stayed for good. He recalled:

"My mother had said I couldn't go on the boat to England because I couldn't swim and I walked in my sleep. She thought it was a fatal combination. But Paddy O'Connor, one of the Christian Brothers at my school who taught football, told her not to worry. He had a few words at the quayside with some people who were sailing on the same boat. I went down to dinner on the first evening and found myself sharing a table with nine priests, returning from mission stations in the Belgian Congo."

After 14 days under their watchful eyes, Foreman arrived in England on 15 February 1952, en route to Brighton & Hove Albion. News of his arrival made a paragraph in the papers, although it was somewhat overshadowed by the blanket coverage of King George VI's funeral. As Foreman came down the gangplank, carrying four cricket bats – he would play cricket for Sussex for 16 years – his new manager, Billy Lane, chirped up: "I hope you realise we're a football club."

Foreman, a winger, played more than 200 times for Brighton before a knee injury curtailed his career. After hanging up his boots, he became a cricket coach and sports teacher. He retired, aged 60, in 1993 and now spends his days coaching football and cricket in Brighton. His most memorable Brighton moments include playing for Jimmy Seed's South African XI against Scotland, and also a trip to Anfield in September 1958, a few months after Brighton had won the Third Division (South) title. They travelled with high hopes of an encouraging result at their new higher level. Liverpool won 5–0.

They were bittersweet times for many players, as summed up by Eddie Firmani. He described the day in February 1955 when he scored five goals for Charlton in a 6–1 win against Aston Villa. No other player had or has ever scored five League goals in a top division game for the club.

"I was very proud that I went to England and did the things people expected me to do," he said. "I made the grade and that's the best you can do."

He talked about that game at length, almost 48 years later. He recalled that it was played almost five years to the day since he'd arrived as a 16-year-old from South Africa. His parents had been at The Valley to see it happen, to watch their son achieve this thing they'd had the faith in him to achieve.

"It was one of the highlights of my life to see them in the stands on their only trip to see me," he said. He paused. He paused for a long time. And then he said, quietly: "I should've gone home more often."

CHAPTER FOUR

Two POWs And One World Cup Qualifier

Whatever success I have enjoyed in English football could not have been achieved without the co-operation, tolerance and sympathetic encouragement of the man who represents the backbone of your great national game – the chap on the popular side with his cloth cap and muffler, and penetrating voice. To him and his lady I owe more than I can hope to repay... Thank you to supporters all over the country for their many kindnesses to a German stranger in what was once an alien land.

Bert Trautmann, Footballer of the Year, 1956

AT NEWCASTLE United's Christmas party in 1998, some 53 years after the end of the Second World War, the German midfielder Dietmar Hamann unwrapped a gift from his colleagues – a copy of *Mein Kampf*.

Other presents handed out that day also reflected the humour of the dressing room. The Italian defender Alessandro Pistone was handed a sheep's heart, fresh from the butcher's and still dripping with blood. He was told:

"Here's a heart because you haven't got one."

How he laughed, all the way to arbitration.

Alan Shearer, the local hero who was once the most expensive footballer in the world, was given a Mary Poppins doll to reflect his 'goody two shoes' image. Stuart Pearce, another England international veteran, then aged 36, was given a Zimmer frame. Duncan Ferguson, a former Scotland international whose relationship with his country's Football Association disintegrated when he served time in prison for an on-field assault, was given a convict's outfit.

Dietmar Hamann's defining characteristic, the elementary peg on which his gift was hung, was his nationality. Two World Wars, one World Cup. Have a book by Hitler. What a thoroughly modern Premiership.

It was little surprise that Hamann left Newcastle after less than a year. While he was there he played in an FA Cup final, only the second German to do so. But the period was otherwise marked down to unpleasant experience. At his next club, Liverpool, he would fare much better, being part of a team who won a treble of domestic and European trophies in 2001. Before that, he had secured another significant victory, scoring the only goal for Germany against England at Wembley in a World Cup qualifier in October 2000. It was the old stadium's last ever international fixture.

That match signalled the end of two eras, for Wembley and for Kevin Keegan, who promptly resigned as the England manager. It was the latest dramatic episode in a history of Anglo-German football relations chock full of them. Keegan himself is the only English footballer to have won the European Footballer of the Year award twice. He did so while playing in Germany for SV Hamburg in the 1970s. The English national team's greatest success – indeed England's only success in a major event – came at Wembley in 1966, against West Germany. In 1970, in the quarter-final of the next World Cup, England lost, against West Germany. England also lost to West Germany, on penalties, in the semi-final of the 1990 World Cup in Italy. And again on penalties against Germany, in the semi-final of Euro 96, at Wembley. Then there was the acrimonious contest to stage the 2006 World Cup. England lost out to Germany.

Even England's most celebrated international performance of recent years, the 5–1 win in Munich in September 2001, was undeniably sweeter to the average supporter because it was the Germans who were drubbed.

Antipathy within the Anglo-German relationship has been mirrored in football since the first decades of the 20th Century. The experiences of Max Seeburg, the Football League's first German-born player (see Chapter One) were testament to that. As were some of the struggles encountered by the founding nations of FIFA.

In some cases history has served only to instil discord into events where there was none originally. To this day, the famous antique photographs of the German Graf Zeppelin flying over Wembley are routinely captioned to reflect menace. The craft is invariably described as 'looming', 'hovering', 'ominous', as if to hint at sinister encroachment on the heart of English football, indeed England. Such presentation is distortion. Yes, the Zeppelin was used in bombing raids in the Great War. Undoubtedly it had been a token of German aggression. But the photographs were taken in 1930 on the day of the FA Cup final. By then, the Zeppelin was a commercial aircraft on a legitimate peacetime pleasure flight. It was not unfamiliar. The pilot had descended to 2,000ft to give his passengers a better view as Arsenal beat Huddersfield Town 2–0.

But to acknowledge that would be to diminish the hostility still inherent in English society everywhere from tabloid caricature to jibes about Germans and their sun-loungers. The same hostility perpetuates the casual use of phrases such as 'little Hitler' and 'acting like a Nazi'. Even the language of stereotype has been crafted from the rhetoric of battle. In England, German efficiency is still invariably described as 'ruthless', implementation 'clinical', resistance 'stubborn'. Almost 60 years after the end of the Second World War, these terms are applied across all walks of life, from finance and business to politics and sport.

Living with the enemy

Two Germans arrived in England as prisoners of that war, yet went on to have long careers in English professional football – Bert Trautmann and Alec Eisentrager.

On his arrival in England, Trautmann was officially classified as a Nazi. More than any other footballer in England before him, he had to rally against being defined by what he represented as opposed to who he actually was. He toiled in English fields and in English bomb-disposal units, succeeded in settling peacefully into his adopted community and proved his worth in local football. Yet, when he moved into professional football with Manchester City, he had to prove himself all over again.

He did prove himself, for 15 years, not only as a great goalkeeper but as an innovator in a team which took risks in search of progress. He was part of the team who won the FA Cup in 1956, playing for the last 15 minutes with a broken neck. Six weeks before he'd been voted Footballer of the Year, the first foreign player to win the award. He became a hero far beyond the boundaries of Maine Road, offering the ultimate proof that nationality need never be a bar to becoming a fans' favourite, whatever the prevailing political and social conditions.

But he also paid a price for his nationality, enduring hostility, suspicion and cynicism throughout a career that was also littered with personal traumas and tragedy. Had he been an Englishman, he would arguably have been one of the most celebrated figures in British sporting history. As it was, he set a benchmark for foreign footballers in England. When you do well you're a good player and no-one cares where you're from. When you don't, or when you step out of line, you're a lousy foreigner.

Eisentrager's story is less well-known outside the West Country, where he enjoyed immense popularity, playing hundreds of times for Bristol City. Trautmann arrived in England as a hardened, 21-year-old 'Nazi' veteran; Eisentrager, who arrived first, was a 17-year-old novice soldier when captured. His classification, as an 'ordinary' combatant, was less severe. He had his ups and downs – some because he pined for home, some because he was German – but his ascension to League football and his innovation when he got there were, when set against Trautmann's exploits, barely noticed.

Most of the reasons were self-evident. Trautmann was tall, blond, strapping, tough, single-minded and vociferous, the epitome of the stereotypical German soldier. He also moved to a big club and made a big impression on the biggest stages. Eisentrager, on the other hand, was 5ft 6in, slight, cheeky, brown-haired, boyish. He played in the Third Division (South).

Promotion to the Second Division was a pinnacle for him. His personal life was not sensational. But ultimately, it was their formative years and wartime lives that led to Trautmann and Eisentrager's different classifications, and their experiences in England.

Battling to Bristol

Eisentrager was barely out of his childhood when he left the family home to fight. The son of a Polish mother, Appolonia, and a German father, Oscar Johannes, the young Alois – a name later anglicised to Alec – had only ever wanted to play football. He'd been a junior player for SV Hamburg, the biggest club in his home town, and but for the war, he would likely have stayed there into adulthood.

But at 16 it became obvious he would be drafted into the services.

"My mother said it would be better to enrol voluntarily in the air force than wait to be conscripted to the infantry," he recalled. "She said if I was conscripted they'd probably send me to the Russian front. But if I joined the air force then they'd have to teach me to fly, and by the time they'd done that the war would be over."

No such luck. In July 1944, the week before his 17th birthday, he was called up and sent on a three-month infantry pioneer course. Eisentrager wasn't cut out for soldiering. Almost immediately he was in trouble, for licking a gherkin container. He spent three days in the cells. He celebrated his release with a cigarette. He smoked it in a barn full of hay; another six days in the slammer. Later, in a billet full of soldiers, a potential target for bombing, he neglected to extinguish his lamp overnight. Another two days in detention. Not that any of these slip-ups meant he would avoid the hostilities. He was dispatched to defend the front line in Belgium in October 1944. Less than two weeks later his war was over – he was captured near Breda in The Netherlands.

"All the best troops had been sent back to Germany to defend the Rhine. The rest of us had been told to defend the line with our last bullet. But we had a smart Lance Corporal who said, 'I'm responsible for you, I want to make sure you come home with your lives. When the British come I'll put out the white flag.' And he did.

"There were 10 of us. The British soldiers were very good with us on the front. The further back we got, the more they pinched everything we had – cigarettes, photographs. It didn't seem fair, even the pictures of my parents were destroyed."

After a short stay in a POW camp in Belgium and four months in a holding camp in Ostend – 4,000 prisoners held in open kilns in a derelict brick factory – he was taken to Tilbury Docks in the hold of a ship. Naturally, the war was dominating all aspects of life in England. Almost every story, every day, in every newspaper carried news of the war, from reports about Field-Marshall Montgomery's latest initiative to the newest Nazi advances to the consequences of bombing raids. The consequences were always terrible in England and successful in Germany.

A photo-story on the front page of *The Daily Mirror* in January 1945 summed up the English attitude towards Germans. The caption read:

> This German soldier was wounded
> by American shelling in Belgium. He
> fell into the snow and the bitter cold
> stiffened his upraised arm as he died.

It was accompanied by a picture of a dead German soldier, as described, with the headline: 'Heil Hitler!'

But Eisentrager's first impressions were not of hostility.

"We were amazed at the quality of the trains," he said. "We weren't used to it, second-class seats with upholstery. We thought 'Blimey, this is smart'. The other thing we couldn't understand was women smoking on the streets – amazing! In Germany some women smoked but not on the streets. But the most surprising thing when we got to the next holding camp, at Kempton Park, were the hot showers. The first one I had was like someone giving me £1,000."

After initial interrogation, he was moved to Nottingham.

"That was the first time we played any football, 6,000 of us in a championship."

Further moves, to a second camp in Nottingham, then to one in Ashford, Kent, also featured football as the main activity. On official release in 1948, he took up the offer of civil agricultural work in Herne Bay, where he played a few times for the local football side. And then in summer 1948 he was transferred to Chippenham in Wiltshire where he was assigned to hay-making:

"I cut all the wrong things so they put me in the kitchens. I wasn't any good there either. I never wanted to do anything except play football."

The chance emerged through the efforts of a fellow former prisoner, Bert Meyer. (In old photographs Meyer bears a striking resemblance to a young Sven Goran Eriksson.) He designated himself as Eisentrager's agent and wrote on his behalf to the most prominent local team, Trowbridge Town. Word got out and the local newspapers began carrying reports that Ted Long, the Trowbridge manager, wanted to sign a German. The Wiltshire FA intervened to say Long was not allowed to sign an alien. Long appealed to the Football Association in London, who replied that Eisentrager could join them as long as he was only an amateur.

A deal was struck. Officially, Eisentrager was an agricultural worker and paid £4 10s per week for his labours, playing football in his spare time.

"But Trowbridge actually fixed it that I didn't have to work on the land. I trained full-time."

The investment paid dividends, with Eisentrager, a forward, scoring 38 goals in the 1948–49 season. His play quickly attracted attention, and not just in England. A job offer arrived from 1860 Munich, one of Germany's biggest clubs, as early as October 1948. News of Eisentrager's progress had been reported in newspapers and magazines back home. Although Munich officials could not offer much of a salary, a letter sent to Eisentrager said he could be otherwise compensated.

> I'm thinking in terms of a coat, a suit,
> shirts, etc and in addition a one-off
> sum direct to you of DM 1000 [*about
> £80*]

wrote Robert Engels, a senior club official. Engels also offered to help Eisentrager find a house and a job in his chosen profession.

> I think I can promise you'll do well
> here. The players of the first team are
> all good, decent people. One is a

> builder, another a shopkeeper and others are office workers... I hope you'll soon be coming back to your native land.

But Eisentrager had settled well at Trowbridge and was happy in his digs and with the surrogate parental attentions of his landlady, Mrs Sartin, and her husband. They'd lost their own son in the war when he crashed his plane. It seems plausible that they responded so warmly to Eisentrager because of that fact, not in spite of it.

"They treated me like their own son," he said.

Life at the football club was also good. The management and directors were eager to keep their prolific young talent happy, even paying for his parents to make a trip from Hamburg to visit him. The supporters had also showed, from day one, that they backed him. Ted Long initially put Eisentrager in the reserves because he was afraid of a negative reaction to fielding a German in the first team. A deluge of letters to the club and the local press rapidly brought his promotion.

With Eisentrager in such good form, it was inevitable a League club would come in for him. That club was Bristol City...

"A scout came along and said did I want to join them. He said they'd see me right. I had no formal links to Trowbridge in terms of contract so I went. After the way I'd been treated so well I did feel guilty, like I'd done the dirty on them. But City sent a team down for a friendly and Trowbridge got a crowd of 6,000 for that."

So it was, in June 1949, that Alec Eisentrager, on an amateur contract with Bristol City, became the first German national, born and raised in Germany, to join a League club. On the day he signed, he said:

"I'm only 21 years old and my biggest wish is to play in the highest English league. I'm not interested in the money."

He played as an amateur until 1950, by which time he'd been a civilian resident for two years and could sign professional terms. He stayed with the club for a further eight years, playing 229 League games and bringing something new to the supporters in the process.

The bicycle kick

At first glance many fans had fears that such a diminutive figure would not last long in the tough environs of the League. But what Eisentrager lacked in stature he made up for in application. He could control the ball in a manner rarely seen at that level, picking it smoothly from the air with his foot and stopping it dead. He had flicks and tricks and could dribble. He was a schemer and liked to shoot from a distance. And his *pièce de resistance*, a version of the bicycle kick, was something most observers had never seen.

"It was like a scissor kick," he said. "I remember we had instruction films from the FA telling us not to use it because it was dangerous and not very effective. The FA policy was to wait and hit the ball on the volley. But I always felt you were quicker to the ball with the scissor. And it was pretty accurate. I scored goals with it. I even passed with it."

During Eisentrager's time there, Bristol City's greatest success was winning promotion to the Second Division in 1955, although he played only 11 games that season. His personal high point had come early, in September 1949, when he scored four in a 6–0 win against Newport County.

Away from the pitch he was as popular as any other player. Photographs of his wedding to a local girl, Olwyn, show large crowds of fans, draped in City colours and scarves and showering the couple with confetti. His nationality had been no problem for his wife's family despite four of her brothers being ex-servicemen and one of them having been a former POW under the Japanese.

"I think there was more compassion in people then, full stop," Eisentrager said. "People had had a hard time in the war and they knew that others had had a hard time too, wherever they came from."

Bert Trautmann, he added, probably had things tougher because he'd been a paratrooper.

Eisentrager eventually left Bristol to play non-league football in Wales before retirement from the game in 1960s. He later worked as a salesman and in printing and then spent 19 years as a machinist with a Bristol engineering firm. He retired in 1988 and still lives in the area, where his sons have been heavily involved in West Country football.

"I had ups and downs," Eisentrager said of his career, after sporadically detailing prejudice. He mentioned opposition fans at Trowbridge who had persisted in saying he "fiddled with the ball" because of who he was. He mentioned times at City when an opponent would run past and say "I'll get you, you little Hitler". He recalled how he got on well with his team-mates despite their regular jokes about him paying for the bomb damage to their city. And he talked about the time when he walked into a pub in London and someone started having a go at him because he was German.

"But I can honestly say I had no problems because of my nationality," he said.

Trautmann did, both en route to the League and when he arrived.

The making of a legend

Trautmann was born in Bremen in 1923, the son of Carl, who worked in a chemical plant, and Frieda, a housewife. He excelled at sport, especially Volkerball, a throwing game where the basic aim was to hit a member of the opposing team with a ball. His agility allowed him to dodge incoming shots – a key element in the game – while his power and accuracy gave him a useful throw. He also played football, either as a forward or a defender, both positions where his height and strength were advantageous.

When he was nine he joined Tura, a publicly-funded club where young people were encouraged to play a range of sports. The same year he joined the Jungvolk, a boys' organisation where hiking, organised games and lectures on a variety of subjects prepared him for full entry to the Hitler Youth Movement at 14. It was a natural progression for Trautmann and his friends to make, unaware of the political significance of their actions.

After leaving school, Trautmann began a two-year apprenticeship as a motor mechanic which ended in early 1941. By then he was 17 and Adolf Hitler had invaded Poland and started the Second World War. Many of Trautmann's friends had already joined the forces and in March 1941 he followed suit. He volunteered for the Luftwaffe as a wireless operator and was posted to Schwerin-in-Mecklenburg near the Baltic Sea. The following month he was reassigned to a paratrooper unit in

Berlin and four weeks later was sent to Zamos in Poland. Germany then declared war on Russia, and at 4am one morning in June 1941 his unit was dispatched to western Ukraine. He was to spend three years on the Russian front.

War, and no peace of mind

It was early in this period that Trautmann was court-martialled for sabotage. Having advanced to Berdichev, a town reached over rough terrain that took a heavy toll on the German vehicles, a lorry was sent back to Warsaw for spare parts. It took more than two weeks to return. In the interim, the troops in Berchidev were ordered to advance, although a few drivers and mechanics – Trautmann included – were told to wait for the spares to arrive and then catch up. The sergeant in command of this group did not want to be left without a vehicle during the wait. Trautmann was therefore persuaded to alter the timing of a working car to ensure it would not start when the majority of the troops moved on. The sergeant's theory was that Trautmann could reverse the damage later, thereby providing them with transport. The plan failed when the advance party took the car anyway by towing it. It burst into flames, burning a staff sergeant.

Some 10 days later, after the spare parts had arrived from Warsaw and the repair group had caught up with their unit, Trautmann was arrested. The sergeant who had asked him to sabotage the car had confessed to the injured soldier, who'd reported the matter. Potential punishments included the firing squad. In the event, Trautmann was sentenced to nine months in prison, later reduced to three on the grounds of his youth and inexperience.

He was put in a cell with two SS officers who were serving time for killing a Russian civilian. Shortly after his arrival, a stomach pain that had been nagging for a fortnight became so severe that Trautmann collapsed. The prison commander initially thought he was angling for sympathy. His genuine agony was soon obvious. Trautmann was transferred to the army hospital where he was diagnosed with acute appendicitis and underwent emergency surgery. The doctor told him he had been within an hour of death. Trautmann spent the rest of his sentence in the hospital.

He emerged to the routine horrors of war. He killed and saw comrades killed. He was caught by the Russians but escaped. He got drunk one Christmas and punched a staff sergeant. He avoided a second court martial only after an unofficial overnight incarceration in a potato-storage pit. His experiences, he said, were no worse and no better than those of millions of others:

"There was tragedy and there was humour, as there was on every battle front."

By 1944, Trautmann was serving in France as part of the Odenwald paratroop unit, where he was captured by French Resistance fighters. After 30 hours tied up in a forest, he wriggled free. He described it as an effective but unspectacular exit. A more dramatic escape came that October, around his 21st birthday. An Allied bombing raid on the German town of Kleve killed hundreds. Trautmann sheltered in a school with many others, but when it was bombed only he and a handful of others survived.

A month earlier he had been at Arnhem as countless Allied paratroopers had fallen from the sky into a hail of bullets. The slaughter diminished any appetite for further battle.

The grim winter of 1944 turned into the no-more-hopeful spring of 1945. The Germans were in permanent retreat and Trautmann's regiment had split up. He was part of a small detachment stationed near the German town of Krefeld. By March, desertions were commonplace, as were the subsequent executions, meted out by the SS. Morale was non-existent. Trautmann decided to make the 100-mile journey north to his home town.

Unfortunately, finding his way home proved difficult, and he ended up hopelessly lost and fell into the hands of some American soldiers. He was questioned and then led into a field under moonlight. He was told to stand against a tree with his hands on his head. He heard guns being cocked and then a shout in English. No shots came. He ran across fields. He jumped over hedges. He landed in the middle of a British field-telephone unit having a tea break. After four years of combat that had seen him honoured five times for bravery, including with the Iron Cross (First Class), his war was over.

Classified a Nazi

After two weeks in the derelict brick factory near Ostend, with no sanitation and little food, it was almost a relief, at the end of the first week of April 1945, to be transported via landing craft to Tilbury Docks in Essex. From there he was moved to Kempton Park, where his status was classified. Prisoners were put into three categories: A, B and C. Those who could prove they were ideologically opposed to Nazism were 'A' prisoners. Those who were judged by intelligence specialists to be essentially non-political and non-Nazi were 'B' prisoners. Soldiers who had known nothing but Nazi indoctrination from childhood, most of them SS or paratroopers, were 'C' prisoners. Trautmann was one of them, officially a Nazi.

After a week at Kempton Park, Trautmann was transferred to a camp in Cheshire, where 3,300 prisoners, all German, were divided into two sections, East and West. The East section was for non-Nazis. Trautmann was put in the West. Football was the major pastime. The camp's only pitch was on the East side so all the West's games were played away from home – adversity dogged him, even in kickabouts.

In early June 1945 Trautmann was moved again, this time to a camp in Ashton-in-Makerfield in Lancashire, where he lived until his release in March 1948, working as a driver for the camp's commanding officer. It was in Ashton-in-Makerfield that he first played as a goalkeeper, deputising for an injured team-mate. He was a natural and was soon the regular No1 in a camp team who faced local sides, including Wigan, Orrell and Haydock, in charity fixtures.

Through these games the Germans forged friendships with local people, whom they were allowed to visit on Sundays, as long as they remained within a three-mile radius of the camp. Through these trips, Trautmann met his first girlfriend, Marion Greenall, although the relationship ended in acrimony when Marion fell pregnant and Trautmann declined to marry her. The paternity suit over the baby, a daughter, Freda, was one of many personal issues he would have to deal with in England.

Settling in England

Official release from captivity came in February 1948. Like Eisentrager, Trautmann took up the option of doing civil agricultural work in a nation short of labour. He had no immediate prospects in Germany so he decided to stay and was posted to a farm in Westmorland. It was during a visit back to Ashton-in-Makerfield during this period that he was invited by a local friend, Cliff Knowles, to attend a trial at St Helens Town football club.

The St Helens manager, George Fryer, asked him to play in a Liverpool County Combination game. He was an instant hit, and commuted to matches every weekend until late 1948. At Christmas that year Jack Friar, the secretary of St Helens, invited Trautmann to meet his family, including his daughter Margaret. She had announced that she did not like Germans and would go out if he came round. She kept that pledge but later became Trautmann's first wife. Her objections to his nationality would resurface.

At the start of 1949, Trautmann moved to Huyton near Liverpool as a member of a bomb-disposal squad. It meant he no longer had to travel so far at weekends to play football and he became a regular face around St Helens. He was evidently already popular. At the end of January, the British Government paid for all former prisoners of war to make a trip home to see their families. Before Trautmann departed, the St Helens supporters' club invited him to a meeting. He was presented with an envelope containing £50 and a trunk full of sugar, cakes, ham and other items that were scarcer in Germany even than in England.

On returning to England in March 1949, he moved in with the Friars, briefly, before he was posted to a new bomb-disposal unit in Bristol. It was there that he and Eisentrager had their one and only meeting. It did not last long, as Eisentrager recalled...

"Bert Trautmann came along to Bristol City, where I'd just started playing," he said. "I got a message that some German fella wanted to speak to me and that he'd like a trial. Would it be possible for me to ask the manager to see him? I went to the club secretary to say that he was there but he told me 'We've got three keepers on our books already. We don't need any more.' And that was it. They lost out on the best goalkeeper in the world. I'd not met Bert before and I haven't met him since. I think the next time I saw him was on the TV in the 1956 FA Cup final."

With Trautmann soon pining for Lancashire, and St Helens pining for a goalkeeper who lived closer to home, Jack Friar engaged the help of his local MP to get Trautmann posted back to Huyton. He signed another amateur contract, for the

1949–50 season, but it quickly became apparent he was heading to a higher level. Doncaster, Wrexham, Bolton, Grimsby, Liverpool and Everton were among clubs who made inquiries or sent people to watch him play.

His stature was impressive enough, a formidable physical presence with big, capable hands. His agility, despite his size, also marked him out, and he also had an innovative approach to the game. The goalkeeper's traditional remit was to stop shots and then hoof the ball away as far as possible. Trautmann, remarkably for the time, read the game ahead of him and actually tried to aim his clearances.

By the end of September 1949, the rumour mill was working overtime. First Division Burnley were making final plans for an offer and believed Trautmann would be arriving at their Turf Moor ground for negotiations in October. St Helens had already decided that if their goalkeeper wanted to leave there was little they could do to stop him. They were prepared to meet interested parties for talks. The most intense interest, however, came from Manchester City, who were seeking a replacement for their veteran custodian, Frank Swift.

Public debate

Before officials from St Helens had even met their counterparts from City, the newspapers in Manchester began receiving letters of protest.

> As a Jew, I feel very sore that Manchester City should contemplate signing on a German

wrote one correspondent in a letter that appeared in the *Manchester Evening News* on Thursday 6 October.

> The Germans killed six million of my brothers and sisters in the last war and the English public must have a very short memory if they can forget the thousands of women and children killed in air raids in this country... I have sent a telegram to the directors of the Manchester City Football Club informing them that if they sign this German goalkeeper

> I will organise a boycott... I myself
> have been a City supporter for
> 45 years.

Another correspondent, who'd served in the Second World War
and had used his rare leave to watch City play wartime football,
wrote:

> I did not think that one day Frank
> Swift's place would be taken by an
> individual who was at that time an
> enemy.

Such sentiments were echoed over and over again.

City were undeterred. That evening, 6 October 1949, Jack
Friar kept an appointment at a Manchester hotel, where he had
been led to believe he would meet City officials. It was never
confirmed who at Maine Road had phoned his office to tell him
to be there. Meanwhile, back at his house, City's manager, Jock
Thompson, and a director, Walter Smith, arrived unannounced
to see Trautmann, who was in bed with flu. Unhindered by Friar,
they persuaded him to sign there and then.

With the transfer official, the story took on wider
significance. It made the front pages of the national newspapers
on 8 October, when the player's name was less important than
the fact he'd been a German paratrooper. (He was initially
named as 'Berg' Trautmann despite having been called Bernhard
by his parents and Bert almost from day one of his arrival in
England.) The newspapers said former servicemen were
threatening a boycott of City. They said representatives from
Manchester's sizeable Jewish community had made their
opposition clear. They said City were taking an enormous risk.

The letters' pages of newspapers reflected the divide in
public opinion. Large numbers of people believed there was no
place for a Nazi in English football. Others felt the bitterness
of the war should be set aside. If Trautmann was a good
goalkeeper and seemed to be a good man, why not allow him to
make his living in peace?

> I don't give a damn what you are or
> where you come from as long as you
> can play football and can put some
> life into this City team

wrote one supporter in a personal letter.

> Best of luck, and take no notice of
> these miserable buggers.

The official view from City was similar.

> People can boycott or not, as they
> like [*said Bob Smith, the club's
> chairman*]. I am very glad we have
> signed Trautmann. From what I have
> heard of him he is not a good
> goalkeeper, he is a superb goalkeeper.
> We had to get him in quickly or other
> teams would have taken him from
> under our noses.

Trautmann met his team-mates, including the City captain, Eric Westwood, who had served in Normandy during the war, on 11 October. His career in League football was underway.

'Good lad, you'll do'

His debut, for the City reserves, came on 15 October 1949 in a 1–0 defeat at Barnsley. One national newspaper reported:

> Berg Trautmann, the young German
> goalkeeper, gave a promising show.
> One cat-like leap had the stamp of
> class, although there were other times
> when his handling and impetuosity
> did not inspire complete confidence.
> With coaching he should do well.

He made five reserve appearances before his League debut at Bolton on 19 November 1949. City lost 3–0 but Trautmann, who'd heard the first 'Heil Hitler' chants ring out that afternoon, took heart from Frank Swift's assessment. "Good lad, you'll do," said the outgoing keeper. From a man who'd served City for 16 years and was about to embark on a new career as a respected newspaper correspondent, it provided solace.

"In some ways I'd been lucky when all the controversy broke about me joining City," Trautmann recalled. "I'd been in St Helens, away from the centre of it. And I'd already been playing for St Helens so I knew that it was possible that supporters could take to me. St Helens showed a lot of kindness. They showed friendship.

"That game at Barnsley was the first time I actually saw people protesting against me. But within a month, a lot of those same people who'd been against me were having a go at anyone having a go at me. It changed very quickly. When I signed for City the papers were full of discriminating headlines along the lines of 'If City sign a Nazi, what next?'. And then people realised I'd been digging unexploded bombs in their country. They started to see me as a person with a mother and father. It was all about the human touch."

Trautmann's first few months saw some contrasting results. His home debut ended in a 4–0 win over Birmingham. The following week, City lost 7–0 at Derby. But the match that long stood out for Trautmann came on 14 January 1950 when City travelled to Fulham and he played in London for the first time.

The capital still resembled a giant bomb site, destroyed by years of German attacks. More than the inhabitants of any other English city, Londoners were still faced, on a daily basis, with the evidence of conflict. Throw in the traditional north-south rivalries of football and two sides struggling for consistency and the easiest target for abuse was the German goalkeeper.

"Jack Friar, who was about to become my father-in-law, told me before I left for London how important the game would be for me personally," Trautmann recalled. "He said I needed to play better than ever because I'd be the focus of all the attention. He said I wasn't just playing against Fulham, I was playing against London. I needed to make a good impression to get the national press on my side, and he told me he expected we could lose 7–0 or 8–0."

Trautmann gave the performance of his fledgling City career against a backdrop of abuse that grew quieter with every brilliant save in a 1–0 defeat. At the end, led by the home side, all the players formed a line of honour and applauded him down the players' tunnel. The crowd began to join in.

"In London, at that time, that was a testimony," he recalled of a day he still remembers as one of the proudest of his life.

The 1949–50 season ended with relegation for City but Trautmann, personally, had settled. Away from the pitch, he had married Margaret Friar, who was expecting the couple's first son, John. On the pitch, his goalkeeping was often the only thing that had kept some of City's scorelines respectable. He was also developing a reputation as a penalty specialist, something confirmed by career statistics that showed he saved six in every ten.

New division, new season, new manager

When City dropped to the Second Division, manager Jock Thompson departed. He was replaced by Les McDowall, an Indian-born son of a British church minister. McDowall had been the captain at City before the war. He had an immediate impact as manager. City started the 1950–51 season by going 10 games unbeaten and ended it promoted in second place behind Preston. Trautmann played every League game, earning £5 a week for doing so. The law dictated that former prisoners were only allowed to play football if they also had another job, so technically these wages were for his other job as a mechanic in a local garage.

Trautmann's pay increased to £12 per week at the start of the 1951–52 season as McDowall began to build his team in earnest. His most significant move was the purchase of the inside-forward Don Revie from Hull for £29,000, a huge sum at the time. Revie was a tactician, as was Trautmann, and although at the end of their first season playing together the team finished mid-table – and with Trautmann starting to wonder whether his future lay in Germany – it would be a key acquisition.

Plotting an exit, asking for trouble

In the summer of 1952 City toured Spain, playing against the likes of Barcelona, Seville and Zaragoza, the last of those managed by a Hungarian, Emilio Berkessy.

"He was a man with revolutionary ideas who would have made his presence felt in England," Trautmann noted.

In the late 1950s, Berkessey agreed to take up a position in England, with Grimsby Town, but the move fell through because he was refused a work permit on the grounds that he would be taking the job of a British worker.

Trautmann ended the 1952 summer tour with a trip home to Germany on a mission that would have lasting repercussions.

He had decided, for several reasons, that he was open to offers from German clubs. The economic situation at home had improved for a start, and if he were to have any chance of playing for his country he would have to live there. So without telling anyone in England – not even his wife, let alone Manchester City – he held unofficial talks with Schalke04, who offered wages of £100 a month and also a garage business for Trautmann to run. He believed a deal could be agreed through official channels and told Schalke it was now up to them. There's no doubt his complicity was naïve, but the row that followed highlighted again the suspicions that clung to him because of his nationality.

When he arrived back in Manchester, he began to let slip he was homesick. Schalke, meanwhile, contacted City and said that a delegation, including their trainer Fritz Szepan, would like to visit Maine Road at the end of November 1952 with the aim of studying British football. Unbeknownst to City, they were also preparing a bid of around £1,000 for Trautmann. The German transfer system then worked on the basis that bids should equal a year of the player's proposed salary.

The Schalke delegation duly arrived in Manchester. They accepted City's warm hospitality and then announced they'd like to buy Trautmann for the price they'd assumed would be suitable. City's chairman, Bob Smith, was not only surprised but annoyed. He replied that Trautmann "is worth 20 times that amount". Although Smith had not intended to say so, the Germans returned home to report that there was an astronomical figure of £20,000 on Trautmann's head – an amount unheard of for a goalkeeper.

For Trautmann it was a turbulent time, partly of his own making. Margaret was livid. City were outraged because they were roundly criticised for effectively stopping Trautmann, who had served them well in difficult circumstances, from leaving. Trautmann then went public with his feelings, writing an open letter in the *Manchester Evening Chronicle* in December 1952, saying he was homesick and his mother was ill. He also wrote to the English FA, asking them to intercede on his behalf. In Germany, the popular press said it was a cruel joke that England had discovered this German and now the English were stopping him playing in Germany. Public opinion in Manchester was largely behind Trautmann but the anti-German minority also made their feelings known.

City said he wasn't going anywhere. He knew they wouldn't budge. He also came to realise that he'd helped create this uncomfortable situation and it needed resolving. He continued to play, making progressively less noise about moving. By the April of 1953 the fuss had died down. Trautmann had decided to stay put and City escaped relegation by a whisker.

The incident was an early example of the disproportionate amount of disdain that has always been heaped upon 'want away' foreigners. Was it greed that motivated Trautmann? Or genuine ambition? Was it a heartfelt yearning for home? Or did he want to leave because he was unsettled? If so, was that because he lacked character and commitment? Or because there was money to be made? The alien, by his very nature (and because accurate detail is harder to establish across borders) has always been subject to greater scepticism. That fact remains true today.

Trautmann's two mistakes in the Schalke episode were acting in secrecy in the first place and then trying to justify himself publicly in a way that was less than totally honest. Alec Eisentrager also wanted to leave England at one point but was more straightforward in the way he tried to engineer the move. He opened his heart to a Hamburg newspaper, a strategy that he correctly assumed would have no repercussions in England if his bid to leave was unsuccessful (as it turned out to be).

The resulting feature, which appeared in Germany after he'd been with Bristol City for five years, was spread over several pages and carried the headline: 'Homesick for Germany, but will he be successful?'. The plea for a new club could not have been more direct.

"I would like to go back to Germany. The finances are looking better there," he reportedly said. "A German club could offer me a better job and raise my income."

The article then recapped the earlier Trautmann-Schalke affair, quoting the goalkeeper's value at DM 240,000 (£20,000) and Eisentrager's at DM 60,000.

> It shouldn't be forgotten that the pair only cost their clubs DM 120 each for registering them. With this they became the property of the clubs.

The feature was accompanied by a series of photographs of Eisentrager, including one of him with the Bristol City squad, one of him saying hello to a fan in the street, one of him in action, one playing snooker, one with his wife and daughter taking a walk, one of his mother in Hamburg awaiting his return and one of him doing the dishes at home in Bristol. The last carried the caption:

> Doing the dishes without being asked points to good honour in a husband. Just like Alex Eisentrager. Wife Olwyn is happy about that. By the way, anglican husbands are much more natural with the dishes than ours.

There was even a quote from Olwyn saying:

> I would like to live in Germany. The Germans are much funnier – they know how to live.

Ultimately, the appeal failed, just as Trautmann's attempted move to Schalke had failed. Both players stayed put to become part of winning teams. In Trautmann's case, it was in dramatic fashion as an indirect result of an event a few months after his doubts of the 1952–53 season had been resolved.

That event, significant for English football as well as for Trautmann personally, came on 25 November 1953. The 'Magical Magyars' of Hungary came to Wembley and won 6–3, handing England their first-ever home loss against Continental opposition.

Inspiration for the Revie Plan

The result was achieved, above all, through the individual brilliance of Hungary's key players, the forwards Ferenc Puskas, Nandor Hidegkuti and Sandor Kocsis, and the mainspring right-half, Jozsef Bozsik. But it was the way that their collective talents allowed their coach, Gustav Sebes, to deploy Hidegkuti as a 'deep-lying' centre-forward that left a lasting impression and would ultimately help Manchester City to their 1956 FA Cup win.

Hideguti's role was so revolutionary because of what had passed for tactical innovation in England until that time. In the

65 years since the start of the Football League, there had been only one major tactical advance in the way the game had been played. From 1888 to 1925, the so-called 'pyramid' system (the 2–3–5 formation) was prevalent. In front of the goalkeeper were two full-backs, dedicated to guarding the box. Ahead of them were three-half backs, positioned left, right and centre. That trio were all link players, with the central half-back – the centre-half – having the most flexibility to go forward. The five forwards attacked in a line.

The big tactical change came after the offside law was changed before the start of the 1925–26 season. Up until then a player was deemed offside unless three opponents, including the goalkeeper, were ahead of him in their own half when the ball was played forward. Attacks could effectively be stifled by using an offside trap which saw the two full-backs advance to the halfway line. A forward would either run into the 'trap' and be adjudged offside, or spring the trap but have two men immediately chasing him down. When the offside law was changed – dictating that only two instead of three opponents were needed to play a forward onside – the initiative was handed back to the attacking players. Forwards saw the difficulty of springing the offside trap halved at a stroke and the total number of goals in the League rocketed from 4,700 to 6,373 in a season.

It became evident that a dedicated defensive line consisting of only two full-backs could not cope under the new rules. If they stuck together when trying to execute the offside trap, a forward only had to beat one of them to stay onside. If they spread themselves to cut that danger, they left a gap through the middle. That gap needed filling and it was Herbert Chapman, Arsenal's manager at the time, who pioneered the method that did so. A rare beacon of strategic thought who had just won two titles with Huddersfield, he made the centre-half into a defensive player, creating a line of three at the back. The wide half-backs stayed in place, assisted by the two inside-forwards, who took on some of the former centre-half duties. Spearheading the attack was the centre-forward, who was flanked by the two wide attackers. The so-called WM formation was born, establishing the blueprint 3–4–3 formation (strictly 3–2–2–3) that proved a huge success and became the widespread system of choice for 30 years. Later, in different guises, it would metamorphose to 4–2–4 and 4–3–3 and then 4–4–2 or

3–5–2 but in 1953 it was still essentially Chapman's WM 3–4–3. This only served to help Hungary.

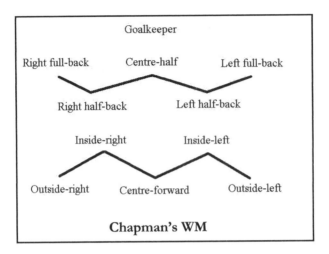

The English game, as its broad conservatism had showed, had been based around rigid tactical ideas that took major events to shift. Managers deployed the given system because it was the way the game was played. Full stop. Goalkeepers kept goal and then got rid of the ball. Full-backs cleared the ball upfield. Centre-halves were the big men who stood firm and mopped up. They were programmed to mark the opposing No9, the centre-forward. Faced with a system where the opposing No9 did something a bit different, there was instant confusion.

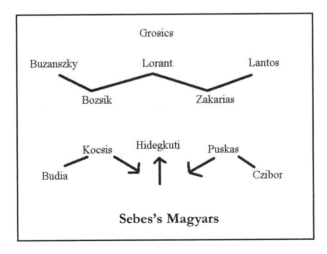

S. NICOLAS CHAPEL, LANCING CHAPEL

POST CARD

Printed in Great Britain

ADDRESS

FOR CORRESPONDENCE

— JARROLD & SONS LTD., NORWICH —

GUARANTEED REAL PHOTOGRAPH

POST CARD

Printed in Great Britain

FOR CORRESPONDENCE

ADDRESS

— JARROLD & SONS LTD., NORWICH —

POST CARD

Printed in Great Britain

FOR CORRESPONDENCE

ADDRESS

— JARROLD & SONS LTD., NORWICH —

THE CRYPT, LANCING CHAPEL

POST CARD

Printed in Great Britain

FOR CORRESPONDENCE

ADDRESS

— JARROLD & SONS LTD., NORWICH —

And what confusion the Hungarians caused that day, simply by deploying Hidegkuti as a deep-lying centre-forward who roamed at will behind his two inside-forwards, Puskas and Kocsis. They in turn were left to run free onto the wonderful passing of Bozsik or pick up passes from Bozsik via Hidegkuti. England's centre-half, Harry Johnston, was torn between trying to stay with Hidegkuti (which drew him out of position leaving a gap) or staying in position, leaving Hidegkuti unattended. England's full-backs, Alf Ramsey and Bill Eckersley, were pressed into providing cover in the centre, leaving Puskas and Kocsis more space in which to work.

Given the result and the method of success, that match has taken on an almost mythical status, as if it were a singular turning point for the game. In fact it was about some exceptional Hungarian players, with only one man deployed unconventionally, playing fluid, varied, communicative football towards the best of their abilities. Hidegkuti scored a hat-trick, Puskas got two and Bozsik one.

Watching the game on the television in Manchester, Bert Trautmann and Don Revie were as stunned as any other football fans.

"That game mattered," Trautmann said. "Before then managers had made assumptions about how opposing players were going to behave. They'd say 'the player in that position will play like this and therefore you need to try doing that to stop him'. They did not think how to counter individual styles."

Nor did managers do much to encourage players to use them. McDowall was about to, inspired by what'd he'd seen. He began to experiment with a system based around a deep-lying forward in City's reserve team during the 1953–54 season. At the start of the 1954–55 season he decided to try it with his first team. Revie would play the Hidegkuti role, hence McDowall's experiment became known as the Revie Plan in the national media, who were keen to follow its progress.

The debut of the Plan was inauspicious. City lost 5–0 to Preston, who had Tom Finney in fine form. But McDowall was adamant that his best team had not been available that day and he needed to persevere for at least a month. In the next game, Ken Barnes, who McDowall had acquired from non-league Stafford Rangers shortly after taking over from Jock Thompson, was played in the Bozsik role at right-half, a crucial link to the deep-lying Revie. City beat Sheffield United 5–2 and suddenly the Plan wasn't such a stupid idea after all.

Trautmann's role became more and more important. Both Revie and Barnes knew what an exceptional goalkeeper he was, mentally, because he liked to read the game and distribute the ball intelligently. He could throw the ball a long way with accuracy and because the Plan's effectiveness was reliant on quick progression forward, via accurate passing, a goalkeeper who could get involved from his own line was a huge bonus. Gyula Grosics in Hungary's goal had played similarly. Now Trautmann could look up the pitch, gauge almost instinctively which of his team-mates was best placed to receive, and distribute it to his feet more often than not.

The season, by and large, was a success. City topped the table for a while before ending in seventh place, only two points adrift of the runners-up spot. Trautmann had a personal down moment when he was suspended – for a week – for the first time in his career. He'd taken exception to the referee in a game against Charlton and when he was booked for derogatory comments about the official, he gave his name as Stanley Matthews. After the match, the referee was tripped in the tunnel by an unidentified player and stumbled into Trautmann, who pushed him away, brushing his face with his cap. The incident, as usual with any containing controversy, brought strong criticism of the German. But the season also saw brought a good FA Cup run all the way to the final.

Trautmann's first taste of Wembley

City beat Derby, Manchester United and Luton on the way to a sixth-round meeting at Birmingham, which resulted in a 1–0 win and Trautmann making two saves that were heralded as amongst the best of the season. The semi-final, against Sunderland at Villa Park, was settled with a single goal. Trautmann was on his way to Wembley to face Newcastle in the final on 7 May.

The teams emerged from the tunnel after the traditional rendition of *Abide With Me* and lined up to meet the Duke of Edinburgh, in attendance with the Queen. Roy Paul, the City captain, made the introductions, telling the Duke that Trautmann was the first German ever to play in a Cup final at Wembley. "Sehr gut," said the Duke, shaking the goalkeeper's hand. Trautmann admitted to being so stunned that he began bowing, much to his team-mates' surprise.

The jollity lasted for all of 50 seconds once the action started, Newcastle's Jackie Milburn heading his side into the lead. City's attacking game-plan was already in disarray even before a 19th-minute injury to their right-back, Jimmy Meadows. He couldn't continue, thereby reducing City to 10 men for more than 70 minutes. Somehow Bobby Johnstone, recently signed by McDowall, equalised after some accomplished goalkeeping by Trautmann had kept his side in contention. But two second-half Newcastle goals meant the Cup was going back to St James' Park for the third time in five years.

Trautmann spent the evening at a gala dinner at London's Café Royal, where his parents, who had been flown over from Germany by the *Manchester Evening Chronicle*, were special guests. They also attended the civic reception at Manchester Town Hall on the following Monday, where they were quite overwhelmed at the reaction their son received as he took his bow from the balcony. His father, Carl, seemed strangely quiet as he watched so Trautmann asked him if anything was the matter.

"They seem to be very fond of you and you must never forget them and what they have done for you," he told his son. "Hitler never had a reception quite like that."

Putting the boot in

The 1955–56 season followed a similar pattern to the previous campaign. It began with innovation, albeit only the introduction of a new boot for Trautmann. A friend from Germany, Adolf 'Adi' Dassler had asked him if he'd be interested in becoming a sales agent for his sportswear range in England. Trautmann declined but was still the first player to wear the Adidas boot in England.

City also had another decent season in the League, finishing in fourth place. Trautmann was outstanding, never more so than with a masterclass of keeping on a bog of a pitch against Southend in the fourth round of the FA Cup. City snatched a 1–0 win.

There was also controversy for Trautmann, accused of a foul on Tottenham's outside-left, George Robb, in the FA Cup semi-final at Villa Park. City won 1–0 but only after Robb had been denied a penalty after Trautmann grabbed his leg. The incident led to a renewal of abuse about his nationality, not least in sackloads of letters from London. The balance was provided by an equally large correspondence from people who believed his "honest accident" version of events. The people of Manchester made their feelings clear by voting Trautmann their Player of the Year. Shortly afterwards the prestigious Football Writers' Association voted him Footballer of the Year.

Down to the crunch

So to another FA Cup final. There were less than 15 minutes left when Peter Murphy, Birmingham City's inside-left, surged forward towards the Manchester City goal. Birmingham had reached the final as favourites by winning five consecutive away games, scoring 18 goals and conceding only two. But now, in the last act of the Wembley showpiece, they trailed 3–1.

The ball had been headed into Murphy's path. He was inside the box. He seemed certain to score. Trautmann thought otherwise. He was in no mind to lose two finals in two years. He threw himself forward and to the right and somehow took the ball in his hands. Murphy, his left leg outstretched and the full weight of his body already on course for a collision, had no chance of avoiding him. Trautmann lost consciousness still holding the ball.

The first words he heard as he came round were from the City trainer, Laurie Barnett. "Only 14 minutes left," he said. "That was the last thing I remember," Trautmann told reporters after the whistle, having continued, dazed and in pain. It took four days of inaccurate diagnoses before the extent of the injury was confirmed:

Trautmann's neck was BROKEN

said one typically incredulous headline. Trautmann's second vertebrae had cracked in two while the third vertebrae had wedged against it, holding the pieces together. Surgery was required to bore two holes in Trautmann's head through which calipers were bolted to support his spine and neck, which was encased in plaster.

He stayed in hospital for two weeks but almost as soon as he was released disaster struck. Having been confined to bed for a fortnight he'd decided he deserved a break and accepted an invitation to be a special guest at a Germany versus England game in Berlin. While he was away his son John was knocked down and killed in a road accident.

Such tragedy on the back of his existing misfortune inevitably took its toll, not least on Trautmann's already troubled marriage. It would take years to fall apart completely but it was not abnormal even then for Trautmann's wife to make derogatory comments about his nationality. He was not a perfect husband but this, combined with a continuous suspicion surrounding him – for years he underwent 'routine' post-war de-briefings and assessment by intelligence officers – would have impacted on anyone's state of mind.

And yet by December of 1956, Trautmann was back playing reserve football, a month after having his calipers removed. Not surprisingly there were doubts about his comeback. His obvious lack of fitness and form saw costly errors in a string of defeats. But McDowall urged him to continue with his programme of recovery and he played 21 League games that season as City finished fifth from bottom.

The following season, 1957–58, he played 34 games as City finished fifth from top, the first team ever to score and concede 100 goals in the same season. City's campaign that year, in common with English football as a whole, was overshadowed by the Munich air disaster, which claimed the lives of more than half the 40 people aboard. The death of Trautmann's predecessor and City hero Frank Swift, on the plane on assignment with his newspaper, was among the first to be confirmed. Another of those killed was Eddie Colman, the best friend of Steve Fleet, who had been covering for Trautmann during his rehabilitation, still not complete.

But Trautmann, who had proved time and again he was made of stern stuff, was nowhere near the end of his career. He played 41 League games in 1958–59 as City finished third from bottom, escaping relegation in the last game of season. He played the same number of games the next season, during which City shattered the British transfer record by signing Denis Law for £55,000 but could only finish 16th. Trautmann played 40 League games in 1960–61, by which time he was the players' union representative at Maine Road.

It proved to be a breakthrough season for players in general as the maximum wage was abolished. It was also momentous for

Trautmann, although not for financial reasons. In October 1960, two weeks short of his 37th birthday and shortly after the Football League had decided to include non-English players in its representative teams for the first time, he was chosen as the captain as the English League played their Irish counterparts in Blackpool. He was the only non-international player as England won 5–2.

Trautmann could evidently still do a job for City and assumed, at the start of the 1961–62 season, that would be rewarded well because of the abolition of the maximum wage. Fulham's Johnny Haynes was earning £100 per week. Trautmann was offered £30 and accepted it only reluctantly. It increased to £35 in 1962–63, by which time he was the second-choice goalkeeper. City were relegated, Trautmann having played fewer games than in any season since he'd joined, including the year he broke his neck. Les McDowall resigned following relegation and the 1963–64 season was Trautmann's last at Manchester City. His final League game at Maine Road was a 5–0 win over Norwich in March 1964. He played his last League game the next day in a defeat at Preston. The official crowd number given at his testimonial match in April 1964 was almost 48,000 but was probably closer to 60,000. Trautmann banked £9,000 and started thinking about the future.

Initially it lay in general management at Stockport County of the Fourth Division, between 1964 and 1966, by which time relations with the club owner had become strained. A summer spent as the official attaché to the German World Cup squad brought some relief but by October 1966 Trautmann had resigned. Having been re-election fodder when he arrived, Stockport went on to win the Fourth Division a few months after Trautmann left.

Two spells in management with minor German teams followed, exacerbating Trautmann's domestic problems as Margaret stayed in England with the couple's two boys, both born after John's death. The marriage finally broke down in 1971, the same year Trautmann's mother died. At one stage he went missing and Interpol were involved in the search for him. He ended up working in a friend's garage in Germany before joining a German FA scheme that sent managers to Third World countries to assist with the development of the game.

He had accomplished stints in Burma (where he met his second wife, Ursula), Tanzania, Liberia and Pakistan before a spell back in Germany. There he split up with Ursula and met Marlys, who later became his third wife, before spending the mid-1980s working in Yemen and Malta. He retired in 1988 and now lives in Valencia.

> This German-born player owes so much of his popularity to his cheerful demeanour on the field and his determination to do well whatever the odds

wrote Sir Stanley Rous, then the secretary of the FA, in the foreword to Trautmann's 1955 autobiography, *Steppes to Wembley*. Without irony, Rous added:

> It is typical of football in this country that not only have we accepted Trautmann as a player but we have come to praise his splendid goalkeeping and to admire his rich personality.

Almost 40 years after his playing career with City ended, Trautmann felt that his good times in England exceeded the bad. But he remained unsure whether the Anglo-German relationship had progressed; or whether in fact, it had actually always been too intimate, and therefore hostile:

"England and Germany are like two poles pushing each other away," he said. "But even in those days [*the 1940s and 1950s*] you had to ask whether this was because they were actually so similar."

Trautmann remained a regular visitor to Maine Road into retirement and took a keen interest as compatriots including Hamann, and before him Jurgen Klinsmann, made their impact in England. In 1995, when Klinsmann won the Footballer of the Year award – the second and last German to date to do so – Trautmann was the guest of honour at the presentation dinner. He was also the City of Manchester's guest of honour during Euro 96, when Germany (and Klinsmann, their captain) were based there during the tournament.

Klinsmann

Klinsmann's two spells with Tottenham, for the duration of the 1994–95 season and for the second half of the 1997–98 season, were an unqualified successes for the player and a boon for the club. This was entirely down to Klinsmann's ability to turn a potentially awkward situation around very quickly and persuade potential detractors of his value before they even had the chance to criticise.

The backdrop to his initial move to White Hart Lane from Monaco was not exactly promising. Despite having shown exquisite form in the 1994 World Cup, he had a reputation in England as a 'dirty' Continental who was expert in the dark arts of diving. He had also been an integral part of the German team who'd ended England's interest in the 1990 World Cup, which hardly endeared him to the average fan.

Spurs's off-field situation in the summer of 1994 also did nothing to inspire confidence. After being found guilty of financial irregularities by the FA, they'd been docked 12 points and banned from the FA Cup before the season even kicked off. These punishments were subsequently rescinded but when Klinnsman signed in July 1994, the day before his 30th birthday, they seemed threatening indeed.

Klinsmann won respect, with a little self-mockery, before a ball was kicked. "Is there a diving school in London?" he asked the assembled media in his first press conference. In his first-team debut, in the opening game of the season, he scored the winning goal, a stunning header, in a 4–3 win at Sheffield Wednesday. He celebrated by diving to the ground with a huge grin. His team-mates promptly copied and then mobbed him.

He scored seven goals in his first seven Premier League games, and 20 altogether in 41 League games that season, which was disrupted by the sacking of manager Ossie Ardiles. He added four more in the Coca-Cola Cup and another five in an FA Cup run that went as far as the semi-finals. Away from the pitch he was a complete professional in every sense of the word. He trained well, he ate well, he was a good example to his young – and not so young – team-mates. He turned up, on time, for interviews. He was engaging company. And there was nothing flashy about his lifestyle, despite the assumption that he was the highest-paid player in England at the time. He drove a VW Beetle because he'd always driven one and he liked it.

At the end of the season, Spurs finished seventh, which meant they'd failed to qualify for the following season's UEFA Cup. Klinsmann said he wanted to leave because there was no prospect of European football and moved to Bayern Munich. Spurs's chairman, Alan Sugar, made public his disgust by throwing Klinnsman's shirt away on television. Even two years later, berating what he saw as a general trend of money-grabbing foreigners, Sugar said: "They come here for a year to better themselves and for personal gain because they saw what happened with us and Jurgen Klinsmann."

Many Tottenham fans begged to differ in Klinsmann's case.

Klinsmann returned to England for Euro 96, a tournament Germany won with him as captain, although he missed the semi-final against England through injury. He returned again to Spurs as a player in December 1997, a surprise not least because it was Sugar, on a breakfast TV show, who made the announcement. During this stay Klinsmann played in only 15 Premier League games but scored nine times to end the season as Spurs's top scorer in a dire year. In the penultimate game of the season, when a victory against Wimbledon was needed to all but ensure safety from relegation, he scored four times in a 6–2 win.

After the 1998 World Cup he retired from football and moved to California.

"I still feel a great affinity with the fans in England and the Spurs fans in particular, who were the best I ever played for," he said later. "Many of the greatest experiences of my career were in London where I was very happy."

21st Century targets

Dietmar Hamann's experiences in Liverpool have been a vast improvement on his days with Newcastle. The treble of major trophies in 2001 was supplemented in March 2003 with another success in the Worthington Cup final. Liverpool beat Manchester United 2–0 in Hamann's first match of the season in that competition. Injury problems had curtailed his involvement between December and February.

Evidence still existed, however, that his nationality was an issue, if not with his team-mates or Liverpool fans, then with some opposition supporters. During a Premier League game at Charlton in December 2002, he fell victim to the abuse of a Charlton follower who was subsequently charged in court with using "racially aggravated threatening words and behaviour".

The perpetrator was a 30-year-old manager at a company that provided stewards and security at several of London's football clubs. He was found guilty of racially abusing Hamann and given a three-year conditional discharge. He was ordered to pay £50 in costs. By the time of his court appearance, Charlton, a family-orientated club with a friendly reputation, had already banned him from their ground for life. They were surprised that the courts did not ban him from attending all football matches.

The case showed once again how a German player was targeted for abuse simply because of his nationality. There is ultimately no bar to whom supporters will adore. It just makes it easier if they're not German, or, if they are, that they're like Klinsmann, and not only confound the stereotype from day one but are tremendously successful on the pitch as well.

CHAPTER FIVE

Extreme Prejudice

A number of key themes emerged:

1) Racism is evil and needs to be eliminated

2) Its origins lie outside football in wider society

3) To extinguish it co-operation is needed from all interested bodies, inside and outside football

4) Long term planning is essential for success

IN AUGUST 2001 the official news bulletin of FIFA, football's world governing body, carried an article about the 'Conference Against Racism' it had recently organised in Buenos Aires. Several hundred delegates from national associations, confederations and non-governmental organisations had gathered to debate ways and means to eliminate racism from football. The article reported that FIFA's president, Joseph S. Blatter, had congratulated the conference on addressing the problem. Blatter had concluded, arguably 30 years late: "Now the moment has come to start working on this issue." The FIFA bulletin highlighted the 'key themes' that had emerged from the conference, reproduced at the top of this page. The headline above the article said: 'Approved resolution to eradicate widespread evil.'

If only.

During the 2002–03 season, two of England's black players, Emile Heskey and Ashley Cole, were racially abused throughout an international match in Slovakia.

"In 2002, you'd have thought that everyone's minds would have changed by now but it's still the same," Heskey said. "It's very sad and it came as a shock."

He added that he would never consider taking his family to watch England play overseas.

Two Ipswich players, Marcus Bent and Finidi George, were racially abused when they played against Sartid in Yugoslavia. They were taunted and spat on. "It's not the worst I've had," said George, "but it was still pretty bad."

During a match in Eindhoven against PSV in the Champions' League, Arsenal's Thierry Henry was abused by opposition fans and pelted with coins as he took corners. This incident happened only a few days after Heskey, playing for Liverpool, had suffered a similar fate against Valencia. Two of Fulham's players, Rufus Brevett and Steve Marlet, had also been targeted that week when playing in Europe against Hadjuk Split.

In England during the same season, Chelsea's Dutch striker, Jimmy Floyd Hasselbaink, reported racist chanting from a minority of Newcastle fans who had travelled to a game at Stamford Bridge. Peter Ndlovu, Sheffield United's Zimbabwean forward, reportedly received racial abuse during a match at Brighton, a week before an anti-racism awareness week started. Ndlovu later said he heard no abuse but the match referee that day, Phil Prosser, stated in his official report to the FA that both Ndlovu and himself had been racially abused.

"The racial abuse towards me was at the end of the game when I was leaving the pitch," he said. "I don't know where it was from, but I know what I heard and the facts have been reported to the FA."

A survey conducted by BBC Radio Five also indicated that racism was still prevalent in English football. It found that the clubs in the Premier League and Nationwide League had banned 122 fans between them for racist chanting in the previous five years. That figure raised two immediate questions: How come only 122 when many supporters could testify to regular racism at matches? And how come so few cases – a handful at most – ever got anywhere near prosecution? Racist chanting at football matches is illegal.

A poll by the Football Association also showed that racist abuse was deterring black and Asian fans from attending matches. Some 83 per cent of Asian fans and 77 per cent of African-Caribbean fans said that racist abuse discouraged people from minority ethnic groups from going to games. A majority of white fans agreed that racist abuse still existed in domestic football. And this in 'enlightened' times when anti-racism initiatives have been funded and backed to the hilt by the likes of the Professional Footballers' Association, the Kick It Out campaign and the FA for years.

The careers of English football's non-white pioneers knew no such initiatives or understanding. To many people in the 1970s and earlier, racism was an alien concept – no pun intended – and political correctness was something to do with the House of Commons.

Many of those pioneers were born and raised in Britain. Walter Tull was born in Folkestone in 1888 and played for Tottenham in the League. He was the first black outfield player in England's top division and later the first black combat soldier to fight – and die – for Britain. He was killed in the Great War. Hong Ying Soo, aka Frank Soo, was born in Buxton, Derbyshire in 1914 of a Chinese father and English mother. He played for Stoke and Luton and became the first non-white player to represent England, albeit in unofficial wartime internationals. Mike Trebilcock, born in Cornwall in 1944, was the first black player to score in an FA Cup final, when he did so twice for Everton as the Merseysiders beat Sheffield Wednesday 3–2 in 1966. And Viv Anderson, born in Nottingham in 1956, was the first black player to win a full England cap, in 1978 against Czechoslovakia.

These home-grown players were all subject to the routine prejudice that came with the colour of their skin. For those non-white players from overseas down the decades, there were also the added hardships and uncertainties of physical displacement in a foreign land. Arthur Wharton found this in the late 19th Century as did Tewfik Abdallah (Chapter One) in the 1920s and Lindy Delapenha from the late 1940s (see Chapter Two). And so did some of the most influential black players from the late 1950s onwards, including Albert Johanneson from South Africa, Clyde Best from Bermuda, Ces Podd from St Kitts, Brendon Batson from Grenada,

Luther Blissett from Jamaica and Cyrille Regis from French Guyana. Such figures helped pave the way for every non-white player, British and otherwise, since.

But there have also been plenty of cases where talented non-white players found a life in English football too much to bear. Some, it will never be known how many, decided not to come in the first place. Others came and left. The experiences of the ones who got away tell their own stories.

The incredible Kalamazoo

The career of Steve 'Kalamazoo' Mokone, the first black South African footballer to play outside that country, offers one extraordinary example. In 1956, he swapped Pretoria for Coventry in the Third Division (South). He later rejected Real Madrid before becoming a highly-paid headliner in a title-winning team in The Netherlands. He guest-starred around Europe, including appearing against Pele's Santos, before, improbably, moving back to Britain with Cardiff. He moved to Barcelona but never played for them, then spent time in France, Rhodesia and Australia. He married in London and then caused a stir for Torino in Italy.

Later, in America, he was sent to prison for crimes he denied committing. On release, he emerged to start a charitable foundation for promising athletes and then retired because of cardiac trouble. Approaching his 71st birthday, in spring 2003, he was living in America, awaiting a heart transplant.

Mokone was born in Doornfontein in March 1932, the son of Paul Mokone, who had once studied to be a Methodist minister but who ended up the proprietor of a taxi firm. The family moved to Kilnerton, north of Pretoria, when Mokone was six, and he was later sent to school in Durban. Paul Mokone hoped that his son's studies would keep his mind away from football but before Steve was 16 he was making a name for himself with Bush Bucks FC. At 16 he played for a black South African XI and was attracting attention from touring English managers.

Stan Cullis of Wolverhampton Wanderers, who would steer his side to FA Cup victory in 1949 and three League titles in the 1950s, was one who was rebuffed. "My father said no, I was too young, I had to finish at school first," Mokone recalled. An offer from Stan Seymour of Newcastle, who would win three FA Cups between 1951 and 1955, was also turned down.

"My father asked afterwards if Seymour spoke English because he couldn't understand his accent."

It was only in the mid 1950s, with the intervention of Charlie Buchan, that Mokone left South Africa. Buchan had been a prolific striker either side of the Great War, playing for Sunderland, Arsenal and England. He remains Sunderland's all-time leading goalscorer. He is also credited by some historians as being a major influence in Herbert Chapman's decision to deploy one of his half-backs as a central defender. When his playing days were over he found a new career as a journalist, publishing *Charles Buchan's Football Monthly* for many years. It was in that capacity that he met Mokone and helped fund his passage to England.

"He came to see me and said that a lot of teams were interested," Mokone said. "He knew people at Coventry and thought it might be a good place to start. They were in the Third Division and the idea was I could work my way up."

It took more than a year for the South African authorities and police to make what they deemed to be sufficient investigations into Mokone's past to issue a passport. Operating under the apartheid regime, initiated in 1948 by Daniel Malan's National Party, any black person wanting to travel overseas was viewed as a threat. When the passport was issued in 1955, Mokone went to collect it and was told: "Stay out of politics, or else."

It was assumed that anti-apartheid activity was always one aim of such trips. And in one sense, for Mokone, it was. He was not overtly political but knew some senior ANC figures, including Dr William Nkomo, a close associate of Nelson Mandela.

"The night before I left South Africa in 1956, Dr Nkomo, who was like a second father to me, said that every goal I scored would be one more goal towards independence. As the days had drawn closer to leaving I had become a bit sceptical about what I was doing. There were doubts and fears, I had reservations. But this was the chance of a lifetime to show that South Africa was not a bad place."

The culture shock started as soon as he stepped off the plane in London. "I'd never been in an all-white environment before. I had no-one as a mentor. I had no-one to talk to, no-one to confide in. It was a very lonely experience to begin with. Even the hotel I found shocking. It was the first time I had ever stayed in a hotel and I remember it clearly, the Strand Palace Hotel.

There were white people serving me in the restaurant and white people making my bed. It was a total culture shock."

Mokone recalled that during his first few days in London he had the chance to meet with another black South African sportsman, the boxer Jake N'tuli, better known in Britain as Jake Tuli. The fighter had become the first black South African to win an Empire boxing title, at flyweight, in his first fight abroad in Newcastle in 1952, and had been rated among the best in the world of his era. Tuli was training in London when Mokone arrived and provided a friendly face for a few hours. But even their meeting ended with panic.

"After walking Jake back to his tube station at Piccadilly Circus I went to buy a newspaper and got lost. I emerged at the wrong exit. I couldn't work out where I was. I saw a policeman but there was a psychological block to approaching him and asking for help. In South Africa as a young black man you developed a scent for policemen. It was an almost instinctive ability to sense danger, to know there was a police vehicle a street away."

Eventually Mokone approached the policeman and announced he was lost.

"What's the name of your hotel?" asked the policeman.

"I don't know."

"That's bloody helpful, that is. How will I know where your hotel is if you don't even know its name?"

A supervisor was called.

"What's the name of your hotel?"

"I don't know."

"Why are you in London?"

"I'm a soccer player and I'm going to Coventry City."

The supervisor departed to make some enquiries and returned shortly afterwards.

"I know who you are now. You're Stephen Mokone. Your arrival was mentioned on the television earlier. And you're staying at the Strand Palace."

The surprises kept coming, including the television set in Mokone's hotel room. Britain had been hit by television hysteria over the previous four years, with church leaders, doctors and even the BBC becoming alarmed at the effect it was having on ordinary folk as they sat by their firesides. In the early 1950s, one screen appearance by a homeless mongrel dog, Smokey, led to the whole of Britain's GPO telephone lines being jammed as thousands of people offered a home for him. There were also concerns that viewers were confusing characters with real people and some actors and TV personalities had received death threats. That hysteria was abating by 1956 but Mokone had never even seen a television set before. "I didn't know how it worked or even how to switch it on."

More confusing was the concept of room service. "There was a lady who came to make the bed and she took my shoes away afterwards. I thought 'Why the hell is she taking my shoes away?' But I couldn't say anything because she was white and because I was afraid of the implications of confrontation. When the cleaning supervisor came round I told her that my shoes had been taken away. They were brought back but the next day they were taken away again. I just could not understand why they were doing this. The cleaning lady told me they took them away to polish them and I didn't believe her. After that I took them and hid them under the bed. I just wasn't sure."

Mokone spent a long time contemplating whether he was being subjected to racism. "In one sense I expected it. I assumed all white people were racist. But because I wanted to play football, I thought England would give me that chance. A reporter back home had told me that the British weren't racist but then he also said there were no black people in Britain."

There certainly weren't many, if any, prominent black sportsmen. The USA had produced some who were well known in Britain, most often boxers or track athletes. But there were few others outside this narrow range. The mere presence on the women's tennis tour of the black American, Althea Gibson, was still newsworthy in 1956, the year Mokone arrived in Coventry. When Gibson became the first black woman to win Wimbledon, in 1957, it was a defining moment. Yet comparable success for black footballers in the English game was still many years away. It was certainly something Mokone would never experience.

After his introduction to London, he was taken to see England's second city, Birmingham, which impressed him. Then he was taken to Coventry. He recalled that the city seemed less proud of its football than its statue of Lady Godiva. Her longevity and resilience seemed to be a constant talking point. The first weeks were nothing if not disconcerting.

"I was confused and I was homesick. Children ran up to me and touched me and ran away. The first time I went to a Coventry game people just stared at me. I was sitting with the manager, Harry Warren, and the chairman. All these people were staring at me. It made me uncomfortable. When they started smiling it only made me more suspicious. But I said to myself that I've got to make it."

Coventry found him lodgings with a devout Christian family who were involved in the anti-apartheid movement.

"It still felt uncomfortable, using the same cups and the same toilet as a white family. But I know now that these were problems of my own making. That was my cultural baggage and it was not their fault in any way."

Mokone judged with hindsight that moving to Coventry was "a terrible mistake", if only because the approach to the game was so different.

"If you start in a poor division, you only make things more difficult for yourself. It worked against you all the time, trying to use skill and thought when the standard wasn't great. It didn't work and you didn't make progress."

His ability became a potential burden from day one. After one of his first training sessions, he noticed a group of players practising penalties against goalkeeper Reg Matthews. One of the local newspaper reporters suggested Mokone have a go, which he did, reluctantly, unsure how his new team-mate might react if beaten. Matthews, despite playing in the Third Division South, was the England goalkeeper at the time.

Mokone stepped up to the ball and feigned as if to hit it to Matthews's left – Matthews dived in that direction – but actually placed the ball to his right. The delighted reporters laughed and asked him to do it again. He did the same thing, reversing the feint. Two nil. More laughter. The reporters asked for one more shot, as did Matthews, and Mokone scored a third time. Uncomfortable, he refused to take any more penalties and headed for the bath. Matthews found him and congratulated him to ease his anxiety, and would later be the only player to invite Mokone to his house. Few of the others showed such warmth.

"It was my first professional team and I hadn't realised there were cliques. The players did invite me out but whenever they were in bars they took it in turns to pick up the tab. I was earning £5 a week, and that was for my work in the club office because technically I was on extended trial to begin with. It was half, less than half what the others were earning. After my rent, tax, travel costs, food, clothes, I just didn't have the money. I couldn't go out for a beer because I couldn't pick up the tab."

Mokone's closest associate in Coventry was the Irish boyfriend of a West Indian woman who lived in the area. Once he'd seen her around, he felt it was natural to make her acquaintance because she was black.

"One day this Irish guy got badly beaten up in pub. A few days later he went back to same pub. I was very naïve. I said 'Why on earth are you going back to the same pub? Why don't you go somewhere else?' I'll remember his reply for the rest of my life.

"He said 'It won't make any difference. The fucking English discriminate against the Irish'. I just could not understand what he was saying. I could not understand it at all. It confused me absolutely. I thought blacks had a monopoly on being discriminated against."

Back at the club, Mokone was soon elevated to the first-team squad, as his talent demanded. An outside-right, he possessed the pace and dribbling skills that good wingers required. What marked him out was his touch and trickery, exemplified to best effect later in his career, elsewhere. Such artistry was of limited use in the hurly-burly of the Third Division. And when he did do well, he recalled, he was often unsure whether his team-mates were too impressed.

There was one practice game when he recalled scoring twice despite the pitch being shrouded in fog.

"In the dressing room afterwards someone said well done for my goals and then another player, I did not see who it was, said 'You should have had a hat-trick. It was so murky out there no-one would've seen you'. It was a huge joke that I interpreted as racism whether it was meant that way or not."

Not long afterwards, in conversation with a newspaper reporter who had been following his progress closely, it was suggested to Mokone that his services were worth a lot more than

£5 a week. He was advised to give the club an ultimatum: either you make me a professional or I'll look for another club that will. When he went to the club with his proposition he was told: "That's the trouble with you people, you're never satisfied".

"The phrase 'you people' had so many connotations for me," Mokone recalled, certain in his own mind that he was being treated differently because he was black. The ultimatum paid dividends, however. He was offered a professional contract the following day. Signing the deal ultimately proved to be about as good as things got. He played just four League games in the 1956–57 season, scoring one goal.

Even a good relationship with Coventry's coach, George Raynor, did little to improve matters. Raynor was well-travelled and broad-minded. A former player, he'd been a physical training instructor for the British army in Iraq during the Second World War. His work at Aldershot FC soon afterwards led to a recommendation to the Swedish FA, who appointed him as their national team manager. He led Sweden to the Olympic title in 1948 and then took them to third place in the 1950 World Cup. Hans Jeppson, later of Charlton (see Chapter Two) played under him in that tournament. Raynor then coached in Italy at Juventus and Lazio before becoming the coach at Coventry under Harry Warren. He would later take charge of Sweden again, leading them to the 1958 World Cup final on home turf, which they lost 5–2 to Brazil, and the emerging superstar, Pele.

But in the 1956–57 season, Raynor's remit was to mould a team to cope in the Third Division South.

"My style just didn't fit," said Mokone. "It was the long-ball game and I was used to short passing. I felt I had a good awareness of where people were and how to build play. And if I couldn't find a way forward then I'd pass backwards. But at Coventry I was told not to do that. They said it was the wrong way to play.

"And some of the training, I couldn't understand at all. We had to climb ropes like we were in the marines. We could only train with the balls one day a week. We were told they were like fish and chips. If you had them Monday, Tuesday, Wednesday, Thursday and Friday you'll have no appetite for Saturday when you're meant to enjoy them. I found it completely baffling."

A year that started with paranoia and culture shock stretched into one of isolation, frustration and loneliness. Mokone did have a brief friendship with another immigrant black player – the Nigerian Teslim Balogun, who was playing in London for Queen's Park Rangers and was featured alongside Mokone in an issue of Charlie Buchan's magazine – but one season was all he lasted at Coventry. The Midlands club agreed that things had not worked out and said Mokone could leave without a transfer fee if he wished.

In the summer of 1957, he was considering returning to South Africa but was also made aware that other European clubs had shown an interest. Mokone travelled to Spain to investigate the possibility of a trial with Real Madrid.

"But I couldn't speak a word of Spanish. They told me it wouldn't be a problem because they had a secretary who spoke English but when I was introduced it was obvious she only spoke movie English. She just had phrases like 'See you later, alligator'."

He didn't see her later, or ever again.

Back in London, a telegram had arrived from a Dutch club, Heracles, saying they were interested in meeting him. Another black South African winger, Gerry Francis, who had just signed professionally with Leeds United, encouraged Mokone to take his chance in The Netherlands.

Heracles, based in the small town of Almelo, about 10 miles from the border with Germany, had once been a leading Dutch side, winning the country's top division in 1927 and 1941. But the introduction of professional football in the mid-1950s had caused a polarisation that ultimately helped the larger clubs prosper and the smaller ones struggle. By 1957, Heracles had fallen from the Premier Division, down through the regional second tier (the First Division) and into the third tier (the Second Division). They were intent on reviving their fortunes. Mokone went to see what was on offer.

"Heracles said they wanted to play me in a trial that weekend in a pre-season game against Eintracht Frankfurt. They offered me $1,000 [*then worth £360*] for one game."

He played and scored twice in a 4–3 win. Heracles asked him to stay and play again the following Sunday for the same fee. He did, and scored again. News of his appearances was good for business and a lucrative contract was rapidly offered and accepted. It was worth upwards of £3,500 a year but proved good value for Heracles. The population of Almelo was only 35,000 people but in the 1957–58 season, the club regularly drew crowds of 20,000, travelling from far and wide to see Mokone play.

His first season was sensational. He played almost every match and scored 15 goals from the wing, a decent return from any wide player. More significantly, he provided countless assists to the striker Joop Schuman, who scored an astonishing 43 League goals during that season. Schuman went on to become Dutch football's all-time highest goalscorer. Heracles won the Second Division title and Mokone's place in the club's history and the annals of Dutch football was secure. His second season, in the First Division in 1958–59, was also regarded as a success, although an ankle injury limited his appearances as the club finished seventh in the table.

Mokone's time in Almelo was recounted in detail in *De Zwarte Meteoor* (The Black Meteor), written by the Dutch football commentator and journalist Tom Egbers in the late 1990s. The book was made into a film in 2000. There is also a street named after Mokone in Almelo and one of the stands in Heracles's home, the Polman Stadion, is also named after him.

Mokone's decision to leave Heracles was based on three factors. First, he believed that he could play at a higher level. His reputation in The Netherlands and beyond saw bigger clubs invite him to play for them as a guest in major one-off friendlies. On this basis, he once played for PSV Eindhoven against the touring Brazilian side, Botafogo. He also played against Santos of Brazil, who had Pele in the team. Mokone scored during a defeat.

Second, he had a disagreement with Heracles about his terms of employment. Most of the players were semi-professional and also had other jobs. Mokone chose to work as an entertainer and singer in the local theatre. Heracles said that he should stop singing and concentrate on his football. He did not agree. Third, and most improbably, Mokone received an invitation to return to the Football League, with Second Division Cardiff City.

"I'd been disappointed not to achieve something at Coventry and still hoped be able to make it in the English League," he said.

Mokone's nomadic career ultimately showed he was not destined to settle in one place for long, but neither did British football seem intent on encouraging him to do so. He made his League debut for Cardiff on 22 August 1959 at home against Liverpool, scoring the opening goal in 3–2 win in front of a crowd of 23,744. In the next match, four days later against Middlesbrough, he played well in a 2–0 home win but sustained a knock to his ankle. Having damaged the same leg while at Heracles he was reticent about being picked for the trip to Charlton three days later, but was selected and told he should get on with it.

"My ankle was hurting like hell. I didn't do well in the game and got criticised. I said 'What do you expect when I'm not fully fit?' They weren't happy and it was all downhill from there."

Mokone did not play for Cardiff again, seeing out the rest of the 1959–60 season from the sidelines. Cardiff won promotion almost entirely without him.

He left the Football League for a second time. His next deal saw another strange twist. "I agreed to join Barcelona but because they already had their full quota of foreign players, was loaned indefinitely to Marseille," he said. He never made an appearance for either club, but occupied himself in the south of France by running a small factory that made football boots, sold under the brand name 'Mokone'. At the end of the 1960–61 season, one of little playing activity, he ended up back in England, where he joined the third and final Football League club of his career, Third Division Barnsley. It was the briefest of associations. Mokone made one first-team appearance, in a first-round League Cup win against Southport on 13 September 1961.

There was one other significant event during Mokone's time in England, his marriage to Joyce Maaga, a South African he met in London. After the couple had spent a year in Rhodesia, where Mokone played for Salisbury, they moved in autumn 1962 to Italy, where he would play for his last European team, Torino of Serie A.

He made an early impact, as was his forte. In one match against Verona, he scored four goals, leading to a huge front-page headline that compared him favourably with Eusebio. It was praise indeed. The Mozambique-born Eusebio had won the European Cup with Benfica of Portugal against Real Madrid in 1962 and would go on to be the top scorer in the Portuguese league for nine consecutive seasons. Representing Portugal, he would also be the leading goalscorer at the 1966 World Cup finals.

Yet ask about Mokone in modern-day Italy, even in Turin, and it is likely you will be met with scepticism that he ever played there at all. Only by physically searching the shelves in the archives at newspapers such as *Gazzetta Dello Sport*, where an old envelope of cuttings about Mokone sits gathering dust, can you be certain he even passed through. By the mid-1960s he had also passed through Canada, where he ended his football career, before settling in America.

It was there that his story took another series of extraordinary twists. In 1966, he and his wife had a daughter who would become the subject of a bitter custody battle in the mid-1970s. By that time Mokone had gained a degree, a masters degree and a doctorate and was an assistant professor of psychiatry. His wife was a nurse who lived in hospital digs. Steve Mokone won the custody battle.

Three violent assaults followed. Mokone himself was attacked in a parking lot by three unidentified assailants. Next Joyce Mokone's lawyer was attacked with acid. Then Joyce Mokone herself was attacked in an almost identical assault. Mokone was arrested, charged and faced separate trials for the attacks on each of the women. He maintained his innocence but was convicted and sent to prison in New York for a term dictated as '8 to 12 years'. He served eight and was released in 1988.

Numerous people offered support. One was the Reverend Desmond Tutu, whom Mokone had studied alongside at college in South Africa in the early 1950s. Rev Tutu even wrote to the New York Supreme Court in 1984 to plead Mokone's case and ask that he be set free. He described Mokone in his letter as "a gentle man. He speaks for kindness and compassion among humans".

Another believer in Mokone's integrity was Tom Egbers, who only discovered Mokone's history as a convicted criminal after he had written *De Zwarte Meteoor*. Having spent a lot of time talking to Mokone and having established what he assumed was a solid friendship, he was "stunned" to be informed that Mokone had been convicted of two assaults.

"Steve had never mentioned it," said Egbers. "I confronted him, only to be told that he did not want to talk about it. Steve said he was innocent and that he would rather leave it behind him. It was in his past."

But Egbers wanted to know, for his own peace of mind, what had happened. He went to America to investigate.

His findings were published in 2002 in the book *Twaalf Gestolen Jaren* (Twelve Stolen Years), which, like *De Zwarte Meteoor*, was only released in Dutch. Egbers uncovered evidence, including previously undisclosed documents and tapes relating to the cases, that made the verdicts questionable. This evidence included a suggestion that a key prosecution witness had been coerced to testify against Mokone and that the jury in the second trial had seen prejudicial material from the first.

Egbers also unearthed letters from the period from the shadowy Department of Internal Affairs in South Africa and the American CIA that called for Mokone to be brought to heel. Egbers concluded there was a strong case that Mokone had been framed. In the mid-1970s Mokone had had pre-existing ties to the ANC and had become increasingly political in America, in his outlook and his writing. He had also been blacklisted as a member of a terrorist organisation, the ANC.

In 2002, Egbers took his findings to all the protagonists in the cases who were still alive. Some of them, including one lawyer, claimed never to have heard of Steve Mokone or the case.

"I know I wasn't guilty," said Mokone, whose conviction still stands.

After Mokone left prison – where he ran the library and also organised a football team – he worked for four years and then retired with heart trouble in 1992. He continued in his duties as a goodwill ambassador for the South African tourist board in New York and also helped found a charitable institution that assisted young South Africans with a talent for sport in finding places in further education, including in America.

He also maintained a close interest in world football, using his contacts of several decades to assist in the career paths of promising young footballers, including the South African international striker, Benni McCarthy, who has played for Ajax in The Netherlands and Celta Vigo in Spain and has been linked several times with moves to England.

Mokone's story is one of a gifted footballer who ultimately found that English football could not accommodate him. His talents were better utilised in countries more receptive to foreign players and new ideas. Unlike English football, he moved on.

Barefoot and brilliant

Teslim Balogun, the first Nigerian to play in the League, stayed slightly longer. He'd first come to England in 1949 as part of a Nigerian touring side who earned plaudits for their flair and gasps of wonder for the fact they played in bare feet. The lanky forward – 6ft 2in in his non-stockinged feet – spent the next six years back at home, winning the Nigerian Challenge Cup with three of the six teams he played for. He was then asked back to England in 1955 for a trial with Peterborough United of the Midlands League. He stayed with them a year as a regular in the reserves, simultaneously working for a printing firm to gain experience in a useful trade.

Balogun was popular with the Peterborough fans and it came as a surprise when he was released by the club in 1956. Unsubstantiated rumours of recreational drug use, never proven since, had been doing the rounds but no reason for his departure was ever made public. The following season started with a short spell at non-League Skegness in Lincolnshire before his move to QPR in September 1956. He stayed with the London side for one season, 1956–57, scoring three times in 13 League games and twice more in two FA Cup matches. It was during this time that he and Mokone occasionally visited each other during free weekends or days off.

London was not to Balogun's liking and he headed back to rural Lincolnshire with non-League Holbeach. His best performance came in a match against Peterborough reserves when he scored four times against the club who had let him go. Within a year he was back home in Nigeria and by his early 30s was establishing himself as a coach. He returned briefly to England in 1964 to take a Football Association coaching course and went on to become one of the most influential figures in Nigerian coaching in the 1960s. He died in 1973, aged 42, although his legacy lives on today, with a stadium in Lagos named in his honour.

The second Nigerian in the League was Elkanah Onyeali, who arrived in England in summer 1960 to study electrical engineering at a technical college in Birkenhead on Merseyside. As with Balogun, his primary aim was to learn a useful trade but he also wanted to continue his football career. It was with this in mind, shortly after his 21st birthday, that he went to see Peter Farrell, the manager of Tranmere Rovers, then in the Third Division.

Onyeali, an inside-forward, told Farrell he had played in all of Nigeria's international matches the previous season and had scored 14 of their 26 goals. The information was hard to verify. Indeed even in 2002 the Nigerian FA was unable to confirm such historic details, although other sources do mention Onyeali as a prolific goalscorer in the months after his reported Nigeria debut in October 1959.

Farrell was touched by the player's enthusiasm and organised a private trial match. Onyeali scored twice to earn himself a one-year part-time contract. A second trial game was opened to the public, who immediately took Onyeali – known variously by the nicknames 'Al', 'Barrington' and 'Englishman' – to their hearts.

His reserve debut, against Stockport, was a revelation. The Tranmere supporters had rarely, if ever, seen a player try to juggle the ball and flick it during a game, let alone dash with such verve around markers. The slightly-built Onyeali also scored twice. On his next outing, three days later, he scored again, and the crowd started calling for his promotion to the first team. They got what they wanted and he made his League debut on 3 September 1960 at home to Bournemouth.

Tranmere were 3–2 down and seemingly heading for defeat when he effortlessly side-stepped his marker and then picked his spot for the equaliser. When he scored his second, which turned out to be the winner, there were few doubts Farrell had got himself a gem. Two days later, Onyeali scored again, in a 2–1 win over Southend. He announced that his studies were his priority and that football must not be allowed to get in the way.

He continued to play, although not in midweek games, appearing in 13 League games that season. He scored eight League goals and once in three FA Cup ties. Quite why his time at Tranmere proved so short is open to debate.

Onyeali made it clear from the start that his main objective was study and that training and games came second. But another view was that as the season wore on, he became more reluctant to play on heavy pitches, in freezing weather and in a situation where he was increasingly a target for crude, damaging tackles. He was also reported on several occasions to be suffering from flu, although it later transpired that after one bout he'd spent his recovery time in Nigeria playing for his international side.

That mattered little to the Tranmere fans, who had enjoyed a thrilling if brief glimpse of his exotic talents. At the end of the 1960–61 season, they were more concerned that their side had been relegated and that Walter Galbraith, appointed as Farrell's successor mid-season, did not want to retain Onyeali's services. He was given a free transfer, playing occasionally for non-League Holyhead Town before his studies took him to America.

Another player who ended up across the Atlantic, in Canada, was Gerry Francis, the second black South African in the League after Steve Mokone. He'd paid his own way to England with money earned repairing shoes in Johannesburg and joined Leeds. Francis was initially signed as an amateur but became a professional in summer 1957. Leeds were then managed by Raich Carter and had recently returned to the First Division after nine long years away.

By the time Francis made his first-team debut, in October 1959, the Yorkshire club had seen Carter depart, his successor Bill Lambton had come and gone, and Jack Taylor was in charge. Francis's debut season, during which he did not feature prominently, ended in relegation. The following year, 1960–61, saw the large share of his 46 Leeds League appearances and some fine goals from the right wing. Arguably of more significance that season was the part he played in orchestrating Leeds's signing of his compatriot Albert Johanneson, another black winger, in April 1961.

The pair were close friends – Johanneson was the best man at Francis's wedding – but their appearances together were limited. Six months after attracting huge attention for becoming the first pair of black wingers in the same League side, when Leeds drew 0–0 with Stoke in the month Johanneson joined, Francis was transferred to Fourth Division York City. He played 20 times then moved to the non-League game. In the 1970s he emigrated to settle in Canada.

Johanneson spent considerably longer at Elland Road than Francis, staying from 1961 until summer 1970, when he too moved to York City. His time at Leeds can be split into two distinct periods, before and after the 1965 FA Cup final, when he became the first black player to appear in the showcase event.

His best years unquestionably came in the first half of his stay. The statistics tell their own story. From April 1961 to May 1965 he played an average of 33 League games per season. He scored most of his 48 League goals in that period. Between the 1965 Cup final and his departure he played an average of eight games a season.

This was, to some degree, due to the emergence in 1965 of a rival in his position, Eddie Gray, who went on to become one of Leeds and Scotland's most admired players. But the Cup final marked a symbolic downturn for Johanneson. He was physically sick before the game. As his former team-mate John Giles recalled: "The occasion got to him. He just didn't play."

Leeds had gone into the final, their first, as favourites. They lost to Liverpool, who took their first FA Cup, 2–1. All the goals came in extra time.

Johanneson's decline, argued Giles, had really started when Leeds won promotion in 1964. In Johanneson's first two full seasons he'd been a firm fixture in Don Revie's resurgent team in the Second Division. He was Leeds's top scorer as they won it.

"He was a fairly orthodox winger," recalled Giles. "He had good control, pace, he was well balanced, he could beat people at close quarters and he finished well. I remember playing with him in my first match and seeing him go for a ball where he was clearly second favourite. He got it. Even in the cross country he'd leave the rest of us standing. When we won promotion he played brilliantly. I thought he was going to be a real star.

"I think he had difficulties with the First Division. It was only my impression, I never talked to him about it, but I think the grounds and the crowds, the bigger names, places like Manchester United, got to him. He just didn't play as well. It seemed partly his mind, a psychological barrier. And maybe partly it was the absence of the usual transition that other players had. He wouldn't have been brought up with the same background in terms of joining a youth team [*at a League club*], staying there a few years, moving to the reserves, acclimatising there, breaking into the first team. He went into the first team, did brilliantly in the Second Division and then couldn't seem to cope with the First Division."

Johanneson's problems on the pitch followed him off it. He drank too much towards the end of his playing days and more than too much when they ended. It cost him his marriage and children. He had planned to return to South Africa as a coach and spent a short time back there exploring the possibilities. But he returned to Leeds, lost his battle against alcoholism and died alone, age 53. It was several days before his body was discovered in his flat in a tower block in Headingley.

England's exclusive agenda

The experiences of Steve Mokone, Gerry Francis and Albert Johanneson in English football ultimately proved dispiriting but the decades since have seen numerous successful black South African-born footballers. The prolific forward Mark Stein played from 1984 onwards for a host of League clubs, including Luton, Aldershot, Stoke, Chelsea and Ipswich, and continued to give value service in the non-League game with the likes of Dagenham.

With the dawning of the post-apartheid South Africa and its re-emergence on the international stage in the 1990s came the likes of Phil Masinga and Lucas Radebe, following Francis and Johanneson at Leeds. Others included Shaun Bartlett at Charlton and Quinton Fortune at Manchester United.

South Africa aside, however, the majority of nations with colonial ties are not and never have been major providers of non-white players to Britain. Nations such as France, who won the 1998 World Cup with a multi-racial side that reflected her colonial past, and The Netherlands, where Surinam is found on the birth certificates of some of its most lauded players, including Ruud Gullit, have always tended towards greater sporting inclusiveness. But this has not been the case in England. This is most evident when considering the Subcontinent, which has had close ties to Britain for centuries and is home to a fifth of the world's population.

Football has never been especially popular in India (or Pakistan or Bangladesh in their various incarnations since partition in 1947) and the political, social, cultural and historical reasons for this would fill a book of their own. But it remains statistically remarkable that the first Indian-born player with no parental links to Britain to play in the English League did not arrive until Bhutia Baichung signed for Bury of the Second Division in the last months of the 20th century.

And only a smattering of Indian-born players with any Indian heritage had played League football before him. Among them

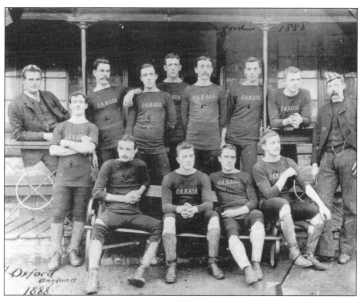

Walter Bowman (standing, fourth from left, No3) was the first foreign player in the Football League. He initially arrived in England in 1888 as part of a Canadian international touring side, pictured above in Oxford, and later played for Accrington and then Ardwick, who became Manchester City.

Arthur Wharton, born in Ghana in 1865, was a champion sprinter and superb all-round athlete. He played League football for Rotherham Town, Sheffield United and Stockport.

Hassan Hegazi, an Egyptian international forward, spent several seasons with non-league Dulwich Hamlet and also played League football for Fulham in 1911.

Nils Middleboe captained Denmark to the Olympic Games football final of 1912 and then played League football for Chelsea from 1913.

Tewfik Adballah, an Egyptian international, was the cover star of *Topical Times* magazine after joining Derby County in 1920. He also played for Hartlepools and Cowdenbeath before forging a long playing and coaching career in America.

Eugene Langenove was the first French footballer in the English League when he joined Walsall in 1922. He had been banned from playing in France after kicking an opponent in the eye during a friendly. A string of Cantona-esque incidents marred his career.

Charles Sutcliffe (top left), a solicitor from Lancashire, had a lengthy and influential career in football administration that ultimately led him to the presidency of the League. A dogged campaigner against foreign players, he was appalled in 1930 when Arsenal signed a Dutch goalkeeper, **Gerry Keizer** (above right, in action for The Netherlands). The subsequent brouhaha led to an effective ban on foreigners that would last for 47 years. Players coming from countries with colonial ties to Britain were mostly exempt from the ban. They included **Alf Charles** (left) from Trinidad, who arrived in England on a West Indies cricket tour and played one League match for Southampton in 1937.

Chile's **George Robledo** (far right) with his Newcastle United team-mates in April 1952, a few days before he scored the winning goal against Arsenal in the FA Cup final, a match that also featured his brother **Ted** (second left).

George Robledo (right) rushes in to challenge Blackpool's goalkeeper, George Farm, in the 1951 FA Cup final at Wembley Stadium. Robledo set up the opening goal for Jackie Milburn in Newcastle's 2–0 win.

In 1948, goalkeeper **Rolando Ugolini** (above left) became the first Italian to feature in the Football League when he signed for Middlesbrough, where he spent six years in the same team as **Lindy Delapenha** (above right), the first Jamaican in the League. Delapenha had previously played for Portsmouth, where he had become the first black player to be part of a title-winning side.

Joe Marston (below left) was the first Australian to play in an FA Cup final when he appeared for Preston against West Bromwich Albion in 1954.

Hans Jeppson, a Swedish international forward (below right) enjoyed one of the most remarkable cameo stints in League history when he single-handedly saved Charlton from relegation in 1951 with nine crucial goals in 11 games, including a hat-trick against Arsenal at Highbury.

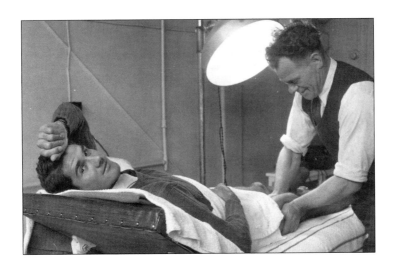

John Hewie (above left) receives treatment from Charlton's trainer, Jimmy Trotter, in October 1953. Hewie, a defender (also below, far left), was one of 12 South Africans who played League football for Charlton between the end of the Second World War and the early 1960s. Hewie made 495 League starts for the club, a record for any overseas-born outfielder at one club. Two other South African record breakers at The Valley were forwards **Stuart Leary** (below, third from left) and **Eddie Firmani** (fourth from left). Leary scored 153 League goals for Charlton, still a club record. When Firmani was sold to Sampdoria in 1955 he attracted a fee of £35,000, then a record for a British club.

Blackpool's captain, Harry Johnston (above, holding the FA Cup) has his left leg supported by **Bill Perry**, the South African forward who had just scored the winning goal in the 1953 FA Cup final. The game was nicknamed the 'Matthews final' in honour of Stanley Matthews (being held aloft, right), who is sharing a word with Stan Mortensen, who scored a hat-trick in the 4–3 win over Bolton.

Denis Foreman (left) moved to England from South Africa in 1952, aged 19, to begin a lengthy career as a footballer with Brighton and a cricketer with Sussex. Numerous other imports from the period, especially from South Africa and Australia, played both football and cricket professionally.

Manchester City's German goalkeeper, **Bert Trautmann** (bowing), is introduced by his captain, Roy Paul, to Prince Philip, The Duke of Edinburgh, before the 1955 FA Cup final against Newcastle United, which Trautmann's team lost 3–1

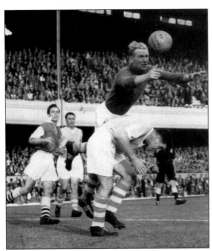

Trautmann leaps to make a save during a 0–0 draw against Arsenal at Highbury in September 1955. Manchester City finished the 1955–56 season fourth in the League and also won the FA Cup final, during which Trautmann broke his neck but played on. He had been voted Footballer of the Year six weeks previously. The next German to win that award was Tottenham's **Jurgen Klinsmann** (below) in 1995. Trautmann was the guest of honour at the presentation dinner.

were Roy Smith, born in Rawalpindi, then in India, who played at West Ham from 1955 and later with Portsmouth. Bud Houghton, born in Madras, signed for Bradford from non-League Cambridge in 1955 and also played for Birmingham, Southend, Oxford and Lincoln.

Kevin Keelan, the goalkeeper son of a British army officer and an Indian-Portuguese mother, played at Aston Villa, Stockport and Wrexham before embarking, in 1963, on a 17-year career with Norwich. He played 571 League games for them. No overseas-born player has ever made more appearances for one League club.

Keelan's family had left India in 1948, discontent with post-partition uncertainty. Wilf Heppolette, whose son Ricky became a star at Preston in the late 1960s, moved to England from Delhi for similar reasons in 1952, when Ricky was three. Heppolette Jnr, a fiesty midfielder, grew up in Bolton and signed for Preston as an apprentice at 15. He played 149 League matches for them before moving on to Orient, Crystal Palace, Chesterfield and Peterborough.

The main reason for the dearth of non-white players from former colonies was British officialdom's attitude to non-white people at large. In the years between 1952, when the Football Association's non-racial but stringent anti-foreigner regulations were tightened again (see Chapter Two) and 1978, when the effective ban on foreign players was lifted, around 120 foreign-born players made League debuts in England.

The majority were white. They hailed from nations with colonial ties such as South Africa, Canada and Australia. They had no trouble entering Britain. Others were born in European nations like Italy or Germany but had either moved to Britain as children or were the sons of servicemen. A few more were refugees. Some had come to England for other reasons and qualified to play via residency. Others had been allowed to play on short-term amateur terms, having been deemed of sufficient insignificance as to merit no threat.

And then there was a group of black players from countries with colonial or Commonwealth links. They arrived, often with their parents, in a society undergoing profound change. It was a period that started with the self-interested inclusiveness of the *1948 British Nationality Act* but witnessed growing institutional aversion to non-white immigrants. Football mirrored what was happening in society.

When the 1948 Act was passed, enshrining the right of Commonwealth citizens to enter the UK, settle, work and bring their families, it quickly became apparent that the Government had never actually intended to be welcoming. The arrival at Tilbury of the Empire Windrush in 1948, carrying 492 Jamaicans, signalled the start of pronouncements and legislation to prove the fact.

In 1949, the Royal Commission on Population argued that immigrants should only be encouraged if they were of 'good human stock'. Reading between the lines was hardly necessary. Another sign of the times came in 1950, when a Private Member's Bill to outlaw racial discrimination failed. Another bill, to outlaw racial discrimination in public, would also fail in 1956.

Six years later, the Government effectively reversed the 1948 Act by passing the *1962 Commonwealth Immigrants Act*. This restricted the admission of Commonwealth immigrants with the introduction of employment vouchers. Cabinet papers from 1961 detail how these vouchers were conceived by the Conservative Government specifically to restrict non-white immigrants. The scheme was presented as non-discriminatory on the grounds of race and colour but in practice operated on non-whites almost exclusively.

Racial tension was evident in Britain either side of the 1962 Act, from violent street attacks on black people in Nottingham and London in the late 1950s to the election slogan of one Conservative candidate in Birmingham in the 1964 election: 'Nigger for your neighbour? Vote Labour.'

Labour won the election and set about reducing the number of entry vouchers for immigrants in 1965, the same year the *Race Relations Act* finally made some acts of racial discrimination unlawful. The most deceitful episode followed with the *Commonwealth Immigrant Act of 1968*. The anti-discrimination laws were widened to include housing and employment but measures were introduced to exclude Kenyan Asians who held UK passports from entering the country. The Act was described as "racist, inhuman and degrading" by the European Human Rights Commission. Enoch Powell, meantime talked of "rivers of blood" if immigration continued. Three years later, the

1971 Immigration Act moved away from work vouchers and towards a new system based on stringent conditions aimed implicitly at ending primary migration.

Bermuda's Best

It was against this backdrop that footballers such as Ces Podd, born in St Kitts, and Brendon Batson, born in Grenada, grew up. Racism had been an issue for players like Mokone and Johanneson but it was to become much more widespread, blatant and vitriolic for their successors. Podd and Batson both arrived in England as nine-year-olds in the early 1960s and first played League football in the early 1970s. Before either of them debuted came Clyde Best from Bermuda, who arrived in 1968, aged 17, with the sole intention of playing professional football. Their stories are significant not just because of the longevity and direction of their careers – Podd and Best both became international managers, and Batson the most high-profile black administrator in English football – but because of the doors they helped open for generations of non-white players later.

"It was only a long time after I left England that I came to appreciate what my time there meant to other players later," said Best. "Players like Cyrille Regis, Ian Wright, they've specifically told me what I meant to them, how I made it easier, saying they're grateful that I played."

Best was recommended to West Ham's manager, Ron Greenwood, by Graham Adams, the English manager of the Bermudan national side.

"Ron Greenwood deserves a lot of credit over many years, for his football and his humanity," said Best. "If he hadn't given me a chance then perhaps there'd be a lot less black players now."

Other black players at West Ham at the time included the Charles brothers, John and Clive. Best lived as part of their family when he first arrived.

In seven years with the club, Best played 188 League games and scored 47 League goals. He endured constant racial abuse, which had become widespread during the previous decade on and off the pitch. His footballing approach, despite being 6ft 1in and powerful, was built around technique rather than traditional brawn. This also earned him criticism from those who thought he just wasn't tough enough to cope.

"What people forgot to realise was that just because you couldn't run through a brick wall didn't mean you couldn't play. Give some of those big guys the ball and they didn't know what to do with it. They'd have failed abroad in a more sophisticated environment. My technique was as good as anyone's.

"People said that I wasn't strong enough or willing to assert myself physically. They also said that black players couldn't play in cold weather. Total nonsense. Every time I went on the field I tried to give it 100 per cent. I looked at players like Billy Bonds and I tried to emulate his work rate. He'd run himself into the ground. I worked hard to do the same. The West Ham fans were knowledgeable people and they liked people who worked."

Away from home was where the racist abuse was at its worst.

"It was a bit more brutal," said Best. "But you couldn't let them upset you. You can't be selfish in those situations. If it affects you, you let people down. If there'd been no-one to consider but myself then maybe I wouldn't have stuck it out. But I was also playing for people at home, the people behind me.

"I was lucky because Mrs Charles took me in and treated me as part of her family. 'Don't listen to it', she said. 'It happens. Don't dwell on it. Look what you're trying to achieve. Be conscious of what you're doing.' I also thought that people of colour had dominated world football for so long – Pele, Garrincha, Eusebio – that abuse and ignorance wasn't going to stop me playing football. All sorts of things go through your head but you have to stick it out."

He stuck it out until 1976, by which time he'd helped dispel the myth that a black footballer couldn't cope with life in the top division. What he couldn't cope with, in the end, were the off-field pressures. More accurately, he made a conscious decision that he shouldn't have to cope any more. He moved to America, where he played for the Tampa Bay Rowdies and the Portland Timbers.

"I'd visited America before 1976 and I liked the lifestyle. The standard of living was better in the US, there was less pressure. In England, you couldn't go to a chip shop or a pub without people bombarding you. I didn't mind too much if it was people asking for autographs but if you're having a meal with your wife and they come up and start having a go, it gets a bit much."

America also became the country of choice for Emment Kapengwe and Freddie Mwila, the first two Zambians to play in the English League. There were recruited from Africa to the North American Soccer League in 1967 by Phil Woosnam. He was a former Welsh international who had been coaching in the NASL and later became its long-serving Commissioner. Kapengwe and Mwila both had brief spells at Aston Villa, one of Woosnam's former clubs, in the 1969–70 season but both returned to the United States. Mwila later managed at international level with Botswana and his own country.

When Clyde Best's playing days were over he settled in California. He maintained a close interest in the game, not least in Bermuda, where his success had been an inspiration. In 1997, he was asked to return home and become the national team manager. He went, staying in the post three years before being sacked for failing to achieve the Bermudan FA's unrealistic targets of regional dominance.

At the start of 2003, Best, the son of a prison warder, was working in a half-way house in Bermuda, helping to rehabilitate offenders.

"If I got the right offer, I'd like to get back into football in England," he said, talking on the day in January when West Ham announced the signing from Leeds of Lee Bowyer.

"I could sit down with Bowyer, for example, tell him he's got to grow up now. Someone needs to tell him he's supposed to be a role model," Best said.

Bowyer had a history of using racial abuse, on one occasion during a violent outburst in a London McDonald's restaurant. He had also been involved in events leading to a vicious attack on an Asian student although was subsequently cleared of all charges at trial.

"The fact we're still talking about racism in football tells me we're still some way off [*eradicating it*]," said Best.

A Bradford hero

Cyril 'Ces' Podd, like Best, played when racism in football was an everyday occurrence. He moved to England from St Kitts in 1962, age nine, with his mother and father, Georgina and Cyril Snr, and his five brothers and sisters. Cyril Snr had worked as a clerk in St Kitts but worked on the buses in the family's new home town, Leeds. Ces recalled with laughter one of his early preoccupations in England:

"I remember at school sitting in class looking at other kids flicking their hair. I just sat there thinking 'Mine won't move'."

But the fact he was black meant he was a target for racism. He described it as "persistent casual abuse", from direct name-calling to being expected to laugh at television jokes about black people, invariably 'niggers'.

"Either you became strong and ignored it or you fought it. I became strong. I didn't talk to anyone about it. I kept it to myself. I didn't want to upset my parents. I didn't tell them to protect them. Without realising it, I was dealing with a lot more than I should've been at that age. Having said that there were lots of good people in our neighbourhood who completely accepted us even though we were the only black family."

Podd had "hardly even heard of football" before coming to England, let alone played in an organised team. That quickly changed. He was soon playing for his school and the local church team. And after watching Albert Johanneson at Leeds United in the early 1960s, he decided a career was possible.

"Johanneson was an inspiration, just the fact that he was black and playing."

While playing for the church team Podd was spotted by a scout for Wolverhampton Wanderers. They offered him a trial.

"I was the only black kid, and the only kid who didn't get a follow-up. The same thing happened at Manchester United."

At a trial with Bradford City he was also the only black kid.

"I was a right-winger but the only position available at the trial was at full-back. I said 'I'm a full-back'. I got in."

He stayed in, as a defender, making 502 League appearances between 1970 and 1984. No overseas-born outfielder has played more for one club. Only Charlton's John Hewie, from South Africa, started more League games for one club – 495 to Podd's 494 – with Podd pipping him overall through substitute appearances.

"I went through some tough times," said Podd, recalling the systematic abuse of the 1970s. "Everything was thrown at me, from bananas to saliva. I almost got arrested once for reacting to a situation at Crewe. It was the end of a game, I was absolutely shattered, walking off the pitch taking gulps of air. My mouth was open and this guy spat in it."

Podd argued that wider prejudice within the game also halted black players' advancement.

"Some clubs seemed to question whether black players were able to cope with the physical side. In the end it didn't matter to me. I was happy at Bradford. That was my incentive to stay. I played under a lot of managers there and at least four of them called me in at some point to say there was interest from elsewhere. West Ham showed interest. And I could've gone to Portsmouth but when I looked on the map it was a million miles away. I got on so well with the Bradford fans. They were my security. I was adored."

Despite never playing outside the bottom two divisions, his standing in the game was recognised with the strength of the invitational side who turned out for his 1981 testimonial. Podd assembled an all-black team comprising the likes of Cyrille Regis, Luther Blissett, Justin Fashanu and Brendon Batson. Tottenham's Garth Crooks also turned up despite Spurs telling him he shouldn't play because they had an important First Division game a few days later against Everton. "He came on at half-time anyway," said Podd.

After leaving Bradford, Podd played for Halifax and was the assistant manager at Scarborough. He moved on to Leeds, where he played an integral part in setting up their innovative community programme. By the late 1990s, it was offering a wide range of educational and outreach projects to local children from its hub in a purpose-built centre at Elland Road.

After the 1998 World Cup, and the success of Jamaica's Reggae Boyz in reaching the finals, the Football Association of St Kitts & Nevis asked Podd if he could be the architect of another Caribbean dream.

"Everyone wants to manage their own country. I took the job."

He was in charge of the 'Sugar Boyz' for two and a half years from 1999, blending a team of talented locals with players from Britain and Europe who he discovered were qualified to play for him. They won the Leeward Islands championship and more importantly progressed through the early regional qualifying rounds for the 2002 World Cup.

For a country with only 46,000 people it was a decent achievement. But failure to make the World Cup finals was deemed a failure by an over-expectant FA and Podd resigned. He returned to England to work for the Leeds-based HN Sport, an agency that brokers contracts and looks after the interests of footballers, including Gary Speed and David Batty.

Gotta lotta bottle

Brendon Batson, like Podd, played the majority of his football in the 1970s. He had arrived from the Caribbean aged nine, in 1962. He and his elder brother lived with their uncle and aunt in Tilbury until their mother and sister moved over to join them two years later.

"We came over in April and I remember it was bloomin' cold," Batson said. "Having never seen snow before I was really looking forward to the winter of 1962–63. It turned out to be the worst winter in 30 years. There was so much snow I hated it. I still do. Other than that it was a big adventure. Kids are quite resilient, I took it in my stride."

Batson stood out in the town. Indeed all the Batsons stood out.

"We were the only black family in Tilbury. When you went out no-one needed to ask your name because you were a Batson. Everyone knew it. My aunt was a midwife and she'd delivered half of Tilbury."

Like Podd, Batson was subjected to persistent casual racism. He fought against it, often literally, into his teens. By then he'd fallen in love with football, a game he had never seen before moving to England. He was spotted playing Sunday football by Arsenal, signed as a schoolboy and became intent on making his way as a player.

"Arsenal was a fantastic club to grow up in. Football was the dominant factor in my life. And Bertie Mee, the manager, had a way of developing people not just players but as men."

Batson progressed to the first team but only made six starts in an Arsenal shirt. He felt he "hit a brick wall" in terms of his progress and asked for a transfer. In 1974, he moved down to the Third Division with Cambridge United, where manager Bill Leithers was soon replaced by Ron Atkinson. When Big Ron's managerial career continued its upward trajectory and he moved on to West Bromwich Albion in 1977, Batson followed soon afterwards.

At The Hawthorns he was one third of the black trio Atkinson famously nicknamed his 'Three Degrees', the others being Cyrille Regis and Lawrie Cunningham. Batson recalls the label as a publicity stunt typical of his ebullient manager. He best remembers those times for getting on with his job and doing so in an exciting era for the club.

"I don't think we realised the impact or significance," he said, talking about his position as a role model and forerunner to generations of non-white players. "I was just a player making my way. You were aware of a constant whispering campaign about black players, people saying 'They don't like training, they're lazy, they've got no bottle'. I just wanted to prove people wrong.

"I thought as the number of black players increased the abuse would ease. It got worse before it got better. You got it in all forms, monkey chants, bananas, I was surprised by nothing except the scale of it. If you're walking down the street and someone says something it's bad enough. If you're running down a football pitch towards a whole bank of supporters shouting things, it's something else. That deterred a lot of people coming to games. Even today you don't see the percentage of black players reflected among the supporters. That all stems back. The time to capture those supporters was then but they were lost to football."

The same was undoubtedly true of some players, although as late 1970s turned to the mid-1980s, the number of prominent black players increased and colour became less of an issue, albeit slowly. Others who made an impact at that time included Luther Blissett, born in Jamaica, and Regis, born in French Guyana, both of whom starred for England. Blissett later became a coach and then a TV pundit. Regis now works as an agent.

Another full international of the era was Nigeria's John Chiedozie. His father, fleeing the Biafran war, moved to east London to work in a car plant. Chiedozie joined him in 1972, aged 12, his childhood having been disrupted by war. He was unable to speak English and couldn't write. Four years of intensive assistance from a sympathetic teacher remedied that, although it took less time to make progress on the pitch. He was spotted playing for a Sunday team at 14 and went on to have a lengthy professional career involving five clubs, including Tottenham in the era of Hoddle, Ardiles and Crooks. When he retired from the game, he moved to Hampshire to run a children's entertainment company, providing bouncy castles and the like. In the summer of 2002, he also started a small-scale coaching programme for local children.

After Batson's playing days were curtailed by injury in the early 1980s, he went on to work for the Professional Footballer's Association, becoming the deputy chief executive to Gordon Taylor. From his experiences as a player and with the PFA, where he worked on numerous anti-racism campaigns, he believes football is now "a good example of an integrated industry", albeit one that mirrors society and must guard against any complacency.

The PFA, he added, was a progressive organisation when Taylor asked him to be his deputy and it remains a progressive organisation today. Batson himself only left the PFA to take up a new job as managing director at his former club, West Brom.

Gordon Taylor remains the PFA's chief executive, a post he has held since 1978, a year when English football underwent one of the biggest changes in its history.

CHAPTER SIX

The Barriers Come Down: 1978–79

World Cup final

Sunday, 25 June 1978

Monumental, Buenos Aires

Argentina (1) 3 Netherlands (0) 1 (*after extra time*)

Attendance: 76,609

KEITH BURKINSHAW, the manager of Tottenham Hotspur, was sitting in his office at White Hart Lane a few days after the 1978 World Cup final. He had less than two months to prepare for the start of the new season. Spurs were returning to the First Division after a year away. Bill Nicholson, Burkinshaw's most eminent predecessor, the man who'd overseen Spurs's glory days of the early 1960s, had joined him for a chat. There was plenty to discuss.

While they were talking the phone rang. Nicholson answered it.

"Hello Bill, it's Harry Haslam."

Haslam was the manager of Sheffield United and a friend of Burkinshaw's.

"Hello Harry, what can we do for you?" asked Nicholson.

"Would Keith be interested in signing Osvaldo Ardiles?" said Haslam.

Nicholson turned around to Burkinshaw.

"Harry Haslam's on the phone and he wants to know if you're interested in signing Osvaldo Ardiles," he said.

"Is he pulling your leg or what?" said Burkinshaw.

Ossie Ardiles, a 25-year-old midfielder, had been one of the stars of the World Cup. He defied the stereotype of the bustling, long-haired Latin. He was 5ft 6in, slightly built, and had a short coiffure that resembled a beret. He could also play like a dream. A right-sided midfielder with his Buenos Aires club, Huracan, he'd been the perceptive, thoughtful architect of much of Argentina's best play. Not that he dawdled, he could ease past opponents. And his ball control and passing were brilliant.

He'd been there in the starting line-up on 2 June as Argentina had taken to the pitch amid a blur of flags, lights and tickertape for their first World Cup finals match on home soil. Argentina beat Hungary 2–1. He'd been there again, darting nimbly past defenders as they beat France 2–1 in the next game. He'd done well in the defeat to Italy, and then excelled next time out against Poland, setting up the second goal with his playmaker's touch. Against Brazil, he'd lasted only 45 minutes, replaced by his friend Ricardo 'Ricky' Villa. And he'd missed the 6–0 win over Peru, a result that whiffed of a fix and saw Argentina to the semi-finals on goal difference at the expense of Brazil. But he was back for the final, part of the team who brought rapture to a nation living in the shadow of a military junta.

Ardiles was a shoe-in in almost every pundit's team of the tournament, including that of Ron Greenwood, the England manager. Greenwood had only been in South America as a spectator, England having failed to qualify for the World Cup finals for a second time on the bounce. That Harry Haslam was suggesting Ardiles was available for a move to north London was incredible. But he was.

In the next 12 months there was a revolution in the English game. The barriers preventing foreign players from moving freely to England came down. Established international names from Europe and further afield brought their talent to the League.

These players entered a tough, physical environment and found a tactical approach that was often one-dimensional. The emphasis was on bravery and strength and getting the ball upfield quickly. With few exceptions it was route one stuff. The tempo was helter skelter. 'Fitness regimes' meant laying off the booze the night before a game. 'Dietary sophistication' was the timing of your pre-match steak and chips.

There was never any prospect that a few dozen imports could achieve radical transformation overnight, or even in a season or two. But what did happen, from 1978 onwards, was that English football started to appreciate and utilise a more continental approach. Midfield became a place to pass through not bypass. This required better technical ability, which players like Ardiles possessed. Mental application became more important, which suited Ardiles. He regarded the game as an intellectual exercise as well as his sporting passion.

The Football League had not been without British-born thinkers and players of extraordinary technical ability. Herbert Chapman had been a visionary coach and an astute tactician at Huddersfield and Arsenal in the 1920s and 1930s. Stanley Matthews, the Wizard of the Dribble, the first ever European Footballer of the Year, in 1956, became football's first global star. He also took care of himself, playing until he was 50. John Charles of Wales, known as the 'Gentle Giant' in an Italy he mesmerised, earned lifelong adulation with his delicate, sumptuous style. Jimmy Greaves possessed a speed of thought to match his feet and became his generation's most natural goalscorer. Northern Ireland's George Best, who at his peak was the greatest British player ever, had it all.

But such giants of the game marked themselves out as exceptional. They were not products of a system that had deliberately set out to encourage and nurture their genius. They and other home-grown innovators either swam against the tide because they believed wholeheartedly in progress, like Chapman, or were uniquely gifted, like Matthews and Charles, or were trend-bucking mavericks with all the good and bad that entailed, like Greaves and Best.

It was not until later that coaches began to move in numbers towards an holistic approach where detail mattered, from diet to training to sports science to technique to instilling a sense that football could be a genuinely intellectual as well as a physical profession. But if Arsène Wenger at Arsenal would set new standards of excellence in this way in the late 1990s, the seeds were sown for him to do so in 1978. There were a few kicks and screams along the way, not least from the government and the PFA, still edgy about the consequences of a 'foreign invasion' but still there were glimpses of what the best of footballing travellers could bring, to the pitch and to the attendance figures alike.

The political decision that ultimately allowed them to come had been taken on 23 February 1978 in an anonymous meeting room in Brussels. It was on that day the European Community declared that the football associations of nations within the EC must modify their regulations to fall in line with the *Treaty of Rome*.

> According to the new EC ruling, there may be no restriction in future on the number of players from EC states signed on by clubs in other EC states

announced the official monthly bulletin of UEFA, the governing body of the European game, in March 1978, reporting the EC's February decision. The news nestled at the bottom of page 18 of the bulletin under the headline 'EC lifts restrictions on foreign players'.

The purpose of the EC in introducing this new legislation was to extend the scope of the Rome Treaty on the freedom of workers' movement to football. It followed an earlier decision by the EC's Court of Justice determining the professional footballer in the status of an employee. The National Associations of the member states of the European Community (West Germany, France, Italy, The Netherlands, Belgium, Luxembourg, Denmark, the Republic of Ireland, England, Scotland, Wales and Northern Ireland) had to change their regulations accordingly by the start of the 1978–79 season if they had not already done so.

At its AGM in the summer of 1978, the Football League had no choice but to accept the decision and amend its rules, thereby reversing the effective ban on foreign players that had been implemented in 1931 (see Chapter One) and strengthened in 1952 (see Chapter Two). Foreign players, and not just those from Europe, the League decided, were free to come to England. The only stipulation was that no more than two foreign players be fielded in one team. Over time, such quotas would expand and in most cases disappear.

"I said to Bill 'Is he pulling your leg or what?'" Burkinshaw recalled of that June day in 1978. "I'd watched the World Cup on TV. Of course the Argentinians were a very good team. Ardiles took my eye and there was one game when Ricky Villa came on as a sub and I thought what a big strong lad he was. But that was it. I hadn't actually been out to see it.

"I went on the phone for a chat. Harry said he was going out to Argentina to look at some players. He couldn't afford Ardiles but he knew he was available. I said I couldn't believe it was true, that I'd just be able to go there and just sign someone of that calibre, but I said I'd go along. I had nothing to lose."

Haslam mentioned that Terry Neill, who'd managed Tottenham immediately before Burkinshaw and was then the manager of Arsenal, was also interested in travelling to Argentina. Neill was considering a bid for Ricky Villa.

"I wasn't too keen on that," Burkinshaw said. "Going on a trip for players with another manager could get complicated. But of course I was still interested. On the next Monday or Tuesday Harry rang back and said Arsenal weren't interested any more. We left that week and arrived in Buenos Aires on the Saturday morning."

Sensational signings

Harry Haslam's interest in South Americans had stemmed from contacts built via one of his senior coaching staff, Oscar Arce, an Argentinian. Burkinshaw knew this, and that Haslam already had a rudimentary scouting network in place across in Argentina. He was still a little taken aback when he disembarked in Buenos Aires on Saturday 8 July 1978 to be met off the plane by Antonio Rattin.

Rattin had captained Argentina in the most notorious game of the 1966 World Cup finals, the ill-tempered quarter-final against England. During the first half hour of the game, which England won 1–0, Rattin committed a series of fouls, contested almost every decision and spat in front of the referee. He was shown the red card after 36 minutes but refused to leave the pitch. There was uproar as he stood his ground and it took eight minutes to persuade him to go. He even tried to sit on the touchline and was eventually escorted away by the police.

Geoff Hurst, England's goalscorer that day, talked afterwards of feeling as though he would be mugged at any moment. There had been high tackles, kicking, tugging and poking from both sides. Nobby Stiles memorably said: "Apart from the violence, I came through with no problems." Alf Ramsey, England's manager, described the Argentineans as "animals". The infamy of Rattin and his team was sealed.

"But Rattin was a tremendous guy," Burkinshaw said of their meeting in 1978. "We were there for four or five days and he was a great fella. He escorted us everywhere, he made all the introductions, he was wonderful."

Before leaving for Argentina, Burkinshaw had been in touch with the Football League, the Football Association and the Department of Employment about signing Ardiles. The League and the FA had said that under the new rules they could foresee no problems with a deal. The Department of Employment, which issued work permits, had also made positive noises. Permits were issued to workers – in any business, not just football – who had a confirmed job offer from an employer who had tried and failed to recruit suitable talent at home. There seemed little chance that Spurs would fail to meet the criteria. England was not awash with World Cup-winning midfielders.

Burkinshaw met Ardiles at a Buenos Aires hotel within hours of arriving in Argentina. Considering the impact the deal would have, it was concluded more smoothly than Burkinshaw could ever have anticipated.

"I asked Ossie if he'd be interested in signing for Tottenham. He said yes, but he'd have to come back with his wife, Sylvia. He did. Twenty minutes into that second meeting he said 'Give me the form and I'll sign it'. Then he said 'Would you like to sign Ricky Villa?'

"I rang Tottenham. The chairman [*Sidney Wale*] told me to go ahead if that's what I wanted. I met Ricky the next day and five minutes later he was a Tottenham player."

News of the signings reached England on Monday 10 July. 'Sensational' appeared in numerous headlines. It was claimed to be the first time two foreign players had ever signed for one League club at the same time. This was not strictly accurate because Charlton's Jimmy Seed had made a habit of signing South Africans in pairs in the 1950s. But it was certainly the first time two overseas players with no Commonwealth or colonial ties had signed together. Bookmakers responded instantly by cutting Tottenham's odds of winning the First Division from 66–1 to 25–1.

Sidney Wale, Tottenham's chairman, went public on the reasons for his purchases:

"The [*financial*] situation is certainly right for signing players out there," he said.

The pair had cost around £750,000 between them. Ardiles, already the holder of more than 40 caps, had cost £325,000 from Huracan. Villa, despite having less international experience, cost marginally more from Racing Club. Burkinshaw said:

"It proves that Tottenham think big and want to be the best club in the country."

Peter Taylor, Tottenham's England winger, added: "The arrival of Ardiles and Villa is magical news. It's bound to affect attendances and create interest everywhere we go."

Ron Greenwood added: "I congratulate Tottenham on their enterprise."

Not everyone was convinced. Having completed the deals and left Villa and Ardiles to start their packing, Burkinshaw arrived back in London on Wednesday 12 July to find objections from the players' union.

"It is a situation that cannot be dismissed lightly," said Cliff Lloyd, the secretary of the PFA. "Seeing these two could whet people's appetites and we could be caught up in something that is detrimental to the game in this country as a whole... The position had got to be looked at very carefully. One has got to consider the game in this country at all levels, right up to the England team and what sort of effect it will have."

Lloyd also questioned whether Ardiles and Villa would be able to cope in England.

"These two will find it a different kettle of fish playing in our conditions and with our commitments. It is a long, arduous season and these players still have to prove themselves under our conditions."

Tottenham's new signings flew to England on Sunday 16 July. Despite transport delays that kept them from their beds until the early hours of Monday morning, they were at White Hart Lane a few hours later to meet the press. They were asked why they'd chosen to come to England when the rate of taxation was so high. Surely anywhere else in Europe would have been more profitable? Villa, speaking through a translator, diplomatically said that England was the home of football, and that that was an obvious attraction.

Interviewed for this book in 2002, Ardiles's recollection is that they signed for Spurs because Tottenham were the first European club to make an offer.

"It had never crossed my mind for a second that I might go to England," he said. "I'd thought about maybe Spain, Italy or even France, people had talked about this around the World Cup. But when we got home there was nothing whatsoever. The first person who came out to Argentina to see us was Keith Burkinshaw. Suddenly he was there. He wanted me and Ricky, he put the offer on the table. The rest is history."

Neither player, on arrival, knew much about the English game beyond some basic knowledge of the international team. They knew most about Kevin Keegan, who was playing in Germany for SV Hamburg. Otherwise they could name Bobby Charlton, Bobby Moore and Gordon Banks, all from the 1966 World Cup team, as examples of prominent English players.

Neither Ardiles nor Villa had heard of Brian Clough, the outspoken manager of Nottingham Forest, who had led his side to the First Division title in May that year. Forest would be Spurs's first opponents in the forthcoming season.

Ardiles's and Villa's arrival received plenty of positive coverage in the newspapers on Tuesday 18 July. It was rare at the time for such news to spread beyond the ghetto of the sports pages but the pair soon found themselves on the news and features pages. There they shared space with other items of international interest, including the countdown to the birth of the world's first test-tube baby, which was a week away. There was also news of the death in Russia of Fyodor Kulakov, who'd been tipped as a likely successor to Leonid Brezhnev, and the 60th birthday of Nelson Mandela, who'd spent a third of his life in prison. Mandela's wife, Winnie, said that her husband, locked away on Robben Island, was inspired by the hope that he might live to see black South Africans free from apartheid. It seemed an unlikely aim.

The barriers come down

Within two days of Ardiles and Villa's arrival came news that a third Argentinian, Alex Sabella, was coming to England. Harry

Haslam signed the 23-year-old midfielder from River Plate for £160,000, a record fee for Sheffield United. "I've seen him play and he has a lot of skill and flair," said Haslam. "I think he can fit in well at Bramall Lane."

Gordon Taylor, a member of the PFA's executive committee, reacted by saying:

"If a trickle of foreign players becomes a flow, it would be detrimental to our members. Whatever way you look at it, there could already be two English players out of a job at Tottenham because of the Argentinians."

His statement did nothing to deter other clubs from looking abroad. Manchester City confirmed they were interested in signing Legia Warsaw's Kazimierz Deyna, who was Poland's most capped player. City had earlier declined the opportunity to travel to Argentina to meet Ardiles and Villa and had failed in an attempt to sign Kevin Keegan from Hamburg for £500,000. Elsewhere, Birmingham were interested in Alberto Tarantini, another Argentinian and Southampton had already done a deal to sign the Yugoslav defender, Ivan Golac. Lawrie McMenemy, Southampton's manager at the time, recalled:

"The same time I signed him Tottenham were getting all the publicity for their big-money Argentinian deals, it overshadowed my little fifty-thousand-pounder. But Ivan was a terrific fella and terrific value for money."

There were still some hurdles to clear before these transfers could be rubber-stamped with long-term work permits, however. Although the Football League accepted the registrations of Ardiles, Villa and Sabella on 30 July, the Government, at the behest of the PFA, then stepped in. From 31 July, League clubs were temporarily banned from buying non-Common Market players. The ban lasted until 28 September, when a compromise plan was drawn up by the Sports Minister, Denis Howell, and the Minister of Employment, John Grant. To allay the fears of the PFA, they and football's governing bodies agreed that only 'established' foreign players would be given work permits. 'Established' meant players who had been capped by their countries and who could make a "distinctive contribution to the national game". The Department of Employment would make these judgments on a case by case basis, often in consultation with the PFA.

Ivan Golac had already played six League games for Southampton before 28 September after receiving special dispensation to do so by the Home Office. His full work permit was the first to be ratified under the 'compromise' rules. Alberto Tarantini was also issued with a permit and he made his League debut for Birmingham on 14 October 1978. The game ended in a 1–0 defeat at White Hart Lane against Tottenham, who had Ossie Ardiles in their side.

By that time, Ardiles and Villa had both been playing in the First Division for two months, as had the Dutchman Arnold Muhren, who had joined Bobby Robson's Ipswich from Twente Enschede in August. Ron Greenwood had already seen enough to reiterate his positive stance on foreign players.

"They have acted as a stimulant on our soccer," the England manager said. "They have created a feeling of expectancy, excitement and glamour."

The 1978–79 season brought much more. English football was attracting some famous foreign names and was on the verge of some landmark events. Kazimierz Deyna completed his move to Maine Road in November, the same month that Gordon Taylor stepped up to become the chief executive of the PFA. Kevin Keegan of Hamburg became the European Footballer of the Year in December, the first Englishman to do so since Bobby Charlton in 1966. Trevor Francis became Britain's first £1m footballer when he moved from Birmingham to Nottingham Forest in February 1979. This came a few days before Ipswich signed a second Dutchman, Frans Thijssen from Twente Enschede.

Other foreign signings that season included Middlesbrough's purchase of the Yugoslavian striker Bozo Jankovic in February and Chelsea's acquisition of the Yugoslavian goalkeeper Petar Borota in March. Bristol City signed the Dutch winger Gert Meijer and the Finnish midfielder Pertti Jantunen. Bolton signed the Polish winger Tadeusz Nowak. Decades later, in the Premier League era, such signings would become so routine that a player's nationality would not be an issue. When Bolton fielded their first starting line-up entirely of non-British players, in March 2003, it warranted the merest of mentions. But in 1978–79, every foreign signing was a big deal, worthy of special scrutiny.

Before that season was finished, there were signs that the newcomers would not all acclimatise. Birmingham, heading for relegation, sold Tarantini back to an Argentinian club, Talleres, after only six months and 23 League games. (And even that was a successful tenure compared to that of another Argentinian, Pedro Verde, the uncle of Juan Sebastian Veron, who played only 10 League games for Sheffield United in 1979–80.)

But there were also signs that the foreign players were bringing benefits. Ardiles and Villa attracted huge crowds as Tottenham finished 11th in the table. Ipswich enjoyed a purple patch after signing Thijssen, winning 10, drawing six and losing only one of their 17 League games after his arrival. They also reached the quarter-final of the European Cup-Winners' Cup and were not disgraced in defeat to Barcelona, the eventual winners. Manchester City did not have the best of seasons in the League, but reached the quarter-finals of the UEFA Cup, with Deyna scoring during their European campaign. Like Ipswich, they were defeated by their competition's eventual winners, Borussia Moenchengladbach.

English football was confirmed as a vibrant place to work when Brian Clough's Nottingham Forest won the European Cup on 30 May, the winning goal scored by Trevor Francis. Two days later the AGM of the Football League decided that out-of-season loans of English-based players to the North American Soccer League were to be banned. In the summer of 1978, England had provided 129 players to the NASL. That was more than any other nation, including the USA. Trevor Francis had been one of them. It had meant that he'd only arrived back in England for the start of the 1978–79 League campaign a few hours before kick-off. Evidently it hadn't done him any harm but it had fuelled a season-long debate about conflicts of interests. The outcome was clear. England was now an importing nation, and it also wanted to hold on to its own.

Glory and war – Tottenham's Argentinians

Impact, honours and legacy are the hallmarks of any successful career. Ossie Ardiles and Ricky Villa provided White Hart Lane with all three during playing tenures that lasted a decade and five years respectively. They also brought glamour, a convergence of cultures, and drama. This was never more intense than in the successful FA Cup runs of 1981 and 1982. In the first they both

167

featured to the point of memorable triumph. In the second Spurs ultimately retained the trophy without them in the wake of the Falklands War.

The pair made their first appearances for Tottenham on 8 August 1978 in a pre-season friendly in Belgium against Royal Antwerp.

"They will stretch everyone in the team," Keith Burkinshaw said after the 3–1 win. "And considering they have had only one day's training, they fitted in far better than we could have hoped."

Some 200 travelling Tottenham fans had ticker-taped the pitch before kick-off in the Argentinians' honour. The next match on the pre-season tour, against Bohemians in Ireland, saw scenes of unadulterated frenzy.

"It was crazy," said Burkinshaw. "We had to be escorted everywhere by the police. The ground was absolutely packed. There were people standing on the roof. Everyone wanted to see Ossie and Ricky."

The same was true on their Football League debut, away to the defending champions, Nottingham Forest, on 19 August 1978. So large was the crowd at the City Ground that kick-off had to be delayed while the pitch was cleared of an overspill. The attendance of 41,223 was 10,000 above the average and would only be bettered that season – and by a few hundred – with the visit of Liverpool, who were then on their way to being champions.

The Forest match saw Ricky Villa score the equaliser in a 1–1 draw after Martin O'Neill had put the home side ahead. The headline-grabbing start was not maintained. On the Argentinians' home debut four days later, Spurs suffered a 1–4 drubbing against Aston Villa. Three days after that they were held 2–2 at home by Chelsea and in their next match, in the League Cup, they could only draw at Third Division Swansea. Before the replay, which ended in an embarrassing 3–1 home defeat to the Welsh side, a rampant Liverpool crashed seven goals past Spurs in the League at Anfield for no reply.

But taking these results in isolation, or even Tottenham's League placings of 11th, 14th and 10th in the Argentinians' first three seasons would be to miss the point. Their very presence spoke of ambition. Their flair and individual brilliance said that Burkinshsaw wanted to revive the glory days in glory fashion.

"Tottenham spectators were always looking for top technical players," he said. "They enhanced what we had at the time. They fitted in the way we wanted to play. I thought buying from abroad was a terrific idea at the time. I think what's gone wrong now is that there are so many, there are some teams with virtually no home-grown players. That's too many. They come for the money. Ossie and Ricky didn't come for the money. They were earning as much as our best players but that was it.

"We acquired a big house out near the training ground that took in the two lads and their wives and families and settled them down. Three or four months later they moved to their own houses next door to each other. Having them together made it a success. After six or eight months they had their own friends and settled well.

"Ossie was such a character. He was only small but on the field no-one could boss him. His feet never stopped moving, making positions for himself to receive the ball. He was always very aware of where everyone was. And his passing was unbelievable. So accurate. I'd not seen the like of it before. He was a big influence.

"Ricky was the better technical player. Glenn Hoddle was the best but Ricky wasn't far behind. The only thing I'd say was he wasn't the most consistent. If he started a match well, I knew he'd have a good performance. If not then I wasn't so sure.

"The other good thing is they looked after themselves. It was good for the younger players to see how they behaved. It was a sportsman's life, not the culture of going out and knocking back the pints."

Ardiles contends that it probably wasn't until the 1990s, and the arrival of the likes of Jurgen Klinsmann and Gianfranco Zola, that young home-grown players started deliberately copying the best continental habits in training and preparation.

"Certainly those players have had a major influence. They've brought in new diets, tactics, training, the whole lot. The bigger you are the more influence you have. If someone like Klinsmann runs better, eats better, trains harder, doesn't drink and plays better for it, you copy him. You have to be stupid not to follow the best examples."

But he also acknowledges that he and Villa were more aware of what they ate and drank than their British counterparts 25 years ago.

"When we arrived we never drank anything except Coca-Cola and water, maybe we had one glass of wine once a week with a meal. But the lifestyle [*of British players*], what they ate and drank, I was very surprised.

"The food was terrible. It was chips, sausages, greasy things, it was awful. The pre-match meals were heavy. Steak and chips, bread and butter. And that was on top of a full English breakfast in the morning."

He found the on-pitch fare almost as rudimentary. "I came into a team that was not the best. We had some talented players, like Glenn Hoddle, who was almost South American in his approach, but the style in general was very direct. It was like all the other English clubs at the time, except Liverpool. It bypassed the midfield. English players were fit, never say die, they ran more than us definitely, but there was still a long-ball mentality. I don't think it was unique in Europe, but even within Europe you could differentiate these things.

"In 1978 England was very, very isolated. Italy and Spain were very open to influence from the outside, especially from South America and Brazil. Other countries were more sceptical. England was the head of the sceptics. It took a while [*for Tottenham to improve*]. We were pretty bad. But when we started doing it as an 11 we got better."

The FA Cup final of 1981, which went to a replay against Manchester City, provided evidence of this, albeit after some drama. Ricky Villa was substituted in the initial 1–1 draw and left the pitch in tears.

"I took Ricky off and he didn't like it," Burkinshaw recalled. "I've said to him since 'You were having a stinker' and he's agreed, 'Yes I was.' When it happened I went into that dressing room afterwards and told him straight away that he was playing in the replay and that he needed to be ready."

Villa responded by scoring one of the most memorable goals in FA Cup history. His late winning strike came at the end of a powerful run where he rounded man after man before beating Joe Corrigan to make it 3–2. It was the defining moment in a Tottenham career that Ardiles contends was only ever, in Villa's mind, going to be temporary.

"We were exotic and people loved us for that," he said. "And then we played well, and they loved us for that. I enjoyed it and

I adapted myself a lot quicker than Ricky. Mentally he was different. People said before we came that he would be the one to survive and I'd had no chance because I was smaller.

"But Ricky had an approach where he always seemed to be getting ready for life back in Argentina while he was still in England. If I went out and bought a picture, for example, I'd be thinking 'That'll look good on the wall of my house'. I'd be thinking of my house in England, where I lived. If Ricky did the same he'd be thinking 'That'll look good in my house in Argentina'. He had a big farm there, cattle, it was his home. For me, once I'd arrived here, this was my home."

Conflict and confusion

Ardiles's attachment to his adopted country made the fallout from the Falklands War ever more painful. Keith Burkinshaw recalled how he first heard news of the conflict, on the morning of 3 April 1982.

"We were due to play in the FA Cup semi-final against Leicester at Villa Park that day. When everyone went to bed in the team hotel the night before everything was fine. The next morning the two lads told me that our countries were at war. They'd been up literally all night talking to people back home. They'd hardly slept. I had to make a decision whether or not to play them."

In the event, only Ardiles was picked to start and Spurs won 2–0. Burkinshaw recalled that Ardiles got "some terrible stick" from the crowd.

In the aftermath of the game there was intense media debate about whether or not it was right and proper for the Argentinians to continue playing for Tottenham while Britain was at war with their country. Matters were further complicated because Ardiles was due to return to Argentina to begin pre-World Cup training with his international side. When he left for Buenos Aires after the FA Cup semi-final, his departure was taken in some quarters as a political statement. Burkinshaw insists it was a pre-arranged move that had nothing to do with the Falklands.

"Before the semi-final, I'd already agreed that he could go home to prepare for the World Cup in Spain. The press said at the time it was because of the war. That was wrong. The decision had been made before the war even started."

Villa, who was not involved in the World Cup, stayed in England and played on during the war, although he removed himself from contention from the FA Cup final, played on 22 May while the hostilities were still raging. Spurs beat Queens Park Rangers 1–0 without him.

In early June, Ardiles was back in Europe, although not in England. The doubts still lingered about his future and many observers felt he would never play for Spurs again. Burkinshaw travelled to the Continent to meet him at the training camp where Argentina were preparing for their opening World Cup match on 13 June.

Ardiles told him: "It will not be possible for me to play for Tottenham again. We're at war."

It was an awkward meeting. Barely a month had passed since almost 400 Argentinian crew aboard the cruiser General Belgrano had been killed as their ship was torpedoed by the British outside the war zone, while sailing away from the islands. More recently, the battle of Goose Green had brought multiple deaths and injuries on both sides and reports of bloody hand-to-hand bayonet combat were filtering out. The Argentinians were also stepping up their air attacks on British landing craft, a policy that would claim dozens of lives.

"We're winning," Ardiles told an incredulous Burkinshaw.

"I don't think you are," Burkinshaw replied.

"I don't want to come back," Ardiles said.

"Well I'm not going to sell you," said Burkinshaw. "You can go somewhere on loan for 12 months but I'm not letting you go."

Burkinshaw recalled: "It seemed obvious that he'd been given all kinds of false information back home. The propaganda in Argentina had been drilled into him all the time. And then the war was all over a few days after that. In the end we agreed a loan deal to let him go to Paris St Germain but almost as soon as he got there he was on the phone saying 'Come and get me'."

Ardiles recalls the period as "an incredibly difficult time where it was hard to have an everyday life". He said:

"Tottenham never wanted me to leave but I thought returning to England would be a bad thing to do. My wife wanted to come back, Keith wanted me to come back. But I thought the best thing to do was leave. The scars were open, people had lost sons on both sides. We compromised and I went to France. I don't regret going and I don't regret coming back."

He returned to Tottenham in January 1983 and in his first match, away at Luton, he received vocal abuse from the home supporters. There had also been criticism from Argentina. Within a couple of months, by early March, Ricky Villa had decided to leave England. Ardiles remained, and went on to play for Spurs until March 1988, after which he had a brief playing spells with Blackburn and QPR before taking over as player-manager at Swindon Town. Between 1991 and 1994 he also managed at Newcastle, West Bromwich Albion and Tottenham with a variety of ups and downs. He continued his managerial career in Mexico, Japan (where his Shimizu S-Pulse side won three cups and were runners-up in the league), Croatia, Japan again (where the Yokohama Marinos topped the J-League), Saudi Arabia and Spain. In early 2003 he was managing in Argentina, with Ricky Villa as his assistant. In the summer of 2003 Ardiles moved back to manage in Japan.

Ardiles says that the best of his playing days were spent at Tottenham, not least in the later years, when Spurs finished as high as third in the league on two occasions. The highlight of his time in London though – and the second best moment of his playing career, after the 1978 World Cup – was the 1981 FA Cup win. Although Spurs won the UEFA Cup in 1984, Ardiles only appeared as a substitute in one leg of the final against Anderlecht. And in any case, he recalled that the FA Cup, in 1981 at least, was "the cup in the world. People always say it, but then it was really true. The FA Cup was better to win than the UEFA Cup. Now, it's unequivocally not. The European Champions' League is the cup to win. But then the FA Cup was the most prestigious."

Aside from the high point of 1981 and the low of the war, Ardiles picked out a third-round FA Cup replay win over Manchester United in 1980 as a particularly memorable moment. Many fans remember it best as the time when Glenn Hoddle was drafted in as an emergency goalkeeper in the second half. Ardiles remembers it best for scoring the only and decisive extra-time goal, in the 118th minute.

Away from the pitch, he endeared himself to supporters with his polite and gentle manner and never flinched from extra-curricular activity that might amuse supporters. No student of football songs is ever likely to forget that the 1981 FA Cup final was commemorated in verse beforehand in the genre 'classic', *Ossie's Dream (Spurs are on their way to Wembley)*, sung by the squad and accompanied by Chas n' Dave.

Surely no foreign player has, before or since, been honoured in such a way. The song began with the lines 'Ossie's going to Wembley/His knees have gone all trembly' and contained the following verse, in which Ardiles memorably sang the final – heavily accented – line:

In our ranks there's Ossie Ardiles

He's had a dream for a year or two

That one day he's gonna play at Wembley

Now his dream is coming true

Ossie we're gonna be behind you

All together, man for man

We know you're gonna play a blinder

In the cup for Tott-ing-ham!

In retrospect, the verse that included the lines 'We are the boys from Keithy's army/And we're marching off to war/We're sending our soldiers to Wembley/Under General Burkinshaw' was never one that Ardiles would be singing a year later, but it seemed light enough at the time.

War was a recurring theme for Ardiles in 1981. It was also the year he starred in John Huston's cult football movie, *Escape To Victory*, with such venerable acting talent as Michael Caine and Sylvester Stallone and alongside footballers including Pele, Bobby Moore, Mike Summerbee, Kazimierz Deyna and what seemed like half of Ipswich Town.

Legacy

Ardiles and Villa's footballing legacy was that they ushered in the era of the passing game. Keith Burkinshaw says:

"Now it's better than ever, more accurate, not just forwards but sideways and backwards, and with patience. That's one legacy."

Ardiles agrees, although he says it took "a long, long time" to happen.

Burkinshaw adds: "But there are other things we've lost. We've lost wingers, we've lost people with the ability to dribble, we don't run with the ball at people. At one time there'd be a lot of players like that, causing a threat."

The greatest intangible legacy lies in the memories of supporters, both of Tottenham and of football at large. Keith Palmer, a lifelong Spurs fan, said:

"I look back at those years with extreme reverence – a meeting of two worlds, a meeting of two peoples. The strong, cold, physical world of the northern hemisphere, and the flamboyant, skilful style of two South Americans who will remain in the hearts of Tottenham fans all over the world forever. Individual games did not matter as much as the effect their mere presence brought with them, and in an era before the English Premiership became the world's largest temp agency."

Steven Bridge, a Charlton fan and chronicler of the game through his photography for several decades, said:

"I'll never forget the slow motion footage of Ardiles doing this flick with the heel of his foot with the ball going up in the air. It was out of this world, and certainly not out of England. I'd never seen such a trick. Years later Ossie was to repeat it in *Escape To Victory.*"

Bridge recalled going to a Charlton match away at Everton in August 2000. One of the other Charlton fans travelling with him was a 17-year-old, Pete, who'd recently seen a video of Ardiles's party piece for the first time.

"We arrived on the coach early. We saw loads of kids playing football on Stanley Park. We fancied a bit of footy before the real thing, and so we challenged five teenagers to a game. During the game, at full speed, Pete did the Ardiles flick over their goalkeeper, rounded him, only to hit the post with his shot. But twenty years on, Ardiles's South American magic lived on and his influence was felt by a lad not even born when Ardiles entered English shores.

"I'm a Charlton fan through and through but I went to Ardiles's testimonial at White Hart Lane in 1986, paid good money to see a great player grace our game in England. Ardiles signed my programme. That's the test. I went the extra mile to get the autograph."

Bobby Robson's double Dutch

Bobby Robson had already transformed the fortunes of Ipswich Town by 1978, winning the FA Cup that year, having forged a successful team who regularly finished in the top six in the First Division. His side boasted England internationals including Mick Mills, Brian Talbot, Paul Mariner and Trevor Whymark as well as the youthful but experienced Scots, George Burley and John Wark. The club had played regular European football from 1973 onwards and there was plenty of evidence that Robson was becoming one of the leading managers in the country.

Yet the style of play was still essentially English, with an emphasis on getting the ball as quickly as possible from the defence to the attack. 'Total Football' it was not, but as a keen follower of the Dutch game, where Rinus Michels had pioneered that philosophy based on fluid movement and versatility, Robson aspired to try something new.

"I built some good teams at Ipswich but we did play quite direct football, from back to front, quite often," he recalled. "Get the ball up to Mariner, get the ball up to Whymark. That was all right but it used to break down a lot of the time so we used to bypass the midfield. I knew for us to improve and be a better team altogether we had to play a different form of football than we'd ever played. Through the midfield, with the midfield, passing the ball in sequence and get it up to the strikers in a better, more controlled way. And to do that you need to have top-class players, midfield players who can command the ball, turn on the ball, can accept the ball, deal with it."

His solution, once the transfer barrier came down, was to turn to The Netherlands. In particular he turned to Frans Thijssen and Arnold Muhren, two midfield players he'd first seen in action when they'd played against Ipswich for Twente Enschede in the UEFA Cup in 1973–74 and 1974–75.

Muhren arrived first, in August 1978, and was followed by Thijssen six months later. They were outstanding buys and would encapsulate all the benefits and none of the pitfalls of buying foreign talent. They were cheap, relatively speaking, being purchased for a combined total of £350,000, which was £100,000 less than the going rate for one English player of a similar quality at the time. In later years, managers would champion the purchase of foreign players on the grounds of cost. It had already been a factor since the 1970s.

The Dutchmen at Ipswich offered something different in their approach, mentally, physically and technically. England had few home-grown players with such lavish technical gifts and those that did exist, like Glenn Hoddle at Tottenham, were rare and expensive. Muhren and Thijssen also brought dedicated professionalism and good training and dietary habits.

"I just thought they were wonderful players," said Robson. "Highly technical players. Muhren was a beautiful passer of the ball, very educated left foot. Not a great defender but in possession he was outstanding. He could hit every pass in the book. Thijssen was a great dribbler. They were just what I needed to make my team."

Robson made his approach for Muhren after a lengthy period of solo clandestine scouting.

"I could get from Ipswich to Norwich by car in 40 minutes. I could get on a plane from Norwich and be in Amsterdam quickly and from there I could get anywhere. We played on a Saturday, then on the Sunday I could go into Holland, watch a Dutch game and I'd be back that night. I could get to Amsterdam quicker than I could get to Leicester or Nottingham, certainly quicker than I could be in Liverpool or Manchester... I didn't tell anybody, just got on a plane and I used to go and watch Dutch football. So I saw them play independent of our games against them."

Cost was a significant factor in the transfers.

"I saw in those two they'd be two ideal players. And they were cheap. I sold Talbot to Arsenal for £450,000, which was a large sum of money then. We'd just beaten Arsenal in the FA Cup in 1978 and Talbot had been outstanding. Terry Neill wanted to buy him and in the meantime I'd identified these two players so we sold Talbot for £450,000. We paid £150,000 for Muhren and £200,000 for Thijssen and put £100,000 in the bank and we brought two crème de la crème players to the club.

"They were sensational. They adapted themselves to the English style of football, which was a bit more rugged, a bit more competitive. They loved the English way of life, the English way of training. They adapted very well. They spoke English, as most Dutch people do, so that wasn't a problem. So their adaptation into the town wasn't too difficult. They just clicked. They just went straight in. I bought Muhren at the beginning of the season and Thijssen in the February. I tried to get them both together but they wouldn't sell. Then FC Twente had a bad year, the bad weather came along and they didn't play for six or seven weeks so the Dutch clubs weren't getting the money in so I went in and they were willing to sell Thijssen for £200,000. It was wonderful, and that was it. I'd seen them play and I was sure about them. They were just what we wanted. Two big pieces in a jigsaw.

"They were two players we didn't have. They were two players we couldn't get in England anyway. We didn't have two players like that in England. And if there was anyone else of that quality in the market, we couldn't afford it."

In the season before the Dutch moved to Suffolk, Ipswich finished 18th in the First Division. When Thijssen arrived, they were 13th but rallied to finish in 6th. They finished third in 1979–1980. The following season they were runners-up behind Aston Villa, won the UEFA Cup and reached the semi-final of the FA Cup before elimination by Manchester City. City would lose the final to the Tottenham of Ardiles and Villa. Ipswich players made a clean sweep of the end-of-year awards, with Thijssen winning the Football Writers' Footballer of the Year award, the first foreigner to do so since Bert Trautmann in 1956. Robson recalled:

"In 1981, that lovely Ipswich side that I created was brilliant but those two were marvellous architects of the way we played. They brought a different dimension to our game. They brought a different way of playing. They were terrific pros. They were non-drinkers, they were great trainers, they conducted themselves very well.

"Arnold Muhren could speak six languages. He could speak Dutch, English, German, French, Italian and Spanish. And he could switch from one language to another just like that. I said, 'How do you do that?'. He said, 'My upbringing'. He spoke *six* languages! And they were good lads. They loved our training, which was hard, and they loved the English type of game, more competitive, more pace, more power. They were great pros, punctual on the bus or train or reporting for training. Their application on the training ground was marvellous. They'd been brought up right. They'd had a good education in terms of preparation for football. Their diet, the way they ate, they looked after themselves… I wasn't conscious of what we were doing in the grand scheme of things. I didn't know it would be the beginning of a fleet of players. What I was doing was bringing two artists to the club."

Ipswich achieved another runners-up spot in the First Division in 1982, this time behind Liverpool, before Robson became the manager of England and Muhren moved on to Manchester United under Ron Atkinson. There, he was part of the FA Cup-winning side of 1983, scoring a penalty in the replay of the final against Brighton. He would demonstrate his longevity by returning, aged 34, to The Netherlands with Ajax, where he won the European Cup-Winners' Cup in 1987. He was also an integral part of a magnificent Dutch team – including Marco Van Basten and Ruud Gullit – who won the European Championship in 1988, beating England 3–1 along the way.

Thijssen left Ipswich in 1983 for a brief spell with Nottingham Forest before moving to Canada with the Vancouver Whitecaps. He returned to The Netherlands in the mid-1980s and continued playing until 1991, later becoming a manager. In April 2003, he was coming towards the end of a one-year coaching assignment with Al Whada, a club in the United Arab Emirates, and was planning to return to The Netherlands. Muhren, who had been running coaching clinics for promising players and had been attached to the development set-up at Ajax, was still involved in youth coaching.

A Pole apart

When the transfer barrier came down, two eastern European nations, Poland and Yugoslavia, become prominent providers of players throughout Europe. In Poland's case, this led to a renewal of the export relationship with England that had briefly flourished immediately after the Second World War (see Chapter Two). In Yugoslavia's case, the new rules led to players from that country coming to England for the first time.

The most prominent Pole to arrive in England in 1978–79 was Kazimierz Deyna, Poland's World Cup captain. The most prominent Yugoslav was the international defender, Ivan Golac. Deyna's time in the League was largely unfruitful. He played 38 First Division games for Manchester City and scored 12 goals in a two-year stay. Golac fared much better. He played more than 170 times for Southampton, where his swashbuckling style made him a fans' favourite. He also had loan spells at Bournemouth, Manchester City and Portsmouth before hanging up his boots and moving on to management. Both men's stories throw light on how England's search for international talent functioned at the time and also how one successful or prominent move could lead to the 'cluster effect' of several subsequent others.

Deyna's transfer was unwittingly inspired by the words of the BBC television commentator, Barry Davies, and the intervention of a Manchester-based football reporter. The reporter, John Roberts, was working for *The Guardian* at the time of the 1978 World Cup, a tournament he watched on television in England. During one of Poland's early games Davies made an off-the-cuff comment that Deyna would be interested in playing club football in Western Europe.

Roberts thought nothing more about it until he saw a news agency report, a few days after the World Cup, linking Manchester City with a possible move for Ossie Ardiles and Ricky Villa. To check out the story, he located City's chairman Peter Swales – who was on a trip to the theatre – and phoned him. Swales went to the box office to take Roberts's call and explained he'd been given an option to buy Ardiles and Villa but had not been entirely happy with the deal and had let it pass. He then invited Roberts to lunch.

"He told me City were looking for a midfield player and asked if I knew any who might be available," recalled Roberts. "I mentioned Deyna because I'd heard that BBC commentary."

Swales was interested. Since ending England's hopes of qualifying for the 1974 World Cup finals, costing Sir Alf Ramsey his job as manager, the Poles had established themselves as an international force. Swales also thought their style was similar enough to make the assimilation of a Polish player smooth.

Swales asked Roberts how City could go about making an approach and Roberts offered to talk to the Polish international coach, Jacek Gmoch. Roberts had met Gmoch when the latter had travelled to Manchester United to study training methods. Gmoch confirmed Deyna's interest. He told Roberts:

"I do not think there would be a great problem for a club like Manchester City to have Deyna. I know he would like to move and Manchester City seems to me to be the kind of club which would suit him. In my opinion, Deyna has enough stamina and ability to be able to offer at least two seasons in the highest grade of football anywhere in the world. He was feeling down, psychologically, after the World Cup finals, but that was to be expected and he is now as enthusiastic as ever."

City thus called upon the services of another Pole already at the club, a catering manager called George Bergier, to act as a go-between and interpreter. A complex series of negotiations began. City had to deal with, in turn, the Polish FA, the Polish Government, and the Polish army. The army had to agree to demobilise Lieutenant Deyna, a member of the army club, Legia Warsaw, for whom he had scored almost 200 goals in nearly 500 games. He eventually moved to Manchester in November 1978 in a deal that cost City around £100,000, comprising photo-copying machines, medical instruments and US dollars, which the Poles used to send their athletes abroad to prepare for the 1980 Moscow Olympics.

There was no doubt that Deyna was a skilful player. He was technically accomplished and had won a record 102 caps for his country at a time when the team was respected throughout Europe. But the culture shock of the bagatelle style in England did not suit him, or ultimately, City. When Malcolm Allison returned to Maine Road as the manager to succeed Tony Book, who'd signed Deyna, the Pole found himself playing in the reserves. This prompted him to say:

"City play ping-pong football. I don't need Malcolm Allison to tell me I am a great player. Pele told me I am a great player."

Although he outlasted Allison, who departed in 1980, the next manager, John Bond, also rejected his talents, selling him to the San Diego Sockers in January 1981. As Alan Durban, then the manager of First Division Stoke, said at the time:

"The problem is, Deyna's on a different wavelength. He's tuned to Radio Four, and the others are on Radio Luxemburg."

Deyna continued to play professionally until 1987 before becoming a coach in the US. He was killed in a car crash in California in 1989.

Following Deyna's move to Maine Road, a number of other well-known Poles were given permission to play abroad, which was unusual at the time. Tadeusz Nowak, a winger, joined First Division Bolton from Legia Warsaw in March 1979 but was unable to prevent relegation in 1979–80 and made just 24 League appearances over three seasons. Lower down the divisions, Ryszard Kowenicki, a midfielder, joined Oldham, while the international defender, Adam Musial, spent three seasons with Hereford from 1980.

The Yugoslavs

A more high-profile cluster of players, and at bigger clubs, came from Yugoslavia in the wake of Ivan Golac, the first player from that country in the League when he joined Southampton. The attraction for the English clubs was that they were hiring proven players at affordable prices. The lure for the players was partially money – they could earn more in England – but also the opportunity for career advancement. This often came within football, as the subsequent coaching careers of several showed, but also in other professions. Many of the migrant Yugoslav footballers were highly-educated men, and several went on to pursue careers as lawyers.

Among the cluster of players who moved to England in the late 1970s and early 1980s were the internationals Bozo Jankovic, Petar Borota, Raddy Avramovic and Raddy Antic.

Jankovic, a striker, joined Middlesbrough in February 1979. He took a while to adapt but was Boro's leading scorer in 1980–81. He later moved to France with Metz before becoming a coach back home and then the president of his first club, Zeljeznicar. He had trained to be a lawyer throughout his playing career but had to abandon his law practice in war-torn Sarajevo in the early 1990s. He died in 1993.

Borota, an extrovert goalkeeper, joined Chelsea from Partizan Belgrade in March 1979. He broke Peter Bonetti's record of 16 clean sheets in a season in 1980–81. He was also voted Player of the Year, twice, at Stamford Bridge. But his unpredictability was sometimes a little unsettling for his team-mates. He was even known to back-heel the ball to a team-mate in his own box to liven up a dull match, or move upfield for corners.

Avramovic, another goalkeeper, joined Notts County in August 1979 and was a key figure as they regained their First Division place in 1981 after an absence of 55 years. He was later released in a cost-cutting exercise and played briefly in Canada before joining Coventry in 1983. He was sacked after some poor displays and returned home to become a lawyer.

Raddy Antic, a midfielder, joined Luton Town in 1980 and helped them to win the Second Division title in 1981–82, then scored Luton's winner at Manchester City on the last day of the following season to preserve their top-flight status at City's expense. When his playing days were over, he embarked on a managerial career which by early 2003 had taken him to one of the world's most high-profile jobs in club football, at Barcelona.

Other Yugoslavs of the era in England included Nikola Jovanovic at Manchester United, Ivan Katalinic at Southampton, Dragoslav Stepanovic at Manchester City, Anton Mirocevic at Sheffield Wednesday, and Dzemal Hadziabdic and Ante Rajkovic at Swansea.

Ivan Golac stands out not just for his success with Southampton but for his later managerial success in Scotland. The high points in his career at The Dell included reaching the League Cup final of 1979, being voted the club's Player of the Year in 1980–81 and being part of the Saints' most successful ever League season, in 1983–84. Having returned to Yugoslavia in 1983, he rejoined Southampton during the title run-in during the spring of 1984. The team were in fifth place on the day of his first game back but his return to the defence inspired eight clean sheets in the last eleven games and only one goal conceded in each of the other three. Southampton finished second in the League, three points behind champions Liverpool.

Lawrie McMenemy, who signed Golac for Southampton, recalls the 1978 World Cup as a time "when everyone was getting a flavour for international football. It just seemed to have more impact".

McMenemy worked on the BBC's expert panel during the 1978 tournament. Shortly after it ended, he took a call from a friend, Tom Lawrence, who was an agent.

"Except he wasn't a football agent, they hardly existed in those days. He was a travel agent. He had this company offering tours abroad and he had a connection with a fella in Yugoslavia. The [*football*] system over there said players couldn't leave until they were 28 and they also had to be internationals. Golac fitted the bill.

"He came over and played in a pre-season friendly and I more or less had to make my mind up on that one game. I knew at half-time that I'd take him. He cost £50,000. By the end of the game we'd pretty much sorted out all the paperwork."

McMenemy recalls the post-match meal when Golac and his representative – who wore a cream suit and was therefore nicknamed 'The Ice Cream Man' – came over to his table and "stood to attention".

"They asked if we could go out for a walk to discuss things. It was very amusing, so formal. But it made an impression. Nowadays people take a lot of chances buying players but I always put a lot of store by character. Ivan had a wife and kids, was a good family man, you weigh all those things up. He was totally in awe of the British game. And he had one of the best record collections around. He loved pop music."

Aside from Golac's quality on the field, which he proved, the value for money he gave Southampton was also significant.

"The first day we went up to training we were driving past some houses in town," said McMenemy. "They were basic terrace houses with six-inch gardens and Ivan said how he impressed he was. I thought 'He'll not be hard to please'.

"It didn't take long for the standing to attention to wear off and his taste in houses soon changed but we never had any problem with his contracts. He was delighted just to come to England and he didn't get massive money for it. Pound for pound those players were better value than nowadays. Now there are players being pushed all over Europe and they're often mercenaries. The English Premier League is popular [*for football*] but don't let's kid ourselves, it also pays well."

Golac's managerial career began with Partizan Belgrade, whom he steered to the Yugoslav League and cup double in 1989. He briefly managed Torquay in 1992 and then made history in 1993 when he took over at Dundee United, becoming the first coach born outside Britain or Ireland to take charge of a Scottish League side. He won huge acclaim from the fans by guiding his side to their first ever Scottish FA Cup win in 1994, when they beat Rangers 1–0 in the final. He also endeared himself to supporters and players alike with his novel approach. On one occasion, after a 5–0 defeat, he fined every member of his team, and himself, £100 for the poor performance. He was sacked in 1995 but went on to coach elsewhere in Europe, including back in Yugoslavia. In December 2002, he took over as the manager of FC Karpaty Lviv in Ukraine.

If the British careers of players such as Golac and Raddy Antic ultimately prepared them for management, they also helped inspire later generations of east Europeans to move to England. Such players included Sergei Baltacha of the USSR, who became the first Soviet in the League when he moved to Ipswich in 1989. Baltacha's son, Sergei Jnr, who grew up in Suffolk and Scotland, has since played for the Scotland Under-21 side. His daughter, Elena, is ranked No1 in British women's tennis at the time of writing. Ipswich also had the first Bulgarian player in the League, Bontcho Guentchev, in 1992.

Other 'firsts' from eastern Europe and the Balkans included the Czech Republic's Ludek Miklosko, who first entered the League with West Ham in 1990, Romania's Stefan Iovan (who first arrived at Brighton in 1991), Croatia's Igor Stimac (Derby, 1995), Georgia's Georgi Kinkladze (Manchester City, 1995), Slovakia's Vladimir Kinder (Middlesbrough, 1997), Slovenia's Ales Krizan and Macedonia's Georgi Hristov (both Barnsley, 1997) and Moldova's Ivan Tistimetanu (Bristol City, 1998).

By the end of the 1990s, the English Leagues were the most diversely staffed in the world thanks to a process that started in 1978. Foreign players no longer stood out simply because they were foreign. They had to make a special impact to do that, as the following chapters show.

Seven Shades
Of Eric

"When the seagulls follow the trawler it is because they
think sardines will be thrown into the sea. Thank you."

Eric Cantona, March 1995

"If a Frenchman goes on about seagulls,
trawlers and sardines he is called a philosopher.
I'd just be called a short Scottish bum talking crap."

Gordon Strachan, a former team-mate, in response

ERIC CANTONA polarised opinion like no other footballer before
him.

Devotees were in thrall to his Rimbaud-reading, expressionist-
painting, philosophy-espousing ways. They adored his unique
talent, both as a player and as the inspiration who underpinned
a glorious decade at Manchester United. They appreciated that
he eschewed the trappings of success to live in modest
accommodation with his wife and two children. They warmed
to his generosity and humility.

Cantona's critics said he was a pretentious, garbage-spouting
lout. They said he was too volatile to be reliable. They said he
couldn't tackle and was useless in the hothouse of European
football. They said he was a head-case who deserved a jail

sentence because he couldn't control his temper. They asked why, if he was really so humble and uninterested in cashing-in on his fame, he exploited Rimbaud in Eurostar commercials and accepted the Nike dollar with such gusto? And as for humility, they asked 'What humility?'.

It was a trait not widely attributed to a man, nicknamed 'Le Dieu', who took to the pitch with upturned collar, the epitome of arrogance. A different story is told by those who got close to him, including Alex Fynn, who worked for Saatchi & Saatchi and was involved in the blueprint for the Premier League. A writer on the business of football, he also worked as a consultant for Manchester United, and was asked to help Cantona with two projects in 1996.

"Eric was obliged to produce a book and a video as part of his contract with Manchester United," Fynn recalled. "My job was to make it as painless as possible for him. I hired a commercials director to do the video, which took a couple of afternoons. For the book, [*Cantona On Cantona*] I sat down with him and asked him questions, in French. He replied and then the answers were translated later."

It was a simple enough exercise and was proceeding steadily when at one point Fynn wondered whether Cantona was enjoying the process.

"In the middle of the conversation I stopped and asked him 'Do you like me?' "

Cantona, slightly nonplussed, replied: "Yes."

"Is it because you've found someone who speaks French worse than you speak English?" Fynn asked.

Cantona was not renowned for his use of English. He could speak it, certainly, although former team-mates tell how he would underplay his ability if he felt uncommunicative. It had been, at times, a touchy subject.

"But he just laughed," Fynn said. "Some people had this image of a pompous individual but he wasn't like that."

At a later meeting, Fynn discovered that Cantona seemed genuinely reluctant to milk his image for cash.

"He was such a commodity it would have been easy for him to transcend the game. I did one presentation for him about how he could become a brand, much the same way Ayrton Senna had become a brand, popular well outside the boundaries of his own sport. After the presentation we had a discussion and Eric said he didn't need the money or the hassle."

Regardless of the divergence of opinion, there is no doubt that during Cantona's five years at Old Trafford the landscape of English football changed beyond recognition and that he was a major catalyst. His first season at United, 1992–93, ended in triumph with the club's first title for 26 years. His second season, 1993–94, ended with United's first League and FA Cup Double. Had he not kung-fu kicked an opposition supporter in January 1995, earning himself an eight-month worldwide ban, a back-to-back Double would have been probable. Instead the second Double came in 1996, followed by another League title in 1997. It was Cantona's fifth title in six years because he'd also won the League with Leeds in 1992.

The hard facts of his influence were plain to see, domestically at least. His playing record, examined in detail later in this chapter, shows that United were a better team when he was on the pitch. They were more likely to win. They scored more goals per game. They conceded fewer. Those margins matter in football and Cantona was influential by a margin. Even in the period after his ban, when the statistics show his ability to turn a game was on the wane, one purple patch saw him almost single-handedly drive United to the 1996 Double with goal after match-winning goal.

Manchester United's torrent of success established them as the No1 football club in England and the most valuable in the world. It was a heady transition. As recently as 1989, the self-styled 'millionaire property tycoon' Michael Knighton had been on the verge of buying United for £20m plus the promise that he'd invest another £10m, badly needed for investment in facilities and the squad. The deal fell through because the money failed to materialise but it acted as a marker of where United – and football – stood in the immediate post-Hillsbrough era. A decade later, after years of success, kick-started by Cantona, United were the most successful club in the world's richest league and were being courted by billionaire media moguls. They were also well on the way to being the first £1bn sports club in history.

"He was born to play for United," Alex Ferguson once said of his French captain. "Some players, with respected and established reputations, are cowed and broken by the size and expectations. Not Eric. He swaggered in, stuck his chest out, raised his head and surveyed everything as if to ask: 'I'm Cantona, how big are you? Are you big enough for me?' "

Cantona was not the first Frenchman in the League, nor even the first to land a ban for hot-headed kicking. Eugene Langenove (see Chapter One) fulfilled both those criteria in the 1920s. But he was the first Frenchman to win anything in England. And he was the first foreign player ever to be voted Footballer of the Year by his peers when he won the PFA's version of that award in 1994.

He brought a new dimension to the English game. He blazed a trail for French football, which by 2003 had comfortably overtaken every other nation as the largest provider of players to the League. His accomplishments proved the value it was possible to win from a gamble on a foreigner.

The irony of his achievements in England is that he only ever crossed the Channel because he felt unable to function in France. He rebelled against the system that would go on to produce a golden generation of World Cup and European champions. Instead he took the burning desire of his singular approach to the English game. It collided with a monolithic culture and won.

Shades of Eric No1: Accommodating l'étranger

"Eric gives interviews on art, philosophy and politics.
A natural room-mate for David Batty, I thought immediately."
Howard Wilkinson, manager of Leeds, after hiring Cantona in 1992

"We're a team who shout a lot and at the moment Eric is
not getting all the messages. He's an excellent player –
it's just a pity he wasn't born in Barnsley."
Howard Wilkinson, on adjusting to Cantona

"Eric likes to do what he likes, when he likes, because he
likes it, and then fuck off – we'd all like a bit of that."
Howard Wilkinson, post-Cantona

When Cantona arrived in England, he arrived with 'previous'. A trawler-load of previous. Trouble was as common as trophies. In a career where few years saw nothing for the mantelpiece, that was saying something. Only his first three seasons, from his debut for Auxerre, aged 17 in 1983, until the last year of his tenure there, were largely uncontroversial.

He built a gritty reputation – attributed in part to his Marseille upbringing – that would earn the first of 43 French caps in 1987, the year he paid his first heavy fine. His crime had been to punch a goalkeeper in the face, giving him a black eye. The fine would probably have been bigger if his victim hadn't been his own goalkeeper.

He moved to Marseille in July 1988 for a then-record fee of 22m francs (£2.2m). Despite a decent start, in August he was left out of Henri Michel's next international squad. Cantona reacted by calling Michel a "sac à merde" (sack of shit). It would have been wiser not to do this on television. Cantona was suspended from the French team for a year.

Five months later he was suspended indefinitely by Marseille after having a tantrum in a European game against Torpedo Moscow. After being substituted, he kicked the ball into the crowd, took off his shirt, threw it to the ground and left the pitch with his head held high. He joined Bordeaux on loan, briefly, before transferring to Montpellier for a seventh of the fee that had taken him to Marseille.

A series of disputes at Montpellier culminated in a 10-day suspension after Cantona smashed his boots into the face of a team-mate, Jean-Claude Lemoult. The pair put the incident behind them and went on to win the French Cup that year although Cantona returned to Marseille soon afterwards. He made a good start to the 1990–91 season, scoring nine goals in 12 matches under the coaching guidance of Franz Beckenbauer. A knee injury then curtailed his season and when he returned to action, he found himself on the bench, from where he watched Marseille lose the 1991 European Cup final on penalties.

In 1991 he moved to Nîmes, newly promoted to the French First Division. He was attracted by the prospect of joining a dynamic young team but poor results frustrated him. On 7 December in a match with St Etienne, he flew into a rage after what he perceived to be a poor refereeing decision. He threw the ball in the official's face. He walked off the pitch before the inevitable red card was shown. He was banned for three games. At his disciplinary hearing, he walked up to each member of the committee in turn and said "Idiot". His ban was increased to two months and he responded by announcing his retirement from football.

His exile did not last long. By January 1992 he was in England, having a trial with Sheffield Wednesday. His rationale was that a new country, any new country, would give him a chance to wipe the slate clean. He had been at Hillsborough for a week when the manager, Trevor Francis, suggested he spend another seven days being assessed. He promptly left to join Leeds, managed by Howard Wilkinson.

Cantona made his League debut on 8 February 1992 as his new side, who were in a neck-and-neck battle for the title with Manchester United, lost 2–0 at Oldham. He went on to make 15 consecutive appearances until the end of the season. Manchester United faltered, losing three of their last four games, to finish runners-up. Leeds won the title. In Cantona's first season in England they were the last team, to date, to win the title with an English manager.

At the start of the inaugural season of the Premier League in 1992–93, Cantona scored a hat-trick in the Charity Shield and then six more goals in 13 games in the League. His relationship with Wilkinson had soured however, and by December 1992, Cantona had been sold to Manchester United for £1.2m.

Shades of Eric No2: Becoming an Old Trafford talisman

"One minute I'm thinking 'Who's that ugly, French, one-eyebrowed git?'. Then one trip over the Pennines and suddenly there's this dark, brooding, Heathcliff-type figure on the horizon."
Lizzie from Bolton, a Manchester United fan, in an article entitled 'One for the Ladies', in the United fanzine, *Red Issue*

"He certainly deserves the captaincy of France as far his talent is concerned but I'm not sure about his cultural knowledge, which seems pretty basic to me."
Claude Simonet, president of the French FA, 1994

"The only English I've heard from him is 'Goal!' "
Steve Bruce, team-mate of Cantona at United

"No-one should have any doubt about the massive
influence made by Eric Cantona. He brought priceless
presence and style to the team."

Alex Ferguson, manager of Manchester United

At the end of one of his first training sessions with Manchester
United, Cantona approached Alex Ferguson and asked if he
could borrow a couple of players – he wanted to continue
practising and it was helpful to have someone crossing the ball
and someone in goal to make the session a little more realistic.
It was a key moment in the manager's relationship with his new
player, the moment he felt vindicated about his potentially risky
purchase.

Within days of his first extended training session, Cantona
was being accompanied not by youngsters drafted in to help
him, but by volunteers including David Beckham, Ryan Giggs,
Paul Scholes and the Neville brothers, who would go on to be
the spine of United's team in later years.

"Players like myself, the Nevs, Butty, Scholes and Becks stay
behind and practise, things like free-kicks and shooting," said
Giggs in an interview the year after Cantona left United. "We've
always done it because that was what Eric always used to do. We
just learned from his actions, the way he played and trained."

As Ferguson wrote in his autobiography:

> Many people have justifiably acclaimed
> Cantona as a catalyst who had a crucial
> impact on our successes... but nothing
> he did in matches meant more than
> the way he opened my eyes to the
> indispensability of practice.

It said much about the English game in the early 1990s that one
player should stand out so prominently simply by doing more than
was required in training. But then he also made a huge impact on
the pitch, at domestic level at least. Specifically, what stood out was
his imagination, his control, his passing, his long-range shots, his
clinical touch close up and his ability to squeeze the best from a
small amount of space in no time at all. Not to mention his utter
commitment to winning. The back-heeled passes, the chips, the
lobs and the volleys on turn were the icing on the cake.

Ask Manchester United fans to name special or important
goals between 1993 and 1997 and several of Cantona's 80 will

almost certainly feature. A breathtaking volley against Wimbledon in the FA Cup run of 1994, perhaps. Or his two penalties in the final against Chelsea the same year. Or the two goals in the first Manchester derby of that season, that helped turn a 2–0 half-time deficit to a 3–2 full-time win. Or both goals in the reverse fixture, which ended 2–0 to United.

There was a delicate chip that defied the wind of Bramall Lane against Sheffield United the following year. Cantona stood, a trademark statue, as the home fans watched in disbelief. And then there was the purple patch of 1995–96. On his return from his eight-month ban, facing Liverpool, he made the first goal for Nicky Butt and then scored the equaliser from a penalty in a 2–2 draw. Five months later he embarked on a six-match run of scoring in every League game, including, crucially, in a 1–0 win at title rivals Newcastle. Two months after that he scored the only goal in the FA Cup final against Liverpool.

The downside was Cantona's disciplinary record and occasional lapses into reckless, even callous, challenges. Bookings were frequent and he was the only United player, up to 1997 (the year of his departure), to be dismissed in consecutive matches. That pair of red cards came against Swindon, when he inexplicably stamped on John Moncur, and then against Arsenal, for two bookable offences. He had also seen red in Europe, at Galatasaray, after calling into question the referee's honesty. His most notorious transgression, however, arguably the most notorious in English football had ever seen, involved neither a player nor an official.

Shades of Eric No3: The kick

Four minutes into the second half of Manchester United's League game at Crystal Palace on 25 January 1995, Cantona kicked an opponent, Richard Shaw, and was sent off. Walking towards the dressing rooms, he suddenly jumped into the crowd. He leapt feet first in kung fu style, kicking an abusive Palace supporter, Matthew Simmons, a 21-year double-glazing fitter, in the chest. As soon as he was back on his feet Cantona started raining punches on the supporter, until dragged away. The event and its repercussions became headline news around the world for weeks.

The following day, Simmons made an official complaint against Cantona to the police. The Football Association released a statement saying it was appalled by the incident, which it said brought shame on those involved and on the game. Cantona was given 14 days to answer charges of bringing the game into disrepute.

Former players, pundits, commentators and even people who knew nothing of football began calling for the Frenchman to be banned from the English game for life.

"Pressure was no excuse," said Sir Stanley Matthews, who was never booked during his career. "I would take any amount of personal abuse for £10,000 a week."

"He's nothing more than a brat," said Jimmy Hill.

"He's a genius but there is this other side to him," said Chris Waddle, who'd played alongside Cantona at Marseille. "Maybe he needs someone to examine him, a psychiatrist or something."

"What I don't understand is how a Frenchman can be playing for Manchester United," said Lord Denning. "He's not even from England. They employ him to play football for them, not to go round hitting people."

The reaction in France varied from philosophical to disgusted. An editorial in *Le Monde* said:

> In leaping the barrier, boots first, Eric Cantona attacked English football in its most sensitive spot. The British have succeeded in eliminating football violence to the point where the hideous metal fences supposed to protect the players have disappeared from their grounds. Now they have to acknowledge that the hooligans are on the pitch, threatening the public.

Another newspaper, *Le Provençal*, stated:

> We're no longer interested in his escapades, his pseudo philosophical bragging, his crudeness and the state of his soul. He lives his life and we live ours and we don't miss him.

Manchester United maintained their silence until 27 January, when they announced that they had suspended Cantona for four months, until the end of the season, and had fined him the maximum allowed, two weeks' wages, or £20,000. The same day, the French FA announced Cantona had been stripped of his captaincy of the national side. Simmons meanwhile, who had been revealed as having a conviction for assault and close ties to far-right groups, was banned from Crystal Palace for the season.

Cantona took his family on holiday to the Caribbean but remained front-page news. In one incident he allegedly attacked a reporter from ITN News, sent to track him down in Guadeloupe. The reporter, Terry Lloyd, a veteran war correspondent who died in a 'friendly fire' incident in the 2003 war on Iraq, said after his run-in with Cantona that he had "never been so frightened". He said he was put into a headlock and was then on the receiving end of a kick similar to that meted out to Simmons. After the Guadeloupe episode, Cantona's lawyers said they were considering suing ITN for invasion of privacy.

Those weeks in early 1995 were a tawdry time for the English game and its relationship with foreign players. Arsenal sacked their manager, George Graham, for "failing to act in the interests of the club", having accepted undeclared payments from the Norwegian agent, Rune Hauge, after buying foreign players. These events would later be scrutinised in a 'bungs' inquiry that would shake football. Graham's sacking came on the day Cantona was charged with common assault for his attack on Simmons.

Not long afterwards, in a completely unrelated inquiry, three footballers – the Zimbabwean goalkeeper, Southampton's Bruce Grobbelaar, the Dutch goalkeeper, Wimbledon's Hans Segers, and John Fashanu, a team-mate of Segers – were arrested on claims of match-fixing masterminded by a Far Eastern betting syndicate. They were eventually cleared in 1997 after two trials that lasted 17 weeks and cost the British taxpayers £12m but in 1995 the game's reputation was mud.

Before that trio's arrest came Cantona's disciplinary hearing with the FA, on 24 February. Cantona had already written to the FA, giving his side of the story, saying that Simmons had insulted him racially, causing him to react impulsively. He had asked the FA to take into account his regret and his club's punishment.

Simmons, during his own later trial for using threatening language and behaviour at the Manchester United game, claimed:

"I was shouting 'Off, off, off!', and I was pointing towards the dressing room 'cos that's what you do at football games. At no time was I doing anything else than pointing. I did not use any language of this kind. At no stage did I swear and I am quite certain of that. As far as I am concerned I was doing nothing wrong to deserve these actions. I was teasing Cantona but there is a big difference between a criminal offence and what you would call banter at a football match."

Simmons was subsequently found guilty of two charges of using threatening words and behaviour during the Cantona incident. When he appeared for sentence he was jailed for seven days for contempt of court for attacking a lawyer during those proceedings. As police overpowered him, he tried to attack the prosecuting counsel, he shouted: "I am innocent. I swear on the Bible. You Press. You are scum!"

It was never officially established what Simmons had said to Cantona, although it was thought to be derogatory about his nationality, and rather 'industrial'. A friend of Simmons was quoted in *The Guardian* newspaper as saying:

"He [*Cantona*] should be deported. We were giving him verbals. It was just the usual stuff about him being French. That's why you pay your £20."

None of this had any bearing on Cantona's FA hearing. The FA Commission's task was simply to consider the evidence before them in February and decide how to proceed. Graham Kelly, the FA's chief executive and an admirer of Cantona's football, was acutely aware that the spotlight was on his organisation and how they handled the issue. He did not, however, want to see Cantona lost to the English game so contacted him privately before the hearing to give him some advice. He advised Cantona that he had to make it clear he was sorry. Although he did not say so to Cantona, there could be no repeat of the "Idiots" situation of years before in France.

The hearing Commission included a director of Oldham, Ian Stott, who caused mirth among the Manchester United contingent at one point by asking Cantona: "Isn't it a fact that you're a kung fu expert?"

Cantona was confused by the question but his representatives stepped in to say that no, he was not.

The proceedings had been going for more than three hours when Cantona was called to speak. Kelly recalled how Cantona said that he wanted to apologise to all concerned, including Manchester United, his team-mates, the United fans and the FA. And then, right at the end, in a gesture that showed he wasn't quite ready to bow and scrape completely, he added: "And I want to apologise to the prostitute who shared my bed last evening."

The Commission doubled the ban that United had handed out to eight months. They also fined Cantona £10,000. A month later, after his court case for assault, he was sentenced to two weeks in jail. He was bailed pending appeal, which he subsequently won. His sentence was commuted to 120 hours' community service on 31 March. On hearing the news he hosted a press conference. He sat down, said one sentence about seagulls, a trawler and prawns, sipping water for dramatic effect after the first three words. He added "Thank you" and left.

A surreal afternoon – during which this French anti-hero had talked nonsense having had a jail sentence rescinded after kicking a loutish football supporter – was completed when a 13-year-old boy, a fan from Kent called Sebastian Pennells, handed Cantona a greeting card on his way out. Inside it was the message: 'Eric is an idol, Eric is a star, If my mother had her way, He would also be my Pa.' While David Beckham can claim a strange existence in 2003, Cantona had his share of bizarre moments.

After some doubts over whether he would stay in England, he signed a new three-year contract with United on 28 April 1995, a couple of weeks before United ceded the League title to Blackburn Rovers on the final day of the season by a single point. Blackburn actually lost their last match against Liverpool but United, without Cantona, could only draw at West Ham and failed to overtake them. A Cantona-less United also lost in the FA Cup final that year, 1–0 to Everton.

"Nobody in the history of football has been punished as hard as Eric but he has never said a word about it or complained. He is so mild mannered when the volcano is not erupting inside him."

Alex Ferguson, during Cantona's ban

"Wasn't it good to see Eric Cantona back in action?
Let's hope this time he remembers that kicking people
in the teeth is the Tory Government's job."

Tony Blair, as leader of the opposition, addressing the Labour Party
conference of 1995, shortly after Cantona's ban ended

"I'd hesitate to say that what happened was a mistake,
or that it was foolish or silly. It was far too complicated
to be characterised in such a way."

Cantona, 1996, reflecting on 'The kick'

Shades of Eric No4: Renaissance

Between 22 January and 5 May 1996, Manchester United played
15 Premiership games, winning 13, drawing one and losing one.
Cantona played in every one, scoring in nine of them. At one
stage he scored vital goals in six consecutive League games.
He also played in all seven of United's FA Cup games between
6 January and 11 May, scoring in five of them, including the only
goal of the final against Liverpool.

In May 1996, Cantona was voted the Footballer of the Year
by the Football Writers' Association, becoming the fourth
foreign player – and the first Frenchman – to win the award.
He followed in the footsteps of Bert Trautmann (1956), Frans
Thijssen (1981) and Jurgen Klinsmann (1994).

A purple patch for the King – 20 games in 1996

Date	Comp	Scoreline				Cantona goals
22 January	PL	West Ham	0	Man Utd	1	1
27 January	FAC (4r)	Reading	0	Man Utd	3	1
3 February	PL	Wimbledon	2	Man Utd	4	2
10 February	PL	Man Utd	1	Blackburn	0	–
18 February	FAC (5r)	Man Utd	2	Man City	1	1
21 February	PL	Man Utd	2	Everton	0	–
25 February	PL	Bolton	0	Man Utd	6	–
4 March	PL	Newcastle	0	Man Utd	1	1
11 March	FAC (6r)	Man Utd	2	Southampton	0	1
16 March	PL	QPR	1	Man Utd	1	1
20 March	PL	Man Utd	1	Arsenal	0	1
24 March	PL	Man Utd	1	Tottenham	0	1
31 March	FAC (sf)	Chelsea	1	Man Utd	2	–
6 April	PL	Man City	2	Man Utd	3	1
8 April	PL	Man Utd	1	Coventry	0	1
13 April	PL	Southampton	3	Man Utd	1	–
17 April	PL	Man Utd	1	Leeds	0	–
28 April	PL	Man Utd	5	Nottm Forest	0	1
5 May	PL	Middlesbrough	0	Man Utd	3	–
11 May	FAC (final)	Liverpool	0	Man Utd	1	1

PL= Premier League match; FAC= FA Cup match

Shades of Eric No5: Statistics, success and the sticky issue of Europe

Throughout Eric Cantona's time at Old Trafford, Manchester United played 250 games combined in the Premiership, the Coca-Cola Cup, the FA Cup and in Europe. Cantona played in 182 of them, scoring 80 goals, or 0.44 goals per game. In his peak season in the Premier League, in 1994–95 before his ban, he scored 0.57 goals per game. He eclipsed that figure in the FA Cup, scoring 0.59 goals per game over four years in 17 matches, only one of which United lost. His worst season in the Premier League was his last, when he scored 0.31 goals per game, the same strike rate he achieved in European competition.

Statistically, Cantona was a positive influence over the length of his United career. During that time, the club won 5.8 per cent more games when he played, drew 3.6 per cent more and lost 9.4 per cent less. They scored 0.26 goals per game more when he played and conceded 0.06 goals per game fewer.

The effect of his ban can be broadly seen by United's statistics 'pre-kick' and 'post-kick'. Between signing for the club and that fateful day at Selhurst Park, United won 12.6 per cent more games when Cantona was in the team, drew 9.2 per cent more and lost 21.8 per cent less. They scored almost half a goal per game more and conceded almost a quarter of a goal per game less. After his return, the 'Cantona effect' was actually slightly detrimental overall. There are, of course, lies, damned lies and statistics, because the 'post-kick' era also contained the purple patch of 1996. But the following details should give some indication of quite how valuable Cantona was to United.

Manchester United's Record During The Cantona Era

The summary

Premier League winners: 1993, 1994, 1996, 1997

Premier League runners-up: 1995 (Cantona suspended from Jan 1995 to end of season)

FA Cup winners: 1994, 1996

FA Cup runners-up: 1995 (while Cantona was suspended)

Other FA Cup runs: 1992–93, United were knocked out in fifth round by Sheffield United, Cantona was not playing. 1996–1997, United were knocked out by Wimbledon in a fourth-round replay. Cantona played. It was the only FA Cup match he lost from 17 contested

Coca-Cola Cup runners-up: 1994 (Cantona played five of the six Coca-Cola Cup games of his career during that season. The defeat in the final to Aston Villa was his only Coca-Cola Cup defeat)

European Cup/Champions' League

1993–94: Second-round exit to Galatasaray (Cantona was sent off at the end of the second leg)

1994–95: Eliminated after group stage (Cantona was serving a European suspension for four of six games)

1996–97: Semi-final exit to Borussia Dortmund (Cantona played 10 games during the campaign)

UEFA Cup

1995–96: First-round exit to Rotor Volgograd (Cantona was not playing, still suspended after 'The kick')

The statistics

OVERALL: Premier League, FA Cup, Coca-Cola Cup & European Cup

	P	W	D	L	F	A	
Man Utd	250	154	58	38	469	225	
without Cantona	68	39	14	15	115	64	
with Cantona	182	115	44	23	354	161	(80 Cantona goals)

	% Won	% Drawn	% Lost	Goals per game
without Cantona	57.4	20.6	22	F: 1.69 A: 0.94
with Cantona	63.2	24.2	12.6	F: 1.95 A: 0.88
The Cantona effect	+5.8	+3.6	-9.4	+0.26 -0.06

PREMIER LEAGUE

1992–93	P	W	D	L	F	A	
Man Utd	25	17	6	2	49	19	9 Cantona goals =
with Cantona	22	15	6	1	44	16	0.41 goals per game

1993–94	P	W	D	L	F	A	
Man Utd	42	27	11	4	80	38	18 Cantona goals =
with Cantona	34	23	10	1	72	31	0.53 goals per game

1994–95	P	W	D	L	F	A	
Man Utd	42	26	10	6	77	28	12 Cantona goals =
with Cantona	21	13	5	3	40	17	0.57 goals per game

1995–96	P	W	D	L	F	A	
Man Utd	38	25	7	6	73	35	14 Cantona goals =
with Cantona	30	19	6	5	58	27	0.47 goals per game

1996–97	P	W	D	L	F	A	
Man Utd	38	21	12	5	76	44	11 Cantona goals =
with Cantona	36	20	11	5	73	42	0.31 goals per game

The statistics (continued)

FA CUP: Five seasons, 1992–93 to 1996–97 inclusive

	P	W	D	L	F	A	
Man Utd	27	20	4	3	55	18	10 Cantona goals =
with Cantona	17	14	2	1·	34	8	0.59 goals per game

COCA-COLA CUP: Cantona played during two seasons, 1993–94 and 1995–96

	P	W	D	L	F	A	
Man Utd	16	10	1	5	28	19	1 Cantona goal =
with Cantona	6	4	1	1	10	6	0.17 goals per game

EUROPEAN CUP: Three seasons, 1993–94, 1994–95 & 1996–97

	P	W	D	L	F	A	
Man Utd	22	8	7	7	31	24	5 Cantona goals =
with Cantona	16	7	3	6	23	14	0.31 goals per game

Before and after 'The kick'

Before 'The kick'	P	W	D	L	F	A	
Man Utd	126	81	29	16	242	112	47 Cantona goals =
without Cantona	31	17	5	9	49	33	
with Cantona	95	64	24	7	193	79	0.49 goals per game

	% Won	% Drawn	% Lost	Goals per game
without Cantona	54.8	16.1	29.1	F: 1.58 A: 1.06
with Cantona	67.4	25.3	7.3	F: 2.03 A: 0.83
The Cantona effect	+12.6	+9.2	-21.8	+0.45 -0.23

After 'The kick'	P	W	D	L	F	A	
Man Utd	124	73	29	22	227	113	33 Cantona goals =
without Cantona	37	22	9	6	66	31	
with Cantona	87	51	20	16	161	82	0.38 goals per game

	% Won	% Drawn	% Lost	Goals per game
without Cantona	59.5	24.3	16.2	F: 1.78 A: 0.84
with Cantona	58.6	23	18.4	F: 1.85 A: 0.94
The Cantona effect	-0.9	-1.3	+1.8	+0.07 +0.1

The sticky issue of Europe

	P	W	D	L	F	A	
Man Utd	22	8	7	7	31	24	5 Cantona goals
with Cantona	16	7	3	6	23	14	0.31 goals per game
without Cantona	6	1	4	1	8	10	

	% Won	% Drawn	% Lost	Goals per game
without Cantona	16.7	66.6	16.7	F: 1.33 A: 1.67
with Cantona	43.7	18.7	37.6	F: 1.44 A: 0.88
The Cantona effect	+27	-47.9	+20.9	+0.11 -0.79

Cantona played in 16 European matches for Manchester United over three European Cup campaigns, in 1993–94, 1994–95 and 1996–97. There is no doubt he failed to make his mark, as his goal contribution, let alone his performances, showed. The first of those campaigns saw an aggregate preliminary-round win over Kispest Honved (in which Cantona scored), and then a defeat, on away goals, to Galatasaray. The second leg of that tie saw a lacklustre Cantona display and ended with him being sent off after the final whistle. A four-game ban from Europe followed.

By the time he returned to the European stage, United had already played four games from six in the Champions' League group stage of the 1994–95 competition. They had won one, drawn two and lost one, making the next match, against Gothenburg, crucial. Cantona was ineffective, meaning that even though the last game ended in a 4–0 win, United were eliminated on goal difference.

Cantona did not play in Europe the following season as United were knocked out of the UEFA Cup by Rotor Volgograd. He was still serving his ban for 'The kick'. Which left only one other European campaign in his United career, the 1996–97 European Cup, when his side reached the semi-final.

In the group stage, he scored twice, once at home to Rapid Vienna and once away in Fenerbahce. The latter goal was scored in what was probably his best European performance. At least United played as expected against moderate opponents and Cantona played his part. But in four other games in that year's competition, he played below par. Two of them were in group-stage losses to Juventus. The other two, crucially, were in the semi-final against Borussia Dortmund. He featured as a marginal figure in the 1–0 away leg and was hustled off the ball for the Germans' goal. In the home leg, which United also lost 1–0, he was sluggish and missed chances he would normally have been expected to convert.

In short, in the key games, against Galatasary, against Gothenburg and especially against Dortmund, he failed to make an impact. It was to his great credit that he rarely, if ever, failed to make an impact domestically and to United's regret that he failed to make that impact on Europe's biggest stage. His exclusion from his national side, which coincided with his worst displays in Europe, probably had something to do with his inability to cope in international club football.

Alex Ferguson admitted that there was "perhaps some kind of mental block" that stopped him from playing at his best at the highest level.

> There was an element in his nature that seemed to prevent him from realising the full potential of his incredible gifts.

Shades of Eric No6: Departure

The morning after Manchester United's European Cup semi-final defeat to Dortmund, Cantona told Alex Ferguson he wanted to retire from football. As the season drew to a close, Ferguson leaned towards agreement with the decision. As he wrote in his autobiography:

> Seeing the dullness in his eyes, and the changing outline of his physique, I had to acknowledge that perhaps he was right to terminate his career before blatant decline became an insult to the fierce pride that burned in him.

Cantona made his decision final a few days after United won their fourth title in five years. The club announced the decision on Sunday 18 May 1997. Cantona had gone before the news broke, leaving only a note. It said:

"I have played professional football for 13 years, which is a long time. I now wish to do other things."

Ferguson faced the press, telling them:

"It's a sad day for United that he has decided to retire. He has been a fantastic player."

The Cantona era was over.

> "The danger with games is that you can get tired of them.
> That's why I swapped soccer for cinema in the way a
> child takes up playing Cluedo when he is sick of Monopoly.
> But I'm still interested in football. It is like when you
> leave a woman and you don't cry when she goes off
> with someone else."
>
> Eric Cantona, 1998

"He's a footballer, a thug and he's French."
Gavin Stamp, art critic, on why there would be no portrait of
Cantona in the National Portrait Gallery, 1997

Shades of Eric No7: Legacy

In 2002, in a BBC documentary about Sir Alex Ferguson, Cantona accused Manchester United of treating him "like a shit". Ferguson had said in his autobiography that Cantona had given two reasons for his departure. One was a perceived lack of ambition by the club's board in the purchase of players. The second was that he felt he had become a pawn of United's marketing department.

These explanations needed to be digested with care. Firstly, Ferguson's autobiography was published in 1999, a time when the manager was flexing his muscles in his own struggles with the board. Any suggestion that a club hero such as Cantona had said the club was not ambitious enough would only serve to back his argument in wrangles over transfer cash. Secondly, Cantona apparently did not acknowledge to Ferguson when he quit that he felt his influence on the pitch was waning. He was under no obligation to do so, of course, but to suggest that marketing quarrels were more influential than a slipping of his own high standards seemed strange. And anyway, later in 1997, in an interview with *GQ magazine*, Cantona said:

"I stopped playing football because I'd done as much as I could."

This was backed up in April 2003, on the day he was named the Overseas Player of the Decade at a ceremony to mark the first 10 seasons of the Premier League.

"I loved the game," he said of his retirement, "but I no longer had the passion to go to bed early, not to go out with my friends, not to drink, and not to do a lot of other things – the things you like in life."

The exploitation of his image while at the club had clearly rankled, however. In the BBC documentary in 2002 he said that he had agreed a deal whereby he would share the profits for the use of his image.

"[*But*] I signed a contract and they did not respect anything," he said. "At that time they thought that merchandising was more important than the team and players. When the business is more important than the football I just give up, rather than be treated like a pair of socks, a shirt or a shit. I am not a shit at all."

The current generation of players, who looked up to Cantona and learned from him, would testify to that. As would the supporters. They can still be seen wearing Cantona shirts and plastic face masks, waving French flags, even carrying toy parrots that say: 'Ooh Aah Cantona'. Many still travel around the world to watch their hero, now pursuing a film career, play on the international beach football tour.

"Without exception, he always has the time to talk and thank those travelling," said Oli Swinton, a United supporter. "Everything about him was different."

"1966 was a great year for English football.
Eric was born."
Advert for Nike

"Cantona is a great player, but only in the context of English football."
Robert Louis-Dreyfus, president of Marseille, 1997

"For my next film role I would love to play a psychopath or an unpleasant person."
Cantona, 2000

CHAPTER EIGHT

Northern Rock

Peter Schmeichel's honours with Manchester United

1991–1992
League Cup winner
(played six games of eight, including the final)

1992–1993
Premier League winner (42 games of 42)

1993–1994
(The Double)
Premier League winner (40 games of 42)
FA Cup winner (seven games of seven)

1995–1996
(The Double)
Premier League winner (36 games of 38)
FA Cup winner (six games of seven, including the final)

1996–1997
Premier League winner (36 games of 38)

1998–1999
(The Treble)
Premier League winner (34 games of 38)
FA Cup winner (eight games of eight)
European Cup winner (13 games of 13)

WHEN THE day of reckoning dawned on Peter Schmeichel's playing career, the Danish goalkeeper could lay his medals on the table. It was a sizeable table, naturally, befitting a man lauded as one of the greatest custodians football has ever seen.

In a 19-year, six-club odyssey that started in 1984 with Hvidovre in his native Denmark and ended with Manchester City, he won 15 major trophies with his clubs as well as a European Championship with his country and an assortment of personal awards. He retired because his 39-year-old body had taken enough – and given enough.

"His success was a magnificent achievement," said a 79-year-old Bert Trautmann shortly before Schmeichel's last game for City on 11 May 2003. It was the last ever match played at Maine Road, the venue where Trautmann had spent the majority of his own goalkeeping days.

"When you consider the amount of games you play, over 15 years in my case, that's about 30,000 falls on your hips, your knees, your shoulders," said Trautmann. "Throw in training and that could be 60,000. It took something special for Schmeichel to remain a world-class goalkeeper for so long. And to have spent eight years with Manchester United in the era he did, it says everything."

Amid a barrage of eye-catching statistics from Schmeichel's days of blocking, bawling and diving, one stands testament to his influence. During the most successful decade in Manchester United's history they won 10 major trophies. Schmeichel had a pair of big hands in them all.

When he announced his retirement he acknowledged two other men as being the instigators of United's success in that period. The first was Alex Ferguson, the manager who had signed him and who had later hailed that deal as "one of the bargains of the century". The second was Eric Cantona. Schmeichel said:

"He had a massive influence on our performances. He is the one who has to take the credit."

But if Cantona was a catalyst for success, and Ireland's Roy Keane later the thundering heartbeat who sustained it, Schmeichel proved to be the bedrock. His contribution to the cause was massive in all senses. At 6ft 4in, his physical presence between the posts was enhanced by his foghorn exhortations to his team-mates. His shot-stopping ability was second to none.

He was unrivalled in the one-on-one, capable, as all great goalkeepers are, of 'making himself big' in the eyes of an oncoming striker. His particular method of body expansion was a star-shaped jump which involved hurling each limb as far from his core as possible, thereby covering as much of the target area as possible. This he did on countless occasions having already charged out to narrow the angle.

Schmeichel was also possessed by an attacking instinct that manifested itself in his own penalty area and the opposition's. Like Trautmann at Maine Road in the 1950s, he understood the value of the long, accurate throw as a crucial starting point for assaults on goal. "He can throw the ball further than I go on holiday," the perma-tanned Ron Atkinson once said.

The Dane also liked to go forward for corners, sometimes to spectacular effect. This was never truer than in his last game for Manchester United, when his madcap run into Bayern Munich's area in the dying seconds of the 1999 European Cup final helped spread the confusion that led to United's crucial equaliser.

The ingredient that underpinned Schmeichel's career was commitment.

"It has to be everything or nothing," he said, just before telling Kevin Keegan, his manager at Manchester City, that he would be hanging up his gloves. "Everybody has days when they don't want to go to work. As a footballer you cannot think like that, you cannot cut corners."

The 'half-way' option, of continuing to play but not in every game, was dismissed.

"There are no short cuts, you have to perform up to a certain level. Having the option of saying that you don't feel up to it [so] the manager can put someone else in is not for me. I could not work like that."

At Manchester United that attitude helped win five Premier League titles, three FA Cups, a League Cup and a European Cup. Only one other foreign player has ever won more medals in England. That was another goalkeeper, Bruce Grobbelaar, who won 13 major honours with Liverpool. But Schmeichel also won three league titles and an FA Cup in Denmark before arriving in England, as well as a Portuguese title with Sporting Lisbon in 2000. He also played a crucial part in Denmark's European Championship win in 1992.

Safety (and in numbers)

Some 300 footballers from the so-called 'Northern Countries' of Denmark, Sweden, Norway, Finland and Iceland have played in England's professional leagues since the first, Nils Middleboe, in 1913. A Danish Olympian and strategist, Middleboe showed the League that Scandinavia had something to offer and that the region's footballers could acclimatise. In the late 1940s and 1950s he was followed by Sweden's Dan Ekner and Hans Jeppson, Iceland's Albert Gudmundsson and Finland's Mauno Rintanen. They each offered glimpses of flair and thought during cameo stints that might have been longer but for the rules that dictated they could play only as amateurs.

Viggo Jensen was resident long enough to overcome that hurdle and set a new benchmark for reliable Danes, playing at Hull through most of the 1950s. Ben Arentoft, a midfielder, maintained that tradition at Newcastle and Blackburn in the late 1960s and early 1970s. In the 1980s came another Danish pair, Allan Simonsen and Jan Molby, whose contrasting stays in England are detailed later in this chapter.

Other notable Danes included Jesper Olsen, bought by Manchester United in 1984. He'd made his name at Ajax and had scored for his country against England. He played in United's FA Cup-winning side of 1985. Although his impact declined as the tempo of English game took its toll, he stayed at Old Trafford until moving to France in 1988. He later became an agent.

At United, Olsen played for a short while alongside a compatriot, Johnny Sivebaek, who lasted only 29 League games. Sivebaek later played for Denmark alongside Schmeichel in the European Championships of 1992, a tournament that featured numerous Scandinavians who had played in England or would later do so. Denmark's Kent Nielsen, John Jensen and Torben Piechnik fell into that category, as did Sweden's Roland Nilsson, Patrik Andersson, Tomas Brolin, Anders Limpar, Stefan Schwarz and Martin Dahlin.

They had diverse experiences. Nilsson, a cultured right-back, won promotion with Sheffield Wednesday in the same year, 1991, that his club won the League Cup. He was also part of the side who lost both domestic cup finals to Arsenal in 1993 and later played for, and briefly managed, Coventry.

Brolin moved to Leeds United in 1995 for £4.5m from Parma. He was dogged by injury, his weight fluctuated and he became a figure of fun at Elland Road and later at Crystal Palace. When news came through in 1999, after his retirement, that he'd been involved in a non-serious road collision with an elk, it only cemented the image. He said, without irony: "I am very lucky not to have been injured."

Given the huge number of Scandinavians who've worked in the English game, it is not surprising there have been flops. But they have been consistently outnumbered by cheap, jobbing professionals who rarely had problems with the language, the climate or the style of play. In the post-Bosman years, the migration across the North Sea only intensified.

The sheer numbers and specific successes tell their own stories. Denmark's Allan Nielsen moved to England in 1996 and scored the injury-time winner in the 1999 League Cup final. Thomas Sorensen, who succeeded Schmeichel as Denmark's goalkeeper, kept a record 30 clean sheets as Sunderland won the First Division the same year. Thomas Gravesen played a key role in Everton's renaissance after joining in 2000, the same year Jesper Gronkjaer arrived at Chelsea.

Prominent Swedes were also prevalent in the 1990s, following in the footsteps of Glenn Hysen, who played in Liverpool's defence in the title-winning side of 1989–90. They included Coventry's international goalkeeper, Magnus Hedman, and the striker Andreas Andersson, who played for Newcastle in the 1998 FA Cup final defeat against Arsenal. A few months after that match, Arsenal signed Freddie Ljungberg, who would be a Double winner in 2002, while Manchester United signed the former Swedish Player of the Year, Jesper Blomqvist, who would be involved in the Treble of 1999.

Iceland provided English football with the likes of the prolific striker Eidur Gudjohnsen and the stalwart defender Hermann Hreidarsson. That country also provided Stoke City – owned by an Icelandic consortium – with a squad list featuring the likes of Gudjonsson, Gunnlaugsson, Gunnarsson, Danielsson, Dadason, Gislason, Kristinsson, Thordarson and Marteinsson. Almost every team shirt had a 'son' on its back, if not a son of the City inside it.

Similar Northern Country influence – from Norway – saw a comparably Nordic feel to team sheets at Wimbledon and Hartlepool around the same time.

From the end of the 1990s, Finland started exporting players to England in numbers, notably No1s. Three Finnish goalkeepers – Jussi Jaaskelainen, Peter Enckelman and Antti Niemi – played in the Premier League in 2002–03, for Bolton, Aston Villa and Southampton. Niemi arrived in England via Scotland, the workplace of numerous Scandinavians from the Second World War onwards. Finland also provided Liverpool with Sami Hyypia and, briefly, Jari Litmanen. Other Finnish internationals found work further down the English leagues, from Aki Riihilati at Crystal Palace to Petri Helin and Jarkko Wiss at Stockport County.

Norwegians have made a big impact, on and off the pitch. The dealings of the agent Rune Hauge (detailed later) became notorious, while the service provided by some of his compatriot clients, including Henning Berg, Ronny Johnsen and Ole Gunnar Solskjaer has been more glorious. That trio are among the most prolific medal-winning foreign players ever to play in England, each having been involved in multiple title successes as well as domestic and European Cup wins.

But no single Scandinavian in England has yet eclipsed the value for money, the durability, the professionalism or the single-minded will to win of Peter Schmeichel, Manchester United's northern rock.

Bargain of the century

Schmeichel was approaching his 28th birthday when Alex Ferguson signed him for £505,000 in the summer of 1991. The canny Scot had first spotted him training in Spain, where United used the same warm-weather training facilities as those used by Schmeichel's club at the time, Brøndby. Ferguson's scouts soon confirmed what a special talent he was.

The people of Denmark already knew. After starting at an amateur team with his hometown club, Gladsaxe, Schmeichel made his debut for Hvidovre in 1984. He stayed three years, scoring six goals in the process to prove he was no ordinary keeper. In 1987 he signed for Brøndby, where he won three league titles, the Danish cup and the first of his 129 international caps. In 1990 he was voted Denmark's Footballer of the Year.

At the start of the 1991–92 season, Schmeichel went straight into United's team as a replacement for Jim Leighton. He played 40 games in the League that year as Leeds United took the final title of the pre-Premier League era. He also played in six of United's eight matches in the League Cup, then sponsored by Rumbelows, a chain of electrical stores. The spark still existed in the tournament and winning it was a cause for celebration, even for a club of United's pedigree.

The summer of 1992 brought another title for Schmeichel, when his nation won the European Championship. Denmark only played as 11th-hour replacements for Yugoslavia. Schmeichel was a key figure in the success. England and The Netherlands were among those thwarted en route to the final against Germany, which saw some vital saves in a combative match. The opening goal in Denmark's 2–0 win was scored by John Jensen, whose subsequent move to Arsenal that August would trigger the 'bungs' inquiry of the 1990s.

Back in England, in the first season of the Premier League, 1992–93, Leeds sold Eric Cantona to Manchester United, who won the title. Schmeichel played in every match. Schmeichel's team lost their first two games of the season – 2–1 at Sheffield United and 3–0 at home to Everton but it wasn't the start of a trend; Manchester United lost only four more games in the next forty, and never by more than a single goal. Schmeichel kept 18 clean sheets in the League.

The following season brought another title, with United losing only four League games, one at home. Schmeichel kept 15 League clean sheets. United reached two domestic cup finals. Without Schmeichel – who had been suspended – United lost the League Cup 1–0. They won the FA Cup 4–0 against Chelsea. A remarkable match at Liverpool the same season became the focus of intense debate on the day and well beyond.

United quickly established a 3–0 lead only to capitulate and draw 3–3. When Bruce Grobbelaar, Liverpool's goalkeeper that day, was later accused of match-fixing, that fixture, and the three goals he conceded, became the focal point of the jury's attention. The three goals Schmeichel conceded became the focal point of his manager's anger immediately after the game.

"He wasn't just livid, he was absolutely hysterical," Schmeichel said later of Alex Ferguson's reaction. "He didn't just criticise my kicking, he more or less heaped derision on just about everything I had done in the entire game." Schmeichel hit back with a tirade of his own. "It reached such a personal level that neither of us was interested in, or capable of, backing down. I said the most awful things. I questioned his capabilities as a manager. I accused him of having a suspect personality. Ferguson did not keep anything back either and at one point he threatened to throw a cup of tea in my face."

Ferguson decided the only appropriate course of action was to sack his goalkeeper for impudence. Such steely resolve was a feature of his management style, as later players, such as Jaap Stam, found out. Despite being a formidable presence in the heart of defence in the Treble-winning side of 1999, the Dutchman was quickly sold by Ferguson soon after publishing an autobiography, which included an anecdote about his manager's temper.

Schmeichel survived because he apologised to his team-mates for his outburst, an act of contrition that Ferguson overheard. There is no doubt that the goalkeeper's value to the club was also taken into consideration.

That value was apparent when Schmeichel was absent due to injury for an eight-game stretch in the League in the middle of the 1994–95 season. Those eight games included a 2–1 home defeat to Nottingham Forest, a 1–1 home draw with Leicester and a 2–2 draw at Southampton. Something was missing. A single extra point from any of those matches would have handed the title to United, who eventually lost out by one point to Blackburn, who had an inferior goal difference.

The evidence suggests that with Schmeichel present the extra point necessary would have come from either the home game against Forest or the one against Leicester. United conceded goals in both of these, something they were not in the habit of doing at home when Schmeichel was between the posts. He did not concede a single League goal at Old Trafford between 23 April 1994 and 7 May 1995. In fact, United only conceded four at home in the whole of the 1994–95 season, and three of those hit the back of their net when Schmeichel wasn't in front of it. Even the fourth, on 10 May against Southampton, which brought the Dane's astounding run of home invincibility to an end, came in a 2–1 win for United.

Ferguson's problems continued almost as soon as Schmeichel returned from injury – Cantona kung fu kicked his way to an eight-month ban shortly afterwards. United certainly missed the Frenchman's influence, both in the title run-in and the FA Cup final, which they lost to Everton, but Schmeichel's temporary loss had also taken its toll.

Boxing clever, saving the day

The defining moments in a goalkeeper's career tend to be the crucial saves in the biggest matches. Schmeichel was no different, but his involvement in the opposition box also proved memorable. His first and only goal for Manchester United came on 26 September 1995 in a UEFA Cup match at Old Trafford. He headed the late equaliser against Rotor Volgograd of Russia that preserved United's record of never having lost a European tie at home. His only other goal in England came for Aston Villa at Everton in October 2001 in a 3–2 defeat. On that occasion, Schmeichel belted it with his foot, earning a standing ovation from the Goodison Park crowd.

The most significant – and final – upfield foray of Schmeichel's career also ended in a goal, the injury-time equaliser in the 1999 European Cup final. Though he did not score it, his presence in the penalty area helped create confusion in the Bayern Munich defence. David Beckham's corner flew into the box and fell to a rattled Thorsten Fink, who could only scramble a clearance to Ryan Giggs. The Welshman's shot was steered in by Teddy Sheringham.

In the absence of Roy Keane, Schmeichel was the United captain that day, in his last match for United. After the equaliser he barely had time to settle back on his own line before United had scored again to complete the most astonishing last-gasp comeback the European Cup has ever seen.

"Not even Hans Christian Andersen could have written a fairytale like that," Schmeichel said. "Of course you believe you have a chance until the final whistle goes and I never stopped believing we had a chance – although I admit, not much of one. But the late goals exemplified our team spirit. One thing I have learnt throughout my time at United is that we never give up and we proved that."

Supersub Solskjaer

Norway's Ole Gunnar Solskjaer scored the winner that day after coming on as an 80th-minute substitute. Waiting on the bench for most of the game, only to come on and deliver this kind of crucial input, has been Solskjaer's trademark. Earlier that season, in February, he had come on as a substitute 18 minutes from the end of a League game at Nottingham Forest. He scored his first goal of the game on 80 minutes and added another three before the final whistle, claiming the record for the fastest ever hat-trick (let alone four-goal haul) by a substitute.

"Good job they didn't put him on earlier," said Ron Atkinson, then Forest's manager, who'd just watched his side lose 8–1.

If the European Cup final and the Forest game exemplified the essence of Solskjaer, then Schmeichel's United career was encapsulated by 45 minutes at St James' Park on the evening of Monday 4 March 1996.

The occasion pitted the League leaders Newcastle, under the irrepressible guidance of Kevin Keegan, against second-placed Manchester United, a team in transition. Key figures from a year before, including Paul Ince, Mark Hughes and Andrei Kanchelskis had gone from United's set-up. The likes of David Beckham, Paul Scholes, the Neville brothers and Nicky Butt were in their first full season as regular starters. Schmeichel needed to be a big presence. He was.

The match was pivotal in the title race. Keegan's side had let slip a seemingly unassailable 12-point lead at the top of the table but were still six ahead of United before kick-off. A win would have re-opened the gap to nine. A defeat would have left the visitors with only three to catch up and a game in hand.

Keegan's starting XI was typically brimming with attacking options, with Les Ferdinand and Faustino Asprilla a potent Anglo-Colombian blend up front, supplemented by the scampering of Peter Beardsley and the flair of David Ginola in his pomp. Newcastle had not lost at home for almost a year and they showed why by laying siege to their visitors' goal with mesmerising waves of attack. They were thwarted by one man.

Specific saves included marvellous reaction stops to shots by Ferdinand, Ginola and Robert Lee. Time after time the Dane narrowed the angle, made himself big, refused to countenance that he could be beaten. A Newcastle goal seemed inevitable. It never came. Eric Cantona scored, making it 1–0 to him and Schmeichel, whose sheer belief gave his team-mates the confidence to hold out.

216

Another notable performance – specifically one save – also came in 1996, in the away leg of a Champions' League match against Rapid Vienna in December. Somehow, after a seemingly unstoppable shot from Rene Wagner, Schmeichel reached the ball after diving to his right. He spooned it over the bar. It was reminiscent of Gordon Banks's save from Pele in 1970.

Yet another memorable stop came in the FA Cup semi-final of the Treble-winning season against Arsenal in the best semi-final in the Cup's history. The football was bewitching: drama, tension, a sending off, and a last-gasp extra-time decider by Ryan Giggs that was one of finest goals in the tournament's history. He only had a platform for his 70-yard, 13-touch wondergoal, however, because Schmeichel had saved a penalty during stoppage time at the end of the regulation 90 minutes. Having already denied Dennis Bergkamp with a full-stretch save in open play, he produced a world-class save from the Dutchman's spot kick.

And the winner is...

The 1998–99 Treble brought Schmeichel's trophy tally at United to ten. His time at Old Trafford was punctuated by other landmarks. In September 1997, he became the first goalkeeper to keep 100 clean sheets in the Premier League. The 100th came 11 months after Schmeichel's most testing spell, during which he was beaten 11 times in two games. Those five goals against Newcastle and six against Southampton had critics asking if his career was over. United responded by winning the title again.

In 1998 Schmeichel played in all five of Denmark's games at the World Cup finals, winning his 100th cap in the process. In the same year, he was voted the best goalkeeper in Europe by the 24 coaches of the quarter-finalists in the three major European competitions. He was also rated the best in Europe in four of his Manchester United years – 1992, 1993, 1997 and 1999 – by dint of being the highest-ranked goalkeeper in *France Football*'s 'Ballon D'Or' rankings.

Even while he was in Portugal (1999–2001), winning a title with Sporting Lisbon, their first for 17 years, he picked up another gong in England, an honorary MBE in January 2001.

A Wright debacle

No-one ever accused Schmeichel of being quiet or retiring on a football pitch. His team-mates' eardrums would regularly take a battering. But to be accused of racially abusing an opponent, as Schmeichel was in the 1996–97 season, was something that appalled him.

The accusation came from the Arsenal striker, Ian Wright, initially after a League match at Old Trafford in November 1996 which Arsenal lost 1–0. It did not take the form of an official complaint. "We've had absolutely no complaint from Ian, and he's certainly not someone afraid to voice his opinion," said an FA spokesman at the time.

Instead, after the match, on the basis of a lip reader's interpretation of a video of the game, it was suggested in the press that Schmeichel had called Wright a "black bastard". Without ever explicitly saying that Schmeichel had called him that, Wright then used his column in *The Sun* newspaper to say:

> I've seen a video of the incident and to put it politely it isn't nice [*he added*]. I'm not in the habit of getting my fellow professionals into trouble. I've said things myself in the heat of the moment that have got me into trouble, and I'm sure that's the case with Peter Schmeichel. But what he's done is there for everyone to see... I don't want to get involved any more. Other people must deal with it.

Racism in football was – and still is – something that the game's authorities want to eliminate; the Wright–Schmeichel incident had an import beyond a spat between two players. Consequently, Wright's evasion in not making his accusation clear was taken in some quarters as unsatisfactory.

Even *The Voice*, a newspaper aimed at Britain's black community, said, in December 1996:

> Wright has a duty, if he believes the remark was made, to say so clearly and unambiguously so that the

authorities can investigate the matter
properly. But he also has a duty if the
remark wasn't made, and that's a duty
to Peter Schmeichel. The goalkeeper
categorically denies making a racist
slur and if Wright knows that's true
he must stand up and clear
Schmeichel's name. The odium that
the tag 'racist' attracts must be
reserved for those whose actions
deserve it. Wright will show himself
to be a bigger man if he comes out
clearly and gives his version of
events. The current fudge helps
no-one.

The 'current fudge' was further complicated by the fact that an
Arsenal supporter at the match had made an official complaint
about Schmeichel's alleged abuse. This prompted an
investigation by the Crown Prosecution Service. Even if
Schmeichel had felt like conceding that he'd used abusive
language – and he never did – to do so would have been to invite
a prosecution.

The matter remained unresolved. Wright made no
unequivocal complaint, and no complaint at all to the
authorities. Schmeichel maintained he had nothing to apologise
for. It was against this backdrop that the reverse fixture between
United and Arsenal took place in February 1997. United won
2–1 in a game in which Wright made a crude double-footed
lunge at Schmeichel. The pair had a verbal spat after the game
and scuffled in the tunnel, prompting Wright to say, via a
newspaper, he had been racially abused again. No formal
complaint was made.

Alex Ferguson denied Schmeichel had racially abused Wright
and said the claim was a slur on Manchester United.

"We can categorically deny any racist remark whatsoever
from Peter Schmeichel, I can assure you of that," Ferguson said.
"Two years ago we were coaching in the townships of South
Africa and Peter was part of that. We have supporters
everywhere in the world. We place great store in our reputation,
so it's a big slur on us."

The FA summoned representatives of Arsenal and Manchester United to a meeting to sort out the issue, which filled acres of newsprint and hours of airtime on radio and television. Ruud Gullit, then Chelsea's manager, said: "If someone calls me a black so-and-so, I don't take it as a racist thing because I am black." Arsenal's manager, Arsène Wenger, indicated that whatever had been said between the two was worthy of nothing more than a handshake and acceptance that football matches sometimes become heated. "I think it will be good to bring this to an end because I think so much has been created from such a small thing," he said.

Mediation by the FA brought no definitive apologies from either side. Graham Kelly, the FA's chief executive wrote letters to the players asking for a public reconciliation.

In his letter to Schmeichel, he wrote:

> I have to decide what is best for English football. I have to be aware that both you and Ian Wright are public figures, idolised by millions of football fans at home and abroad. Your example is vitally important. That is why I ask you, in the interests of the game as a whole, to make a public statement of reconciliation with Ian Wright as soon as possible. In doing so, you can be a power for bringing the game together, not dividing it. In current circumstances, a drawn-out disciplinary procedure with uncertain results would not be helpful. I want to avoid it unless you and Ian Wright leave me no alternative.

The letter was sent on the same day the Crown Prosecution Service announced that no charges would be made against Schmeichel relating to the incident in November. Wright revealed that he had been approached three times by the CPS to make a complaint or statement based on video evidence. He said he had not done so "for the benefit of football and everybody concerned with our national game".

Eventually, the FA was able to release a statement – albeit without apologies – saying that the pair had confirmed there was no feud between them. Schmeichel, who would later play alongside Wright's son, Shaun, at Manchester City, steadfastly maintained that he was not a racist. On that he stood firm. He always stood firm.

Wheeling and dealing: Rune Hauge

Rune Hauge had a role in the majority of the deals involving Scandinavian player-moves to England in the early 1990s. He represented some of the key figures of the era, Schmeichel included. There is no suggestion that Schmeichel's move from Brøndby to Manchester United, or indeed many others involving Hauge were 'dodgy' in any way. But several transfers *did* involve irregular payments, leading to the 'bungs' inquiry that cast a shadow over the game in the mid-1990s and beyond. In essence, Hauge paid money to various people to smooth some of the transfers involving 'his' players. The buying clubs were the losers because money they believed was going to the selling club was actually being paid as 'palm-greasers' to other parties.

Hauge, an accountant by training, first became involved in the business of football in the 1970s in Germany. He established a company, Proman, which sold pitch-side advertising space. He worked closely with FC Nuremburg, the club in the town where he studied in the 1970s. By the early 1980s, he was back in his native Norway, working as an advertising executive at a small club, Bryne FK, but retained his links with Germany. He began to buy up the registrations of low-profile Norwegian players and then sell them on at a profit to overseas clubs, mostly in Germany.

His earliest big-money deal with an English club involved brokering the move in the late 1980s of a Norwegian goalkeeper, Erik Thorstvedt. Hauge initially offered the player to Arsenal, who thought the £60,000 fee was good value. The London side could not obtain a work permit, however, because Thorstvedt was not an international. The player moved instead to Sweden with IFK Gothenburg, and then, in December 1988 – after a year and an international call-up – to Tottenham, then managed by Terry Venables, for around £600,000.

In 1989 Hauge enlisted the services of Steve Burtenshaw, who would later become the chief scout at Arsenal, to introduce him to English managers, coaches and scouts. Burtenshaw signed a deal with Proman that would pay him 25 per cent of the profits from any business he put Hauge's way, net of any 'paybacks' (undeclared payments, or bungs) that would be necessary to facilitate those deals. Through Burtenshaw, Hauge forged links with more than 20 managers, coaches and scouts in England. To most of them, Hauge was just another agent, albeit one with a good eye for a valuable player, and they dealt with him accordingly.

From late 1989, Hauge was involved in a string of player-moves to England. The Norwegian defender, Erland Johnsen, moved to Chelsea in December 1989. In the same month, a 'dodgy' deal brought Toddi Orlygsson, an Icelandic midfielder, from Akureyri in his native country to Nottingham Forest, then managed by Brian Clough. It was later revealed during the bungs inquiry that Ronnie Fenton, Clough's assistant, had received a £45,000 backhander as part of the Orlygsson move. Fenton collected the money in Hull, where it arrived on a trawler stashed in a fish box.

In 1990, Hauge was involved as Anders Limpar moved to Arsenal. In 1991, he oversaw Schmeichel's move to Manchester United, and before that, helped in the negotiations that led the winger, Andrei Kanchelskis, to move from Shakhtar Donetsk in Ukraine to Old Trafford, initially for £650,000. United paid Hauge a £35,000 fee for 'professional services', one of which was helping with the Schmeichel and Kanchelskis transfers. This breached the rules on payments to agents but an FA inquiry established no bungs had been paid.

The Kanchelskis move would evolve into a saga – not involving Hauge – that was so murky that it even made Hauge's transgressions look tame. When Kanchelskis signed in 1991, United's deal with Shakhtar included a clause which said United would pay additional sums, amounting to an extra £550,000, depending on the player's appearances and whether he renewed his contract. United later paid this money in good faith into a Swiss bank account but it did not reach Shakhtar. The club's president, Aleksandr Bragin, was suspected of diverting the money. He and five bodyguards were killed by a remote-controlled bomb triggered by persons unknown in October 1995.

Whether the events detailed below contributed to that assassination will never be known but suspicions about Bragin had built up during the previous year. Kanchelskis had signed a new contract at United in 1994, brokered by an agent, Grigori Yesaulenko. That contract had a clause stating that Kanchelskis would receive a third of any sell-on fee if he left United. Shortly after it was signed, Yesaulenko handed £40,000 in cash in a wrapped box to United's manager, Alex Ferguson, in a hotel car park. Ferguson, shocked upon opening the box, reported the matter to his club. The money remained in United's safe for almost a year until Yesaulenko next visited Old Trafford.

As Ferguson wrote in his autobiography:

> If I had been able to foresee the dramas that were still to be enacted in the Kanchelskis saga, I might have wondered if the cash was meant to be not so much a thank-you for past assistance as an encouragement towards co-operation in the future.

That 'co-operation' was probably expected by Kanchelskis's connections in 1995 when he announced he wanted to leave Old Trafford. This presented United with two problems. The player's 1994 contract said he was entitled to a third of the sell-on fee. Additionally, a clause in United's original 1991 contract with Shakhtar had stipulated the Ukrainian club was also entitled to a third of any sell-on fee.

United clearly did not want to sell Kanchelskis and then give away two-thirds of the proceeds (a third to the player and a third to his former club). After United's chairman, Martin Edwards, had said as much, he received death threats. Edwards then explained to Yesaulenko that he just could not sanction a sale if United had to pay Shakhtar a third. A fax on Shakhtar notepaper, dated 13 July 1995, waiving this payment, arrived soon afterwards. Kanchelskis was then sold to Everton for £6m.

The matter was still not closed. In September 1995, United received a letter from Bragin and his deputy saying that the author of the July fax, a director called Kolotsei, had not known what he was doing. They wrote:

> Mr Kolotsei signed... text in the English language prepared by Mr Yesaulenko... only because

> Mr Yesaulenko requested and
> explained that this fax was necessary
> exclusively for helping Andrei
> Kanchelskis to solve private
> problems...

It was only when other senior figures associated with Shakhtar started looking into the Kanchelskis deal that they realised the club had been due £550,000 in performance payments under the 1991 contract and that the money had never arrived. Bragin was killed shortly afterwards for reasons unconfirmed.

Shakhtar remained in dispute with United over monies due to them until March 1996, when United made a £770,000 settlement payment. Both parties signed a confidentiality agreement relating to the deal.

After the Kanchelskis and Schmeichel deals, Hauge's next major sale to an English club was that of Pal Lydersen, a Denmark-born Norwegian defender, to Arsenal in November 1991. After the deal went through Hauge gave Arsenal's manager, George Graham, £140,000 in used £50 notes.

In August 1992 came the deal that would prove to be Graham's undoing. Hauge arranged the transfer of the Danish international John Jensen to Arsenal for £1.57m from Brøndby. The bungs inquiry report would later conclude:

> From a transfer fee of £1,570,000
> paid by Arsenal, Brøndby paid
> approximately £392,500 to HSV
> Hamburg [*Jensen's former club*],
> approximately £739,433 to InterClub
> Ltd [*Hauge's company*] and retained
> approximately £438,067. From the
> amount InterClub received, we know
> it paid £285,000 into a bank account
> opened for Mr Graham's benefit.

The scam was initially uncovered by a Danish reporter, Henrik Madsen, although an Inland Revenue inquiry following a tip-off actually led to Graham being fingered.

Graham always maintained that the two payments – totalling £425,000 – that he received from Hauge were unsolicited gifts. Hauge backed him up. The authorities did not agree and in 1995 Graham was banned from football for a year and fined £50,000.

He repaid Arsenal the total amount of his 'unsolicited gifts' from Hauge, plus interest. Hauge was banned by FIFA for life from being an agent, a punishment that was commuted to a two-year ban on appeal.

Hauge brokered a raft of other deals, before and after his ban. The most prominent and longest-serving Scandinavians involved included Stig Inge Bjornebye, Henning Berg, Lars Bohinen, Alf-Inge Haaland, Gunnar Halle, Ole Solskjaer, Ronny Johnsen and Tore Andre Flo. With the exception of Haaland's move to Nottingham Forest in 1994, after which Ronnie Fenton received another £45,000, there was no evidence that any of the other deals were anything but legitimate, above-board moves. Indeed George Graham even had the confidence to use Hauge's services to provide players for him at Leeds after their respective bans elapsed.

Seventeen games of wonder (then a decade of despair)

Football and money have never mixed well but few deals have led to such a catastrophic outcome for one club than that which took Allan Simonsen to Charlton in 1982. The bare facts hardly convey the enormity of the move. Simonsen, a Danish forward, had been the European Footballer of the Year in 1977. By 1982, he was playing at Barcelona when he swapped the Nou Camp for Charlton, then mid-table in the English Second Division. An equivalent move in 2003 might have seen Zinedine Zidane, European Footballer of the Year five years before, swap Real Madrid for Burnley (mid-table in the division below the Premier League). Unthinkable.

Charlton's chairman, Mark Hulyer, was able to persuade Simonsen to move by offering a lucrative two-year contract worth £82,000 a year, an enormous sum at the time. Hulyer believed that Simonsen would not only increase attendances dramatically but help lift Charlton to the top division. Hulyer also agreed to pay Simonsen a share of sponsorship deals he was sure would materialise through the Dane's presence. The attraction for Simonsen – 29 at the time and not past his peak – was that he was struggling to hold his place in the Barcelona side. Crucially, Charlton also had a former Denmark international coach, Ernst Netuka, working for their manager Lennie Lawrence. Two other Danish players, Viggo Jacobsen and Johnny Ostergaard, had recently had spells at the club.

On-off negotiations between Charlton and Barcelona dragged on through the late summer and early autumn of 1982. Simonsen eventually moved in November for a fee of £324,000, not that Charlton were able to pay it all up front. With hindsight, it was obvious they could never afford the deal in the first place.

Steven Bridge, a 'long suffering' Charlton fan even before 1982, was among the crowd when Simonsen made his first appearance in a Charlton shirt. It came on 10 November 1982, in a reserve match against Swansea City.

"It was such an event that I took my wife," recalled Bridge. "Simo had scored for Borussia Monchengladbach against the winners Liverpool in the 1977 European Cup Final and he'd won the European Cup-Winners' Cup with Barcelona only six months before signing for Charlton.

"The average attendance for a Charlton reserve game was 419 at the time. Me and my wife were two among the 2,578 who went to see if it really was true. Then in typical Charlton let-you-down style, Simo wasn't in the team. Nor was he on the bench. He wasn't there. An announcement was made that he was stuck in traffic. He made it for a second-half appearance. The wait until his first-team debut was unbearable. Three days. I was like one of the disciples of Jesus waiting for the resurrection. The restoration of Charlton's fortunes, that's what it was going to be."

The first-team debut came on 13 November 1982 at The Valley against Middlesbrough. Simonsen scored once in a 3–2 defeat in front of 10,807 people, which was about double the usual attendance.

His next game was on 4 December against Newcastle, who also had a former European Footballer of the Year on their books, Kevin Keegan, who did not play that day. Charlton won 2–0 and Simsonsen scored again. He went on to play another 14 League games and one FA Cup match, scoring nine times altogether. But despite Mark Hulyer's best intentions, crowds settled to average around 5,000 (half the level anticipated), there were no major sponsorship deals to share and, crucially, no vast improvement in Charlton's on-pitch fortunes.

Nick Riley, a Charlton fan since 1965, recalled:

"Simonsen was so good it was frightening, but the players around him were very poor, it didn't do us any good. Simonsen

Alec Eisentrager (centre, top, playing for Bristol City against Ipswich) was a teenaged conscript in the German army when he became a POW in the Second World War. He remained in England after hostilities ceased and went on to have a 10-year career as a forward at Ashton Gate. His wedding to a local girl, Olwyn (above) drew hundreds of fans who'd been charmed by his on-field showmanship and off-field demeanour. In a magazine feature printed in Germany in the 1950s, his willingness to do the dishes (right) was seen as a positive effect of life in his adopted homeland.

Teslim Balogun was the first Nigerian to play in the League when he signed for QPR in 1956. He had first travelled to England in 1949 (above) as part of a Nigerian touring side who inspired awe with their flair and bare feet. Balogun, whose nickname was 'Thunder' in honour of his powerful shot, also played for Peterborough before their ascension to the Football League.

Steve Mokone (above) was the first black South African to play professional football outside South Africa when he joined Coventry City in the Third Division (South), in the 1956–57 season. He also had brief stints at Cardiff and Barnsley but enjoyed the greatest success of a nomadic career in the Netherlands. Mokone's compatriot **Albert Johanneson** (below) was the first black player to appear in an FA Cup final, for Leeds in 1965. He was at Elland Road for nine years and later played for York but met a tragic end after a decline into alcoholism.

Ces Podd from St Kitts (above, right, on a training run with Bryan Edwards, his manager at Bradford City, in 1971) moved to England as a nine-year-old in the early 1960s, as did Brendon Batson (below, right), who was born in Grenada. Podd played more than 500 times in defence for Bradford. Batson, an apprentice at Arsenal, hit the big time with West Bromwich Albion in the late 1970s and later went on to become the most senior black official in English football as the deputy chief executive of the PFA. Clyde Best, a Bermudan striker (below, left), travelled to England as a 17-year-old in 1968 and became a hero at West Ham and a trailblazer for non-white players in the English game.

Ossie Ardiles (above, outside White Hart Lane) joined Tottenham in the summer of 1978 shortly after helping Argentina win the World Cup on home soil. He arrived as one half of a sensational double signing brokered by the Spurs manager, Keith Burkinshaw (below, centre), that brought Ardiles (below, right) and his fellow Argentina midfielder, **Ricky Villa** (below, left) to north London at the start of a landmark season for the English game.

Southampton's **Ivan Golac** (above, right), the first Yugoslavian to play in the League, attempts to win the ball from Manchester City's Trevor Francis in a match in 1981. Golac moved to England at the start of the 1978–79 season, the year that Francis became Britain's first £1m footballer when he moved from Birmingham to Nottingham Forest.

Kazimierz Deyna, Poland's most capped international, moved to Manchester City from Legia Warsaw in 1978 as a result of the BBC TV commentator Barry Davies making an on-screen, off-the-cuff remark about him wanting to play in western Europe. In the same season that Deyna moved to Manchester, the Ipswich manager, Bobby Robson, signed the Dutch midfield pair **Frans Thijssen** (below, left) and **Arnold Muhren** (below, right).

The most trophy-laden decade in Liverpool's history, the 1980s, involved key contributions from several foreign players, not least the South African-born Zimbabwean goalkeeper **Bruce Grobbelaar** (above, letting off steam in training in 1991), the South Africa-born Australian striker **Craig Johnston** (below, left with Ian Rush) and the Danish international midfielder, **Jan 'Scouser' Molby** (below, right). The trio remain among the most bemedalled foreign footballers to have played in England. Grobbelaar won 13 major honours while at Anfield, the clear record for any foreigner in England, although his reputation was later tarnished by allegations of match-fixing.

France's **Eric Cantona** (above) was widely acknowledged as the catalyst for Manchester United's domination of English football in the mid-1990s. His No7 shirt (left) was later taken by David Beckham (below, left), one of a crop of United youngsters who grew up learning all about the art of thorough preparation from the Frenchman.

could spot things the other players just didn't read. Exquisite defence-splitting passes went nowhere. Magical runs into space went unnoticed by his colleagues. He was some player but completely wasted at Charlton at that time."

Another supporter, Dave Rodden, recalled:

"Supporting Charlton for 40 years has produced many a surreal moment, but watching one of Europe's all-time greats line up alongside the likes of Les Berry took the proverbial hob-nob. The defining moment of this bizarre episode came in a match at The Valley against Leicester. With the exception of the incredibly talented Simmo, we had a remarkably average team, and perhaps the most average of the ingredients was a certain Don McAllister. Twenty minutes in, with Simonsen yet to see a ball played to him within viewing distance, let alone along the ground, the ball was lobbed towards McAllister in the right-back position, tight on the touchline and with Simonsen ten yards in front of him. Don, with that sturdy right boot of his, smashed the ball on the volley, at 150 mph, straight at the diminutive Dane's thyroid. An average player would have been killed. A really good player would have got out of the way. Simonsen, astonishingly, caught the ball on his chest so that it dropped to his feet, took a quick look up, and rolled it back along the ground to McAllister. He swung that trusty right boot again, and sliced the ball viciously into the main stand. You knew at that moment that this was never going to work out."

The transfer quickly took its toll on the club's balance sheet. Simonsen's wages were becoming a burden and Charlton failed to pay him on time. On 26 February 1983, the Dane refused to board the team bus before a game at Burnley. After persuasion he relented but Charlton lost the game 7–1. The next day Charlton announced that signing Simonsen had been a "costly error" and that he would be sold. Barcelona were also pressing for £180,000 still owed on the transfer. Simonsen was put up for sale at that price. His last game was on 19 March and then he headed back to Denmark, joining Vejle BK for an undisclosed but probably small sum.

Charlton's financial tailspin eventually ended in bankruptcy. In 1985, they lost their ground, playing in exile for seven years at Crystal Palace's Selhurst Park and West Ham's Upton Park. Extinction was a real threat and it was only after years of faith and dogged campaigning by fans that the club returned to The

Valley in 1992. Rightly, no-one ever blamed Simonsen, it was not his fault. But his time at Charlton tipped the club over the edge.

Despite the years of turmoil, few if any Charlton fans have anything but positive memories of Simonsen himself or of the kudos that his astonishing cameo briefly brought.

"Worth every penny," said Steven Bridge.

And Simonsen's time at Charlton did attract new followers. One of them, Andy Bishop, recalled:

"I was 13 years old and I'd never really supported a team properly apart from liking who my friends liked, i.e. Liverpool. So when I saw Charlton had signed Allan Simonsen I went along to The Valley for the first time. I remember going up to the turnstiles and seeing the admission fee of £3.20. I didn't have enough money so I pretended to be 12 and got in for £1.80. Charlton lost 3–2 but Simonsen scored with a deflected free-kick. That afternoon I fell in love with The Valley and that was it. I became a Charlton supporter. Twenty years on I'm still a loyal fan."

Simonsen returned to London six months after he left, but only to represent Denmark against England in a European Championship qualifier at Wembley. He scored the only goal of the game.

When his playing days were over, he moved into management. He spent eight years as the national coach of the Faroe Islands before moving to the equivalent post in Luxembourg in late 2001.

Liverpool legend: A Danish Scouser

In contrast to Simonsen's four months at Charlton was the 14-year League playing career of his compatriot Jan Molby, who moved to Liverpool from Ajax in 1984. In his prime, he was, as his former Liverpool team-mate and manager Kenny Dalglish said, "one of the finest midfield players of his generation".

His first successes with Liverpool, and arguably his greatest, came with the Double in 1985–86. The FA Cup final that year, the first all-Merseyside final, became a showcase for his major strengths, which were his vision and his passing. Everton took a 1–0 lead through Gary Lineker but Molby exerted his influence to turn the game on its head. He created the equaliser, setting up Ian Rush. He provided the cross for Craig Johnston to make it

2–1. He also started the attack that led to Rush getting his second of the game for 3–1. Dalglish, in his first season in management, had done the Double.

Anfield's record-breaking foreigners

The Liverpool team that day included three overseas players who are still, to date, among the most successful foreigners, by medal count, ever to have played in England. Johnston, a South African-born Australian striker, won nine major honours. When his playing career ended he embarked on a successful business career that included the invention and development of the Predator football boot.

Bruce Grobbelaar, who produced a world-class save in the 1986 FA Cup final, won 13 major honours with Liverpool between 1982 and 1992. His haul comprised League titles in 1982, 1983, 1984, 1986, 1988 and 1990, FA Cup wins in 1986, 1989 and 1992, a hat-trick of League Cups between 1982 and 1984 and the European Cup in 1984. Only Peter Schmeichel has yet come even within three major trophies of matching Grobbelaar's 13 although the latter ended his time in England with a tarnished reputation.

Born in South Africa in 1957, Grobbelaar was actually a Zimbabwean citizen and represented Zimbabwe internationally. He started his professional career in Canada with the Vancouver Whitecaps before a first spell in England in 1979–80 with Crewe. He went back to Canada before Bob Paisley bought him for Liverpool for £250,000 in March 1981 as an understudy to the England goalkeeper Ray Clemence.

When Clemence left for Tottenham that summer, Grobbelaar became Anfield's No1. "He was a phenomenal athlete," recalled Jan Molby. "He was quick off his line, he provided good cover for crosses, he was always very fit. As a person he was a character 24 hours a day. He had fun. He enjoyed himself. He made some high-profile mistakes, as all goalkeepers do, but he made some fantastic saves as well."

Although Grobbelaar's clowning became a trademark, his record speaks for itself. He made more than 600 appearances in 13 years with Liverpool and then went on to play for Stoke, Southampton, Plymouth, Oldham, Bury, Lincoln and in the non-League game, finally hanging up his boots in his early 40s.

Arguably his most successful piece of theatrics came in the 1984 European Cup final against Roma, which ended with a penalty shoot-out. Steve Nicol hit Liverpool's first kick over the bar. 0–0. Roma scored. 1–0. Phil Neal scored. 1–1. Roma missed. 1–1. Graeme Souness scored. 1–2. Roma scored. 2–2. Ian Rush scored. 2–3. Then as Roma's Francesco Graziani stepped up to the spot, Grobbelaar stood on his line wobbling his legs like manic spaghetti. Graziani missed, meaning if Ray Kennedy scored the game was beyond the Italians. He did.

But if Grobbelaar's on-field antics were controversial for their eccentricity, they were nothing compared to the match-fixing accusations levelled against him by *The Sun* in November 1994. The newspaper had secretly filmed Grobbelaar in a meeting with a former business partner, Chris Vincent. It was alleged that Grobbelaar had conspired to fix specific matches dating back to 1992. Malaysian betting syndicates were said to be behind the scam. These matches included games when Grobbelaar was playing for Liverpool and Southampton, not least the 3–3 draw in 1994 between Liverpool and Manchester United that had earned Peter Schmeichel his massive rollicking from Alex Ferguson.

The Sun's claims led to two trials in 1997, when Grobbelaar, plus fellow players Hans Segers and John Fashanu, and a businessman, Richard Lim, were acquitted. Grobbelaar sued *The Sun* for libel and won £85,000 in damages in 1999.

"It was not the money I was after, I was just trying to clear my name in football," he said.

In January 2001, Appeal Court judges sensationally overturned the 1999 verdict, saying the jury's verdict had been "a miscarriage of justice". Grobbelaar then asked the House of Lords for permission to appeal.

In October 2002, he won that appeal but his original damages were cut from £85,000 to £1. Lord Bingham, who presided over the Law Lords said:

> It would be an affront to justice if a court of law were to award substantial damages to a man shown to have acted in such flagrant breach of his legal and moral obligations.

It was judged that Grobbelaar had accepted bribes but that *The Sun* had failed to show that he actually let in goals to fix the matches under scrutiny.

Undoubtedly Grobbelaar accepted money from Vincent. By doing so his legacy in England was soiled. But there were – and remain – plenty of people within football who never thought that Grobbelaar had actually thrown games. As Jan Molby said: "Not in a million years."

England, his England

After Molby won the 1986 Double, he added another League title in 1990, having played a bit-part role in the title of 1988 in between. He also won another FA Cup winners' medal in 1992 and played in the successful Cup run of 1988–89, although not in the final. His clinical penalties – he had a success rate of 40 from 42 – also earned him a place in the record books in November 1986 with a spot-kick hat-trick against Coventry in a League Cup game. Molby's other major acquisition was his remarkable Scouse accent, which did much to endear him to fans in Liverpool and beyond.

When he left Anfield, he embarked on a managerial career, firstly with Swansea from 1996, and then with Kidderminster, whom he steered to promotion from the non-League Conference to the Football League in 2000. For that he won the Conference Manager of the Year award and a new four-year contract. He resigned from Kidderminster in 2002 and took up a short-lived post at Hull City soon after. In a pressured environment where immediate promotion from the Third Division was expected, he was sacked after 16 games. In the spring of 2003, he was living back in his 'native' Liverpool, doing media work and waiting for an opportunity to get back into the game.

"Settling in England was never a problem for me," he recalled. "Liverpool was a very relaxing place, a great club to go to. The difficult part was the football, at least to start with. It was different to what I'd been used to, more physical. There were a lot of old-fashioned sides around whose aim was just to get the ball forward however they could. That wasn't true of Liverpool but we still had to cope against teams who did it. Having played in Holland for two years that took some getting used to, as did the pace. There was pace in Dutch football but only in the final third."

Molby described the 1986 Double as unexpected, not least because Everton were a "super side" that year. "And really we should have done the Double again, in 1988 and 1989." Instead Wimbledon beat Liverpool's 1988 League title winners in the FA Cup final that year and Arsenal pipped Liverpool's FA Cup-winning side of 1989 in the final dramatic game of that League campaign.

Such sporting setbacks were put firmly in perspective for Molby by other events in his time at Anfield. He fought a constant battle with injuries and then, as a result of a series of subsequent lay-offs, with his weight. Grahame Lloyd, who collaborated with Molby on his 1999 autobiography, *Jan The Man*, noted: "It's often said that Jan Molby peaked too soon and achieved too little." It was something that many, including Molby, agreed with.

Molby's wife, Mandy, described as "heart-breaking" watching her husband cope with injuries, put on weight, lose it, hope the next season would mean a fresh start and then be thwarted again. Molby himself admitted: "I wasn't as careful with food and drink as somebody of my size should have been when not playing. I thought I could lose weight as easily as I'd put it on and I now regret not taking much more care of my body."

Ironically, one of the times his Liverpool team-mates saw him at his slimmest and fittest was after he had failed to take care elsewhere. He was arrested in 1988 for reckless driving and spent six weeks in prison as a result. He felt he was victimised because he was a high-profile footballer with a flashy car. The press vilified him and there were calls for him to be sacked and even banished from England. Some of his fellow prisoners were given cameras and offered large sums of money to snatch photographs of him for the newspapers. It was, he said, "the worst time in my life, not just my career". He served his time and got back to his football.

Hillsborough

Within a few months, in April 1989, came a tragedy on a scale that English football had never seen before. Ninety-six people lost their lives at Hillsborough. Molby was there, as he had been at Heysel in 1985 when 39 people were crushed to death by a falling wall at the European Cup final.

"Immediately after Hillsborough happened on the Saturday, we players were a bit distant from it, we got on the coach back to Liverpool, went home," Molby said. "Then the magnitude of what happened began to dawn. People came to see you, relatives, a father or a daughter of someone who'd died, just to talk about it. There was no hiding place, and no-one wanted to hide."

Liverpool made sure that at least one player, past or present, attended the funeral of every victim. Molby went to eight.

"All of those players at the time feel a particularly strong bond to the city," he said. "Not many cities would have responded in the way that Liverpool did. There was unity from everyone, Liverpool, Everton. It brought home that there's nothing more important than your football club. I thought people who'd lost relatives might've said 'That's it, I'm never going back'. But they turned to their football club for support and inspiration. People came in their hundreds of thousands just to walk around the pitch and lay flowers. The players and Kenny Dalglish, we just did whatever we could. We had to, and wanted to. It was the least we could do."

Despite everything – because of everything? – Molby remains a resident of Liverpool to this day.

"Without actually being English," he said, "you couldn't be any more English than me."

CHAPTER NINE

Samba On Tees

"It would be strange to play in England
but not play for Middlesbrough."

Juninho, February 2003

SHORTLY AFTER 11am on Monday 16 October 1995, a private jet
en route from London to Teesside dipped beneath the clouds
and made its final approach to the runway. Its exotic cargo, small
but priceless, leaned into the window and took a look at his new
home town below. And so Juninho, Brazil's No10, came to
earth, sending local expectations into orbit.

No transfer to the Premier League had ever resonated with
such possibilities. Pele's heir, aged 22 and with his best years
ahead of him, had swapped South America not for Madrid or
Milan but Middlesbrough. Had he joined Arsenal or Manchester
United, the move would still have been huge news. But he
hadn't. In the eyes of some, he'd shunned footballing affluence
for industrial effluence. And if Boro – unfashionable,
unsuccessful, unloved Boro – could lure so lavish a talent to the
banks of the Tees, then what limits were there for the rest of the
English game?

True, Juninho was not the first big-name foreign signing to
the cash-rich League. In the summer of 1995 Arsenal had paid
£7.5m to Internazionale of Italy to make the Dutchman Dennis
Bergkamp their record signing. And Jurgen Klinsmann had
already come and gone at Tottenham, taking the Footballer of
the Year award with him. But Arsenal were a rich club with a

history to match and Spurs had used all their glory, glory heritage as well as a huge salary to attract a player aged 30 on arrival. Both those clubs had also used the playground of London as enticement.

Juninho's move to Middlesbrough – who had never won a major trophy – was widely instructive for several reasons, not least why he migrated there, how he settled and how he forged such a bond that even when he was forced away – twice – he kept coming back for more. The details of the transfer, and how it almost collapsed, also throw light on the complexities of the international market and the pitfalls for a club on the rise.

The move said that Premier League football, for its own sake, could persuade a golden boy from Brazil, the most glamorous and successful nation in the world game, to England. It said the League was going places and that talent would go to unlikely places to be part of it.

It said that money needn't be the be-all and end-all. Yes, Juninho was handsomely rewarded for decamping to north-east England. But he could have pocketed much more elsewhere. And the affinity he would develop with Teesside would show that a player's horizons don't always shift with the weight of cash stacked upon them.

The move also showed that there wasn't necessarily an unbridgeable gulf between contrasting footballing cultures. In 1995, much was made of the juxtaposition between the Copacabana and Teesside: how the sun-kissed magician could only fail to cope in cold, grey England. Portraying the move in black and white was an easy device to employ at that time. Never mind that Juninho actually came from Sao Paulo, a city every bit as industrialised as Middlesbrough, and much poorer. But even the salient point in the argument, that a Brazilian would struggle with the physical, sometimes crude, approach in England, ended up scotched. Juninho showed that the samba style need not be snuffed out, even though he was as slight as Puck.

On the other hand, the move *did* emphasise other less palatable facts. Juninho shone because he was brilliant but the sheen was brighter because most of those around him in the League weren't from the same school, let alone in his class.

And in the end – or rather at the end of Juninho's first tenure (of three) – Middlesbrough found that one diamond was not enough. It was a close-run thing, but success proved elusive.

Worse, it was replaced by failure, via relegation from the Premier League and defeats in two Wembley cup finals. And worse still, instead of being universally applauded for their coup, the club and its town felt a nasty backlash of 'told you so'. Middlesbrough was painted by some not as a place trying to make good, but a town acting above its station. Even as the League sought to attract an international cast, the parochial bickering remained.

Juninho's story, and that of Middlesbrough from the mid-1990s onwards, says much about the impact that one foreign player could make.

Precedents

Only three Brazilian-born footballers had played in England before Juninho. Two of them, Edward Laxton and Marques Isaias, weren't even Brazilian. The birthplace of Laxton, who played for Norwich from 1919, was down to his father's work as an engineer. Isaias, who joined Coventry in the summer of 1995, was raised in Portugal and was a Portuguese national.

The only previous bona fide Brazilian had been Mirandinha, who'd spent two seasons with Newcastle from August 1987. On arrival, he was heralded as a prolific striker. Though popular with fans, the evidence was sporadic. He scored 20 goals in 47 League starts before falling out with his manager, Jim Smith. He departed when Newcastle were relegated.

A couple of Brazilians had been employed in the Scottish league but neither had made an impression. The first, who joined St Mirren in 1965, was Fernando Jose de Azvedo Parreiras Horta, also known – to the great relief of the stadium announcer – as Nando. He played a couple of matches and livened up a few half-time breaks with some ball juggling before finding the climate too harsh and going home. In 1994–95, Dundee United signed a forward, Sergio, who played 15 first-team games that season. He was prevented from returning for the 1995–96 season by a passport problem, spotted in Portugal after a pre-season training trip. He never made it back to Scotland.

This backdrop of experiences made the capture of Juninho all the more remarkable.

Pre-Juninho Middlesbrough

In May 1992, Middlesbrough won promotion from the old Second Division to become north-east England's only representatives in the inaugural season of the Premier League. Their home was Ayresome Park, a shabby old ground, and their team was mediocre at best. They lasted a season before being relegated.

The pattern of non-achievement irked Steve Gibson, a local businessman and lifelong fan, and he yearned to do something about it. "I felt that the club had always had this history of mediocrity and we needed to make a statement to the town and the football world that we had ambition and we meant business," he recalled. Backed by the millions he'd accrued from his haulage business, he took over as chairman, aged 36, in September 1993. Boro were attracting crowds of less than 7,000 as they languished in mid-table in the First Division.

Gibson's revolution involved a new manager, Bryan Robson, the former captain of Manchester United and England, who was hired in May 1994. Robson led Boro to promotion in his first season. The next step was a new £20m stadium, the Riverside, built during the promotion year. With perfect timing, it was ready for life back in the Premier League in 1995–96, which only left a squad to grace it. Enter Juninho.

"To bring in Juninho, the rising star of world football, was symbolic for us," Gibson said. "It was only afterwards that we realised the wider significance of him coming to England rather than an Italian or Spanish club. The English could finally compete. No Italian or Spanish player of consequence had ever played in England and suddenly we had Juninho, Brazil's Player of the Year, at Middlesbrough. In retrospect it was probably the start of the reassessment of English football."

Signing Boy Wonder

Oswaldo Giroldo Jnr, aka Juninho, was born in Sao Paulo in February 1973. He started his career at a junior club, Ituano, where Tele Santana spotted his potential. Santana was the manager of Sao Paulo FC, the big boys of Brazil in more ways than one. Juninho, when he signed in 1993, was 5ft 1in and skinny. On Santana's advice, he expanded his diet to six meals a day. He grew four inches, filled out – to eight and a half stone –

and waltzed to his first batch of honours. In 1993, he helped Sao Paulo win the Recopa, the Super Copa and the World Club Championship, with Milan being vanquished in the latter.

The next year Sao Paulo won the Recopa again and then the Conmebol Cup, with Juninho, as bedazzling as he was committed, taking the Golden Boot. As his mother Lucia later recalled, there had only ever been one game for her son.

"We'd give him toys, model cars, you name it, but he never touched them. All he ever played with was a ball," she said. "I'm so proud of him, that God gave me a son like this. He's a simple boy and humble."

In 1995 Juninho was voted Brazil's best player and made his first visit to England. The occasion was the Umbro Cup, a four-nation tournament featuring the host country plus Japan, Sweden and Brazil. Juninho dazzled as his side beat Sweden 1–0 and Japan 3–0 but it was against England that he really caught the eye.

At the time, Bryan Robson, as well as being Middlesbrough's manager, was acting as an assistant to the England coach, Terry Venables. He watched from the bench as Juninho scored a sensational free-kick in Brazil's 3–1 win over England.

"Bryan was absolutely mesmerised by him," said Gibson. "He just thought 'What a player!' and we followed it up by finding out as much as we could about him. We went and watched him play for his club in Brazil and decided to make a move for him."

Robson and Boro's chief executive, Keith Lamb, flew to Sao Paulo in July 1995.

"I had no idea of the wheeling and dealing of the clubs out there," Gibson said. "Oswaldo Snr appointed an Italian guy as Juninho's agent. It was long-winded. First we had to deal with Sao Paulo, but they didn't own all of his registration, so there was the previous club to consider as well. Then there was the father, the agent and the player. We had to deal with this cauldron of ties. But we entered negotiations and bit by bit by bit it started to stack up."

It wasn't until September 1995 that Juninho finally decided he wasn't going to renew his contract at Sao Paulo. Robson and Lamb flew to Brazil again at the start of October. Neither had yet had a one-to-one meeting with the player. They spent days around the negotiating table with a multitude of interested parties. Matters became more complicated when Arsenal and Internazionale both faxed confirmations of firm interest. But by the evening of Friday 6 October, Sao Paulo had agreed to sell Juninho to Middlesbrough. Robson met Juninho for the first time a few hours later.

"It was surprising for me that after only two years with Sao Paulo I was able to move to Europe," Juninho recalled. "No-one in Brazil really knew about English football because we didn't watch it much on television. People said to me 'Don't go, it's too hard, it's hard football. They play mostly long balls over there and that will make it difficult for you'.

"I was also being told by people at home 'Wait, wait until tomorrow, wait until the next day, because agents are talking to other clubs that could be better for you'. I said to them: 'The most important thing for me is the manager, not the president, not the directors.' And after talking with Bryan, I just said to them 'I'm going. I'd like to play in England'.

"I'd only seen videos of Bryan before but I knew that he was a big name in English football, he'd been the captain of the national team and of Manchester. He took trouble to come to Brazil to see me and show me how he wanted me to play. That was very good, very important. That's why I made my decision.

"I didn't ask him about the place because the most important thing for me was the football. If you are happy with the way the team's playing, never mind the place, you can adapt to the place."

Juninho's only prior knowledge of Boro was that they were based somewhere in rainy northern England and that the team played in red, his lucky colour.

"I didn't know much about Middlesbrough but Bryan told me how we were going to play. He showed me the ambition of the club and I moved because I trusted Bryan.

"I was young and when you're young you're just thinking about playing and that's all. Once I'd decided to move to England I never thought I wasn't going to adapt. People said it would be cold, very different weather from Brazil. But I think it's better to play in the cold than the heat. It's easier to warm up than cool down."

Steve Gibson believes that a combination of factors helped secure Juninho's signature. Robson's relationship with the player was crucial.

"When they sat down there was an instant recognition and respect and they genuinely liked each other."

He felt Juninho was lured by the 'great adventure' of England, a 'mythical place' in the history of the game.

Juninho's family situation was an important factor. Middlesbrough would care for them en masse: mum and dad, sister, granny, and a variety of visiting friends.

"And then there was the security that we were offering," Gibson said. "When you look at the average income, we were making Juninho and his family secure for life."

Contract details at Middlesbrough, as at all English clubs, are private matters. Gibson has never breached that privacy to reveal details. But it is thought Juninho was earning £13,000 a week in 1995, an era when the £10,000-a-week pay packet was still a rare thing, even in the Premier League. Juninho also received 15 per cent of the transfer fee, a lump sum of around £660,000. The transfer fee was around £4.4m. The deal overall was an eye-opener for Gibson.

"The way that things work in South America is so complex that you can never work them out," he said. At one stage there was a suggestion that an unlicensed agent might have been involved in Brazil. A Football Association investigation established that Boro had acted entirely by the book. The whole process showed South America could be a complex place to do business.

"They had grooming schools there where players are taken at an early age and a guy owns 10 per cent [*of a player*]," Gibson said. "One club owns something, another owns something, [*the player*] owns something. So where it [*the fee paid for Juninho*] all ended up, I can't be certain… We paid it all into the Brazilian FA and then it was distributed wherever by the Brazilian FA. But that was none of our business really."

On the brink

One startling aspect of Juninho's transfer was never made public. The whole deal was almost scuppered at the 11th hour by a winding-up petition served on Middlesbrough. Such petitions are legal tools used by creditors to exert pressure on debtors. The tacit aim of using one is to force a suspension of trading. They necessarily disrupt business. They lead to bank accounts being frozen and can force companies to the wall. A winding-up petition was hanging over Boro when they signed Juninho, although the club's fans and the media were oblivious at the time.

The man who issued the petition against Middlesbrough was Albert Dicken, a local businessman. Dicken, by his own admission, had never been a huge football fan. He'd been involved with a small-scale sponsorship deal at Boro in 1986–87 but had no special affinity with the club. His attentions were primarily focused on his business interests, which included a chain of DIY stores and some retail outlets in the north-east. He became involved with Middlesbrough again in the mid-1990s because he saw it as a good way to boost the profile of the Dicken's DIY chain.

Boro did a deal by which Dicken would sponsor the club in the 1994–95 and 1995–96 seasons. The deal was agreed while Boro were in the First Division and before the Riverside stadium – which was central to Steve Gibson's grand plan for the club – was built. After Bryan Robson made such a successful start to his tenure and as the stadium became reality, Boro's ambition grew. Steve Gibson was pouring millions into a venture that was boosting local morale. He wanted to continue building the dream, of which Juninho would become a crucial part.

"The deal in financing the stadium was that we brought in a top-quality sponsor, not a local parochial guy who could pay us tens of thousands but a club sponsor who would sponsor the shirts and the stadium and would pay the club millions," Gibson said. "And we pulled off this deal with BT Cellnet which was a fantastic deal."

British Telecom agreed to pay £3m for 'naming rights' to the Riverside so that its Cellnet brand would become synonymous with the venue. The company agreed to pay another £1m a year for five years to sponsor Middlesbrough's shirts. The only problem for Boro was that the deals needed to start with the 1995–96 season and Dicken already had a deal for that year.

Boro approached Dicken in May 1995 to ask him to waive his right to sponsor the club in 1995–96. The club asked him to do this 'in the interests of the community' and said they were prepared to pay him substantial compensation, far in excess of his original investment of around £35,000 a year.

Dicken, interviewed in April 2003, said he had disagreed with the notion that Boro's expansion was being pursued for the good of the community. "It was business," he said. He added he was "very concerned and upset" about being asked to step aside. "You should always honour your contracts, regardless." He entered a process of tough negotiation to secure as big a pay-off as possible. Gibson said Boro's opening offer was £250,000. Dicken declined, in 2003, to say precisely how much he eventually settled for but said it was "compensation we were happy with".

In September 1995, he was evidently still not happy with Middlesbrough. After negotiating his sponsorship pay-off he claimed the club had reneged on a deal to rent space in some of his retail outlets. On 25 September 1995, his lawyers issued a winding-up petition against Middlesbrough. Dicken said that the petition sought a "substantial" six-figure sum from Boro.

The timing was terrible for Boro. After buying Nick Barmby from Tottenham for £5.5m that summer, the team had won their first League game at the new Cellnet Riverside, beating Chelsea 2–0. They'd then won two and drawn two of their first four games in September and were seventh in the table. On top of this, amid a lot of rumour on Teesside, they were progressing towards the conclusion of the Juninho coup.

Steve Gibson believed that Dicken was trying to make as much money from Boro as possible and that the imminent Juninho transfer was being used as a lever.

"What we wanted was a surprise announcement [*about Juninho*] but these things never stay private. It began to leak," Gibson recalled. "Because of the press speculation Mr Dicken decided to put as much pressure as possible on Middlesbrough Football Club."

In April 2003, Dicken said he had been unaware at that time that his legal action would jeopardise the signing of Juninho. He also said he had been unaware of the precise measures his lawyers had taken against Boro.

The winding-up petition was issued against Middlesbrough on 25 September 1995 in a court in Newcastle.

"Immediately that that happens you have to appear in court," Gibson said. "But that court thing can take 14 days and in that 14 days the banks have no option other than to freeze your accounts. Mr Dicken could see we were about to make a major coup by signing Juninho. The whole town was up for it, all the community supported it. We'd delivered Bryan Robson, we'd delivered promotion to the Premiership, we'd delivered on the new stadium. We'd brought in Nick Barmby for five and half million and strengthened the team and we were riding high, seventh in the Premier League. To bring in Juninho would just keep that momentum going. And this guy comes along and sticks a winding-up petition on the club."

On 6 October 1995, the football world thought that Juninho's transfer had been sealed. It was actually far from complete. Boro's accounts had been frozen and the transfer fee had not been paid. Only after Boro took swift legal action to free their finances could the deal be rushed through before Juninho's unveiling. The petition had almost thwarted the biggest signing in Boro's history. "It nearly did," said Gibson. "It nearly stopped us signing Juninho."

The petition was subsequently 'struck out' by a court in Newcastle on 2 November 1995, effectively underlining that it had been an invalid claim. Dicken and Boro remained at legal loggerheads until 1999, when they resolved their differences. Dicken said Boro made a donation to a local hospice as part of the settlement.

The episode underlined some of the hazards of the football business. Dicken had almost ruined a transfer that, as Gibson rightly asserted, had led to many people reassessing English football. Amid all the excited gossip about Juninho's arrival, very few people had been aware of the price Gibson was paying. Boro, thinking big, had been stymied by a bloke who owned the local DIY store.

A one-man band

Juninho eventually flew into Teesside on 16 October 1995. The following day Boro threw a welcoming party in his honour. The samba band was fake but the pint-sized messiah was the real deal. As a 50-piece ensemble from the local Stockton and Billingham College knocked out tunes on upturned bins, some 4,000 fans turned the Riverside into a sea of adoring yellow. Brazilian flags and shirts were as numerous as wide-eyed kids playing hookey. Some schools had closed until lunchtime and those that hadn't weren't surprised by their absentees. They knew their pupils would be learning an important lesson at The Riverside. Middlesbrough had something to shout about.

The local papers had been shouting for weeks. The signing had 'brought the town to life' said the *Evening Gazette*. Juninho was front-page news day after day before he'd even put pen to paper. There were huge queues for season tickets, prompting Boro's spokesman, Dave Allan, to announce:

> Juninho-mania is underway. I would recommend that any supporters who want to watch the team regularly should buy a season ticket because if they don't they risk disappointment. Credit is available and fans can pay monthly if they wish.

The club increased its season-ticket quota to 26,500, equivalent to almost 90 per cent of capacity. They sold out. Local shirt suppliers ran out of Brazil shirts. The *Gazette* ran beginners' guides to Portuguese, telling its readers how to communicate with Juninho with such phrases as 'I like football', 'Is this your first time in England?', 'Would you like to come to dinner?' and 'I have three sisters'. Juninho had demonstrated the extent of his English in an interview with *The Independent* newspaper before he left Brazil. He'd mastered just one phrase – "You is beautiful. I love you, sweet honey".

In 2003, during his third spell at Boro, Juninho had become fluent enough to recall the welcome he'd been given almost eight years before.

"It was incredible. I didn't know that people would know me. I had a great reception, even before I'd played. Each country has a different presentation of players and what happened in Middlesbrough was a surprise to me. In Brazil they just introduce you to the press and that's it, you don't get introduced to the supporters. In Spain it's different again, there's a game to introduce you to your team-mates and the fans. England was great for me because I'd never had an opportunity of being welcomed like that. I'll never forget it."

Steve Gibson will never forget his first meeting with Juninho on the day the player arrived on Teesside.

"I couldn't believe it when I met the guy, he was so small," he said. "We even had to get special boots that were small enough, something like size five or six. I said to Bryan Robson 'Are you sure about this? He looks so small he'll get kicked to death in the Premiership'. But Juninho proved he could cope. I remember watching him with the ball. The tricks, the confidence. He was quite charismatic in a very quiet way. He could never be described as extrovert but he was a presence."

That presence had done enough to stir jibes from elsewhere, not least London and the *Evening Standard* newspaper, which had a dig at Teesside after Arsenal had failed to win Juninho's signature. The gist of what was said can be gleaned easily enough from the response in Middlesbrough.

'Don't believe a word of it' an *Evening Gazette* front-page headline told Juninho. The story said:

> Proud Teessiders today rounded on a London newspaper after an astonishing attack on our area. The *Evening Standard* article commenting on Boro's coup in signing Brazilian soccer superstar Juninho MOCKS the way we speak, IMPLIES our women are unattractive, DAMNS the area as polluted and ugly.

Though the *Standard*'s attack was probably tongue-in-cheek, it touched a nerve and had repercussions.

"Something that was so positive – getting a Brazilian international to come to Middlesbrough – actually worked the other way for us," said Gibson. "It was great PR within the town but outside the town people concentrated on the things that were wrong. Comments along the lines of cloth caps, whippets, coal miners, ugly women. It was horrid. It became a negative factor for the club for quite some time. But the fact is Juninho had come to Middlesbrough and people adored him."

The affection became mutual.

Country life

Middlesbrough offered Juninho a choice of four houses in which to live. He opted for a property in Ingleby Barwick, a village within easy reach of the club. He shared it, at various times, with his mother and father, his sister Gislene, his grandmother Rosa, and an assortment of friends and relatives who travelled from South America for a taste of the English countryside.

"In Brazil I lived in a big city, 20 million people, so of course it was different but I ended up getting on very well with the local people," Juninho recalled. "Whenever I went out they were very welcoming to me. I never thought I wasn't going to adapt. And anyway it's impossible not to adapt to a place where the people are so polite.

"My family decided to come with me because we're close and because it was good for me. I didn't go out that much but we got on well with the neighbours. Everyone was nice to me."

Steve Gibson added: "Possibly because of the bad press the whole town was more motivated to make the whole family feel welcome."

One of the main concerns for the family, not least Juninho's mother and grandmother, was food, and specifically a supply of decent coffee and the right pulses to make an authentic feijoada (pork and bean casserole), Juninho's favourite dish. A small community of ex-pat Brazilians who worked for a local Brazilian-owned engineering firm was on hand to offer advice. Supply lines were soon established.

Middlesbrough's priority was to keep the family happy. Doing so would keep Juninho happy. Gibson enrolled them all at the language-learning unit at the local headquarters of ICI, then a major shareholder in Boro. They received one-to-one tuition and help with any day-to-day problems.

"It's relatively easy for foreign players to settle because they're busy," Gibson said. "It's more difficult for the families because the wives and children don't speak English and they're trying to settle into a new culture. How do they get a plumber if they need one? What if they need help with a bank account? You need to take care of all that."

At ICI the Giroldo clan struck up a particularly close relationship with one tutor, Zelia Knight, a Brazilian who was married to a local man. Gibson's response was to make her a full-time employee at Middlesbrough. "She joined us with the sole aim of looking after the family."

A routine was quickly established. Juninho went to work, his week filled not only with training and playing but a whole range of engagements befitting the most popular man in town.

The number of requests to Middlesbrough for Juninho to make public appearances outstripped the total for the rest of the squad combined. He visited schools, hospitals, coaching clinics. He was the guest of honour at numerous functions and would rarely if ever say no to a shirt-signing session. "There were a lot of invitations and I did my best to talk to everyone," he said.

"Off the pitch, he never said no," said Gibson. "It got to the stage where we had to protect him, ask him not to do so much because nearly all the requests were for him. Left to himself he'd have done them all."

Zelia, meanwhile, took Juninho's family out shopping or sightseeing and arranged trips to different parts of Britain, when they were in England.

"They'd go back and forwards to Brazil, disappear for a while, come back for a month, but there was always someone here with Juninho," Gibson said.

In 2003, Zelia was still with the club, performing the same role for other players and their families.

Getting stuck in

Juninho played 21 League games during the 1995–96 season, scoring only twice as he got to grips with England and its rough-and-tumble game. But if that bedding-in period was pocked with inconsistency, so was Middlesbrough's form. At one stage they lost eight consecutive games in a 13-match winless run that ruined any hopes of qualification for Europe the next year. There was still no doubting the Brazilian's work-rate nor his repertoire of speed, trickery and skill.

"He worked his socks off in training," Gibson said. "And he had a willingness to learn and a desire to learn. And this in someone who had skills that you can't coach. They were God-given, natural talent."

Juninho himself had no doubts that he would be able to cope, despite his size, once he'd spent time acclimatising. He said: "You have to be strong. Never mind your size. Your legs have to be strong. My legs have always been strong so I don't need to be tall to play. If it was basketball or volleyball, sure you need to be tall. But not with football. You have to know how to play. You have to be quick and then you don't have to try to make contact with the other players.

"I knew that for one-on-one challenges for the ball I was going to lose out on size alone. But I try to get there first, make my feet do the work beforehand. It was incredible at first because, when you're watching English football on television, you think there is no space to play. But when you compete you can find space when you're on the pitch. To me there's a very big difference between watching and playing."

Triumphs and tears

No Middlesbrough supporter is ever likely to forget the 1996–97 season. It was the year in which their club was relegated despite having won enough points to stay up. It was the year their team reached two Wembley finals and lost both. It was the year that a posse of foreign players arrived but one made his mark above everyone. For better or worse, it was Juninho's year.

"My enduring memory of that year was whereas one or two of the other foreign players looked to blame everyone else for the club's plight, Juninho just gave it everything he had," said Steve Gibson. "And that's what the fans loved about him as well. He gave everything he could for the football club."

The season had started with a bang when Boro's new £7m Italian striker Fabrizio Ravanelli scored a hat-trick on his debut on the opening day against Liverpool. The only downside was that Liverpool also scored three times to take a point. Boro's next match ended in defeat, 1–0 to Chelsea. This was followed by a 1–1 draw at Nottingham Forest, Juninho getting the goal.

Ten more goals followed in three games as Boro beat West Ham 4–1, Coventry 4–0 and Everton 2–1 at Goodison Park. Juninho, starting to sparkle, scored twice against Coventry and the winner at Everton. He was establishing himself as a danger in the area and the creative hub of the side. His portfolio of jinking runs, twists and turns, bursts of speed and slide-rule passes were the key to Boro's best performances.

Though Juninho was standing out, the team then faltered, securing only four points from four draws, in their next dozen League games. Juninho was absent, injured, for three of them, including the season's biggest defeat, 5–1 at Liverpool. On his return to the side on Boxing Day 1996, he scored twice in a 4–2 win over Everton.

A few days earlier Bryan Robson had made a decision that would, unbeknownst to him or anyone else, prove fatal to Boro's season. Due to an injury and illness crisis that had sidelined 23 of the club's players – Juninho included – Boro had unilaterally cancelled their game at Blackburn on 22 December. The following month, after a Premier League inquiry, Middlesbrough would be docked three points and fined £50,000 for this 'illegal' act. At the end of the season, the three-point deduction meant they were relegated, in 19th place on 39 points. Without the deduction, they would have had 42 points, enough for a 16th-place finish and safety.

That did not become apparent until later, of course. Juninho, in the interim, illuminated the season in the three domestic competitions. Aside from his intrinsic entertainment value, he provided 38 goal assists, mostly for Ravanelli, as well as scoring 15 times himself. He scored a dazzling 90th-minute goal against Sheffield Wednesday after a lightning dribble from the touchline. He was instrumental in four successive League wins in March as Boro beat Derby 6–1, Leicester 3–1, Blackburn 2–1 and Chelsea 1–0. He scored in the last three of those games, including Boro's Goal of the Season against Chelsea, a move he orchestrated from midfield and then finished with a diving header.

Two cup runs led to two Wembley finals. In the Coca-Cola Cup, Hereford were despatched 10–0 on aggregate, before Boro beat Huddersfield, Newcastle, Liverpool and Stockport en route to the final against Leicester, which went to a replay and ended in defeat.

In the FA Cup Boro beat Chester 6–0, then non-League Hednesford, Manchester City (Juninho scored the only goal), Derby (Juninho scored) and Chesterfield, after a replayed semi-final. The end-of-season showpiece final, against Chelsea on 17 May, ended in another defeat.

Six days earlier had come the most poignant of the season's reverses when Middlesbrough were relegated following a 1–1 draw at Leeds. The home side had taken a 77th-minute lead through Brian Deane. Juninho equalised two minutes later. A win – and another two points – would have been enough for safety. It was not to be. At the final whistle, Juninho sank to his knees and wept.

The season had been a personal triumph and was recognised as such when Juninho was voted the Premier League Player of the Year by the tournament's sponsors and runner-up in the

Footballer of the Year award handed out by the Football Writers' Association. He was also the Middlesbrough fans' Player of the Year, with 98 per cent voting for him. (A search party is still looking for the other two per cent.)

But as Juninho knelt on the Elland Road turf, he knew his time at The Riverside was over.

"He didn't want to leave but he was pressured into leaving by the Brazilian national team coach [*Mario Zagalo*], following relegation," said Keith Lamb. "Zagalo knew how desperate Juninho was to go to the World Cup in 1998 and said, 'If you're not playing in the Premier League it will put severe pressure on my ability to pick you for the Brazilian squad'. And so he was almost forced away from the club. I'm sure he would have been the first to stand up to get us back into the Premier League from the First Division. It wasn't as if he hadn't given his all."

Juninho's tears had been genuine, a fact evident even six years later, in 2003, when he recalled how upset he'd been.

"I was, I was. I'd learned to love the club. They'd been very good to me. I was very involved with the club so I didn't want to leave. I was happy. Maybe if we'd won one of the cups it would have been different…

"It was an incredible season because we went twice to Wembley and that meant a lot to the supporters. But at the same time we went down. The fans still say it was the best season ever but it should've been better. We had a lot of opportunities to stay up and we didn't do it. That was the little punch."

Agony in exile

Once the decision had been made that Juninho was leaving, Boro needed to secure the best move for themselves and the player. That meant finding a top-flight club somewhere in Europe. Tottenham's chairman, Alan Sugar, wanted it to be Spurs and he made an offer.

"Spurs fans were quite cynical about Alan Sugar's approach but I know it was a genuine approach," Gibson said. "Alan Sugar rang me and made me a significant offer and the offer was actually better than the one we eventually received from Atletico Madrid."

Juninho went to Madrid and not Spurs for two reasons. After a season of such raw emotion, he could not envisage playing in

England for a team other than Boro. And Boro preferred that he went abroad. That would make it easier to negotiate a first option on a buy-back later. It would also reduce the chances that Juninho would ever have to play *against* Boro.

"We had a preference not to have him staying in England," Gibson said. "Alan Sugar acted with integrity and made an offer acceptable to Middlesbrough Football Club [*but*] there would have been quite a lot of pressure on us, locally, if we'd allowed him to go to another English club. When Atletico made a derisory offer, I told them we had another offer. In the end they matched it. Actually it fell short, but only just short, and Juninho went."

Atletico paid around £12m and agreed to give Boro first refusal if they decided to sell Juninho later.

Within five months of leaving England, Juninho was back, briefly, playing for Atletico in the UEFA Cup against Leicester. The Brazilian gained a small measure of revenge for his Coca-Cola Cup final defeat five months earlier by scoring as the Spaniards ended Leicester's European adventure.

It was a rare positive moment in a wretched time in Madrid. Juninho had re-arranged his life to suit Zagalo but then suffered a broken leg in Spain that kept him out of the 1998 World Cup anyway. The injury, the result of a tackle by Celta Vigo's Michel Salgado, also effectively ended Juninho's career at Atletico Madrid. By the time he was recovering, the manager who'd signed him, Raddy Antic, was gone. Juninho was overlooked by Antic's successor, Arrigo Sacchi, and then also by Sacchi's replacement, Claudio Ranieri.

Trouble and strife from across the Atlantic

Although Juninho had an unhappy time in Madrid, Spain has always had a good record of assimilating Brazilians and other South Americans. The same has not been true of England. The appendices of this book tell their own story of hit-and-miss flings with players from a variety of nations. It is especially evident that players from South and Central America have struggled to settle (or been tough to accommodate).

Middlesbrough found out as much with three other Brazilians in the late 1990s. Branco, a vastly experienced international defender, played only two League games. He failed to settle or to impress and left eight months before his contract was due to expire. Emerson, a huge – and hugely talented – midfielder, played for the best part of two seasons, including all of 1996–97. At one stage he went awol in Brazil after his girlfriend had described Middlesbrough as a "strange, terrible place". He was reluctantly sold.

Then there was Fabio, who was Emerson's girlfriend's brother-in-law. He was ostensibly brought in, along with his wife, as company for Emerson and his partner. He was also given a trial. He'd played a bit of local football in Brazil and had a Spanish passport, which made signing him easy, and he actually ended up getting a chance in the first team. He was outstanding in his one and only match, a First Division game against Huddersfield in October 1997. He never hit such heights, or indeed played, again.

A variety of other players from South America arrived in the north-east around the same time. Among them were Bolivia's Jaime Moreno and Colombia's Hamilton Ricard at Middlesbrough and a range of players from Chile, Paraguay and Argentina at Newcastle. By 2003, St James' Park's most durable South American was Nolberto Solano of Peru, who'd joined the Tynesiders in 1998, giving consistently good service thereafter.

Newcastle fans had previously delighted in the two-year stay of Faustino Asprilla between February 1996 and January 1998. The flamboyant Colombian striker possessed all the attacking verve associated with Kevin Keegan, the manager who signed him. He was part of the side who finished as Premier League runners-up in 1997 and his personal high point came with a European hat-trick against Barcelona. But his ultimate return of nine goals in 48 League matches was a moderate tally and he left for Parma.

The football-crazy north-east witnessed a farcical postscript to the Asprilla story in the 2002–2003 season when Darlington of the Third Division said they were going to stun the football world by signing the Colombian. Darlington's owner, George Reynolds, appeared live on television to announce the great news. Asprilla even appeared with him, smiling and laughing. Within hours he'd boarded a plane and fled, leaving Reynolds understandably fuming. The episode did nothing to dispel the notion that players from the region were a bit of gamble.

It was a theory that had been bolstered by numerous signings across England. Sunderland signed the Honduran Milton

Nunez for £1.6m in March 2000 in the belief he was coming from a top-flight Uruguayan club. He'd actually played for a small Third Division team. He made one substitute appearance at Sunderland before being released for nothing.

Derby paid around £1.9m for an Argentinian, Esteban Fuertes, in 1999 after protracted negotiations. He scored once in eight League games. Passport irregularities were then discovered at Heathrow Airport as he returned from a mid-season break in Portugal. Fuertes was deported, his English sojourn over.

In 2001, Aston Villa paid a club-record fee of £9m to buy the Colombian international striker Juan Pablo Angel. It proved another poor investment when he failed to live up to his transfer fee. Agustin Delgado, a striker from Ecuador, was even more of a disappointment at Southampton. He made one League appearance in his first season after joining in November 2001. By the end of the 2002–2003 season, dogged by injuries and under a cloud after a series of spats and walk-outs, he was no closer to being a regular starter.

Another popular boy from Brazil

There have been some heroes from the region, but local heroes, cult figures at their clubs and not much beyond. Into that category came the Brazilian striker, Edinho, who joined Bradford City of the First Division in 1997. Though his goals were important – he was the joint-top scorer in 1997–98 – his relationship with the supporters cemented his place in local lore. He was known to drive through town, honking his car horn and waving when he saw someone in a Bradford replica shirt. Tales of his generosity abounded, such as the occasion when some fans spotted him dining alone in a local restaurant. He invited them over, paid their bill and engaged in lengthy discourse, despite having mastery only of the words 'yes' and 'thank you'. He lost his place in the team in late 1998 and was loaned to Dunfermline in Scotland before moving to Portugal.

Costa Rica's Paulo Wanchope was briefly adored at Derby County after joining in March 1997. He scored on a memorable League debut as his side inflicted a rare defeat on Manchester United at Old Trafford. His gangling, almost random, runs endeared him to fans although he fared less well after moving to West Ham and later Manchester City.

Of the South Americans who arrived at the Premier League's leading clubs from the late 1990s, Uruguay's Gustavo Poyet was among the most productive. He joined Ruud Gullit's Chelsea legionnaires in the summer of 1997. He excelled as a probing, attack-minded midfielder who maintained consistency at a club renowned for doing the opposite.

Poyet's influence was often underrated but he was badly missed when absent. This was never more apparent than in the middle of the 1998–99 season, when Chelsea's first league title since 1955 seemed attainable. On Boxing Day 1998, with Chelsea at the top of the table, Poyet fell victim to a horrible, damaging tackle by Patrick Colleter, a French Southampton defender. The resultant injury kept him out for 10 games. When Poyet returned, Chelsea were third, having dropped vital points in various games, including those against Manchester United and Arsenal, teams who eventually finished first and second in the title race, five points and four points ahead of Chelsea.

Recovery for Poyet – and Chelsea – came too late on that occasion but the Uruguayan helped win silverware before and after. He was part of the European Cup-Winners' Cup-winning team in 1998 and the FA Cup-winning team of 2000.

Boxing Day 1999 and another significant match. Back at Southampton with Chelsea, a year to the day after the Colleter tackle, Poyet was part of the first all-foreign XI ever to start a League match in England.

By the end of the 2002–03 season, the jury was still out on some of the other major South American migrants to England. Brazil's Gilberto Silva, a World Cup winner in 2002, had been a qualified success during one campaign at Arsenal. Argentina's Juan Sebastian Veron, who'd become British football's record signing when he joined Manchester United for £28m in 2001, had yet to find a role that best utilised his undoubted abilities. The same was true of Uruguay's Diego Forlan, who became an Old Trafford striker in January 2002 but saw his chances to strike quite limited.

Juninho's second coming

Juninho endured his own period of frustration at Atletico Madrid while recovering from his broken leg. By the start of the 1999–2000 season, he was desperate to get back to fitness and felt he needed to be playing matches. Middlesbrough had kept in touch and Steve Gibson, Keith Lamb and Bryan Robson flew out to Spain to meet Oswaldo Snr. He indicated his son wanted to move back to Boro and a short-term loan, from September 1999 to May 2000, was arranged with Atletico.

Back at the Riverside, some things had not changed. Juninho resumed occupation of the same house in Ingleby Barwick and took up where he left off in his rapport with the fans. But the Boro squad – and approach – had seen some significant alterations. Brian Deane, who'd scored for Leeds on Juninho's first Middlesbrough debut and then again on the fateful day in 1997 when they were relegated, was wearing the Brazilian's No10 shirt. Fabrizio Ravanelli was long gone, as was Emerson. The new-look squad – less cavalier, more intent on solidity – now featured the likes of Paul Ince and Gary Pallister, both former Manchester United men like Bryan Robson.

Steve Gibson's assessment was that Juninho had less freedom to show his flair in a side primarily concerned with re-establishing itself back in the Premiership. Certainly he did not thrive as in 1996–97. Robson also felt the recovery from the broken leg was not as it should be. The skill was still there, but the pace and final touch were not back to their best. After nine months, 28 League games and four goals, Juninho's second spell at Boro came to an end.

"We had an option to buy him back," said Gibson. "Despite all the heart strings saying we should keep him, we had to be quite ruthless and we had to let him go. We felt that the injury was showing in his performances."

Renaissance, Ronaldinho and glory

Juninho returned to Atletico in May 2000. Still out of favour, he went home on loan to Brazil's Vasco da Gama. It was the perfect move, leading to success in the Mercosur Cup and more importantly, a recall to the Brazilian squad. By the 2002 World Cup, he was firmly re-established as an international regular.

Before that tournament, many pundits thought the winning nation of 1958, 1962, 1970 and 1994 might struggle to become champions for a record-extending fifth time. France were expected to do well and build on their World Cup win of 1998 and their European Championship success of 2000. Argentina were joint-favourites for the title. Italy, as ever, were fancied to be resilient. Spain, as ever, were touted as having a team who could finally achieve something on the biggest stage. Brazil, while not being written off, arrived unburdened by great expectations. The mood inside the camp was upbeat.

"There was an incredible atmosphere in our group," Juninho said. "We had a lot of difficulties in qualification and didn't play so well. But then we met together only one or two days before each match. When we had the chance to train for a month and a half, we got it together.

"When we arrived at the World Cup our mental [*attitude*] was very sharp. The press didn't know that so that's why they thought we wouldn't do so well. They were surprised when we played our first three games. And then they started to believe us that we could play very well. Because our mental was strong."

Brazil won all their group games, beating Turkey, China and Costa Rica; Juninho featured in each match. They beat Belgium in the second round, with Juninho playing for 57 minutes before being substituted with a non-serious knock.

The quarter-final pitted Brazil against England, whose coach, Sven Goran Eriksson, had Steve McClaren, by then the Middlesbrough manager, as a coaching assistant. Juninho, still recovering from the Belgium match, did not play, although he was involved in the build-up and watched from the bench.

On a sweltering June afternoon in Shizuoka, England took the lead in the 23rd minute through Michael Owen. On the cusp of half-time Brazil equalised. David Beckham, England's captain, who was still recovering from a broken bone in his foot, had jumped out of the way of a challenge near the half-way line. Before he had the chance to say 'holy metatarsal!', a swift counter attack was concluding with Rivaldo scoring for 1–1.

Five minutes after the break, Brazil were ahead after a goal that would cause intense debate for months afterwards. The South Americans won a free kick some 40 yards from the England goal on the right-hand side of the pitch. Ronaldinho, an attacker-midfielder who played his club football in France, stepped up to the ball and lofted it high across the box. As David Seaman, England's goalkeeper, watched on incredulously, the ball floated over his head. He tried to move backwards, arm outstretched, to no avail. The ball dipped into the top left corner of the net. Game over.

Ronaldinho was later sent off but England, resorting to a long-ball game of little wit and no imagination, could not get back on terms. At the final whistle, as Seaman wept, the embodiment of a broken man, the arguments started over whether Ronaldinho had intended his 'freak' goal or not. A question mark would hang over Seaman's international future thereafter.

The winning goal was a major talking point within the Brazilian squad after the match. Ronaldinho and Juninho discussed it. Ronaldinho revealed it was a fluke.

"He said he tried to put the ball in the opposite angle to where it went, the other corner," Juninho recalled. "He could see Seaman. Seaman thought that Ronaldinho was going to cross the ball to the area and Ronaldino tried to surprise Seaman by putting it on the other angle. He mis-hit it. In the end it was lucky. In football you have to be lucky sometimes."

England's reaction after the Ronaldinho goal surprised the Brazilians. "England should've attacked Brazil more when we were down to 10 players," Juninho said. "England didn't go forward. Maybe they were afraid to get another goal. But they should have done that. They tried to use the long balls but our defenders were strong in the air."

Brazil beat Turkey in the World Cup semi-final, for which Juninho was rested, and then beat Germany in the final. Ronaldo, the former World Player of the Year, capped a tournament of personal salvation by scoring both goals in a 2–0 win. After a few unhappy years himself, Juninho – on the pitch as a late substitute for Ronaldinho – achieved his own personal redemption.

Before the World Cup had even started, Steve Gibson had decided he wanted Juninho back at Middlesbrough. The subject had been discussed with Steve McClaren, who agreed that if Juninho had recovered to be anywhere near the player he'd been in 1996–97, he was worth buying.

Gibson thus organised his hectic schedule to combine some business with a trip to the World Cup. He made contact with Juninho's father a couple of days before the quarter-final with England. The conversation started with small talk and catching up on family news. Then Gibson told Oswaldo Snr: "The reason I'm ringing you is because I'm interested in bringing Juninho home."

Juninho's father said his son could be interested. It was all Gibson needed to know so he could make an official approach to Atletico Madrid, to whom Juninho was still contracted. The deal was done and the player moved 'home' to Teesside for around £6m.

"When I was in Spain I always said I wanted to go back to English football," said Juninho, when he was interviewed for this book in February 2003. His third term at Boro had had an inauspicious start because he'd sustained serious knee ligament damage in a friendly before the 2002–03 season and had been sidelined for seven months. But as he talked, he was feeling fit and well and was within days of making his comeback. "It would be strange to play in England but not play for Middlesbrough. That's why I'm here for the third time. And this time I deserve to win something."

The comeback came in a reserve match against Bradford at The Riverside on 25 February 2003. The presence of Juninho drew a staggering 20,000-strong crowd, a record for a second-XI match. He scored once in a 9–0 win. Three days later he made his Premier League re-appearance, against Everton. It was his first competitive match since the World Cup final and his first League match for Middlesbrough since 14 May 2000. The opponents that day had been Everton and Juninho had bid farewell with a goal. He scored against them again to mark his return.

England evidently suited Juninho. Few other leading Brazilians had felt similarly. Spain and Italy were the European destinations of choice for the biggest names, although in February 2003 Juninho sensed that could change. Gilberto Silva, his World Cup-winning team-mate, had moved to Arsenal in 2002, after all. And transfer gossip had frequently linked the likes of Ronaldinho, Rivaldo and even Ronaldo with moves to England.

Of his international colleagues Juninho said: "They've changed their minds about English football. All the players in Europe know now it's exciting. If [permit] controls were more open then there are a lot of South Americans who want to come to England."

He added that the likes of Ronaldo and Rivaldo had been tempted by the Premier League, just not quite tempted enough. "They haven't found the right move. They want to go to a club that's going to play in the Champions' League all the time, and a club fighting for a title. And maybe in England no-one appropriate showed an interest."

It's possible, sometime around the year 2020, that someone in England could be showing an interest in Juninho's son. Lucas Giroldo can already claim to have made the most important debut of his life in Middlesbrough. He was born at the town's James Cook University Hospital in October 2002, shortly after Juninho signed for Boro for a third time. Lucas's first family home was in Yarm, Teesside, where Juninho moved when he returned, bringing his wife, Juliana, and a daughter, Brunna, with him. Juninho had specifically wanted Lucas to be born in England. "That was Juliana's present for me," he said.

As for the future, Lucas will be qualified to play for England. "Yes," said Juninho, grinning. "If he's not good enough to play for Brazil."

CHAPTER TEN

Sublime And Ridiculous

DIAMOND TALENT glints in various shades, from the brilliant orange of Dennis Bergkamp and Ruud Van Nistelrooy to the rhapsody in blue of Gianfranco Zola.

The Dutchmen have played pivotal roles in title-winning teams at Arsenal and Manchester United respectively, pirouetting and galloping to glory and goals. Zola, as enduring as he is magical, has set new standards for his Chelsea team-mates, on and off the pitch. The impact, honours and legacy of these three players are examined later.

But such stars have been hugely outnumbered by other, less stellar, legionnaires. Some have been farcical, others fictional. Many have been ordinary, others simply mercenary. Some have been good enough to shine in major international tournaments but not deemed good enough to rise to England's top division. Others have evidently not been good enough to play there but have managed to do so anyway.

So what? There have been good and bad home-grown players at all levels of the game as long as football has existed. Why should it matter now where players come from? Why should it matter that foreign players are no longer primarily big names at big clubs but routine acquisitions at every club from Carlisle to Wigan, Burnley to Scunthorpe, Millwall to Bournemouth to Plymouth?

On one level, the PFA would argue, it matters because the quest for cheaper, more exotic, crowd-pulling labour has changed the make-up of the player pool too radically. In 1990, of the country's 3,000 professionals, a few dozen came from overseas. By 2003, some 1,200 more had followed. To the displaced natives and their union, that's simply too many. They say mediocre imports have taken the jobs of home-grown players. They say this will damage the long-term development of the domestic game at club and international level. That whole argument can be saved for later.

On another level, the influx matters because of the effects of its rapidity and scale. The clubs have contributed to this, wittingly and otherwise. They have paid enormous salaries to lure leading players from overseas. This has been necessary in many cases to compete with the richest continental clubs. And there is nothing wrong with paying the going rate if you can afford it and you think you're getting value for money.

But many clubs have paid high, unsustainable wages to very ordinary players, justifying that expenditure with claims that in the post-Bosman era, savings have been made on transfer fees. These claims have been made throughout the divisions. In reality, these savings have often been cancelled out by the costs of higher salaries. Worse, by paying high wages – either to lure players or because no transfer fee was paid – clubs have helped create crippling wage inflation.

This wage inflation has only increased the attraction of England as a place of work, not just for players but for middle men and agents. If their clients are earning more, they are earning more. And if their clients are moving around, so much the better. Fees to agents for a few days' work arranging a move can run to hundreds of thousands of pounds.

So the range and the number of newcomers have continued to grow, leading to fundamental changes in the recruitment process. These are intrinsically linked to the process of dealing with foreign markets. Clubs rely, more heavily than ever before, on third-party brokers. Basic information on background and ability is often left to people with vested interests to verify on trust. Sometimes such details are never verified at all. Haphazard hiring, sometimes solely on video evidence, is far from unknown.

In essence, the process that has brought some wonderful, innovative footballers has also brought some absolute duds.

It has brought hoaxers, whose antics can be seen as amusing, and shadowy opportunists whose mendacity, scamming – and occasional threats of violence – cannot.

In 1999 Gordon Taylor, the chief executive of the PFA, revealed that up to a fifth of foreign players seeking working permits in England had had their requests refused in the previous five years because of suspicions that deals were being brokered by unscrupulous agents.

"I'm talking about players from places such as Eastern Europe, Africa and South America," he said. "With those deals, I'd estimate that in 10 to 20 per cent of cases there have been too many grounds for caution to allow the deals to go through." Taylor said the PFA had been concerned that buying clubs had been asked to pay fees to third parties rather than to the selling clubs. "If we're not careful, the game will be run by agents. Without proper controls, you can't be sure who's getting paid for what."

Anecdotal evidence within the game suggests such problems have not gone away. The difficulty for investigators, not least the football authorities, is that the evidence has remained mostly that – anecdotal. Administrators and senior club figures, interviewed anonymously for this book, talked about offers of bungs and corrupt middle men, including one agent who showed up with heavies and threatened extreme violence unless his client was allowed to move.

A chairman and a manager at one club had both been offered bungs, which they said were declined. One senior executive talked about going overseas to negotiate a deal. An agent mistook him for another middle man instead of the major shareholder he was. "This guy said he'd open a Swiss bank account for my slice of the action. I told him he was suggesting I nick my own money. Then I told him to f-off."

So did all these incidents get reported? No. The reason? Lack of evidence. As one executive said: "If you're in the clear yourself and you don't get involved in that, how can you prove something that *didn't* happen? And if you did report it, there's the possibility that it gets out that you're helping with an investigation. And then everyone thinks you're 'at it' anyway."

But back to the players. Into the blend of the sublime and the ridiculous, you can also throw plenty of decent jobbing professionals, of myriad nationalities, who have simply tried to make their way. They have arrived in England, settled happily in towns and cities up and down the country, become firm local favourites and played, productively, for years. The whole ensemble has helped to change the English football landscape.

What can never be known for certain is whether a newcomer will settle, whether he will succeed, whether he will have that X factor that wins games and hearts. This is as true of those who have already been successful and famous elsewhere as it is of those who are unknown. Players who have cost millions have flopped. Others who have cost nothing have excelled. But every new arrival, on debut day at least, speaks of hope: for the clubs, for the fans, and for the players themselves.

Before considering some of the more extreme cases of transfer madness and recruitment mayhem, here are a few snapshots from a cosmopolitan age. The winners and losers are not always easy to distinguish.

1995

Jesus, Bob and Izzy, Wigan Athletic's 'Three Amigos', all made their League debuts in a Third Division game at Gillingham on 12 August 1995. The trio had been imported from Spain for free. The following weekend three Dutchmen – Dennis Bergkamp, Marc Boogers, and Ruud Gullit – made debuts respectively for Arsenal, West Ham and Chelsea in the Premier League.

The Spaniards, aka Jesus Seba, Roberto Martinez and Isidro Diaz, went on to become the darlings of Wigan, although Seba made fewer than 10 starts and Diaz's wages eventually priced him away, to Wolves. He failed to impress, returned to Wigan and failed to resettle. Martinez had staying power, and was Wigan's longest serving player and a local hero when the club released him, against his will, in 2001.

By that time Gullit, a former World Footballer of the Year, had been gone from English football for almost two years having been a player and manager at Chelsea and then manager at Newcastle. Boogers, who only ever made four substitute appearances, was a distant and laughable memory. (He was one of 19 foreign players signed by West Ham between 1995 and 1997, eleven of whom made fewer than 10 starts for the club.) Bergkamp had won one Double, was on his way to another and had been the 1998 Footballer of the Year.

1996

Stephane Pounewatchy, an amiable, saxophone-playing French defender, made his League debut for Carlisle United in a Third Division game at Doncaster on 17 August 1996. He had cost nothing, having previously played in France for Gueugnon, with whom he'd been relegated. The next day Gianluca Vialli, who'd won the European Cup with Juventus that year and then joined Chelsea for nothing, made his Premier League debut in a 0–0 draw at Southampton. In November 1996, Vialli was joined at Stamford Bridge by compatriot Gianfranco Zola, who cost £4.5m from Parma. The weekend after Zola's first game, another Premier League debutant, Ali Dia, was making his bow for Southampton.

Pounewatchy went on to help Carlisle win promotion in his first season and was part of the side who were relegated the next. He moved to Dundee in Scotland on an insecure monthly contract and lasted three games before playing twice on the same terms for Port Vale. He next had a short spell at Colchester. (Colchester incidentally, had employed seven overseas-born goalkeepers alone by that point in their history. Very few clubs have never had at least one foreign keeper, while the likes of Chelsea, Crewe, Fulham, Liverpool and Manchester United have all matched or bettered Colchester's seven.)

Pounewatchy's last club in England was Scunthorpe. He never made a League appearance for them but was part of the set-up when they were relegated in 2000. By that point Vialli was entering his last few months of management at Chelsea, where he'd won the FA Cup as a player (1997) and manager (2000), and the League Cup and European Cup-winners' Cup (both 1998) while the player-manager. He was sacked. Dia, who only ever made that one appearance for Southampton, as a substitute who was substituted, was another distant and laughable memory. Zola had won two FA Cups, a League Cup, a European Cup-Winners' Cup and had been the 1997 Footballer of the Year.

1998

On 15 September 1998, millions of people in China sat glued to their television sets, waiting for a man called Graham to blow a whistle in Bury and signify a defining moment in their nation's sporting history. Graham Laws, a Football League referee, duly signalled the start of a Worthington Cup second-round, first-leg game between Bury and Crystal Palace. There were no live pictures of the match in China but news bulletins provided a massive audience with in-depth updates. The reason? Palace's Fan Zhiyi and Sun Jihai had just become the first Chinese players to make first-team debuts in English football. Palace lost 3–0.

Four days later, Fan Zhiyi became the first of the Chinese to make a League debut, in a 4–0 defeat at Barnsley. The Palace team that day also included an Argentinian debutant, Walter Del Rio. In Palace's next match, a mid-table First Division encounter with Sheffield United on 27 September, Fan Zhiyi and Del Rio both featured. Unlikely though it sounds, it was one of the most eagerly anticipated matches in the world that weekend. It was screened live in China, attracting an audience of millions on subscriber and pay-per-view channels.

Fan Zhiyi, China's international captain, went on to play for Palace for three years before moving to Dundee in 2001, where the manager at the time was Ivano Bonetti, an Italian. Bonetti had been one of 18 foreign arrivals – including Fan Zhiyi and Sun Jihai – at Crystal Palace between August 1997 and November 1998.

Fan Zhiyi's time in Dundee was cut short when the football authorities in China ordered he move back home to Shanghai in March 2002 to prepare for the forthcoming World Cup. He did so, and both he and Sun Jihai, who'd left Palace to go back to China in 1999, played for their country in that tournament. In early 2003, Fan Zhiyi was playing for Second Division Cardiff City and Sun Jihai was at Manchester City. At Crystal Palace, Walter Del Rio was a distant and not-so-funny memory. His time at the club had been restricted to the two games mentioned above. He'd been released against his will when the club was in financial meltdown in 1999. He joined Bonetti's Dundee a year later and then dropped out of the British game at the end of the 2001–02 season.

2000

Eddie Lewis, an American international winger, joined First Division Fulham from San Jose Earthquakes for £1.3m and made his League debut in March 2000. It seemed to be the start of a great adventure. A few weeks later, Ruud Van Nistelrooy, then a prolific striker with PSV Eindhoven, announced he was signing for Manchester United. Within a few days United announced that the Dutch international would not, in fact, be joining them, because his medical had shown a problem with his medial ligaments. The deal was called off and Van Nistelrooy, within days, had broken down in training with a serious knee injury. His dream move was in doubt, if not over.

By the end of the 2001–02 season, Lewis had made a total of 16 League games for Fulham in 26 months with the London club. He had made only one appearance in the previous year. In the summer of 2002 he played for the United States as they reached the quarter-finals of the World Cup, an event Van Nistelrooy missed because The Netherlands had failed to qualify. Lewis spent the 2002–03 season with Preston as the First Division side tried to reach mid-table. Van Nistelrooy, who'd eventually joined Manchester United in 2001, spent the season scoring goals for fun as his side won their eighth Premier League title in 11 years.

Movers and fakers

Southampton's Ali Dia was the antithesis of Ruud Van Nistelrooy. Calling him a one-hit wonder would be inaccurate. He didn't hit the target and the only thing wondrous about his Premier League 'career' was how he ever made it on the pitch in the first place.

His one game for the Saints came in 1996. He had apparently been recommended to the Saints manager, Graeme Souness, by Liberia's George Weah, a superstar at Milan and the World Footballer of the Year.

According to some of Southampton's players, including Francis Benali and Matt Le Tissier, Dia had seemed strangely reluctant to exert himself in training. No-one made a big issue of the fact. Weah wouldn't recommended duds, would he? And anyway, it was reasoned, Dia hadn't been at the club long and was probably still acclimatising. Souness put him on the bench for the Leeds game on 23 November.

The match was 32 minutes old when Le Tissier suffered a groin strain and limped off. Dia was sent on in his place. Within seconds he had a first opportunity for glory. Eyal Berkovic, Southampton's Israeli playmaker, surged forward from the halfway line. Dia ran ahead of him and peeled off to the right. Berkovic slipped a pass to his feet, all of 12 yards from goal.

With time and space to pick his spot, Dia kicked the ball straight at the goalkeeper, Nigel Martyn.

It was the high point in Dia's afternoon. In the second half it became obvious he was out of his depth. He struggled for position, wasted possession of the ball and tired quickly. This was a problem and became serious when Leeds' Gary Kelly scored the first goal of the game in the 82nd minute. If Southampton wanted to take anything from the contest they needed to score. Dia was clearly not going to do that. The substitute was substituted five minutes from the end. He had been on the pitch for 53 minutes. He was replaced up front by Ken Monkou, a defender. Leeds scored again, the game finished.

Little fuss was made the next day. A poor debut was an unremarkable event. According to newspaper reports, which concentrated on the simple details of who Dia was, the newcomer was a 30-year-old Senegalese international striker. (He was actually 31.) It was reported that Dia had been available on a free transfer after leaving Bologna in Italy, and that he'd been a former team-mate of Weah's at Paris St Germain. Souness was quoted as saying: "When someone the calibre of George Weah calls to recommend a player you tend to sit up and take notice."

It took a few weeks for Dia's true credentials to be revealed. Several lower division clubs, having seen him on TV against Leeds, announced they'd been approached before Southampton. Second Division Peterborough and Bournemouth had both considered him because he had a French passport and a move would've been free of red tape. Trials proved unconvincing.

First Division Port Vale admitted they'd been surprised to hear from Weah but weren't the kind of club to look a gift horse in the mouth. Vale had actually played Dia in a reserve match in September before deciding he wasn't going to fit in. Tony Pullis, the manager at Second Division Gillingham, was more forthright in his appraisal. He'd also taken a phone call from 'Weah' and then given Dia a trial. "The lad was rubbish," Pullis said.

Belated checks into Dia's past revealed he was not an international. George Weah, asked about the player, said he did not know anyone of that name and had certainly not made calls on his behalf. Bologna and PSG had never heard of him. The whole background was fabrication.

Dia, whose professional experience actually stretched no further than a few months with lowly Lubeck in Germany, said he was innocent. He said that an agent he'd employed in England had been claiming to be Weah without his knowledge. After a few setbacks, it had been relatively simple to get a game in the Premier League. Dia subsequently moved to non-League Gateshead, where he scored two goals in 10 games in a three-month stay. He later took a business degree at the University of Northumbria, graduating in 2001. Weah played briefly for Chelsea and Manchester City in 2000, making more impact than Dia had done at Southampton. But not that much more.

While Dia's appearance in the League was the result of a few lies and some institutional complacency, at least he had existed in the real world. The same wasn't true of Didier Baptiste, who seemed on course for a move to Liverpool in 1999. At least that's what the readers of *The Times* could have been forgiven for thinking.

In the daily round-up of Premier League news on 23 November 1999, the newspaper reported:

> Liverpool are interested in signing Didier Baptiste, the left-back, who is a France Under-21 international and plays for AS Monaco. He would cost £3.5m.

The story had been taken from a seemingly authoritative source, Liverpool's Clubcall service, an official premium-rate telephone hotline that promised the inside line from Anfield for 60p a minute. Unfortunately, the inside line had been anything but. Clubcall had taken the story from the previous day's *News of the World*.

On the 21 November 1999, the newspaper had told its readers:

> Liverpool boss Gérard Houllier wants Monaco's £3.5m rated French U-21 international Didier Baptiste after losing out to Manchester United in his bid to sign Mickael Silvestre earlier this season. But he faces stiff competition from Arsène Wenger who wants a long-term replacement for Nigel Winterburn at Arsenal.

On the same day, *The Observer* reported:

> Liverpool are close to signing French
> U21 star Didier Baptiste from
> Monaco.

The story had been taken in good faith from a news agency, Hayter's. The agency had acquired it, in good faith but without independent checks, after it had appeared on an unofficial website. Baptiste, it seemed, had confided that he might be moving to play "in England for a French manager".

Herein lay the problem. Baptiste was not real but a character on *Dream Team*, Sky TV's football soap opera. In the storyline he was moving from Monaco to fictional Harchester United. Tom Redhill, the actor who played Baptiste, had indeed uttered the line about playing in England for a French manager. But in the fantasy land of English football, a false whisper to a news agency had become hard news.

Two Sunday newspapers had picked it up and run with it. Liverpool's Clubcall service had no reason to doubt such voices of authority. *The Times* had no reason to doubt Liverpool. News outlets around the world had no reason to doubt any of them. That's why a paper as far removed as *The Waikato Times* in New Zealand found itself having to tell readers on 26 November 1999:

> Oops. Now here's a trap for New
> Zealand-based soccer fans who try to
> bring you the latest UK news.

The Baptiste affair, amusing and harmless though it was, was illustrative of the state of the game. In an industry where hundreds of stories each week linked unknown players to clubs, fiction could pass as fact. The cross-border trade had made verification not only tricky but evidently, in some cases, unnecessary.

Arguably the Baptiste blooper was only spotted – and gloated over by those not involved – because the error was prominent and could be traced. There was also irony in the fact that *The Times* and the *News of the World* were both owned by the same company that owned Sky TV, which made *Dream Team* and had exclusive rights to Premier League football. But if another fictional name had been inserted into a similar story about a less high-profile club and nothing had come of it, it's easy to believe it would have passed largely unnoticed.

Believing what you're told is not abnormal. Southampton believed Ali Dia was a peer of George Weah's. Sunderland believed Milton Nunez was a top Honduran player. West Ham believed, on the basis of an edited video, that Marco Boogers was worth an investment in his transfer fee and wages. Crystal Palace believed the same of Walter Del Rio and others.

Third Division Bury believed, in 1993, that David Adekola was an experienced Nigerian international striker with 16 caps and a good track record in the French league. It seemed touching rather than bizarre when he said he wanted to join Bury rather than Marseille because his girlfriend lived nearby.

Unlike Ali Dia later, Adekola made a great start to his League career. Bury won six of the first seven League matches he played for them. He scored in his second game and got two more in his fourth. He scored again his fifth and nabbed a hat-trick in his sixth. This was ample reason for the fans to delight in the coup.

Adekola went on to play a total of 48 League games while attached to six different clubs over four years. Most of his appearances – 35 of them – came for Bury, where his early blaze of form petered out by his second season. Only later, after investigations by *The Observer*, did it emerge that Adekola's caps could not be traced and that clubs in France who he had supposedly been attached to had never heard of him. Did it matter to the Bury fans, who'd warmed to his character and relished his goals? Not really. Why should it?

Trouble at Palace

The story of Crystal Palace in the 1998–1999 season provided one of the most emphatic examples of what can go wrong when scrutiny is thrown out the window. The hiring of a posse of foreign players was a significant part of the problem. Indeed when the club went into administration in March 1999 with debts of £20m, contractual liabilities alone – not least to 'star' foreign names – stood at around £14m. Another £5.4m was owed to foreign clubs in unpaid transfer fees. And the owner of Palace, Mark Goldberg, who ended up bankrupt, was still pondering quite how he'd managed to sanction some rather bizarre signings.

Goldberg first showed an interest in owning Palace in 1997, when the then owner, Ron Noades, placed an advert in the *Financial Times* seeking interested buyers. Goldberg phoned Noades and told him he was a lifelong fan and had plans to transform the club. Noades had never heard of Goldberg but discovered he was a moderately wealthy businessman who owned a recruitment company, MSB, that mainly dealt with IT specialists.

Noades did a deal whereby Goldberg would buy 10 per cent of Palace for £3m in November 1997 with an option to buy the rest when he'd raised the money. He struggled to do so and sold more than £20m of shares in MSB to raise the funds. He paid Noades £22.8m for the club, but this did not include Palace's ground, Selhurst Park, to which Noades retained the freehold. As even Noades acknowledged: "It was a stupid deal for him to do."

Even before Goldberg had taken a controlling interest in Palace, he helped to broker a deal which took the Italian midfielder, Attilio Lombardo, from Juventus on a contract worth an astronomical £14,000 per week. Goldberg thought that by assembling a glittering array of international names he'd be able to steer Palace to the upper echelons of the Premier League and market the Palace brand worldwide.

By the time Goldberg had completed his takeover in the summer of 1998, Palace had been relegated, taking Lombardo (and his wage bill) into the First Division. Undaunted, Goldberg hired Terry Venables as his new manager. He offered the former England manager a package including a salary worth £750,000 a year after tax, an unsecured interest-free loan of £500,000, a house worth £650,000 and a Mercedes. It was little surprise that Venables accepted. Why wouldn't he if that's what Goldberg was prepared to pay?

Between July and November 1998, Palace signed nine foreign players. They included an Australian defender, Craig Moore, signed on a four-year contract on a starting wage of £10,705 per week; a Yugoslav defender, Gordan Petric, who signed on a four-year deal that paid £5,000 a week; an Israeli defender, David Amsalem, signed on video evidence, on a three-year contract worth £6,500 a week; a Swedish forward, Mathias Svensson, signed on a four-year contract worth £3,500 per week; and Craig Foster, an Australian midfielder, signed on a weekly wage of £3,000, contracted to rise to £4,000, plus an annual loyalty bonus of £100,000.

To give some idea of how big these deals were, a survey of footballers' salaries in April 2000, compiled by *The Independent* in association with the PFA, showed the average wage in the First Division was less than £2,500 per week. Yet Palace had been paying, in some cases, up to four or five times as much 18 months earlier.

Three of Palace's other foreign signings in the period July–November 1998 caused ripples that went beyond the balance sheet. They were those of the Chinese pair, Fan Zhiyi and Sun Jihai (who had initial wages of £3,500 a week each) and the Argentinian Walter Del Rio (£2,500 a week).

Goldberg's grand plan behind signing Fan and Sun was to make Palace a force in the enormous market of China. This never happened. Some of Palace's games were screened there but the money from the rights deals wasn't huge and anyway went into a central Football League pot for distribution to all the 72 clubs below the Premier League. There was no Chinese stampede for Palace shirts and souvenirs, there were no lucrative spin-off deals and no Palace-mania. By the time Goldberg was on his way out of Selhurst Park, licking his wounds after blowing some £30m, all he'd amassed was nightmares.

The original deal to bring Fan and Sun to London had been troublesome. In August 1998 Palace agreed to pay £1.35m for the two players. In November 1998 it was revealed that the authorities in China were expecting only $1.5m, or £400,000 less than the figure Palace were paying. Somewhere in the deal, £400,000 seemed to be unaccounted for. Shijun Liu, the London-based Chinese representative in the deal, said he could not comment because of a confidentiality clause in the deal.

In mid-November, Palace released a statement saying:

> At today's board meeting, it was confirmed that the board had requested an FA-assisted inquiry into the destination of monies paid by the club to a Chinese FA bank account in London, authorised by its London representative Shijun Liu, for its two Chinese players.

No action was taken after an investigation and the two sides reportedly resolved their differences. No explanation of what happened to the missing money was ever made public.

Another transfer that Goldberg was unhappy with was David Amsalem's. Aside from the player's £6,500-per-week wages, Palace had agreed to pay a fee of £850,000 for him, or about £600,000 more than Goldberg thought he was worth. The gamble didn't pay off. After six League starts and four substitute appearances Amsalem was released. His original move had been problematic after the selling club, Maccabi Neve Alom, had complained they hadn't received all the money they thought was due. It was around this time that Goldberg said he would support any moves within the football industry "for improved regulatory procedures governing the transfer of foreign players".

If one single move summed up that era at Palace it was that of Del Rio. The transaction that saw him move from Argentina in the summer of 1998 was typically confused. His arrival was announced in the club programme along with that of two other young compatriots, Pablo Rodrigues and Cristian Ledesma. Rodrigues subsequently failed a medical and went home while Ledesma was unhappy with the deal he was offered and left without playing too.

Del Rio remained, alone, although how much he cost was uncertain, even to those within Palace's hierarchy. In 1999, a leaked letter from Palace's former chief executive, Jim McAvoy, who'd resigned in dismay at the club's situation earlier that year, said: "The Argentinian escapade cost £448,769 in agent fees and £187,000 in transfer fees." No transfer fee should have been payable for Del Rio because he was out of contract when Palace signed him. English football clubs are loath to disclose how much they pay for players or how much agents receive. It was subsequently revealed that a British agency, First Artist, had made £91,000 commission on the Del Rio deal. But as with the Chinese transfers, Palace never explained publicly the full facts surrounding the Argentinians.

Del Rio's personal plight showed the insecurity and pitfalls of being a young player abroad. From being a 22-year-old squad player with Boca Juniors in Buenos Aires, he'd gambled on his future and eight months later found himself with no job and no income, living in Croydon, south London. Instead of coaching sessions at home that had featured guest appearances by his hero, Diego Maradona, he ended up excluded from Palace training and running around a field by himself to keep fit.

During an interview with Del Rio at the time, the player said he had only travelled to England after being told Venables had been impressed by watching a video of him in action: "I was very excited to have the chance to play for Crystal Palace," he said. He made his debut in a 4–0 defeat at Barnsley in September and was then used as a late substitute in the next game against Sheffield United. The club's coach, Terry Fenwick, went onto the pitch afterwards, put his arm around Del Rio, and said: "You did very well today. Well done." It was Del Rio's last appearance. "But no-one ever talked to me or told me why," he said.

In March 1999, with Palace in a parlous financial state, Del Rio received a two-sentence letter signed by the club secretary, Michael Hurst.

> This is to confirm that Crystal Palace Football Club have given you a free transfer. You have the club's authority to seek future employment with any other club.

Del Rio was not paid that month. A second letter, dated 13 April, said:

> I, as secretary, acting with the authority and on behalf of the Club, hereby give notice that the Club will cancel your contract on 30 June 1999.

It was also signed by Hurst. The club had every right to cancel the contract – it was only due to run a year – but Palace had also stopped paying him. He went to training every day so they could not claim that he'd failed to turn up. He ran around by himself.

"I'm very worried," he said at the time. "It's very difficult. I sent my last pay home and now I have no money." Del Rio's wages made a big difference to his widowed mother and two brothers. At the time he also had concerns over whether the bailiffs would arrive to evict him from his flat in Croydon, which the club paid the rent for, or whether his car would be repossessed. In the end he went home and returned to British football the following year with Dundee.

One of the most ironic aspects of that era was how much was actually done to meet the needs of the Palace players.

275

Among other personnel, Goldberg hired a broadcasting manager, an IT manager, a human resources manager, an Internet specialist, a variety of PR executives, a full-time doctor, a fitness expert and team of three personal trainers, a nutritionist, five physiotherapists, a masseur, extra office staff and a cook. But no-one specifically to meet players from the airport. Or see them off again.

Local heroes

The flipside to the unhappy, short-lived stays of the likes of Walter Del Rio can be found in the stories of men like Alex Calvo-Garcia from Spain.

"He's considered to be something of a local hero," said John Staff, an historian and lifelong fan of Scunthorpe United. "He was the first foreign player to join us who had no previous ties with England. He came over because he wanted to make it in the Football League. When he arrived he spoke limited English but with a lot of hard work, on the pitch and in the language classroom, he made it into the first team."

In 1996 Calvo-Garcia, a midfielder, was playing for a small club, Eibar, located in northern Spain between Bilbao and San Sebastian. He was 24 at the time and felt he wanted to try living abroad. His agent told him Scunthorpe were holding trials. He knew nothing about Scunthorpe, or indeed where it was, but he travelled anyway and was immediately offered a contract.

By the end of the 2002–03 season, he'd completed almost seven seasons with the club, having made more than 200 League starts and scored some vital goals. None was more important than the only goal of Scunthorpe's Third Division play-off final at Wembley Stadium in 1999. "There was even talk of naming a street after him after that," said Staff.

Although Calvo-Garcia broke his leg during the 1999–2000 season, spending a long and painful year on the sidelines, he fought back to fitness and returned to the side. Away from the club, he'd bought a house in the town with his Spanish wife, Leira, and taken up snooker as a hobby. It wasn't a game he'd ever played at home but a lot of his Scunthorpe team-mates played.

"He's extremely popular with the fans and can easily be spotted around town," said John Staff. "But then his car is the only one in Scunthorpe with a Spanish registration plate."

Despite standing out, Calvo-Garcia believes England to be a more peaceful place to make a living than Spain. The fans are more loyal, he said, and it is easier to go about daily life without being pestered all the time.

Another player who acclimatised well was Canada's Carlo Corazzin, a striker. By the end of the 2002–03 season he'd spent almost 10 years in England providing decent service at each of his four clubs, Cambridge, Plymouth, Northampton and Oldham. He'd made more than 300 League starts and scored more than 100 goals. Despite never making it into the Premier League, he'd enjoyed a triumphant career as part of the most successful national side in Canada's history.

In February 2000, while making a living at Third Division Northampton Town, he won the Golden Boot at the Gold Cup, an event that Canada won after beating the likes of Mexico and Colombia. He scored in the final against the latter and received his Golden Boot from Sir Bobby Charlton afterwards. "Winning it was an honour but it was almost as much of an honour to be presented it by him," he said.

After the Gold Cup Corazzin went back to Northampton and ended that season by helping them to win promotion to the Second Division. He hoped at the time that an offer might come in from a First Division club – or even one of the smaller Premier League sides – but nothing materialised and he moved to Oldham.

Corazzin's international colleague, Jason De Vos, a defender, spent the 2002–03 season not far away, at Wigan. He'd previously played at Dundee United. Before that he'd been at Darlington, where he gave locals something to celebrate by becoming the first player in the club's history to win international honours while attached to them. He achieved the feat when he played for Canada against Iran in August 1997. It probably wasn't the kind of fixture that many Darlo followers would have imagined would excite them a decade before, but it showed the positives of the foreign invasion.

Other full internationals who have played hundreds of times for English clubs without ever making it to the top division include Australia's Andy Bernal (Reading), Tim Cahill (Millwall) and Shaun Murphy (Notts County, West Brom, Sheffield United and Crystal Palace); Bermuda's Kyle Lightbourne (nine different clubs); and St Vincent's Rodney Jack (Torquay and Crewe).

Numerous others have started at lower clubs and worked up – including Australia's Lucas Neill and the United States' Kasey Keller – while many more will undoubtedly follow.

Others have gone in at the top with the sole intention of staying there, not least two brilliant Dutchmen and a pint-sized Italian.

Brilliant orange

The greatest strikers need to have a hunger that success doesn't sate. A hunger for the game for its own sake, a hunger for the ball, a hunger for goals and a hunger for improvement. Ruud Van Nistelrooy has the hunger of a horse.

At the end of the 2002–03 season he'd won a Premier League winners' medal, a Golden Boot and broken or equalled another set of records. By scoring against Everton on the last day of the season, he'd taken his Manchester United tally for the season to 44. Twelve of those had come in the Champions' League (a tournament record) and 25 in the Premier League (which won him the Golden Boot).

His goal at Goodison Park made him the first United player to score in 10 consecutive games – eight in the League and two in Europe – and equalled his own record of scoring in eight successive Premier League matches. His scintillating form had brought two goals for The Netherlands, meaning he'd racked up 17 goals (including two hat-tricks and one brace) in the final 12 matches of his football year.

These were remarkable feats even by his own standards. In the 2001–02 season, his first at United after recovering from a serious injury, he'd scored 'only' 35 goals, including 23 in the Premier League (enough for the Golden Boot) and 10 in Europe (the highest in the competition).

And yet in May 2003 he was already talking of new targets.

"What I really want is to get at least 150 goals or more," he said. "For a foreign player to score that many times for Manchester United would be a truly remarkable achievement. What happened to us last season [*not winning any competition*] was a total sickener for me. I'm not used to a season finishing without a trophy and it felt bad."

In December 2002, while United's form had been fluctuating, Van Nistelrooy had been reluctant to talk numbers but had shown a yearning for improvement.

"My goal for this year is to become the complete striker... I'm always looking to be a better player and that's why I try to do more in training and in games as well. That's what it's all about.

"I'm 26 and I didn't come to Manchester United to say 'That's it, I've made it now, I don't need to work hard, I can't improve any more'. You're going to be a worse player if you say that. So it's all about trying to improve and working hard in training on the things you want to do in a game. Having shown people what I could do last season I now have to work even harder this year. I'm very confident that things will work out for me."

Evidence of hunger can be found throughout Van Nistelrooy's career. Rewind to 23 April 2003. United were playing the second leg of their Champions' League quarter-final against Real Madrid at Old Trafford. It had been billed as a clash of the titans. In reality it was a contest between one of the best two teams in England and a side from another planet featuring Zinedine Zidane, Ronaldo, Luis Figo et al.

United started the game trailing 3–1 from the first leg in Spain, which had been a sumptuous exhibition of the art of football by Real Madrid, and a goal by Van Nistelrooy. Real Madrid went 1–0 up through Ronaldo in the second leg to make it 4–1 on aggregate. Then Van Nistelrooy scored just before half-time to make 1–1 on the night and 4–2 overall. Most of United's players, if not lethargic in their celebrations, acted as though the goal was a consolation not a comeback. But there was Van Nistelrooy, following the ball into the net to retrieve it and return it to the centre circle for the restart. He wanted to play ball.

In the end Real won 6–5 on aggregate after a superb Ronaldo hat-trick. But it wasn't through lack of effort by United's Dutchman.

Rewind again, to 16 April 2003. The race for the League title had reached the crunch. Manchester United were top of the table with five games left. Arsenal were three points behind with a game in hand, a better goal difference and a seemingly easier run-in. United were playing at Arsenal.

In the 24th minute Van Nistelrooy exchanged passes with Ryan Giggs, eased past Sol Campbell and Martin Keown like they were part-timers not England internationals and bore down on goal. He waited just long enough for the goalkeeper to start going down then chipped in for 0–1. Thierry Henry scored twice, the second in the 62nd minute to make it 2–1 to Arsenal. Giggs equalised a minute later and ran off to celebrate. And there was Van Nistelrooy, following the ball into the net to retrieve it and return it to the centre circle for the restart. He wanted to play ball.

The game ended 2–2, which at the season's end proved good enough. Some effort from United's Dutchman.

Rewind again, to 21 April 2000. Ruud Van Nistelrooy was sitting at a table in The Netherlands in front of banks of television cameras and dozens of reporters. He'd called a unilateral press conference to announce he was leaving PSV Eindhoven to become a Manchester United player. This was real hunger, risky hunger.

"I'm glad I'm in a position to play for Manchester United," he said. "It is an honour for any player to play for them and I'm very happy. United made contact with me two weeks ago and on Thursday it was finished. It was very quick."

United were not as certain as the player that the move was a done deal. Van Nistelrooy was so happy he wanted to tell the world. In Manchester, United's assistant secretary, Ken Ramsden, said:

"The two clubs have agreed terms and we have agreed terms with the player and he will now come over next week for a medical. Hopefully that will go well and there will then be a press conference some time next week to announce the completion of the transfer."

The word 'hopefully' hung in the air like a dark cloud for four days.

On 25 April, United announced that Van Nistelrooy's move had been put on indefinite hold. The club's doctors had been unhappy with a recurring knee problem. They wanted to open it up and examine the ligaments but Van Nistelrooy preferred they didn't because he was hungry to play for his country on home turf in Euro 2000 that summer.

Three days later, Van Nistelrooy launched himself into a routine jump for a ball on a PSV training pitch. As he landed he snapped the cruciate ligament in his suspect knee. There was career-threatening damage and his move to Old Trafford was plunged further into doubt.

He banished negative thoughts and got on with his rehabilitation. He spent months undergoing physiotherapy, unable to train or even run properly. Instead he swam for hours on end and did weights to increase his upper-body strength. It was an area he had wanted to improve and it seemed a good time to do it. He eventually returned to action at the tail end of the 2000–01 season, scoring two goals in 10 games for PSV. His move to United was resurrected and the paperwork was completed in April 2001. After signing, he said, wide-eyed:

"Manchester United. It is no longer a dream. I just shook hands with Bobby Charlton – Sir Bobby Charlton."

The moment was so sweet because the opportunity – indeed his career – had almost been snatched away. Now he had finally made it to one of the biggest clubs in the world.

Van Nistelrooy had not always been so focused about what he wanted. Not before he was shown how to be hungry. Rewind to the summer of 1997, when he'd been a big name only on his birth certificate. Rutgerus Johannes Martinius Ruud Van Nistelrooy had just moved from his first professional club, FC Den Bosch of the Dutch Second Division, to Heerenveen of the First. At Den Bosch he'd hinted at his scoring abilities, netting 17 times in 69 games in four years, primarily from a midfield position. But at Heerenveen he would transform into a bona fide striker.

The man responsible for the metamorphosis was the astute Heerenveen technical director, Foppe de Haan, who would become the Dutch Coach of the Year in 1998. He knew Van Nistelrooy possessed enormous natural talent, great technical skills and finesse. "Ruud has the same feeling in his feet that other people have in their hands," he said at the time.

But De Haan also knew that if Van Nistelrooy wanted to be ranked alongside his hero, the great Marco Van Basten, he needed to study and he needed to be made aware how important the game was to him.

De Haan solved the latter problem by keeping Van Nistelrooy guessing about his place in the team. When he got the nod, after being told De Haan was having doubts about his role, he grabbed it with both feet and didn't look back.

As for the learning process, De Haan took Van Nistelrooy to watch Dennis Bergkamp, then enjoying a wonderful season at

Arsenal. Van Nistelrooy continued the studies on his own, watching how Bergkamp moved, how he timed his runs, how he used the ball, where he went when he wasn't in possession. "I wrote things down, I studied him in every detail," he said. The year at Heerenveen marked the turning point in Van Nistelrooy's career.

On his 22nd birthday he signed for PSV Eindhoven for £4.2m, a record for the club. Bobby Robson was his coach in his first season there, 1998–99. He scored 60 goals in 57 games in his first two seasons, winning his first international cap in November 1998 and the Dutch Player of the Year award in 1999.

Alex Ferguson had been interested in Van Nistelrooy for some time and had sent his brother Martin, United's European scout, to watch him play for PSV on numerous occasions. On one trip, while him was still with PSV, Martin Ferguson bumped into him at the airport on his way home. Robson told Martin Ferguson that United should buy the striker because of his 'immense' talent. Alex Ferguson had already made up his mind.

When United subsequently agreed to pay £18.5m for him in April 2000, the only reason that Robson, then the manager at Newcastle, did not bid was because he couldn't afford him. "I knew all about him and I knew his ability," he said. "I would've loved to have brought him to Newcastle, but we didn't have the money."

The player Manchester United eventually acquired in 2001 had all the attributes Alex Ferguson could have wished for. He had a hunger to play at Old Trafford and a hunger for the game that had only intensified after seeing his career hang in the balance. And he certainly had talent, supplementing a lethal touch in the area with commitment, work-rate and powerful, clever, running.

"I knew he was going to become a great player," Ferguson said after winning the 2003 title. "But I didn't know quite how good he was going to become, I must say that, because he has surprised me almost every week."

There was even talk, from Van Nistelrooy's team-mate Gary Neville, among others, that the Dutchman could become the greatest forward United had ever had. Among the pantheon he will need to displace to achieve that is Denis Law, who set

United's scoring record for a season in 1963–64 with 46 goals. If that tally is ever to be beaten, it would be fitting if Van Nistelrooy were the man to beat it. He did learn, after all, from watching Dennis Bergkamp, whose football-mad parents named him in honour of Law.

Before Van Nistelrooy's arrival Bergkamp's had undoubtedly made the biggest impact of any of the Dutchmen to have played in England – and there had been more than 100 in the League by the 2002–03 season.

Of the others, Ruud Gullit's premium days were behind him when he arrived at Chelsea, although he was still influential both as a player and manager. Bryan Roy and Pierre Van Hooijdonk made impressions at Nottingham Forest in the 1990s, although Roy's was not lasting and Van Hooijdonk's tenure ended in farce when he went on strike and walked out.

Marc Overmars was a key figure in Arsenal's 1998 Double but departed after 100 League games. Jimmy Floyd Hasselbaink had a terrific strike rate at Leeds in the late 1990s but left on terrible terms. His return to England with Chelsea in the summer of 2000 showed he could still be influential. It also showed he could still be temperamental as several 'Will he stay?/Won't he stay?' episodes showed.

Jaap Stam at Manchester United was the best example among many hard-working, no-nonsense Dutch defenders, playing a key role in Manchester United's 1999 Treble. But he eventually departed after being erased from his manager's plans. The same fate befell the Dutch international goalkeeper Sander Westerveld at Liverpool. Westerveld won three major honours in 2001 only to find himself surplus to Gérard Houllier's requirements.

The non-flying Dutchman

Bergkamp has outlasted them all. It is a tribute to both his own efforts and to those of the elite educational establishment that nurtured him at Ajax. He was well aware of the standards required when he entered their youth system as a 12-year-old. This was the Ajax of legend, a club who'd been captained to a hat-trick of European Cups by Johan Cruyff in the early 1970s under the managerial guidance of Rinus 'Total Football' Michels. Cruyff was back as the manager by the time Bergkamp made his debut.

The young player knew that making the grade would be tough and that 100 youngsters would fall by the wayside for every one who made it to the first team. But he was utterly dedicated, realising from his teenage years onwards that going to bed early and staying away from off-field distractions would make him a better footballer.

"What's so great about smoking, drinking and partying?" he later wrote on his website at icons.com. (Even his utilisation of that forum shows attention to detail. In the internet age, when many players' websites are little more than bland, agent-driven shopfronts to sell merchandise, Bergkamp's has stood out for his personal input.)

As he matured into his teens, it was clear he had outstanding technical ability – a prerequisite at Ajax. He made his debut in European competition at 17 and won a European Cup-Winners' Cup medal in 1987 three days before his 18th birthday. He came on as a substitute in the final against Lokomotiv Leipzig, a game won by a single goal from Marco Van Basten. Bergkamp later won another European trophy with Ajax, the 1992 UEFA Cup, with Liverpool among those eliminated en route.

After scoring 103 goals in 185 games in seven seasons with Ajax, he moved to Internazionale in Milan in the summer of 1993. In hindsight it was an error. Inter had promised they'd make other adventurous signings and change the way they played to accommodate him. But instead ·of becoming exponents of free-flowing football – which had never been likely in the land of defensive strategy – they stayed truer to *catenaccio* tradition, locking up at the back when ahead.

Bergkamp's 11 goals in two years in Italy's Serie A was some comedown. The move did not work out, even though Inter won the UEFA Cup in 1995 with Bergkamp their leading scorer in Europe. Critics said Bergkamp had failed. Away from the easy pickings of the Dutch League, they said, he couldn't make his mark. Bergkamp himself admitted that in such a stifling football culture – on the pitch where defending was an art form, and off it where footballers were public property – he found it tough.

His move to Arsenal in 1995 was his road back to freedom of expression. Arguments are always likely to rage about the essential characteristics of English football. One man's high-tempo, rough 'n' tumble pinball is another man's idea of merit-heavy, attack-based entertainment. But there is no doubt it suited Bergkamp, who was soon finding plenty of space in which to make his runs and lots of chances to craft delicious, tricksy goals.

He has also got himself into trouble, by resorting, on occasion, to a tough physical approach, including crude tackling and a forceful use of his arms or elbows. This has landed him several red cards, an FA fine of £5,000 for improper conduct and a variety of tongue-lashings from various opponents, pundits and managers (although never, in public, from Arsenal's Arsène Wenger).

Depending on your point of view, his misdemeanours have either been a result of hot-headed petulance or the over-stretching of a necessary application of force to cope with the conditions. The truth probably lies somewhere in between. It's arguable that several of England's leading foreign imports have been able to 'mix it' when necessary, not least Arsenal's Patrick Vieira, one of the best and most influential midfielders in the world. Van Nistelrooy is no shrinking violet in the one-on-one challenge either.

One thing is certain. Bergkamp is clearly capable of feeling a burning sense of injustice when things don't work out the way he plans. He admitted as much when talking about his reaction to being the *victim* of a foul.

"I accept that I do quite often sit on the ground after a foul, with my hands in the air calling on the referee to make a decision my way," he said. "It must be frustrating for the fans when they see that because even though I've been fouled, they must wish I could just get on with it. But it's just so frustrating because you have the whole picture of the move in your head and then you get pushed or pulled and no-one sees it."

These are the words of someone who eats, sleeps and above all thinks about the game, right down to how he's going to finish a move once he's split a defence or found a gap in which to work.

Arsenal's Double-winning campaign of 1997–98 saw him at his peak. It was a year of glory for the club and personal highs for him. Although he missed the FA Cup final, injured, he ended the season as Arsenal's leading scorer in the League and in both domestic cups. Some of his goals were mesmerising and he achieved a unique treble when a hat-trick against Leicester secured him first, second and third places in the BBC's Goal of the Month competition. He also achieved a personal 'double' by being voted the player of the year both by his peers and by the Football Writers' Association.

He then capped a decent World Cup at France 98 by scoring a breathtaking 89th-minute quarter-final winner for The Netherlands against Argentina. Not only was it a classy volley under pressure but it was Bergkamp's 36th international goal and broke The Netherlands' record tally of 35, reached by Fas Wilkes in 1961. Talk about a year of flying high.

Not that Bergkamp flew anywhere that year, literally speaking. He gave up travelling by plane in 1995 after making a decision that remains intriguing to many, if not the player himself. He has said that it bores him and annoys him when well-intentioned people offer advice about how his fear can be conquered. As far as he's concerned, he made a decision for his own reasons and that is the end of the matter. If it affects his chances of playing in faraway locations, so be it.

All he has ever said publicly on the subject is that he reached a point when the thought of flying was affecting him so much his game was suffering. He would worry for days before a flight to a game. On the pitch he would fret about the flight home. Around the time he moved to Arsenal, he decided never to fly again.

"I felt free again after I'd made that decision," he said. "I believe it's not a coincidence that I've played the best football of my career at Arsenal, since I made that decision."

So where *did* the fear originate? It is a question worth asking if only because Bergkamp is convinced that removing the fear – by eradicating the possibility of it – had such an effect on his game. Imagine the possibilities of removing fear and recreating results like that.

He has never said why he stopped flying. In fact he's said that there was no specific reason. Various theories have done the rounds, including one that he was shaken by an on-board bomb scare while in America at the 1994 World Cup. But privately he says this was not the reason.

There are few other clues, although one entry in his website biography does make interesting reading. It comes in a section where he writes about his favourite goals at Ajax and a particular goal against RKC on 4 October 1992.

It says:

> It was a very good goal for me even
> though it wasn't an important goal
> because we were already four or
> five goals ahead. The movement
> leading to it was excellent and the
> goal itself was a great chip. That's my
> speciality...

So far, so normal. He doesn't mention it in the biography but he actually scored a hat-trick that day in a 5–0 win. On the day of the game, an El Al Boeing 747 crashed into an Amsterdam apartment block shortly after take-off from Schipol Airport, killing 43 people, most of them on the ground. Bergkamp's diary entry above is completed:

> ...I have mixed memories of that day
> because straight after that match, we
> heard about the infamous 747 plane
> crash in Amsterdam. I tend to
> remember those two things together
> so I have a great memory from the
> goal but a bitter, sad memory of the
> plane crash.

Whether that incident had any effect on him whatsoever is open to speculation. It's quite possible it didn't, although his reminiscence does confirm a strong link between that game and that day's events. Did he somehow subconsciously equate on-field brilliance – ie the scoring of a wonderful goal, one of a hat-trick – with air disaster? That's one for the shrinks to argue over.

But Bergkamp did not score another hat-trick for almost six years, until after he'd given up using planes. Only then did he start flying on the pitch again.

Rhapsody in blue

Gianfranco Zola, Italy's Peter Pan, has been flying all his footballing life, from the day he made his debut aged 18 for Nuorese of the Italian Fourth Division to a thrilling 2002–03 season when he continued, aged 36, to defy the years and shine for Chelsea.

At 5ft 6in, he's been a giant in a diminutive frame with a heart the size of his native Sardinia. His passion for football, and the example he has set to others, have made him one of the most valuable foreign players England has ever seen.

His body of work, measured strictly by honours, is impressive enough. He won the Italian title and Super Cup with Napoli, where he became Diego Maradona's successor. He won the UEFA Cup with Parma, for whom he scored 49 goals in 102 matches in the tight confines of Serie A. Six months after joining Chelsea in the 1996–97 season he was voted England's Footballer of the Year. By 2003, after six and a half years at Stamford Bridge, he'd won the FA Cup twice, the European Cup-Winners' Cup and the League Cup.

Beyond that he'd also won admirers for his grace, his technique, his deceptive toughness and his sportsmanship.

"I've been watching Chelsea for 37 years and Zola, without doubt, is by far the greatest player ever to have graced the hallowed turf of Stamford Bridge," said Billy Black, a Chelsea fan. "He is everything you would or could want from a player. He's got skill, motivation, integrity. He's got a gentle nature but can tackle strongly. He is the model that all players should aspire to. It's difficult to pick out one match that he made a difference to, because 99 per cent of his performances contain some moment most other players can only dream of."

Evidently many Chelsea fans feel the same. In 2003, they voted him the greatest player, from any nation, ever to represent the club. Here's what Zola's team-mate, Frank Lampard said, shortly after that award was announced…

"You can talk about people like Dennis Bergkamp and Eric Cantona, and I think Cantona would be the one nearest to Franco for his influence on Manchester United as a club, but Franco is definitely the best.

"He's got individual skill, has helped Chelsea win trophies and the way that he holds himself makes people respect him. No-one ever has a bad word to say about him. Franco is a great ambassador for kids to look up to and he always has time to sign autographs and help younger players. That makes him not only a great player but also a great man."

What sets Zola apart is that he's also touched buttons far beyond the fringes of partisanship.

As Alex Ferguson confided towards the end of the 2002–03 season:

"I just love the wee man. Even some of the greatest players cheat, but he never does. Aye, I love him."

To paraphrase the famous Nike advert about Eric Cantona: '1966 was a great year for English football. Gianfranco Zola was born.'

He was certainly born to last. Despite being only six weeks younger than Cantona, by 2003 he'd played at the top level until he was six *years* past Cantona's retirement age. And unlike Cantona, with Zola there has been no dark side, no tortured exposition of the soul, no torn-apart heart on the sleeve. The Italian's heart has been in his work, and in his tireless desire to *play*, in the most literal sense, with a smile on his face.

"Whatever you do, you have to do it with passion," Zola told BBC Radio London in April 2003, as he pondered whether to extend his stay at Chelsea another year. "That has been the key to my success so far. I've done whatever I've done because I've just enjoyed it so much that I've never felt tired with what I was doing. That will be the same when I do something else."

The measure of any player's contribution is ultimately his legacy. As Lampard and numerous others have testified, Zola has led by example. There are striking parallels listening to him talk about the players who inspired *him*. He names three who he especially admired in Italy: Zico, often called the best Brazilian since Pele, who spent time at Udinese; Michel Platini of France, who played for Juventus; and Diego Maradona of Argentina, Zola's one-time team-mate at Napoli and also his ultimate hero.

"For me, I don't think there will be a player like him in the future," said Zola. "He was simply amazing, a great inspiration."

The common thread is that Zico, Platini and Maradona, like Zola in England, were players from another country, another world. They inspired first and foremost through their ability. But they also inspired – Maradona above all – because they were shrouded in otherworldliness but were simultaneously down to earth. Here's how Zola explains the effect Maradona had on him...

"When you think of great games of football, like Real Madrid against Manchester United [*in the 2003 Champions' League quarter-finals*], it was a game where you thought 'I just have to go and play football'. It was so good, it gave you a charge. Just watching

Maradona training had the same effect for me. I wanted to go and do that. That's the feeling I got from him. He was a lovely guy... the first time I met him I was shaking and speechless, I didn't know what to say. But he was so easy to talk to, he put me at my ease. I've always been impressed by that."

Replace the name 'Maradona' with 'Zola' and history has repeated itself for any number of young English players. Zola acknowledges the impact that he and other foreign players have had.

"Young players want to look up to them, pick up something from them. The foreign players have brought better preparation. The way they look after themselves off the pitch is just as important as what they do *on* the pitch. It's a matter of education, of professionalism, what you achieve. If I hadn't been so professional during my life then I wouldn't have been able to play for so long."

Of the changes in playing style in England since he arrived, Zola added:

"I'd say that [*in 1996*] about 80 per cent of teams played the long-ball game, passed it over the midfield. Now it's completely changed. More teams go for passing. It makes you a better player, it's a better way to play. I always look at the Brazilians, the best in the world, and that's the way they play. English football has improved so much. And the young English players have improved so much, they have good technical knowledge."

Zola said that England has been an education for him too, not least the discovery of the importance of the FA Cup. He rated Chelsea's success in 1997 as his proudest moment in England.

"It came as a surprise, honestly. It was a big achievement. The Cup-Winners' Cup [*of 1998*] was very prestigious, because we won in Europe, but that first FA Cup was special because it was something I didn't expect. I'll never forget the day after we won, going down the King's Road on a bus, completely surrounded by thousands of supporters; I felt great. The fans made me feel like I was someone very important.

"I was totally not prepared for what the FA Cup meant. I'd played in the Italian Cup and that's not very, very important and I thought the same would be true in England. But I learned about the history. It's so great that small teams can compete. Everyone plays in the FA Cup. That's what it's all about, players from small towns being able to play against Theirry Henry and Ruud Van Nistelrooy. That is real football."

Expanding the theme of his admiration for England, he added: "The thing I enjoy most is the way the fans live for football. I really like the passion they have for their club, no matter. If the club is successful, good, if not, they still keep close to the club all the time."

Zola has won admirers for making an effort all the time, be it in a pre-season friendly, a vital international or major European game. His work-rate is not swayed by arenas, it seems, only by the task in hand. And whichever task that is, it is always the most important.

Three examples. He scored for Italy in 1997 as they inflicted England's first ever World Cup match defeat at Wembley. He scored twice for Chelsea against Reading in a pre-season friendly later the same year. He came off the bench to find the winner in the European Cup-Winners' Cup in 1998. It was hard to differentiate at any given moment in any of those games which meant more. The point was that they all meant everything.

"The moment which most sums the wee man up in my book came at the end of the 2001–02 season," said Dan Davies, a Chelsea fan. "We were playing West Ham at reserve level on a Monday evening. The crowd was sparse, it was a non-event. With two or three minutes to go, we were 2–0 up and I was making my way behind the goal that we were attacking on my way out of the ground. We got a throw-in level with the edge of the West Ham penalty area. Not only did Franco run across the box to receive the throw, he was jinking and turning, spinning in a desperate attempt to give him that half yard of space to receive the ball. Nothing came of the move, but to see the level of effort and application that he was putting in under such mundane circumstances said it all."

In a class of his own

Set against Zola's benchmark, no other Italian in England has come close in terms of class or legacy. Giorgio Chinaglia, born in Italy and raised in Wales, played for Swansea in the 1960s but was not a star until he played prolifically for Lazio and later the New York Cosmos. Fabrizio Ravanelli scored goals for Middlesbrough but was temperamental and did little for his team-mates.

Chelsea's aristocratic Gianluca Vialli did plenty, as a player and manager, although his transformation from one to the other caused rifts that led to his leaving. Roberto Di Matteo secured a place in history with the fastest ever goal in an FA Cup final, scoring in 43 seconds as Chelsea beat Middlesbrough 2–0. He scored the winner in the 2000 FA Cup final too but then his career was cut short when he sustained a broken leg in a European defeat to St Gallen of Switzerland.

Chelsea's other Italians have had mixed experiences. Pierluigi Casiraghi sustained a knee injury that curtailed his career shortly after his move from Lazio in 1998. Luca Percassi and Sam Dalla Bona were signed the same year but only the latter made the transition from youth hopeful to regular. Later, Christian Panucci did not even make it to the end of a loan spell. Goalkeeper Carlo Cudicini, the son of the former Italian national goalkeeper, Fabio, stayed long after his own loan, which was initially for one year from August 1999. By the end of the 2002–03 season he had established himself as one of the best custodians in the Premier League.

Away from Stamford Bridge, the Italian who consistently grabbed the most headlines during his time in the League was Paolo Di Canio, although often for the wrong reasons. A transient striker who pledged undying allegiance at various stages during a career at Lazio, Ternana, Juventus, Napoli, Milan, Sheffield Wednesday and West Ham, his ability – a delight at times – was beyond question.

He had a knack of scoring vital goals, as he did against Zola's Chelsea in the penultimate game of the 2002–03 season. That gave West Ham a glimmer of hope that they might not be relegated, as did an 89th-minute equaliser in their last game against Birmingham. Ultimately it was a hope unrealised. West Ham – and Di Canio – had failed to do enough earlier in the season to avoid the drop.

Di Canio was always a jumble of contradictions. Of Benito Mussolini, Di Canio wrote in his autobiography:

> What fascinates me, and this is probably where Mussolini and I are very different, is the way he was able to go against his morals to achieve his goals.

And yet despite frequent talk of playing his heart out for his team, he was capable of behaviour detrimental to it.

This was never truer than when he earned an 11-match ban in 1998, when he was playing for Sheffield Wednesday, for shoving the referee Paul Alcock to the ground. In mitigation he said: "I could push my eight-year-old daughter Ludovica that way and she wouldn't fall over... My first reaction was that somebody must have been crouching behind him, like in one of those old slapstick comedies. That is the only way it is humanly possible to fall over like that."

And then there was 'fair play' Di Canio, the persona who won a FIFA prize for an outstanding act of sportsmanship in a game between West Ham and Everton in 2001. With a clear opportunity to score but with the Everton goalkeeper Paul Gerrard in obvious need of treatment, he caught the ball and stopped play.

But there was also street-fighting Di Canio, the character who grew up supporting Lazio and used to be member of the club's notorious *Irriducibili* hooligan mob. (One recollection from his 'ultra' days was: "So I kicked the Padova fan while he was lying on the ground. Two or three times, I don't remember how many... I was high from the adrenalin rush.")

Di Canio's footballing abilities meant that he was not the kind of player teams liked to face. But then his inconsistencies often made it tough for his managers to guarantee him a place.

Zola, by great contrast, has always worked for the team, setting an example while not stooping to judge those who have not followed it. Even his less fruitful periods, such as the second season at Chelsea when injuries and squad rotation disrupted his flow, he remained patient and dignified. Again this set him apart. His raison d'être has always been to ask the most from himself and not be dissatisfied when others don't deliver.

"Zola is just fantastic," said Claudio Ranieri, his Chelsea manager, after yet another fine all-round display in 2003, a win over lowly Shrewsbury in the FA Cup. "He is always the same, he always wants to give his best. We treated this game as if it was in the Premiership, and that is the way Zola always plays. He is an example to everybody."

The 2002–03 season was all the more remarkable because Zola had seriously considered returning to Sardinia for good before it started. Instead, he took a holiday, worked hard to keep fit, and then capitalised when Chelsea's first-choice strikers Jimmy Floyd Hasselbaink and Eidur Gudjohnsen succumbed to early injuries.

"I wasted no time and took advantage," Zola said in April 2003. "I scored goals and that gave me confidence. I put the manager [*Claudio Ranieri*] in a situation where he couldn't take me out. This season has probably been the most consistent of my career. When you work on something and it pays off it's a great feeling... Nothing comes by itself. You have to help yourself. I put in a lot of effort and it worked."

At some stage Zola will return and settle in Sardinia, of that he is certain. "If you're born on an island there's something stuck in your DNA. You feel that one day you'll go back there. Whether that's the food or the air, I don't know. One day I'm going to be there."

English football can be grateful that he dropped by, on that there is unanimous agreement. Here's Gordon Taylor, speaking at the end of the 2002–03 season...

"Pound for pound, foreign players hardly come much better than Gianfranco Zola. He has been absolutely brilliant, not just this season but ever since he arrived at Chelsea. He continues to be a joy to watch – a tremendous professional and a thoroughly nice gentleman to boot.

"Claudio Ranieri likes to use all sorts of words to describe Franco – little genius, magician, wizard – and they are all applicable. When he is in possession he comes alive and makes the ball talk. To still be playing at the top level at his age, and to be enjoying arguably his best-ever season in a Chelsea shirt, is a remarkable achievement and a testimony to his supreme professionalism and dedication. He has shown this season that he is as good as anyone else on display in the Premiership and you could not find a better role model."

So said the chief executive of the English PFA.

CHAPTER ELEVEN

French Connections

ARSENE WENGER, the master of minutiae, turned English football on its head by using his brain. And that, when you strip it to the bones, is what the so-called, French Revolution, has been all about: attention to detail, studious application, and *thought*.

The type of game played by Wenger's Arsenal, and indeed the French sides that lifted the World Cup in 1998 and the European Championship in 2000, has been characterised by the same guiding principles. On the pitch there's been a strong preference for progressive full-backs, an influential holding midfielder paired with a probing partner, pace on the flanks and creativity in attack. Whether the players line up 4–4–2 or 4–2–3–1 or anywhere in between is not as important as fluidity and ability to switch with the play.

Off the pitch, minute attention has been paid to all areas of preparation, from diet to training to individual mentoring. Technical improvements have been hastened through physiological conditioning. The appliance of science has been taken as read. *Vive la différence.*

As Wenger said a few minutes after Arsenal won the 2003 FA Cup final against Southampton: "When you win a cup or a championship, it's down to very small things."

He was talking about moments that can turn a game, for better or worse, be it using an extra half yard of pace, finding a few extra inches in a jump or possessing a split-second advantage in awareness. Such moments, as he'd said before, can be influenced by small things in preparation. And Arsène Wenger is a god of small things.

Not that grooming ends with the body. Wenger views football as a cerebral exercise. He wants his players to win, certainly, but he wants them to win by expressing themselves, by enjoying the pursuit of perfection. He wants them to feel that every game is important but none is more important than the next one. When a game is gone, its only worth is what it has taught. By extension, when a career is gone it is too late to change it. So take care of yourself *now*. Carpe diem.

Wenger's other Latin motto, in practice at least, is the one historically inscribed on Arsenal's official badge: *Victoria concordia crescit*. Although this was dropped from the badge in 2002 after 'corporate re-branding', the sentiment lives on: Victory through harmony.

One of the hallmarks of Wenger's career has been the promotion of a team ethic, an all-for-one and one-for-all mentality that starts at the top and works down. He never – ever – criticises his players in public, on the basis that what happens within a club stays within a club. Maybe this explains why he always claims not to have seen contentious incidents involving his players. The unity of the team is paramount. The development of his players – as men as well as athletes – is part and parcel of the same aim. In this respect he is not just a manager but a teacher.

Wenger's erudite approach was evident from the moment he started his debut press conference at Highbury in September 1996. He expounded a philosophy: "I like real, modern football," he said. "Football made of compact lines, of zones, of pressure. And football of quick, co-ordinated movements with a good technical basis."

He laid down an agenda in clear and simple terms: "I believe in discipline," he said. "But the best discipline is always when a player understands it's in his best interests. Success today relies on discipline on and off the field."

He tipped a nod to England's place in the history of football.

"The main reason for coming is that I love English football, the roots of the game are here."

Easy to say, but this detail was sincere and it mattered. It told his ultimate audience – the players and fans – that he came with respect for his new home.

And then he acknowledged that his move to north London was also inspired by self interest. "For my career, it can be another improvement, a further step for my personal development," he said. It was a shrewd statement, a deliberate message. It said: 'My fate is tied to Arsenal's. I want Arsenal to improve under me.'

He added: "There are two challenges. The first is for me to adapt to the team and the qualities of English players. The second is for them to adapt to my ideas. I want to improve the squad with my ideas."

Ideas. They didn't so much as tumble out as queue up and stride forth. He wanted to blend an English fighting mentality with a sophisticated technical style. He wanted to bring players in who would be young and have their best years ahead of them. He said he wanted to do "quality work" and after that "hope for the best". Some hope. Some realisation.

Wenger's 1996 debut press conference marked him out for several reasons. A traditional English debut press conference deals with the basics. A bit like traditional English football, in fact. Journalists, looking for a line, want an incoming manager to say 'This is the biggest challenge of my life' or 'This club has the potential to challenge for honours'. It is routine fare. It makes for easy headlines. If a manager will also throw in some information about his transfer kitty, the players he wants to buy and a prediction for where his team will be at the end of the season, so much the better. But you don't, as a matter of course, expect talk of compact lines, of zones, of discipline being in a player's interests, of the manager's personal development.

Of course it was different with Wenger because he was the first Frenchman ever to manage in England. Few people knew much about him and there was an element of starting from scratch. But Wenger also stood out because he was full of ideas and expressed them.

Revolutionary fruit

Measured by honours alone, the French have had an enormous impact in England. By the end of 2002–03, Wenger had won Doubles in 1998 and 2002, a third FA Cup in 2003 and had never finished lower than second in the Premier League. Gérard Houllier at Liverpool won a treble of the FA Cup, League Cup and UEFA Cup in 2001 and added a second League Cup in 2003.

Between 1996 and 2003, the Footballer of the Year award went to Frenchmen in four years from eight, with the recipients being Eric Cantona (1996), David Ginola (1999), Robert Pires (2002) and Thierry Henry (2003). Cantona alone won five Premier League titles and two FA Cups. More than 20 other French players have played some role in winning at least one major domestic or European trophy with an English club in the last six years.

In terms of numbers, France has now provided England with more players than any country outside of Britain and Ireland. By 2003, the figure stood at more than 150, with the vast majority arriving since 1997. A bandwagon effect on the back of France's international successes can account for journeymen Frenchmen at League clubs of all sizes – Barnet to Carlisle, Colchester, Darlington, Oldham, Orient, Swansea, Stockport and Tranmere to name a few. But there has also been a high number of internationals, past, present and in-the-making.

Eric Cantona raged and rampaged to brilliant effect, not so much opening the door for his compatriots as ripping it off its hinges. David Ginola's stylish skipping down the wing at Newcastle and Tottenham made it easier for fans to part with their ticket money. Because he was worth it.

They were followed by Patrick Vieira, who blossomed to become one of the world's best midfielders; Nicolas Anelka, who caused a stir, on and off the pitch; Emmanuel Petit, whose telepathic relationship with Vieira led to honours for club and country; and Marcel Desailly, one of the world's great defenders.

Others who have chosen England in their prime include Sylvain Wiltord, Pires and Henry at Arsenal, Mikael Silvestre at Manchester United and William Gallas, who played no small part in securing a 2003–04 Champions' League qualifying place for Chelsea. Among those who still felt they had something to offer late in their careers were the likes of Laurent Blanc, Didier Deschamps, Yourri Djorkaeff and Christophe Dugarry. The last two were influential in helping Bolton and Birmingham respectively to stay in the Premier League in 2003.

Without doubt the epicentre of England's French revolution has been at Arsenal under Wenger, whose annual battle with Manchester United's Alex Ferguson has developed into one of the most compelling rivalries in British sport. Without Wenger, would Arsenal have consistently pressured United to raise their own standards to stay on top? Would the recent two-horse race for the title actually have been more like a walkover for the northern reds?

But even if Wenger had never come to England, he would still have played his part in reshaping the English game. It was under his managerial guidance at Monaco in the late 1980s that Glenn Hoddle first had thoughts of becoming a manager himself. Hoddle later signed Ruud Gullit for Chelsea. Gullit made them multi-national, hiring, among others, Gianluca Vialli, who continued the trend and ended up fielding the first all-foreign XI in English League history.

By the same token, Wenger might have to claim some responsibility for Southampton's signing of the hoaxer Ali Dia, who only got a game by trading on the name of George Weah. And where did Weah blossom from being a rookie Liberian teenager into a sublime talent who became the World Footballer of the Year? At Monaco, under Wenger.

"Arsène is the best coach I have ever played for," Weah said when Wenger joined Arsenal. "He brought the best out of me as a footballer."

Take your pick of any prominent French footballer of the last decade and many will echo the sentiment, not least Henry, Vieira and Pires. And if they don't cite Wenger, the chances are they'll mention Gérard Houllier, England's second French manager. It was under Houllier, at various points in time, that many of France's golden generation were nurtured, directly or indirectly.

As well as managing France's senior and junior teams, Houllier has long had close ties to the Clairefontaine national coaching centre, located south-west of Paris, which has been the physical and spiritual heart of that country's footballing renaissance. Wenger, Houllier and the ethos of Clairefontaine have all helped reshape English football. So has another Frenchman, one who wasn't even born in France.

Genesis of a revolution

The French Revolution started not in France but in Algeria. Or more precisely in Kouba, a suburb of Algiers. Because that was the birthplace, on 1 October 1923, of Fernand Sastre, who pioneered the Clairefontaine project and later organised France 98, where the graduates of Clairefontaine lifted the World Cup.

The story of how Sastre, the son of a *pied noir* farmer, masterminded those triumphs and others is instructive to English football. It speaks of inclusiveness, open-mindedness, long-term planning, attention to detail and thought. It tells how Sastre was influential not only at Clairefontaine but also, tacitly, in the careers of Houllier, Wenger and a generation of French players.

Without Sastre, it is possible that France would not have produced, in their contemporary forms, either Houllier or Wenger. Both men evolved as managers within a French footballing structure put in place largely under Sastre's administration. Both have benefited as managers from the players that that system has produced. And both, like Sastre, have been guided by principles that encourage freedom of expression, equality of opportunity regardless of background, and team spirit. (Or *'liberté, égalité, fraternité'*, as the French might say.)

Sastre, Wenger and Houllier all grew up believing that football was no mere distraction but an integral part of life. In doing so they followed in the tradition of another French football addict, Albert Camus – philosopher, writer, goalkeeper.

He, like Sastre, was born into a working-class *pied noir* family in Algeria (in 1913) and was involved in local football. But whereas Sastre spent his twenties in coaching and development in Kouba, Camus concentrated on actually playing the game, for the Racing University club in Algiers (RUA) among others. Camus's days as a keeper were just ending as Sastre became involved with Kouba FC a few miles away.

One oft (mis)quoted phrase from Camus states: "All I know about morality and the obligations of man, I owe to football." It was not quite what he said. He did not specify football. His exact observation, made in an essay for *France Football* magazine in 1957 – the year, incidentally, that he won the Nobel Prize for Literature – was:

> What I most surely know in the long run about morality and the obligations of men, I owe to sport:
> I learned that at RUA.

Still, the message was the same: football, a moral and sporting conundrum.

Sastre, Houllier and Wenger all travelled widely to broaden their experience. Sastre, a tax inspector by trade, ascended to mainland France in 1962, the year Algeria gained independence. He later travelled extensively on government and football business. Houllier travelled to England in the late 1960s, to work as a teacher in Liverpool (where he watched football from the Kop) and then around the world as a coach. Wenger travelled to Cambridge, albeit briefly, to study English, and then around France as a coach before moving to Japan and then to Arsenal.

The salient point for English football is how their careers converged at various times, and how they all influenced the French game. Understanding *their* history helps explain how they have been able to influence England's football history.

Sastre's involvement in the administration of the French game, from his arrival in the country in 1962 onwards, was a natural progression. He had worked his way up the ladder in the Algerian game, becoming an influential figure in Algiers. His rise in France was nonetheless swift. In 1969, after seven years in France, he became the secretary general of the French Football Federation and then in 1973 he became the FFF president. He retained that post until 1984, when he became an honorary life president.

France experienced some pivotal moments during Sastre's 11 years in day-to-day charge. On 27 June 1984, the nation won its first international competition, the European Championship, with a 2–0 victory over Spain on home turf at the Parc des Princes. The winning team included Jean Tigana and the three-times European Football of the Year Michel Platini, who scored the first goal in the final to add to the eight others he'd scored in the tournament. Sastre, the chief organiser of the event, was among the first on the pitch afterwards to congratulate Platini, with whom he forged a long friendship based on mutual admiration.

Sastre delighted in Platini's brilliance as a footballing architect. Platini, a strategist in all areas of his life, appreciated Sastre's meticulous approach in mapping the future of the game, not least his proposal, put forward in 1976, that France needed a national training centre. Sastre also wanted a network of regional centres of excellence to work in coordination with it. This was long-term thinking, and took a long time to achieve, but 1976 was a significant year for beginnings.

The same year, Gérard Houllier, then 30, who'd been a youth coach at Arras, took up his first job as a head coach, at Third Division Noeux Les Mines. He spent six years there, winning promotion with his senior side, several titles with his youth sides and a reputation as a shrewd developer of talent.

When Houllier took over at Noeux Les Mines, Arsène Wenger, heading for his 27th birthday, hadn't even made his playing debut at professional level, let alone taken up coaching. Like Sastre and Houllier, he was never an exceptional footballer. He'd grown up in an Alsace village, Duttlenheim, located outside Strasbourg. Of his prowess on the pitch, he later said, with self-deprecation: "I was the best." [*Pause*] "In the village." [*Pause*] "And it was a small village."

Wenger's priorities in life were academic. He gained a degree in economics and sociology from Strasbourg University and played amateur football for Mutzig, Mulhouse and Vauban before a brief professional career – less than a dozen first-team games – in the late 1970s with Strasbourg. He played three times in their title-winning season in 1978–79. It was only after that, as he hit 30, that he took a manager's diploma in Paris.

In 1982, by which time he was the youth coach at Strasbourg, the FFF, under Sastre's guidance, finally chose a location for a national training centre, at Clairefontaine. Houllier, meanwhile, moved from Noeux Les Mines to Lens, with whom he won the French title in 1986. By then Wenger's career was advancing swiftly, as was the Clairefontaine project. Wenger had become the player-coach at Cannes in 1983 and then the coach of Nancy in 1984. The FFF had put the final touches to their Clairefontaine designs, been granted planning permission and arranged funding. In 1985, as Sastre stepped down from the day-to-day presidency of the FFF, the first bricks were laid at the national coaching centre.

In 1987, as Wenger took over at Monaco, Clairefontaine was being fitted out and decorated. It opened for business on 1 January 1988, a few months before Wenger led Monaco to the French title. That summer Houllier was appointed as the technical director of the French national team, as an assistant to the French national coach, Platini. Their base was Clairefontaine.

The integrated revolution was underway in earnest. Promising young players were identified for enrolment at academies around the country, linked to Clairefontaine. A strong emphasis was put on uniform standards for players' development. Sastre's work was coming to fruition in the hands of his friend Platini as well as other national-level coaches like Houllier and club coaches like Wenger, who was constantly refining his own methods.

By 1992 those methods were paying dividends. Wenger's stock rose as he took Monaco to the final of the European Cup-Winners' Cup that year. Two months later Houllier was appointed as the manager of France, succeeding Platini, who moved into administration at the FFF. By November 1992, Platini and Sastre were co-chairmen of the organising committee for France 98.

After Monaco reached the semi-finals of the European Champions' League in 1994, Wenger was offered the job as the French national coach. Houllier had resigned in 1993 – after France missed out on qualifying for the 1994 World Cup – but stayed on as the FFF technical director. Wenger was also offered a job at Bayern Munich. He turned down both the FFF and the Germans, saying he could not walk out on his Monaco contract. A few months into the 1994–95 season, he was sacked.

In January 1995, Wenger moved to Japan to become the coach of Nagoya Grampus Eight, where he turned his new club from relegation fodder into league runners-up and cup winners by 1996. The same year Houllier became the coach of the French under-18 team, which included the likes of Thierry Henry (who had played at Monaco as a 17-year-old under Wenger) and Nicolas Anelka.

By 1997, when Houllier was the coach of the French under-20 side (including Henry, Anelka, Mikael Silvestre and William Gallas), Wenger was the manager of Arsenal. His recruitment drive included buying Anelka in March 1997 and then Emmanuel Petit and Gilles Grimandi (who had both played for him at Monaco) that summer.

In the spring of 1998 Arsenal won their first Double of the Wenger era with Anelka, Petit and Patrick Vieira (signed in 1996 from his former club, Cannes) all prominent. Houllier, meanwhile, was a few months away from a move to Liverpool but first spent the summer watching the Clairefontaine dream realised as France lifted the World Cup.

At the end of France's semi-final win over Croatia, the French manager, Aime Jacquet, turned to Houllier and said: "This is our victory." By the time Brazil had been beaten in the final it really was. It was also Sastre's victory, Clairefontaine's victory and a victory for Wenger's players, past, present and future. Among the triumphant French squad were Henry, Vieira, Pires and Petit, who scored the third goal of the final, France's 1000th in international competition.

It was also a victory for the rainbow nation of France, featuring players born as far afield as Senegal (Vieira), New Caledonia (Christian Karembeu) and Ghana (Marcel Desailly) as well as Henry and other second-generation immigrants. And the talisman of the side, the scorer of France's first two goals in the final, was Zinedine Zidane, whose family roots lay in Algeria, the birthplace of Fernand Sastre.

Sastre had been overjoyed to bring the World Cup finals to France and was justifiably proud of his role – often in the background – in developing the team who won it. But he was not there to see Les Bleus lift the trophy. A few hours after their first match of the tournament, a 3–0 win over South Africa, he had died, aged 74, his life's work done.

His legacy lives on.

The ethos of Clairefontaine

On 17 July 1998, France's flagship coaching facility was renamed in honour of the man who conceived it. Though everyone still knows it as Clairefontaine, its official name is now the Fernand Sastre National Technical Centre (CTNFS).

It was established with clear objectives, principally to produce players for the national team at all levels; to be the training base and pre-match base for all France's national teams; to be the focal point of France's nationwide academy system; and to be an educational centre for coaches.

It is also home to the most promising young players in the country, aged 13 to 15, who each spent two years there being groomed. They live within the grounds from Sunday evening to Friday evening, spending the mornings doing academic work and the afternoons training. The emphasis is always on technique and on exercises that will mean something in the context of real matches. All training for the national teams, up to the highest level, is conducted on the same basis.

The Clairefontaine complex includes seven pitches of competition standard and two synthetic surfaces, one indoor and one outdoor. Tennis courts offer another sporting diversion. There's accommodation for 300 people, a gymnasium, stretch rooms and saunas. There are 16 dressing rooms where it's not unusual to find coaches explaining tactics via laptop simulations. Follow-up work is done in seminar rooms. A full-time staff of 60 includes coaches, physios, fitness specialists, nutritionists and physiological assessors who monitor everything from heartbeats to fat levels to the state of the players' teeth.

In short, Clairefontaine has all the facilities that the English FA would like to have at its own proposed national centre in Burton, Staffordshire, if and when the finances allow. (And if and when the powers-that-be accept that sustained international success stems from long-term preparation, not a hit-and-miss hope that a crop of good players will spontaneously emerge.)

The ethos of Clairefontaine is relevant to England. Lessons can be learnt from it. Dozens of players at English clubs have been shaped by it. And at Arsenal, Arsène Wenger has developed his own version of it. Considering the problems at Highbury before he arrived, the job he's done has been all the more remarkable, as a quick glance backwards shows.

Wenger's way

The boozing had to stop. That was Arsène Wenger's most emphatic message in his first few weeks at Arsenal.

"I will not ban beer completely, because one pint helps relax people. But I do not want the players drinking 15 beers, because that is bad," he said at the end of September 1996. "A footballer's body is his work. If he then destroys that with bad habits like drinking, it's silly. My players will have to change their social habits."

And with that, Wenger set about changing the culture of Arsenal. It needed changing. For every strength there seemed to be a damaging weakness.

First: the club had an illustrious history and noble tradition but was reeling after the sacking of Bruce Rioch and then the resignation of his temporary successor, Stuart Houston.

Second: Arsenal were comparatively wealthy and should have been at the forefront of innovation but they didn't even own their own training facilities.

Third: the team's famous defenders – Lee Dixon, Steve Bould, Martin Keown, Nigel Winterburn and Tony Adams – were the best in the business, their cohesion unrivalled, but the linchpin and club captain, Adams, had just admitted he was fighting alcoholism.

Fourth: The club was replete with decent players but self-discipline was in short supply. In the same squad as the health fanatic Dennis Bergkamp, there was Paul Merson, who had problems with gambling, cocaine and alcohol; John Hartson, who was fond of his pints and his partying; and a group of others – Bould, Ray Parlour and Winterburn among them – who had been in trouble at one stage or another for drink-related misdemeanours. Ian Wright was also a loose cannon. Though the problems of Adams and Merson attracted huge attention, Arsenal were not atypical. English football had long been a professional game lacking a professional approach.

Wenger's ideas, utilised to rapid effect at both Monaco and Grampus, made all the difference at Highbury. What the players ate and drank was of great importance.

"I think in England you eat too much sugar and meat and not enough vegetables," Wenger said. "I lived in Japan and it was the best diet I ever had. The whole way of life there is linked to health. The people there are known to work harder than anywhere else and they have the highest life expectancy. Their diet is basically boiled vegetables, fish and rice. No fat, no sugar."

Japan had a big effect on Wenger beyond the food he ate. In many ways he had more freedom to experiment with his philosophies and methods than in any previous job. The Japanese have always been happy to borrow ideas and then sell them back to the world. Grampus were really just borrowing a fresh perspective from Europe. They allowed Wenger the scope to do whatever he wanted. It helped that the J-League was in its infancy – and therefore everything was relatively new. It also helped that Wenger was a success.

In turn Wenger took away new ideas about food, about a work ethic, and about succeeding on his own terms in an environment traditionally suspicious of individuality. Japanese society – from the playground to the boardroom – is arranged

Denmark's **Peter Schmeichel** (above) won 10 major honours with Manchester United during the 1990s, starting with the League Cup, in 1992, and ending with the European Cup, part of an historic Treble in 1999. His compatriot, **Allan Simonsen** (below), could not have had a more contrasting time in England. The former European Footballer of the Year's tenure at cash-strapped Charlton in the 1982–83 season lasted just 17 games after an ill-fated move from Barcelona. Simonsen is pictured on his debut for Charlton on 13 November 1982, which ended in a 3–2 home defeat to Middlesbrough.

Manchester United have signed considerably fewer foreign players (25) during the Premier League era than the likes of Arsenal (44), Chelsea (48) and Liverpool (35) but those who *have* moved to Old Trafford have mostly made a big impact. Above, Norway's **Ole Gunnar Solskjaer** celebrates scoring the dramatic last-gasp winner in the 1999 European Cup final, sharing his joy with **Dwight Yorke** (Trinidad & Tobago, behind), **Ronny Johnsen** (Norway, front) and **Jaap Stam** (Netherlands, right). Below, **Ruud Van Nistelrooy** of the Netherlands celebrates scoring yet another goal during a prolific first two seasons at Old Trafford, the second of which ended with the 2003 League title and the Golden Boot.

Middlesbrough's Brazilian little and large duo, **Juninho** (above, left) and **Emerson** (right), nervously await kick-off in the 1997 FA Cup final, a match they went on to lose to Chelsea, compounding the misery of relegation and a League Cup final defeat the same season. Below, in happier times, they celebrate after Juninho had scored the winner in a match against Everton in September 1996.

Argentina's **Juan Sébastian Veron** (above) became the most expensive signing in British football history when he moved from Lazio to Manchester United in the summer of 2001 for £28m. Italy's **Gianluca Vialli** (below, left) cost Chelsea nothing when he moved to Stamford Bridge on a 'Bosman' free from Juventus in 1996. He won four major trophies with them, three as manager, when his players included **Gianfranco Zola** (right-hand picture below, left) and **Tore Andre Flo** (right-hand picture below, right) shaking hands after playing against each other for Chelsea and Sunderland respectively in November 2002.

Gianfranco Zola, England's Player of the Year in 1997, was voted Chelsea's best player ever by the club's fans in 2003 and is widely regarded as one of England's most successful foreign imports, on and off the pitch.

Chelsea's French midfielder **Emmanuel Petit** (left) attempts to close down Arsenal's Dutch striker, **Dennis Bergkamp**, during the 2002 FA Cup final, which Arsenal won. That game came four years after the pair had played alongside each other in Arsenal's League and Cup Double-winning team of 1998.

Arsenal's French manager, **Arsène Wenger** (above, background) and Liverpool's French manager, **Gérard Houllier** (above, foreground) pace the touchline during the 2001 FA Cup final, which was won by Liverpool. Wenger and Houllier have both been major players in England's so-called French Revolution, as has Chelsea's World Cup-winning defender, **Marcel Desailly** (below left, outjumping Manchester United's Andy Cole in the 2000 Charity Shield). France's **Emmanuel Petit** and **Patrick Vieira** (below, right, celebrating Arsenal's FA Cup win in 1998) were both influential in Arsenal's Double-winning side that year and France's World Cup win that summer.

France and Arsenal's **Thierry Henry** (left), **Robert Pires** (centre) and **Sylvain Wiltord** (right) celebrate after Henry scored against Newcastle United in 2003, a year that Henry had to settle for 'only' a League runners-up medal, an FA Cup-winners medal, the PFA Player of the Year award and the Football Writers' Player of the Year award.

Arsenal's French midfielder **Robert Pires** (above, left), England's Player of the Year in 2002, tries to tackle Everton's Chinese international **Li Tie** (right) in a Premier League match in March 2003.

Brazil's **Ronaldo** (left) and **Gilberto Silva** (right) kiss the World Cup trophy; Ronaldo scored both goals in the 2002 tournament final against Germany in Japan. Gilberto moved to Arsenal shortly afterwards as Ronaldo moved from Internazionale of Italy to Real Madrid.

to encourage conformity. The company is every salaryman's ultimate master. Something as simple as going out for a drink after work can become a minefield of manners. If you don't drink enough, it can be seen as a sign you're not on board. If you drink too much, you risk embarrassing the firm. There is always pressure to be seen to be doing the right thing.

In Japan, although most *gaijin* – foreigners – are subject to fewer of these pressures, they still exist. So the way Wenger coped was interesting. He worked tirelessly, which is the measure of a company man in Japan. And because he was bookish, multi-lingual, methodical and evidently very clever, he was viewed as something of a *sensei* (teacher). While every Japanese teacher is *sensei* (eg: Mr Sugimoto, the geography teacher, is known to his pupils as Sugimoto-*sensei*), the term *sensei* is also used in honorific fashion to show deep respect to any mentor. Wenger-*sensei* pulled off the tricky feat of doing things on his own terms, and succeeding, while maintaining – indeed increasing – the respect people had for him. Whether the experience strengthened his belief that he could impose his ideas in other arenas resistant to change (ie English football) is something only he knows.

Back to Arsenal's diet in 1996. Out went the steak and chips and booze. In came pasta, lean meat, fish, vegetables and plenty of water. As Ian Wright said at the time: "He's put me on grilled fish, grilled broccoli, grilled everything. Yuk!"

But it worked, as did the widespread introduction of vitamin injections and dietary supplements, such as creatine.

Longer training sessions were introduced, with the focus being drills and exercises to hone technique, tone specific parts of the body and build muscle memory. The stopwatch was never far from Wenger's hand as he controlled the precise length of sessions and monitored exactly how much his charges were improving. The importance of warming-up and warming-down was stressed, as was the need for enough rest.

"It's silly to work hard the whole week and then spoil it by not preparing properly before the game," Wenger said. "You can point out what is wrong. Some players act the wrong way because they are not strong enough to fight temptation. Some act the wrong way just because they don't know what the right way is. As a coach I can teach the players the things they're doing wrong without knowing it."

After making it clear to the players that he expected them to look after themselves, Wenger made it clear to the Arsenal board that the club needed training facilities fit for champions. The hierarchy agreed and Wenger went on a fact-finding mission to borrow ideas from leading institutions in France, Germany and Japan to blend with his own.

Arsenal invested more than £10m in a brand new complex at Shenley in Hertfordshire, which opened in 1999 complete with 10 pitches (indoor and outdoor), a gym, a warm-up room, a steam room, a swimming pool, a hydro-therapy pool, treatment rooms, a doctor's office, a canteen serving all the right foods and a common room. It has become the heart of Wenger's Arsenal operation, a place if not of seclusion then of focus on excellence. Visiting international sides who've borrowed the facility – including Brazil – have come away with nothing but admiration.

That Wenger took such a hands-on role in the design said much about his attention to detail and obsession with his job. And he is obsessed, as he has admitted himself. These days, he says, he thinks about football for *only* 90 per cent of the time. He expects at least as much dedication from his players. How he has succeeded – or failed – to achieve that aim is best examined through the stories of his players.

The making of Vieira

Wenger has earned a reputation at Arsenal as a talent spotter *par excellence*. He is the shrewdest of traders who brings players to the club who either become committed to the cause and offer superb value, or who end up leaving but not without profit. Nicolas Anelka was bought for £500,000 and sold for £23m. Emmanuel Petit and Marc Overmars were bought for £9.5m between them and sold for £30m. The trio all provided something on the pitch and then left something in the bank.

Freddie Ljungberg (bought for £3m), Thierry Henry (£10m) and Robert Pires (£6m) all fall into the category of players who had potential but only realised it fully under Wenger. Their values have rocketed accordingly. As David Dein, Arsenal's vice-chairman, is fond of saying:

"Arsène makes an average player into a good player, a good player into a very good player, and a very good player into a world-class player."

Arsenal under Wenger have also gained a reputation for lacking discipline, however, not in how they look after themselves, but on the pitch. They have been awarded more red cards during his time in charge than any other top-flight team. Their total in the Premier League alone between 1996 and May 2003 was 32. The overall tally is now ticking towards 50. In the same time period Manchester United received 13 red cards in the League.

Patrick Vieira has exemplified both Wenger's judgement of a player, and Arsenal's incautious approach. The two are not mutually exclusive. Vieira was signed because Wenger believed he could play in English conditions. By being tough on the pitch, he has been hugely influential. Of course Wenger would have preferred that he hadn't got himself in so much trouble. But then that's probably why he made Vieira his captain for 2002–03, and why the player has matured so much since, "as a player and as a man".

"I go on the pitch with the same commitment but I had to improve the way I acted," he said in early 2003. "I made some mistakes and I learned. Now I am captain I don't react like I used to because I have to be an example. Tackles are part of the game. I give them and have to accept them."

A précis of Vieira's charge sheet since 1996 does not make light reading. He was twice charged with misconduct in 1998 and was fined £3,000 for a scuffle, then £20,000 for a gesture at an opposition crowd. In 1999 he was given a six-match ban and a £30,000 fine for spitting, and a two-match ban and a £15,000 fine for a confrontation with a police officer. He has been charged with misconduct for kicking an opponent (in 2000), for an elbowing offence (in 2001, of which he was subsequently cleared), and, in 2002, for using 'abusive and/or insulting words' to a match official. (He told referee Andy D'Urso that he had no personality.) For the latter he received a two-match ban and a £25,000 fine. He had also, by May 2003, been sent off eight times for Arsenal, seven times in the League.

And yet Vieira has been Arsenal's consistently most influential player for six years, with Wenger's team almost always enhanced by his presence and weakened by his absence. His height (6ft 4in) and power are assets in themselves but it is his energy, his commitment to winning the ball and his distribution that make him special. He was signed at Wenger's behest, for what now seems an absolute steal of £3.5m, before the manager even took over. He made his debut on the day Wenger's arrival in London was officially confirmed and has been at the heart of two Double-winning sides and a team in 2002–03 who played some of the most attractive football Highbury has ever seen.

Even Vieira's history of hints at departure – which have rarely been subtle and sometimes downright rude – can be offset against the amount of work he does. In the 2001–02 season, which ended with France's unsuccessful World Cup odyssey, he played 66 times in 11 months for club and country, often after long journeys abroad. As for his disciplinary record, statistics show that while he is no saint, he has been more likely to be been a victim than a perpetrator of fouls. Arsène Wenger has been unhappy with his side's red card count but there is some evidence that opponents tend to take a physical approach to thwart and rile them. The seasons ending in 2001, 2002 and 2003 respectively saw three, six and three Arsenal sendings-off in the League, but their opponents collectively racked up seven, eight and nine.

Team-mates are always quick to praise Vieira, with Thierry Henry calling him the best defensive midfielder in the world. Wenger has said Vieira is the umbilical cord connecting him with his team. And his disciplinary record has improved since becoming captain, with only one red card last season and that for two bookable offences.

Vieira is a natural fighter. He was born in Dakar, Senegal, and moved, aged eight, to France, where he settled with his mother and brothers in Dreux, a small town 40 miles west of Paris. At the time Dreux was a National Front stronghold. Vieira has developed a mentality – particularly strong among France's rainbow nation – of making the most of his opportunities. A recurring theme is that the opportunities matter more because in childhood they were infrequent, even unlikely. Vieira's heritage is a common reference point, as is his desire to reflect the spirit of his country of birth. "I'm a French product with an African's hunger," he said in 2003 to illustrate what drives him.

Wenger has been crucial in helping Vieira see his dreams realised. Milan saw enough potential in the 19-year-old version to sign him from Cannes, his first club, in late 1995, but he played just twice in Serie A that season. Wenger bought him and moulded him into a World Cup-winning player. The key has been letting his players know he believes in them, and that he will stand by them.

"He knows the team and what we can do and that's really important," said Vieira last season. "The belief he has in us is fantastic and to see the manager put so much faith in the players is really good. He really believes in the team."

In the run-up to the 2003 FA Cup final, the seemingly endless speculation about Vieira's future started again. His contract, due to expire in summer 2004, became a focal point of attention. Would he stay? Would he go to Real Madrid, as had been suggested on more than one occasion? His public statements were par for the course for a player in negotiations.

"I have always said I would not quit this club," he said. "I will be here next season. My contract finishes in 2004. I want to stay, the club want me to stay, so that is a good start. If we can find a solution I will be here."

Wenger has always shown a determination to retain Vieira, whose input has far outweighed his shortcomings. Vieira, in turn, has frequently talked about feeling at home at Highbury. "I have found what I am looking for, a club which wants to be big in Europe, which wants to win trophies, where the fans love the players and the players have respect from everyone," he said. "It is fantastic to be in an environment where you can really enjoy your job. England is a country where you can enjoy your football.

"The fans are fantastic. They are real supporters. They support you even if you lose. That is important for players. In Italy or France it is completely different. I like it when, even if I meet a Man United fan or Tottenham fan, they say: 'I don't support your team but the team plays good football.' It is nice to hear that. It shows the respect the fan has for the footballer. You don't find that in other countries."

Enfant térrible

Nicolas Anelka was a month short of his 18th birthday when Arsène Wenger signed him for £500,000 from Paris St Germain in February 1997. He was a 20-year-old Double winner and a formidable striking talent when Wenger sold him to Real Madrid in August 1999 for a profit of £22.5m.

In Anelka's turbulent career it says a lot that his best – most consistent, most productive – playing days to date were those at Arsenal. And it says a lot that even after big-money moves to Spain (where he won the European Cup with Real), and France (where he had two mediocre years back at PSG), that he yearned to return to England. Gérard Houllier ultimately decided not to sign him for Liverpool after a five-month loan in 2001–02 so he moved to Manchester City instead, for £13m.

Under Kevin Keegan, he had a decent 2002–03 season although whether he continues to mature remains to be seen. He may have been 'Made in England', as the cover of *France Football* magazine proclaimed in January 2002, but whether he can make it in England again is a different matter. Wenger knows he has the ability, as he said before Arsenal hosted Manchester City last season.

"Perhaps having a huge fee on his shoulders at the age of 19 was a bit too flashy for him," he said. "That's maybe why it did not work out at Paris St Germain. But I have kept a check on Nicolas's career and I feel he has gone through a needed evolution. Mentally he has taken a big step forward now. He has matured. There has never been any doubt about his football ability."

The question of Anelka's maturity has risen time and again. It earned him his Arsenal nickname of the 'Incredible Sulk'. Towards the end of his days at Highbury he became more and more outspoken about his team-mates. In February 1999, during a season in which he was Arsenal's top goalscorer, he made public his disdain for Marc Overmars.

"It's the absolute truth that Overmars plays exclusively for his own benefit and that he never gives a scoring pass," Anelka raged to *L'Equipe* of the Dutch winger. "Why shouldn't I say that? There's no reason why I should shut up about having to run like a bird-dog after the missiles that he aims out to the wings, where I'm left with no choice but to put them back into the centre so that he can take advantage of them to shine all by himself, which was his aim all along."

Matters deteriorated to the extent that Anelka demanded that he be allowed to leave. There was talk of him unilaterally breaking his Arsenal contract if he wasn't given a move. His brothers, Claude and Didier, who looked after the business side of his career, were portrayed as the puppeteers behind this perceived outrage but there was evidently something unsettled about the player himself. At Real Madrid he fell out with his coach, Vicente del Bosque, refused to train and was suspended by his club. He returned to shine in the Champions' League success of 2000 (and in Euro 2000 for France) but struggled at PSG and then failed to persuade Houllier – who'd mentored him at junior international level – to give him a Liverpool contract.

Soon after signing Anelka, Keegan clearly felt that he could be the manager who would finally get the best out of the player over a sustained period. "He's already got the total respect of the other players," he said. "His work rate is good, his energy is good and he works very hard. At 23, he has got a lot ahead of him still. Nicolas has been an absolute dream to train. I have to take him off the pitch and the only other player I have had to do that with was David Beckham [*when I was the manager*] with England."

Anelka himself has said that he is happy in England, indeed happier than in any other country. As Wenger has said: "He realises that it is a paradise for footballers here. The big following, the commitment of the fans, you get it here more than anywhere in the world. Every player needs to be loved."

And maybe therein lies the reason why his early professional years were so turbulent. He knew he was *valued*, because the price on his head told him. But after two years' estrangement from his non-footballing friends while at Clairefontaine, and then a high-profile move to Arsenal as a 17-year-old, it's possible he felt more like a commodity than a kid who happened to be a good footballer.

He'd wanted to succeed. He'd accepted that leaving home at 13 was part of that. He knew his career was important to his parents, Jean-Philippe and Marguerite, who'd swapped Martinique in the 1970s for a life in high-rise, south-west Paris. But none of that changed the fact that he was a teenager living in a strange country under a constant media spotlight.

Certainly there are those who can testify that even in his phase as Le Sulk of Highbury, he was actually still bemused by the attention and lifestyle his work handed him. Like every famous footballer, Anelka was bombarded with offers of free goodies by manufacturers eager to have their name associated with him. Patrick McAleenan was a PR consultant for one such company, a well-known clothing label. McAleenan, who knew nothing about football, had no idea who Anelka was when he was detailed to take the player shopping in 1999. He only found out when a work-mate pointed out newspaper stories of Anelka's supposed attitude problem.

"He was actually quite shy," McAleenan said. "There was nothing remotely arrogant or stroppy about him. I think the clothes thing was something an agent had told him to do. He came along and we gave him some gear. He picked out a few things he liked, not huge amounts of stuff. And he was very grateful. He kept saying thank you. It was as though he was surprised that we were interested in working with him."

Pitfalls of youth

If anything can be learnt from Anelka's teenage years, it is that importing young players comes with potential hazards for both parties. The players face the obvious risks of dislocation for no guaranteed reward. Most are happy to take the chance that they'll make it at the top level. But academies all over England now have foreign youngsters who won't. David Grondin, a friend of Anelka's, arrived at Highbury as an 18-year-old in 1998. Five years and one League appearance later he was still attached to the club in May 2003, albeit out on loan in Scotland with Dunfermline. Perhaps after a while as cannon fodder in the Scottish Premier League – he was part of the side trounced 6–1 by Rangers on the last day of the 2002–03 SPL season – he'll emerge a strong and successful player.

But there have been loud protests from France about the movement of teenagers who the French authorities believe should spend their developing years at home. The biggest brouhaha came in January 1999 when Arsène Wenger announced he was going to sign a young striker, Jeremie Aliadière. The player was two months short of his 16th birthday when the announcement was made. Arsenal had already taken flak that year over the signing of the 15-year-old England schoolboy Jermaine Pennant from Notts County amid accusations that they were using their financial muscle to turn Pennant's head.

The Aliadière affair caused an altogether bigger rumpus in France. "It's a disgrace," said Noel Le Graet, the president of the French league. "[*Aliadière's*] coaches, his teachers and his parents should ask themselves a few questions about this auction of a child of 15... Here is a boy, educated and coached within the national structures of French football, who leaves for the highest bidder. What happened is obvious. Let's call a spade a spade. Arsène Wenger has an employee stalking the corridors of the Institute [*at Clairefontaine*]."

Wenger responded by saying: "We have done nothing wrong. We are happy with what we have done. It's better than bringing someone all the way from Nigeria."

Aliadière moved with little subsequent fuss and by 2002–03 was on the fringes of the first team. Pennant was also starting to make his mark, and scored his first Premier League hat-trick, against Southampton, towards the end of the season. Rather than losing their way they appeared to be finding their feet.

Maybe, going into the 2003–04 season, Arsenal are close to producing their first crop of Shenley-reared youngsters under Wenger. The lack of academy products in his first-team line-ups has been glaring since 1996. "When I first joined the club I could not really look at the younger players coming through, I had to buy players," he said towards the end of the 2002–03 season.

It is possible that Pennant and Aliadière will become established stars alongside the likes of their cosmopolitan peers of 2003. They range from the genuinely home-grown players, such as Ryan Garry and Jerome Thomas, to the 'home-grown' foreign players, like Sebastian Svard and Moritz Volz, who have already been at Arsenal for three or four years.

In December 2002 Wenger also reached an agreement with Servette of Switzerland to sign the Swiss youth international, Philippe Senderos, on a deal starting in July 2003. Wenger, who beat the likes of Real Madrid, Bayern Munich, Roma and Lens to the player's signature, is expecting big things of Senderos, a central defender who turned 18 in February 2003.

One night in February

If one match on English soil summed up the French Revolution in progress at the end of the 20th century it was the friendly fixture between England and France at Wembley stadium on 10 February 1999. Nicolas Anelka scored France's first-ever goal at the venue and then the second as the visitors won 2–0. Even to the most sceptical English minds it was obvious: France's World Cup win had been no fluke. The World Champions really did have strength in depth. What other conclusion was there when

Anelka, who hadn't even made it to France 98, had put England to the sword so stylishly?

Roger Lemerre, France's coach, said afterwards that the result had gone some way to dismantling the 'myth of Wembley'. He said: "When I go to watch Arsenal, Liverpool, Manchester United and Chelsea the fervour is still there. But at Wembley it is not as great. When the crowd are all behind England it's 10 times harder. Perhaps in some way it's the myth of Wembley disappearing." It was certainly the might of France being sustained.

Four names in the England starting line-up were notable: Seaman, Dixon, Keown, Adams. Aside from Chelsea's Graeme Le Saux at left-back, the home back-five were from Arsène Wenger's Arsenal. And they were torn to pieces by Arsène Wenger's Anelka.

The rest of the French players in action that day were as follows: Barthez (Monaco), Thuram (Parma), Desailly (Chelsea), Blanc (Marseille), Lizarazu (Bayern Munich), Deschamps (Juventus), Petit (Arsenal), Djorkaeff (Internazionale), Zidane (Juventus), Pires (Marseille), Leboeuf (Chelsea), Dugarry (Marseille), Wiltord (Bordeaux), Vieira (Arsenal).

With Thuram, Desailly, Blanc and Lizarazu solid at the back, a two-man central midfield pairing of Deschamps and Petit played distribution and holding roles. The pace of Pires, the genius of Zidane and the passing of Djorkaeff in the line ahead of them allowed incision with a touch of class. Anelka finished with poise, netting three times, one of which was disallowed. The substitutes were stylish window dressing.

With the exception of Thuram, Lizarazu and Zidane, every starting player and most of the squad had, by 2003, moved to England. Barthez and Blanc went to Manchester United, Deschamps to Chelsea, Djorkaeff to Bolton, Pires and Wiltord to Arsenal and Dugarry to Birmingham.

The French squad that night is not a bad snapshot of France's influence in England. Desailly, who was at the very top of his game with Milan, was nonetheless an important figure at Chelsea afterwards. Significantly, he has been influential in the careers of William Gallas and a generation of young players at Stamford Bridge, not to mention Arsenal's Patrick Vieira (while he was at Milan). Desailly was also part of the Chelsea side, along with compatriots Frank Leboeuf and Didier Deschamps, who won the last FA Cup staged at the old Wembley Stadium, in 2000.

Petit, before and after 1999, was of great importance alongside his close friend Vieira in Arsenal's midfield. After an unsuccessful spell in Barcelona, he has started to make an impression at Chelsea as well.

And then there's Pires, the star of the show in Arsenal's 2002 Double, at least until he ruptured the cruciate ligaments in his knee at the tail end of the season. Not that that stopped him walking away with a personal Double of the PFA and Football Writers' player of the year awards.

"I think that I have succeeded in coming to terms a little with English football," he said in understatement after winning the FWA award. "When I first came to London I was surprised by the speed of the Premiership and the ferocity of the tackling. For a few months I was a little disconcerted; but I looked, I observed and realised that in order to succeed you have to match it. The team does seem more together than it was last year; in just about every match the spirit is there. We have to be combative because you can't compete in England without it."

Almost without exception, French players marvel at the spirit of the English game and the fact that supporters follow one club – and passionately, regardless of results – for their whole lives. Those factors both made an impression on someone who *wasn't* in the French team in 1999 but has since become England's most prolific French goalscorer.

Va va voom

Thierry Henry moves around a football pitch with such ease that it sometimes appears that his feet aren't touching the ground. Watch him from high in the stadium, where the viewpoint is aerial, and his movement can mimic a tornado. It's the not speed per se that catches the eye, although there is that. And it's not the force because he looks so easy. It's the virtual certainty that whatever falls in his path he will find a way around it. In practice he drops a shoulder and then dips past on the other side, or knocks the ball beyond himself, loses his marker and catches up again. But it can be so fluid on occasion that it seems like he's levitating.

His timing is superb. He can stop a ball dead and then wait for the precise fraction of a second to pass before a lay-off or shot. He does a lot of lay-offs, and crosses, and running. He also scores a lot of goals, more than one every other game since he's been in the Premier League. In all competitions by the end of May 2003, he'd netted 112 times for Arsenal, making him the most prolific Frenchman ever to play for an English club bar none.

These are a few of the reasons he was voted the player of the year in 2003 by his peers *and* the Football Writers' Association. It was a close call. Ruud Van Nistelrooy had an extremely strong case because he turned on the determination when it mattered, scored a hat-load of goals and helped Manchester United win the title. But Henry was not an undeserving winner of either award. He graced the season.

Among a strong cast of contenders, Henry has the potential to be Arsène Wenger's greatest success story. Patrick Vieira is way up there while Robert Pires and Freddie Ljungberg have claims. But Henry, from being a failure at Juventus, has enjoyed a renaissance to become one of the best footballers in the world.

The rise has more than an echo of Patrick Vieira about it. Henry too was brought up in a Parisian suburb, the son of immigrant parents, Antoine, who came from Guadeloupe, and Maryse, who hailed from Martinique. They instilled a work ethic in their son and made him determined that he would not let failure envelop him.

That he failed at Juventus is something he has admitted himself. Here, he is talking about the pain endured by childhood friends who also wanted to be footballers but failed to make the grade. "No-one thinks about the possibility of failure. That's why when you do fail it is so difficult mentally. You can have it in your mind from eight to 21 that you're going to be a professional. Thirteen years of dreams and then you fail.

"Your family crying their eyes out because you've failed. That feeling when you go home and say 'Sorry, I didn't make it'. Everyone fears that feeling. That's what drives me. That's why I'm running my socks off, not to have that feeling. I failed at Juventus. To lose I can accept but to fail I can't. Failure is at my front door every day. People should remember that."

What Arsène Wenger did, in buying Henry for Arsenal, was restore the player's faith in himself and his ability. Wenger knew all about the latter, having been the manager at Monaco who fast-tracked a 17-year-old Henry into his side without even stopping off at the reserves. When Wenger was sacked and left for Japan he knew that one day, if possible, he'd be reacquainted with his protégé. In 1999 he was, and Henry will never forget it.

"I will stay at Arsenal as long as they want to keep me," he said on Cup final day 2003 after announcing he had signed a contract extension until 2007. "I want to make it clear I am very happy to stay, which has always been the case. I want to do well for this club both domestically and, hopefully, in Europe.

"People are keen to say that foreign players are only here in England for the money. Of course, in some cases, this may be true. But I have enjoyed some good years at Arsenal and I want to give something back. Hopefully I will have a long stay here as I am so comfortable. I did not feel at home in Italy. To come to Arsenal was the best thing I ever did."

Two days earlier, at the prize-giving dinner to pick up his FWA Footballer of the Year award, he had voiced similar sentiments. But he'd also made another point: foreign players have contributed a lot to English football but English football has given a lot back. "The commitment, desire and passion for the game in England is something amazing," he said.

Henry's achievements in England have been all the more remarkable because when he arrived he was a winger who did not consider himself proficient up front. "When he first came to us Thierry was not totally convinced that he could score goals, but in every big career you need to have someone who believes in you," Wenger said. "I believed in him and I think everyone now knows, including himself, that he is a big, big player.

"He is so strong and powerful, and what's more he's very intelligent. He understands quickly and he deserves great credit for his contributions to this team. He is very important to us. He has everything you need to be a top player. The question is how far does he want to go? He has everything to be the best of the best."

An Anfield academic

At some stage in the 2003–04 season, Gérard Houllier is confident that two incoming French teenagers will serve notice that they can be the best of the best. The Liverpool manager signed Florent Sinama–Pongolle and Anthony Le Tallec in 2001 for £6m from Le Havre. His aim was that they would move to Anfield in summer 2003, by which time they would both be 18.

The pair were the undisputed stars of the Under-17 World Cup for France in September 2001. Sinama-Pongolle, a striker, scored nine goals in that tournament while Le Tallec, likened to a young Zinedine Zidane, had the honour of being voted the joint-best player.

Houllier overcame competition from dozens of other managers around the world, including Manchester United's Alex Ferguson, to sign the pair. The Frenchman's connections with Clairefontaine and in his home country ultimately made the difference. He and Arsène Wenger – and Jean Tigana when he was the manager at Fulham – have had this obvious advantage in being able to attract French players. In the post-Cantona age, Ferguson has arguably lost out on some of the fruits of the French Revolution for this reason.

Speaking about Sinama-Pongolle and Le Tallec in May 2003, Houllier said: "They may need six months or a year to play in the reserves and to get used to football before they are ready for the first team. They are two gems, I can tell you that, but remember they are still only 18."

After doing the 2001 deal to buy the pair, they were immediately loaned back to Le Havre so they could continue their education at home in a first-team environment. Houllier had considered allowing them to stay there into the 2003–04 season but with Le Havre being relegated from France's top division in May 2003, it seemed likely their English careers would start soon afterwards. Only time will tell whether they have what it takes to make the grade.

Aside from investment in French teenagers, Houllier's managerial tenure at Anfield since his arrival in July 1998 has had several parallels with Wenger's at Arsenal. He took an academic and disciplined approach, cleared out the dead wood and boozers and set about building his own side.

Like Wenger, he invested in a lot of foreign players. The roll call of hits and misses includes Kippe, Ferri, Song, Traoré, Hyypia, Camara, Henchoz, Westerveld, Smicer, Meijer, Hamann, Babbel, Diomede, Arphexad, Ziege, Vignal, Sjolund, Biscan, Arne Riise, Litmanen, Dudek, Baros, Xavier, El-Hadji Diouf, Cheyrou, Diarra, Luzi and Diao.

The nurturing of those who still remain will be key to Liverpool's future, as will the continuing development of a strong English contingent featuring Michael Owen, Steven Gerrard, Danny Murphy, Emile Heskey and Chris Kirkland. The club has already made great strides.

At the end of the 1999–2000 season, Houllier's first full season in sole charge (he started as co-manager with Roy Evans in an experiment that failed), Liverpool finished fourth in the Premier League, qualifying for the UEFA Cup of 2000–01. He signed a five–year contract in the summer of 2000 and then embarked on his most successful season to date.

On 25 February 2001, Liverpool won their first trophy in six years by beating Birmingham 5–4 on penalties in the League Cup final. On 12 May, they added the FA Cup after two goals from Owen were enough to see off the challenge of Wenger's Arsenal, 2–1. On 16 May an historic Treble was completed when Houllier's side won the UEFA Cup, claiming it after a golden goal had given them a remarkable 5–4 win over Alaves in Dortmund. Three days later Liverpool secured third place in the Premier League behind Manchester United and Arsenal to claim a Champions' League qualifying slot for 2001–02.

The Treble-winning team had key foreign elements, notably Germany's Dietmar Hamann as a vital holding player ahead of a central defence of Sami Hyypia and Stephane Henchoz. The English personnel – Owen, Gerrard, Heskey, Murphy, Robbie Fowler – were supplemented by the wise old Scottish head of Gary McAllister, who was hugely influential.

Liverpool and Houllier had a life-affirming 2001–02. After major heart surgery in October 2001, Houllier's mere return to work in March 2002 was a triumph. His team, in the hands of Phil Thompson, went on to finish runners-up in the League behind Arsenal, thereby consigning Manchester United to their first finish outside the top two since 1991. Houllier's side, it seemed, were ready for the final push to break the Arsenal-United duopoly at the top.

The 2002–03 season started well, with Liverpool topping the table after 10 games but then came a slump that ruined not only their title chances but their hopes of qualifying for the Champions' League in 2003–04. It was a close thing, eventually coming down to one match at the end of the season against

Chelsea, but the Londoners prevailed to win a place at Europe's top table.

As Houllier said in January 2003, when Liverpool hit the 'blip' that undermined their season:

"We have to keep strong. But this is an ideal opportunity to tell people that at the end of the season the strong will be even stronger, but the weak will have to go. The more difficult the period is, the more you get out of it and the strong personalities and top players will emerge stronger, bigger and more clever.

"The weaker ones will disappear – sometimes you need that sort of crisis to sort out what is going on. Over the last four years we have changed a lot of things at the club and managed to win five trophies. I would not jeopardise that for a blip that has lasted a couple of months."

In the same week he said:

"I would be disappointed to leave this club without a championship trophy."

His aim is to build, to work for the future, to see his young team achieve their potential within the next three years. It is a common aim among French managers.

The best team in England?

Arsène Wenger stood surrounded by journalists, hands in his pockets, talking quietly about his pleasure at winning the 2003 FA Cup. And amid all a barrage of questions about whether David Seaman would or wouldn't be staying at the club, whether he had transfer targets earmarked for the summer, whether Arsenal could 'recover' after winning 'only' one major honour and finishing as runners-up in the League, he said: "Things went against us in the last two months and maybe we were not strong enough to deal with it."

In that sentence he acknowledged the work that needed to be done. Arsenal had lost the title after failing to hold onto the lead in crucial games. Their heads had dropped after elimination from the Champions' League. They had missed the presence of Patrick Vieira when he was injured in the run-in. They had failed to bring about the 'shift of power' that Wenger had hoped was around the corner a year earlier.

No doubt he went away to spend the summer working on the detail but the shortcomings (a relative term) had become evident enough. Wenger has never adequately replaced Arsenal's famous old defence. In the Cup final, with Pascal Cygan (yet to prove himself) injured and Sol Campbell suspended after picking up another red card to add to the Highbury collection (shortcoming), he had had to field Oleg Luzhny alongside Martin Keown (age 36) in central defence.

As it transpired, Luzhny had his best game in an Arsenal shirt. But there was no strength in depth within the rearguard, highlighted by the fielding of Lauren as a makeshift right-back. No doubt Wenger went away intending to solve that problem and hoping that Philippe Senderos will be a revelation. The Arsenal manager said that he hoped to bring in between one and three players in the summer.

"I've learnt a lot about the bonding and the character of the team," he said. "There are some boys here you can rely on. What I've learnt is that this group has a future."

CHAPTER TWELVE

A New World Order

AS FOOTBALL'S new world order was unfolding around them, Sven Goran Eriksson's team resorted to the long ball approach. The opponents were Brazil. The occasion was the 2002 World Cup, the biggest stage on the planet. England hoofed themselves off it.

So much for the promise of the barmy day in September 2001 when Eriksson's men had travelled to Germany and won 5–1. So much for the way that Argentina had been marvellously held at bay and then defeated in the Sapporo Dome. England were on their way home, unable to claim a place among the genuinely upwardly mobile.

The 2002 tournament was full of upsets as emerging nations prospered and giants toppled lamely over. Senegal struck an early blow for Africa, stunning the reigning champions France 1–0 in the opening match. Pape Diop scored the winner, which had supporters of Norwich City reaching for their record books. Was that *really* the same Senegalese Pape Diop who was at Carrow Road for seven games in the 1999–2000 season? (No, it was a different Senegalese Pape Diop, but that's the international market for you.)

The USA beat Portugal in the group phase. So did South Korea. The USA and South Korea marched to the second round, Portugal went home. England beat Argentina, who could only draw with Sweden. Argentina went home early, as did France. Croatia beat Italy but failed to advance. Then Italy drew with Mexico and failed to win their group. After going unbeaten, Japan won theirs. So to the second round.

Senegal beat Sweden. The USA beat Mexico. South Korea stunned Italy. Japan bowed out to Turkey. So to the quarter-finals. Turkey beat Senegal. South Korea stunned Spain. Germany scraped past the USA. Ronaldinho saw off England.

Only in the semi-finals was a semblance of order restored. Brazil crept past Turkey by a single goal as Germany ended South Korea's dream by the same small margin. The rest was Ronaldo's story.

So was it a good tournament for England? Yes and no for Eriksson's team. Yes, because getting there in the first place had been an achievement after a terrible qualifying start under Kevin Keegan. And no, because of the nature of the defeat to Brazil.

In a wider sense, it was definitely a good tournament for England – as an advert for a footballing nation as opposed to an advert for a national team. Among the combined ranks of the 32 participating countries at the start of the event, one in every seven players (or 105 from 736) was contracted to an English League club at the time. They included seven Swedes, eight Frenchmen, six Danes, six Americans, quartets from Cameroon and Croatia and an assortment of players from 15 other countries including China, Belgium, Ecuador, Slovenia and Nigeria (as well as England and the Republic of Ireland). No other league in the world was as widely represented. Italy was next best with 74 players, including all 23 members of the Italian squad.

In addition to the 105 who earned a living in England at the time, there were plenty of others who had played in England in the past. They included Brazil's Juninho, Croatia's Davor Suker, Denmark's Jon Dahl Tomasson, France's Frank Leboeuf, Nigeria's Taribo West, Saudi Arabia's Sami Al Jaber, Costa Rica's Mauricio Solis and the USA's Cobi Jones. And there were more again who were about to move to England for the first time, including Senegal's El Hadji Diouf, Salif Diao and Aliou Cisse, Nigeria's Jay-Jay Okocha and Joseph Yobo, China's Li Weifeng and Li Tie, Slovenia's Milenko Acimovic and Brazil's Gilberto Silva.

And the point is?

The point is that many observers looked at the topsy-turvy results and the early exits of some of the strong favourites and concluded that the biggest nations played too much football. That, they said, was why the major names from the likes of

France and Argentina had failed. Because they were tired. It was a legitimate point. It was particularly evident in specific cases such as Zinedine Zidane's. Long domestic seasons and fatigue certainly were factors.

But they cannot have been the only factors. Brazil won the trophy with a squad that included numerous players who'd had lengthy club campaigns at home or in Italy's Serie A or in Spain's La Liga (not to mention in the Champions' League).

Germany reached the final with a squad including five players from Bayer Leverkusen who'd gone to the World Cup on the back of a phenomenally draining season. Within 11 days in May 2002 Leverkusen were pipped to the Bundesliga title, lost the German FA Cup final and then lost the Champions' League final to Real Madrid. And yet their quintet of German internationals subsequently reached the World Cup final.

It is arguable that what happened in Korea and Japan in the summer of 2002 was not just a fluke of exhaustion but a result of the internationalisation of the game. Due mainly to television, players and coaches are more familiar than ever before with the day-to-day details of leagues around the world. But most significantly a huge number of players who featured in the World Cup had played alongside or against their opponents at club level. Taking the argument to its logical conclusion, such familiarity is bound to start levelling the playing field.

The majority of Argentina's squad at the World Cup played their club football in Spain, Italy or France. The same was true of the backbone of Brazil's triumphant team. Senegal's squad were au fait with European football because 21 of them (out of 23) played their club football in France, unlike France's squad, the majority of whom then played in Italy or Spain or England. Denmark's squad members were variously attached to clubs in The Netherlands, Italy, Scotland, Sweden, Greece and Germany as well as Denmark and England. Nigeria's squad then played for clubs in Switzerland, Ukraine, France, The Netherlands, Belgium, Greece, Israel, Saudi Arabia, Nigeria and England. The list went on but England was there, time and again, as the biggest single melting pot.

Sven Goran Eriksson and his side were not able to win the World Cup for England but English football played a sizeable role in the event.

By the first World Cup of the 21st century England's most successful export ever – football – had really come home. The motherland, historically a reluctant host to outsiders, had gone cosmopolitan. Even the national team was coached by a Swede.

Svengali?

By the end of the 2002–03 domestic season in England, the national team's only competitive defeat under Sven Goran Eriksson had been the one to Brazil in the World Cup quarter-finals. And yet he had already begun to face a barrage of questions about his suitability for the job.

The turning point probably came in the run-up to Japan when his aura of studious calm was damaged by revelations about his private life (an affair) and by details of how he'd been cashing-in on commercial opportunities (lending his name to a CD compilation of classical music). These 'misdemeanours' in themselves should not have been, and weren't, serious enough to warrant calls for his head. But they started a media feeding frenzy that threatened to drive him away from England.

They also helped to dismantle the persona he had established. Previously he had seemed to be quietly professional, unencumbered by the weight of emotional attachment to his country of employment. This was no bad thing because his objectivity was rarely in question. Afterwards he was seen as someone who couldn't resist a quick buck. Or fling.

Most damaging, however, was that when England played Brazil and needed something magical (as they'd found against Germany in the 5–1 win, and against Argentina in Sapporo) there was nothing there except another long ball upfield. After that, everything was open to question, especially everything on the pitch.

The post-World Cup answers were mixed. England laboured to a 2–1 win in Slovakia in a qualifying game for Euro 2004 and then managed only a 2–2 draw against Macedonia. Then came a 3–1 friendly defeat to Australia in February 2003.

The reason Australia were rated as such underdogs says much about the mentality the English are capable of adopting. Despite the Aussies fielding a team predominantly comprising Premier League-quality players, they were deemed 7–1 outsiders to win. In the event they scored three times to England's once, their middle goal courtesy of Harry Kewell of Leeds. Kewell and his club-mate Mark Viduka have spearheaded Australia's contribution to the modern English game.

The fixture became farcical when Eriksson substituted his entire team in the second half. In mitigation, he had reached the point when he was under pressure not to use certain players for more than half a match. This was at the request of various club managers. He was under added pressure to play – and watch – as many players as possible in action because his friendly experiments were so limited in number. He'd passed up the opportunity of others, knowing that the powerful Premier League clubs would only kick up a fuss about releasing their players.

After Australia came Liechtenstein, in the next Euro 2004 qualifier, at the end of March. A professional job was required and ultimately delivered although not with comfort. If nothing else the fixture showed that the 'no easy games in international football' mantra is increasingly true.

It also showed that a job in English football is now regarded as a feasible and desirable aim for players from anywhere. This was apparent by talking to Liechtenstein's national team manager, Ralf Loose. His name is pronounced 'loser' which seems appropriate given Liechtenstein's record of one competitive win in their history. But his attitude to his work was refreshing.

"We normally expect to lose," he said. "You start every game equal at 0–0 and you never know what might happen. We don't concentrate on the result. Our aim is to play with heart and courage."

He then detailed the sparse nature of his playing resources. Although his star striker, Mario Frick, played in Italy in Serie B, and his goalkeeper, Peter Jehle, played professionally in Switzerland, most of his international squad were either attached to lowly FC Vaduz in Liechtenstein's capital or were amateurs. Among the latter was Harry Zech, a wine producer, who had been known to cry off international duty because his grapes were ripening.

Loose's idea of a 'quality' performance was a recent 1–1 draw with Macedonia and a 5–0 defeat to Turkey. The latter had been especially pleasing because Turkey, World Cup semi-finalists in 2002, had had to wait until the last two minutes to get their fourth and fifth goals against his side. Liechtenstein had also created some chances.

"In the past we played with the sole intention of keeping down the number of goals scored against us," Loose said. "This time we are more offensive."

Loose's ultimate aim was not to actually qualify for a major event (he was being realistic) but to gradually increase the number of professionals in his national side.

"The qualifier against England is a good opportunity for my players," he said. "Because maybe if they play well they'll get the chance to move to England. Not in the Premier League or even First Division, but perhaps in the Second or Third Division."

On the evidence of his side's match against England, in which they had chances to score, it did not seem an unreasonable aim. No Liechtensteiner had ever played in the English League at any level by the end of the 2002–03 season, however.

England's next match after Liechtenstein was another Euro 2004 qualifier in April against Turkey. England won 2–0. The crowd at Sunderland's Stadium of Light went bonkers (typically, nastily so in the case of some idiots who racially abused the Turkish players and fans). The general consensus was that England had done well. The critical view was that after losing to Australia and only beating Liechtenstein 2–0, any win was a superb win. Eriksson lived to fight another day, his results ultimately what mattered.

The final match of spring 2003 came in May with a controversial friendly in South Africa. The football itself – which was only one reason for the trip – ended with England winning 2–1. The peripheral activities were what caused ructions. England were invited to meet Nelson Mandela and most of the squad travelled to do so. But several players remained at their hotel, preferring to rest rather than take an internal flight. Their decision in some quarters was seen as a snub.

The other controversy was why England had agreed to go to South Africa in the first place. It was hardly a convenient jaunt. Basically the South African FA had wanted England to help publicise their bid to stage the 2010 World Cup. A photo opportunity with Mandela and David Beckham certainly did that. The natural quid pro quo was that England's profile rose on the continent of Africa. It was a commercially sensible trip to make.

Commercial thinking could yet become common in every area of the game, right down to the players who are hired.

Looking East

Li Weifeng was a member of China's 2002 World Cup team. Playing in the tournament was a great achievement for the 23-year-old, a defender with Shenzen Ping'an. But a few weeks after returning home he found out he'd achieved something else equally fantastic without even knowing.

"I was in Shanghai with Shenzhen Ping'an in preparation for tomorrow's match against Shanghai SVA," he told local reporters on 18 July 2002. "Last night I had a good sleep, making no dreams. And this morning when I got up, I was told that I have been loaned to Everton. Even now I cannot calm myself down. When I was a child I dreamed that one day I could go to play in the Premiership. And now it suddenly comes true. I need some time to let it sink in."

The move had come about because Everton had signed a sponsorship contract with a Chinese company, Kejian, who made mobile phones. The deal involved Everton wearing shirts with the company's name on the front and Kejian paying Everton to do so. There was also the small matter that Kejian would send a player to Everton for a year on loan. The logic was straightforward enough. If a Chinese player managed to get into Everton's team, it would be big news in China, where the audience for English football is huge. And if Everton were attracting a sizeable audience in China, then Kejian would be reaching new customers via the advert on Everton's shirts.

The financial arrangements of the deal were not revealed because they were 'commercial secrets' according to the Chinese media. It is thought that Kejian paid Everton around £1m, some of which was spent on a loan fee to Li Weifeng's club and some of which was spent on his salary.

By January 2003, after one appearance in the Premier League, Li Weifeng was back home. "He has joined a club in China and on behalf of everyone at Everton we wish him all the very best with his future career," David Moyes, Everton's manager, said.

"I lost my way, my confidence went when I was off the pitch and not playing in the first team," Li himself said, back in China. "I am afraid I cannot get that back if I play for the reserve team for a long time, that is the reason why I would not come back.

I really wanted to play for the first team, but there are a lot of quality players in the same position and it is very difficult to get into the side."

He added: "Everton was like a home for me. The manager is brilliant and all my team-mates were friendly and accommodating and tried to help me settle. I have got many benefits from my experience at Everton. It's not only improved my football skill, but also gave me a lot of fresh ideas."

Li Weifeng's departure still left Everton with one Chinese player, Li Tie, who, according to reports in China, was originally supposed to be the sole player involved in the deal. Except he was withdrawn from the process late in the day and Li Weifeng was drafted in as a replacement. Then Li Tie was reinstated in the deal and both players moved to Goodison Park.

Speculation in China suggested that Li Tie's Chinese club, Liaoning, had been unhappy about his move to Everton because Liaoning's main sponsor was Bird, a mobile phone manufacturer and a major rival to Kejian. Allowing their player to go to England and win new business for Kejian was not an attractive idea. Evidently the sticking point was resolved and both players moved.

In the summer of 2002 it seemed that David Moyes was not exactly thrilled at having two players imposed on him. Kejian's president, Hao Jianxue, had made it clear that Everton ultimately decided which player they wanted, but the bottom line was that Everton had to take a player as part of a commercial deal. Talking about Li Tie, Moyes seemed cool about the chances of either player actually getting a game.

"Li is, I feel, the best player that the Chinese national team has to offer but we really mustn't get carried away," he said. "He will have a great deal of work to do and progress to make if he's to break into our first team."

In the event, Li Tie had a good pre-season and became a fixture in Everton's side in 2002–03, playing 29 League games in Everton's midfield. At the end May 2003, Moyes said he would like to sign Li Tie permanently but added: "Li Tie's club seem to want too much for him now so we will try to get another year's loan."

On the face of it, it makes commercial sense for any club to strike a deal like the one Everton did with Kejian. The club makes money and cracks a new market, the company gets exposure and the player gets a chance in England if he's good enough.

Whether such details remain harmless as clubs seek to expand further into new Asian markets – primarily China, Japan and South Korea – remains to be seen. There seems an obvious risk of clubs hiring 'emerging market' players in deals that stipulate he must play in a certain number of televised games. The moment that happens, the game will lose what's left of its sporting integrity.

There is no suggestion that Everton's tie-up with Kejian involved any such agreement. The deal is a straightforward plugging opportunity for Kejian and no more, as the company's chief marketing officer, Samuel Lam, told the *China Daily* newspaper in November 2002.

"It is a great breakthrough for Kejian to sponsor Everton as part of our brand strategy," Lam said. "It is expected that Kejian will become an everlasting and world-famous brand. Everton is a famous football club in the United Kingdom with a history of more than a century. In this respect, Everton matches Kejian's strategy in seeking to become a long-lasting brand. This was why it was chosen by us."

The *China Daily* concluded:

> Everton matches are now a 90-minute advertisement for Kejian. The image and fame of Kejian have been dramatically boosted.

One club who evidently did not feel there was much potential for exploiting an Asian market with a player deemed unsuitable by their manager was Arsenal. After Junichi Inamoto had warmed the bench for a year, Arsène Wenger decided not to retain him in 2002. He shone at the World Cup and then moved to Fulham.

Tottenham also seemed keen in 2003 to recruit players from the Far East. They signed Kazuyuki Toda, a Japanese World Cup midfielder, on a one-year loan in January. Then at the start of March they released a statement:

> The club is delighted to announce that we have agreed terms with Chinese international striker Qu Bo.

Terms have been agreed with both the player and his club, FC Qingdau Yizhong. He will join us for the start of pre-season training when we hope to complete the formalities of a medical and obtaining a work permit. Qu Bo, 21, has won 19 caps for China and impressed in testimonial games against Crystal Palace and Watford in a short spell at the club last summer.

The Qu Bo deal had not been completed by the end of the 2002–03 season due to delays over a work permit.

Majority legionnaires

One thing is certain as the 2003–04 season progresses: England's top division will continue to have more foreign personnel involved in games, week in, week out, than players who are eligible for England's international team. Possibly, by the time Euro 2004 comes around, the number of foreign players will outnumber the number from all the home nations combined.

The other certainty is that a major football administrator, probably within FIFA, UEFA, a players' union or at a club somewhere in Europe, will propose that the number of foreign players should be limited.

When the Premier League's 20 clubs kicked off the 2002–03 season, only 88 players of the 220 in the starting line-ups were English. The other 132 came from 42 other countries. Of those, 101 hailed from outside Britain and Ireland.

"I would never have expected to see so many nationalities plying their trade in England," said Gordon Taylor, the chief executive of the PFA. "It's a two-way process because a lot of the players who come in from abroad can vastly improve our youngsters. But I just hope that they don't block the way for the next generation of Steven Gerrards and Joe Coles.

"A lot of money is going out of the game to bring new players in from abroad and clubs must strike the correct balance. We still have to produce players for World Cups and that's why we need youngsters to be given the chance to succeed."

At the start of 2002–03, Arsène Wenger's Arsenal had the most foreign players, with 24. Next came Claudio Ranieri's Chelsea (23), then Houllier's Liverpool (22); next was Kevin Keegan's Manchester City (18) and Jean Tigana's Fulham (15). Sunderland had 15, Bolton had 13 (and fielded an all-foreign XI by the end of the season), Middlesbrough had 13, Everton 12, Southampton 12, Aston Villa 11, Manchester United 11, Tottenham 11 and West Ham 11. Only six clubs – Blackburn, Newcastle, Charlton, Birmingham, Leeds and West Brom – had 10 or fewer.

The basic case for restricting the numbers of foreign players has moved on from the simplistic 'they take our jobs' line. Instead the national interest is invoked, with claims that national teams will suffer if the leading club sides are staffed primarily by overseas players. Scotland is often used as an example.

The other main argument is that the long-term general health of the game depends on local youngsters getting a chance. If clubs have no incentive to nurture young players because there is a constant stream of 'Bosman frees', they will eventually stop doing so.

This was the gist of what FIFA and UEFA said in October 2002 when they announced they were looking – again – at limiting the number of foreign players in domestic leagues.

"One idea is that six players on a team should at all times be eligible for the national team, in order to protect the young players in all countries," said Markus Siegler, FIFA's communications director.

A UEFA spokesman said that the European Commission, which shapes European Law, would be highly unlikely to make any ruling based on nationality because it would be challenged in court. "We have instead suggested an idea where a certain number of players developed through a club's youth system must be part of their first-team squad," the spokesman said. "We have taken the lead in this and have had initial discussions with the EC about this."

The theme recurs. In May 2003, Franz Beckenbauer, the supervisory chairman of Bayern Munich, became the latest big name to state he was in favour of reducing the number of foreign players. The former World Cup-winning player and coach said: "There are teams that go out with 11 foreigners. Even Bayern have had games with nine foreigners. I certainly have nothing against foreigners but we should think about a limit."

He added that he had doubts about whether Germany would have enough home-grown talent in 2006 to mount a serious challenge for the World Cup it will be staging on home soil.

Many managers and coaches, past and present, support some kind of controls. Eddie Firmani, a former player and manager with Charlton from the 1950s onwards, and later a successful manager in America, holds a not atypical view. "How are you going to develop an England team when there are 10 foreign players or more at one club?" said the South African ex-Italy striker.

"When I was playing you could go to the north-east and from Newcastle, Sunderland and Middlesbrough alone you could pick two decent teams for England. You could go to Sheffield and the Midlands and pick another. In London, you could pick two more. Now you can barely pick one."

Newcastle's Sir Bobby Robson was unequivocal in his praise for the "best foreign players"...

"They've enhanced our Premiership. No doubt about it. They've enhanced our Premiership. They've made it better, more attractive, better football, spurred us on and entertained the crowds. It's been great for the public. Henry, Vieira, Bergkamp, all the top players, Van Nistelrooy..."

Robson was a little taken aback at the volume of imports in the last six years, which stands at around 800. "I can't believe it," he said. "I cannot believe it. I cannot believe it. I can't believe it. What you're telling me is staggering. I cannot believe it."

But he added: "They've enhanced it, they've been brilliant for us [for England as a whole]. What we have to be careful about is we don't bring ordinary players. We have to bring players who we haven't got the likes of in this country. Bring in ordinary players and it's obviously denying our own players the chance of progressing and we mustn't do that. And I think that has happened, to be honest.

"We've brought in players for the sake of bringing in a player, probably got him a bit cheaper than an English player but not better than what we've got and that's what we've got to guard against. Because obviously if we are denying English players a chance of playing English football that will ultimately affect the English side, won't it? If we shorten the base, that's less players being produced for England."

The former England manager's team-building at Newcastle has been conspicuous for the number of British players he has bought and used. In 2002–03, Newcastle regularly fielded more British and Irish players than any other top-flight side.

Real standards

English football has been radically reshaped in the last decade. The style and substance of the football on offer has improved by leaps and bounds (and flicks and tricks and deft little lay-offs).

And yet, to date, few of the world's very best footballers have chosen to come to England in their prime. There's been no Roberto Baggio, Hristo Stoitchkov, Matthias Sammer, Ronaldo, Zinedine Zidane, Rivaldo or Luis Figo. All of them have been European Footballer of the Year since 1993. Italy and Spain have been the destinations of choice.

There's been no Gabriel Batistuta, Oliver Bierhoff, Roberto Carlos, Hernan Crespo or Edgar Davids. Maybe they think England's still unsophisticated.

No Alessandro Del Piero, Fernando Hierro, Patrick Kluivert, Paolo Maldini. Maybe there hasn't been the right offer.

No Raul, Marcelo Salas, Andrei Shevchenko, Lilian Thuram, Christian Vieri.

Not yet.

All-time Bests

'OF THE 1,700 overseas-born footballers to have featured in the English League since 1888, which players, from any point in history, would you choose to select in a fantasy XI?'

That question is answered in the following pages by a panel of 20 senior football figures who were asked to contribute their 'All-time best foreign XIs' especially for this book. The 20 were chosen because they have direct links to the story of foreign footballers in England and/or because of their broad experience in the game.

The only rules for their team selections were:

i) Each chosen player must have appeared in at least one League game in England.

ii) Each XI must have a goalkeeper and 10 outfielders, with no less than two players in each of the defence, the midfield and the attack.

Before considering the selections of the panel, here are some other ways of exploring the question 'Who is the best?'

If 'best' is determined solely by major trophies won with English clubs, then Zimbabwe's Bruce Grobbelaar (13 major medals with Liverpool) has been the best foreign player so far followed by Denmark's Peter Schmeichel (10), Australia's Craig Johnston (9), France's Eric Cantona (7) and Norway's Ole Gunnar Solskjaer (7). More than 30 other foreign players have won between three and six major trophies.

If durability and loyalty (ie: most appearances with one club) are the decisive factors then Kevin Keelan, an Anglo-Indian-Portuguese goalkeeper born in India has been the best, with 571 League outings for Norwich. He's followed by Germany's Bert Trautmann (508 League games for Manchester City), St Kitts's Ces Podd (502 League games for Bradford), South Africa's John Hewie (495 League games for Charlton) and Grobbelaar (440 League games for Liverpool alone).

If the number of goals denotes greatness, then South Africa's Gordon Hodgson has been the best with 294 League goals. Another 21 overseas-born footballers have scored 100 League goals or more with Bermuda's Shaun Goater (194) the leading contemporary player. Hodgson has scored the most for one club, his 232 at Liverpool from 1925 onwards coming at a rate of 0.65 per game. In comparison, Arsenal's Frenchman Thierry Henry had scored 82 Premier League goals in 136 League games (0.6 per game) by May 2003 while Manchester United's Dutchman Ruud Van Nistelrooy had scored 48 goals in 66 League games (0.73 per game).

If international caps are a hallmark of quality then the likes of Schmeichel and France's Marcel Desailly are among the best foreign players, having passed the 100 mark for Denmark and France respectively. But then so is Sami Al-Jaber, once of Wolves, who was capped 149 times by Saudi Arabia.

If crowd-pulling feats are the measure of the man, then Trautmann and Chile's George Robledo were among the greatest successes of the 1950s, as were Argentina's Ossie Ardiles and Ricky Villa from 1978, as was Brazil's Juninho in 1995 and beyond. Juninho's re-appearance after injury in 2003 attracted 20,000 people to a Middlesbrough reserve match.

But back to the all-time XIs, where the only thing that matters is the opinion of the selectors, free to nominate whoever they wanted to, for whatever reasons. The 11 players who gained the most nominations comprised one goalkeeper, two defenders, five midfielders and three strikers. They are displayed on the page opposite in the 2–5–3 line-up their positions suggest.

A more conventional 4–4–2 line-up, based on the most-often nominated players capable of playing in each position, would be as follows:

Goalkeeper: Peter Schmeichel (14 votes)

Right-back: Ivan Golac or Roland Nilsson (5 votes each)

Central defence: Marcel Desailly (17 votes) plus Sami Hyypia or Jaap Stam (7 votes each)

Left-back: Mikael Silvestre (12 votes)

Right midfield: Robert Pires (10 votes)

Central midfield: Ossie Ardiles (14 votes) and Patrick Vieira (17 votes)

Left midfield: Arnold Muhren (11 votes)

Forwards: Thierry Henry (17 votes) plus Gianfranco Zola or Eric Cantona (9 votes each)

So who's the best of the best? Three players won the votes of 17 members of the 20-man panel. They were Marcel Desailly, Patrick Vieira and Thierry Henry.

The panel members were also invited to select a captain for their teams. Ruud Gullit and Vieira were nominated most often (four times each) followed by Desailly and Cantona (three times each). Jurgen Klinsmann and Ardiles were also nominated.

Using the captaincy issue as the tie-breaker between Desailly, Vieira and Henry, Vieira becomes the experts' best of the best. Let the debate begin.

All-time best foreign XI in England

(Players with most votes from a panel of 20 selectors)

	Peter Schmeichel (14)	
Marcel Desailly (17)		Mikael Silvestre (12)
Robert Pires (10)	Ruud Gullit (8)	Arnold Muhren (11)
	Ossie Ardiles (14)	Patrick Vieira (17)
Gianfranco Zola (9)	Eric Cantona (9)	Thierry Henry (17)

Supplementary members of a 25-man all-time squad (includes all other players with three or more votes, plus reserve goalkeepers): **Goalkeepers:** Bert Trautmann (2), Bruce Grobbelaar (2), Carlo Cudicini (2). **Defenders:** Sami Hyypia (7), Jaap Stam (7), Ivan Golac (5), Roland Nilsson (5), John Hewie (3), Celestine Babayaro (3), Lucas Radebe (3), Laurent Blanc (3). **Midfielder:** Juninho (5). **Forwards:** Ruud Van Nistelrooy (6), Jurgen Klinsmann (4), Dennis Bergkamp (3).

Jimmy Armfield's XI

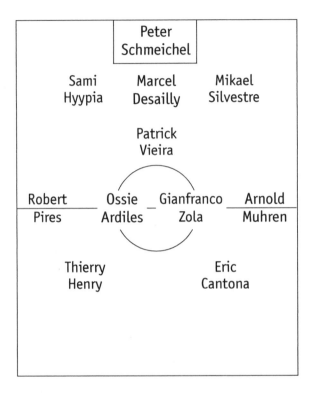

Peter
Schmeichel

Sami   Marcel   Mikael
Hyypia   Desailly   Silvestre

Patrick
Vieira

Robert   Ossie   Gianfranco   Arnold
Pires   Ardiles   Zola   Muhren

Thierry   Eric
Henry   Cantona

Jimmy Armfield was Blackpool's right-back between 1954 and 1971. He won 43 England caps and also captained his country. He managed at Bolton and Leeds in the 1970s before pursuing a media career. He is currently the technical director of the PFA's coaching department and works for BBC Radio Five Live as an expert summariser.

Brendon Batson's XI

Peter
Schmeichel

Albert   Marcel   Lucas   Celestine
Ferrer   Desailly   Radebe   Babayaro

Ossie   Patrick   Arnold
Ardiles   Vieira   Muhren

Eric   Thierry   Gianfranco
Cantona   Henry   Zola

Brendon Batson moved to England from the West Indies as a boy in 1962. He made his League debut for Arsenal but spent the majority of his career at Cambridge and then West Brom. When his playing days were over he worked for the PFA, rising to deputy chief executive. He left the PFA to return to West Brom as the managing director.

Craig Brown's XI

Craig Brown played for Rangers, Dundee and Falkirk before coaching at Motherwell and Clyde. He also worked as a teacher and lecturer before joining Scotland's coaching staff for the 1986 World Cup. He amassed a wealth of experience in the international game as the Scotland coach between 1989 and 2001. He became the manager at Preston in 2002.

Keith Burkinshaw's XI

Keith Burkinshaw played for Liverpool, Workington and Scunthorpe before moving into coaching at Newcastle in 1968. He became the first-team coach at Tottenham in 1975 and was the manager between 1976 and 1984. In the summer of 1978 he sensationally signed the Argentinean World Cup-winning midfielders Ossie Ardiles and Ricky Villa.

Barry Davies's XI

Barry Davies is a veteran BBC football commentator, having spent the majority of his broadcasting career with the corporation since joining in 1963. A spell at ITV included covering the 1966 World Cup. He was back at the BBC for the 1978 World Cup, when an off-the-cuff on-screen comment led to Poland's Kazimierz Deyna moving to England.

Sir Tom Finney's XI

Sir Tom Finney, one of England's greatest and most versatile footballers, played 433 League games for Preston between 1940 and 1960, during which time he was twice voted England's Player of the Year. He won 76 England caps and was once England's most prolific scorer, with 30 international goals. The archetypal 'Gentleman Footballer' he was never booked and never sent off. He is a life president at Preston.

John Giles's XI

John Giles won the FA Cup with Manchester United in 1963 before moving to Leeds. There he won the League title twice as well as the League Cup, the FA Cup and two Fairs Cups before a short spell at West Brom. He won 59 caps for Ireland, whom he also managed. He also coached in the USA, Cananda and Ireland and managed West Brom twice. He is now a respected and authoritative columnist and pundit.

Ron Greenwood's XI

Ron Greenwood was a centre-half with Bradford Park Avenue, Brentford, Chelsea and Fulham in a playing career that ended in 1956. He was the manager of West Ham between 1961 and 1977 and his signings included Clyde Best. He was then the England manager for five years, stepping down after the 1982 World Cup, a tournament where his team were eliminated despite being unbeaten.

Graham Kelly's XI

Graham Kelly joined the Football League as an accounts clerk in the late 1960s, rising to becoming the general secretary of the League in 1979. In 1988 he became the chief executive of the Football Association, in which post he oversaw the inception of the Premier League. He resigned from the FA in 1998 and is now a writer and broadcaster.

Gary McAllister's XI

Peter
Schmeichel

| Albert | Marcel | Jaap | Mikael |
| Ferrer | Desailly | Stam | Silvestre |

| Robert | Patrick | Arnold | David |
| Pires | Vieira | Muhren | Ginola |

Eric
Cantona

Thierry
Henry

Gary McAllister played for Motherwell, Leicester, Leeds, Coventry and Liverpool and won 57 caps for Scotland. He won the League title with Leeds in 1992 alongside Eric Cantona and was an influential figure as Liverpool won a treble of major trophies in 2001 under Gérard Houllier. He became the manager of Coventry in April 2002.

Lawrie McMenemy's XI

Lawrie McMenemy's coaching career started at Gateshead in 1961. He was the manager at Doncaster and Grimsby before taking over at Southampton in 1973. He guided the Saints to FA Cup success in 1976 and signed Ivan Golac in 1978. He later managed Sunderland and Northern Ireland and has also been the assistant manager of England.

Jan Molby's XI

Jan Molby joined Liverpool from Ajax in 1984 and starred in Liverpool's first ever Double-winning side, in 1985–86. He added further League and Cup wins in a long Anfield career before leaving for spells at Barnsley, Norwich and Swansea. He started his managerial career at Swansea in 1996 and has also managed Kidderminster and Hull.

John Motson's XI

John Motson started work as a local newspaper journalist in London, moving on to cover football for the *Morning Telegraph* in Sheffield. After branching out into radio, he got a job as a sports presenter on Radio 2. In 1971 he became a junior member of BBC television's *Match Of The Day* team. He has since commentated on more than 1,500 matches, domestically and internationally.

Michael Parkinson's XI

Bert Trautmann

Celestine Babayaro   Marcel Desailly   Sami Hyypia   Mikael Silvestre

Ossie Ardiles   Ruud Gullit   Patrick Vieira

Thierry Henry   Ruud Van Nistelrooy   Gianfranco Zola

Michael Parkinson was born near Barnsley and his boyhood football heroes included Chile's George Robledo, who played at Oakwell in the 1940s. A newspaper journalist by training, 'Parky' began a long association with television as a producer at Granada TV but has written about sport, including several books on football, throughout his career. Now writing for the *Daily Telegraph*, in 2003 he was voted the Columnist of the Year by the Sports Writers' Association.

Claudio Ranieri's XI

Carlo
Cudicini

Jaap   Laurent   Marcel   Mikael
Stam   Blanc   Desailly   Silvestre

Ruud   Patrick   Emmanuel   Robert
Gullit   Vieira   Petit   Pires

Ruud Van   Thierry
Nistelrooy   Henry

Claudio Ranieri began his managerial career with
Campania in his native Italy, moving on to manage
Cagliari, Napoli, Fiorentina, Valencia and Atletico
Madrid before taking over at Chelsea in September
2000. After two sixth-place Premier League
finishes in his first two seasons, he guided
Chelsea to fourth place (and a Champions' League
qualifying slot) in 2003.

Sir Bobby Robson's XI

Peter Schmeichel

John Hewie   Marcel Desailly   Jaap Stam   Mikael Silvestre

Frans Thijssen   Ruud Gullit   Patrick Vieira   Robert Pires

Thierry Henry   Eric Cantona

Bobby Robson was an inside-forward with Fulham, West Brom and England (20 caps) in the 1950s and 1960s. His managerial career started as player-coach with Vancouver Whitecaps in 1967. He managed Fulham and Ipswich (where he signed Arnold Muhren and Frans Thijssen) before managing England for eight years, taking them to the semi-final of the 1990 World Cup. He then managed PSV Eindhoven, Sporting Lisbon, Porto, Barcelona and PSV again before taking over at his hometown club, Newcastle, in 1999.

Graham Taylor's XI

Graham Taylor played as a full-back for Grimsby and Lincoln in the 1960s and early 1970s before managing at Lincoln, Watford (twice), Aston Villa (twice) and Wolves. He succeeded Bobby Robson as the England manager, a post he resigned from after failing to qualify for the 1994 World Cup. He was instrumental in the formation of the League Managers' Association when he was the England coach.

Peter Taylor's XI

Peter Taylor was a winger in the League with Southend, Crystal Palace, Tottenham (alongside Ossie Ardiles and Ricky Villa), Orient, Oldham and Exeter. He was also capped by England. His managerial career started in 1993 at Southend and has taken him to Gillingham, Leicester, Brighton and Hull via the England Under-21 job and one match as England's stand-in manager, in which post he made David Beckham the England captain.

Martin Tyler's XI

Martin Tyler played as a centre-forward for Corinthian Casuals while studying for a Masters degree in Sociology at university in the late 1960s. He worked for Marshall Cavendish as an author on football before moving into television commentating in the 1970s. He joined Sky Sports in 1991 and has been synonymous with the channel's live Premier League coverage for more than a decade.

Howard Wilkinson's XI

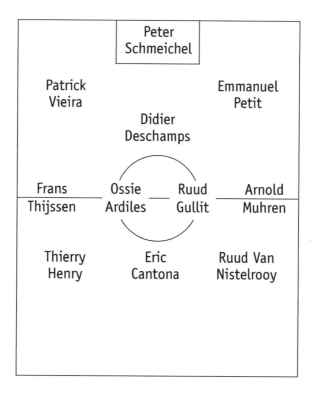

Peter
Schmeichel

Patrick
Vieira

Emmanuel
Petit

Didier
Deschamps

Frans
Thijssen

Ossie
Ardiles

Ruud
Gullit

Arnold
Muhren

Thierry
Henry

Eric
Cantona

Ruud Van
Nistelrooy

Howard Wilkinson was the last Englishman to manage a League-winning side in England when he did so in 1992 with Leeds. That came a few months after he'd given Eric Cantona his first job in English football. A player with Sheffield Wednesday and Brighton, Wilkinson has also managed Notts County, Wednesday and Sunderland. He was the technical director of the FA for five years and is the only man to have had two spells as the England manager, both as a stand-in, in 1999 and then 2000.

Bibliography

Cantona On Cantona by Eric Cantona and Alex Fynn. London: Manchester United Books. (1996).

Colouring Over The White Line: The History Of Black Footballers in Britain by Phil Vasili. Edinburgh: Mainstream. (2000).

Complete Book Of The World Cup 2002 by Cris Freddi. London: Collins Willow. (2002).

Everton: The Official Centenary History by John Roberts. London: Mayflower Books (1978).

Football League Players' Records: 1888 to 1939 by Michael Joyce. Nottingham: SoccerData Publications. (2002).

Football With The Millionaires by Eddie Firmani. London: Sportsmans Book Club. (1960).

For The Good Of The Game: The Official History Of The PFA by John Harding. London: Robson Books. (1991).

Jan The Man: From Anfield To Vetch Field by Jan Molby with Grahame Lloyd. London: Orion. (1999).

Managing My Life: My Autobiography by Alex Ferguson with Hugh McIlvanney. London: Hodder & Stoughton. (1999).

Moving With The Ball: The Migration Of Professional Footballers by Pierre Lanfranchi and Matthew Taylor. Oxford: Berg. (2001).

Paolo Di Canio: The Autobiography by Paolo Di Canio with Gabriele Marcotti. London: Collins Willow. (2000).

Premiership: Lifting The Lid On A National Obsession by Chris Horrie. London: Pocket Books. (2002).

Rothmans Football Yearbooks [1970–71 to 2002–03 inclusive] Herts: Queen Anne Press (until 1992) and then London: Headline.

Schmeichel: The Autobiography by Peter Schmeichel with Egon Balsby. London: Virgin Books. (2000).

Steppes To Wembley by Bert Trautmann. London: Sportsmans Book Club. (1957).

Sven Goran Eriksson by Joe Lovejoy. London: Collins Willow. (2002).

Sweet F.A: A Fascinating Insight Into Football's Corridors Of Power by Graham Kelly with Bob Harris. London: Collins Willow. (1999).

The Book Of Football Quotations by Phil Shaw. London: Ebury Press (2003).

The First Black Footballer: Arthur Wharton 1865–1930 by Phil Vasili. London: Frank Cass. (1998).

The First World Atlas Of Football by Radovan Jelinek and Jiri Tomes. Prague: Infokart. (2000).

The Jimmy Seed Story by Jimmy Seed. London: Sportsmans Book Club. (1958).

The PFA Premier & Football League Players' Records 1946-1998 by Barry Hugman. Herts: Queen Anne Press. (1998).

The Professor: Arsène Wenger at Arsenal by Myles Palmer. London: Virgin Books (2002).

The Story Of Football by Martin Tyler. London: Marshall Cavendish. (1976).

Trautmann: The Biography by Alan Rowlands. Derby: Breedon Books. (1990).

Twaalf Gestolen Jaren by Tom Egbers. Amsterdam: Uitgeverij Thomas Rap. (2002).

Credits

THANKS TO the following people for the help, co-operation, advice and information they provided in the compilation of this book and its appendices: Paul Agnew, Dave Allan, David Allen, Barry Baker, David Barber, Ivan Barnsley, Professor Peter Beck, Kath Begley, Andy Bishop, Mike Blackstone, David Bowler, Rob Briggs, Keith Brookman, Billy Brown, Jim Brown, Tony Brown, Ian Burnden, Cliff Butler, Tim Carder, Jean-Michel Cazal, Gary Chalk, Steve Chu, Ian Cook, Nicolas Cornu, James Corrigan, Mike Davage, Dan Davies, Reg Davies, Andrew Dewhurst, Albert Dicken, Jason Dickinson, Stephen Done, David Downes, Sheila Drake, Sébastien Duret, Soren Elbech & Jimmie Thomsen, official statisticians to the Danish FA (www.danskfodbold.dk), Michell Eyl, Chris Evans, Mick Everett, David Farmer, Harold Finch, Brian Fraser, Ed Furniss, John Garrett, Helen Giles, Harry Glaspar, Pat Godbold, Osvaldo José Gorgazzi, Frank Grande, Colin Groves, Mark Hannen, Roger Harrison, Phil Haynes, Sergio Hernandez, Dag T Hoelseth, Susan Hoffman, Judith Horey, Andrew Howe, Andy Howland, Matt Hudson, Gary James, Victor H Kurhy, Claudia Leati, Barry Leeming, David Litterer, Roberto Mamrud, Simon Marland, Tony Matthews, Paddy McAleenan, Pawel Mogielnicki, Mohammed Safi, Molde FC, Gerald Mortimer, Kevin Mullen, Paul Mullen, Donald Nannestad, Tom Nichol, Richard Owen, Keith Palmer, Ben Parker, Jenny Parker, Geraint Parry, Mark Pearson, Mike Petersen, Malcolm Porter, Matt Porter, Norman Renouf, Ian Rigby, Nick Riley, Chas Robinson, Dave Rodden, David Ross, Rev Nigel Sands, Christian Savill, Richard Shepherd, Ray Simpson, Ken Smales, Ómar Smárason, Ray Simpson, Dave Smith, Rob Smith, John Staff, David Steele, Greg Stock, Snorre Strand, Dave Sullivan, Matt Taylor, Paul Taylor, Jorge Teixeira, Ian Thomas, Trevor Thompson, Dennis Turner, Frank Tweddle, Gilbert Upton, Oli Winton, Neil Vacher, Remco van Dam, Peter Walter, Roger Wash, Bob Weeks, Margaret Weeks (née Seeburg), Paul Wright, Mark Wylie.

Picture credits

THANK YOU TO The Waterloo Historical Society in Canada for the photo of Walter Bowman; to Dulwich Hamlet FC for the photo of Hassan Hegazi; to the Dutch FA for the photo of Gerry Keizer; to Gary Chalk for the photo of Alf Charles; to Alec Eisentrager and the Bristol Evening Post for the photos of Alec; to Steven Bridge for his photo of Peter 'Northern Rock' Schmeichel; and to Denis Foreman for his picture.

Thank you to Jen Little at EMPICS, who supplied the following: Arthur Wharton; Eugene Langenove; George Robledo in action in the 1951 FA Cup final; Rolando Ugolini; Lindy Delapenha; Joe Marston; Hans Jeppson; Bill Perry in the 'Matthews final'; Bert Trautmann with Prince Philip; Jurgen Klinsmann; Teslim Balogun; Steve Mokone; Albert Johanneson; Ces Podd; Brendon Batson; Clyde Best; Ossie Ardiles; Ricky Villa, Keith Burkinshaw and Ossie Ardiles; Ivan Golac; Kazimierz Deyna; Frans Thijssen and Arnold Muhren; Bruce Grobbelaar; Craig Johnston and Jan 'Scouser' Molby; three shots of Eric Cantona; Allan Simonsen; Ole Gunnar Solskjaer, Dwight Yorke, Ronny Johnsen and Jaap Stam; Ruud Van Nistelrooy; Juninho with Emerson; Juninho in action, September 1996; Juan Sebastian Veron; Gianluca Vialli; Gianfranco Zola with Tore Andre Flo; Gianfranco Zola; Emmanual Petit and Dennis Bergkamp during the 2002 FA Cup final; Arsène Wenger with Gérard Houllier; Marcel Desailly with Andy Cole; Emmanual Petit and Patrick Vieira; Thierry Henry, Robert Pires and Sylvain Wiltord; Robert Pires in action with Li Tie; Ronaldo and Gilberto Silva with the 2002 World Cup.

Thank you to the Hulton Getty archive for the following: Nils Middleboe; George and Ted Robledo with the team bus; John Hewie on the treatment table; Stuart Leary and Eddie Firmani in the bath; Bert Trautmann in action against Arsenal.

APPENDICES

Appendix One:
Foreign players in England since 1888 – Country by Country

Appendix Two:
Foreign players in England since 1888 – Club by Club

Appendix Three:
Foreign players in England since 1888 – A to Z

Abbreviations: Countries

Alb Albania; **Alg** Algeria; **Ang** Angola; **Ant** Antigua; **Arg** Argentina; **Aus** Australia; **Aut** Austria; **Bar** Barbados; **Bel** Belgium; **Ber** Bermuda; **Blr** Belarus; **Bol** Bolivia; **Bos** Bosnia-Herzogovina; **Bra** Brazil; **Brit** Great Britain; **Bul** Bulgaria; **Bur** Burma; **Cam** Cameroon; **Can** Canada; **Chi** Chile; **Chn** China; **Col** Colombia; **CoRi** Costa Rica; **Cro** Croatia; **Cyp** Cyprus; **CzRep** Czech Republic; **Den** Denmark; **Dom** Dominica; **DRC** Democratic Republic of Congo (formerly Zaire); **Ecu** Ecuador; **Egy** Egypt; **Eng** England; **Est** Estonia; **Far** Faroes; **Fin** Finland; **Fr** France; **FrGu** French Guiana; **Gab** Gabon; **Geo** Georgia; **Ger** Germany; **Gha** Ghana; **Gib** Gibraltar; **Grk** Greece; **Grn** Grenada; **Guad** Guadeloupe; **Gui** Guinea; **GuB** Guinea Bissau; **Guy** Guyana; **Herz** Herzogovina; **HK** Hong Kong; **Hon** Honduras; **Hun** Hungary; **Ice** Iceland; **Ind** India; **Ire** Republic of Ireland; **Irn** Iran; **Isr** Israel; **It** Italy; **IvCo** Ivory Coast; **Jam** Jamaica; **Jap** Japan; **Kaz** Kazakhstan; **Ken** Kenya; **Lat** Latvia; **Lbr** Liberia; **Lby** Libya; **Lith** Lithuania; **Mac** Macedonia; **Mad** Madagascar; **Mal** Malta; **Mau** Mauritania; **Mex** Mexico; **Mli** Mali; **Mly** Malaya/Malaysia; **Mol** Moldova; **Mor** Morocco; **Moz** Mozambique; **Mrt** Martinique; **N Ire** Northern Ireland; **NCal** New Caledonia; **Neth** The Netherlands; **Nig** Nigeria; **Nor** Norway; **NZ** New Zealand; **Par** Paraguay; **Per** Peru; **Pol** Poland; **Por** Portugal; **Reu** Reunion; **Rom** Romania; **Rus** Russia; **SA** South Africa; **Sau** Saudi Arabia; **Sco** Scotland; **Sen** Senegal; **Sey** Seychelles; **SiLe** Sierra Leone; **Sing** Singapore; **SL** Sri Lanka; **Slo** Slovenia; **Sp** Spain; **StK** St Kitts-Nevis; **StL** St Lucia; **StV** St Vincent and the Grenadines; **Sur** Surinam; **Svk** Slovakia; **Swe** Sweden; **Swit** Switzerland; **Tan** Tanzania; **Tgo** Togo; **Tob** Tobago; **Trin** Trinidad & Tobago; **Tun** Tunisia; **Tur** Turkey; **Uga** Uganda; **Ukr** Ukraine; **Uru** Uruguay; **USA** United States; **Ven** Venezuela; **Wal** Wales; **Yug** Yugoslavia; **Zai** Zaire (now Democratic Republic of Congo; **Zam** Zambia; **Zim** Zimbabwe (formerly Rhodesia)

Abbreviations: Clubs

Acc Stanley Accrington Stanley; **A Villa** Aston Villa; **Birmingham** Birmingham City; **Blackburn** Blackburn Rovers; **Bolton** Bolton Wanderers; **B&B Ath** Bournemouth & Boscombe Athletic; **Bradford** Bradford City; **Bradford PA** Bradford Park Avenue; **Brighton** Brighton & Hove Albion; **Bristol C** Bristol City; **Bristol R** Bristol Rovers; **Cambridge** Cambridge United; **Cardiff** Cardiff City; **Carlisle** Carlisle United; **Charlton** Charlton Athletic; **Cheltenham** Cheltenham Town; **Chester** Chester City; **Clapton O** Clapton Orient; **Colchester** Colchester United; **Coventry** Coventry City; **Crewe** Crewe Alexandra; **C Palace** Crystal Palace; **Derby** Derby County; **Doncaster** Doncaster Rovers; **Grimsby** Grimsby Town; **Halifax** Halifax Town; **Hartlepool** Hartlepool United; **Hereford** Hereford United; **Huddersfield** Huddersfield Town; **Hull** Hull City; **Ipswich** Ipswich Town; **Kidderminster** Kidderminster Harriers; **Leeds** Leeds United; **Leicester** Leicester City; **Lincoln** Lincoln City; **Luton** Luton Town; **Macclesfield** Macclesfield Town; **Maidstone** Maidstone United; **Man City** Manchester City; **Man Utd** Manchester United; **Mansfield** Mansfield Town; **N Brighton** New Brighton; **NB Tower** New Brighton Tower; **Newcastle** Newcastle United; **Newport** Newport County; **Northampton** Northampton Town; **Nottm For** Nottingham Forest; **Notts Co** Notts County; **Norwich** Norwich City; **Oldham** Oldham Athletic; **Orient** Leyton Orient/Orient; **Oxford** Oxford United; **Peterborough** Peterborough United; **Plymouth** Plymouth Argyle; **Preston** Preston North End; **QPR** Queen's Park Rangers; **Rotherham** Rotherham United; **Rushden & D** Rushden & Diamonds; **Scunthorpe** Scunthorpe United; **Sheff Utd** Sheffield United; **Sheff Wed** Sheffield Wednesday; **Shrewsbury** Shrewsbury Town; **Southend** Southend United; **Stockport** Stockport County; **Stoke** Stoke City; **Swansea** Swansea Town/City; **Swindon** Swindon Town; **Torquay** Torquay United; **Tottenham** Tottenham Hotspur; **Tranmere** Tranmere Rovers; **WBA** West Bromwich Albion; **West Ham** West Ham United; **Wigan Ath** Wigan Ath; **Wigan Bor** Wigan Borough; **Wolves** Wolverhampton Wanderers; **Wycombe** Wycombe Wanderers; **York** York City

Foreign players in England since 1888

Country by Country

Overseas-born players in English League history by country of origin in chronological order of arrival/first appearance (1888–May 2003 inclusive)

Key: DOB = Date of birth. Nat = Nationality/footballing nationality. i) These appendices do not include any players born within Britain or Ireland, for example players who are British nationals but represent countries outside Britain and Ireland. ii) If an overseas-born player has represented one of the home nations or is otherwise identifiable as English, Scottish, Welsh or Northern Irish as opposed to simply British, it is specified. Joined/first played, in this context, means the month from which the player was employed by the club and usually refers to the month he signed his contract. In some cases (loans, non-contract deals, instances when it has not been possible to establish precisely when the contract was signed) the month here refers to the player's debut. In many instances, a player leaves one club on loan, plays for another and returns to play for his original club. This is only listed as two separate spells at the original club when the player has severed his ties and then returned.

The number in brackets after each country is the number of players born there. (+1) denotes how many other players born outside that country have the nationality of that country.

SURNAME, NAME	DOB	PLACE OF BIRTH	NAT	CLUB(S) JOINED/FIRST PLAYED
ALBANIA (1)				
Kuqi, Shefki	10 Nov 1976	Vuqitern	Alb/Fin	Stockport (Jan 2001); Sheff Wed (Jan 2002)
ALGERIA (2+1)				
Saib, Moussa	5 Mar 1969	Theniet-el-Had	Alg	Tottenham (Feb 1998)
Benarbia, Ali	8 Oct 1968	Oran	Alg	Man City (Sep 2001)
Qualified for Algeria but born outside Algeria				
Belmadi, Djamel	27 Mar 1976	Champigny, Fr	Alg	Man City (Jan 2003)
ANGOLA (6)				
Paulo, Pedro	21 Nov 1973	Angola	Por	Darlington (Aug 1995)
Quitongo, Jose	18 Nov 1974	Luanda	Ang	Darlington (Sep 1995)
Helder, Rodrigues	21 Mar 1971	Luanda	Por	Newcastle (Nov 1999)
Batista, Jordao	30 Aug 1971	Malanje	Por	WBA (Aug 2000)
Da Silva, Lourenco	5 Jun 1983	Luanda	Por	Bristol C (Mar 2001); Oldham (Aug 2002)
Garrocho, Carlos	26 Jan 1974	Benguela	Ang	Walsall (Jul 2001)
ANTIGUA (1)				
Carr, Everton	11 Jan 1961	Antigua	Ant	Leicester (Jan 1979); Halifax (Aug 1981); Rochdale (Mar 1983)
ARGENTINA (35+1)				
Peed, Frank	27 Jul 1905	Vernado Tuerto	Brit	B&B Ath (Jun 1930); Norwich (Oct 1930); Newport (Aug 1931); Barrow (Nov 1933)
Ardiles, Ossie	3 Aug 1952	Cordoba	Arg	Tottenham (Jul 1978); Blackburn (Mar 1988); QPR (Aug 1988); Swindon (Jul 1989)
Villa, Ricky	18 Aug 1952	Buenos Aires	Arg	Tottenham (Jul 1978)
Sabella, Alex	5 Nov 1954	Buenos Aires	Arg	Sheff Utd (Aug 1978); Leeds (Jun 1980)
Tarantini, Alberto	3 Dec 1955	Buenos Aires	Arg	Birmingham (Oct 1978)
Verde, Pedro	12 Mar 1952	Buenos Aires	Arg	Sheff Utd (Aug 1979)
Marangoni, Claudio	17 Nov 1954	Rosario	Arg	Sunderland (Dec 1979)
Lorenzo, Nestor	28 Feb 1966	Buenos Aires	Arg	Swindon (Oct 1990)
Taricco, Mauricio	10 Mar 1973	Buenos Aires	Arg	Ipswich (Sep 1994); Tottenham (Dec 1998)
Mendez, Gabriel	12 Mar 1973	Buenos Aires	Aus	Notts Co (Mar 1997)
Di Lella, Gustavo	6 Oct 1973	Buenos Aires	Arg	Darlington (Dec 1997); Hartlepool (Mar 1998)
Carbonari, Horacio	2 May 1973	Rosario	Arg	Derby (Jul 1998); Coventry (ADD)
Cobian, Juan	11 Sep 1975	Buenos Aires	Arg	Sheff Wed (Aug 1998); Swindon (Jul 2000)
Vivas, Nelson	18 Oct 1969	San Nicolas	Arg	Arsenal (Aug 1998)
Del Rio, Walter	16 Jun 1976	Buenos Aires	Arg	C Palace (Sep 1998)
Caballero, Fabian	31 Jan 1978	Misiones	Arg	Arsenal (Oct 1998)
Otta, Walter	20 Dec 1973	Cordoba	Arg	Walsall (Nov 1998)

SURNAME, NAME	DOB	PLACE OF BIRTH	NAT	CLUB(S) JOINED/FIRST PLAYED
Fuertes, Esteban	26 Dec 1976	Colonel Dorredo	Arg	Derby (Aug 1999)
Marinelli, Carlos	28 Aug 1980	Buenos Aires	Arg	Middlesbrough (Oct 1999)
Padula, Gino	11 Jul 1976	Buenos Aires	Arg	Walsall (Nov 1999); Wigan Ath (Jul 2000); QPR (Aug 2002)
Bassedas, Chistian	16 Feb 1973	Buenos Aires	Arg	Newcastle (Jul 2000)
Arca, Julio	31 Jan 1981	Quilmes Bernal	Arg	Sunderland (Aug 2000)
Cordone, Daniel	6 Nov 1974	General Rodriguez	Arg	Newcastle (Aug 2000)
Mazzina, Nicolas	31 Jan 1979	Buenos Aires	Arg	Swansea (Jul 2001); York (Sep 2002)
Veron, Juan S	9 Mar 1975	La Plata	Arg	Man Utd (Jul 2001)
Bonvin, Pablo F	15 Apr 1981	Concepcion	Arg	Sheff Wed (Aug 2001)
Peralta, Sixto	16 Apr 1979	Chubut	Arg	Ipswich (Aug 2001)
Caceres, Adrian	20 Jan 1982	Buenos Aires	Aus	Brentford (Sep 2001), Hull (Mar 2002)
Zavagno, Luciano	6 Aug 1977	Rosario	Arg	Derby (Oct 2001)
Biagini, Leo	13 Apr 1977	Arroyo Seco	Arg	Portsmouth (Feb 2002)
Colusso, Cristian	7 Feb 1977	Rosario	Arg	Oldham (Feb 2002)
Sava, Facundo	3 Jul 1974	Ituzaingo	Arg	Fulham (Jul 2002)
Medina, Nicolas	17 Feb 1982	Buenos Aires	Arg	Sunderland (Jan 2003)
Sara, Juan	13 Oct 1978	Buenos Aires	Arg	Coventry (Jan 2003)
Herrera, Martin	13 Sep 1970	Rio Puerto	Arg	Fulham (Feb 2003)

Other players qualified for Argentina but born outside Argentina

Corbo, Mateo	21 Apr 1976	Montevideo, Uru	Arg	Barnsley (Aug 2000)

AT SEA (1)

Wilcox, Tom	1879	At sea	Brit	Blackpool (May 1906); Man Utd (Aug 1907); Huddersfield (Jan 1911)

AUSTRALIA (91+6)

Cuffe, John	26 Jun 1880	Sydney	Aus	Glossop (Jul 1905)
Higginbotham, Harry	27 Jul 1897	Sydney	Aus	South Shields (Aug 1919); Luton (Jul 1920); Clapton O (Feb 1923); Nelson (Oct 1923); Reading (May 1924)
Baines, Peter	11 Sep 1919	Australia	Aus	Wrexham (Apr 1943); Crewe (Nov 1946); Hartlepool (Jun 1947); N Brighton (Oct 1947)
Mitchell, Frank	3 Jun 1922	Goulbourn	Aus	Birmingham (Sep 1943); Chelsea (Jan 1949); Watford (Aug 1952)
Grieves, Ken	27 Aug 1925	Sydney	Aus	Bury (Apr 1947); Bolton (Dec 1951); Stockport (Jul 1957)
Horsfall, George	19 Sep 1924	Perth	Aus	Southampton (May 1947); Southend (Jun 1949)
Cornock, Wally	1 Jan 1921	Bondi	Aus	Rochdale (Nov 1947)
Marston, Joe	7 Jan 1926	Sydney	Aus	Preston (Feb 1950)
Fraser, Willie	24 Feb 1929	Melbourne	Sco	Sunderland (Mar 1954); Nottm For (Dec 1958)
Tolson, Max	18 Jul 1945	Wollongong	Aus	Workington (Feb 1966)
Roberts, John	24 Mar 1944	Cessnock	Aus	Blackburn (Apr 1966); Chesterfield (Aug 1967); Bradford (Aug 1968); Southend (Jan 1971); Northampton (Jul 1972)
Kosmina, John	17 Aug 1956	Adelaide	Aus	Arsenal (Mar 1978)
Dorigo, Tony	31 Dec 1965	Melbourne	Eng	A Villa (Jul 1983); Chelsea (Jul 1987); Leeds (Jun 1991); Derby (Oct 1998); Stoke (Jul 2000)
Davidson, Alan	1 Jun 1960	Melbourne	Aus	Nottm For (Nov 1984)
Oldfield, David	30 May 1968	Perth	Eng	Luton (May 1986); Man City (Mar 1989); Leicester (Jan 1990); Millwall (Feb 1995); Luton (Jul 1995); Stoke (Jul 1998); Peterborough (Mar 2000); Oxford (Aug 2002)
Bernal, Andy	16 May 1966	Canberra	Aus	Ipswich (Sep 1987); Reading (Jul 1994)
Kearton, Jason	9 Jul 1969	Ipswich	Aus	Everton (Oct 1988); Blackpool (Jan 1992); Stoke (Aug 1991); Notts Co (Jan 1995); Crewe (Oct 1996)
Petterson, Andy	26 Sep 1969	Fremantle	Aus	Luton (Dec 1988); Ipswich (Mar 1993); Charlton (Jul 1994); Bradford (Dec 1994); Colchester (Mar 1996); Ipswich (Sep 1995); Plymouth (Jan 1996); Portsmouth (Jul 1999); Torquay (Mar 2001); Brighton (Aug 2002)
Bosnich, Mark	13 Jan 1972	Fairfield	Aus	Man Utd (Jun 1989); A Villa (Feb 1992); Man Utd (Jun 1999); Chelsea (Jan 2001)
Hughes, Zacari	6 Jun 1971	Bentley	Aus	Rochdale (Aug 1989)
Edwards, Alistair	21 Jun 1968	Whyalla	Aus	Brighton (Nov 1989); Millwall (Dec 1994)
Greer, Ross	23 Sep 1967	Perth	Aus	Chester (Nov 1989)
Bradley, Pat	27 Apr 1972	Sydney	Aus	Bury (Jul 1990)
Lovell, Stuart	9 Jan 1972	Sydney	Aus	Reading (Jul 1990)
Farina, Frank	5 Sep 1964	Queensland	Aus	Notts Co (Mar 1992)
Johnson, Richard	27 Jul 1974	Kurri Kurri	Aus	Watford (May 1992); Northampton (Feb 2003)
Ollerenshaw, Scott	9 Feb 1968	Sydney	Aus	Walsall (Aug 1992)
Murphy, Shaun	5 Nov 1970	Sydney	Aus	Notts Co (Sep 1992); WBA (Dec 1996); Sheff Utd (Jul 1999); C Palace (Feb 2002)
Talia, Frank	20 Jul 1972	Melbourne	Aus	Hartlepool (Dec 1992); Swindon (Sep 1995); Sheff Utd (Sep 2000); Wycombe (Aug 2002)
Filan, John	8 Feb 1970	Sydney	Aus	Cambridge (Mar 1993); Coventry (Mar 1995); Blackburn (Jul 1997); Wigan Ath (Dec 2001)
Hodgson, Doug	27 Feb 1969	Frankston	Aus	Sheff Utd (Jul 1994); Plymouth (Aug 1995); Burnley (Oct 1996); Oldham (Feb 1997); Northampton (Oct 1998)

370

| --- | --- | --- | --- | --- |
Veart, Carl	21 May 1970	Whyalla	Aus	Sheff Utd (Jul 1994); C Palace (Mar 1996); Millwall (Dec 1997)
Van Blerk, Jason	16 Mar 1968	Sydney	Aus	Millwall (Sep 1994); Man City (Aug 1997); WBA (Mar 1998); Hull (Jan 2002); Stockport (Aug 2001); Shrewsbury (Aug 2002)
Seal, David	26 Jan 1972	Penrith	Aus	Bristol C (Oct 1994); Northampton (Aug 1997)
Agostino, Paul	9 Jun 1975	Woodville	Aus	Bristol C (Jul 1995)
Corica, Steve	24 Mar 1973	Cairns	Aus	Leicester (Aug 1995); Wolves (Feb 1996); Walsall (Feb 2002)
Knight, Jason	16 Sep 1974	Melbourne	Aus	Doncaster (Aug 1995)
McDermott, Andy	24 Mar 1977	Sydney	Aus	QPR (Aug 1995); WBA (Mar 1997); Notts Co (Aug 2000)
Zelic, Ned	4 Jul 1971	Australia	Aus	QPR (Aug 1995)
Lazaridis, Stan	16 Aug 1972	Perth	Aus	West Ham (Sep 1995); Birmingham (Jul 1999)
Kalac, Zeljko	16 Dec 1972	Sydney	Aus	Leicester (Oct 1995)
Neill, Lucas	9 Mar 1978	Sydney	Aus	Millwall (Nov 1995); Blackburn (Sep 2001)
Kewell, Harry	22 Sep 1978	Smithfield	Aus	Leeds (Dec 1995)
Coyne, Chris	20 Dec 1978	Brisbane	Aus	West Ham (Jan 1996); Brentford (Aug 1998); Southend (Mar 1999); Luton (Sep 2001)
Johnson, Glenn	16 Jul 1972	Sydney	Aus	Cardiff (Mar 1996)
Mautone, Steve	10 Aug 1970	Myrtleford	Aus	West Ham (Mar 1996); Crewe (Sep 1996); Reading (Feb 1997); C Palace (Nov 1999); Gillingham (Mar 2000)
Riches, Steve	6 Aug 1976	Sydney	Aus	Orient (Sep 1996)
Schwarzer, Mark	6 Oct 1972	Sydney	Aus	Bradford (Nov 1996); Middlesbrough (Feb 1997)
Cahill, Tim	6 Dec 1979	Sydney	Aus	Millwall (Jul 1997)
Harries, Paul	19 Nov 1977	Sydney	Aus	Carlisle (Jul 1997); Portsmouth (Sep 1997); Torquay (Feb 1999); Exeter (Sep 2002)
Aloisi, John	5 Feb 1976	Adelaide	Aus	Portsmouth (Aug 1997); Coventry (Dec 1998)
Kalogeracos, Vas	21 Mar 1975	Perth	Aus	Stockport (Aug 1997)
Thorp, Hamilton	21 Aug 1973	Darwin	Aus	Portsmouth (Aug 1997)
Zabica, Robert	9 Apr 1964	Perth	Aus	Bradford (Apr 1997)
Foster, Craig	15 Apr 1969	Melbourne	Aus	Portsmouth (Sep 1997); C Palace (Oct 1998)
Enes, Robbie	22 Aug 1975	Victoria	Aus	Portsmouth (Oct 1997)
Ilic, Sasa	18 Jul 1972	Melbourne	Yug	Charlton (Oct 1997); West Ham (Feb 2000); Portsmouth (Sep 2001)
Kyratzoglou, Alex	27 Aug 1974	Armitale	Aus	Oldham (Oct 1997)
Robertson, Mark	6 Apr 1977	Sydney	Aus	Burnley (Oct 1997); Swindon (Aug 2000)
Tiatto, Danny	22 May 1973	Melbourne	Aus	Stoke (Nov 1997); Man City (Jul 1998)
Edds, Gareth	3 Feb 1981	Sydney	Aus	Nottm For (Feb 1998); Swindon (Aug 2002)
Zois, Peter	21 Apr 1978	Melbourne	Aus	Cardiff (Feb 1998)
Brady, Jon	14 Jan 1975	Newcastle	Aus	Rushden & D (Jul 1998)
Miotto, Simon	5 Sep 1969	Tasmania	Aus	Hartlepool (Jul 1998)
Rizzo, Nicky	9 Jun 1979	Sydney	Aus	C Palace (Jul 1998)
Allsopp, Danny	10 Aug 1978	Melbourne	Aus	Man City (Aug 1998); Notts Co (Nov 1999); Wrexham (Feb 2000); Bristol R (Oct 2000); Notts Co (Nov 2000)
Garcia, Richard	4 Sep 1981	Perth	Aus	West Ham (Sep 1998); Orient (Aug 2000)
Moore, Craig	12 Dec 1975	Canterbury	Aus	C Palace (Oct 1998)
Howells, Lee	14 Oct 1968	Freemantle	Aus	Cheltenham (Aug 1999)
Panopoulos, Mike	9 Oct 1976	Melbourne	Grk	Portsmouth (Sep 1999)
Viduka, Mark	9 Oct 1975	Melbourne	Aus	Leeds (Jul 2000)
Blatsis, Con	6 Jul 1977	Melbourne	Aus	Derby (Aug 2000); Sheff Wed (Dec 2000); Colchester (Mar 2002)
Burns, Jacob	21 Apr 1978	Sydney	Aus	Leeds (Aug 2000)
Invincible, Danny	31 Mar 1979	Brisbane	Aus	Swindon (Aug 2000)
McDonald, Scott	21 Aug 1983	Melbourne	Aus	Southampton (Aug 2000); Huddersfield (Aug 2002); Bournemouth (Mar 2003)
Okon, Paul	5 Apr 1972	Sydney	Aus	Middlesbrough (Aug 2000); Watford (Jan 2002); Leeds (Nov 2002)
Stergiopoulos, Marcus	12 Jun 1973	Melbourne	Grk	Lincoln (Aug 2000)
Mansley, Chad	13 Nov 1980	Newcastle	Aus	Orient (Nov 2000)
Foxe, Hayden	23 Jun 1977	Canberra	Aus	West Ham (Mar 2001); Portsmouth (Aug 2002)
Guyett, Scott	20 Jan 1976	Ascot	Aus	Oxford (May 2001)
Colosimo, Simon	8 Jan 1979	Melbourne	Aus	Man City (Jul 2001)
Popovic, Tony	4 Jul 1973	Sydney	Aus	C Palace (Aug 2001)
Hews, Chay	30 Sep 1976	Belmont	Aus	Carlisle (Sep 2001)
Pogliacomi, Les	3 May 1976	Australia	Aus	Oldham (Aug 2002)
Zdrilic, David	14 Apr 1974	Sydney	Aus	Walsall (Aug 2002)
Reid, Paul	6 Jul 1979	Sydney	Aus	Bradford (Sep 2002)
McMaster, Jamie	29 Nov 1982	Sydney	Aus	Leeds (Sep 2002); Coventry (Nov 2002)
Cansdell-Sheriff, Shane	10 Nov 1982	Sydney	Aus	Rochdale (Nov 2002)
Milosevic, Danny	26 Jun 1978	Carlton	Aus	Plymouth (Nov 2002); Crewe (Jan 2003)
Theoklitos, Michael	11 Feb 1981	Melbourne	Aus	Blackpool (Nov 2002)
Cooney, Sean	31 Oct 1983	Australia	Aus	Coventry (Apr 2003)

Other players qualified for Australia but born outside Australia

SURNAME, NAME	DOB	PLACE OF BIRTH	NAT	CLUB(S) JOINED/FIRST PLAYED
Johnston, Craig	8 Dec 1960	Johannesburg	Aus	Middlesbrough (Feb 1978); Liverpool (Apr 1981)
Banovic, Yakka	12 Nov 1956	Bihac (Bos, ex-Yug)	Aus	Derby (Sep 1980)
Bozinoski, Vlado	30 Mar 1964	Skopje, Mac	Aus	Ipswich (Dec 1992)
Kulcsar, George	12 Aug 1967	Budapest, Hun	Aus	Bradford (Mar 1997); QPR (Dec 1997)

SURNAME, NAME	DOB	PLACE OF BIRTH	NAT	CLUB(S) JOINED/FIRST PLAYED
Mendez, Gabriel	12 Mar 1973	Buenos Aires, Arg	Aus	Notts Co (Mar 1997)
Caceres, Adrian	20 Jan 1982	Buenos Aires, Arg	Aus	Brentford (Sep 2001), Hull (Mar 2002)

AUSTRIA (9)

Manninger, Alex	4 Jun 1977	Salzburg	Aut	Arsenal (Jun 1997)
Hiden, Martin	11 Mar 1973	Stainz	Aut	Leeds (Oct 1997)
Dorner, Mario	21 Mar 1970	Baden	Aut	Darlington (Oct 1997)
Resch, Franz	4 May 1969	Vienna	Aut	Darlington (Oct 1997)
Mayrleb, Christian	8 Jun 1972	Leonding	Aut	Sheff Wed (Jan 1998)
Laudrup, Brian	22 Feb 1969	Vienna	Den	Chelsea (Jun 1998)
Breitenfelder, Friedrich	16 Jun 1980	Vienna	Aut	Luton (Aug 2000)
Macho, Jurgen	24 Aug 1977	Vienna	Aut	Sunderland (Jul 2000)
Haas, Bernt	8 Apr 1978	Vienna	Swit	Sunderland (Aug 2001)

BARBADOS (5)

Kingsley, Alf	25 Oct 1891	Barbados	Bar	Charlton (Jul 1921); Fulham (Jan 1922); Millwall (Sep 1923)
Alleyne, Andy	19 May 1951	Springtown	Bar	Reading (Nov 1972)
Corbin, Kirk	12 Mar 1955	Barbados	Bar	Cambridge (Jan 1978)
Welch, Micky	21 May 1958	Barbados	Bar	Wimbledon (Nov 1984); Southend (Feb 1985)
Goodridge, Greg	10 Jul 1971	Barbados	Bar	Torquay (Mar 1994); QPR (Aug 1995); Bristol C (Aug 1996); Cheltenham (Feb 2001); Torquay (Nov 2001)

BELARUS (5)

Gotsmanov, Sergei	17 Mar 1959	Minsk (then USSR)	USSR	Brighton (Feb 1990); Southampton (Aug 1990)
Gurinovich, Igor	5 Mar 1960	Minsk (then USSR)	USSR	Brighton (Nov 1990)
Yanushevski, Victor	23 Jan 1960	Minsk (then USSR)	USSR	Aldershot (Mar 1991)
Kachouro, Petr	2 Aug 1972	Minsk (then USSR)	Blr	Sheff Utd (Jul 1996)
Shtaniuk, Sergei	11 Jan 1972	Minsk (then USSR)	Blr	Stoke (Jul 2001)

BELGIUM (30+2)

Van Den Eynden, Ike	c.1890	Belgium	Bel	Clapton O (Feb 1914)
Bryant, Billy	1 Mar 1899	Belgium	Bel	Millwall (Jul 1925)
Gaillard, Marcel	15 Jan 1927	Charleris	Bel	C Palace (Feb 1948); Portsmouth (Feb 1951)
Van Den Hauwe, Pat	16 Dec 1960	Dendermonde	Wal	Birmingham (Aug 1978); Everton (Sep 1984); Tottenham (Aug 1989); Millwall (Sep 1993)
McDonough, Darron	7 Nov 1962	Antwerp	Brit	Oldham (Jan 1980); Luton (Sep 1986); Newcastle (Mar 1992)
Van Gool, Roger	1 Jun 1950	Belgium	Bel	Coventry (Mar 1980)
Van der Elst, Francois	1 Dec 1954	Opwyk	Bel	West Ham (Dec 1981)
Claesen, Nico	1 Oct 1962	Leut	Bel	Tottenham (Oct 1986)
Albert, Philippe	10 Aug 1967	Bouillon	Bel	Newcastle (Aug 1994); Fulham (Jan 1999)
Degryse, Marc	4 Sep 1965	Roeslare	Bel	Sheff Wed (Aug 1995)
Genaux, Reggie	31 Aug 1973	Charleroi	Bel	Coventry (Aug 1996)
Clement, Philippe	22 Mar 1974	Antwerp	Bel	Coventry (Jul 1998)
Ngonge, Michel	10 Jan 1967	Huy	DRC	Watford (Jul 1998); Huddersfield (Mar 2000); QPR (Dec 2000)
Vaesen, Nico	28 Sep 1969	Hasselt	Bel	Huddersfield (Jul 1998); Birmingham (Jun 2001)
Walschaerts, Wim	5 Nov 1972	Antwerp	Bel	Orient (Jul 1998)
Delorge, Laurent	21 Jul 1979	Leuven	Bel	Coventry (Nov 1998)
Bakalli, Adrian	22 Nov 1976	Brussels	Bel	Watford (Jan 1999); Swindon (Mar 2001)
De Bilde, Gilles	9 Jun 1971	Zellik	Bel	Sheff Wed (Jul 1999); A Villa (Oct 2000)
Gysbrechts, Davy	20 Sep 1972	Heusden	Bel	Sheff Utd (Aug 1999)
Camilieri-Gioia, Carlo	14 May 1975	Brussels	Bel	Mansfield (Sep 1999)
Roussel, Cedric	6 Jan 1978	Mons	Bel	Coventry (Oct 1999); Wolves (Feb 2001)
Kinet, Christophe	31 Dec 1974	Huy	Bel	Millwall (Feb 2000)
Nilis, Luc	25 May 1967	Hasselt	Bel	A Villa (Jul 2000)
Peeters, Tom	25 Sep 1978	Bornem	Bel	Sunderland (Jul 2000)
Verhoene, Kenny	14 Apr 1973	Ghent	Bel	C Palace (Mar 2001)
Malbranque, Steed	6 Jan 1980	Mouscron	Fr	Fulham (Aug 2001)
Van Deurzen, Jurgen	26 Jan 1974	Genk	Bel	Stoke (Aug 2001)
Blondel, Jonathan	3 Apr 1984	Belgium	Bel	Tottenham (Aug 2002)
Bulent, Akin	28 Aug 1979	Brussels	Tur	Bolton (Oct 2002)
Oyen, Davy	17 Jul 1975	Bilzen	Bel	Nottm For (Feb 2003)

Other players qualified for Belgium but born outside Belgium

Smeets, Axel	12 Jul 1974	Karawa, DRC	Bel	Sheff Utd (Jul 1999)
Strupar, Branko	9 Feb 1970	Zagreb, Cro	Bel	Derby (Dec 1999)

BERMUDA (8)

Woollard, Arnold	24 Aug 1930	Bermuda	Ber	Northampton (Jun 1949); Newcastle (Dec 1952); B&B Ath (Jun 1956); Northampton (Mar 1962)
Symonds, Calvin	29 Mar 1932	Bermuda	Ber	Rochdale (Oct 1954)
Mallory, Richard	10 Aug 1942	Bermuda	Ber	Cardiff (May 1963)
Best, Clyde	24 Feb 1951	Bermuda	Ber	West Ham (Mar 1969)
Goater, Shaun	25 Feb 1970	Hamilton	Ber	Rotherham (Oct 1989); Notts Co (Nov 1993); Bristol C (Jul 1996); Man City (Mar 1998)
Jennings, Jed	15 Oct 1971	Bermuda	Ber	Hereford (Aug 1991)
Wade, Meshach	23 Jan 1973	Bermuda	Ber	Hereford (Aug 1991)

SURNAME, NAME	DOB	PLACE OF BIRTH	NAT	CLUB(S) JOINED/FIRST PLAYED
Lightbourne, Kyle	29 Sep 1968	Bermuda	Ber	Scarborough (Dec 1992); Walsall (Sep 1993); Coventry (Jul 1997); Fulham (Jan 1998); Stoke (Feb 1998); Cardiff (Feb 2001); Swindon (Jan 2001); Macclesfield (Jul 2001); Hull (Mar 2002)

BOLIVIA (1)

Moreno, Jaime	19 Jan 1974	Santa Cruz	Bol	Middlesbrough (Sep 1994) & (Dec 1997)

BOSNIA- HERZEGOVINA (8)

Jankovic, Bozo	22 May 1951	Sarajevo (Bos, then Yug)	Yug	Middlesbrough (Feb 1979)
Banovic, Yakka	12 Nov 1956	Bihac (Bos, then Yug)	Aus	Derby (Sep 1980)
Rajkovic, Anto	17 Aug 1952	Sarajevo (Bos, then Yug)	Yug	Swansea (Mar 1981)
Milosevic, Savo	2 Sep 1973	Bijeljina (Bos, then Yug)	Yug	A Villa (Jul 1995)
Mavrak, Darko	19 Jan 1969	Mostar (Bos, then Yug)	Bos	Walsall (Jan 1999)
Konjic, Muhamed	14 May 1970	Tuzla (Bos, then Yug)	Bos	Coventry (Feb 1999)
Stanic, Mario	10 Apr 1972	Sarajevo (Bos, then Yug)	Cro	Chelsea (Jul 2000)
Boksic, Alen	21 Jan 1970	Makarska (Herz, then Yug)	Cro	Middlesbrough (Aug 2000)

BRAZIL (24)

Laxton, Edward	1896	Brazil	Brit	Norwich (Dec 1919)
Mirandinha, Francisco	2 Jul 1959	Fortaleza	Bra	Newcastle (Aug 1987)
Isaias, Marques	17 Nov 1963	Rio de Janeiro	Por	Coventry (Aug 1995)
Juninho	22 Feb 1973	Sao Paulo	Bra	Middlesbrough (Oct 1995); (Sep 1999); (Aug 2002)
Branco	4 Apr 1964	Bage	Bra	Middlesbrough (Mar 1996)
Emerson	12 Apr 1972	Rio de Janeiro	Bra	Middlesbrough (Jun 1996)
Edinho, Amaral	21 Feb 1967	Brazil	Bra	Bradford (Feb 1997)
Moreira, Fabio	14 Mar 1972	Rio de Janeiro	Bra	Middlesbrough (Feb 1997)
Marcelo	11 Oct 1969	Niteroi	Bra	Sheff Utd (Oct 1997); Birmingham (Oct 1999); Walsall (Feb 2002)
Thome, Emerson	30 Mar 1972	Porto Alegre	Bra	Sheff Wed (Mar 1998); Chelsea (Dec 1999); Sunderland (Sep 2000)
Fumaca, Jose	15 Jul 1976	Belem	Bra	Colchester (Mar 1999); C Palace (Sep 1999); Newcastle (Sep 1999)
Miglioranzi, Stefani	20 Sep 1977	Pocos de Caldas	USA	Portsmouth (Jun 1999); Swindon (Aug 2002)
Silvinho, Silvio	12 Apr 1974	Sao Paulo	Bra	Arsenal (Jul 1999)
Di Giuseppe, Bica	12 Mar 1972	Sao Paulo	Bra	Sunderland (Sep 1999); Walsall (Oct 1999)
Edu	16 May 1978	Sao Paulo	Bra	Arsenal (Jan 2001)
Herivelto, Moreira	23 Aug 1975	Tres Rios	Bra	Walsall (Jul 2001)
Duarte, Juan Maldondo	6 Feb 1982	Sao Paulo	Bra	Arsenal (Aug 2001)
Ferrari, Carlos	19 Feb 1979	Londrina	Bra	Birmingham (Aug 2001)
Silva, Gilberto	7 Oct 1976	Lagoa da Prata	Bra	Arsenal (Aug 2002)
Carvalho, Rogerio	28 May 1980	Brazil	Bra	York (Aug 2002)
Gaia, Marcio	8 Sep 1978	Sao Mateus	Bra	Exeter (Aug 2002)
Junior, Jose Luis	15 Jun 1979	Fortaleza	Bra	Walsall (Aug 2002)
Rodrigo, Juliano	7 Aug 1976	Santos	Bra	Everton (Aug 2002)
Doriva, Guidoni	28 May 1972	Landeara	Bra	Middlesbrough (Apr 2003)

BULGARIA (4)

Guentchev, Bontcho	7 Jul 1964	Tchoshevo	Bul	Ipswich (Dec 1992); Luton (Aug 1995)
Mikhailov, Bobby	12 Feb 1963	Sofia	Bul	Reading (Sep 1995)
Kishishev, Radostin	30 Jul 1974	Burgas	Bul	Charlton (Aug 2000)
Todorov, Svetoslav	30 Aug 1978	Dobrich	Bul	West Ham (Jan 2001); Portsmouth (Mar 2002)

BURMA (1)

Mitten, Charlie	17 Jan 1921	Rangoon	Brit	Man Utd (Jan 1938); Fulham (Jan 1952); Mansfield (Feb 1956)

CAMEROON (14+2)

Pagal, Jean-Claude	15 Sep 1964	Cameroon	Cam	Carlisle (Feb 1998)
Misse-Misse, Jean-Jacques	7 Aug 1968	Yaounde	Cam	Chesterfield (Mar 1998)
Ipoua, Guy	14 Jan 1976	Douala	Fr	Bristol R (Aug 1998); Scunthorpe (Aug 1999); Gillingham (Mar 2001)
Foe, Marc-Vivien	1 May 1975	Nkolo	Cam	West Ham (Jan 1999); Man City (Aug 2002)
Song, Rigobert	1 Jul 1976	Nkenlicock	Cam	Liverpool (Nov 1999); West Ham (Nov 2000)
Lauren	19 Jan 1977	Lodhji Kribi	Cam	Arsenal (Jun 2000)
Mamoun, Blaise	25 Dec 1979	Bamenda	Cam	Scunthorpe (Aug 2000)
Medou-Otye, Parfait	29 Nov 1976	Ekoundendi	Cam	Kidderminster (Nov 2000)
Suffo, Patrick	17 Jan 1978	Ebolowa	Cam	Sheff Utd (Nov 2000)
Mettomo, Lucien	19 Apr 1977	Douala	Cam	Man City (Sep 2001)
Atangana, Simon	10 Jul 1979	Yaounde	Cam	Port Vale (Jan 2002); Colchester (Nov 2002)
Mboma, Patrick	15 Nov 1970	Douala	Cam	Sunderland (Feb 2002)
Geremi	20 Dec 1978	Batousam	Cam	Middlesbrough (Aug 2002)
Wome, Pierre	23 Mar 1979	Douala	Cam	Fulham (Sep 2002)
Other players qualified for Cameroon but born outside Cameroon				
Job, Joseph-Desire	1 Dec 1977	Venissieux, Fr	Cam	Middlesbrough (Aug 2000)
Moreau, Fabrice	7 Oct 1967	Paris, Fr	Cam	Notts Co (Mar 2001)

CANADA (43+4)

Bowman, Walter W	c.1862	Ontario	Can	Accrington (Aug 1891); Ardwick (Feb 1893)
Dalton, James	c.1865	Ontario	Can	Sunderland (Sep 1891)

SURNAME, NAME	DOB	PLACE OF BIRTH	NAT	CLUB(S) JOINED/FIRST PLAYED
Fursdon, Roy	1 Sep 1918	Saskatchewan	Can	Torquay (Aug 1938)
McMahon, Doug	c.1915	Winnipeg	Can	Wolves (Aug 1938)
Whittaker, Fred	12 Oct 1923	Vancouver	Can	Notts Co (Aug 1946)
Killin, Roy	18 Jul 1929	Toronto	Can	Lincoln (Aug 1952)
Kirk, John	13 Mar 1930	Winnipeg	Can	Acc Stanley (Mar 1953)
Burgess, Mike	17 Apr 1932	Montreal	Can	Orient (Jul 1953); Newport (Feb 1956); B&B Ath (Jun 1957); Halifax (Jul 1961); Gillingham (Mar 1963); Aldershot (Nov 1965)
Pidcock, Fred	29 Jun 1933	Canada	Can	Walsall (Sep 1953)
Crossan, Errol	6 Oct 1930	Montreal	Can	Gillingham (Jul 1955); Southend (Aug 1957); Norwich (Sep 1958); Orient (Jan 1961)
Newman, Mick	2 Apr 1932	London, Ontario	Can	West Ham (Feb 1957)
Sharp, Ronnie	22 Nov 1932	Montreal	Can	Doncaster (Oct 1958)
Emmerson, Wayne	2 Nov 1947	Canada	Can	Crewe (Jul 1968)
Johnson, Glenn	22 Apr 1951	Vancouver	Can	WBA (Oct 1969)
Twamley, Bruce	23 May 1952	Victoria	Can	Ipswich (Oct 1969)
Lenarduzzi, Bob	1 May 1955	Vancouver	Can	Reading (May 1973)
Nicholl, Jimmy	28 Dec 1956	Hamilton	N Ire	Man Utd (Feb 1974); Sunderland (Dec 1981); WBA (Nov 1984)
Sweetzer, Gordon	27 Jan 1957	Toronto	Can	Brentford (Jul 1975); Cambridge (Apr 1978); Brentford (Jan 1982)
Ferguson, Don	2 Jan 1963	Toronto	Can	Wrexham (Jan 1986)
Kerr, John	6 Mar 1965	Toronto	USA	Portsmouth (Aug 1987); Peterborough (Dec 1987); Millwall (Feb 1993); Walsall (Nov 1995)
Forrest, Craig	20 Sep 1967	Vancouver	Can	Colchester (Mar 1988); Ipswich (Aug 1988); Chelsea (Mar 1997); West Ham (Jul 1997)
Sharp, Kevin	19 Sep 1974	Sarnia, Ontario	Can	Leeds (Oct 1992); Wigan Ath (Nov 1995); Wrexham (Oct 2001); Huddersfield (Aug 2002)
Peschisolido, Paul	25 May 1971	Pickering, Ontario	Can	Birmingham (Nov 1992); Stoke (1994-95); Birmingham (Mar 1996); WBA (Jul 1996); Fulham (Oct 1997); Norwich (Mar 2001); QPR (Nov 2000); Sheff Utd (Jul 2001)
Aunger, Geoff	4 Feb 1968	Red Deer	Can	Luton (Sep 1993); Chester (Dec 1994); Stockport (Dec 1997)
Watson, Mark	8 Sep 1970	Vancouver	Can	Watford (Nov 1993); Oxford (Dec 1998); Oldham (Sep 2000)
Corazzin, Carlo	25 Dec 1971	New Westminster	Can	Cambridge (Dec 1993); Plymouth (Mar 1996); Northampton (Jul 1998); Oldham (Jul 2000)
Brennan, Jim	8 May 1977	Toronto	Can	Bristol C (Oct 1994); Nottm For (Oct 1999); Huddersfield (Mar 2001)
Heald, Oliver	13 Mar 1975	Vancouver	Can	Scarborough (Aug 1995)
De Vos, Jason	2 Jan 1974	Appin, Ontario	Can	Darlington (Nov 1996); Wigan Ath (Jul 2001)
Nash, Martin	27 Dec 1975	Regina	Can	Stockport (Nov 1996); Chester (Sep 1999); Macclesfield (Jan 2003)
Dickinson, Patrick	6 May 1978	Vancouver	Can	Hull (Jul 1997)
Papaconstantinou, Loukas	10 May 1974	Toronto	Can	Darlington (Jul 1997)
Giumarra, Willy	26 Aug 1971	Ontario	Can	Darlington (Aug 1997)
Larkin, Jim	23 Oct 1975	Ontario	Can	Cambridge (Jan 1998)
Xausa, Davide	10 Mar 1976	Vancouver	Can	Stoke (Feb 1998)
Rogers, Mark	3 Nov 1975	Guelph	Can	Wycombe (Dec 1998)
Dunfield, Terry	20 Feb 1982	Vancouver	Can	Man City (May 1999); Bury (Aug 2002)
Busby, Hubert	18 Jun 1969	Kingston	Can	Oxford (Aug 2000)
Hume, Iain	31 Oct 1983	Brampton	Can	Tranmere (Nov 2000)
Bent, Jason	8 Mar 1977	Bramton	Can	Plymouth (Sep 2001)
Godfrey, Elliott	22 Feb 1983	Toronto	Can	Watford (Mar 2003)
Hirschfeld, Lars	17 Oct 1978	Edmonton	Can	Luton (Feb 2003)
Lynch, Simon	19 May 1982	Montreal	Sco	Preston (Jan 2003)
Other players qualified for Canada but born outside Canada				
Bunbury, Alex	18 Jun 1967	Guyana	Can	West Ham (Dec 1992)
Hooper, Lyndon	30 May 1966	Guyana	Can	Birmingham (Sep 1993)
Samuel, Randy	23 Dec 1963	Trinidad	Can	Port Vale (Nov 1995)
Radzinski, Tomasz	14 Dec 1973	Poznan, Pol	Can	Everton (Jul 2001)

CHILE (4)

Robledo, George	14 Apr 1926	Iquique	Chi	Barnsley (Apr 1943); Newcastle (Jan 1949)
Robledo, Ted	26 Jul 1928	Iquique	Chi	Barnsley (Mar 1946); Newcastle (Jan 1949); Notts Co (Sep 1957)
Margas, Javier	10 May 1969	Santiago	Chi	West Ham (Aug 1998)
Acuna, Clarence	8 Feb 1975	Coya Rancagua	Chi	Newcastle (Oct 2000)

CHINA (5)

Jihai, Sun	30 Sep 1977	Dalian	Chn	C Palace (Sep 1998); Man City (Feb 2002)
Zhiyi, Fan	22 Jan 1970	Shanghai	Chn	C Palace (Sep 1998); Cardiff (Dec 2002)
Enhua, Zhang	28 Apr 1973	Dalian	Chn	Grimsby (Dec 2000)
Li Tie	18 Sep 1977	China	Chn	Everton (Aug 2002)
Li Weifeng	26 Jan 1978	China	Chn	Everton (Nov 2002)

COLOMBIA (3)

Asprilla, Faustino	10 Nov 1969	Tulua	Col	Newcastle (Feb 1996)
Ricard, Hamilton	12 Jan 1974	Choco	Col	Middlesbrough (Mar 1998)
Angel, Juan Pablo	24 Oct 1975	Medellin	Col	A Villa (Jan 2001)

COSTA RICA (2)

SURNAME, NAME	DOB	PLACE OF BIRTH	NAT	CLUB(S) JOINED/FIRST PLAYED
Wanchope, Paulo	31 Jan 1976	Heredia	CoRi	Derby (Mar 1997); West Ham (Jul 1999); Man City (Aug 2000)
Solis, Mauricio	13 Dec 1972	Heredia	CoRi	Derby (Mar 1997)

CROATIA (11+3)

SURNAME, NAME	DOB	PLACE OF BIRTH	NAT	CLUB(S) JOINED/FIRST PLAYED
Stimac, Igor	6 Sep 1967	Metkovic	Cro	Derby (Oct 1995); West Ham (Sep 1999)
Bilic, Slaven	11 Sep 1968	Split	Cro	West Ham (Feb 1996); Everton (Jul 1997)
Asanovic, Aljosa	14 Dec 1965	Split	Cro	Derby (Jun 1996)
Jerkan, Nikola	8 Dec 1964	Sinj	Cro	Nottm For (Jun 1996)
Maric, Silvio	20 Mar 1975	Zagreb	Cro	Newcastle (Feb 1999)
Suker, Davor	1 Jan 1968	Osijek	Cro	Arsenal (Aug 1999); West Ham (Jul 2000)
Brkovic, Ahmet	23 Sep 1974	Dubrovnik	Cro	Orient (Oct 1999); Luton (Oct 2001)
Strupar, Branko	9 Feb 1970	Zagreb	Bel	Derby (Dec 1999)
Biscan, Igor	4 May 1978	Zagreb	Cro	Liverpool (Dec 2000)
Bunjevcevic, Goran	17 Feb 1973	Karlovac	Yug	Tottenham (Jun 2001)
Balaban, Bosko	15 Oct 1978	Rijeka	Cro	A Villa (Aug 2001)

Other players qualified for Croatia but born outside Croatia

SURNAME, NAME	DOB	PLACE OF BIRTH	NAT	CLUB(S) JOINED/FIRST PLAYED
Stanic, Mario	10 Apr 1972	Sarajevo, then Yug	Cro	Chelsea (Jul 2000)
Boksic, Alen	21 Jan 1970	Makarska, Herz	Cro	Middlesbrough (Aug 2000)
Prosinecki, Robert	12 Jan 1969	Schweminger, Ger	Cro	Portsmouth (Aug 2001)

CYPRUS (8)

SURNAME, NAME	DOB	PLACE OF BIRTH	NAT	CLUB(S) JOINED/FIRST PLAYED
Orhan, Yilmaz	13 Mar 1955	Nicosia	Cyp	West Ham (Oct 1972)
Young, Charlie	14 Feb 1958	Nicosia	Brit	A Villa (Nov 1975); Gillingham (Mar 1978)
Salman, Danis	12 Mar 1960	Famagusta	Eng	Brentford (Aug 1977); Millwall (Aug 1986); Plymouth (Mar 1990); Peterborough (Mar 1992); Torquay (Sep 1992)
Goss, Jerry	11 May 1965	Oekolia	Wal	Norwich (Mar 1983)
Bedrossian, Ara	2 Jun 1967	Nicosia	Cyp	Fulham (Mar 1993)
O'Sullivan, Wayne	25 Feb 1974	Akrotiri	Ire	Swindon (May 1993); Cardiff (Aug 1997); Plymouth (Jul 1999)
Papavasiliou, Nicky	31 Aug 1970	Limassol	Cyp	Newcastle (Jul 1993)
Constantinou, Costas	24 Sep 1968	Limassol	Cyp	Barnet (Oct 1996)

CZECH REPUBLIC (8)

SURNAME, NAME	DOB	PLACE OF BIRTH	NAT	CLUB(S) JOINED/FIRST PLAYED
Miklosko, Ludek	9 Dec 1961	Ostrava	CzRep	West Ham (Feb 1990); QPR (Oct 1998)
Stejskal, Jan	15 Jan 1962	Czechoslavakia	CzRep	QPR (Oct 1990)
Srnicek, Pavel	10 Mar 1968	Ostrava	CzRep	Newcastle (Feb 1991); Sheff Wed (Nov 1998)
Poborsky, Karel	30 Mar 1972	Jindrihuv-Hradec	CzRep	Man Utd (Jul 1996)
Berger, Patrik	10 Nov 1973	Prague	CzRep	Liverpool (Aug 1996)
Smicer, Vladimir	24 May 1973	Decin	CzRep	Liverpool (Jul 1999)
Repka, Tomas	2 Jan 1974	Slavicin Zlin	CzRep	West Ham (Sep 2001)
Baros, Milan	28 Oct 1981	Valassake Mezirici	CzRep	Liverpool (Dec 2001)

DEMOCRATIC REPUBLIC OF CONGO (Formerly ZAIRE) (8+1)

SURNAME, NAME	DOB	PLACE OF BIRTH	NAT	CLUB(S) JOINED/FIRST PLAYED
Kandol, Tresor	30 Aug 1981	Banga	Brit	Luton (Sep 1998); Bournemouth (Oct 2001); Cambridge (Aug 2001)
Lua-Lua, Lumana Tresor	28 Dec 1980	Kinshasa	DRC	Colchester (Sep 1998); Newcastle (Sep 2000)
Smeets, Axel	12 Jul 1974	Karawa	Bel	Sheff Utd (Jul 1999)
Bolima, Cedric	26 Sep 1979	Kinshasa	DRC	Rotherham (Oct 2000)
Itonga, Carlin	11 Dec 1982	Kinshasa	DRC	Arsenal (Aug 2001)
M'Bombo, Doudou	11 Sep 1980	Kinshasa	DRC	QPR (Aug 2001)
Yulu, Christian	26 Jan 1978	Kinshasa	Fr	Coventry (Feb 2003)
Zakuani, Gaby	31 May 1986	Kinshasa	DRC	Orient (Mar 2003)

Other players qualified for DRC but born outside DRC

SURNAME, NAME	DOB	PLACE OF BIRTH	NAT	CLUB(S) JOINED/FIRST PLAYED
Ngonge, Michel	10 Jan 1967	Huy, Bel	DRC	Watford (Jul 1998); Huddersfield (Mar 2000); QPR (Dec 2000)

DENMARK (78+4)

SURNAME, NAME	DOB	PLACE OF BIRTH	NAT	CLUB(S) JOINED/FIRST PLAYED
Middleboe, Nils	5 Oct 1887	Copenhagen	Den	Chelsea (Nov 1913)
Hansen, Edvin	21 Jan 1920	Koge	Den	Grimsby (Dec 1946)
Jensen, Viggo	29 Mar 1921	Skagen	Den	Hull (Oct 1948)
Arentoft, Ben	1 Nov 1942	Copenhagen	Den	Newcastle (Mar 1969);Blackburn (Sep 1971)
Thorup, Borge	4 Oct 1943	Copenhagen	Den	C Palace (Mar 1969)
Bartram, Per	8 Jan 1944	Odense	Den	C Palace (Aug 1969)
Jacobsen, Viggo	11 Aug 1953	Denmark	Den	Charlton (Nov 1979)
Ostergaard, Johnny	6 Feb 1955	Denmark	Den	Charlton (Nov 1979)
Simonsen, Allan	15 Dec 1952	Vejle	Den	Charlton (Nov 1982)
Olsen, Jesper	20 Mar 1961	Fakse	Den	Man Utd (Jul 1984)
Molby, Jan	4 Jul 1963	Kolding	Den	Liverpool (Aug 1984); Barnsley (Sep 1995); Norwich (Dec 1995); Swansea (Feb 1996)
Christensen, Tommy	20 Jul 1961	Aarhus	Den	Leicester (Nov 1985); Portsmouth (Nov 1985)
Bakholt, Kurt	12 Aug 1963	Odense	Den	QPR (Jan 1986)
Sivebaek, John	25 Oct 1961	Vejle	Den	Man Utd (Feb 1986)
Pingel, Frank	9 May 1964	Resskov	Den	Newcastle (Jan 1989)
Kristensen, Bjorn	10 Oct 1963	Malling	Den	Newcastle (Mar 1989); Bristol C (Mar 1993); Portsmouth (Nov 1992)
Nielsen, Kent	28 Dec 1961	Frederiksberg	Den	A Villa (Jun 1989)
Elstrup, Lars	24 Mar 1963	Rarby	Den	Luton (Aug 1989)
Mortensen, Henrik	12 Feb 1968	Odder	Den	Norwich (Oct 1989)

SURNAME, NAME	DOB	PLACE OF BIRTH	NAT	CLUB(S) JOINED/FIRST PLAYED
Schmeichel, Peter	18 Nov 1968	Gladsaxe	Den	Man Utd (Aug 1991); A Villa (Jul 2001); Man City (Aug 2002)
Lydersen, Pal	10 Sep 1965	Odense	Nor	Arsenal (Nov 1991)
Jensen, John	3 May 1965	Copenhagen	Den	Arsenal (Aug 1992)
Piechnik, Torben	21 May 1963	Copenhagen	Den	Liverpool (Sep 1992)
Rieper, Marc	5 Jun 1968	Rodoure	Den	West Ham (Jun 1994)
Thomsen, Claus	31 May 1970	Aarhus	Den	Ipswich (Jun 1994); Everton (Jan 1997)
Ekelund, Ronnie	21 Aug 1972	Glostrup	Den	Southampton (Sep 1994); Coventry (Dec 1995); Man City (Dec 1995); Walsall (Dec 2000)
Vilstrup, Johnny	27 Feb 1969	Copenhagen	Den	Luton (Sep 1995)
Haddaoui, Riffi	24 Mar 1971	Copenhagen	Den	Torquay (Mar 1996)
Laursen, Jacob	6 Oct 1971	Vejle	Den	Derby (Jul 1996); Leicester (Jan 2002)
Frandsen, Per	6 Feb 1970	Copenhagen	Den	Bolton (Aug 1996); Blackburn (Sep 1999); Bolton (Jul 2000)
Gall, Benny	14 Mar 1971	Copenhagen	Den	Shrewsbury (Aug 1996)
Johansen, Michael	22 Jul 1972	Golstrup	Den	Bolton (Aug 1996)
Nielsen, Tommy	25 Mar 1972	Aarhus	Den	Shrewsbury (Aug 1996)
Beck, Mikkel	12 May 1973	Aarhus	Den	Middlesbrough (Sep 1996); Derby (Mar 1999); Nottm For (Nov 1999); QPR (Feb 2000)
Nielsen, Allan	13 Mar 1971	Esbjerg	Den	Tottenham (Sep 1996); Wolves (Mar 2000); Watford (Aug 2000)
Nielsen, John	7 Apr 1972	Aarhus	Den	Southend (Sep 1996)
Dursun, Peter	8 Jan 1975	Aarhus	Den	Southend (Nov 1996)
Pedersen, Per	30 Mar 1969	Aalborg	Den	Blackburn (Feb 1997)
Willer-Jensen, Thomas	19 Sep 1968	Copenhagen	Den	Swansea (Mar 1997)
Johansen, Martin	22 Jul 1972	Golstrup	Den	Coventry (Jun 1997)
Tomasson, Jon Dahl	29 Aug 1976	Copenhagen	Den	Newcastle (Jun 1997)
Koogi, Anders	8 Sep 1979	Roskilde	Den	Peterborough (Jul 1997)
Nielsen, Martin	24 Mar 1973	Aarhus	Den	Huddersfield (Mar 1998)
Andersen, Soren	31 Jan 1970	Aarhus	Den	Bristol C (Jul 1998)
Jensen, Claus	29 Apr 1977	Nykobing	Den	Bolton (Jul 1998); Charlton (Jul 2000)
Sorensen, Thomas	12 Jun 1976	Fredericia	Den	Sunderland (Aug 1998)
Thogersen, Thomas	2 Apr 1968	Copenhagen	Den	Portsmouth (Aug 1998); Walsall (Oct 2001)
Dabelsteen, Thomas	6 Mar 1973	Copenhagen	Den	Scarborough (Nov 1998)
Goldbaek, Bjarne	6 Oct 1968	Nykobing Falster	Den	Chelsea (Nov 1998); Fulham (Jan 2000)
Andersen, Bo	26 Mar 1976	Slagelse	Den	Bristol C (Dec 1998)
Degn, Peter	6 Apr 1977	Aarhus	Den	Everton (Feb 1999)
Hansen, Bo	16 Jun 1972	Jutland	Den	Bolton (Feb 1999)
Fredgaard, Carsten	20 May 1976	Hillesod	Den	Sunderland (Jul 1999); WBA (Feb 2000); Bolton (Nov 2000)
Hogh, Jes	7 May 1966	Aalborg	Den	Chelsea (Jul 1999)
Hyldgaard, Morten	26 Jan 1978	Herning	Den	Coventry (Jul 1999); Scunthorpe (Jan 2000); Coventry (Aug 2002)
Jorgensen, Claus	27 Apr 1976	Holstebro	Den	Bournemouth (Jul 1999); Bradford (Jul 2001)
Skovbjerg, Thomas	25 Oct 1974	Esbjerg	Den	Kidderminster (Aug 1999)
Hjorth, Jesper	3 Apr 1975	Denmark	Den	Darlington (Nov 1999)
Jensen, Brian	8 Jun 1975	Copenhagen	Den	WBA (Mar 2000)
Nedergaard, Steen	25 Feb 1970	Aalborg	Den	Norwich (Jul 2000)
Gravesen, Thomas	11 Mar 1976	Vejle	Den	Everton (Aug 2000)
Heiselberg, Kim	21 Sep 1977	Tarm	Den	Swindon (Aug 2000)
Risom, Henrik	24 Jul 1968	Vildbjerg	Den	Stoke (Aug 2000)
Svard, Sebastian	15 Jan 1983	Hvidovre	Den	Arsenal (Aug 2000)
Jorgensen, Henrik	12 Jan 1979	Bogense	Den	Notts Co (Oct 2000)
Nielsen, David	1 Dec 1976	Sonderberg	Den	Grimsby (Oct 2000); Wimbledon (Mar 2001); Norwich (Dec 2001)
Bidstrup, Stefan	24 Feb 1975	Helsinger	Den	Wigan Ath (Nov 2000)
Gronkjaer, Jesper	12 Aug 1977	Nuuk	Den	Chelsea (Dec 2000)
Moller, Peter	23 Mar 1972	Gistrup	Den	Fulham (Jan 2001)
Johnsson, Julian	24 Feb 1975	Denmark	Far	Hull (Jun 2001)
Pedersen, Henrik	10 Jun 1975	Copenhagen	Den	Bolton (Jul 2001)
Gaardsoe, Thomas	23 Nov 1979	Randers	Den	Ipswich (Aug 2001)
Sand, Peter	19 Jul 1972	Aalborg	Den	Barnsley (Oct 2001)
Henriksen, Bo	7 Feb 1975	Roskilde	Den	Kidderminster (Nov 2001)
Jensen, Niclas	17 Aug 1974	Copenhagen	Den	Man City (Jan 2002)
Tofting, Stig	14 Aug 1969	Aarhus	Den	Bolton (Feb 2002)
Bischoff, Mikkel	3 Mar 1982	Denmark	Den	Man City (Sep 2002)
Timm, Mads	31 Oct 1984	Odense	Den	Man Utd (Oct 2002)

Other players qualified for Denmark but born outside Denmark

SURNAME, NAME	DOB	PLACE OF BIRTH	NAT	CLUB(S) JOINED/FIRST PLAYED
Kjeldbjerg, Jakob	21 Oct 1969	Fredrikstad, Nor	Den	Chelsea (Aug 1993)
Melvang, Lars	3 Apr 1969	Seattle, USA	Den	Watford (Aug 1997)
Laudrup, Brian	22 Feb 1969	Vienna, Aut	Den	Chelsea (Jun 1998)
Hansen, John	17 Sep 1973	Mannheim, Ger	Den	Cambridge (Feb 2000)

DOMINICA (2)

SURNAME, NAME	DOB	PLACE OF BIRTH	NAT	CLUB(S) JOINED/FIRST PLAYED
Cooke, Joe	15 Feb 1955	Dominica	Dom	Bradford (May 1972); Peterborough (Jan 1979); Oxford (Aug 1979); Exeter (Jun 1981); Bradford (Jan 1982); Rochdale (Jul 1984); Wrexham (Jul 1986)
Henry, Liburd	29 Aug 1967	Roseau	Dom	Watford (Nov 1987); Halifax (Sep 1988); Maidstone Utd (Jun 1990); Gillingham (Jun 1992); Peterborough (Aug 1994)

376

SURNAME, NAME	DOB	PLACE OF BIRTH	NAT	CLUB(S) JOINED/FIRST PLAYED
ECUADOR (2)				
Delgado, Agustin	23 Dec 1974	Ibarra	Ecu	Southampton (Nov 2001)
De La Cruz, Ulises	2 Aug 1974	Piqulucho	Ecu	A Villa (Aug 2002)
EGYPT (3)				
Hegazi, Hassan	14 Sep 1891	Cairo	Egy	Fulham (Nov1911)
Abdallah, Tewfik	23 Jun 1897	Cairo	Egy	Derby (Sep 1920); Hartlepools (Mar 1924)
Georgeson, Roddy	31 Jul 1948	Shubra	Brit	Port Vale (Jan 1966)
ESTONIA (1)				
Poom, Mart	3 Feb 1972	Tallinn	Est	Portsmouth (Aug 1994); Derby (Mar 1997); Sunderland (Apr 2003)
FAROES (0+1)				
Qualified for the Faroes but born outside the Faroes				
Johnsson, Julian	24 Feb 1975	Denmark	Far	Hull (Jun 2001)
FINLAND (27+3)				
Rintanen, Mauno	28 Apr 1925	Helsinki	Fin	Hull (Sep 1956)
Jantunen, Pertti	25 Jun 1952	Lahti	Fin	Bristol C (Mar 1979)
Lahtinen, Aki	31 Oct 1958	Oulu	Fin	Notts Co (Sep 1981)
Rantanen, Jari	31 Dec 1961	Helsinki	Fin	Leicester (Sep 1987)
Paatelainen, Mixu	3 Feb 1967	Helsinki	Fin	Bolton (Jul 1994); Wolves (Aug 1997)
Moilanen, Tepi	12 Dec 1973	Oulu	Fin	Preston (Dec 1995); Scarborough (Dec 1996); Darlington (Jan 1997)
Kottila, Mika	22 Sep 1974	Helsinki	Fin	Hereford (Nov 1996)
Vanhala, Jari	29 Aug 1965	Helsinki	Fin	Bradford (Dec 1996)
Jaaskelainen, Jussi	17 Apr 1975	Mikkeli	Fin	Bolton (Nov 1997)
Heinola, Antti	20 Mar 1973	Helsinki	Fin	QPR (Jan 1998)
Enckelman, Peter	10 Mar 1977	Turku	Fin	A Villa (Feb 1999)
Viljanen, Ville	2 Feb 1971	Helsinki	Fin	Port Vale (Feb 1999)
Hyypia, Sami	7 Oct 1973	Porvoo	Fin	Liverpool (Jul 1999)
Vanninen, Jukka	31 Jan 1977	Riihimaki	Fin	Exeter (Dec 1999)
Valakari, Simo	28 Apr 1973	Helsinki	Fin	Derby (Jul 2000)
Wiss, Jarkko	17 Apr 1972	Tampere	Fin	Stockport (Aug 2000)
Tuomela, Marko	3 Mar 1972	Helsinki	Fin	Swindon (Sep 2000)
Helin, Petri	13 Dec 1969	Helsinki	Fin	Luton (Nov 2000); Stockport (Jul 2001)
Salli, Janne	14 Dec 1977	Seinajoki	Fin	Barnsley (Nov 2000)
Tihinen, Hannu	1 Jul 1976	Keminmaa	Fin	West Ham (Dec 2000)
Litmanen, Jari	20 Feb 1971	Lahti	Fin	Liverpool (Jan 2001)
Pilvi, Tero	21 Feb 1976	Vihti	Fin	Cambridge (Mar 2001)
Riihilahti, Aki	9 Sep 1976	Helsinki	Fin	C Palace (Mar 2001)
Viander, Jani	18 Aug 1975	Tuusula	Fin	Bolton (Nov 2001)
Niemi, Antti	31 May 1972	Oulu	Fin	Southampton (Sep 2002)
Heikkinen, Markus	13 Oct 1978	Finland	Fin	Portsmouth (Feb 2003)
Petrescu, Tomi	24 Jul 1986	Jyvaskyla	Fin	Leicester (May 2003)
Other players qualified for Finland but born outside Finland				
Forssell, Mikael	15 Mar 1981	Steinfurt, Ger	Fin	Chelsea (Dec 1998); C Palace (Feb 2000)
Johansson, Jonatan	16 Aug 1975	Stockholm, Swe	Fin	Charlton (Aug 2000)
Kuqi, Shefki	10 Nov 1976	Vuqitern, Kosovo	Alb/Fin	Stockport (Jan 2001); Sheff Wed (Jan 2002)
FRANCE (158+25)				
Langenove, Eugene	1898	Paris	Fr	Walsall (Oct 1922)
Praski, Josef	22 Jan 1926	France	Fr	Notts Co (Mar 1949)
Six, Didier	21 Aug 1954	Lille	Fr	A Villa (Oct 1984)
Bernardeau, Olivier	19 Aug 1962	Bourges	Fr	Chesterfield (Aug 1986)
Cantona, Eric	24 May 1966	Nimes	Fr	Leeds (Feb 1992); Man Utd (Nov 1992)
Cantona, Joel	26 Oct 1967	Paris	Fr	Stockport (Mar 1994)
Ginola, David	25 Jan 1967	Gossin	Fr	Newcastle (Jul 1995); Tottenham (Jul 1997); A Villa (Aug 2000); Everton (Feb 2002)
Rolling, Franck	23 Aug 1968	Colmar	Fr	Leicester (Sep 1995); Bournemouth (Aug 1997); Gillingham (Sep 1998)
Prunier, William	14 Aug 1967	Montreuil	Fr	Man Utd (Dec 1995)
Leboeuf, Frank	22 Jan 1968	Marseille	Fr	Chelsea (Jul 1996)
Darras, Frederic	19 Aug 1966	Calais	Fr	Swindon (Aug 1996)
Garde, Remi	3 Apr 1966	L'Arbresle	Fr	Arsenal (Aug 1996)
Perez, Lionel	24 Apr 1967	Bagnols Ceze	Fr	Sunderland (Aug 1996); Scunthorpe (Oct 1999); Cambridge (Jun 2000)
Pounewatchy, Stephane	10 Feb 1968	Paris	Fr	Carlisle (Aug 1996); Port Vale (Aug 1998); Colchester (Feb 1999)
Romano, Serge	25 May 1964	Metz	Fr	Wolves (Aug 1996)
Barbara, Daniel	12 Oct 1974	France	Fr	Darlington (Dec 1996)
Anelka, Nicolas	14 Mar 1979	Versailles	Fr	Arsenal (Mar 1997); Liverpool (Dec 2001); Man City (Aug 2002)
Laurent, Pierre	13 Dec 1970	Tulle	Fr	Leeds (Mar 1997)
Blondeau, Patrick	27 Jan 1968	Marseille	Fr	Sheff Wed (Jun 1997); Watford (Jul 2001)
Grimandi, Gilles	11 Nov 1970	Gap	Fr	Arsenal (Jun 1997)
Petit, Emmanuel	22 Sep 1970	Dieppe	Fr	Arsenal (Jun 1997); Chelsea (Jul 2001)
Terrier, David	4 Aug 1973	Verdun	Fr	West Ham (Jun 1997)
Valery, Patrick	3 Jul 1969	Brignoles	Fr	Blackburn (Jun 1997)
Bonalair, Thierry	14 Jun 1966	Paris	Fr	Nottm For (Jul 1997)

SURNAME, NAME	DOB	PLACE OF BIRTH	NAT	CLUB(S) JOINED/FIRST PLAYED
Remy, Christophe	6 Aug 1971	Besancon	Fr	Oxford (Jul 1997)
Cuervo, Phillipe	13 Aug 1969	Ris-Orangis	Fr	Swindon (Aug 1997)
Peron, Jeff	11 Oct 1965	St Omer	Fr	Walsall (Aug 1997); Portsmouth (Sep 1998); Wigan Ath (Nov 1999)
Coulbault, Regis	12 Aug 1972	Brignoles	Fr	Southend (Oct 1997)
Croci, Laurent	8 Feb 1964	Montbeliard	Fr	Carlisle (Oct 1997)
Lama, Bernard	7 Apr 1963	St-Symphorien	Fr	West Ham (Dec 1997)
Madar, Mickael	8 May 1968	Paris	Fr	Everton (Dec 1997)
Charvet, Laurent	8 May 1973	Beziers	Fr	Chelsea (Jan 1998); Newcastle (Jul 1998); Man City (Oct 2000)
Ismael, Valerien	28 Sep 1975	Strasbourg	Fr	C Palace (Jan 1998)
Sissoko, Habib	24 May 1971	Juvisy-sur-Orge	Fr	Preston (Feb 1998); Torquay (Aug 2000)
Eydelie, Jean-Jacques	3 Feb 1966	Angouleme	Fr	Walsall (Mar 1998)
Tholot, Didier	2 Apr 1964	Feurs	Fr	Walsall (Mar 1998)
Dacourt, Olivier	25 Sep 1974	Montreuil-sous-Bois	Fr	Everton (Jun 1998); Leeds (Jul 2000)
D'Jaffo, Laurent	5 Nov 1970	Bazas	Fr	Bury (Jul 1998); Stockport (Aug 1999); Sheff Utd (Feb 2000)
Grondin, David	8 May 1980	Paris	Fr	Arsenal (Jul 1998)
Guivarc'h, Stephane	6 Sep 1970	Concameau	Fr	Newcastle (Jul 1998)
Keller, Marc	14 Jan 1968	Colmar	Fr	West Ham (Jul 1998); Blackburn (Jan 2001); Portsmouth (Sep 2000)
Perez, Sebastien	24 Nov 1973	Saint-Chamond	Fr	Blackburn (Jul 1998)
Santos, Georges	15 Aug 1970	Marseille	Fr	Tranmere (Jul 1998); WBA (Mar 2000); Sheff Utd (Jul 2000); Grimsby (Oct 2002)
Wallemme, Jean-Guy	10 Aug 1967	Naubeuge	Fr	Coventry (Jul 1998)
Bacque, Herve	13 Jul 1976	Bordeaux	Fr	Luton (Aug 1998)
Leoni, Stephane	1 Sep 1976	Metz	Fr	Bristol R (Aug 1998)
Mirankov, Alex	2 Dec 1967	Grenoble	Fr	Scarborough (Aug 1998)
Garcia, Tony	18 Mar 1972	Pierre Patte	Fr	Notts Co (Sep 1998)
Louis-Jean, Mathieu	22 Feb 1976	Mont St Aignan	Fr	Nottm For (Sep 1998)
Thetis, Manuel	5 Nov 1971	Dijon	Fr	Ipswich (Sep 1998); Wolves (Aug 2000); Sheff Utd (Mar 2001)
Simba, Amara	23 Dec 1961	Paris	Fr	Orient (Oct 1998)
Bonnot, Alex	31 Jul 1973	Boissy	Fr	Watford (Nov 1998); QPR (Aug 2001)
Horlaville, Christophe	1 Mar 1969	Rouen	Fr	Port Vale (Nov 1998)
Colleter, Patrick	6 Nov 1965	Brest	Fr	Southampton (Dec 1998)
Ferri, Jean-Michel	7 Feb 1969	Lyon	Fr	Liverpool (Dec 1998)
Keller, Francois	27 Oct 1973	Colmar	Fr	Fulham (Dec 1998)
L'Helgoualch, Cyrille	25 Sep 1970	St Nazaire	Fr	Mansfield (Dec 1998)
Diawara, Kaba	16 Dec 1975	Toulon	Fr	Arsenal (Jan 1999); Blackburn (Aug 2000); West Ham (Sep 2000)
Domi, Didier	2 May 1979	Sarcelles	Fr	Newcastle (Jan 1999)
Saha, Louis	8 Aug 1978	Paris	Fr	Newcastle (Jan 1999); Fulham (Jun 2000)
Traore, Djimi	1 Mar 1980	St Ouen	Fr	Liverpool (Feb 1999)
Germain, Steve	22 Jun 1981	Cannes	Fr	Colchester (Mar 1999)
Huck, Willie	11 Mar 1979	Paris	Fr	Bournemouth (Mar 1999)
Richard, Fabrice	16 Aug 1973	Saintes	Fr	Colchester (Mar 1999)
Simb, Jean-Pierre	4 Sep 1974	Paris	Fr	Torquay (Mar 1999)
Anselin, Cedric	24 Jul 1977	Lens	Fr	Norwich (Apr 1999)
Deschamps, Didier	15 Oct 1968	Bayonne	Fr	Chelsea (Jun 1999)
Dumas, Franck	9 Jan 1968	Bayeux	Fr	Newcastle (Jun 1999)
De Blasiis, Jean-Yves	25 Sep 1973	Bordeaux	Fr	Norwich (Jul 1999)
Diaf, Farid	19 Apr 1971	Carcassonne	Fr	Preston (Jul 1999)
Goma, Alain	5 Oct 1972	Sault	Fr	Newcastle (Jul 1999); Fulham (Mar 2001)
Luntala, Tresor	31 May 1982	Dreux	Fr	Birmingham (Jul 1999)
Pinault, Thomas	4 Dec 1981	Grasse	Fr	Colchester (Jul 1999)
Henry, Thierry	17 Aug 1977	Paris	Fr	Arsenal (Aug 1999)
Roy, Eric	26 Sep 1967	Nice	Fr	Sunderland (Aug 1999)
Pamarot, Louis Noe	14 Apr 1979	Paris	Fr	Portsmouth (Sep 1999)
Pollet, Ludo	18 Jun 1970	Vieux-Conde	Fr	Wolves (Sep 1999); Walsall (Nov 2002)
Rodriguez, Bruno	25 Dec 1972	Bastia	Fr	Bradford (Sep 1999)
Silvestre, Mickael	9 Aug 1977	Chambray-les-Tours	Fr	Man Utd (Sep 1999)
Bossu, Bert	14 Oct 1980	Calais	Fr	Barnet (Oct 1999)
Fradin, Karim	2 Feb 1972	St Martin d'Hyeres	Fr	Stockport (Nov 1999)
Gravelaine, Xavier	5 Oct 1968	Tours	Fr	Watford (Nov 1999)
Passi, Franck	28 Mar 1966	Bergerac	Fr	Bolton (Nov 1999)
Kaprielian, Mickael	6 Oct 1980	Marseille	Fr	Bolton (Jan 2000)
Aliadiere, Jeremie	30 Mar 1983	Rambouillet	Fr	Arsenal (Mar 2000)
Kanoute, Frederic	2 Sep 1977	Sainte Foy-les-Lyon	Fr	West Ham (Mar 2000)
Barthez, Fabien	28 Jun 1971	Lavelanet	Fr	Man Utd (Jun 2000)
Diomede, Bernard	23 Jan 1974	Saint-Douichard	Fr	Liverpool (Jul 2000)
Pires, Robert	29 Oct 1973	Reims	Fr	Arsenal (Jul 2000)
Bassila, Christian	5 Oct 1977	Paris	Fr	West Ham (Aug 2000)
Bouanane, Emad	22 Nov 1976	Paris	Fr	Wrexham (Aug 2000)
Fernandes, Fabrice	29 Oct 1979	Aubervilliers	Fr	Fulham (Aug 2000); Southampton (Dec 2001)
Javary, Jean-Phillipe	10 Jan 1978	Montpelier	Fr	Brentford (Aug 2000); Plymouth (Feb 2001); Sheff Utd (Mar 2002)
Job, Joseph-Desire	1 Dec 1977	Venissieux	Cam	Middlesbrough (Aug 2000)
Mawene, Youl	16 Jul 1979	Caen	Fr	Derby (Aug 2000)
Menetrier, Mickael	23 Sep 1978	Reims	Fr	Bournemouth (Aug 2000)
Weber, Nicolas	28 Oct 1970	Metz	Fr	Sheff Utd (Aug 2000)

SURNAME, NAME	DOB	PLACE OF BIRTH	NAT	CLUB(S) JOINED/FIRST PLAYED
Wiltord, Sylvain	10 May 1974	Neuilly-sur-Marne	Fr	Arsenal (Aug 2000)
Dagnogo, Moussa	30 Jan 1972	Paris	Fr	Bristol R (Sep 2000)
Lemarchand, Stephane	6 Aug 1971	Saint-Lo	Fr	Carlisle (Sep 2000); Rotherham (Nov 2000)
Vignal, Gregory	19 Jul 1981	Montpelier	Fr	Liverpool (Sep 2000)
Zeghdane, Lehit	3 Oct 1977	Revin	Fr	Darlington (Sep 2000)
Bernard, Olivier	14 Oct 1979	Paris	Fr	Newcastle (Oct 2000); Darlington (Mar 2001)
Cadiou, Frederic	20 Apr 1969	Paris	Fr	Orient (Oct 2000)
Romo, David	7 Aug 1978	Nimes	Fr	Swansea (Oct 2000)
Sahnoun, Nicolas	3 Sep 1980	Bordeaux	Fr	Fulham (Oct 2000)
Friio, David	17 Feb 1973	Thionville	Fr	Plymouth (Nov 2000)
Larrieu, Romain	31 Aug 1976	Mont-de-Marsan	Fr	Plymouth (Nov 2000)
Martin, Lilian	28 May 1971	Valreas	Fr	Derby (Nov 2000)
Schemmel, Sebastien	2 Jun 1975	Nancy	Fr	West Ham (Jan 2001)
Vasseur, Emmanuel	3 Sep 1976	Calais	Fr	Orient (Jan 2001)
Fabiano, Nicolas	8 Feb 1981	Courbevoie	Fr	Swansea (Feb 2001)
Opinel, Sacha	9 Apr 1977	Bourg-Saint-Maurice	Fr	Orient (Feb 2001)
Verschave, Matthias	24 Dec 1977	Lille	Fr	Swansea (Feb 2001)
Carteron, Patrice	30 Jul 1970	St Brieux	Fr	Sunderland (Mar 2001)
Cau, Jean-Michel	27 Oct 1980	Ajaccio	Fr	Darlington (Mar 2001)
Epesse-Titi, Steeve	5 Sep 1979	Bordeuax	Fr	Exeter (Mar 2001)
Forge, Nicolas	13 May 1977	Roanne	Fr	Orient (Mar 2001)
Jeannin, Alex	30 Dec 1977	Troyes	Fr	Darlington (Mar 2001)
Moreau, Fabrice	7 Oct 1967	Paris	Cam	Notts Co (Mar 2001)
Gallas, William	17 Aug 1977	Asnieres	Fr	Chelsea (May 2001)
Laslandes, Lilian	4 Sep 1971	Pauillac	Fr	Sunderland (Jun 2001)
Sabin, Eric	22 Jan 1975	Sarcelles	Fr	Swindon (Jun 2001)
Bellion, David	27 Nov 1982	Paris	Fr	Sunderland (Jul 2001)
Libbra, Marc	5 Aug 1972	Toulon	Fr	Norwich (Jul 2001)
Ben Askar, Aziz	30 Mar 1976	Chateau Gontier	Fr	QPR (Aug 2001)
Biancalani, Frederic	21 Jul 1974	Villerupt	Fr	Walsall (Aug 2001)
Blanc, Laurent	19 Nov 1965	Ales	Fr	Man Utd (Aug 2001)
Courtois, Laurent	11 Sep 1978	Lyon	Fr	West Ham (Aug 2001)
Legwinski, Sylvain	10 Jun 1973	Clermont-Ferrand	Fr	Fulham (Aug 2001)
Marlet, Steve	1 Oct 1974	Pithiviers	Fr	Fulham (Aug 2001)
Distin, Sylvain	16 Dec 1977	Bagnolet	Fr	Newcastle (Sep 2001); Man City (Aug 2002)
N'Gotty, Bruno	10 Jun 1971	Lyon	Fr	Bolton (Sep 2001)
One, Armand	15 Mar 1983	Paris	Fr	Cambridge (Sep 2001); Northampton (Sep 2003)
Valois, Jean-Louis	15 Oct 1973	Saint-Priest	Fr	Luton (Sep 2001)
Baudet, Julien	13 Jan 1979	Grenoble	Fr	Oldham (Oct 2001)
Ducrocq, Pierre	18 Dec 1976	Pontoise	Fr	Derby (Oct 2001)
Queudrue, Franck	27 Aug 1978	Paris	Fr	Middlesbrough (Oct 2001)
Skora, Eric	20 Aug 1981	Metz	Fr	Preston (Oct 2001)
Grenet, Francois	8 Mar 1975	Bordeaux	Fr	Derby (Nov 2001)
Le Pen, Ulrich	21 Jan 1974	Auray	Fr	Ipswich (Nov 2001)
Carasso, Cedric	30 Dec 1981	Avignon	Fr	C Palace (Dec 2001)
Debeve, Mickael	1 Dec 1970	Abbeville	Fr	Middlesbrough (Feb 2002)
Djorkaeff, Youri	9 Mar 1968	Lyon	Fr	Bolton (Feb 2002)
Espartero, Mario	17 Jan 1978	Frejus	Fr	Bolton (Feb 2002)
Cheyrou, Bruno	10 May 1978	Suresnes	Fr	Liverpool (Aug 2002)
Cisse, Edouard	30 Mar 1978	Pau	Fr	West Ham (Aug 2002)
Mendy, Bernard	20 Aug 1981	Evreux	Fr	Bolton (Aug 2002)
Cygan, Pascal	19 Apr 1974	Lens	Fr	Arsenal (Sep 2002)
Berthelin, Cedric	25 Dec 1976	Courriers	Fr	Luton (Oct 2002); C Palace (Jan 2003)
Lopes, Osvaldo	6 Apr 1980	Fregus	Fr	Plymouth (Sep 2002)
Debec, Fabien	18 Jan 1976	Lyon	Fr	Coventry (Sep 2002)
Dugarry, Christophe	24 Mar 1972	Bordeaux	Fr	Birmingham (Jan 2003)
Belmadi, Djamel	27 Mar 1976	Champigny	Alg	Man City (Jan 2003)
Andre, Pierre-Yves	14 May 1974	Lannion	Fr	Bolton (Feb 2003)
Laville, Florent	7 Aug 1973	Valence	Fr	Bolton (Feb 2003)
Antoine-Curier, Mickael	5 Mar 1983	Orsay	Fr	Brentford (Mar 2003)
Pericard, Vincent	3 Oct 1982	Epko	Fr	Portsmouth (Apr 2003)

Other players qualified for France but born outside France

SURNAME, NAME	DOB	PLACE OF BIRTH	NAT	CLUB(S) JOINED/FIRST PLAYED
Vieira, Patrick	23 Jun 1976	Dakar, Sen	Fr	Arsenal (Aug 1996)
Horace, Alain	4 Dec 1971	Madagascar	Fr	Hartlepool (Oct 1996)
Lambourde, Bernard	11 May 1971	Pointe-a-Pitre, Guad	Fr	Chelsea (Jul 1997); Portsmouth (Sep 2000)
Arphexad, Pegguy	18 May 1973	Abymes, Guad	Fr	Leicester (Aug 1997); Liverpool (Jul 2000); Stockport (Sep 2001)
Boli, Roger	26 Sep 1965	Adjame, IvCo	Fr	Walsall (Aug 1997); Bournemouth (Oct 1998)
Abou, Samassi	4 Aug 1973	Gagnoa, IvCo	Fr	West Ham (Nov 1997); Ipswich (Dec 1998); Walsall (Oct 1999)
Berthe, Mohamed	12 Sep 1972	Conakry, Gui	Fr	Bournemouth (Jul 1998)
Darcheville, Jean-Claude	25 Jul 1975	Sinnamary, FrGu	Fr	Nottm For (Jul 1998)
Desailly, Marcel	17 Sep 1968	Accra, Gha	Fr	Chelsea (Jul 1998)
Ipoua, Guy	14 Jan 1976	Douala, Cam	Fr	Bristol R (Aug 1998); Scunthorpe (Aug 1999); Gillingham (Mar 2001)
Allou, Bernard	19 Jun 1975	Cocody, IvCo	Fr	Nottm For (Mar 1999)
Hodouto, Kwami	31 Oct 1974	Lome, Tgo	Fr	Huddersfield (Sep 1999)
Sigere, Jean-Michel	26 Jan 1977	Martinique	Fr	Rushden & D (Mar 2000)
Gueret, Willy	3 Aug 1973	St Claude, Guad	Fr	Millwall (Jul 2000)
Joseph, David	22 Nov 1976	Guad	Fr	Notts Co (Aug 2000)

SURNAME, NAME	DOB	PLACE OF BIRTH	NAT	CLUB(S) JOINED/FIRST PLAYED
Karembeu, Christian	3 Dec 1970	Lifou, NCal	Fr	Middlesbrough (Aug 2000)
Gope-Fenepej, John	6 Nov 1978	Noumea, NCal	Fr	Bolton (Sep 2000)
Sidibe, Mamady	18 Dec 1979	Mali	Fr	Swansea (Jul 2001); Gillingham (Aug 2002)
Gnohere, Arthur	20 Nov 1978	Yamoussoukro, IvCo	Fr	Burnley (Aug 2001)
Malbranque, Steed	6 Jan 1980	Mouscron, Bel	Fr	Fulham (Aug 2001)
Robert, Laurent	21 May 1975	Saint-Benoit, Reu	Fr	Newcastle (Aug 2001)
Negouai, Christian	20 Jan 1975	Fort-de-France, Mrt	Fr	Man City (Nov 2001)
Djetou, Martin	15 Feb 1972	Brogohio, IvCo	Fr	Fulham (Oct 2002)
Sommeil, David	10 Aug 1974	Point-a-Pitre, Guad	Fr	Man City (Jan 2003)
Yulu, Christian	26 Jan 1978	Kinshasa, DRC	Fr	Coventry (Feb 2003)

FRENCH GUYANA (2)

SURNAME, NAME	DOB	PLACE OF BIRTH	NAT	CLUB(S) JOINED/FIRST PLAYED
Regis, Cyrille	9 Feb 1958	Mariapousoula	Eng	WBA (May 1977); Coventry (Oct 1984); A Villa (Jul 1991); Wolves (Aug 1993); Wycombe (Aug 1994); Chester (Aug 1995)
Darcheville, Jean-Claude	25 Jul 1975	Sinnamary	Fr	Nottm For (Jul 1998)

GABON (1)

SURNAME, NAME	DOB	PLACE OF BIRTH	NAT	CLUB(S) JOINED/FIRST PLAYED
Nzamba, Guy	13 Jul 1970	Port Gentil	Gab	Southend (Sep 1997)

GEORGIA (6)

SURNAME, NAME	DOB	PLACE OF BIRTH	NAT	CLUB(S) JOINED/FIRST PLAYED
Kinkladze, Georgi	6 Jul 1973	Tbilisi	Geo	Man City (Aug 1995); Derby (Jun 2000)
Kavelashvili, Mikhail	22 Jul 1971	Tbilisi	Geo	Man City (Mar 1996)
Ketsbaia, Temuri	18 Mar 1968	Gali	Geo	Newcastle (Jul 1997); Wolves (Aug 2000)
Shelia, Murtaz	25 Mar 1969	Tbilisi	Geo	Man City (Nov 1997)
Tskhadadze, Kakhaber	7 Sep 1968	Rustavi	Geo	Man City (Feb 1998)
Aleksidze, Rati	3 Aug 1978	Tbilisi	Geo	Chelsea (Feb 2000)

GERMANY (73+3)

SURNAME, NAME	DOB	PLACE OF BIRTH	NAT	CLUB(S) JOINED/FIRST PLAYED
Seeburg, Max	19 Sep 1884	Leipzig	Ger	Tottenham (May 1907); Burnley (Jan 1910); Grimsby (Jul 1911)
Gunn, Alf	11 Jul 1924	Germany	Ger	Nottm For (Feb 1947)
Eisentrager, Alec	20 Jul 1927	Hamburg	Ger	Bristol C (Jul 1949)
Trautmann, Bert	22 Oct 1923	Bremen	Ger	Man City (Oct 1949)
Bruck, Dietmar	19 Apr 1944	Danzig	Ger	Coventry (May 1962); Charlton (Oct 1970); Northampton (Jun 1972)
Smit(h), Wilf	3 Sep 1946	Neumunster	Ger	Shef Wed (Sep 1963); Coventry (Aug 1970); Brighton (Oct 1974); Millwall (Jan 1975); Bristol R (Mar 1975); Chesterfield (Nov 1976)
Tunks, Roy	21 Jan 1951	Wuppertall	Brit	Rotherham (Mar 1968); York (Jan 1969); Preston (Nov 1974); Wigan Ath (Nov 1981); Hartlepool (Jul 1988); Preston (Nov 1988)
Berry, George	19 Nov 1957	Rostrup	Wal	Wolves (Nov 1975); Stoke (Aug 1982); Doncaster (Aug 1984); Peterborough (Jul 1990); Preston (Aug 1991); Aldershot (Nov 1991)
MacDonald, Ian	30 Aug 1953	Rinteln	Brit	Carlisle (May 1976)
Lee, Alan	19 Jun 1960	Wegburg	Brit	Leicester (Feb 1979)
Casey, Paul	6 Oct 1961	Rinteln	Brit	Shef Utd (Jun 1979); Lincoln (Mar 1988)
Phillips, David	29 Jul 1963	Wegburg	Brit	Plymouth (Aug 1981); Man City (Aug 1984); Coventry (Jun 1986); Norwich (Jul 1989); Nottm For (Aug 1993); Huddersfield (Nov 1997); Lincoln (Mar 1999)
Rober, Jurgen	25 Dec 1953	Gernrode	Ger	Nottm For (Dec 1981)
Galloway, Steve	13 Feb 1963	Hanover	Brit	C Palace (Oct 1984); Cambridge (Mar 1986)
Sanderson, Mike	26 Oct 1966	Germany	Brit	Darlington (Mar 1986)
Kruszynski, Detsi	14 Oct 1961	Divschav	Ger	Wimbledon (Dec 1988); Brentford (Aug 1992); Coventry (Sep 1993); Peterborough (Dec 1993)
Short, Chris	9 May 1970	Munster	Brit	Scarborough (Jul 1988); Notts Co (Sep 1990); Huddersfield (Dec 1994); Shef Utd (Dec 1995); Stoke (Jul 1998)
Hauser, Thomas	10 Apr 1965	Schopfhain	Ger	Sunderland (Feb 1989)
Taylor, Robin	14 Jan 1971	Rinteln	Brit	Wigan Ath (Oct 1989)
Barnard, Darren	30 Nov 1971	Rinteln	Wal	Chelsea (Jul 1990); Reading (Nov 1994); Bristol C (Oct 1995); Barnsley (Aug 1997); Grimsby (Apr 2003)
Lomas, Steve	18 Jan 1974	Hanover	N Ire	Man City (Jan 1991); West Ham (Mar 1997)
Neilson, Alan	26 Sep 1972	Wegburg	Wal	Newcastle (Feb 1991); Southampton (Jun 1995); Fulham (Nov 1997); Grimsby (Oct 2001); Luton (Feb 2002)
Moylon, Craig	16 Oct 1972	Munster	Brit	Preston (Jul 1991)
Beinlich, Stefan	13 Jan 1972	Berlin	Ger	A Villa (Oct 1991)
Breitkreutz, Matthias	12 May 1971	Crivitz	Ger	A Villa (Oct 1991)
Tierling, Lee	25 Oct 1972	Wegburg	Brit	Fulham (May 1992)
Kitchen, Sam	11 Jun 1967	Rinteln	Brit	Orient (Aug 1992); Doncaster (Feb 1994)
Craven, Peter	30 Jun 1968	Hanover	Ger	Halifax (Mar 1993)
Thirlby, Anthony	4 Mar 1976	Berlin	Brit	Exeter (Jul 1993); Torquay (Feb 1997)
Hartenberger, Uwe	1 Feb 1968	Leuterecken	Ger	Reading (Sep 1993)
Rosler, Uwe	15 Nov 1968	Attenburg	Ger	Man City (Feb 1994); Southampton (Jul 2000); WBA (Oct 2001)
Karl, Steffen	3 Feb 1970	Hohenm-Oelsen	Ger	Man City (Mar 1994)
Klinsmann, Jurgen	30 Jul 1964	Goppingen	Ger	Tottenham (Aug 1994); Tottenham (Dec 1997)

SURNAME, NAME	DOB	PLACE OF BIRTH	NAT	CLUB(S) JOINED/FIRST PLAYED
Gaudino, Maurizio	12 Dec 1966	Brule	Ger	Man City (Dec 1994)
Fuchs, Uwe	23 Jul 1966	Kaiserslautern	Ger	Middlesbrough (Jan 1995); Millwall (Jul 1995)
Taylor, Maik	4 Sep 1971	Hildesheim	N Ire	Barnet (Jun 1995); Southampton (Jan 1997); Fulham (Nov 1997)
Jones, Ian	26 Aug 1976	Germany	Brit	Cardiff (Jul 1995)
Immel, Eike	27 Nov 1960	Marburg Lahn	Ger	Man City (Aug 1995)
Frontzeck, Michael	26 Mar 1964	Moenchengladbach	Ger	Man City (Jan 1996)
Lenhart, Sascha	16 Dec 1973	Cologne	Ger	Leicester (Sep 1996)
Dowe, Jens	1 Jun 1968	Rostock	Ger	Wolves (Oct 1996)
Hey, Tony	19 Sep 1970	Berlin	Ger	Birmingham (Jun 1997)
Leese, Lars	18 Aug 1969	Cologne	Ger	Barnsley (Jul 1997)
Mendez, Alberto	24 Oct 1974	Nuremburg	Sp	Arsenal (Jul 1997)
Riedle, Karl-Heinz	16 Sep 1965	Weiler	Ger	Liverpool (Aug 1997); Fulham (Sep 1999)
Newell, Justin	8 Feb 1980	Germany	Ger	Torquay (Sep 1997)
Sobiech, Jorg	15 Jan 1969	Gelsenkirchen	Ger	Stoke (Mar 1998
Schnoor, Stefan	24 Apr 1971	Neumunster	Ger	Derby (Jul 1998)
Hamann, Dietmar	27 Aug 1973	Waldasson	Ger	Newcastle (Aug 1998); Liverpool (Jul 1999)
Hebel, Dirk	24 Nov 1972	Cologne	Ger	Brentford (Aug 1998)
Lehmann, Dirk	16 Aug 1971	Aachen	Ger	Fulham (Aug 1998); Brighton (Jun 2001)
Forssell, Mikael	15 Mar 1981	Steinfurt	Fin	Chelsea (Dec 1998); C Palace (Feb 2000)
Freund, Steffen	19 Jan 1970	Brandenburg	Ger	Tottenham (Dec 1998)
Unger, Lars	30 Sep 1972	Eutin	Ger	Southend (Feb 1999)
Jermyn, Mark	16 Apr 1981	Germany	Ger	Torquay (Mar 1999)
Wright, Ben	1 Jul 1980	Munster	Ire	Bristol C (Mar 1999)
Helmer, Thomas	21 Apr 1965	Herford	Ger	Sunderland (Jul 1999)
Malz, Stefan	15 Jun 1972	Ludwigshafen	Ger	Arsenal (Jul 1999)
Ziege, Christian	1 Jan 1972	Berlin	Ger	Middlesbrough (Aug 1999); Liverpool (Aug 2000); Tottenham (Jul 2001)
Schwinkendorf, Jorn	27 Jan 1971	Hamburg	Ger	Cardiff (Nov 1999)
Volz, Moritz	21 Jan 1983	Siegen	Ger	Arsenal (Jan 2000); Wimbledon (Feb 2003)
Hansen, John	17 Sep 1973	Mannheim	Den	Cambridge (Feb 2000)
Babbel, Markus	8 Sep 1972	Munich	Ger	Liverpool (Jul 2000)
Hitzlsperger, Thomas	5 Apr 1982	Munich	Ger	A Villa (Aug 2000); Chesterfield (Oct 2001)
Macdonald, Gary	25 Oct 1979	Iselone	Brit	Peterborough (Feb 2001)
Cennamo, Luigi	7 Feb 1980	Munich	It	Burnley (Jul 2001)
Canham, Marc	11 Sep 1982	Wefburg	Brit	Colchester (Aug 2001)
Formann, Pascal	16 Nov 1982	Werne	Ger	Nottm For (Aug 2001)
Prosinecki, Robert	12 Jan 1969	Schweminger	Cro	Portsmouth (Aug 2001)
Huth, Robert	18 Aug 1984	Berlin	Ger	Chelsea (Feb 2002)
Konstantinidis, Kostas	31 Aug 1972	Schorndorf	Gre	Bolton (Mar 2002)
Pelzer, Marc	24 Sep 1980	Trier	Ger	Blackburn (Jun 2002)
Camara, Ben	19 Jun 1985	Bonn	Brit	Torquay (Mar 2003)

Other players qualified for Germany but born outside Germany

SURNAME, NAME	DOB	PLACE OF BIRTH	NAT	CLUB(S) JOINED/FIRST PLAYED
Niestroj, Robert	2 Dec 1974	Oppeln, Pol	Ger	Wolves (Nov 1998)
Bopp, Eugene	5 Sep 1983	Kiev, Ukr	Ger	Nottm For (Aug 2001)
Bobic, Fredi	30 Oct 1971	Maribor, Slo	Ger	Bolton (Jan 2002)

GHANA (13)

SURNAME, NAME	DOB	PLACE OF BIRTH	NAT	CLUB(S) JOINED/FIRST PLAYED
Wharton, Arthur	28 Oct 1865	Accra	Gha	Rotherham T (Jul 1893); Sheff Utd (Jul 1894); Rotherham T (Jul 1895); Stockport (Jul 1901)
Laryea, Benny	20 Mar 1962	Ghana	Gha	Torquay (Mar 1984)
Grant, Kim	25 Sep 1972	Sekondi-Takaradi	Gha	Charlton (Mar 1991); Luton (Mar 1996); Millwall (Aug 1997); Notts Co (Dec 1998); Scunthorpe (Aug 2001)
Okai, Stephen	3 Dec 1973	Ghana	Brit	Orient (Apr 1992)
Lamptey, Nii	10 Dec 1974	Accra	Gha	A Villa (Aug 1994); Coventry (Aug 1995)
Yeboah, Tony	6 Jun 1966	Kumasi	Gha	Leeds (Jan 1995)
Agogo, Junior	1 Aug 1979	Accra	Gha	Sheff Wed (Oct 1996); Oldham (Jul 1999); Chester (Sep 1999); Chesterfield (Nov 1999); Lincoln (Dec 1999)
Boateng, George	5 Sep 1975	Nkawkaw	Neth	Coventry (Dec 1997); A Villa (Jul 1999); Middlesbrough (Aug 2002)
Desailly, Marcel	17 Sep 1968	Accra	Fr	Chelsea (Jul 1998)
Hammond, Elvis	6 Oct 1980	Accra	Gha	Fulham (Jul 1999); Bristol R (Aug 2001)
Nyarko, Alex	15 Oct 1973	Accra	Gha	Everton (Aug 2000)
Asamoah, Derek	1 May 1981	Accra	Brit	Northampton (Jul 2001)
Awuah, Jones	10 Jul 1983	Ghana	Gha	Gillingham (Sep 2002)

GIBRALTAR (5)

SURNAME, NAME	DOB	PLACE OF BIRTH	NAT	CLUB(S) JOINED/FIRST PLAYED
Hill, Reg	1907	Gibraltar	Brit	Carlisle (Jul 1930); Tranmere (Dec 1932); Hartlepools (Jan 1933); Darlington (Feb 1937)
Macedo, Tony	22 Feb 1938	Gibraltar	Brit	Fulham (Oct 1955); Colchester (Sep 1968)
Devereux, Tony	6 Jan 1940	Gibraltar	Brit	Aldershot (Nov 1958)
Houston, Graham	24 Feb 1960	Gibraltar	Brit	Preston (Mar 1978); Wigan (Aug 1986); Carlisle (Oct 1987)
McEvoy, Ricky	6 Aug 1967	Gibraltar	Ire	Luton (Aug 1985); Cambridge (Feb 1987)

GREECE (12+5)

SURNAME, NAME	DOB	PLACE OF BIRTH	NAT	CLUB(S) JOINED/FIRST PLAYED
Donis, George	29 Oct 1969	Greece	Grk	Blackburn (Jul 1996); Sheff Utd (Mar 1999); Huddersfield (Jun 1999)
Borbokis, Vassilis	10 Feb 1969	Serres	Grk	Sheff Utd (Jul 1997); Derby (Mar 1999)

SURNAME, NAME	DOB	PLACE OF BIRTH	NAT	CLUB(S) JOINED/FIRST PLAYED
Dellas, Traianos	31 Jan 1976	Salonika	Grk	Sheff Utd (Aug 1997)
Zagorakis, Theo	17 Oct 1971	Kavala	Grk	Leicester (Feb 1998)
Dabizas, Nicos	3 Aug 1973	Ptolemaida	Grk	Newcastle (Mar 1998)
Vlachos, Michalis	20 Sep 1967	Athens	Grk	Portsmouth (Jun 1998); Walsall (Feb 2000)
Kyzeridis, Nicos	20 Apr 1971	Salonika	Grk	Portsmouth (Jul 1998)
Georgiadis, Georgios	8 Mar 1972	Kavala	Grk	Newcastle (Aug 1998)
Michopoulos, Nik	20 Feb 1970	Karditsa	Grk	Burnley (Aug 2000); C Palace (Sep 2002)
Syros, George	8 Feb 1976	Athens	Grk	Bury (Aug 2001)
Tavlaridis, Stathis	25 Jan 1980	Serres	Grk	Arsenal (Sep 2001); Portsmouth (Jan 2003)
Koumantarakis, George	27 Mar 1974	Athens	SA	Preston (Jan 2003)

Other players qualified for Greece but born outside Greece

Panopoulos, Mike	9 Oct 1976	Melbourne, Aus	Grk	Portsmouth (Sep 1999)
Stergiopoulos, Marcus	12 Jun 1973	Melbourne, Aus	Grk	Lincoln (Aug 2000)
Bertos, Leo	20 Dec 1981	Wellington, NZ	Grk	Barnsley (Sep 2000)
Papadopoulos, Dimitrios	20 Sep 1981	Kazakhstan	Grk	Burnley (Jul 2001)
Konstantinidis, Kostas	31 Aug 1972	Schorndorf, Ger	Grk	Bolton (Mar 2002)

GRENADA (1)

Batson, Brendan	6 Feb 1953	St George's	Eng	Arsenal (Jun 1971); Cambridge (Jan 1974); WBA (Feb 1978)

GUADELOUPE (5)

Lambourde, Bernard	11 May 1971	Pointe-a-Pitre	Fr	Chelsea (Jul 1997); Portsmouth (Sep 2000)
Arphexad, Pegguy	18 May 1973	Abymes	Fr	Leicester (Aug 1997); Liverpool (Jul 2000); Stockport (Sep 2001)
Gueret, Willy	3 Aug 1973	St Claude	Fr	Millwall (Jul 2000)
Joseph, David	22 Nov 1976	Guadeloupe	Fr	Notts Co (Aug 2000)
Sommeil, David	10 Aug 1974	Point-a-Pitre	Fr	Man City (Jan 2003)

GUINEA (4+1)

Berthe, Mohamed	12 Sep 1972	Conakry	Fr	Bournemouth (Jul 1998)
Camara, Titi	7 Nov 1972	Donka	Gui	Liverpool (Jun 1999); West Ham (Dec 2000)
Camara, Mohamed	25 Jul 1975	Conakry	Gui	Wolves (Aug 2000)
Oulare, Souleymane	16 Oct 1972	Conakry	Gui	Stoke (Dec 2001)

Other players qualified for Guinea but born outside Guinea

Diallo, Drissa	4 Jan 1973	Nouadhibou, Mau	Gui	Burnley (Jan 2003)

GUINEA BISSAU (1)

Forbes, Boniek	30 Sep 1983	Guinea Bissau	GuB	Orient (Sep 2002)

GUYANA (5)

Maynard, Mike	7 Jan 1947	Guyana	Brit	Peterborough (Jul 1967)
Quamina, Mark	25 Nov 1969	Guyana	Guy	Wimbledon (Jul 1988); Plymouth (Jul 1991)
Griffith, Cohen	26 Dec 1962	Georgetown	Brit	Cardiff (Oct 1989)
Bunbury, Alex	18 Jun 1967	Plaisance	Can	West Ham (Dec 1992)
Hooper, Lyndon	30 May 1966	Georgetown	Can	Birmingham (Sep 1993)

HONDURAS (3)

Nunez, Milton	30 Oct 1972	Zambocreek	Hon	Sunderland (Mar 2000)
Guerrero, Ivan	30 Nov 1977	Comayagua	Hon	Coventry (Oct 2000)
Martinez, Jairo	14 May 1978	Yoro	Hon	Coventry (Oct 2000)

HONG KONG (6)

Edwards, Gerald	c.1919	Hong Kong	Brit	Luton (Jan 1931)
Harris, Alex	22 Oct 1934	Hong Kong	Brit	Blackpool (Nov 1951)
Cheung, Chi Doy	30 Jul 1941	Hong Kong	Brit	Blackpool (Oct 1960)
Anderson, Doug	29 Aug 1963	Hong Kong	Brit	Oldham (Sep 1980); Tranmere (Aug 1984); Plymouth (Aug 1987); Cambridge (Sep 1988); Northampton (Dec 1988)
Hunter, Chris	18 Jan 1964	Hong Kong	Brit	Preston (Sep 1981); Preston (Sep 1984)
Williamson, Davey	15 Dec 1975	Hong Kong	Brit	Cambridge (Aug 1996)

HUNGARY (7)

Nagy, Mick	1 May 1929	Budapest	Hun	Swindon (Aug 1951)
Olah, Bela	8 Jun 1938	Oyd	Hun	Northampton (Dec 1958)
Haasz, Johnny	7 Jul 1934	Budapest	Hun	Swansea Town (Sep 1960); Workington (Jul 1961)
Kozma, Istvan	3 Dec 1964	Paszto	Hun	Liverpool (Feb 1992)
Kulcsar, George	12 Aug 1967	Budapest	Aus	Bradford (Mar 1997); QPR (Dec 1997)
Sebok, Vilmos	13 Jun 1973	Budapest	Hun	Bristol C (Jan 1999)
Bukran, Gabor	16 Nov 1975	Eger	Hun	Walsall (Aug 1999); Wigan Ath (ADD)

ICELAND (29)

Gudmundsson, Albert	5 Oct 1923	Reykjavik	Ice	Arsenal (Sep 1946)
Jonsson, Siggi	27 Sep 1966	Akranes	Ice	Sheff Wed (Feb 1985); Barnsley (Jan 1986); Arsenal (Jul 1989)
Bergsson, Gudni	21 Jul 1965	Reykjavik	Ice	Tottenham (Dec 1988); Bolton (Mar 1995)
Orlygsson, Toddi	2 Aug 1966	Odense	Ice	Nottm For (Dec 1989); Stoke (Aug 1993); Oldham (Dec 1995)
Torfason, Gunnar	13 Dec 1961	Westann Isles	Ice	Doncaster (Jul 1994)
Sigurdsson, Larus	4 Jun 1973	Akuveyni	Ice	Stoke (Oct 1994); WBA (Sep 1999)

SURNAME, NAME	DOB	PLACE OF BIRTH	NAT	CLUB(S) JOINED/FIRST PLAYED
Gunnlaugsson, Arnie	6 Mar 1973	Akranes	Ice	Bolton (Aug 1997); Leicester (Feb 1999); Stoke (Mar 2000)
Hreidarsson, Hermann	11 Jul 1974	Reykjavik	Ice	C Palace (Aug 1997); Brentford (Sep 1998); Wimbledon (Oct 1999); Ipswich (Aug 2000)
Gislason, Valur	8 Sep 1977	Reykjavik	Ice	Brighton (Oct 1997)
Gudmundsson, Johann	7 Dec 1977	Reykjavik	Ice	Watford (Mar 1998); Cambridge (Nov 2000)
Gudjohnsen, Eidur	15 Sep 1978	Reykjavik	Ice	Bolton (Aug 1998); Chelsea (Jul 2000)
Larusson, Bjarni	11 Mar 1976	Vestmannaeyjar	Ice	Walsall (Sep 1998); Scunthorpe (Sep 2000)
Danielsson, Helgi	13 Jul 1981	Reykjavik	Ice	Peterborough (Oct 1998)
Eyjolfsson, Siggi	1 Dec 1973	Reykjavik	Ice	Walsall (Jan 1999); Chester (Jan 2000)
Gunnlaugsson, Bjarke	6 Mar 1973	Akranes	Ice	Preston (Sep 1999)
Ingimarsson, Ivar	20 Aug 1977	Reykjavik	Ice	Torquay (Oct 1999); Brentford (Nov 1999); Wolves (Aug 2002); Brighton (Feb 2003)
Danielsson, Einer Thor	19 Jan 1970	Reykjavik	Ice	Stoke (Nov 1999)
Gislason, Siggi	25 Jun 1968	Akranes	Ice	Stoke (Nov 1999)
Einarsson, Gunnar	7 Jul 1976	Reykjavik	Ice	Brentford (Jan 2000)
Gunnarsson, Brynjar	16 Oct 1975	Reykjavik	Ice	Stoke (Jan 2000)
Helguson, Heidar	22 Aug 1977	Akureyri	Ice	Watford (Jan 2000)
Gudjonsson, Bjarni	26 Feb 1979	Akranes	Ice	Stoke (Mar 2000)
Thordarson, Stefan	27 Mar 1975	Reykjavik	Ice	Stoke (Jun 2000)
Gottskalksson, Ole	12 Mar 1968	Keflavik	Ice	Brentford (Jul 2000)
Dadason, Rikki	26 Apr 1972	Reykjavik	Ice	Stoke (Oct 2000)
Kristinsson, Birkir	15 Aug 1964	Vestmannaeyjar	Ice	Stoke (Nov 2000)
Gudjonsson, Thordur	14 Oct 1973	Akranes	Ice	Derby (Mar 2001); Preston (Jan 2002)
Marteinsson, Petur	14 Jul 1973	Reykjavic	Ice	Stoke (Nov 2001)
Gudjonsson, Joey	25 May 19980	Akranes	Ice	A Villa (Jan 2003)

INDIA (40)

SURNAME, NAME	DOB	PLACE OF BIRTH	NAT	CLUB(S) JOINED/FIRST PLAYED
Pass, Jimmy	6 Nov 1883	Juffulpore	Brit	Stockport (Aug 1903)
Donaghy, Charles	c.1885	India	Brit	Chelsea (Aug 1905)
Hunter, George	Aug 1886	Peshawar	Brit	A Villa (Feb 1908); Oldham (Jan 1912); Chelsea (Feb 1913); Man Utd (Mar 1914)
Dolby, Hugh	c.1885	Agra	Brit	Chelsea (Jul 1908)
O'Donnell, Rudolph	Aug 1888	Madras	Brit	Fulham (Dec 1909)
Chandler, Robert	Sep 1894	Calcutta	Brit	A Villa (Aug 1913)
Wagstaffe, Thomas	c.1890	Dinapore	Brit	Sunderland (Mar 1923); Crewe (Sep 1926)
Quantrill, Alf	22 Jan 1897	Punjab	Eng	Derby (Aug 1914); Preston (Jul 1921) Bradford PA (Sep 1924); Nottm For (May 1930)
Mills, Paddy	23 Feb 1900	Multan	Brit	Hull (Aug 1920); Notts Co (Mar 1926); Birmingham (Feb 1929); Hull (Dec 1929)
Armand, Jack	11 Aug 1898	Sabathu	Brit	Leeds (Dec 1922); Swansea Town (May 1929); Newport (Aug 1932)
Preedy, Charlie	11 Jan 1900	Neemuch	Brit	Charlton (Dec 1922); Wigan Bor (Jul 1928); Arsenal (May 1929); Bristol R (Jul 1933); Luton (Aug 1934)
Bellis, George	8 Jun 1904	Khadki	Brit	Southport (Aug 1923); Wrexham (May 1927); Wolves (Jun 1929); Burnley (Dec 1932); B&B Ath (Jul 1935)
Ashton, Hubert	13 Feb 1898	Calcutta	Brit	Bristol R (Jul 1924); Clapton O (Aug 1926)
Tricker, Reg	5 Oct 1905	Karachi	Brit	Luton (Jul 1924); Charlton (Aug 1925); Arsenal (Mar 1927); Clapton O (Feb 1929)
Price, Johnny	4 Dec 1903	Mhow	Brit	Brentford (Apr 1928); Fulham (Jun 1928); Port Vale (May 1937)
Callachan, Harry	9 Apr 1903	Madras	Brit	Leicester (Sep 1929)
Mills, Arthur	1906	Karachi	Brit	Luton (Jul 1932); Gillingham (Jul 1933)
McDowall, Les	25 Oct 1912	Gunga Pur	Brit	Sunderland (Dec 1932); Man City (Mar 1938); Wrexham (Nov 1949)
Dugnolle, Jack	24 Mar 1914	Peshawar	Brit	Brighton (Oct 1934); Plymouth (Feb 1939); Brighton (Aug 1946)
Lancelotte, Eric	26 Feb 1917	India	Brit	Charlton (May 1935); Brighton (Feb 1948)
Court, Dick	23 Oct 1916	India	Brit	Aldershot (Jun 1937)
Dolding, Len	13 Dec 1922	Nundydroog	Brit	Chelsea (Jul 1945); Norwich (Jul 1948)
Garwood, Len	28 Jul 1923	Ranikwet	Brit	Tottenham (May 1946)
Leslie, Maurice	19 Aug 1923	India	Brit	Swindon (Jun 1947)
Pickett, Reg	6 Jan 1927	India	Brit	Portsmouth (Mar 1949); Ipswich (Jun 1957)
Bluck, Dave	31 Jan 1930	India	Brit	Aldershot (Aug 1951)
Stiffle, Nelson	30 Jul 1928	India	Brit	Chester (Dec 1951); Chesterfield (Mar 1954); B&B Ath (May 1955); Exeter (Mar 1958); Coventry (Jul 1960)
Fleming, Mike	23 Feb 1928	India	Brit	Tranmere (Sep 1953)
Smith, Roy	19 Mar 1936	Rawalpindi	Brit	West Ham (Jun 1955); Portsmouth (Jan 1962)
Houghton, Bud	1 Sep 1936	Madras	Brit	Bradford PA (Oct 1955); Birmingham (Oct 1957); Southend (Oct 1958); Oxford (Mar 1961); Lincoln (Oct 1963)
Huggins, Joe	24 Feb 1930	India	Brit	Aldershot (Dec 1955)
Porteous, Jack	12 Jan 1933	India	Brit	Aldershot (Dec 1955)
Keelan, Kevin	5 Jan 1941	Calcutta	Brit	A Villa (Jul 1958); Stockport (Apr 1961); Wrexham (Nov 1961); Norwich (Jul 1963)
Thorpe, Arthur	31 Jul 1939	Lucknow	Brit	Scunthorpe (Sep 1960); Bradford (Jul 1963)

SURNAME, NAME	DOB	PLACE OF BIRTH	NAT	CLUB(S) JOINED/FIRST PLAYED
Chadwick, Dave	19 Aug 1943	Ooctamund	Brit	Southampton (Oct 1960); Middlesbrough (Jul 1966); Halifax (Jan 1970); Bournemouth (Feb 1972); Torquay (Dec 1972); Gillingham (Sep 1974)
Heppolette, Ricky	8 Apr 1949	Bhusawal	Brit	Preston (Sep 1964); Orient (Dec 1972); C Palace (Oct 1976); Chesterfield (Feb 1977); Peterborough (Aug 1979)
Methven, Colin	10 Dec 1955	India	Brit	Wigan Ath (Oct 1979); Blackpool (Jul 1986); Carlisle (Sep 1990); Walsall (Nov 1990)
Payne, Mark	2 Sep 1966	Bombay	Brit	Swindon (Sep 1984)
Cooper, Neale	24 Nov 1963	Darjeeling	Sco	A Villa (Jul 1986); Reading (Jul 1991)
Bhutia, Baichung	15 Jun 1976	Gangtok	Ind	Bury (Sep 1999)

IRAN (1)

SURNAME, NAME	DOB	PLACE OF BIRTH	NAT	CLUB(S) JOINED/FIRST PLAYED
Bagheri, Karim	20 Feb 1974	Abbasi	Iran	Charlton (Aug 2000)

ISRAEL (14)

SURNAME, NAME	DOB	PLACE OF BIRTH	NAT	CLUB(S) JOINED/FIRST PLAYED
Cohen, Avi	14 Nov 1956	Tel Aviv	Isr	Liverpool (Jul 1979)
Gariani, Moshe	18 Jun 1957	Tiberias	Isr	Brighton (Jun 1980)
Cohen, Jacob	25 Sep 1956	Israel	Isr	Brighton (Oct 1980)
Fadida, Aharon	20 Sep 1961	Israel	Isr	Aldershot (Dec 1985)
Pisanti, David	27 May 1962	Israel	Isr	QPR (Sep 1987)
Rosenthal, Ronny	4 Oct 1963	Haifa	Isr	Liverpool (Jun 1990); Tottenham (Jan 1994); Watford (Aug 1997)
Berkovic, Eyal	2 Apr 1972	Haifa	Isr	Southampton (Oct 1996); West Ham (Jun 1997); Blackburn (Feb 2001); Man City (Jul 2001)
Zohar, Itzhak	31 Oct 1970	Tel Aviv	Isr	C Palace (Aug 1997)
Hazan, Alon	14 Sep 1967	Ashdod	Isr	Watford (Jan 1998)
Amsalem, David	4 Sep 1971	Israel	Isr	C Palace (Aug 1998)
Badir, Walid	12 Mar 1974	Kafr Kasm	Isr	Wimbledon (Aug 1999)
Ghrayib, Naguyan	30 Jan 1974	Nazareth	Isr	A Villa (Aug 1999)
Nimni, Avi	26 Apr 1972	Tel Aviv	Isr	Derby (Nov 1999)
Tal, Idan	13 Sep 1975	Petach-Tikva	Isr	Everton (Oct 2000)

ITALY (58+2)

SURNAME, NAME	DOB	PLACE OF BIRTH	NAT	CLUB(S) JOINED/FIRST PLAYED
Ugolini, Rolando	4 Jun 1924	Lucca	It	Middlesbrough (May 1948);Wrexham (Jun 1957)
Besagni, Remo	22 Apr 1935	Italy	It	C Palace (Oct 1952)
Kemp, Fred	27 Feb 1946	Salerno	Brit	Wolves (Jun 1963); Southampton (Jun 1965); Blackpool (Nov 1970); Halifax (Dec 1971); Hereford (Jul 1974)
Derko, Franco	22 Dec 1946	Italy	It	Mansfield (Jan 1965)
Sartori, Carlo	10 Feb 1948	Calderzone	It	Man Utd (Feb 1965)
Chinaglia, Giorgio	24 Jan 1947	Carrara	It	Swansea Town (Apr 1965)
Masiello, Luciano	2 Jan 1951	Italy	It	Charlton (Jan 1969)
Fiocca, Paul	13 Jan 1955	Italy	It	Swindon (Jan 1973)
Sperti, Franco	28 Jan 1955	Italy	It	Swindon (Jan 1973)
Ponte, Raimondo	4 Apr 1954	Naples	It	Nottm For (Aug 1980)
Silenzi, Andrea	10 Feb 1966	Rome	It	Nottm For (Aug 1995)
Bonetti, Ivano	1 Aug 1964	Brescia	It	Grimsby (Sep 1995); Tranmere (Aug 1996); C Palace (Oct 1997)
Bolesan, Mirko	6 May 1975	Genoa	It	Cardiff (Oct 1995)
Gambaro, Enzo	23 Feb 1966	Genoa	It	Grimsby (Mar 1996)
Ravanelli, Fabrizio	11 Dec 1968	Perugia	It	Middlesbrough (Jun 1996); Derby (Jul 2001)
Vialli, Gianluca	9 Jul 1964	Cremona	It	Chelsea (Jul 1996)
Carbone, Benito	14 Aug 1971	Bagnara Calabra	It	Sheff Wed (Oct 1996); A Villa (Oct 1999); Bradford (Aug 2000); Derby (Oct 2001); Middlesbrough (Feb 2002)
Zola, Gianfranco	5 Jul 1966	Oliena	It	Chelsea (Nov 1996)
Festa, Gianluca	15 Mar 1969	Cagliari	It	Middlesbrough (Jan 1997); Portsmouth (Aug 2002)
Eranio, Stefano	29 Dec 1968	Genoa	It	Derby (Jul 1997)
Pistone, Alessandro	27 Jul 1975	Milan	It	Newcastle (Jul 1997); Everton (Jul 2000)
Baiano, Francesco	24 Feb 1968	Naples	It	Derby (Aug 1997)
Lombardo, Attilio	6 Jan 1966	St Maria la Fossa	It	C Palace (Aug 1997)
Di Canio, Paolo	9 Jul 1968	Rome	It	Sheff Wed (Aug 1997); West Ham (Jan 1999)
Padovano, Michele	28 Aug 1966	Turin	It	C Palace (Nov 1997)
Berti, Nicola	14 Apr 1967	Salsomaggiore Terme	It	Tottenham (Jan 1998)
Branca, Marco	6 Jan 1965	Grosseto	It	Middlesbrough (Feb 1998)
Bruno, Pasquale	19 Jun 1962	Lecce	It	Wigan Ath (Feb 1998)
Billio, Patrizio	19 Apr 1974	Treviso	It	C Palace (Mar 1998)
Sanetti, Francesco	11 Jan 1979	Rome	It	Sheff Wed (Apr 1998)
Fabio, Ferraresi	25 May 1979	Fano	It	A Villa (Jun 1998)
Tramezzani, Paolo	30 Jul 1970	Reggio-Emilia	It	Tottenham (Jun 1998)
Casiraghi, Pierluigi	4 Mar 1969	Monza	It	Chelsea (Jul 1998)
Materazzi, Marco	19 Aug 1973	Perugia	It	Everton (Jul 1998)
Bortolazzi, Mario	10 Jan 1965	Verona	It	WBA (Aug 1998)
Maresca, Enzo	10 Feb 1980	Pontecagnano	It	WBA (Aug 1998)
Percassi, Luca	25 Aug 1980	Milan	It	Chelsea (Aug 1998)
Pinamonte, Lorenzo	9 May 1978	Verona	It	Bristol C (Sep 1998); Brentford (Feb 2000); Brighton (Dec 1999); Orient (Feb 2000)
Dalla Bona, Sam	6 Feb 1981	San Dona di Piave	It	Chelsea (Oct 1998)

SURNAME, NAME	DOB	PLACE OF BIRTH	NAT	CLUB(S) JOINED/FIRST PLAYED
Marcolin, Dario	28 Oct 1971	Brescia	It	Blackburn (Oct 1998)
Gioacchini, Stefano	25 Nov 1976	Rome	It	Coventry (Jan 1999)
Cudicini, Carlo	6 Sep 1973	Milan	It	Chelsea (Jun 1999)
Nuzzo, Raffaele	21 Feb 1973	Monza	It	Coventry (Jul 1999)
Ambrosetti, Gabriele	7 Aug 1973	Varese	It	Chelsea (Aug 1999)
Mannini, Moreno	15 Aug 1962	Imola	It	Nottm For (Aug 1999)
Matrecano, Salvatore	5 Oct 1970	Naples	It	Nottm For (Aug 1999)
Petrachi, Gianluca	14 Jan 1969	Lecce	It	Nottm For (Aug 1999)
Taibi, Massimo	18 Feb 1970	Palermo	It	Man Utd (Sep 1999)
Di Piedi, Michele	4 Dec 1980	Palermo	It	Sheff Wed (Aug 2000); Bristol R (Feb 2003)
Panucci, Christian	12 Apr 1973	Savona	It	Chelsea (Aug 2000)
Morini, Emanuele	31 Jan 1982	Rome	It	Bolton (Sep 2000)
Mancini, Roberto	27 Nov 1964	Jesi	It	Leicester (Jan 2001)
Grabbi, Corrado	29 Jul 1975	Turin	It	Blackburn (Jun 2001)
Galli, Filippo	19 May 1963	Monza	It	Watford (Jul 2001)
Zamperini, Alessandro	15 Aug 1982	Rome	It	Portsmouth (Jul 2001)
Daino, Daniele	8 Sep 1979	Alessandria	It	Derby (Aug 2001)
Sereni, Matteo	11 Feb 1975	Parma	It	Ipswich (Aug 2001)
Maccarone, Massimo	9 Sep 1979	Galliate	It	Middlesbrough (Aug 2002)
Qualified for Italy but born outside Italy				
Di Matteo, Roberto	29 May 1970	Sciaffusa, Swit	It	Chelsea (Jul 1996)
Cennamo, Luigi	7 Feb 1980	Munich, Ger	It	Burnley (Jul 2001)

IVORY COAST (10)

Boli, Roger	26 Sep 1965	Adjame	Fr	Walsall (Aug 1997); Bournemouth (Oct 1998)
Abou, Samassi	4 Aug 1973	Gagnoa	Fr	West Ham (Nov 1997); Ipswich (Dec 1998); Walsall (Oct 1999)
Bakayoko, Ibrahima	31 Dec 1976	Seguela	IvCo	Everton (Oct 1998)
Zahana-Oni, Landry	8 Aug 1976	Abidjan	IvCo	Luton (Jan 1999)
Allou, Bernard	19 Jun 1975	Cocody	Fr	Nottm For (Mar 1999)
Tebily, Olivier	19 Dec 1975	Abidjan	IvCo	Sheff Utd (Mar 1999); Birmingham (Mar 2002)
Gnohere, Arthur	20 Nov 1978	Yamoussoukro	Fr	Burnley (Aug 2001)
Toure, Kolo	19 Mar 1981	Adidjan	IvCo	Arsenal (Aug 2002)
Djetou, Martin	15 Feb 1972	Brogohio	Fr	Fulham (Oct 2002)
Diabate, Lassina	16 Sep 1974	Bouake	IvCo	Portsmouth (Oct 2002)

JAMAICA (22)

Delapenha, Lindy	25 May 1927	Kingston	Jam	Portsmouth (Apr 1948); Middlesbrough (Apr 1950); Mansfield (Jun 1958)
Phillips, Brendon	16 Jul 1954	St Catherine	Jam	Peterborough (Aug 1973); Mansfield (Aug 1980)
Gardner, Don	30 Aug 1955	Kingston	Jam	Wolves (Aug 1973)
Blissett, Luther	1 Feb 1958	Falmouth	Eng	Watford (Jul 1975); Watford (Aug 1984); Bournemouth (Nov 1988); Watford (Aug 1991); WBA (Oct 1992); Bury (Aug 1993); Mansfield (Dec 1993)
Williams, Everton	1 Feb 1957	Blackrod	Jam	Wrexham (Jul 1975)
Richards, Lloyd	11 Feb 1958	Kingston	Jam	Notts Co (Feb 1976); York (Jun 1980)
Streete, Floyd	5 May 1959	Kingston	Jam	Cambridge (Jul 1976); Derby (Oct 1984); Wolves (Oct 1985); Reading (Jul 1990)
Hazell, Bob	14 Jun 1959	Kingston	Eng	Wolves (Mar 1977); QPR (Sep 1979); Leicester (Sep 1983); Wolves (Sep 1985); Reading (Nov 1986); Port Vale (Dec 1986)
Cunningham, Tony	12 Nov 1957	Kingston	Brit	Lincoln (May 1979); Barnsley (Sep 1982); Sheff Wed (Nov 1983); Man City (Jul 1984); Newcastle (Feb 1985); Blackpool (Jul 1987); Bury (Jul 1989); Bolton (Mar 1991); Rotherham (Aug 1991); Doncaster (Jul 1993); Wycombe (Mar 1994)
Blake, Noel	12 Jan 1962	Kingston	Brit	A Villa (Aug 1979); Shrewsbury (Mar 1982); Birmingham (Sep 1982); Portsmouth (Apr 1984); Leeds (Jul 1988); Stoke (Feb 1990); Bradford (Jul 1992); Exeter (Aug 1995)
Barnes, John	7 Nov 1963	Kingston	Eng	Watford (Jul 1981); Liverpool (Jun 1987); Newcastle (Aug 1997); Charlton (Feb 1999)
Richards, Carl	1 Dec 1960	St Mary's	Brit	Bournemouth (Jul 1986); Birmingham (Oct 1988); Peterborough (Jul 1989); Blackpool (Jan 1990); Maidstone (Oct 1991)
Johnson, David	15 Aug 1976	Kingston	Jam	Bury (Jul 1995); Ipswich (Nov 1997); Nottm For (Jan 2001); Sheff Wed (Feb 2002); Burnley (Mar 2002)
Jack, Rodney	28 Sep 1972	Kingston	StV	Torquay (Oct 1995); Crewe (Aug 1998)
Moncrieffe, Prince	27 Feb 1977	Kingston	Jam	Doncaster (Jul 1997)
Gardner, Ricardo	25 Sep 1978	St Andrews	Jam	Bolton (Aug 1998)
Boyd, Walter	1 Jan 1972	Kingston	Jam	Swansea (Oct 1999)
Goodison, Ian	21 Nov 1972	St James	Jam	Hull (Oct 1999)
Whitmore, Theo	21 Nov 1972	St James	Jam	Hull (Oct 1999)
Fuller, Ricardo	31 Oct 1979	Kingston	Jam	C Palace (Feb 2001); Preston (Aug 2002)
Lowe, Onandi	2 Dec 1973	Kingston	Jam	Port Vale (Feb 2001); Rushden & D (Nov 2001)
Johnson, Jermaine	25 Jun 1980	Kingston	Jam	Bolton (Sep 2001)

SURNAME, NAME	DOB	PLACE OF BIRTH	NAT	CLUB(S) JOINED/FIRST PLAYED
JAPAN (5)				
Atkins, Arthur	21 Feb 1925	Tokyo	Brit	Birmingham (Nov 1948); Shrewsbury (Jun 1954)
Inamoto, Junichi	18 Sep 1979	Kagoshima	Jap	Arsenal (Jul 2001); Fulham (Jul 2002)
Nishizawa, Akinori	18 Jun 1976	Shizuoka	Jap	Bolton (Jul 2001)
Kawaguchi, Yoshikatsu	15 Aug 1975	Shizuoka	Jap	Portsmouth (Oct 2001)
Toda, Kazuyuki	30 Dec 1977	Tokyo	Jap	Tottenham (Apr 2003)
KAZAKHSTAN (1)				
Papadopoulos, Dimitrios	20 Sep 1981	Kazakhstan	Grk	Burnley (Jul 2001)
KENYA (4)				
Thompson, Peter	25 Jul 1942	Kenya	Brit	Peterborough (Mar 1964)
McBride, Andy	15 Mar 1954	Kenya	Brit	C Palace (Oct 1971)
Rafferty, Kevin	9 Nov 1960	Kenya	Brit	Crewe (Nov 1978)
Johnstone, Glenn	5 Jun 1967	Kenya	Brit	Preston (Jan 1993)
LATVIA (7+1)				
Freimanis, Eddie	22 Feb 1920	Latvia	Lat	Northampton (May 1948)
Astafjevs, Vitalis	3 Apr 1971	Riga	Lat	Bristol R (Jan 2000)
Bleidelis, Imants	16 Aug 1975	Latvia	Lat	Southampton (Feb 2000)
Kolinko, Alex	18 Jun 1975	Latvia	Lat	C Palace (Sep 2000)
Stepanovs, Igors	21 Jan 1976	Ogre	Lat	Arsenal (Sep 2000)
Rubins, Andrejs	26 Nov 1978	Latvia	Lat	C Palace (Oct 2000)
Stolcers, Andrejs	8 Jul 1974	Latvia	Lat	Fulham (Dec 2000)
Qualified for Latvia but born outside Latvia				
Pahars, Marian	5 Aug 1976	Chernevol, Ukr	Lat	Southampton (Mar 1999)
LIBERIA (4)				
Wreh, Christopher	14 May 1975	Monrovia	Lbr	Arsenal (Aug 1997); Birmingham (Oct 1999)
Andreasson, Marcus	13 Jul 1978	Monrovia	Swe	Bristol R (Jul 1998)
Sarr, Mass	6 Feb 1973	Unification Town	Lbr	Reading (Jul 1998)
Weah, George	1 Oct 1966	Monrovia	Lbr	Chelsea (Jan 2000); Man City (Aug 2000)
LIBYA (1)				
Muntasser, Jehad	26 Jul 1978	Tripoli	Lby	Arsenal (Jun 1997)
LITHUANIA (2+1)				
Bookman, Louis	1890	Zagaren	Brit	Bradford City (Jul 1911); West Brom (Feb 1914); Luton (Aug 1920); Port Vale (Jul 1923)
Tereskinas, Andrejus	10 Jul 1970	Telsiai	Lith	Macclesfield (Nov 2000)
Qualified for Lithuania but born outside Lithuania				
Danilevicius, Tomas	18 Jul 1978	Moscow, Rus	Lith	Arsenal (Sep 2000)
MACEDONIA (3)				
Bozinoski, Vlado	30 Mar 1964	Skopje	Aus	Ipswich (Dec 1992)
Hristov, Georgi	30 Jan 1976	Bitola	Mac	Barnsley (Jul 1997)
Sedloski, Goce	10 Apr 1974	Golemo Konjari	Mac	Sheff Wed (Mar 1998)
MADAGASCAR (1)				
Horace, Alain	4 Dec 1971	Madagascar	Fr	Hartlepool (Oct 1996)
MALAYSIA (3)				
Mordey, Henry	4 May 1911	Kuala Lumpur	Brit	Charlton (Jul 1936)
Cruickshank, George	22 Jul 1931	Malaysia	Brit	Carlisle (Aug 1957)
Edge, Declan	18 Sep 1965	Malacca	NZ	Notts Co (Dec 1985)
MALI (1)				
Sidibe, Mamady	18 Dec 1979	Mali	Fr	Swansea (Jul 2001); Gillingham (Aug 2002)
MALTA (14)				
Hogan, Cornelius	1878	Malta	Brit	NB Tower (May 1899); Burnley (Nov 1901)
Dwane, Eddie	17 Jul 1896	Malta	Brit	Lincoln (Jul 1920)
McNeill, Hamilton	13 May 1910	Malta	Brit	Hull (May 1937); Bury (Feb 1939)
Shanks, Wally	1 May 1923	Malta	Brit	Luton (Dec 1946)
Cini, Joe	20 Nov 1936	Malta	Mal	QPR (Aug 1959)
Cutbush, John	28 Jun 1949	Malta	Brit	Fulham (Jul 1972); Sheff Utd (Mar 1977); Sheff Utd (Aug 1979)
Liddle, David	21 May 1957	Malta	Brit	Northampton (May 1975)
Eames, Billy	20 Sep 1957	Malta	Brit	Portsmouth (Sep 1975); Brentford (Aug 1978)
Strutt, Brian	21 Sep 1959	Malta	Mal	Sheff Wed (Sep 1977)
Geard, Glen	25 Feb 1960	Malta	Brit	Brighton (Feb 1978)
Stevens, Ian	21 Oct 1966	Malta	Brit	Preston (Nov 1984); Bolton (Mar 1987); Stockport (Oct 1986); Bury (Jul 1991); Shrewsbury (Aug 1994); Carlisle (May 1997); Cheltenham (Mar 2000); Wrexham (Jul 1999); Carlisle (Aug 2000)
Buttigieg, John	15 Oct 1963	Malta	Mal	Brentford (Nov 1988); Swindon (Sep 1990)
Kerr, Dylan	14 Jan 1967	Malta	Brit	Leeds (Feb 1989); Blackpool (Dec 1991); Doncaster (Aug 1991); Reading (Jul 1993); Carlisle (Sep 1996); Kidderminster (Sep 2000); Exeter (Aug 2001)

SURNAME, NAME	DOB	PLACE OF BIRTH	NAT	CLUB(S) JOINED/FIRST PLAYED
Tisdale, Paul	14 Jan 1973	Malta	Brit	Southampton (Jun 1991); Northampton (Mar 1992); Huddersfield (Nov 1996); Bristol C (Jun 1997); Exeter (Dec 1997)

MARTINIQUE (2)

Sigere, Jean-Michel	26 Jan 1977	Martinique	Fr	Rushden & D (Mar 2000)
Negouai, Christian	20 Jan 1975	Fort-de-France	Fr	Man City (Nov 2001)

MAURITANIA (1)

Diallo, Drissa	4 Jan 1973	Nouadhibou	Gui	Burnley (Jan 2003)

MEXICO (2)

Burton, Frank	1891	Luapagno	Brit	West Ham (Aug 1919); Charlton (Jul 1921)
Lopez, Carlos	18 Apr 1970	Mexico City	Mex	Wycombe (Jan 2002)

MOLDOVA (1)

Tistimetanu, Ivan	27 Apr 1974	Moldova	Mol	Bristol C (Dec 1998)

MOROCCO (11)

Nayim, Mohamed	5 Nov 1968	Ceuta	Mor	Tottenham (Nov 1988)
Mettioui, Ahmed	3 Nov 1965	Tangier	Mor	Crewe (Jul 1992)
Moussaddik, Chuck	23 Feb 1970	Meknes	Mor	Wycombe (Sep 1995)
Kachloul, Hassan	19 Feb 1973	Agadir	Mor	Southampton (Oct 1998); A Villa (Jun 2001)
Chippo, Youssef	10 Jun 1973	Boujaad	Mor	Coventry (Jul 1999)
Hadji, Mustapha	16 Nov 1971	Ifrane	Mor	Coventry (Aug 1999); A Villa (Jul 2001)
El Khalej, Tahar	16 Jun 1968	Marrakesh	Mor	Southampton (Mar 2000); Charlton (Feb 2003)
Chalqi, Khalid	28 Apr 1971	Oujda	Mor	Torquay (Nov 2000)
Ouaddou, Abdeslam	1 Nov 1978	Ksar-Askour	Mor	Fulham (Aug 2001)
Safri, Youssef	1 Mar 1977	Casablanca	Mor	Coventry (Aug 2001)
El Karkouri, Talal	8 Jul 1976	Casablanca	Mor	Sunderland (Feb 2003)

MOZAMBIQUE (2)

Xavier, Abel	30 Nov 1972	Nampula	Por	Everton (Sep 1999); Liverpool (Jan 2002)
Cadete, Jorge	27 Aug 1968	Porto Amélia	Por	Bradford (Feb 2000)

THE NETHERLANDS (107+18)

Keizer, Gerry	18 Aug 1910	Amsterdam	Neth	Arsenal (Aug 1930); Charlton (Jul 1931)
Warburton, George	1916	Netherlands	Brit	Chester (Nov 1938)
Schroeder, Nico	19 Nov 1947	Netherlands	Neth	Swansea (Jul 1976)
Muhren, Arnold	2 Jun 1951	Volendam	Neth	Ipswich (Aug 1978); Man Utd (Aug 1982)
Thijssen, Frans	23 Jan 1952	Heumen	Neth	Ipswich (Feb 1979); Nottm For (Oct 1983)
Meijer, Geert	15 Mar 1951	Amsterdam	Neth	Bristol C (Mar 1979)
Ursem, Loek	7 Jan 1958	Amsterdam	Neth	Stoke (Jul 1979); Sunderland (Mar 1982)
De Goey, Len	29 Feb 1952	Amsterdam	Neth	Sheff Utd (Aug 1979)
Koenen, Frans	4 Nov 1958	Waalwijk	Neth	Newcastle (Aug 1980)
Brocken, Bud	12 Sep 1957	Tilburg	Neth	Birmingham (Aug 1981)
Kaiser, Rudi	26 Dec 1960	Amsterdam	Neth	Coventry (Aug 1981)
Otto, Heine	24 Aug 1954	Amsterdam	Neth	Middlesbrough (Aug 1981)
Van Mierlo, Toine	24 Aug 1957	Sorendonk	Neth	Birmingham (Aug 1981)
Jol, Maarten	16 Jan 1956	Den Haag	Neth	WBA (Oct 1981); Coventry (Jul 1984)
Lohman, Jan	18 Feb 1959	Dussen	Neth	Watford (Oct 1981)
Van Breukelen, Hans	4 Oct 1956	Utrecht	Neth	Nottm For (Sep 1982)
Van Wijk, Dennis	16 Dec 1962	Oostzaan	Neth	Norwich (Oct 1982)
Kraay, Hans	22 Dec 1959	Utrecht	Neth	Brighton (Feb 1984)
Metgod, Johnny	27 Feb 1958	Amsterdam	Neth	Nottm For (Aug 1984); Tottenham (Jul 1987)
Segers, Hans	30 Oct 1961	Eindhoven	Neth	Nottm For (Aug 1984); Stoke (Feb 1987); Sheff Utd (Nov 1987); Wimbledon (Sep 1988); Wolves (Feb 1998); Tottenham (Aug 1998)
Cheetham, Mike	30 Jun 1967	Amsterdam	Brit	Ipswich (Oct 1988); Cambridge (Oct 1989); Colchester (Mar 1995); Chesterfield (Jul 1994)
Atteveld, Ray	8 Sep 1966	Amsterdam	Neth	Everton (Aug 1989); Bristol C (Mar 1992); West Ham (Feb 1992)
Van der Laan, Robin	5 Sep 1968	Schiedam	Neth	Port Vale (Feb 1991); Derby (Aug 1995); Wolves (Oct 1996); Barnsley (Jul 1998)
Jalink, Nico	22 Jun 1964	Rotterdam	Neth	Port Vale (Jul 1991)
Essers, Pierre	20 Feb 1959	Holland	Neth	Walsall (Sep 1991)
Hoekman, Danny	21 Sep 1964	Nijmegen	Neth	Man City (Oct 1991)
Van Rossum, Erik	27 Mar 1963	Nijmegen	Neth	Plymouth (Jan 1992)
Vonk, Michel	28 Oct 1968	Alkmaar	Neth	Man City (Mar 1992); Oldham (Dec 1995); Sheff Utd (Nov 1995)
Dijkstra, Meindert	28 Feb 1967	Eindhoven	Neth	Notts Co (Aug 1992)
Goulooze, Richard	16 Nov 1967	Alkmaar	Neth	Derby (Sep 1992)
Keizerweerd, Orpheo	2 Nov 1968	Holland	Neth	Oldham (Mar 1993)
Groenendijk, Alfons	17 May 1964	Leiden	Neth	Man City (Jul 1993)
Nijholt, Luc	29 Jul 1961	Zaandam	Neth	Swindon (Jul 1993)
Boere, Jeroen	18 Nov 1967	Arnheim	Neth	Portsmouth (Mar 1994); West Ham (Sep 1993); WBA (Sep 1994); C Palace (Sep 1995); Southend (Mar 1996)
Dijkstra, Sieb	20 Oct 1966	Kerkrade	Neth	QPR (Jul 1994); Bristol C (Sep 1995); Wycombe (Mar 1996)
Roy, Bryan	12 Feb 1969	Amsterdam	Neth	Nottm For (Aug 1994)

SURNAME, NAME	DOB	PLACE OF BIRTH	NAT	CLUB(S) JOINED/FIRST PLAYED
Sneekes, Richard	30 Oct 1968	Amsterdam	Neth	Bolton (Aug 1994); WBA (Mar 1996); Hull (Nov 2001); Stockport (Sep 2001)
Van Heusden, Arjan	11 Dec 1972	Alphen	Neth	Port Vale (Aug 1994); Oxford (Sep 1997); Cambridge (Aug 1998); Exeter (Jul 2000); Mansfield (Sep 2002); Torquay (Nov 2002)
De Wolf, John	10 Dec 1962	Schiedam	Neth	Wolves (Dec 1994)
Helder, Glenn	28 Oct 1968	Leiden	Neth	Arsenal (Feb 1995)
Witschge, Richard	20 Sep 1969	Amsterdam	Neth	Blackburn (Mar 1995)
Bergkamp, Dennis	18 May 1969	Amsterdam	Neth	Arsenal (Jul 1995)
Boogers, Marco	12 Jan 1967	Dordrecht	Neth	West Ham (Jul 1995)
Holwyn, Jermaine	16 Apr 1973	Amsterdam	Neth	Port Vale (Jul 1995)
Willems, Ron	20 Sep 1966	Epe	Neth	Derby (Jul 1995)
De Zeeuw, Arjan	16 Apr 1970	Castricum	Neth	Barnsley (Nov 1995); Wigan Ath (Jul 1999); Portsmouth (Aug 2002)
Griemink, Bart	29 Mar 1972	Groningen	Neth	Birmingham (Nov 1995); Peterborough (Oct 1996); Swindon (Mar 2000)
Bos, Gijsbert	22 Mar 1973	Spakenburg	Neth	Lincoln (Mar 1996); Rotherham (Aug 1997)
Ten Heuvel, Laurens	6 Jun 1976	Duivendrecht	Neth	Barnsley (Mar 1996); Sheff Utd (Aug 2002); Bradford (Mar 2003)
Van der Velden, Carel	3 Aug 1972	Arnhem	Neth	Barnsley (Mar 1996); Scarborough (Aug 1997)
Petta, Bobby	6 Aug 1974	Rotterdam	Neth	Ipswich (Jun 1996)
Regtop, Erik	16 Feb 1968	Emmen	Neth	Bradford (Jul 1996)
Sas, Marco	16 Feb 1971	Vlaardingden	Neth	Bradford (Jul 1996)
Van der Gouw, Raimond	24 Mar 1963	Oldenzaal	Neth	Man Utd (Jul 1996)
Cruyff, Jordi	9 Feb 1974	Amsterdam	Neth	Man Utd (Aug 1996)
Trustfull, Orlando	4 Aug 1970	Amsterdam	Neth	Sheff Wed (Aug 1996)
Molenaar, Robert	27 Feb 1969	Zaandam	Neth	Leeds (Jan 1997); Bradford (Dec 2000)
Koordes, Rogier	13 Jun 1972	Haarlem	Neth	Port Vale (Feb 1997)
Van Hooijdonk, Pierre	29 Nov 1969	Steenbergen	Neth	Nottm For (Mar 1997)
Gentile, Marco	24 Aug 1968	Den Haag	Neth	Burnley (Jun 1997)
Schreuder, Jan-Dirk	2 Aug 1971	Barneveld	Neth	Stoke (Jun 1997)
Sepp, Dennis	5 Jun 1973	Apeldoorn	Neth	Bradford (Jun 1997)
Zoetebier, Ed	7 May 1970	Purmerend	Neth	Sunderland (Jun 1997)
Overmars, Marc	29 Mar 1973	Emst	Neth	Arsenal (Jul 1997)
De Goey, Ed	20 Dec 1966	Gouda	Neth	Chelsea (Jul 1997)
Wiekens, Gérard	25 Feb 1973	Tolhuiswyk	Neth	Man City (Jul 1997)
Van Dulleman, Ray	6 May 1973	Gravenhage	Neth	Northampton (Aug 1997)
Snijders, Mark	12 Mar 1972	Alkmaar	Neth	Port Vale (Sep 1997)
Smeets, Jorg	5 Nov 1970	Bussum	Neth	Wigan Ath (Oct 1997); Chester (Mar 1999)
Holster, Marco	4 Dec 1971	Weesp	Neth	Ipswich (Jul 1998)
Stam, Jaap	17 Jul 1972	Kampen	Neth	Man Utd (Jul 1998)
Jonk, Wim	12 Oct 1966	Volendam	Neth	Sheff Wed (Aug 1998)
Kromheer, Elroy	15 Jan 1970	Amsterdam	Neth	Reading (Aug 1998)
Van der Kwaak, Peter	12 Oct 1968	Haarlem	Neth	Reading (Aug 1998); Carlisle (Feb 2000)
Achterberg, John	8 Jul 1971	Utrecht	Neth	Tranmere (Sep 1998)
Zwijnenberg, Clemens	18 May 1970	Enschede	Neth	Bristol C (Sep 1998)
Korsten, Willem	21 Jan 1975	Baxtel	Neth	Leeds (Jan 1999); Tottenham (Jul 1999)
Kuipers, Michel	26 Jun 1974	Amsterdam	Neth	Bristol R (Jan 1999); Brighton (Jul 2000)
Westerveld, Sander	23 Oct 1974	Enschede	Neth	Liverpool (Jun 1999)
Meijer, Erik	2 Aug 1969	Meersen	Neth	Liverpool (Jun 1999); Preston (Oct 2000)
Melchiot, Mario	4 Nov 1976	Amsterdam	Neth	Chelsea (Jul 1999)
Sibon, Gerald	19 Apr 1974	Dalen	Neth	Sheff Wed (Jul 1999)
Karelse, John	17 May 1970	Kapelle	Neth	Newcastle (Aug 1999)
Derveld, Fernando	22 Oct 1976	Vlissingen	Neth	Norwich (Mar 2000); WBA (Feb 2001)
De Waard, Raimond	27 Mar 1973	Rotterdam	Neth	Norwich (Mar 2000)
Reuser, Martijn	1 Feb 1975	Amsterdam	Neth	Ipswich (Jun 2000)
Abidallah, Nabil	5 Aug 1982	Amsterdam	Neth	Ipswich (Jul 2000)
Kaak, Tom	31 Mar 1978	Winterswijk	Neth	Darlington (Jul 2000)
Van der Geest, Frank	30 Apr 1973	Beverwijk	Neth	Darlington (Aug 2000)
Van der Linden, Antoine	10 Mar 1976	Rotterdam	Neth	Swindon (Aug 2000)
Bogarde, Winston	22 Oct 1970	Rotterdam	Neth	Chelsea (Sep 2000)
Hernandez, Dino	27 May 1971	Amersfoort	Neth	Wigan Ath (Nov 2000)
Willems, Menno	3 Oct 1977	Amsterdam	Neth	Grimsby (Nov 2000)
Van Nistelrooy, Ruud	1 Jul 1976	Oss	Neth	Man Utd (Apr 2001)
Van Bronckhorst, Giovanni	5 Feb 1975	Rotterdam	Neth	Arsenal (Jun 2001)
Cas, Marcel	30 Apr 1972	Breda	Neth	Notts Co (Jul 2001)
Hoekstra, Peter	4 Apr 1973	Assen	Neth	Stoke (Jul 2001)
Busscher, Robbie	23 Nov 1982	Leichendan	Neth	Grimsby (Aug 2001)
De Vogt, Wilko	17 Sep 1975	Breda	Neth	Sheff Utd (Aug 2001)
Moor, Reinier	12 Jun 83	The Hague	Ire	Exeter (Aug 2001)
Van der Sar, Edwin	29 Oct 1970	Voorhout	Neth	Fulham (Aug 2001)
Zenden, Boudewijn	15 Aug 1976	Maastricht	Neth	Chelsea (Aug 2001)
Evans, Michael	21 Jul 1976	Venlo	Neth	York (Sep 2001)
Ommel, Sergio	2 Sep 1977	The Hague	Neth	Bristol R (Nov 2001)
Postma, Stefan	10 Jun 1976	Utrecht	Neth	A Villa (Jul 2002)
Loran, Tyrone	29 Jun 1981	Amsterdam	Neth	Tranmere (Jan 2003)
Cas, Marcel	30 Apr 1972	Breda	Neth	Sheff Utd (Feb 2003)

Other players qualified for The Netherlands but born outside The Netherlands

SURNAME, NAME	DOB	PLACE OF BIRTH	NAT	CLUB(S) JOINED/FIRST PLAYED
Zondervan, Romeo	4 Mar 1959	Surinam	Neth	WBA (Mar 1982); Ipswich (Mar 1984)
Wilson, Ulrich	5 May 1964	Surinam	Neth	Ipswich (Dec 1987)

SURNAME, NAME	DOB	PLACE OF BIRTH	NAT	CLUB(S) JOINED/FIRST PLAYED
Monkou, Ken	29 Nov 1964	Surinam	Neth	Chelsea (Mar 1989); Southampton (Aug 1992); Huddersfield (Aug 1999)
Verveer, Etienne	22 Sep 1967	Surinam	Neth	Millwall (Dec 1991); Bradford (Feb 1995)
De Freitas, Fabian	28 Jul 1972	Surinam	Neth	Bolton (Aug 1994); WBA (Aug 1998)
Gullit, Ruud	1 Sep 1962	Surinam	Neth	Chelsea (Jul 1995)
Uhlenbeek, Gus	28 Aug 1970	Surinam	Neth	Ipswich (Aug 1995); Fulham (Jul 1998); Sheff Utd (Aug 2000); Walsall (Mar 2002); Bradford (Aug 2002)
Blinker, Regi	4 Jun 1969	Surinam	Neth	Sheff Wed (Mar 1996)
Van Gobbel, Ulrich	16 Jan 1971	Surinam	Neth	Southampton (Oct 1996)
Wilsterman, Brian	19 Nov 1966	Surinam	Neth	Oxford (Feb 1997); Rotherham (Jul 1999)
Hasselbaink, Jimmy Floyd	27 Mar 1972	Surinam	Neth	Leeds (Jul 1997); Chelsea (Jul 2000)
Boateng, George	5 Sep 1975	Nkawkaw, Gha	Neth	Coventry (Dec 1997); A Villa (Jul 1999); Middlesbrough (Aug 2002)
Wijnhard, Clyde	9 Nov 1973	Surinam	Neth	Leeds (Jul 1998); Huddersfield (Jul 1999); Preston (Mar 2002); Oldham (Aug 2002)
Wilnis, Fabian	23 Aug 1970	Surinam	Neth	Ipswich (Jan 1999)
Faerber, Winston	23 Jul 1971	Surinam	Neth	Cardiff (Aug 1999)
Gorre, Dean	10 Sep 1970	Surinam	Neth	Huddersfield (Sep 1999); Barnsley (Jul 2001)
Wooter, Nordin	24 Aug 1976	Surinam	Neth	Watford (Sep 1999)
Koejoe, Sammy	17 Aug 1974	Surinam	Neth	QPR (Nov 1999)

NEW CALEDONIA (2)

Karembeu, Christian	3 Dec 1970	Lifou, NCal	Fr	Middlesbrough (Aug 2000)
Gope-Fenepej, John	6 Nov 1978	Noumea, NCal	Fr	Bolton (Sep 2000)

NEW ZEALAND (15+1)

Moorhead, George	27 May 1895	Christchurch	Ire	Southampton (Aug 1920); Brighton (Aug 1922)
Rush, Jon	13 Oct 1961	Wellington	NZ	Blackpool (Nov 1979)
Herbert, Ricki	10 Apr 1961	Auckland	NZ	Wolves (Oct 1984)
Evans, Ceri	2 Oct 1963	Christchurch	NZ	Oxford (Feb 1989)
Ngata, Harry	24 Aug 1971	Wanganui	NZ	Hull (Jul 1989)
Zoricich, Chris	3 May 1969	Auckland	NZ	Orient (Feb 1990)
Smith, Scott	6 Mar 1975	Christchurch	NZ	Rotherham (Oct 1993)
Norfolk, Lee	17 Oct 1975	Dunedin	NZ	Ipswich (Jul 1994)
Viljoen, Nik	3 Dec 1976	Auckland	NZ	Rotherham (Jun 1995)
Fallon, Rory	20 Mar 1982	Gisbourne	NZ	Barnsley (Mar 1999); Shrewsbury (Dec 2001)
Killen, Chris	8 Oct 1981	Wellington	NZ	Man City (Mar 1999); Wrexham (Sep 2000); Port Vale (Sep 2001); Oldham (Aug 2002)
Hay, Danny	15 May 1975	Auckland	NZ	Leeds (Aug 1999); Walsall (Aug 2002)
Bertos, Leo	20 Dec 1981	Wellington	Grk	Barnsley (Sep 2000)
Christie, Jeremy	22 May 1983	Whangarie	NZ	Barnsley (Dec 2001)
Pearce, Allan	7 Apr 1983	Wellington	NZ	Lincoln (Dec 2002)

Qualified for New Zealand but born outside New Zealand

Edge, Declan	18 Sep 1965	Malacca, Mly	NZ	Notts Co (Dec 1985)

NIGERIA (39)

Balogun, Tesilim	27 Mar 1931	Lagos	Nig	QPR (Sep 1956)
Onyeali, Elkanah	7 Jun 1939	Port Harcourt	Nig	Tranmere (Aug 1960)
Coker, Ade	19 May 1954	Lagos	Nig	West Ham (Dec 1971); Lincoln (Dec 1974)
Chiedozie, John	18 Apr 1960	Owerri	Nig	Orient (Apr 1977); Notts Co (Aug 1981); Tottenham (Aug 1984); Derby (Aug 1988); Chesterfield (Mar 1990); Notts Co (Jan 1990)
Nwajiobi, Emeka	25 May 1959	Nibo Awka	Nig	Luton (Dec 1983)
Salako, John	11 Feb 1969	Lagos	Eng	C Palace (Nov 1986); Swansea (Aug 1989); Coventry (Aug 1995); Bolton (Mar 1998); Fulham (Jul 1998); Charlton (Aug 1999); Reading (Nov 2001)
Iorfa, Dominic	1 Oct 1968	Lagos	Nig	QPR (Mar 1990); Peterborough (Oct 1992); Southend (Aug 1994); Southend (Dec 1998)
Salako, Andy	8 Nov 1972	Lagos	Nig	Charlton (Apr 1991)
Okenla, Foley	9 Oct 1967	Nigeria	Nig	Birmingham (Aug 1991)
Adekola, David	18 May 1968	Lagos	Nig	Bury (Jan 1993); Exeter (Feb 1994); Bournemouth (Sep 1994); Wigan Ath (Oct 1994); Cambridge (Aug 1995); Brighton (Oct 1996)
Adebola, Dele	23 Jun 1975	Lagos	Nig	Crewe (Mar 1993); Birmingham (Feb 1998); Oldham (Mar 2002); C Palace (Aug 2002)
Obebo, Godfrey	16 Apr 1966	Lagos	Nig	Halifax (Mar 1993)
Okorie, Chima	8 Oct 1968	Izombe	Nig	Grimsby (Sep 1993); Torquay (Mar 1994)
Amokachi, Daniel	30 Dec 1972	Kaduna	Nig	Everton (Aug 1994)
Emenalo, Michael	14 Jul 1965	Aba	Nig	Notts Co (Aug 1994)
Omoyimni, Manny	28 Dec 1977	Nigeria	Nig	West Ham (May 1995); Bournemouth (Sep 1996); Orient (Mar 1999); Gillingham (Sep 1999); Scunthorpe (Dec 1999); Barnet (Feb 2000); Oxford (Jul 2000)
Ayorinde, Sammy	20 Oct 1974	Lagos	Nig	Orient (Apr 1996)
Bankole, Ade	9 Sep 1969	Abeokuta	Nig	Crewe (Sep 1996); QPR (Jul 1998); Crewe (Jul 2000)
Babayaro, Celestine	29 Aug 1978	Kaduna	Nig	Chelsea (Jun 1997)
Okafar, Sam	17 Mar 1982	Xtiam	Nig	Colchester (Aug 1998)

389

SURNAME, NAME	DOB	PLACE OF BIRTH	NAT	CLUB(S) JOINED/FIRST PLAYED
Ameobi, Shola	12 Oct 1981	Zaria	Eng	Newcastle (Oct 1998)
Ifejiagwa, Emeka	30 Oct 1977	Aba	Nig	Brighton (Oct 1998)
Iroha, Ben	29 Nov 1969	Aba	Nig	Watford (Dec 1998)
Kanu, Nwankwo	1 Aug 1976	Owerri	Nig	Arsenal (Feb 1999)
Opara, Kelechi	21 Dec 1981	Oweri	Nig	Colchester (Aug 1999); Orient (Dec 2000)
Abbey, George	20 Oct 1978	Port Harcourt	Nig	Macclesfield (Aug 1999)
Etuhu, Dixon	8 Jun 1982	Kano	Nig	Man City (Dec 1999); Preston (Jan 2002)
Odejayi, Kay	21 Feb 1982	Ibadon	Brit	Bristol C (Jul 2000)
Olaoye, Dele	17 Oct 1982	Lagos	Nig	Port Vale (Aug 2000)
West, Taribo	26 Mar 1974	Port Harcourt	Nig	Derby (Nov 2000)
Shittu, Danny	2 Sep 1980	Lagos	Nig	Blackpool (Feb 2001); QPR (Oct 2001)
Foyewa, Amos	26 Dec 1981	Nigeria	Nig	Bournemouth (Jul 2001)
Ofodile, Adolphus	15 Dec 1979	Fungu	Nig	Walsall (Jul 2001)
George, Finidi	15 Apr 1971	Port Harcourt	Nig	Ipswich (Aug 2001)
Okocha, Jay-Jay	14 Aug 1973	Enugu	Nig	Bolton (Aug 2002)
Okoli, James	11 Jan 1976	Nigeria	Nig	York (Aug 2002)
Yobo, Joseph	6 Sep 1980	Kano	Nig	Everton (Sep 2002)
Ayegbini, Yakubu	22 Nov 1982	Nigeria	Nig	Portsmouth (Jan 2003)
Udeze, Ifeanyi	21 Jul 1980	Lagos	Nig	WBA (Jan 2003)

NORWAY (77+2)

SURNAME, NAME	DOB	PLACE OF BIRTH	NAT	CLUB(S) JOINED/FIRST PLAYED
Hansen, Karl	4 Jul 1921	Denmark	Nor	Huddersfield (Jan 1949)
Aas, Einar	12 Oct 1955	Moss	Nor	Nottm For (Mar 1981)
Hareide, Aage	23 Sep 1953	Hareide	Nor	Man City (Oct 1981); Norwich (Jun 1983)
Osvold, Kjetil	5 Jun 1961	Aalesund	Nor	Nottm For (Mar 1987); Leicester (Dec 1987)
Thorstvedt, Erik	28 Oct 1962	Stavanger	Nor	Tottenham (Dec 1988)
Andersen, Vetle	20 Apr 1964	Kristiansand	Nor	WBA (Dec 1989)
Johnsen, Erland	5 Apr 1967	Fredrikstad	Nor	Chelsea (Dec 1989)
Halle, Gunnar	11 Aug 1965	Larvik	Nor	Oldham (Feb 1991); Leeds (Dec 1996); Bradford (Jun 1999); Wolves (Mar 2002)
Bjornebye, Stig Inge	11 Dec 1969	Elverum	Nor	Liverpool (Dec 1992); Blackburn (Jun 2000)
Berg, Henning	1 Sep 1969	Eidsvell	Nor	Blackburn (Jan 1993); Man Utd (Aug 1997); Blackburn (Sep 2000)
Ingebrigtsen, Kaare	11 Nov 1965	Rosenborg	Nor	Man City (Jan 1993)
Strandli, Frank	16 May 1972	Norway	Nor	Leeds (Jan 1993)
Fjortoft, Jan Aage	10 Jan 1967	Aalesund	Nor	Swindon (Jul 1993); Middlesbrough (Mar 1995); Sheff Utd (Jan 1997); Barnsley (Jan 1998)
Flo, Jostein	3 Oct 1964	Eid	Nor	Sheff Utd (Aug 1993)
Kjeldbjerg, Jakob	21 Oct 1969	Fredrikstad	Den	Chelsea (Aug 1993)
Pedersen, Tore	29 Sep 1969	Fredrikstad	Nor	Oldham (Oct 1993); Blackburn (Sep 1997); Wimbledon (Jun 1999)
Bohinen, Lars	8 Sep 1969	Vadso	Nor	Nottm For (Nov 1993); Blackburn (Oct 1995); Derby (Mar 1998)
Nilsen, Roger	8 Aug 1969	Tromso	Nor	Sheff Utd (Nov 1993); Tottenham (Mar 1999)
Haaland, Alf-Inge	23 Nov 1972	Stavanger	Nor	Nottm For (Jan 1994); Leeds (Jul 1997); Man City (Jun 2000)
Hansen, Vergard	8 Aug 1969	Drammen	Nor	Bristol C (Nov 1994)
Leonhardsen, Oyvind	17 Aug 1970	Kristiansund	Nor	Wimbledon (Nov 1994); Liverpool (Jun 1997); Tottenham (Aug 1999); A Villa (Sep 2002)
Hovi, Tom	15 Jan 1972	Gjovik	Nor	Charlton (Jan 1995)
Riseth, Vidar	21 Apr 1972	Levanger	Nor	Luton (Oct 1995)
Rushfeldt, Siggi	11 Dec 1972	Vadso	Nor	Birmingham (Oct 1995)
Belsvik, Petter	2 Oct 1967	Lillehammer	Nor	Southend (Nov 1995)
Andersen, Leif	19 Apr 1971	Fredrikstad	Nor	C Palace (Jan 1996)
Johnsen, Ronny	10 Jun 1969	Sandefjord	Nor	Man Utd (Jul 1996); A Villa (Sep 2002)
Solskjaer, Ole Gunnar	26 Feb 1973	Kristiansund	Nor	Man Utd (Jul 1996)
Grodas, Frode	24 Oct 1964	Sogndal	Nor	Chelsea (Sep 1996)
Ostenstad, Egil	2 Jan 1972	Haugesund	Nor	Southampton (Oct 1996); Blackburn (Aug 1999); Man City (Feb 2001)
Henriksen, Tony	25 Apr 1973	Hammel	Nor	Southend (Oct 1996)
Knarvik, Tommy	1 Nov 1979	Bergen	Nor	Leeds (Nov 1996)
Lundekvam, Claus	22 Feb 1973	Austevoll	Nor	Southampton (Nov 1996)
Sundgot, Ole	21 Mar 1972	Olsumd	Nor	Bradford (Nov 1996)
Heidenstrom, Bjorn	15 Jan 1968	Porsgrunn	Nor	Orient (Dec 1996)
Iversen, Steffen	10 Nov 1976	Oslo	Nor	Tottenham (Dec 1996)
Kvarme, Bjorn Tore	17 Jun 1972	Trondheim	Nor	Liverpool (Jan 1997)
Nevland, Erik	10 Nov 1977	Stavanger	Nor	Man Utd (Jul 1997)
Soltvedt, Trond Egil	15 Feb 1967	Voss	Nor	Coventry (Jul 1997); Southampton (Aug 1999); Sheff Wed (Feb 2001)
Flo, Tore Andre	15 Jun 1973	Stryn	Nor	Chelsea (Aug 1997); Sunderland (Nov 2002)
Hjelde, Jon Olav	30 Jul 1972	Levanger	Nor	Nottm For (Aug 1997)
Pedersen, Jan Ove	12 Nov 1968	Oslo	Nor	Hartlepool (Oct 1997)
Rudi, Petter	17 Sep 1973	Kristiansund	Nor	Sheff Wed (Oct 1997)
Solbakken, Stale	27 Feb 1968	Kongsvinger	Nor	Wimbledon (Oct 1997)
Fuglestad, Erik	13 Aug 1974	Randaberg	Nor	Norwich (Nov 1997)
Hollund, Martin	11 Aug 1974	Stord	Nor	Hartlepool (Nov 1997)
Myhre, Thomas	16 Oct 1973	Sarpsborg	Nor	Everton (Nov 1997); Birmingham (Mar 2000); Tranmere (Nov 2000); Sunderland (Oct 2002)
Larsen, Stig Olav	29 Sep 1973	Bergen	Nor	Hartlepool (Dec 1997)
Johansen, Stig	13 Jun 1972	Svolvær	Nor	Bristol C (Feb 1998); Southampton (Aug 1997)
Heggem, Vegard	13 Jul 1975	Trondheim	Nor	Liverpool (Jul 1998)

SURNAME, NAME	DOB	PLACE OF BIRTH	NAT	CLUB(S) JOINED/FIRST PLAYED
Alsaker, Paul	6 Nov 1973	Stord	Nor	Stockport (Aug 1998)
Kval, Frank	17 Jul 1974	Bergen	Nor	Burnley (Oct 1998)
Vindheim, Rune	18 May 1972	Hoyanguer	Nor	Burnley (Oct 1998); Hartlepool (Sep 1999)
Berntsen, Robin	10 Jul 1970	Tromso	Nor	Port Vale (Nov 1998)
Andreassen, Svein	3 Jul 1968	Hadsel	Nor	Portsmouth (Dec 1998)
Jacobsen, Anders	18 Apr 1968	Oslo	Nor	Sheff Utd (Dec 1998); Stoke (Aug 1999); Notts Co (Sep 2000)
Flo, Havard	4 Apr 1970	Volda	Nor	Wolves (Jan 1999)
Kippe, Frode	17 Jan 1978	Oslo	Nor	Liverpool (Jan 1999); Stoke (Dec 1999)
Stensaas, Stale	7 Jul 1971	Trondheim	Nor	Nottm For (Jan 1999)
Bakke, Eirik	13 Sep 1977	Sogndal	Nor	Leeds (Jul 1999)
Andersen, Trond	6 Jan 1975	Kristiansund	Nor	Wimbledon (Aug 1999)
Normann, Runar	1 Mar 1978	Harstad	Nor	Coventry (Aug 1999)
Tennebo, Thomas	19 Mar 1975	Bergen	Nor	Hartlepool (Aug 1999)
Bergersen, Kent	8 Feb 1967	Oslo	Nor	Stockport (Sep 1999)
Andresen, Martin	2 Feb 1977	Oslo	Nor	Wimbledon (Oct 1999)
Berntsen, Tommy	18 Dec 1973	Oslo	Nor	Portsmouth (Nov 1999)
Tessem, Jo	28 Feb 1972	Orlandet	Nor	Southampton (Nov 1999)
Lund, Andreas	7 May 1975	Kristiansand	Nor	Wimbledon (Feb 2000)
Bragstad, Bjorn Otto	5 Jan 1971	Trondheim	Nor	Derby (Aug 2000); Birmingham (Sep 2001)
Sperrevik, Tim	2 Mar 1976	Bergen	Nor	Hartlepool (Aug 2000)
Fostervold, Anders	4 Oct 1971	Molde	Nor	Grimsby (Nov 2000)
Johansen, Rune	1 Apr 1978	Oslo	Nor	Bristol R (Nov 2000)
Karlsen, Kent	17 Feb 1973	Oslo	Nor	Luton (Nov 2000)
Soma, Ragnvald	10 Nov 1979	Bryne	Nor	West Ham (Jan 2001)
Riise, John Arne	29 Sep 1980	Molde	Nor	Liverpool (Jun 2001)
Rovde, Marius	26 Jun 1972	Trondheim	Nor	Wrexham (Jan 2002)
Capaldi, Tony	12 Aug 1981	Porsgrunn	N Ire	Plymouth (May 2003)

Other players qualified for Norway but born outside Norway

Lydersen, Pal	10 Sep 1965	Odense, Den	Nor	Arsenal (Nov 1991)
Baardsen, Espen	7 Dec 1977	San Rafael, USA	Nor	Tottenham (Jul 1996); Watford (Aug 2000); Everton (Jan 2003)

PARAGUAY (1)

Gavilan, Diego	1 Mar 1980	Ascuncion	Par	Newcastle (Feb 2000)

PERU (3)

Solano, Nolberto	12 Dec 1974	Lima	Per	Newcastle (Aug 1998)
Zuniga, Ysrael	27 Aug 1976	Lima	Per	Coventry (Mar 2000)
Labarthe, Gianfranco	20 Sep 1984	Lima	Per	Huddersfield (Feb 2003)

POLAND (20+1)

Kubicki, Eryk	18 Aug 1925	Hadjuki	Pol	York (Oct 1946)
Wojtczak, Edouard	29 Apr 1921	Poland	Pol	York (Oct 1946)
Gerula, Stan	21 Feb 1914	Dzikow	Pol	Orient (May 1948)
Kapler, Konrad	25 Feb 1925	Tychy	Pol	Rochdale (May 1949)
Starocsik, Felix	20 May 1920	Silesia	Pol	Northampton (Jul 1951)
Wasilewski, Adam	1925	Poland	Pol	Rochdale (Jul 1953)
Deyna, Kazimierz	23 Oct 1947	Starograd	Pol	Man City (Nov 1978)
Nowak, Tadeusz	28 Nov 1948	Trzcinsko	Pol	Bolton (Mar 1979)
Kowenicki, Ryszard	22 Dec 1948	Lodz	Pol	Oldham (Dec 1979)
Musial, Adam	18 Dec 1948	Wieliczka	Pol	Hereford(Aug 1980)
Warzycha, Robert	20 Jun 1963	Wielun	Pol	Everton (Mar 1991)
Kubicki, Dariusz	6 Jun 1963	Kozuchow	Pol	A Villa (Aug 1991); Sunderland (Mar 1994); Tranmere (Mar 1998); Wolves (Aug 1997); Carlisle (Jul 1998); Darlington (Oct 1998)
Dziekanowski, Jackie	30 Sep 1962	Warsaw	Pol	Bristol C (Jan 1992)
Wdowczyk, Dariusz	21 Sep 1962	Warsaw	Pol	Reading (Aug 1994)
Niestroj, Robert	2 Dec 1974	Oppeln	Ger	Wolves (Nov 1998)
Radzinski, Tomasz	14 Dec 1973	Poznan	Can	Everton (Jul 2001)
Dudek, Jerzy	23 Mar 1973	Rybnik	Pol	Liverpool (Aug 2001)
Adamczuk, Darius	20 Oct 1969	Szczecinek	Pol	Wigan (Aug 2001)
Bak, Arkadiusz	6 Jan 1974	Szczecinek	Pol	Birmingham (Dec 2001)
Swierczewski, Piotr	8 Apr 1972	Nowy Sacz	Pol	Birmingham (Feb 2003)

Qualified for Poland but born outside Poland

Kloner, Hymie	23 May 1929	Jo-burg, SA	Pol	Birmingham (Nov 1950)

PORTUGAL (26+7)

Dominguez, Jose	16 Feb 1974	Lisbon	Por	Birmingham (Mar 1994); Tottenham (Aug 1997)
Andrade, Jose-Manuel	1 Jun 1970	Gaboverde	Por	Stoke (Mar 1995); Stoke (Aug 1997)
Neves, Rui	10 Mar 1965	Vinhais	Por	Darlington (Aug 1995)
Carvalho, Dani	2 Nov 1976	Lisbon	Por	West Ham (Feb 1996)
Futre, Paulo	26 Feb 1966	Montijo	Por	West Ham (Jun 1996)
Moreira, Joao	30 Jun 1970	Oporto	Por	Swansea (Jun 1996)
Nelson, Fernando	5 Nov 1971	Lisbon	Por	A Villa (Jun 1996)
Cavaco, Luis Miguel	1 Mar 1972	Almada	Por	Stockport (Aug 1996)
Da Costa, Hugo	4 Nov 1973	Tramagal	Por	Stoke (Aug 1996)
Porfirio, Hugo	29 Sep 1973	Lisbon	Por	West Ham (Sep 1996); Nottm For (Jan 1999)
Pinto, Sergio	8 Jan 1973	Escudos	Por	Bradford (Oct 1996)
Kiko, Manuel	24 Oct 1976	Cedofeita	Por	Stockport (Dec 1996)
Oliveira, Raul	26 Aug 1972	Lisbon	Por	Bradford (Mar 1997)

SURNAME, NAME	DOB	PLACE OF BIRTH	NAT	CLUB(S) JOINED/FIRST PLAYED
Boa Morte, Luis	4 Aug 1977	Lisbon	Por	Arsenal (Jun 1997); Southampton (Aug 1999); Fulham (Jun 2001)
Ribeiro, Bruno	22 Oct 1975	Setubal	Por	Leeds (Jul 1997); Sheff Utd (Oct 1999)
Alves, Paulo	10 Feb 1969	Mateus Villareal	Por	West Ham (Nov 1997)
Rodrigues, Dani	3 Mar 1980	Madeira	Por	Bournemouth (Oct 1998); Southampton (Mar 1999); Bristol C (Oct 2000); Walsall (Aug 2002)
Costa, Ricardo	10 Jan 1973	Lisbon	Por	Darlington (Jan 1999)
Almeida, Marco	4 Apr 1977	Lisbon	Por	Southampton (Jul 1999)
Rocha, Carlos	4 Dec 1974	Lisbon	Por	Bury (Aug 1999)
Leitao, Jorge	14 Jan 1974	Oporto	Por	Walsall (Aug 2000)
Andre, Carlos	28 Nov 1971	Lisbon	Por	Walsall (Aug 2001)
Miranda, Jose	2 Apr 1974	Lisbon	Por	Rotherham (Sep 2001)
Costa, Jorge	14 Oct 1971	Porto	Por	Charlton (Dec 2001)
Viana, Hugo	15 Jan 1983	Barcelos	Por	Newcastle (Aug 2002)
De Oliveira, Filipe	27 May 1984	Braga	Por	Chelsea (Sep 2002)
Other players qualified for Portugal but born outside Portugal				
Isaias, Marques	17 Nov 1963	Rio de Janeiro, Bra	Por	Coventry (Aug 1995)
Paulo, Pedro	21 Nov 1973	Angola	Por	Darlington (Aug 1995)
Xavier, Abel	30 Nov 1972	Nampula, Moz	Por	Everton (Sep 1999); Liverpool (Jan 2002)
Helder, Rodrigues	21 Mar 1971	Luanda, Ang	Por	Newcastle (Nov 1999)
Cadete, Jorge	27 Aug 1968	Porto Amélia, Moz	Por	Bradford (Feb 2000)
Batista, Jordao	30 Aug 1971	Malanje, Ang	Por	WBA (Aug 2000)
Da Silva, Lourenco	5 Jun 1983	Luanda, Ang	Por	Bristol C (Mar 2001); Oldham (Aug 2002)

REUNION (1)

Robert, Laurent	21 May 1975	Saint-Benoit	Fr	Newcastle (Aug 2001)

ROMANIA (6)

Iovan, Stefan	23 Aug 1960	Bucharest	Rom	Brighton (Mar 1991)
Dumitrescu, Ilie	6 Jan 1969	Bucharest	Rom	Tottenham (Aug 1994); West Ham (Mar 1996)
Petrescu, Dan	22 Dec 1967	Bucharest	Rom	Sheff Wed (Aug 1994); Chelsea (Nov 1995); Southampton (Aug 2000); Bradford (Aug 2000)
Popescu, Gica	9 Oct 1967	Calafat	Rom	Tottenham (Sep 1994)
Raducioiu, Florin	17 Mar 1970	Bucharest	Rom	West Ham (Jun 1996)
Moldovan, Viorel	8 Jul 1972	Bistrita	Rom	Coventry (Jan 1998)

RUSSIA (3)

Kharine, Dimitri	16 Aug 1968	Moscow	Rus	Chelsea (Dec 1992)
Kulkov, Vasili	11 Jun 1966	Moscow	Rus	Millwall (Jan 1996)
Danilevicius, Tomas	18 Jul 1978	Moscow	Lith	Arsenal (Sep 2000)

SAUDI ARABIA (1)

Al-Jaber, Sami	11 Dec 1972	Riyadh	Sau	Wolves (Sep 2000)

SENEGAL (14)

Vieira, Patrick	23 Jun 1976	Dakar	Fr	Arsenal (Aug 1996)
Dia, Ali	20 Aug 1965	Dakar	Sen	Southampton (Nov 1996)
N'Diaye, Sada	27 Mar 1975	Dakar	Sen	Southend (Oct 1997)
Diop, Pape Seydou	12 Jan 1979	Dakar	Sen	Norwich (Aug 1999)
Mendy, Jules	4 Sep 1973	Pikine	Sen	Torquay (Aug 2000)
N'Diaye, Seyni	1 Jun 1973	Dakar	Sen	Tranmere (Mar 2001)
Diawara, Djibril	3 Jan 1975	Dakar	Sen	Bolton (Jun 2001)
Sall, Abdou	1 Nov 1980	Dakar	Sen	Kidderminster (Aug 2001); Oxford (Dec 2002)
Diallo, Cherif	28 Aug 1971	Dakar	Sen	Exeter (Sep 2001)
Cisse, Aliou	24 Mar 1976	Zinguinchor	Sen	Birmingham (Aug 2002)
Diao, Salif	10 Jan 1977	Kedougou	Sen	Liverpool (Aug 2002)
Diouf, El Hadji	15 Jan 1981	Dakar	Sen	Liverpool (Aug 2002)
Sonko, Ibrahima	22 Jan 1981	Bignola	Sen	Brentford (Aug 2002)
Coly, Ferdinand	10 Sep 1973	Dakar	Sen	Birmingham (Jan 2003)

SEYCHELLES (1)

Betsy, Kevin	20 Mar 1978	Seychelles	Sey	Fulham (Sep 1998); Bournemouth (Sep 1999); Hull (Nov 1999); Barnsley (Mar 2002)

SIERRA LEONE (2)

Dillsworth, Eddie	16 Apr 1946	Freetown	SiLe	Lincoln (Mar 1967)
Bart-Williams, Chris	16 Jun 1974	Freetown	Brit	Orient (Jul 1990); Sheff Wed (Nov 1991); Nottm For (Jul 1995); Charlton (Dec 2001)

SINGAPORE (6)

Twissell, Charlie	16 Dec 1932	Singapore	Eng	Plymouth (Aug 1955); York (Nov 1958)
Butcher, Terry	28 Dec 1958	Singapore	Eng	Ipswich (Aug 1976); Coventry (Nov 1990); Sunderland (Jul 1992)
Callaghan, Nigel	12 Sep 1962	Singapore	Eng	Watford (Jul 1979); Derby (Feb 1987); A Villa (Feb 1989); Derby (Sep 1990); Watford (Mar 1991); Huddersfield (Jan 1992)
Young, Eric	25 Mar 1960	Changi	Wal	Brighton (Nov 1982); Wimbledon (Jul 1987); C Palace (Aug 1990); Wolves (Sep 1995)
Atkinson, Paddy	22 May 1970	Singapore	Brit	Hartlepool (Aug 1988); York (Nov 1995); Scarborough (Aug 1998)

SURNAME, NAME	DOB	PLACE OF BIRTH	NAT	CLUB(S) JOINED/FIRST PLAYED
Carmichael, Matt	13 May 1964	Singapore	Brit	Lincoln (Aug 1989); Scunthorpe (Jul 1993); Barnet (Sep 1994); Preston (Mar 1995); Darlington (Feb 1996); Doncaster (Aug 1995); Mansfield (Aug 1995)

SLOVAKIA (6)

Kinder, Vladimir	9 Mar 1969	Bratislava	Svk	Middlesbrough (Jan 1997)
Varga, Stanislav	8 Oct 1972	Lipany	Svk	Sunderland (Aug 2000); WBA (Mar 2002)
Balis, Igor	5 Jan 1970	Zalozinik	Svk	WBA (Dec 2000)
Nemeth, Szilard	8 Aug 1977	Komarno	Svk	Middlesbrough (Jul 2001)
Labant, Vladimir	8 Jun 1974	Zilina	Svk	West Ham (Jan 2002)
Gresko,Vratislav	24 Jul 1977	Pressburg	Svk	Blackburn (Jan 2003)

SLOVENIA (5)

Krizan, Ales	25 Jul 1971	Maribor	Slo	Barnsley (Jul 1997)
Rudonja, Mladen	26 Jul 1971	Koper	Slo	Portsmouth (Aug 2000)
Karic, Amir	31 Dec 1973	Oramovica Ponja	Slo	C Palace (Mar 2001); Ipswich (Sep 2000)
Bobic, Fredi	30 Oct 1971	Maribor	Ger	Bolton (Jan 2002)
Acimovic, Milenko	15 Feb 1977	Ljubljana	Slo	Tottenham (Aug 2002)

SOUTH AFRICA (121+1)

Waller, Wilfred	27 Jul 1877	South Africa	SA	Bolton (Mar 1900)
Bell, Alec	1882	Cape Town	Sco	Man Utd (Jan 1903); Blackburn (Jul 1913)
Whitson, Anthony	c.1880	Cape Town	SA	Newcastle (Feb 1905)
Gibson, Fred	8 Dec 1888	Pilgrim's Rest	SA	Sunderland (May 1909); Coventry (May 1919)
Mackrill, Percy	19 Oct 1894	Wynberg	SA	Coventry (Jul 1919); Halifax (Jul 1921); Torquay (Jul 1925)
Osborne, Frank	14 Oct 1896	Wynberg	Eng	Fulham (Nov 1921); Tottenham (Jan 1924); Southampton (Jun 1931)
Osborne, Reg	23 Jul 1898	Wynberg	Eng	Leicester (Feb 1923)
King, Charlie	18 May 1897	Johannesburg	SA	Southport (May 1923)
Osborne, Harold	2 Apr 1904	Wynberg	SA	Norwich (Sep 1924)
Riley, Arthur	26 Dec 1903	Boksburg	SA	Liverpool (Jul 1925)
Murray, David	1902	Wynberg	SA	Everton (Aug 1925); Bristol C (Oct 1926); Bristol R (1928); Swindon (Jun 1930); Rochdale (Aug 1931)
Hodgson, Gordon	16 Apr 1904	Johannesburg	Eng	Liverpool (Nov 1925); A Villa (Jan 1936); Leeds (Mar 1937)
Martin, Sydney	c.1910	Durban	SA	Gillingham (Jul 1929)
Mandy, Aubrey	c.1910	Transvaal	SA	Leicester (Oct 1929)
Crawford, Ronald	c.1910	South Africa	SA	Thames (Jul 1930); Rotherham (Jul 1931)
Richardson, John	1909	Johannesburg	SA	Bristol R (Aug 1930)
Carr, Lance	18 Feb 1910	Johannesburg	SA	Liverpool (Aug 1933); Newport (Oct 1936); Newport (Jul 1938); Bristol R (Aug 1946)
Nieuwenhuys, Berry	5 Nov 1911	Boksburg	SA	Liverpool (Sep 1933)
Bunch, Arthur	30 Sep 1909	Bloemfontein	SA	Aldershot (Jun 1934)
Clarke, Bruce	4 Oct 1910	Johannesburg	SA	Fulham (Jun 1934)
Brown, Lennox	24 Nov 1910	South Africa	SA	Millwall (Nov 1935)
Kemp, Dick	15 Oct 1913	Cape Town	SA	Liverpool (Jul 1936)
Van Den Berg, Herman	21 Mar 1918	Cape Town	SA	Liverpool (Jul 1937)
Wienand, Tolley	1912	East London	SA	Huddersfield (Jul 1937); Hull (Oct 1938)
Lindsay, Denis	1916	Benoni	SA	Huddersfield (Aug 1937)
Woolf, Levi	28 Jan 1916	Johannesburg	SA	Southampton (Sep 1937)
Fish, Kenneth	c.1915	Cape Town	SA	Port Vale (Nov 1937)
Milligan, Dudley	7 Nov 1916	Johannesburg	N Ire	Chesterfield (Nov 1938); B&B Ath (Aug 1947); Walsall (Oct 1948)
Malan, Norman	23 Nov 1923	Johannesburg	SA	Middlesbrough (Oct 1945); Scunthorpe (Jun 1950); Bradford PA (Jul 1956)
Priday, Bob	29 Mar 1925	Cape Town	SA	Liverpool (Dec 1945); Blackburn (Mar 1949); Acc Stanley (Dec 1952); Rochdale (Aug 1953)
Strauss, Bill	6 Jan 1916	Transvaal	SA	Plymouth (Jul 1946)
Kelly, Pat	9 Apr 1918	Johannesburg	N Ire	Barnsley (Oct 1946); Crewe (Feb 1952)
Forbes, Dudley	19 Apr 1926	Cape Town	SA	Charlton (Dec 1947)
O'Linn, Syd	5 May 1927	Oudtschoorn	SA	Charlton (Dec 1947)
Havenga, Willie	6 Nov 1924	Bloemfontein	SA	Birmingham (Jul 1948); Luton (May 1950); Ipswich (Jan 1952)
Arnison, Joseph	27 Jun 1924	Johannesburg	SA	Luton (Aug 1948)
Uytenbogaardt, Albert	5 Mar 1930	Cape Town	SA	Charlton (Oct 1948)
Nielson, Norman	6 Nov 1928	Johannesburg	SA	Charlton (Jul 1949); Derby (Sep 1951); Bury (May 1954); Hull (Apr 1957)
Williams, Stan	1 May 1919	South Africa	SA	Plymouth (Aug 1949)
Falconer, Andy	27 Jun 1925	South Africa	SA	Blackpool (Sep 1949)
Hewie, John	13 Dec 1927	Pretoria	Sco	Charlton (Oct 1949)
Perry, Bill	10 Sep 1930	Johannesburg	SA	Blackpool (Nov 1949); Southport (Jun 1962)
Firmani, Eddie	7 Aug 1933	Cape Town	SA	Charlton (Feb 1950); Charlton (Oct 1963); Southend (Jun 1965); Charlton (Mar 1967)
Leary, Stuart	30 Apr 1933	Cape Town	SA	Charlton (Feb 1950); QPR (Dec 1962)
Ackerman, Alf	5 Jan 1929	Pretoria	SA	Hull (Jul 1950); Norwich (Aug 1951); Hull (Oct 1953); Derby (Mar 1955); Carlisle (Nov 1956); Millwall (Jan 1959)

SURNAME, NAME	DOB	PLACE OF BIRTH	NAT	CLUB(S) JOINED/FIRST PLAYED
Purdon, Ted	1 Mar 1930	Johannesburg	SA	Birmingham (Aug 1950); Sunderland (Jan 1954); Workington (Mar 1957); Barrow (Mar 1958); Bristol R (Aug 1960)
Carr, John	10 Jun 1926	Durban	SA	Huddersfield (Oct 1950)
Kloner, Hymie	23 May 1929	Jo-burg, SA	Pol	Birmingham (Nov 1950)
Miller, George	17 Oct 1927	South Africa	SA	Leeds (Nov 1950); Workington (Mar 1952)
Stuart, Eddie	12 May 1931	Johannesburg	SA	Wolves (Jan 1951); Stoke (Jul 1962); Tranmere (Aug 1964); Stockport (Jul 1966)
Davies, Roy	23 Aug 1924	Cape Town	SA	Luton (May 1951)
Kirsten, Ken	28 Oct 1922	South Africa	SA	Aldershot (Aug 1951)
Oelofse, Ralph	12 Nov 1926	Johannesburg	SA	Chelsea (Oct 1951); Watford (Jul 1953)
Stewart, Gordon	7 Aug 1927	Durban	SA	Leeds (Oct 1951)
Chamberlain, Ken	30 Jun 1926	Durban	SA	Charlton (Oct 1951)
Foreman, Denis	1 Feb 1933	Cape Town	SA	Brighton (Mar 1952)
Gerhardt, Hugh	5 May 1933	South Africa	SA	Liverpool (Aug 1952)
Hastie, Ken	6 Sep 1928	Cape Town	SA	Leeds (Aug 1952)
Miller, Graham	25 Aug 1927	South Africa	SA	Workington (Dec 1952)
Firmani, Peter	14 Feb 1936	Cape Town	SA	Charlton (Sep 1953)
Oosthuizen, Ron	16 Mar 1936	South Africa	SA	Charlton (Sep 1953); Carlisle (Sep 1959)
Tulloch, Roland	15 Jul 1932	South Africa	SA	Hull (Dec 1953)
McEwan, Peter	23 May 1933	Roodepoort	SA	Luton (Feb 1954)
Rudham, Doug	3 May 1926	Johannesburg	SA	Liverpool (Nov 1954)
Hauser, Peter	20 Apr 1934	Kimberley	SA	Blackpool (Nov 1955); Chester (Aug 1963)
Hewkins, Ken	30 Oct 1929	Pretoria	SA	Fulham (Nov 1955)
Kennon, Sandy	26 Nov 1933	Johannesburg	Zim	Huddersfield (Aug 1956); Norwich (Feb 1959); Colchester (Mar 1965)
Hodge, Eric	3 Apr 1933	Cape Town	SA	Brighton (Oct 1956); Aldershot (Jun 1959)
Mokone, Steve	23 Mar 1932	Pretoria	SA	Coventry (Oct 1956); Cardiff (Jun 1959); Barnsley (Aug 1961)
Peterson, Brian	20 Oct 1936	Durban	SA	Blackpool (Oct 1956)
Horne, Des	12 Dec 1939	Johannesburg	SA	Wolves (Dec 1956); Blackpool (Mar 1961)
Lightening, Arthur	1 Aug 1936	Durban	SA	Nottm For (Dec 1956); Coventry (Nov 1958); Middlesbrough (Aug 1962)
Le Roux, Daniel	25 Nov 1933	Port Shepstone	SA	Arsenal (Feb 1957)
Durandt, Cliff	16 Apr 1940	Johannesburg	SA	Wolves (Jun 1957); Charlton (Mar 1963)
Cubie, Neil	3 Nov 1932	South Africa	SA	Hull (Jul 1957)
Francis, Gerry	6 Dec 1933	Johannesburg	SA	Leeds (Jul 1957); York (Oct 1961)
Kichenbrand, Don	13 Aug 1933	Johannesburg	SA	Sunderland (Mar 1958)
Tennant, Roy	12 Sep 1936	Durban	SA	Workington (Jul 1958)
Hubbard, John	16 Dec 1930	Pretoria	SA	Bury (Apr 1959)
Tocknell, Brian	21 May 1937	Pretoria	SA	Charlton (Jul 1959)
Smethurst, Peter	8 Aug 1940	Durban	SA	Blackpool (Feb 1960)
Johanneson, Albert	12 Mar 1940	Johannesburg	SA	Leeds (Apr 1961); York (Jul 1970)
Viljoen, Colin	20 Jun 1948	Johannesburg	SA	Ipswich (Mar 1967); Man City (Aug 1978); Chelsea (Mar 1980)
Smethurst, Derek	24 Oct 1947	Durban	SA	Chelsea (Dec 1968); Millwall (Sep 1971)
Collins, Mike	27 Jul 1953	Johannesburg	SA	Swindon (Jul 1973)
Vernon, John	2 Mar 1956	South Africa	SA	Stockport (Apr 1975)
Backos, Des	13 Nov 1950	Wynberg	SA	Stoke (Oct 1977)
Stein, Brian	19 Oct 1957	Cape Town	Eng	Luton (Oct 1977); Luton (Jul 1991); Barnet (Aug 1992)
Johnston, Craig	8 Dec 1960	Johannesburg	Aus	Middlesbrough (Feb 1978); Liverpool (Apr 1981)
Parkinson, Andy	5 May 1959	Johannesburg	SA	Newcastle (Mar 1978); Peterborough (Aug 1979)
D'Avray, Mich	19 Feb 1962	Johannesburg	Eng	Ipswich (May 1979); Leicester (Feb 1987)
Grobbelaar, Bruce	6 Oct 1957	Durban	Zim	Crewe (Dec 1979); Liverpool (Mar 1981); Stoke (Mar 1993); Southampton (Aug 1994); Plymouth (Aug 1996); Oldham (Dec 1997); Bury (Sep 1998); Lincoln (Dec 1998)
Nebbeling, Gavin	15 May 1963	Johannesburg	SA	C Palace (Aug 1981); Northampton (Oct 1985); Fulham (Jul 1989); Hereford(Dec 1991); Preston (Jul 1993)
Stein, Edwin	28 Jun 1955	Cape Town	Brit	Barnet (Jul 1982)
Stein, Mark	28 Jan 1966	Cape Town	Eng	Luton (Jan 1984); Aldershot (Jan 1986); QPR (Jun 1988); Oxford (Sep 1989); Stoke (Nov 1991); Chelsea (Oct 1993); Stoke (Aug 1996); Bournemouth (June 1998); Ipswich (Aug 1997); Luton (Jul 2000)
Wegerle, Roy	19 Mar 1964	Johannesburg	USA	Chelsea (Jun 1986); Swindon (Mar 1988); Luton (Jul 1988); QPR (Dec 1989); Blackburn (Mar 1992); Coventry (Mar 1993)
McMillan, Andy	22 Jun 1968	Bloemfontein	SA	York (Jul 1987)
Paskin, John	1 Feb 1962	Cape Town	SA	WBA (Aug 1988); Wolves (Jun 1989); Stockport (Sep 1991); Birmingham (Nov 1991); Shrewsbury (Feb 1992); Wrexham (Feb 1992); Bury (Jul 1994)
Leitch, Grant	31 Oct 1972	South Africa	SA	Blackpool (Aug 1990)
Aspinall, Brendan	22 Jul 1975	Johannesburg	SA	Mansfield (Jul 1994)
Masinga, Phil	28 Jun 1969	Johannesburg	SA	Leeds (Aug 1994)
Radebe, Lucas	12 Apr 1969	Johannesburg	SA	Leeds (Sep 1994)
Stephenson, Ashlyn	6 Jul 1974	South Africa	SA	Darlington (Sep 1995)
Williams, Mark	11 Aug 1966	Johannesburg	SA	Wolves (Sep 1995)

SURNAME, NAME	DOB	PLACE OF BIRTH	NAT	CLUB(S) JOINED/FIRST PLAYED
Goodhind, Warren	16 Aug 1977	Johannesburg	SA	Barnet (Jul 1996); Cambridge (Sep 2001)
Harris, Andy	26 Feb 1977	Springs	Brit	Southend (Jul 1996); Orient (Jul 1999)
Tinkler, Eric	30 Jul 1970	Roodepoort	SA	Barnsley (Jul 1997)
Arendse, Andre	27 Jun 1967	Cape Town	SA	Fulham (Aug 1997); Oxford (Jul 1999)
Fish, Mark	14 Mar 1974	Cape Town	SA	Bolton (Sep 1997); Charlton (Nov 2000)
Dundee, Sean	7 Dec 1972	Durban	SA	Liverpool (Jun 1998)
Arber, Mark	9 Oct 1977	Johannesburg	Brit	Barnet (Sep 1998); Peterborough (Dec 2002)
O'Brien, Burton	10 Jun 1981	South Africa	Brit	Blackburn (Feb 1999)
Fortune, Quinton	21 May 1977	Cape Town	SA	Man Utd (Aug 1999)
Hardy, Adam	22 Feb 1983	Uitenhage	SA	Bradford (Sep 2000)
Bartlett, Shaun	31 Oct 1972	Cape Town	SA	Charlton (Dec 2000)
Byrne, Paul	26 Nov 1982	Natal	Brit	Port Vale (Apr 2001)
Greyling, Anton	5 Dec 1977	Pretoria	SA	Torquay (Aug 2001)
Issa, Pierre	11 Aug 1975	Johannesburg	SA	Watford (Sep 2001)
Roberts, Sean	2 Jan 1983	Johannesburg	SA	Sheff Wed (Oct 2001)
Miller, Justin	16 Dec 1980	Johannesburg	SA	Orient (Sep 2002)
Evans, Paul	28 Dec 1973	Newcastle	SA	Sheff Wed (Mar 2003)

Other players qualified for South Africa but born outside South Africa

Koumantarakis, George	27 Mar 1974	Athens, Grk	SA	Preston (Jan 2003)

SPAIN (30+1)

Aldecoa, Emilio	30 Nov 1922	Bilbao	Sp	Coventry (Dec 1945)
Gallego, Jose	8 Apr 1923	San Sebastian	Sp	Brentford (Jan 1947); Southampton (May 1948); Colchester (Aug 1950)
Gallego, Tony	2 Jun 1924	San Sebastian	Sp	Norwich (Mar 1947)
Diaz, Isidro	15 May 1972	Valencia	Sp	Wigan Ath (Jul 1995); Wolves (Aug 1997); Wigan Ath (Aug 1997); Rochdale (Aug 1998)
Martinez, Roberto	13 Jul 1973	Balaguer Lerida	Sp	Wigan Ath (Jul 1995); Walsall (Aug 2002); Swansea (Feb 2003)
Seba, Jesus	11 Apr 1974	Zaragoza	Sp	Wigan Ath (Aug 1995)
Mateu, Jose-Luis	15 Jan 1966	Castellon	Sp	Torquay (Sep 1995)
Doncel, Antonio	31 Jan 1967	Lugo	Sp	Hull (Aug 1996)
San Miguel, Xavier	7 May 1971	Bilbao	Sp	Cambridge (Aug 1996)
Calvo-Garcia, Alex	1 Jan 1972	Ordizia	Sp	Scunthorpe (Oct 1996)
Segura, Victor	30 Mar 1973	Zaragoza	Sp	Norwich (Aug 1997)
Garcia Sanjuan, Jesus	22 Aug 1971	Zaragoza	Sp	Wolves (Sep 1997)
Merino, Carlos	15 Mar 1980	Bilbao	Sp	Nottm For (Sep 1997)
Ferrer, Albert	6 Jun 1970	Barcelona	Sp	Chelsea (Aug 1998)
Gomez, Fernando	11 Sep 1965	Valencia	Sp	Wolves (Aug 1998)
Matias, Pedro	11 Oct 1973	Madrid	Sp	Macclesfield (Dec 1998); Tranmere (Aug 1999); Walsall (Oct 1999)
Mori Cuesta, Francisco	10 Nov 1970	Canea de Onis	Sp	Barnsley (Mar 1999)
Elena, Marcelino	26 Sep 1971	Gijon	Sp	Newcastle (Jul 1999)
Aranalde, Zigor	28 Feb 1973	Guipuzcoa	Sp	Walsall (Aug 2000)
Counago, Pablo	9 Aug 1979	Potevedra	Sp	Ipswich (May 2001)
Juanjo, Carricondo	4 May 1977	Barcelona	Sp	Bradford (Oct 2001)
Sanchez-Lopez, Carlos	22 Jul 1979	Madrid	Sp	Bristol R (Feb 2002)
Yordi	14 Sep 1974	San Fernando	Sp	Blackburn (Feb 2002)
De Lucas, Enrique	17 Aug 1978	Llobregat	Sp	Chelsea (Aug 2002)
Dixon, Jonny	16 Jan 1984	Muria	Brit	Wycombe (Aug 2002)
Campo, Ivan	21 Feb 1974	San Sebastian	Sp	Bolton (Sep 2002)
Lopez, Ricardo	30 Dec 1971	Madrid	Sp	Man Utd (Sep 2002)
Ballesta, Salva	22 May 1975	Paese	Sp	Bolton (Feb 2003)
Bravo, Raul	14 Apr 1981	Gandia	Sp	Leeds (Feb 2003)
Engonga, Vincente	20 Oct 1969	Barcelona	Sp	Coventry (Feb 2003)

Other players qualified for Spain but born outside Spain

Mendez, Alberto	24 Oct 1974	Nuremburg, Ger	Sp	Arsenal (Jul 1997)

SRI LANKA (1)

Butler, Jack	14 Aug 1894	Colombo	Brit	Arsenal (Jan 1914); Torquay (May 1930)

ST KITTS-NEVIS (4)

Podd, Ces	7 Aug 1952	St Kitts	StK	Bradford (Aug 1970); Halifax (Aug 1984); Scarborough (Jul 1986)
Bowery, Bert	29 Oct 1954	St Kitts	StK	Nottm For (Jan 1975); Lincoln (Feb 1976)
Benjamin, Tristan	1 Apr 1957	St Kitts	StK	Notts Co (Mar 1975); Chesterfield (Jul 1987)
Walwyn, Keith	17 Feb 1956	Nevis	Brit	Chesterfield (Nov 1979); York (Jul 1981); Blackpool (Jun 1987); Carlisle (Jul 1989)

ST LUCIA (2)

Marshall, Dwight	3 Oct 1965	St Lucia	Brit	Plymouth (Aug 1991); Middlesbrough (Mar 1993); Luton (Jul 1994); Plymouth (Oct 1998)
Jean, Earl	9 Oct 1971	St Lucia	StL	Ipswich (Dec 1996); Rotherham (Jan 1997); Plymouth (Aug 1997)

ST VINCENT (2+1)

Ambrose, Leroy	22 Jun 1960	St Vincent	StV	Charlton (Aug 1979)
Kelly, Errington	8 Apr 1958	Sandy Bay	StV	Bristol R (Sep 1981); Lincoln (Jan 1983); Bristol C (Feb 1983); Peterborough (Mar 1984); Peterborough (Dec 1986)

SURNAME, NAME	DOB	PLACE OF BIRTH	NAT	CLUB(S) JOINED/FIRST PLAYED
Other players qualified for St Vincent but born outside St Vincent				
Jack, Rodney	28 Sep 1972	Kingston, Jam	StV	Torquay (Oct 1995); Crewe (Aug 1998)

SURINAM (17)

SURNAME, NAME	DOB	PLACE OF BIRTH	NAT	CLUB(S) JOINED/FIRST PLAYED
Zondervan, Romeo	4 Mar 1959	Surinam	Neth	WBA (Mar 1982); Ipswich (Mar 1984)
Wilson, Ulrich	5 May 1964	Surinam	Neth	Ipswich (Dec 1987)
Monkou, Ken	29 Nov 1964	Surinam	Neth	Chelsea (Mar 1989); Southampton (Aug 1992); Huddersfield (Aug 1999)
Verveer, Etienne	22 Sep 1967	Surinam	Neth	Millwall (Dec 1991); Bradford (Feb 1995)
De Freitas, Fabian	28 Jul 1972	Surinam	Neth	Bolton (Aug 1994); WBA (Aug 1998)
Gullit, Ruud	1 Sep 1962	Surinam	Neth	Chelsea (Jul 1995)
Uhlenbeek, Gus	28 Aug 1970	Surinam	Neth	Ipswich (Aug 1995); Fulham (Jul 1998); Sheff Utd (Aug 2000); Walsall (Mar 2002); Bradford (Aug 2002)
Blinker, Regi	4 Jun 1969	Surinam	Neth	Sheff Wed (Mar 1996)
Van Gobbel, Ulrich	16 Jan 1971	Surinam	Neth	Southampton (Oct 1996)
Wilsterman, Brian	19 Nov 1966	Surinam	Neth	Oxford (Feb 1997); Rotherham (Jul 1999)
Hasselbaink, Jimmy Floyd	27 Mar 1972	Surinam	Neth	Leeds (Jul 1997); Chelsea (Jul 2000)
Wijnhard, Clyde	9 Nov 1973	Surinam	Neth	Leeds (Jul 1998); Huddersfield (Jul 1999); Oldham (Aug 2002)
Wilnis, Fabian	23 Aug 1970	Surinam	Neth	Ipswich (Jan 1999)
Faerber, Winston	23 Jul 1971	Surinam	Neth	Cardiff (Aug 1999)
Gorre, Dean	10 Sep 1970	Surinam	Neth	Huddersfield (Sep 1999); Barnsley (Jul 2001)
Wooter, Nordin	24 Aug 1976	Surinam	Neth	Watford (Sep 1999)
Koejoe, Sammy	17 Aug 1974	Surinam	Neth	QPR (Nov 1999)

SWEDEN (54+3)

SURNAME, NAME	DOB	PLACE OF BIRTH	NAT	CLUB(S) JOINED/FIRST PLAYED
Ekner, Dan	5 Feb 1927	Sweden	Swe	Portsmouth (1949-50)
Jeppson, Hans	10 May 1925	Gothenburg	Swe	Charlton (Jan 1951)
Moller, Jan	17 Sep 1953	Malmo	Swe	Bristol C (Dec 1980)
Gough, Richard	5 Apr 1962	Stockholm	Sco	Tottenham (Aug 1986); Nottm For (Mar 1999); Everton (Jun 1999)
Rehn, Stefan	22 Sep 1966	Stockholm	Swe	Everton (Jun 1989)
Hysen, Glenn	30 Oct 1959	Gothenburg	Swe	Liverpool (Jul 1989)
Nilsson, Roland	27 Nov 1963	Helsingborg	Swe	Sheff Wed (Nov 1989); Coventry (Jul 1997) & (Jul 2001)
Limpar, Anders	24 Sep 1965	Solna	Swe	Arsenal (Aug 1990); Everton (Mar 1994); Birmingham (Jan 1997)
Andersson, Patrik	18 Aug 1971	Borgeby	Swe	Blackburn (Dec 1992)
Shail, Mark	15 Oct 1963	Sandviken	Brit	Bristol C (Mar 1993); Kidderminster (Jul 2000)
Wirmola, Jonas	17 Jul 1969	Vaxjo	Swe	Sheff Utd (Aug 1993)
Schwarz, Stefan	18 Apr 1969	Malmo	Swe	Arsenal (May 1994); Sunderland (Aug 1999)
Ingesson, Klas	20 Aug 1968	Odeshog	Swe	Sheff Wed (Sep 1994)
Brolin, Tomas	29 Nov 1969	Hudiksvall	Swe	Leeds (Nov 1995); C Palace (Jan 1998)
Kaamark, Pontus	5 Apr 1969	Vasteras	Swe	Leicester (Nov 1995)
Sahlin, Dan	18 Apr 1967	Falum	Swe	Birmingham (Nov 1995)
Gudmundsson, Niklas	29 Feb 1972	Sweden	Swe	Blackburn (Dec 1995); Ipswich (Mar 1997)
Pehrsson, Magnus	25 May 1976	Malmo	Swe	Bradford (Oct 1996)
Jansson, Jan	26 Jan 1968	Kalmar	Swe	Port Vale (Nov 1996)
Svensson, Mathias	24 Sep 1974	Boras	Swe	Portsmouth (Dec 1996); C Palace (Sep 1998); Charlton (Jan 2000)
Ottosson, Ulf	2 Jul 1968	Degefors	Swe	Norwich (Jan 1997)
Eriksson, Jan	24 Aug 1967	Sundsvall	Swe	Sunderland (Jan 1997)
Rahmberg, Marino	7 Aug 1974	Orebro	Swe	Derby (Jan 1997)
Andersson, Anders	15 Mar 1974	Tomelilla	Swe	Blackburn (Jun 1997)
Dahlin, Martin	16 Apr 1968	Udevalla	Swe	Blackburn (Jul 1997)
Hedman, Magnus	19 Mar 1973	Stockholm	Swe	Coventry (Jul 1997)
Steiner, Rob	20 Jun 1973	Finsprong	Swe	Bradford (Jul 1997); QPR (Jul 1998); Walsall (Mar 1999); QPR (Jul 1999)
Markstedt, Peter	11 Jan 1972	Vasteras	Swe	Barnsley (Nov 1997)
Alexandersson, Niclas	29 Dec 1971	Halmstad	Swe	Sheff Wed (Dec 1997); Everton (Jul 2000)
Andersson, Andreas	10 Apr 1974	Osterhoninge	Swe	Newcastle (Jan 1998)
Blomqvist, Jesper	5 Feb 1974	Tavelsjo	Swe	Man Utd (Jul 1998); Everton (Nov 2001); Charlton (Sep 2002)
Ljungberg, Freddie	16 Apr 1977	Halmstad	Swe	Arsenal (Sep1998)
Mattsson, Jesper	18 Apr 1968	Visby	Swe	Nottm For (Dec 1998)
Pringle, Martin	18 Nov 1970	Gothenburg	Swe	Charlton (Jan 1999); Grimsby (Feb 2002)
Lundin, Pal	21 Nov 1964	Osby	Swe	Oxford (Mar 1999)
Axeldahl, Jonas	2 Sep 1970	Holm	Swe	Ipswich (Jul 1999); Cambridge (Aug 2000)
Bengtsson, Robert	4 Jun 1968	Gothenburg	Swe	Barnsley (Nov 1999)
Gustafsson, Tomas	7 May 1973	Stockholm	Swe	Coventry (Dec 1999)
Hansson, Mikael	15 Mar 1968	Norrkoping	Swe	Stoke (Dec 1999)
Bryngelsson, Fredrik	10 Apr 1975	Sweden	Swe	Stockport (Jul 2000)
Johansson, Jonatan	16 Aug 1975	Stockholm	Fin	Charlton (Aug 2000)
Karlsson, Par	29 May 1978	Gothenburg	Swe	Wimbledon (Sep 2000)
Traore, Demba	22 Apr 1982	Stockholm	Swe	Cambridge (Dec 2000)
Svensson, Anders	17 Jul 1976	Gothenburg	Swe	Southampton (Jun 2001)
Mellberg, Olof	3 Sep 1977	Gullspang	Swe	A Villa (Jul 2001)
Johansson, Nils-Eric	13 Jan 1980	Stockholm	Swe	Blackburn (Oct 2001)
Mild, Hakan	14 Jun 1971	Trollhattan	Swe	Wimbledon (Nov 2001)
Bjorklund, Joachim	15 Mar 1971	Vaxjo	Swe	Sunderland (Jan 2002)

SURNAME, NAME	DOB	PLACE OF BIRTH	NAT	CLUB(S) JOINED/FIRST PLAYED
Linderoth, Tobias	21 Apr 1979	Stockholm	Swe	Everton (Jan 2002)
Allback, Marcus	5 Jul 1973	Gothenburg	Swe	A Villa (Jul 2002)
Svensson, Michael	25 Nov 1975	Sweden	Swe	Southampton (Aug 2002)
Shaaban, Rami	30 Jun 1975	Stockholm	Swe	Arsenal (Nov 2002)
Lucic, Teddy	15 Apr 1973	Biskopsgaard	Swe	Leeds (Oct 2002)
Tidman, Ola	11 May 1979	Sweden	Swe	Stockport (Jan 2003)

Other players qualified for Sweden but born outside Sweden

Andreasson, Marcus	13 Jul 1978	Monrovia, Lbr	Swe	Bristol R (Jul 1998)
Avdiu, Kemajl	22 Dec 1976	Kosovo, Yug	Swe	Bury (Aug 1998)
Djordjic, Bojan	6 Feb 1982	Belgrade, Yug	Swe	Man Utd (Feb 1999); Sheff Wed (Dec 2001)

SWITZERLAND (10+1)

Steffen, Willi	17 Mar 1925	Berne	Swit	Chelsea (Nov 1946)
Hottiger, Marc	7 Nov 1967	Lausanne	Swit	Newcastle (Aug 1994); Everton (Mar 1996)
Mazzarelli, Giuseppe	14 Aug 1972	Uster	Swit	Man City (Mar 1996)
Di Matteo, Roberto	29 May 1970	Sciaffusa	It	Chelsea (Jul 1996)
Vega, Ramon	14 Jun 1971	Olten	Swit	Tottenham (Jan 1997); Watford (Jun 2001)
Pascolo, Marco	9 May 1966	Sion	Swit	Nottm For (Jun 1997)
Henchoz, Stephane	7 Sep 1974	Billens	Swit	Blackburn (Jul 1997); Liverpool (Jul 1999)
Giallanza, Gaetano	6 Jun 1974	Dornach	Swit	Bolton (Mar 1998); Norwich (Mar 2000)
Konde, Oumar	19 Aug 1979	Binnengen	Swit	Blackburn (Nov 1998)
Foletti, Patrick	27 May 1974	Sorengo	Swit	Derby (Feb 2002)

Other players qualified for Switzerland but born outside Switzerland

Haas, Bernt	8 Apr 1978	Vienna, Aut	Swit	Sunderland (Aug 2001)

TANZANIA (1)

Chine, Athumani	12 Mar 1967	Dar es Salaam	Tan	Walsall (Mar 1992)

TOGO (1)

Hodouto, Kwami	31 Oct 1974	Lome	Fr	Huddersfield (Sep 1999)

TRINIDAD AND TOBAGO (18)

Charles, Alf	11 Jul 1909	Trinidad	Trin	Southampton (Jan 1937)
Auguste, Joe	24 Nov 1955	Trinidad	Trin	Exeter (Jun 1981)
Granville, John	6 May 1956	Tobago	Trin	Millwall (Oct 1985); Aldershot (Aug 1991)
Yorke, Dwight	3 Dec 1971	Canaan	Trin	A Villa (Dec 1989); Man Utd (Aug 1998); Blackburn (Jul 2002)
Samuel, Randy	23 Dec 1963	Trinidad	Can	Port Vale (Nov 1995)
Marcelle, Clint	9 Nov 1968	Port of Spain	Trin	Barnsley (Aug 1996); Scunthorpe (Oct 1999); Darlington (Feb 2001); Hull (Sep 2000)
Rougier, Tony	17 Jul 1971	Tobago	Trin	Port Vale (Jan 1999); Reading (Aug 2000); Brighton (Feb 2003)
Ince, Clayton	13 Jul 1972	Trinidad	Trin	Crewe (Sep 1999)
Samuel, J Lloyd	29 Mar 1981	Trinidad	Brit	A Villa (Feb 1999); Gillingham (Oct 2001)
John, Stern	30 Oct 1976	Tunapuna	Trin	Nottm For (Nov 1999); Birmingham (Feb 2002)
Eve, Angus	23 Feb 1972	Trinidad	Trin	Chester (Dec 1999)
Laird, Kamu	23 Dec 1975	Port of Spain	Trin	Chester (Dec 1999)
Pierre, Nigel	2 Jun 1979	Port of Spain	Trin	Bristol R (Feb 2000)
Edwards, Carlos	24 Oct 1978	Port of Spain	Trin	Wrexham (Aug 2000)
Sam, Hector	25 Feb 1978	Mount Murray	Trin	Wrexham (Aug 2000)
Lawrence, Denis	1 Aug 1974	Port of Spain	Trin	Wrexham (Mar 2001)
Norville, Jason	9 Sep 1983	Trinidad	Brit	Watford (Oct 2001)
Rahim, Brent	8 Aug 1978	Diego Martin	Trin	Northampton (Jan 2003)

TUNISIA (1)

Karaa, Roch	3 Apr 1964	Tunisia	Tun	Darlington (Mar 1985)

TURKEY (4+1)

Alpay Ozalan	29 May 1973	Karisyaled	Tur	A Villa (Jul 2000)
Tugay Kerimoglu	24 Aug 1970	Istanbul	Tur	Blackburn (Jul 2001)
Hakan Unsal	14 May 1973	Sinop	Tur	Blackburn (Mar 2002)
Hakan Sukur	1 Sep 1971	Sakarya	Tur	Blackburn (Dec 2002)

Other players qualified for Turkey but born outside Turkey

Bulent, Akin	28 Aug 1979	Brussels, Bel	Tur	Bolton (Oct 2002)

UGANDA (3)

Baugh, John	23 Feb 1956	Uganda	Uga	Exeter (Feb 1977)
Iga, Andrew	9 Dec 1977	Kampala	Brit	Millwall (Jun 1995)
Kitamirike, Joel	5 Apr 1984	Uganda	Uga	Chelsea (Apr 2001)

UKRAINE (9)

Baltacha, Sergei	17 Feb 1958	Kiev	USSR	Ipswich (Jan 1989)
Kanchelskis, Andrei	23 Jan 1969	Kirowograd	Ukr	Man Utd (Mar 1991); Everton (Aug 1995); Man City (Jan 2001); Southampton (Sep 2002)
Yuran, Sergei	11 Jun 1969	Kiev	Ukr	Millwall (Jan 1996)
Evtushok, Alex	11 Jan 1970	Kiev	Ukr	Coventry (Feb 1997)
Pahars, Marian	5 Aug 1976	Chernevol	Lat	Southampton (Mar 1999)
Luzhny, Oleg	5 Aug 1968	Kiev	Ukr	Arsenal (Jul 1999)
Rebrov, Sergei	3 Jun 1974	Gorlovka	Ukr	Tottenham (Jun 2000)
Bopp, Eugene	5 Sep 1983	Kiev	Ger	Nottm For (Aug 2001)
Baltacha, Sergei Jnr	28 Jul 1979	Kiev, Ukr	Sco	Millwall (Jan 2003)

SURNAME, NAME	DOB	PLACE OF BIRTH	NAT	CLUB(S) JOINED/FIRST PLAYED
URUGUAY (6)				
Villazan, Rafael	19 Jul 1956	Montevideo	Uru	Wolves (May 1980)
Perdomo, Jose	6 Jan 1965	Montevideo	Uru	Coventry (Aug 1990)
Paz, Adrian	9 Sep 1968	Montevideo	Uru	Ipswich (Sep 1994)
Poyet, Gustavo	15 Nov 1967	Montevideo	Uru	Chelsea (Jul 1997); Tottenham (Jul 2001)
Corbo, Mateo	21 Apr 1976	Montevideo	Arg	Barnsley (Aug 2000)
Forlan, Diego	19 May 1979	Montevideo	Uru	Man Utd (Jan 2002)
USA (47+4)				
Andrews, Billy	1886	Kansas City	N Ire	Oldham (Aug 1908); Stockport (Mar 1909); Grimsby Town (Jul 1912)
Lester, Hugh	1891	USA	Brit	Liverpool (Aug 1911); Oldham (Aug 1914)
Gibson, Jock	23 Mar 1898	Philadelphia	Sco	Sunderland (Nov 1920); Hull (May 1922); Sheff Utd (Mar 1929); Luton (Jul 1933)
Donoghue, John	22 Jan 1903	New York	USA	Wrexham (Jul 1930)
Aspinall, Wilf	22 Sep 1910	Hartford	USA	Stockport (Jun 1934); Southport (Jul 1935)
McLaughlin, William	31 Jan 1918	USA	USA	Crewe (Oct 1946)
Kirkby, John	29 Nov 1929	USA	USA	Stoke (Dec 1946); Wrexham (Aug 1951)
Boyd, John	10 Sep 1926	USA	USA	Bristol C (Dec 1950)
Turner, Alf	26 Dec 1929	USA	Brit	N Brighton (Feb 1951)
Clelland, Crawford	3 Dec 1930	New Jersey	USA	Plymouth (Jun 1955)
Baker, Gerry	11 Apr 1938	New York	Brit	Man City (Nov 1960); Ipswich (Dec 1963); Coventry (Nov 1967); Brentford (Oct 1969)
Potts, Steve	7 May 1967	Hartford	Eng	West Ham (May 1984)
Goulet, Brent	19 Jun 1964	Tacoma	USA	Crewe (Jan 1988); Bournemouth (Nov 1987)
Pittman, Steve	18 Jul 1967	North Carolina	USA	Shrewsbury (Mar 1989)
Bruce, Marcelle	15 Mar 1971	Detroit	USA	Colchester (Jul 1989)
Meola, Tony	21 Feb 1969	Belleville	USA	Brighton (Aug 1990)
Harkes, John	8 Mar 1967	Kearny	USA	Sheff Wed (Oct 1990); Derby (Aug 1993); West Ham (Oct 1995); Nottm For (Jan 1999)
Sommer, Jurgen	27 Feb 1964	New York	USA	Luton (Sep 1991); Brighton (Nov 1991); Torquay (Oct 1992); QPR (Aug 1995); Bolton (Feb 2001)
Keller, Kasey	27 Nov 1969	Washington	USA	Millwall (Feb 1992); Leicester (Aug 1996); Tottenham (Aug 2001)
Murray, Bruce	25 Jan 1966	Washington	USA	Millwall (Aug 1993); Stockport (Mar 1994)
Barada, Taylor	14 Aug 1972	Charlottesville	USA	Colchester (Mar 1994)
Stackman, Scott	16 Nov 1975	Arizona	USA	Northampton (Mar 1994)
McDougald, Junior	12 Jan 1975	Big Spring	Brit	Brighton (May 1994); Chesterfield (Mar 1996); Rotherham (Jul 1996); Millwall (Jul 1998); Orient (Oct 1998)
Ammann, Mike	8 Feb 1971	California	USA	Charlton (Jul 1994)
Jones, Cobi	16 Jun 1970	Detroit	USA	Coventry (Sep 1994)
Feuer, Ian	20 May 1971	Las Vegas	USA	Peterborough (Feb 1995); Luton (1995-96); West Ham (Feb 2000); Wimbledon (Jun 2000); Derby (Oct 2001); Tranmere (Aug 2002)
Crawford, Jimmy	1 May 1973	Chicago	Ire	Newcastle (Mar 1995); Rotherham (Sep 1996); Reading (Mar 1998)
Lapper, Mike	28 Aug 1970	California	USA	Southend (Aug 1995)
Santos, Ali	n/a	New Jersey	USA	Bournemouth (Aug 1995)
Caldwell, Garrett	6 Nov 1973	Princeton	USA	Colchester (Sep 1995)
Baardsen, Espen	7 Dec 1977	San Rafael	Nor	Tottenham (Jul 1996); Watford (Aug 2000); Everton (Jan 2003)
Melvang, Lars	3 Apr 1969	Seattle	Den	Watford (Aug 1997)
Friedel, Brad	18 May 1971	Lakewood	USA	Liverpool (Dec 1997); Blackburn (Nov 2000)
Hahnemann, Marcus	15 Jun 1972	Seattle	USA	Fulham (Jul 1999); Rochdale (Oct 2001); Reading (Dec 2001)
Rachubka, Paul	21 May 1981	San Luis	USA	Man Utd (Jul 1999); Oldham (Nov 2001)
Carver, Joe	11 Jun 1971	Illinois	USA	Chester (Sep 1999)
Moore, Joe-Max	23 Feb 1971	Tulsa	USA	Everton (Dec 1999)
Lewis, Eddie	17 May 1974	Cerritos	USA	Fulham (Mar 2000); Preston (Sep 2002)
McBride, Brian	19 Jun 1972	Arlington Heights	USA	Preston (Sep 2000); Everton (Jan 2003)
Olsen, Ben	3 May 1977	Harrisburg, PA	USA	Nottm For (Oct 2000)
Berhalter, Gregg	8 Jan 1973	Tenafly	USA	C Palace (Feb 2001)
Joy, Ian	14 Jul 1981	San Diego	USA	Kidderminster (Aug 2001)
Kirovski, Jovan	18 Mar 1976	Escondido	USA	C Palace (Aug 2001); Birmingham (Sep 2002)
Thorrington, John	17 Oct 1979	Palos Verdes	USA	Huddersfield (Aug 2001)
Reyna, Claudio	20 Jul 1973	New Jersey	USA	Sunderland (Dec 2001)
Myhill, Boaz	9 Nov 1982	California	Eng	Bradford (Nov 2002)
Sagere, Jake	5 Apr 1980	USA	USA	Grimsby (Apr 2003)
Other players qualified for USA but born outside USA				
Wegerle, Roy	19 Mar 1964	Johannesburg, SA	USA	Chelsea (Jun 1986); Swindon (Mar 1988); Luton (Jul 1988); QPR (Dec 1989); Blackburn (Mar 1992); Coventry (Mar 1993)
Kerr, John	6 Mar 1965	Toronto, Can	USA	Portsmouth (Aug 1987); Peterborough (Dec 1987); Millwall (Feb 1993); Walsall (Nov 1995)
Radosavljevic, Preki	24 Jun 1963	Belgrade, Yug	USA	Everton (Aug 1992); Portsmouth (1994-95)
Miglioranzi, Stefani	20 Sep 1977	Pocos de Caldas, Bra	USA	Portsmouth (1998-99); Swindon (Aug 2002)

SURNAME, NAME	DOB	PLACE OF BIRTH	NAT	CLUB(S) JOINED/FIRST PLAYED

USSR (7)

Five of these players also listed under Belarus

SURNAME, NAME	DOB	PLACE OF BIRTH	NAT	CLUB(S) JOINED/FIRST PLAYED
Baltacha, Sergei	17 Feb 1958	Kiev (then USSR)	USSR	Ipswich (Jan 1989)
Cherednik, Alexei	12 Dec 1960	Pamir (then USSR)	USSR	Southampton (Feb 1990)
Gotsmanov, Sergei	17 Mar 1959	Minsk (then USSR)	USSR/Blr	Brighton (Feb 1990); Southampton (Aug 1990)
Gurinovich, Igor	5 Mar 1960	Minsk (then USSR)	USSR/Blr	Brighton (Nov 1990)
Yanushevski, Victor	23 Jan 1960	Minsk (then USSR)	USSR/Blr	Aldershot (Mar 1991)
Kachouro, Petr	2 Aug 1972	Minsk (then USSR)	Blr	Sheff Utd (Jul 1996)
Shtaniuk, Sergei	11 Jan 1972	Minsk (then USSR)	Blr	Stoke (Jul 2001)

VENEZUELA (3)

SURNAME, NAME	DOB	PLACE OF BIRTH	NAT	CLUB(S) JOINED/FIRST PLAYED
De Ornelas, Fernando	29 Jul 1976	Caracas	Ven	C Palace (Sep 1999); QPR (Oct 2001)
Savarese, Giovanni	14 Jul 1971	Caracas	Ven	Swansea (Oct 2000); Millwall (Jul 2001)
Nacca, Franco	9 Nov 1982	Venezuela	Ven	Cambridge (Sep 2002)

YUGOSLAVIA (31+1)

Eight of these players also listed under Bosnia-Herzogovina

SURNAME, NAME	DOB	PLACE OF BIRTH	NAT	CLUB(S) JOINED/FIRST PLAYED
Golac, Ivan	15 Jun 1950	Kuprivnica	Yug	Southampton (Nov 1978); Bournemouth (Nov 1982); Man City (Mar 1983); Southampton (Mar 1984); Portsmouth (Jan 1985)
Jankovic, Bozo	22 May 1951	Sarajevo (Bos, then Yug)	Yug	Middlesbrough (Feb 1979)
Borota, Petar	5 Mar 1952	Belgrade	Yug	Chelsea (Mar 1979)
Avramovic, Raddy	29 Nov 1949	Rijeka	Yug	Notts Co (Aug 1979); Coventry (Sep 1983)
Stepanovic, Dragoslav	30 Aug 1948	Rekovac	Yug	Man City (Aug 1979)
Jovanovic, Nikola	18 Sep 1952	Cetinje	Yug	Man Utd (Jan 1980)
Katalinic, Ivan	17 May 1951	Yugoslavia	Yug	Southampton (Feb 1980)
Antic, Raddy	22 Nov 1949	Zitiste	Yug	Luton (Jul 1980)
Hadziabdic, Dzemal	25 Jul 1953	Yugoslavia	Yug	Swansea (Aug 1980)
Banovic, Yakka	12 Nov 1956	Bihac (Bos, then Yug)	Aus	Derby (Sep 1980)
Muzinic, Drazen	25 Jan 1953	Yugoslavia	Yug	Norwich (Sep 1980)
Mirocevic, Ante	6 Aug 1952	Titograd	Yug	Sheff Wed (Oct 1980)
Dusan, Nikolic	23 Jan 1953	Belgrade	Yug	Bolton (Oct 1980)
Rajkovic, Anto	17 Aug 1952	Sarajevo (Bos, then Yug)	Yug	Swansea (Mar 1981)
Petrovic, Vladimir	1 Jul 1955	Belgrade	Yug	Arsenal (Dec 1982)
Radosavljevic, Preki	24 Jun 1963	Belgrade	USA	Everton (Aug 1992); Portsmouth (Jul 1994)
Milosevic, Savo	2 Sep 1973	Bijeljina (Bos, then Yug)	Yug	A Villa (Jul 1995)
Curcic, Sasa	14 Feb 1972	Belgrade	Yug	Bolton (Oct 1995); A Villa (Aug 1996); C Palace (Mar 1998)
Stefanovic, Dejan	28 Oct 1974	Belgrade	Yug	Sheff Wed (Dec 1995)
Kovacevic, Darko	18 Nov 1973	Kovin	Yug	Sheff Wed (Dec 1995)
Bosancic, Jovo	7 Aug 1970	Novi Sad	Yug	Barnsley (Aug 1996)
Avdiu, Kemajl	22 Dec 1976	Kosovo	Swe	Bury (Aug 1998)
Petric, Gordan	30 Jul 1969	Belgrade	Yug	C Palace (Nov 1998)
Mavrak, Darko	19 Jan 1969	Mostar (Bos, then Yug)	Bos	Walsall (Jan 1999)
Konjic, Muhamed	14 May 1970	Tuzla (Bos, then Yug)	Bos	Coventry (Feb 1999)
Djordjic, Bojan	6 Feb 1982	Belgrade	Swe	Man Utd (Feb 1999); Sheff Wed (Dec 2001)
Milovaijevic, Goran	11 Apr 1967	Kraljevo	Yug	Chester (Sep 1999)
Stanic, Mario	10 Apr 1972	Sarajevo (Bos, then Yug)	Cro	Chelsea (Jul 2000)
Boksic, Alen	21 Jan 1970	Makarska (Herz, then Yug)	Cro	Middlesbrough (Aug 2000)
Jokanovic, Slavisa	16 Aug 1968	Novi Sad	Yug	Chelsea (Oct 2000)
Bunjevcevic, Goran	17 Feb 1973	Karlovac (Cro, then Yug)	Yug	Tottenham (Jun 2001)

Qualified for Yugoslavia but born outside Yugoslavia

SURNAME, NAME	DOB	PLACE OF BIRTH	NAT	CLUB(S) JOINED/FIRST PLAYED
Ilic, Sasa	18 Jul 1972	Melbourne, Aus	Yug	Charlton (Oct 1997); West Ham (Feb 2000); Portsmouth (Sep 2001)

ZAMBIA (9)

SURNAME, NAME	DOB	PLACE OF BIRTH	NAT	CLUB(S) JOINED/FIRST PLAYED
Mwila, Freddie	6 Jul 1946	Kasama	Zam	A Villa (Jun 1969)
Kapengwe, Emment	27 Mar 1943	Zambia	Zam	A Villa (Sep 1969)
Hesford, Iain	4 Mar 1960	Ndola	Eng	Blackpool (Aug 1977); Fulham (Jan 1985); Notts Co (Nov 1985); Sunderland (Aug 1986); Hull (Dec 1988); Maidstone United (Aug 1991)
Gregory, Neil	7 Oct 1972	Ndola	Brit	Chesterfield (Feb 1994); Scunthorpe (Aug 1994); Ipswich (Mar 1995); Torquay (Nov 1996); Peterborough (Nov 1997); Colchester (Jan 1998)
Rice, Gary	29 Sep 1975	Zambia	Brit	Exeter (Jul 1994)
Whitley, Jim	14 Apr 1975	Ndola	N Ire	Man City (Aug 1994); Blackpool (Aug 1999); Norwich (Aug 2000); Swindon (Dec 2000); Northampton (Feb 2001); Wrexham (Oct 2001)
Whitley, Jeff	28 Jan 1979	Ndola	N Ire	Man City (Feb 1996); Wrexham (Jan 1999); Notts Co (Mar 2002)
Earnshaw, Robert	6 Apr 1981	Zambia	Wal	Cardiff (Aug 1997)
Haarhoff, Jimmy	27 May 1981	Lusaka	Zam	Birmingham (Jun 1998)

ZIMBABWE (6+2)

SURNAME, NAME	DOB	PLACE OF BIRTH	NAT	CLUB(S) JOINED/FIRST PLAYED
Law, Cecil	10 Mar 1930	Salisbury	Brit	Derby (Aug 1951); Bury (May 1954)
Gibbs, Peter	24 Aug 1956	Chingola	Brit	Watford (Jul 1975)
Statham, Brian	21 May 1969	Harare	Eng	Tottenham (Aug 1987); Reading (Mar 1991); Bournemouth (Nov 1991); Brentford (Jan 1992); Gillingham (Aug 1997)
Robinson, John	29 Aug 1971	Bulawayo	Wal	Brighton (Apr 1989); Charlton (Sep 1992)

SURNAME, NAME	DOB	PLACE OF BIRTH	NAT	CLUB(S) JOINED/FIRST PLAYED
Ndlovu, Peter	25 Feb 1973	Bulawayo	Zim	Coventry (Aug 1991); Birmingham (Jul 1997); Huddersfield (Dec 2000); Sheff Utd (Feb 2001)
McKop, Henry	8 Jul 1967	Bulawayo	Zim	Bristol C (Feb 1994)

Other players qualified for Zimbabwe but born outside Zimbabwe

Kennon, Sandy	26 Nov 1933	Johannesburg, SA	Zim	Huddersfield (Aug 1956); Norwich (Feb 1959); Colchester (Mar 1965)
Grobbelaar, Bruce	6 Oct 1957	Durban, SA	Zim	Crewe (Dec 1979); Liverpool (Mar 1981); Stoke (Mar 1993); Southampton (Aug 1994); Plymouth (Aug 1996); Oldham (Dec 1997); Bury (Sep 1998); Lincoln (Dec 1998)

APPENDIX TWO:
Foreign players in England since 1888
Club by Club

Overseas-born players in English League history, club-by-club, in chronological order of arrival

Key:
LgAp = league starts + substitute appearances. LgG = league goals. OthAp = all other competitive appearances, including FA Cup, League Cup, play-off matches and European club games. OthG = all other goals. Born = country of birth (nationality, where it differs, in brackets after surname). Pos = playing position (gk = goalkeeper; fb = full-back; ch = centre-half; d = defender; wh = wing-half; w = winger; m = midfielder; f = forward). From = the month of signing or month of first appearance. (1) (2) (3) Number in brackets next to a player's name denotes separate playing spells at the club.

SURNAME	NAME	BORN	POS	FROM	LgAp	LgG	OthAp	OthG
ACCRINGTON (1)								
Bowman	Walter	Can	wh	Aug 1891	5	3	0	0
ACCRINGTON STANLEY (2)								
Priday	Bob	SA	w	Dec 1952	5	0	0	0
Kirk	John	Can	f	Mar 1953	14	1	0	0
ALDERSHOT (14)								
Bunch	Arthur	SA	f	Jun 1934	16	3	4	2
Court (Brit)	Dick	Ind	f	Jun 1937	10	1	3	3
Bluck (Brit)	Dave	Ind	wh	Aug 1951	1	0	0	0
Kirsten	Ken	SA	fb	Aug 1951	5	0	0	0
Huggins (Brit)	Joe	Ind	f	Dec 1955	6	5	0	0
Porteous (Brit)	Jack	Ind	f	Feb 1956	1	0	0	0
Devereux (Brit)	Tony	Gib	fb	Nov 1958	132	0	14	0
Hodge	Eric	SA	ch	Jul 1959	17	0	1	0
Burgess	Mike	Can	f/ch	Nov 1965	6	0	1	0
Fadida	Aharon	Isr	f	Dec 1985	9+5	6	1	0
Stein (Eng)	Mark	SA	f	Jan 1986	2	1	0	0
Yanushevski	Victor	USSR	d	Mar 1991	6	1	0	0
Granville	John	Trin	gk	Aug 1991	30	0	3	0
Berry (Wal)	George	Ger	d	Nov 1991	25	1	1	0
ARSENAL (56)								
Butler (Eng)	Jack	SL	ch	Jan 1914	267	7	29	1
Tricker (Brit)	Reg	Ind	f	Mar 1927	12	5	0	0
Preedy (Brit)	Charlie	Ind	gk	May 1929	37	0	2	0
Keizer	Gerry	Neth	gk	Aug 1930	12	0	0	0
Gudmundsson	Albert	Ice	f	Sep 1946	2	0	0	0
Le Roux	Daniel	SA	w	Feb 1957	5	0	0	0
Batson (Eng)	Brendan	Grn	fb	Jun 1971	6+4	0	0	0
Kosmina	John	Aus	f	Mar 1978	0+1	0	1+2	0
Petrovic	Vladimir	Yug	m	Dec 1982	10+3	2	9	1
Jonsson	Siggi	Ice	m	Jul 1989	2+6	1	1+1	0
Limpar	Anders	Swe	w	Aug 1990	76+20	17	19	3
Lydersen (Nor)	Pal	Den	fb	Nov 1991	12+3	0	1	0
Jensen	John	Den	m	Aug 1992	93+5	1	35+3	0
Schwarz	Stefan	Swe	m	May 1994	34	2	13	2
Helder	Glenn	Neth	f	Feb 1995	27+12	1	6+4	0
Bergkamp	Dennis	Neth	f	Jul 1995	204+30	73	69+11	31
Garde	Remi	Fr	m	Aug 1996	19+12	0	8+4	0
Vieira (Fr)	Patrick	Sen	m	Aug 1996	211+7	20	95+2	4
Anelka	Nicolas	Fr	f	Mar 1997	50+15	23	22+2	4
Manninger	Alex	Aut	gk	Jun 1997	38+1	0	24	0

401

SURNAME	NAME	BORN	POS	FROM	LgAp	LgG	OthAp	OthG
Boa Morte	Luis	Por	f	Jun 1997	6+19	0	7+5	4
Grimandi	Gilles	Fr	d	Jun 1997	85+29	4	42+12	2
Petit	Emmanuel	Fr	m	Jun 1997	82+3	9	30+1	2
Muntasser	Jehad	Lby	m	Jun 1997	0	0	0+1	0
Overmars	Marc	Neth	w	Jul 1997	91+9	25	35+6	15
Mendez (Sp)	Alberto	Ger	m	Jul 1997	1+3	0	5+2	2
Wreh	Christopher	Lbr	f	Aug 1997	10+18	3	8+9	1
Grondin	David	Fr	d	Jul 1998	1	0	3	0
Vivas	Nelson	Arg	d	Aug 1998	14+26	0	15+14	1
Ljungberg	Freddie	Swe	m	Sep 1998	100+17	31	54+11	13
Caballero	Fabian	Arg	f	Oct 1998	0+1	0	0+2	0
Diawara	Kaba	Fr	f	Jan 1999	2+10	0	1+2	0
Kanu	Nwankwo	Nig	f	Feb 1999	60+49	29	34+30	11
Luzhny	Oleg	Ukr	d	Jul 1999	58+17	0	33+1	0
Malz	Stefan	Ger	m	Jul 1999	2+4	1	4+4	1
Silvinho	Silvio	Bra	fb	Jul 1999	46+9	3	19+5	2
Henry	Thierry	Fr	f	Aug 1999	121+15	82	58+10	30
Suker	Davor	Cro	f	Aug 1999	8+14	8	7+10	3
Volz	Moritz	Ger	d	Jan 2000	0	0	1+1	0
Aliadiere	Jeremie	Fr	f	Mar 2000	0+4	1	0+2	0
Lauren		Cam	m	Jun 2000	68+4	5	39+6	3
Pires	Robert	Fr	m	Jul 2000	77+10	27	46+5	10
Svard	Sebastian	Den	d	Aug 2000	0	0	2+1	0
Wiltord	Sylvain	Fr	f	Aug 2000	70+24	28	39+21	17
Stepanovs	Igors	Lat	d	Sep 2000	17	0	12+2	1
Danilevicius (Lith)	Tomas	Rus	f	Dec 2000	0+2	0	0+1	0
Edu		Bra	m	Jan 2001	22+15	3	15+8	3
Van Bronckhorst	Giovanni	Neth	m	Jun 2001	22+19	2	17+5	0
Inamoto	Junichi	Jap	m	Jul 2001	0	0	2+2	0
Duarte	Juan Maldondo	Bra	d	Aug 2001	0	0	2	0
Itonga	Carlin	DRC	f	Aug 2001	0	0	0+1	0
Tavlaridis	Stathis	Grk	d	Sep 2001	0+1	0	4	0
Silva	Gilberto	Bra	m	Aug 2002	32+3	0	12+3	2
Toure	Kolo	IvCo	d	Aug 2002	9+17	2	7+6	0
Cygan	Pascal	Fr	d	Sep 2002	16+2	1	11+2	0
Shaaban	Rami	Swe	gk	Nov 2002	3	0	2	0

ASTON VILLA (46)

SURNAME	NAME	BORN	POS	FROM	LgAp	LgG	OthAp	OthG
Hunter (Brit)	George	Ind	wh	Feb 1908	91	1	6	0
Chandler (Brit)	Robert	Ind	gk	Aug 1913	1	0	0	0
Hodgson (Eng)	Gordon	SA	f	Jan 1936	28	11	0	0
Keelan (Brit)	Kevin	Ind	gk	Jul 1958	5	0	0	0
Mwila	Freddie	Zam	f	Jun 1969	1	0	0	0
Kapengwe	Emment	Zam	f	Sep 1969	3	0	0	0
Young (Brit)	Charlie	Cyp	d	Nov 1975	9+1	0	1	0
Blake (Brit)	Noel	Jam	d	Aug 1979	4	0	0	0
Dorigo (Eng)	Tony	Aus	fb	Jul 1983	106+5	1	21+1	0
Six	Didier	Fr	w	Oct 1984	13+3	2	1+1	0
Cooper (Sco)	Neale	Ind	m	Jul 1986	19+1	0	2	1
Callaghan (Eng)	Nigel	Sing	w	Feb 1989	24+2	1	3+2	0
Nielsen	Kent	Den	d	Jun 1989	74+5	4	16+1	1
Yorke	Dwight	Trin	f	Dec 1989	195+36	73	51+4	24
Regis (Eng)	Cyrille	FrGu	f	Jul 1991	46+6	12	8+3	0
Kubicki	Dariusz	Pol	fb	Aug 1991	24+1	0	7+1	0
Beinlich	Stefan	Ger	m	Oct 1991	7+9	1	0	0
Breitkreutz	Matthias	Ger	m	Oct 1991	10+3	0	0+1	0
Bosnich	Mark	Aus	gk	Feb 1992	179	0	48+1	0
Lamptey	Nii	Gha	m	Aug 1994	1+5	0	2+1	3
Milosevic	Savo	Yug	f	Jul 1995	84+6	28	26+1	5
Nelson	Fernando	Por	d	Jun 1996	54+5	0	11+4	0
Curcic	Sasa	Yug	m	Aug 1996	20+9	3	3+2	1
Fabio	Ferraresi	It	m	Jun 1998	0	0	0+1	0
Enckelman	Peter	Fin	gk	Feb 1999	51+1	0	14+1	0
Samuel (Brit)	J Lloyd	Trin	d	Feb 1999	56+17	0	12+3	0
Boateng (Neth)	George	Gha	m	Jul 1999	96+7	4	31+1	1
Ghrayib	Naguyan	Isr	d	Aug 1999	1+4	0	1	0
Carbone	Benito	It	f	Oct 1999	22+2	3	6	5
Nilis	Luc	Bel	f	Jul 2000	3	1	2	1
Ozalan	Alpay	Tur	d	Jul 2000	52	0	13	0
Ginola	David	Fr	w	Aug 2000	14+18	3	5+4	2
Hitzlsperger	Thomas	Ger	m	Aug 2000	0+1	0	0	0
De Bilde	Gilles	Bel	f	Oct 2000	4	0	0	0
Angel	Juan Pablo	Col	f	Jan 2001	41+12	14	6+5	6
Kachloul	Hassan	Mor	m	Jun 2001	17+5	2	8+2	0
Hadji	Mustapha	Mor	m	Jul 2001	24+10	2	7+6	1
Schmeichel	Peter	Den	gk	Jul 2001	29	1	7	0
Mellberg	Olof	Swe	d	Jul 2001	70+1	0	10	0
Balaban	Bosko	Cro	f	Aug 2001	0+8	0	2+1	0
Allback	Marcus	Swe	f	Jul 2002	9+11	5	3+2	1
Postma	Stefan	Neth	gk	Jul 2002	5+1	0	3	0
De La Cruz	Ulises	Ecu	d/m	Aug 2002	12+8	1	3+1	1

SURNAME	NAME	BORN	POS	FROM	LgAp	LgG	OthAp	OthG
Johnsen	Ronny	Nor	d	Sep 2002	25+1	0	3	0
Leonhardsen	Oyvind	Nor	m	Sep 2002	13+6	3	3+1	0
Gudjonsson	Joey	Ice	m	Jan 2003	9+2	2	0	0

BARNET (9)

SURNAME	NAME	BORN	POS	FROM	LgAp	LgG	OthAp	OthG
Stein (Brit)	Edwin	SA	m	Jul 1982	0+1	0	0	0
Stein (Eng)	Brian	SA	f	Aug 1992	17+23	8	2	0
Carmichael (Brit)	Matt	Sing	f	Sep 1994	2+1	0	0	0
Taylor (N Ire)	Maik	Ger	gk	Jun 1995	70	0	12	0
Goodhind	Warren	SA	d	Jul 1996	73+20	3	9+2	1
Constantinou	Costas	Cyp	d	Oct 1996	1	0	0	0
Arber (Brit)	Mark	SA	d	Sep 1998	123+2	15	9	1
Bossu	Bert	Fr	gk	Oct 1999	0	0	0+1	0
Omoyimni	Manny	Nig	f	Feb 2000	1+5	0	0	0

BARNSLEY (30)

SURNAME	NAME	BORN	POS	FROM	LgAp	LgG	OthAp	OthG
Robledo	George	Chi	f	Apr 1943	105	45	9	2
Robledo	Ted	Chi	wh	Mar 1946	5	0	0	0
Kelly (N Ire)	Pat	SA	gk	Oct 1946	144	0	3	0
Mokone	Steve	SA	w	Aug 1961	0	0	1	0
Cunningham (Brit)	Tony	Jam	f	Sep 1982	40+2	11	3	0
Jonsson	Siggi	Ice	m	Jan 1986	5	0	0	0
Molby	Jan	Den	m	Sep 1995	5	0	0	0
De Zeeuw	Arjan	Neth	d	Nov 1995	138	7	26	0
Ten Heuvel	Laurens	Neth	f	Mar 1996	1+7	0	0+1	0
Van der Velden	Carel	Neth	m	Mar 1996	7+2	0	1	0
Bosancic	Jovo	Yug	m	Aug 1996	30+12	3	8+2	0
Marcelle	Clint	Trin	f	Aug 1996	37+32	8	9+6	1
Hristov	Georgi	Mac	f	Jul 1997	18+26	8	4+7	3
Krizan	Ales	Slo	d	Jul 1997	13	0	6	0
Tinkler	Eric	SA	m	Jul 1997	78+21	9	18+1	1
Leese	Lars	Ger	gk	Jul 1997	16+1	0	4	0
Barnard (Wal)	Darren	Ger	m	Aug 1997	151+19	28	28+3	8
Markstedt	Peter	Swe	f	Nov 1997	8+1	0	1+1	0
Mori Cuesta	Francisco	Sp	m	Mar 1999	2	0	0	0
Fjortoft	Jan Aage	Nor	f	Jan 1998	21+13	9	5+1	4
Van der Laan	Robin	Neth	m	Jul 1998	52+15	5	11+2	4
Fallon	Rory	NZ	f	Mar 1999	21+15	7	2+1	0
Bengtsson	Robert	Swe	d	Nov 1999	0	0	2	0
Corbo	Mateo	Uru	d	Aug 2000	10+8	0	2+1	1
Bertos (Grk)	Leo	NZ	f	Sep 2000	4+8	1	0+1	0
Gorre (Neth)	Dean	Sur	m	Jul 2001	32+14	2	2	0
Salli	Janne	Fin	d	Nov 2000	6+1	0	1	0
Sand	Peter	Den	m	Oct 2001	4+2	1	1+1	0
Christie	Jeremy	NZ	m	Dec 2001	0+1	0	0+1	0
Betsy	Kevin	Sey	m	Mar 2002	42+6	6	2	0

BARROW (2)

SURNAME	NAME	BORN	POS	FROM	LgAp	LgG	OthAp	OthG
Peed (Brit)	Frank	Arg	f	Nov 1933	38	15	0	0
Purdon	Ted	SA	f	Mar 1958	37	12	0	0

BIRMINGHAM CITY (42)

SURNAME	NAME	BORN	POS	FROM	LgAp	LgG	OthAp	OthG
Mills (Brit)	Paddy	Ind	f	Feb 1929	13	3	0	0
Mitchell	Frank	Aus	wh	Sep 1943	93	6	13	2
Havenga	Willie	SA	f	Jul 1948	1	0	0	0
Atkins (Brit)	Arthur	Jap	ch	Nov 1948	97	0	8	0
Purdon	Ted	SA	f	Aug 1950	64	27	6	3
Kloner (Pol)	Hymie	SA	wh	Nov 1950	1	0	0	0
Houghton (Brit)	Bud	Ind	f	Oct 1957	4	1	0	0
Van Den Hauwe (Wal)	Pat	Bel	fb	Aug 1978	119+4	1	17	0
Tarantini	Alberto	Arg	d	Oct 1978	23	1	1	0
Brocken	Bud	Neth	m	Aug 1981	17	0	2	0
Van Mierlo	Toine	Neth	w	Aug 1981	44	4	3	0
Blake (Brit)	Noel	Jam	d	Sep 1982	76	5	20	0
Richards (Eng)	Carl	Jam	f	Oct 1988	18+1	2	0	0
Okenla	Foley	Nig	m	Aug 1991	2+5	1	1+3	0
Paskin	John	SA	f	Nov 1991	8+2	3	0+1	0
Peschisolido (1)	Paul	Can	f	Nov 1992	37+6	16	2+1	1
Hooper (Can)	Lyndon	Guy	m	Sep 1993	1+4	0	1	0
Dominguez	Jose	Por	w	Mar 1994	15+20	3	3+3	0
Rushfeldt	Siggi	Nor	f	Oct 1995	3+4	0	1	1
Griemink	Bart	Neth	gk	Nov 1995	20	0	4	0
Sahlin	Dan	Swe	f	Nov 1995	0+1	0	0	0
Peschisolido (2)	Paul	Can	f	Mar 1996	7+2	1	0	0
Limpar	Anders	Swe	w	Jan 1997	3+1	0	1	0
Hey	Tony	Ger	m	Jun 1997	8+1	0	2	1
Ndlovu	Peter	Zim	f	Jul 1997	78+29	22	22+5	5
Adebola	Dele	Nig	f	Feb 1998	86+43	31	16+7	11
Haarhoff	Jimmy	Zam	f	Jun 1998	0+1	0	0	0
Luntala	Tresor	Fr	d/m	Jul 1999	9+6	0	1	0
Lazaridis	Stan	Aus	w	Jul 1999	91+33	6	14+9	0
Wreh	Christopher	Lbr	f	Oct 1999	6+1	1	0	0

SURNAME	NAME	BORN	POS	FROM	LgAp	LgG	OthAp	OthG
Marcelo		Bra	f	Oct 1999	47+30	24	6+9	2
Myhre	Thomas	Nor	gk	Mar 2000	7	0	2	0
Vaesen	Nico	Bel	gk	Jun 2001	49+1	0	6	0
Ferrari	Carlos	Bra	f	Aug 2001	0+4	0	0	0
Bragstad	Bjorn Otto	Nor	d	Sep 2001	3	0	0	0
Bak	Arkadiusz	Pol	m	Dec 2001	2+2	0	1	0
John	Stern	Tri	f	Feb 2002	35+10	12	4+1	5
Tebily	Olivier	IvCo	d	Mar 2002	19	0	4	0
Cisse	Aliou	Sen	m	Aug 2002	21	0	0	0
Kirovski	Jovan	USA	f	Sep 2002	5+12	2	2+1	0
Coly	Ferdinand	Sen	d	Jan 2003	1	0	1	0
Dugarry	Christophe	Fr	f	Jan 2003	16	5	0	0
Swierczewski	Piotr	Pol	m	Feb 2003	0+1	0	0	0

BLACKBURN ROVERS (40)

SURNAME	NAME	BORN	POS	FROM	LgAp	LgG	OthAp	OthG
Bell (Sco)	Alec	SA	wh	Jul 1913	11	0	1	0
Priday	Bob	SA	w	Mar 1949	44	11	1	0
Roberts	John	Aus	gk	Apr 1966	3	0	0	0
Arentoft	Ben	Den	m	Sep 1971	94	3	14	0
Ardiles	Ossie	Arg	m	Mar 1988	5	0	1+1	0
Wegerle (USA)	Roy	SA	f	Mar 1992	20+14	6	7+4	6
Andersson	Patrik	Swe	d	Dec 1992	7+5	5	3	1
Berg (1)	Henning	Nor	d	Jan 1993	154+5	4	34	0
Witschge	Richard	Neth	m	Mar 1995	1	0	0	0
Bohinen	Lars	Nor	m	Oct 1995	40+18	7	5+3	2
Gudmundsson	Niklas	Swe	f	Dec 1995	1+5	0	0	0
Donis	George	Grk	m	Jul 1996	11+11	2	2+1	0
Pedersen	Per	Den	f	Feb 1997	6+5	1	1+1	0
Andersson	Anders	Swe	m	Jun 1997	1+3	0	3+1	1
Valery	Patrick	Fr	d	Jun 1997	14+1	0	3+1	0
Filan	John	Aus	gk	Jul 1997	61+1	0	11	0
Henchoz	Stephane	Swit	d	Jul 1997	70	0	11+1	0
Dahlin	Martin	Swe	f	Jul 1997	13+13	4	2+2	2
Pedersen	Tore	Nor	d	Sep 1997	3+2	0	3	0
Perez	Sebastien	Fr	m	Jul 1998	4+1	1	3	1
Marcolin	Dario	It	m	Oct 1998	5+5	1	5	0
Konde	Oumar	Swit	d/m	Nov 1998	0	0	0+1	0
O'Brien (Brit)	Burton	SA	f	Feb 1999	0	0	0+1	0
Ostenstad	Egil	Nor	f	Aug 1999	38+24	12	10+9	2
Frandsen	Per	Den	m	Sep 1999	26+5	5	4	1
Bjornebye	Stig Inge	Nor	d	Jun 2000	53+3	1	11+1	0
Diawara	Kaba	Fr	f	Aug 2000	1+4	0	1	1
Berg (2)	Henning	Nor	d	Sep 2000	90+1	3	10+1	0
Friedel	Brad	USA	gk	Nov 2000	100	0	25	0
Keller	Marc	Fr	m	Jan 2001	0+2	0	0+3	0
Berkovic	Eyal	Isr	m	Feb 2001	4+7	2	3	0
Grabbi	Corrado	It	f	Jun 2001	11+14	2	4+5	3
Tugay	Kerimoglu	Tur	m	Jul 2001	64+6	4	18+3	0
Neill	Lucas	Aus	d/m	Sep 2001	65	1	15	0
Johansson	Nils-Eric	Swe	d	Oct 2001	34+16	0	15+2	2
Yordi		Sp	f	Feb 2002	5+3	2	0+1	0
Hakan Unsal		Tur	m	Mar 2002	7+1	0	0	0
Pelzer	Marc	Ger	d	Jun 2002	0	0	1	0
Hakan Sukur		Tur	f	Dec 2002	7+2	2	0	0
Yorke	Dwight	Trin	f	Jul 2002	25+8	8	10	5
Gresko	Vratislav	Svk	m	Jan 2003	10	0	0	0

BLACKPOOL (22)

SURNAME	NAME	BORN	POS	FROM	LgAp	LgG	OthAp	OthG
Wilcox (Brit)	Tom	At sea	gk	May 1906	37	0	1	0
Falconer	Andy	SA	f	Sep 1949	4	0	0	0
Perry	Bill	SA	w	Nov 1949	397	119	42	10
Harris (Brit)	Alex	HK	w	Nov 1951	15	4	0	0
Hauser	Peter	SA	wh	Nov 1955	83	10	14	1
Peterson	Brian	SA	f	Oct 1956	101	16	8	1
Smethurst	Peter	SA	f	Feb 1960	1	0	0	0
Cheung	Chi Doy	HK	f	Oct 1960	2	1	0	0
Horne	Des	SA	w	Mar 1961	117+1	17	19	4
Kemp (Brit)	Fred	It	m	Nov 1970	19+2	1	3	0
Hesford (Eng)	Iain	Zam	gk	Aug 1977	202	0	28	0
Rush	Jon	NZ	gk	Nov 1979	11	0	0	0
Methven (Brit)	Colin	Ind	d	Jul 1986	166+7	11	26+1	2
Walwyn (Brit)	Keith	Jam	f	Jun 1987	51+18	16	10+2	1
Cunningham (Brit)	Tony	Jam	f	Jul 1987	71	17	13	5
Richards (Eng)	Carl	Jam	f	Jan 1990	32+9	8	2+2	0
Leitch	Grant	SA	f	Aug 1990	13+12	1	1+1	0
Kerr (Brit)	Dylan	Mal	d	Dec 1991	12	1	0	0
Kearton	Jason	Aus	gk	Jan 1992	14	0	0	0
Whitley (N Ire)	Jim	Zam	m	Aug 1999	7+1	0	1	0
Shittu	Danny	Nig	m	Feb 2001	15+2	2	2	0
Theoklitos	Michael	Aus	gk	Nov 2002	2	0	1	0

SURNAME	NAME	BORN	POS	FROM	LgAp	LgG	OthAp	OthG
BOLTON WANDERERS (47)								
Waller	Wilfred	SA	gk	Mar 1900	6	0	0	0
Grieves	Ken	Aus	gk	Dec 1951	49	0	1	0
Nowak	Tadeusz	Pol	w	Mar 1979	22+2	1	1+2	0
Dusan	Nikolic	Yug	w	Oct 1980	22	2	3	0
Stevens (Brit)	Ian	Mal	f	Mar 1987	26+21	7	5+3	2
Cunningham (Brit)	Tony	Jam	f	Mar 1991	9	4	3	0
Paatelainen	Mixu	Fin	f	Jul 1994	58+11	15	12+2	3
Sneekes	Richard	Neth	m	Aug 1994	51+4	7	13+1	4
De Freitas (Neth)	Fabian	Sur	f	Aug 1994	24+16	7	3+6	2
Bergsson	Gudni	Ice	d	Mar 1995	263+7	23	43+4	4
Curcic	Sasa	Yug	m	Oct 1995	28	4	5	3
Frandsen (1)	Per	Den	m	Aug 1996	129+1	17	22+2	5
Johansen	Michael	Den	m	Aug 1996	112+25	16	28+5	5
Gunnlaugsson	Arnie	Ice	m	Aug 1997	24+18	13	7+4	2
Fish	Mark	SA	d	Sep 1997	102+1	3	23+1	1
Jaaskelainen	Jussi	Fin	gk	Nov 1997	166+1	0	17	0
Giallanza	Gaetano	Swit	f	Mar 1998	0+3	0	0	0
Salako (Eng)	John	Nig	m	Mar 1998	0+7	0	0	0
Jensen	Claus	Den	d	Jul 1998	85+1	8	23	2
Gudjohnsen	Eidur	Ice	f	Aug 1998	48+7	18	16+2	8
Gardner	Ricardo	Jam	m	Aug 1998	132+22	15	23+5	4
Hansen	Bo	Den	m	Feb 1999	64+32	15	14+9	2
Passi	Franck	Fr	m	Nov 1999	21+17	0	9+2	0
Kaprielian	Mickael	Fr	m	Jan 2000	0+1	0	0	0
Frandsen (2)	Per	Den	m	Jul 2000	94+8	12	6+4	1
Morini	Emanuele	It	m	Sep 2000	1+1	0	1	0
Gope-Fenepej (Fr)	John	NCal	d	Sep 2000	0+2	0	0	0
Fredgaard	Carsten	Den	m	Nov 2000	1+4	0	0	0
Sommer	Jurgen	USA	gk	Feb 2001	0	0	1	0
Diawara	Djibril	Sen	d	Jun 2001	4+5	0	2	0
Nishizawa	Akinori	Jap	f	Jul 2001	0	0	3	1
Pedersen	Henrik	Den	f	Jul 2001	36+8	7	3+2	2
Johnson	Jermaine	Jam	m	Sep 2001	4+8	0	4+1	0
N'Gotty	Bruno	Fr	d	Sep 2001	47+2	2	3+1	0
Viander	Jani	Fin	gk	Nov 2001	0	0	1	0
Bobic (Ger)	Fredi	Slo	f	Jan 2002	14+2	4	0	0
Tofting	Stig	Den	m	Feb 2002	8+6	0	3	0
Djorkaeff	Youri	Fr	f	Feb 2002	48	11	1	0
Espartero	Mario	Fr	m	Feb 2002	0+3	0	0	0
Konstantinidis (Grk)	Kostas	Ger	m	Mar 2002	3	0	0	0
Mendy	Bernard	Fr	d	Aug 2002	20+1	0	2	0
Okocha	Jay-Jay	Nig	m	Aug 2002	26+5	7	0+1	0
Campo	Ivan	Sp	d	Sep 2002	28+3	2	3	0
Bulent (Tur)	Akin	Bel	m	Oct 2002	0+1	0	2	0
Andre	Pierre-Yves	Fr	f	Feb 2003	0+9	0	0	0
Ballesta	Salva	Sp	f	Feb 2003	1+5	0	0	0
Laville	Florent	Fr	d	Feb 2003	10	0	0	0
BOURNEMOUTH (27)								
Peed (Brit)	Frank	Arg	f	Jun 1930	2	0	0	0
Bellis (Brit)	George	Ind	ch	Jul 1935	56	0	4	0
Milligan (N Ire)	Dudley	SA	f	Aug 1947	45	25	3	2
Stiffle (Brit)	Nelson	Ind	w	May 1955	36	7	6	1
Woollard	Arnold	Ber	fb	Jun 1956	157	0	15	0
Burgess	Mike	Can	f/ch	Jun 1957	104	34	9	2
Chadwick (Brit)	Dave	Ind	w	Feb 1972	29+7	4	1	0
Golac	Ivan	Yug	fb	Nov 1982	9	0	1	0
Richards (Eng)	Carl	Jam	f	Jul 1986	57+14	16	9+3	2
Goulet	Brent	USA	f	Nov 1987	1+2	0	0	0
Blissett (Eng)	Luther	Jam	f	Nov 1988	121	56	18	4
Statham (Eng)	Brian	Zim	d/m	Nov 1991	2	0	0	0
Adekola	David	Nig	f	Sep 1994	0	0	0+1	0
Santos	Ali	USA	f	Aug 1995	0+3	0	0	0
Omoyimni	Manny	Nig	f	Sep 1996	5+2	0	0	0
Rolling	Franck	Fr	d	Aug 1997	26+4	4	2+2	1
Stein (Eng)	Mark	SA	f	Jun 1998	90	30	17	9
Berthe (Fr)	Mohamed	Gui	m	Jul 1998	12+3	2	5	0
Boli (Fr)	Roger	IvCo	f	Oct 1998	5+1	0	0+3	0
Rodrigues	Dani	Por	f	Oct 1998	0+5	0	0	0
Huck	Willie	Fr	m	Mar 1999	11+29	0	0+6	1
Jorgensen	Claus	Den	m	Jul 1999	77+10	14	12	1
Betsy	Kevin	Sey	m	Sep 1999	1+4	0	0	0
Menetrier	Mickael	Fr	gk	Aug 2000	12+1	0	2	0
Foyewa	Amos	Nig	f	Jul 2001	1+8	0	0+3	0
Kandol (Brit)	Tresor	DRC	f	Oct 2001	3+9	0	0+2	0
McDonald	Scott	Aus	f	Mar 2003	3+4	1	0+1	0
BRADFORD CITY (34)								
Bookman (Brit)	Louis	Lith	w	Jul 1911	32	2	2	0
Thorpe (Brit)	Arthur	Ind	w	Jul 1963	81	17	9	0

SURNAME	NAME	BORN	POS	FROM	LgAp	LgG	OthAp	OthG
Roberts	John	Aus	gk	Aug 1968	44	0	4	0
Podd	Ces	StK	fb	Aug 1970	494+8	3	63+1	1
Cooke (1)	Joe	Dom	d/f	May 1972	184+20	62	25+1	9
Cooke (2)	Joe	Dom	d/f	Jan 1982	61+1	6	10	2
Blake (Brit)	Noel	Jam	d	Jul 1992	44+1	3	7+1	1
Petterson	Andy	Aus	gk	Dec 1994	3	0	0	0
Verveer (Neth)	Etienne	Sur	m	Feb 1995	9	1	0	0
Regtop	Erik	Neth	f	Jul 1996	5+3	1	2	0
Sas	Marco	Neth	d	Jul 1996	31	3	3	0
Pehrsson	Magnus	Swe	m	Oct 1996	1	0	0	0
Pinto	Sergio	Por	m	Oct 1996	7+11	0	1+1	0
Schwarzer	Mark	Aus	gk	Nov 1996	13	0	3	0
Sundgot	Ole	Nor	f	Nov 1996	11+14	6	0+1	0
Vanhala	Jari	Fin	f	Dec 1996	0+1	0	0	0
Edinho	Amaral	Bra	f	Feb 1997	50+9	15	3+1	1
Oliveira	Raul	Por	d	Mar 1997	2	0	0	0
Kulcsar (Aus)	George	Hun	d	Mar 1997	23+3	1	0	0
Sepp	Dennis	Neth	f	Jun 1997	0+3	0	0	0
Steiner	Rob	Swe	f	Jul 1997	40+12	14	5	2
Zabica	Robert	Aus	gk	Aug 1997	3	0	1	0
Halle	Gunnar	Nor	d	Jun 1999	78+5	1	9+1	1
Rodriguez	Bruno	Fr	f	Sep 1999	0+2	0	1+2	0
Cadete (Por)	Jorge	Moz	f	Feb 2000	2+5	0	0	0
Carbone	Benito	It	f	Aug 2000	39+3	10	3+1	2
Petrescu	Dan	Rom	m	Aug 2000	16+1	1	2+1	0
Hardy	Adam	SA	m	Sep 2000	0	0	0+1	0
Molenaar	Robert	Neth	d	Dec 2000	70+1	1	5+1	0
Jorgensen	Claus	Den	m	Jul 2001	41+9	12	3+1	0
Juanjo	Carricondo	Sp	f	Oct 2001	7+19	1	2+1	0
Uhlenbeek (Neth)	Gus	Sur	d	Aug 2002	42	1	2	0
Reid	Paul	Aus	m	Sep 2002	7+1	2	0	0
Myhill (Eng)	Boaz	USA	gk	Nov 2002	2	0	0	0
Ten Heuvel	Laurens	Neth	f	Mar 2003	4+1	0	0	0

BRADFORD PARK AVENUE (3)

SURNAME	NAME	BORN	POS	FROM	LgAp	LgG	OthAp	OthG
Quantrill (Eng)	Alf	Ind	w	Sep 1924	191	58	11	1
Houghton (Brit)	Bud	Ind	f	Oct 1955	28	7	3	3
Malan	Norman	SA	gk	Jul 1956	24	0	2	0

BRENTFORD (20)

SURNAME	NAME	BORN	POS	FROM	LgAp	LgG	OthAp	OthG
Price (Brit)	Johnny	Ind	f	Apr 1928	1	1	0	0
Gallego	Jose	Sp	w	Jan 1947	6	0	0	0
Baker (Brit)	Gerry	USA	f	Oct 1969	8	2	0	0
Sweetzer (1)	Gordon	Can	f	Jul 1975	68+4	40	7	4
Salman (Eng)	Danis	Cyp	d	Aug 1977	316+9	8	34+2	0
Eames (Brit)	Billy	Mal	f	Aug 1978	2	1	0	0
Sweetzer (2)	Gordon	Can	f	Jan 1982	8+1	1	0	0
Buttigieg	John	Mal	d	Nov 1988	24+16	0	3+2	0
Statham (Eng)	Brian	Zim	d/m	Jan 1992	148+18	1	23	0
Kruszynski	Detsi	Ger	m	Aug 1992	13+1	0	1	0
Coyne	Chris	Aus	d	Aug 1998	7	0	1	0
Hebel	Dirk	Ger	m	Aug 1998	6+9	0	2+1	0
Hreidarsson	Hermann	Ice	d	Sep 1998	41	6	4	1
Ingimarsson	Ivar	Ice	m	Nov 1999	109+4	10	12	0
Einarsson	Gunnar	Ice	d	Jan 2000	1+2	0	0	0
Pinamonte	Lorenzo	It	f	Feb 2000	8+15	2	1+1	1
Gottskalksson	Ole	Ice	gk	Jul 2000	73	0	9	0
Javary	Jean-Phillipe	Fr	m	Aug 2000	4+2	0	2	0
Caceres (Aus)	Adrian	Arg	m	Sep 2001	5	0	0	0
Sonko	Ibrahima	Sen	d	Aug 2002	37	5	6	0
Antoine-Curier	Mickael	Fr	f	Mar 2003	11	3	0	0

BRIGHTON & HOVE ALBION (28)

SURNAME	NAME	BORN	POS	FROM	LgAp	LgG	OthAp	OthG
Moorhead (Ire)	George	NZ	ch	Aug 1922	1	0	0	0
Dugnolle (Brit)(1)	Jack	Ind	ch	Oct 1934	7	0	0	0
Dugnolle (Brit)(2)	Jack	Ind	ch	Aug 1946	59	0	6	0
Lancelotte (Brit)	Eric	Ind	f	Feb 1948	60	14	1	0
Foreman	Denis	SA	w	Mar 1952	211	63	8	6
Hodge	Eric	SA	ch	Oct 1956	4	0	0	0
Smit(h)	Wilf	Ger	fb	Oct 1974	5	0	0	0
Geard	Glen	Mal	m	Feb 1978	0	0	1	0
Gariani	Moshe	Isr	m	Jun 1980	0+1	0	0	0
Cohen	Jacob	Isr	d	Oct 1980	3+3	0	0	0
Young (Wal)	Eric	Sing	d	Nov 1982	126	10	19+1	1
Kraay	Hans	Neth	m/d	Feb 1984	19+4	3	0	0
Robinson (Wal)	John	Zim	m	Apr 1989	57+5	6	7+3	2
Edwards	Alistair	Aus	f	Nov 1989	1	0	0	0
Gotsmanov (Blr)	Sergei	USSR	f	Feb 1990	14+2	4	0	0
Meola	Tony	USA	gk	Aug 1990	1	0	1	0
Gurinovich (Blr)	Igor	USSR	f	Nov 1990	3+1	1	1	1
Iovan	Stefan	Rom	d	Mar 1991	4+2	0	3	0

SURNAME	NAME	BORN	POS	FROM	LgAp	LgG	OthAp	OthG
Sommer	Jurgen	USA	gk	Nov 1991	1	0	0	0
McDougald (Brit)	Junior	USA	f	May 1994	71+7	14	12	5
Adekola	David	Nig	f	Oct 1996	1	0	0	0
Gislason	Valur	Ice	m	Oct 1997	7	0	0	0
Ifejiagwa	Emeka	Nig	d	Oct 1998	2	1	0	0
Pinamonte	Lorenzo	It	f	Dec 1999	8+1	2	0	0
Kuipers	Michel	Neth	gk	Jul 2000	94	0	7	0
Lehmann	Dirk	Ger	f	Jun 2001	3+4	0	1+1	0
Petterson	Andy	Aus	gk	Aug 2002	6+1	0	2	0
Ingimarsson	Ivar	Ice	m	Feb 2003	15	0	0	0
Rougier	Tony	Trin	m/f	Feb 2003	5+1	2	0	0

BRISTOL CITY (32)

SURNAME	NAME	BORN	POS	FROM	LgAp	LgG	OthAp	OthG
Murray	David	SA	f	Oct 1926	16	0	0	0
Eisentrager	Alec	Ger	f	Jul 1949	228	47	11	0
Boyd	John	USA	w	Dec 1950	31	6	1	0
Jantunen	Pertti	Fin	m	Mar 1979	7+1	1	3+1	1
Meijer	Geert	Neth	w	Mar 1979	12+3	2	1+1	0
Moller	Jan	Swe	gk	Dec 1980	48	0	13	0
Kelly	Errington	StV	w	Feb 1983	4+1	1	0	0
Dziekanowski	Jackie	Pol	f	Jan 1992	40+3	7	5+1	2
Atteveld	Ray	Neth	d/m	Mar 1992	9+5	1	0	0
Kristensen	Bjorn	Den	d	Nov 1992	4	0	0	0
Shail (Brit)	Mark	Swe	d	Mar 1993	117+11	4	18+1	1
McKop	Henry	Zim	d	Feb 1994	2+3	0	0	0
Brennan	Jim	Can	fb	Oct 1994	51+4	3	7	0
Seal	David	Aus	f	Oct 1994	24+27	10	5+2	3
Hansen	Vergard	Nor	fb	Nov 1994	36+1	0	7	0
Agostino	Paul	Aus	f	Jul 1995	63+21	19	10+3	7
Dijkstra	Sieb	Neth	gk	Sep 1995	8	0	0	0
Barnard (Wal)	Darren	Ger	m	Oct 1995	77+1	15	12	2
Goater	Shaun	Ber	f	Jul 1996	67+8	40	14	2
Goodridge	Greg	Bar	w	Aug 1996	76+43	14	15+7	2
Tisdale (Brit)	Paul	Mal	m	Jun 1997	2+3	0	2+1	0
Johansen	Stig	Nor	f	Feb 1998	2+1	0	0	0
Andersen	Soren	Den	f	Jul 1998	26+13	10	3+1	1
Pinamonte	Lorenzo	It	f	Sep 1998	3+4	1	1+2	0
Zwijnenberg	Clemens	Neth	d	Sep 1998	1+2	0	1	0
Andersen	Bo	Den	gk	Dec 1998	10	0	0	0
Tistimetanu	Ivan	Mol	d	Dec 1998	23+12	2	4+1	0
Sebok	Vilmos	Hun	d	Jan 1999	18+5	0	4	0
Wright (Ire)	Ben	Ger	f	Mar 1999	0+2	0	0	0
Odejayi (Brit)	Kay	Nig	f	Jul 2000	0+6	0	0	0
Rodrigues	Dani	Por	f	Oct 2000	3+5	0	0	0
Da Silva (Por)	Lourenco	Ang	m	Mar 2001	1+2	1	0	0

BRISTOL ROVERS (22)

SURNAME	NAME	BORN	POS	FROM	LgAp	LgG	OthAp	OthG
Ashton (Brit)	Hubert	Ind	d	1924	1	0	0	0
Murray	David	SA	f	1928	39	12	5	1
Richardson	John	SA	f	1930	8	0	0	0
Preedy (Brit)	Charlie	Ind	gk	1933	39	0	3	0
Carr	Lance	SA	f	Aug 1946	42	8	1	0
Purdon	Ted	SA	f	Aug 1960	4	1	2	0
Smit(h)	Wilf	Ger	d	Mar 1975	54	2	8	0
Kelly	Errington	StV	m	Sep 1981	12+6	3	2+1	0
Andreasson	Marcus	Swe	d	Jul 1998	14+1	1	4	0
Ipoua (Fr)	Guy	Cam	f	Aug 1998	15+9	3	4+2	0
Leoni	Stephane	Fr	m	Aug 1998	27+11	0	5+1	1
Kuipers	Michels	Neth	gk	Jan 1999	1	0	0	0
Astafjevs	Vitalis	Lat	m	Jan 2000	87+22	16	14+1	1
Pierre	Nigel	Trin	f	Feb 2000	1+2	0	0	0
Andreasson	Marcus	Swe	d	Mar 2000	9	1	2	0
Dagnogo	Moussa	Fr	f	Sep 2000	0+2	0	0	0
Allsopp	Danny	Aus	f	Oct 2000	4+2	0	0	0
Johansen	Rune	Nor	m	Nov 2000	0+2	0	1	0
Hammond	Elvis	Gha	f	Aug 2001	3+4	0	0+1	0
Ommel	Sergio	Neth	f	Nov 2001	18+5	8	2+1	1
Sanchez-Lopez	Carlos	Sp	m	Feb 2002	6	0	0	0
Di Piedi	Michele	It	m	Feb 2003	3+2	0	0	0

BURNLEY (14)

SURNAME	NAME	BORN	POS	FROM	LgAp	LgG	OthAp	OthG
Hogan (Brit)	Cornelius	Mal	f	Nov 1901	43	17	3	2
Seeburg	Max	Ger	f	Jan 1910	17	0	1	0
Bellis (Brit)	George	Ind	ch	Dec 1932	86	0	5	0
Hodgson	Doug	Aus	d	Oct 1996	1	0	0	0
Gentile	Marco	Neth	d	Jun 1997	0	0	1	0
Robertson	Mark	Aus	m	Oct 1997	27+9	1	1+2	0
Vindheim	Rune	Nor	m	Oct 1998	8	2	1	0
Kval	Frank	Nor	gk	Oct 1998	0	0	1	0
Michopoulos	Nik	Grk	gk	Aug 2000	85	0	8	0
Cennamo (It)	Luigi	Ger	gk	Jul 2001	0	0	0+1	0

SURNAME	NAME	BORN	POS	FROM	LgAp	LgG	OthAp	OthG
Papadopoulos (Grk)	Dimitrios	Khz	f	Jul 2001	7+33	3	2+6	3
Gnohere (Fr)	Arthur	IvCo	d	Aug 2001	62+5	5	10	0
Johnson	David	Jam	f	Mar 2002	8	5	0	0
Diallo (Gui)	Drissa	Mau	m	Jan 2003	14	1	4	1

BURY (19)

SURNAME	NAME	BORN	POS	FROM	LgAp	LgG	OthAp	OthG
McNeill (Brit)	Hamilton	Mal	f	Feb 1939	18	7	0	0
Grieves	Ken	Aus	gk	Apr 1947	59	0	4	0
Law	Cecil	Zim	w	May 1954	44	5	3	0
Nielson	Norman	SA	ch	May 1954	100	5	7	0
Hubbard	John	SA	w	Apr 1959	109	29	11	3
Cunningham (Brit)	Tony	Jam	f	Jul 1989	55+3	17	7	1
Bradley	Pat	Aus	d	Jul 1990	0+1	0	0	0
Stevens	Ian	Mal	f	Jul 1991	100+10	38	7+3	0
Adekola	David	Nig	f	Jan 1993	21+14	12	3+1	0
Blissett (Eng)	Luther	Jam	f	Aug 1993	8+2	1	2	1
Paskin	John	SA	f	Jul 1994	15+23	8	4+3	1
Johnson	David	Jam	f	Jul 1995	72+25	18	9+3	4
D'Jaffo	Laurent	Fr	f	Jul 1998	35+2	8	5+1	1
Avdiu (Swe)	Kemajl	Yug	m	Aug 1998	8+19	1	0+2	0
Grobbelaar (Zim)	Bruce	SA	gk	Sep 1998	1	0	0	0
Rocha	Carlos	Por	f	Aug 1999	0+3	0	0	0
Bhutia	Baichung	Ind	m	Sep 1999	20+17	3	4+3	0
Syros (Grk)	George	Grk	d	Aug 2001	9+1	1	0+1	0
Dunfield	Terry	Can	m	Aug 2002	28+1	2	3	0

CAMBRIDGE UNITED (25)

SURNAME	NAME	BORN	POS	FROM	LgAp	LgG	OthAp	OthG
Batson (Eng)	Brendan	Grn	fb	Jan 1974	162+1	6	17	0
Streete (Brit)	Floyd	Jam	d	Jul 1976	111+14	19	13+4	1
Sweetzer	Gordon	Can	f	Apr 1978	9	3	0	0
Corbin	Kirk	Bar	fb	Jan 1978	3	0	0	0
Galloway (Brit)	Steve	Ger	f	Mar 1986	0+1	0	0	0
McEvoy (Ire)	Ricky	Gib	m	Feb 1987	10+1	1	0	0
Anderson (Brit)	Doug	HK	m	Sep 1988	8	2	0	0
Cheetham	Mike	Neth	m	Oct 1989	123+9	22	30+1	4
Filan	John	Aus	gk	Mar 1993	68	0	9	0
Corazzin	Carlo	Can	f	Dec 1993	104+1	39	9	2
Adekola	David	Nig	f	Aug 1995	1+4	1	2	0
San Miguel	Xavier	Sp	m	Aug 1996	0+1	0	1	0
Larkin	Jim	Can	gk	Jan 1998	1	0	0	0
Williamson (Brit)	Davey	HK	d	Aug 1996	2+4	0	2	0
Van Heusden	Arjan	Neth	gk	Aug 1998	41+1	0	7	0
Hansen (Den)	John	Ger	m	Feb 2000	19+9	3	1+2	1
Perez	Lionel	Fr	gk	Jun 2000	87+1	0	7	0
Axeldahl	Jonas	Swe	f	Aug 2000	12+6	2	3	1
Gudmundsson	Johann	Ice	m	Nov 2000	3	0	0	0
Traore	Demba	Swe	f	Dec 2000	2+6	0	1	0
Pilvi	Tero	Fin	m	Mar 2001	3+2	0	0	0
Kandol (Brit)	Tresor	DRC	f	Aug 2001	2+2	0	0	0
Goodhind	Warren	SA	d	Sep 2001	45+6	0	6	0
One	Armand	Fr	f	Sep 2001	18+14	4	0+2	0
Nacca	Franco	Ven	d	Sep 2002	9+8	0	1+5	0

CARDIFF CITY (13)

SURNAME	NAME	BORN	POS	FROM	LgAp	LgG	OthAp	OthG
Mokone	Steve	SA	w	Jun 1959	3	1	0	0
Mallory	Richard	Ber	w	May 1963	3	0	1	0
Griffith (Brit)	Cohen	Guy	m/f	Oct 1989	205+29	39	27+2	5
Jones (Brit)	Ian	Ger	d	Jul 1995	3	0	0	0
Bolesan	Mirko	It	f	Oct 1995	0+1	0	0	0
Johnson	Glenn	Aus	f	Mar 1996	1+4	0	0	0
Earnshaw (Wal)	Robert	Zam	f	Aug 1997	93+35	63	18+4	14
O'Sullivan (Ire)	Wayne	Cyp	m	Aug 1997	78+7	4	11+2	1
Zois	Peter	Aus	gk	Feb 1998	1	0	0	0
Faerber (Neth)	Winston	Sur	d	Aug 1999	31+2	1	8+1	0
Schwinkendorf	Jorn	Ger	m	Nov 1999	5	0	1	0
Lightbourne	Kyle	Ber	f	Feb 2001	2+1	0	0	0
Zhiyi	Fan	Chn	d	Dec 2002	6	0	0	0

CARLISLE UNITED (19)

SURNAME	NAME	BORN	POS	FROM	LgAp	LgG	OthAp	OthG
Hill (Brit)	Reg	Gib	wh	Jul 1930	5	0	0	0
Ackerman	Alf	SA	f	Nov 1956	97	61	10	12
Cruickshank (Brit)	George	Mly	w	Aug 1957	14	0	0	0
Oosthuizen	Ron	SA	w	Sep 1959	1	0	0	0
MacDonald (Brit)	Ian	Ger	d	May 1976	186+1	7	32	2
Houston	Graham	Gib	m	Oct 1987	8+8	1	0	0
Walwyn (Brit)	Keith	Jam	f	Jul 1989	59+3	15	8	2
Methven (Brit)	Colin	Ind	d	Sep 1990	12	0	3	0
Pounewatchy	Stephane	Fr	d	Aug 1996	81	3	12	0
Kerr (Brit)	Dylan	Mal	d	Sep 1996	0+1	0	0	0
Stevens (1)	Ian	Mal	f	May 1997	64+14	26	4	1
Harries	Paul	Aus	f	Jul 1997	6+14	2	1	1

SURNAME	NAME	BORN	POS	FROM	LgAp	LgG	OthAp	OthG
Croci	Laurent	Fr	m	Oct 1997	1	0	0	0
Pagal	Jean-Claude	Cam	d	Feb 1998	1	0	0	0
Kubicki	Dariusz	Pol	fb	Jul 1998	7	0	2	0
Van der Kwaak	Peter	Neth	gk	Feb 2000	2	0	0	0
Stevens (2)	Ian	Mal	f	Aug 2000	64+3	19	8	5
Lemarchand	Stephane	Fr	f	Sep 2000	4+1	1	0	0
Hews	Chay	Aus	m	Sep 2001	4+1	2	0	0

CHARLTON ATHLETIC (47)

SURNAME	NAME	BORN	POS	FROM	LgAp	LgG	OthAp	OthG
Burton (Brit)	Frank	Mex	fb	Jul 1921	97	0	10	0
Kingsley	Alf	Bar	w	Jul 1921	20	2	0	0
Preedy (Brit)	Charlie	Ind	gk	Dec 1922	131	0	9	0
Tricker (Brit)	Reg	Ind	f	Aug 1925	41	17	2	1
Keizer	Gerry	Neth	gk	Jul 1931	17	0	0	0
Lancelotte (Brit)	Eric	Ind	f	May 1935	40	6	1	1
Mordey (Brit)	Henry	Mly	fb	Jul 1936	10	0	1	0
O'Linn	Syd	SA	f	Dec 1947	187	32	7	1
Forbes	Dudley	SA	wh	Dec 1947	57	1	3	0
Uytenbogaardt	Albert	SA	gk	Oct 1948	6	0	0	0
Nielson	Norman	SA	ch	Jul 1949	1	0	0	0
Hewie (Sco)	John	SA	fb	Oct 1949	495	37	35	1
Firmani (1)	Eddie	SA	f	Feb 1950	100	50	6	1
Leary (Eng)	Stuart	SA	f	Feb 1950	376	153	27	10
Jeppson	Hans	Swe	f	Jan 1951	11	9	0	0
Chamberlain	Ken	SA	ch	Oct 1951	42	0	2	0
Firmani	Peter	SA	fb	Sep 1953	31	2	4	0
Oosthuizen	Ron	SA	w	Sep 1953	1	0	0	0
Tocknell	Brian	SA	wh	Jul 1959	199	14	21	1
Durandt	Cliff	SA	w	Mar 1963	36	4	0	0
Firmani (2)	Eddie	SA	f	Oct 1963	55	32	6	0
Firmani (3)	Eddie	SA	f	Mar 1967	10	6	0	0
Masiello	Luciano	It	w	Jan 1969	6	0	2	1
Bruck	Dietmar	Ger	fb	Oct 1970	54+2	0	6	0
Ambrose	Leroy	StV	m	Aug 1979	28+5	1	1	0
Jacobsen	Viggo	Den	m	Nov 1979	9	0	0	0
Ostergaard	Johnny	Den	f	Nov 1979	8+4	1	0+2	0
Simonsen	Allan	Den	f	Nov 1982	16	9	1	0
Grant	Kim	Gha	f	Mar 1991	74+49	18	11+14	6
Salako	Andy	Nig	d	Apr 1991	1	0	1+1	0
Robinson	John	Zim	m	Sep 1992	296+36	35	39+8	8
Petterson	Andy	Aus	gk	Jul 1994	68+4	0	11	0
Ammann	Mike	USA	gk	Jul 1994	28+2	0	1	0
Hovi	Tom	Nor	m/d	Jan 1995	0+2	0	0	0
Ilic (Yug)	Sasa	Aus	gk	Oct 1997	51	0	8	0
Pringle	Martin	Swe	f	Jan 1999	28+30	8	5	0
Barnes (Eng)	John	Jam	f	Feb 1999	2+10	0	0	0
Salako (Eng)	John	Nig	f	Aug 1999	10+37	2	4+6	1
Svensson	Mathias	Swe	f	Jan 2000	41+26	7	2+5	1
Jensen	Claus	Den	m	Jul 2000	85+6	12	8	0
Bagheri	Karim	Iran	m	Aug 2000	0+1	0	0	0
Johansson (Fin)	Jonatan	Swe	f	Aug 2000	58+34	19	8+1	5
Kishishev	Radostin	Bul	d	Aug 2000	52+12	2	6+1	0
Fish	Mark	SA	d	Nov 2000	72	2	6	0
Bartlett	Shaun	SA	f	Dec 2000	51+12	12	7+1	0
Bart-Williams (Brit)	Chris	SiLe	m	Dec 2001	17+12	2	3+1	0
Costa	Jorge	Por	d	Dec 2001	22+2	0	2	0
Blomqvist	Jesper	Swe	m	Sep 2002	0+3	0	1	0
El Khalej	Tahar	Mor	d	Feb 2003	2+1	0	0	0

CHELSEA (64)

SURNAME	NAME	BORN	POS	FROM	LgAp	LgG	OthAp	OthG
Donaghy (Brit)	Charles	Ind	w	Aug 1905	2	1	1	0
Dolby (Brit)	Hugh	Ind	w	Jul 1908	2	0	0	0
Hunter (Brit)	George	Ind	wh	Feb 1913	30	2	2	0
Middleboe	Nils	Den	hb	Nov 1913	41	0	5	0
Dolding (Brit)	Len	Ind	w	Jul 1945	26	2	1	0
Steffen	Willi	Swit	fb	Nov 1946	15	0	5	0
Mitchell	Frank	Aus	wh	Jan 1949	75	1	10	0
Oelofse	Ralph	SA	wh	Oct 1951	8	0	0	0
Smethurst	Derek	SA	f	Dec 1968	14	4	4+1	1
Borota	Petar	Yug	gk	Mar 1979	107	0	7	0
Viljoen	Colin	SA	m	Mar 1980	19+1	0	3	0
Wegerle (USA)	Roy	SA	f	Jun 1986	15+8	3	1+1	1
Dorigo (Eng)	Tony	Aus	fb	Jul 1987	146	11	21	0
Monkou (Neth)	Ken	Sur	d	Mar 1989	92+2	2	15	0
Johnsen	Erland	Nor	d	Dec 1989	135+10	1	31+3	0
Barnard (Wal)	Darren	Ger	m	Jul 1990	18+11	2	2+2	0
Kharine	Dimitri	Rus	gk	Dec 1992	118	0	28	0
Kjeldbjerg (Den)	Jakob	Nor	d	Aug 1993	52	2	13+1	0
Stein (Eng)	Mark	SA	f	Oct 1993	46+4	21	11+2	4
Gullit (Neth)	Ruud	Sur	m	Jul 1995	37+12	4	13+2	3
Petrescu	Dan	Rom	m	Nov 1995	134+16	18	52+5	6

SURNAME	NAME	BORN	POS	FROM	LgAp	LgG	OthAp	OthG
Di Matteo (It)	Roberto	Swit	m	Jul 1996	108+11	15	44+9	11
Leboeuf	Frank	Fr	d	Jul 1996	142+2	17	55+2	7
Vialli	Gianluca	It	f	Jul 1996	46+12	21	23+6	19
Grodas	Frode	Nor	gk	Sep 1996	20+1	0	6	0
Zola	Gianfranco	It	f	Nov 1996	185+44	59	72+8	21
Forrest	Craig	Can	gk	Mar 1997	2+1	0	0	0
Babayaro	Celestine	Nig	d	Jun 1997	110+12	4	48+6	3
Lambourde (Fr)	Bernard	Guad	d	Jul 1997	29+11	2	14+6	1
Poyet	Gustavo	Uru	m	Jul 1997	79+26	36	29+8	12
De Goey	Ed	Neth	gk	Jul 1997	123	0	52+1	0
Flo	Tore Andre	Nor	f	Aug 1997	59+53	34	35+15	16
Charvet	Laurent	Fr	d	Jan 1998	7+4	2	0+2	0
Laudrup (Den)	Brian	Aut	f	Jun 1998	5+2	0	3	1
Casiraghi	Pierluigi	It	f	Jul 1998	10	1	2+2	0
Desailly (Fr)	Marcel	Gha	d	Jul 1998	141+2	6	52	1
Percassi	Luca	It	d	Aug 1998	0	0	0+2	0
Ferrer	Albert	Sp	d	Aug 1998	71+5	0	33+3	1
Dalla Bona	Sam	It	m	Oct 1998	42+13	6	9+9	0
Goldbaek	Bjarne	Den	m	Nov 1998	15+14	5	6+5	0
Forssell (Fin)	Mikael	Ger	f	Dec 1998	6+26	5	5+13	7
Cudicini	Carlo	It	gk	Jun 1999	87+2	0	29+1	0
Deschamps	Didier	Fr	m	Jun 1999	24+3	0	20	1
Hogh	Jes	Den	d	Jul 1999	6+3	0	5+3	0
Melchiot	Mario	Neth	d	Jul 1999	97+10	2	22+2	0
Ambrosetti	Gabriele	It	f	Aug 1999	9+7	0	2+5	1
Thome	Emerson	Bra	d	Dec 1999	19+2	0	1	0
Weah	George	Lbr	f	Jan 2000	9+2	3	4	2
Aleksidze	Rati	Geo	m	Feb 2000	0+2	0	0+1	0
Gudjohnsen	Eidur	Ice	f	Jul 2000	63+34	34	19+11	12
Hasselbaink (Neth)	Jimmy Floyd	Sur	f	Jul 2000	97+9	57	26	12
Stanic (Cro)	Mario	Yug	m	Jul 2000	39+18	7	14+3	3
Panucci	Christian	It	d	Aug 2000	7+1	0	2	1
Bogarde	Winston	Neth	d	Sep 2000	2+7	0	2+1	0
Jokanovic	Slavisa	Yug	m	Oct 2000	19+20	0	9+5	0
Gronkjaer	Jesper	Den	m	Dec 2000	37+20	5	9+5	3
Bosnich	Mark	Aus	gk	Jan 2001	5	0	2	0
Gallas	William	Fr	d	May 2001	63+5	5	21	1
Kitamirike	Joel	Uga	d	Apr 2001	0	0	1	0
Petit	Emmanuel	Fr	m	Jul 2001	49+2	2	18	1
Zenden	Boudewijn	Neth	m	Aug 2001	24+19	4	6+10	0
Huth	Robert	Ger	d	Feb 2002	2+1	0	2+1	0
De Lucas	Enrique	Sp	m	Aug 2002	17+8	0	4+2	0
De Oliveira	Filipe	Por	f	Sep 2002	0+3	0	0+2	0

CHELTENHAM TOWN (3)

SURNAME	NAME	BORN	POS	FROM	LgAp	LgG	OthAp	OthG
Howells	Lee	Aus	f	Aug 1999	112	6	11	2
Stevens (Brit)	Ian	Mal	f	Mar 2000	1	0	0	0
Goodridge	Greg	Bar	w	Feb 2001	10+1	1	0	0

CHESTER CITY (14)

SURNAME	NAME	BORN	POS	FROM	LgAp	LgG	OthAp	OthG
Warburton	George	Neth	w	Nov 1938	11	3	0	0
Stiffle (Brit)	Nelson	Ind	w	Dec 1951	7	2	0	0
Hauser	Peter	SA	wh	Aug 1963	117+4	3	16	0
Greer	Ross	Aus	f	Nov 1989	2	0	1	0
Aunger	Geoff	Can	d/m	Dec 1994	1+4	0	0	0
Regis (Eng)	Cyrille	FrGu	f	Aug 1995	29	7	4	0
Smeets	Jorg	Neth	m	Mar 1999	1+2	0	0	0
Agogo	Junior	Gha	f	Sep 1999	10	6	0	0
Carver	Joe	USA	f	Sep 1999	1+1	0	0	0
Eve	Angus	Trin	f	Dec 1999	9+5	4	0	0
Laird	Kamu	Trin	f	Dec 1999	2+1	1	0	0
Milovaijevic	Goran	Yug	m	Sep 1999	11+1	0	5	0
Nash	Martin	Can	m	Sep 1999	12+4	0	3+1	0
Eyjolfsson	Siggi	Ice	f	Jan 2000	9	3	0	0

CHESTERFIELD (15)

SURNAME	NAME	BORN	POS	FROM	LgAp	LgG	OthAp	OthG
Milligan (N Ire)	Dudley	SA	f	Nov 1938	49	19	4	1
Stiffle (Brit)	Nelson	Ind	w	Mar 1954	38	9	1	0
Roberts	John	Aus	gk	Aug 1967	46	0	3	0
Smit(h)	Wilf	Ger	fb	Nov 1976	26+1	2	0+1	0
Heppolette (Brit)	Ricky	Ind	m	Feb 1977	46+1	3	5	1
Walwyn (Brit)	Keith	Jam	f	Nov 1979	3	1	1+2	0
Bernardeau	Olivier	Fr	m	Aug 1986	5+4	0	0+1	0
Benjamin	Tristan	StK	d	Jul 1987	32+2	0	0	0
Chiedozie	John	Nig	w	Mar 1990	5+2	0	3	1
Gregory (Brit)	Neil	Zam	f	Feb 1994	2+1	1	0	0
Cheetham	Mike	Neth	m	Jul 1994	5	0	2	1
McDougald (Brit)	Junior	USA	f	Mar 1996	9	3	0	0
Misse-Misse	Jean-Jacques	Cam	f	Mar 1998	1	0	0	0
Agogo	Junior	Gha	f	Nov 1999	3+1	0	0	0
Hitzlsperger	Thomas	Ger	m	Oct 2001	5	0	0	0

SURNAME	NAME	BORN	POS	FROM	LgAp	LgG	OthAp	OthG
COLCHESTER UNITED (21)								
Gallego	Jose	Sp	w	Aug 1950	4	0	0	0
Kennon	Sandy	SA	gk	Mar 1965	76	0	6	0
Macedo (Brit)	Tony	Gib	gk	Sep 1968	38	0	2	0
Forrest	Craig	Can	gk	Mar 1988	11	0	0	0
Bruce	Marcelle	USA	gk	Jul 1989	28+1	1	2	0
Barada	Taylor	USA	gk	Mar 1994	1	0	0	0
Cheetham (Brit)	Mike	Neth	m	Mar 1995	33+4	3	3	1
Caldwell	Garrett	USA	gk	Sep 1995	6	0	2	0
Petterson	Andy	Aus	gk	Mar 1996	5	0	0	0
Gregory (Brit)	Neil	Zam	f	Jan 1998	41+12	11	5	0
Okafar	Sam	Nig	m	Aug 1998	0+1	0	0	0
Lua-Lua (DRC)	Lumana Tresor	DRC	f	Sep 1998	37+24	15	5	5
Pounewatchy	Stephane	Fr	d	Feb 1999	15	1	0	0
Fumaca	Jose	Bra	m	Mar 1999	1	0	0	0
Richard	Fabrice	Fr	d	Mar 1999	23+1	0	1+1	0
Germain	Steve	Fr	f	Mar 1999	2+7	0	0	0
Pinault	Thomas	Fr	m	Jul 1999	73+20	5	6+1	0
Opara	Kelechi	Nig	f	Aug 1999	2+17	0	1	0
Canham (Brit)	Marc	Ger	m	Aug 2001	2+2	0	0	0
Blatsis	Con	Aus	d	Mar 2002	7	0	0	0
Atangana	Simon	Cam	f	Nov 2002	1+5	0	0+1	0
COVENTRY CITY (58)								
Gibson	Fred	SA	w	May 1919	54	5	0	0
Mackrill	Percy	SA	fb	Jul 1919	1	0	0	0
Aldecoa	Emilio	Sp	w	Dec 1945	29	0	2	0
Mokone	Steve	SA	w	Oct 1956	4	1	0	0
Lightening	Arthur	SA	gk	Nov 1958	150	0	10	0
Stiffle (Brit)	Nelson	Ind	w	Jul 1960	15	2	3	0
Bruck	Dietmar	Ger	fb	May 1962	181+8	7	27+1	1
Baker	Gerry	USA	f	Nov 1967	27+4	5	3	1
Smit(h)	Wilf	Ger	fb	Aug 1970	132+3	1	18	1
Van Gool	Roger	Bel	w	Mar 1980	17	0	2	0
Kaiser	Rudi	Neth	w	Aug 1981	11+5	3	3	0
Avramovic	Raddy	Cro	gk	Sep 1983	18	0	6	0
Jol	Maarten	Neth	m	Jul 1984	15	0	0	0
Regis (Eng)	Cyrille	FrGu	f	Oct 1984	231+6	47	39+1	15
Phillips (Brit)	David	Ger	m	Jun 1986	93+7	8	17	1
Perdomo	Jose	Uru	m	Aug 1990	4	0	2	0
Butcher (Eng)	Terry	Sing	d	Nov 1990	6	0	1	0
Ndlovu	Peter	Zim	f	Aug 1991	141+36	37	15+4	4
Wegerle (USA)	Roy	SA	f	Mar 1993	46+7	9	8+2	2
Kruszynski	Detsi	Ger	m	Sep 1993	1+1	0	1	0
Jones	Cobi	USA	m	Sep 1994	16+5	2	2+2	0
Filan	John	Aus	gk	Mar 1995	15+1	0	2	0
Isaias (Por)	Marques	Bra	m	Aug 1995	9+3	2	2	0
Lamptey	Nii	Gha	f	Aug 1995	3+3	0	3+2	2
Salako (Eng)	John	Nig	f	Aug 1995	68+4	4	13	4
Genaux	Reggie	Bel	d	Aug 1996	3+1	0	0	0
Evtushok	Alex	Ukr	d	Feb 1997	3	0	0	0
Johansen	Martin	Den	m/f	Jun 1997	0+2	0	1	0
Hedman	Magnus	Swe	gk	Jul 1997	134	0	17	0
Lightbourne	Kyle	Ber	f	Jul 1997	1+6	0	3	0
Nilsson (1)	Roland	Swe	fb	Jul 1997	60	0	9	0
Soltvedt	Trond Egil	Nor	m	Jul 1997	47+10	3	6+6	1
Boateng	George	Gha	m	Dec 1997	43+4	5	11	2
Moldovan	Viorel	Rom	f	Jan 1998	5+5	1	2+2	1
Clement	Philippe	Bel	m	Jul 1998	6+6	0	2+2	0
Wallemme	Jean-Guy	Fr	d	Jul 1998	4+2	0	2	0
Chippo	Youssef	Mor	m/f	Jul 1999	100+22	6	10+1	4
Delorge	Laurent	Bel	f	Nov 1998	23+7	4	1+3	0
Aloisi	John	Aus	f	Dec 1998	18+24	10	2+3	3
Gioacchini	Stefano	It	f	Jan 1999	0+3	0	0	0
Konjic	Muhamed	Bos	d	Feb 1999	94+2	2	11+1	0
Hyldgaard	Morten	Den	gk	Jul 1999	27	0	4	0
Hadji	Mustapha	Mor	m/f	Aug 1999	61+1	12	7+1	1
Normann	Runar	Nor	m	Aug 1999	3+10	1	1+1	0
Nuzzo	Raffaele	It	gk	Jul 1999	0	0	1	0
Roussel	Cedric	Bel	f	Oct 1999	28+11	8	3+1	3
Gustafsson	Tomas	Swe	d	Dec 1999	10+5	0	1+2	0
Zuniga	Ysrael	Per	f	Mar 2000	11+18	3	2	1
Guerrero	Ivan	Hon	d	Oct 2000	6+1	0	1	0
Martinez	Jairo	Hon	f	Oct 2000	5+6	3	1+1	0
Nilsson (2)	Roland	Swe	fb	Jul 2001	9	0	1	0
Safri	Youssef	Mor	m	Aug 2001	56+4	1	4	0
Carbonari	Horacio	Arg	d	Mar 2002	5	0	0	0
Debec	Fabien	Fr	gk	Sep 2002	11	0	2	0
McMaster	Jamie	Aus	m	Nov 2002	2	0	0	0
Sara	Juan	Arg	f	Jan 2003	1+2	1	0+1	0
Engonga	Vincente	Sp	m	Feb 2003	5+3	0	0	0

411

SURNAME	NAME	BORN	POS	FROM	LgAp	LgG	OthAp	OthG
Yulu (Fr)	Christian	DRC	m	Feb 2003	1+2	0	0	0
Cooney	Sean	Aus	d	Apr 2003	0+1	0	0	0

CREWE ALEXANDRA (16)

SURNAME	NAME	BORN	POS	FROM	LgAp	LgG	OthAp	OthG
Wagstaffe (Brit)	Thomas	India	f	Sep 1926	3	1	0	0
McLaughlin	William	USA	wh	Oct 1946	1	0	0	0
Baines	Peter	Aus	f	Nov 1946	8	0	0	0
Kelly (N Ire)	Pat	SA	gk	Feb 1952	38	0	0	0
Emmerson	Wayne	Can	f	Jul 1968	6+2	1	1	1
Rafferty (Brit)	Kevin	Ken	gk	Nov 1978	22	0	4	0
Grobbelaar (Zim)	Bruce	SA	gk	Dec 1979	24	1	0	0
Goulet	Brent	USA	f	Jan 1988	2+1	3	0	0
Mettioui	Ahmed	Mor	m	Jul 1992	1+2	0	1	0
Adebola	Dele	Nig	f	Mar 1993	98+26	39	18+5	5
Bankole (1)	Ade	Nig	gk	Sep 1996	6	0	1	0
Mautone	Steve	Aus	gk	Sep 1996	3	0	0	0
Kearton	Jason	Aus	gk	Oct 1996	190+1	0	25	0
Jack (StV)	Rodney	Jam	f	Aug 1998	140+23	33	20+2	5
Ince	Clayton	Trin	gk	Sep 1999	61+3	0	10	0
Bankole (2)	Ade	Nig	gk	Jul 2000	51+1	0	6+2	0
Milosevic	Danny	Aus	gk	Jan 2003	1	0	0	0

CRYSTAL PALACE (49)

SURNAME	NAME	BORN	POS	FROM	LgAp	LgG	OthAp	OthG
Gaillard	Marcel	Bel	w	Feb 1948	21	3	0	0
Besagni	Remo	It	f	Oct 1952	2	0	0	0
Thorup	Borge	Den	fb	Mar 1969	0+1	0	0	0
Bartram	Per	Den	f	Aug 1969	8+2	2	1+1	1
McBride (Brit)	Andy	Ken	d	Oct 1971	1	0	0	0
Heppolette (Brit)	Ricky	Ind	m	Oct 1976	13+2	0	3	0
Nebbeling	Gavin	SA	d	Aug 1981	145+6	8	13+1	0
Galloway (Brit)	Steve	Ger	f	Oct 1984	3+2	1	0+1	0
Salako (Eng)	John	Nig	f	Nov 1986	172+43	23	39+5	9
Young (Wal)	Eric	Sing	d	Aug 1990	161	15	35	1
Boere	Jeroen	Neth	f	Sep 1995	0+8	1	0	0
Andersen	Leif	Nor	d	Jan 1996	19+11	1	5	0
Veart	Carl	Aus	m	Mar 1996	41+16	6	8+3	5
Hreidarsson	Hermann	Ice	d	Aug 1997	32+5	2	11	1
Zohar	Itzy	Isr	m	Aug 1997	2+4	0	2	0
Lombardo	Attilio	It	m	Aug 1997	40+3	8	5	2
Bonetti	Ivano	It	m	Oct 1997	0+2	0	0	0
Padovano	Michele	It	f	Nov 1997	8+4	1	0	0
Brolin	Tomas	Swe	m	Jan 1998	13	0	3	0
Ismael	Valerien	Fr	m	Jan 1998	13	0	3	0
Billio	Patrizio	It	m	Mar 1998	1+2	0	0	0
Curcic	Sasa	Yug	m	Mar 1998	10+13	5	3	0
Rizzo	Nicky	Aus	m	Jul 1998	15+21	1	2+3	1
Amsalem	David	Isr	d	Aug 1998	6+4	0	1+1	0
Del Rio	Walter	Arg	d	Sep 1998	1+1	0	0+1	0
Jihai	Sun	Chn	d	Sep 1998	22+1	0	2	0
Svensson	Mathias	Swe	f	Sep 1998	26+6	10	3	0
Zhiyi	Fan	Chn	d	Sep 1998	87+1	4	14	2
Moore	Craig	Aus	d	Oct 1998	23	3	1	0
Foster	Craig	Aus	m	Oct 1998	47+5	3	2	0
Petric	Gordan	Yug	d	Nov 1998	18	1	0	0
Fumaca	Jose	Bra	m	Sep 1999	2+1	0	2	0
De Ornelas	Fernando	Ven	m	Sep 1999	5+4	0	0	0
Mautone	Steve	Aus	gk	Nov 1999	2	0	0	0
Forssell (Fin)	Mikael	Ger	f	Feb 2000	44+8	16	9+1	2
Kolinko	Alex	Lat	gk	Sep 2000	79+3	0	17	0
Rubins	Andrejs	Lat	m	Oct 2000	17+14	0	5+1	2
Berhalter	Gregg	USA	d	Feb 2001	10+9	1	1+1	0
Fuller	Ricardo	Jam	f	Feb 2001	2+6	0	0	0
Karic	Amir	Slo	d	Mar 2001	3	0	0	0
Riihilahti	Aki	Fin	m	Mar 2001	69+10	7	8+1	1
Verhoene	Kenny	Bel	d	Mar 2001	0+1	0	0	0
Kirovski	Jovan	USA	f	Aug 2001	25+11	5	3	0
Popovic	Tony	Aus	d	Aug 2001	56	5	10	1
Carasso	Cedric	Fr	g	Dec 2001	0+1	0	0	0
Murphy	Shaun	Aus	d	Feb 2002	11	0	0	0
Adebola	Dele	Nig	f	Aug 2002	32+7	5	9	2
Michopoulos	Nik	Grk	gk	Sep 2002	5	0	1+1	0
Berthelin	Cedric	Fr	gk	Jan 2003	9	0	2+1	0

DARLINGTON (26)

SURNAME	NAME	BORN	POS	FROM	LgAp	LgG	OthAp	OthG
Hill (Brit)	Reg	Gib	wh	Feb 1937	12	0	0	0
Karaa	Roch	Tun	gk	Mar 1985	1	0	0	0
Sanderson (Brit)	Mike	Ger	m	Mar 1986	1	0	0	0
Neves	Rui	Por	f	Aug 1995	3+2	0	2	0
Paulo	Pedro	Por	m	Aug 1995	4+2	0	1+1	0
Quitongo	Jose	Ang	f	Sep 1995	1	0	0	0
Stephenson	Ashlyn	SA	gk	Sep 1995	1	0	0	0

SURNAME	NAME	BORN	POS	FROM	LgAp	LgG	OthAp	OthG
Carmichael (Brit)	Matt	Sing	f	Feb 1996	11+2	2	2+1	0
De Vos	Jason	Can	d	Nov 1996	43+1	5	7	1
Barbara	Daniel	Fr	f	Dec 1996	1+5	1	0	0
Moilanen	Tepi	Fin	gk	Jan 1997	16	0	0	0
Papaconstantinou	Loukas	Can	gk	Jul 1997	1	0	0	0
Giumarra	Willy	Can	m	Aug 1997	0+4	0	0	0
Resch	Franz	Aut	d	Oct 1997	15+2	1	1+2	0
Dorner	Mario	Aut	f	Oct 1997	34+15	13	6+1	2
Di Lella	Gustavo	Arg	m	Dec 1997	0+5	0	0	0
Kubicki	Dariusz	Pol	d	Oct 1998	2+1	0	0	0
Costa	Ricardo	Por	f	Jan 1999	0+3	1	0	0
Hjorth	Jesper	Den	f	Nov 1999	16+29	7	6+4	0
Kaak	Tom	Neth	f	Jul 2000	7+1	2	0+2	0
Van der Geest	Frank	Neth	gk	Aug 2000	2	0	2	0
Zeghdane	Lehit	Fr	f	Sep 2000	1+2	0	0+2	0
Marcelle	Clint	Trin	f	Feb 2001	8+7	0	0	0
Bernard	Olivier	Fr	m	Mar 2001	9+1	2	0	0
Cau	Jean-Michel	Fr	f	Mar 2001	0+1	0	0	0
Jeannin	Alex	Fr	d	Mar 2001	22	0	0	0

DERBY COUNTY (47)

SURNAME	NAME	BORN	POS	FROM	LgAp	LgG	OthAp	OthG
Quantrill (Eng)	Alf	Ind	w	Aug 1914	72	5	4	0
Abdallah	Tewfik	Egy	f	Sep 1920	15	1	0	0
Law (Brit)	Cecil	Zim	w	Aug 1951	33	2	0	0
Nielson	Norman	SA	ch	Sep 1951	57	8	3	1
Ackerman	Alf	SA	f	Mar 1955	36	21	0	0
Banovic (Yug)	Yakka	Aus	gk	Sep 1980	35	0	3	0
Streete (Brit)	Floyd	Jam	d	Oct 1984	35	0	5	0
Callaghan (Eng)(1)	Nigel	Sing	w	Feb 1987	76	10	7	1
Chiedozie	John	Nig	w	Aug 1988	2	0	0	0
Callaghan (Eng) (2)	Nigel	Sing	w	Sep 1990	12	1	0	0
Goulooze	Richard	Neth	d	Sep 1992	7+5	0	1+1	0
Harkes	John	USA	m	Aug 1993	67+7	2	8	0
Willems	Ron	Neth	f	Jul 1995	41+18	13	6+2	3
Van der Laan	Robin	Neth	m	Aug 1995	61+4	8	9+3	3
Stimac	Igor	Cro	d	Oct 1995	84	3	9	0
Asanovic	Aljosa	Cro	m	Jun 1996	37+1	7	5	0
Laursen	Jacob	Den	d/m	Jul 1996	135+2	3	16	0
Rahmberg	Marino	Swe	f	Jan 1997	0+1	0	0	0
Poom	Mart	Est	gk	Mar 1997	143+3	0	20	0
Solis	Mauricio	CoRi	m	Mar 1997	3+8	0	1+2	0
Wanchope	Paulo	CoRi	f	Mar 1997	65+7	23	10+1	5
Eranio	Stefano	It	m	Jul 1997	83+12	7	13	3
Baiano	Francesco	It	f	Aug 1997	52+12	16	11	3
Bohinen	Lars	Nor	m	Mar 1998	47+9	1	5	0
Carbonari	Horacio	Arg	d	Jul 1998	89+1	9	12	0
Schnoor	Stefan	Ger	d	Jul 1998	48+12	2	7+2	0
Dorigo (Eng)	Tony	Aus	fb	Oct 1998	37+4	1	8	2
Beck	Mikkel	Den	f	Mar 1999	11+7	2	2+1	1
Borbokis	Vassilis	Grk	d	Mar 1999	9+7	0	4	1
Fuertes	Esteban	Arg	f	Aug 1999	8	1	2	1
Nimni	Avi	Isr	m	Nov 1999	2+2	1	1	0
Strupar (Bel)	Branko	Cro	f	Dec 1999	32+9	16	2	0
Kinkladze	Georgi	Geo	m	Jun 2000	60+33	7	5+2	1
Valakari	Simo	Fin	m	Jul 2000	20+6	3	4	0
Blatsis	Con	Aus	d	Aug 2000	2	0	0	0
Bragstad	Bjorn Otto	Nor	d	Aug 2000	10+2	0	4	2
Mawene	Youl	Fr	d	Aug 2000	24+1	1	5	0
Martin	Lilian	Fr	d	Nov 2000	7+2	0	2+1	0
West	Taribo	Nig	d	Nov 2000	18	0	2	0
Gudjonsson	Thordur	Ice	m	Mar 2001	2+8	1	0	0
Ravanelli	Fabrizio	It	f	Jul 2001	46+4	14	3	2
Daino	Daniele	It	d	Aug 2001	2	0	1+1	0
Carbone	Benito	It	f	Oct 2001	13	1	1	0
Ducrocq	Pierre	Fr	m	Oct 2001	19	0	0	0
Feuer	Ian	USA	gk	Oct 2001	2	0	0	0
Zavagno	Luciano	Arg	d	Oct 2001	32+3	2	1+1	0
Grenet	Francois	Fr	d	Nov 2001	14+4	0	1	0
Foletti	Patrick	Swit	g	Feb 2002	1+1	0	1+1	0

DONCASTER ROVERS (9)

SURNAME	NAME	BORN	POS	FROM	LgAp	LgG	OthAp	OthG
Sharp	Ronnie	Can	w	Oct 1958	58	11	8	3
Berry (Wal)	George	Ger	d	Aug 1984	1	0	1	0
Kerr (Brit)	Dylan	Mal	d	Aug 1991	7	1	0	0
Cunningham (Brit)	Tony	Jam	f	Jul 1993	19+6	1	3+1	0
Kitchen (Brit)	Sam	Ger	d	Feb 1994	21+1	1	1	0
Torfason	Gunnar	Ice	f	Jul 1994	1+3	0	1+1	1
Carmichael (Brit)	Matt	Sing	f	Aug 1995	19+8	4	0+2	1
Knight	Jason	Aus	m	Aug 1995	1+3	0	0	0
Moncrieffe	Prince	Jam	f	Jul 1997	30+8	8	3	0

413

SURNAME	NAME	BORN	POS	FROM	LgAp	LgG	OthAp	OthG
EVERTON (37)								
Murray	David	SA	f	Aug 1925	3	1	0	0
Van Den Hauwe (Wal)	Pat	Bel	fb	Sep 1984	134+1	2	55	1
Kearton	Jason	Aus	gk	Oct 1988	3+3	0	2	0
Rehn	Stefan	Swe	w	Jun 1989	1+3	0	1+1	0
Atteveld	Ray	Neth	d/m	Aug 1989	41+10	1	12+2	1
Warzycha	Robert	Pol	w	Mar 1991	51+21	6	5+5	0
Radosavljevic (US)	Preki	Yug	w	Aug 1992	22+24	4	3+4	0
Limpar	Anders	Swe	w	Mar 1994	51+15	5	12+3	1
Amokachi	Daniel	Nig	f	Aug 1994	34+9	10	8+3	4
Kanchelskis	Andrei	Ukr	w	Aug 1995	52	20	8	2
Hottiger	Marc	Swit	fb	Mar 1996	13+4	1	1	0
Thomsen	Claus	Den	m	Jan 1997	17+7	1	1	0
Bilic	Slaven	Cro	d	Jul 1997	26+2	0	4	0
Myhre	Thomas	Nor	gk	Nov 1997	70	0	12	0
Madar	Mickael	Fr	f	Dec 1997	17+2	6	0+1	0
Dacourt	Olivier	Fr	m	Jun 1998	28+2	2	6	1
Materazzi	Marco	It	d	Jul 1998	26+1	1	6	1
Bakayoko	Ibrahima	IvCo	f	Oct 1998	17+6	4	3+2	3
Degn	Peter	Den	m	Feb 1999	0+4	0	1	0
Gough (Sco)	Richard	Swe	d	Jun 1999	38	1	3+1	0
Xavier (Por)	Abel	Moz	d	Sep 1999	39+4	0	6	0
Moore	Joe-Max	USA	f	Dec 1999	22+30	8	5+7	2
Alexandersson	Niclas	Swe	m	Jul 2000	49+9	4	6+2	1
Pistone	Alessandro	It	d	Jul 2000	40+7	1	4	0
Gravesen	Thomas	Den	m	Aug 2000	82+8	5	5+1	0
Nyarko	Alex	Gha	m	Aug 2000	19+3	1	2	0
Tal	Idan	Isr	m	Oct 2000	13+16	2	1+3	0
Radzinski (Can)	Tomasz	Pol	f	Jul 2001	50+7	17	5+1	1
Blomqvist	Jesper	Swe	m	Nov 2001	10+5	1	2+1	0
Linderoth	Tobias	Swe	m	Jan 2002	6+7	0	3+1	0
Ginola	David	Fr	w	Feb 2002	2+3	0	2	0
Li Tie		Chn	m	Aug 2002	28+1	0	3+1	0
Rodrigo	Juliano	Bra	m	Aug 2002	0+4	0	0	0
Yobo	Joseph	Nig	d	Sep 2002	22+2	0	2	0
Li Weifeng		Chn	d	Nov 2002	1	0	1	0
Baardsen (Nor)	Espen	USA	gk	Jan 2003	1	0	0	0
McBride	Brian	USA	f	Jan 2003	7+1	4	0	0
EXETER CITY (17)								
Stiffle (Brit)	Nelson	Ind	w	Mar 1958	94	17	4	2
Baugh	John	Uga	gk	Feb 1977	20	0	4	0
Cooke	Joe	Dom	d/f	Jun 1981	17	3	4	2
Auguste	Joe	Trin	f	Sep 1983	7+3	0	1	0
Thirlby (Brit)	Anthony	Ger	m	Jul 1993	27+12	2	2+3	0
Adekola	David	Nig	f	Feb 1994	1+2	1	0	0
Rice (Brit)	Gary	Zam	d	Jul 1994	31+13	0	3	0
Blake (Brit)	Noel	Jam	d	Aug 1995	135+12	10	12	0
Tisdale (Brit)	Paul	Mal	m	Dec 1997	10	1	0	0
Vanninen	Jukka	Fin	m	Dec 1999	3+2	0	0	0
Van Heusden	Arjan	Neth	gk	Jul 2000	74	0	6	0
Epesse-Titi	Steeve	Fr	d	Mar 2001	5+1	0	0	0
Kerr (Brit)	Dylan	Mal	d	Aug 2001	5	1	1	0
Moor (Ire)	Reinier	Neth	f	Aug 2001	2+17	3	1+3	1
Diallo	Cherif	Sen	f	Sep 2001	0+2	0	0	0
Gaia	Marcio	Bra	d	Aug 2002	33	1	5	1
Harries	Paul	Aus	f	Sep 2002	0+1	0	0+1	0
FULHAM (47)								
O'Donnell (Brit)	Rudolph	Ind	gk	Dec 1909	3	0	0	0
Hegazi	Hassan	Egy	f	Nov 1911	1	1	0	0
Kingsley	Alf	Bar	w	Jan 1922	29	2	2	0
Osborne (Eng)	Frank	SA	f	Nov 1921	67	18	3	0
Price (Brit)	Johnny	Ind	f	Jun 1928	189	49	15	4
Clarke	Bruce	SA	wh	Jun 1934	112	1	2	0
Mitten (Brit)	Charlie	Bur	wh	Jan 1952	154	32	6	1
Macedo (Brit)	Tony	Gib	gk	Oct 1955	346	0	45	0
Hewkins	Ken	SA	gk	Nov 1955	38	0	3	0
Cutbush (Brit)	John	Mal	fb	Jul 1972	131+3	3	26	0
Hesford (Eng)	Iain	Zam	gk	Jan 1985	3	0	0	0
Nebbeling	Gavin	SA	d	Jul 1989	85+3	2	8	0
Tierling (Brit)	Lee	Ger	m	May 1992	7+12	0	1	0
Bedrossian	Ara	Cyp	m	Mar 1993	34+8	1	1+1	0
Arendse	Andre	SA	gk	Aug 1997	6	0	3	0
Peschisolido	Paul	Can	f	Oct 1997	69+26	24	18+2	6
Neilson (Wal)	Alan	Ger	d	Nov 1997	24+5	2	8+2	0
Taylor (N Ire)	Maik	Ger	gk	Nov 1997	183+1	0	46	0
Lightbourne	Kyle	Ber	f	Jan 1998	4	2	0	0
Salako (Eng)	John	Nig	f	Jul 1998	7+3	1	4+2	1
Uhlenbeek (Neth)	Gus	Sur	d	Jul 1998	22+17	1	7+3	0
Lehmann	Dirk	Ger	f	Aug 1998	16+10	2	7+2	3

SURNAME	NAME	BORN	POS	FROM	LgAp	LgG	OthAp	OthG
Betsy (Brit)	Kevin	Sey	m	Sep 1998	3+12	1	2+2	0
Keller	Francois	Fr	m	Dec 1998	0+1	0	0	0
Albert	Philippe	Bel	d	Jan 1999	12+1	2	0	0
Hahnemann	Marcus	USA	gk	Jul 1999	2	0	2	0
Hammond	Elvis	Gha	f	Jul 1999	3+7	0	0+1	0
Riedle	Karl-Heinz	Ger	f	Sep 1999	16+19	6	1	0
Goldbaek	Bjarne	Den	m	Jan 2000	73+12	6	12+5	1
Lewis	Eddie	USA	f	Mar 2000	8+8	0	6	1
Saha	Louis	Fr	f	Jun 2000	80+16	40	17+8	8
Fernandes	Fabrice	Fr	m	Aug 2000	23+6	2	5+2	2
Sahnoun	Nicolas	Fr	m	Oct 2000	2+5	0	2	0
Stolcers	Andrejs	Lat	f	Dec 2000	8+17	2	2+4	2
Moller	Peter	Den	f	Jan 2001	2+3	1	0	0
Goma	Alain	Fr	d	Mar 2001	64+1	0	23	0
Boa Morte	Luis	Por	f	Jun 2001	61+30	21	22+6	7
Legwinski	Sylvain	Fr	m	Aug 2001	63+5	7	19+3	4
Malbranque (Fr)	Steed	Bel	m	Aug 2001	68+6	14	23+4	9
Marlet	Steve	Fr	f	Aug 2001	49+5	10	20+3	8
Ouaddou	Abdeslam	Mor	d	Aug 2001	13+8	0	15+2	0
Van der Sar	Edwin	Neth	gk	Aug 2001	56	0	15	0
Inamoto	Junichi	Jap	m	Jul 2002	9+10	2	6+8	4
Sava	Facundo	Arg	f	Jul 2002	13+7	5	10+2	1
Wome	Pierre	Cam	m	Sep 2002	13+1	1	3+2	0
Djetou (Fr)	Martin	IvCo	d	Oct 2002	22+3	1	8+2	0
Herrera	Martin	Arg	gk	Feb 2003	1+1	0	0	0

GILLINGHAM (15)

SURNAME	NAME	BORN	POS	FROM	LgAp	LgG	OthAp	OthG
Martin	Syd	SA	f	Jul 1929	2	0	1	0
Mills (Brit)	Arthur	Ind	w	Jul 1933	33	12	2	1
Crossan	Errol	Can	w	Jul 1955	76	16	4	1
Burgess	Mike	Can	f/ch	Mar 1963	109+1	2	10	0
Chadwick (Brit)	Dave	Ind	w	Sep 1974	35	3	1	0
Young (Brit)	Charlie	Cyp	d	Mar 1978	27+1	1	6	1
Henry	Liburd	Dom	f	Jun 1992	37+5	2	6+1	1
Statham (Eng)	Brian	Zim	d/m	Aug 1997	16+4	0	2	0
Rolling	Franck	Fr	d	Sep 1998	1	0	0	0
Mautone	Steve	Aus	gk	Mar 2000	1	0	0	0
Omoyimni	Manny	Nig	f	Sep 1999	7+2	3	2	0
Ipoua (Fr)	Guy	Cam	f	Mar 2001	42+40	12	6+6	3
Samuel	JLloyd	Trin	d	Oct 2001	7+1	0	0	0
Sidibe (Fr)	Mamady	Mli	f	Aug 2002	24+6	3	3+1	1
Awuah	Jones	Gha	f	Sep 2002	1+3	0	0	0

GLOSSOP (1)

SURNAME	NAME	BORN	POS	FROM	LgAp	LgG	OthAp	OthG
Cuffe	John	Aus	fb	Jul 1905	282	3	9	0

GRIMSBY TOWN (16)

SURNAME	NAME	BORN	POS	FROM	LgAp	LgG	OthAp	OthG
Seeburg	Max	Ger	f	Jul 1911	20	0	1	0
Andrews (N Ire)	Billy	USA	wh	Jul 1912	105	2	3	0
Hansen	Edvin	Den	f	Dec 1946	1	0	0	0
Okorie	Chima	Nig	f	Sep 1993	0+5	0	0+1	1
Bonetti	Ivano	It	m	Sep 1995	19	3	3	1
Gambaro	Enzo	It	d	Mar 1996	0+1	0	0	0
Nielsen	David	Den	f	Oct 2000	16+1	5	1+1	1
Fostervold	Anders	Nor	d	Nov 2000	9+1	0	0	0
Willems	Menno	Neth	f	Nov 2000	44+10	2	5	0
Enhua	Zhang	Chn	d	Dec 2000	16+1	3	0	0
Busscher	Robbie	Neth	m	Aug 2001	0+1	0	0	0
Neilson (Wal)	Alan	Ger	d	Oct 2001	8+2	0	2	0
Pringle	Martin	Swe	f	Feb 2002	2	0	0	0
Santos	Georges	Fr	m	Oct 2002	24+2	1	1	1
Sagere	Jake	USA	f	Apr 2003	1	0	0	0
Barnard (Wal)	Darren	Ger	m	Apr 2003	21+8	2	1	0

HALIFAX TOWN (9)

SURNAME	NAME	BORN	POS	FROM	LgAp	LgG	OthAp	OthG
Mackrill	Percy	SA	fb	Jul 1921	57	0	5	0
Burgess	Mike	Can	f/ch	Jul 1961	34	3	2	0
Chadwick (Brit)	Dave	Ind	w	Jan 1970	95	15	8	1
Kemp (Brit)	Fred	It	m	Dec 1971	106+5	10	8	1
Carr	Everton	Ant	fb	Aug 1981	49+4	0	5	0
Podd	Ces	StK	fb	Aug 1984	52+5	0	6+1	0
Henry	Liburd	Dom	f	Sep 1988	1+4	0	0	0
Craven	Peter	Ger	w	Mar 1993	7	0	0	0
Obebo	Godfrey	Nig	f	Mar 1993	0+3	0	0	0

HARTLEPOOL UNITED (15)

SURNAME	NAME	BORN	POS	FROM	LgAp	LgG	OthAp	OthG
Abdallah	Tewfik	Egy	f	Mar 1924	11	1	0	0
Hill (Brit)	Reg	Gib	wh	Jan 1933	139	6	13	0
Baines	Peter	Aus	f	Jun 1947	9	1	0	0
Tunks (Brit)	Roy	Ger	gk	Jul 1988	5	0	0	0
Atkinson (Brit)	Paddy	Sing	fb	Aug 1988	9+12	3	2+2	0
Talia	Frank	Aus	gk	Dec 1992	14	0	0	0

SURNAME	NAME	BORN	POS	FROM	LgAp	LgG	OthAp	OthG
Horace (Fr)	Alain	Mad	m	Oct 1996	0+1	0	0	0
Pedersen	Jan Ove	Nor	m	Oct 1997	17	1	1	1
Hollund	Martin	Nor	gk	Nov 1997	117	0	9	0
Larsen	Stig Olav	Nor	f	Dec 1997	0+4	0	0	0
Di Lella	Gustavo	Arg	m	Mar 1998	22+9	4	4+1	1
Miotto	Simon	Aus	gk	Jul 1998	5	0	0	0
Tennebo	Thomas	Nor	d	Aug 1999	6+7	0	1+2	0
Vindheim	Rune	Nor	m	Sep 1999	7	0	1	0
Sperrevik	Tim	Nor	f	Aug 2000	4+11	1	1	0

HEREFORD UNITED (6)

SURNAME	NAME	BORN	POS	FROM	LgAp	LgG	OthAp	OthG
Kemp (Brit)	Fred	It	m	Jul 1974	12+1	2	3	0
Musial	Adam	Pol	d	Aug 1980	44+2	0	2	0
Jennings	Jed	Ber	fb	Aug 1991	11+5	0	0	0
Wade	Meshach	Ber	m	Aug 1991	13+4	0	5	0
Nebbeling	Gavin	SA	d	Dec 1991	3	0	1	0
Kottila	Mika	Fin	f	Nov 1996	11+2	1	0	0

HUDDERSFIELD TOWN (24)

SURNAME	NAME	BORN	POS	FROM	LgAp	LgG	OthAp	OthG
Wilcox (Brit)	Tom	At sea	gk	Jan 1911	2	0	0	0
Wienand	Tolley	SA	m	Jul 1937	28	3	4	0
Lindsay	Denis	SA	gk	Aug 1937	1	0	0	0
Hansen	Karl	Nor	f	Jan 1949	15	2	0	0
Carr	John	SA	w	Oct 1950	1	0	0	0
Kennon	Sandy	SA	gk	Aug 1956	78	0	2	0
Callaghan (Eng)	Nigel	Sing	w	Jan 1992	8	0	0	0
Short (Brit)	Chris	Ger	d	Dec 1994	6	0	0	0
Tisdale (Brit)	Paul	Mal	m	Nov 1996	1+1	0	0	0
Phillips (Brit)	David	Ger	m	Nov 1997	44+8	3	7	0
Nielsen	Martin	Den	d	Mar 1998	0+3	0	0	0
Vaesen	Nico	Bel	gk	Jul 1998	134	0	19	0
Donis	George	Grk	m	Jun 1999	10+10	0	3+2	0
Wijnhard (Neth)	Clyde	Sur	f	Jul 1999	51+11	16	8	1
Monkou (Neth)	Ken	Sur	d	Aug 1999	21	1	4	0
Gorre (Neth)	Dean	Sur	m	Sep 1999	49+13	6	5+1	1
Hodouto (Fr)	Kwami	Tgo	d	Sep 1999	1+1	0	1	0
Ngonge (DRC)	Michel	Bel	f	Mar 2000	0+4	0	0	0
Ndlovu	Peter	Zim	f	Dec 2000	6	4	0	0
Brennan	Jim	Can	d	Mar 2001	0+2	0	0	0
Thorrington	John	USA	m	Aug 2001	45+17	7	2+3	0
McDonald	Scott	Aus	f	Aug 2002	7+6	1	0+1	0
Sharp	Kevin	Can	d	Aug 2002	38+1	0	3	0
Labarthe	Gianfranco	Per	f	Feb 2003	0+3	0	0	0

HULL CITY (23)

SURNAME	NAME	BORN	POS	FROM	LgAp	LgG	OthAp	OthG
Mills (Brit) (1)	Paddy	Ind	f	Aug 1920	173	76	11	7
Gibson	Jock	USA	fb	May 1922	210	0	8	0
Mills (Brit) (2)	Paddy	Ind	f	Dec 1929	96	25	11	2
McNeill (Brit)	Hamilton	Mal	f	May 1937	52	27	0	0
Wienand	Tolley	SA	w	Oct 1938	15	3	0	0
Jensen	Viggo	Den	d/m	Oct 1948	308	51	27	3
Ackerman (1)	Alf	SA	f	Jul 1950	34	21	3	0
Ackerman (2)	Alf	SA	f	Oct 1953	58	28	8	2
Tulloch	Roland	SA	wh	Dec 1953	3	0	0	0
Rintanen	Mauno	Fin	gk	Sep 1956	4	0	0	0
Nielson	Norman	SA	ch	Apr 1957	25	0	3	0
Cubie	Neil	SA	wh	Jul 1957	4	0	0	0
Hesford (Eng)	Iain	Zam	gk	Dec 1988	91	0	9	0
Ngata	Harry	NZ	f	Jul 1989	8+17	0	1+1	0
Doncel	Antonio	Sp	d	Aug 1996	30+8	2	6+1	0
Dickinson	Patrick	Can	m	Jul 1997	2+2	0	1	0
Goodison	Ian	Jam	d	Oct 1999	67+3	1	9+1	0
Whitmore	Theo	Jam	m	Oct 1999	63+14	9	10+1	1
Betsy	Kevin	Sey	m	Nov 1999	1+1	0	0	0
Marcelle	Clint	Trin	f	Sep 2000	16+7	2	2	0
Johnsson (Far)	Julian	Den	m	Jun 2001	38+2	4	4	1
Sneekes	Richard	Neth	m	Nov 2001	17+5	0	0+1	0
Van Blerk	Jason	Aus	m	Jan 2002	10	1	0	0
Caceres (Aus)	Adrian	Arg	m	Mar 2002	1+3	0	0	0
Lightbourne	Kyle	Ber	f	Mar 2002	3+1	0	0	0

IPSWICH TOWN (45)

SURNAME	NAME	BORN	POS	FROM	LgAp	LgG	OthAp	OthG
Havenga	Willie	SA	f	Jan 1952	19	3	0	0
Pickett (Brit)	Reg	Ind	wh	Jul 1957	140	3	6	0
Baker	Gerry	USA	f	Dec 1963	135	58	16	8
Viljoen	Colin	SA	m	Mar 1967	303+2	45	59+3	9
Twamley	Bruce	Can	fb	Oct 1969	2	0	0	0
Butcher (Eng)	Terry	Sing	d	Aug 1976	271	16	80	5
Muhren	Arnold	Neth	m	Aug 1978	161	21	53	8
Thijssen	Frans	Neth	m	Feb 1979	123+2	10	44+1	6
D'Avray (Eng)	Mich	SA	f	May 1979	170+41	37	29+10	9
Zondervan (Neth)	Romeo	Sur	m	Mar 1984	270+4	13	37+2	5

SURNAME	NAME	BORN	POS	FROM	LgAp	LgG	OthAp	OthG
Bernal	Andy	Aus	d	Sep 1987	4+5	0	0	0
Wilson (Neth)	Ulrich	Sur	d	Dec 1987	5+1	0	0	0
Baltacha (Ukr)	Sergei	USSR	d	Jan 1989	22+6	1	1	0
Cheetham	Mike	Neth	m	Oct 1988	1+3	0	0+1	0
Forrest	Craig	Can	gk	Aug 1988	263	0	35	0
Bozinoski (Aus)	Vlado	Mac	m	Dec 1992	3+6	0	1+2	0
Guentchev	Bontcho	Bul	m	Dec 1992	39+22	6	12+2	5
Petterson (1)	Andy	Aus	gk	Mar 1993	1	0	0	0
Gregory (Brit)	Neil	Zam	f	Aug 1994	18+27	9	3+5	0
Norfolk	Lee	NZ	m	Jul 1994	1+2	0	0	0
Paz	Adrian	Uru	f	Sep 1994	13+4	1	0+1	0
Taricco	Mauricio	Arg	fb	Sep 1994	134+3	4	30	3
Thomsen	Claus	Den	m	Jun 1994	77+4	7	13	1
Petterson (2)	Andy	Aus	gk	Sep 1995	1	0	0	0
Uhlenbeek (Neth)	Gus	Sur	d	Aug 1995	77+12	4	12+7	0
Gudmundsson	Niklas	Swe	f	Mar 1997	2+6	2	1+1	1
Jean	Earl	StL	f	Dec 1996	0+1	0	0	0
Petta	Bobby	Neth	m	Jun 1996	55+15	9	16+3	0
Johnson	David	Jam	f	Nov 1997	121+10	55	27	7
Stein (Eng)	Mark	SA	f	Aug 1997	6+1	2	3+1	1
Abou (Fr)	Samassi	IvCo	f	Dec 1998	5	1	0	0
Holster	Marco	Neth	m	Jul 1998	1+9	0	0+2	0
Thetis	Manuel	Fr	d	Sep 1998	44+3	2	9+1	1
Wilnis (Neth)	Fabian	Sur	d	Jan 1999	113+18	5	25+4	0
Axeldahl	Jonas	Swe	f	Jul 1999	1+15	0	0+4	0
Reuser	Martijn	Neth	f	Jun 2000	39+35	11	9+10	3
Abidallah	Nabil	Neth	m	Jul 2000	0+2	0	0+1	0
Hreidarsson	Hermann	Ice	d	Aug 2000	101+1	2	26	1
Karic	Amir	Slo	d	Sep 2000	0	0	0+3	0
Gaardsoe	Thomas	Den	m	Aug 2001	40+1	5	5+3	2
George	Finidi	Nig	f	Aug 2001	24+11	7	6+5	1
Counago	Pablo	Sp	f	May 2001	29+23	17	12+3	4
Le Pen	Ulrich	Fr	m	Nov 2001	0+1	0	0+2	0
Peralta	Sixto	Arg	m	Aug 2001	16+6	3	5+2	2
Sereni	Matteo	It	gk	Aug 2001	25	0	8	0

KIDDERMINSTER HARRIERS (7)

Skovbjerg	Thomas	Den	m	Aug 1999	7+5	1	0	0
Shail (Brit)	Mark	Swe	d	Jul 2000	40	1	5	0
Kerr (Brit)	Dylan	Mal	d	Sep 2000	0+1	0	0	0
Medou-Otye	Parfait	Cam	d	Nov 2000	18+1	0	1	0
Joy	Ian	USA	d	Aug 2001	15+7	0	0+1	0
Sall	Abdou	Sen	d	Aug 2001	31	2	1	0
Henriksen	Bo	Den	f	Nov 2001	60+2	28	4	0

LEEDS UNITED (38)

Armand (Brit)	Jack	Ind	f	Dec 1922	74	23	5	1
Hodgson (Eng)	Gordon	SA	f	Mar 1937	82	51	4	2
Miller	George	SA	f	Nov 1950	13	1	1	0
Stewart	Gordon	SA	f	Oct 1951	9	2	2	0
Hastie	Ken	SA	f	Aug 1952	4	2	0	0
Francis	Gerry	SA	w	Jul 1957	48	9	4	0
Johanneson	Albert	SA	w	Apr 1961	170+2	48	27+1	19
Sabella	Alex	Arg	m	Jun 1980	22+1	2	4	0
Blake (Brit)	Noel	Jam	d	Jul 1988	51	4	6+1	0
Kerr (Brit)	Dylan	Mal	d	Feb 1989	6+7	0	3	0
Dorigo (Eng)	Tony	Aus	fb	Jun 1991	168+3	5	35+1	0
Cantona	Eric	Fr	f	Feb 1992	18+10	9	6	2
Sharp	Kevin	Can	d	Oct 1992	11+6	0	0+1	0
Strandli	Frank	Nor	f	Jan 1993	5+9	2	1+1	0
Masinga	Phil	SA	f	Aug 1994	20+11	5	6+2	6
Radebe	Lucas	SA	d	Sep 1994	168+15	0	55+6	3
Yeboah	Tony	Gha	f	Jan 1995	44+3	24	17+2	8
Brolin	Tomas	Swe	m	Nov 1995	17+2	4	3+3	0
Kewell	Harry	Aus	m	Dec 1995	169+12	45	58+3	18
Knarvik	Tommy	Nor	m	Nov 1996	0	0	0+1	0
Halle	Gunnar	Nor	d	Dec 1996	65+5	4	13+2	0
Molenaar	Robert	Neth	d	Jan 1997	47+4	5	13+1	1
Laurent	Pierre	Fr	f	Mar 1997	2+2	0	0	0
Haaland	Alf-Inge	Nor	m	Jul 1997	57+17	8	15+3	0
Hasselbaink (Neth)	Jimmy Floyd	Sur	f	Jul 1997	66+3	34	18	8
Ribeiro	Bruno	Por	m	Jul 1997	35+7	4	8+2	2
Hiden	Martin	Aut	d	Feb 1998	25+1	0	6	0
Wijnhard (Neth)	Clyde	Sur	f	Jul 1998	11+7	3	3+4	1
Korsten	Willem	Neth	f	Jan 1999	4+3	2	2+1	0
Bakke	Eirik	Nor	m	Jul 1999	99+20	7	45+4	12
Hay	Danny	NZ	d	Aug 1999	2+2	0	1+1	0
Dacourt	Olivier	Fr	m	Jul 2000	53+4	3	25	0
Viduka	Mark	Aus	f	Jul 2000	96+4	48	35	12
Burns	Jacob	Aus	m	Aug 2000	5+1	0	4+1	0
McMaster	Jamie	Aus	m	Sep 2002	0+2	0	0	0

SURNAME	NAME	BORN	POS	FROM	LgAp	LgG	OthAp	OthG
Lucic	Teddy	Swe	d	Oct 2002	16+1	1	3+1	0
Okon	Paul	Aus	d	Nov 2002	15	0	6	0
Bravo	Raul	Sp	d	Feb 2003	5	0	1	0

LEICESTER CITY (23)

SURNAME	NAME	BORN	POS	FROM	LgAp	LgG	OthAp	OthG
Osborne (Eng)	Reg	SA	fb	Feb 1923	240	2	9	0
Callachan (Brit)	Harry	Ind	fb	Sep 1929	3	0	0	0
Mandy	Aubrey	SA	gk	Oct 1929	3	0	0	0
Carr	Everton	Ant	fb	Jan 1979	11+1	0	2	0
Lee (Brit)	Alan	Ger	w	Feb 1979	6	0	0	0
Hazell (Eng)	Bob	Jam	d	Sep 1983	41	2	5	0
Christensen	Tommy	Den	f	Nov 1985	1+1	0	0	0
D'Avray (Eng)	Mich	SA	f	Feb 1987	3	0	0	0
Rantanen	Jari	Fin	f	Sep 1987	10+3	3	2+1	1
Osvold	Kjetil	Nor	m	Dec 1987	3+1	0	0	0
Oldfield (Eng)	David	Aus	m/f	Jan 1990	163+25	26	20+5	4
Corica	Steve	Aus	m	Aug 1995	16	2	2	0
Rolling	Franck	Fr	d	Sep 1995	18	0	5+1	0
Kalac	Zeljko	Aus	gk	Oct 1995	1	0	1+1	0
Kaamark	Pontus	Swe	d	Nov 1995	60+5	0	11+1	0
Keller	Kasey	USA	gk	Aug 1996	99	0	27	0
Lenhart	Sascha	Ger	m	Sep 1996	0	0	0+1	0
Arphexad (Fr)	Pegguy	Guad	gk	Aug 1997	17+4	0	7+1	0
Zagorakis	Theo	Grk	m	Feb 1998	34+16	3	11+7	0
Gunnlaugsson	Arnie	Ice	m	Feb 1999	10+20	3	3+7	1
Mancini	Roberto	It	f	Jan 2001	3+1	0	1	0
Laursen	Jacob	Den	d/m	Jan 2002	10	0	0	0
Petrescu	Tomi	Fin	f	May 2003	0+1	0	0	0

LEYTON ORIENT (33)

SURNAME	NAME	BORN	POS	FROM	LgAp	LgG	OthAp	OthG
Van Den Eynden	Ike	Bel	ch	Feb 1914	12	0	0	0
Higginbotham	Harry	Aus	f	Feb 1923	19	1	0	0
Ashton (Brit)	Hubert	Ind	fb	Aug 1926	5	0	0	0
Tricker (Brit)	Reg	Ind	f	Feb 1929	131	60	6	3
Gerula	Stan	Pol	gk	May 1948	30	0	1	0
Burgess	Mike	Can	f/ch	Jul 1953	31	12	5	2
Crossan	Errol	Can	w	Jan 1961	8	2	2	0
Heppolette (Brit)	Ricky	Ind	m	Dec 1972	113+10	9	0	0
Chiedozie	John	Nig	w	Apr 1977	131+14	20	15	3
Zoricich	Chris	NZ	d	Feb 1990	53+9	1	6+3	0
Bart-Williams (Brit)	Chris	SiLe	m	Jul 1990	34+2	2	4	0
Okai (Brit)	Stephen	Gha	m	Apr 1992	11+14	4	2+2	0
Kitchen (Brit)	Sam	Ger	d	Aug 1992	35+8	1	6	0
Ayorinde	Sammy	Nig	f	Apr 1996	7+6	2	2+1	0
Riches	Steve	Aus	m	Sep 1996	2+3	0	0	0
Heidenstrom	Bjorn	Nor	d/m	Dec 1996	3+1	0	0	0
Walschaerts	Wim	Bel	m	Jul 1998	120+5	9	22+1	2
McDougald (Brit)	Junior	USA	f	Oct 1998	3+5	0	1+1	0
Simba	Amara	Fr	f	Oct 1998	27+10	13	8+4	1
Omoyimni	Manny	Nig	f	Mar 1999	3+1	1	0	0
Harris (Brit)	Andy	SA	m	Jul 1999	143+6	2	21+1	0
Brkovic	Ahmet	Cro	m	Oct 1999	59+10	8	7+4	2
Garcia	Richard	Aus	f	Aug 2000	18	4	3	0
Cadiou	Frederic	Fr	f	Oct 2000	0+3	0	0	0
Mansley	Chad	Aus	f	Nov 2000	0+1	0	0+1	0
Opara	Kelechi	Nig	f	Dec 2000	3+3	0	2	0
Vasseur	Emmanuel	Fr	m	Jan 2001	0+2	0	0	0
Opinel	Sacha	Fr	d	Feb 2001	9+2	1	0	0
Pinamonte	Lorenzo	It	f	Feb 2001	5+6	2	0	0
Forge	Nicolas	Fr	d	Mar 2001	1	0	0	0
Forbes	Boniek	GuB	f	Sep 2002	0+3	0	0+1	0
Miller	Justin	SA	d	Sep 2002	19	0	3	0
Zakuani	Gaby	DRC	d	Mar 2003	0+1	0	0	0

LINCOLN CITY (16)

SURNAME	NAME	BORN	POS	FROM	LgAp	LgG	OthAp	OthG
Dwane (Brit)	Eddie	Mal	wh	Jul 1920	46	2	2	0
Killin	Roy	Can	fb	Aug 1952	7	0	3	0
Houghton (Brit)	Bud	Ind	f	Oct 1963	54	22	7	3
Dillsworth	Eddie	SL	wh	Mar 1967	2	0	0	0
Coker	Ade	Nig	f	Dec 1974	6	1	1	0
Bowery	Bert	StK	f	Feb 1976	2+2	1	0	0
Cunningham (Brit)	Tony	Jam	f	May 1979	111+12	32	18+1	8
Kelly	Errington	StV	w	Jan 1983	0+2	0	0	0
Casey (Brit)	Paul	Ger	d/m	Mar 1988	44+5	4	4	0
Carmichael (Brit)	Matt	Sing	f	Aug 1989	113+20	18	13+2	1
Bos	Gijsbert	Neth	m	Mar 1996	28+6	6	7	4
Grobbelaar (Zim)	Bruce	SA	gk	Dec 1998	2	0	0	0
Phillips (Brit)	David	Ger	m	Mar 1999	15+2	0	1+1	0
Agogo	Manuel	Gha	f	Dec 1999	3	1	0	0
Stergiopoulos (Grk)	Marcus	Aus	m	Aug 2000	2+5	0	1+1	1
Pearce	Allan	NZ	f	Dec 2002	9+7	1	0	0

SURNAME	NAME	BORN	POS	FROM	LgAp	LgG	OthAp	OthG
LIVERPOOL (53)								
Lester	Hugh	USA	wh	Aug 1911	2	0	0	0
Hodgson (Eng)	Gordon	SA	f	Nov 1925	359	232	19	8
Riley	Arthur	SA	gk	Jul 1925	322	0	16	0
Carr	Lance	SA	w	Aug 1933	31	8	2	0
Nieuwenhuys	Berry	SA	w	Sep 1933	239	74	21	5
Kemp	Dirk	SA	gk	Jul 1936	30	0	3	0
Van Den Berg	Herman	SA	w	Jul 1937	22	4	0	0
Priday	Bob	SA	w	Dec 1945	34	6	6	1
Gerhardt	Hugh	SA	f	Aug 1952	6	0	0	0
Rudham	Doug	SA	gk	Nov 1954	63	0	3	0
Cohen	Avi	Isr	fb	Jul 1979	16+2	1	5+1	0
Grobbelaar (Zim)	Bruce	SA	gk	Mar 1981	440	0	169	0
Johnston (Aus)	Craig	SA	w	Apr 1981	165+25	30	59+12	9
Molby	Jan	Den	m	Aug 1984	195+23	44	55+8	14
Barnes (Eng)	John	Jam	f	Jun 1987	310+4	84	89	22
Hysen	Glenn	Swe	d	Jul 1989	70+2	2	19	1
Rosenthal	Ronny	Isr	f	Jun 1990	32+42	21	8+13	1
Kozma	Istvan	Hun	m	Feb 1992	3+3	0	0+3	0
Piechnik	Torben	Den	d	Sep 1992	16+1	0	7	0
Bjornebye	Stig Inge	Nor	d	Dec 1992	132+7	2	43+2	2
Berger	Patrik	CzRep	f	Aug 1996	106+42	28	30+17	7
Kvarme	Bjorn Tore	Nor	d	Jan 1997	39+6	0	9	0
Leonhardsen	Oyvind	Nor	m	Jun 1997	34+3	7	8+4	0
Riedle	Karl-Heinz	Ger	f	Aug 1997	34+26	11	8+8	4
Friedel	Brad	USA	gk	Dec 1997	25	0	5+1	0
Dundee	Sean	SA	d	Jun 1998	0+3	0	0+2	0
Heggem	Vegard	Nor	d	Jul 1998	38+16	3	8+3	0
Ferri	Jean-Michel	Fr	d/m	Dec 1998	0+2	0	0	0
Kippe	Frode	Nor	d	Jan 1999	0	0	0+2	0
Song	Rigobert	Cam	d	Jan 1999	27+7	0	3+1	0
Traore	Djimi	Fr	d	Feb 1999	38+2	0	20+3	0
Camara	Titi	Gui	f	Jun 1999	22+11	9	2+2	1
Westerveld	Sander	Neth	gk	Jun 1999	75	0	26	0
Hamann	Dietmar	Ger	m	Jul 1999	113+6	6	46+5	1
Henchoz	Stephane	Swit	d	Jul 1999	117	0	54	0
Hyypia	Sami	Fin	d	Jul 1999	146	11	64	5
Meijer	Erik	Neth	f	Jul 1999	7+17	0	3	2
Smicer	Vladimir	CzRep	m	Jul 1999	52+39	7	37+14	7
Diomede	Bernard	Fr	m	Jul 2000	1+1	0	3	0
Arphexad (Fr)	Pegguy	Guad	gk	Jul 2000	1+1	0	4	0
Babbel	Markus	Ger	d	Jul 2000	42	3	27+1	3
Ziege	Christian	Ger	m	Aug 2000	11+5	1	9+7	1
Vignal	Gregory	Fr	d	Sep 2000	7+4	0	7+2	0
Biscan	Igor	Cro	m	Dec 2000	15+9	0	10+8	1
Litmanen	Jari	Fin	f	Jan 2001	12+14	5	7+10	4
Riise	John Arne	Nor	d	Jun 2001	65+10	13	31+3	0
Dudek	Jerzy	Pol	gk	Aug 2001	65	0	28+1	0
Anelka	Nicolas	Fr	f	Dec 2001	13+7	4	2	1
Baros	Milan	CzRep	f	Dec 2001	17+10	9	5+10	3
Xavier (Por)	Abel	Moz	d	Jan 2002	13+1	1	6	1
Cheyrou	Bruno	Fr	m	Aug 2002	8+11	0	6+3	1
Diao	Salif	Sen	m	Aug 2002	13+13	1	9+5	1
Diouf	El Hadji	Sen	f	Aug 2002	21+8	3	13+4	3
LUTON TOWN (42)								
Higginbotham	Harry	Aus	f	Jul 1920	80	26	8	4
Bookman (Brit)	Louis	Lith	w	Aug 1920	72	4	5	1
Tricker (Brit)	Reg	Ind	f	Jul 1924	4	0	1	0
Edwards	Gerald	HK	gk	Jan 1931	2	0	0	0
Mills	Arthur	Ind	w	Jul 1932	37	14	4	0
Gibson	Jock	USA	fb	Jul 1933	3	0	0	0
Preedy (Brit)	Charlie	Ind	gk	Aug 1934	5	0	0	0
Shanks (Brit)	Wally	Mal	wh	Dec 1946	264	6	11	0
Arnison	Joseph	SA	f	Aug 1948	44	19	2	2
Havenga	Willie	SA	f	May 1950	18	6	1	1
Davies	Roy	SA	w	May 1951	150	24	16	2
McEwan	Peter	SA	f	Feb 1954	26	11	0	0
Stein (Eng) (1)	Brian	SA	f	Oct 1977	378+10	126	63	21
Antic	Raddy	Yug	m	Jul 1980	54+40	9	5+3	1
Nwajiobi	Emeka	Nig	f	Dec 1983	59+13	17	11+4	3
Stein (Eng) (1)	Mark	SA	f	Jan 1984	41+13	19	13+1	3
McEvoy (Brit)	Ricky	Gib	m	Aug 1985	0+1	0	0	0
Oldfield (Eng) (1)	David	Aus	m/f	May 1986	21+8	4	4+3	2
McDonough (Brit)	Darron	Bel	d	Sep 1986	88+17	5	19+2	2
Wegerle (USA)	Roy	SA	f	Jul 1988	39+6	10	11	8
Petterson	Andy	Aus	gk	Dec 1988	16+3	0	2	0
Elstrup	Lars	Den	f	Aug 1989	50+10	19	7	7
Stein (Eng) (2)	Brian	SA	f	Jul 1991	32+7	3	2+1	0
Sommer	Jurgen	USA	gk	Sep 1991	82	0	17	0
Aunger	Geoff	Can	d/m	Sep 1993	5	1	0	0

SURNAME	NAME	BORN	POS	FROM	LgAp	LgG	OthAp	OthG
Marshall (Brit)	Dwight	Jam	f	Jul 1994	90+38	28	16+4	7
Oldfield (Eng) (2)	David	Aus	m/f	Jul 1995	99+18	18	15	5
Guentchev	Bontcho	Bul	m	Aug 1995	40+22	10	7+4	0
Feuer	Ian	USA	gk	Sep 1995	97	0	15	0
Vilstrup	Johnny	Den	m	Sep 1995	6+1	0	0	0
Riseth	Vidar	Nor	d/m	Oct 1995	6+5	0	0	0
Grant	Kim	Gha	f	Mar 1996	18+17	5	4+3	2
Bacque	Herve	Fr	f	Aug 1998	2+5	0	1+2	0
Kandol (Brit)	Tresor	DRC	f	Sep 1998	9+12	3	3+1	2
Zahana-Oni	Landry	IvCo	f	Jan 1999	4+5	0	0	0
Stein (Eng) (2)	Mark	SA	f	Jul 2000	19+11	3	4+1	1
Breitenfelder	Friedrich	Aut	m	Aug 2000	2+3	0	0	0
Helin	Petri	Fin	d	Nov 2000	23	1	3	0
Karlsen	Kent	Nor	d	Nov 2000	4+2	0	2	0
Coyne	Chris	Aus	d	Sep 2001	67+4	0	3	0
Valois	Jean-Louis	Fr	m	Sep 2001	32+2	6	0	0
Brkovic	Ahmet	Cro	m	Oct 2001	46+11	4	4	3
Neilson (Wal)	Alan	Ger	d	Feb 2002	29+5	0	1+3	0
Berthelin	Cedric	Fr	gk	Oct 2002	9	0	0	0
Hirschfeld	Lars	Can	gk	Feb 2003	5	0	0	0

MACCLESFIELD TOWN (5)

SURNAME	NAME	BORN	POS	FROM	LgAp	LgG	OthAp	OthG
Matias	Pedro	Sp	m	Dec 1998	21+1	2	1	0
Abbey	George	Nig	d	Aug 1999	56+19	1	6+5	0
Tereskinas	Andrejus	Lith	d	Nov 2000	0+1	0	0	0
Lightbourne	Kyle	Ber	f	Jul 2001	61+12	15	6	3
Nash	Martin	Can	m	Jan 2003	1+4	0	0	0

MAIDSTONE UNITED (3)

SURNAME	NAME	BORN	POS	FROM	LgAp	LgG	OthAp	OthG
Henry	Liburd	Dom	f	Jun 1990	61+6	9	3+1	1
Hesford (Eng)	Iain	Zam	gk	Aug 1991	42	1	4	0
Richards (Eng)	Carl	Jam	f	Oct 1991	4	2	0	0

MANCHESTER CITY (59)

SURNAME	NAME	BORN	POS	FROM	LgAp	LgG	OthAp	OthG
Bowman	WW	Can	ch	Feb 1893	47	3	2	0
McDowall (Brit)	Les	Ind	ch	Mar 1938	120	8	9	0
Trautmann	Bert	Ger	gk	Nov 1949	508	0	37	0
Baker	Gerry	USA	f	Nov 1960	37	14	2	0
Viljoen	Colin	SA	m	Aug 1978	25+2	0	10+1	1
Deyna	Kazimierz	Pol	f	Nov 1978	34+4	12	4+1	1
Stepanovic	Dragoslav	Yug	d	Aug 1979	14+1	0	4	0
Hareide	Aage	Nor	d	Oct 1981	17+7	0	0+1	0
Golac	Ivan	Yug	fb	Mar 1983	2	0	0	0
Cunningham (Brit)	Tony	Jam	f	Jul 1984	16+2	1	5+1	3
Phillips (Brit)	David	Ger	m	Aug 1984	81	13	13	0
Oldfield (Eng)	David	Aus	m/f	Mar 1989	18+8	6	2+1	2
Lomas (N Ire)	Steve	Ger	m	Jan 1991	102+9	8	25+1	3
Hoekman	Danny	Neth	m	Oct 1991	0+1	0	0+2	0
Vonk	Michel	Neth	d	Jun 1992	87+4	4	9+3	2
Ingebrigtsen	Kaare	Nor	m	Jan 1993	4+11	0	2	3
Groenendijk	Alfons	Neth	m	Jul 1993	9	0	3	0
Karl	Steffen	Ger	d/m	Mar 1994	4+2	1	0	0
Rosler	Uwe	Ger	f	Feb 1994	141+11	50	24+1	14
Whitley (N Ire)	Jim	Zam	m	Aug 1994	27+11	0	5+2	1
Gaudino	Maurizio	Ger	m	Dec 1994	17+3	3	4+1	1
Immel	Eike	Ger	gk	Aug 1995	42	0	8	0
Kinkladze	Georgi	Geo	m	Aug 1995	105+1	20	15	2
Ekelund	Ronnie	Den	f	Dec 1995	2+2	0	1+1	0
Frontzeck	Michael	Ger	d	Jan 1996	19+4	0	2	0
Whitley (N Ire)	Jeff	Zam	m	Feb 1996	96+27	8	14+3	0
Kavelashvili	Mikhail	Geo	f	Mar 1996	9+19	3	0+1	0
Mazzarelli	Giuseppe	Swit	m	Mar 1996	0+2	0	0	0
Wiekens	Gerard	Neth	d	Jul 1997	167+15	10	27+3	0
Van Blerk	Jason	Aus	fb	Aug 1997	10+9	0	0+2	0
Shelia	Murtaz	Geo	d	Nov 1997	15	2	2	0
Tskhadadze	Kakhaber	Geo	d	Feb 1998	12	2	1	1
Goater	Shaun	Ber	f	Mar 1998	164+20	84	25+3	19
Tiatto	Danny	Aus	d	Jul 1998	111+24	3	13+1	1
Allsopp	Danny	Aus	f	Aug 1998	3+26	4	0+8	1
Killen	Chris	NZ	f	Mar 1999	0+3	0	0	0
Dunfield	Terry	Can	m	May 1999	0+1	0	0	0
Etuhu	Dixon	Nig	m	Dec 1999	11+1	0	1	0
Haaland	Alf-Inge	Nor	m	Jun 2000	35+3	3	8+1	0
Wanchope	Paulo	CoRi	f	Aug 2000	39+3	21	7	2
Weah	George	Lbr	f	Aug 2000	5+2	1	2	3
Charvet	Laurent	Fr	d	Oct 2000	19+4	0	0+1	0
Kanchelskis	Andrei	Urk	w	Jan 2001	7+3	0	1	1
Ostenstad	Egil	Nor	f	Feb 2001	1+3	0	0	0
Berkovic	Eyal	Isr	m	Jul 2001	47+5	7	6+2	0
Colosimo	Simon	Aus	d	Jul 2001	0+6	0	1	0
Benarbia	Ali	Alg	m	Sep 2001	59+12	11	7	0

SURNAME	NAME	BORN	POS	FROM	LgAp	LgG	OthAp	OthG
Mettomo	Lucien	Cam	d	Sep 2001	20+7	1	3+1	0
Negouai (Fr)	Christian	Mart	m	Nov 2001	2+3	1	1+1	0
Jensen	Niclas	Den	m	Jan 2002	48+3	2	5	0
Toure	Alioune	Fr	f	Sep 2001	0+1	0	0+1	0
Jihai	Sun	Chn	d	Feb 2002	27+8	2	3	0
Anelka	Nicolas	Fr	f	Aug 2002	38	14	3	0
Distin	Sylvain	Fr	d	Aug 2002	34	0	2	0
Foe	Marc-Vivien	Cam	m	Aug 2002	35	9	3	0
Schmeichel	Peter	Den	gk	Aug 2002	29	0	2	0
Bischoff	Mikkel	Den	d	Sep 2002	1	0	0	0
Belmadi (Alg)	Djamel	Fr	m	Jan 2003	2+6	0	0	0
Sommeil (Fr)	David	Guad	d	Jan 2003	14	1	0	0

MANCHESTER UNITED (37)

SURNAME	NAME	BORN	POS	FROM	LgAp	LgG	OthAp	OthG
Bell (Sco)	Alec	SA	wh	Jan 1903	278	10	28	0
Wilcox (Brit)	Tom	At sea	gk	Aug 1907	2	0	0	0
Hunter (Brit)	George	Ind	wh	Mar 1914	22	2	1	0
Mitten (Brit)	Charlie	Bur	w	Jan 1938	142	50	19	11
Sartori	Carlo	It	m	Feb 1965	26+13	4	14+2	2
Nicholl (N Ire)	Jimmy	Can	fb	Feb 1974	188+9	3	46+4	3
Jovanovic	Nikola	Yug	d	Jan 1980	20+1	4	5	0
Muhren	Arnold	Neth	m	Aug 1982	65+5	13	27	5
Olsen	Jesper	Den	f	Jul 1984	119+20	21	29+7	3
Sivebaek	John	Den	d	Feb 1986	29+2	1	3	0
Bosnich (1)	Mark	Aus	gk	Jun 1989	3	0	0	0
Kanchelskis	Andrei	Urk	w	Mar 1991	96+27	28	33+2	8
Schmeichel	Peter	Den	gk	Aug 1991	292	0	100	1
Cantona	Eric	Fr	f	Nov 1992	142+1	64	39	16
Prunier	William	Fr	d	Dec 1995	2	0	0	0
Poborsky	Karel	CzRep	m	Jul 1996	18+14	5	10+5	1
Johnsen	Ronny	Nor	d	Jul 1996	85+14	7	43+5	1
Solskjaer	Ole Gunnar	Nor	f	Jul 1996	135+65	84	49+53	30
Van der Gouw	Raimond	Neth	gk	Jul 1996	26+11	0	20+1	0
Cruyff	Jordi	Neth	m	Aug 1996	15+19	8	9+8	0
Nevland	Erik	Nor	f	Jul 1997	0+1	0	2+3	1
Berg	Henning	Nor	d	Aug 1997	49+17	2	29+4	1
Blomqvist	Jesper	Swe	m	Jul 1998	20+5	1	9+4	0
Stam	Jaap	Neth	d	Jul 1998	79	1	39+1	0
Yorke	Dwight	Trin	f	Aug 1998	80+16	48	37+13	16
Djordjic (Swe)	Bojan	Yug	m	Feb 1999	0+1	0	1	0
Bosnich (2)	Mark	Aus	gk	Jun 1999	23	0	8	0
Rachubka	Paul	USA	gk	Jul 1999	1	0	0+1	0
Fortune	Quinton	SA	m	Aug 1999	23+13	5	10+9	0
Silvestre	Mickael	Fr	d	Sep 1999	120+10	2	49+6	1
Taibi	Massimo	It	gk	Sep 1999	4	0	0	0
Barthez	Fabien	Fr	gk	Jun 2000	92	0	45	0
Veron	Juan Sebastian	Arg	m	Jul 2001	45+6	7	30+1	4
Van Nistelrooy	Ruud	Neth	f	Apr 2001	62+4	48	31+3	31
Blanc	Laurent	Fr	d	Aug 2001	44+4	1	27	3
Forlan	Diego	Uru	f	Jan 2002	13+25	6	9+16	3
Lopez	Ricardo	Sp	gk	Sep 2002	0+1	0	3+1	0
Timm	Mads	Den	f	Oct 2002	0	0	0+1	0

MANSFIELD TOWN (10)

SURNAME	NAME	BORN	POS	FROM	LgAp	LgG	OthAp	OthG
Mitten (Brit)	Charlie	Bur	w	Feb 1956	100	25	6	2
Delapenha	Lindy	Jam	f	Jun 1958	115	27	5	0
Derko	Franco	It	fb	Jan 1965	1	0	0	0
Phillips	Brendon	Jam	m	Aug 1980	17	0	6	0
Blissett (Eng)	Luther	Jam	f	Dec 1993	4+1	1	0	0
Aspinall	Brendan	SA	d	Jul 1994	13+7	0	5+1	1
Carmichael (Brit)	Matt	Sing	f	Aug 1995	1	1	0	0
L'Helgoualch	Cyrille	Fr	m	Dec 1998	3+1	1	0	0
Camilieri-Gioia	Carlo	Bel	m	Sep 1999	0+2	0	0	0
Van Heusden	Arjan	Neth	gk	Sep 2002	5	0	0	0

MIDDLESBROUGH (41)

SURNAME	NAME	BORN	POS	FROM	LgAp	LgG	OthAp	OthG
Malan	Norman	SA	gk	Oct 1945	2	0	0	0
Ugolini	Rolando	It	gk	May 1948	320	0	15	0
Delapenha	Lindy	Jam	f	Apr 1950	260	90	10	3
Lightening	Arthur	SA	gk	Aug 1962	15	0	3	0
Chadwick (Brit)	Dave	Ind	w	Jul 1966	100+2	3	13+1	1
Johnston (Aus/Eng)	Craig	SA	w	Feb 1978	61+3	16	9+4	0
Jankovic	Bozo	Yug	f	Feb 1979	42+8	16	10+2	2
Otto	Heine	Neth	m	Aug 1981	163+3	24	21	4
Marshall (Brit)	Dwight	Jam	f	Mar 1993	0+3	0	0	0
Moreno (1)	Jaime	Bol	m	Sep 1994	8+13	1	3+1	0
Fuchs	Uwe	Ger	f	Jan 1995	13+2	9	0	0
Fjortoft	Jan Aage	Nor	f	Mar 1995	37+4	9	7+2	3
Juninho (1)		Bra	m	Oct 1995	54+2	14	18	3
Branco		Bra	f	Mar 1996	6+3	0	2	2
Emerson		Bra	m	Jun 1996	53	9	17	3

SURNAME	NAME	BORN	POS	FROM	LgAp	LgG	OthAp	OthG
Ravanelli	Fabrizio	It	f	Jun 1996	35	17	15	15
Beck	Mikkel	Den	f	Sep 1996	66+25	24	19+6	7
Festa	Gianluca	It	d	Jan 1997	132+6	10	32+1	2
Kinder	Vladimir	Svk	d	Jan 1997	29+8	5	10+1	0
Schwarzer	Mark	Aus	gk	Feb 1997	203	0	28	0
Moreira	Fabio	Bra	m	Feb 1997	1	0	0	0
Moreno (2)	Jaime	Bol	m	Dec 1997	1+4	1	2	0
Branca	Marco	It	f	Feb 1998	11+1	9	2	1
Ricard	Hamilton	Col	f	Mar 1998	92+23	33	17+2	10
Juninho (2)		Bra	m	Sep 1999	24+4	4	5	1
Ziege	Christian	Ger	m	Aug 1999	29	6	4+1	1
Marinelli	Carlos	Arg	m	Oct 1999	17+25	2	6+4	1
Boksic (Cro)	Alen	Herz	f	Aug 2000	59+9	22	5+4	0
Job (Cam)	Joseph-Desire	Fr	f	Aug 2000	33+11	7	2+2	0
Karembeu (Fr)	Christian	NCal	m	Aug 2000	31+2	4	2+1	0
Okon	Paul	Aus	d	Aug 2000	24+4	0	2	0
Nemeth	Szilard	Svk	f	Jul 2001	26+23	10	6+2	3
Wilkshire	Luke	Aus	m	Aug 2001	13+8	0	3	0
Queudrue	Franck	Fr	d	Oct 2001	57+2	3	8	1
Carbone	Benito	It	f	Feb 2002	13	1	0	0
Debeve	Mickael	Fr	m	Feb 2002	1+3	0	1+1	0
Boateng (Neth)	George	Gha	m	Aug 2002	28	0	0	0
Juninho (3)		Bra	m	Aug 2002	9+1	3	0	0
Maccarone	Massimo	It	f	Aug 2002	26+8	9	0	0
Geremi		Cam	d/m	Aug 2002	33	7	1	0
Doriva	Guidoni	Bra	m	Apr 2003	3+2	0	0	0

MILLWALL (29)

SURNAME	NAME	BORN	POS	FROM	LgAp	LgG	OthAp	OthG
Kingsley	Alf	Bar	w	Sep 1923	44	2	3	0
Bryant	Billy	Bel	ch	Jul 1925	132	30	7	0
Brown	Lennox	SA	f	Nov 1935	1	0	0	0
Ackerman	Alf	SA	f	Jan 1959	81	35	3	0
Smethurst	Derek	SA	f	Sep 1971	66+4	9	7+2	4
Smit(h)	Wilf	Ger	fb	Jan 1975	5	0	0	0
Granville	John	Trin	gk	Oct 1985	6	0	0	0
Salman (Eng)	Danis	Cyp	d	Aug 1986	85+8	4	12+1	1
Verveer (Neth)	Etienne	Sur	m	Dec 1991	46+10	7	6	2
Keller	Kasey	USA	gk	Feb 1992	176	0	24	0
Kerr (USA)	John	Can	f	Feb 1993	21+22	8	2+2	0
Murray	Bruce	USA	f	Aug 1993	7+6	2	0+1	1
Van Den Hauwe (Wal)	Pat	Bel	fb	Sep 1993	27	0	8	0
Van Blerk	Jason	Aus	fb	Sep 1994	68+5	2	11+1	0
Edwards	Alistair	Aus	f	Dec 1994	3+1	0	3+1	0
Oldfield (Eng)	David	Aus	m/f	Feb 1995	16+1	6	0	0
Iga (Brit)	Andrew	Uga	gk	Jun 1995	0+1	0	0	0
Fuchs	Uwe	Ger	f	Jul 1995	21+11	5	2+2	0
Neill	Lucas	Aus	d/m	Nov 1995	124+28	13	12+1	0
Kulkov	Vasili	Rus	d/m	Jan 1996	6	0	0	0
Yuran	Sergei	Ukr	f	Jan 1996	13	1	0	0
Cahill	Tim	Aus	m	Jul 1997	172+5	43	15+3	1
Grant	Kim	Gha	f	Aug 1997	35+20	11	3+1	1
Veart	Carl	Aus	m	Dec 1997	7+1	1	0	0
McDougald (Brit)	Junior	USA	f	Jul 1998	0+1	0	0	0
Kinet	Christophe	Bel	m	Feb 2000	39+28	7	6+7	1
Gueret (Fr)	Willy	Guad	gk	Jul 2000	11+1	0	1	0
Savarese	Giovanni	Ven	f	Jul 2001	0+1	0	0	0
Baltacha (Sco)	Sergei Jnr	Ukr	m	Jan 2003	1+1	0	0+1	0

NELSON (1)

SURNAME	NAME	BORN	POS	FROM	LgAp	LgG	OthAp	OthG
Higginbotham	Harry	Aus	f	Oct 1923	4	0	0	0

NEW BRIGHTON (2)

SURNAME	NAME	BORN	POS	FROM	LgAp	LgG	OthAp	OthG
Baines	Peter	Aus	f	Oct 1947	2	0	0	0
Turner	Alf	USA	f	Feb 1951	4	0	0	0

NEW BRIGHTON TOWER (1)

SURNAME	NAME	BORN	POS	FROM	LgAp	LgG	OthAp	OthG
Hogan	Cornelius	Mal	f	May 1899	18	1	0	0

NEWCASTLE UNITED (50)

SURNAME	NAME	BORN	POS	FROM	LgAp	LgG	OthAp	OthG
Whitson	Tony	SA	fb	Feb 1905	124	0	21	0
Robledo	George	Chi	f	Jan 1949	146	82	18	9
Robledo	Ted	Chi	wh	Feb 1949	37	0	8	0
Woollard	Arnold	Ber	fb	Dec 1952	8	0	2	0
Arentoft	Ben	Den	m	Mar 1969	46+4	2	13+1	1
Parkinson	Andy	SA	f	Mar 1978	0+3	0	0	0
Koenen	Frans	Neth	m	Aug 1980	11+1	1	2	0
Cunningham (Brit)	Tony	Jam	f	Feb 1985	37+10	4	3	2
Mirandinha	Francisco	Bra	f	Aug 1987	47+7	20	8+1	3
Pingel	Frank	Den	f	Jan 1989	13+1	1	0	0
Kristensen	Bjorn	Den	d	Mar 1989	69+11	4	11	0
Neilson (Wal)	Alan	Ger	d	Feb 1991	35+7	1	4	0

SURNAME	NAME	BORN	POS	FROM	LgAp	LgG	OthAp	OthG
Srnicek	Pavel	CzRep	gk	Feb 1991	148+1	0	31+1	0
McDonough (Brit)	Darron	Bel	d	Mar 1992	2+1	0	0	0
Papavasiliou	Nicky	Cyp	m	Jul 1993	7	0	0	0
Albert	Philippe	Bel	d	Aug 1994	87+9	8	36+5	4
Hottiger	Marc	Swit	d	Aug 1994	38+1	1	14+1	1
Crawford (Ire)	Jimmy	USA	d/m	Mar 1995	0+2	0	0+1	0
Ginola	David	Fr	m	Jul 1995	54+4	6	16+1	1
Asprilla	Faustino	Col	f	Feb 1996	36+12	9	14	9
Tomasson	Jon Dahl	Den	f	Jun 1997	17+6	3	10+2	1
Ketsbaia	Temuri	Geo	f	Jul 1997	41+37	8	16+15	6
Pistone	Alessandro	It	d	Jul 1997	45+1	1	16+1	0
Barnes (Eng)	John	Jam	f	Aug 1997	22+5	6	11+2	1
Andersson	Andreas	Swe	f	Jan 1998	21+6	4	4+1	0
Dabizas	Nicos	Grk	d	Mar 1998	119+11	10	44+2	3
Charvet	Laurent	Fr	d	Jul 1998	37+3	1	13	0
Guivarc'h	Stephane	Fr	f	Jul 1998	2+2	1	0	0
Hamann	Dietmar	Ger	m	Aug 1998	22+1	4	8	1
Georgiadis	Georgios	Grk	m	Aug 1998	7+3	0	1+2	1
Solano	Nolberto	Per	m	Aug 1998	150+10	29	49+5	8
Ameobi (Eng)	Shola	Nig	f	Oct 1998	24+39	7	14+9	8
Saha	Louis	Fr	f	Jan 1999	5+6	1	1	1
Domi	Didier	Fr	d	Jan 1999	44+11	3	11+4	1
Maric	Silvio	Cro	f	Feb 1999	12+11	0	5+3	2
Dumas	Franck	Fr	d	Jun 1999	6	0	1	0
Goma	Alain	Fr	d	Jul 1999	32+1	1	8	0
Elena	Marcelino	Sp	d	Jul 1999	15+2	0	4+1	0
Karelse	John	Neth	gk	Aug 1999	3	0	0	0
Fumaca	Jose	Bra	m	Sep 1999	1+4	0	0+1	0
Helder (Por)	Rodrigues	Ang	d	Nov 1999	8	1	4	0
Gavilan	Diego	Par	m	Feb 2000	2+5	1	0+1	0
Bassedas	Chistian	Arg	m	Jul 2000	18+6	1	7+2	0
Cordone	Daniel	Arg	f	Aug 2000	12+9	2	1+5	1
Lua-Lua	Lumana Tresor	DRC	f	Sep 2000	12+40	5	6+19	4
Acuna	Clarence	Chi	m	Oct 2000	35+11	6	9+4	1
Bernard	Olivier	Fr	m	Oct 2000	28+18	5	14+5	0
Robert (Fr)	Laurent	Reu	m	Aug 2001	59+4	13	16+3	2
Distin	Sylvain	Fr	d	Sep 2001	20+8	0	7	0
Viana	Hugo	Por	m	Aug 2002	11+12	2	6+5	2

NEWPORT COUNTY (4)

SURNAME	NAME	BORN	POS	FROM	LgAp	LgG	OthAp	OthG
Peed (Brit)	Frank	Arg	f	Aug 1931	13	4	1	0
Armand (Brit)	Jack	Ind	f	Aug 1932	3	1	1	0
Carr (1)	Lance	SA	f	Oct 1936	25	5	2	0
Carr (2)	Lance	SA	f	Jul 1938	39	9	10	1
Burgess	Mike	Can	f/ch	Feb 1956	24	7	0	0

NORTHAMPTON TOWN (20)

SURNAME	NAME	BORN	POS	FROM	LgAp	LgG	OthAp	OthG
Freimanis	Eddie	Lat	f	May 1948	19	4	0	0
Woollard (1)	Arnold	Ber	fb	Jun 1949	3	0	0	0
Starocsik	Felix	Pol	m	Jul 1951	49	19	1	0
Olah	Bela	Hun	m	Dec 1958	42	8	1	0
Woollard (2)	Arnold	Ber	fb	Mar 1962	28	0	3	0
Bruck	Dietmar	Ger	fb	Jun 1972	41	0	3	0
Roberts	John	Aus	gk	Jul 1972	13	0	0	0
Liddle (Brit)	David	Mal	d	May 1975	28+3	3	7	0
Nebbeling	Gavin	SA	d	Oct 1985	11	0	0	0
Anderson (Brit)	Doug	HK	m	Dec 1988	4+1	0	0	0
Tisdale (Brit)	Paul	Mal	m	Mar 1992	5	0	0	0
Stackman	Scott	USA	d	Mar 1994	0+1	0	0	0
Seal	David	Aus	f	Aug 1997	35+8	12	5+3	2
Van Dulleman	Ray	Neth	f	Aug 1997	0+1	0	0+1	0
Corazzin	Carlo	Can	f	Jul 1998	63+15	30	8+2	1
Hodgson	Doug	Aus	d	Oct 1998	7+1	1	2	0
Whitley (N Ire)	Jim	Zam	m	Feb 2001	13	0	0	0
Asamoah (Brit)	Derek	Gha	f	Jul 2001	23+59	7	2+5	1
Rahim	Brent	Trin	m	Jan 2003	6	1	0	0
Johnson	Richard	Aus	m	Feb 2003	5+1	1	0	0
One	Armand	Fr	f	Sep 2003	6	1	0+1	0

NORWICH CITY (30)

SURNAME	NAME	BORN	POS	FROM	LgAp	LgG	OthAp	OthG
Laxton	Edward	Bra	w	Dec 1919	16	0	0	0
Osborne	Harold	SA	w	Sep 1924	1	0	0	0
Peed (Brit)	Frank	Arg	f	Oct 1930	17	4	2	2
Gallego	Tony	Sp	gk	Mar 1947	1	0	0	0
Dolding (Brit)	Len	Ind	w	Jul 1948	12	1	0	0
Ackerman	Alf	SA	f	Aug 1951	66	31	4	4
Crossan	Errol	Can	w	Sep 1958	102	28	14	4
Kennon	Sandy	SA	gk	Feb 1959	213	0	42	0
Keelan (Brit)	Kevin	Ind	gk	Jul 1963	571	0	88	0
Muzinic	Drazen	Yug	d	Sep 1980	15+4	0	2+2	0
Van Wijk	Dennis	Neth	d/m	Oct 1982	109+9	3	31+1	1

SURNAME	NAME	BORN	POS	FROM	LgAp	LgG	OthAp	OthG
Goss (Wal)	Jerry	Cyp	m	Mar 1983	155+33	14	34+7	6
Hareide	Aage	Nor	d	Jun 1983	38+2	1	14	1
Phillips (Brit)	David	Ger	m	Jul 1989	152	18	26	1
Mortensen	Henrik	Den	f	Oct 1989	12+6	0	0+1	1
Molby	Jan	Den	m	Dec 1995	3	0	2	1
Ottosson	Ulf	Swe	f	Jan 1997	4+3	1	0+1	0
Segura	Victor	Sp	d	Aug 1997	24+5	0	4	0
Fuglestad	Erik	Nor	d	Nov 1997	71+3	2	5+1	0
Anselin	Cedric	Fr	m	Apr 1999	22+4	1	3	0
De Blasiis	Jean-Yves	Fr	m	Jul 1999	28+7	0	2+1	0
Diop	Pape Seydou	Sen	d/m	Aug 1999	2+5	0	1+2	0
Derveld	Fernando	Neth	d	Mar 2000	20+2	1	3	0
De Waard	Raimond	Neth	m	Mar 2000	4+6	0	1+2	0
Giallanza	Gaetano	Swit	f	Mar 2000	7+7	2	3+1	3
Nedergaard	Steen	Den	d	Jul 2000	81+9	5	5+2	0
Whitley (N Ire)	Jim	Zam	m	Aug 2000	7+1	1	0	0
Peschisolido	Paul	Can	f	Mar 2001	3+2	0	0	0
Libbra	Marc	Fr	f	Jul 2001	17+17	7	3+1	0
Nielsen	David	Den	f	Dec 2001	33+23	14	7	0

NOTTINGHAM FOREST (46)

SURNAME	NAME	BORN	POS	FROM	LgAp	LgG	OthAp	OthG
Quantrill (Eng)	Alf	Ind	m	May 1930	15	2	0	0
Gunn	Alf	Ger	f	Feb 1947	2	0	0	0
Lightening	Arthur	SA	gk	Dec 1956	6	0	0	0
Fraser (Sco)	Willie	Aus	gk	Dec 1958	2	0	0	0
Bowery	Bert	StK	f	Jan 1975	2	2	2	0
Ponte	Raimondo	It	m	Aug 1980	17+4	3	5+3	4
Aas	Einar	Nor	d	Mar 1981	20+1	1	3	0
Rober	Jurgen	Ger	m	Dec 1981	21+1	3	3	1
Van Breukelen	Hans	Neth	gk	Sep 1982	61	0	14	0
Thijssen	Frans	Neth	m	Oct 1983	17	3	2	0
Metgod	Johnny	Neth	m	Aug 1984	113+3	15	23	2
Segers	Hans	Neth	gk	Aug 1984	58	0	9	0
Davidson	Alan	Aus	fb	Nov 1984	3	0	2	0
Osvold	Kjetil	Nor	m	Mar 1987	5+2	0	0+1	0
Orlygsson	Toddi	Ice	m	Dec 1989	31+6	2	6+1	2
Phillips (Brit)	David	Ger	m	Aug 1993	116+10	5	29+3	0
Bohinen	Lars	Nor	m	Nov 1993	59+5	7	10+1	3
Haaland	Alf-Inge	Nor	m	Jan 1994	66+9	7	9+6	0
Roy	Bryan	Neth	f	Aug 1994	70+15	24	23+2	4
Bart-Williams (Brit)	Chris	SiLe	m	Jul 1995	200+7	30	37+1	5
Silenzi	Andrea	It	f	Aug 1995	4+8	0	4+4	2
Jerkan	Nikola	Cro	d	Jun 1996	14	0	0	0
Van Hooijdonk	Pierre	Neth	f	Mar 1997	68+3	36	4+2	5
Pascolo	Marco	Swit	gk	Jun 1997	5	0	1	0
Bonalair	Thierry	Fr	m	Jul 1997	58+13	5	7+2	0
Hjelde	Jon Olav	Nor	d	Aug 1997	136+21	4	16+1	2
Merino	Carlos	Sp	m	Sep 1997	3+6	0	1+2	0
Edds	Gareth	Aus	m	Feb 1998	11+5	1	1	0
Darcheville (Fr)	Jean-Claude	FrGu	f	Jul 1998	14+2	2	1+2	0
Louis-Jean	Mathieu	Fr	d	Sep 1998	129+6	2	15+2	0
Mattsson	Jesper	Swe	d	Dec 1998	5+1	0	0	0
Harkes	John	USA	m	Jan 1999	3	0	0	0
Porfirio	Hugo	Por	m	Jan 1999	3+6	1	0	0
Stensaas	Stale	Nor	d	Jan 1999	6+1	0	0	0
Allou (Fr)	Bernard	IvCo	m	Mar 1999	1+5	1	2+2	1
Gough (Sco)	Richard	Swe	d	Mar 1999	7	0	0	0
Mannini	Moreno	It	d	Aug 1999	7+1	0	1	0
Matrecano	Salvatore	It	d	Aug 1999	11	0	2	0
Petrachi	Gianluca	It	m	Aug 1999	10+3	0	2	0
Brennan	Jim	Can	m	Oct 1999	117+6	1	14	0
Beck	Mikkel	Den	f	Nov 1999	5	1	0	0
John	Stern	Trin	f	Nov 1999	49+23	18	7+1	2
Olsen	Ben	USA	m	Oct 2000	14+4	2	0	0
Johnson	David	Jam	f	Jan 2001	76+7	30	7+1	4
Bopp (Ger)	Eugene	Ukr	m	Aug 2001	22+10	3	2+2	0
Oyen	Davy	Bel	d	Feb 2003	0+4	0	0	0

NOTTS COUNTY (29)

SURNAME	NAME	BORN	POS	FROM	LgAp	LgG	OthAp	OthG
Mills (Brit)	Paddy	Ind	f	Mar 1926	76	35	3	1
Whittaker	Fred	Can	f	Aug 1946	10	2	0	0
Praski	Josef	Fr	w	Mar 1949	3	0	0	0
Robledo	Ted	Chi	wh	Sep 1957	2	0	0	0
Benjamin	Tristan	StK	d	Mar 1975	296+15	4	46+1	0
Richards	Lloyd	Jam	m	Feb 1976	7+2	0	1+1	0
Avramovic	Raddy	Cro	gk	Aug 1979	149	0	18	0
Chiedozie (1)	John	Nig	m	Aug 1981	110+2	15	19	4
Lahtinen	Aki	Fin	d	Sep 1981	37+8	2	7+1	0
Hesford (Eng)	Iain	Zam	gk	Nov 1985	10	0	0	0
Edge (NZ)	Declan	Mly	f	Dec 1985	7+3	2	3	0
Chiedozie (2)	John	Nig	m	Jan 1990	0+1	0	0	0

SURNAME	NAME	BORN	POS	FROM	LgAp	LgG	OthAp	OthG
Short (Brit)	Chris	Ger	d	Sep 1990	77+17	2	13+1	0
Farina	Frank	Aus	f	Mar 1992	1+2	0	0	0
Dijkstra	Meindert	Neth	gk	Aug 1992	27+2	1	4+1	0
Murphy	Shaun	Aus	d	Sep 1992	100+9	5	14+2	0
Goater	Shaun	Ber	f	Nov 1993	1	0	0	0
Emenalo	Michael	Nig	d	Aug 1994	7	0	0	0
Kearton	Jason	Aus	gk	Jan 1995	10	0	0	0
Mendez (Aus)	Gabriel	Arg	m	Mar 1997	2+1	0	0	0
Garcia	Tony	Fr	m	Sep 1998	10+9	2	3+2	0
Grant	Kim	Gha	f	Dec 1998	6	1	0	0
Allsopp (1)	Danny	Aus	f	Nov 1999	3	1	0	0
Joseph (Fr)	David	Guad	f	Aug 2000	13+14	4	3+2	0
McDermott	Andy	Aus	m	Aug 2000	20+5	0	5	0
Jacobsen	Anders	Nor	d	Sep 2000	27+2	2	5	0
Jorgensen	Henrik	Den	d	Oct 2000	3+4	0	0+3	0
Allsopp (2)	Danny	Aus	f	Nov 2000	97+8	42	11	8
Moreau (Cam)	Fabrice	Fr	m	Mar 2001	2+3	0	0	0
Cas	Marcel	Neth	m	Jul 2001	49+9	8	6	0
Whitley (N Ire)	Jeff	Zam	m	Mar 2002	18	0	1	0

OLDHAM ATHLETIC (25)

Andrews (N Ire)	Billy	USA	wh	Aug 1908	9	3	0	0
Hunter (Brit)	George	Ind	wh	Jan 1912	40	1	6	0
Lester	Hugh	USA	wh	Aug 1914	1	0	0	0
Kowenicki	Ryszard	Pol	m	Dec 1979	40+2	5	5	1
McDonough (Brit)	Darron	Bel	d	Jan 1980	178+5	14	17	3
Anderson (Brit)	Doug	HK	m	Sep 1980	4+5	0	0+2	0
Halle	Gunnar	Nor	d	Feb 1991	185+3	17	24	4
Keizerweerd	Orpheo	Neth	f	Mar 1993	0+1	0	0	0
Pedersen	Tore	Nor	d	Oct 1993	7+3	0	1+1	0
Vonk	Michel	Neth	d	Nov 1995	5	1	0	0
Orlygsson	Toddi	Ice	m	Dec 1995	65+11	1	10+2	0
Hodgson	Doug	Aus	d	Feb 1997	33+8	4	3+2	0
Kyratzoglou	Alex	Aus	m	Oct 1997	0+1	0	0	0
Grobbelaar (Zim)	Bruce	SA	gk	Dec 1997	4	0	0	0
Agogo	Junior	Gha	f	Jul 1999	2	0	0	0
Corazzin	Carlo	Can	f	Jul 2000	82+27	21	11+7	3
Watson	Mark	Can	d	Sep 2000	1+1	0	1	0
Baudet	Julien	Fr	d	Oct 2001	34+10	3	4+2	0
Rachubka	Paul	USA	gk	Nov 2001	16	0	0	0
Colusso	Cristian	Arg	m	Feb 2002	6+7	2	0	0
Adebola	Dele	Nig	f	Mar 2002	5	0	0	0
Da Silva (Por)	Lourenco	Ang	m	Aug 2002	1+6	1	1+1	0
Killen	Chris	NZ	f	Aug 2002	11+16	3	3+3	1
Pogliacomi	Les	Aus	gk	Aug 2002	37	0	6	0
Wijnhard (Neth)	Clyde	Sur	f	Aug 2002	24+1	10	6	3

OXFORD UNITED (15)

Houghton (Brit)	Bud	Ind	f	Mar 1961	53	17	5	2
Cooke	Joe	Dom	d/f	Aug 1979	71+1	13	7	0
Evans	Ceri	NZ	d	Feb 1989	113+3	3	14	0
Stein (Eng)	Mark	SA	f	Sep 1989	72+10	18	6+1	0
Wilsterman (Neth)	Brian	Sur	d	Feb 1997	28+14	2	3	0
Remy	Christophe	Fr	d	Jul 1997	23+5	1	5+3	0
Van Heusden	Arjan	Neth	gk	Sep 1997	11	0	2	0
Watson	Mark	Can	d	Dec 1998	57+1	0	10	0
Lundin	Pal	Swe	gk	Mar 1999	28+1	0	5	0
Arendse	Andre	SA	gk	Jul 1999	13	0	5+1	0
Omoyimni	Manny	Nig	f	Jul 2000	31+33	9	3+4	0
Busby	Hubert	Can	gk	Aug 2000	0+1	0	0	0
Guyett	Scott	Aus	d	May 2001	20+2	0	2	0
Oldfield	David	Aus	m/f	Aug 2002	19+9	2	4	1
Sall	Abdou	Sen	d	Dec 2002	0+1	0	0+1	0

PETERBOROUGH UNITED (21)

Thompson	Peter	Ken	w	Mar 1964	79+6	15	9	3
Maynard	Mike	Guy	fb	Jul 1967	2+1	0	1	0
Phillips	Brendon	Jam	m	Aug 1973	1	0	0	0
Cooke	Joe	Dom	d/f	Jan 1979	18	5	0	0
Heppolette (Brit)	Ricky	Ind	m	Aug 1979	5	0	3	0
Parkinson	Andy	SA	f	Aug 1979	12+1	5	5	1
Kelly (1)	Errington	StV	w	Mar 1984	59+13	22	9+2	4
Kelly (2)	Errington	StV	w	Dec 1986	36+10	6	3+2	1
Kerr (USA)	John	Can	f	Dec 1987	10	1	0	0
Richards (Eng)	Carl	Jam	f	Jul 1989	16+4	5	4+1	2
Berry (Wal)	George	Ger	d	Jul 1990	28+4	6	1	0
Salman (Eng)	Danis	Cyp	d	Mar 1992	1	0	0	0
Iorfa	Dominic	Nig	f	Oct 1992	27+33	9	5+3	0
Kruszynski	Detsi	Ger	m	Dec 1993	2+1	0	2	0
Henry	Liburd	Dom	f	Aug 1994	22+10	7	2+1	1
Feuer	Ian	USA	gk	Feb 1995	16	0	0	0

SURNAME	NAME	BORN	POS	FROM	LgAp	LgG	OthAp	OthG
Griemink	Bart	Neth	gk	Oct 1996	58	0	5	0
Koogi	Anders	Den	m	Jul 1997	0+2	0	0	0
Gregory (Brit)	Neil	Zam	f	Nov 1997	2+1	1	0	0
Danielsson	Helgi	Ice	m	Oct 1998	38+17	2	4	1
Oldfield (Eng)	David	Aus	m/f	Mar 2000	68+10	4	14+2	1
Macdonald (Brit)	Gary	Ger	d	Feb 2001	13+4	1	3+1	0
Arber (Brit)	Mark	SA	d	Dec 2002	24+1	2	0	0

PLYMOUTH ARGYLE (24)

SURNAME	NAME	BORN	POS	FROM	LgAp	LgG	OthAp	OthG
Dugnolle (Brit)	Jack	Ind	ch	Feb 1939	5	0	0	0
Strauss	Bill	SA	w	Jul 1946	158	40	8	2
Williams	Stan	SA	w	Aug 1949	35	4	2	1
Twissell (Eng)	Charlie	Sing	w	Apr 1955	41	9	1	0
Clelland	Crawford	USA	f	Jun 1955	2	0	0	0
Phillips (Brit)	David	Ger	m	Aug 1981	65+8	15	14+2	0
Anderson (Brit)	Doug	HK	m	Aug 1987	17+2	1	2	0
Salman (Eng)	Danis	Cyp	d	Mar 1990	71+3	4	8	1
Quamina	Mark	Guy	m/d	Jul 1991	4+1	0	0	0
Marshall (Brit)(1)	Dwight	StL	f	Aug 1991	93+6	27	17+2	6
Van Rossum	Erik	Neth	d	Jan 1992	9	0	0	0
Hodgson	Doug	Aus	d	Aug 1995	3+2	0	0	0
Petterson	Andy	Aus	gk	Jan 1996	6	0	0	0
Corazzin	Carlo	Can	f	Mar 1996	61+13	22	4+4	1
Grobbelaar (Zim)	Bruce	SA	gk	Aug 1996	36	0	5	0
Jean	Earl	StL	f	Aug 1997	37+28	7	9	2
Marshall (Brit)(2)	Dwight	StL	f	Oct 1998	25+3	12	1+2	0
O'Sullivan (Ire)	Wayne	Cyp	d	Jul 1999	83+2	3	11	0
Friio	David	Fr	m	Nov 2000	100+3	19	8+2	3
Larrieu	Romain	Fr	gk	Nov 2000	102+1	0	10	0
Javary	Jean-Phillipe	Fr	m	Feb 2001	4	0	0	0
Bent	Jason	Can	m	Sep 2001	39+7	4	3+2	1
Lopes	Osvaldo	Fr	m	Sep 2002	4+5	0	2	0
Milosevic	Danny	Aus	gk	Nov 2002	1	0	0	0
Capaldi (N Ire)	Tony	Nor	d	Mar 2003	1	0	0	0

PORTSMOUTH (47)

SURNAME	NAME	BORN	POS	FROM	LgAp	LgG	OthAp	OthG
Delapenha	Lindy	Jam	f	Apr 1948	7	0	1	1
Pickett	Reg	Ind	wh	Mar 1949	123	3	2	0
Ekner	Dan	Swe	f	Nov 1949	5	0	0	0
Gaillard	Marcel	Bel	w	Feb 1951	58	7	6	6
Smith	Roy	Ind	f	Jan 1962	8	3	1	2
Eames (Brit)	Billy	Mal	f	Sep 1975	9+3	1	4+2	2
Blake (Brit)	Noel	Jam	d	Apr 1984	144	10	24	3
Golac	Ivan	Yug	fb	Jan 1985	8	0	0	0
Christensen	Tommy	Den	f	Nov 1985	3	2	1	0
Kerr (USA)	John	Can	f	Aug 1987	2+2	0	0+1	0
Kristensen	Bjorn	Den	d	Mar 1993	56+15	1	13+1	3
Boere	Jeroen	Neth	f	Mar 1994	4+1	0	0	0
Radosavljevic (USA)	Preki	Yug	w	Jul 1994	30+10	5	4+1	2
Poom	Mart	Est	gk	Aug 1994	4	0	3	0
Svensson	Mathias	Swe	f	Dec 1996	34+11	10	4+2	2
Aloisi	John	Aus	f	Aug 1997	55+5	25	7	3
Thorp	Hamilton	Aus	d	Aug 1997	0+7	0	1+1	1
Foster	Craig	Aus	m	Sep 1997	13+3	2	2	2
Harries	Paul	Aus	f	Sep 1997	0+1	0	0	0
Enes	Robbie	Aus	m	Oct 1997	1+4	0	0	0
Vlachos	Michalis	Grk	d	Jun 1998	55+2	0	7	1
Kyzeridis	Nicos	Grk	m	Jul 1998	2+2	0	2	0
Thogersen	Thomas	Den	m	Aug 1998	95+13	8	10+1	0
Peron	Jeff	Fr	m	Sep 1998	46+2	3	6	0
Andreassen	Svein	Nor	m	Dec 1998	0+2	0	1	0
Miglioranzi (USA)	Stefani	Bra	m	Jun 1999	25+10	2	3+4	0
Petterson	Andy	Aus	gk	Jul 1999	32	0	1+1	0
Pamarot	Louis Noe	Fr	d	Sep 1999	1+1	0	0+1	0
Panopoulos (Grk)	Mike	Aus	m	Sep 1999	45+9	7	4	0
Berntsen	Tommy	Nor	d	Nov 1999	1+1	0	0	0
Rudonja	Mladen	Slo	f	Aug 2000	4+10	0	2+2	0
Keller	Marc	Fr	gk	Sep 2000	3	0	0	0
Lambourde (Fr)	Bernard	Guad	d	Sep 2000	6	0	0	0
Zamperini	Alessandro	It	d	Jul 2001	16	2	1	0
Prosinecki (Cro)	Robert	Ger	m	Aug 2001	30+3	9	2	0
Ilic (Yug)	Sasa	Aus	gk	Sep 2001	7	0	0	0
Kawaguchi	Yoshikatsu	Jap	gk	Oct 2001	11+1	0	1	0
Biagini	Leo	Arg	f	Feb 2002	6+2	2	0	0
Todorov	Svetoslav	Bul	f	Mar 2002	46+2	27	3	0
De Zeeuw	Arjan	Neth	d	Aug 2002	35+3	1	1	0
Festa	Gianluca	It	d	Aug 2002	27	1	2	0
Foxe	Hayden	Aus	d	Aug 2002	30+2	1	1	0
Diabate	Lassina	Iv Co	m	Oct 2002	16+9	0	1	0
Ayegbini	Yakubu	Nig	f	Jan 2003	12+2	7	0	0
Tavlaridis	Stathis	Grk	d	Jan 2003	3+1	0	1	0

SURNAME	NAME	BORN	POS	FROM	LgAp	LgG	OthAp	OthG
Heikkinen	Markus	Fin	d	Feb 2003	0+2	0	0	0
Pericard	Vincent	Fr	f	Apr 2003	18+14	9	1+2	1

PORT VALE (23)

SURNAME	NAME	BORN	POS	FROM	LgAp	LgG	OthAp	OthG
Bookman (Brit)	Louis	Lith	w	Jul 1923	10	0	1	0
Fish	Kenneth	SA	f	Nov 1937	5	1	1	0
Price (Brit)	Johnny	Ind	f	May 1937	13	2	0	0
Georgeson	Roddy	Egy	f	Jan 1966	26+1	6	1	0
Hazell (Eng)	Bob	Jam	d	Dec 1986	81	1	12	0
Van der Laan	Robin	Neth	m	Feb 1991	154+22	24	23+2	2
Jalink	Nico	Neth	m	Jul 1991	20+8	1	3	0
Van Heusden	Arjan	Neth	gk	Aug 1994	27	0	4	0
Holwyn	Jermaine	Neth	d	Jul 1995	5+2	0	0	0
Samuel (Can)	Randy	Trin	d	Nov 1995	9	1	0	0
Jansson	Jan	Swe	m	Nov 1996	37+14	6	3+1	0
Koordes	Rogier	Neth	m	Feb 1997	29+9	0	0+1	0
Snijders	Mark	Neth	d	Sep 1997	46+9	2	5	0
Pounewatchy	Stephane	Fr	d	Aug 1998	2	0	0	0
Berntsen	Robin	Nor	d	Nov 1998	1	0	0	0
Horlaville	Christophe	Fr	f	Nov 1998	1+1	0	0+1	0
Rougier	Tony	Trin	m/f	Jan 1999	41+10	8	3	1
Viljanen	Ville	Fin	f	Feb 1999	26+8	6	3	0
Olaoye	Dele	Nig	f	Aug 2000	0+1	0	0	0
Byrne (Brit)	Paul	SA	m	Apr 2001	8+3	0	0	0
Lowe	Onandi	Jam	f	Feb 2001	4+1	1	0	0
Atangana	Simon	Cam	f	Jan 2002	1+1	0	0	0
Killen	Chris	NZ	f	Sep 2001	8+1	6	0	0

PRESTON NORTH END (26)

SURNAME	NAME	BORN	POS	FROM	LgAp	LgG	OthAp	OthG
Quantrill (Eng)	Alf	Ind	w	Jul 1921	64	7	1	0
Marston	Joe	Aus	ch	Feb 1950	185	0	15	0
Heppolette (Brit)	Ricky	Ind	m	Sep 1964	149+5	13	20	1
Tunks (Brit) (1)	Roy	Ger	gk	Nov 1974	277	0	36	0
Houston	Graham	Gib	m	Mar 1978	90+38	11	19+1	1
Hunter (1)	Chris	HK	f	Sep 1981	0+1	0	0	0
Hunter (2)	Chris	HK	f	Sep 1984	3+3	0	0+1	1
Stevens	Ian	Mal	f	Nov 1984	9+2	2	0	0
Tunks (Brit) (2)	Roy	Ger	gk	Nov 1988	25	0	1	0
Moylon (Brit)	Craig	Ger	m	Jul 1991	0+1	0	0	0
Berry (Wal)	George	Ger	d	Aug 1991	4	0	1+1	0
Johnstone (Brit)	Glenn	Ken	gk	Jan 1993	10	0	0	0
Nebbeling	Gavin	SA	d	Jul 1993	22	4	5	0
Carmichael (Brit)	Matt	Sing	f	Mar 1995	7+3	3	0	0
Moilanen	Tepi	Fin	gk	Dec 1995	155+3	0	23+1	0
Sissoko	Habib	Fr	f	Feb 1998	4+3	0	0	0
Diaf	Farid	Fr	m	Jul 1999	1+2	0	0+1	0
Gunnlaugsson	Bjarke	Ice	f	Sep 1999	17+28	2	3+4	1
McBride	Brian	USA	f	Sep 2000	8+1	1	2	0
Meijer	Erik	Neth	f	Oct 2000	9	0	0	0
Skora	Eric	Fr	m	Oct 2001	32+8	0	5	2
Gudjonsson	Thordur	Ice	m	Jan 2002	4+3	0	0+1	0
Wijnhard (Neth)	Clyde	Sur	f	Mar 2002	6	3	0	0
Etuhu	Dixon	Nig	m	Jan 2002	49+6	9	5	0
Fuller	Ricardo	Jam	f	Aug 2002	18	9	1+1	2
Lewis	Eddie	USA	f	Sep 2002	34+4	5	4+1	1
Koumantarakis (SA)	George	Grk	f	Jan 2003	10	3	0	0
Lynch (Sco)	Simon	Can	f	Jan 2003	6+11	1	0	0

QUEENS PARK RANGERS (32)

SURNAME	NAME	BORN	POS	FROM	LgAp	LgG	OthAp	OthG
Balogun	Tesilim	Nig	f	Sep 1956	13	3	2	2
Cini	Joe	Mal	w	Aug 1959	7	1	0	0
Leary (Eng)	Stuart	SA	f	Dec 1962	94	29	10	3
Hazell (Eng)	Bob	Jam	d	Sep 1979	100+6	8	17+1	1
Bakholt	Kurt	Den	m	Jan 1986	0+1	0	0	0
Pisanti	David	Isr	m	Sep 1987	16+5	0	7+1	1
Stein (Eng)	Mark	SA	f	Jun 1988	20+13	4	6+1	3
Ardiles	Ossie	Arg	m	Aug 1988	4+4	0	2+1	0
Wegerle (USA)	Roy	SA	f	Dec 1989	71+4	29	16	2
Iorfa	Dominic	Nig	f	Mar 1990	1+7	0	1	0
Stejskal	Jan	CzRep	gk	Oct 1990	107+1	0	14	0
Dijkstra	Sieb	Neth	gk	Jul 1994	11	0	1	0
Goodridge	Greg	Bar	w	Aug 1995	0+7	1	0+2	0
Sommer	Jurgen	USA	gk	Aug 1995	66	0	5	0
Zelic	Ned	Aus	fb	Aug 1995	3+1	0	0	0
McDermott	Andy	Aus	m	Aug 1995	6	2	0	0
Kulcsar (Aus)	George	Hun	d	Dec 1997	42+14	1	2+2	0
Heinola	Antti	Fin	d	Jan 1998	23+11	0	4+1	0
Steiner	Rob	Swe	f	Jul 1998	29+7	9	3	0
Miklosko	Ludek	CzRep	gk	Oct 1998	57	0	6+2	0
Koejoe (Neth)	Sammy	Sur	f	Nov 1999	13+21	3	4+4	0
Bankole	Ade	Nig	gk	Jul 1998	0+1	0	0	0

SURNAME	NAME	BORN	POS	FROM	LgAp	LgG	OthAp	OthG
Beck	Mikkel	Den	f	Feb 2000	10+1	4	0	0
Peschisolido	Paul	Can	f	Nov 2000	5	1	0	0
Ngonge (DRC)	Michel	Bel	f	Dec 2000	7+6	3	0+2	0
Agogo	Junior	Gha	f	Aug 2001	0+2	0	0	0
Ben Askar	Aziz	Fr	d	Aug 2001	18	0	1	0
Bonnot	Alex	Fr	m	Aug 2001	17+5	1	2	0
De Ornelas	Fernando	Ven	m	Oct 2001	1+1	0	0	0
M'Bombo	Doudou	DRC	f	Aug 2001	23+23	3	2+1	0
Shittu	Danny	Nig	d	Oct 2001	11	1	0	0
Padula	Gino	Arg	d	Aug 2002	17+4	1	3+1	0

READING (22)

Higginbotham	Harry	Aus	f	May 1924	24	3	1	0
Alleyne	Andy	Bar	fb	Nov 1972	46+2	2	5	0
Lenarduzzi	Bob	Can	d	May 1973	63+4	2	3+1	0
Hazell (Eng)	Bob	Jam	d	Nov 1986	4	1	0	0
Lovell	Stuart	Aus	f	Jul 1990	177+50	58	24+9	9
Streete (Brit)	Floyd	Jam	d	Jul 1990	38	0	5	0
Statham (Eng)	Brian	Zim	d/m	Mar 1991	8	0	0	0
Cooper (Sco)	Neale	Ind	m	Jul 1991	6+1	0	2	0
Kerr (Brit)	Dylan	Mal	d	Jul 1993	84+5	5	10+1	1
Hartenberger	Uwe	Ger	f	Sep 1993	8+16	4	0+2	0
Bernal	Andy	Aus	d	Jul 1994	179+8	2	34+2	1
Wdowczyk	Dariusz	Pol	d	Aug 1994	77+5	0	12+1	0
Barnard (Wal)	Darren	Ger	m	Nov 1994	3+1	0	0	0
Mikhailov	Bobby	Bul	gk	Sep 1995	24	0	4	0
Mautone	Steve	Aus	gk	Feb 1997	29	0	5	0
Crawford (Ire)	Jimmy	USA	d/m	Mar 1998	17+4	1	3+2	0
Sarr	Mass	Lbr	f	Jul 1998	18+13	3	2+2	0
Kromheer	Elroy	Neth	d	Aug 1998	11	0	1	0
Van der Kwaak	Peter	Neth	gk	Aug 1998	3+1	0	1	0
Rougier	Tony	Trin	m/f	Aug 2000	47+37	6	4+6	0
Salako (Eng)	John	Nig	f	Nov 2001	64+10	10	1+2	0
Hahnemann	Marcus	USA	gk	Dec 2001	47	0	5	0

ROCHDALE (12)

Murray	David	SA	f	Aug 1931	22	3	1	1
Cornock	Wally	Aus	gk	Nov 1947	1	0	0	0
Kapler	Konrad	Pol	w	May 1949	4	0	0	0
Wasilewski	Adam	Pol	f	Jul 1953	4	1	0	0
Priday	Bob	SA	w	Aug 1953	5	1	0	0
Symonds	Calvin	Ber	f	Oct 1954	1	0	0	0
Carr	Everton	Ant	fb	Mar 1983	9	0	0	0
Cooke	Joe	Dom	d/f	Jul 1984	75	4	9	1
Hughes	Zacari	Aus	d	Aug 1989	2	0	1	0
Diaz	Isidro	Sp	m	Aug 1998	12+2	2	2+2	0
Hahnemann	Marcus	USA	gk	Oct 2001	5	0	0	0
Cansdell-Sheriff	Shane	Aus	d	Nov 2002	3	0	1	0

ROTHERHAM TOWN (1)

Wharton (1)	Arthur	Gha	gk	Jul 1893	19	0	0	0
Wharton (2)	Arthur	Gha	gk	Jul 1895	15	0	0	0

ROTHERHAM UNITED (14)

Crawford	Ronald	SA	fb	Jul 1931	3	0	0	0
Tunks (Brit)	Roy	Ger	gk	Mar 1968	138	0	20	0
Goater	Shaun	Ber	f	Oct 1989	169+40	70	25+7	11
Cunningham (Brit)	Tony	Jam	f	Aug 1991	65+5	24	13	3
Smith	Scott	NZ	d	Oct 1993	30+6	0	4+1	0
Viljoen	Nik	NZ	f	Jun 1995	5+3	2	0	0
McDougald (Brit)	Junior	USA	f	Jul 1996	14+4	2	1	0
Crawford (Ire)	Jimmy	USA	d/m	Sep 1996	11	0	0	0
Jean	Earl	StL	f	Jan 1997	7+11	6	0	0
Bos	Gijsbert	Neth	m	Aug 1997	7+11	4	1+1	0
Wilsterman (Neth)	Brian	Sur	d	Jul 1999	47+5	4	5	0
Bolima	Cedric	DRC	f	Oct 2000	0+1	0	0	0
Lemarchand	Stephane	Fr	f	Nov 2000	0	0	0+1	0
Miranda	Jose	Por	m	Sep 2001	2	0	0+1	0

RUSHDEN & DIAMONDS (3)

Brady	Jon	Aus	m	Jul 1998	9+13	1	3+2	0
Lowe	Onandi	Jam	f	Nov 2001	63+1	34	5+1	0
Sigere (Fr)	Jean-Michel	Mart	f	Mar 2000	4+3	1	1	0

SCARBOROUGH (9)

Podd	Cec	StK	fb	Jul 1986	3	0	0	0
Short (Brit)	Chris	Ger	d	Jul 1988	42+1	1	6	0
Lightbourne	Kyle	Ber	f	Dec 1992	11+8	3	1	0
Heald	Oliver	Can	m	Aug 1995	1+8	1	0+3	0
Moilanen	Tepi	Fin	gk	Dec 1996	4	0	0	0
Van der Velden	Carel	Neth	m	Aug 1997	5+3	1	2	0
Atkinson (Brit)	Paddy	Sing	d	Aug 1998	23+4	0	4	0

SURNAME	NAME	BORN	POS	FROM	LgAp	LgG	OthAp	OthG
Mirankov	Alex	Fr	m	Aug 1998	22	4	3	0
Dabelsteen	Thomas	Den	m	Nov 1998	5	1	0	0

SCUNTHORPE UNITED (13)

SURNAME	NAME	BORN	POS	FROM	LgAp	LgG	OthAp	OthG
Malan	Norman	SA	gk	Jun 1950	136	0	18	0
Thorpe (Brit)	Arthur	Ind	w	Sep 1960	27	5	1	0
Carmichael (Brit)	Matt	Sing	f	Jul 1993	51+11	20	5+4	2
Gregory (Brit)	Neil	Zam	f	Mar 1995	10	7	0	0
Calvo-Garcia	Alex	Sp	m	Oct 1996	197+24	30	34+2	11
Ipoua (Fr)	Guy	Cam	f	Aug 1999	50+15	23	5	4
Marcelle	Clint	Trin	f	Oct 1999	8+2	0	1	0
Perez	Lionel	Fr	gk	Oct 1999	13	0	0	0
Omoyimni	Manny	Nig	f	Dec 1999	6	1	0	0
Hyldgaard	Morten	Den	gk	Jan 2000	5	0	0	0
Mamoun	Blaise	Cam	m	Aug 2000	0+1	0	0	0
Larusson	Bjarni	Ice	m	Sep 2000	33	4	5	0
Grant	Kim	Gha	f	Aug 2001	3+1	1	1	0

SHEFFIELD UNITED (40)

SURNAME	NAME	BORN	POS	FROM	LgAp	LgG	OthAp	OthG
Wharton	Arthur	Gha	gk	Jul 1894	1	0	0	0
Gibson	Jock	USA	fb	Mar 1929	74	0	3	0
Cutbush (1)	John	Mal	fb	Mar 1977	79+2	1	2	0
Sabella	Alex	Arg	m	Aug 1978	76	8	6	0
Casey (Brit)	Paul	Ger	d/m	Jun 1979	23+2	1	0	0
Cutbush (2)	John	Mal	fb	Aug 1979	47+1	0	4	0
De Goey	Len	Neth	m	Aug 1979	33	5	3	0
Verde	Pedro	Arg	f	Aug 1979	9+1	3	2	0
Segers	Hans	Neth	gk	Nov 1987	10	0	0	0
Flo	Jostein	Nor	f	Aug 1993	74+10	19	5+1	3
Wirmola	Jonas	Swe	d	Aug 1993	8	0	1	0
Nilsen	Roger	Nor	d	Nov 1993	157+9	0	20+4	0
Hodgson	Doug	Aus	d	Jul 1994	24+6	0	4+2	0
Veart	Carl	Aus	m	Jul 1994	47+19	15	4+2	2
Short (Brit)	Chris	Ger	d	Dec 1995	40+4	0	11+2	0
Vonk	Michel	Neth	d	Dec 1995	37	2	6	2
Kachouro	Petr	Blr	f	Jul 1996	50+45	19	13+13	4
Fjortoft	Jan Aage	Nor	f	Jan 1997	30+4	19	6+2	4
Borbokis	Vassilis	Grk	d	Jul 1997	55	4	19	5
Dellas	Traianos	Grk	d	Aug 1997	14+12	3	2+3	0
Marcelo		Bra	f	Oct 1997	47+19	24	14+3	8
Jacobsen	Anders	Nor	d	Dec 1998	8+4	0	0+1	0
Donis	George	Grk	m	Mar 1999	5+2	1	0	0
Tebily	Olivier	IvCo	d	Mar 1999	7+1	0	0	0
Murphy	Shaun	Aus	d	Jul 1999	157+1	10	24	2
Smeets (Bel)	Axel	DRC	d	Jul 1999	2+3	0	2+1	0
Gysbrechts	Davy	Bel	d	Aug 1999	9+8	0	2	0
Ribeiro	Bruno	Por	m	Oct 1999	12+13	1	4+1	0
D'Jaffo	Laurent	Fr	f	Feb 2000	45+24	11	1+4	1
Santos	Georges	Fr	m	Jul 2000	37+24	6	3+4	0
Uhlenbeek (Neth)	Gus	Sur	d	Aug 2000	47+4	0	8	0
Weber	Nicolas	Fr	d	Aug 2000	3+1	0	2	0
Talia	Frank	Aus	gk	Sep 2000	6	0	0	0
Suffo	Patrick	Cam	f	Nov 2000	16+20	5	0+2	1
Ndlovu	Peter	Zim	f	Feb 2001	86+13	16	13+3	4
Thetis	Manuel	Fr	d	Mar 2001	0+1	0	0	0
Peschisolido	Paul	Can	f	Jul 2001	27+30	11	4+9	4
De Vogt	Wilko	Neth	gk	Aug 2001	5+1	0	3	0
Javary	Jean-Phillipe	Fr	m	Mar 2002	8+5	1	0+1	0
Ten Heuvel	Laurens	Neth	f	Aug 2002	0+5	0	0+4	0
Cas	Marcel	Neth	m	Feb 2003	3+3	0	0	0

SHEFFIELD WEDNESDAY (40)

SURNAME	NAME	BORN	POS	FROM	LgAp	LgG	OthAp	OthG
Smit(h)	Wilf	Ger	fb	Sep 1963	206	4	27	1
Strutt	Brian	Mal	f	Sep 1977	2	0	0	0
Mirocevic	Ante	Yug	m	Oct 1980	58+3	6	7+2	1
Cunningham (Brit)	Tony	Jam	f	Nov 1983	26+2	5	4+1	0
Jonsson	Siggi	Ice	m	Feb 1985	59+8	4	4+1	2
Nilsson	Roland	Swe	fb	Nov 1989	151	2	32+1	1
Harkes	John	USA	m	Oct 1990	59+22	7	33+1	4
Bart-Williams (Brit)	Chris	SiLe	m	Nov 1991	95+29	16	20+11	7
Petrescu	Dan	Rom	m	Aug 1994	28+9	3	3+2	1
Ingesson	Klas	Swe	m	Sep 1994	12+6	2	3	0
Degryse	Marc	Bel	m	Aug 1995	30+4	8	4	4
Kovacevic	Darko	Yug	f	Dec 1995	8+8	4	1	0
Stefanovic	Dejan	Yug	d	Dec 1995	59+7	4	6	1
Blinker (Neth)	Regi	Sur	f	Mar 1996	24+18	3	3	0
Trustfull	Orlando	Neth	m	Aug 1996	9+10	3	2+1	0
Carbone	Benito	It	f	Oct 1996	86+10	25	10+1	1
Agogo	Junior	Gha	f	Oct 1996	0+2	0	0+1	0
Blondeau	Patrick	Fr	d	Jun 1997	5+1	0	0	0
Di Canio	Paolo	It	f	Aug 1997	39+2	15	7	2

SURNAME	NAME	BORN	POS	FROM	LgAp	LgG	OthAp	OthG
Rudi	Petter	Nor	m	Oct 1997	70+7	8	11+1	2
Alexandersson	Niclas	Swe	m	Dec 1997	73+2	8	12+1	4
Mayrleb	Christian	Aut	f	Jan 1998	0+3	0	0	0
Sedloski	Goce	Mac	d	Mar 1998	3+1	0	0	0
Thome	Emerson	Bra	d	Mar 1998	60+1	1	9+1	1
Sanetti	Francesco	It	f	Apr 1998	1+4	1	0+2	0
Cobian	Juan	Arg	d	Aug 1998	7+2	0	1	0
Jonk	Wim	Neth	m	Aug 1998	69+1	5	11	0
Srnicek	Pavel	CzRep	gk	Nov 1998	44	0	8	0
Thome	Emerson	Bra	d	Mar 1998	54+1	1	9+1	1
De Bilde	Gilles	Bel	f	Jul 1999	50+9	13	9	2
Sibon	Gerald	Neth	d	Jul 1999	98+31	36	18+3	7
Di Piedi	Michele	It	m	Aug 2000	9+30	5	1+4	2
Blatsis	Con	Aus	d	Dec 2000	6	0	2	0
Soltvedt	Trond Egil	Nor	m	Feb 2001	74	2	7	2
Bonvin	Pablo Facundo	Arg	m	Aug 2001	7+16	4	2+5	1
Roberts	Sean	SA	gk	Oct 2001	0+1	0	0	0
Djordjic (Swe)	Bojan	Yug	m	Dec 2001	4+1	0	0	0
Kuqi (Fin)	Shefki	Alb	f	Jan 2002	51+6	14	3	0
Johnson	David	Jam	f	Feb 2002	7	2	0	0
Evans	Paul	SA	gk	Mar 2003	7	0	0	0

SHREWSBURY TOWN (9)

SURNAME	NAME	BORN	POS	FROM	LgAp	LgG	OthAp	OthG
Atkins (Brit)	Arthur	Jap	ch	Jun 1954	16	0	1	0
Blake (Brit)	Noel	Jam	d	Mar 1982	6	0	0	0
Pittman	Steve	USA	fb	Mar 1989	31+1	2	4	0
Paskin	John	SA	f	Feb 1992	1	0	0	0
Stevens	Ian	Mal	f	Aug 1994	98+31	39	6+4	2
Gall	Benny	Den	gk	Aug 1996	34	0	4	0
Nielsen	Tommy	Den	fb	Aug 1996	19+3	1	1+2	0
Fallon	Rory	NZ	f	Dec 2001	8+3	0	0	0
Van Blerk	Jason	Aus	m	Aug 2002	17+6	1	3	1

SOUTHAMPTON (43)

SURNAME	NAME	BORN	POS	FROM	LgAp	LgG	OthAp	OthG
Moorhead (Ire)	George	NZ	ch	Aug 1920	9	0	4	0
Osborne (Eng)	Frank	SA	f	Jun 1931	17	0	3	0
Charles	Alf	Trin	f	Jan 1937	1	0	0	0
Woolf	Levi	SA	f	Sep 1937	1	0	0	0
Horsfall	George	Aus	wh	May 1947	2	0	0	0
Gallego	Jose	Sp	w	May 1948	1	0	0	0
Chadwick (Brit)	Dave	Ind	w	Oct 1960	25	1	1	0
Kemp (Brit)	Fred	It	m	Jun 1965	58+3	10	10+1	1
Golac (1)	Ivan	Yug	fb	Nov 1978	143+1	4	28	0
Katalinic	Ivan	Yug	gk	Feb 1980	48	0	6	0
Golac (2)	Ivan	Yug	fb	Mar 1984	24	0	0	0
Cherednik	Alexei	USSR	d	Feb 1990	19+4	0	4	0
Gotsmanov	Sergei	USSR	f	Aug 1990	2+6	0	4	0
Monkou (Neth)	Ken	Sur	d	Aug 1992	190+8	10	33+1	3
Grobbelaar (Zim)	Bruce	SA	gk	Aug 1994	32	0	8	0
Ekelund	Ronnie	Den	f	Sep 1994	15+2	5	2+1	0
Tisdale (Brit)	Paul	Mal	m	Jun 1991	5+11	1	0+2	0
Neilson (Wal)	Alan	Ger	d	Jun 1995	42+13	0	8	0
Lundekvam	Claus	Nor	d	Sep 1996	219+6	0	38+3	0
Ostenstad	Egil	Nor	f	Oct 1996	80+16	28	12+1	5
Berkovic	Eyal	Isr	m	Oct 1996	26+2	4	6+1	2
Van Gobbel (Neth)	Ulrich	Sur	d	Oct 1996	25+2	1	7	1
Dia	Ali	Sen	f	Nov 1996	0+1	0	0	0
Taylor (N Ire)	Maik	Ger	gk	Jan 1997	18	0	0	0
Johansen	Stig	Nor	f	Aug 1997	3+3	0	1+1	0
Kachloul	Hassan	Mor	m	Oct 1998	73+13	14	9+2	1
Colleter	Patrick	Fr	d	Dec 1998	24	1	3	0
Rodrigues	Dani	Por	f	Mar 1999	0+2	0	0	0
Pahars (Lat)	Marian	Ukr	f	Mar 1999	99+16	40	13+2	2
Almeida	Marco	Por	d	Jul 1999	0+1	0	0	0
Boa Morte	Luis	Por	f	Aug 1999	6+8	1	1+2	0
Soltvedt	Trond Egil	Nor	m	Aug 1999	20+10	2	8+1	3
Tessem	Jo	Nor	m	Nov 1999	66+41	12	11+8	4
Bleidelis	Imants	Lat	m	Feb 2000	0+2	0	1+2	0
El Khalej	Tahar	Mor	d	Mar 2000	48+10	3	3+4	1
Rosler	Uwe	Ger	f	Jul 2000	9+15	0	1+4	1
McDonald	Scott	Aus	f	Aug 2000	0+2	0	1	0
Petrescu	Dan	Rom	m	Jan 2001	8+3	2	0	0
Svensson	Anders	Swe	m	Jun 2001	59+8	6	11+1	4
Delgado	Agustin	Ecu	f	Nov 2001	2+5	0	2	1
Fernandes	Fabrice	Fr	m	Dec 2001	41+7	4	7+2	1
Svensson	Michael	Swe	d	Aug 2002	33+1	2	9	2
Kanchelskis	Andrei	Ukr	m	Sep 2002	0+1	0	0+1	0
Niemi	Antti	Fin	gk	Sep 2002	25	0	8	0

SURNAME	NAME	BORN	POS	FROM		LgAp	LgG	OthAp	OthG
SOUTHEND UNITED (19)									
Horsfall	George	Aus	wh	Jul 1949		1	0	0	0
Crossan	Errol	Can	w	Aug 1957		40	11	5	0
Houghton (Brit)	Bud	Ind	f	Oct 1958		68	32	5	1
Firmani	Eddie	SA	f	Jun 1965		55	24	7	4
Roberts	John	Aus	gk	Jan 1971		47	0	4	0
Welch	Micky	Bar	f	Feb 1985		4	0	0	0
Iorfa (1)	Dominic	Nig	f	Aug 1994		5+7	1	2	0
Lapper	Mike	USA	d	Aug 1995		46+6	1	3	0
Belsvik	Petter	Nor	f	Nov 1995		3	1	0	0
Boere	Jeroen	Neth	f	Mar 1996		61+12	25	5+2	0
Harris (Brit)	Andy	SA	m	Jul 1996		70+2	0	8	0
Nielsen	John	Den	m	Sep 1996		18+11	3	3	1
Dursun	Peter	Den	f	Nov 1996		0+1	0	0	0
Nzamba	Guy	Gab	f	Sep 1997		0+1	0	0	0
Coulbault	Regis	Fr	m	Oct 1997		30+4	4	2	0
Henriksen	Tony	Nor	gk	Oct 1996		0	0	0+1	0
N'Diaye	Sada	Sen	m	Oct 1997		15+2	2	1	0
Iorfa (2)	Dominic	Nig	f	Dec 1998		0+2	0	0	0
Unger	Lars	Ger	m	Feb 1999		14	0	0	0
Coyne	Chris	Aus	d	Mar 1999		0+1	0	0	0
SOUTHPORT (4)									
King	Charlie	SA	ch	May 1923		35	1	4	0
Bellis (Brit)	George	Ind	ch	Aug 1923		41	4	1	0
Aspinall	Wilf	USA	f	Jul 1935		6	0	0	0
Perry	Bill	SA	w	Jun 1962		26	0	3	0
SOUTH SHIELDS (1)									
Higginbotham	Harry	Aus	f	Aug 1919		7	0	0	0
STOCKPORT COUNTY (29)									
Wharton	Arthur	Gha	gk	Jul 1901		6	0	0	0
Pass (Brit)	Jimmy	Ind	f	Aug 1903		59	18	7	1
Andrews (N Ire)	Billy	USA	wh	Mar 1909		13	0	0	0
Aspinall	Wilf	USA	f	Jun 1934		1	1	0	0
Grieves	Ken	Aus	gk	Jul 1957		39	0	4	0
Keelan (Brit)	Kevin	Ind	gk	Apr 1961		3	0	0	0
Stuart	Eddie	SA	d	Jul 1966		77	1	4	0
Vernon	John	SA	w	Apr 1975		4+2	0	0	0
Stevens	Ian	Mal	f	Oct 1986		1+1	0	0+1	0
Paskin	John	SA	f	Sep 1991		3+2	1	0	0
Cantona	Joel	Fr	m	Mar 1994		0+3	0	0	0
Murray	Bruce	USA	f	Mar 1994		2+1	0	0	0
Cavaco	Luis Miguel	Por	f	Aug 1996		19+10	5	10+2	2
Nash	Martin	Can	f	Nov 1996		0+11	0	0+1	0
Kiko	Manuel	Por	f	Dec 1996		0+3	0	0	0
Kalogeracos	Vas	Aus	f	Aug 1997		0+2	0	1	0
Aunger	Geoff	Can	d/m	Dec 1997		0+1	0	0	0
Alsaker	Paul	Nor	f	Aug 1998		1	0	1	0
D'Jaffo	Laurent	Fr	f	Aug 1999		20+1	7	2	1
Bergersen	Kent	Nor	m	Sep 1999		18+8	1	1	0
Fradin	Karim	Fr	m	Nov 1999		72+9	9	6+1	2
Bryngelsson	Fredrik	Swe	d	Jul 2000		7+1	0	2	0
Wiss	Jarkko	Fin	m	Aug 2000		34+7	6	4+2	1
Kuqi (Fin)	Shefki	Alb	f	Jan 2001		32+3	11	3	1
Helin	Petri	Fin	d	Jul 2001		10+3	0	1+2	0
Sneekes	Richard	Neth	m	Sep 2001		8+1	0	1	0
Arphexad (Fr)	Pegguy	Guad	gk	Sep 2001		3	0	0	0
Van Blerk	Jason	Aus	m	Aug 2001		13	0	1	0
Tidman	Ola	Swe	gk	Jan 2003		18	0	0	0
STOKE CITY (43)									
Kirkby	John	USA	fb	Dec 1946		1	0	0	0
Stuart	Eddie	SA	d	Jul 1962		63	2	8	0
Backos	Des	SA	f	Oct 1977		1+1	0	0	0
Ursem	Loek	Neth	w	Jul 1979		32+8	7	4	0
Berry (Wal)	George	Ger	d	Aug 1982		229+8	27	23	1
Segers	Hans	Neth	gk	Feb 1987		1	0	0	0
Blake (Brit)	Noel	Jam	d	Feb 1990		74+1	3	11+1	0
Kearton	Jason	Aus	gk	Aug 1991		16	0	0	0
Stein (Eng) (1)	Mark	SA	f	Nov 1991		94	50	14	9
Grobbelaar (Zim)	Bruce	SA	gk	Mar 1993		4	0	0	0
Orlygsson	Toddi	Ice	m	Aug 1993		86+4	16	13	2
Peschisolido	Paul	Can	f	Aug 1994		59+7	19	9	3
Sigurdsson	Larus	Ice	d	Oct 1994		199+1	7	23+1	0
Andrade (1)	Jose-Manuel	Por	f	Mar 1995		2+2	1	0	0
Stein (Eng) (2)	Mark	SA	f	Aug 1996		11	4	0	0
Da Costa	Hugo	Por	d	Aug 1996		1+1	0	1+1	0
Schreuder	Jan-Dirk	Neth	f	Jun 1997		0	0	0+2	0
Andrade (2)	Jose-Manuel	Por	f	Aug 1997		4+8	1	2	0

SURNAME	NAME	BORN	POS	FROM	LgAp	LgG	OthAp	OthG
Tiatto	Danny	Aus	d	Nov 1997	11+4	1	0	0
Xausa	Davide	Can	f	Feb 1998	1	0	0	0
Lightbourne	Kyle	Ber	f	Feb 1998	83+28	21	12	2
Sobiech	Jorg	Ger	d	Mar 1998	3	0	0	0
Oldfield (Eng)	David	Aus	m/f	Jul 1998	50+15	7	6+1	0
Short (Brit)	Chris	Ger	d	Jul 1998	33+2	0	5+1	0
Jacobsen	Anders	Nor	d	Aug 1999	29+4	2	5+1	0
Danielsson	Einer Thor	Ice	m	Nov 1999	3+5	1	0	0
Gislason	Siggi	Ice	m	Nov 1999	4+4	0	0	0
Hansson	Mikael	Swe	m	Dec 1999	60+5	2	9	0
Kippe	Frode	Nor	d	Dec 1999	30+4	1	2	0
Gunnarsson	Brynjar	Ice	d	Jan 2000	128+3	16	18	3
Gudjonsson	Bjarni	Ice	f	Mar 2000	119+13	11	21+2	3
Gunnlaugsson	Arnie	Ice	m	Mar 2000	19+3	5	4	1
Thordarson	Stefan	Ice	f	Jun 2000	18+33	8	7+3	2
Dorigo (Eng)	Tony	Aus	d	Jul 2000	34+2	0	5	0
Risom	Henrik	Den	m	Aug 2000	9+16	0	3+2	0
Dadason	Rikki	Ice	f	Oct 2000	19+20	10	1+6	1
Kippe	Frode	Nor	d	Oct 2000	15+4	0	2	0
Kristinsson	Birkir	Ice	gk	Nov 2000	18	0	0	0
Shtaniuk	Sergei	Blr	d	Jul 2001	84	5	11	0
Hoekstra	Peter	Neth	f	Jul 2001	46+8	7	5+2	1
Van Deurzen	Jurgen	Bel	m	Aug 2001	44+8	5	5+3	0
Marteinsson	Petur	Ice	m	Nov 2001	9+6	2	1+1	0
Oulare	Souleymane	Gui	f	Dec 2001	0+1	0	0+1	1

SUNDERLAND (42)

SURNAME	NAME	BORN	POS	FROM	LgAp	LgG	OthAp	OthG
Dalton	James	Can	ch	Sep 1891	3	0	0	0
Gibson	Fred	SA	w	May 1909	1	0	0	0
Gibson	Jock	USA	fb	Nov 1920	4	0	1	0
Wagstaffe (Brit)	Thomas	Ind	f	Mar 1923	2	0	0	0
McDowall	Les	Ind	ch	Dec 1932	13	0	1	0
Purdon	Ted	SA	f	Jan 1954	90	39	6	3
Fraser (Sco)	Willie	Aus	gk	Mar 1954	127	0	16	0
Kichenbrand	Don	SA	f	Mar 1958	53	28	1	0
Marangoni	Claudio	Arg	m	Dec 1979	19+1	3	2	0
Ursem	Loek	Neth	w	Mar 1982	0+4	0	0	0
Nicholl (N Ire)	Jimmy	Can	fb	Sep 1982	32	0	8	0
Hesford (Eng)	Iain	Zam	gk	Aug 1986	97	0	9	0
Hauser	Thomas	Ger	f	Feb 1989	22+31	9	3+8	2
Butcher (Eng)	Terry	Sing	d	Jul 1992	37+1	0	4	1
Kubicki	Dariusz	Pol	fb	Jun 1994	135+1	0	14	0
Perez	Lionel	Fr	gk	Aug 1996	74+1	0	9	0
Eriksson	Jan	Swe	d	Jan 1997	1	0	0	0
Zoetebier	Ed	Neth	gk	Jun 1997	0	0	2	0
Sorensen	Thomas	Den	gk	Aug 1998	171	0	26	0
Fredgaard	Carsten	Den	f	Jul 1999	0+1	0	3+1	2
Helmer	Thomas	Ger	d	Jul 1999	1+1	0	0	0
Roy	Eric	Fr	m	Aug 1999	20+7	0	7	1
Schwarz	Stefan	Swe	m	Aug 1999	62+5	3	8	1
Di Giuseppe	Bica	Bra	f	Sep 1999	0	0	0+1	0
Nunez	Milton	Hon	f	Mar 2000	0+1	0	0+1	0
Arca	Julio	Arg	m	Aug 2000	53+9	3	10	3
Macho	Jurgen	Aut	gk	Jul 2000	20+2	0	4+1	0
Peeters	Tom	Bel	m	Jul 2000	0	0	1	0
Thome	Emerson	Bra	d	Sep 2000	43+1	2	9	0
Varga	Stanislav	Svk	d	Aug 2000	18+3	1	10+1	0
Carteron	Patrice	Fr	d	Mar 2001	8	1	0	0
Bellion	David	Fr	f	Jul 2001	5+15	1	3+1	0
Haas	Bernt	Aut	d	Aug 2001	27	0	1+1	0
Laslandes	Lilian	Fr	f	Jun 2001	5+7	0	0+1	1
Reyna	Claudio	USA	m	Dec 2001	28	3	1	1
Bjorklund	Joachim	Swe	d	Jan 2002	30+2	0	1+1	0
Mboma	Patrick	Cam	f	Feb 2002	5+4	1	0	0
Myhre	Thomas	Nor	gk	Oct 2002	1+1	0	1	0
Flo	Tore Andre	Nor	f	Nov 2002	23+6	4	2+1	2
Medina	Nicolas	Arg	m	Jan 2003	0	0	1	0
El Karkouri	Talal	Mor	d	Feb 2003	8	0	0+1	0
Poom	Mart	Est	gk	Apr 2003	4	0	0	0

SWANSEA CITY (18)

SURNAME	NAME	BORN	POS	FROM	LgAp	LgG	OthAp	OthG
Armand (Brit)	Jack	Ind	f	May 1929	54	10	1	0
Haasz	Johnny	Hun	f	Sep 1960	1	0	0	0
Chinaglia	Giorgio	It	f	Apr 1965	4+1	1	1	0
Schroeder	Nico	Neth	gk	Jul 1976	1	0	0	0
Hadziabdic	Dzemal	Yug	fb	Aug 1980	87+2	1	14	1
Rajkovic	Anto	Yug	d	Mar 1981	79+1	2	14	1
Salako (Eng)	John	Nig	f	Aug 1989	13	3	2	1
Molby	Jan	Den	m	Feb 1996	39+2	8	2	0
Moreira	Joao	Por	d	Jun 1996	15	0	7+1	0
Willer-Jensen	Thomas	Den	d	Mar 1997	7	0	0	0

SURNAME	NAME	BORN	POS	FROM	LgAp	LgG	OthAp	OthG
Boyd	Walter	Jam	f	Oct 1999	35+9	10	3+1	0
Romo	David	Fr	m	Oct 2000	31+12	1	2+1	0
Savarese	Giovanni	Ven	f	Oct 2000	28+3	12	0+1	0
Fabiano	Nicolas	Fr	m	Feb 2001	12+4	1	0	0
Verschave	Matthias	Fr	f	Feb 2001	12	3	0	0
Mazzina	Nicolas	Arg	m	Jul 2001	3	0	1	0
Sidibe (Fr)	Mamady	Mli	f	Jul 2001	26+5	7	2+1	1
Martinez	Roberto	Sp	m	Feb 2003	19	2	0	0

SWINDON TOWN (30)

SURNAME	NAME	BORN	POS	FROM	LgAp	LgG	OthAp	OthG
Murray	David	SA	f	Jun 1930	1	0	0	0
Leslie (Brit)	Maurice	Ind	fb	Jun 1947	1	0	0	0
Nagy	Mick	Hun	ch	Aug 1951	2	0	0	0
Fiocca	Paul	It	m	Jan 1973	1	0	0	0
Sperti	Franco	It	fb	Jan 1973	1	0	0	0
Collins	Mike	SA	f	Jul 1973	2+4	0	1	0
Payne (Brit)	Mark	Ind	w	Sep 1984	0+3	0	1	0
Wegerle (USA)	Roy	SA	f	Mar 1988	7	1	0	0
Ardiles	Ossie	Arg	m	Jul 1989	0+2	0	0	0
Buttigieg	John	Mal	d	Sep 1990	2+1	0	0+1	0
Lorenzo	Nestor	Arg	d	Oct 1990	20+4	2	3	0
O'Sullivan (Ire)	Wayne	Cyp	m	May 1993	65+24	3	12+3	1
Fjortoft	Jan Aage	Nor	f	Jul 1993	62+10	28	12+1	11
Nijholt	Luc	Neth	d	Jul 1993	66+1	1	14+2	1
Talia	Frank	Aus	gk	Sep 1995	107	0	11	0
Darras	Frederic	Fr	d	Aug 1996	42+7	0	6	0
Cuervo	Phillipe	Fr	m	Aug 1997	16+19	0	2+1	0
Cobian	Juan	Arg	d	Jul 2000	3+1	0	3	0
Griemink	Bart	Neth	gk	Mar 2000	117+1	0	14	0
Heiselberg	Kim	Den	m	Aug 2000	1	0	1	0
Invincible	Danny	Aus	m	Aug 2000	109+19	22	11+1	3
Van der Linden	Antoine	Neth	d	Aug 2000	17+16	1	3	0
Robertson	Mark	Aus	m	Aug 2000	4+6	1	2+1	0
Tuomela	Marko	Fin	d	Sep 2000	1+1	0	2	0
Whitley (N Ire)	Jim	Zam	m	Dec 2000	2	0	1	0
Lightbourne	Kyle	Ber	f	Jan 2001	2	0	0	0
Bakalli	Adrian	Bel	d	Mar 2001	1	0	0	0
Sabin	Eric	Fr	f	Jun 2001	60+13	9	7	0
Edds	Gareth	Aus	m	Aug 2002	8+6	0	1+1	0
Miglioranzi (USA)	Stefani	Bra	m	Aug 2002	39+2	3	2	0

THAMES (1)

SURNAME	NAME	BORN	POS	FROM	LgAp	LgG	OthAp	OthG
Crawford	Ronald	SA	fb	Jul 1930	3	0	0	0

TORQUAY UNITED (27)

SURNAME	NAME	BORN	POS	FROM	LgAp	LgG	OthAp	OthG
Mackrill	Percy	SA	fb	Jul 1925	6	0	0	0
Butler (Eng)	Jack	SL	d	May 1930	50	2	3	0
Fursdon	Roy	Can	w	Aug 1938	15	2	0	0
Chadwick (Brit)	Dave	Ind	m	Dec 1972	10	0	0	0
Laryea	Benny	Gha	f	Mar 1984	10+2	3	3	1
Salman (Eng)	Danis	Cyp	d	Sep 1992	20	0	2	0
Sommer	Jurgen	USA	gk	Oct 1992	10	0	0	0
Goodridge (1)	Greg	Bar	w	Mar 1994	32+6	4	8+1	2
Okorie	Chima	Nig	f	Mar 1994	32+4	6	8+1	1
Mateu	Jose-Luis	Sp	f	Sep 1995	5+5	1	0+3	1
Jack (StV)	Rodney	Jam	f	Oct 1995	82+5	24	15	4
Haddaoui	Riffi	Den	f	Mar 1996	0+2	0	0	0
Gregory (Brit)	Neil	Zam	f	Nov 1996	5	0	0	0
Thirlby (Brit)	Anthony	Ger	m	Feb 1997	1+2	0	0	0
Newell (Brit)	Justin	Ger	f	Sep 1997	0+1	0	0	0
Harries	Paul	Aus	f	Feb 1999	5	0	0	0
Simb	Jean-Pierre	Fr	f	Mar 1999	4+16	1	0+4	0
Jermyn (Brit)	Mark	Ger	d	Mar 1999	0+1	0	0	0
Ingimarsson	Ivar	Ice	m	Oct 1999	4	1	0	0
Mendy	Jules	Sen	m	Aug 2000	7+14	2	0+4	0
Sissoko	Habib	Fr	f	Aug 2000	7+7	2	2	0
Chalqi	Khalid	Mor	f	Nov 2000	20+1	1	2	1
Petterson	Andy	Aus	gk	Mar 2001	6	0	0	0
Goodridge (2)	Greg	Bar	w	Nov 2001	9+8	1	0	0
Greyling	Anton	SA	m	Aug 2001	0+2	0	0	0
Van Heusden	Arjan	Neth	gk	Nov 2002	15	0	1	0
Camara (Brit)	Ben	Ger	f	Mar 2003	0+2	0	0	0

TOTTENHAM HOTSPUR (41)

SURNAME	NAME	BORN	POS	FROM	LgAp	LgG	OthAp	OthG
Seeburg	Max	Ger	f	May 1907	1	0	0	0
Osborne (Eng)	Frank	SA	f	Jan 1924	210	78	10	4
Garwood (Brit)	Len	Ind	wh	May 1946	2	0	0	0
Ardiles	Ossie	Arg	m	Jul 1978	221+16	16	71+2	9
Villa	Ricky	Arg	m	Jul 1978	124+9	18	44+2	7
Chiedozie	John	Nig	w	Aug 1984	45+8	12	19+3	2
Claesen	Nico	Bel	f	Oct 1986	37+13	18	8+5	5

SURNAME	NAME	BORN	POS	FROM	LgAp	LgG	OthAp	OthG
Gough (Sco)	Richard	Swe	d	Aug 1986	49	2	16	0
Metgod	Johnny	Neth	m	Jul 1987	5+7	0	2	0
Statham (Eng)	Brian	Zim	d/m	Aug 1987	20+4	0	2+1	0
Nayim	Mohamed	Mor	m	Nov 1988	95+17	11	23+9	6
Bergsson	Gudni	Ice	d	Dec 1988	51+20	2	11+5	0
Thorstvedt	Erik	Nor	gk	Dec 1988	171+2	0	45	0
Van Den Hauwe (Wal)	Pat	Bel	fb	Aug 1989	110+6	0	29	0
Rosenthal	Ronny	Isr	f	Jan 1994	55+33	4	10+2	7
Dumitrescu	Ilie	Rom	m	Aug 1994	16+2	4	2	1
Klinsmann (1)	Jurgen	Ger	f	Aug 1994	41	20	9	9
Popescu	Gica	Rom	m	Sep 1994	23	3	5	0
Baardsen (Nor)	Espen	USA	gk	Jul 1996	22+1	0	5+1	0
Nielsen	Allan	Den	m	Sep 1996	78+19	12	16+3	6
Iversen	Steffen	Nor	f	Dec 1996	112+31	36	25+9	11
Vega	Ramon	Swit	d	Jan 1997	53+11	7	17+3	1
Ginola	David	Fr	w	Jul 1997	100	12	26+1	9
Dominguez	Jose	Por	w	Aug 1997	12+33	4	4+9	1
Klinsmann (2)	Jurgen	Ger	f	Dec 1997	15	9	3	0
Berti	Nicola	It	m	Jan 1998	21	3	2	0
Saib	Moussa	Alg	m	Feb 1998	3+10	1	0	0
Segers	Hans	Neth	gk	Aug 1998	1	0	1	0
Freund	Steffen	Ger	m	Dec 1998	92+10	0	29	0
Taricco	Mauricio	Arg	fb	Dec 1998	94+4	1	19	2
Nilsen	Roger	Nor	d	Mar 1999	3	0	0	0
Tramezzani	Paolo	It	d	Jun 1998	6	0	1	0
Korsten	Willem	Neth	f	Jul 1999	12+11	3	1+3	0
Leonhardsen	Oyvind	Nor	m	Aug 1999	46+8	7	13+5	4
Rebrov	Sergei	Ukr	f	Jun 2000	37+22	10	11+5	6
Bunjevcevic	Goran	Yug	d	Jun 2001	36+5	0	3+1	0
Ziege	Christian	Ger	m	Jul 2001	37+2	7	6	2
Keller	Kasey	USA	gk	Aug 2001	47	0	5	0
Poyet	Gustavo	Uru	m	Jul 2001	54+8	15	11	5
Acimovic	Milenko	Slo	m	Aug 2002	4+13	0	1	0
Blondel	Jonathan	Bel	m	Aug 2002	0+1	0	0	0
Toda	Kazuyuki	Jap	m	Apr 2003	2+2	0	0	0

TRANMERE ROVERS (15)

Hill (Brit)	Reg	Gib	wh	Dec 1932	1	0	0	0
Fleming (Brit)	Mike	Ind	f	Sep 1953	115	8	7	0
Onyeali	Elkanah	Nig	f	Aug 1960	13	8	3	1
Stuart	Eddie	SA	d	Aug 1964	83	2	6	0
Anderson (Brit)	Doug	HK	m	Aug 1984	125+1	15	13+1	3
Bonetti	Ivano	It	m	Aug 1996	9+4	1	2	1
Kubicki	Dariusz	Pol	fb	Mar 1998	12	0	0	0
Santos	Georges	Fr	m	Jul 1998	46+1	2	7	0
Achterberg	John	Neth	gk	Sep 1998	135+3	0	25+1	0
Matias	Pedro	Sp	m	Aug 1999	1+3	0	0	0
Hume	Iain	Can	m	Nov 2000	23+39	6	0+5	0
Myhre	Thomas	Nor	gk	Nov 2000	3	0	1	0
N'Diaye	Seyni	Sen	f	Mar 2001	11+8	4	2+1	0
Feuer	Ian	USA	gk	Aug 2002	2	0	0	0
Loran	Tyrone	Neth	d	Jan 2003	16+1	0	0	0

WALSALL (43)

Langenove	Eugene	Fr	f	Oct 1922	2	0	0	0
Milligan (N Ire)	Dudley	SA	f	Oct 1948	5	1	0	0
Pidcock	Fred	Can	gk	Sep 1953	1	0	0	0
Methven (Brit)	Colin	Ind	d	Nov 1990	97	3	9+1	0
Essers	Pierre	Neth	f	Sep 1991	1	0	0	0
Chine	Athumani	Tan	m	Mar 1992	4+1	0	0	0
Ollerenshaw	Scott	Aus	f	Aug 1992	8+12	4	2+4	0
Lightbourne	Kyle	Ber	f	Sep 1993	158+7	65	24+2	14
Kerr (USA)	John	Can	f	Nov 1995	0+1	0	0+1	0
Boli (Fr)	Roger	IvCo	f	Aug 1997	41	12	10	6
Peron	Jeff	Fr	m	Aug 1997	38	1	9	0
Eydelie	Jean-Jacques	Fr	m	Mar 1998	10+1	0	0	0
Tholot	Didier	Fr	f	Mar 1998	13+1	4	0	0
Larusson	Bjarni	Ice	m	Sep 1998	45+14	3	4+1	1
Otta	Walter	Arg	f	Nov 1998	6+2	3	2	0
Eyjolfsson	Siggi	Ice	f	Jan 1999	1+22	2	1+5	3
Mavrak (Bos)	Darko	Cro	m	Jan 1999	13+4	2	1+2	0
Steiner	Rob	Swe	f	Mar 1999	10	3	0	0
Bukran	Gabor	Hun	m	Aug 1999	63+10	4	11+2	3
Abou (Fr)	Samassi	IvCo	f	Oct 1999	7+1	0	0	0
Di Giuseppe	Bica	Bra	f	Oct 1999	0+1	0	0	0
Matias	Pedro	Sp	m	Oct 1999	98+27	23	13+6	3
Padula	Gino	Arg	d	Nov 1999	23+2	0	2	0
Vlachos	Michalis	Grk	d	Feb 2000	11	1	0	0
Aranalde	Zigor	Sp	d	Aug 2000	126+3	5	22	1
Leitao	Jorge	Por	f	Aug 2000	107+19	37	20+1	7
Ekelund	Ronnie	Den	f	Dec 2000	2+7	1	0+1	0

SURNAME	NAME	BORN	POS	FROM	LgAp	LgG	OthAp	OthG
Herivelto	Moreira	Bra	m	Jul 2001	10+10	3	2+1	1
Garrocho	Carlos	Ang	m	Jul 2001	2+2	0	0+1	0
Herivelto	Moreira	Bra	m	Jul 2001	11+17	5	3+2	1
Ofodile	Adolphus	Nig	f	Jul 2001	0+1	0	1	0
Biancalani	Frederic	Fr	d	Aug 2001	13+5	2	2+1	0
Thogersen	Thomas	Den	m	Oct 2001	7	2	0	0
Andre	Carlos	Por	m	Dec 2001	5	0	2	0
Corica	Steve	Aus	m	Feb 2002	46+8	7	5+2	0
Marcelo		Bra	f	Feb 2002	9	1	0	0
Uhlenbeek (Neth)	Gus	Sur	d	Mar 2002	5	0	0	0
Rodrigues	Dani	Por	f	Aug 2002	0+1	0	0	0
Hay	Danny	NZ	d	Aug 2002	26+3	0	6	0
Junior	Jose Luis	Br	f	Aug 2002	28+8	15	6	1
Martinez	Roberto	Sp	m	Aug 2002	1+5	0	0	0
Zdrilic	David	Aus	f	Aug 2002	9+15	3	1+4	2
Pollet	Ludo	Fr	d	Nov 2002	5	0	0	0

WATFORD (33)

SURNAME	NAME	BORN	POS	FROM	LgAp	LgG	OthAp	OthG
Mitchell	Frank	Aus	wh	Aug 1952	193	0	12	0
Oelofse	Ralph	SA	wh	Jul 1953	15	0	0	0
Blissett (Eng)(1)	Luther	Jam	f	Jul 1975	222+24	95	43+1	16
Gibbs	Peter	Zim	gk	Jul 1975	4	0	0	0
Callaghan (Eng) (1)	Nigel	Sing	w	Jul 1979	209+13	41	51+4	8
Barnes (Eng)	John	Jam	f	Jul 1981	232+1	65	58	18
Lohman	Jan	Neth	m	Oct 1981	51+12	6	12+3	3
Blissett (Eng)(2)	Luther	Jam	f	Aug 1984	113+14	44	25+4	13
Henry	Liburd	Dom	f	Nov 1987	8+2	1	4	0
Callaghan (Eng) (2)	Nigel	Sing	w	Mar 1991	6+6	1	0	0
Blissett (Eng)(3)	Luther	Jam	f	Aug 1991	34+8	9	5	3
Johnson	Richard	Aus	m	May 1992	210+32	20	29+3	2
Watson	Mark	Can	d	Nov 1993	18	0	1+2	0
Melvang (Den)	Lars	USA	f	Aug 1997	4	1	1	0
Rosenthal	Ronny	Isr	f	Aug 1997	25+5	8	7+2	3
Hazan	Alon	Isr	m	Jan 1998	15+18	2	1+4	0
Gudmundsson	Johann	Ice	m	Mar 1998	7+15	2	1+3	0
Ngonge (DRC)	Michel	Bel	f	Jul 1998	29+18	9	7+3	2
Bonnot	Alex	Fr	m	Nov 1998	8+8	0	0	0
Iroha	Ben	Nig	d	Dec 1998	8+2	0	1	0
Bakalli	Adrian	Bel	d	Jan 1999	0+2	0	0	0
Wooter (Neth)	Nordin	Sur	m	Sep 1999	37+26	3	5+2	0
Gravelaine	Xavier	Fr	m	Nov 1999	7	2	0	0
Helguson	Heidar	Ice	f	Jan 2000	76+37	31	7+9	4
Baardsen (Nor)	Espen	USA	gk	Aug 2000	41	0	5	0
Nielsen	Allan	Den	m	Aug 2000	95+6	19	9+3	0
Blondeau	Patrick	Fr	d	Jul 2001	24+1	0	3	0
Vega	Ramon	Swit	d	Jun 2001	23+4	1	6	2
Galli	Filippo	It	d	Jul 2001	27+1	1	1	0
Issa	Pierre	SA	d	Sep 2001	12+3	1	3	0
Norville (Brit)	Jason	Trin	f	Oct 2001	6+7	0	0+1	0
Okon	Paul	Aus	d	Jan 2002	14+1	0	0	0
Godfrey	Elliott	Can	f	Mar 2003	0+1	0	0	0

WEST BROMWICH ALBION (29)

SURNAME	NAME	BORN	POS	FROM	LgAp	LgG	OthAp	OthG
Bookman (Brit)	Louis	Lith	w	Feb 1914	16	1	0	0
Johnson	Glenn	Can	f	Oct 1969	2+2	0	0	0
Regis (Eng)	Cyrille	FrGu	f	May 1977	233+4	82	62+1	27
Batson (Eng)	Brendan	Gda	fb	Feb 1978	172	1	46	1
Jol	Maarten	Neth	m	Oct 1981	63+1	4	15	0
Zondervan (Neth)	Romeo	Sur	m	Mar 1982	82+2	5	11	0
Nicholl (N Ire)	Jimmy	Can	fb	Nov 1984	56	0	9	0
Paskin	John	SA	f	Aug 1988	14+11	5	1+2	0
Andersen	Vetle	Nor	d	Dec 1989	0+1	0	0	0
Blissett (Eng)	Luther	Jam	f	Oct 1992	3	1	0	0
Boere	Jeroen	Neth	f	Sep 1994	5	0	0	0
Sneekes	Richard	Neth	m	Mar 1996	208+19	30	23+3	4
Peschisolido	Paul	Can	f	Jul 1996	36+9	18	5+1	3
Murphy	Shaun	Aus	d	Dec 1996	60+11	7	7	0
McDermott	Andy	Aus	fb	Mar 1997	49+3	1	4+1	1
Van Blerk	Jason	Aus	fb	Mar 1998	106+3	3	11+1	0
Bortolazzi	Mario	It	m	Aug 1998	25+10	2	1	0
De Freitas (Neth)	Fabian	Sur	f	Aug 1998	34+27	8	6+1	2
Maresca	Enzo	It	m	Aug 1998	28+19	5	3+3	0
Sigurdsson	Larus	Ice	d	Sep 1999	99+12	1	10+2	0
Fredgaard	Carsten	Den	m	Feb 2000	5	0	0	0
Jensen	Brian	Den	gk	Mar 2000	46	0	4	0
Santos	Georges	Fr	m	Mar 2000	8	0	0	0
Batista (Por)	Jordao	Ang	m	Aug 2000	47+16	6	5+3	2
Balis	Igor	Svk	f	Dec 2000	60+9	4	3+3	0
Derveld	Fernando	Neth	d	Feb 2001	1+1	0	0	0
Rosler	Uwe	Ger	f	Oct 2001	5	1	0	0

SURNAME	NAME	BORN	POS	FROM	LgAp	LgG	OthAp	OthG
Varga	Stanislav	Svk	d	Mar 2002	3+1	0	0	0
Udeze	Ifeanyi	Nig	d	Jan 2003	7+4	0	0	0

WEST HAM (56)

SURNAME	NAME	BORN	POS	FROM	LgAp	LgG	OthAp	OthG
Burton (Brit)	Frank	Mex	fb	Aug 1919	64	2	5	0
Smith (Brit)	Roy	Ind	f	Jun 1955	6	1	0	0
Newman	Mick	Can	f	Feb 1957	7	2	0	0
Best	Clyde	Ber	f	Mar 1969	178+8	47	32	11
Coker	Ade	Nig	f	Dec 1971	9+1	3	1	0
Orhan	Yilmaz	Cyp	f	Oct 1972	6+2	0	1	0
Van der Elst	Francois	Bel	m	Dec 1981	61+1	14	7+1	3
Potts (Eng)	Steve	USA	d	May 1984	362+37	1	87+5	0
Miklosko	Ludek	CzRep	gk	Feb 1990	315	0	50	0
Atteveld	Ray	Neth	d/m	Feb 1992	1	0	2	0
Bunbury (Can)	Alex	Guy	f	Dec 1992	2+2	0	0+1	0
Boere	Jeroen	Neth	f	Sep 1993	15+10	6	3+1	1
Omoyimni	Manny	Nig	f	May 1995	1+8	2	1+3	0
Rieper	Marc	Den	d	Jun 1994	83+7	5	10+1	0
Boogers	Marco	Neth	m	Jul 1995	0+4	0	0	0
Lazaridis	Stan	Aus	w	Sep 1995	53+16	3	15+3	0
Harkes	John	USA	m	Oct 1995	6+5	0	1+1	0
Coyne	Chris	Aus	d	Jan 1996	0+1	0	0	0
Bilic	Slaven	Cro	d	Feb 1996	48	2	6	1
Dumitrescu	Ilie	Rom	m	Mar 1996	5+5	0	2+1	0
Mautone	Steve	Aus	gk	Mar 1996	1	0	2	0
Carvalho	Dani	Por	f	Feb 1996	3+6	2	0	0
Futre	Paulo	Por	f	Jun 1996	4+5	0	0	0
Raducioiu	Florin	Rom	f	Jun 1996	6+5	2	1	1
Porfirio	Hugo	Por	m	Sep 1996	15+8	2	3+1	2
Lomas (N Ire)	Steve	Ger	m	Mar 1997	156+3	9	32+1	3
Berkovic	Eyal	Isr	m	Jun 1997	62+3	10	13+1	2
Terrier	David	Fr	m	Jun 1997	0+1	0	0	0
Forrest	Craig	Can	gk	Jul 1997	26+4	0	8	0
Abou (Fr)	Samassi	IvCo	f	Nov 1997	14+8	5	5+4	1
Alves	Paulo	Por	f	Nov 1997	0+4	0	0	0
Lama	Bernard	Fr	gk	Dec 1997	12	0	2	0
Keller	Marc	Fr	m	Jul 1998	36+8	5	11+1	2
Margas	Javier	Chi	d	Aug 1998	21+3	1	5+1	0
Garcia	Richard	Aus	f	Sep 1998	2+6	0	0+3	0
Di Canio	Paolo	It	f	Jan 1999	114+4	47	23	4
Foe	Marc-Vivien	Cam	m	Jan 1999	38	1	9+1	1
Wanchope	Paulo	CoRi	f	Jul 1999	33+2	12	10+2	3
Stimac	Igor	Cro	d	Sep 1999	43	1	9	0
Feuer	Ian	USA	gk	Feb 2000	3	0	0	0
Ilic (Yug)	Sasa	Aus	gk	Feb 2000	1	0	0	0
Kanoute	Frederic	Fr	f	Mar 2000	79+5	29	8	4
Suker	Davor	Cro	f	Jul 2000	7+4	2	1+1	1
Bassila	Christian	Fr	d	Aug 2000	0+3	0	0+1	0
Diawara	Kaba	Fr	f	Sep 2000	6+5	0	0	0
Song	Rigobert	Cam	d	Nov 2000	23+1	0	3	0
Camara	Titi	Gui	f	Dec 2000	5+6	0	2+1	0
Tihinen	Hannu	Fin	d	Dec 2000	5+3	0	2	0
Schemmel	Sebastien	Fr	d	Jan 2001	60+3	1	9+1	0
Soma	Ragnvald	Nor	d	Jan 2001	3+4	0	1+1	0
Foxe	Hayden	Aus	d	Mar 2001	7+4	0	0+1	0
Todorov	Svetoslav	Bul	f	Jan 2001	4+10	1	1+1	1
Courtois	Laurent	Fr	m	Aug 2001	5+2	0	0+1	0
Labant	Vladimir	Svk	d	Jan 2002	7+6	0	0+2	0
Repka	Tomas	CzRep	d	Sep 2001	63	0	4+1	0
Cisse	Edouard	Fr	m	Aug 2002	18+7	0	0	0

WIGAN (21)

SURNAME	NAME	BORN	POS	FROM	LgAp	LgG	OthAp	OthG
Methven (Brit)	Colin	Ind	d	Oct 1979	295+1	21	45	7
Tunks (Brit)	Roy	Ger	gk	Nov 1981	245	0	41	0
Houston	Graham	Gib	m	Aug 1986	16+1	4	3	0
Taylor (Brit)	Robin	Ger	m	Oct 1989	0+1	0	0	0
Adekola	David	Nig	f	Oct 1994	1+3	0	0+1	0
Diaz	Isidro	Sp	m	Jul 1995	58+20	16	6+2	3
Martinez	Roberto	Sp	m	Jul 1995	148+39	17	26+4	5
Seba	Jesus	Sp	f	Aug 1995	8+13	3	2+3	0
Sharp	Kevin	Can	d	Nov 1995	156+22	10	21+5	1
Smeets	Jorg	Neth	m	Oct 1997	10+14	3	1+2	0
Bruno	Pasquale	It	d	Feb 1998	1	0	0	0
De Zeeuw	Arjan	Neth	d	Jul 1999	126	6	19	0
Peron	Jeff	Fr	m	Nov 1999	19+4	0	1+1	0
Bidstrup	Stefan	Den	m	Nov 2000	10+5	2	2	1
Hernandez	Dino	Neth	m	Nov 2000	0	0	1	0
Padula	Gino	Arg	d	Jul 2000	2+2	0	2+1	0
Nuzzo	Raffaele	It	gk	Mar 2001	0	0	0	0
Adamczuk	Darius	Pol	m	Aug 2001	3	0	1	0
Bukran	Gabor	Hun	m	Aug 2001	1	0	0	0

SURNAME	NAME	BORN	POS	FROM	LgAp	LgG	OthAp	OthG
De Vos	Jason	Can	d	Jul 2001	62+1	13	7	0
Filan	John	Aus	gk	Dec 2001	71	0	8	0

WIGAN BOROUGH (1)

Preedy (Brit)	Charlie	Ind	gk	Jul 1928	41	0	0	0

WIMBLEDON (18)

Welch	Micky	Bar	f	Nov 1984	2+2	0	0	0
Young (Wal)	Eric	Sing	d	Jul 1987	96+3	9	19+1	1
Quamina	Mark	Guy	m/d	Jul 1988	1	0	0	0
Segers	Hans	Neth	gk	Sep 1988	265+2	0	48	0
Kruszynski	Detsi	Ger	m	Dec 1988	65+6	4	10+1	0
Leonhardsen	Oyvind	Nor	m	Nov 1994	73+3	13	24+2	3
Solbakken	Stale	Nor	m	Oct 1997	4+2	1	1+1	0
Pedersen	Tore	Nor	d	Jun 1999	6	0	0	0
Andersen	Trond	Nor	m	Aug 1999	136+10	6	21	2
Badir	Walid	Isr	m	Aug 1999	12+9	1	3+1	0
Andresen	Martin	Nor	m	Oct 1999	4+10	1	1+1	0
Hreidarsson	Hermann	Ice	d	Oct 1999	25	1	2	0
Lund	Andreas	Nor	f	Feb 2000	10+2	2	0	0
Karlsson	Par	Swe	m	Sep 2000	10+16	0	6	1
Nielsen	David	Den	f	Mar 2001	15+8	4	1	0
Feuer	Ian	USA	gk	Jun 2000	2+2	0	3	0
Mild	Hakan	Swe	m	Nov 2001	8+1	0	0	0
Volz	Moritz	Ger	d	Feb 2003	10	1	0	0

WOLVERHAMPTON WANDERERS (38)

Bellis (Brit)	George	Ind	ch	Jun 1929	42	0	1	0
McMahon	Doug	Can	f	Aug 1938	1	0	0	0
Stuart	Eddie	SA	d	Jan 1951	287	1	32	0
Durandt	Cliff	SA	w	Jun 1957	43	9	5	0
Horne	Des	SA	w	Dec 1956	40	16	11	2
Kemp (Brit)	Fred	It	m	Jun 1963	3	0	1	0
Gardner	Don	Jam	m	Aug 1973	1+2	0	0	0
Berry (Wal)	George	Ger	d	Nov 1975	124	4	36	2
Hazell (Eng) (1)	Bob	Jam	d	May 1977	32+1	1	3	0
Villazan	Rafael	Uru	d	May 1980	20+3	0	4	0
Herbert	Ricki	NZ	d	Oct 1984	44+1	0	3	0
Hazell (Eng) (2)	Bob	Jam	d	Sep 1985	1	0	0	0
Streete (Brit)	Floyd	Jam	d	Oct 1985	157+2	6	20	0
Paskin	John	SA	f	Jun 1989	21+13	3	4+1	0
Regis (Eng)	Cyrille	FrGu	f	Aug 1993	8+11	2	1+2	0
De Wolf	John	Neth	d	Dec 1994	27+1	5	5	0
Williams	Mark	SA	f	Sep 1995	5+7	0	3+1	1
Young (Wal)	Eric	Sing	d	Sep 1995	31	2	9	0
Corica	Steve	Aus	m	Feb 1996	80+20	5	8+2	0
Romano	Serge	Fr	d	Aug 1996	1+3	0	1	0
Dowe	Jens	Ger	m	Oct 1996	5+3	0	0	0
Van der Laan	Robin	Neth	m	Oct 1996	7	0	0	0
Diaz	Isidro	Sp	m	Aug 1997	1	0	0	0
Kubicki	Dariusz	Pol	fb	Aug 1997	12	0	4	0
Paatelainen	Mixu	Fin	f	Aug 1997	10+13	0	8+2	5
Garcia Sanjuan	Jesus	Sp	m	Sep 1997	4	0	2+1	1
Segers	Hans	Neth	gk	Feb 1998	11	0	2	0
Gomez	Fernando	Sp	f	Aug 1998	17+2	2	3	0
Niestroj (Ger)	Robert	Pol	m	Nov 1998	2+4	0	1	0
Flo	Havard	Nor	f	Jan 1999	27+11	9	3+2	1
Pollet	Ludo	Fr	d	Sep 1999	74+4	7	7+1	1
Nielsen	Allan	Den	m	Mar 2000	7	2	0	0
Camara	Mohamed	Gui	d	Aug 2000	27+18	0	5+2	0
Ketsbaia	Temuri	Geo	f	Aug 2000	14+10	3	4+1	1
Thetis	Manuel	Fr	d	Aug 2000	3	0	0	0
Al-Jaber	Sami	Sau	f	Sep 2000	0+4	0	1	0
Roussel	Cedric	Bel	f	Feb 2001	9+17	2	0+2	0
Halle	Gunnar	Nor	d	Mar 2002	4+1	0	2	0
Ingimarsson	Ivar	Ice	m	Aug 2002	10+3	2	2	0

WORKINGTON (6)

Miller	George	SA	f	Mar 1952	11	0	0	0
Miller	Graham	SA	f	Dec 1952	10	1	0	0
Purdon	Ted	SA	f	Mar 1957	33	9	3	1
Tennant	Roy	SA	ch	Jul 1958	151	1	13	0
Haasz	Johnny	Hun	f	Jul 1961	50	13	5	2
Tolson	Max	Aus	f	Feb 1966	29+2	6	4	0

WREXHAM (22)

Bellis (Brit)	George	Ind	ch	May 1927	82	5	6	0
Donoghue	John	USA	wh	Jul 1930	67	2	4	0
Baines	Peter	Aus	f	Apr 1943	6	2	0	0
McDowall	Les	Ind	ch	Nov 1949	3	0	1	0
Kirkby	John	USA	fb	Aug 1951	5	0	0	0
Ugolini	Rolando	It	gk	Jun 1957	83	0	4	0

SURNAME	NAME	BORN	POS	FROM	LgAp	LgG	OthAp	OthG
Keelan (Brit)	Kevin	Ind	gk	Nov 1961	68	0	4	0
Williams	Everton	Jam	f	Jul 1975	1+1	0	0	0
Ferguson	Don	Can	gk	Jan 1986	20	0	0	0
Cooke	Joe	Dom	d/f	Jul 1986	49+2	4	11	1
Paskin	John	SA	f	Feb 1992	28+23	11	1+3	2
Whitley (N Ire)	Jeff	Zam	m	Jan 1999	9	2	0	0
Stevens	Ian	Mal	f	Jul 1999	14+2	4	3+1	0
Allsopp	Danny	Aus	f	Feb 2000	3	4	0	0
Bouanane	Emad	Fr	m	Aug 2000	13+4	0	1	0
Edwards	Carlos	Trin	m	Aug 2000	84+22	17	5+2	1
Sam	Hector	Trin	f	Aug 2000	34+41	16	6+1	0
Killen	Chris	NZ	f	Sep 2000	11+1	3	0	0
Lawrence	Denis	Trin	d	Mar 2001	60+7	3	2+1	0
Sharp	Kevin	Can	d	Oct 2001	12+3	0	0	0
Whitley (N Ire)	Jim	Zam	m	Oct 2001	78	1	4	0
Rovde	Marius	Nor	g	Jan 2002	12	0	0	0

WYCOMBE WANDERERS (8)

Cunningham (Brit)	Tony	Jam	f	Mar 1994	4+1	0	0	0
Regis (Eng)	Cyrille	FrGu	f	Aug 1994	30+5	9	3	1
Moussaddik	Chuck	Mor	gk	Sep 1995	1	0	0+1	0
Dijkstra	Sieb	Neth	gk	Mar 1996	13	0	0	0
Rogers	Mark	Can	d	Dec 1998	108+16	4	19+1	2
Lopez	Carlos	Mex	d	Jan 2002	1	0	0	0
Dixon (Brit)	Jonny	Sp	f	Aug 2002	14+8	5	0	0
Talia	Frank	Aus	gk	Aug 2002	35	0	2	0

YORK CITY (14)

Kubicki	Eryk	Pol	w	Oct 1946	5	0	0	0
Wojtczak	Edouard	Pol	gk	Oct 1946	8	0	0	0
Twissell (Eng)	Charlie	Sing	w	Nov 1958	53	8	3	0
Francis	Gerry	SA	w	Oct 1961	16	4	4	1
Tunks (Brit)	Roy	Ger	gk	Jan 1969	4	0	0	0
Johanneson	Albert	SA	w	Jul 1970	26	3	7	2
Richards	Lloyd	Jam	m	Jun 1980	17+1	1	4	1
Walwyn(Brit)	Keith	Jam	f	Jul 1981	245	119	42	20
McMillan	Andy	SA	fb	Oct 1987	409+12	5	50	0
Atkinson (Brit)	Paddy	Sing	fb	Nov 1995	36+5	0	3+1	0
Evans	Michael	Neth	f	Sep 2001	1+1	0	0	0
Carvalho	Rogerio	Bra	f	Aug 2002	0+4	0	0+1	0
Okoli	James	Nig	d	Aug 2002	1+2	0	0	0
Mazzina	Nicolas	Arg	m	Sep 2002	0+3	0	0	0

Foreign players in England since 1888

A–Z

League club(s) for each player in alphabetical, not chronological, order

NAME (Born) (Nationality, if differs)	LEAGUE CLUB(S)
A	
Aas, Einar (Nor)	Nottm For
Abbey, George (Nig)	Macclesfield
Abdallah, Tewfik (Egy)	Derby, Hartlepool
Abidallah, Nabil (Neth)	Ipswich
Abou, Samassi (IvCo) (Fr)	Ipswich, Walsall, West Ham
Achterberg, John (Neth)	Tranmere
Acimovic, Milenko (Slo)	Tottenham
Ackerman, Alf (SA)	Carlisle, Derby, Hull, Millwall, Norwich
Acuna, Clarence (Chi)	Newcastle
Adamczuk, Dariusz (Pol)	Wigan
Adebola, Dele (Nig)	Birmingham, Crewe, C Palace Oldham
Adekola, David (Nig)	Bournemouth, Brighton, Bury, Cambridge, Exeter, Wigan
Agogo, Junior (Gha)	Chester, Chesterfield, Lincoln, Oldham, Sheff Wed
Agostino, Paul (Aus)	Bristol C
Albert, Philippe (Bel)	Fulham, Newcastle
Aldecoa, Emilio (Sp)	Coventry
Aleksidze, Rati (Geo)	Chelsea
Alexandersson, Niclas (Swe)	Everton, Sheff Wed
Aliadiere, Jeremie (Fr)	Arsenal
Al-Jaber, Sami (Sau)	Wolves
Allback, Marcus (Swe)	A Villa
Alleyne, Andy (Bar)	Reading
Allou, Bernard (IvCo) (Fr)	Nottm For
Allsopp, Danny (Aus)	Bristol R, Man City, Notts Co, Wrexham
Almeida, Marco (Por)	Southampton
Aloisi, John (Aus)	Coventry, Portsmouth
Alsaker, Paul (Nor)	Stockport
Alves, Paulo (Por)	West Ham
Ambrose, Leroy (StV)	Charlton
Ambrosetti, Gabriele (It)	Chelsea
Ameobi, Shola (Nig) (Eng)	Newcastle
Ammann, Mike (USA)	Charlton
Amokachi, Daniel (Nig)	Everton
Amsalem, David (Isr)	C Palace
Andersen, Bo (Den)	Bristol C
Andersen, Leif (Nor)	C Palace
Andersen, Soren (Den)	Bristol C
Andersen, Trond (Nor)	Wimbledon
Andersen, Vetle (Nor)	WBA
Anderson, Doug (HK) (Brit)	Cambridge, Northampton, Oldham, Plymouth, Tranmere
Andersson, Anders (Swe)	Blackburn
Andersson, Andreas (Swe)	Newcastle
Andersson, Patrik (Swe)	Blackburn
Andrade, Jose-Manuel (Por)	Stoke

NAME (Born) (Nationality, if differs)	LEAGUE CLUB(S)
Andre, Carlos (Por)	Walsall
Andre, Pierre-Yves (Fr)	Bolton
Andreassen, Svein (Nor)	Portsmouth
Andreasson, Marcus (Swe)	Bristol R
Andresen, Martin (Nor)	Wimbledon
Andrews, Billy (USA) (N Ire)	Grimsby, Oldham, Stockport
Anelka, Nicolas (Fr)	Arsenal, Liverpool, Man City
Angel, Juan Pablo (Col)	A Villa
Anselin, Cedric (Fr)	Norwich
Antic, Raddy (Yug)	Luton
Antoine-Curier, Mickael (Fr)	Brentford
Aranalde, Zigor (Sp)	Walsall
Arber, Mark (SA) (Brit)	Barnet, Peterborough, Tottenham
Arca, Julio (Arg)	Sunderland
Ardiles, Ossie (Arg)	Blackburn, QPR, Swindon, Tottenham
Arendse, Andre (SA)	Fulham, Oxford
Arentoft, Ben (Den)	Blackburn, Newcastle
Armand, Jack (Ind) (Brit)	Leeds, Newport, Southport, Swansea Town
Arnison, Joseph (SA)	Luton
Arphexad, Pegguy (Guad) (Fr)	Leicester, Liverpool, Stockport
Asamoah, Derek (Gha) (Brit)	Northampton
Asanovic, Aljosa (Cro)	Derby
Ashton, Hubert (Ind) (Brit)	Bristol R, Clapton O
Aspinall, Brendan (SA)	Mansfield
Aspinall, Wilf (USA)	Southport, Stockport
Asprilla, Faustino (Col)	Newcastle
Astafjevs, Vitalis (Lat)	Bristol R
Atangana, Simon (Cam)	Colchester, Port Vale
Atkins, Arthur (Jap) (Brit)	Birmingham, Shrewsbury
Atkinson, Paddy (Sing) (Brit)	Hartlepool, Scarborough, Sheff Utd, York
Atteveld, Ray (Neth)	Bristol C, Everton, West Ham
Auguste, Joe (Trin)	Exeter
Aunger, Geoff (Can)	Chester, Luton, Stockport
Avdiu, Kemajl (Yug) (Swe)	Bury
Avramovic, Raddy (Cro)	Coventry, Notts Co
Awuah, Jones (Gha)	Gillingham
Axeldahl, Jonas (Swe)	Cambridge, Ipswich
Ayegbini, Yakubu (Nig)	Portsmouth
Ayorinde, Sammy (Nig)	Orient
B	
Baardsen, Espen (USA) (Nor)	Everton, Tottenham, Watford
Babayaro, Celestine (Nig)	Chelsea
Babbel, Markus (Ger)	Liverpool
Backos, Des (SA)	Stoke
Bacque, Herve (Fr)	Luton
Badir, Walid (Isr)	Wimbledon
Bagheri, Karim (Irn)	Charlton

D

Da Costa, Hugo (Por)	Stoke
Da Silva, Lourenco (Ang) (Por)	Bristol C, Oldham
Dabelsteen, Thomas (Den)	Scarborough
Dabizas, Nicos (Grk)	Newcastle
Dacourt, Olivier (Fr)	Everton, Leeds
Dadason, Rikki (Ice)	Stoke
Dagnogo, Moussa (Fr)	Bristol R
Dahlin, Martin (Swe)	Blackburn
Daino, Daniele (It)	Derby
Dalla Bona, Sam (It)	Chelsea
Dalton, James (Can)	Sunderland
Danielsson, Einer Thor (Ice)	Stoke
Danielsson, Helgi (Ice)	Peterborough
Danilevicius, Tomas (Rus) (Lith)	Arsenal
Darcheville, Jean-Claude (FrGu) (Fr)	Nottm For
Darras, Frederic (Fr)	Swindon
Davidson, Alan (Aus)	Nottm For
Davies, Roy (SA)	Luton
D'Avray, Mich (SA) (Eng)	Ipswich, Leicester
De Bilde, Gilles (Bel)	A Villa, Sheff Wed
De Blasiis, Jean-Yves (Fr)	Norwich
De Freitas, Fabian (Sur) (Neth)	Bolton, WBA
De Goey, Ed (Neth)	Chelsea
De Goey, Len (Neth)	Sheff Utd
De La Cruz, Ulises (Ecu)	A Villa
De Lucas, Enrique (Sp)	Chelsea
De Oliveira, Filipe (Por)	Chelsea
De Ornelas, Fernando (Ven)	C Palace, QPR
De Vogt, Wilko (Neth)	Sheff Utd
De Vos, Jason (Can)	Darlington, Wigan
De Waard, Raimond (Neth)	Norwich
De Wolf, John (Neth)	Wolves
De Zeeuw, Arjan (Neth)	Barnsley, Portsmouth, Wigan
Debec, Fabien (Fr)	Coventry
Debeve, Mickael (Fr)	Middlesbrough
Degn, Peter (Den)	Everton
Degryse, Marc (Bel)	Sheff Wed
Del Rio, Walter (Arg)	C Palace
Delapenha, Lindy (Jam)	Mansfield, Middlesbrough, Portsmouth
Delgado, Agustin (Ecu)	Southampton
Dellas, Traianos (Grk)	Sheff Utd
Delorge, Laurent (Bel)	Coventry
Derko, Franco (It)	Mansfield
Derveld, Fernando (Neth)	Norwich, WBA
Desailly, Marcel (Gha) (Fr)	Chelsea
Deschamps, Didier (Fr)	Chelsea
Devereux, Tony (Gib) (Brit)	Aldershot
Deyna, Kazimierz (Pol)	Man City
Di Canio, Paolo (It)	Sheff Wed, West Ham
Di Giuseppe, Bica (Bra)	Sunderland, Walsall
Di Lella, Gustavo (Arg)	Darlington, Hartlepool
Di Matteo, Roberto (Swit) (It)	Chelsea
Di Piedi, Michele (It)	Bristol R, Sheff Wed
Dia, Ali (Sen)	Southampton
Diabate, Lassina (IvCo)	Portsmouth
Diaf, Farid (Fr)	Preston
Diallo, Cherif (Sen)	Exeter
Diallo, Drissa (Mau) (Gui)	Burnley
Diao, Salif (Sen)	Liverpool
Diawara, Djibril (Sen)	Bolton
Diawara, Kaba (Fr)	Arsenal, Blackburn, West Ham
Diaz, Isidro (Sp)	Rochdale, Wigan, Wolves
Dickinson, Patrick (Can)	Hull
Dijkstra, Meindert (Neth)	Notts Co
Dijkstra, Sieb (Neth)	Bristol C, QPR, Wycombe
Dillsworth, Eddie (SiLe)	Lincoln
Diomede, Bernard (Fr)	Liverpool
Diop, Pape Seydou (Sen)	Norwich
Diouf, El Hadji (Sen)	Liverpool

Distin, Sylvain (Fr)	Man City, Newcastle
Dixon, Jonny (Sp) (Brit)	Wycombe
D'Jaffo, Laurent (Fr)	Bury, Sheff Utd, Stockport
Djetou, Martin (IvCo) (Fr)	Fulham
Djordjic, Bojan (Yug) (Swe)	Man Utd, Sheff Wed
Djorkaeff, Youri (Fr)	Bolton
Dolby, Hugh (Ind) (Brit)	Chelsea
Dolding, Len (Ind) (Brit)	Chelsea, Norwich
Domi, Didier (Fr)	Newcastle
Dominguez, Jose (Por)	Birmingham, Tottenham
Donaghy, Charles (Ind) (Brit)	Chelsea
Doncel, Antonio (Sp)	Hull
Donis, George (Grk)	Blackburn, Huddersfield, Sheff Utd
Donoghue, John (USA)	Wrexham
Dorigo, Tony (Aus) (Eng)	A Villa, Chelsea, Derby, Leeds, Stoke
Doriva, Guidoni (Bra)	Middlesbrough
Dorner, Mario (Aut)	Darlington
Dowe, Jens (Ger)	Wolves
Duarte, Juan Maldondo (Bra)	Arsenal
Ducrocq, Pierre (Fr)	Derby
Dudek, Jerzy (Pol)	Liverpool
Dugarry, Christophe (Fr)	Birmingham
Dugnolle, Jack (Ind) (Brit)	Brighton, Plymouth
Dumas, Franck (Fr)	Newcastle
Dumitrescu, Ilie (Rom)	Tottenham, West Ham
Dundee, Sean (SA)	Liverpool
Dunfield, Terry (Can)	Bury, Man City
Durandt, Cliff (SA)	Charlton, Wolves
Dursun, Peter (Den)	Southend
Dusan, Nikolic (Yug)	Bolton
Dwane, Eddie (Mal) (Brit)	Lincoln
Dziekanowski, Jackie (Pol)	Bristol C

E

Eames, Billy (Mal) (Brit)	Brentford, Portsmouth
Earnshaw, Robert (Zam) (Wal)	Cardiff
Edds, Gareth (Aus)	Nottm For, Swindon
Edge, Declan (Mly) (NZ)	Notts Co
Edinho, Amaral (Bra)	Bradford
Edu (Bra)	Arsenal
Edwards, Alistair (Aus)	Brighton, Millwall
Edwards, Carlos (Trin)	Wrexham
Edwards, Gerald (HK) (Brit)	Luton
Einarsson, Gunnar (Ice)	Brentford
Eisentrager, Alec (Ger)	Bristol C
Ekelund, Ronnie (Den)	Coventry, Man City, Southampton, Walsall
Ekner, Dan (Swe)	Portsmouth
El Karkouri, Talal (Mor)	Sunderland
El Khalej, Tahar (Mor)	Charlton, Southampton
Elena, Marcelino (Sp)	Newcastle
Elstrup, Lars (Den)	Luton
Emenalo, Michael (Nig)	Notts Co
Emerson (Bra)	Middlesbrough
Emmerson, Wayne (Can)	Crewe
Enckelman, Peter (Fin)	A Villa
Enes, Robbie (Aus)	Portsmouth
Engonga, Vincente (Sp)	Coventry
Enhua, Zhang (Chn)	Grimsby
Epesse-Titi, Steeve (Fr)	Exeter
Eranio, Stefano (It)	Derby
Eriksson, Jan (Swe)	Sunderland
Espartero, Mario (Fr)	Bolton
Essers, Pierre (Neth)	Walsall
Etuhu, Dixon (Nig)	Man City, Preston
Evans, Ceri (NZ)	Oxford
Evans, Michael (Neth)	York
Evans, Paul (SA)	Sheff Wed
Eve, Angus (Trin)	Chester
Evtushok, Alex (Ukr)	Coventry
Eydelie, Jean-Jacques (Fr)	Walsall
Eyjolfsson, Siggi (Ice)	Chester, Walsall

F

NAME (Born) (Nationality, if differs)	LEAGUE CLUB(S)
Fabiano, Nicolas (Fr)	Swansea
Fabio, Ferraresi (It)	A Villa
Fadida, Aharon (Isr)	Aldershot
Faerber, Winston (Sur) (Neth)	Cardiff
Falconer, Andy (SA)	Blackpool
Fallon, Rory (NZ)	Barnsley, Shrewsbury
Farina, Frank (Aus)	Notts Co
Ferguson, Don (Can)	Wrexham
Fernandes, Fabrice (Fr)	Fulham, Southampton
Ferrari, Carlos (Bra)	Birmingham
Ferrer, Albert (Sp)	Chelsea
Ferri, Jean-Michel (Fr)	Liverpool
Festa, Gianluca (It)	Middlesbrough, Portsmouth
Feuer, Ian (USA)	Derby, Luton, Peterborough, Tranmere, West Ham, Wimbledon
Filan, John (Aus)	Blackburn, Cambridge, Coventry, Wigan
Fiocca, Paul (It)	Swindon
Firmani, Eddie (SA)	Charlton, Southend
Firmani, Peter (SA)	Charlton
Fish, Kenneth (SA)	Port Vale
Fish, Mark (SA)	Bolton, Charlton
Fjortoft, Jan Aage (Nor)	Barnsley, Middlesbrough, Sheff Utd, Swindon
Fleming, Mike (Ind) (Brit)	Tranmere
Flo, Havard (Nor)	Wolves
Flo, Jostein (Nor)	Sheff Utd
Flo, Tore Andre (Nor)	Chelsea, Sunderland
Foe, Marc-Vivien (Cam)	Man City, West Ham
Foletti, Patrick (Swit)	Derby
Forbes, Boniek (GuB)	Orient
Forbes, Dudley (SA)	Charlton
Foreman, Denis (SA)	Brighton
Forge, Nicolas (Fr)	Orient
Forlan, Diego (Uru)	Man Utd
Formann, Pascal (Ger)	Nottm For
Forrest, Craig (Can)	Chelsea, Colchester, Ipswich, West Ham
Forssell, Mikael (Ger) (Fin)	Chelsea, C Palace
Fortune, Quinton (SA)	Man Utd
Foster, Craig (Aus)	C Palace, Portsmouth
Fostervold, Anders (Nor)	Grimsby
Foxe, Hayden (Aus)	Portsmouth, West Ham
Foyewa, Amos (Nig)	Bournemouth
Fradin, Karim (Fr)	Stockport
Francis, Gerry (SA)	Leeds, York
Frandsen, Per (Den)	Bolton, Blackburn
Fraser, Willie (Aus) (Sco)	Nottm For, Sunderland
Fredgaard, Carsten (Den)	Bolton, Sunderland, WBA
Freimanis, Eddie (Lat)	Northampton
Freund, Steffen (Ger)	Tottenham
Friedel, Brad (USA)	Blackburn, Liverpool
Friio, David (Fr)	Plymouth
Frontzeck, Michael (Ger)	Man City
Fuchs, Uwe (Ger)	Middlesbrough, Millwall
Fuertes, Esteban (Arg)	Derby
Fuglestad, Erik (Nor)	Norwich
Fuller, Ricardo (Jam)	C Palace, Preston
Fumaca, Jose (Bra)	Colchester, C Palace, Newcastle
Fursdon, Roy (Can)	Torquay
Futre, Paulo (Por)	West Ham

G

NAME (Born) (Nationality, if differs)	LEAGUE CLUB(S)
Gaardsoe, Thomas (Den)	Ipswich
Gaia, Marcio (Bra)	Exeter
Gaillard, Marcel (Bel)	C Palace, Portsmouth
Gall, Benny (Den)	Shrewsbury
Gallas, William (Fr)	Chelsea
Gallego, Jose (Sp)	Brentford, Colchester, Southampton
Gallego, Tony (Sp)	Norwich
Galli, Filippo (It)	Watford
Galloway, Steve (Ger) (Brit)	Cambridge, C Palace
Gambaro, Enzo (It)	Grimsby
Garcia, Richard (Aus)	Orient, West Ham
Garcia, Sanjuan Jesus (Sp)	Wolves
Garcia, Tony (Fr)	Notts Co
Garde, Remi (Fr)	Arsenal
Gardner, Don (Jam)	Wolves
Gardner, Ricardo (Jam)	Bolton
Gariani, Moshe (Isr)	Brighton
Garrocho, Carlos (Arg)	Walsall
Garwood, Len (Ind) (Brit)	Tottenham
Gaudino, Maurizio (Ger)	Man City
Gavilan, Diego (Par)	Newcastle
Geard, Glen (Mal)	Brighton
Genaux, Reggie (Bel)	Coventry
Gentile, Marco (Neth)	Burnley
George, Finidi (Nig)	Ipswich
Georgeson, Roddy (Egy) (Brit)	Port Vale
Georgiadis, Georgios (Grk)	Newcastle
Geremi (Cam)	Middlesbrough
Gerhardt, Hugh (SA)	Liverpool
Germain, Steve (Fr)	Colchester
Gerula, Stan (Pol)	Orient
Ghrayib, Naguyan (Isr)	A Villa
Giallanza, Gaetano (Swit)	Bolton, Norwich
Gibbs, Peter (Zim)	Watford
Gibson, Jock (Brit)	Hull, Luton, Sheff Utd, Sunderland
Gibson, Fred (SA)	Coventry, Sunderland
Ginola, David (Fr)	A Villa, Everton, Newcastle, Tottenham
Gioacchini, Stefano (It)	Coventry
Gislason, Valur (Ice)	Brighton
Gislason, Siggi (Ice)	Stoke
Giumarra, Willy (Can)	Darlington
Gnohere, Arthur (IvCo) (Fr)	Burnley
Goater, Shaun (Ber)	Bristol C, Man City, Notts Co, Rotherham
Godfrey, Elliott (Can)	Watford
Golac, Ivan (Yug)	Bournemouth, Man City, Portsmouth, Southampton
Goldbaek, Bjarne (Den)	Chelsea, Fulham
Goma, Alain (Fr)	Fulham, Newcastle
Gomez, Fernando (Sp)	Wolves
Goodhind, Warren (SA)	Barnet, Cambridge
Goodison, Ian (Jam)	Hull
Goodridge, Greg (Bar)	Bristol C, Cheltenham, QPR, Torquay
Gope-Fenepej, John (NCal) (Fr)	Bolton
Gorre, Dean (Sur) (Neth)	Barnsley, Huddersfield
Goss, Jerry (Cyp) (Wal)	Norwich
Gotsmanov, Sergei (USSR) (Blr)	Brighton, Southampton
Gottskalksson, Ole (Ice)	Brentford
Gough, Richard (Swe) (Sco)	Everton, Nottm For, Tottenham
Goulet, Brent (USA)	Bournemouth, Crewe
Goulooze, Richard (Neth)	Derby
Grabbi, Corrado (It)	Blackburn
Grant, Kim (Gha)	Charlton, Luton, Millwall, Notts Co, Scunthorpe
Granville, John (Trin)	Aldershot, Millwall
Gravelaine, Xavier (Fr)	Watford
Gravesen, Thomas (Den)	Everton
Greer, Ross (Aus)	Chester
Gregory, Neil (Zam) (Brit)	Chesterfield, Colchester, Ipswich, Peterborough, Scunthorpe, Torquay
Grenet, Francois (Fr)	Derby
Gresko, Vratislav (Svk)	Blackburn
Greyling, Anton (SA)	Torquay
Griemink, Bart (Neth)	Birmingham, Peterborough, Swindon
Grieves, Ken (Aus)	Bolton, Bury, Stockport

NAME (Born) (Nationality, if differs)	LEAGUE CLUB(S)
Griffith, Cohen (Guy) (Brit)	Cardiff
Grimandi, Gilles (Fr)	Arsenal
Grobbelaar, Bruce (SA) (Zim)	Bury, Crewe, Lincoln, Liverpool, Oldham, Plymouth, Southampton, Stoke
Grodas, Frode (Nor)	Chelsea, Tottenham
Groenendijk, Alfons (Neth)	Man City
Grondin, David (Fr)	Arsenal
Gronkjaer, Jesper (Den)	Chelsea
Gudjohnsen, Eidur (Ice)	Bolton, Chelsea
Gudjonsson, Bjarni (Ice)	Stoke
Gudjonsson, Joey (Ice)	A Villa
Gudjonsson, Thordur (Ice)	Derby, Preston
Gudmundsson, Albert (Ice)	Arsenal
Gudmundsson, Johann (Ice)	Cambridge, Watford
Gudmundsson, Niklas (Swe)	Blackburn, Ipswich
Guentchev, Bontcho (Bul)	Ipswich, Luton
Gueret, Willy (Guad) (Fr)	Millwall
Guerrero, Ivan (Hon)	Coventry
Guivarc'h, Stephane (Fr)	Newcastle
Gullit, Ruud (Sur) (Neth)	Chelsea
Gunn, Alf (Ger)	Nottm For
Gunnarsson, Brynjar (Ice)	Stoke
Gunnlaugsson, Arnie (Ice)	Bolton, Leicester, Stoke
Gunnlaugsson, Bjarke (Ice)	Preston
Gurinovich, Igor (USSR) (Blr)	Brighton
Gustafsson, Tomas (Swe)	Coventry
Guyett, Scott (Aus)	Oxford
Gysbrechts, Davy (Bel)	Sheff Utd

H

NAME (Born) (Nationality, if differs)	LEAGUE CLUB(S)
Haaland, Alf-Inge (Nor)	Leeds, Man City, Nottm For
Haarhoff, Jimmy (Zam)	Birmingham
Haas, Bernt (Aut)	Sunderland
Haasz, Johnny (Hun)	Swansea Town, Workington
Haddaoui, Riffi (Den)	Torquay
Hadji, Mustapha (Mor)	A Villa, Coventry
Hadziabdic, Dzemal (Yug)	Swansea
Hahnemann, Marcus (USA)	Fulham, Reading, Rochdale
Hakan Sukur (Tur)	Blackburn
Hakan Unsal (Tur)	Blackburn
Halle, Gunnar (Nor)	Bradford, Leeds, Oldham, Wolves
Hamann, Dietmar (Ger)	Liverpool, Newcastle
Hammond, Elvis (Gha)	Bristol R, Fulham
Hansen, Bo (Den)	Bolton
Hansen, Edvin (Den)	Grimsby
Hansen, John (Ger) (Den)	Cambridge
Hansen, Karl (Nor)	Huddersfield
Hansen, Vergard (Nor)	Bristol C
Hansson, Mikael (Swe)	Stoke
Hardy, Adam (SA)	Bradford
Hareide, Aage (Nor)	Man City, Norwich
Harkes, John (USA)	Derby, Nottm For, Sheff Wed, West Ham
Harries Paul (Aus)	Carlisle, Exeter, Portsmouth, Torquay
Harris, Alex (HK) (Brit)	Blackpool
Harris, Andy (SA) (Brit)	Orient, Southend
Hartenberger, Uwe (Ger)	Reading
Hasselbaink, Jimmy Floyd (Sur) (Neth)	Chelsea, Leeds
Hastie, Ken (SA)	Leeds
Hauser, Peter (SA)	Blackpool, Chester
Hauser, Thomas (Ger)	Sunderland
Havenga, Willie (SA)	Birmingham, Ipswich, Luton
Hay, Danny (NZ)	Leeds, Walsall
Hazan, Alon (Isr)	Watford
Hazell, Bob (Jam) (Eng)	Leicester, Port Vale, QPR, Reading, Wolves
Heald, Oliver (Can)	Scarborough
Hebel, Dirk (Ger)	Brentford
Hedman, Magnus (Swe)	Coventry
Hegazi, Hassan (Egy)	Fulham
Heggem, Vegard (Nor)	Liverpool
Heidenstrom, Bjorn (Nor)	Orient
Heikkinen, Markus (Fin)	Portsmouth
Heinola, Antti (Fin)	QPR
Heiselberg, Kim (Den)	Swindon
Helder, Glenn (Neth)	Arsenal
Helder, Rodrigues (Ang) (Por)	Newcastle
Helguson, Heidar (Ice)	Watford
Helin, Petri (Fin)	Luton, Stockport
Helmer, Thomas (Ger)	Sunderland
Henchoz, Stephane (Swit)	Blackburn, Liverpool
Henriksen, Tony (Nor)	Southend
Henriksen, Bo (Den)	Kidderminster
Henry, Liburd (Dom)	Gillingham, Halifax, Maidstone, Peterborough, Watford
Henry, Thierry (Fr)	Arsenal
Heppolette, Ricky (Ind) (Brit)	Chesterfield, C Palace, Orient, Peterborough, Preston
Herbert, Ricki (NZ)	Wolves
Herivelto, Moreira (Bra)	Walsall
Hernandez, Dino (Neth)	Wigan
Herrera, Martin (Arg)	Fulham
Hesford, Iain (Zam) (Eng)	Blackpool, Fulham, Hull, Maidstone, Notts Co, Sunderland
Hewie, John (SA) (Sco)	Charlton
Hewkins, Ken (SA)	Fulham
Hews Chay (Aus)	Carlisle
Hey, Tony (Ger)	Birmingham
Hiden, Martin (Aut)	Leeds
Higginbotham, Harry (Aus)	Luton, Nelson, Orient, Reading, South Shields
Hill, Reginald (Gib) (Brit)	Carlisle, Darlington, Hartlepool, Tranmere
Hirschfeld, Lars (Can)	Luton
Hitzlsperger, Thomas (Ger)	A Villa, Chesterfield
Hjelde, Jon Olav (Nor)	Nottm For
Hjorth, Jesper (Den)	Darlington
Hodge, Eric (SA)	Aldershot, Brighton
Hodgson, Doug (Aus)	Burnley, Northampton, Oldham, Plymouth, Sheff Utd
Hodgson, Gordon (SA) (Eng)	A Villa, Leeds, Liverpool
Hodouto, Kwami (Tgo) (Fr)	Huddersfield
Hoekman, Danny (Neth)	Man City
Hoekstra, Peter (Neth)	Stoke
Hogan, Cornelius (Mal)	Burnley, NB Tower
Hogh, Jes (Den)	Chelsea
Hollund, Martin (Nor)	Hartlepool
Holster, Marco (Neth)	Ipswich
Holwyn, Jermaine (Neth)	Port Vale
Hooper, Lyndon (Guy) (Can)	Birmingham
Horace, Alain (Mad) (Fr)	Hartlepool
Horlaville, Christophe (Fr)	Port Vale
Horne, Des (SA)	Blackpool, Wolves
Horsfall, George (Aus)	Southampton, Southend
Hottiger, Marc (Swit)	Everton, Newcastle
Houghton, Brian (Ind) (Brit)	Birmingham, Bradford PA, Lincoln, Oxford, Southend
Houston, Graham (Gib) (Brit)	Carlisle, Preston, Wigan
Hovi, Tom (Nor)	Charlton
Howells, Lee (Aus)	Cheltenham
Hreidarsson, Hermann (Ice)	Brentford, C Palace, Ipswich, Wimbledon
Hristov, Georgi (Mac)	Barnsley
Hubbard, John (SA)	Bury
Huck, Willie (Fr)	Bournemouth
Huggins, Joe (Ind) (Brit)	Aldershot
Hughes, Zacari (Aus)	Rochdale
Hume, Iain (Can)	Tranmere

NAME (Born) (Nationality, if differs)	LEAGUE CLUB(S)
Hunter, Chris (HK) (Brit)	Preston
Hunter, George (Ind) (Brit)	A Villa, Chelsea, Man Utd, Oldham
Huth, Robert (Ger)	Chelsea
Hyldgaard, Morten (Den)	Coventry, Scunthorpe
Hysen, Glenn (Swe)	Liverpool
Hyypia, Sami (Fin)	Liverpool

I

Ifejiagwa, Emeka (Nig)	Brighton
Iga, Andrew (Uga) (Brit)	Millwall
Ilic, Sasa (Aus) (Yug)	Charlton, Portsmouth, West Ham
Immel, Eike (Ger)	Man City
Inamoto, Junichi (Jap)	Arsenal, Fulham
Ince, Clayton (Trin)	Crewe
Ingebrigtsen, Kaare (Nor)	Man City
Ingesson, Klas (Swe)	Sheff Wed
Ingimarsson, Ivar (Ice)	Brentford, Brighton, Torquay, Wolves
Invincible, Danny (Aus)	Swindon
Iorfa, Dominic (Nig)	Peterborough, QPR, Southend
Iovan, Stefan (Rom)	Brighton
Ipoua, Guy (Cam) (Fr)	Bristol R, Gillingham, Scunthorpe
Iroha, Ben (Nig)	Watford
Isaias, Marques (Bra) (Por)	Coventry
Ismael, Valerien (Fr)	C Palace
Issa, Pierre (SA)	Watford
Itonga, Carlin (DRC)	Arsenal
Iversen, Steffen (Nor)	Tottenham

J

Jaaskelainen, Jussi (Fin)	Bolton
Jack, Rodney (Jam) (StV)	Crewe, Torquay
Jacobsen, Anders (Nor)	Notts Co, Sheff Utd, Stoke
Jacobsen, Viggo (Den)	Charlton
Jalink, Nico (Neth)	Port Vale
Jankovic, Bozo (Yug)	Middlesbrough
Jansson, Jan (Swe)	Port Vale
Jantunen, Pertti (Fin)	Bristol C
Javary, Jean-Phillipe (Fr)	Brentford, Plymouth, Sheff Utd
Jean, Earl (StL)	Ipswich, Plymouth, Rotherham
Jeannin, Alex (Fr)	Darlington
Jennings, Jedd (Ber)	Hereford
Jensen, Brian (Den)	WBA
Jensen, Claus (Den)	Bolton, Charlton
Jensen, John (Den)	Arsenal
Jensen, Niclas (Den)	Man City
Jensen, Viggo (Den)	Hull
Jeppson, Hans (Swe)	Charlton
Jerkan, Nikola (Cro)	Nottm For
Jermyn, Mark (Ger) (Brit)	Torquay
Jihai, Sun (Chn)	C Palace, Man City
Job, Joseph-Desire (Fr) (Cam)	Middlesbrough
Johanneson, Albert (SA)	Leeds, York
Johansen, Martin (Den)	Coventry
Johansen, Michael (Den)	Bolton
Johansen, Rune (Nor)	Bristol R
Johansen, Stig (Nor)	Bristol C, Southampton
Johansson, Jonatan (Swe) (Fin)	Charlton
Johansson, Nils-Eric (Den)	Blackburn
John, Stern (Trin)	Birmingham, Nottm For
Johnsen, Erland (Nor)	Chelsea
Johnsen, Ronny (Nor)	Man Utd, A Villa
Johnson, David (Jam)	Burnley, Bury, Ipswich, Nottm For, Sheff Wed
Johnson, Glenn (Aus)	Cardiff
Johnson, Glenn (Can)	WBA
Johnson, Richard (Aus)	Northampton, Watford
Johnson, Jermaine (Jam)	Bolton

NAME (Born) (Nationality, if differs)	LEAGUE CLUB(S)
Johnsson, Julian (Den) (Far)	Hull
Johnston, Craig (SA) (Aus)	Liverpool, Middlesbrough
Johnstone, Glenn (Ken) (Brit)	Preston
Jokanovic, Slavisa (Yug)	Chelsea
Jol, Maarten (Neth)	Coventry, WBA
Jones, Cobi (USA)	Coventry
Jones, Ian (Ger) (Brit)	Cardiff
Jonk, Wim (Neth)	Sheff Wed
Jonsson, Siggi (Ice)	Arsenal, Barnsley, Sheff Wed
Jorgensen, Claus (Den)	Bournemouth, Bradford
Jorgensen, Henrik (Den)	Notts Co
Joseph, David (Guad) (Fr)	Notts Co
Jovanovic, Nikola (Yug)	Man Utd
Joy, Ian (USA)	Kidderminster
Juanjo, Carricondo (Sp)	Bradford
Juninho (Bra)	Middlesbrough
Junior, Jose Luis (Bra)	Walsall

K

Kaak, Tom (Neth)	Darlington
Kaamark, Pontus (Swe)	Leicester
Kachloul, Hassan (Mor)	A Villa, Southampton
Kachouro, Petr (Blr)	Sheff Utd
Kaiser, Rudi (Neth)	Coventry
Kalac, Zeljko (Aus)	Leicester
Kalogeracos, Vas (Aus)	Stockport
Kanchelskis, Andrei (Ukr)	Everton, Man City, Man Utd, Southampton
Kandol, Tresor (DRC) (Brit)	Bournemouth, Cambridge, Luton
Kanoute, Frederic (Fr)	West Ham
Kanu, Nwankwo (Nig)	Arsenal
Kapengwe, Emment (Zam)	A Villa
Kapler, Konrad (Pol)	Rochdale
Kaprielian, Mickael (Fr)	Bolton
Karaa, Roch (Tun)	Darlington
Karelse, John (Neth)	Newcastle
Karembeu, Christian (NCal) (Fr)	Middlesbrough
Karic, Amir (Slo)	C Palace, Ipswich
Karl, Steffen (Ger)	Man City
Karlsen, Kent (Nor)	Luton
Karlsson, Par (Swe)	Wimbledon
Katalinic, Ivan (Yug)	Southampton
Kavelashvili, Mikhail (Geo)	Man City
Kawaguchi, Yoshikatsu (Jap)	Portsmouth
Kearton, Jason (Aus)	Blackpool, Crewe, Everton, Notts Co, Stoke
Keelan, Kevin (Ind) (Brit)	A Villa, Norwich, Stockport, Wrexham
Keizer, Gerry (Neth)	Arsenal, Charlton
Keizerweerd, Orpheo (Neth)	Oldham
Keller, Francois (Fr)	Fulham
Keller, Kasey (USA)	Leicester, Millwall, Tottenham
Keller, Marc (Fr)	Blackburn, Portsmouth, West Ham
Kelly, Errington (StV)	Bristol C, Bristol R, Lincoln, Peterborough
Kelly, Pat (SA) (N Ire)	Barnsley, Crewe
Kemp, Dirk (SA)	Liverpool
Kemp, Fred (It) (Brit)	Blackpool, Halifax, Hereford, Southampton, Wolves
Kennon, Sandy (SA)	Colchester, Huddersfield, Norwich
Kerr, Dylan (Mal) (Brit)	Blackpool, Carlisle, Doncaster, Exeter, Kidderminster, Leeds, Reading
Kerr, John (Can) (USA)	Millwall, Peterborough, Portsmouth, Walsall
Ketsbaia, Temuri (Geo)	Newcastle, Wolves
Kewell, Harry (Aus)	Leeds
Kharine, Dimitri (Rus)	Chelsea

NAME (Born) (Nationality, if differs)	LEAGUE CLUB(S)
Pelzer, Marc (Ger)	Blackburn
Peralta, Sixto (Arg)	Ipswich
Percassi, Luca (It)	Chelsea
Perdomo, Jose (Uru)	Coventry
Perez, Lionel (Fr)	Cambridge, Scunthorpe, Sunderland
Perez, Sebastien (Fr)	Blackburn
Pericard, Vincent (Fr)	Portsmouth
Peron, Jeff (Fr)	Portsmouth, Walsall, Wigan
Perry, Bill (SA)	Blackpool, Southport
Peschisolido, Paul (Can)	Birmingham, Fulham, Norwich, QPR, Sheff Utd, Stoke, WBA
Peterson, Brian (SA)	Blackpool
Petit, Emmanuel (Fr)	Arsenal, Chelsea
Petrachi, Gianluca (It)	Nottm For
Petrescu, Dan (Rom)	Bradford, Chelsea, Sheff Wed, Southampton
Petrescu, Tomi (Fin)	Leicester
Petric, Gordan (Yug)	C Palace
Petrovic, Vladimir (Yug)	Arsenal
Petta, Bobby (Neth)	Ipswich
Petterson, Andy (Aus)	Bradford, Brighton, Charlton, Colchester, Ipswich, Luton, Plymouth, Portsmouth, Torquay
Phillips, Brendon (Jam)	Mansfield, Peterborough
Phillips, David (Ger) (Brit)	Coventry, Huddersfield, Lincoln, Man City, Norwich, Nottm For, Plymouth
Pickett, Reg (Ind) (Brit)	Ipswich, Portsmouth
Pidcock, Fred (Can)	Walsall
Piechnik, Torben (Den)	Liverpool
Pierre, Nigel (Trin)	Bristol R
Pilvi, Tero (Fin)	Cambridge
Pinamonte, Lorenzo (It)	Brentford, Brighton, Bristol C, Orient
Pinault, Thomas (Fr)	Colchester
Pingel, Frank (Den)	Newcastle
Pinto, Sergio (Por)	Bradford
Pires, Robert (Fr)	Arsenal
Pisanti, David (Isr)	QPR
Pistone, Alessandro (It)	Everton, Newcastle
Pittman, Steve (USA)	Shrewsbury
Poborsky, Karel (CzRep)	Man Utd
Podd, Cyril (StK)	Bradford, Halifax, Scarborough
Pogliacomi, Les (Aus)	Oldham
Pollet, Ludo (Fr)	Walsall, Wolves
Ponte, Raimondo (It)	Nottm For
Poom, Mart (Est)	Derby, Portsmouth, Sunderland
Popescu, Gica (Rom)	Tottenham
Popovic, Tony (Aus)	C Palace
Porfirio, Hugo (Por)	Nottm For, West Ham
Porteous, Jack (Ind) (Brit)	Aldershot
Postma, Stefan (Neth)	A Villa
Potts, Steve (USA) (Eng)	West Ham
Pounewatchy, Stephane (Fr)	Carlisle, Colchester, Port Vale
Poyet, Gustavo (Uru)	Chelsea, Tottenham
Praski, Josef (Fr)	Notts Co
Preedy, Charlie (Ind) (Brit)	Arsenal, Bristol R, Charlton, Luton, Wigan Borough
Price, Johnny (Ind) (Brit)	Brentford, Fulham, Port Vale
Priday, Bob (SA)	Blackburn, Liverpool, Rochdale, Acc Stanley
Pringle, Martin (Swe)	Charlton, Grimsby
Prosinecki, Robert (Cro)	Portsmouth
Prunier, William (Fr)	Man Utd
Purdon, Ted (SA)	Barrow, Birmingham, Bristol R, Sunderland, Workington

Q

Quamina, Mark (Guy)	Plymouth, Wimbledon
Quantrill, Alf (Ind) (Eng)	Bradford PA, Derby, Nottm For, Preston
Queudrue, Franck (Fr)	Middlesbrough
Quitongo, Jose (Ang)	Darlington

R

Rachubka, Paul (USA)	Man Utd, Oldham
Radebe, Lucas (SA)	Leeds
Radosavljevic, Preki (Yug) (USA)	Everton, Portsmouth
Raducioiu, Florin (Rom)	West Ham
Radzinski, Tomasz (Pol) (USA)	Everton
Rafferty, Kevin (Ken) (Brit)	Crewe
Rahim, Brent (Trin)	Northampton
Rahmberg, Marino (Swe)	Derby
Rajkovic, Anto (Yug)	Swansea
Rantanen, Jari (Fin)	Leicester
Ravanelli, Fabrizio (It)	Derby, Middlesbrough
Rebrov, Sergei (Ukr)	Tottenham
Regis, Cyrille (FrGui) (Eng)	A Villa, Chester, Coventry, WBA, Wolves, Wycombe
Regtop, Erik (Neth)	Bradford
Rehn, Stefan (Swe)	Everton
Reid, Paul (Aus)	Bradford
Remy, Christophe (Fr)	Oxford
Repka, Tomas (CzRep)	West Ham
Resch, Franz (Aut)	Darlington
Reuser, Martijn (Neth)	Ipswich
Reyna, Claudio (USA)	Sunderland
Ribeiro, Bruno (Por)	Leeds, Sheff Utd
Ricard, Hamilton (Col)	Middlesbrough
Rice, Gary (Zam) (Brit)	Exeter
Richard, Fabrice (Fr)	Colchester
Richards, Carl (Jam) (Brit)	Birmingham, Blackpool, Bournemouth, Maidstone, Peterborough
Richards, Lloyd (Jam)	Notts Co, York
Richardson, John (SA)	Bristol R
Riches, Steve (Aus)	Orient
Riedle, Karl-Heinz (Ger)	Fulham, Liverpool
Rieper, Marc (Den)	West Ham
Riihilahti, Aki (Fin)	C Palace
Riise, John Arne (Nor)	Liverpool
Riley, Arthur (SA)	Liverpool
Rintanen, Mauno (Fin)	Hull
Riseth, Vidar (Nor)	Luton
Risom, Henrik (Den)	Stoke
Rizzo, Nicky (Aus)	C Palace
Rober, Jurgen (Ger)	Nottm For
Robert, Laurent (Fr)	Newcastle
Roberts, Sean (SA)	Sheff Wed
Roberts, John (Aus)	Blackburn, Bradford, Chesterfield, Nothampton, Southend
Robertson, Mark (Aus)	Burnley, Swindon
Robinson, John (Zim) (Wal)	Brighton, Charlton
Robledo, George (Chi)	Barnsley, Newcastle
Robledo, Ted (Chi)	Barnsley, Newcastle, Notts Co
Rocha, Carlos (Por)	Bury
Rodrigo, Juliano (Bra)	Everton
Rodrigues, Dani (Por)	Bournemouth, Bristol C, Southampton, Walsall
Rodriguez, Bruno (Fr)	Bradford
Rogers, Mark (Can)	Wycombe
Rolling, Franck (Fr)	Bournemouth, Gillingham, Leicester
Romano, Serge (Fr)	Wolves
Romo, David (Fr)	Swansea
Rosenthal, Ronny (Isr)	Liverpool, Tottenham, Watford
Rosler, Uwe (Ger)	Man City, Southampton, WBA

Index